Television Western Players of the Fifties

ALSO BY EVERETT AAKER

Encyclopedia of Early Television Crime Fighters: All Regular Cast Members in American Crime and Mystery Series, 1948–1959 (McFarland, 2006)

Television Western Players of the Fifties

A Biographical Encyclopedia of All Regular Cast Members in Western Series, 1949–1959

by EVERETT AAKER

McFarland & Company, Inc., Publishers
Jefferson, North Carolina, and London

The present work is a reprint of the library bound edition of Television Western Players of the Fifties: A Biographical Encyclopedia of All Regular Cast Members in Western Series, 1949–1959, *first published in 1997 by McFarland.*

LIBRARY OF CONGRESS CATALOGUING-IN-PUBLICATION DATA

Aaker, Everett.
Television western players of the fifties : a biographical encyclopedia of all regular cast members in western series, 1949–1959 / by Everett Aaker.
p. cm.
Includes filmographies, bibliographical references, and index.

ISBN-13: 978-0-7864-3087-1
(softcover : 50# alkaline paper) ∞

1. Western television programs—United States. 2. Television actors and actresses—United States—Biography—Dictionaries.
I. Title.
PN1995.9.W4A24 2007
791.45'6278'03—dc21
[B] 97-13647

On the cover: Cast of *Gunsmoke* ca. 1974 (CBS-TV, 1955–75) CBS/Photofest; background ©2007 Photodisc

Manufactured in the United States of America

McFarland & Company, Inc., Publishers
Box 611, Jefferson, North Carolina 28640
www.mcfarlandpub.com

This book is dedicated to

Will Hutchins
Don Diamond
Sean McClory
Jan Merlin

ACKNOWLEDGMENTS

Thanks are due to the following people:

David Ragan

The late Leslie Halliwell

Bob and Janette Anderson

Dennis Howells, Michael Selby, Trevor Brown,
John Buttery, Robin Ray, Brian Beard
and the other members of "The Black Bird Club"

Bob and Janet Ainsley and the "Burton Manor" crowd

Boyd Magers

Bill Cappello

Jim and Tom Goldrup

Valerie Caine

Susan Poole

Andrew and Suzanne Hight

John Andrew

My father and my sister

All of the players who supplied me with information

The majority of the photographs in this book were supplied by

The Cinema Shop, San Francisco, California

The Bijou Collectibles, Fullerton, California

Stephen Sally, New York

Ed Mason, The King's Road, Chelsea, London, England

POVERTY ROW STUDIOS 1929-1940

PITTS, MICHAEL   McFARLAND 1997

SWEETHEARTS of THE SAGE

RAINEY, BUCK   McFARLAND 1992

THOSE GREAT COWBOY SIDEKICKS

ROTHEL, DAVID   SCARECROW PRESS. 1984

Deanna Brewster

COMMUNITY MEETINGS

Joshua Farrar, Ashland Town Manager, will host five community meetings during the months of April & May. The following topics will be discussed at the meetings: May 2020 Town Council elections and updates on Town happenings. In addition, residents will have ample opportunity to discuss other Town related issues with Mr. Farrar. All meetings start at 6:00 PM.

29 April Pride of Hanover

30 April Ashland Woods

6 May Sedgefield

8 May Patrick Henry YMCA

16 May Ashland Library

www.AshlandVA.gov

TABLE OF CONTENTS

INTRODUCTION

Since the appearance of the first Western series shot expressly for the small screen (*The Lone Ranger* in 1949), more than 150 Westerns have aired on television. Nearly 50 percent of these made their debut between 1955 and 1960. Eighteen Westerns started in 1958 alone, when 12 out of the top 25 highest-rated shows were Westerns (including seven out of the top ten). The genre reached its peak in 1959, when 32 Westerns were shown weekly on prime-time television. In no other decade were Westerns as popular as during the 1950s.

Television Western Players of the Fifties attempts to chart the careers and appearances of every actor and actress who had a regular role in a Western series, network or syndicated, between September 15, 1949, and December 31, 1959. Where possible—which usually means where a series star is discussed—there are biographical and family details; an account of how the player first went into show business; a record of marriages and offspring; details of the role which the individual played in the Western series; in some cases what his or her contemporaries thought of the actor as a person (and, perhaps more importantly, what the actor thought of himself or herself or the series); what motivated each to make the choices he or she did; and details of the actor's subsequent career, whether he or she went on to even greater triumphs or slid into obscurity.

For actors no longer alive, an account is given of the circumstances of their deaths together with some indication of personal wealth if known. For those who were alive at the time of this writing, entries note where they live today and whether they are still professionally active or have moved on to other areas of endeavor.

In the case of supporting actors or bit players in a series, the entries tend to be less detailed, usually consisting of the player's dates (if known) together with information about the character he or she played in the series. A short entry indicates that comparatively little information has been published or obtained about an individual; that the person could not be traced; that he or she has failed to respond to inquiries; or that the person has politely declined to answer.

The primary source of information about a television series has been press releases issued at the time the series was first aired. Although the book does contain important information about the series (particularly in the Appendix), the primary focus is on the players themselves.

Biographical information has been culled from numerous encyclopedias and magazines, from press releases, and from the individuals themselves. Additional information, much of it never previously published, has been provided by interviews with the artists, face to face, by telephone, or by correspondence. When actors have not responded to inquiries, the author has often had to fall back on secondary material.

If any artist feels that he or she has been unjustly neglected or omitted altogether, the author would be very pleased to hear from that individual or from any of his or her relatives, friends or professional colleagues who can supply additional information about the subject. (The author can be reached care of McFarland.) In the case of any player who is deceased but is not denoted as such in the entry, the author would like to hear from anyone who has the details.

Each entry is complete with what the author hopes is a full list of film and serial credits, together with a list of miniseries and television series. In the case of television series, the name of the character whom the performer played is also included to facilitate identification. These lists are in some cases the most complete ever published and were compiled with help from the artists themselves. A number of very obscure credits were located by modern technological means. Nevertheless, the writer cannot guarantee that every bit part in every direct-to-video release or obscure spaghetti western is represented here.

It is doubtful whether any general conclusions can be drawn from the entries contained in this book. Some of the players whom one might have assumed had it made for life are now to be found on Skid Row, while others who do not appear to have worked creatively in years or who have had erratic careers are living the lives of millionaires. Some players were very reticent, while others were disarmingly frank about themselves and their contemporaries. Some players were genuine Westerners born and brought up on a ranch, while others were classically trained stage actors who by chance found themselves cast in Western television series. Researching such varied and interesting lives has been a most rewarding effort that has turned up some fascinating anecdotes, some of which are recounted here for the first time.

The definition of the Western in this book is broad, which explains the presence of stars from series only marginally concerned with Western themes such as *Northwest Passage* and *Circus Boy*. The only series omitted from this volume are a couple of marginal Westerns where the Western element was so greatly outweighed by the crime element that the series seem more properly to belong to a companion volume on detective players; any series that was only shown locally or live and that did not come out of Hollywood; series that were merely rehashes of old Western movies with minimal contemporary input; and *Red Ryder*. Although this alleged series of 39 episodes starring Allan "Rocky" Lane is contained in some volumes, more authoritative historians have indicated that the series never went beyond the pilot stage. No one has any recollection of having seen an episode nor of it being in any television buff's collection.

With the advent of satellite and cable television and home video players, many of these series have become newly available to the public. Thus viewers have the opportunity either to meet the players for the first time, or to make their reacquaintance.

Since I do not approve of books written by committee, I compiled all of this book myself. It therefore follows that any mistakes or omissions are mine. This book is primarily intended to inform and entertain and to be the definitive reference work on the artists contained herein, a purpose which this writer hopes it fulfills.

EVERETT AAKER
1997

THE PLAYERS

LEE AAKER

The child actor was born Lee William Aaker in Inglewood, California, on September 25, 1943. He has one brother named Dee (born in 1942) who also acted. His mother, later Mrs. Miles Wilbour, was a dance teacher who enrolled him at a dancing academy in Inglewood. He was educated by private tutors on the set and at the William Kelsoe Elementary School in Inglewood. He made his screen debut in a bit role in *Louisiana* (1947). In December 1948 he performed a song and dance routine at the Orpheum Theatre in Los Angeles. His first major role was in *Benjy* (1950), a semidocumentary in which he played a crippled boy in a Los Angeles hospital.

His most memorable film role was as Johnny, the son of Geraldine Page in the Western *Hondo* (1953). Around this time it was said that his earnings were all being saved for him and he planned to buy his parents a new house. In the studio or on location, his tutor went with him and said that his charge was a bright student. He is best remembered as Corporal Rusty in the Western television series *The Adventures of Rin Tin Tin* (1954–1959). Rusty was orphaned in an Indian raid. He and his faithful canine companion Rin Tin Tin were adopted and made honorary troopers by the cavalry soldiers of Fort Apache, Arizona. They assisted the cavalry and townspeople in the nearby town of Mesa Grande to establish and maintain justice on the frontier. Each episode was shot in two to two-and-a-half days on a budget of $25,000.

Aaker also appeared in many anthology series of the 1950s. His last recorded acting credit was an episode of *The Lucy Show* in 1963. He later became a production assistant on the television series *Route 66*, but was forced to stop when he developed panic attacks. This led to him becoming reclusive and being unable to either fly in a plane or face live audiences. He developed an alcohol problem, but has been sober since the late 1970s. He stayed for 14 months with close friend Paul Petersen to get his life back together. Afterwards his profession was carpentry, which he basically enjoyed, although he says that he is now retired from this. Recently he has taught ski school to handicapped children. He resides in Northridge, California. He has been married and divorced, but has no children. In 1993 he stepped out of obscurity to expose an impostor who had been impersonating him at conventions for the past five years.

Lee Aaker Filmography

1947: *Louisiana.*
1950: *Benjy.*
1952: *My Son John, The Atomic City, No Room for the Groom, O. Henry's Full House* ("Ransom of Red Chief" segment), *The Greatest Show on Earth, Something to Live For.*
1953: *Jeopardy, Take Me to Town, Arena, Mister Scoutmaster, Hondo, Desperate Search.*
1954: *Ricochet Romance, Destry.*
1956: *Bigger Than Life.*

Television Series

1954–1959: *The Adventures of Rin Tin Tin* as Corporal Rusty.

Sources

Best, Marc. *Their Hearts Were Young and Gay.* South Brunswick and New York: Barnes, 1975.
Dye, David. *Child and Youth Actors: Filmographies of Their Entire Careers, 1914–1985.* Jefferson, NC: McFarland, 1988.
Magers, Boyd. *Western Clippings* magazine, 1993.

Lee Aaker in *The Adventures of Rin Tin Tin.*

Perry, Jeb H. *Screen Gems: A History of Columbia Pictures Television from Cohn to Coke, 1948–1983.* Metuchen NJ: Scarecrow, 1991.

Picture Show Annual. London: Amalgamated Press, 1954.

NICK ADAMS

Nick Adams was an actor whose life and achievements were somewhat overshadowed by the bizarre manner in which he met his death. He rather defied being placed in any category because he was not handsome enough to be a movie leading man, nor old enough to be called a character actor. He once said, "My goal is to be a good actor rather than a personality." Considering his lack of formal education and dramatic training, he was extremely tenacious in his pursuit of elusive stardom. While he appeared in 30 films, his greatest success came on television when he essayed the role of a Civil War veteran in *The Rebel.*

Nick Adams was born Nicholas Aloysius Adamschock in Nanticoke, Pennsylvania, on July 10, 1931, the son of Peter Adamschock, a Ukrainian coal miner, and his wife, Catherine. He had a brother, Andrew D. Adams, whom he put through college and who became a doctor. His limited education was obtained at St. Peter's College. He was a devout Roman Catholic. While he was still a teenager his family relocated to Jersey City, where his parents became janitors of an apartment complex. While on a bus, he read a story about an unknown becoming a Hollywood star. This fired in him the desire to study acting. He found the theatrical district in Manhattan, but enjoyed no luck. He haunted New York book shops. While he was browsing in one, another actor whose day job was a salesman in the store told him that a company was auditioning for a play in the Carnegie Hall building. Adams went to the auditions, and while there he encountered Jack Palance, another hopeful from a similar ethnic background. They both won roles in the play *The Silver Tassie.* Although he subsequently appeared in several other non–Equity plays, his earnings were negligible and most of his income came from being a Jersey City pool hustler.

When Palance found fame in the movies in 1950, Adams hitchhiked across the country to Hollywood. He found a place to live in a boiler room (in exchange for mowing the lawn) and obtained an agent. He did menial jobs such as dishwasher in an ice cream parlor, truck driver, gas station attendant and usher-cum-maintenance man at a Beverly Hills theater. He was drafted in 1952 and served as a radio officer on a Coast Guard frigate along the California coast. While there in June 1954 he read in a newspaper that director John Ford was casting for the motion picture *Mister Roberts* at Warner Bros.

He rode to the studio on a bus, found the casting room office and introduced himself to Solly Biano, head of Warners' casting, who took him to see Ford; Adams explained that he was a radio man with enough leave to make a motion picture. An impressed Ford cast him in the movie, and Adams soon found himself on the plane to Hawaii with the cast and crew of *Mister Roberts.* He engineered a 90-day leave to complete the role.

Adams made a number of movies for Warner Bros., of which one of the best remembered was *Rebel Without a Cause* (1955). James Dean became his idol and best friend. Adams also became very friendly with Natalie Wood and her mother. Allegedly he was personally asked by Wood's mother to teach Natalie the facts of life when she was 14. He also accompanied her and Robert Wagner on their first honeymoon. In 1959 Adams met and married actress Carol Nugent, by whom he had two children (Allyson Lee Adams, born in 1960, and Jeb Stuart Adams, born in 1962).

Adams wrote to Andrew J. Fenady, a writer and producer, about a project which subsequently came to nothing. The two men met for lunch and became friends. Adams visited the producer's house and asked if he could announce during an upcoming chat show appearance that they were going to do a television series. This evolved into the series *The Rebel.* In it Adams played Johnny Yuma, an

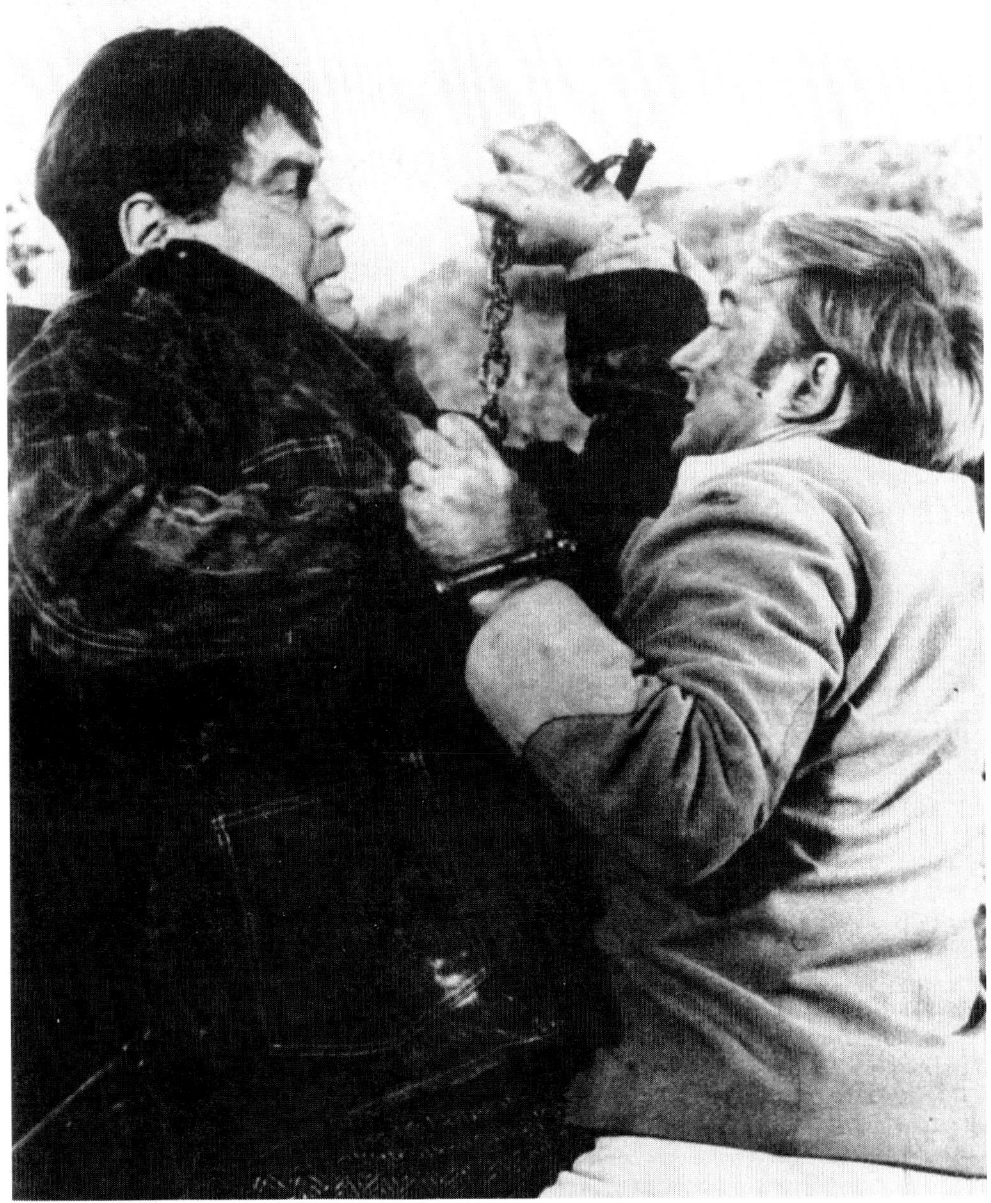

Nick Adams (right) wrestles with guest-star Frank Overton in *The Rebel*.

ex–Confederate Cavalry officer who turns troubleshooter in the Wild West. Yuma took the South's defeat personally and searched the West to find peace. In doing this, Adams created a truly tragic hero. This Western was unique because it showed the aftermath of the Civil War as a period of great hardship and uncertainty rather than as a pool for the talents of Civil War veterans.

It was originally intended to be shown as an episode of *Dick Powell's Zane Grey Theater*. Instead it fell into the hands of producers Mark Goodson and Bill Todman, who loved the concept and invested their own money in a pilot. Fenady shared a production credit with them. The memorable theme song *Johnny Yuma* was sung by Johnny Cash. The shooting schedule for each half-hour episode was three days, each episode cost approximately $40,000 and Adams was paid $5,000 a show. The series ran successfully for two years. It was a very highly rated program which was scuttled by network politics rather than poor audience response. Adams subsequently followed it up with a contemporary series called *Saints and Sinners* in which he played a crusading reporter. This was a short-lived flop.

He guest-starred in episodes of many series and made a number of movies of which his most memorable contribution was *Twilight of Honor* (1963) as an accused killer. After spending $8,000 of his own money campaigning for one, he received an Oscar nomination as Best Supporting Actor. After that his movie career began to disintegrate and he was forced to go abroad to make money and play leading roles in films. All of them were in Grade Z fare with ridiculous titles. He also occasionally essayed the lead in some American B features.

The low-quality films in which he appeared had more to do with the depressing climate of the American movie industry during the 1960s and the low number of films being shot in the United States than with Adams' ability. There were many talented former and future stars who found the going very rough during that period.

Adams was involved in a bitter custody battle over his children after his marriage ended in divorce in 1966. He won this, but during Carol Nugent's visitation period, her new boyfriend Paul Rapp tried to discipline the children. Adams obtained a court order that henceforth his ex-wife could visit the children but not with non-related male adults. Adams was under such stress during this period that he was prescribed paraldehyde, an anti-depressant normally used to treat alcoholics with D.T.s, although Adams was only a light social drinker.

Adams went to Italy to make a movie for which he was paid $50,000, first class travel and all his expenses. Upon his return he made an arrangement to meet Ervin "Tip" Roeder, his attorney and business manager on February 5, 1968.

During the intervening weekend, Adams had been seen in the grounds of his home at 2126 El Roble Lane in the exclusive Trousdale Estates area of Beverly Hills with his children. Eyewitnesses later testified that he had been in excellent spirits. Adams never showed up to keep the appointment with Roeder. After persistent telephone calls to his house went unanswered, Roeder drove to investigate. When he arrived late on February 7, 1968, the house was in darkness. Roeder was forced to break open a back window in order to obtain access. He eventually found his way to Adams' bedroom where he discovered the 36-year-old actor dead, fully clothed and propped against a wall in a sitting position with his eyes wide open. A telephone was within easy reach, but not any of the equipment deemed necessary to have injected himself with the instantaneous fatal dose of paraldehyde and other drugs.

This has strengthened suspicion over the years that he was murdered. This theory was given increased weight when it was discovered that most of Adams' memorabilia from his career together with family effects were missing from his home. There was no suicide note. Roeder had links with the underworld. In June 1981 he and his wife, the vivacious 39-year-old former actress Jenny Maxwell (who appeared with Elvis Presley in 1961's *Blue Hawaii* and with Adams on television), were mysteriously gunned down outside their Beverly Hills condominium. This was widely believed to be an underworld hit especially since Maxwell had revealed an intention the previous day of informing the authorities how Adams had really met his end.

Nick Adams was buried at S.S. Cyril and Methodius Cemetery at Berwick, Pennsylvania, not far from where he was born.

Nick Adams Filmography

1952: *Somebody Loves Me.*
1955: *Mister Roberts, Strange Lady in Town, I Died a Thousand Times, Rebel Without a Cause, Picnic.*
1956: *The Last Wagon, A Strange Adventure, Our Miss Brooks.*
1957: *Sing Boy Sing!, Fury at Showdown.*
1958: *The FBI Story, No Time for Sergeants, Teacher's Pet.*
1959: *Pillow Talk.*
1962: *The Interns, Hell Is for Heroes!*
1963: *The Young Lovers, Twilight of Honor, The Hook, A Girl Named Tamiko.*

1965: *Young Dillinger, Frankenstein Conquers the World, Monster Zero.*
1966: *Die Monster Die, Don't Worry We'll Think of a Title.*
1967: *Fever Heat, The Killing Bottle.*
1968: *Mission Mars.*

Television Series

1959–1961: *The Rebel* as Johnny Yuma.
1962–1963: *Saints and Sinners* as Nick Alexander.

Sources

Adams, Nick. *Film Show Annual.* London: Robinson, 1958.
Anderson, Bob. "Branded with the Fenady Touch." *Trail Dust* magazine, spring 1995.
Austin, John. *More of Hollywood's Unsolved Mysteries.* New York: Shapolsky, 1991.
Parish, James Robert. *Hollywood Death Book.* Las Vegas, NV: Pioneer, 1992.
Rovin, Jeff. *TV Babylon.* New York: Signet, 1987.
Schessler, Ken. *This Is Hollywood.* Published privately, 1995.

JOHN ALDERSON

Born in England in 1916, John Alderson was active in U.S. movies and television from the early 1950s. A familiar character actor, his only regular series role was as a cavalry sergeant in *Boots and Saddles*. The actor modestly admits, "Westerns were only about ten percent of my work." In 1965 he briefly returned to England for "The Gunfighters" episodes of the classic BBC sci-fi serial *Dr. Who*. In this, ironically, he played Wyatt Earp in a version of the Gunfight at the OK Corral. Alderson currently resides in retirement in Glendale, California.

John Alderson Filmography

1952: *Against All Flags.*
1953: *The Desert Rats, South Sea Woman.*
1954: *King Richard and the Crusaders, Casanova's Big Night, Living It Up.*
1955: *To Catch a Thief, Moonfleet, Violent Saturday, The Scarlet Coat, Target Zero.*
1957: *Shootout at Medicine Bend, Spoilers of the Forest, Don't Go Near the Water, The Last Stagecoach West.*
1958: *Wolf Larsen, The Young Lions.*
1959: *No Name on the Bullet, Pork Chop Hill.*
1961: *Romanoff and Juliet.*
1964: *My Fair Lady.*
1965: *I Deal in Danger, The War Lord.*
1967: *Double Trouble.*
1968: *The Hellfighters, The Molly Maguires.*
1969: *The Dubious Patriots.*
1970: *The Deserter, You Can't Win 'Em All.*
1974: *The Klansman.*
1975: *The Log of the Black Pearl* (TV).
1976: *The Duchess and the Dirtwater Fox.*
1977: *Candleshoe.*
1978: *The Cat from Outer Space.*
1981: *Ragtime.*
1982: *Evil Under the Sun.*
1990: *Young Guns II.*

Television Series

1957–1958: *Boots and Saddles—The Story of the Fifth Cavalry* as Sergeant Bullock.

Sources

Correspondence between Alderson and the author.

REX ALLEN

The "Arizona Cowboy" was born Rex Elvie Allen in Willcox, Arizona, on December 31, 1920. His father was born at Fort Chadnorne, Texas, and moved to Arizona when aged 15. He became a rancher who endured problems similar to those depicted in many Western films. Rex Allen lived for the first five years of his life on a ranch about 40 miles north of Willcox. When his brother was bitten by a rattlesnake and died, the family moved into the town itself. They lived there for about 12 months before moving to a ranch about five miles outside Willcox where he attended school.

For a few years he lived the life of an average ranch boy milking cows, branding cattle and repairing fences. For a hobby his father played a fiddle and needed a guitarist as a backup, so he bought his son a guitar together with a book of instructions. While at high school he sang and played at glee clubs and church choirs. When he graduated from high school in 1939, he was offered a scholarship to the University of Arizona. Instead he won a statewide talent contest by giving a guitar solo which obtained him a job singing on the radio in Phoenix. He joined a rodeo on the East Coast which nearly ended his career prematurely when he was thrown from a bull. When he recovered in 1943 his first daily radio program was on a small station in Trenton, New Jersey. For two years he worked in a rubber mill during the day and on the radio at night.

Subsequently he obtained a job with a group called the Sleepy Hollow Gang at Allentown, Pennsylvania. While there, several of the acts featured on the prestigious radio show *National Barn Dance* appeared at the big outdoor park. At the suggestion of one of the acts, Allen went to Chicago to audition for the show. He passed the audition with flying colors and within three months in 1945 he was being starred on the show. He was stricken with an optical problem which delicate corrective surgery overcame. During that time he sang to over five million people and had several hit records.

Over the years he was approached by several studios and personalities to do a Western film series. Paramount, who still owned the rights to the *Hopalong Cassidy* series, planned on starring Allen as a replacement for William Boyd in a new feature film series. Gene Autry had an option at Columbia to produce a series of Western features and planned to star Allen. Roy Rogers intended to leave Republic for 20th Century–Fox and wanted Allen as his costar. But none of these deals amounted to anything.

Rex Allen in *Frontier Doctor.*

One day he received a telephone call from Herbert J. Yates, President of Republic Studios, who was in Chicago and had seen and heard him on *National Barn Dance*. Yates wanted to talk to him in person. Allen went and talked to him. Republic flew him to Hollywood for a screen test which was successful and signed him to a seven-year contract to star in his own series of Westerns. His contract expressly stated that he was not allowed to do television.

His screen debut came in the appropriately titled *The Arizona Cowboy* (1950), which set the pattern for the mixture of humor, songs and adventure which comprised his subsequent 18 features for Republic. When Allen left Chicago to join Republic Pictures, Phillips Petroleum (one of his radio sponsors) moved his program *The Rex Allen Show* to Hollywood where it played over CBS. *The Rex Allen Show* was a spin-off from *National Barn Dance*.

His films were normally shot for between $50,000 and $60,000 in black and white in five days. The songs were usually very successfully integrated into the action. Although his films were not nearly so elaborate as those of Roy Rogers, by 1951 he was one of the top five Western stars in movies. His famous horse Koko, which he did not ride in his first movie, was a stud horse bought by horse trainer Glen Randall and originally intended for Dale Evans. The horse was believed to be half Morgan and half Quarter. Allen later traveled with that horse over half a million miles on the rodeo circuit. The original Koko died in 1968, aged 28. Allen's favorite of his own movies is *The Rodeo King and the Señorita* (1951), a reworking of *The Cowboy and the Lady* (1938) which starred Gary Cooper. His favorite director was William Witney.

Despite fighting television for many years, Republic was eventually forced to capitulate to it. An executive decision was made to ease themselves into television while still maintaining some feature film production. Allen, who was still under contract to them, stayed to do *Frontier Doctor* (1958), a syndicated television series, and to appear in a couple of big-budget movies (which were never made).

Frontier Doctor was devised by the star and sold to the studio. It was set in Rising Springs, Arizona, in the early 1900s. Allen played Dr. Bill Baxter, a medico who struggles to enforce neglected medical laws and assist pioneers against Indians and badmen. One novel feature of this series was that Baxter did not carry a gun, although he was not slow to use his fists when the occasion demanded. When Republic became locked in confrontation with the Screen Actors Guild because Herbert J. Yates refused to pay residuals, Yates was blacklisted and disbarred from any further production. He sold the studio to CBS, which effectively ended the Allen series.

One night shortly after that, Allen was telephoned at home by a gentleman who turned out to be Walt Disney. Disney asked Allen if he would care to work for him and Allen replied in the affirmative. He subsequently went on to narrate numerous nature films and to do character voices in cartoons. He appeared at numerous rodeos and fairs and did commercials, notably for dog food. He is also an extremely successful songwriter, with over 300 published songs to his credit. He owns a 20-acre spread called The Diamond X in Lancaster, California, and currently resides in Sonita, Arizona, a few miles from the Rex Allen Museum which houses his memorabilia. He lost his right eye in an accident and wears a glass replacement.

In 1945 he married Bonnie Linder (from Newhawka, Nebraska), whom he met when she appeared with him on the radio in Chicago. They have three sons: Rex, Jr., born in 1947; twins Curtis Lee and Mark Wayne, born in 1950; and a daughter, Bonita. They were wed until 1978. He has since wed twice more, the latest time in 1992.

Rex Allen Filmography

1950: *The Arizona Cowboy, Hills of Oklahoma, Redwood Forest Trail, Under Mexicali Stars, Trail of Robin Hood.*
1951: *Silver City Bonanza, Thunder in God's Country, The Rodeo King and the Señorita, Utah Wagon Train.*
1952: *Colorado Sundown, The Last Musketeer, Border Saddlemates, Old Oklahoma Plains, South Pacific Trail.*
1953: *Old Overland Trail, Iron Mountain Trail, Down Laredo Way, Shadows of Tombstone, Red River Shore.*
1954: *The Phantom Stallion.*
1960: *For the Love of Mike.*
1961: *The Tomboy and the Champ.*
1976: *The Secret of Navajo Cave.*

Television Series

1957–1958: *Frontier Doctor* as Dr. Bill Baxter.

Sources

Copeland, Bobby J. "Meet Rex Allen the Arizona Cowboy." *Films of the Golden Age* magazine, winter 1996.

Courneau, Ernest N. *The Hall of Fame of Western Film Stars.* North Quincy, MA: Christopher, 1969.

McClure, Arthur F. and Jones, Ken D. *Heroes, Heavies and Sagebrush.* South Brunswick and New York: Barnes, 1972.

Miller, Lee O. *The Great Cowboy Stars of Movies and Television.* New Rochelle, NY: Arlington House, 1979.

Rothel, David. *The Singing Cowboys.* San Diego, CA: Barnes, 1978.

Speed, F. Maurice. *The Western Film and Television Annual.* London: MacDonald, 1957.

BOB ANDERSON

This supporting actor played the part of the town blacksmith in the Western television series *Wichita Town*. Mr. Anderson is understood to be deceased, but the details do not appear to have been recorded.

Bob Anderson Filmography

1937: *Wings Over Honolulu.*
1943: *Gildersleeve on Broadway, The Mexican Spitfire's Blessed Event, The Adventures of a Rookie, Higher and Higher, Tender Comrade, The Iron Major.*
1944: *The Falcon Out West, Action in Arabia, Marine Raiders.*
1945: *Uncle Harry, Johnny Angel, West of the Pecos, Bride by Mistake.*
1946: *Nocturne, Without Reservation.*
1947: *The Bishop's Wife, The Woman on the Beach.*
1948: *Kidnapped.*
1949: *Undertow, Francis.*
1950: *Winchester '73, The Desert Hawk.*
1951: *Two of a Kind, Bright Victory, Silver City, The Mob.*
1952: *Rancho Notorious, Untamed Frontier.*
1953: *Born to the Saddle, Take Me to Town, The Lawless Breed, Miss Sadie Thompson.*
1954: *The Outlaw Stallion, The Long Long Trailer.*
1956: *Fury at Gunsight Pass, Showdown at Abilene, Forbidden Planet, Toy Tiger.*
1957: *Pal Joey, The Phantom Stagecoach, The Tall T, The Night Runner.*
1958: *The Man Who Died Twice, The Left Handed Gun, Buchanan Rides Alone.*
1961: *The Gambler Wore a Gun.*
1962: *Stagecoach to Dancer's Rock.*
1964: *Advance to the Rear.*
1969: *Young Billy Young.*

Television Series

1959–1960: *Wichita Town* as Aeneas MacLinahan.

Sources

Summers, Neil. *The Official TV Western Book Volume #2.* Vienna, WV: Old West Shop Publishing, 1989.
Thomas, Tony. *Joel McCrea—Riding the High Country.* Burbank, CA: Riverwood Press, 1991.

JOHN ANDERSON

John Anderson was born on a farm in Clayton, Illinois, on October 20, 1922, and was raised in the larger town of Quincy, Illinois. He was interested in acting from childhood. After graduating from high school, he moved to St. Louis, Missouri, where he was hired as a radio announcer. He was fired from this job, but almost immediately was hired as an actor aboard a Mississippi showboat called "Goldenrod," where he performed in melodramas for about six months in 1942.

He was drafted into the Coast Guard during World War II. Afterwards he took advantage of the G.I. Bill Of Rights and obtained an M.A. in drama from the University of Iowa. He did not wish to pursue a career as an academic in the theater, so immediately upon graduation he joined a summer stock theater in Buffalo, New York. When the summer was over, he joined the Cleveland Playhouse, a prestigious resident company.

After discussing the situation with his wife, Anderson left the Cleveland Playhouse after one season in 1950 and journeyed to New York with the hope of landing a role in a Broadway play. Instead, for the next six years he played in off-Broadway shows; played in stock theater in the winter; did industrial shows; and had small roles on live television. He tried without success to win a role in a play on the Great White Way, but he supported himself as a professional actor with no other income throughout this period. In 1956 he finally landed his first Broadway role (as Gooper) in the play *Cat on a Hot Tin Roof,* an enormous hit. He also toured with this play.

While touring in Los Angeles, he was approached by an agent who told him to look him up if he was interested in relocating. When the play folded, Anderson returned to Hollywood where his first role was as a crazy heavy in an episode of *Gunsmoke* in 1956. This caused a sensation and made Anderson an in-demand actor. Doors were opened to him and he chalked up large numbers of television appearances in a relatively short space of time. He played about 20 different characters in episodes of *The Rifleman* alone. His sole regular role was as Virgil Earp, the brother of Wyatt Earp, in *The Life and Legend of Wyatt Earp* (1959–1961). When Hugh O'Brian left the series, it was proposed to continue the series with the Virgil Earp character as the lead, but it did not materialize. Of his 700 television roles, his two favorites were an episode of *Here Come the Brides,* in which he played a charming conman who romanced Joan Blondell, and an episode of *Thriller* in which he played a grave robber. In the 1980s he had a recurring role as the title character's father on the *MacGyver* television series.

He is also well remembered from the movie *Psycho* (1960), in which he played an inquisitive used car salesman. He also made a specialty of playing Abraham Lincoln in three television programs, two films and two Los Angeles stage plays; he also toured twice in a stage production of *The Lincoln-Douglas Debates.* One of his biggest career disappointments was when he played Sylvus Hammond in *Ride the High Country* (1962). This film, which was one of his favorites, did not receive the promotion or distribution it deserved. He was awarded the Western Heritage Award by the National Cowboy Hall Of Fame in 1967.

John Anderson died of a heart attack suffered in Sherman Oaks, California, on August 7, 1992, at age 69. He was survived by two sisters; two children (Jeffrey and Kelsey); five grandchildren; and a great-grandson. At the time of his death he was preparing a Broadway production of *In the Sweet By and By,* which he had performed in the Los Angeles Back Alley Theater in the early 1980s.

John Anderson Filmography

1958: *The True Story of Lynn Stuart.*

1959: *Last Train from Gun Hill.*

1960: *Psycho.*

1962: *Ride the High Country, Geronimo, A Walk on the Wild Side.*

1965: *The Satan Bug, The Hallelujah Trail.*

1966: *Scalplock* (TV), *Namu the Killer Whale, The Fortune Cookie, A Covenant with Death.*

1967: *Welcome to Hard Times.*

1968: *Massacre Harbor, 5 Card Stud, Day of the Evil Gun.*

1969: *A Man Called Gannon, Heaven with a Gun, Young Billy Young, The Great Bank Robbery, Set This Town on Fire* (TV).

1970: *Soldier Blue, Cotton Comes to Harlem, The Animals.*

1971: *The Stepmother.*

1972: *Man and Boy, Molly and Lawless John.*

1973: *Call to Danger* (TV), *Brock's Last Case* (TV), *Il Consigliore (*a.k.a. *The Counselor), Executive Action.*

1974: *The Dove, Heatwave* (TV), *Smile Jenny You're Dead* (TV), *Manhunter* (TV).

1975: *Dead Man on the Run* (TV), *Death Among Friends* (TV), *The Specialist.*

1976: *The Dark Side of Innocence* (TV), *Bridger: The 40th Day* (TV).

1977: *Tail Gunner Joe* (TV), *Peter Lundy and the Medicine Hat Stallion* (TV), *The Last Hurrah* (TV), *The Lincoln Conspiracy.*

1978: *Donner Pass: The Road to Survival* (TV), *The Deerslayer* (TV).

1979: *In Search of Historic Jesus.*

1980: *Smokey and the Bandit II, Zoot Suit.*

1982: *The First Time* (TV), *Missing Children: A Mother's Story* (TV).

1983: *Lone Wolf McQuade.*

1986: *Never Too Young to Die, Scorpion (*a.k.a. *The Summons).*

1987: *American Harvest* (TV).

1988: *Eight Men Out.*

1989: *Full Exposure: The Sex Tapes Scandal* (TV).

1990: *Follow Your Heart* (TV).

1991: *In Broad Daylight* (TV), *Babe Ruth* (TV), *Daddy* (TV).

1992: *Bed of Lies* (TV).

Television Series

1959–1961: *The Life and Legend of Wyatt Earp* as Virgil Earp.

Miniseries

1976: *Once an Eagle.*
1976–1977: *Rich Man Poor Man—Book II.*
1979: *Backstairs at the Whitehouse.*
1985: *North and South.*
1986: *Dream West.*

Sources

Goldrup, Jim and Tom Goldrup. *Feature Players: The Stories Behind the Faces Volume #2.* Published privately, 1992.
Jarvis, Everett G. *Final Curtain: Deaths of Noted Movie and TV Personalities.* New York: Citadel, 1995.
Jones, Ken D., Arthur F. McClure and Alfred E. Twomey. *Character People.* Secaucus, NJ: Citadel, 1979.
Quinlan, David. *Illustrated Directory of Film Character Actors.* London: Batsford, 1995.

Portrait of John Anderson, who appeared in *The Life and Legend of Wyatt Earp*.

STANLEY ANDREWS

Stanley Andrews was born in Chicago, Illinois on August 28, 1891, although his parents emigrated from Cornwall, England. He was a successful radio actor (notably playing "Daddy Warbucks" on the *Little Orphan Annie* show) before making his screen debut in the 1930s. He achieved his greatest fame quite late in life when he played "The Old Ranger," the host and narrator of the highly successful syndicated television series *Death Valley Days.*

The factual stories told of the legends and folklore of Death Valley. It began as a radio series in 1930 to promote 20 Mule Team Borax. It was the creation of Ruth Woodman, a New York writer, who ironically at the time had never visited the location of the stories. The atmosphere was enhanced by the opening bugle call together with the scene of the 20 Mule Team hauling the borax wagons out of the desert. The radio series lasted from 1930 to 1945. The television series commenced in 1952 but there were a variety of hosts during its 20-year run; Andrews was the first and lasted until 1965. *Death Valley Days* received a single Emmy award nomination in 1954 as Best Western or Adventure Series in the only year that category existed.

Stanley Andrews died in Hollywood on June 23, 1969, at age 77.

Stanley Andrews Filmography

1933: *Roman Scandals.*
1934: *Evelyn Prentice.*
1935: *Wings in the Dark, College Scandal, Mississippi, All the King's Horses, Private Worlds,*

People Will Talk, The Crusades, Nevada, Wanderer of the Wasteland, Drift Fence, Hold 'Em Yale, Escape from Devil's Island, The Big Broadcast of 1936, She Gets Her Man, Alias Mary Dow, Goin' to Town, Men Without Names, Murder Man, She Couldn't Take It, Stolen Harmony, It's in the Air, After Office Hours.

1936: *Wild Brian Kent, Desire, In His Steps, Happy Go Lucky, The Texas Rangers, Mr. Deeds Goes to Town, Sins of the Children, Pennies from Heaven, Drift Fence, Alibi for Murder, Dangerous Intrigue, Florida Special.*

1937: *John Meade's Woman, High Wide and Handsome, The Devil's Playground, Easy Living, The Man Who Found Himself, Nancy Steele Is Missing, She's Dangerous, The Man Who Cried Wolf, Double or Nothing, Madame X, Big City.*

1938: *The Buccaneer, Cocoanut Grove, Spawn of the North, The Mysterious Rider, Prairie Moon, When G-Men Step In, Blondie, Adventure in Sahara, Alexander's Ragtime Band, I'll Give a Million, Kentucky, The Lone Ranger* (serial), *Stablemates, Forbidden Valley, Hold That Co-ed, Juvenile Court, Shine On Harvest Moon, The Lady Objects, The Higgins Family.*

1939: *Andy Hardy Gets Spring Fever, Mr. Smith Goes to Washington, Homicide Bureau, Beau Geste, Union Pacific, Geronimo, Hotel Imperial, The Green Hornet* (serial), *The Lady's from Kentucky, Coast Guard, Golden Boy.*

1940: *King Of The Royal Mounted* (serial), *The Blue Bird, Little Old New York, Brigham Young, Kit Carson, The Westerner, Maryland, The Man Who Wouldn't Talk, Colorado.*

1941: *In Old Colorado, Play Girl, Meet John Doe, Strange Alibi, Mr. and Mrs. North, Wild Geese Calling, Time Out for Rhythm, Borrowed Hero, Dead Men Tell.*

1942: *To the Shores of Tripoli, Valley of the Sun, North to the Klondike, The Fleet's In, Reap the Wild Wind, The Major and the Minor, Canal Zone, My Gal Sal, The Postman Didn't Ring, Ten Gentlemen from West Point, In Old Oklahoma (*a.k.a. *War of the Wildcats).*

1943: *Dixie, Riding High, Daredevils of the West* (serial), *Crash Dive, The Ox-Bow Incident, Flight for Freedom, True To Life, Canyon City.*

1944: *The Man from Frisco, Murder My Sweet, Tucson Raiders, The Princess and the Pirate, Sensations of 1945, Follow the Boys, Lake Placid Serenade, The Hitler Gang, A Wing and a Prayer, Rosie the Riveter, Vigilantes of Dodge City, Faces In the Fog.*

1945: *Keep Your Powder Dry, Practically Yours, Trail to Vengeance, Road to Utopia, Adventure, Atlantic City, The Daltons Ride Again, Steppin' in Society.*

1946: *The Hoodlum Saint, The Virginian, California, Till the Clouds Roll By, Smoky, Wake Up and Dream, Bad Bascomb, It's a Wonderful Life.*

1947: *Desire Me, Road to Rio, Easy Come Easy Go, Trail Street, Robin Hood of Texas, Michigan Kid, Blaze Of Noon, Sea of Grass, Framed, Scared to Death, Killer Dill, Millie's Daughter, The Fabulous Texan.*

1948: *Montana Belle, Adventures of Frank and Jesse James* (serial), *The Return of Wildfire, Last of the Wild Horses, State of the Union, Sinister Journey, The Dead Don't Dream, The Valiant Hombre, Docks of New Orleans, The Paleface, Northwest Stampede, My Dear Secretary, The Fuller Brush Man, I Remember Mama, Mr. Blandings Builds His Dream House, Perilous Waters, Jinx Money, Best Man Wins, Leather Gloves.*

1949: *Blondie's Big Deal, Brothers in the Saddle, Man from Colorado, Trail of the Yukon, The Last Bandit, Brimstone, Tough Assignment, Fighting Fools.*

1950: *Copper Canyon, Colt .45, Where Danger Lives, Across the Badlands, Arizona Cowboy, Blonde Dynamite, Mule Train, The Nevadan, Outcast of Black Mesa, Salt Lake Raiders, Short Grass, Streets of Ghost Town, Trigger Junior, Two Flags West, Tyrant of the Sea, Under Mexicali Stars, West of Wyoming, Rock Island Trail.*

1951: *The Lemon Drop Kid, Al Jennings of Oklahoma, Saddle Legion, Silver Canyon, Utah Wagon Train, Vengeance Valley, Stage to Tucson, The Texas Rangers, Hot Lead.*

1952: *The Bad and the Beautiful, The Greatest Show on Earth, Carson City, Fargo, Kansas Territory, The Man from the Black Hills, Talk About a Stranger, Thundering Caravans, Waco, And Now Tomorrow, Woman of the North Country, Lone Star.*

1953: *Canadian Mounties Vs. Atomic Invaders* (serial), *Appointment in Honduras, Dangerous Crossing. El Paso Stampede, Ride Vaquero! Ride the Man Down.*

1954: *Dawn at Socorro, Southwest Passage, The Steel Cage.*

1955: *Treasure of Ruby Hills, The Twinkle in God's Eye.*
1956: *Frontier Gambler.*
1958: *Cry Terror!*

Television Series

1952–1965: *Death Valley Days* as "The Old Ranger."

Sources

McClure, Arthur F. and Ken D. Jones. *Heroes, Heavies and Sagebrush.* South Brunswick and New York: Barnes, 1972.
Parish, James Robert. *Hollywood Character Actors.* New Rochelle, NY: Arlington House, 1978.
Picture Show's Who's Who on Screen. London: Amalgamated Press, c. 1956.

TOD ANDREWS

He was born Tod Andrews in Buffalo, New York, on November 10, 1920, the son of Henry Rowland Andrews and Lynda Anderson. He was educated at Washington State College. His ambition was to be a mining engineer until he appeared in a school play. He studied for the stage at the Pasadena Playhouse and with Sanford Meisner at the Neighborhood Playhouse. He made his debut under the name of Michael Ames at Pasadena Community Playhouse, California, in 1940 as Cass in *Winterset.* He made his New York debut at the Guild Theater in 1940 as Fitzgerald in *Quiet Please.* He next appeared as Future Admiral in *My Sister Eileen* in 1940 in New York. When under contract to Warner Bros. and Monogram during the 1940s he continued to use the name of Michael Ames in motion pictures.

He resumed his stage career in 1944 as Dougie in *Storm Operation* in New York. Under the name of Tod Andrews he appeared at the Margo Jones Repertory Theater in Dallas from 1946 to 1948. He appeared as John Buchanan, Junior, in the world premiere of *Summer and Smoke* at the Music Box Theater, New York, in 1948. Director Ida Lupino saw him in the play and decided he was just the actor to play the role of the minister in a controversial film about rape she was shooting called *Outrage* (1950). In late 1950 he took over from Henry Fonda in the play *Mister Roberts* in the title role and toured in this part from 1951 to 1953. In 1954 he took over the part of Linus Larrabee, Jr., in *Sabrina Fair,* and toured America in 1956 in a recital called *The Best of Steinbeck.*

He played a leading role in the small-screen soap opera *First Love* in the mid–1950s, but his greatest television success came with the series *The Gray Ghost* (1957–1958). In it Andrews played the title role of Major John Singleton Mosby. Mosby was a real-life character who had originally been on the Union side in the Civil War, but switched allegiance and became a hero when he staged a series of well-executed raids on Union strongholds. He acquired the tag of "The Gray Ghost" because of his uncanny ability to remain at large.

Advertisers were very skeptical about the advisability of having a Confederate hero at a time of Civil Rights unrest, and the CBS network for whom it was originally intended failed to find a sponsor. Eventually CBS syndicated it to local stations and it became a surprising success. Andrews, who had become something of an authority on the real-life person, toured the South where he was greeted with enormous enthusiasm and warmth. Even so, the series only lasted 39 episodes.

The rest of Andrews' career was spent playing leads in minor movies such as the notorious *From Hell It Came* (1957), bits in major motion pictures and guest-starring roles on television. He played Henry II in *Becket* on stage in Chicago in 1962 and Frank Elgin in *The Country Girl* in Pennsylvania in 1965. In 1969–1970 he appeared in Canada in a revival of *Plaza Suite.* He had a regular role on the soap opera *Bright Promise* during the early 1970s. One of his last roles was as President of the United States Jeremy Haines in the disappointing telemovie *The President's Plane Is Missing* (1971). Tod Andrews died in Beverly Hills on November 6, 1972, at age 51, of a heart

Tod Andrews (center) with Phil Chambers (left) and Ron Hagerthy in *The Gray Ghost.*

attack. His marriages to Gloria Folland and Alice Hooker had ended in divorce, but he was survived by his third wife, Karolyn Rainwater.

Tod Andrews Filmography

1941: *Murder in the Big House, Dive Bomber, They Died with Their Boots On, International Squadron, Dangerously They Live, The Body Disappears.*
1942: *I Was Framed; Captain of the Clouds; Bullet Scars; The Male Animal; Now, Voyager; Spy Ship.*
1943: *Truck Busters, Heaven Can Wait.*
1944: *The Last Ride, Voodoo Man, Return of the Ape Man.*
1950: *Outrage.*
1956: *Between Heaven and Hell.*
1957: *From Hell It Came.*
1965: *In Harm's Way.*
1968: *Hang 'Em High.*
1969: *Changes.*
1970: *Beneath the Planet of the Apes, Weekend of Terror* (TV).
1971: *The President's Plane Is Missing, Believe in Me* (TV).
1973: *The Baby.*

Television Series

1954–1955: *First Love* as Zach James.
1957–1958: *The Gray Ghost* as Major John Singleton Mosby.
1959: *Counterthrust* as Agent.
1969–1972: *Bright Promise* as Henry Pierce.

Sources

Picture Show Annual. London: Amalgamated Press, 1953.
Summers, Neil. *The Official TV Western Book Volume #4.* Vienna, WV: Old West Shop Publishing, 1992.
Truitt, Evelyn Mack. *Who Was Who on Screen Illustrated Edition.* New York: Bowker, 1984.
Who's Who in the Theatre 15th Edition. London: Pitman, 1970.

ANNA-LISA

She was born Ana-Lisa Ruud in Oslo, Norway, in 1934 and was a familiar guest on many television series from 1958 to about 1966. Her only regular role in a series was in *Black Saddle* as Nora Travers, the owner of the Marathon Hotel where Clay Culhane (Peter Breck) decides to stay and set up his law practice. She was the focal point of the first episode ("Client: Travers"), in which a vengeful rancher buys up all the land and property in a town except that owned by one strong-minded widow, Nora Travers, who refuses to sell. Culhane comes to her rescue. Anna-Lisa appeared in a couple of feature films. They were in the sci-fi genre and she played scientists in both.

Anna-Lisa Filmography

1959: *Have Rocket—Will Travel.*
1960: *12 to the Moon.*

Television Series

1959–1960: *Black Saddle* as Nora Travers.

Sources

Hirschhorn, Clive. *The Columbia Story.* London: Pyramid, 1989.
Inman, David. *The TV Encyclopedia.* New York: Perigee, 1991.
Yoggy, Gary A. *Riding the Video Range: The Rise and Fall of the Western on Television.* Jefferson, NC: McFarland, 1995.

MICHAEL ANSARA

Michael Ansara was born in a small village in Syria on April 15, 1922, and came to the U.S. with his American parents at the age of two, living in New England until the family's relocation to California ten years later. Although playing Indians was a career specialty, he is of Lebanese extraction. Intending to become a doctor, he took a pre-medical course at Los Angeles City College. In an attempt to overcome his crippling shyness, he added theater arts to his pre-med curriculum and found artistic satisfaction from the classes. This caused him to leave City College and enroll at the Pasadena Playhouse.

His studies were interrupted by World War II, in which he served as an army medic. After an honorable discharge, he joined a Shakespearean stock company. He also worked as a rookie cop, drove a taxi cab, sold carpets and worked for a collection agency. He made his motion picture debut in a minor role in *Action in Arabia* (1944), but he only played bits in this decade. His big break came while starring on stage in a Playhouse production of *Monserrat,* where a talent scout from Warner Bros. caught his performance. He was signed to play Tuscos in the film *Only the Valiant* (1951), the first though not the last time he would be called upon to play an American Indian. He appeared in a number of spear and sandal movies in which he usually played some cruel Eastern despot. The actor himself cites Judas in *The Robe* (1953) as the role which established him as a serious and accomplished actor.

Many films followed in which he nearly always played the villain. His image did not change until he won the lead in the television series *Broken Arrow,* playing the noble Indian Cochise. In this series Tom Jeffords (John Lupton) was originally an army officer given the assignment of moving the U.S. mail safely through Apache country in Arizona. Unlike his contemporaries, Jeffords sought peace with the Indians by riding into their territory and meeting Cochise. Impressed with his bravery, Cochise allowed the mail to go through untouched and the two men became blood brothers. This brought an uncertain peace in the region which eventually led to Jeffords becoming an Indian agent for the Chiricahua Reservation. Later he married the beautiful Indian maiden Sonseeray (Sue England), but she was murdered by Indian-hating white men soon after the marriage. This only strengthened Jeffords' resolve to accomplish his mission as Indian agent of bringing permanent peace between the two races.

Most of the location shooting was done at the Fox Ranch in Malibu Canyon and Vasquez Rocks. Ansara's chief recollection of the series was the uncomfortable wig and costume which he wore at the height of the summer, although when the weather turned wintry, he was glad of both. Ansara has gone on record as saying that he enjoyed playing in the series because Cochise was a civilized man and not a savage. The series also gave him wide public exposure. Ansara read assiduously about the legendary character before undertaking the role. Although he and John Lupton hardly knew each other before the series began, they became good friends and played sports together. After the series ended, their friendship became dormant. They met only once in later years, but it was still an amicable relationship.

Ansara's second Western series, *Law of the Plainsman,* had its origins in an episode of *The Rifleman* screened in 1959. It scored such high ratings that the NBC network ordered a series (produced by Four Star Television), which debuted on October 1, 1959. The plainsman was a unique Western hero because U.S. Marshal Sam Buckhart, played by Ansara, was also a Red Indian. Born an Apache, his name amongst his own people was Buck Heart. When a cavalry captain was badly wounded in an Indian skirmish, he had been found and nursed back to health by Buck Heart. When the captain died a couple of years later, he left the Indian who saved him sufficient funds for an education at a fine school and Harvard University.

Once he had acquired this education, Buck Heart greatly admired the flag, the laws and the constitution of the white man, but nevertheless returned to the troubled New Mexico Territory of the 1880s with the intention of becoming a marshal. One dimension which made this series unique was that in addition to overcoming varmints, Buckhart also had to deal with the strong elements of racial prejudice. He became a deputy under U.S. Marshal Andy Morrison (Dayton Lummis) in Santa Fe while residing in the rooming house run by Martha Commager (Nora Marlowe). The other lady in his life was eight-year-old Tess Logan (Gina Gillespie), whom he rescued after a stagecoach accident. The leading character of the series was extremely interesting and the series was well made, but in the face of stiff competition, it only lasted for 30 half-hour black and white episodes, ending in September 1960.

Once asked if these two series might typecast him, he replied, "It will give us all a chance to find out." Two decades later he was again playing an Indians in the miniseries *Centennial.* He had become one of the most familiar guest-stars on American television. He did Westerns such as *Rawhide*, crime series such as *The Name of the Game* and was particularly memorable in the title role in the "Soldier" episode of the classic sci-fi anthology series *The Outer Limits* in 1964. In the sci-fi television series *Buck Rogers in the 25th Century*, he played the evil henchman of Princess Ardala.

He continued to obtain plenty of work in feature films through the 1970s and 1980s in such diverse roles as Walt Disney's children's film *The Bears and I* (1974); many low-budget horror movies such as *The Day of the Animals* (1976), the "rampaging baby" cult film *It's Alive* (1974), and the very weird *The Manitou* (1977), in which Susan Strasberg has a 400-year-old Indian growing out of her neck; and the historical drama *Mohammed, Messenger Of God* (1976).

He married and divorced actress Jean Byron during the 1950s. *How to Marry a Millionaire,* starring Barbara Eden, was a syndicated sitcom being shot at 20th Century–Fox at the same time as *Broken Arrow.* As a publicity gimmick, Eden met Ansara. The couple married in January 1958, and had a son, Matthew, born in 1965. They lived in a ranch house in Sherman Oaks and appeared together in two films, *Voyage to the Bottom of the Sea* (1961) and *Quick, Let's Get Married* (1964). While her career took off and gave her regular employment (particularly in the situation comedy *I Dream Of Jeannie),* he could not land another series and endured stretches of unemployment. He guest-starred as the Blue Djinn and King Kamehameha in her series. To compound matters in 1971, the actress miscarried. To compensate, Eden threw herself into her career, so the couple separated and divorced in 1973. He told reporters, "I'm confused. I never did any of those things that women can't forgive. I don't drink excessively, gamble or run around with other girls ... perhaps she suddenly felt she didn't need me any more. It is so unbelievably sad. I've been married to Barbara for 15 years and I still love her." He has since remarried.

Ansara kept trim by bicycling, swimming, bowling and playing tennis and golf. He is also a keen painter. He resides in Calabasas, California.

Michael Ansara Filmography

1944: *Action in Arabia.*
1947: *Intrigue.*
1949: *South Sea Sinner.*
1950: *Kim, The Desert Hawk.*
1951: *My Favorite Spy, Smuggler's Island, Only the Valiant, Soldiers Three, Bannerline.*
1952: *Yankee Buccaneer, The Golden Hawk, Diplomatic Courier, Brave Warrior, Road to Bali, The Lawless Breed.*
1953: *White Witch Doctor, Julius Caesar, Serpent of the Nile, The Robe, Bandits of Corsica, Slaves of Babylon, The Diamond Queen.*
1954: *Sign of the Pagan, The Egyptian, Three Young Texans, Princess of the Nile, The Saracen Blade, Bengal Brigade.*
1955: *Diane, New Orleans Uncensored, Abbott and Costello Meet the Mummy, Jupiter's Darling.*
1956: *The Ten Commandments, Pillars of the Sky, The Lone Ranger, Gun Brothers.*
1957: *Last of the Badmen, The Tall Stranger, The Sad Sack, Quantez.*
1961: *The Comancheros, Voyage to the Bottom of the Sea.*
1964: *The Confession (*a.k.a. *Quick! Let's Get Married).*
1965: *Harum Scarum, The Greatest Story Ever Told.*
1966: *...And Now Miguel, The Destructors, Texas Across the River, How I Spent My Summer Vacation (*a.k.a. *Deadly Roulette).*
1967: *The Pink Jungle, Sol Madrid.*
1968: *Daring Game.*
1969: *Guns of the Magnificent Seven, The Phynx, How to Make It (*a.k.a. *Target Harry), The Phynx.*
1971: *Powderkeg* (TV).
1972: *Stand Up and Be Counted, Dear Dead Delilah.*
1973: *It's Alive!, The Doll Squad, Call To Danger* (TV), *Ordeal* (TV).
1974: *Shootout in a One-Dog Town* (TV), *The Bears and I.*
1975: *Barbary Coast* (TV).
1976: *Day of the Animals, The Message (*a.k.a. *Mohammed, Messenger of God).*
1977: *The Manitou, Kino The Padre on Horseback.*
1981: *The Guns and the Fury.*
1982: *Bayou Romance.*
1983: *The Fantastic World of DC Collins* (TV).
1984: *Access Code, Lethal (*a.k.a. *KGB: The Secret War), Knights of the City.*
1987: *Assassination.*
1989: *Border Shootout.*
1996: *Johnny Mysto the Boy Wonder.*

Television Series

1956–1958: *Broken Arrow* as Cochise.
1959–1960: *Law of the Plainsman* as Deputy U.S. Marshal Sam Buckhart.
1979–1980: *Buck Rogers in the 25th Century* as Kane.

Miniseries

1978–1979: *Centennial* as Lame Beaver.

Sources

Brooks, Tim. *The Complete Directory to Prime Time TV Stars.* New York: Ballantine Books, 1987.
Interview with John Lupton, 1993.
Skinner, John Walter. *Who's Who on the Screen.* Worthing, England: Madeleine, 1983.
Smith, Ronald L. *Sweethearts of '60s TV.* New York: St. Martin's Press, 1989.
Summers, Neil. *The First Official TV Western Book.* Vienna, WV: Old West Shop Publishing, 1987.
Summers, Neil. *The Official TV Western Book Volume #2.* Vienna, WV: Old West Publishing, 1989.
Additional biographical information provided by "Also Starring" agency.

JAMES ARNESS

A lawmaker from Kansas once gave a speech in the United States Senate in which he named Wyatt Earp, Bat Masterson and Matt Dillon as among the great lawmen of the frontier era. It was soon pointed out to him that Matt Dillon was a fictitious character played by actor James Arness. The lawmaker smiled and replied, "Does any man in this august body have the courage to state to his children or grandchildren that Matt Dillon never existed?"

Arness, who created the role on television, played the character throughout the run of the *Gunsmoke* series. Arness was Matt Dillon in the same way that William S. Hart and Randolph Scott became indistinguishable from their onscreen personas. His monolithic face, granite jaw and massive physique merged everyone's memories of frontier lawmen of the Old West so that he became a single, definitive, towering good guy.

Of his offscreen personality he has become known as one of Hollywood's most famous recluses, never appearing in public or on other programs of any kind. He once said, "Aloneness is absolutely essential to my life. I can't see how people don't need it occasionally. I feel a need for it regularly." Friends of the actor attribute his standoffishness in part to shyness, adding, "There's not much emotion in him. When that little bit of openness closes up, it really closes." On the other hand, it has been said that he continued to star in the series for the last few seasons simply because so many craftsmen depended upon it for work.

James Arness, who is of Norwegian descent, was born James King Aurness on a farm near Minneapolis, Minnesota, on May 26, 1921. His parents were Ruth Duesler Salisbury and Rolf Aurness, who divorced in 1948. His father, who retired as a medical supplies representative, later ran a cattle ranch that his son owned in California. His mother remarried to businessman Maurice Salisbury and resided in Carmel, California.

Arness lived in Minneapolis for the first 18 years of his life. His first attempts at acting came in his schooldays, and he also particularly enjoyed singing. He sang in the Hennepin Avenue Church choir and in choral groups at John Burroughs Grade School, Ramsey Junior High School and West High School in Minneapolis. Each summer he would be off to the woods of Minnesota for months of fishing, hunting and sailing interrupted only by an occasional job at a nearby resort.

In 1942 he enrolled at Beloit College in Wisconsin, but was drafted during his freshman year and soon found himself involved as a combat infantryman of the Third Infantry Division in the bitter fighting of the Italian campaign. Machine gun bullets shattered his right leg below the knee during the battle for Anzio Beach. It took the doctors a year to put his leg back together, but it did not mend properly, leaving him with a slight, permanent limp. (As a result of his wounds, in later years he had to use stepladders to mount his horse.) He was honorably discharged in 1945.

He returned to his home town for a try at radio announcing. He worked as a substitute radio announcer at station WLOL in Minneapolis for six months. He also took part in local dramatics on stage which led to a decision that he would try and make a career for himself as an actor, so he left for Hollywood. He was given a screen test with Warner Bros. but flopped. While acting at the Bliss-Hayden Theater in Beverly Hills, he was discovered by agent Leon Lance, who introduced him to film producer Dore Schary. He made his screen debut as Peter in Schary's production *The Farmer's Daughter* (1947) starring Loretta Young.

With the money he earned from this he ventured to Mexico only to return to Hollywood several months later, broke. The following weeks were the worst he could remember. He became a beach bum, slept in the back of an old car, worked part-time as a salesman and carpenter and collected veteran's benefits and unemployment insurance. For some years he was unable to find a decent job in Hollywood. Leading men who worked predominantly in Westerns refused to let Arness appear in their movies because at 6'6" he rode taller and looked more rugged than they did. Things looked black until he decided he would settle down to a more conscientious approach to act-

James Arness in *Gunsmoke.*

ing. He devoted all his time to improving his technique. This finally paid off when MGM gave him the role of a marine in the war movie *Battleground* (1949). He recalled, "I guess you might say this film was the turning point in my life because after this things started to go a little more smoothly for me." Two of his best remembered films were the classic science fiction *The Thing from Another World* (1951), in which he played the title role, and *Them!*

(1954), about giant ants, in which he played FBI agent Robert Graham. In 1952 Charles Marquis Warren, later producer-director of *Gunsmoke,* gave him a part in *Hellgate*, a film that was written, produced and directed by Warren. As a result of his performance in this film, Arness was signed to a contract with John Wayne's company and appeared in four movies with him. Wayne was one of the few stars around who was so big and rugged that he had no objection to surrounding himself with other strapping actors like James Arness.

Gunsmoke had its genesis in 1952 when writers Norman MacDonnell and John Meston decided to write a Western for radio which would be aimed squarely at adults. They originally called their concept *Jeff Spain*. When they submitted their script to CBS radio, it was rejected because it was believed that audiences would never accept it since it was too radical. Fortunately the people at CBS radio could not find a conventional Western series to go with. They decided to go with *Jeff Spain*. The name of the hero became Matt Dillon and the title of the program was changed to *Gunsmoke*. It soon shot to the top of the ratings chart and stayed there with the booming voice of William Conrad as Marshal Matt Dillon.

CBS wanted to transfer the series to television, but producer/director Charles Marquis Warren felt that Conrad lacked all the physical attributes so vital for the role. The first choice for the part was John Wayne, but he was so popular in films that there was no question at that time of him starring in a weekly television series. Twenty-four other actors were tested and rejected for the role. John Wayne suggested Arness for the part, saying, "Jim will get the job done for you. He's big and he can be mean. What more do you want?"

As Arness later recalled, "I have to thank John Wayne in many ways for the chance of playing Dillon. He had signed me to a contract with his own company when the offer of playing Dillon came up. ... When I was first approached about it, I had to say no because of a film commitment. I was asked again when I finished the film I was making. I was very interested in the offer, but I had a contract with Wayne."

Allegedly Wayne was furious at the ingratitude which Arness displayed about the offer. He asked Arness over to his house to talk about it. The two big men sat across a table with a bottle between them, arguing into the night. Arness's objection was that a part in a television Western series (particularly an adult one) would probably flop and torpedo his flourishing film career. But Wayne was a very determined man and pressured Arness into it by tearing up his contract in May 1955, and offering to introduce the first episode himself (guaranteeing a large audience on the first night). As one company executive expressed it, "It was a wonderful gesture by John Wayne. He has tremendous admiration for Arness, both as a man and as an actor."

Gunsmoke premiered on September 10, 1955, only four days after another landmark adult Western, *The Life and Legend of Wyatt Earp*. It was set in Dodge City, Kansas, around 1880. The other key characters were limping Chester Goode (Dennis Weaver), the loyal deputy; crusty, kindly town physician Doc Adams (Milburn Stone); and Kitty Russell (Amanda Blake), who started out as one of the hostesses of the Long Branch Saloon and later became its owner. In the radio version it was strongly implied that she was a prostitute.

In that first episode Marshal Dillon had a confrontation on the main street with a hired killer from Texas. Dillon brushed Kitty aside and reached for his gun. Then, in violation of every cliché in Western television, the bad guy outdrew Dillon, shot him and left him for dead in the dust. Subsequently Dillon recovered, rode after the varmint and overpowered him. In one episode *Gunsmoke* had established itself as an adult Western. It changed the course of the television Western. The plots were generally more mature and avoided the undiscriminating action sequences so common in juvenile Westerns. Dillon had to reason as well as fight and shoot. He acted with tact and sensitivity and used his Colt only as a last resort. The great appeal of *Gunsmoke* lay in the competence and rapport of the actors. Aside from that, it reflected a grimy, gritty version of the reality of frontier life. From the show's inception, Matt Dillon dressed in plain work clothes minus the flamboyant garb that adorned a previous generation of Western heroes. Above all, he never professed any deep love for his horse.

Gunsmoke was an instant hit, ranking first in the Nielsen ratings in 1957 and remaining among the top ten shows annually thereafter.

Arness himself was three times nominated for an Emmy Award (in 1956, 1957 and 1958–1959), but lost out on each occasion. *Gunsmoke* won an Emmy in 1957 as Best Dramatic Series with Continuing Characters. During the first six seasons when the series was 30 minutes long, scripts from the radio series were used and most were written by either John Meston or Les Crutchfield. Each episode interspersed elements of gunplay and compelling human interest. It was expanded to a full hour in 1960. Gradually the series became an anthology with the central character focus changing from episode to episode so that Arness could be given more time to relax off camera. As Norman MacDonnell explained, "Expanding *Gunsmoke* to a full hour allows us more time to develop the plot and characters, giving the show new scope. We can now spend more time on various key people in the show, letting them get involved in situations, problems and events which might not have been possible in the shorter 30-minute version."

John Mantley replaced Norman MacDonnell as the show's producer in 1966 and became executive producer two years later. When *Gunsmoke* dropped to 34th place in the ratings following the 1966–1967 season, it was canceled. John Mantley recalled the trouble began with the antiviolence campaign which followed the assassination of President John Kennedy. Virtually every other producer of an action adventure series was in terrible trouble, but Mantley was riding on air because he had four marvelous characters and all he had to do was write stories around them. This turned out to be Mantley's single biggest mistake in show business. Since the essence of drama is conflict, he found it impossible to create conflict amongst them. They were characters who were genuinely very fond of each other, thought much alike and shared a similar sense of humor. He discovered the way out of his dilemma was to bring a guest-star with a problem into the middle of the action, have that character take center stage and play off the regular characters. Mantley drew repeatedly on 20th century issues which were transferred to a frontier context.

There was a national outcry following the cancelation, so William S. Paley, Board Chairman at CBS, intervened and reinstated it at the start of the 1967–1968 season. His courage was rewarded when the show's popularity began to revive shortly afterwards. After moving to Monday evenings in 1967, the series returned to the Top Ten and remained there until its demise. In a further attempt to bring realism to the series, the producers insisted on as much location shooting as possible. This necessitated location trips to Utah with the stars and a crew of 50 technicians. "Personally I prefer filming outdoors," Arness once said. "The setting and the atmosphere get a hold of you more than it does when you're inside a studio on a stuffy, hot stage. I like the open air." The series, which was the longest-running dramatic show in the history of television, eventually ended after 633 episodes over a 20-year period in 1975. It was appropriately the last Western left on network television by that time. Once asked why it ended, Arness explained, "I attribute this antiviolence thing as the reason our show had to end; otherwise we might have lasted another two or three seasons. But the ban imposed on violence, even when it was essential to our script, is what ruined things."

Arness teamed with executive producer John Mantley on a miniseries entitled *How The West Was Won* in 1977. He played Zeb Macahan, a rugged mountain man, who spent the decade in the Dakota Territory before returning to Virginia, where his brother's family were preparing to move West. When the Civil War broke out, Zeb's brother Timothy returned East and his wife Kate was subsequently killed in an accident, leaving the four Macahan children in Zeb's care. The eldest was Luke (Bruce Boxleitner), who had killed three men in self defense and was on the run from the marshal; Laura (Kathryn Holcomb), who was on the brink of womanhood; Jessie (Vicki Schreck), a precocious 12-year-old; and Josh (William Cullen), a younger brother. Aunt Molly (Fionnula Flanagan), Kate's widowed sister, accompanied them on the hazardous journey. After an initial series which rose as high as 11th in the ratings, the series returned in 1979 with 11 new two-hour episodes which told of the Macahans homesteading a ranch in the Tetons and raising Appaloosa horses. A particularly attractive feature of this series was the stunning location photography of Utah, Colorado, Arizona and Southern California.

With the character of Zeb Macahan,

Arness was not reprising the role of Matt Dillon. He was creating a completely new character. He was a mountain man, a type who frequently signified a threat to the precarious establishment of law and order in the days of the Old West. They were frequently mean and drunken. During the course of the narrative, the life of Zeb Macahan declines. Ironically one of his nephews almost becomes like a young Matt Dillon, a man ready to accept responsibility and enforce it on others. John Mantley recalled enormous network interference from ABC on this series, primarily over whether running times should be one, two or three hours. He was forced by over-tight editing to destroy his own best work; some of the concurrent storylines became incomprehensible. Audiences generally remained loyal but confused.

Arness's final stab at series television came with NBC and *McClain's Law* (1981–1982), his only later foray into contemporary life and his least successful series. He played Detective Jim McClain, who retired from the San Pedro, California, police in the late 1960s after being injured in the leg. He later worked as a fisherman living in a houseboat. When his partner was robbed and murdered, McClain obtained reinstatement with the force in order to apprehend the murderer. He proved quite capable in the modern hi-tech world of police procedure as well as the old-fashioned rough-house methods of catching criminals. He ingratiated himself with other members of the force, but not with the viewing audience, who adamantly refused to warm to him in this guise. The show was not renewed for a second season.

Since then Arness has reprised the Matt Dillon character in some telemovies which are generally considered to be a travesty of the original series, with lethargic performances and badly fatigued stories. He has also stepped into his mentor John Wayne's boots by appearing in a couple of very inferior, low-budget television reworkings of Wayne's warmly remembered films (namely *The Alamo: 13 Days To Glory* [1987] and *Red River* [1988]). Arness's contribution was probably best expressed by L.Q. Jones (who appeared along with a lot of other veteran talent in *Red River)* when he said, "A nice feller but John Wayne he ain't."

Arness married Virginia Chapman, whom he met when they were both students appearing in the play *Candida* at the Pasadena Playhouse theatre in 1948. They divorced in 1960, and she later died of a drug overdose. They had three children: Craig, born in 1947, who was a child of Chapman's by an earlier marriage and adopted by Arness; Jennie Lee Arness, born in 1951, who committed suicide in 1975 by a drug overdose after splitting up with rock star Gregg Allman; and a son Rolf, who was born in 1952 and became a world surfing champion. In the late 1970s Arness married another actress, Janet Surtees. Arness became a multimillionaire through *Gunsmoke* and he invested his money wisely. He owns a house in Hawaii; one in Pacific Palisades, California; a California ranch; and two other homes in California. For recreation he enjoys piloting his two planes and other outdoor pursuits. His younger brother is the actor Peter Graves, who was born in 1925.

James Arness Filmography

1947: *The Farmer's Daughter, Roses Are Red.*
1948: *The Man from Texas.*
1949: *Battleground.*
1950: *Sierra, Two Lost Worlds, Wyoming Mail, Wagon Master, Double Crossbones, Stars in My Crown.*
1951: *Cavalry Scout, Belle Le Grand, Iron Man, The People Against O'Hara, The Girl in White, The Thing from Another World.*
1952: *Carbine Williams, Horizons West, Big Jim McLain, Hellgate.*
1953: *Lone Hand, Ride the Man Down, The Veils of Bagdad, Hondo, Island in the Sky.*
1954: *Her Twelve Men, Them!*
1955: *Many Rivers to Cross, The Sea Chase, Flame of the Islands.*
1956: *The First Traveling Saleslady, Gun the Man Down.*
1976: *The Macahans* (TV).
1987: *The Alamo: 13 Days to Glory* (TV), *Gunsmoke: Return to Dodge* (TV).
1988: *Red River* (TV).
1990: *Gunsmoke II: The Last Apache* (TV).
1992: *Gunsmoke III: To The Last Man* (TV).
1993: *Gunsmoke IV: The Long Ride* (TV).
1994: *Gunsmoke V: One Man's Justice* (TV).

Television Series

1955–1975: *Gunsmoke* as Matt Dillon.

1977–1979: *How The West Was Won* as Zeb Macahan.
1981–1982: *McClain's Law* as Detective Jim McClain.

Sources

Current Biography Yearbook. New York: The H.W. Wilson Company, 1973.
Hayward, Anthony and Deborah Hayward. *TV Unforgettables.* Enfield, England: Guinness, 1993.
Miller, Lee O. *The Great Cowboy Stars of Movies & Television.* New Rochelle, NY: Arlington House, 1979.
Newcomb, Horace and Robert S Alley. *The Producer's Medium.* London and Oxford: Oxford University Press, 1983.
Speed, F. Maurice. *The Western Film and TV Annual.* London: MacDonald, 1957, 1959 and 1960.
Thomey, Tedd. *The Glorious Decade.* New York: Ace, 1971.

Note

James Arness appeared in early films billed under his real name.

JAN ARVAN

Born in 1913, he was a busy character actor in television and films. He appeared as an escaped political prisoner in the *Zorro* television series and was frequently seen in support of Red Skelton. He died of a heart attack on May 24, 1979, at age 66, in Los Angeles, California, survived by his widow, a son and a daughter.

Jan Arvan Filmography

1950: *The Desert Hawk.*
1954: *The Other Woman, Trade, Tom of the China Seas* (serial).
1955: *The Cobweb, Abbott and Costello Meet the Mummy.*
1957: *Designing Woman, Istanbul, 20 Million Miles to Earth.*
1958: *Some Came Running, Curse of the Faceless Man.*
1960: *Three Came to Kill, The Sign of Zorro, Gunfighters of Abilene, A Noose for a Gunman.*
1961: *Frontier Uprising.*
1964: *The Brass Bottle.*
1966: *The Spy With My Face.*
1967: *Winchester '73* (TV).
1972: *The Screaming Woman* (TV), *The Poseidon Adventure.*
1973: *The Stone Killer.*
1977: *The Other Side Of Midnight.*

Television Series

1957–1959: *Zorro* as Nacho Torres.

Sources

Willis, John. *Screen World Annual.* London: Muller, 1980.
Yoggy, Gary A. *Riding the Video Range: The Rise and Fall of the Western on Television.* Jefferson, NC: McFarland, 1995.

ROSCOE ATES

The rubber-faced, pop-eyed, stuttering, perennial Western comic was born in Grange, Mississippi, on January 20, 1892. He became a soda fountain attendant and motion picture projectionist before going to the Dana Musical Institute in Ohio. He stuttered badly but discovered that he had no stammer when he sang, so he recited song lyrics and tongue twisters in front of a mirror. He had long since cured himself of the stutter which he put to such good use in his films. His ambition was to be a concert violinist, but somehow he became sidetracked into vaudeville where he performed for 15 years prior to making his screen debut in 1929. He came to the attention of director Wesley Ruggles, who cast him as Jess Rickey in *Cimarron* (1931).

During World War II he was a major in the Army Air Corps for two years. He was placed on inactive service in 1944, but continued as an entertainer in Special Services. He is best remembered for being sidekick Soapy Jones to Eddie Dean in a series of 15 films for Producers Releasing Corporation in the 1940s. He later supported Russell Hayden and Eddie Dean separately in a perfunctory live Western series, *The Marshal Of Gunsight Pass* (1950). This was regarded as primitive even by the standards of those days and quickly disappeared. This was Ates's only shot at a regular role in series television, although he remained an active television performer until the end of the 1950s (notably in Westerns and episodes of *Alfred Hitchcock Presents)*. Will Hutchins, who worked with him on the "MacBrewster the Bold" episode of *Sugarfoot*, said of him, "I loved working with Roscoe Ates. He kept hiking up the kilts of the Scotsmen, much to the director's dismay." His final motion picture was a bit in *The Errand Boy* (1961).

His first wife was Ethel Rogers, with whom he had a daughter Dorothy (1917–1982), who had been in show business. After divorcing Rogers, in 1922 he wed Clara Callaghan Adrian, but they divorced in 1935. In 1938 he wed actress Lenora Bell, known professionally as Barbara Ray (1914–1955). They divorced in 1944, but remarried in 1949. She died of leukemia in 1955. In the same year his fiancée Sandy Reeves beat him up with the heel of a spiked shoe. In 1958, 24-year-old showgirl Reba Sandborn overdosed in his apartment. He married the former Mrs. Beatrice Martinez in Las Vegas in December 1960, when he was 68 and she was 26. In 1961 he was fined on a drunk driving charge after an argument they had while driving. In the same year he spent six weeks in hospital suffering from lung cancer. He was discharged in a satisfactory condition, but readmitted in February 1962. He died at West Valley Community Hospital Encino, California, on March 1, 1962, at age 70. He is buried at Forest Lawn in Glendale. Although he earned top dollar as a character actor, he spent lavishly and died broke.

Roscoe Ates Filmography

1929: *South Sea Rose.*

1930: *The Lone Star Ranger, Reducing, Caught Short, The Big House, City Girl, Billy the Kid, Love in the Rough.*

1931: *The Great Lover, Cracked Nuts, The Big Shot, The Champ, A Free Soul, Cimarron, Politics, Too Many Cooks.*

1932: *Freaks, Ladies of the Jury, The Rainbow Trail, Young Bride (*a.k.a. *Love Starved* and *Veneer), Roadhouse Murder, Hold 'Em Jail!, Come On Danger, Deported.*

1933: *Renegades of the West, The Past of Mary Holmes, The Cheyenne Kid, Golden Harvest, Alice in Wonderland, What No Beer!, Scarlet River, Lucky Devils.*

1934: *Woman in the Dark, She Made Her Bed, The Merry Wives of Reno.*

1935: *The People's Enemy.*

1936: *God's Country and the Woman, Fair Exchange.*

1938: *Riders of the Black Hills, The Great Adventures of Wild Bill Hickok* (serial).

1939: *Three Texas Steers, Gone with the Wind, Rancho Grande.*

1940: *Cowboy from Sundown, Captain Caution, Untamed, I Want a Divorce, Chad Hanna.*

1941: *Ziegfeld Girl, I'll Sell My Life, Birth of the Blues, Mountain Moonlight, She Knew All the Answers, Sullivan's Travels, Robin Hood of the Pecos, Reg'lar Fellers, Badmen of Missouri, One Foot in Heaven.*

1942: *The Palm Beach Story, The Affairs of Jimmy Valentine.*

1944: *Can't Help Singing.*

1946: *Colorado Serenade, Down Missouri Way, Driftin' River, Tumbleweed Trail, Stars Over Texas, Wild West.*

1947: *Wild Country, Range Beyond the Blue, West to Glory, Black Hills, Shadow Valley.*

1948: *Check Your Guns, Tornado Range, Inner Sanctum, The Westward Trail, The Hawk of Powder River, Prairie Outlaws, The Tioga Kid, Thunder in the Pines.*

1950: *The Hills of Oklahoma, Father's Wild Game.*

1951: *Honeychile.*

1952: *The Blazing Forest.*
1953: *Those Redheads from Seattle, The Stranger Wore a Gun.*
1955: *Lucy Gallant, Abbott and Costello Meet the Keystone Kops.*
1956: *Come Next Spring, The Birds and the Bees, The Kettles in the Ozarks, Meet Me in Las Vegas.*
1957: *Run of the Arrow, The Big Caper, Short Cut to Hell.*
1958: *The Sheepman.*
1961: *The Silent Call, The Ladies' Man, The Errand Boy.*

Television Series

1950: *The Marshal of Gunsight Pass* as Deputy Roscoe.

Sources

Jones, Ken D., Arthur F. McClure and Alfred E. Twomey, *Character People.* Secaucus, NJ: Citadel, 1979.
The Picturegoer's Who's Who and Encyclopedia. London: Odhams Press, 1933.
Quinlan, David. *Illustrated Directory of Film Comedy Stars.* London: Batsford, 1992.
Rothel, David. *Those Great Cowboy Sidekicks.* Waynesville, NC: World of Yesterday Publications, 1984.
Smith, Ronald L. *Comic Support.* New York: Citadel, 1993.
Correspondence between Will Hutchins and the author.

GENE AUTRY

Gene Autry was Hollywood's first major singing cowboy star whose exciting screen exploits endeared him to millions of young fans from the late 1930s to the early 1950s. In more than 80 films, the white-hatted, guitar-strumming Autry preached honesty and goodness and even introduced The Ten Cowboy Commandments which advocated fair play, truthfulness, patriotism, purity of thought and respect for the elderly. Romance was rarely allowed to interrupt the action and music in his movies, and when he did kiss a girl he was usually nudged on by his horse, Champion.

Autry is not among the silver screen's best actors, but he is reputed to be amongst the richest. Of his legendary wealth he said, "Money doesn't bring happiness, but it is a necessity of life. I know what it is like to be very poor because I had nothing until I started making records in my 20s. I usually work three days a week. I don't need to work, but I like to keep my mind busy so that I don't become stale, old or cranky."

Lady luck frequently smiled on him and he was in the right place at the right time on more than one occasion. His career has been the work of more people than just the performer himself. As an actor he had a somewhat awkward manner which initially enhanced his appeal. He has demonstrated commercial progress and the value of American broadcasting and business enterprise more than any of his contemporaries. Autry also made a major contribution as both producer and performer to the style of the television Western in the early 1950s.

Orvon Gene Autry was born in Tioga, Texas, on September 29, 1907. He was the son of Delbert Autry, a struggling horse and cattle dealer, and his wife Elnora Ozmont Autry and was one of four children. His sisters were Velda and Wilma and his brother was Dudley. When he was still a child, his family moved to Achille, Oklahoma, where he was raised on his father's cattle ranch. His grandfather William T. Autry, who was a Baptist minister, was the first to notice Gene's voice and placed him in the church choir. At 12 he bought his first guitar from a Sears, Roebuck catalogue.

Although he sang in local nightspots and briefly joined a traveling medicine show, Autry became interested in railways and telegraphs. He learned Morse code and after graduating from Ravia Community School in 1925 was employed as a telegrapher for the Frisco Line in Chelsea, Oklahoma, earning $35 as a trainee and up to $150 as a professional. One morning while he was playing his guitar and singing in the office, a stranger came in to send a telegram and said, "I think you may have something. Work hard at it and you may get somewhere." It was only after the stranger had left that Autry glanced at the name on the wire and realized the stranger was Will Rogers.

In 1928 Autry quit the railroad, went to New York and tried to obtain a break in the recording field. In the reception room at Victor Records he sang an impromptu audition which was overheard by Nat Shilkret, an executive who advised him to seek experience on the radio, giving him a letter of introduction. He obtained a job singing on radio station KVOO in Tulsa, Oklahoma, and soon his popularity became statewide. He was invited back to New York to make a record. While there he became acquainted with Arthur Satherley, who had just started to work for the American Record Corporation. Autry decided to sign with him. He was fortunate enough to secure a major hit from his first recording session: "That Silver Haired Daddy of Mine," a song he had written in the Oklahoma telegraph office with a friend named Jimmy Long. In 1930 it sold 30,000 copies in the first month of its release.

A major outlet for his records was the Sears, Roebuck catalogue and stores. The company decided that the young Autry would be an invaluable asset selling their wares on their WLS (World's Largest Store) radio station in Chicago. Until 1935 Sears presented *The Gene Autry Program,* for which he was paid the lowly salary of $35 a week. Simultaneously Autry appeared in the enormously popular *National Barn Dance* radio show and also toured with the performers. It was here that he first teamed with Smiley Burnette, his most frequent prewar sidekick.

One day in New York in 1934, three influential men entered into a discussion. The first was Nat Levine, an independent producer who owned Mascot Pictures. The second was Herbert J. Yates, who owned Consolidated Film Laboratories and later Republic Pictures. Levine intended to make a regular Western, but then the third man (Moe Siegel, president of the American Record Corporation) suggested that Levine make a musical Western and that Autry would be the ideal star. Levine met Autry in Chicago and spoke to him about the idea but nothing further seemed to develop. A little later Autry had an offer from Monogram Pictures, so he wrote to Levine informing him that he intended to go with Monogram. Levine wrote back, informing him that he was shooting a movie called *In Old Santa Fe* (1934) with Ken Maynard and offering him a role.

In Autry's first film he sang a few Western ballads and awkwardly delivered a few lines. Upon seeing himself for the first time, Autry was appalled, but was talked out of returning to Chicago by his wife. The reception accorded to him by patrons, however, was very positive, the only complaint being that he was underused in the movie. Producer-writer Wallace MacDonald went to have a tooth extracted and, while he was under gas, he dreamed up the idea of a 12-chapter serial to star Autry which would be a bizarre meeting of the science fiction and Western genres. The resultant serial, *The Phantom Empire,* was shot for $70,000. The basic plot for each of the chapters called for Autry to escape from the clutches of the subterranean world of Murania and get back to Radio Ranch in time to sing "That Silver Haired Daddy of Mine" in his next radio broadcast. Autry also used his own name on screen.

At the time, Autry was under contract to Mascot and was being paid $150 per week. The reaction to *The Phantom Empire* was so strong that it convinced Nat Levine of the potential of a series of Western features starring Autry, the first of which was *Tumbling Tumbleweeds* (1935). This set the pattern for most of the Autry features that followed. Although a few films were set in the Old West, almost all of them were located in the modern West where cars, radios, machine guns and airplanes were standard. Autry would also sing between five and eight times in a film. His most familiar sidekick during these years was Smiley Burnette.

From 1937 to 1942 Autry placed first in the Motion Picture Herald Poll of Top Money Making Western Stars. From 1947 to 1954 Autry was placed second behind Roy Rogers. His horse (featured in all his films) was called Champion. It was a dark sorrel with a blazeface from Oklahoma. The original Champion died during World War II. This horse appeared

Gene Autry in *The Gene Autry Show.*

in his movies while the horse Autry used in personal appearances was called Lindy and resembled Champion. Lindy was born in Oklahoma on May 20, 1927, and died in 1944. The mount Autry used in the postwar years was called Champion, Jr. There were in fact two Champion Jrs., of which the better remembered debuted in *Strawberry Roan* (1948). Champion, Jr. (who starred in television's *Champion the Wonder Horse*) died in 1976.

The business ability of Gene Autry which has become legendary over the years first manifested itself when the actor, still earning only $150 per week, demanded a raise. His movies, which cost from $50,000 to $75,000, were grossing over three times that amount. Herbert J. Yates introduced new singing cowboy Roy Rogers as a threat, but Autry refused to perform in his next scheduled movie. Instead he went on personal appearance tours in the South, where he was immensely popular. Republic capitulated in the end. They were desperate to have him back because they could only sell their other films on the strength of Autry's name.

Autry settled for making six to eight films a year for $12,500 a film. Merchandising tie-ins at that time netted him approximately $25,000 per annum. In 1940 he began a weekly Sunday evening radio program called *Melody Ranch* for which his salary eventually rose to $5,000 a show. He also earned substantial royalties from his records. In 1940 he did his only outside film, *Shooting High,* for Twentieth Century–Fox, in which he played a character other than Gene Autry. For this he was paid a flat fee of $25,000. He made this film at the request of his costar Jane Withers. In 1939 he was reliably reported to be receiving a record 50,000 fan letters per month.

In July 1942, Autry volunteered for military duty. Initially he was used for recruiting drives, entertaining the troops and selling war bonds. Winning his pilot's wings, he was ordered to the Air Ferry Command, ferrying cargo planes of men and materiel to Africa and Asia. In 1942 his annual income was $500,000. During the war he earned only $150 per month. The check for merchandising royalties enabled him to stay afloat financially, but this indoctrinated in him the need after the war to become a businessman as well as an actor.

In 1946 he was discharged and returned to Republic to resume his career, but was unhappy with the financial position there. He wanted to establish his own production company so that he could have a percentage of the profits. When Herbert J. Yates refused to consider it, Autry entered into negotiations with Columbia Pictures. In 1947 he signed a very lucrative contract with them and moved his center of operations over to that studio where he produced and starred in 32 features, many of which were of high quality. *The Last Roundup* (1947) is reported to be his favorite of his own movies and the first one which he made under his own banner.

Autry began the ascent to business tycoon at the end of the 1940s when his holdings were reported to include his own movie production company; a radio company; various radio stations; a publishing company; a rodeo; ownership of movie theaters; record royalties; a California flying school; and a grocery store. His net income in 1948 was estimated to be $600,000.

Generally Autry's garb in these later films was less flamboyant and more workmanlike. The action content was stepped up while the musical interludes took a back seat. The last of his B Westerns was *The Last of the Pony Riders* (1953). In the course of his career his records sold 40,000,000 ("Rudolph the Red Nosed Reindeer" accounted for more than 10,000,000). Autry's favorites of his own songs were "That Silver Haired Daddy of Mine," "South of the Border" and his theme song, "Back in the Saddle Again."

In the early 1950s Autry diversified into television. He and his staff made extensive preparations for the new medium. First they created a new organization called "Flying A Productions." Armand Schaefer, Autry's longtime motion picture associate, became the producer in charge. Original scripts written especially for television filming were purchased from various Western writers, and an initial schedule of 26 films was put in front of the cameras.

Special filming techniques, devised with the home viewer in mind, were adopted. Long shots were eliminated and close-up action shots were increased to give the viewer maximum intimacy with the players. In riding sequences, horsemen were photographed at closer range and shown traveling across the screen rather than towards the camera. More whites and lighter shades were emphasized and darker portions of the picture were kept deep gray rather than flat black. The first television film music was licensed by the American Federation of Musicians to "Flying A Productions" and the Autry company made good use of it. During 80 percent of each film's action, background music helped to set the mood. Each episode was complete in itself, running exactly

27 minutes, with at least one song integrated into the plot.

There were 108 half-hour segments of *The Gene Autry Show* produced for CBS between 1950 and 1956; Gene, his sidekick Pat Buttram and Champion rode from town to town in the Southwest helping to maintain law and order. The episodes were shot at a place called Pioneertown, situated in the Californian desert about 50 miles from Palm Springs. Two half-hour episodes were shot each week, and the last 13 were in color. He recalled, "We used to shoot two shows at the same time. While we were making these, the director was planning two more. Shooting two films at once, the director always looked at the possibilities of switching a shot so it could be used in two films. If, for instance, the camera filmed a rider coming down the side of a mountain, it might also reshoot him going up the mountain for another film." Autry was also heavily into producing other series such as *Annie Oakley, The Range Rider, Buffalo Bill, Jr.*, and *Champion the Wonder Horse.* After 1956, when *The Gene Autry Show* turned to reruns and the radio show *Melody Ranch* went off the airwaves, Autry made the metamorphosis completely from cowboy to business tycoon with a vast empire of holdings in just about every enterprise imaginable. In 1961, for instance, he bought the California Angels baseball franchise.

In 1932 Autry married Ina Mae Spivey (the niece of his original cosongwriter Jimmy Long) when she was a student at Teacher's Training College in St. Louis. They wed on April 1, 1932. They were married for 48 years until his wife died on May 20, 1980, at their home in Palm Springs, California. On July 19, 1981, Autry married Jacqueline Ellam, age 38, the vice-president of a bank, at the First United Methodist Church in Burbank, California. Of her he said, "She was my banker in Palm Springs. She's a lovely person and a very good businesswoman. She has filled a void and we have an awful lot in common." Autry is a bastion of the Republican Party

Gene Autry Filmography

1934: *In Old Santa Fe, Mystery Mountain* (serial).

1935: *Phantom Empire* (serial), *Tumbling Tumbleweeds, Melody Trail, Singing Vagabond, The Sagebrush Troubador.*

1936: *Red River Valley, Comin' Round the Mountain, The Singing Cowboy, Guns and Guitars, Oh Susanna, Ride Ranger Ride, The Big Show, The Old Corral.*

1937: *Roundup Time in Texas, Git Along Little Dogies, Rootin' Tootin' Rhythm, Yodelin' Kid from Pine Ridge, Public Cowboy No. 1, Boots and Saddles, Manhattan Merry-Go-Round* (guest), *Springtime in the Rockies.*

1938: *The Old Barn Dance, Gold Mine in the Sky, Man from Music Mountain, Prairie Moon, Rhythm of the Saddle, Western Jamboree.*

1939: *Home on the Prairie, Mexicali Rose, Blue Montana Skies, Mountain Rhythm, Colorado Sunset, In Old Monterey, Rovin' Tumbleweeds, South of the Border.*

1940: *Rancho Grande, Shooting High, Gaucho Serenade, Carolina Moon, Ride Tenderfoot Ride, Melody Ranch.*

1941: *Ridin' on a Rainbow, Back in the Saddle, The Singing Hills, Sunset in Wyoming, Under Fiesta Stars, Down Mexico Way, Sierra Sue.*

1942: *Cowboy Serenade, Heart of the Rio Grande, Home in Wyomin', Stardust on the Trail, Call of the Canyon, Bells of Capistrano.*

1946: *Sioux City Sue.*

1947: *Trail to San Antone, Twilight on the Rio Grande, Saddle Pals, Robin Hood of Texas, The Last Round-Up.*

1948: *The Strawberry Roan.*

1949: *Loaded Pistols, The Big Sombrero, Riders of the Whistling Pines, Rim of the Canyon, The Cowboy and the Indians, Riders in the Sky.*

1950: *Sons of New Mexico, Mule Train, Cow Town, Beyond the Purple Hills, Indian Territory, The Blazing Sun.*

1951: *Gene Autry and the Mounties, Texans Never Cry, Whirlwind, Silver Canyon, Hills of Utah, Valley of Fire.*

1952: *The Old West, Apache Country, Barbed Wire, Wagon Team, Blue Canadian Rockies, Night Stage to Galveston.*

1953: *Winning of the West, On Top of Old Smoky, Goldtown Ghost Riders, Pack Train, Saginaw Trail, Last of the Pony Riders.*

1968: *The Silent Treatment* (guest).

Television Series

1950–1956: *The Gene Autry Show* as Gene Autry.

Sources

Barton, Dick. "Where Are They Now?" *Sunday Express* newspaper, 1984.
Courneau, Ernest N. *The Hall of Fame of Western Film Stars.* North Quincy, MA: Christopher, 1969.
Merlock, Ray. *Shooting Stars.* "Gene Autry and the Coming of Civilization." Bloomington and Indianapolis: Indiana University Press, 1987.
Miller, Lee O. *The Great Cowboy Stars of Movies & Television.* New Rochelle, NY: Arlington House, 1979.
Parish, James Robert. *Great Western Stars.* New York: Ace, 1976.
Rothel, David. *The Singing Cowboys.* San Diego, CA: Barnes, 1978.
Speed, F. Maurice. *The Western Film Annual.* London: MacDonald, 1951 and 1955.
Tuska, Jon. *The Filming of the West.* Garden City, NY: Doubleday, 1976.

Note

Gene Autry is credited by some authorities with an appearance in *Alias Jesse James* (1959), but this appears to be erroneous.

JIMMY BAIRD

Born in 1948, this child actor played the role of Joey Newton's friend Pee Wee on *Fury*.

Jimmy Baird Filmography

1954: *There's No Business Like Show Business.*
1955: *The Seven Little Foys.*
1958: *The Return of Dracula.*
1959: *The Black Orchid.*
1960: *A Dog's Best Friend.*
1961: *Operation Eichmann.*

Television Series

1955–1958: *Fury* as Pee Wee.

Sources

Dye, David. *Child and Youth Actors: Filmographies of Their Entire Careers, 1914–1985.* Jefferson, NC: McFarland, 1988.
Lance, Steven. *Written Out of Television: A TV Lover's Guide to Cast Changes 1945–1994.* Lanham, MD: Madison, 1996.

JIM BANNON

Jim Bannon was notorious for making wrong decisions. When he told his first wife Bea Benaderet he was going to play Western hero "Red Ryder," she shouted at him, "You had a hell of a career as a radio announcer going, but you walked away from that. At Columbia you've done dress clothes pictures for three years with a couple of Westerns thrown in. You've doubled a bunch of people. You ride a horse like a maniac who's not afraid of anything. But somehow that doesn't seem to me to be enough." Bannon was rather too much of a maverick to be entirely successful in Hollywood. He did not appear to play the Hollywood game too well and probably should have stayed in radio. Towards the end of his days in the limelight, he appeared in *The Adventures of Champion*. Even then he was third billed beneath an animal and a child!

Physically he could be intimidating. On one occasion while shooting *The Man from Colorado* in 1947, director Charles Vidor (who

Jim Bannon as "Red Ryder." He later appeared in *The Adventures of Champion.*

was later fired) refused to let him leave the set after being told that Bannon's pregnant wife had been injured in a fall. Since he didn't budge, Bannon belted him and Vidor went down. Bannon stepped over him and went to aid his wife. He was also physically robust. On another occasion he played the lead in a television soap opera unaware that he was suffering from bronchial pneumonia.

Jim Bannon was born in Kansas City, Missouri, on April 9, 1917. He was the son of Lala and William Bannon and was of Irish extraction. He had one older brother, John Francis Bannon, who was a Jesuit Priest and eventually head of the history department at St. Louis University and who died in 1986. Bannon was educated at Rockhurst College where he was a star athlete in baseball and football, but the lead in a couple of college plays convinced him that his future lay in show business.

Radio became his target and he was added to the crew of announcers of a small station owned by the local newspaper *The Kansas City Kansan* in Kansas City, Kansas. After three months he headed for St. Louis and went to work for station KMOX, owned by the CBS network. After a year of this he flipped a coin and decided to head for California, where he arrived in June 1937. After a struggle he picked up a spot at the KHJ Mutual Network Station. There he first met half-Jewish, half-Irish radio actress Bea Benaderet (1906–1968), who became his first wife in August 1938. They had two children; son Jack, who was born on June 14, 1940, became an actor. Their daughter Maggie was born in 1947. Benaderet was instrumental in having him obtain a better job as a staff announcer at KFI. He also became a network announcer (primarily on NBC) on several prestigious radio shows such as those with Edgar Bergen and Charlie McCarthy and Joe Penner.

When it became likely that he would be drafted in 1942, Bannon returned to Kansas City, Missouri, to learn to fly so that he could enter the Air Transport Command rather than end up a casualty in the infantry. After logging sufficient hours to obtain a license, he flew back to California where he was ironically declared 4F by all branches of the services because of an ulcer. Instead he became a civilian instructor in November 1942, at Condor Field, a glider base in the Mojave Desert. This turned out to be a total waste of his time and talent.

When he resigned and returned to Hollywood in March 1943, his career as a radio announcer really picked up in the absence of much competition. The most significant assignment was *I Love a Mystery* (written by Carleton E. Morse) which ran five days a week. He was offered tests at MGM and 20th Century-Fox which he declined. Max Arnow, head of the talent department at Columbia Pictures, asked him to test for Columbia, which he did in April 1944. He did a successful test opposite Janis Carter, but this meant that he had to trade in his successful career as a radio announcer for a shot at a branch of show business he knew nothing about. He signed with Columbia because producer Wallace MacDonald was going to make a series of films based on the *I Love a Mystery* radio series and wanted Bannon to play Jack Packard since Mike Raffetto (the radio lead) looked nothing like the character.

Bannon's first film for them was *The Soul of A Monster* (1944), a low budget B movie which he hated. Max Arnow tried to persuade him to change his name, but Bannon refused. Since he had built up a reputation on radio under his real name, he was not about to change it. Conflicting schedules also put a considerable strain on his marriage. He played a role in a William Boyd Western, *Riders Of The Deadline* (1943). On account of his athletic prowess and horsemanship, he also doubled for one of the leads. He played the hero in the Western musical *The Gay Señorita* (1945), but his singing was so indifferent that he realized he would never make it as a singing cowboy.

When *I Love a Mystery* (1945) eventually became a movie and then a short-lived series, it was a disappointment. The problem was that Carleton E. Morse was not allowed to write the scripts. Instead the staff writers were turned loose on them, with disastrous results. Bannon also played supporting roles on some of the studio's bigger-budgeted features of which *Renegades* (1946) was the one he enjoyed most. In July 1947, he obtained a release from his contract because Columbia was not offering him the roles he wanted and had done little to promote him.

On the advice of his then-agents at MCA, he decided to freelance. Within a few weeks it became obvious that he was not going to make the grade as a star of any major production and he and MCA parted company. Antrim Short, a small-time agent, approached him with an offer to represent him which Bannon accepted with alacrity. Short secured him the lead in a 12-episode chapterplay at Republic called *Dangers of the Canadian Mounted* (1948). Elsewhere, however, the pickings were lean.

Over breakfast one morning in May 1948, he announced to his startled family that he proposed to become a Western star. To this end he painted his Buick convertible white and then had it decorated with steer horns. From that time onward he dressed exclusively in Western garb. This ploy paid off in August 1948, when he signed with a small outfit Equity Pictures to play "Red Ryder." (The rights to the character had originally been owned by Republic Pictures, but they let their option lapse and Equity Pictures acquired them.)

Equity Pictures was an outfit owned by Jerry Thomas, his father Harry and a silent partner named Jack Schwartz, whom Bannon intensely disliked. Prior to the interview, Bannon had his natural hair dyed red, which deceived the Thomas father and son into hiring him on the spot. They hired a talented youngster named Little Brown Jug Reynolds, who used the screen name Don Kay Reynolds, to play Little Beaver and veteran Emmett Lynn to play Buckskin, Ryder's sidekick. They shot the first two movies (1949's *Ride, Ryder, Ride* and *Roll, Thunder, Roll)* back to back. Thunder was the name of the black horse Bannon rode. He did most of his own stunts. He did many personal appearance tours and worked up a sharpshooting act in conjunction with the series.

"Red Ryder," however, was terminated after only four movies because Jack Schwartz made other feature films with stars who had no box office power. Exhibitors refused to book these turkeys unless the moneymaking "Red Ryder"s were given to them at a reduced rate. Equity Pictures barely made production costs back on the "Red Ryder" series. Bannon shot an inept pilot for a Red Ryder television series which came to nothing when the producers refused to hire Little Brown Jug Reynolds because he was too expensive. It became so frustrating that the company eventually folded in 1950.

Tom Parks, a wrestling promoter from St. Louis, hired Bannon to headline in a circus. The amount of time he had spent on the road since assuming the role of "Red Ryder" caused his marriage to fail and Bea Benaderet filed for divorce in September 1950. He tried to reactivate their relationship once in 1955, but it was dead and buried. Ironically, Benaderet in her last years enjoyed the kind of success on television with *Petticoat Junction* that Bannon craved. He had become so much associated with the character of "Red Ryder" that, in spite of reverting back to normal clothes and car, most producers and directors in Hollywood refused to have him in their movies. Even when Bannon was in heavy disguise, directors like Henry Hathaway and Roy Del Ruth would not cast him. Both personally and professionally, he reached his lowest ebb in 1950.

He was rescued from obscurity when an offer came from an outfit called Wilding Pictures to shoot a commercial/industrial film in Chicago in 1950 for Swift and Company with actor Milburn Stone. Normally film actors tended to regard commercials as beneath their dignity, but Bannon found the experience very rewarding, especially because of the integrity of the production company. While doing this, he was approached by Mary Dooling, who operated Talent Inc., a large agency. Dooling offered to represent him if he cared to relocate.

He returned to California where Antrim Short was approached by producer Vincent Fennelly with an offer to costar Bannon in the Whip Wilson Western series he was producing at Monogram. The series was dying and Fennelly figured that the addition of a couple of new characters (Bannon and Fuzzy Knight) would give it a new lease on life. Bannon regarded the scripts as appalling and personally disliked Whip Wilson, whom he considered untalented. Director Lewis Collins shared his views, refused to direct Wilson and treated Bannon as the star. Bannon shot five segments and was happy to walk away.

With no further movie offers forthcoming, he relocated to Chicago where he signed with Mary Dooling. She negotiated for him to appear in a regular role in the live television soap opera *Hawkins Falls* for the NBC network. He did this for five years. It was a non-exclusive deal so this left him free to take other offers (mainly to do several commercials, radio announcing and to appear in the occasional feature film). Romantically his name was linked with actress Janis Carter.

He made a whirlwind trip of three days to Hollywood in April 1955, and was written out of *Hawkins Falls* for that period. The purpose of his visit was to shoot the pilot for a Western television series called *The Adventures of Champion*. The production company was "Flying A" (owned by Gene Autry) and the deal was packaged by Mitch Hamilburg, Autry's agent. Champion was the name of Autry's horse. In this he was the leader of a herd of wild horses who befriends a little boy, Ricky North (Barry Curtis). Bannon played Sandy North, his uncle.

The pilot was accepted, which turned out to be a blessing because *Hawkins Falls* finished soon afterwards. Between August and November 1955, 26 episodes of *The Adventures of Champion* were made. The series was shot on location at Pioneertown, which had excellent production facilities but nothing else to recommend it. Accommodations consisted of one motel, and boredom reigned supreme. When Bannon accidentally rode into a cactus on one occasion, there was no First Aid kit, so the medical treatment he received was rudimentary. When the series ended, he was more relieved than saddened.

Bannon once again became active as a radio announcer in New York and occasionally in Chicago. In March 1961, he married Barbara Cork, a 20-year-old part-time Marshall Fields model and college student. By coincidence, she was also half-Jewish and half-Irish. By her he raised a second family, vowing, "This time I won't screw it up." He spent time in Pleno, Texas, but eventually died in obscurity in Ojai, California, on July 28, 1984, age 67.

Jim Bannon Filmography

1943: *Riders of the Deadline.*

1944: *The Soul of a Monster, Sergeant Mike, The Missing Juror.*

1945: *Tonight and Every Night, I Love a Mystery, The Gay Señorita, Out of the Depths.*

1946: *Renegades, The Devil's Mask, The Unknown.*

1947: *Johnny O'Clock, Framed, The Corpse Came C.O.D., The 13th Hour, T-Men.*

1948: *The Man from Colorado, Miraculous Journey, Dangers of the Canadian Mounted* (serial), *Frontier Revenge, Trail to Laredo.*

1949: *Daughter of the Jungle, Ride Ryder Ride. Roll Thunder Roll, The Fighting Redhead.*

1950: *Kill the Umpire!, Jiggs and Maggie Out West, The Cowboy and the Prizefighter.*

1951: *Riding the Outlaw Trail, Sierra Passage, Canyon Raiders, Nevada Badmen, Lawless Cowboys, Stagecoach Driver, Wanted Dead or Alive, Unknown World, The Texas Rangers.*

1952: *Rodeo, The Black Lash.*

1953: *Jack Slade, The Great Jesse James Raid, War Arrow, The Command.*

1957: *Chicago Confidential.*

1959: *They Came to Cordura, Inside the Mafia.*

1962: *40 Pounds of Trouble.*

1963: *A Gathering of Eagles, Man's Favorite Sport?*

1964: *Good Neighbor Sam.*

1966: *Madame X.*

Television Series

1951–1955: *Hawkins Falls.*

1955–1956: *The Adventures of Champion* as Sandy North.

Sources

Bannon, Jim. Collected letters of Jim Bannon 1937–1961, published privately.

Corneau, Ernest N. *The Hall of Fame of Western Film Stars.* N. Quincy, MA: Christopher, 1969.

Picture Show Annual. London: Amalgamated Press, 1947.

TREVOR BARDETTE

Trevor Bardette was born in Nashville, Arkansas, on November 19, 1902. He relocated to Denver in 1907 and to Los Angeles in 1915. He was educated at Oregon University and

Northwestern University where he studied mechanical engineering. He became fascinated with drama while at college. Upon graduation he gravitated to New York, where he won a role in a musical called *Flossie* because of his fluency in Spanish.

He appeared with numerous stock companies until 1936, when he headed for Hollywood and made his screen debut. He went on to appear in numerous films (usually playing villains) and later on television. One of his most popular film portrayals was as the villainous Pegleg in the serial *Overland with Kit Carson* (1939). His best-remembered television role was as Old Man Clanton in the Western series *The Life and Legend of Wyatt Earp* during its last two seasons. He later retired and went to live in Arizona. Bardette died on November 28, 1977, at age 75.

Trevor Bardette Filmography

1937: *They Won't Forget, The Great Garrick, Borderland, White Bondage.*
1938: *Mystery House, In Old Mexico, Topa Topa, Stand Up and Fight.*
1939: *Let Freedom Ring, The Oklahoma Kid, Charlie Chan at Treasure Island, Overland with Kit Carson* (serial).
1940: *Girl From Havana, The Westerner, The Refugee, Abe Lincoln in Illinois, The Dark Command, Wagons Westward, Three Faces West, Killers of the Wild, Young Buffalo Bill, Winners of the West* (serial), *Torrid Zone.*
1941: *Romance of the Rio Grande, Topper Returns, Mystery Ship, Doomed Caravan, Buy Me That Town, Wild Bill Hickok Rides, Red River Valley, Jungle Girl* (serial).
1942: *Flight Lieutenant, Henry and Dizzy, The Apache Trail, The Secret Code* (serial).
1943: *The Moon Is Down, The Deerslayer, The Chance of a Lifetime.*
1944: *None Shall Escape, The Whistler, Tampico, The Black Parachute, U-Boat Prisoner, Faces in the Fog.*
1945: *Counter-Attack, Dick Tracy.*
1946: *The Hoodlum Saint, The Big Sleep, The Man Who Dared, Sing While You Dance, Dragonwyck.*
1947: *The Sea of Grass, Slave Girl, Wyoming, The Last Round-up, Marshal of Cripple Creek, Ramrod, T-Men, The Beginning or the End.*
1948: *The Loves of Carmen, Secret Service Investigator, Alias a Gentleman, Sword of the Avenger, Adventures in Silverado, Return of the Whistler, Black Eagle, Sundown at Santa Fe, Marshal of Amarillo, Behind Locked Doors, The Gallant Region.*
1949: *The Blazing Trail, Renegades of the Sage, Sheriff of Wichita, Hellfire, Song of India, Omoo Omoo the Shark God, The Wyoming Bandit, San Antone Ambush, Apache Chief.*
1950: *The Palomino, Hills of Oklahoma, A Lady Without Passport, Gun Crazy (*a.k.a. *Deadly Is The Female), Union Station.*
1951: *The Texas Rangers, Gene Autry and the Mounties, Fort Savage Raider, Fort Dodge Stampede, The Barefoot Milkman, Lorna Doone, Flight to Mars, Honeychile.*
1952: *Lone Star, The San Francisco Story, Montana Territory, Macao.*
1953: *Ambush at Tomahawk Gap, Thunder Over the Plains, Bandits of the West, The Desert Song, The Outlaw Stallion, A Perilous Journey, Red River Shore, The Sun Shines Bright.*
1954: *Destry, Johnny Guitar.*
1955: *Run for Cover, The Man from Bitter Ridge.*
1956: *Red Sundown, The Rack.*
1957: *Shoot-Out at Medicine Bend, The Monolith Monsters, Dragoon Wells Massacre, The Hard Man.*
1958: *Thunder Road, The Saga Of Hemp Brown.*
1959: *The Mating Game.*
1963: *Papa's Delicate Condition.*
1964: *The Raiders.*
1967: *The Way West.*
1969: *Mackenna's Gold.*
1975: *Run for the Roses.*

Television Series

1959–1961: *The Life and Legend of Wyatt Earp* as Old Man Clanton.

Sources

Inman, David. *The TV Encyclopedia.* New York: Perigee, 1991.
McClure, Arthur F. and Ken D. Jones. *Heroes, Heavies and Sagebrush.* South Brunswick and New York: Barnes, 1972.
Truitt, Evelyn Mack. *Who Was Who on Screen Illustrated Edition.* New York: Bowker, 1984.

GENE BARRY

The name of Gene Barry has become synonymous with a kind of sartorial elegance. Even when he played television Western hero Bat Masterson, he was not the gritty, grimy Westerner depicted in so many films and television series. Instead he was debonair, sophisticated and fastidious. He dressed nattily and carried a gold-topped cane. Bat Masterson was not, however, a sissy. He was a crack shot and a force to be reckoned with. Barry later became even more successful on television with the series *Burke's Law* before abandoning television in later years for the world of the stage, particularly musicals, where his star shone very brightly indeed.

Gene Barry was born Eugene Klass in Manhattan on June 14, 1921, the son of Martin Klass, a jeweler who died in 1969, and Eva Conn. He is the eldest of five children and was educated at New Utrecht High School, Brooklyn. Physically robust, he enjoyed football, but found early fame as a violin player, being something of a prodigy (he appeared in public and was entertaining audiences at the age of six). His potential as a concert violinist was shattered when he broke his arm while playing football.

He then decided to switch to singing while in school. He made such considerable progress that in his final term, he won a major singing contest and was awarded a scholarship to the Chatham Square School of Music. "When I'd broken my arm," he recalled, "my father told me that things always happen for the best. I couldn't understand this, but I guess he was right, because if I had not taken up singing, I would never have become an actor." Both his parents were delighted with his choice of career because they were frustrated thespians themselves.

A local radio station eventually signed him to a weekly show. One night he was heard by bandleader Teddy Powell, who offered him a job with his band doing one-night stands. The job of dance band vocalist led him to a meeting with Max Reinhardt, a famous stage producer. This resulted in an offer to play the role of The Bat in a spectacular Broadway presentation of the musical *Rosalinda* (1942). He stayed with the *Rosalinda* production for nearly two years and then went into *The Merry Widow* (1943). One night Mike Todd came backstage to see him. Todd wanted him for a role opposite Mae West in *Catherine Was Great* (1944) and offered to pay him twice as much as he was being paid for *The Merry Widow*.

He accepted Todd's offer. While he was appearing with West, he received an offer to do a musical, *Glad To See You*, at double the salary Todd was paying him. He talked matters over with the dynamic Todd, who informed him that he would not stand in his way if he wanted to go, but the choice was his. He surprised Todd by saying that he would accept the other offer. He recalled, "When I left, Mike gave me a look which said that I'd made a terrible mistake. In one way I did, because the show didn't do so well, but if I'd not left Mike, I would never have met my wife!"

Her stage name was Julie Carson and she was costarring with Ethel Barrymore in *The Corn Is Green* when they were introduced at Sardi's. Her real name was Betty Claire Kalb. She was an ex-high school jumping champion who had also been a sculptor and a writer of jingles and poetry. They immediately began dating and married on October 22, 1944 (three weeks after their introduction). Of her he says, "She is still the most important person in my life." They have two sons, Michael Lewis, born in 1946, and Fredric James, born in 1953, together with an adopted daughter, Elizabeth.

Despite his personal happiness, his career nosedived. Work became very hard to come by and things began to turn desperate. "I didn't know where my next job was coming from," he said. In order to make ends meet he obtained jobs in other fields such as working for a jeweler and then as a salesman. "Those years were pretty dark," he recalled, "and just when everything seemed to be going so well. But if it hadn't been for Betty, I would not have been able to retain faith in myself. She was my inspiration. She kept believing. She kept encouraging. We matured side by side through those dark years from nothingness to success. That's why we're so close."

The tide began to turn again in his favor

Gene Barry in *Bat Masterson*.

when he was performing in an Equity Library Theater production of *Idiot's Delight*. An agent sitting in the audience one night encouraged him to move to the West Coast after seeing him perform. He became a busy television actor in New York during the early days of live television. He, his wife and son arrived in Hollywood in a beat-up jalopy to audition unsuccessfully for a role in the motion picture *The Turning Point*. Nevertheless in 1951 he was signed to a contract with Paramount which began a career in movies, frequently in villainous roles. About these, he observed, "I've played so many heavies in my time and I've died so often in films that I was beginning to wonder what it was people didn't like about me!"

Bat Masterson was produced by Ziv Television Programs Incorporated. It was a half-hour television series of 108 episodes shot in black and white for NBC about a sheriff who cleaned up Dodge City in the early days of the West. It was based on an authentic character with a slightly exaggerated reputation. A former professional gambler, Bat Masterson was the Beau Brummell of the West. He wore a derby, white collar and tie, a neat blue suit and polished shoes and kissed women's hands. Barry was picked for the role by Ziv chairman Fred W. Ziv himself after 23 other actors had been tested for the part.

When he was asked to play Bat Masterson in 1957, he initially declined. "I didn't want to do a Western as I preferred to stay in films. But the producers explained the character was a different kind of cowboy ... one who wore a derby hat and carried a cane. The idea then became much more appealing and I agreed to play the role." After three years in the part he said that he had had enough. "A television show becomes a factory, grinding out so many products in so many days. The pace is killing. I hate factories." He reprised the role of Bat Masterson in the *Paradise* series in 1989 and in *The Gambler Returns: The Luck Of The Draw* in 1990.

Subsequently Barry enjoyed his greatest professional success in the series *Burke's Law* (1963–1965) as Amos Burke, a millionaire homicide detective who drove around in his Rolls-Royce solving crimes. The series was a male forerunner of *Murder She Wrote*. Its most notable asset was the endless roll call of famous Hollywood names who appeared as suspects in every episode. Its biggest demerit was that the formula was not as pat as *Murder She Wrote* and the scripts were not especially ingenious or original.

When he was searching for his Amos Burke, the show's producer Aaron Spelling said, "Amos Burke is a man who is positively smothered with women. The actor I'll choose will be worthy of that privilege. He'll be no ordinary being, whoever he is. The accent of the show is on pure glamour and lavish entertainment, with a hero every man dreams of emulating and every woman admires." When he was first approached to play the role, Barry resisted, but as soon as he read a script, he was hooked. He enjoyed playing Burke despite the hard work the part called for. The series was later transformed into *Amos Burke—Secret Agent* (1966) in which Burke became a James Bond–type spy. This was a dreadful flop and only lasted half a season. The CBS network together with Spelling-TV resurrected the series *Burke's Law* in the 1990s with Barry reprising his original role, now with a young son to do the legwork. He is played by Peter Barton, best-known for the CBS daytime soap opera *The Young and the Restless*.

Barry starred as newspaper magnate Glenn Howard in the 90-minute series *The Name of the Game* (1968–1971), rotating with Robert Stack and Tony Franciosa. He was also the star of the short-lived television series *The Adventurer* (1972), shot in Europe. This was his weakest series, in which he played a highly unlikely spy with the cover of being a movie star! After this Barry abandoned television series for musical theatrical productions. He starred in *Kismet, No No Nanette, Annie Get Your Gun* and *Fiddler on the Roof*. In 1983 he was nominated for a Tony Award as the best male lead in a musical for his role as Georges in *La Cage Aux Folles*, a part with which he is particularly associated. He appeared in this until 1986. He has also had one of the slickest cabaret acts of any Hollywood actor. His act (entitled *Gene Barry in One)* included singing, dancing, telling jokes and projecting an amiable, witty, relaxed personality.

He has actively campaigned for John F. and Robert Kennedy, Lyndon Johnson and Hubert Humphrey. In 1970 he was urged to run for the United States Senate, but declined. He has interests in several businesses including mining and construction and had his own company, Barbety Enterprises. He lives in an extremely elegant colonial house in Hollywood, lavishly decorated and complete with a beautiful swimming pool. He designed and built the house to his own specification.

Gene Barry Filmography

1952: *The Atomic City, The War of the Worlds.*
1953: *The Girls of Pleasure Island, Those Redheads from Seattle.*
1954: *Alaska Seas, Red Garters, Naked Alibi.*
1955: *Soldier Of Fortune, The Purple Mask.*

1956: *The Houston Story, Back from Eternity.*
1957: *The 27th Day, China Gate, Forty Guns.*
1958: *Hong Kong Confidential, Thunder Road.*
1967: *Maroc 7.*
1968: *Prescription: Murder* (TV), *Istanbul Express* (TV).
1969: *Subterfuge.*
1970: *Do You Take This Stranger* (TV).
1971: *The Devil and Miss Sarah* (TV).
1974: *The Second Coming of Suzanne* (also produced).
1977: *Ransom for Alice* (TV).
1979: *Guyana: The Crime of the Century.*
1980: *A Cry for Love* (TV), *The Girl, the Gold Watch and Dynamite* (TV).
1981: *The Adventures of Nellie Bly* (TV).
1987: *Perry Mason: The Case of the Lost Love* (TV).
1989: *Turn Back the Clock* (TV).

Television Series

1955–1956: *Our Miss Brooks* as Gene Talbot.
1958–1961: *Bat Masterson* as Bat Masterson.
1963–1965: *Burke's Law* as Police Captain Amos Burke.
1966: *Amos Burke—Secret Agent* as Amos Burke.
1968–1971: *The Name of the Game* as Glenn Howard.
1972: *The Adventurer* as Gene Bradley.
1993–1995: *Burke's Law* as Amos Burke.

Miniseries

1977: *Aspen.*
1990: *The Gambler Returns: The Luck of the Draw.*

Sources

Contemporary Theater, Film and Television Volume 12. Detroit, MI: Gale, 1994.
Ferguson, Ken. *Television Stars Annual.* London: Purnell, 1966.
Hyem, Janette. "Presenting Mr. Gene Barry." *TV Scene* magazine 1990.
Meyers, Richard. *TV Detectives.* San Diego CA: Barnes, 1981.
Picture Show Annual. London: Amalgamated Press, 1954.
Speed, F. Maurice. *The Western Film and Television Annual.* London: MacDonald, 1959.

BILLY BARTY

Billy Barty was born in Millsboro, Pennsylvania, on October 25, 1924. He is a midget, but his parents were normal sized. His family relocated to California in 1927. He made his screen debut at the age of three in a short called *Wedded Blisters.* He appeared as Mickey Rooney's kid brother in the *Mickey McGuire* shorts between 1927 and 1934. One of his most notable appearances was as the all-knowing child in *Gold Diggers of 1933.* During the 1930s and early 1940s he worked in vaudeville with his sisters and did impressions of leading entertainers such as James Cagney and Jimmy Durante.

He temporarily retired in 1942 and finished high school with the intention of becoming a sports journalist via college. Instead, show business dragged him back. By 1948 he was doing a variety act with a partner. From 1952 to 1960 he was a member of Spike Jones's City Slickers, scoring his biggest hit with a hilarious parody of Liberace's "I'm in the Mood for Love" in 1954.

He was active in television work from its embryo days. He played the midget in the marginal Western series *Circus Boy.* After playing host of a children's show in Los Angeles during the early 1960s, he resumed his film career. He continued to be active on television, mainly in children's shows in the 1960s and 1970s. In the short-lived sitcom *Ace Crawford Private Eye* he played Inch the diminutive bartender. In real life a tireless worker on behalf of midgets, he founded two organizations to help them, "The Little People Of America" in 1957 and later "The Billy Barty Foundation." He is married and has a son, born in 1970.

Billy Barty Filmography

1931: *Daddy Long Legs.*
1933: *Gold Diggers of 1933, Out All Night, Roman Scandals, Footlight Parade, Alice in Wonderland.*
1934: *Gift of Gab.*
1935: *A Midsummer Night's Dream, Bride of Frankenstein.*
1937: *Nothing Sacred, Hollywood Hotel.*
1942: *Here We Go Again.*
1950: *Pygmy Island.*
1952: *The Clown.*
1957: *The Undead.*
1962: *Billy Rose's Jumbo.*
1964: *Roustabout.*
1965: *Harem Scarum.*
1970: *Pufnstuf.*
1973: *The Godmothers.*
1974: *The Day of the Locust, Punch and Jody* (TV).
1975: *Won Ton Ton, The Dog Who Saved Hollywood.*
1976: *Twin Detectives* (TV), *The Amazing Dobermans, W. C. Fields and Me.*
1977: *The Happy Hooker Goes to Washington.*
1978: *Foul Play, Lord of the Rings* (voice only).
1979: *Firepower, Skatetown USA.*
1980: *Hardly Working.*
1981: *Being Different, Under the Rainbow.*
1984: *Night Patrol.*
1985: *Legend.*
1986: *Tough Guys.*
1987: *Masters of the Universe, Crazylegs (*a.k.a. *Off the Mark), Rumpelstiltskin, Body Slam, Snow White.*
1988: *Willow.*
1989: *UHF, Lobster Man from Mars.*
1990: *Wishful Thinking, The Rescuers Down Under* (voice only), *Diggin' Up Business.*
1991: *Life Stinks.*
1992: *The Naked Truth.*
1994: *The Princess and the Pea, The Legend of D. B. Taggart.*

Television Series

1951–1952: *Ford Festival.*
1954: *The Spike Jones Show.*
1956–1958: *Circus Boy* as Little Tom.
1957: *The Spike Jones Show.*
1958: *The Club Oasis.*
1974–1976: *Sigmund and the Sea Monsters.*
1983: *Ace Crawford Private Eye* as Inch.

Sources

Goldrup, Tom and Jim. *Feature Players: The Stories Behind the Faces Volume One.* Published privately, 1986.
Quinlan, David. *Illustrated Directory of Film Character Actors Second Edition.* London: Batsford, 1995.
Smith, Ron. *Comic Support.* New York: Citadel, 1993.

HAL BAYLOR

Hal Baylor was born Hal Bittan in San Antonio, Texas, on December 10, 1918. His parents divorced when he was very young. He relocated with his mother to Vallejo, California, where she ran a beauty salon and married again to Walter Fieberling; Hal Bittan adopted the name Hal Fieberling. He was very keen on sports so he studied physical education at Chico State University in 1938 and then transferred on a sports scholarship to Washington State University, where he studied business administration. While at Chico State he made his screen debut as one of the band of Robin Hood in *The Adventures of Robin Hood* (1938) because the movie was shot on location there. Nevertheless, he had no plans to pursue an acting career.

He became a successful professional boxer, losing only five out of 57 bouts. In 1942 he entered the Marine Corps, serving in World War II and being discharged in 1946. Afterwards he tried to return to professional boxing, but his family objected. Instead he enrolled in medical school in Oakland, California, where

Hal Baylor in *The Life and Legend of Wyatt Earp*.

he studied to become a chiropractor. He proved to be unsuited to this profession so he returned to Hollywood to resume boxing for a living. While there he ran into actor Joe Kirkwood (whom he had known in the armed forces), who used him in one of his *Joe Palooka* boxing pictures. He had one day's work and earned $300.

Art Cohn had written a script which was eventually filmed as *The Set-Up* (1949). He knew Hal Fieberling from his previous boxing days and suggested that he should play Robert Ryan's opponent in the film. Fieberling won the part and spent four weeks working on the movie at $400 a week, which convinced him that his future lay as an actor. On the strength of this he was signed by an agent, but he had no formal acting training. In the early 1950s he changed his name to Hal Baylor since Fieberling was difficult to spell and pronounce. The surname Baylor he derived from his great-grandfather, who founded Baylor University. He sometimes used the Christian name Steve.

After a while he signed with a more prestigious agency which sometimes found him so much work that he was shooting two features simultaneously. Once producers discovered that he could ride, he became a mainstay of television Western series. He has calculated that he has appeared in over a thousand episodes, in most of which he was cast as the heavy, a guise he much prefers. One of the few features in which he played a romantic role was *This Is My Love* (1954), which starred Linda Darnell. He had a semi-regular role for the first season in *The Life and Legend of Wyatt Earp* as Billy Thompson, one of a pair of outlaw brothers.

He continued to be active in show business until 1983, when he had encountered one too many young people who were running the business. They simply neither knew his work nor cared about his credits, so he retired. An outdoor type, his hobbies are hunting, fishing and golf. He resides with his wife Shirley in Los Angeles.

Hal Baylor Filmography

1938: *The Adventures of Robin Hood.*
1948: *Joe Palooka in Winner Take All.*
1949: *The Set-Up, The Crooked Way, Yes Sir That's My Baby, Sands of Iwo Jima.*
1950: *Destination Big House, Dial 1119, For Heaven's Sake, Joe Palooka in the Squared Circle.*
1951: *The Guy Who Came Back, Jim Thorpe All American.*
1952: *Big Jim McLain, Fort Osage, One Minute to Zero, The Wild Blue Yonder.*
1953: *Champ for a Day, Breakdown, Flight Nurse, Hot News, Island in the Sky, The Sun Shines Bright, Woman They Almost Lynched.*
1954: *Prince Valiant, River of No Return, This Is My Love, Tobor the Great, Black Tuesday.*
1955: *Outlaw Treasure.*
1956: *Away All Boats, The Burning Hills.*
1957: *Kiss Them for Me.*
1958: *The Young Lions.*
1959: *Operation Petticoat.*
1960: *Pepe*
1963: *Johnny Cool.*
1964: *Quick Before It Melts.*
1966: *Lord Love a Duck.*
1967: *The Gnome-Mobile.*
1970: *The Cheyenne Social Club, WUSA.*
1971: *The Barefoot Executive, Evel Knievel, The Grissom Gang.*
1972: *Pick-up on 101.*
1973: *Emperor of the North Pole, One Little Indian.*
1974: *The Bears and I.*
1975: *Hustle, A Boy and His Dog.*
1976: *The Macahans* (TV), *The New Daughters of Joshua Cabe* (TV).

Television Series

1955–1956: *The Life and Legend of Wyatt Earp* as Billy Thompson.

Sources

Anderson, Bob. "And In This Corner," winter 1995, and "The Winner and Still Champ." *Trail Dust* magazine, spring 1996.
Goldrup, Tom and Jim Goldrup. *Feature Players The Stories Behind the Faces Volume Two.* Published privately, 1992.
Picture Show Annual. London: Amalgamated Press, 1956.
Picture Show's Who's Who on Screen. London: Amalgamated Press, c. 1956.

NOAH BEERY, JR.

Noah Beery, Jr., was born on August 10, 1913, the son of actor Noah Beery and Marguerite Lindsey. Wallace Beery was his uncle. The nickname "Pidge" was given to him by Josie Cohan, the sister of George M. Cohan, shortly after he was born in New York City, where Beery, Sr., was appearing on stage. Initially after moving to California, the family lived in a house on Vine Street in Hollywood, but later relocated to the San Fernando Valley. He was educated at Curtis School, Los Angeles Urban Military Academy, Harvard Military Academy, the Hollywood High School for Girls and North Hollywood High School. Although he made his screen debut as a child in *The Mark Of Zorro* (1920), it was only after he graduated from school that he embarked on a career as a professional actor.

Carl Laemmle, Jr., signed him to a contract at Universal and proceeded to groom him carefully by giving him small parts preparatory to promoting him to starring roles. In some of his earlier films he was the hero, but with *Tailspin Tommy* (1934) he settled into the rut of being the hero's sidekick which he seemed to prefer. He did play leads from time to time, but most of these were in bucolic comedies. Although many of his films were low-budgeters, he did appear in a few classics. His favorite film was *Red River* (1948), and Buck Jones and John Wayne were the stars he rated the highest.

When television came along, he appeared as a regular in several series, but continued to play supporting roles in feature films. In the marginal Western series *Circus Boy*, he played the part of Joey the Clown, the surrogate father of the title character (Mickey Braddock). When conflict was being experienced between the stars of the *Riverboat* series, which led to the departure of one of the leads, Beery was one of the actors drafted in to replace him for the aborted second season. Beery became best known as "Rocky," the genial, folksy father of hard-luck private eye Jim Rockford (James Garner) in TV's *The Rockford Files*. He was unavailable for the pilot because he was shooting the shortlived series *Doc Elliot* at the time, but was substituted when the series was picked up. The role earned him two Emmy nominations in 1977 and 1980. He rented a place at Malibu while filming his scenes.

An unpretentious man, Beery became disillusioned with urban encroachment on his home in the San Fernando Valley in the mid-1950s and moved to the Clear Creek-B Ranch outside of Tehachapi, California. There he enjoyed the simple life being with nature and tending livestock. His other main hobby was sculpting, examples of which were sold in Western art galleries. He was in poor health after suffering a stroke in the mid–1980s. In mid-September 1994, he underwent an operation for bleeding in his brain. Although he survived the operation, he never fully recovered and died at his home on November 1, 1994, at age 81.

Noah Beery, Jr., married Maxine Jones, the only child of cowboy star Buck Jones, in the late 1930s. They had three children (Maxine, Buckland and Melissa) before divorcing in 1966. His first wife died in 1990 of cancer. In 1969 he married his second wife Lisa, who had two children by a previous marriage. She was at his side when he died.

Noah Beery, Jr. Filmography

1920: *The Mark of Zorro.*
1922: *Penrod.*
1923: *Penrod and Son.*
1929: *Father and Son.*
1932: *Heroes of the West* (serial), *The Jungle Mystery* (serial).
1933: *The Three Musketeers* (serial), *Fighting With Kit Carson* (serial), *Rustlers' Roundup.*
1934: *The Trail Beyond, Tailspin Tommy* (serial), *Tailspin Tommy in the Great Air Mystery* (serial).
1935: *Call of the Savage* (serial), *Stormy, Five Bad Men, Devil's Canyon.*
1936: *Parole, Ace Drummond* (serial).
1937: *The Road Back, Some Blondes Are Dangerous, The Mighty Treve.*
1938: *Girl's School, Trouble at Midnight, Outside the Law, Forbidden Valley.*
1939: *Only Angels Have Wings, Flight at Midnight, Of Mice and Men, Parents on Trial, Bad Lands.*

1940: *Twenty Mule Team, A Little Bit of Heaven, The Carson City Kid, The Light of Western Stars, Passport to Alcatraz.*
1941: *Sergeant York, Tanks a Million, Riders of Death Valley* (serial), *All-American Coed, Two in a Taxi.*
1942: *Overland Mail* (serial), *Dudes Are Pretty People, 'Neath Brooklyn Bridge, Hay Foot, Tennessee Johnson.*
1943: *Calaboose, What a Woman!, Prairie Chickens, Corvette K-225, Pardon My Gun, Gung Ho!, We've Never Been Licked, Top Man, Frontier Badmen.*
1944: *See My Lawyer, Follow the Boys, Weekend Pass, Allergic to Love, Hi Beautiful!.*
1945: *Under Western Skies, Her Lucky Night, The Daltons Ride Again, The Beautiful Cheat, The Crimson Canary.*
1946: *The Cat Creeps.*
1948: *Red River, Indian Agent.*
1949: *The Doolins of Oklahoma.*
1950: *Two Flags West, Davy Crockett—Indian Scout, Rocketship X-M, The Savage Horde.*
1951: *The Last Outpost, The Texas Rangers.*
1952: *The Story of Will Rogers, Wagons West, The Cimarron Kid.*
1953: *Wings of the Hawk, War Arrow, Tropic Zone.*
1954: *The Black Dakotas, Yellow Tomahawk.*
1955: *White Feather.*
1956: *Jubal, The Fastest Gun Alive.*
1957: *Decision at Sundown.*
1959: *Escort West.*
1960: *Guns of the Timberland, Inherit the Wind.*
1964: *Seven Faces of Dr. Lao.*
1966: *Incident at Phantom Hill.*
1967: *Hondo and the Apaches* (TV).
1968: *Journey to Shiloh.*
1969: *Heaven with a Gun, Little Fauss and Big Halsy, The Cockeyed Cowboys of Calico County (*a.k.a. *A Woman for Charlie).*
1973: *The Alpha Caper, The Petty Story (*a.k.a. *Smash-up Alley), Walking Tall.*
1974: *The Spikes Gang, Savages* (TV), *Sidekicks* (TV).
1976: *Walking Tall Part Two.*
1977: *Francis Gary Powers—The True Story of the U-2 Incident* (TV).
1978: *The Bastard* (TV).
1980: *The Great American Traffic Jam* (TV), *Gridlock* (TV).
1981: *The Capture of Grizzly Adams* (TV).
1982: *The Best Little Whorehouse in Texas, Mysterious Two* (TV).
1983: *Waltz Across Texas.*

Television Series

1956–1958: *Circus Boy* as Joey the Clown.
1960–1961: *Riverboat* as Bill Blake.
1967: *Hondo* as Buffalo Baker.
1974: *Doc Elliot* as Barney Weeks.
1974–1980: *The Rockford Files* as Joseph "Rocky" Rockford.
1982: *The Quest* as Art Henley.
1983–1984: *The Yellow Rose* as Luther Dillard.

Sources

Courneau, Ernest N. *The Hall of Fame of Western Film Stars.* N. Quincy, MA: Christopher, 1969.
Lentz, Harris M. *Obituaries in the Performing Arts, 1994.* Jefferson, NC: McFarland, 1996.
Miller, Lee O. *The Great Cowboy Stars of Movies & Television.* New Rochelle, NY: Arlington House, 1979.
Quinlan, David. *Illustrated Directory of Film Character Actors Second Edition.* London: Batsford, 1995.

JAMES BELL

James Harllee Bell was born in Suffolk, Virginia, on December 1, 1891, the son of James C. Bell and his wife Cartie Inez Harllee. He was educated at Virginia Polytechnic Institute and afterwards was employed for some years as an electrical engineer. He made his first stage appearance at the Globe Theater Atlantic City in June 1920, as Venustiano in *The Bad Man,* continuing in the same part in New York. From 1922 to 1927 he was engaged in stage management. He resumed his acting career in *A Free Soul* in 1928 and went on to appear in many other plays.

He made his screen debut as Red in *I Am a Fugitive from a Chain Gang* (1932). Although he made an abortive attempt to enter films in the 1930s, he remained primarily a stage actor both in New York and on the road throughout the 1930s and early 1940s until he permanently relocated to California in 1943. Most of his Westerns date from the postwar period. He also appeared on television and had a semiregular role as the foreman of the Flying Crown Ranch on the modern Western series *Sky King*. His hobbies were woodworking and farming, and he was a member of The Players Club in New York. James Bell died on October 26, 1973, at age 81. He was married to actress Joyce Arling.

James Bell Filmography

1932: *I Am a Fugitive from a Chain Gang.*
1933: *King's Vacation, Infernal Machine, Private Detective 62, Day of Reckoning, White Woman, Storm at Daybreak.*
1935: *The Lives of a Bengal Lancer.*
1943: *I Walked with a Zombie, My Friend Flicka, Gangway for Tomorrow, The Leopard Man, So Proudly We Hail!*
1944: *I Love a Soldier, Step Lively, Secret Mission.*
1945: *Thunderhead Son of Flicka, Blood on the Sun, The Girl of the Limberlost.*
1946: *The Spiral Staircase, The Unknown.*
1947: *Dead Reckoning, Blind Spot, The Sea of Grass, Brute Force, The Romance of Rosy Ridge, Driftwood, Killer McCoy, Philo Vance's Secret Mission, The Millerson Case.*
1948: *I Jane Doe, Sealed Verdict, Black Eagle.*
1949: *Streets of Laredo, Roughshod.*
1950: *Dial 1119, The Company She Keeps, Buckaroo Sheriff of Texas, The Violent Hour.*
1951: *The Dakota Kid, Flying Leathernecks, Arizona Manhunt, Red Mountain.*
1952: *Japanese War Bride, Wild Horse Ambush, Ride the Man Down, Million Dollar Mermaid.*
1953: *Devil's Canyon, All the Brothers Were Valiant, The Last Posse.*
1954: *The Glenn Miller Story, Riding Shotgun, Crime Wave, About Mrs. Leslie, Black Tuesday.*
1955: *Marty, Strategic Air Command, Lay That Rifle Down, Teenage Crime Wave, Sincerely Yours, A Lawless Street, Texas Lady.*
1956: *Huk, Four Girls in Town, The Search for Bridey Murphy, Tribute to a Bad Man.*
1957: *The Lonely Man, Back from the Dead, Johnny Trouble, The Tin Star.*
1958: *In Love and War.*
1959: *The Oregon Trail, -30-.*
1961: *Claudelle Inglish, Posse from Hell.*
1963: *Twilight of Honor.*

Television Series

1951–1954: *Sky King* as the foreman of the Flying Crown Ranch.

Sources

McClure, Arthur F. and Jones, Ken D. *Heroes, Heavies and Sagebrush.* South Brunswick and New York: Barnes, 1972.
Truitt, Evelyn Mack. *Who Was Who on Screen Illustrated Edition.* New York: Bowker 1984.
Who's Who in the Theater 10th Edition. London: Pitman, 1947.

Note

Many reference books erroneously credit Bell with the part played by Walter Baldwin in *Stranger on Horseback* (1955).

FRANCES BERGEN

Frances Bergen was born Frances Westerman in Birmingham, Alabama, in 1922, the daughter of William and Lilly Mae Westerman. She came from an extremely affluent family.

Her father was vice-president of an interior decorating company. She was educated at Robert E. Lee Junior High School until she was ten, when her beloved father died of tuberculosis after a three-month stay in a sanitarium. Both mother and daughter were distraught. Her mother insisted on them relocating to California where they could begin a new life.

Although the family had been left extremely well provided for, her mother had not been tutored in business and lost a lot of money. This was compounded when she remarried a man named Parry Boyd, who came from a good New England family but was a wastrel and squandered what remained of their fortune. He then walked out on them. Her mother was forced to work for the first time in her life, waitressing in a boarding house.

Frances Westerman grew up with a good voice and figure, but there was no longer any money for her education and singing lessons. When she graduated from Los Angeles High School, she first worked as a filing clerk and then as a model for a department store. She was torn between dual ambitions of being a singer or a John Robert Powers model, but elected to try her luck in New York as soon as she had saved some money.

She first met ventriloquist Edgar Bergen when she was 19 in 1941 and had gone to one of his radio broadcasts with a friend who was the wife of his head writer. She went backstage, where they were introduced. The following day he invited her to go flying in his private plane. Despite the fact that there was an instant attraction, she still went to New York as planned where she was quickly signed by the John Robert Powers agency. Although she deeply desired to be a high fashion model, her healthy Californian appearance was not the one that was in vogue with the high command of the magazine world, so her ambition was thwarted.

Nevertheless she became a success as a lingerie and swimsuit model. Her greatest fame came from being the Chesterfield cigarette girl on billboards. Despite his misgivings about their age difference and the warnings of his lawyers who dismissed her as a gold digger, she and Edgar Bergen conducted a long-distance courtship which culminated in their marriage in Mexico on June 28, 1945. Their daughter, who became actress Candice Bergen, was born on May 8, 1946, and their son Kris Edgar, who later became a film editor, was born on October 12, 1961.

As his assistant, she appeared alongside her husband when he performed on stage in nightclubs and for G.I.s stationed in Berlin after World War II and later in Vietnam. During the 1950s she rehearsed and performed a nightclub act of her own in the United States and Canada. Her repertoire consisted of comfortable songs and clever patter. She appeared in a couple of feature films and on television in the semi-regular role of Madame Francine, the stunning and vibrant proprietor of the nitery frequented by title character Jock Mahoney in *Yancy Derringer*.

Her marriage (one of Hollywood's happiest unions) ended with Edgar Bergen's death on September 30, 1978. Shortly afterwards, Frances Bergen was contacted by a casting agent who wanted her to test for a part in *American Gigolo*. Since appearing in that 1980 hit, she has played in a handful of feature films; appeared in the miniseries *Hollywood Wives* with daughter Candice (a role which she won on her own merits); and performed in the national touring company of *On Your Toes*. Frances Bergen continues to reside in Beverly Hills.

Frances Bergen Filmography

1953: *Titanic*.
1954: *Her Twelve Men*.
1957: *Interlude*.
1980: *American Gigolo*.
1981: *Rich and Famous*.
1982: *Bare Essence* (TV).
1983: *The Star Chamber*.
1984: *The Muppets Take Manhattan* (cameo).
1986: *The Morning After*.
1990: *Eating*.
1993: *Made in America*.

Television Series

1958–1959: *Yancy Derringer* as Madame Francine.

Miniseries

1985: *Hollywood Wives*.
1987: *Nutcracker Money, Madness and Murder*.

Sources

Brooks, Tim. *The Complete Directory to Prime Time TV Stars 1946–Present.* New York: Ballantine Books, 1987.

Holt, Georgia, Phyllis Quinn and Sue Russell. *Star Mothers: The Moms Behind the Celebrities.* New York: Simon and Schuster, 1988.

AMANDA BLAKE

Whenever Marshal Matt Dillon faced problems in television's longest running Western series *Gunsmoke*, he knew he could always obtain comfort from Miss Kitty, alias actress Amanda Blake, the titian-haired, golden-hearted owner of Dodge City's Long Branch saloon.

Amanda Blake was born Beverly Louise Neill in Buffalo, New York, on February 20, 1929, of mixed English and Scottish descent. She began her acting career at the age of seven in a school play. She attended grammar and high school in Buffalo and when she moved to Claremont, California, enrolled at Claremont High, from which she graduated. She also attended Pomona College. Upon graduation she worked as a telephone operator at $40 a week. Her diction brought her radio work in her home town and she also did dramatic readings for women's clubs. She launched herself on a full acting schedule that found her doing summer stock in New England and "little theater" activity. She graced such plays as *You Can't Take It with You, George Washington Slept Here, The Corn Is Green, Macbeth, Antigone* and *Parlor Story.* She was signed by MGM, without a conventional test, as a potential successor to Greer Garson and made her screen debut in *Stars In My Crown* (1950). MGM farmed her out to other studios where she occasionally essayed the lead in B movies like *Miss Robin Crusoe* (1954).

She made her television debut as the lead in the "Double Exposure" episode of *Schlitz Playhouse* in the early 1950s. The role helped to establish her as a top performer and led to starring roles in such anthology series as *General Electric Theater, Four Star Playhouse, Cavalcade of America* and *Lux Video Theater.* In 1955 she began her 19-year role as Kitty Russell in *Gunsmoke,* the most famous adult Western television series. As the owner of the Long Branch saloon, Blake's quiet style and banked fires romance with Marshal Dillon struck a responsive chord and won her a large and loyal following. "The question I'm always being asked," she said, "is what the relationship is between Kitty and Matt. My reply is always the same—their relationship is unresolved. Whatever the viewer thinks, that's it." When she took over the role, she devised her own biography of Kitty in order to help with the characterization. She goes to Dodge City after suffering a broken romance in New Orleans. In Dodge she finds the kind of life she is looking for, running the town's saloon. When CBS threatened to cancel the series in 1967, outraged fans forced the network to bring it back and it ran for another seven years.

Between them, Matt, Kitty, Chester (Dennis Weaver) and Doc (Milburn Stone) managed to solve just about every crisis which confronted them in the episodes of *Gunsmoke.* They were among the most popular stars on television. They were equally close off-screen. With Weaver and Stone she also teamed up in a vaudeville act based on *Gunsmoke.* These three stars barnstormed the country entertaining full-house audiences during a break in filming at weekends. "I'd never sung a note until Milburn convinced me I could," she said, "and when I tried I found my voice lower than Dennis's. I sang a number called 'Long Branch Blues' which told the story of Kitty's life and her relationship with Matt Dillon. It was great fun."

Of her role she said, "I've loved every minute of it." In 1959 she was nominated for an Emmy Award for Best Supporting Actress in a Dramatic Series. Reportedly her favorite episode was one where Matt was shot in the back in the opening scene and Doc labored all night to save his life. Always before when this had happened, Kitty had acted as nurse assisting Doc. This time she was standing at the back of the room looking ashen and shaken and not participating at all. Finally after what appeared to be an all-night operation, Doc straightened up, took a deep breath and said, "Well, he's going to make it!" Kitty did not say a word. She just turned and went out.

It was nighttime. She made straight for the Long Branch, filled a glass full of bourbon and belted it back. She poured another one, at which point Doc entered and said, "What's the matter with you? I told you he's going to be all right!" She downed the second drink, looked at Doc and said, "Great! What can you tell me about the next time! Eleven times up in that room I've watched you dig bullets out of that man's body, never knowing whether he was going to live or die, and I've had all I can take. I love him, but I can't live with it any more." The next morning there was a "For Sale" sign on the saloon and Kitty was gone. The whole crux of the story was whether Matt would go after her and bring her back. Finally, of course, he did go after her. She came back and agreed to live with the problem, recognizing it was his problem as well as hers. Producer John Mantley recalled, "Amanda thought it was a hell of a show. We all did."

Through *Gunsmoke* she became very wealthy. Over the ten years following the demise of the series, her television appearances were infrequent. She played guest roles on *Edge of Night, Hart to Hart, The Love Boat* and *The Quest.* In the CBS telefilm *The Betrayal* (1974), she had the lead role of Helen Mercer, a lonely widow who hires a young woman companion, unaware that the girl and her boyfriend are killer extortionists planning to make her their next victim. One of her costars in this film was Dick Haymes. She was reunited with James Arness in the slow and sadistic two-hour special *Gunsmoke: Return to Dodge* (1987). She looked emaciated. Her final role was in *B.O.R.N.* (1989). It stood for Body Organ Replacement Network and was a "Z" movie in the genre of director Michael Crichton's *Coma.* She played the role of Rosie, and the film was praised for its veteran cast and old-fashioned professionalism.

Off-screen she lived in a spacious eight-room ranch-style house in the Woodland Hills section of the San Fernando Valley with her five dogs and three cats. She excelled at fencing and swimming. For a hobby she bred cheetahs in Arizona and sold them to American zoos. She said, "Cheetahs were facing extinction and I felt I wanted to do something to help. I adore their looks; they're magnificent animals." She also spent much of her time exploring places like the Galapagos Islands and Kenya.

In her last years she lived near Sacramento with Pat Derby and Ed Stewart. They owned a 20-acre ranch for retired show business animals. Blake devoted her spare time to their charity PAWS (Performing Animal Welfare Society). She had no children. Her five marriages to Jack Shea, TV director Don Whitman, rancher Jason Day, Frank Gilbert and Mark Spaeth all ended in divorce. She once said, "I'm not very good at marriage. I never found out what it's all about." A former smoker who had oral cancer surgery in 1977, Blake made a number of appearances on behalf of the American Cancer Society. In 1984 the society gave Blake its "Courage" award.

After a visit to Africa in late 1988, she returned looking haggard. When she died in Sacramento on August 16, 1989, at 7:15 P.M. at age 60, it was initially said that she had throat cancer. On August 13, 1989, she had changed her will to leave PAWS her entire estate. Her major asset was the house (estimated to be worth $400,000) which she had left empty when she went to live with Derby and Stewart. Blake's sister and two cousins, with whom she had been out of touch for years, contested the will, claiming that she was suffering from head and neck cancer and was not of sound and disposing mind. Two months later her physician Dr. Lou Nishimura admitted, "She did have throat cancer, but that wasn't the reason she died. She died of AIDS-related complications."

She had contracted the disease from fifth husband Mark Spaeth, a Texas real estate developer and Austin City councilman, whom she had married in 1984 and divorced within 12 months. The bisexual Spaeth reportedly died of AIDS in 1985. Although Blake had informed her housekeeper that the marriage had never been consummated, she was lying.

Amanda Blake with (left-right) Milburn Stone, Dennis Weaver, and James Arness in *Gunsmoke*.

The marriage fell apart after she discovered that Spaeth had the illness and had known about it for two months before they were married. Details of her sickness were kept secret from her closest friends. After the Africa trip she had gone to see Dr. Nishimura. Tests were performed which confirmed that she had AIDS. Although she was treated with AZT, she became progressively worse. In July she entered Mercy General Hospital in Sacramento where she died. She was admitted under her real name and died with her dog Butterfly at her side. Subsequently the court did not alter the terms of her will and as a tribute to her, the elephant dwelling at the PAWS ranch was called "Lake Amanda." In November 1991, memorabilia from her estate were auctioned off in North Hollywood, with proceeds going to

PAWS. James Arness recalled of her recently, "I do miss her. It's difficult sometimes doing these specials because her presence is always there. Amanda was a major and integral part of that 20 year period."

Amanda Blake Filmography

1950: *Stars in My Crown, Battleground, Duchess of Idaho.*
1951: *Criminal Lawyer, Counterspy Meets Scotland Yard, Sunny Side of the Street, Smugglers' Gold.*
1952: *Scarlet Angel, Cattle Town.*
1953: *Lili, Sabre Jet.*
1954: *The Adventures of Hajji Baba, A Star Is Born, Miss Robin Crusoe, About Mrs. Leslie.*
1955: *The Glass Slipper, High Society.*
1974: *The Betrayal (*a.k.a. *The Companion)* (TV).
1987: *Gunsmoke: Return to Dodge* (TV).
1988: *The Boost.*
1989: *B.O.R.N.*

Television Series

1955–1974: *Gunsmoke* as Miss Kitty Russell.

Sources

Daily Telegraph newspaper. "Actress's Death Linked to AIDS," November 1989.
Ferguson, Ken. *The Boys Western Film and TV Annual.* London: Purnell, 1963.
Where Are They Now? Globe Special. Boca Raton, Florida: Globe International, 1993.
Green, James. "Where Are They Now?" *Sunday Express* newspaper. December 1985.
Variety. Obituary, August 1989.
Newcomb, Horace, and Robert S. Alley. *The Producer's Medium: Conversations with Creators of American TV.* New York and Oxford: Oxford University Press, 1983.
Picture Show Annual. London: Amalgamated Press, 1951.
Parish, James Robert. *The Hollywood Death Book.* Las Vegas, NV: Pioneer, 1992.
Rovin, Jeff. *TV Babylon II.* New York: Signet, 1991.

Note

The *High Society* mentioned in the filmography is not the MGM musical but a Bowery Boys comedy released by Allied Artists in 1955 with the same title. Amanda Blake played the role of Clarissa.

DAN BLOCKER

Dan Blocker was a perfect example of how a heavyweight with a benign countenance could find a niche for himself on the range. People the world over never tired of watching this gentle giant perform simple acts like sitting down in a rickety chair or straightening his hat. His characterization of Hoss Cartwright in *Bonanza* was so convincing that many viewers believed he had a low intellect in real life. Nothing could have been further from the truth. He was once asked whether his size handicapped his career as an actor. "Well, figure it this way, friend," he replied, "I ain't gonna play Romeo." He was a giant among actors in more ways than one.

Dan Blocker was born in grinding poverty on a ranch in the Dust Bowl country of Texas on December 10, 1928. At 14 pounds he was said to have been the largest baby ever born in Bowie County. He spent his boyhood in patched overalls and shirts which had been laundered so many times they were threadbare. At the age of ten he worked side by side with grown men unloading grain trucks. When he entered Texas Military Institute at 12, he stood six feet tall and weighed 200 pounds. His main juvenile pastime was fighting. They called him "the big 'un," roped off the streets of O'Donnell, Texas, where he was raised and matched him against the local toughs. He never lost a fight and eventually ran out of opponents. By the time he was fully grown he stood six-foot-four and weighed 280 pounds.

Determined to make something of him-

Left-right: Dan Blocker, Lorne Greene, Pernell Roberts and Michael Landon in *Bonanza*.

self, Blocker worked night and day putting himself through Sul Ross State College in Alpine, Texas, earning high grades and bachelor's and master's degrees. His first taste of acting came in a college production of the black comedy *Arsenic and Old Lace* when the producers needed someone strong enough to carry out the bodies. Since he was the football team's biggest lineman, he won the part. This hooked him, and after directing a college production of *Mr. Roberts* with the football team in the cast, he switched his major from physical education to drama. At college he won outstanding reviews for the title role in *Othello*, but it was his part as De Lawd in *Green Pastures* which won him the national award for Best College Acting in 1949. It was while acting in this play that he met his future wife Dolphia Lee Parker. She had a small role.

In 1950 he performed in stock in Boston and appeared on Broadway in *King Lear*. Shortly afterwards he was drafted into the Korean War, but was nearly killed on Christmas Eve 1951, which gave him a lifelong hatred of guns and caused him to drift away from acting for a while. Shortly after being discharged from the armed forces in 1952, he married. He taught school while simultaneously obtaining his master's degree in Shakespeare at Sul Ross. For six years he taught history, politics, drama and English in Texas and New Mexico high schools. In 1956 he relocated to California where he enrolled at the University of California at Los Angeles intending to study for his doctorate.

He was introduced to a Hollywood talent agent who took one look at his size and exclaimed, "I think I can get you a job on television this week!" "I'm sorry, sir, but I don't believe that's possible," Blocker replied politely. The agent made a couple of phone calls and the next morning Blocker reported to the *Gunsmoke* set where he was given a bit part. When he discovered that he could earn more in four days as an actor than in a month as a teacher, he withdrew from UCLA and devoted himself entirely to thesping. He soon landed his first continuing role in *Cimarron City*, which starred

George Montgomery. It was, however, his role as a sympathetic deaf mute in an episode of *The Restless Gun* which convinced producer David Dortort in 1959 to cast him on *Bonanza* as Hoss, a role he continued to play for the next 13 years.

Hoss was supposed to be five years younger than Adam. He was a colossus of a man, broad and powerful as an ox. Yet Hoss was gentle and good-hearted and a little shy in the company of ladies. He felt more at home with the horses. Hoss was Little Joe's protector. His real name was Eric. Once when asked how he got the name Hoss, Blocker replied, "I suppose it was because of his great love of animals. He used to take better care of his horse than himself." The hat which he wore in the series was his pride and joy. It was made for a Bob Hope movie. One day Blocker popped it on his head for a joke. Producer Dortort saw him wearing it, liked the idea and Blocker wore it ever afterwards.

In real life Blocker could out-argue anyone in defense of his democratic principles. There were various things which "bugged the hell out of him," including cruelty, color prejudice, people who tormented children or animals and the more extreme comments of Republican politicians. A peaceloving man, he did not like displays of brute strength. He made personal appearances as Hoss in shows throughout the United States. He refused to appear in the segregated halls of the South. In one Mississippi town where he told the sponsors this, they assured him he had nothing to worry about. When he arrived at the theater, he discovered he had been duped. It took him all of six minutes to case the joint, decide he did not like what he saw, let rip with a verbal tornado and announce he was flying back to Hollywood immediately.

One person who befriended the actor was Frank Sinatra, who gave him roles in a couple of his pictures. He played the hulking Gronsky in *Lady in Cement* (1968), the second of two films in which Frank Sinatra played private eye Tony Rome. This one was basically a reworking of Raymond Chandler's *Farewell My Lovely* with Blocker in the Moose Malloy role. One highly amusing in-joke is where Gronsky is hiding out in a massage parlor, switches on the television and happily settles down to watch *Bonanza*. At the time of his death Blocker was set to play Roger Wade in the 1973 movie version of *The Long Goodbye* which owed more to director Robert Altman than to writer Raymond Chandler. Sterling Hayden replaced him in the Elliott Gould-starring film which was dedicated to Dan Blocker's memory.

He also sandwiched a few other features in between his *Bonanza* commitments, most notably 1968's *Something for A Lonely Man* (the title of which is a quotation from Ralph Waldo Emerson). In this Western fable Blocker starred as John Killibrew, an illiterate blacksmith who tries to atone to the townsfolk who followed him West and built a town later bypassed by the railroad. Finally he finds a way with the love of Mary Duran (Susan Clark), a book of Emerson's essays and a derailed steam engine.

At his peak he earned $20,000 an episode from *Bonanza*. Amongst other businesses, he had shares in a fertilizer company and a barbecue food company. His hobby was race cars and he was a partner in a firm called Vinegaroon Racing Associates. He canceled all engagements to attend the Indy 500 every year. He lived with his wife in a rambling Western house in the San Fernando Valley with their two sons, Dirk and David, and twin daughters Danna and Debra. On May 1, 1972, Dan Blocker underwent routine gall bladder surgery at Centinela Valley Hospital in Inglewood. His recovery was so swift that he was sent home early. On Saturday, May 13, he found himself short of breath and in agony. He was rushed to Daniel Freeman Hospital, also in Inglewood. By 4 P.M. that afternoon he was dead. The official cause of death was pulmonary embolus, a blood clot on the lung, after an internal operation. He was 43. His wife and one of their twin daughters were at the bedside. He is buried at Woodmen Cemetery in DeKalb, Texas.

Dan Blocker Filmography

1957: *Gunsight Ridge.*
1961: *The Errand Boy* (cameo).
1963: *Come Blow Your Horn.*
1968: *Lady in Cement, Something for a Lonely Man* (TV).
1969: *The Cockeyed Cowboys of Calico County* (a.k.a. *A Woman for Charley).*

Television Series

1958–1959: *Cimarron City* as Tiny Budinger.
1959–1972: *Bonanza* as Hoss Cartwright.

Sources

Daily Mirror newspaper. Obituary, May 1972.
Mitchum, John. *Them Ornery Mitchum Boys.* Pacifica, CA: Creatures at Large Press, 1989.
Shapiro, Melany. *Bonanza.* Las Vegas, NV: Pioneer, 1993.
Zec, Donald. "Hoss: The Heart and Mind of Dan Blocker." *Daily Mirror* newspaper, July 17, 1964.

WARD BOND

"I'm in charge of this wagon train and I'm going to get you all to California. That's what I'm paid to do and you're all going to take orders from me." The voice unmistakably is that of the gruff, authoritarian Wagon Master Seth Adams played by Ward Bond in the phenomenally successful Western series *Wagon Train.* Adams was the kind of hero Americans revere the most. He was 6-foot-three and weighed 220 pounds. He was coarse, poorly educated and enjoyed a rough house. Despite this he exuded the confidence of a natural leader of men but had a tender side. This rugged-faced, burly cowboy with a potbelly was the sort of father figure who many wished would lead them from the misery of their own lives to a land of opportunity.

Prior to playing Seth Adams, Ward Bond had for many years been one of Hollywood's most seasoned character actors, appearing in over 200 features, but it is certain that his career did not depend upon his looks. Actress Maureen O'Hara recalls, "In the morning, when we'd come in we'd say, 'Who's in the barrel today?' This meant, who's going to get hell today from the old man, John Ford? And sometimes I'd be in the barrel, sometimes Duke would be in the barrel, but Ward Bond was always in the barrel." Harry Carey, Jr., added, "He was a character. By being in the barrel constantly, he saved the rest of us."

Wardell Bond was born either in Bendelman, Nebraska, or Denver, Colorado, on April 9, 1903. He was the son of John W. Bond and his wife Mabel. He had one sister, Bernice. After attending the Colorado School of Mines, he won a football scholarship to the University of Southern California as a tackle, where he played alongside John Wayne. In 1928 John Ford went to the USC campus to obtain extras to play Annapolis naval cadets for a movie called *Salute* (1929), which starred George O'Brien. He hired Bond because of his resemblance to Victor McLaglen.

The day the cast and crew assembled at Santa Fe railroad station in Los Angeles ready to depart for the location, Ward Bond turned up. He and John Wayne had never been friends. "What the hell are you doing here?" Duke asked Bond. "You're too damn ugly to be in movies." Bond strode past him and boarded the train. When the train pulled out of the station, they were enemies. Months later, upon finishing the movie, they were great friends. They were founding members of the Young Men's Purity, Total Abstinence and Yachting Association, a fraternity devoted to carousing and consuming vast quantities of alcohol. Bond was a premedical student at the time, but ironically he received screen credit in *Salute* (1929) while Wayne did not. Years later, when Bond would roar with explosive anger against Hollywood, Wayne would answer, "I did my damnedest to keep you the hell out of the picture business. But you had to shove your fat butt into the train, so you only got yourself to blame."

Graduating with a B.S. degree in engineering in 1931, Bond decided to try a career in movies and landed a job as a stunt man. Within a short time he was playing villains in low-budget Westerns starring Buck Jones, Ken Maynard, Tim McCoy and John Wayne. Wayne was also responsible for getting Ward a part in his first starring film, *The Big Trail* (1930), a forerunner of *Wagon Train*. At the time it was an expensive failure, but a recent video reissue shows that it holds up very well today. Contrary to most published reviews, Wayne was not incompetent. He was much the same as usual except that he was younger and slimmer. Bond had a minor role as the son of one of the pioneers. Bond had become a drinking buddy of both Wayne and Ford. He was very rapidly accepted into Ford's elite circle of friends, but unlike Wayne he was never excommunicated. He believed throughout the course of his life that he and not Wayne should have been a movie star, a feature of his personality which Ford was not slow to exploit.

Throughout the 1930s Bond was one of Hollywood's busiest supporting actors, making dozens of appearances in features that usually had him playing tough, bullying characters with few if any redeeming features. It was only Ford who enabled him to show what he could really do by giving him roles in such films as Yank in *The Long Voyage Home* (1940), and as Lov Bensey in the alternately comic and moving *Tobacco Road* (1941). Through Ford's influence, Bond finally broke away from these stereotyped roles and obtained bigger, more important assignments. He could sometimes be quite moving, notably in *The Sullivans* (1944), directed by Lloyd Bacon. This was based on the true story of the five brothers from Waterloo, Iowa, who were lost in the sinking of the Juneau off Guadalcanal. Anne Baxter played the widow of the youngest. In this unremittingly sad film Bond played the naval officer who delivered the tragic news to the rest of the family.

John Ford claimed that he would have made superior films on location if he had not spent so much time playing practical jokes on Bond. When Ford was shooting *They Were Expendable* (1945), he hired a pretty waitress to serve his company and primed her to become infatuated with Bond. She told him that he was her favorite actor and begged him for a signed photograph. When she waited table, she would take Bond's order first and let everyone else wait until he had been served.

She told him that her husband worked on the Atchison, Topeka and Santa Fe railroad and that he was away on an assignment. He would, however, soon be returning and she would only have one more night alone. She arranged for Bond to show up at her bungalow with a six-pack of beer and a watermelon. Beforehand Ford, Wayne and those of the cast and crew who were in on the joke waited in the darkness of the bungalow. As Bond crept up with the six-pack and the watermelon, they began firing pistols loaded with blanks and setting off firecrackers. Believing the husband had returned prematurely, Bond dropped the six-pack. He lit out across the porch, leapt the rail and ran for his life, still clutching the watermelon.

On another occasion at Ford's house, Bond bet Wayne that Duke could not hit him off a newspaper. Wayne accepted the bet. Bond lowered the newspaper in the middle of doorway. Then he closed the door between them, shouting, "Hit me now, you dumb son of a bitch." Wayne punched clean through the closed door, shattering it and knocking Bond off his feet. One of Wayne's best films, *Tall in the Saddle* (1944), features a dandy no-holds-barred fistfight between them which was very excitingly filmed.

Bond was an outspoken advocate against the spread of Communism within the motion picture industry. He was a charter member of the Motion Picture Alliance for the Preservation of American Ideals. This stance made him extremely unpopular in some quarters. Triple-threat writer/producer/director Carl Foreman labeled him "Ward 'The Hangman' Bond who could smell a Commie-Jew a mile away." The equally talented Irving Brecher was another who actively disliked him. Two fellow producers had submitted Brecher's name as one of questionable loyalty to get themselves off the hook. Although Brecher continued to make ends meet through his participation in television series such as *The Life of Riley*, for a two-year period the phone did not ring. Brecher recalled bitterly, "Ward Bond, that prick, and Roy Brewer of the Carpenter's Union. You had to write them a letter explaining your past associations. They would either clear you or condemn you to death. And I wrote them a letter—the worst job I ever did. The day after the letter was delivered, I was off the list."

Bond played important roles in many John Ford films. He was Boots Mulcahey in *They Were Expendable* (1945); Morgan Earp in *My Darling Clementine* (1946); El Gringo in

Ward Bond (right) with Robert Horton in *Wagon Train*.

The Fugitive (1947); Sgt. Major O'Rourke in *Fort Apache* (1948); Buck Sweet in *Three Godfathers* (1948); Father Peter Lonergan in *The Quiet Man* (1952); Tyrone Power's West Point commanding officer Captain Herman J. Koehler in *The Long Gray Line* (1955); and C.P.O. Dowdy in *Mister Roberts* (1955). He played a thinly disguised parody of John Ford under the name of John Dodge in *The Wings Of Eagles* (1957), in which John Wayne starred as Frank "Spig" Wead, a pioneer World War One aviator who subsequently became a successful Hollywood screenwriter. Of Bond's imitation of him Ford recalled, "I didn't intend it that way, but he did. I woke up one morning and my good hat was gone, my pipe and everything else; and they'd taken all the Academy Awards and put them in the office set." Bond's best film role was as Captain Reverend Samuel Clayton in Ford's celebrated *The Searchers* (1956). His most touching scene in this film is when Ethan Edwards' (John Wayne) brother's wife Martha (Dorothy Jordan), who is in love with Ethan, picks up his coat and caresses it. Bond, who is finishing breakfast, spies this, but silently turns his eyes forward and continues eating. He would rather die than reveal what he has seen.

More important from the viewpoint of his later career was *Wagon Master* (1950). Directed by Ford and allegedly one of his favorite films, it costarred Ben Johnson and Harry Carey, Jr., as leaders of a Mormon wagon train. Bond played the elder Wiggins. When Ford was casting this film, he said to Carey, Jr., "That means I can use you and dammit I suppose Ward!" This film led to an outgrowth which spawned the television series *Wagon Train*.

After his anti-Communist activities Bond was finding it difficult to obtain employment in films. He was offered the lead in this series, but turned it down because of the constant pressures it would impose on him. However, he recognized that under American tax laws at the time he could earn as much by making the series as John Wayne could in a feature. (At that time Wayne was paid $500,000 a film.) That tax angle clinched his acceptance of the *Wagon Train* lead. He agreed to recreate the part of Major Seth Adams in September 1957, providing that his two pals Wooster (Frank McGrath) and Hawks (Terry Wilson) could be accommodated. Their parts were subsequently expanded.

The setting was a California-bound wagon train in the post–Civil War days, starting out each season from St. Joseph, Missouri, and making its way West until reaching California in the spring. The series was basically a character study with one or more guests taking center stage each week. Each episode cost the then-staggering sum of $100,000 to produce. It took a season to become popular, but came close to capturing the essence of the pioneer spirit, which was a key factor in its success. In its second season it made the Top Ten in the ratings. After three years of being placed a close second to *Gunsmoke*, it finally became the number one program on U.S. television during the 1961–1962 season. Possibly the most distinguished episode was *The Colter Craven Story* (1960) because it was directed by John Ford. John Wayne had a cameo, billed under his real name, as General Sherman. The episode aired three weeks after Bond's death. *The Seth Adams Story,* a two-parter which allegedly told of Adams's life before and during the Civil War and which included a highly unlikely romance with Virginia Grey, was one of the least convincing episodes. Bond with boot-polished hair and a paunch simply was not convincing as a romantic leading man. In one of the funniest episodes, rambunctious Cassie Tanner (Marjorie Main) set her cap at him so he spent an episode keeping out of her way.

Bond continued to appear in films. He did a cameo as Seth Adams in the amusing Bob Hope spoof western *Alias Jesse James* (1959). His final role was as Pat Wheeler, the friend of Sheriff John T. Chance (John Wayne), who tries to come to his assistance in the classic Howard Hawks Western *Rio Bravo* (1959), but is shot in the back for his pains. Even at the end of his career his films fluctuated in quality. *Dakota Incident* (1956) stands out as one of his worst.

One night during the early 1940s he was hit by a car on Hollywood Boulevard. His left leg was hurt so badly that doctors threatened to amputate, but John Wayne prevented this. It eventually healed, but was never the same again. Bond was forced to wear a brace from then on. This injury was compounded by another one much later. For a while in the series Bond was seen hobbling around on crutches. It was explained that Seth Adams had sprained his back in heaving a covered wagon out of the mud at some point in the trek West. What happened in real life was even more dramatic. Bond twisted his hip while saving a film extra from what might have been a nasty accident. A horse broke loose on location and headed for an extra who failed to notice the danger. Bond leaned down from his own mount and pulled the extra out of the way. Then as he sat back in the saddle, the loose horse came alongside his own and trapped his leg. He twisted his hip so badly that there was talk of him being written out of the series until he was better. Bond was so keen on the part that he insisted on carrying on.

For several years while filming *Wagon Train*, Bond was in rotten health. He suffered from chronic stomach ulcers and was so highly strung that at the least provocation his Olympian rage would erupt in full glorious Technicolor. His blood pressure was so low towards the end that he drank an estimated 45 cups of coffee every day in order to keep his energy up. Nevertheless he habitually went on personal appearance tours because he loved the power of fame. On these hellraising trips he drank, played poker, chain smoked and partied until dawn. Then he flew back to Hollywood where he resumed working nonstop on *Wagon Train*.

On November 5, 1960, he was scheduled to make a personal appearance during halftime at the Cotton Bowl football game in Dallas, Texas. It was one rendezvous he was destined never to keep. He suffered a heart attack and died instantly in his motel room as he stepped out of the shower. He was 57 years old. John McIntire eventually replaced him as Wagon Master Chris Hale.

In 1936 Bond married Doris Sellers Childs, whom he divorced in 1944. In 1954 he wed Mary Louise May, a talent agent who was born in 1915. Mary Lou, as she was known, remarried but perished in a fire at her home in Vista, California, on January 28, 1988. Ward bequeathed a .20 gauge shotgun to John Wayne. He owned two ranches in Kern County, California. He lies buried at Forest Lawn Memorial Park in Glendale.

Ward Bond Filmography

1929: *Salute, Words and Music.*

1930: *Born Reckless, The Big Trail.*

1931: *Arrowsmith.*

1932: *Virtue, Hello Trouble, Rackety Rax, White Eagle, High Speed, Air Mail, The Trial of Vivienne Ware.*

1933: *Heroes for Sale, Wild Boys of the Road, When Strangers Marry, College Coach, The Wrecker, Police Car No. 17, Whirlpool, The Sundown Rider, Unknown Valley, Obey the Law.*

1934: *Straightaway, Most Precious Thing in Life, The Poor Rich, Frontier Marshal, Broadway Bill, It Happened One Night, The Defense Rests, Fighting Ranger, Here Comes the Groom, Chained, The Affairs of Cellini, The Fighting Code, A Voice in the Night, A Man's Game, The Crime of Helen Stanley, Kid Millions, Against the Law, Girl in Danger, The Human Side, Tall Timber, The Crimson Trail.*

1935: *Western Courage, Devil Dogs of the Air, She Gets Her Man, His Night Out, Black Fury, Fighting Shadows, Little Big Shot, The Last Days of Pompeii, G-Men, Go Into Your Dance, Calm Yourself, The Informer, Guard That Girl, Murder in the Fleet, Waterfront Lady, The Headline Woman, Justice of the Range, Men of the Night, Too Tough to Kill.*

1936: *Cattle Thief, Muss 'Em Up, The Bride Walks Out, Second Wife, Without Orders, Crash Donovan, They Met in a Taxi, The Legion of Terror, Conflict, The Man Who Lived Twice, Fury, The Leathernecks Have Landed, Avenging Waters, Pride of the Marines, The Gorgeous Hussy, Colleen, Fatal Lady, White Fang.*

1937: *You Only Live Once, Dead End, The Devil's Playground, A Fight to the Finish, The Wildcatter, 23½ Hours Leave, Escape by Night, Night Key, Park Avenue Lodger, The Go Getter, Mountain Music, The Singing Marine, Music for Madame.*

1938: *Born to Be Wild, The Law West of Tombstone, Reformatory, Professor Beware, Gun Law, Hawaii Calls, Flight Into Nowhere, Mr. Moto's Gamble, The Amazing Doctor Clitterhouse, Over the Wall, Numbered Woman, Prison Break, Bringing Up Baby, You Can't Take It with You, Of Human Hearts, Penitentiary, The Adventures of Marco Polo, Going Places, Fugitive for a Night, Submarine Patrol.*

1939: *Dodge City, Made for Each Other, Son of Frankenstein, They Made Me a Criminal, Waterfront, Trouble in Sundown, The Return of the Cisco Kid, Gone with the Wind, Young Mr. Lincoln, Frontier Marshal, The Kid from Kokomo, The Oklahoma Kid, The Girl from Mexico, Drums Along the Mohawk, Dust Be My Destiny, Heaven with a Barbed Wire Fence, Mr. Moto in Danger Island, Confessions of a Nazi Spy, Pardon Our Nerve.*

1940: *Santa Fe Trail, Buck Benny Rides Again, Little Old New York, Virginia City, The Cisco Kid and the Lady, The Grapes of Wrath, The Mortal Storm, The Long Voyage Home, Sailor's Lady, Kit Carson.*

1941: *The Shepherd of the Hills, A Man Betrayed, Tobacco Road, Swamp Water, Sergeant York, Manpower, Doctors Don't Tell, Wild Bill Hickok Rides, The Maltese Falcon.*

1942: *In This Our Life, Gentleman Jim, The Falcon Takes Over, Sin Town, Ten Gentlemen from West Point, A Night to Remember.*

1943: *A Guy Named Joe, They Came to Blow Up America, Hitler—Dead Or Alive, Cowboy Commandos, Hello Frisco Hello, Slightly Dangerous.*
1944: *Home in Indiana, The Sullivans, Tall In the Saddle.*
1945: *Dakota, They Were Expendable.*
1946: *Canyon Passage, It's a Wonderful Life!, My Darling Clementine.*
1947: *The Fugitive, Unconquered.*
1948: *Fort Apache, Three Godfathers, The Time of Your Life, Joan Of Arc, Tap Roots.*
1950: *Wagon Master, Riding High, Singing Guns, Kiss Tomorrow Goodbye.*
1951: *The Great Missouri Raid, Operation Pacific, Only the Valiant, On Dangerous Ground.*
1952: *The Quiet Man, Thunderbirds, Hellgate.*
1953: *Blowing Wild, The Moonlighter, Hondo.*
1954: *Gypsy Colt, The Bob Mathias Story, Johnny Guitar.*
1955: *The Long Gray Line, Mister Roberts, A Man Alone.*
1956: *The Searchers, Dakota Incident, Pillars of the Sky.*
1957: *The Wings of Eagles, The Halliday Brand.*
1958: *China Doll.*
1959: *Alias Jesse James* (cameo), *Rio Bravo.*

Television Series

1957–1960: *Wagon Train* as Major Seth Adams.

Sources

Carey, Harry, Jr. *Company of Heroes.* Metuchen, NJ: Scarecrow, 1994.
Corneau, Ernest N. *The Hall of Fame of Western Film Stars.* North Quincy, MA: Christopher, 1969.
Server, Lee. *Screenwriter Words Become Pictures.* Pittstown, NJ: The Main Street Press, 1987.
Shepherd, Donald, Robert Slatzer and Dave Grayson. *Duke.* London: Sphere, 1985.
Speed, F. Maurice. *The Western Film and TV Annual.* London: MacDonald, 1959.
Thomey, Tedd. *The Glorious Decade.* New York: Ace, 1971.
Tuska, Jon. *The Filming of the West.* Garden City, NY: Doubleday, 1976.
Wayne, Pilar and Alex Thorleifson. *My Life with the Duke.* London: New English Library, 1988.

RICHARD BOONE

While making *The War Lord*, Charlton Heston noted somewhat crossly in the December 18, 1964, entry in his journals *The Actor's Life (1956–1976)*, "Dick Boone had gone off on an unauthorized departure to Hawaii yesterday without clearance, so we had to shoot around him." Richard Boone had the face of a rugged Westerner, drawn like a map of the Grand Canyon. His craggy features most naturally lent themselves to villainy. If television hadn't changed the path of his career, he would have spent the greater part of it playing bad guys. His greatest success was in the role of Paladin in *Have Gun Will Travel.* He was voted Best Actor three times by American television critics and nominated for an Emmy award five times by the National Academy of Television Arts and Sciences.

He had a reputation for being tough to work with. He was a perfectionist. He said, "I can't stand incompetence. And I can't stand being disturbed when I'm working. That's why I hate visitors on a set. I refuse to let them wander round on a set on which I'm filming. That's why most of my sets are barred to intruders." It was once reported that he hired an armed guard to keep away autograph hunters who invaded the privacy of a studio restaurant where he dined daily. "It isn't that I'm a prima donna," he explained, "but until I hired the guard, people were making me slop soup all over the place by nudging me and demanding I sign their books. I have a high respect for my fans. And I'm delighted to talk with them, sign their books when I'm relaxed and not tensed up."

Richard Boone in *Have Gun Will Travel.*

Subtlety was not his strong suit. Sometimes, particularly towards the end of his career, his performances were wretchedly over the top. He spent a lifetime rebelling against authority and finally became totally intractable. Ironically, he was chosen by Dr. Laurence J. Peter as one of 15 showbiz personalities who fulfilled the Peter Principle of rising to the level of his own incompetence. The cream rose until it went sour. Actress Catherine McLeod recalled him as one of three actors whom she had hoped never to encounter again. Drink also played a significant role in his downfall. As Harry Carey, Jr., once said about him, "We all of us drank. It was just that Boone never stopped."

He was born Richard Allen Boone in Los Angeles, California, on June 18, 1917, the second of three children to Kirk Boone, a successful corporation attorney, and Cecile Beckerman. He was allegedly a seventh generation nephew of the legendary pioneer Daniel Boone. From 1929 to 1932 he received his primary education at the Army and Navy Academy in San Diego. During summer vacations he enrolled as a crewman on a chartered fishing boat operating between San Diego and Mexico. He was expelled from school for walking out of an open window when a lecture bored him. He attended California's Stanford University from 1934 to 1937, coupling studies with boxing. In 1936 and 1937 he was college amateur light heavyweight boxing champion.

In a Theta Xi fraternity practical joke, Boone and his fellow fraternity members created a life-sized dummy out of rags and bottles, covered it with tomato ketchup and placed it in front of a fraternity house to be knocked down by the first motorist who passed. After the faked accident, Boone ran into the street screaming and crying, "You've killed my brother!" at the innocent driver. The driver turned out to Mrs. Herbert Hoover and she had sprained her ankle in the fracas. Like Queen Victoria she was not amused, so Boone was expelled.

His father hoped that he would become a lawyer, but as Boone recalled in later years, "It wasn't that I didn't respect and admire my father. I just didn't want to be a lawyer." Instead he worked as a laborer in the oil fields of California. Then Boone and his first wife moved to Carmel, the California arts colony, where Boone wrote short stories and painted both unsuccessfully. He said, "I remember becoming almost obsessed to make my living as a painter, but World War Two put paid to that." He did some scene design for summer theater which in turn involved him in acting. He enlisted in the U.S. Navy as an aerial gunner in a torpedo squadron which patrolled the Pacific area from 1941 to 1945. He recalled of this period, "I guess I'm really lucky to be alive. The Japs certainly had it in for me. I was torpedoed on a carrier, 'Intrepid'; bombed on the 'Enterprise'; and finally kamikazed on the 'Hancock.' Somehow I came through."

When he was given an honorable discharge in 1946, he set about the task of furthering his acting interests. He moved to New York after the war and financed his theatrical studies under the G.I. Bill of Rights. He studied acting at the Neighborhood Playhouse with Sanford Meisner and at the Actors' Studio with Elia Kazan and Lee Strasberg from 1945 to 1947. He also studied modern dance with Martha Graham and joined Nina Fonaroff's dance company. Boone's stage debut was as a soldier and understudy to John Gielgud's Jason in *Medea* on Broadway in 1947. He did two other plays on Broadway. One of them was *Macbeth* starring Michael Redgrave; Boone was fired, allegedly because of his antipathy to the star. He also toured as Yank in *The Hasty Heart.*

While at the Actors' Studio in 1950, Boone was asked by a student actress about to take a screen test for Twentieth Century–Fox to read a few lines from *The Glass Menagerie* by Tennessee Williams as she took the test. Although Boone's face did not appear on camera, his voice so impressed the veteran Hollywood director Lewis Milestone that he brought Boone to Hollywood to play a nerve-wracked colonel in *The Halls of Montezuma* (1950). Elia Kazan directed the screen test, which resulted in a contract with Fox and a permanent move to Los Angeles. In 1954 when his contract expired, he decided to go freelance.

NBC's *Medic* television series (1954–56) first brought Boone to public attention in a big way. Cases from the files of the Los Angeles County Medical Association were dramatized. Dr. Konrad Styner (Boone) hosted and narrated as well as often participating in the cases. His introduction to each episode always included this description of the doctor: "...guardian of birth, healer of the sick and comforter of the aged." The show's theme song "Blue Star" was a hit in 1955. Boone's characterization was so authentic and appealing that he received an enormous quantity of fan mail from women seeking medical advice. It was produced by Worthington Miner, a veteran of live television, and mainly written by James Moser, who later created *Ben Casey*. In its efforts to present the practice of medicine in as gritty and realistic a way as possible, *Medic* was shot at real hospitals and clinics, and often used real doctors and nurses as part of the cast. Blood was frequently part of the wardrobe; one episode even showed the birth of a baby. The series was criticized at times for going overboard to depict the seamy side of life. Boone left the series to avoid being typecast.

His greatest opportunity came when ex-radio writers Sam Rolfe and Herb Meadows created the character of Paladin, named after the knights-errant who attended the court of Charlemagne. Boone was second choice to play the role after Randolph Scott turned it down because of movie commitments. *Have Gun Will Travel* (in which Boone played Paladin) was one of the most popular programs of the late 1950s. Paladin was different from other gunslingers. He was college-educated, having attended West Point in pursuit of a military career. After serving in the Civil War he headed west to become a high-priced "gun for hire." He operated out of the plush Hotel Carlton in San Francisco. He was distinguished by two trademarks, namely a black leather holster that bore the symbol of the white chess knight (called a Paladin) and a calling card that read, "Have Gun Will Travel...Wire Paladin, San Francisco."

Paladin was something of a dandy, a gourmet and a man of culture who spouted literary classics. He underwent a transformation when on assignment. Then he dressed all in black and could be extremely frightening. He was however a man of principle, which occasionally led him to seek out the very people who had hired him in the first place if they were the guilty parties. By definition a Paladin is one who undertakes a noble cause. He came to the aid of an Indian marshal, sided with a Chinese detective, defended a woman doctor and shot a black bad guy. He was a man of ingenuity and resources. Once he was stranded defenseless in the Canadian Rockies. Most men would have died. Paladin, however, was not cut from common cloth. He fashioned a deadly weapon based on a design used by 18th-century Eskimos. He not only destroyed his enemies, but made it back for opening night at the San Francisco Opera House in the company of a beautiful and stylish lady.

Paladin was one hero who shot to kill. He usually succeeded and sent his opponent into the next world with a bullet and a short eulogy from Shakespeare or a Roman poet. Boone was right at home working with Paladin's belt derringer, six shooter, saddle rifle and self-styled machine gun. He played the role of Paladin with relish, explaining that "he's an intriguing sort of a guy with an air of mystery about him." The series was so popular that a radio version was developed, reversing the usual trend of successful radio shows like *Gunsmoke* and *The Lone Ranger* that were adapted for television. It was broadcast from 1958 to 1960. Boone also directed several episodes of the television series and was to assume the director's chores again on some segments of the later *The Richard Boone Show*.

Hey Boy (Kam Tong), the Oriental working at the Hotel Carlton, was seen at the beginning of most episodes bringing a message to Paladin from a likely client. During the 1960–1961 season while Kam Tong was involved in a bigger role in another series *(The Garlund Touch)*, he was temporarily replaced by Hey Girl (Lisa Lu). He returned to *Have Gun Will Travel* after his new venture bit the dust. *Have Gun Will Travel* was a smash hit, ranking among the top five programs during its first season on the air. From 1958 to 1961 it was the number three program on American television behind two other westerns *(Gunsmoke* and *Wagon Train)*. In 1960 CBS paid Boone $1,100,000, spread over three years for tax purposes, to retain his services for the following season. Its theme song, "The Ballad of Paladin," was a hit single in the early 1960s. *Have Gun Will Travel* debuted on CBS in September 1957. It lasted through 225 half-hour episodes and was sent to Boot Hill in September 1963.

Boone also accepted a number of assignments as a freelance in anthology series like *Playhouse 90* and *U.S. Steel Hour* which showed his versatility and enhanced his reputation with fans and critics alike. Boone accelerated his shooting schedule as Paladin and accepted an invitation from producer Cheryl Crawford to do *The Rivalry* by Norman Corwin on Broadway. It opened at the Bijou Theater on February 7, 1959. Although Boone impressed the critics as Abraham Lincoln during the period of the Lincoln-Douglas debates, the play closed after 81 performances and lost an estimated $65,000. He was invited to read the Gettysburg Address at the Lincoln Memorial in Washington D.C. on the 150th anniversary of Lincoln's birth on February 12, 1959.

Boone wanted to turn his back on television. He asserted, "I'm through unless something comes along so exciting that I can't turn it down." Something did come along which fired his imagination. Boone used his wealth and influence to develop *The Richard Boone Show,* which presented a repertory theater in television. Acting as host, Boone starred in half the episodes and played featured roles in the others. He became "the man of many faces" playing parts as diverse as a retired gangster, an 80-year-old tyrant of a Great Lakes shipping company, a Korean war veteran, a Los Angeles policeman, a successful, hard-driving prosecuting attorney, a former French resistance fighter and an American storekeeper in a Mexican village.

Each of the regulars had an opportunity to star in at least one of the episodes in addition to having supporting roles in many of them. This hour-long series of 25 shows made its debut on NBC in September 1963. Boone explained, "I studied carefully the difficulties of doing a different play every week and discovered that anthologies, even good ones like Dick Powell's might have fair ratings, but never anything steady or solid. That's when I realized that a repertory company, a group of stock players who would appear in different roles from week to week, might be a greater attraction than a continuing television series. I thought that viewers might become interested in seeing what role Harry Morgan or Lloyd Bochner or Bethel Leslie would be doing in their next appearance..." Some of the scripts, particularly those by Clifford Odets, carried rather heavy messages. It was cancelled by the network after one season because it gained only half the viewers of the CBS competition *Petticoat Junction.* It seems strange in retrospect, with the wealth of drama inherent in the Western and other traditional genres, that Boone only felt fulfilled if he was appearing in an offbeat project like this which never began to look like a winner.

Boone's subsequent move to Hawaii prompted rumors that he was angry with the program's premature cancellation, but he replied that he wanted to provide a better environment for his son. In Hawaii he formed a movie production company, Pioneer Productions, to start a fledgling movie industry there. The project did not materialize beyond one film, *Kona Coast* (1968). He became a partner in a saloon on the Kona Coast where he proceeded to drink most of the stock; taught drama in a poor Hawaiian neighborhood; and contemplated running for Governor of Hawaii.

He left Hawaii to make the telemovie *In Broad Daylight* (1971) because he liked the script. It did well in the ratings and led to producer Jack Webb offering Boone the leading role in a new series *(Hec Ramsey)* as a righteous but slovenly deputy sheriff. Boone and Webb had met and become close friends when they both appeared in *The Halls of Montezuma.* In 1901 Ramsey was a grizzled old ex-gunfighter who decided to settle down on the side of the law in New Prospect, Oklahoma. He had become interested in the newfangled science of criminology and had spent years studying it. He still carried a gun and upon occasion used it, but to appease the anti-violence lobby he was quicker to extract his fingerprinting equipment and magnifying glass.

Hec soon discovered that Sheriff Oliver B. Stamp (Richard Lenz) was very young and inexperienced. Stamp, fearing that Hec's legendary fast gun would attract trouble, was uncertain about his new partner, but they eventually learned to compromise and to make good use of Hec's novel methods. *Hec Ramsey* spent two seasons (from October 1972 to August 1974) as one of the four rotating elements of the *NBC Sunday Mystery Movie.* There were ten made, mostly for a two-hour slot. It was generally believed that the concept was not strong enough to survive without the violence which had been an integral part of *Have Gun Will Travel.* This led to several angry outbursts from the star along the lines of, "I think the whole country's going effeminate—conned into it by antiviolence Milquetoasts, be they viewers, producers or advertisers."

Richard Boone made approximately 50 movies. Occasionally he was good, more often he was evil, always he was tough. In *The Tall T* (1957), one of the famous series of taut Westerns which starred Randolph Scott and were directed by Budd Boetticher, he plays Frank Usher, leader of an outlaw gang who hold Doretta Mims (Maureen O'Sullivan) and Pat Brennan (Randolph Scott) hostage for ransom. At one point he even discusses with Brennan the possibility of release, but is not taken aback when Brennan points out he would certainly return to kill him. "Yeah," Usher chuckles, "silly even to talk about it, ain't it?" Even though Usher eventually obtains the money, Brennan gets the drop on him at his camp and he is forced to ride out without it. He returns rifle blazing, but is shot out of the saddle by Brennan.

He had scarcely reformed on screen by the time he came to play the part of John Fain in *Big Jake* (1971). He kidnaps the grandson of Jake McCandles (John Wayne) for ransom and lives to regret it, but not for long. In Wayne's final film, *The Shootist* (1976), Boone played Sweeney who hates J.B. Books (John Wayne) because Books killed his brother years ago. He joins two other gunslingers and tries to gun Books down in a saloon in revenge, but Books is too smart for them and dispatches them instead. Wayne liked Boone, but Boone was continuously drunk while filming *The Shootist*. However, he was punctual and knew his lines, so Wayne kept quiet. Boone was offered the role of Doyle Lonnegan in *The Sting* (1973), but allegedly was so drunk that he never even bothered to reply. Robert Shaw subsequently played the part.

From 1972 onwards Boone made his permanent residence at St. Augustine, Florida, the birthplace of his third wife. He became Florida's "cultural ambassador." He lectured on acting at Flagler College and returned to his first love, painting. Richard Boone died on January 10, 1981, at age 63 at his Florida home of throat cancer. He married Jane Hopper, a painter, in 1937. They divorced in 1940. He then married singer Mimi Kelly in 1949. They divorced in 1950. On April 27, 1951, he wed the former Claire McAloon, an American ex-ballet dancer whom he met in Australia while shooting *Kangaroo* for director Lewis Milestone. Their son Peter was born on August 22, 1953. Peter later graduated from Stanford University as a music major. Richard Boone was survived by his third wife and son. He was cremated and his ashes were scattered over the Hawaiian islands which he loved.

Richard Boone Filmography

1950: *Halls of Montezuma*.
1951: *Call Me Mister, The Desert Fox*.
1952: *Kangaroo, Red Skies of Montana, Return of the Texan*.
1953: *Way of a Gaucho, Beneath the Twelve Mile Reef, City of Bad Men, Man on a Tightrope, The Robe, Vicki*.
1954: *The Raid, Dragnet, The Siege at Red River*.
1955: *Man Without a Star, Robbers' Roost, Ten Wanted Men, The Big Knife* (narrated only).
1956: *Battle Stations, Away All Boats, Star in the Dust*.
1957: *The Garment Jungle, Lizzie, The Tall T*.
1958: *I Bury the Living*.
1960: *The Alamo*.
1961: *A Thunder of Drums*.
1964: *Rio Conchos*.
1965: *The War Lord*.
1967: *Hombre*.
1968: *Kona Coast, Night of the Following Day*.
1969: *The Arrangement, The Kremlin Letter*.
1970: *Madron*.
1971: *Big Jake, Hec Ramsey: The Century Turns* (TV), *In Broad Daylight* (TV).
1972: *Goodnight My Love* (TV), *Deadly Harvest* (TV).
1974: *The Great Niagara* (TV).
1976: *Against a Crooked Sky, The Shootist*.
1977: *Winter Kills, God's Gun, The Last Dinosaur* (TV).
1978: *The Big Sleep, The Bushido Blade*.

Television Series

1954–1956: *Medic* as Dr. Konrad Styner.
1957–1963: *Have Gun Will Travel* as Paladin.
1963–1964: *The Richard Boone Show*.
1972–1974: *Hec Ramsey* as Hec Ramsey.

Sources

The Annual Obituary. Detroit, MI: St. James Press, 1981.
Current Biography Yearbook. New York: H.W. Wilson, 1964.
Fireman, Judy. *TV Book The Ultimate Television Book*. New York: Workman, 1977.
Heston, Charlton. *The Actor's Life Journals 1956–1976*. London: Allen Lane, 1979.
Miller, Lee O. *The Great Cowboy Stars of Movies & Television*. New Rochelle, NY: Arlington House, 1979.
Shepherd, Donald, Robert Slatzer and Dave Grayson. *Duke*. London: Sphere, 1985.

Speed, F. Maurice. *The Western Film and TV Annual.* London: Macdonald, 1960.
Television Star Book. London: Purnell, 1964.
Star TV and Film Annual. London: Odhams, 1966.
Willis, John. *Screen World.* London: Muller, 1982.

WILLIS BOUCHEY

Willis Bouchey was born William Bouchey in 1895. After years of experience in stock and on Broadway, this character actor relocated to Hollywood where he carved a solid niche for himself. In films he was frequently seen as a Western sheriff, banker, military officer or other official. On television he had a semi-regular role as the Mayor of Velardi in the Western series *Johnny Ringo.* Willis Bouchey died in Burbank, California, on September 28, 1977, at age 82.

Willis Bouchey Filmography

1951: *Elopement.*
1952: *Red Planet Mars, Carbine Williams, Just for You, Assignment Paris, Don't Bother to Knock, Million Dollar Mermaid, Washington Story, Deadline USA.*
1953: *Gun Belt, The Big Heat, The I Don't Care Girl, The President's Lady, Pick-Up on South Street, From Here to Eternity, Dangerous Crossing.*
1954: *The Battle of Rogue River, The Bridges at Toko-Ri, Suddenly, Drum Beat, Them!, The Long Gray Line, Executive Suite, Fireman Save My Child, A Star Is Born.*
1955: *The Violent Men, I Cover the Underworld, Battle Cry, The Spoilers, The McConnell Story, Big House USA, The Eternal Sea.*
1956: *Hell on Frisco Bay, Pillars of the Sky, Johnny Concho, Forever Darling, Magnificent Roughnecks.*
1957: *Mister Cory, The Garment Jungle, The Night Runner, The Wings of Eagles, Last of the Badmen, Beau James, Zero Hour, Last Stagecoach West.*
1958: *Darby's Rangers, The Sheepman, The Last Hurrah.*
1959: *No Name on the Bullet, The Horse Soldiers.*
1960: *Sergeant Rutledge.*
1961: *Saintly Sinners, Five Guns to Tombstone, Two Rode Together, You Have to Run Fast, Pocketful of Miracles.*
1962: *Incident in an Alley, The Man Who Shot Liberty Valance, Panic in Year Zero!*
1963: *How the West Was Won.*
1964: *Cheyenne Autumn, Where Love Has Gone, Apache Rifles.*
1965: *McHale's Navy Joins the Air Force.*
1966: *Return of the Gunfighter, Follow Me Boys.*
1968: *Support Your Local Sheriff.*
1969: *Young Billy Young, The Love God?*
1970: *Dirty Dingus Magee, The Intruders* (TV).
1971: *Support Your Local Gunfighter, Lawman, Shootout.*

Television Series

1959–1960: *Johnny Ringo* as the Mayor Of Velardi.

Sources

Quinlan, David. *Illustrated Directory of Film Character Actors Second Edition.* London: Batsford, 1995.
Truitt, Evelyn Mack. *Who Was On Screen Illustrated Edition.* New York: Bowker, 1984.

Willis Bouchey (right) with Don Durant in *Johnny Ringo*.

WILLIAM BOYD

In this day and age it is not uncommon for thespians who play hardcases or bitches on television to be consumed by the characters they portray and develop the same traits in real life. One actor who went in the reverse direction was William Boyd, a notorious playboy and hellraiser who, once he began playing Hopalong Cassidy, changed his personality and became a good guy. His portrayal of Hopalong (who wore a black suit and hat and rode a snow-white horse named Topper) was the longest running characterization in Hollywood history.

Hoppy, a character half conceived by writers and half by Boyd, didn't smoke, drink, swear or kiss girls. He captured villains rather than shot them. Of Hoppy, Boyd once said, "He's part philosopher, part doctor, part minister—he's everything." "When you've got kids looking up to you," he added, "when you've got parents who say what a wonderful guy Hoppy is, what the hell do you do? You have to be a wonderful guy." Rand Brooks, who played Lucky Jenkins for a while in the film series, recalled, "The players got along beautifully during filming. William Boyd was a gentleman, always on time, always much the good worker."

William Lawrence Boyd was born on June 5, 1895, either at Cambridge or Hendrysburg, Ohio. He was one of five children born to William Charles Boyd, a laborer and Lida Alberta Wilkins. His early years were spent in abject poverty. By the age of ten in 1905, the family had relocated to Tulsa, Oklahoma, where he attended school until he was 13. His father was killed in 1909 while rescuing fellow workers who had been trapped by an explosion on a construction job, so young Boyd quit school to work to support the family. He originally intended to be an engineer, but worked as a tool dresser, surveyor and automobile salesman before starting out at the age of 20 for California. By the time he reached Globe, Arizona, he had run out of money, so he sawed wood in a lumber camp. When World War I broke out, he tried to enlist, but was rejected because of an injury sustained as a lumberjack. He earned sufficient cash to take him as far as Orange, some 30 miles from Hollywood. In 1918 while on a train, he met Bryant Washburn, a famous film star, who persuaded him to try films because he was photogenic. He then worked as an orange picker and oil driller to earn enough money for clothes which would equip him for his ambition to become a motion picture actor.

Even in those days Boyd had prematurely grey hair and this feature, together with his rugged physique and handsome face, won him a place as an extra in films like *Old Wives For New* (1918) and *Why Change Your Wife?* (1919). This brought him to the attention of director Cecil B. DeMille. Boyd signed a contract with Famous Players–Lasky at $25.00 a week. In 1922 his contract was not renewed. After a period resting he appeared as the villain in a Buck Jones western on the Fox lot. A broken ankle terminated this activity prematurely. His best early opportunities came when DeMille cast him as Feodor in *The Volga Boatmen* (1926) and as Simon of Cyrene in *King Of Kings* (1927).

He had no difficulty making the transition to talkies because of his well-modulated speaking voice. In 1932 RKO Radio Pictures gave Boyd a contract which paid him $2,500 weekly with star billing. He also acquired tastes which went with his high salary. He owned a mansion in Beverly Hills, a beach house in Malibu and a ranch. He was a heavy drinker and a high-rolling gambler. In 1932 an actor with an identical name called William "Stage" Boyd was arrested for organizing a Hollywood beach party in which everyone did drugs, gambled with loaded equipment, consumed bootleg liquor and participated in a sex orgy. The following day newspapers across the land printed photographs of the wrong William Boyd. Although retractions were later printed, the public stayed away from his movies. RKO Radio, invoking a morals clause in his contract, voided it, leaving him broke and unemployed. For two years he received very little work in the movies.

In 1934 producer Harry "Pop" Sherman bought the screen rights to six of Clarence E. Mulford's books about the cowpuncher Hopalong Cassidy. Boyd was chosen to play Buck Peters, the dull ranch owner, in two of the films. Boyd not only persuaded Sherman to let him play Peters' sidekick, but also signed a contract for a series of six movies at a blanket salary of $30,000. Ironically it was originally intended that James Gleason should play the role of the hard-drinking hellraiser who limped because of a bullet injury. Boyd was so successful that he continued to play Cassidy, shooting six movies in a year. After the first film, *Hopalong Cassidy* (1935), Boyd eliminated the limp from his characterization. Mulford was a Brooklyn license clerk who had never been west of Chicago until he had written several of the books. Later Sherman bought the motion picture rights to the character and employed screenwriters to create new stories around him.

The Cassidy films were very popular because of their picturesque locations and plentiful action. After 1936 Boyd exclusively played the character. He also surprised many by becoming a skilled horseman. From 1936–1948 he was ranked high in the *Motion Picture Herald*'s lists of top Western stars. In 1938 Boyd's salary rose to $100,000 a year. A dispute began between Boyd and Sherman when Boyd returned $40,000 of his year's salary for the employment of better writing and creative personnel. Boyd had a permanent falling out with Sherman when he accused the latter of employing more staff than necessary, all of whom wanted to contribute. He walked out in a high dudgeon. The first 41 films were distributed by Paramount and the remainder by United Artists, who refused to accept a substitute actor. After an 18-month negotiation, Sherman turned over to the actor a ten-year lease on a sub-royalty basis of $25,000 a year for the motion picture rights to the character.

Boyd, who had spent two years touring with circuses, then formed Hopalong Cassidy Productions, which from 1946 to 1948 was responsible for releasing 12 new Cassidy vehicles through United Artists. His various partners were Benedict Bogeaus, Lewis Rachmil and Carl Lesserman. Each of the new vehicles was budgeted at $100,000 with a two-week shooting schedule. They lacked the production values which his early vehicles had benefited from. The yearly series of six was made during four consecutive months, leaving Boyd free from acting and production work during eight months of the year.

By 1948 the Cassidy series had ceased production, but television rode to the rescue. Boyd astutely saw the chance to make a fortune. He sold his ranch, borrowed every cent he could and mortgaged himself to the hilt. He bought all the remaining rights to the character from Mulford. He rejected a role in *Duel in the Sun* (1946) even though he needed the money because he was afraid it would detract from the Hoppy characterization. Although at one point he was reduced to living in a two-room shack and teetered on the brink of bankruptcy, the gamble paid off handsomely.

In 1949 when 54 of the Sherman-produced Cassidy films became available for television, the NBC network paid Boyd $250,000 for the weekly video presentation of an edited film. It made its debut on June 24, 1949, three months before *The Lone Ranger* and three days ahead of *Captain Video*. The films (originally televised in 39 cities) proved to be very popular with audiences of all ages. As the program's popularity grew, NBC commissioned 52 new half-hour episodes which Boyd produced as well as starred in. Twenty-six episodes of *Hopalong Cassidy* were broadcast during the 1952–1953 season and 26 during the 1953–1954 season. The first 12 were edited versions of the last 12 *Hopalong Cassidy* features which Boyd had produced between 1946 and 1948. Thus, Boyd only shot 14 new episodes for the first season, making 40 fresh episodes in total. It took about three days to shoot every 30-minute episode at Placeritos Ranch near Newhall, California. When its prime time network run ended in 1951, the series aired in syndication for another three years. Occasionally Boyd's old personality traits did surface, most notably when the time came to cast his sidekick in the series. He had promised the role to Andy Clyde, who turned down offers of work in the meantime. Instead he chose Edgar Buchanan and left Clyde to read about it in the pages of *Variety*.

Cassidy was first heard on the radio and seen in a comic strip in January 1950. The Sunday afternoon broadcast over Mutual network could be heard on 496 stations by an audience estimated at about 25 million. The comic strip, syndicated by the Los Angeles *Mirror*, was bought at the outset by some 50 newspapers.

Hopalong also reached the public in comic books, 15,000,000 of which were distributed in 1949; records, 50,000 of which were sold in a month; and 50 novelties which paid five percent royalties. In a coast-to-coast tour of 26 cities, he was greeted by more than 1,000,000 fans. In 1950 Boyd had consolidated his five Hollywood offices into two—one for his merchandising operation, the other a clearing house for his miscellaneous products. The character, the products and the films grossed $70 million in 1952 when Cassidy mania was at its peak. Boyd recalled, "I was broke. I couldn't get my pictures rereleased in theaters, but today I'm the richest cowboy in America. When I die, my wife will never have to worry about having money."

Boyd's final cinema job was for Cecil B. DeMille, who had shown confidence in him in the first place: He did a cameo as himself in *The Greatest Show On Earth* (1952). DeMille once admitted that Boyd had been his second choice of lead for *The Ten Commandments* (1923) and *The Plainsman* (1936). In 1958 Boyd sold Hopalong Cassidy Productions to William Boyd Enterprises for $8 million. When his horse Topper died in 1960 and was followed three weeks later by his groom, Boyd took this as a premonition of disaster. "Disasters," he told his wife, "come in threes. I'm not going to go for that third one." He retired almost immediately.

His health began to fail seriously in the 1960s. He suffered from Parkinson's disease and cancer. After an operation to remove a tumor from his lymph gland in 1968, he refused interviews on the grounds that the public would be shocked at the difference in his appearance. He lived quietly at his winter home in Palm Desert, California, and summer home at Dana Point, California. He eventually died at South Coast Community Hospital in Laguna Beach, California, on September 12, 1972, at age 77. A hospital spokesman said that Boyd had died from complications of Parkinson's disease and congestive heart failure. He is buried in the Sanctuary Of Sacred Promise at Forest Lawn Memorial Parks, Glendale, in a large marble crypt.

Some controversy exists over the number of marriages which Boyd had. There appears to be no concrete information available over whether he was married four or five times. His first reported wife was Diana Ruth Miller (1903–1981), a Boston heiress and actress, whom Boyd met when he was her chauffeur. He wed her in 1921 and divorced her in 1924. By her he had his only child, a son who died when he was nine months old. He next married actress Elinor Fair (1903–1957) in Santa Ana, California, on January 13, 1926. She was his leading lady in *The Volga Boatmen* (1926). They divorced in 1930. He next wed Dorothy Sebastian (1905–1957), his leading lady in *His First Command* (1929). They wed in 1930, but she divorced him in Los Angeles on May 29, 1936, charging him with cruelty. On June 5, 1937, he wed actress Grace Bradley, who was born in 1913. She admitted that she had had a crush on him since childhood. They wed three weeks after they first met and their marriage endured. At last report she taught Tai Chi in South Laguna, California. She still receives 500 letters a year from Hoppy fans all over the world.

William Boyd Filmography

1918: *Old Wives for New.*

1919: *Why Change Your Wife?*

1920: *A City Sparrow.*

1921: *Brewster's Millions, Moonlight and Honeysuckle, The Affairs of Anatol, Exit the Vamp, A Wise Fool.*

1922: *Bobbed Hair, Nice People, The Young Rajah, Manslaughter, On the High Seas.*

1923: *Enemies of Children, The Temple of Venus, Michael O'Halloran, Hollywood.*

1924: *Tarnish, Changing Husbands, Triumph.*

1925: *Forty Winks, The Road to Yesterday, The Golden Bed, The Midshipman.*

1926: *The Last Frontier, Eve's Leaves, Her Man O'War, The Volga Boatmen, Steel Preferred.*

1927: *Two Arabian Knights, King of Kings, Dress Parade, Wolves of the Air, Jim the Conqueror, Yankee Clipper.*

1928: *The Night Flyer, Power, Skyscraper, The Cop.*

1929: *High Voltage, Lady of the Pavements, The Flying Fool, The Leatherneck, Wolf Song.*

1930: *Those Who Dance, Officer O'Brien, His First Command, The Storm.*

1931: *The Gang Buster, The Painted Desert, Beyond Victory, The Big Gamble, Suicide Fleet.*

1932: *Carnival Boat, Men of America, The Wiser Sex, Madison Sq. Garden.*

William Boyd in *Hopalong Cassidy*.

1933: *Lucky Devils, Emergency Call.*
1934: *Port of Lost Dreams, Cheaters, Flaming Gold.*
1935: *Racing Luck, Hop-a-Long Cassidy, Bar 20 Rides Again, Eagle's Brood, Call of the Prairie, Go Get 'Em Haines.*
1936: *Three on the Trail, Federal Agent, Burning Gold, Heart of the West, Hopalong Cassidy Returns, Trail Dust, Borderland.*
1937: *Hills of Old Wyoming, North of the Rio Grande, Rustlers' Valley, Hopalong Rides Again, Texas Trail, Partners of the Plains, Cassidy of Bar 20.*
1938: *Bar 20 Justice, Heart of Arizona, In Old Mexico, The Frontiersman, Pride of the West, Sunset Trail.*
1939: *Silver on the Sage, Law of the Pampas, Range War, Renegade Trail.*

1940: *Santa Fe Marshal, Showdown, Hidden Gold, Stagecoach War, Three Men from Texas.*
1941: *In Old Colorado, Doomed Caravan, Pirates on Horseback, Border Vigilantes, Wide Open Town, Secrets of the Wasteland, Stick to Your Guns, Twilight on the Trail, Outlaws of the Desert, Riders of the Timberline.*
1942: *Undercover Man, Lost Canyon.*
1943: *Leather Burners, Hoppy Serves a Writ, Border Patrol, False Colors, Colt Comrades, Bar 20, Riders of the Deadline.*
1944: *Texas Masquerade, Lumberjack, Forty Thieves, Mystery Man.*
1946: *The Devil's Playground, Fools' Gold, Unexpected Guest, Dangerous Venture.*
1947: *Hoppy's Holiday, The Marauders.*
1948: *Silent Conflict, The Dead Don't Dream, Strange Gamble, Sinister Journey, False Paradise, Borrowed Trouble.*
1952: *The Greatest Show on Earth* (cameo).

Television Series

1949–1954: *Hopalong Cassidy* as Hopalong Cassidy

Sources

Current Biography Yearbook. New York: H.W. Wilson, 1950.
Duncan, Lee O. *The Great Cowboy Stars of Movies & Television.* New Rochelle, NY: Arlington House, 1979.
Katchmer, George. *Eighty Silent Film Stars: Biographies and Filmographies of the Obscure to the Well Known.* Jefferson, NC: McFarland, 1991.
Parish, James Robert. *Great Western Stars.* New York: Ace, 1976.
Parish, James Robert. *The Hollywood Death Book.* Las Vegas, NV: Pioneer, 1992.
Tuska, Jon. *The Filming of the West.* Garden City, NY: Doubleday, 1976.
Wollman, Jane. "William Boyd: Hoppy at Last." *Memories* magazine, June/July, 1989.
Yoggy, Gary A. *Riding the Video Range: The Rise and Fall of the Western on Television.* Jefferson, NC: McFarland, 1995.

MICKEY BRADDOCK (DOLENZ)

Mickey Braddock was born George Michael Dolenz, Jr., in Los Angeles on March 8, 1945, but from an early age he was known as Mickey. He was the son of actor and restaurateur George Dolenz (1908–1963) and Janelle Johnson, a former showgirl and actress who was born in 1923. He has three younger sisters: Gemma Marie (nicknamed "Coco"), Deborah and Gina. Initially they lived on a chicken ranch in Tarzana, California, later on Bing Crosby's old ranch at Toluca Lake, and still later in a more modest home in the San Fernando Valley. Initially he was educated at Eunice Knight Saunders School in the San Fernando Valley.

When Mickey was ten, his father's agent arranged for him to go on an interview for the title role in a television series called *Circus Boy.* This was one of several interviews for similar series which he attended. After the interview he was invited back for a screen test. Then his parents took him to the Marquis restaurant, which his father owned, where he was told by Norman Blackburn, one of the producers, that *Circus Boy* had been sold to NBC and that he was playing the leading role. The stipulations were that his naturally brown hair should be dyed blond and that he should change his surname to Braddock (derived from one of his ancestors). This was in order to avoid confusion with his father and because it was deemed more American.

This series dealt with a traveling circus on the Western frontier at the turn of the century as seen through the eyes of a 12-year-old orphan named Corky. His parents had been trapeze artists, but while performing they had an accident and were killed. After this he lived with the other circus artists. Corky's best friend was an elephant named Bimbo for whom he was a water boy. The other leading characters in the series were Joey the Clown (Noah Beery, Jr.)

Mickey Braddock (center) with Noah Beery, Jr. (left), and Robert Lowery in *Circus Boy*.

and Big Tim Champion (Robert Lowery), who owned the circus and found a place for Corky. Stories centered around the larger-than-life circus performers and the characters whom they meet as they pass through different towns.

This NBC series made its bow on September 23, 1956. It was shot mainly at Corriganville, deep in the heart of the San Fernando Valley. Since he was required in nearly every scene, Braddock had a private tutor on the set. He also undertook personal appearance tours with the elephant and developed a singing act. The series lasted for 49 half-hour, black and white episodes before the big top was dismantled for the final time on September 11, 1958. It was a production of Screen Gems, the television arm of Columbia Pictures.

Even though he was offered another series, his parents removed him from the show business environment to concentrate on his education. Eventually he enrolled at Valley Junior College, but when his father died he dropped out and drifted into petty crime. Becoming interested in acting again, he signed with an agent and did a few television guest shots. Around this time he enrolled in architectural school with a view to opening his own remodeling business. He studied guitar and sang at amateur talent events. One night at the Red Velvet Nightclub he was approached by an agent of sorts who signed him as part of a group called Micky and the One-Nighters which lived up to its name. Later it changed its name to The Missing Links, but by this time *he* had become the missing link because he was ousted.

About this time, a couple of young, hip producers named Bob Rafelson and Bert Schneider were seeking to make a series about a group called the Monkees, which was to be representative of all the groups playing in clubs across the land at the time. They were backed by an American television company, again Screen Gems. Dolenz has flatly denied that the group was in any way modeled on the Beatles. Allegedly he attended an open audition in 1965 for this group, but the actor has stated that he did not see the original newspaper advertisement for this and that he had a private audition. Although there were over 500 hopefuls, he was chosen to be one of the four. He was now using the name Mickey Dolenz. Although he had acting experience, he had no musical background other than his guitar studies, so the producers gave him a crash course as a drummer and he also sang vocals with Peter Tork, Michael Nesmith and Davy Jones.

Surprisingly, the Monkees were a success in their own right. The Monkees broke into the pop charts in September 1966, with the hit "Last Train To Clarksville." It was followed by over a dozen more Top Ten hits before the group broke up in 1970. The zany and surreal television series lasted for two seasons and the group also shot the feature film *Head* (1968), which flopped because it lacked a proper story structure and was deemed to contain material offensive to the general public. When the series ended Dolenz was very solvent, mainly because of royalties from the records.

Mickey Dolenz had occasional guest roles on prime time series during the 1970s and did voices for Hanna-Barbera cartoons for the rest of the decade. He auditioned for but did not win the role of Fonzie on *Happy Days*. His image worked against him for general acting roles. He started a small production company and began producing and directing some local commercials. He toured with Davy Jones for a while and did a musical in Sacramento called *The Adventures of Tom Sawyer*. In 1975 he was invited to costar with Davy Jones in a limited run of *The Point* at the Mermaid Theater in London, England. He and his erstwhile friend and partner had a spectacular falling out which led him to stay in England for 15 years.

An agent offered to represent him, and on the strength of his directing reel, he was offered a shot at directing an episode of a BBC series called *Premiere* designed to showcase new talent. He became a successful producer of children's comedy series, notably *Luna* (1980) and *Metal Mickey* (1979–1981). He also wrote and directed the English theatrical version of *Bugsy Malone* in 1982. There was a successful Monkees revival tour in 1986 and again in Britain in 1990, but only with three of the original group. Michael Nesmith, the only one to achieve solo success was not interested.

Mickey Dolenz married Britisher Samantha Juste in 1968. She was cohost of the English pop show *Top of the Pops*, and they met on an English tour in 1966. With her Dolenz had a daughter, Ami, born on January 8, 1969. Dolenz and Juste divorced in 1975. Throughout the 1980s Dolenz lived with his second wife, English-born model Trina Dow, in a £1,000,000 manor house in Nottinghamshire, England. They had three daughters, Charlotte, Emily and Georgia, all born during the 1980s. The pressures of touring led to an acrimonious divorce in 1991. After the divorce he returned to television work in the United States. He now lives alone in Los Angeles.

In January 1995, the four original Monkees met at the Hard Rock Cafe in Beverly

Hills to launch the rerelease of the band's first three albums by the record company Rhino, which is also putting all their 58 television shows on video.

Mickey Dolenz Filmography

1968: *Head.*
1970: *Keep Off My Grass.*
1971: *The Brother.*
1992: *Deadfall.*

Television Series

1956–1958: *Circus Boy* (under the name Mickey Braddock) as Corky.
1966–1968: *The Monkees* as Mickey Dolenz.

Sources

Brooks, Tim. *The Complete Directory to Prime Time TV Stars 1946–Present.* New York: Ballantine Books, 1987.
Dolenz, Micky and Mark Bego. *I'm a Believer.* New York: Hyperion, 1993.
"Hey, Hey, We're the Monkees for the Nineties." *Daily Mail* newspaper, January 1995.
"Monkee Speaks at Last." *Daily Mail* newspaper, August 1994.
Perry, Jeb H. *Screen Gems: A History of Columbia Pictures Television from Cohn to Coke 1948–1983.* Metuchen, NJ: Scarecrow, 1991.
Picture Show Annual. London: Amalgamated Press, 1953.

Note

All the reference books list him as spelling Mickey with an "e" but his autobiography uses the spelling Micky throughout.

PAT BRADY

Pat Brady was born Robert Ellsworth Patrick Aloysious O'Brady in Toledo, Ohio, on December 31, 1914, the son of John and Lucille O'Brady, vaudeville performers. He was an only child. From infancy he toured with his parents and made his stage debut at four in *Mrs. Wiggs of the Cabbage Patch.* When he was 12 his parents separated and he went to live with his father, who relocated to California.

He was briefly a rodeo rider. As a teenager he became a proficient bass player with a bias towards pop and jazz music. By 1935 he was appearing as one of a quartet at a nightclub in Sunset Beach. One night Len Slye dropped into the club for a drink and introduced himself to Pat Brady. Slye was part of the Sons of the Pioneers, a Western musical group. In 1937 Slye won a contract to star in a series of Westerns for Republic under the name of Roy Rogers. A replacement needed to be found for him with his singing group, so he suggested Brady. Since Bob Nolan was already a member of the group, it was not considered to be appropriate for there to be two Bobs in the same outfit, so Brady adopted the Christian name of Pat. He joined the Sons of the Pioneers on October 16, 1937.

From 1937 to 1941 this musical group were regulars in the series of Westerns which Charles Starrett shot for Columbia. Brady made his screen debut in *Outlaws of the Prairie* (1937). He proved to have a natural flair for comedy and sometimes did sketches in these Westerns. In 1941 the Sons of the Pioneers quit Columbia to join the Republic stable as a backup for Roy Rogers. They appeared with Rogers in 41 films beginning with *Red River Valley* (1941) and finishing with *Night Time in Nevada* (1948).

Brady was not with them throughout this entire period. He quit and joined the armed forces for a three-year period during World War II. Most of his time was spent with Patton's Third Army in France where he served with gallantry, being awarded several medals including two Purple Hearts. After the war, when Roy Rogers lost his most recent sidekick Andy Devine to other offers, he asked Brady

Pat Brady (right) with Roy Rogers on *The Roy Rogers Show.*

to take over. Pat Brady essayed the role of Sparrow Biffle in five of Rogers' films. He acted as comic relief and frequently sang a novelty song in these films. *The Golden Stallion* (1949) was a seminal film because it introduced Brady's mode of transportation, a Jeep with a mind of its own called Nellybelle. This was Rogers' idea and he actually owned and built the Jeep.

When Rogers began his television series which lasted from 1951 to 1957, he retained the Jeep for the series and Pat Brady to provide the comedy. There was also a place in the Jeep for a hidden driver, so that the various antics which became so integral a part of the series could be performed. Brady made numerous personal appearances in the same guise with his Jeep until 1959 when he was asked to rejoin the Sons of the Pioneers, which he did, remaining with them until 1967. He was also a regular on *The Roy Rogers and Dale Evans Show*, a variety show of 1962.

In 1967 he left the group and relocated to Colorado Springs, Colorado, where he became manager of a guest ranch. He later did promotional work, some of it involving Nellybelle, for a furniture store and the local Ford dealer in that area. He also created and performed with a musical group which played clubs. Early in 1972 he admitted himself to The Ark, a rehabilitation center in Green Mountain Falls, Colorado. One day later, on February 27, 1972, he was dead. Although the cause of death was reported to be a heart attack, it is known that years of heavy drinking were a major contributory factor. On March 1, 1972, he was buried at the Evergreen Cemetery while some members of the Sons of the Pioneers sang a selection of his favorite Westerns ballads. He was survived by his wife Carol, from whom he was separated, and a son.

Pat Brady Filmography

1937: *Outlaws of the Prairie.*
1938: *West of Cheyenne, South of Arizona, Rio Grande, Western Caravans, Texas Stagecoach.*
1939: *Man from Sundown.*
1940: *Two Fisted Rangers, The Durango Kid, Thundering Frontier, West of Abilene.*

1941: *The Pinto Kid, Outlaws of the Panhandle, Red River Valley.*
1942: *The Man from Cheyenne, South of Santa Fe, Sunset on the Desert, Romance on the Range, Call of the Canyon.*
1943: *Song of Texas, The Man from Music Mountain, Silver Spurs.*
1945: *Along the Navajo Trail.*
1949: *Down Dakota Way, The Golden Stallion.*
1950: *Bells of Coronado, Trigger Jr., Twilight in the Sierras.*
1951: *South of Caliente.*

Television Series

1951–1957: *The Roy Rogers Show* as Pat Brady.
1962: *The Roy Rogers and Dale Evans Show* as Himself.

Sources

McClure, Arthur F. and Ken D. Jones. *Heroes, Heavies and Sagebrush.* South Brunswick and New York: Barnes, 1972.

Rothel, David. *Those Great Cowboy Sidekicks.* Waynesville, NC: World of Yesterday Publications, 1984.

SCOTT BRADY

Scott Brady was the star of the syndicated television Western series *Shotgun Slade* (1959–1961). He was a handsome but hard-living actor who later, as a fat and balding character actor, did some sterling work. Like many of the films he made, his television series was neither a big hit nor a failure. Brady's background and physique dictated that he acquit himself well in physical rather than cerebral roles. He was not an actor of much depth in his starring days and admitted that he did not spend time analyzing the characters nor the screenplays in which he appeared. He changed his name from Gerry Tierney to Scott Brady because he did not want to cash in on his older brother's fame. The name Scott Brady derived from a short story which a friend of the actor wrote about a fictitious boxer hero with that name.

Scott Brady was born Gerald Kenneth Tierney in Brooklyn, New York, on September 13, 1924, the son of Lawrence and Maria Tierney. His father was a police chief who died in 1964. His mother died in 1960. He had one older brother, actor Lawrence Tierney, who was born on March 15, 1919, and one younger brother, Edward. Scott Brady grew up in Westchester where he attended Roosevelt and St. Michael's high schools. He was a star athlete whose ambition was to be a football coach. Upon graduation he enlisted in the navy, where he served as a naval aviation mechanic aboard the U.S.S. Norton Sound. He became light heavyweight boxing champion at his naval base during his gunnery training at Pensacola, Florida.

He was discharged from the Navy in California in April 1945. He was not intending to become an actor, but he did want to look up his brother Lawrence. He did a number of menial jobs before being spotted in a drugstore by producer Hal B. Wallis, who offered him a screen test. The test was a flop but it gave direction to his life, so he enrolled at the Bliss-Hayden drama school in Beverly Hills under the G.I. Bill. He was also squired around town by his brother Lawrence. Brady made his screen debut in *Born to Kill* (1947), which starred brother Lawrence.

While Scott Brady was appearing in a drama school production of *Heaven Can Wait*, agent Johnny Darrow caught the play. Darrow took him on as a client and arranged for Poverty Row company Eagle-Lion to sign him. He made four movies for them at a salary of $300 a movie. They were shot in only ten days apiece, but Brady registered strongly in them. He and his agent decided to buy up his contract, but the company obtained an injunction preventing him from working elsewhere. Once the affair was settled, Brady immediately signed a non-exclusive contract with Universal for two movies a year. In 1951 he inked a simultaneous deal with 20th Century–Fox to make one movie a year at a salary of $25,000. What might have been his most prestigious assign-

Scott Brady in *Shotgun Slade*.

ment, the role of Turk Fisher in *Come Back Little Sheba* (1952), he had to nix because of other acting commitments.

When his contract with Universal expired, he signed limited pact deals with 20th Century–Fox, Lippert, Republic and Columbia. At Republic he appeared in his two best remembered films: as Dancin' Kid in *Johnny Guitar* (1954) with Joan Crawford, and as the Sundance Kid in *The Maverick Queen* (1956) opposite Barbara Stanwyck, his favorite leading lady. When his film work diminished in the late 1950s he turned to stage and television. He played the title role in *Shotgun Slade*, a syndicated Western series, which lasted for 78 black and white episodes. The pilot played as a single episode of *Schlitz Playhouse*. Slade was an investigator working for Wells Fargo and various insurance companies. He relied on a unique weapon, a two-in-one shotgun. The series had a snappy jazz score and plenty of beautiful women. One interesting feature of the series was the casting of offbeat actors and sportsmen in the supporting roles.

Surprisingly for a predominantly film-oriented actor, he proved reasonably successful on stage, notably in *The Moon Is Blue* and in touring companies of *Picnic*, *The Best Man* and *Detective Story*. He made his Broadway debut as a ruthless cardsharp in the musical version of *Destry* (1959) and earned favorable reviews. This and the television series marked a strong dividing line in his career because thereafter he was primarily seen in character parts in films and television. He enjoyed doing stage work, but did more film and television because they paid better.

A second projected television series, *The World Of Floyd Gibbons*, a spin-off from a 1962 episode of *The Untouchables*, did not materialize. Instead he appeared in supporting roles in a number of minor films including A. C. Lyles' 1960s Westerns for Paramount. Several low-budget films went direct to television or were drive-in fodder. His most prestigious assignments were for Mike Frankovitch, a personal friend for whom he appeared in *Marooned* (1970), *$* (1971) and *Doctors' Wives* (1971). He also had good roles in *The China Syndrome* (1979) and *Gremlins* (1984).

He played in numerous television series, most notably a semi-regular role on the successful anthology series *Police Story* (1974–1978). His real-life girlfriend for many years was Dorothy Malone. Many expected them to wed, but instead he married former model Mary Elizabeth (Lisa) Tirony in 1967. They had two sons, Timothy and Terrence. Once quizzed on why he appeared in so many small roles on television, he replied, "I can't afford to turn down many parts, not with the kids to send to college."

Scott Brady died in Woodland Hills, California, on April 16, 1985, at age 60, of respiratory failure. He was survived by his wife, sons and brothers. He is buried at Holy Cross Cemetery and Mausoleum, Culver City, California.

Scott Brady Filmography

1947: *Born to Kill.*
1948: *Montana Belle, In This Corner, Canon City, He Walked by Night.*
1949: *Port of New York, The Gal Who Took the West, Undertow, I Was a Shoplifter.*
1950: *Kansas Raiders, Undercover Girl.*
1951: *The Model and the Marriage Broker.*
1952: *Bloodhounds of Broadway, Untamed Frontier, Yankee Buccaneer, Bronco Buster.*

1953: *A Perilous Journey, El Alamein, Three Steps to the Gallows* (released in the U.S. in 1955 as *White Fire*).
1954: *The Law Versus Billy the Kid, Johnny Guitar.*
1955: *They Were So Young, Gentlemen Marry Brunettes, The Vanishing American.*
1956: *Terror at Midnight, The Maverick Queen, Mohawk.*
1957: *The Storm Rider, The Restless Breed.*
1958: *Ambush at Cimarron Pass, Blood Arrow.*
1959: *Battle Flame.*
1963: *Operation Bikini.*
1964: *Stage to Thunder Rock, John Goldfarb Please Come Home.*
1965: *Black Spurs, They Ran for Their Lives.*
1966: *Destination Inner Space, Castle of Evil.*
1967: *Red Tomahawk, Fort Utah, Journey to the Center Of Time.*
1968: *Arizona Bushwackers.*
1969: *Nightmare in Wax, Cain's Way, The Road Hustlers, Hell's Bloody Devils (*a.k.a. *Smashing the Crime Syndicate), The DA: Murder One* (TV).
1970: *Marooned, Five Bloody Graves, Satan's Sadists.*
1971: *Doctors' Wives, The Mighty Gorga, $.*
1972: *The Loners, The Night Strangler* (TV), *The Leo Chronicles, Bonnie's Kids.*
1973: *Wicked Wicked.*
1975: *Roll Freddy Roll, Kansas City Massacre* (TV).
1976: *Law and Order* (TV).
1978: *Suddenly Love* (TV), *Streets of Fear* (TV), *Pressure Point* (TV), *When Every Day Was the Fourth of July* (TV).
1979: *The China Syndrome, The Last Ride of the Dalton Gang* (TV).
1981: *Dead Kids, Shadowland.*
1983: *This Girl For Hire* (TV).
1984: *Gremlins.*

Television Series

1959–1961: *Shotgun Slade* as Shotgun Slade.

Miniseries

1978: *Wheels.*
1983: *The Winds of War.*

Sources

Clark, Al. *The Film Yearbook Volume 4.* London: Virgin, 1986.
Parish, James Robert and Lennard DeCarl. *Hollywood Players The Forties* New Rochelle, NY: Arlington House, 1976.
Picture Show Annual. London: Amalgamated Press, 1951 and 1955.

JOLENE BRAND

Born in Los Angeles in 1935, this starlet was best known for playing the romantic interest of Zorro and for being a female foil of Ernie Kovacs. She also appeared in various other television series and pilots until circa 1966.

Jolene Brand Filmography

1958: *Giant from the Unknown*

Television Series

1958–1959: *Zorro* as Anna Maria Verdugo.
1960–1961: *Guestward Ho!* as Pink Cloud.
1961–1962: *The New Ernie Kovacs Show.*

Sources

Inman, David. *The TV Encyclopedia.* New York: Perigee, 1991.
Yoggy, Gary A. *Riding the Video Range: The Rise and Fall of the Western on Television.* Jefferson, NC: McFarland, 1995.

X BRANDS

He was born Jay X Brands in Kansas City, Missouri, on July 24, 1927, of German, Irish and English descent. The middle letter X is his name, not an initial. Since 1743 in Braeden, Germany, where his family originated, there has been a tradition of having one male member known as X. In 1936 his family relocated to Glendale, California. By the time he was old enough to ride, he had been given his own horse. He became an expert rider, competing in a number of rodeos.

He was conscripted into the Navy during World War II and also served during the Korean conflict. Upon his honorable discharge, he used the G.I. Bill to enroll with the Ben Bard Players, a drama school where he was a full-time student for two years. His spare time was spent at the Hitching Post Cafe, a favorite rendezvous point for Western stuntmen. When a Columbia casting director dropped by looking for tall actors who could ride a motorcycle, X Brands applied. He made his screen debut as one of Marlon Brando's gang of riders in *The Wild One* (1954).

Mainly, however, he worked as an extra and did bits. His earliest employers were Screen Gems and Gene Autry's Flying A Productions. His first steady work was doubling and stunting for Bill Williams on the television series *The Adventures of Kit Carson*. Commencing with *Hondo* (1953) he began an association with John Wayne which continued for a long time. By the mid–1950s he had begun to obtain speaking parts. His biggest break came when he was cast as the Pawnee Indian Pahoo-Ka-Ta-Wah, literally Wolf Who Stands in Water, in the television series *Yancy Derringer*.

He had been working on a B western at Columbia playing an Indian chief. Since he had a gap between his front teeth, a dentist had made him a rubber insert to disguise this. While reciting some dialogue, he accidentally spat out the insert. Despite an intensive search, no one could find it. When he arrived home in the middle of the afternoon, his agent called and told him he was to audition immediately for the role of Pahoo. Brands refused to go because he had lost the insert, but his agent insisted, adding that he would do all the talking. Brands went to the audition but refused to answer any questions. He stared fixedly ahead and let his agent do the talking. Finally Brands walked out without saying a word. Jock Mahoney, the designated star of the series, came after him and congratulated him on having found the character. Pahoo did not speak or change expression during the series. Two days after the audition, Brands found himself shooting the pilot episode.

Derringer and Pahoo originally met when Yancy Derringer went West. Alone on the prairie, Derringer was attacked by a small war party of the Sioux, a tribe which were deadly enemies of the Pawnee. The Sioux had him trapped when Pahoo rode up and rescued him. The two men became lifelong friends. (In real life, too, Brands and Mahoney had a high regard for one another.) Pahoo's trademarks were the flick knife he carried on a sheath at the base of the neck and a double-barreled shotgun which he wore by his side. He also wore a peace medal which had been given to him in Washington by the president. Pahoo used sign language in the series rather than speech. This was authentic because Brands obtained and read a book on the subject so that he could translate his dialogue in the scripts into sign language. He did all of his own stunts in the series. In one episode, he fell from a rope attached to a crane. He sprained both ankles and had to be carried off the set in agony.

It took three days to shoot each episode, and two episodes were shot back-to-back. Interiors were shot at the Selznick Studios at Culver City, with exteriors shot at Bronson Canyon. Although the series was very popular, it only lasted for 34 episodes. It was a textbook example of a series with limitless potential killed off by network politics. The CBS network had bought a new studio in North Hollywood which became CBS Television Center. They went to the four producers of the show and told them to shift the shooting of the series to their new location, adding that they wanted a percentage of the profits as well. The producers indignantly refused. They knew they had a top quality series and intended to air it

Left-right: X Brands, Frances Bergen, and Jock Mahoney in *Yancy Derringer*.

on another network, but it was too late because all the airtime had been taken for the following season. Their sponsor, Johnson's Wax, had given the nod for the following season, but when CBS cancelled their contract for the series, Johnson's Wax refused to cooperate as well.

The Pawnee nation were very enamored of Brands' characterization, however, and he was invited to be Grand Marshal of their homecoming in Pawnee, Oklahoma, in 1959. His agent warned him that he had become so typecast that he would not be considered for other roles. The actor was completely happy about this state of affairs until native American groups became a vociferous minority and complained about Caucasian actors such as Brands being cast as Indians. Since Westerns on television began to die out and the number of Western feature films were being drastically reduced, X Brands found himself unemployable in Hollywood. The chronic insecurity led him to develop a drinking problem, but he has been sober since 1968. About a year later it was suggested to him by a colleague that since flying was his hobby, he might obtain another type of employment as a flying instructor.

By 1971 he had flown thousands of miles, subsequently becoming Chief Flight Instructor and Pilot Examiner at Van Nuys Airport. He has done little acting work since then, three of his last appearances being segments of *The FBI* and *Dynasty* in which, appropriately, he played a pilot. Rather ruefully he has admitted, "I didn't desert show business. It deserted me!" X Brands has been twice married and twice divorced.

X Brands Filmography

1954: *The Wild One.*
1956: *The Naked Gun.*
1957: *Young and Dangerous, She Devil.*
1959: *Escort West, Gunmen from Laredo.*
1960: *Oklahoma Territory.*
1966: *Beau Geste.*
1973: *Santee.*
1978: *Avalanche.*
1979: *The Rebels.*

Television Series

1958–1959: *Yancy Derringer* as Pahoo-Ka-Ta-Wah.

Sources

Anderson, Bob. "Pahoo Ka-Ta-Wah: Wolf Who Stands in Water." *Trail Dust* magazine, fall/winter 1993.

Inman, David. *The TV Encyclopedia.* New York: Perigee, 1991.

Lamparski, Richard. *Whatever Became Of? Eleventh Series.* New York: Crown, 1989.

PETER BRECK

Peter Breck once said, "When the public gets tired of the various film themes in vogue, they always return to the Western." He added that his ambition was to follow in the footsteps of such Western greats as John Wayne, James Stewart and Randolph Scott. Indeed it was a laudable ambition, but despite *Black Saddle* and *The Big Valley*, it was never realized.

Peter Breck was born in Rochester, New York, on March 13, 1929. His father was a bandleader and his mother was a dancer. At one time in his career, he appeared in nightclubs as a singer, dancer and comedian, but later he determined to be an actor. After his discharge from the navy, he enrolled as a drama major at the University of Texas. He appeared in an estimated 140 legit productions in 36 states and Canada. Robert Mitchum saw him give a wonderful performance in a play staged in Washington. Mitchum was so impressed that he cast Breck in the role of Stacey Gouge in the film *Thunder Road* (1958). When the North Carolina locations were finished, he was called to Hollywood to post-synch some of his lines. "I owe Bob a lot for my break into movies," he said. "After the picture was released, I started getting many other offers, mostly heavy parts. I was always the villain!"

Black Saddle started out as an episode of *Dick Powell's Zane Grey Theater* in 1959. Chris Alcaide played the role of an ex-gunfighter who is shot and taken to the home of a judge to recover. The availability of law books and his respect for the judge make him decide to study law and become an attorney. The pilot was sold and Alcaide was cast in the lead. A week before production was due to start, Alcaide was removed from the series because the sponsor believed that he had become too familiar as a villain, and Peter Breck was substituted. It could be argued that Breck was in danger of being similarly typed, but his was a fresher face.

In the series (called *Black Saddle*), Breck played a character called Clay Culhane who was a member of a family of gunslingers. After his brothers are killed in a shoot-out, he rejects violence and turns towards the law, qualifying as an attorney. He rode through the New Mexico territory during the years immediately after the Civil War, helping those in need of legal assistance. Since his law books were in his saddle bags, this justified the title of *Black Saddle*. U.S. Marshal Gib Scott (Russell Johnson), who doubted that Culhane had reformed, dogged his trail. Culhane operated out of Latigo, New Mexico, residing at the Marathon Hotel owned by Nora Travers (Anna-Lisa). *Black Saddle* made its debut on the NBC network on January 10, 1959. It switched to ABC on October 5, 1959, but ended on September 30, 1960. A Four Star Production, it consisted of 44 half-hour, black and white episodes. It was intended as a prestigious Western series which would launch Breck as a star, but the ratings were only average and the network did not renew it after the first season.

When the series ended, Breck became a contract player with Warner Bros. television. This he came to regard as a retrograde step because he had established himself as a star with *Black Saddle*, whereas he was one of the lesser lights at Warners where the pay was also lower. His tenure at Warners was unusual because he quickly became one of their most dependable actors, turning up in numerous Western and detective episodics. Oddly, he did not star in a series of his own for them, nor did this ever appear to be a possibility.

When he quit Warner Bros., he briefly returned to films, most notably as the protagonist Johnny Barratt in Sam Fuller's *Shock Corridor* (1963). He played a crime reporter who has himself committed to an asylum to discover who committed a murder there. His motive is to win a Pulitzer Prize, but the outcome is ironic. Breck's first love, however, was Westerns, and he built himself a three-acre ranch some 40 miles from Hollywood where he enjoyed the outdoor life.

He was cast as the spirited, hot-tempered, rough-edged Nick Barkley in the Western series *The Big Valley*, which was set in the rich San Joaquin Valley in California in the 1870s. Victoria Barkley (Barbara Stanwyck) owned the sprawling ranch assisted by her offspring, of whom Nick was one. The series began on the ABC network on September 15, 1965, and ended on May 19, 1969, after 112 color episodes. Allegedly Breck was not impressed when he discovered that Richard Long was to be billed above him in the series. Long had also been a Warner Bros. contract player. Breck's agent warned him not to be too vocal in his protests. The reason became apparent when his agent extracted two documents. One was a copy of Richard Long's contract, the other a copy of Breck's. When he compared the two, he discovered that his negotiated salary was twice that of Long.

Unlike the other stars of *The Big Valley* who all maintained a high profile after the demise of the series, Breck's career declined precipitously. He logged only a handful of credits thereafter. He played the ambitious but evil Jess Keller in the shortlived NBC serial *Secret Empire* (1979), which attempted unsuccessfully to revive cliffhangers on television. One of his last recorded appearances was the "King Of The Cowboys" episode of *The Fall Guy* in 1984, which reunited him with *Big Valley* costar Lee Majors and a number of television Western stars. He currently resides in Vancouver, Canada, where he operates a couple of drama schools.

Peter Breck Filmography

1946: *Deadline at Dawn*.
1957: *Slim Carter*.
1958: *Thunder Road, I Want to Live!*
1959: *The Wild and the Innocent*.
1961: *Portrait of a Mobster*.
1962: *Lad: A Dog*.
1963: *Shock Corridor, Hootenanny Hoot, The Crawling Hand*.
1965: *The Glory Guys*.
1969: *Barquero*.
1974: *Benji*.
1982: *The Sword and the Sorcerer*.
1990: *Terminal City Ricochet*.
1991: *Yes Virginia There Is a Santa Claus* (TV), *I Still Dream of Jeannie* (TV), *Highway 61*.
1992: *The Unnamable Returns: The Statement Of Randolph Carter*.
1993: *Sworn To Vengeance* (TV).

1995: *Decoy.*
1996: *Lulu.*

Television Series

1959–1960: *Black Saddle* as Clay Culhane.
1965–1969: *The Big Valley* as Nick Barkley.
1979: *The Secret Empire* as Jess Keller.

Miniseries

1978: *Black Beauty.*

Sources:

Ferguson, Ken. *Television Stars.* London: Purnell, 1966.
Ferguson, Ken. *Western Stars of Television and Film.* London: Purnell, 1967.
Yoggy, Gary A. *Riding the Video Range: The Rise and Fall of the Western on Television.* Jefferson, NC: McFarland, 1995.

Left: **Peter Breck in** ***Black Saddle.***

PAUL BRINEGAR

Paul Brinegar played different characters in five separate television series. He appeared in 216 episodes of *Rawhide*; 51 episodes of *Lancer*; 38 episodes of *Wyatt Earp*; 13 episodes of *Matt Houston*; and 10 episodes of *Code R.* Clearly the best remembered of these characters was his role as "Wishbone" in the seven-year television run of *Rawhide.* "Wishbone" was the bewhiskered and comedic chuckwagon driver played with finesse by Brinegar. When quizzed about the secret or talent he possessed that placed him in comedic roles, he replied, "I'm not a comedian. I'm a serious actor whose roles were exaggerated reality in such a way that the situations I portrayed were funny because they were out of context."

Paul Brinegar was born in Tucumcari, New Mexico, on December 19, 1917. While being raised in Santa Fe, he found himself enjoying roles in high school plays and developed a career desire to be a professional actor. Relocating to Pasadena in 1935, he enrolled in what is now known as Pasadena City College, where he pursued his ambition.

Interrupted by the outbreak of World War II, he spent four years in the U.S. Navy in the South Pacific serving as chief radioman. Following the end of the war, he worked as a radio repairman to support himself and found as many roles as he could, performing at night to pursue his acting career. Taking bit parts in movies and in local theaters, he was looking for the proverbial "big break" every entertainer hopes to find.

The entertainment industry and movie studios were entering into the television era in the late 1940s and early 1950s. A busy actor or actress who worked in movies feared the stigma of television, and those who worked in television were not regarded as serious contenders for important movie parts. Confusion did not reign supreme in the entertainment

Left-right: Paul Brinegar, guest-star Gail Kobe, and Eric Fleming in *Rawhide*.

industry, but misapprehension was a facet of everyday life for someone in Brinegar's position. Taking the plunge, he became a television pioneer by accepting parts in early television series such as *Dragnet* and *Racket Squad*. He was not afraid of the adverse reaction he might be creating for himself on movie lots.

The "break" he was searching for came to him in 1956–1957 with the television series *Wyatt Earp*, in which he portrayed Mayor Kelly, the feisty mayor of Dodge City. "After that series," he said, "it just opened up for me." Following the *Wyatt Earp* series, he appeared with Joel McCrea in Charles Marquis Warren's movie production of *Cattle Empire* (1958), a role that prompted producers of the *Rawhide* series to select him to portray the character of "Wishbone" for seven years. He was the trail drive cook. In episodes such as "The Prairie Elephant," his character had the most footage of the regulars. Asked what he thought of his costars in this series, he replied succinctly, "All great guys."

In 1968–1969 he appeared as a ranch handyman on the CBS series *Lancer*, which was modeled along the lines of *Bonanza*, starring Andrew Duggan and James Stacey. In 1977 Brinegar found himself in the *Code R* television series for one season. Of the *Matt Houston* television series, he said, "The producers didn't know what to do with two old cowboys, so [they] dropped us." In all, his regular television series roles totaled 328 episodes. Later he had a recurring role as Francis Killbridge on the *Adventures Of Brisco County Jr.* series.

In 1989 he participated in what may have been the last-ever event of its kind in America, the Montana Cattle Drive. He appeared on a Reba McEntire music video; in supporting or guest-star roles in over 100 other series from the early 1950s; and in numerous television commercials. He was Honorary Sheriff and Fire Chief of Granada Hills, where by all accounts he did an excellent job of keeping the territory safe and law-abiding. He was once asked if he would have done anything differently if he could choose. "No," he said simply, "I wouldn't change anything. I have enjoyed my work completely and found wonderful friends through the years." In 1994 he was awarded a Golden Boot at the annual ceremony.

Paul Brinegar married Shirley Talbott, former actress and model, on December 29, 1962. They had two sons, Paul III (born January 3, 1964) and Mark (born on July 4, 1967). One son has been a psychology student attending Humboldt State College and the other is employed in the San Fernando Valley. Brinegar and his wife lived from the early 1960s in a modest house in the Granada Hills area of the North San Fernando Valley. Their home was filled with memorabilia and paintings, the latter the product of his talented wife's brush.

At 77, Paul Brinegar died in Los Angeles on March 27, 1995 of emphysema.

Paul Brinegar Filmography

1948: *Larceny.*
1949: *The Gal Who Took the West, Sword in the Desert, Take One False Step.*
1950: *Storm Warning.*
1951: *Journey into Light.*
1952: *The Captive City, Here Come the Nelsons, Pat and Mike.*
1953: *Fast Company, So Big.*
1954: *Human Desire, Rogue Cop, Dawn at Socorro, The Rocket Man, Phantom of the Rue Morgue.*
1955: *I Died a Thousand Times.*
1956: *World Without End, Flight to Hong Kong.*
1957: *The Vampire, Hell on Devil's Island, Copper Sky, The Spirit of St. Louis.*
1958: *Cattle Empire, How to Make a Monster.*
1966: *Country Boy.*
1969: *Charro!*
1973: *High Plains Drifter.*
1977: *Crisis in Sun Valley* (TV).
1981: *The Creature Wasn't Nice.*
1983: *The Gambler Part II: The Adventure Continues* (TV).
1984: *Chattanooga Choochoo.*
1987: *Independence* (TV).
1991: *Life Stinks.*
1994: *Maverick, Wyatt Earp: Return to Tombstone* (TV).

Television Series

1956–1958: *The Life and Legend of Wyatt Earp* as Jim "Dog" Kelly.
1959–1966: *Rawhide* as "Wishbone."
1969–1970: *Lancer* as Jelly Hoskins.
1977: *Code R.*
1982–1983: *Matt Houston* as Lamar Pettybone.

Sources

Correspondence between Brinegar and the author.

Lentz, Harris M. III. *Obituaries in the Performing Arts, 1995.* Jefferson, NC: McFarland, 1996.

STEVE BRODIE

Born Johnny Stevens in Wichita or Eldorado, Kansas, on November 25, 1919, he began his career in stock. He had contracts with MGM and later RKO Radio, where he did some of his best work. With his lived-in face, it seemed that he might have made a success as the offbeat kind of hero that television sometimes favors. His appearances as a series regular were limited to a two-season stint on *The Life and Legend of Wyatt Earp,* in which he played the sheriff who was in league with the Clantons, and in an obscure syndicated series called *Everglades.*

Although he was one of television's most prolific guest-stars during the late 1950s and early 1960s, his career later declined, exacerbated by a drink problem which clouded his capacity to recall his lines. He coproduced *Bobbie Jo and the Outlaw* (1976), a low-budget feature in which he did not appear. He was also active at conventions and continued his career in commercial voiceovers. He died in West Hills, California, on January 9, 1992, at age 72, of cancer. Formerly wed to actress Lois Andrews, he was survived by his wife Virginia, two sons—one of whom (Kevin) is a filmmaker—and five stepdaughters.

Steve Brodie Filmography

1944: *Follow the Boys, Ladies Courageous, Thirty Seconds Over Tokyo.*
1945: *A Walk in the Sun, It's in the Bag, The Crimson Canary, This Man's Navy, Anchors Aweigh.*
1946: *Badman's Territory, Criminal Court, Young Widow, The Falcon's Adventure, Sunset Pass.*
1947: *Desperate, Trail Street, Out of the Past, Crossfire, Thunder Mountain, Code of the West.*
1948: *Arizona Ranger, Bodyguard, Station West, Return of the Badmen, Guns of Hate.*
1949: *I Cheated the Law, Rose of the Yukon, Home of the Brave, Massacre River, Treasure of Monte Cristo, The Big Wheel. Tough Assignment, Brothers in the Saddle, The Rustlers.*
1950: *Winchester '73, It's a Small World, Kiss Tomorrow Goodbye, The Admiral Was a Lady, Armored Car Robbery, The Great Plane Robbery, Counterspy Meets Scotland Yard.*
1951: *The Steel Helmet, Fighting Coast Guard, M, Sword of Monte Cristo, Two-Dollar Bettor, Only the Valiant, Joe Palooka in Triple Cross.*
1952: *Army Bound, Bal Tabarin, Three for Bedroom C, Lady in the Iron Mask, The Will Rogers Story.*
1953: *White Lightning, Donovan's Brain, Sea of Lost Ships, The Charge at Feather River, The Beast from 20,000 Fathoms.*
1954: *The Caine Mutiny.*
1955: *The Far Country.*
1956: *The Cruel Tower, The Wild World of Batwoman* (TV series).
1957: *Gun Duel in Durango, The Crooked Circle, Under Fire.*
1958: *Sierra Baron, Spy in the Sky.*
1959: *Arson for Hire.*
1960: *Three Came to Kill.*
1961: *Blue Hawaii.*
1962: *A Girl Named Tamiko.*
1963: *Of Love and Desire, A Bullet for Billy the Kid.*
1964: *Roustabout.*
1969: *Cycle Savages.*
1975: *The Giant Spider Invasion.*
1981: *Frankenstein's Island.*
1984: *Mugsy's Girls.*
1987: *The Wizard of Speed and Time, Code Vengeance.*

Television Series

1959–1961: *The Life and Legend of Wyatt Earp* as Sheriff Johnny Behan.
1961–1962: *Everglades.*

Sources

Inman, David. *The TV Encyclopedia.* New York: Perigee, 1991.
Quinlan, David. *Illustrated Directory of Film Stars Third Edition.* London: Batsford, 1991.
Variety. January 1992.

JOHN BROMFIELD

John Bromfield is best known for his starring role as Frank Morgan in the television series *Sheriff of Cochise* and *U.S. Marshal.* He is one actor who has successfully juggled an acting career and hobbies. He has always been interested in sports, especially fishing. He is also an inveterate traveler who has roamed the world extensively and made documentaries about his adventures. "My wife and I love people, characters—the more different they are the more we enjoy them. It would be a sad world, wouldn't it, if we were all alike? So we are happy for the differences in people and customs," he says.

John Bromfield was born Farron Bromfield in South Bend, Indiana, on June 11, 1922. The famous author Louis Bromfield was his cousin. He came with his family to Venice, California, when he was five years of age and grew up in a home on the beach. As a youth he lived an exciting and pleasant life swimming, surfing and learning to fish. Although he attended Westminster grammar school in Venice, each day he would rise early enough to allow for a little fishing before his walk to school. He made friends with an old fisherman at the beach who took him in hand and taught him the correct way to surf fish. Although his parents were unable to join him in his hobby, they encouraged him and taught him to think like an adult.

As a student at Venice High School, he became interested in various sports. He was an All Western Football League end and also boxed for the Venice Athletic Club. After graduation he was approached by a number of different colleges, but chose St. Marys, home of the Galloping Gaels, where he made first string during a winning season. When World War II broke out, he joined the V-7 program at college with a navy career in mind. Later he took a job on a 500-ton tuna clipper and made two trips into Mexican waters, relishing the rough, hard work. After completing college, he joined the navy in San Diego. After his navy service ended, he advanced his education with the intention of becoming a coach.

He became a commercial fisherman and was actually discovered while mending fish nets on the Santa Monica pier in California. Two producers approached him and asked him if he would like to make a fishing film. He thought they were playing a practical joke. When he showed his father their cards, he encouraged his son to make an appointment with them. He was soon offered a job in a film to be shot on board a whaling boat working the Bering Straits and Alaska. The boat was about 24 feet long, made of walrus hides and was crewed by eight paddlers.

They tried for whales in the Bering Straits, but the weather was too bad, so they cruised into Captain's Bay, seeking calmer waters. In the bay they saw 15 or 20 humpback and finback whales feeding. "For three weeks we went out every day in the small boat, called an oogra, with me in the bow with the harpoon and the eight men paddling," he recalls. "We couldn't get anywhere near a whale. We'd see one up to spout just 30 yards or so away and we'd figure the next time he came up we'd be right on top of him. But he'd always surface way off to port or starboard.

"But one day, all of a sudden I looked straight down into the water over the bow of the oogra. Something that looked like a submarine was coming up right under us. He came up to blow, almost touching the boat and you'd never believe the smell from his spout. The worst bad breath I've ever smelled. The paddlers drove the boat right at him, and the bow hit him in the angle where his left flipper joined his body, and there I was, with this heaving mountain towering over me, and I just slammed the harpoon into him."

The whale took off, towing the boat sometimes at speeds which he estimated as high as 10 or 12 knots. Eight-and-a-half hours later the "Nantucket sleigh ride" ended when the monster gradually slowed its pace, then died. Bromfield continued, "The first thing the Eskimos did was slit his belly open hoping to find a ball of ambergris, the substance used for making perfume which is very valuable, but there wasn't any. By agreement with government agencies which had given them permits to hunt the whales, the film company gave the carcass to the village people for food. The whale was a humpback, measuring 68 feet and weighing an estimated 68 tons."

A few days later, the oogra was sent against an even larger mammal, a finback which measured 74 feet. Again Bromfield struck with his harpoon and this time the whale, although bigger than the first, died in just four hours. He recalls, "I've harpooned broadbill swordfish off California, but then you're up in a bowsprit pulpit ten feet or so above the water and looking down at a fish that weighs a couple of hundred pounds. With a whale, you're down at water level, looking up at a creature that weighs 140,000 pounds. It's terrifying. When it's happening, you have to move so fast you don't think. Afterwards you say to yourself, 'I can't believe this thing.'"

The film was named *Harpoon* and was given its world premiere in New Bedford in 1948. For days the newspapers there were full of stories, interviews and photographs of the star. On his return to California, he was presented with a lifetime membership in the Whaling Society by the New Bedford Port Society of Massachusetts. This publicity attracted the attention of a New York agency and soon he was back in California as a member of the David Selznick drama class. At the end of the year he was cast in *The Furies* (1950). Subsequently he went on to appear in many other films. One of his favorites was *Easy To Love* (1953) with Esther Williams. "It was the first water skiing movie," he recalls. "I had a ball."

In the midst of his busy film career, he was approached by TV's Desilu Productions, a company formed by Desi Arnaz and Lucille Ball. He says, "In 1956 my agent called and said Desi wanted to see me." The meeting was compelling. "You're going to be in a Western," he recalls Arnaz saying, "but you're not going to be in the old days. You're going to be in a station wagon, going all around Arizona solving crimes." The resulting series, *Sheriff of Cochise* (1957–1958), ran to 78 black and white episodes and became a top-rated series. Stan Jones costarred as Deputy Olson. Bromfield adds, "Desi and I were good friends; he was a very talented man. Luci was a jewel and everyone knows how talented she was."

He immediately followed this up with another highly successful series, *U.S. Marshal* (1959–1960). Asked the reason for the format change, he explains, "Anheiser-Busch [Budweiser Beer] was my sponsor and they decided they would like to keep the show and put us into 86 top markets, but change the area where it took place, so Desi Arnaz came up with the idea of killing off the present-day marshal and having me take his place. That was done in a pilot show, where I, the sheriff, happened to be visiting my friend the marshal [Sidney Blackmer] in Tucson when he was killed. I was sworn in upon his dying request that I become the marshal. That's how the show segued from one into the other." Marshal Frank Morgan was given the run of the whole state of Arizona instead of jurisdiction over Cochise County alone. Both series were filmed in Cochise County, Arizona, along the Mexican border. *U.S. Marshal* also had 78 episodes filmed in black and white. James Griffith costarred as Deputy Tom Ferguson. Both series were seen and remain popular in many countries of the world, as well as being number one on many syndicated stations in America. Many young actors who appeared in these series later became well-known stars. Charles Bronson, for example, played the part of an Indian deputy in six of the shows.

In 1959 Bromfield combined his television career with sports and went into "Outdoor Sports Shows." In 1961 he made a film in Japan, a color feature based on the exploits of *Sheriff of Cochise*. Following a period of appearances on radio and television and traveling around the country on personal appearance tours, in 1962 he retired and made up his mind to enjoy his favorite sports. He became a resident of Orange County, California. In 1970 Fenton McHugh of CBS signed him for a one-hour special called *Fisherman's World*. It was shot in the Bahamas. He narrated and played host to Sam Snead, Gary Moore, baseball star Boog Powell, David Wayne and *Playboy* magazine writer Gene Shepard. In 1980 he made a film for British Air shot on safari in Kenya. In 1982 he shot another fishing film on Lake Powell, Utah, for Frank and Dona Delaney.

John Bromfield in *Sheriff of Cochise*.

John Bromfield has been married four times. He has no children. His first marriage was to Grace Landis when he was in college. They were both very young and it was not meant to be. His second and most highly publicized marriage was to sultry French actress Corinne Calvert. It was certainly a union between two of the screen's most physically attractive stars. They married in Boulder City, Nevada, in 1948. She received a divorce in Los Angeles on March 16, 1954. Their careers were as new as they were and made marriage difficult. His third wife, Lari Thomas, was a dancer, a true gypsy who loved dancing more than she loved him and so that did not work. (The two appeared together in *Curucu, Beast of the* Amazon [1956].) On May 5, 1965, he married singer-dancer Mary Ellen Tillotson. Of this marriage he says, "She managed to find it easy to work and love me at the same time. Our likes and dislikes are for the most part the same. Our love today is as fresh and young as it was 30 years ago. I finally did something right!"

John and Mary Bromfield bought a large motor home and travel extensively throughout the U.S.A. They also maintain a small farm in Northern California. In 1992 they bought a home in Lake Havasu City, Arizona, which is coincidentally the home of London Bridge. From their home they have a beautiful view of the surrounding mountains and look down on the city and the lake. They bought a boat and do a lot of fishing. Bisbee, Arizona, was where *Sheriff of Cochise* was centered, and the *U.S. Marshal* series was located in Tucson, so John Bromfield feels as if he has come home.

John Bromfield Filmography

1948: *Harpoon, Sorry Wrong Number.*
1949: *Rope of Sand.*
1950: *The Furies, Paid in Full.*
1951: *The Cimarron Kid.*
1952: *Flat Top, Hold That Line.*
1953: *Easy to Love.*
1954: *The Black Dakotas, Ring of Fear.*
1955: *The Big Bluff, Revenge of the Creature.*
1956: *Crime Against Joe; Curucu, Beast of the Amazon; Frontier Gambler, Hot Cars, Man-fish, Quincannon Frontier Scout, Three Bad Sisters.*

Television Series

1957–1958: *Sheriff of Cochise* as Sheriff Frank Morgan.
1959–1960: *U.S. Marshal* as Marshal Frank Morgan.

Sources

Correspondence between Bromfield and the author.

RAND BROOKS

Rand Brooks was born Arlington Rand Brooks, Jr., in St. Louis, Missouri, on September 21, 1918. His father was a prosperous jeweler and his mother an actress and singer. The family lived comfortably and traveled until they relocated to California, where his mother sought a career as an actress in movies. He acted in plays while attending Beverly Hills High School, did radio and little theater work, but was not actively seeking a career as an actor. He also became a good rider, competing in amateur rodeos and touring with Clyde Beatty's Circus as a trick rider for about a year. This experience stood him in good stead later when he appeared in Westerns. All of this changed when the family lost their money in the Depression.

He started out working in the Los Angeles Brokerage House and was preparing for a career as a broker, but switched direction when his salary was cut during a recession. By the age of 21 he had several dependents, so he decided the only way he could earn sufficient money for their needs was in motion pictures. He went searching for a job and landed a test at MGM during which he went to pieces. Nevertheless he persevered, offering to rehearse for free opposite starlets. This led to another test at MGM for *Love Finds Andy Hardy* in 1938. On the strength of this MGM gave him a scene.

Director Mervyn LeRoy liked his bit and insisted that the studio hire him for the juvenile lead in *Dramatic School* (1938). MGM then signed him to a contract as a featured player. They loaned him to David O. Selznick to play the small but important role of Charles Hamilton in the classic film *Gone with the Wind* (1939), which is still the part for which he is best remembered. It was, however, two others, *Balalaika* and *The Son of Monte Cristo,* which rank as his favorites of his own movies.

Sometimes he landed quite important roles in major films which were drastically

Clockwise from top left: James L. Brown, Rand Brooks, Joe Sawyer, and Lee Aaker in *The Adventures of Rin Tin Tin.*

edited by the time the movies were released. Twice he was cast in movies to be directed by Cecil B. DeMille, but on both occasions conflicting schedules meant that he could not appear and the roles were recast. He stayed under contract to MGM, who loaned him out to other studios on several occasions. When World War II broke out, the studio dropped him and he was conscripted into the Air Corps.

When he had been in the Air Corps for about a year, he contracted meningitis of the spine and was grounded. The armed forces refused to discharge him on medical grounds and instead he was kept under observation. He returned home from overseas and was discharged a fortnight after VJ Day. Although he received a hero's welcome, he was without a job for months. One day while delivering an electrical appliance to a studio, he was spotted by a producer who remembered him from his rodeo days. The producer told him that William Boyd was starting up as an independent producer of the *Hopalong Cassidy* series and was looking for a young lead who could ride. Brooks fit the bill, landed the part of Lucky Jenkins and appeared in the last dozen features in which Boyd played the character until 1948. Brooks has no fond memories of either the character he played or the films, but did like working with Andy Clyde.

From the early 1950s onwards he became very active in television. He landed the featured role of Corporal Boone in the series *The Adventures of Rin Tin Tin* for six years. This was one of the most popular boy-and-canine Western programs. The shooting was arduous, but Brooks was a professional and the production was made easier by the camaraderie amongst the cast, who remained friends after the show was taken off the air.

He had ambitions to be a director and slowly built up a portfolio via little theater work and being a dialogue director on television. This however proved to be his undoing because he finally landed the chance to produce and direct a feature called *Bearheart* in 1966. It was an animal feature with proven commercial appeal. A substantial part of his own money was invested in it, but one of the backers absconded with the funds. The movie was never released theatrically, left him very short of cash and added to his growing disenchantment with the movie industry.

He decided to retire temporarily and instead started a private paramedic and ambulance provider business in Glendale in 1966. This grew slowly but steadily until by the 1980s the company was the largest provider of paramedics in Los Angeles County. This took over completely from his acting and he never returned to his former profession.

Rand Brooks was married and divorced from Lois Laurel, the daughter of comedian Stan Laurel, and has two children and three grandchildren. Currently married to Hermine Anne Brooks, at last report he was residing in Glendale, California.

Rand Brooks Filmography

1938: *Love Finds Andy Hardy, Dramatic School.*
1939: *Balalaika, Babes in Arms, The Old Maid, Gone with the Wind.*
1940: *And One Was Beautiful, Laddie, Florian, The Girl from Avenue A, The Son of Monte Cristo.*
1941: *Life with Henry, Cheers for Miss Bishop, Double Date, Lady Scarface, Niagara Falls.*
1942: *Cowboy Serenade, Sombrero Kid, Valley of Hunted Men, The Affairs of Jimmy Valentine.*
1943: *High Explosive.*
1944: *Lady in the Dark.*
1946: *The Devil's Playground, Fools Gold, Unexpected Guest.*
1947: *Dangerous Venture, Hoppy's Holiday, The Marauders, Kilroy Was Here.*
1948: *Silent Conflict, The Dead Don't Dream, Strange Gamble, Sinister Journey, False Paradise, Sundown in Santa Fe, Joan of Arc, Ladies of the Chorus.*
1949: *The Wyoming Bandit, Black Midnight.*
1950: *Riding High, The Vanishing Westerner.*
1951: *The Heart of the Rockies, The Cimarron Kid, Yukon Manhunt.*
1952: *Waco, The Maverick, Montana Incident, Man from the Black Hills, The Gunman, The Steel Fist.*
1953: *The Charge at Feather River.*
1955: *To Hell and Back.*
1958: *The Last Hurrah.*
1960: *Comanche Station.*
1962: *Stagecoach to Dancer's Rock.*
1965: *Requiem for a Gunfighter.*
1966: *Bearheart.*
1973: *Double Indemnity* (TV).
1974: *The Sex Symbol* (TV)

Television Series

1954–1959: *The Adventures of Rin Tin Tin* as Corporal Boone.

Sources

Eleventh Annual Golden Boot Awards Program. August 1993.

Goldrup, Tom, and Jim Goldrup. *Feature Players The Stories Behind The Faces Volume I.* Published privately, 1986.

Lamparski, Richard. *Whatever Became Of? Eighth Series.* New York: Crown, 1982.

SALLIE BROPHY

Born in Phoenix, Arizona, on December 14, this actress first came to prominence as the heroine Julie Fielding of the ill-fated soap *Follow Your Heart,* which only lasted a few months on television but enjoyed a healthy six-year run on radio. She made little impact in films, but had one regular role in the prime-time television series *Buckskin*, a shortlived Western. She played Annie O'Connell, who lived in the town of Buckskin, Montana, in the 1880s with her ten-year-old son Jody (Tommy Nolan). She was a widow who ran the local boarding house which became a hive of social life within the community.

She had been posted as one of the lost players of the screen until an accidental encounter with former costar Michael Lipton on a street in New York during the early 1990s. When he introduced himself to her again, she revealed that she had been married and divorced from a show business executive and had been teaching drama in New York for several years under her real name of Sallie Brophy.

Sallie Brophy Filmography

1956: *Storm Center.*
1957: *The Green Eyed Blonde.*

Television Series

1953–1954: *Follow Your Heart* as Julie Fielding.
1958–1959: *Buckskin* as Mrs. Annie O'Connell.

Sources

Brooks, Tim. *The Complete Directory to Prime Time TV Stars 1946–Present.* New York: Ballantine Books, 1987.

Interview with Michael Lipton, March 1995.

JAMES L. BROWN

From debutante's delight to manufacturer of bodybuilding equipment, James L. Brown was both. Nevertheless, he is still best remembered by television Western fans as Lt. Rip Masters in the long-running juvenile Western series *The Adventures of Rin Tin Tin* (1954–1959). Brown had strong views about the series in which he appeared. He said, "Our stories simply taught that right was right and wrong was wrong. You don't get those kind of values on television anymore." Of his offscreen personality, Tommy Farrell (who played Corporal Carson) recalled, "He was Lt. Masters. Everything Lt. Masters stood for, Jim Brown stood for. I never heard anything bad said about him. He was the ultimate professional ...

James L. Brown with young fans and canine companion in *The Adventures of Rin Tin Tin.*

he knew his dialogue ... he was the first one on the set and the last to leave. Oh, how he loved to tell stories and laugh. One hell of a good guy."

Jim Brown fervently believed that his plebeian name hampered the progress of his career. His agent, Henry Willson, begged Paramount to rechristen him when Jim Brown signed with them, but to no avail. Ironically Willson (who had something of a fetish for dubbing pretty boy actors with memorable tags such as Rock Hudson) went in the reverse direction by renaming one of his clients John Smith! After *The Adventures of Rin Tin Tin* ended, Jim Brown wanted to change his name to Rip Masters, but the producer refused to hear of it. Subsequently Brown was billed as James L. Brown to avoid confusion with soul singer James Brown and black actor Jim Brown.

James Lefty Brown was born on March 22, 1920, in Desdemona, Texas, a tent town which mushroomed during the oil boom. He came from a poor background and his family moved to Waco, Texas, when he was about a year old. He was the second of four children, one of whom died in infancy. There were three boys and an older sister. After his mother and father were divorced, his mother became a beautician. Brown was educated at the Schriner Military School in Kearville and for two years at Baylor University. He was a championship tennis player who originally went to California to compete in the Pacific Southwest Tournament. He earned money by playing exhibition matches along the way and was staked to some degree by his mother. He roomed at the home of a tennis playing friend. When a photograph of him taken at the tournament with a debutante came to the attention of the notorious agent Henry Willson, Brown chose Willson to represent him. 20th Century–Fox and Columbia tested him and he came very close to landing the role of Billy the Kid in *The Outlaw* (the role subsequently went to Jack Buetel). The lure of playing varsity tennis at Baylor University was greater, so he returned to Texas.

When Brown gate-crashed Hollywood again the following year, there was little doing so he accepted a temporary job as a vocalist for a dance band at $25 a week. Meanwhile Willson wangled him a test at Paramount and he signed a contract the following day. He was groomed as a replacement for Sterling Hayden. Although *Young and Willing* (1943) was shot first, *Air Force* (1943), a loan-out to Warner Bros., really put him over with the fans. The movie was directed by Howard Hawks, Brown's favorite director.

Our Hearts Were Young and Gay (1944) was shot back-to-back with its sequel, *Our Hearts Were Growing Up*, which stayed on the shelf for a couple of years. Simultaneously he worked on *Going My Way* (1944),a film of which he was especially proud. He would work half a day on each film. He admired director Leo McCarey and his impromptu approach, which meant distributing fresh pages of the script on the set. Although initially he was happy to be under contract to a major studio, subsequently he found himself unhappy with their cavalier treatment of him. He proved to be a very personable young actor, but his youth worked against him. He was tested for a lead in *So Proudly We Hail* (1943), but Claudette Colbert refused him as her leading man because he looked so young. He was replaced by Sonny Tufts. He was announced to essay a lead in a 1946 remake of *The Virginian*, but was again replaced by Tufts. He inked a simultaneous pact with Warner Bros. for one feature a year, but the role he coveted in *Destination Tokyo* (1943) was played by John Garfield. Brown did however make several movies at the Burbank studio, of which the best remembered is *Objective Burma* (1945), which gave the erroneous impression that Errol Flynn won the country singlehanded. Brown worked on this movie for 17 weeks in the role of Sgt. Treacy. MGM requested his services for *Thirty Seconds Over Tokyo* (1944), but Paramount refused to loan him.

He spent five frustrating years at Paramount during which he and his agent repeatedly tried to extricate him from his contract to take advantage of the more lucrative offers outside. Paramount started turning him down for loanouts, but neither did they use him. He went for a year without making a film. One day in Bing Crosby's dressing room, he expressed his unhappiness to the veteran entertainer. The following day Paramount called his agent and told him they were giving Brown his release. Unfortunately his freedom coincided with the postwar slump in motion picture production so that he, along with several other semi-names, found the pickings lean.

The first Western he shot was *The Fabulous Texan* (1947), filmed on location in Sedona, Arizona. He bluffed his way into the part by claiming that he could ride, but the reality was that he had never ridden in his life. One of the location wranglers helped him to the degree that by the time the shooting ended, he had become quite a proficient rider.

He subsequently came to regard the release from his Paramount contract as a mistake. This view was reinforced by his experience over *High Noon* (1952). He and Lloyd Bridges were cast as Gary Cooper's deputies. The film originally lasted over two hours and was previewed disastrously. The movie was drastically reedited and his entire role ended up on the cutting room floor. The movie reemerged at a trim 85 minutes with a catchy Tex Ritter theme, became a classic and won a clutch of Oscars. A single, solitary reference to Brown's role remains where one of the characters notes that in the days when Will Kane (Gary Cooper) arrested Frank Miller, he had half a dozen deputies. Now he has only two! The second deputy is not referred to again, nor does he appear in the film.

He enjoyed his greatest success on television when he played Lt. Rip Masters in *The Adventures of Rin Tin Tin* (1954–1959). He was summoned for an audition for the series. The producers had him read with Lee Aaker, who had already been cast as Rusty, to determine how well they performed together. He was so impressive that he was hired on the spot. He appeared in all 164 episodes, and during that time he had only one-and-a-half days' vacation. The first year they worked six days a week. They shot two shows a week, averaging two-and-half days a show. He had to learn to ride with an English saddle, which he had never done before. The horse he rode for the first 16 episodes was so frisky it had to be replaced. His favorite episode was "The Legend of the White Buffalo," which was shot at the Santa Ana Buffalo Ranch and was the only episode which took four days to film.

Of this period he once said, "I loved all of it and am still proud of the good stuff we had in these shows for kids, but it was exhausting." Sometimes he did not receive scripts until the night before. He was a fast study who was sometimes learning dialogue for as many as four episodes at a time. Earl Bellamy, who directed about 20 episodes, remembers, "Jim was a pro, he was there on time, always knew his lines and became a good horseman. He loved all the people on the set. He liked to have fun and clowned around; nevertheless he got the work done on time." The series was so popular Brown was brought back 20 years later to film new introductions in Utah to the syndicated series. The central figure of the series was the great grandson of the original Rin Tin Tin (1916–1932), a very popular star of the late silents and early talkies. When the programs were repackaged in sepia in 1976, Brown appeared with Rin Tin Tin VII. Along with several of his contemporaries, he failed to make the economic killing he should have made from the show. This was because he failed to appreciate the value of the merchandising together with residuals from the series.

After the series ended, the Edward Small company contacted his agent and he shot six movies for them in rapid succession. They were low budgeters with shooting schedules of five days apiece. He shot a busted pilot for a television series called *The Venturers* (1961) in which he played the commander of a three-man submarine. During the time *The Venturers* had potentially been a goer as a series, Brown was headhunted by five companies who all wanted him as a series lead. When the pilot was not picked up and the option on his services for *The Venturers* expired, he was again available for work, but the offers dried up. He later appeared in seven episodes of *Route 66*.

He and a partner became successful manufacturers of bodybuilding equipment called "Tune-A-Matic Products." Brown handled the public relations while his partner produced the equipment at a factory in St. Petersburg, Florida. In 1969 they sold their business to Faberge/ Brut for a large sum of money. He moved to St. Petersburg, Florida, for two years. Brut/Faberge hired him as Vice-President in charge of Customer Relations, a post in which he served until 1973. Brut/Faberge decided they wished to enter the business of feature film production and shot *Whiffs* (1975), which starred Elliott Gould and Jennifer O'Neill. The first character actor they signed was Brown. He later enjoyed renewed acting success on television when he played Detective Sgt. Harry McSween, a crooked cop on J.R. Ewing's payroll in *Dallas*. He notched up 50 episodes of the series.

Brown died in Hollywood on April 11, 1992, at age 72, after a short bout with lung cancer. There was a memorial gathering on the grass of the backyard of his home in Woodland Hills, attended by many of his Hollywood friends including Will Hutchins and Efrem Zimbalist, Jr. Rand Brooks, who played Corporal Boone in the series, probably summed up everyone's feelings when he said, "I don't think he had any enemies. He was a wonderful guy with a lot of talent. We did a lot of live shows together—rodeos, Madison Square Gardens, Boston Gardens—traveled a lot. Sweet man. I'll miss him."

James Brown married Verna Knopf, a model and actress under contract to Howard Hughes, in 1942. With her he had three daughters (Beverly, Barbara and Carol) before they divorced in 1947. He was also a grandfather. In 1947 he married a nonprofessional with whom he had no offspring before their divorce in 1971. In 1973 he married again. He had only married his final wife Betty in January 1992, after he was widowed in the late 1980s.

James L. Brown Filmography

1942: *The Forest Rangers, Wake Island.*
1943: *Corvette K-225, The Good Fellows, Air Force, Young and Willing.*
1944: *Going My Way, Our Hearts Were Young and Gay.*
1945: *Duffy's Tavern, Objective Burma!*
1946: *Our Hearts Were Growing Up, The Big Fix.*
1947: *The Fabulous Texan.*
1948: *The Gallant Legion*
1949: *Sands of Iwo Jima, Yes Sir That's My Baby, The Younger Brothers, Brimstone, Anna Lucasta.*
1950: *Montana, The Fireball, Chain Lightning.*
1951: *Missing Women, The Groom Wore Spurs, The Sea Hornet, The Wild Blue Yonder, Father Takes the Air, Starlift.*
1952: *Pride of St. Louis, Springfield Rifle, Man Behind the Gun.*
1953: *Thunder Over the Plains, The Charge at Feather River, Flight Nurse, The Woman They Almost Lynched, Crazylegs, Sea of Lost Ships.*
1954: *A Star Is Born.*
1959: *Inside the Mafia.*
1960: *The Police Dog Story.*
1961: *Five Guns to Tombstone, Gun Fight, Wings of Chance, When the Clock Strikes, 20,000 Eyes.*
1962: *Gunstreet.*
1963: *The Ceremony, Irma La Douce.*
1964: *Rio Conchos.*
1965: *Black Spurs, Town Tamer, Ski Party.*
1968: *Targets.*
1971: *Powderkeg* (TV).
1975: *Whiffs.*
1976: *Adios Amigos, Mean Johnny Barrows.*
1979: *The Rebels* (TV).
1981: *Miracle on Ice* (TV).
1985: *Lady Blue* (TV).

Television Series

1954–1959: *The Adventures of Rin Tin Tin* as Lt. Rip Masters.
1984–1988: *Dallas* as Sergeant Harry McSween.

Sources

Goldrup, Tom, and Jim Goldrup. *Feature Players—The Stories Behind The Faces Volume #2.* Published privately, 1992.
Jarvis, Everett G. *Final Curtain: Deaths of Noted Movie and TV Personalities.* New York: Citadel, 1995.
Lamparski, Richard. *Whatever Became Of? Eleventh Series.* New York: Crown, 1989.
Magers, Boyd. "Empty Saddles." *The Big Reel* magazine, May 1992.
Picture Show Annual. London: Amalgamated Press, 1947.

PETER BROWN

Peter Brown was born Pierre de Lappe in New York City on October 5, 1935. His father died when he was four years old. His mother was a radio and stage actress named Mina Reaume. He appeared on radio in children's programs for two years from the age of seven. His mother subsequently remarried a businessman named Albert Brown, and the family relocated to California. Brown spent a considerable amount of his youth on a California ranch where he developed his riding and rodeo skills.

His education, however, was somewhat fragmented and when he graduated from North Central High School in 1952, he estimated that he had attended 18 different schools. His first real adult acting experience came when he entered the army. While he served as a member of the Second Infantry Division from 1954 to 1956 in Alaska, boredom dictated that he organize a drama group. Subsequently he went on to appear in 23 shows. So enjoyable was the experience that when he was discharged, he enrolled as a theater arts major at the University of Southern California. He also studied drama with Jeff Corey. While trying to break into professional acting, he held a job as a filling station attendant.

His first professional role was at the Horseshoe Theater in *Desire Under the Elms,* followed by *Teach Me How to Cry* at the Gallery Theater. Appearing in the latter, he was spotted by producer Albert McCleery who hired him for four *NBC Matinee Theater* productions. He was tested and hired by Warner Bros. for his first feature, *Darby's Rangers* (1958). He appeared in several of that studio's television Westerns. Producer Jules Schermer was familiar with his work and particularly liked his performance in the film *Onionhead* (1958). Schermer, who was producing *Lawman,* was given his pick of young contract players so he cast Brown as Johnny McKay, deputy to Dan Troop (John Russell), in that Western series. Brown diligently practiced riding and honed his fast draw and equestrian skills. Throughout the duration of the series, he rode his own mount Houdini.

Lawman was the most straightforward of all the Warners Western series, and Brown drew large amounts of fan mail from the start. He won the Most Outstanding Newcomer Award from the Theater Owners Of America, the prize being presented to him by John Wayne. The series premiered on the ABC network on October 5, 1958, and lasted until October 1962. It was shot entirely on the back lot. When it went off the air Brown appeared in two Walt Disney films, *Summer Magic* (1963) and *A Tiger Walks* (1964). He was under contract to Universal from 1965 to 1967. Guesting on multiples of *The Virginian* television series, he went on to enjoy his greatest success when he was cast as Ranger Chad Cooper in the Western series *Laredo* (1965–1967) in which he costarred with three other very tough actors: William Smith, Neville Brand and Philip Carey.

When Westerns declined on the small and big screens, he turned his creative energies toward soaps and has had regular roles on six daytime soap operas. He has also continued to be active on prime time television as a guest-star on numerous series up to the 1990s (including *Baywatch* and *One West Waikiki).* Offscreen he has maintained his riding skills, appearing at rodeos and state fairs. He has organized charity rodeos and produced a penning video, a topic on which he is an acknowledged expert. Most of his hobbies such as golf and tennis tend to be of the outdoor variety. After studying bullfighting with the legendary matador Jaime Bravo, he could sometimes be seen with the cape at Tijuana.

He has been married five times. His best known wife was his first, actress Diane Jergens, whom he married on September 6, 1958, but divorced less than three years later. He has two sons, Matthew and Joshua. Since 1986 he has been wed to his fifth wife Mary, whom he met at a Michael Landon Tennis Tournament in 1984. He divides his time between homes in Santa Fe, New Mexico and Hermosa Beach, California.

Peter Brown Filmography

1958: *Darby's Rangers, Majorie Morningstar, Onionhead.*
1962: *Merrill's Marauders.*
1963: *Summer Magic.*
1964: *A Tiger Walks, Ride the Wild Surf, Kitten with a Whip.*
1968: *Three Guns for Texas* (TV).
1969: *Backtrack* (TV).
1970: *Hunters Are for Killing* (TV).
1971: *Chrome and Hot Leather.*
1972: *Piranha Piranha.*
1974: *Rape Squad (*a.k.a. *Act of Vengeance), Eagles Attack at Dawn, Foxy Brown, Memory of Us.*
1975: *Sunburst.*
1976: *The Gentle Savage.*
1979: *Salvage.*
1980: *The Girl, The Gold Watch and Everything* (TV), *The Top of the Hill* (TV),

1982: *The Concrete Jungle.*
1983: *Teenage Tease.*
1985: *The Aurora Encounter.*
1989: *Demonstone (*a.k.a. *Heartstone).*
1995: *Fists of Iron.*
1996: *Asylum.*

Television Series

1958–1962: *Lawman* as Deputy Johnny McKay.
1965–1967: *Laredo* as Ranger Chad Cooper.
1972–1979: *Days of Our Lives* as Greg Peters.
1981–1982: *The Young and the Restless* as Robert Lawrence.
1983–1984: *Loving* as Roger Forbes.
1984–1986: *General Hospital.*
1986–1987: *One Life to Live* as Charles Sanders.
1990–1992: *The Bold and the Beautiful* as Blake Hayes.

Sources

Correspondence between Brown and the author.
Ferguson, Ken. *Western Stars of Television and Film.* London: Purnell, 1967.
Rout, Nancy E., Ellen Buckley and Barney M. Rout. *The Soap Opera Book: Who's Who in Daytime Drama.* West Nyack, NY: Todd Publications, 1992.
Woolley, Lynn, Robert W. Malsbary and Robert G. Strange. *Warner Bros. Television.* Jefferson, NC: McFarland, 1985.

TOM BROWN

Tom Brown was born Thomas Edward Brown in New York on January 6, 1913, the son of vaudevillian Harry Brown and Marie Francis, a musical comedy actress. His father introduced him to the stage as part of his act when he was carried on at the age of 18 months. From the age of five he was appearing as an extra in silent movies. His proper motion picture debut came in *The Hoosier Schoolmaster* (1924). He was educated at the Professional Children's School and appeared frequently in ads as the Arrow Collar Boy, the Buick Boy and Buster Brown. By the age of 17 when he moved to Hollywood, he had appeared in eight Broadway shows and in more than 3,000 radio episodes.

When he came to Hollywood in December 1931, he was given a test by Universal where he landed a contract for three years. He appeared in numerous films during the 1930s, usually as a kid brother, athlete, boxer or cadet. By coincidence he played a character called Tom Brown in the film *Tom Brown of Culver* (1932). His personal favorite of his films was *Navy Blue and Gold* (1937). During World War II he was a paratrooper and served during the Korean conflict, rising to the rank of lieutenant colonel in the infantry. Although he continued his career after World War II, his films were much fewer and less prestigious. Former

Portrait of Tom Brown, who appeared in *Gunsmoke.*

actress turned producer Helen Mack got him started again by giving him parts in numerous radio dramas.

In 1952 he toured in a play called *Strike a Match*. Then he organized hunting tours in the Pacific Northwest. He became an authority on the metal magnetite and developed a mine and built a hotel complex at Tahoe Donner, California. He credited actor Don Barry and comedian Lou Costello with coming to his professional rescue by opening up a new career for him as a character actor in television. He played rancher Ed O'Connor in *Gunsmoke*; Mr. Lucky's policeman friend on *Mr. Lucky*; crusty Al Weeks on the daytime soap opera *General Hospital*; and Nathan Curtis on another soap opera, *Days of Our Lives*. His hobbies were sailing and helping to run the "Lady Sierra Mine," a mine owned cooperatively by the cast and crew of *General Hospital*. He resided in a modest Hollywood apartment.

Tom Brown died in Woodland Hills, California, on June 3, 1990, of cancer; he was 77 years old. As a freelance in Hollywood during the 1930s, his annual income was estimated to be $125,000, but much of this went in alimony and child support. Divorced three times, he was survived by his two sons, a daughter and five grandchildren.

Tom Brown Filmography

1924: *The Hoosier Schoolmaster.*
1925: *Wrongdoers, Children of the Whirlwind.*
1926: *That Old Gang of Mine.*
1929: *A Lady Lies.*
1930: *Queen High.*
1932: *Fast Companions (*a.k.a. *The Information Kid), Tom Brown of Culver, Hell's Highway, The Famous Ferguson Case.*
1933: *Laughter in Hell, Destination Unknown, Central Airport, Three Cornered Moon, Crossfire.*
1934: *Two Alone, Anne of Green Gables, This Side of Heaven, Judge Priest, Bachelor of Arts, The Witching Hour, Hat Coat and Glove.*
1935: *Mary Jane's Pa, Freckles, Sweepstakes Annie, Black Sheep, Annapolis Farewell, Gentle Julia, And Sudden Death, I'd Give My Life, Rose Bowl.*
1936: *The Man Who Cried Wolf, Her Husband Lies, Jim Harvey Detective.*
1937: *Maytime, That Man's Here Again, Navy Blue and Gold.*
1938: *Swing That Cheer, In Old Chicago, The Duke of West Point, Merrily We Live, Goodbye Broadway, The Storm.*
1939: *Big Town Czar, These Glamour Girls, Sergeant Madden, Ex-Champ.*
1940: *Sandy Is a Lady, Ma He's Making Eyes at Me, Oh Johnny How You Can Love, Margie.*
1941: *Three Sons o' Guns, Niagara Falls, Hello Sucker!*
1942: *Sleepy Time Gal, There's One Born Every Minute, Hello Annapolis, Let's Get Tough, Youth on Parade, The Pay-Off.*
1943: *The Adventures of Smilin' Jack* (serial).
1944: *Once Upon a Time.*
1945: *The House on 92nd Street.*
1947: *Buck Privates Come Home.*
1948: *Slippy McGee.*
1949: *The Duke of Chicago, Ringside.*
1950: *Operation Haylift.*
1954: *Fireman Save My Child!.*
1956: *The Naked Gun, I Killed Wild Bill Hickok.*
1957: *The Quiet Gun.*
1958: *The Notorious Mr. Monks.*
1962: *The Choppers.*
1970: *Cutter's Trail* (TV).

Television Series

1955–1975: *Gunsmoke* as Ed O'Connor.
1959–1960: *Mr. Lucky* as Lt. Rovacs.
1975–1979: *General Hospital* as Al Weeks.
1975–1976: *Days Of Our Lives* as Nathan Curtis.

Sources

Dye, David. *Child and Youth Actors: Filmographies of Their Entire Careers, 1914–1985.* Jefferson, NC: McFarland, 1988.
Lamparksi, Richard. *Whatever Became Of? Fifth Series.* New York: Crown, 1974.
Picture Show Annual. London: Amalgamated Press, 1934.
Raddatz, Leslie. "The Dodge City Gang." *Radio Times* magazine, June 15, 1972.
Willis, John. *Screen World.* London: Hutchinson, 1991.

WALLY BROWN

Wally Brown was born in Malden, Massachusetts, on October 9, 1898, and was educated at the University of Chicago. He spent 15 years in vaudeville acquiring an enormous amount of experience in many different shows before signing a contract with RKO Radio Pictures. The ink was scarcely dry on the paper before he was teamed with Alan Carney (1911–1973) in 1943 in a series of comedy films as a cut-price Abbott and Costello. They also went out on the road together and played live on stage doing some clever routines in 1946. Brown was the fast-talking straight man and their partnership lasted through 11 low-budget films until 1946. Their teaming made minimal impact and they are one duo around whom no cult has grown up. Brown later played in another film, *The Absent-Minded Professor* (1961), in which Alan Carney also appeared.

These years under contract turned out to be his halcyon ones although Brown remained active in feature films for the rest of his life in supporting roles. Acquiring a new partner in Jack Kirkwood, he made some two-reel comedies, but they were even less successful than the Brown-Carney combination. Brown appeared in many television series during the 1950s, but his only semi-regular role was that of Jed Flame in *Cimarron City*. He died in Los Angeles on November 13, 1961, at age 63, of a heart attack.

Wally Brown Filmography

1943: *The Adventures of a Rookie* (AC), *Rookies in Burma* (AC), *Gangway for Tomorrow* (AC), *Mexican Spitfire's Blessed Event* (AC), *Petticoat Larceny, The Seventh Victim, Around The World.*
1944: *Step Lively* (AC), *The Girl Rush* (AC), *Seven Days Ashore* (AC), *The Girl in the Case.*
1945: *Radio Stars on Parade* (AC), *Zombies on Broadway* (AC).
1946: *Vacation in Reno* (AC), *Genius at Work* (AC), *Notorious, From This Day Forward.*
1948: *Family Honeymoon.*
1949: *Come to the Stable.*
1951: *As Young As You Feel.*
1954: *The High and the Mighty.*
1956: *The Wild Dakotas.*
1957: *Untamed Youth, The Joker Is Wild.*
1958: *Wink of an Eye, The Left Handed Gun.*
1959: *Holiday for Lovers, Westbound, The Best of Everything.*
1961: *The Absent-Minded Professor.*

Television Series

1958–1959: *Cimarron City* as Jed Flame.

Sources

Brooks, Tim. *The Complete Directory to Prime Time TV Stars 1946-Present.* New York: Ballantine Books, 1987.
Maltin, Leonard. *Movie Comedy Teams.* New York: Signet, 1970.
Quinlan, David. *Illustrated Directory of Film Comedy Stars.* London: Batsford, 1992.

Note

The films with Alan Carney are denoted AC in the filmography.

ROBERT BRUBAKER

The character actor was born in Robinson, Illinois, on October 9, 1916. He attended Robinson Township High School where he first became interested in drama. He then decided that he would like to be an actor although he did not come from a theatrical family. While in high school he won the State Oratory Contest. At the suggestion of a teacher, he enrolled at Northwestern University in Evanston, Illinois, in 1934.

While there he appeared in a highly successful show called *Good News* in which he earned good reviews. In 1936 he quit college and went to work in the government-sponsored Federal Theater where he stayed until the fall of 1937, when he made the decision to go to Hollywood. Arrived there, he enrolled at Ben Bard's acting school where he wound up a teacher to help pay his tuition fees. Simultaneously he also worked as a radio announcer at radio station KMPC.

He appeared in a talent show at Ben Bard's school and was spotted by a representative from Paramount who saw him as their answer to Warners' John Garfield. Unfortunately, a big executive shakeup at Paramount deprived him of this chance. After graduating from Ben Bard's, Brubaker became involved with the Bliss-Hayden little theater. As a result he went to New York playing a lead in the play *Days of Our Youth* in 1941. It was intended to come to Broadway, but the Japanese bombing of Pearl Harbor put an end to that idea.

In 1942 he returned to Hollywood. He volunteered for the U.S. Army Air Force where he became a pilot and an instructor but never saw action overseas. He was given separation papers in December 1945. Returning to Hollywood, he had to reestablish himself from scratch. He did some radio work before heading for New York where he survived a lean time by working in the men's section of a large department store.

He was recalled by the U.S. Army Air Force because he was on the active reserve list. The purpose was to fly the Berlin Airlift in 1949. He flew 130 missions in six months before being assigned to the Strategic Air Command. He subsequently flew 100 missions over Korea before being discharged in 1954. A producer who owned the Barter Theater in Abingdon, Virginia, asked Brubaker to spend the summer at his theater, where he played (among others) Willy Loman in *Death of a Salesman,* which was his happiest experience.

In 1955 he returned to Hollywood where he had a lucky break and began to work in live television almost immediately. One of the biggest disappointments of his career was when he was signed by MGM Television to play the lead in a shortlived 1961 television series based on *The Asphalt Jungle*, but was ousted by a faction from the network who preferred Jack Warden and paid Brubaker off. Brubaker did however play a stagecoach driver and friend of Matt Dillon on the first five years of *Gunsmoke*. He costarred with John Bromfield on *U.S. Marshal* from 1958 to 1959 as Deputy Blake. From 1974 to 1975 he reappeared on *Gunsmoke* as the bartender at the Long Branch Saloon. Subsequently he left show business and became director of sales training at Forest Lawn Cemetery.

Robert Brubaker Filmography

1946: *Blonde Alibi*.
1955: *The Court-Martial of Billy Mitchell.*
1956: *The Girl He Left Behind, Written on the Wind, Battle Hymn.*
1957: *My Man Godfrey, Man of a Thousand Faces.*
1958: *The Gift of Love.*
1964: *Seven Days in May, Apache Rifles.*
1966: *Seconds.*
1967: *40 Guns to Apache Pass.*
1970: *Barquero, Airport.*
1973: *The Sting.*
1974: *A Cry in the Wilderness* (TV).
1979: *Mrs. R's Daughter* (TV).

Television Series

1955–1960: *Gunsmoke* as Jim Buck.
1958–1959: *US Marshal* as Deputy Blake.
1974–1975: *Gunsmoke* as Floyd.

Sources

Goldrup, Tom, and Jim Goldrup. *Feature Players: The Stories Behind the Faces Volume #1.* Published privately, 1986.

Edgar Buchanan in *Judge Roy Bean*.

EDGAR BUCHANAN

"During the 1870s the wildest spot in the United States was the desolate region west of the Pecos River, an area virtually beyond reach of the authorities. The railroads, then pushing their way west, attracted the most vicious characters in the country. It was said that civilization and law stopped at the east bank of the Pecos. It took one man, a lone storekeeper who was sick of the lawlessness to change all this. His name was Judge Roy Bean." During the

1950s the series *Judge Roy Bean* was probably the most memorable characterization of Edgar Buchanan.

For the greater part of his career, Buchanan was typed as a bewhiskered, lovable rogue. He could be a heavy, but usually everyone would be on his side. This typecasting probably reached its apogee with his role as Uncle Joe on the television series *Petticoat Junction*, a part in which he was recognized all over the world. He had the distinct advantage in that his bucolic face was matched by his growling voice.

William Edgar Buchanan, Jr., was born in Humansville, Missouri, on March 21, 1903, the son of Dr. William E. and Rose Kee Buchanan. His father was a dentist. Buchanan, Jr., was studying to become the same at the University of Oregon, but because his grades were so poor, he had to find a subject which would raise his average. His sister suggested play interpretation. He attended the classes, frequently playing Shakespeare's fools. A little later he attended North Pacific Dental College at Portland, Oregon, and joined three little theaters. There he met his wife-to-be, who was also a dentist. After six years of study, he graduated from dental school in 1929. During the last two years he played professional stock with the Henry Duffy Stock Company.

He practiced dentistry from 1929 to 1937 as head of oral surgery at Eugene (Oregon) Hospital. In 1939 he moved his practice to Altadena, California. In the summertime he practiced his profession, while in the winter he would enroll at the Pasadena Playhouse. He was a character actor right from the start. One of the teachers at the Playhouse told him that his voice meant that he would never make it in the theater. Within two weeks he had landed a movie contract for seven years on account of his distinctive voice.

Initially Warner Bros. made a test of him and used him in a few pictures, but did not pick up his option. They offered him a very low salary, and his agent insisted on ten times that amount. Even at that price Columbia was interested and he signed with them for seven years. His first film for them was *Too Many Husbands* (1940), directed by Wesley Ruggles. They became good friends and Ruggles used him on all of his subsequent films. Surprisingly, Buchanan also got along well with Columbia's temperamental head, Harry Cohn.

The film which really put him over was *Texas* (1941), which starred Glenn Ford and William Holden and was directed by George Marshall. This was Buchanan's favorite film because he played a dentist in it. He also enjoyed shooting *Buffalo Bill* (1944), directed by William Wellman on location close to Kanab, Utah. He had a falling-out with Wellman (the director wanted him for a role in *Gallant Journey* [1946] which Buchanan refused) and he did not work for him again.

At the end of his contract in 1947, he refused to sign with Columbia again because at the time he was earning top dollar in radio and the studio wanted 50 percent of his earnings. This decision he later came to regret, because when television entered the arena a couple of years later, it killed radio stone dead. He freelanced with some success for a while and then went into television in a big way during the 1950s. He did some live television which he found harrowing because of the speed of shooting. He was never a great fan of television because it did not allow adequate time for preparation of a character and it overexposed some actors.

His first regular character in series television was Red Connors, sidekick to *Hopalong Cassidy* in 40 half-hour episodes starring William Boyd (originally shown from 1952 to 1954). *Judge Roy Bean* was set in Langtry, Texas, during the 1870s and told of a self-appointed judge (played by Buchanan) and his efforts to maintain law and order in America's most violent region. It was a whitewashed version of the real judge's career and ran for 39 half-hour episodes. It was a syndicated series originally shown between 1955 and 1956.

He finally hit the jackpot with the CBS rural comedy *Petticoat Junction* (1963–1970), which told of the Shady Rest Hotel run by Kate Bradley (Bea Benaderet) and her three beautiful daughters. Buchanan played the rascally but likable Uncle Joe Carson throughout the run of the series. His final regular role was as J.J. Jackson, the cantankerous veteran deputy to Sheriff Sam Cade (Glenn Ford) in the modern Western *Cade's County* (1971–1972).

Buchanan died in Palm Desert, California, on April 4, 1979, at age 76, following brain surgery. He is buried at Forest Lawn cemetery in the Hollywood Hills. His widow, Mildred Spence, and their son Bucky survived him.

Edgar Buchanan Filmography

1939: *My Son Is Guilty, Tear Gas Squad.*
1940: *Three Cheers for the Irish, Too Many Husbands, The Doctor Takes a Wife, When the Daltons Rode, Arizona, Escape to Glory (*a.k.a. *Submarine Zone), The Sea Hawk.*
1941: *Penny Serenade, Her First Beau, Richest Man in Town, Texas, You Belong to Me.*
1942: *Tombstone The Town Too Tough to Die, The Talk of The Town.*
1943: *City Without Men, The Desperadoes, Good Luck Mr. Yates, Destroyer.*
1944: *Buffalo Bill, The Impatient Years, Bride by Mistake.*
1945: *Strange Affair, The Fighting Guardsman.*
1946: *The Bandit of Sherwood Forest, The Walls Came Tumbling Down, Perilous Holiday, If I'm Lucky, Abilene Town, Renegades.*
1947: *The Sea of Grass, Framed.*
1948: *The Swordsman, Wreck of the Hesperus, Adventures in Silverado, Best Man Wins, The Black Arrow, The Untamed Breed, Coroner Creek, The Man from Colorado.*
1949: *The Walking Hills, Red Canyon, Any Number Can Play, Lust for Gold.*
1950: *Cheaper by the Dozen, Cargo to Capetown, The Big Hangover, Devil's Doorway.*
1951: *The Great Missouri Raid, Cave of Outlaws, Rawhide, Silver City.*
1952: *Flaming Feather, The Big Trees, Wild Stallion, Toughest Man in Arizona.*
1953: *It Happens Every Thursday, Shane, Make Haste to Live, She Couldn't Say No.*
1954: *Dawn at Socorro, Human Desire, Destry.*
1955: *Rage at Dawn, Wichita, The Silver Star, The Lonesome Trail.*
1956: *Come Next Spring.*
1957: *Spoilers of the Forest.*
1958: *Day of the Bad Man, The Sheepman.*
1959: *King of the Wild Stallions, It Started with a Kiss, Hound Dog Man, Edge of Eternity.*
1960: *Four Fast Guns, Stump Run, Chartroose Caboose.*
1961: *Cimarron, Devil's Partner, Tammy Tell Me True, The Comancheros.*
1962: *Ride the High Country.*
1963: *Donovan's Reef, Move Over Darling, McLintock!, A Ticklish Affair.*
1965: *The Man from Button Willow* (voice only), *The Rounders.*
1966: *Gunpoint, Welcome to Hard Times.*
1969: *Angel in My Pocket, Something for a Lonely Man* (TV), *The Over-The-Hill Gang* (TV).
1970: *The Over-The-Hill Gang Rides Again* (TV).
1971: *Yuma* (TV).
1974: *Benji.*

Television Series

1952–1954: *Hopalong Cassidy* as Red Connors.
1955–1956: *Judge Roy Bean* as Judge Roy Bean.
1963–1970: *Petticoat Junction* as Uncle Joe Carson.
1971–1972: *Cade's County* as Deputy J.J. Jackson.

Sources

Maltin, Leonard. *The Real Stars.* New York: Curtis Books, 1971.
Parish, James Robert. *Hollywood Character Actors.* New Rochelle, NY: Arlington House, 1978.
Smith, Ron. *Comic Support.* New York: Citadel Press, 1993.
Willis, John. *Screen World.* Obituary. London: Muller, 1980.

JACK BUETEL

Born Jack Beutel on September 5, 1915, in Dallas, Texas, he started out as an insurance clerk while gaining some stage experience with the Dallas Little Theater. He also broadcast on radio and had bits in a couple of movies. After a nationwide search, he and Jane Russell were chosen to star in *The Outlaw* which was produced and later directed by Howard Hughes in 1941. Buetel played Billy the Kid. It was Howard Hughes who changed his name from

Jack Buetel in *Judge Roy Bean.*

Beutel to Buetel because he feared the public would pronounce it "Beetle." Offscreen Russell and Buetel became and remained good friends.

This film might have made him a star, but opposition from the censors was sufficient to cause it to be withdrawn after a couple of perfunctory releases (it was generally released in 1950). Buetel remained on contract to Howard Hughes for a total of 14 years and served in the Navy during World War II. Howard Hawks, who commenced directing *The Outlaw,* allegedly wanted Buetel to play Matthew Garth in his classic film *Red River* (1948), but Hughes refused to loan him. The role made a star of Montgomery Clift. Director Richard L. Bare, who later married Buetel's first wife Ceretha, once said that Buetel was convinced that Hughes killed off his career because he thought Buetel was having an affair with one of his girlfriends.

Buetel had a negligible career in the 1950s including the secondary role of the deputy in *Judge Roy Bean*, a syndicated 1955-56 series. All of his featured roles were in movies of the Western genre. In 1962 Buetel married his third wife, a wealthy widow, and moved to Portland, Oregon, where he became an investment broker. They maintained a second home in Hawaii. His hobby was raising giant schnauzers which he exhibited at dog shows. He died in Portland, Oregon, on June 27, 1989, at age 73, after a long illness. He was survived by a daughter and stepson.

Jack Buetel Filmography

1939: *Gone with the Wind.*
1940: *Congo Maisie.*
1941: *The Outlaw.*
1951: *Best of the Badmen.*
1952: *The Half Breed, Rose of Cimarron.*
1954: *Jesse James' Women.*
1959: *Mustang.*

Television Series

1955–1956: *Judge Roy Bean* as Jeff Taggard.

Sources:

Lamparski, Richard. *Whatever Became Of? Seventh Series.* New York: Bantam, 1977.
Willis, John. *Screen World.* London: Muller, 1990.

DON BURNETT

Donald Burnett was born in Los Angeles on November 4, 1930. His father and mother were British. The son of a commercial artist, he attended Otis Art Institute and UCLA where he studied and worked with Jan Stussy. Between art school, working on a business degree in college and taking time off to surf, he lived in Korea and Japan for three years while serving on active duty as an infantry lieutenant in the U.S. Army.

After college he spent time as an actor. He was an extra when he did a screen test for the

Don Burnett (kneeling) and Keith Larsen in *Northwest Passage.*

John Ford film *The Searchers* (1956). MGM saw the test and put him under contract. He appeared in some films for them and the television series *Northwest Passage* (1958–1959). This was set during the French and Indian War (1754–1759) and told of Rogers' Rangers. The adventures of this group of men fighting the French and the Indians, battling the elements and exploring, provided the background to the series. Burnett played Ensign Langdon

Towne, a Harvard graduate from a wealthy Eastern family, who had become the company map maker. He played the role which in the movie *Northwest Passage* (1940) had been played by Robert Young. When asked how he won the role he replies, "I guess they thought I looked like a Harvard college graduate." Keith Larsen and Buddy Ebsen were his costars in the series. When asked what he thought of them, he says, "Both were great fellows."

He then lived in Europe for two years shooting movies. When asked the reason he turned his back on show business, he replies, "I went to London to do a television series which was never made. While there I went to Stratford and saw a young actor do *The Taming of the Shrew* and the next night *The Merchant of Venice.* His work was so far superior to what I was used to in Hollywood and to what I could do. I decided to go to graduate school and Wall Street. The young actor was Peter O'Toole."

His travels through the countrysides of Italy, France, Spain and England had enriched his palate. Even though he returned to the United States and the investment business, he continued to study and paint. He spent as much of his free time as possible painting landscapes in Southern California. After a successful career in the investment business where he was a partner with a major Wall Street firm, he retired early to devote his full time to painting.

While working on the film *Don't Go Near The Water* (1957), he met actress Gia Scala. They married on August 21, 1959. They moved into his home at Malibu Beach and then later bought a Cape Cod–style house in the Hollywood Hills. It was a very stormy marriage which ended in divorce in September 1970, on the grounds of incompatibility. Scala died on April 30, 1972, at age 38. In 1971 Burnett married the actress Barbara Anderson, a union which has proved to be enduring. They have no children.

Since 1991 they have made their home in Santa Fe, New Mexico, where his landscapes can be seen at the Charleen Cody Gallery.

Don Burnett Filmography

1955: *Hell's Horizon.*
1956: *The Fastest Gun Alive, These Wilder Years, Tea and Sympathy.*
1957: *The Wings of Eagles, Raintree County, Untamed Youth, Don't Go Near the Water.*
1959: *Fury River* (TV:NP), *Frontier Rangers* (TV:NP), *Mission Of Danger* (TV:NP).
1962: *The Triumph of Robin Hood, Damon and Pythias.*

Television Series

1958–1959: *Northwest Passage* as Ensign Langdon Towne.

Sources

Correspondence between Burnett and the author.

Note

Theatrical films which were edited from episodes of the *Northwest Passage* television series for overseas release are denoted TV:NP in the filmography.

PAT BUTTRAM

The life and career of Pat Buttram were characterized by homespun humor and sharp wit, delivered in a half yodel whine, initially on radio and later in films and television. He frequently served as a sidekick to Gene Autry who said of him, "He was just a natural comedian." Later on in his life he forged out a new career for himself as a most sought-after toastmaster and after-dinner speaker. Buttram was another personality, much associated with

Westerns, who could not get along with horses. When quizzed on the subject of stardom, he extracted a dog-eared newspaper clipping dating from the early 1950s when he was almost killed shooting a television episode. The headline read, "Gene Autry almost hurt in explosion."

Pat Buttram was born Maxwell E. Buttram in Addison, Winston County, Alabama, on June 19, 1915, the son of a circuit riding Methodist minister. He had a nomadic childhood, living in several different places. His first stage appearance was made at the age of eight in a church play directed by his father. His early ambition was to be a preacher. His early education was obtained at Mortimer Jordan High School, a rural school where he won a scholarship to study theology at Birmingham-Southern College at Birmingham, Alabama. This lasted for about six months until 1934 when he journeyed to Chicago to see the World's Fair. Radio reporters were interviewing the public to determine their reactions to the event and Buttram was one of the people interviewed. His spontaneous answers to the questions were so hilarious that he was instantly hired. He spent 13 years on the WLS radio show *National Barn Dance,* which was broadcast from Chicago. It was in the course of his work there that he first encountered Gene Autry, with whom he teamed on radio for 15 years (notably on *Melody Ranch).*

He later moved to Hollywood where he appeared in *The Strawberry Roan* (1948) in the minor role of Hank. The star was Autry. When Buttram came to appear in his next film, *Riders In The Sky* (1949), as Chuckwalla Jones, he had risen to become Autry's sidekick. He continued as comic relief in several more of Autry's Westerns at Columbia, sometimes under fictional names and other times using his own. *Mule Train* (1950) was his personal favorite because the sidekick was just as important as the hero. Playing under his own name on the television series *The Gene Autry Show* from 1950 to 1956 on CBS, Buttram helped Autry and his horse Champion keep peace out West for 83 of the episodes. He used his real name in this series because Autry had difficulty remembering any other.

His association with Autry ended dramatically for a while when Buttram was seriously injured in an accident which occurred

Portrait of Pat Buttram, who appeared on *The Gene Autry Show.*

when he was shooting an episode called "The Rainmaker." He played a rainmaker who was supposed to jerk the string on a miniature prop cannon which would fire into the clouds and create rain. Instead the cannon itself exploded and the fragments injured several film personnel. Buttram nearly had his foot blown off and his stomach was ventilated with metal. He spent 12 months in hospital recovering.

Buttram became a favorite of the Hollywood banquet circuit and frequently played benefits. He started out doing this when he was chosen as the emcee for a Western dinner at the Masquer's Club. He was so successful and received such glowing reviews that it started him out on a whole new career. "I used to play a Friar's Club dinner and they'd put me on at the beginning of the speeches," Buttram told the Associated Press in 1963. "I could tell a few jokes and get off. Now they put me on next to the closing following guys like Jack Benny, George Burns, Dean Martin, Frank Sinatra and Joey Bishop. I spend the evening crossing off my jokes because they've already been used." Many of his best vocal routines were recorded in the 1960s comedy album "Off

His Rocker." In 1983 he instigated the Golden Boot Awards, a prestigious annual event which seeks to honor and give recognition to Western personalities of television and film and raise money for charity. He was a recipient of his own Golden Boot in 1984.

He made a considerable amount of money providing voiceovers in commercials. In animated films for Walt Disney he supplied the voice of Napoleon the country dog in *The Aristocats*; the Sheriff Of Nottingham in *Robin Hood*; Luke, a sloshed swamp critter in *The Rescuers*; and the voice of Chief in *The Fox and the Hound*. He provided the voice of a talking bullet in *Who Framed Roger Rabbit*. His best-known television role was as the crafty Mr. Haney on *Green Acres*, which ran on CBS from 1965 to 1971. Haney was the bucolic confidence trickster who sold a rundown farm to unsuspecting businessman Oliver Wendell Douglas (Eddie Albert) and his wife Lisa (Eva Gabor). Buttram made multiple appearances on numerous variety shows of the 1950s. He was also a comedy writer on various radio shows. His final radio appearances were on Los Angeles radio station KMPC from 1990 to 1992.

Buttram met the beautiful actress Sheila Ryan when they appeared in the Western *Mule Train* (1950). They wed in 1952 and had a daughter, Kathleen Kerry, in 1954. Reportedly she is a dead ringer for her mother, but chose to go into banking rather than acting. Sheila Ryan died of a lung ailment in Woodland Hills, California, on November 4, 1975, at age 54. Devastated Pat Buttram suffered a stroke from which he bounced back to go on to enormous triumphs as a toastmaster, emcee and after-dinner speaker. He lived in Sherman Oaks next door to Jock Mahoney. In 1992 he underwent an operation for throat cancer. On January 8, 1994, the 78-year-old actor died at the University of California–Los Angeles Medical Center, of kidney failure. He was survived by a brother, two sisters and his daughter.

Pat Buttram Filmography

1944: *National Barn Dance.*
1948: *The Strawberry Roan.*
1949: *Riders in the Sky.*
1950: *Mule Train, Beyond the Purple Hills, Indian Territory, The Blazing Sun.*
1951: *Gene Autry and the Mounties, Texans Never Cry, Silver Canyon, Hills of Utah, Valley of Fire.*
1952: *The Old West, Night Stage to Galveston, Apache Country, Barbed Wire, Wagon Team, Blue Canadian Rockies.*
1963: *Twilight of Honor.*
1964: *The Hanged Man* (TV), *Roustabout.*
1965: *Sergeant Deadhead.*
1968: *The Sweet Ride.*
1969: *I Sailed to Tahiti with an All Girl Crew, The Gatling Gun (*a.k.a. *King Gun).*
1970: *The Aristocats* (voice only).
1972: *Evil Roy Slade* (TV) (narrator only).
1973: *Robin Hood* (voice only).
1977: *The Rescuers* (voice only).
1979: *The Sacketts* (TV).
1980: *Angels Brigade.*
1981: *The Fox and the Hound* (voice only), *Choices.*
1988: *Who Framed Roger Rabbit* (voice only).
1990: *Back to the Future III, Return to Green Acres* (TV).

Television Series

1950–1956: *The Gene Autry Show* as Pat Buttram.
1965–1971: *Green Acres* as Mr. Haney.

Sources:

Brooks, Tim. *The Complete Directory to Prime Time TV Stars 1946–Present.* New York: Ballantine Books, 1987.
Contemporary Theater, Film and Television Volume 14. Detroit, MI: Gale, 1991.
Cox, Stephen. *The Hooterville Handbook.* New York: St. Martin's Press, 1993.
Eleventh Annual Golden Boot Awards Program. August 1993.
Rothel, David. *Those Great Cowboy Sidekicks.* Waynesville, NC: World of Yesterday Publications, 1984.
Smith, Ron. *Comic Support.* New York: Citadel, 1993.
Speed, F. Maurice. *The Western Film Annual.* London: MacDonald, 1956.
Variety. January 17, 1994.

HOWARD CAINE

Howard Caine was born Howard Cohen in Nashville, Tennessee, on January 2, 1926. At the tender age of two-and-a-half, he played Wheezer in the original silent *Our Gang* comedies. He was probably best known for his recurring role as Gestapo Major Hochstetter in the television series *Hogan's Heroes*. He also appeared in a number of telefilms including *Helter Skelter* as Charles Manson's lawyer; *Marilyn: The Untold Story* as director Billy Wilder; and as Lord Beaverbrook in the miniseries *War and Remembrance*.

He was a regular on the television series *Fair Exchange* and the Western series *The Californians* for one season as Schaab. He made over 750 live and film television appearances. He also appeared on Broadway in five plays including *Damn Yankees* (replacing Ray Walston as Applegate the Devil); as Tad Finney in *Inherit the Wind*; and as Appopolous in *Wonderful Town*. He appeared in numerous musicals in stock, regional and dinner theaters and on radio played in over 300 network shows from New York. In later years he was one of a select band of actors who made a good living from voiceovers and commercials.

He was a longtime board member of the Screen Actors Guild, Actors Equity and the American Federation of Television and Radio Artists. Best known in union circles as a tireless volunteer and outspoken advocate of actors' rights, he served on numerous union committees and was the founding president of Housing for Entertainment Professionals, involved in building low-cost housing in West Hollywood for actors and other industry professionals. "He was very concerned about the average performer, to make sure that nobody was left out," a fellow board member said. "Howard often represented our conscience." He was also a staunch advocate of merging all the performers' unions. In his last run for the AFTRA national board, he campaigned and was reelected on a platform calling for "one union for all performers with full protection for all categories."

Since 1970 he performed folk music at festivals, clubs, temples, churches, schools and universities and at concerts throughout the southland. He received 29 awards for traditional banjo and singing. His concerts included Appalachian Mountain, Delta Blues, Latino and humorous songs with audience participation. The use of a five-string banjo, guitar and Appalachian dulcimer gave a unique sound to his music. He also taught drama at U.S. International University in San Diego and spoke 32 authentic dialects.

Howard Caine, who appeared in *The Californians*.

Caine died at his home in North Hollywood on December 28, 1993, after suffering a heart attack. He was 67. He was survived by his wife actress Valerie Webber Caine; son Lyle Caine; daughter-in-law Gloria Mann; sister Harriet Liss and brother Edmund Caine.

Howard Caine Filmography

1959: *From the Terrace.*
1960: *Pay or Die.*
1961: *Judgment at Nuremberg.*
1962: *Pressure Point.*
1963: *The Man from the Diners' Club.*
1965: *The Loved One.*

1966: *Alvarez Kelly, The Doomsday Flight* (TV).
1970: *Watermelon Man.*
1972: *1776.*
1976: *Helter Skelter* (TV).
1980: *Marilyn: The Untold Story* (TV).
1982: *Forced Vengeance.*
1983: *Trenchcoat.*

Television Series

1957–1958: *The Californians* as Schaab.
1962–1963: *Fair Exchange.*
1966–1971: *Hogan's Heroes* as Major Hochstedder.

Miniseries

1988–1989: *War and Remembrance.*

Sources

Correspondence between Valerie Webber Caine and the author.

RORY CALHOUN

When Victor Mature, the original star of the Spanish Western *Finger on the Trigger,* proved unable to appear, producer-director Sidney Pink was at his wit's end. He did, however, have a good friend in Rory Calhoun. He called him in California and begged him to help out. Calhoun flew to his aid in Spain, shot all his scenes in eight days and dubbed his lines in two. This enabled him to fly back to California to start work on his next film. As Pink expressed it, "I am everlastingly grateful to Rory for pulling me out of that mess." Rory Calhoun has a long association with the Western, including the television series *The Texan.* Given his background it is a miracle that he ever made it at all. As he himself puts it, "I wouldn't change anything. I would have done some of it sooner. If it hadn't all happened, I wouldn't be where and who I am today."

Rory Calhoun was born Francis Timothy McCown in Los Angeles, California, on August 8, 1922. After the early death of his sailor father, he was raised by his stepfather Nathaniel Durgin (whom he hated) and his Spanish mother. He recalls, "For the first 13 years, except for three years in Santa Cruz, we lived a semi-nomadic existence in California. By 1930 things were going badly in the Depression and we moved around. I kinda liked that because I didn't have to go to school much."

He began thieving at 13 and graduated to grand theft auto. He did time in several institutions: Whittier School for Boys; the Preston School of Industry; a federal prison at Springfield, Missouri; and the Federal Reformatory in El Reno, Oklahoma. Quizzed on the reason he turned to crime, he says, "For excitement, I guess. I never remember being hungry or lacking a roof over my head. Funny thing is I later met in Hollywood some of the stars whose cars I had stolen. For instance, I could have told Johnny Weissmuller what had happened to his automobile. My only saving grace was that I never killed anybody and I never carried a weapon of any kind."

He was set on the road to reform by Father Donald J. Kanally, the chaplain at the reformatory in El Reno. He recalls, "I was about to be transferred to Springfield for trying to escape when Father Kanally came running up to me at the railway depot and asked me if I wanted to be baptized. I agreed. He took me into the men's room. I knelt down and was baptized in a sink next to a urinal. Later I was in the train with two armed guards. While one was in the dining car, the other fell asleep. I could easily have reached for his gun. Then I thought, 'Let's ride this one out.'"

He was released in 1944 but was classified 4F, so he did not serve in the armed forces. Instead he did a wide variety of blue collar jobs. Asked how he was discovered he replies, "It was not on a bridle trail by Alan Ladd. I was working in Venice, California, as a forest ranger. On a two-week vacation I was visiting my grandmother. I had spent the day on the beach. I was standing outside MGM studios waiting for a bus when a guy named Pollock came up and asked me, 'Are you an actor?' 'Yes,' I lied. Pollock told me that he believed he could sell me to Sue Carol, once an actress but now a powerful agent and the wife of Alan Ladd. If so, he would give me half. That's what he did. He sold me to Sue Carol for $10,000 and gave me half. It was the easiest $5,000 I ever earned."

He made a few features under his real name. After he signed with agent Henry Willson (who changed his name to Rory Calhoun) his career really took off. He won the role of Teller in *The Red House* (1947), a moody backwoods drama which Edward G. Robinson produced and starred in. He recalls Edward G. with enormous affection. "Every night I went up to his room with him and his wife and he went over my next day's lines with me. It didn't benefit him any, but it helped me a lot."

He signed with 20th Century–Fox and later Universal, where he made Westerns, musicals and comedies. Asked which he likes best he says, "Westerns are the great love of my life. I'm only sorry they are not in vogue right now. I could still play the sheriff or an old cowpoke. Most of the Westerns I made were B movies budgeted at four or five hundred thousand dollars each. They were about six weeks in production." One he remembers with great pride was *Way of a Gaucho* (1952) opposite lovely Gene Tierney. "That was an A Western. A lot of money was spent on it." He produced three Westerns *(Domino Kid, The Hired Gun and Apache Territory)* during 1957–1958. He also contributed to the scripts of *Shotgun* (1955) and *Domino Kid* and penned a Western stageplay, *The Man from Padera.*

Quizzed on how he came to play roving defender of justice Bill Longley in *The Texan* (1958–1960) he recalls, "My partner Vic Orsatti and I met Desi Arnaz who owned Desilu Studios and lived right across the street. He came up with a deal to produce *The Texan.* I was the first actor to produce his own series. I had half the action. Each episode cost $40,000 and we shot two a week." The reference books list 78 episodes. The real Bill Longley was a notorious outlaw who was eventually hanged. The television series borrowed his name, but little else.

Rory Calhoun in *The Texan.*

Asked if any of *The Texan* was actually shot in Texas he explains, "No. We built a Western street at Desilu Studios. For background shots we used a place called 'Pearl Flats' in the Mojave desert." *The Texan* rode as high as #15 in the Nielsen ratings during the 1958–1959 season. After two years it was axed. Asked the reason for its cancelation he says, "I'm a lazy bastard. I needed more leisure time. I had produced the series for two seasons and had an option for a third. I decided to go back into feature films. If I can make enough money, I prefer to work for three months rather than all year round."

He went to Europe where he made a dozen films in Spain, France, Italy and England. Later he produced and directed *Belle Starr* (1969), an ill-fated West End stage musical which starred Betty Grable. It was his most recent visit to London, a city he loves. One little-known facet of his television career is that he hosted and occasionally starred in 68 episodes of the syndicated television series *Death Valley Days* which were rerun under the title *Western Star Theater* (1968–1970).

On August 29, 1948, he wed actress-singer Lita Baron. Their divorce in Santa

Monica in July 1970, was one of the most acrimonious and costly in Hollywood history up to that time. A happy legacy, however, was their three daughters: Cindy Frances (born 1957), Tami Elizabeth (born 1958) and Lorrie Marie (born 1959). For two years after the divorce he did not work at all with the California Community Property Laws applying. On April 20, 1971, in Las Vegas, he married Sue Rhodes Boswell, an Australian journalist, who is several years his junior. They first met when she interviewed him in London at the time of the *Belle Starr* fiasco. In 1971 they welcomed daughter Rorye.

He has appeared in the miniseries *The Rebels* (1979) and *The Blue and the Gray* (1982). He does not have particularly fond memories of the former. "We were shooting up at Tahoe when a blizzard came up. The horses were plunging around. I thought, 'Great, we don't have to shoot in this!' I had visions of warm fires and hot toddies. Instead we went right on shooting, blizzard and all."

Calhoun has made over a thousand television appearances, including 900 as Judson Tyler on the daytime soap *Capitol* (1982–1987). Of the "golden years" he recalls, "There were many Errol Flynns, but some were a little more discreet, that's all. They used to say, 'We had a helluva party. You should have been there.' Nowadays everyone's talking career." The actor, who himself once had a formidable reputation as a hellraiser, has been clean ever since he had a couple of operations a few years back. He says, "Over New Year's I'm one of the most popular guys in town. Whenever the boys are whooping it up, I get to act as chauffeur!"

Rory Calhoun Filmography

1944: *Something for the Boys, Sunday Dinner for a Soldier.*
1945: *Nob Hill, The Great John L, The Bullfighters.*
1947: *The Red House, Adventure Island, That Hagen Girl.*
1948: *Miraculous Journey.*
1949: *Sand, Massacre River.*
1950: *A Ticket to Tomahawk, Return of the Frontiersman, County Fair.*
1951: *I'd Climb the Highest Mountain, Rogue River, Meet Me After the Show.*
1952: *With a Song in My Heart, Way of a Gaucho.*
1953: *The Silver Whip, Powder River, How to Marry a Millionaire.*
1954: *River of No Return, Yellow Tomahawk, A Bullet Is Waiting, Dawn at Socorro, Four Guns to the Border.*
1955: *The Looters, Ain't Misbehavin', Treasure of Pancho Villa, The Spoilers.*
1956: *Red Sundown, Raw Edge, Flight to Hong Kong.*
1957: *Utah Blaine, The Big Caper, The Hired Gun, Ride Out for Revenge, The Domino Kid.*
1958: *The Saga of Hemp Brown, Apache Territory.*
1960: *Thunder in Carolina.*
1961: *Colossus of Rhodes, Secret of Monte Cristo* (a.k.a. *Treasure of Monte Cristo).*
1962: *Marco Polo.*
1963: *The Gun Hawk, The Young and the Brave, Face in the Rain.*
1964: *Operation Delilah.*
1965: *Black Spurs, Young Fury, Finger on the Trigger.*
1966: *Apache Uprising, Our Men in Bagdad.*
1967: *Emerald of Artalama.*
1968: *Dayton's Devils.*
1969: *Operation Cross Eagles.*
1972: *Night of the Lepus.*
1973: *Blood Black and White.*
1975: *Mulefeathers* (a.k.a. *The West Is Still Wild), Won Ton Ton The Dog Who Saved Hollywood.*
1976: *Flight to Holocaust* (TV).
1977: *Kino Padre on Horseback, Love and the Midnight Auto Supply.*
1978: *Bitter Heritage, Flatbed Annie and Sweetiepie: Lady Truckers* (TV).
1979: *The Main Event, Just Not the Same Without You, Okinagan's Day.*
1980: *Motel Hell, Running Hot.*
1982: *Circle of Crime.*
1983: *Angel.*
1984: *Avenging Angel.*
1985: *Half Nelson* (TV).
1987: *Hell Comes to Frogtown.*
1989: *Bad Jim.*
1992: *Pure Country.*

Television Series

1958–1960: *The Texan* as Bill Longley.
1968–1970: *Western Star Theater*—host.
1982–1987: *Capitol* as Judson Tyler.

Miniseries

1979: *The Rebels.*
1982: *The Blue and the Gray.*

Sources

Interview with Calhoun in 1989.
Quinlan, David. *Illustrated Directory Of Film Stars.* London: Batsford, 1991.
Ragan, David. *Movie Stars of the '40s.* Englewood Cliffs NJ: Prentice-Hall, 1985.

HENRY CALVIN

Henry Calvin was born Wimberly Calvin Goodman, Jr., in Dallas, Texas, in 1918. He won scholarships to study opera and was educated at North Texas State College, the University of Southern California, the Chicago Conservatory and Southern Methodist University. After serving as a lieutenant in the artillery during World War II, he became a soloist at the Radio City Music Hall. He landed a major role in the hit Broadway musical *Kismet.* On the strength of this experience he headed for Hollywood determined to be a motion picture actor.

He is best remembered for playing the overweight, buffoonish Sergeant Garcia in the Western series *Zorro* for Walt Disney. He even recorded a version of the theme, but his was not a hit. He worked for Disney in motion pictures such as *Toby Tyler* (1960) and *Babes in Toyland* (1961) in which he formed a comic double act with fellow *Zorro* costar Gene Sheldon. There was a general consensus that their routines were the brightest aspects of these films. After his time with Disney, Calvin was occasionally seen in films and on television, such as "The Cost Of A Vacation" episode of *Mannix* (1967).

Henry Calvin was back in his hometown of Dallas, Texas, when he died of cancer on October 6, 1975, at age 57. He is buried at Grove Hill Memorial Park, Dallas, Texas.

Henry Calvin Filmography

1956: *The Broken Star, Crime Against Joe.*
1960: *Toby Tyler, The Sign of Zorro.*
1961: *Babes in Toyland.*
1965: *Ship of Fools.*

Television Series

1957–1959: *Zorro* as Sergeant Garcia.

Sources

Maltin, Leonard. *The Disney Films.* New York: Crown, 1973.
Truitt, Evelyn Mack. *Who Was Who on Screen Second Edition.* New York: Bowker, 1977.
Yenne, Bill. *The Legend of Zorro.* Greenwich, CT: Brompton, 1991.
Yoggy, Gary A. *Riding the Video Range: The Rise and Fall of the Western on Television.* Jefferson, NC: McFarland, 1995.

Note

The Sign of Zorro is a feature film derived from episodes of the *Zorro* television series.

CLAIRE CARLETON

Claire Carleton was born in New York City on September 28, 1913, the daughter of George Carleton and his wife Marie Louise Zeiner. She was educated in New York and Hollywood. She was prepared for the stage by her father, an actor who managed several stock companies in the United States. Her first stage appearance was in 1918 at the Belasco Theater, Washington, as a butterfly in a ballet. Over several years she acquired substantial stage experience in various stock companies.

She made her first appearance on the New York stage at the Provincetown Theater on June 2, 1932, as Lucy in *Blue Monday*. She toured extensively and appeared on Broadway until 1936. In that year she went to England where she made her first appearance on the London stage at Wyndham's Theater on February 18, 1936, as Mabel in *Three Men on a Horse* in which she had a resounding success. This also ranked as her favorite role. She returned to the United States where she continued her successful stage career, notably playing Crystal Allen in two different versions of *The Women*.

Carleton went to Hollywood in 1940 and was placed under contract by Republic, where she played wisecracking dames. Her studio biography listed her hobbies as riding and eating ice cream sodas. As time went on her facial features hardened and she frequently played floozies who had been around a lot. She also appeared in the short comedies of Leon Errol and Edgar Kennedy. Although she was primarily appearing in films, she did not entirely abandon the stage, touring during 1944 and 1945 in the leading role in *Good Night Ladies*. As late as July 1952, she played Lily Schaeffer in *Time for Elizabeth* at the La Jolla Playhouse.

She had a couple of regular character roles on television, one of which was the Western series *Cimarron City*. She played Alice Purdy opposite her own real-life husband Frederick E. Sherman (playing her husband Burt in the program). She sometimes had some interesting roles in movies, notably *Fort Massacre* (1958), in which she had a supply wagon and sold goods to the hostile Indians. It turned out that she had been able to trade with the Indians because she was one of only a couple of women in the territory who could converse fluently with them in their own language.

Claire Carleton died of cancer on December 11, 1979, at age 66, at her home in Northridge, California. Her husband died in 1969. There were no reported surviving family members.

Claire Carleton Filmography

1940: *The Crooked Road, Sing Dance Plenty Hot, Girl from Havana, Grand Ole Opry, Melody and Moonlight.*

1941: *Petticoat Politics, The Great Train Robbery.*

1943: *Lady of Burlesque, Gildersleeve on Broadway, Rookies in Burma, Around the World.*

1944: *A Night of Adventure, My Pal Wolf, Youth Runs Wild, The Woman in the Window, Show Business.*

1945: *Frontier Gal.*

1946: *Gun Town, That Texas Jamboree, The Crime Doctor's Man Hunt, A Close Call for Boston Blackie, Vacation in Reno.*

1947: *A Double Life, The Senator Was Indiscreet.*

1948: *The Time of Your Life, Ruthless.*

1949: *Sorrowful Jones, The Reckless Moment, Red Light, It's a Great Feeling, Bad Men of Tombstone, Satan's Cradle, Shockproof, The Crime Doctor's Diary, The Barkleys of Broadway.*

1950: *Born Yesterday, Wabash Avenue.*

1951: *Death of a Salesman, Two of a Kind, The Son of Dr. Jekyll, Honeychile.*

1952: *The Fighter, Bal Tabain.*

1953: *Ride the Man Down.*

1954: *Witness to Murder, Jubilee Trail.*

1955: *Love Me or Leave Me.*

1956: *The Black Sleep, Accused of Murder.*

1957: *My Gun Is Quick, The Buster Keaton Story, The Careless Years.*

1958: *Unwed Mother, Fort Massacre.*

1959: *Miracle of the Hills.*

Television Series

1954–1955: *The Mickey Rooney Show* as Mrs. Mulligan.

1958–1959: *Cimarron City* as Alice Purdy.

Sources

Brooks, Tim. *The Complete Directory to Prime Time TV Stars 1946–Present.* New York: Ballantine Books, 1987.

Turner, Steve and Edgar M. Wyatt. *Saddle Gals.* Madison, NC: Empire, 1995.

Who's Who in the Theater Twelfth Edition. London: Pitman, 1957.

Willis, John. *Screen World.* London: Muller, 1980.

RICHARD CARLSON

Richard Carlson always seemed a tad too refined to be a convincing Western hero. With his soft voice and diffident manner, he was much more at home as the intellectual scientist hero of a number of skillfully presented science-fiction films of the early 1950s. It was slightly surprising to see him as the hero of a horse opera television series. He was regarded by his contemporaries as a pleasant man to work with. He was an assured writer and director who knew quite a lot about editing. Generally when he was directing and acting in a film, his own scenes were directed uncredited by others.

Richard Dutoit Carlson was born in Albert Lea, Minnesota, on April 29, 1912, the son of an attorney. Educated at the University of Minnesota, he graduated with an M.A. degree summa cum laude, Phi Beta Kappa and with $2,500 in scholarship money. As a student he wrote, acted and directed two plays which were well-received, and he contributed to *The Minnesota Quarterly.* He was briefly a teacher, but the lure of the footlights proved too strong. He opened a theater in Minneapolis where he invested his cash in writing, directing and acting in three plays which flopped so that he lost all his money. Subsequently he directed and acted in plays at the Pasadena Community Theater before going to New York, where he encountered producer Joshua Logan coming out of Sardi's Restaurant. Within a week he had signed a contract to appear in *Stars in Your Eyes* opposite Ethel Merman on Broadway.

Producer David O. Selznick originally lured Carlson to Hollywood as a writer to contribute to the script of the Janet Gaynor film *The Young in Heart* (1938). After meeting him, Gaynor was so impressed that she insisted he appear in the film instead. His career as an actor took off and he was seen in many films prior to World War II, of which his most important was as David Hewitt in *The Little Foxes* (1941).

Richard Carlson in *Mackenzie's Raiders.*

During war service in the U.S. Navy (1943–1946) he wrote and directed several training films for the government. When he was honorably discharged in 1946, he endeavored to reactivate his career as an actor, starting in England with *So Well Remembered* (1947). Parts were slow in coming, so he supplemented his income by writing articles for national magazines. Among his other business enterprises were theater ticket agencies in Chicago and Hollywood.

His career picked up again with a vengeance in the early 1950s, when he starred in several science-fiction films. The ones he made for Universal, particularly *It Came from Outer Space* (1953) and *Creature from the Black Lagoon* (1954), have achieved classic status. He was very active in television from the early 1950s in anthology series. He also starred in two syndicated series for Ziv. The first of these was the extremely popular and suspenseful *I Led Three Lives* (1953–1956) in which he played the real life Herbert Philbrick, simultaneously a Boston advertising executive and family man/Communist Party member/counterspy for the FBI. This series summed up the Red hysteria so rampant during the 1950s. Carlson was on a percentage deal from this series, so he made a lot of money from it.

His second series was called *Mackenzie's Raiders* (1958–1959) and was also based on fact. He played Col. Ranald Mackenzie, the commander of the U.S. Fourth Cavalry stationed at Fort Clark, Texas, in 1873. Mexican bandits were attacking the local settlers, and Mackenzie's cryptic instructions from the White House were to stop the bandits by chasing them across the Rio Grande into Mexico. Since he had no official jurisdiction across the border, the U.S. Government could not acknowledge him if he were caught. If he was successful, there were neither medals nor glory awaiting him. The series was derived from the book *The Mackenzie Raid* by Col. Russell Reeder. This was a very rugged series in which Carlson acquitted himself much better than in some of his Western films. He was also a very accomplished horseman. It lasted for 39 half-hour black and white episodes.

Carlson had long harbored a desire to direct, an ambition which was fulfilled when he directed Rory Calhoun in *Four Guns to the Border* (1954). He subsequently went on to direct and appear in other films. He also helmed several episodes of television series. Carlson continued as guest-star on several series such as *The FBI, Owen Marshall—Counselor at Law, Cannon,* and *O'Hara United States Treasury.* For some of these he also wrote the scripts. One of his last recorded appearances was an episode of the shortlived series *Khan* in 1975. He also did voiceovers and was president of the Benevolent Actors and Others for Animals Organization.

Carlson lived in the San Fernando Valley where his hobbies were golf and gardening. He died in Encino, California, on November 25, 1977, at age 65. Although the official cause of death was a cerebral hemorrhage, alcoholism was believed to have been a strong contributory factor. He lies buried in the Chapel of the Pines Crematory in Los Angeles. He married model Mona Mayfield in 1939 and was survived by her and two sons, Christopher and Richard Henry. His widow died in Sherman Oaks, California, on January 2, 1990, at age 72.

Richard Carlson Filmography

1938: *The Young in Heart, Duke of West Point.*

1939: *Little Accident, Dancing Co-Ed, These Glamour Girls, Winter Carnival.*

1940: *Beyond Tomorrow, Too Many Girls, The Ghost Breakers, No No Nanette, The Howards of Virginia.*

1941: *West Point Widow, The Little Foxes, Back Street, Hold That Ghost.*

1942: *My Heart Belongs to Daddy, Fly by Night, White Cargo, Highways by Night, The Affairs of Martha.*

1943: *Presenting Lily Mars, Young Ideas, A Stranger in Town, The Man from Down Under.*

1947: *So Well Remembered.*

1948: *Behind Locked Doors.*

1950: *Try and Get Me, King Solomon's Mines.*

1951: *The Blue Veil, Valentino, A Millionaire for Christy.*

1952: *Whispering Smith Hits London (*a.k.a. *Whispering Smith Versus Scotland Yard), Retreat Hell!*

1953: *The Maze, The Magnetic Monster, Flat Top, All I Desire, Seminole, It Came from Outer Space.*

1954: *Riders to the Stars* (also directed), *Creature from the Black Lagoon.*

1955: *The Last Command, Bengazi, An Annapolis Story* (narrator only).

1956: *Three for Jamie Dawn.*

1957: *The Helen Morgan Story.*

1960: *Tormented.*

1965: *Kid Rodelo* (also directed).

1966: *The Doomsday Flight* (TV).
1968: *The Power.*
1969: *The Valley of Gwangi, Change of Habit.*

As director only

1954: *Four Guns to the Border.*
1958: *Appointment With a Shadow, The Saga of Hemp Brown.*

Television Series

1953–1956: *I Led Three Lives* as Herbert Philbrick.
1958–1959: *Mackenzie's Raiders* as Col. Ranald S. Mackenzie.

Sources

Picture Show Annual. London: Amalgamated Press, 1953.
Ragan, David. *Who's Who in Hollywood 1900–1976.* New Rochelle, NY: Arlington House, 1976.
Speed, F. Maurice. *The Western Film and TV Annual.* London: MacDonald, 1959.
Weaver, Tom. *Interviews With B Science Fiction and Horror Movie Makers.* Jefferson, NC: McFarland, 1988.
Willis, John. *Screen World.* London: Muller, 1978.

HOAGY CARMICHAEL

Hoagy Carmichael was not a guy with many namesakes. "Hoagy" was short for Hoagland, which was scarcely any commoner. Hoagland sounds rather like a place, which is appropriate since Carmichael did carve out a "country" of his own, an intriguing mixture of the real and imaginary American south. He was also an actor with an indelible image. Hat low over his eyes, slouched at the piano, tickling the ivories in a smoky roadhouse of the 1940s; this skinny, bat-eared guy with a wayward lock of hair, a lazy, distinctive, burnt coffee voice and a cigarette dangling from his lips epitomized the hero's cynical but sensible best friend in the rich, dark movie melodramas of the period. He was one of the least likely candidates to encounter in a Western series of the 1950s, but he turned up in *Laramie.*

He was born Hoagland Howard Carmichael in Bloomington, Indiana, on November 22, 1899, the son of Howard Clyde Carmichael. At an early age he learned to play the piano from his mother, though he never learned to read music. While attending law school at the University of Indiana, he paid his tuition fees with money he earned from leading a three-piece band. When he graduated with a bachelor of law degree in 1926, he was determined to practice law. He tried to set up a law practice in Florida, but when this did not bring him instant success, he left to head his own band in Indianapolis. When this venture failed, he headed to New York's Tin Pan Alley where he arranged music.

He met and became a close friend of Bix Beiderbecke, the first white musician to become a jazz legend. The influence became ingrained since "Skylark," one of Carmichael's greatest songs of the 1940s, has a serpentine middle section that is in reality a transcription of a Beiderbecke cornet solo. By the end of the 1920s, Carmichael had a reputation as a good pianist who kept more than respectable jazz company and as a competent singer. In 1927 Carmichael cut his first records and later took part in some of the first integrated recording sessions.

Bix Beiderbecke died in 1931 at the age of 29, the year that Carmichael published his biggest hit, "Star Dust." This song, one of the most performed and recorded of the century, started life as a brisk instrumental. Slowed down and given a vernal, contemplative lyric by Mitchell Parish, it made Carmichael's fortune. It was a surprise success since there was nothing hard-sell about it. He wrote the tune while visiting his old college campus in the late 1920s, but had it rejected numerous times. He

Portrait of Hoagy Carmichael, who appeared in *Laramie*.

then went on to write countless other hit melodies including "Georgia On My Mind," which was later adopted as the state anthem.

Jules Glaenzer, vice-president of Cartier's, the famous Fifth Avenue jewelers, gave the best theatrical parties in New York in the 1930s. Whenever George Gershwin was present it epitomized Oscar Levant's phrase: "An evening with Gershwin is a Gershwin evening." He refused to have anyone else's music played with two exceptions: Harold Arlen and Hoagy Carmichael. On some of those evenings Gershwin even asked Carmichael to play "Star Dust."

It seemed inevitable that Carmichael would gravitate to movies. He made his screen debut in *Topper* (1937), in which he sang one of his own compositions, "Old Man Moon." It was several years later that director Howard Hawks, Carmichael's next door neighbor in Hollywood, chanced to see him dressed like a vagrant working in his garden and cast him as Cricket, the baggy-suited honky tonk piano player, in *To Have and Have Not* (1944). He composed the background music for the film and warbled the songs "How Little We Know" and "Hong Kong Blues."

Thereafter he was typed in similar movies, usually contriving to introduce a hit number. As Celestial O'Brien in the deep sea mystery *Johnny Angel* (1945), he sang "Memphis in June," although ironically the location of the film was New Orleans. In 1946 the song "Ole Buttermilk Sky," which he sang in *Canyon Passage,* was nominated for an Oscar. He sang "Here Comes the Bride" and "Among My Souvenirs" in *The Best Years of Our Lives* (1946). He also appeared in *Young Man with a Horn* (1950), an unofficial biography of Bix Beiderbecke. His Hollywood success reached a pinnacle when he shared the Oscar for "In the Cool, Cool, Cool of The Evening" with lyricist Johnny Mercer, regarded by many as Carmichael's most congenial lyricist. This song was sung by Bing Crosby and Jane Wyman in *Here Comes the Groom* (1951), a film in which Carmichael did not appear. His last major hit was "When Love Goes Wrong" from *Gentlemen Prefer Blondes* (1953).

Developing into a theater and cabaret entertainer, in 1951 he was a headliner at the London Palladium. In 1953 he hosted the television series *Saturday Night Revue*, the 90-minute replacement for *Show of Shows,* but it was not popular. His sole regular role on television as an actor was the Western series *Laramie* in which he played Jonesy, the ranch's cook, handyman and loyal backup to Slim Sherman and his brother Andy. Carmichael composed some of the songs and music which were heard in the first season of the series. Throughout the later years of his life, he received a large income from song royalties and profitable investments in Palm Springs and Las Vegas real estate. A keen golfer, he owned a house overlooking a golf course in Palm Springs as well as a penthouse above the Sunset Strip in Hollywood.

Hoagy Carmichael, 82, died in a hospital in Rancho Mirage, California, on December 27, 1981, from heart problems. In 1920 he married Lida Mary Robison, with whom he had a son (Hoagy Bix) born in 1921 and another son (Randy Bob) in 1922. In 1936 he wed Ruth Meinardi, whom he divorced in 1955. In 1977 he married former B picture actress Wanda McKay, who died in 1996. He is buried at Rosehill Cemetery in his native Bloomington, Indiana.

Hoagy Carmichael Filmography

1937: *Topper.*
1945: *To Have and Have Not, Johnny Angel.*
1946: *Canyon Passage, The Best Years of Our Lives.*
1947: *Night Song.*
1949: *Johnny Holiday.*
1950: *Young Man with a Horn.*
1952: *The Las Vegas Story, Belles on Their Toes.*
1955: *Timberjack.*

Television Series

1953: *Saturday Revue*—host.
1959–1960: *Laramie* as Jonesy.

Sources

Adler, Larry. *Daily Express* newspaper. December 29, 1981.
Cushman, Robert. "Stardust Memories. *Radio Times* magazine, October 1, 1988.
Lamparski, Richard. *Whatever Became Of? Third Series.* New York: Crown, 1970.
Picture Show Annual. London: Amalgamated Press, 1953.
Ragan, David. *Movie Stars of the '40s.* Englewood Cliffs, NJ: Prentice-Hall, 1985.
Speed, F. Maurice. *The Western Film and TV Annual.* London: MacDonald, 1960.
The Stage. December 31, 1981.
Willis, John. *Screen World.* London: Muller, 1982.

LEO CARRILLO

Leo Carrillo liked nothing better than to dress up in an elaborate Mexican costume, mount one of his Palomino ponies and ride in the Annual Tournament of Roses Parade. Another favorite activity was his hosting of lavish parties at his home. He had a long and distinguished career in show business, usually in ethnic roles, which lasted from the days of vaudeville and early talkies until long after the Second World War. None of this counted for much after he played the role of Pancho in the *Cisco Kid* films and television series. By common consent his was the definitive interpretation.

Leo Antonio Carrillo was born in Los Angeles, California, on August 6, 1880, the son of Juan J. Carrillo and Francisca Roldan. His father was the first mayor of Santa Monica. His great-grandfather was Carlos Antonio Carrillo, governor of California in 1837. He had two brothers and was of mixed Mexican and Italian ancestry. He attended the University of St. Vincent of Loyola and started out as a cartoonist for the *Los Angeles Examiner.* He made his first recorded stage appearance in 1905 when he appeared in a show sponsored by the San Francisco Press Club. He was allegedly a friend of the writers O. Henry and Jack London.

By 1913 he was appearing in vaudeville as a monologist and in 1915 he made his Broadway debut as Giovanni Gassolini in *Fads and Fancies* at the Knickerbocker Theater. At the Morosco Theater in September 1917, he scored a resounding success as Tito Lombardi in *Lombardi Limited* and toured in this piece all over the United States. He became a familiar player in the legitimate theater.

During 1929-1930 he was touring in California in a few different plays when he scored a hit with one called *Mister Antonio.* The actor re-created his role in the film version in 1929. Thereafter he appeared in films at virtually all of the leading Hollywood studios. Although he was the star of some of his early films, later he headed the supporting cast. He frequently appeared as Latin types, which allowed him to make considerable use of his penchant for dialects and exaggerated gestures. His annual income was listed as $30,333 in 1935 and $57,832 in 1936. He worked exclusively for Universal from 1941 to 1944 and had a role in Universal's million dollar serial *Riders of Death Valley* (1941).

He appeared to be winding down his career when he was offered the role of Pancho, sidekick of the Cisco Kid, in a film series which starred Duncan Renaldo. Initially he refused on the grounds that the part was a caricature. Renaldo persuaded him to accept the role because he argued that it was in the same spirit as Sancho Panza in *Don Quixote.* Carrillo then took the part and went on to play the role in exactly the same stereotyped way which he had originally despised. Renaldo recalled, "He overdid it, but everyone liked him. His accent was so exaggerated that when we finished a picture, no one in the cast or crew could talk normal English." The accents he used in movies and television were entirely assumed. He owned a hacienda at Escondido. From the Mexican janitor there, he borrowed the delivery and mannerisms which he used to play Pancho. Carrillo played the character in five feature films for United Artists and 156 episodes of the television series for Ziv. This was a half-hour, syndicated color series which originally aired between 1950 and 1956. His horse in the series was called Loco.

After the series ended, he assembled and toured in a show entitled *Leo Carrillo and Company* in which he acted as emcee of a group of Hispanic musicians and flamenco guitarists and dancers. He was also a writer. *Western Breezes* was an early volume of verse. In 1961 *The California I Love,* a book which he wrote, was published. On September 10, 1961, he died of cancer at his other home in Santa Monica, at age 81. He was buried at Woodlawn Cemetery, Santa Monica. He had been married to Edith Shakespeare Haeselbarth since 1904. She died in 1953. He was survived by his adopted daughter Marie Antoinette and both his brothers.

Leo Carrillo Filmography

1929: *Mister Antonio, The Dove.*

1931: *Lasca of the Rio Grande, Guilty Generation, Hell Bound, Homicide Squad.*

1932: *Broken Wing, Second Fiddle, Cauliflower Alley, Girl of the Rio, Deception, Men Are Such Fools.*

1933: *Parachute Jumper, City Streets, Moonlight and Pretzels, Obey the Law, Racetrack, Before Morning.*

1934: *Viva Villa!, The Barretts of Wimpole Street, The Gay Bride, Four Frightened People, The Band Plays On, Manhattan Melodrama.*

1935: *The Winning Ticket, In Caliente, If Only You Could Cook, Love Me Forever.*

1936: *It Had to Happen, Moonlight Murder, The Gay Desperado.*

1937: *I Promise to Pay, History Is Made at Night, Hotel Haywire, Manhattan Merry-Go-Round, 52nd Street, The Barrier.*

1938: *Arizona Wildcat, Girl of the Golden West, City Streets, Little Miss Roughneck, Too Hot to Handle, Blockade, Flirting with Fate.*

1939: *The Girl and the Gambler, Society Lawyer, The Chicken Wagon Family, Rio, Fisherman's Wharf.*

1940: *Twenty-Mule Team, Wyoming, One Night in the Tropics, Lillian Russell, Captain Caution.*

1941: *Horror Island, Barnacle Bill, Riders of Death Valley* (serial), *Tight Shoes, The Kid from Kansas, What's Cookin'?*

1942: *Unseen Enemy, Escape from Hong Kong, Men of Texas, Top Sergeant, Danger in the Pacific, Timber, Sin Town, American Empire.*

1943: *Crazy House, Frontier Bad Men, Larceny with Music, Follow the Band, Phantom of the Opera.*

1944: *Babes on Swing Street, Bowery to Broadway, Gypsy Wildcat, Ghost Catchers, Merrily We Sing, Moonlight and Cactus.*

1945: *Crime Inc., Under Western Skies, Mexicana.*

1947: *The Fugitive.*

1948: *The Valiant Hombre* (CK).

1949: *The Gay Amigo* (CK), *The Daring Caballero* (CK), *Satan's Cradle* (CK).

1950: *The Girl from San Lorenzo* (CK), *Pancho Villa Returns.*

Television Series

1950–1956: *The Cisco Kid* as Pancho.

Sources

Corneau, Ernest N. *The Hall of Fame of Western Film Stars.* North Quincy, MA: Christopher, 1969.

Quinlan, David. *Illustrated Directory of Film Character Actors.* London: Batsford, 1995.

Rothel, David. *Those Great Cowboy Sidekicks.* Waynesville, NC: World of Yesterday Publications, 1984.

Smith, Ron. *Comic Support.* New York: Citadel Press, 1993.
Tuska, Jon. *The Filming of the West.* Garden City, NY: Doubleday, 1976.
Who's Who in the Theater Tenth Edition. London: Pitman, 1947.

Note

Films in *The Cisco Kid* series are denoted CK in the filmography.

ALLEN CASE

Born in Dallas, Texas, in 1935, Allen Case was educated at Southern Methodist University for two years before dropping out to pursue a show business career. He obtained a job singing on a local daily television show in Dallas. After touring in such musicals as *South Pacific, Damn Yankees, Company* and *My Fair Lady,* he went to New York to audition for *The Arthur Godfrey Talent Scout Show,* on which he sang for five weeks before making appearances in Miami and Atlantic City niteries. In 1955 he was signed by Columbia Records and appeared in the Marc Blitzstein musical *Reuben, Reuben.* Broadway credits also included *Once Upon a Mattress* and *Hallelujah Baby!*

He appeared in episodes of *Cheyenne, Wagon Train, Have Gun Will Travel* and *Gunsmoke.* It was while appearing in a Broadway show that he was picked to star in the title role of *The Deputy* (1959–1961), an NBC Western series. This series starred Henry Fonda as Chief Marshal Simon Fry, who in the turbulent Arizona Territory of the 1880s found it pretty tough going to maintain law and order in a country which had only just begun to think of a more permanent and orderly way of life than the pattern set by the first rootless pioneers. Fry's job was not made any easier because his deputy Clay McCord (Allen Case), a storekeeper, was a crack shot who did not believe in killing. Stories revolved around the conflict between these two characters and their ideals. McCord frequently served as deputy in Silver City to help older town marshal Herk Lamson (Wallace Ford).

After the series ended, Case combined an acting career with various other activities. His most prominent later role was in another NBC Western series, *The Legend of Jesse James* (1965–1966), in which he played Frank James. In the late 1960s he designed a successful line of fur coats for men and later worked as a photographer, writer and real estate broker. One of his last recorded acting credits was the "Ride the Whirlwind" episode of *CHiPs* in 1979. Later he returned to live in Dallas.

Case was on vacation in Truckee, California, when he collapsed and died on August 25, 1986, of a heart attack. He was 51. Divorced, he was survived by his daughter, mother and sister.

Allen Case Filmography

1973: *The Magician* (TV).
1977: *The Man from Atlantis* (TV).

Television Series

1959–1961: *The Deputy* as Clay McCord.
1965–1966: *The Legend of Jesse James* as Frank James.

Sources

Inman, David. *The TV Encyclopedia.* New York: Perigee, 1991.
Speed, F. Maurice. *The Western Film and Television Annual.* London: MacDonald, 1960.
Variety. August 1986.

MARY CASTLE

Mary Castle was born Mary Ann Noblett in Pampa, Texas, on January 22, 1931. She was originally a model, and it was a bathing suit photograph in a magazine which caught the eye of a talent scout for Columbia, who arranged to test her. When studio executives viewed her screen test, she was promptly signed to a contract and given her first screen role in 1950. She was originally signed with a view to grooming her to replace Rita Hayworth in case that star became temperamental. Although Castle did not supplant her, she did have a modestly successful career of her own.

When Kristine Miller left the syndicated Western television series *Stories of the Century,* Castle assumed the role under a diff-erent name. She played a beautiful undercover railroad detective who apprehends miscreants while working for Matt Clark (Jim Davis). Castle stayed with the series until the end, after which she resumed her movie career until 1960. She is reported to have married Edward Frezza in May 1971, and to reside in Los Angeles. Her studio biography listed her as having red-blonde hair, grey-green eyes and standing 5'6" tall.

Mary Castle Filmography

1948: *Mexican Hayride.*
1950: *The Tougher They Come.*
1951: *Texans Never Cry, Prairie Roundup, When the Redskins Rode, Criminal Lawyer.*
1952: *Eight Iron Men.*
1953: *Gunsmoke, The Lawless Breed, Three Steps to the Gallows* (released in the U.S. in 1955 as *White Fire*).
1956: *Crashing Las Vegas, Yaqui Drums.*
1957: *Last Stagecoach West.*
1960: *The Threat, The Jailbreakers.*

Television Series

1954–1955: *Stories of the Century* as Frankie Adams.

Sources

Picture Show Annual. London: Amalgamated Press, 1952 and 1956.
Ragan, David. *Who's Who in Hollywood.* New York: Facts on File, 1992.
Summers, Neil. *The Official TV Western Book Volume #2.* Vienna, WV: Old West Shop Publishing, 1989.

PEGGIE CASTLE

Warner Bros. was a studio renowned as much for imitation as for innovation. When *Gunsmoke* created a sensation in America, a few years later Warners cloned it with *Lawman* starring John Russell. After a season it was deemed advisable to have some strong feminine interest in the stories to make Dan Troop seem more human. The lady was a saloon owner named Lily Merrill. To play the part, an earthy but classy actress was needed. Warners may not have paid or treated their contract players well, but they were second to none when it came to finding talent. The actress who played the role was Peggie Castle, and to the part she brought a peaches and cream complexion, a knockout figure and a modicum of acting ability. The title of her first movie, of which she was not the focal point, summed her up: *When a Girl's Beautiful.* Peggie Castle was.

She was born Peggie Thomas Blair in Appalachia, Virginia, on December 22, 1926. The daughter of an affluent director of industrial rclations for a large company, she commenced her education at a private school in Pittsburgh, where she began acting in school plays. As a child she had a nomadic life because her father's job took him all over the place. In ten years she lived in no less than 14 cities. This possibly contributed to her problems later on. All this time her ambition never varied, for she wanted to be an actress. The family eventually moved to California where her father became studio manager of the Goldwyn Studios.

As a 14-year-old student at Hollywood High School, she won her first modeling assignment; during the summers she was an usherette at the Hollywood Bowl. Following graduation from high school in 1944, she enrolled at Mills College in Oakland where she majored in drama. She spent two years there, but after that the lure of the arc lights beckoned. She quit college when she won a role on a radio soap opera called *Today's Children* for which she was paid a princely salary of $375 a week. From there she went on to appear on other prestigious radio shows including *Lux Radio Theater.*

Her main ambition was to be a star of the silver screen. One day she was spotted dining in a restaurant by a talent scout from 20th Century–Fox and given a screen test. The test consisted of reading a scene from *Dinner at Eight*. Ironically, the actor whom she shared the test with was a promising contract player called John Russell. She passed the test and was awarded a contract with Fox. She did a bit in one movie, *Mr. Belvedere Goes to College* (1949). When she spontaneously snapped back at waspish star Clifton Webb, her outburst remained in the picture. She was seen by agent Charles Feldman, who arranged for her to be signed by Universal-International.

She was an item with Audie Murphy for a time and accompanied him on promotional trips for *The Kid from Texas* (1950) and *Sierra* (1950). He used his contacts at Universal to secure her her first proper acting roles. However, it was however on loanout to RKO Radio that she played the most important of her early acting roles, as one of Bette Davis's daughters in *Payment On Demand* (1951). She made eight movies at Universal and left there voluntarily in 1951 because she was dissatisfied over her roles.

She made her television debut and appeared on stage in the early 1950s with Groucho Marx in the play *Time for Elizabeth.* She freelanced throughout the decade, appearing for various studios and independent producers. She frequently essayed second leads in more prestigious films and leads in Poverty Row movies. She appeared in as many as six in one year. The films she made were of the escapist variety and divided into three genres: Westerns, thrillers and sci-fi potboilers.

Of the sci-fi potboilers, the most incredible was *Invasion USA* (1952), which starred a quintessential 1950s combination of Gerald Mohr and Castle in the role of Carla. This was produced by veteran schlockmeister Albert Zugsmith and concerned an alleged Russian invasion of the USA! Much of the 73 minute running time consisted of stock footage. The Westerns were generally an uninspiring bunch, but it is worth noting that she appeared for Roger Corman in *The Oklahoma Woman* (1956).

She did her most distinguished movie work in thrillers. She was in two films adapted from the works of Mickey Spillane, *I The Jury* (1953) and *The Long Wait* (1954). In the former she played Charlotte Manning, the fiancée of private eye Mike Hammer (Biff Elliot). She has ambitions to run a crime syndicate and at the end of the movie disrobes. She embraces Hammer while reaching for a hidden gun, and he blasts her in the stomach. "How could you?" she gasps. "It was easy," Hammer snarls in reply. She was also excellent in the film noir *99 River Street* (1953), in which she played the materialistic wife of boxer-turned-cab driver (John Payne). She leaves him for a more exciting boyfriend, but her disloyalty is rewarded with her murder. She went to England to appear in *The Counterfeit Plan* (1957) with Zachary Scott, and to Italy to appear in *The Seven Hills of Rome* (1958) opposite Mario Lanza.

In the early days of Warner Bros. television, she was extremely active guest-starring in episodes of *Cheyenne* and *77 Sunset Strip*. A 1957 episode of *Conflict* entitled "The Money," in which she and Andrew Duggan had the leads, was subsequently revamped and became the basis for the *Bourbon Street Beat* television series.

She shot a couple of busted pilots for television series, but then she joined the cast of the established Western series *Lawman.* She played Lily Merrill, owner of the Birdcage Saloon. A beautiful, strong, self-confident woman, she was introduced in the first episode of the second season of the series in 1959, appropriately entitled "Lily." This was the first time that she and John Russell had appeared together since the screen test ten years earlier, and they clicked. When comparisons were made between Kitty in *Gunsmoke* and Lily in *Lawman,* Warner Bros. personnel denied it. "It is only natural that the lead should have a girlfriend and the best place to put her is in the saloon."

Peggie Castle described Lily Merrill as being "a jolly friendly person with a heart as big as a bus." She continued, "Lily is a real character. She has a kind word and a smile for everyone. This leads some people to think that she's just a woman and not at all intelligent and shrewd. But when she wants to be she is as tough as Dan Troop." After four seasons, the lights dimmed in the Birdcage Saloon for the final time on October 2, 1962, with an episode called "Jailbreak."

It might have been assumed that she would use *Lawman* as a passport to continued television success, possibly in soap opera, but instead her own life began to assume the proportions of a soap opera. She never appeared in another movie, and her last recorded credit was an episode of *The Virginian* called "Morgan Starr" in 1966. Towards the end of *Lawman,* which had been one of the most professionally run of the Warner Bros. programs and one of the most popular, she had begun to drink heavily, boozing away her career. Whether it was because of a secret tragedy or broken romance is unknown. Within the space of a few years she became so hopelessly unprofessional and unpredictable in her behavior that the studio dropped her from contract. No casting director or producer would use her after that.

One day in 1969 a woman was driving around house-hunting in an area of Hollywood that had always held a fascination for her. It was in the hills above the legendary Sunset Strip where there was a panorama of the whole Los Angeles area and a person could see as far as Catalina Island. Another factor which favored the area was that she was especially friendly with a television actor who lived closeby with his wife and whose career was beginning to skyrocket.

A few blocks past his house, she saw a "For Sale" sign on a house which looked ideal. She stopped the car, climbed out and went up to the front door. As she knocked, the front door swung open. It was unlocked. The woman called out several times, but there was no reply. She stepped inside, but as she stood admiring some of the lavish furnishings, the unearthly silence convinced her that something was seriously wrong. As she moved forward, her eyes were drawn to the far side of the living room. As they roamed they took in the claret colored carpet, a shattered glass patio door and a bloodstained hand.

The woman had to escape from there and obtain help. She rushed back to her car and drove away, burning rubber. She made for the home of her actor friend, but found only his wife home. His wife phoned the studio for her husband, who arrived a short while later. The three headed back to the other house. When they arrived, the actor instructed the two women to wait at the door while he went inside to investigate. A couple of minutes elapsed before he reappeared and instructed his wife to phone for an ambulance immediately. While she made the call, he returned to the unconscious woman he had found and proceeded to stop the bleeding. The irony was that when he turned over the woman to administer first aid, he recognized her immediately as an actress he knew.

There was the wail of an approaching siren and soon the patient was being rushed to the UCLA Medical Center in West Los Angeles. One of the ambulance attendants told the actor that he had saved her life and that without him, she would have bled to death. The actor never told the actress of the day's near tragic events, while the actress had no recollection of them. The name of the actor was Chad Everett. The name of the actress was Peggie Castle.

While no record exists in the files of the Los Angeles Police Department of this incident, friends who knew her personal circumstances and the balance of her mind at the time have no doubts that she tried to commit suicide. She had been drinking heavily, taken an overdose of barbiturates and tried to slash her wrists. She sustained her most serious injuries when she fell headlong through the glass doors leading onto the patio. In time she recovered from all her injuries except alcoholism, which even a spell at Camarillo State Hospital did nothing to cure.

In 1945 at the age of 18, Peggie Castle married Los Angeles businessman Revis Call.

Under the name of Peggy Call she made her screen debut in *When a Girl's Beautiful.* She divorced Call in 1950. Then she married Robert H. Rains, a casting director at Universal-International, in Juarez, Mexico, on January 4, 1950. They separated on their third wedding anniversary and were divorced on April 29, 1954. In the same year she married assistant director William McGarry, with whom she had a daughter, but they divorced in 1970. In 1970 she married Arthur Morgenstern, who died in April 1973.

On the night of August 10, 1973, Peggie Castle was found dead by former husband McGarry in a squalid apartment above Hollywood Boulevard, a very far cry from the affluence in which she had once lived. Although the coroner's court initially declared that she died of natural causes, it was subsequently determined that cause of death was due to cirrhosis of the liver and a heart condition. She was 46 years old and survived by daughter Erin McGarry of Huntington Beach. Marc Lawrence recalls, "I directed 18 *Lawman* episodes. Peggie Castle was a pro. I never had any trouble with her, but I felt that she was an extremely unhappy gal."

Peggie Castle Filmography

1947: *When a Girl's Beautiful.*
1949: *Mr. Belvedere Goes to College.*
1950: *I Was a Shoplifter, Shakedown, Woman in Hiding, Buccaneer's Girl.*
1951: *Bright Victory, Payment on Demand, Air Cadet, The Prince Who Was a Thief, The Golden Horde.*
1952: *Invasion USA, Harem Girl, Wagons West.*
1953: *I The Jury, 99 River Street, Cow Country, Son of Belle Starr.*
1954: *The Long Wait, Jesse James' Women, The White Orchid, The Yellow Tomahawk, Overland Pacific, Southwest Passage.*
1955: *Finger Man, Target Zero, Tall Man Riding.*
1956: *Two Gun Lady, Miracle in the Rain, Oklahoma Woman, Quincannon—Frontier Scout.*
1957: *Beginning of the End, The Counterfeit Plan, Hell's Crossroads, Back from the Dead.*
1958: *The Seven Hills of Rome.*

Television Series

1959–1962: *Lawman* as Lily Merrill.

Sources

Ferguson, Ken. *Western Television and Film Annual.* London: Purnell, 1964.
Hogan, David. "Green Eyes Crying." *Filmfax* magazine, #47, Oct./Nov. 1994.
Picture Show Annual. London: Amalgamated Press, 1952.
Vitagliano, Dick. "Chad Everett Saves Actress from Bloody Suicide." *TV Radio Mirror* magazine, May 1971.
Woolley, Lynn, Robert W. Malsbary, and Robert G. Strange, Jr. *Warner Bros. Television.* Jefferson, NC: McFarland, 1985.

Note

Peggie Castle sometimes used the spelling "Peggy" on the credits of some episodes of television series.

PHIL CHAMBERS

This supporting actor had the regular role of Sgt. Miles Magruder, the most trusted and loyal of the disciples of John Singleton Mosby, in the Civil War series *The Gray Ghost.* Phil Chambers died at age 71 on January 16, 1993.

Phil Chambers Filmography

1953: *The Big Heat, Trouble Along the Way, Tumbleweed.*
1954: *Overland Pacific, The Bounty Hunter, Drums Across the River, Rogue Cop, Ricochet Romance, Pushover, Executive Suite.*

1955: *Rage at Dawn, Foxfire, Run for Cover.*
1956: *Backlash, A Day of Fury, The Mole People.*
1957: *Drango, Raintree County, Will Success Spoil Rock Hunter?*
1958: *Good Day for a Hanging.*
1959: *A Summer Place.*
1962: *Six Black Horses.*
1963: *For Love or Money.*

Television Series

1957: *The Gray Ghost* as Lieutenant St. Clair.

Sources

Brooks, Tim. *The Complete Directory to Prime Time TV Stars.* New York: Ballantine Books, 1987.
Films in Review magazine.

LON CHANEY, JR.

Lon Chaney, Jr., lived and died in the shadow of his father, the famous actor of silent films who specialized in grotesques. He was a fine performer in his own right, similar in looks and style to Ernest Borgnine or William Bendix. It was rather shortsighted of Hollywood not to make more of his talents. When the quality of material was high, as in *Of Mice and Men* and *The Wolf Man,* he acquitted himself well, but too often he appeared in inferior rehashes of classic horror films. Drink and illness plagued him in later life, but he was always interesting. *Last of the Mohicans,* a television series of the 1950s in which he appeared, was quite ambitious, and Chaney was convincing in the title role.

He was born Creighton Tull Chaney in Oklahoma City, Oklahoma, on February 10, 1904, son of Lon Chaney and his then-wife, singer Cleva Creighton. His father divorced his mother when the boy was ten in 1914. He won custody of the child and in 1915 wed Hazel Hastings. When Chaney's real mother attempted suicide, Chaney, Sr., lied to his son, telling him that she was dead. This subject caused considerable friction between them later. Chaney, Sr., was an unsuccessful actor for many years, touring in tent shows and rock-bottom stock companies. When he could not work as a hoofer in small shows, Chaney, Sr., worked as a stagehand. Subsequently the family relocated to Los Angeles because Chaney, Sr., heard that there was steady employment in motion pictures.

Chaney, Jr., attended Hollywood High School, an experience he did not enjoy, but during vacations he worked as a fruit picker. When he was rejected as a member of the school football team, he decided to do extra work in movie studios instead. Mentioning this to his father led to a rift. His father transferred him to Commercial Experts Training Institute, since Chaney, Sr., wanted his son to become a businessman with a sound education and career, instead of an actor. Meanwhile, Chaney, Jr., had other jobs such as working in a butcher's shop and at an abattoir. After finishing school, he became a boilermaker at the General Water Heater Corporation, eventually becoming a clerk there.

Lon Chaney, Sr., died at the height of his fame in 1930, age 47. Father and son had been estranged for years, although Chaney, Jr., attended the funeral. Chaney, Sr., left his son only a small inheritance, the balance of his fortune going to his second wife. Chaney, Jr., endured the monotony of his job for two years until a casting director friend persuaded producer David O. Selznick to sign him to a contract at RKO Radio for $200. He made his screen debut in a bit role in *Bird of Paradise* (1932). His first role of any substance was playing the lead in a western serial, *The Last Frontier* (1932). He used the name of Creighton Chaney, but studio executives wanted to rechristen him Lon Chaney, Jr. When he refused, he was dropped from contract.

His career for a long time after that followed a pattern of shooting a couple of quickies, landing a short-term contract and then being unemployed (which led to despair). To survive he did stuntwork. He hoped to equip himself better by enrolling in evening drama classes under an assumed name, but his teachers admitted that as a seasoned professional, they had little to teach him. In desperation in 1935 he finally changed his name to Lon Chaney, Jr., which eventually led to him being signed in 1937 by 20th Century–Fox. In January 1939, after playing bit parts, his contract was not renewed.

After a period of near starvation, he got the news that his agent had won him the chance to audition as Lennie in the West Coast stage production of John Steinbeck's *Of Mice and Men,* which had been a hit on Broadway. Five members of the original New York cast were set to appear in the Los Angeles production. The original Lennie, Broderick Crawford, had signed a movie contract and was therefore unable to appear, so a replacement was sought. Although Chany's reading was not good, the producer and star of the play, Wallace Ford, who played George, believed in Chaney and gave him the role. While he was not a stage-trained actor, Chaney rose each day to learn his lines and went to the theater at 2 P.M. to rehearse. After three weeks he practically knew the part backwards.

The play, which was staged at the El Captain Theater, was a success and Chaney was fine as the hulking Lennie. Later he was desperate to duplicate the role in the film version, which was to be directed by Lewis Milestone. Chaney himself, rather than his agent, went to Milestone and begged for the chance to test. Milestone was so astounded that he agreed. When Milestone was running tests for the other parts, he asked Chaney to read Lennie, assuring him he would have a separate test later. As Milestone recalled, "When it came time to test him, I didn't have to. I couldn't see anybody else in the part." *Of Mice and Men* (1939), which was released through United Artists, was a critical and commercial success in which Chaney earned the best notices of his career.

Universal Studios was riding the crest of the second big horror cycle started by the tremendous success of *Son of Frankenstein* (1939). They signed Chaney to a contract in 1941. During the five years he spent with them, his best film was the horror classic *The Wolf Man* (1941), in which he played Lawrence Talbot, who turns into a lycanthrope after being bitten by a werewolf. The makeup by Jack Pierce, direction by George Waggner and the eerie sequences, particularly on the moors, all combined to make this a big success. Chaney went on to play the Mummy, Dracula and the Frankenstein Monster. He made an oddly tubby Dracula and his Frankenstein Monster lacked Karloff's restrained and sympathetic approach. Many of his other films were pale imitations or sequels to the classic fantasies of the 1930s.

Chaney acquired a real life reputation as a hell-raiser, frequently drinking and battling with burly buddy Broderick Crawford. He also drank heavily with Wallace Ford and Lewis Milestone. He purchased a 1,300-acre ranch in California's Eldorado County which he farmed himself. Chaney starred in the *Inner Sanctum* series of film mysteries, based on a series of dime novels published by Simon and Schuster, with whom Universal had a deal. Although the premise was sound, the low budgets and lack of promotion began to undermine Chaney's career momentum. After the sixth segment of the series, *Pillow of Death* (1945), Chaney's contract was not renewed. His brawls had allegedly cost the studio thousands in trashed sets and dressing rooms, and they were glad to see the back of him.

Immediately afterward, Chaney accepted a role as Harry Brock, the junk king, in the national touring company of *Born Yesterday.* He returned to Hollywood in 1947 where he continued in a number of leading supporting roles. During the 1950s his talents were best utilized by producer Stanley Kramer, who used him in *High Noon* (1952), *Not as a Stranger* (1955) and *The Defiant Ones* (1958).

One of his more unusual assignments during this period was as the Indian Chingachgook in a Canadian television series, *Hawkeye and the Last of the Mohicans,* loosely derived from the novel by James Fenimore Cooper. This series was at best a marginal Western in that Chingachgook, chief of the Mohicans, and his best friend, the legendary scout and hunter Hawkeye, tried to keep peace on the Eastern frontier rather than out West.

The filming took place outside of Toronto, Canada. It was a black and white, half-hour syndicated series which lasted for 39 episodes. Although the series did not impress critics who believed that it was a low-budget travesty of the original novel, it was exciting and was rerun extensively for many years. While the two leading players got along famously off-screen, Chaney's drinking proved to be something of a problem, and it was said that all the serious work had to be done by noon if he was involved because he was useless after a liquid lunch. The series took a year to shoot and during this time, the actors lived in the same apartment building in Toronto.

During the late 1950s and early 1960s, Chaney traveled to many countries to shoot low-budget films. One of his most memorable television assignments was a *Route 66* Halloween episode entitled "Lizard's Leg and Owlet's Wing" in which the characters of the Mummy, the Wolf Man and the Frankenstein Monster were reprised. In the final decade of his career, he played bits and occasional leads in low-budget films.

In 1969 he revealed that for the previous five years he had been battling cancer of the throat (the same illness from which his father died). He was living in a small wooden house in Hollywood at the time and told reporters that he had both spent and given away the fortune he made in his heyday. He underwent an operation, but although he made a successful recovery, he was wracked by a whole series of other ailments including gout, beriberi and hepatitis and underwent surgery for cataracts in April 1973. Ironically, he died on Friday the 13th of July 1973, at age 69, at San Clemente, California. At the time of his death he was planning on touring in a stage revival of *Arsenic and Old Lace.*

In the late 1920s Lon Chaney, Jr., married Dorothy Hinckley, with whom he had two sons, Lon III and Ronald. They divorced in the middle 1930s, which under the California Community Property Laws wiped him out financially. In October 1937, in Colton, California, he wed former professional model Patsy Beck. Their marriage was considered to be one of Hollywood's happiest. She survived him as did his two sons, although both later died prematurely. Since his body was left for medical research, no funeral services were carried out.

Lon Chaney, Jr., Filmography

1931: *The Galloping Ghost* (serial).

1932: *Bird of Paradise, The Last Frontier* (serial).

1933: *Lucky Devils, Scarlet River, Son of the Border, The Three Musketeers* (serial).

1934: *Girl O' My Dreams, The Life of Vergie Winters, Sixteen Fathoms Deep.*

1935: *Captain Hurricane, Accent on Youth, Hold 'Em Yale, Shadow of Silk Lennox, The Marriage Bargain, Scream in the Night.*

1936: *Rose Bowl, Undersea Kingdom* (serial), *The Singing Cowboy, Killer at Large, The Old Corral, Ace Drummond* (serial), *Rhythm on the Range.*

1937: *Secret Agent X-9* (serial), *Midnight Taxi, Angel's Holiday, Wild and Woolly, Wife Doctor and Nurse, Cheyenne Rides Again, Love Is News, Love and Hisses, The Lady Escapes, One Mile from Heaven, This Is My Affair, City Girl, Second Honeymoon, That I May Live, Born Reckless, Thin Ice, Charlie Chan on Broadway, Slave Ship, Checkers, Life Begins in College.*

1938: *Mr. Moto's Gamble, Straight Place and Show, Walking Down Broadway, Alexander's Ragtime Band, Sally Irene and Mary, Passport Husband, Road Demon, Submarine Patrol, Speed to Burn, Happy Landing, Josette.*

1939: *Jesse James, Union Pacific, Frontier Marshal, Charlie Chan in the City of Darkness, Of Mice and Men.*

1940: *One Million B.C., North West Mounted Police.*

1941: *Billy the Kid, San Antonio Rose, Too Many Blondes, Badlands of Dakota, Man Made Monster, The Wolf Man, Riders of Death Valley* (serial).

1942: *The Ghost of Frankenstein, Overland Mail* (serial), *North to the Klondike, The Mummy's Tomb.*

1943: *Frankenstein Meets the Wolf Man, Eyes of the Underworld, Son of Dracula, Frontier Badman, Crazy House, Calling Dr. Death.*

1944: *Follow the Boys, Ghost Catchers, Weird Woman, Cobra Woman, The Mummy's Ghost, Dead Man's Eyes, The Mummy's Curse, House Of Frankenstein.*

1945: *Here Come the Coeds, The Frozen Ghost, House of Dracula, The Daltons Ride Again, Strange Confession, Pillow of Death.*

1947: *My Favorite Brunette.*

1948: *16 Fathoms Deep, Albuquerque, Abbott and Costello Meet Frankenstein, The Counterfeiters.*

1949: *There's a Girl in My Heart, Captain China.*
1950: *Once a Thief.*
1951: *Inside Straight, Only the Valiant, Flame of Araby, Behave Yourself!*
1952: *Bride of the Gorilla, Thief of Damascus, The Battles of Chief Pontiac, Springfield Rifle, High Noon, The Black Castle, The Bushwhackers.*
1953: *A Lion Is in the Streets, Raiders of the Seven Seas, Casanova's Big Night, Bandit Island* (short).
1954: *Jivaro, Passion, The Boy from Oklahoma, The Big Chase, The Black Pirates.*
1955: *Big House USA, I Died a Thousand Times, Not As a Stranger, The Indian Fighter, The Silver Star.*
1956: *Partners, Manfish, Indestructible Man, Daniel Boone—Trail Blazer, The Black Sleep.*
1957: *Cyclops.*
1958: *Money Women and Guns, The Defiant Ones.*
1959: *La Casa del Terror (*a.k.a. *Face of the Screaming Werewolf), The Alligator People, The Devil's Messenger.*
1961: *Rebellion in Cuba.*
1963: *The Haunted Palace, Law of the Lawless.*
1964: *Witchcraft, Stage to Thunder Rock, Young Fury.*
1965: *Black Spurs, House of the Black Death, Town Tamer, Apache Uprising, Spider Baby.*
1966: *Johnny Reno.*
1967: *Welcome to Hard Times, Hillbillys in a Haunted House, Dr. Terror's Gallery of Horrors.*
1968: *Buckskin.*
1969: *Fireball Jungle.*
1971: *Dracula vs. Frankenstein, The Female Bunch.*

Television Series

1956–1957: *Hawkeye and the Last of the Mohicans* as Chingachgook.
1966–1967: *Pistols 'n' Petticoats* as Chief Eagle Shadow.

Sources

Beck, Calvin. *Heroes of the Horrors.* New York: Collier, 1975.
Corneau, Ernest N. *The Hall of Fame of Western Film Stars.* North Quincy, MA: Christopher, 1969.
"I'm Broke, Says Lon." *Sunday Express* newspaper, 1969.
Ragan, David. *Movie Stars of the '40s.* Englewood Cliffs, NJ: Prentice-Hall, 1985.

HARRY V. CHESHIRE

Born in 1892, Harry V. Cheshire was nicknamed "Pappy." He was a veteran of radio and vaudeville before coming to the screen in 1940. His sole regular role on television was in *Buffalo Bill, Jr.,* in which he played the judge who adopts both Bill and his little sister Calamity. The Judge's name was Wiley, and the community in which they live and around which the adventures take place was called Wileyville after him. Harry Cheshire continued to appear in films until the early 1960s. He died on June 16, 1968, at age 76. He is buried at Forest Lawn Cemetery in Los Angeles.

Harry Cheshire Filmography

1940: *Barnyard Follies.*
1942: *Hi Neighbor.*
1943: *Swing Your Partner, O My Darling Clementine.*
1944: *Sing Neighbor Sing.*
1946: *It's a Wonderful Life, The Best Years of our Lives, Smooth as Silk, Child of Divorce, Affairs of Geraldine, Traffic in Crime, If I'm Lucky, Sioux City Sue, Drifting Along.*
1947: *It Happens Every Spring, Nightmare Alley, The Homestretch, The Hucksters, I Wonder Who's Kissing Her Now, The Invisible Wall, Shoot to Kill, Springtime in The Sierras, Sport of Kings, The Tender Years, The Flame, Her Husband's Affairs, The Pilgrim Lady, The Fabulous Tescan.*
1948: *Slippy McGee, Black Eagle, 16 Fathoms Deep, Incident, Moonrise, Adventures of Gallant Bess, For the Love of Mary, Racing Luck, Smoky Mountain Melody.*

1949: *The Lady Takes a Sailor, Bride for Sale, Ma and Pa Kettle, Anna Lucasta, Sand, Riders of the Whistling Pines, It Happens Every Spring, Miss Grant Takes Richmond, I Married a Communist, Fighting Man of the Plains, Brimstone, Chicago Deadline.*
1950: *Paid in Full, A Woman of Distinction, County Fair, Girls' School, The Woman on Pier 13, No Sad Songs for Me, Lucky Losers, Lonely Hearts Bandits, Chain Gang, The Arizona Cowboy, Square Dance Katy, September Affair.*
1951: *Blue Blood, Thunder in God's Country, Bannerline, Rhubarb, As Young As You Feel.*
1952: *Here Come the Nelsons, Phone Call from a Stranger, The Sniper, Dreamboat, Ma and Pa Kettle at the Fair, Flesh and Fury, Woman of the North Country.*
1954: *Phffft, Fireman Save My Child, Pride of the Blue Grass, Dangerous Mission.*
1955: *The Seven Little Foys.*
1956: *The Boss, The First Traveling Saleslady.*
1957: *Loving You, My Man Godfrey, Lure of the Swamp, The Restless Breed.*
1958: *The Big Country.*
1960: *From the Terrace, Heller in Pink Tights, Let's Make Love.*
1961: *The Errand Boy.*
1964: *The Patsy.*

Television Series

1955: *Buffalo Bill, Jr.*, as Judge Ben Wiley.

Sources

Summers, Neil. *The First Official TV Western Book.* Vienna, WV: Old West Shop Publishing, 1987.
Truitt, Evelyn Mack. *Who Was Who On Screen Illustrated Edition.* New York: Bowker, 1984.

TRISTRAM COFFIN

The star of the television series *26 Men* was born in Mammoth, Utah, on August 13, 1909. He had two brothers. His father was the superintendent at Mammoth Mines, a large silver mine. He attended high school in Salt Lake City, where he was raised. He started acting early in high school and became president of the drama club. By 1923 he was a juvenile at the Wills Theater in Salt Lake City. He subsequently played seasons in stock at Portland, Oregon, and Seattle, Washington, before returning to Salt Lake City. At the University of Utah he initially studied medicine, but abandoned this to study journalism at the University of Washington.

He was awarded a scholarship to the Empire School of Theater in Boston. He studied there and at the end of 12 months was appointed an instructor. In the early 1930s he was chosen chief staff announcer at WAB and WAC Radio Stations in Boston, where he also did some acting. He was heard by a scout from RKO Radio Pictures who brought him to Hollywood, made a test of him and signed him to a contract in 1939. He made his screen debut in *The Saint Strikes Back* (1939), which starred George Sanders.

When he was dropped by RKO, he freelanced. After Buck Jones died in 1942, the producers were going to revamp the "Rough Riders" series at Monogram with Tris Coffin in one of the lead roles, but he was drafted and served for three years in the armed forces instead. After the war he made many B Westerns, primarily as a handsome heavy. His best-remembered screen appearance was as Jeff King, the hero of the Republic chapterplay *King of the Rocket Men* (1949).

He shot 78 black and white, half-hour episodes of the television series *26 Men* (1957–1959). Although the series was a syndicated one, it was produced in conjunction with the ABC network, which eventually ran it on their prime time schedule. They were dramatized cases of the Arizona Rangers in which Coffin played the captain. The series was based on historical fact because in 1901 the Arizona Territorial Legislature had authorized an armed force consisting of one captain, one lieutenant, four sergeants and 20 privates to maintain law and order in the Arizona territory. There were 26 because that was all the state could afford. The series was shot in Phoenix and Tucson, Arizona, using a great deal of local talent.

Coffin did many personal appearances around the country to promote the series. He worked a ten- to 12-hour day, six days a week, on the series. His duties included doing many of his own stunts. When the original producer Russell Hayden grew tired of the series, he offered to turn the property over to Coffin and allow him to produce as well as star. The idea came apart when the network refused to sanction a switch to color. Even though he was aided by a photographic memory, Coffin found the work arduous and the series was discontinued.

Towards the end Coffin became disillusioned with the entertainment business, but financially he was secure and did not need to work. He died in obscurity at his home in Santa Monica, California, on March 28, 1990, of lung cancer, at age 80, survived by his widow.

Tristram Coffin Filmography

1939: *The Saint Strikes Back, Irish Luck, Oklahoma Terror, Overland Mail, Dick Tracy's G-Men* (serial).

1940: *Chasing Trouble, Arizona Frontier, Hidden Enemy, The Bowery Boy, Doomed to Die, Meet the Wildcat, The Green Hornet Strikes Again* (serial), *Queen of the Yukon, West of Pinto Basin, The Cowboy from Sundown, Rhythm of the Rio Grande, The Fatal Hour, Melody and Moonlight, On the Spot, Mysterious Dr. Satan* (serial).

1941: *Up in the Air, No Greater Sin, Father Steps Out, You're Out of Luck, Let's Go Collegiate, Arizona Bound, Sailors on Leave, King of Dodge City, Tonto Basin Outlaws, Roaring Frontier, Tuxedo Junction, Forbidden Trails, Wheel of Fortune, Holt of the Secret Service* (serial), *They Met in Bombay, Appointment for Love, Hard Guy, Sky Raiders* (serial), *Blossoms in the Dust, Top Sergeant Mulligan, A Man Betrayed.*

1942: *The Corpse Vanishes, Meet the Mob, Cowboy Serenade, Bells of Capistrano, Dawn on the Great Divide, A Tornado in the Saddle, Prairie Gunsmoke, Devil's Trail, Perils of Nyoka* (serial), *Spy Smasher* (serial), *A Tragedy at Midnight, Police Bullets, Lure of the Islands, Not a Ladies Man, Man with Two Lives* (voice).

1943: *Destroyer, Silver Skates, Bombardier, You Can't Beat the Law (*a.k.a. *Prison Mutiny), Cosmo Jones in Crime Smasher, Idaho, Hoppy Serves a Writ.*

1944: *Lady in the Dark, The Vigilantes Ride, Wyoming Hurricane.*

1945: *The Purple Monster Strikes* (serial; voice only).

1946: *Two Guys from Milwaukee, Dangerous Money, The Gentleman from Texas, The Invisible Informer, Mysterious Mr. Valentine, Sioux City Sioux, Rio Grande Raiders, Under Arizona Skies, Under Nevada Skies, The Gay Cavalier, The Brute Man, G.I. War Brides, Rendezvous With Annie, Shadows Over Chinatown* (voice).

1947: *Land of the Lawless, Valley of Fear, Blackmail, Louisiana, Trail to San Antone, Where the North Begins, The Fabulous Texan, Swing the Western Way, Jesse James Rides Again* (serial), *The Unfaithful, The Voice of the Turtle, Possessed.*

1948: *The Hunted; California Firebrand; Romance on the High Seas; The Gallant Blade; Desperadoes of Dodge City; Federal Agents vs Underworld, Inc.* (serial)*; The Shanghai Chest; Range Justice.*

1949: *The Fountainhead, Bruce Gentry, Daredevil of the Skies* (serial), *Crashing Thru, Desert Vigilante, Riders of the Dusk, King of the Rocket Men* (serial), *Radar Patrol vs. Spy King* (serial), *Lawless Code, My Dream Is Yours, Flamingo Road, Homicide, Angels in Disguise, Duke of Chicago.*

1950: *Pygmy Island, Outrage, Short Grass, The Baron of Arizona, Undercover Girl, The Old Frontier, Square Dance Katy, Pirates of the High Seas* (serial), *The Damned Don't Cry, The Big Hangover, Radar Secret Service.*

1951: *Painting the Clouds with Sunshine, On the Loose, The Lady Pays Off, According to Mrs. Hoyle, Northwest Territory, Buckaroo Sheriff of Texas, The Cimarron Kid, Rodeo King and the Señorita, Mask of the Avenger, The Fat Man, Rhubarb, Queen for a Day, I'll See You in My Dreams, Sirocco, Captain Video* (serial), *Disc Jockey, Indian Uprising, Flight to Mars* (voice).

1952: *Smoky Canyon, The Kid from Broken Gun, At Sword's Point, My Man and I.*

1953: *Combat Squad, Hannah Lee (*a.k.a. *Outlaw Territory), So This Is Love, I Love Melvin, Clipped Wings, Torpedo Alley* (voice), *Law and Order, Salome, City of Bad Men, Latin Lovers, The Eddie Cantor Story.*

1954: *Fireman Save My Child, Dawn at Socorro, A Star Is Born.*

1955: *Creature with the Atom Brain, The Scarlet Coat.*
1956: *Back from Eternity, The Man in the Gray Flannel Suit, The Maverick Queen, Three for Jamie Dawn, The First Traveling Saleslady.*
1957: *Last Stagecoach West, The Night the World Exploded.*
1958: *Kathy O'.*
1960: *Ma Barker's Killer Brood.*
1962: *The Silent Witness.*
1963: *The Crawling Hand.*
1964: *Good Neighbor Sam, Iron Angel.*
1965: *Zebra in the Kitchen.*
1971: *The Barefoot Executive, The Resurrection of Zachary Wheeler.*
1977: *Kino the Padre on Horseback.*

Television Series

1957–1959: *26 Men* as Captain Tom Rynning.

Sources

Goldrup, Tom, and Jim Waldrup. *Feature Players: The Stories Behind the Faces Volume #1.* Published privately, 1986.
Jarvis, Everett G. *Final Curtain: Deaths of Noted Movie and TV Personalities.* New York: Citadel, 1995.
McClure, Arthur F,. and Ken D. Jones. *Heroes, Heavies and Sagebrush.* South Brunswick and New York: Barnes, 1972.

Note

This actor is not the same person as the novelist and political commentator Tristram Coffin.

CHUCK CONNORS

Sportsmen have frequently become movie stars and have done well in certain genres, usually those relying on physical prowess. Some have sunk without a trace after one or two movies, while others have gone on to successful acting careers. One of the more successful was Chuck Connors. Connors was one of Hollywood's archetypal macho men: hard and handsome, with a comic strip hero's prominent jaw atop the well muscled 6'5" physique of a former professional athlete. To millions around the world his enduring fame rests on the television Western series *The Rifleman,* which ran for five years. He always insisted that typecasting as a result of *The Rifleman* series was fine with him. As he expressed it years later, "My whole ability to earn a living derives from that."

Offscreen Connors could be moody and cantankerous, particularly in later years. He said what he felt he should say and was never frightened of speaking out when he felt he was right. Indications are that his heart was basically in the right place. When actor Paul Fix was dying in a hospital, Connors was the only member of the cast who went to visit him regularly. "I've known Chuck Connors for years," said a close friend, "and I've noticed that he has a fear of being known as a softie. He goes out of his way to do things for people, and then he'll work twice as hard to prevent others from knowing it."

He was born Kevin Joseph Aloysius Connors in Bay Ridge, Brooklyn, New York, on April 10, 1921, the son of an Irish immigrant from Newfoundland. He was educated at Seaton Hall College, South Grange, New Jersey, where he first played baseball. "I didn't start out wanting to be an actor," he recalled. "I was crazy about sport and kinda big for my age, and I guess sport came natural to me." He proved to be an outstanding athlete.

He said that his life was greatly influenced by a man named John Flynn, a bank teller. "I was about 13 when this guy came into my life. I remember one afternoon while playing with a ball in the street, I saw these kids, a whole bunch of them, coming down the road carrying gloves, bats and baseballs. So I followed them and found out they called themselves the

Celtics. John Flynn ran the club and was like a father to them. John told me to grab a glove and take part in the game. I joined the club and the months that followed were just great. I treasure those memories very much. John really gave me an anchor. He worked and worked with me, and he had a tremendous influence on my life. He'd explain my mistakes and how to correct them, and he'd even help my dad get a job with the police force.

"In those days, 1935, jobs were scarce, and like a lot of families, we were in trouble, although my sister and I didn't realize it at the time. My dad had been out of a job for a long time. We were on relief and I guess I didn't know any better at the time. I certainly didn't realize how poor we really were. I was so used to it. And then one day it got home to me when another kid told me that I had a hole in my shoe. But my dad held onto the job that John got him from 1935 to 1960, when he retired."

Connors left school to join the army. He served for four years during World War II, primarily as a tank warfare instructor at West Point Military Academy. When he was discharged, he tried professional basketball with the Boston Celtics from 1946 to 1948. He switched to major league baseball for the Brooklyn Dodgers and Chicago Cubs. He caught the eye of fans as much for off-the-diamond clowning as his batting average. Transfer to the Pacific Coast League and the Los Angeles Angels put his name on the Hollywood circuit's party list. In 1952 when Spencer Tracy and Katherine Hepburn made *Pat and Mike* about a sportswoman's affair with her manager, real sportsmen were recruited for minor roles, giving Connors his debut as the police captain. "I had never trained or studied to become an actor," he recalled. "I just stood there in front of those cameras and did what came natural to me. A lot of my baseball player friends told me I was always a great actor on the field. They used to rib me a lot." Acting was an experience he enjoyed and eventually he decided to quit sports for a career in the movies and television. It was a decision he never regretted.

His career did not shoot into orbit until *The Rifleman* television series, which ran on ABC from 1958 to 1963 and was the top-rated new show in its first season. "I've just read your goddamn script," Connors announced to Arnold Laven, the producer of the series, "and I want to play that goddamn part. If anyone else plays it, it's goddamn unfair." Connors won the part. He played New Mexico homesteader Lucas McCain, raising a son by himself and battling villains with the aid of a Winchester rifle with a large ring that he cocked as he drew. According to the scripts, he could fire off a round in three-tenths of a second.

Although successful at first, the series began to decline in its third season. To counteract this, romantic interest in the form of storekeeper Miss Milly (Joan Taylor) arrived and stayed for two seasons. In the final season, hotel keeper Lou Mallory (Patricia Blair) served as the love interest. The series' real attraction, however, was the warmth of the relationship between Lucas and his son Mark (Johnny Crawford). Although violence was present, it was downplayed. Lucas tried to make a man of Mark, which gave him more credibility than many other Western heroes. In most episodes Mark learned something about life on his own or from his father, making the series both an adult Western and one with family appeal. It ended after 168 episodes in 1963.

After the success of *The Rifleman,* Connors appeared regularly on television. He played the part of criminal lawyer John Egan in the ABC series *Arrest and Trial* (1963–1964) with Ben Gazzara. From 1965 to 1966 he starred in the NBC series *Branded* as Captain Jason McCord, a man accused of cowardice in the 1880s. Dismissed from the army, he tried desperately to prove to society that he was a wronged man, but he soon discovered that a branded man was a outcast. His other television shows were *Cowboy in Africa* (1967–1968), *Thrill Seekers* (1972–1974), *The Yellow Rose* (1983–1984) and *Werewolf* (1987–1988). He also appeared regularly in the anthology series *Police Story* in the 1970s. Among his numerous guest-starring roles was a lustful slave owner Tom Moore in the *Roots* miniseries. He appeared on the stage in Chicago in the 1970s in *Mary, Mary* and *My Three Angels.*

Although he was seldom particularly well served by motion pictures, he did have a memorable role in William Wyler's majestic Western *The Big Country* (1958). He played Rafe, the son of Burl Ives. A particularly good scene had Connors and his gang of degenerate trick

Chuck Connors (bottom) with Johnny Crawford in *The Rifleman*.

riders harassing and threatening Gregory Peck in his buggy in a parody of Greek tragedy. In this film Connors showed a gift for sardonic one-liners. This surfaced again in Burt Kennedy's *Support Your Local Gunfighter* (1971), in which he played a sinister bald stranger who when asked where he is heading mutters, "Purgatory." One of the few times he was top-billed in a film was when he played the title role of *Geronimo* (1962), where he put on a brave show of being betrayed by American cavalrymen. His last major film appearance was the self-parodying role of a super-tough ex-army mechanic in the disaster spoof *Airplane II* (1982).

Connors was more flamboyant than the laconic heroes he created. During Soviet leader Brezhnev's 1973 visit to President Reagan's

"Western White House" in San Clemente, California, at a poolside party Connors swept the VIP off his feet and into a crushing bear-hug greeting before presenting him with a pair of ivory-handled Colt revolvers. Brezhnev was so touched that he sent Connors an antique samovar. A long-time Reagan friend and one of his celebrity supporters, Connors (despite pressure) rejected following Reagan's example and entering politics. "From being around so many of them, I became cynical about politicians in general," he admitted.

Unlike many of his contemporaries who had fallen by the wayside, Connors seemed to find no difficulty in obtaining employment in his later years (particularly in television) although his health began to decline. In 1986 he underwent hip surgery. He recovered and lived on an eight-acre ranch at Tehachapi. In October 1992, he was hospitalized with pneumonia. He complained of chest pains, so doctors X-rayed and spotted a deadly blocked coronary artery that needed to be unclogged immediately. Connors said, "They performed an angioplasty procedure right then at 4 A.M." Although he survived this, he was soon diagnosed as terminally ill with lung cancer at Bakersfield Hospital. The 71-year-old Connors was moved to Cedars Sinai Medical Center in Los Angeles, where he died on November 10, 1992. He had just been signed by ESPN for a new series, *American Shooter.*

Over 600 people attended services held at St. Charles Catholic Church in North Hollywood. One of his four sons spoke the eulogy while another sang his favorite song, "My Heroes Have Always Been Cowboys." Johnny Crawford, producer A. C. Lyles, agent Steve Stevens, Alex Cord and producer-director Arnold Laven all spoke. Celebrities attending included Sue Ane Langdon, Neil Summers, Denver Pyle, Leo Gordon, Lee Aaker, Dean Smith, Bob Totten, Michael Dante, Michael Wayne and stuntman Tony Epper (who often doubled Connors). Johnny Crawford told *Entertainment Tonight* following the memorial, "He would include me on camping trips with his sons. Chuck loved the outdoors. He was in many ways the person he played on *The Rifleman.*"

Chuck Connors was married and divorced three times. He was survived by four sons. In 1942 he married Betty Jane Riddle, a model, whom he divorced in 1961. With her he had four sons: Michael (born in 1943), Jeffrey (born in 1944), Steven (born in 1945) and Kevin (born in 1946). In 1963 he wed his *Geronimo* costar Kamala Devi, whom he divorced in 1972.

Chuck Connors Filmography

1952: *Pat and Mike.*
1953: *Trouble Along the Way, Code Two, South Sea Woman.*
1954: *Naked Alibi, Dragonfly Squadron, The Human Jungle.*
1955: *Target Zero, Good Morning Miss Dove, Three Stripes in the Sun.*
1956: *Hold Back the Night, Hot Rod Girl, Walk the Dark Street.*
1957: *Tomahawk Trail, Designing Woman, Death in Small Doses, Old Yeller, The Hired Gun, The Lady Takes a Flyer.*
1958: *The Big Country.*
1962: *Geronimo.*
1963: *Flipper, Move Over Darling.*
1965: *Synanon, Broken Sabre* (made up of episodes of *Branded*).
1966: *Ride Beyond Vengeance.*
1968: *Captain Nemo and the Underwater City, Kill Them All and Come Back Alone.*
1969: *The Profane Comedy (*a.k.a. *Set This Town on Fire)* (TV).
1970: *The Deserter.*
1971: *Support Your Local Gunfighter, The Birdmen* (TV).
1972: *Pancho Villa, Night of Terror* (TV), *Horror At 37,000 Feet* (TV), *Embassy, The Proud and the Damned, The Mad Bomber (*a.k.a. *Police Connection).*
1973: *Soylent Green, Police Story* (TV).
1974: *99 44/100ths Percent Dead, Wolf Larsen.*
1976: *Banjo Hackett* (TV), *Nightmare in Badham County* (TV).
1978: *Tourist Trap, The Night They Took Miss Beautiful* (TV), *Standing Tall* (TV).
1980: *Virus.*
1981: *Day of the Assassin, Red Alert West, Garden of Venus, The Capture of Grizzly Adams* (TV).
1982: *Target Eagle, Airplane II: The Sequel.*
1983: *The Vals.*
1985: *Rattlers, Spenser: For Hire* (TV), *Sakura Killers.*
1986: *Balboa, Summer Camp Nightmare.*
1987: *Werewolf* (TV), *Once Upon a Texas Train* (TV), *Terror Squad.*

1988: *Kill and Enjoy (*a.k.a. *Mania), Trained to Kill, Hell's Heroes, Taxi Killer.*
1989: *Skinheads, Jump, High Desert Kill* (TV).
1990: *Critical Action.*

Television Series

1958–1963: *The Rifleman* as Lucas McCain.
1963–1964: *Arrest and Trial* as John Egan.
1965–1966: *Branded* as Jason McCord.
1967–1968: *Cowboy in Africa* as Jim Sinclair.
1972–1974: *Thrill Seekers*—host/narrator.
1983–1984: *The Yellow Rose* as Jeb Hollister.
1987–1988: *Werewolf* as Janos Skorzeny.

Miniseries

1977: *Roots.*

Sources

The Annual Obituary. Detroit, MI: St. James Press, 1992.
Ferguson, Ken. *Television Stars.* London: Purnell, 1966.
Usher, Shaun. *Daily Mail* newspaper. November 1992.
Variety. November 1992.
Western Clippings magazine. November 1992.

PAT CONWAY

Pat Conway was born in Beverly Hills, California, on January 9, 1930, the son of director Jack Conway and his wife Virginia Bushman. He was the grandson of the famed silent screen star Francis X. Bushman. He spent his childhood on his father's 125-acre ranch in the Pacific Palisades section of Los Angeles. By the age of ten, he knew how to rope and ride and was proficient at tending his father's 150 Angus Cattle. Some accounts of his life state that he appeared in films directed by his father, but this appears to be fiction since he did not make his screen debut until long after his father had retired. He once acted in Shakespeare at the Old Vic in England and studied for a year at the Pasadena Playhouse. Briefly under contract at MGM, Conway got larger parts in the 1950s until he was cast in the lead of Clay Hollister in the series *Tombstone Territory* (1957–1960).

The turbulent history of Tombstone, Arizona, towards the end of the last century was brought to life on the small screen in this series. Every episode of the series was taken from the files of the *Tombstone Epitaph,* the oldest weekly newspaper in the Southwest. Conway was the sheriff and the strong arm of the law, but he received little backing from local businessmen who wanted Tombstone to remain a wide open town so that they could become rich quickly. Richard Eastham played Hollister's sole ally, Harris Claibourne, crusading editor of the *Epitaph.*

The ABC series was produced by Ziv-United Artists Television, made its debut on October 16, 1957, and had its last network showing on October 9, 1959. In a highly unusual situation, new episodes of the series were filmed and shown in syndication after the show stopped being shown on network television. There were 91 half-hour black and white episodes filmed of what was one of the best second-league Western series. Suspense was extremely well generated and maintained. Conway was a highly individualistic actor with an intense style which enhanced the suspense.

A determined bachelor, he lived alone in a small rented house deep in the Hollywood Hills. About himself he said, "I'm a solitary individual. I enjoy being alone. I read a great deal, mainly historical novels, and I love music. Then I have my 23-foot ketch which I keep at Balboa and I go out sailing most weekends. Sometimes I take a friend along, but mostly I go alone." With an eye to the future, he had a manager to handle his financial affairs. One of his interests was a resort motel at Palm Springs which he owned in partnership with Hugh O'Brian, Dennis Weaver and Carolyn Jones.

Conway's name faded very rapidly from the limelight when his series ended. One reason was because he did not employ a press agent to provide him with publicity. The other was because he was an alcoholic who consumed liquor in vast quantities even when he was working, which played havoc with his appearance and career. Two of his last recorded acting roles were in "The Bullet" (1972) and "Endgame" (1975) episodes of the crime series *The Streets of San Francisco.* Pat Conway died prematurely in Santa Barbara, California, in 1981, at age 51.

Pat Conway Filmography

1951: *Westward the Women.*
1952: *Invitation.*
1953: *Above and Beyond.*
1955: *An Annapolis Story.*
1956: *Flight to Hong Kong, Screaming Eagles.*
1957: *Destination 60,000, Undersea Girl (*a.k.a. *Crime Beneath the Sea), The Deadly Mantis.*
1962: *Geronimo.*
1967: *Brighty of the Grand Canyon.*

Television Series

1957–1960: *Tombstone Territory* as Sheriff Clay Hollister.

Pat Conway in *Tombstone Territory.*

Sources

Correspondence between Richard Eastham and the author.
Speed, F. Maurice. *The Western Film and TV Annual.* London: MacDonald, 1960.
Woman's Day. "Looks at TV" article, undated.

JACKIE COOGAN

Jackie Coogan established two distinct personalities. As a child his appearance was marked by enormous brown eyes and a Dutch bob haircut which became his trademark. An expressive, natural mimic, Coogan also possessed a total lack of self-consciousness before the camera. As an adult character actor, he became instantly identifiable as grotesque Uncle Fester in the creepy television comedy series *The Addams Family.* In between he did a considerable amount of television work, including a Western series of the 1950s called *Cowboy G Men.*

Jackie Coogan was born John Leslie Coogan in Los Angeles on October 26, 1914, the son of John Henry Coogan, a vaudeville dancer, and Lillian Rita Dolliver, a hoofer and comedienne known as "Baby Lillian Dolliver." He had one younger brother, Robert (1924–1978), with whom he remained good friends. He allegedly made his first professional appearance accidentally during the summer of 1916 when he wandered onstage at Keith's Riverside in New York while his parents were performing. By the age of four, he was a regular part of their act.

The child was four-and-a-half when Sid Grauman took Charlie Chaplin to Los Angeles Orpheum Theater. Chaplin had been searching for a young boy to use in his new film. He watched Coogan, Sr., do his eccentric dancing act, but at the close he brought on his son, who did a couple of dances which utterly captivated the audience. Chaplin became despondent when he heard that Roscoe "Fatty" Arbuckle had signed Coogan to appear in a movie, but it turned out that Arbuckle had signed the father. Chaplin was able to sign the son the following night.

The Kid (1921) was the film which Chaplin wrote, directed and costarred in with Coogan. It took over a year to shoot, but the result was well worthwhile. In it Chaplin played a likable tramp who picks up an abandoned child (Coogan), learns to love him, but ultimately relinquishes him for the child's own good. Coogan immediately won the hearts of audiences everywhere, and the result was one of Chaplin's most acclaimed films.

Coogan became a top motion picture star with his own production company helmed by his father and a major promotional campaign which saw him advertising and endorsing numerous products. Most of his subsequent films were produced by his father with Sol Lesser as executive producer. His most successful films were released by First National in the three years that followed. He was earning $22,500 per week, from which he received a $6.25 weekly allowance from his parents. By 1924 he had earned at least $2,000,000 from his movies which his father, a canny businessman, had succeeded in doubling through shrewd investments. The same year Coogan signed a contract with MGM, where he continued to make silent films through 1927. He was paid $500,000 merely for inking the contract. His film *Long Live the King* cost over $1,000,000 to make and was considered the most expensive film up to that time. He earned a further $1,000,000 for four pictures. In the summer of 1924 he led a cross-country and transatlantic "Children's Crusade" which raised $35,000,000 worth of food and clothing to assist the children rendered homeless by the Turkish-Greek war of 1922.

During 1930–1931 he appeared in *Tom Sawyer* and *Huckleberry Finn,* but by this stage his vogue had passed. Walter Winchell ran an item in his column to the effect that when a guest in the Coogan home was told by the star's mother that her son was studying with a private tutor, he said to her, "Don't ever teach him arithmetic because someday he's going to wonder where all of his money has gone to." Educated privately until high school, Coogan left the industry to attend Urban Military Academy, and he later studied at Villanova College and the University of Southern California.

In 1935 his father and three others (including young star Junior Durkin) were all killed in a car crash. Jackie Coogan, who was driving, was hurt and was the only survivor. When he came of age to collect the millions he had earned as a child, his mother and Arthur Bernstein, the business manager who subsequently became his stepfather, refused to part with the scant $600,000 which was all that remained. In 1938 he sued both of them for a financial accounting of his earnings over the years. He claimed that when he turned 21, he had been disinherited with only $1,000 and told he could expect no further money. His mother insisted that the law was on her side and that she had the right to all of her son's earnings over the years. The lawsuit dragged on for months amidst an avalanche of publicity. In August 1939, a settlement was reached for $126,000, a small fraction of his original earnings.

The upshot was that the California State Legislature instituted what was formally titled the Child Actors' Bill (known in show business circles as the Coogan Act), which is designed to prevent the exploitation of child actors and provides that at least 20 percent of a minor's earnings be placed in trust funds or long term insurance policies. When the actors reach the age of 21, they are entitled to the proceeds. It is an extremely complicated piece of legislation, but former child star Paul Petersen and the Screen Actors Guild Young Performers Committee are currently doing invaluable work in tracking down one-time child performers who had money placed in trust for them, but who have hitherto failed to claim it. Some of them have not even known that the money was in trust for them.

Jackie Coogan appeared in a few B films during the late 1930s; made a vaudeville tour with Betty Grable, who became his first wife; toured with his own company in *What a Life;* was in *Brother Rat* in New York for seven months; played summer stock; and acted in *Take Me Along* in Buffalo. During World War II he spent nearly five years in the army. He enlisted in the infantry, but was later transferred to the Air Corps (initially as a glider instructor, later as a member of Phil Cochran's First Air Commandos which flew into Burma). Two weeks after his discharge in 1946 he returned to Hollywood where he did an act burlesquing *The Kid* (Coogan dressed as his child self with Ben Blue playing Chaplin). It ran at Slapsie Maxie's nightclub for months. Someone had the bright idea of teaming him and another once-popular child star (Jackie Cooper) in a series of films, but this did nothing to revive either of their careers.

During the embryo days of television, Coogan joined the cast of Irwin Allen's *Hollywood Merry-Go-Round* and was a regular on *Pantomime Quiz*. In 1954 cowboy star Russell Hayden and Henry Donovan were producing a juvenile Western series called *Cowboy G Men* which Hayden starred in. Set in the 1870s, it was based on an idea by Donovan, centering around two undercover agents working for the government. An idea which originated in this series was to have one of them arrive in town ahead of the other. Coogan was hired to play Stoney Crockett. Some regard this as a forerunner to *The Wild Wild West* television series with Coogan in the Ross Martin role. This was a syndicated half-hour black and white series which proved very popular largely because of the unstinting efforts of Hayden and Coogan to barnstorm the country publicizing it. The series lasted through 39 episodes until 1955.

Coogan continued to play bits on television and film. Frequently his movies were of the low-budget or exploitation variety. He had gained considerable weight by this time. He costarred in the shortlived sitcom *McKeever and the Colonel* (1962–1963). During the late 1950s and early 1960s, Coogan was arrested and charged on several occasions for possession of marijuana and the stories were carried in all the newspapers.

He regained his confidence and self-respect, along with some financial stability, when he was chosen to play fat and bald Uncle Fester in the hit comedy series *The Addams Family*, which turned out to be the biggest success of his later career. For the rest of his career he earned between $50,000 and $60,000 annually guest-starring in various television series. In 1972 he was reunited with Charlie Chaplin when the latter returned to the United States

Portrait of Jackie Coogan, who appeared in *Cowboy G Men*.

from his Swiss home to receive an honorary Academy Award. After his retirement in the late 1970s, Coogan resided in Palm Springs with a second home in La Paz, Baja, California.

Coogan, 69, died from cardiac arrest on March 1, 1984, at Santa Monica Hospital. He had been hospitalized for the previous two months and had been in and out of hospitals for the previous six years with a heart condition and kidney problems. He is buried at Holy Cross Cemetery and Mausoleum, Culver City, California.

He married Betty Grable at St. Brendan's Catholic Church in Los Angeles on November 20, 1937. His insolvency led to their divorce in Los Angeles on October 11, 1939. He married showgirl Flower Parry in Gardnerville, Nevada, on August 10, 1941. Son Anthony was born in Los Angeles on March 4, 1942. Flower was granted a divorce in Los Angeles on June 29, 1942, on the grounds of mental cruelty, and awarded custody of their son. On December 26, 1946, Coogan married singer Anne McCormack in Los Angeles. They had a daughter Joan, born in Los Angeles on April 2,

1948. He also became the stepfather of the actor Don Stroud. They were finally divorced in Los Angeles on September 20, 1951, with McCormack being awarded custody of their daughter. In April 1952, Coogan married dancer Dodie Lamphere in Mexico City, but the details were only made public in July 1953. Their daughter Leslie was born in 1953 and their son Christopher was born on July 9, 1967.

Jackie Coogan Filmography

1916: *Skinner's Baby.*
1919: *A Day's Pleasure.*
1921: *The Kid, Peck's Bad Boy.*
1922: *My Boy, Oliver Twist, Trouble.*
1923: *Daddy, Circus Days.*
1924: *Long Live the King, A Boy of Flanders, Little Robinson Crusoe, The Rag Man.*
1925: *Johnny Get Your Gun, Old Clothes.*
1926: *Johnny Get Your Haircut.*
1927: *The Bugle Call, Buttons.*
1930: *Free And Easy* (guest), *Tom Sawyer.*
1931: *Huckleberry Finn.*
1935: *Home on the Range.*
1938: *College Swing.*
1939: *Million Dollar Legs, Sky Patrol.*
1947: *Kilroy Was Here.*
1948: *French Leave.*
1951: *Skipalong Rosenbloom, Varieties on Parade.*
1952: *Outlaw Women.*
1953: *The Actress, Mesa of Lost Women.*
1956: *The Proud Ones.*
1957: *The Buster Keaton Story, The Joker Is Wild, Eighteen and Anxious.*
1958: *High School Confidential!, Lonelyhearts, No Place to Land, The Space Children.*
1959: *Night of the Quarter Moon, The Big Operator, The Beat Generation.*
1960: *Sex Kittens Go to College, Platinum High School, Escape from Terror.*
1964: *John Goldfarb Please Come Home.*
1965: *Girl Happy.*
1966: *A Fine Madness.*
1968: *The Silent Treatment, Rogue's Gallery, The Shakiest Gun in the West.*
1969: *Marlowe.*
1972: *Cool Million* (TV).
1973: *Cahill United States Marshal.*
1974: *The Phantom of Hollywood* (TV).
1975: *The Manchu Eagle Murder Caper Mystery; Won Ton Ton, the Dog Who Saved Hollywood; The Specialists* (TV).
1976: *Sherlock Holmes in New York* (TV).
1979: *Human Experiments.*
1980: *Dr. Heckyl And Mr. Hype.*
1982: *The Escape Artist.*
1983: *The Prey.*

Television Series

1954–1955: *Cowboy G Men* as Stoney Crockett.
1962–1963: *McKeever and the Colonel* as Sgt. Barnes.
1964–1966: *The Addams Family* as Uncle Fester

Sources

Cox, Stephen. *The Addams Chronicles.* New York: Harper Perennial, 1991.
Dye, David. *Child and Youth Actors: Filmographies of Their Entire Careers, 1914–1985.* Jefferson, NC: McFarland, 1988.
McDonald, Archie P. *Shooting Stars.* Bloomington and Indianapolis: Indiana University Press, 1987.
Parish, James Robert. *Great Child Stars.* New York: Ace, 1976.
Willis, John. *Screen World.* New York: Crown, 1985.

RICHARD COOGAN

Richard Coogan was born in Short Hills, New Jersey, on April 14, one of two children. He acquired experience on radio in such programs as *Young Doctor Malone* and also appeared on Broadway during the 1940s. Coogan reached potential stardom when he was the original choice to play the kiddie space hero Captain Video in the series *Captain Video*

Richard Coogan cradles the head of an ailing costar for an episode of *The Californians,* while director Sean McClory looks on.

and His Video Rangers by the Dumont Television Network in 1949. The series was so successful that it went from being a quarter-hour show five days a week to half an hour almost overnight. When Dumont began talking about merchandising, Coogan (fearing typecasting) wanted a percentage of the profits, whereupon he was rapidly replaced by Al Hodge. Ironically, this was probably a lucky break for Coogan because Hodge became virtually unemployable after playing the part.

Coogan appeared in a few feature films. For several years during the 1950s he played a lawyer turned FBI agent in the daytime soap opera *Love of Life* until his character was killed in an aircrash. His best chance came when he was chosen to replace Adam Kennedy in the NBC television Western series *The Californians,* which was set in San Francisco at the peak of the Gold Rush. He arrived part way through the first season as Matt Wayne. Initially Wayne was elected sheriff, but by the second season he had become city marshal, assisted by a newly formed 50-man police force. His love interest was Wilma Fansler (Carole Mathews), a young widow who ran the local saloon. This appeared to be rather a blatant attempt to copy *Gunsmoke,* but there was room for only one Matt on television and it was Dillon rather than Wayne, so the series was sent to Boot Hill after the second season.

From 1960 to 1962 Coogan made several appearances in Western television series such as *Bonanza, Bronco, Cheyenne* and *Laramie.* He also made a return to daytime soap operas in the unsuccessful *Clear Horizon,* which focused on the lives of astronauts and their families stationed at Cape Canaveral, Florida. Coogan himself later became a professional golfer and at last report was residing in Los Angeles.

Richard Coogan Filmography

1954: *Three Hours to Kill.*
1956: *The Revolt of Mamie Stover.*
1960: *Vice Raid.*
1961: *Girl on the Run.*

Television Series

1949–1950: *Captain Video and His Video Rangers* as Captain Video.
1951–1956: *Love of Life* as Paul Raven.
1957–1959: *The Californians* as Marshal Matt Wayne
1960–1962: *Clear Horizon* as Mitchell Corbin.

Sources

Brooks, Tim. *The Complete Directory to Prime Time TV Stars 1946–Present.* New York: Ballantine Books, 1987.
Inman, David. *The TV Encyclopedia.* New York: Perigee, 1991.
Summers, Neil. *The First Official TV Western Book.* Vienna, WV: Old West Shop Publishing, 1987.

ELLEN CORBY

Ellen Corby was born Ellen Hansen in Racine, Wisconsin, on June 3, 1911, of Danish parents. Her parents separated when she was a child, so she moved with her mother to Philadelphia. She entered amateur talent contests as a youngster and later danced in the chorus of an Atlantic City nitery. Then she gravitated to Hollywood in the early 1930s, determined to be a screen actress. Although she played a few bits, she was sidetracked for 12 years as a script girl at various studios and later as a script supervisor at RKO Radio because it gave her a steady income. She cowrote the screenplay of *Twilight on the Trail* for Paramount in 1941.

Her final chore in this capacity was *Murder My Sweet* (1944), which starred Dick Powell. He was instrumental in getting her started as an actress again by casting her in a bit as a French maid in the tough film noir *Cornered* (1945). She studied drama at the Actors' Lab, and when she was cast in the play *Liliom* there, she sent notes to 50 producers and directors she had worked with in her previous job. Some of them came and hired her.

Her demeanor and physical features made her ideal for character roles. Another of these producers, Harriet Parsons, cast Corby in her most notable role as Aunt Trina in *I Remember Mama* (1948), for which she received an Academy Award nomination as Best Supporting Actress. This remains her favorite role. From the mid–1950s onwards she was very active in television. She had a semi-regular role as Henrietta Porter, editor of the Porter, Texas, newspaper, in the Western series *Trackdown.* Most of her other work was overshadowed by her outstanding portrayal of Grandma on *The*

Waltons, for which she received Emmy Awards as Best Supporting Actress in a Drama Series in 1973, 1975 and 1976. In 1976 she suffered a serious stroke and was forced to withdraw from the series for 18 months. She returned for a while in 1978, but her precarious state of health forced her out of the regular series in 1979. She was, however, present for the *Waltons* reunions of the early 1980s.

At last report she was residing in a house in West Hollywood. She authored a novel, *The Pebble Of Gibraltar,* which was published in 1988. She married Francis Corby, a cameraman for Hal Roach, but divorced in 1944.

Ellen Corby and Robert Culp in *Trackdown.*

Ellen Corby Filmography

1933: *Twisted Rails, Little Women.*
1941: *Twilight on the Trail.*
1945: *Cornered.*
1946: *The Dark Corner, From This Day Forward, It's a Wonderful Life, Bedlam, The Locket, In Old Sacramento, Till the End of Time, The Scarlet Horseman* (serial), *Cuban Pete, Crackup, Sister Kenny, Lover Come Back, The Truth About Murder, The Spiral Staircase.*
1947: *Hal Roach Comedy Carnival (*a.k.a. *The Fabulous Joe), Beat the Band, Forever Amber, Railroaded!, Born to Kill, They Won't Believe Me, Driftwood, The Bachelor and the Bobby Soxer.*
1948: *Strike It Rich, I Remember Mama, Fighting Father Dunne, The Dark Past, The Noose Hangs High, If You Knew Susie, I Jane Doe.*
1949: *Little Women, Mighty Joe Young, Rusty Saves a Life, The Judge Steps Out, A Woman's Secret, Madame Bovary, Captain China.*
1950: *Harriet Craig, The Gunfighter, Caged, Peggy, Edge of Doom, Ma and Pa Kettle Go to Town.*
1951: *Goodbye My Fancy, Angels in the Outfield, Here Comes the Groom, The Mating Season, The Sea Hornet, The Barefoot Mailman, On Moonlight Bay.*
1952: *Monsoon, The Big Trees, Fearless Fagan.*
1953: *The Woman They Almost Lynched, Shane, The Vanquished, A Lion Is in the Streets.*
1954: *About Mrs. Leslie, The Bowery Boys Meet the Monsters, Sabrina, Susan Slept Here, Untamed Heiress.*
1955: *Illegal.*
1956: *Slightly Scarlet, Stagecoach to Fury.*
1957: *The Seventh Sin, Night Passage, God Is My Partner, Rockabilly Baby, All Mine to Give.*
1958: *Macabre, Vertigo, As Young As We Are.*
1960: *Visit to a Small Planet.*
1961: *Pocketful of Miracles, Saintly Sinners.*
1963: *The Caretakers, 4 for Texas.*
1964: *Hush ... Hush, Sweet Charlotte, The Strangler.*
1965: *The Family Jewels.*
1966: *The Ghost and Mr. Chicken, The Night of the Grizzly, The Glass Bottom Boat.*
1967: *The Gnome-Mobile.*
1968: *A Fine Pair, The Legend of Lylah Clare.*
1969: *A Quiet Couple* (TV), *Angel in My Pocket.*
1971: *A Tattered Web* (TV), *Support Your Local Gunfighter, The Homecoming* (TV).

1972: *Napoleon and Samantha.*
1974: *The Story of Pretty Boy Floyd* (TV).
1982: *A Day for Thanks on Walton's Mountain* (TV), *Mother's Day on Walton's Mountain* (TV), *A Wedding on Walton's Mountain* (TV).

Television Series

1958–1959: *Trackdown* as Henrietta Porter.
1965–1967: *Please Don't Eat the Daisies* as Martha O'Reilly.
1972–1979: *The Waltons* as Esther (Grandma) Walton.

Sources

Contemporary Theater, Film and Television Volume 9. Detroit, MI: Gale Research Inc., 1991.
Inman, David. *The TV Encyclopedia.* New York: Perigee, 1991.
Lamparski, Richard. *Whatever Became Of? Eleventh Series.* New York: Crown, 1989.
Parish, James Robert. *Hollywood Character Actors.* New Rochelle, NY: Arlington House, 1978.
Quinlan, David. *Illustrated Directory of Film Character Actors.* London: Batsford, 1995.

ROBERT CORNTHWAITE

Robert Cornthwaite was born in St. Helens, Oregon, on April 28, 1917, the son of storekeeper Henry Cornthwaite and his wife, Bessie Eva Graham. He has one older brother. His stage debut was made at the Portland Civic Theater in Portland, Oregon, in July 1935, as Fabian in *Twelfth Night.* His family relocated to California in 1935. He was educated at the University of Southern California, where he graduated Phi Beta Kappa in 1937 with a B.A. degree. Then he worked in radio. His career was interrupted by war service for four years. While serving in the U.S. Army Air Force, he held the rank of sergeant and was awarded the Bronze Star.

When he was honorably discharged from the forces in 1947, he became a radio announcer, but quit when he decided he wanted to be a character actor instead. He made his screen debut as an ambulance driver in *Union Station* (1950). His most memorable film appearance was as Dr. Carrington in the classic sci-fi *The Thing from Another World* (1951). Although the film was a success, initially it did little to further his career because his agent began to demand too much for his services, so he did not work again for nearly a year. With the studio system about to collapse, he turned to television. His television debut came in an episode of the George Raft crime series *I Am the Law* in 1952. He has since appeared in numerous other series, including *Gunsmoke, Lawman, Maverick* and *Wagon Train.* He had the semi-regular role of John James Audubon, the real-life naturalist and artist friend of the hero, in *The Adventures of Jim Bowie.* More recently he was to be found playing Howard Buss in the television series *Picket Fences.*

He made his Broadway debut as Andie in *And a Nightingale Sang* at the Newhouse Lincoln Center in November 1983. His other major stage appearances have been in *Cymbeline* in Hartford, Connecticut, in 1981; in *Mary Stuart* in Los Angeles in 1981; and *The Visions of Simone Marchard* at the La Jolla Playhouse, California, in 1983. He also wrote the play *The Blue* in 1980. He is one actor who prefers the theater because he is more in control.

Among other attributes, he is a fluent speaker of French, German and Italian.

Robert Cornthwaite Filmography

1950: *Union Station, Gambling House.*
1951: *The Thing from Another World, Mark of the Renegade, His Kind of Woman.*
1952: *Something to Live For, Monkey Business.*
1953: *The War of the Worlds.*
1954: *Day of Triumph.*
1955: *Stranger on Horseback, Kiss Me Deadly, The Purple Mask.*
1956: *On the Threshold of Space, The Leather Saint.*

1957: *Hell on Devil's Island, The Spirit of St Louis.*
1959: *Day of the Outlaw, Ten Seconds to Hell.*
1961: *All Hands on Deck.*
1962: *What Ever Happened to Baby Jane?, Reptilicus* (voice only).
1966: *The Ghost and Mr. Chicken.*
1967: *Waterhole #3, The Ride to Hangman's Tree.*
1968: *The Legend of Lylah Clare.*
1969: *Colossus—The Forbin Project.*
1971: *The Peacekillers, Two on a Bench* (TV).
1972: *Journey Through Rosebud, Killer by Night* (TV), *The Longest Night* (TV).
1973: *The Devil's Daughter* (TV), *The Six Million Dollar Man* (TV).
1976: *Futureworld.*
1979: *Love's Savage Fury* (TV).
1983: *Deal of the Century, Dr. Detroit.*
1987: *Disorderlies, Who's That Girl?*
1989: *Time Trackers.*
1992: *Matinee.*
1995: *White Dwarf* (TV).

Television Series

1956–1958: *The Adventures of Jim Bowie* as John James Audubon.
1992–1996: *Picket Fences* as Howard Buss.

Sources

Contemporary Theater, Film and Television Volume I. Detroit, MI: Gale Research Inc., 1982.
Weaver, Tom. *They Fought in the Creature Features: Interviews With 23 Classic Horror, Science Fiction and Serial Stars.* Jefferson, NC: McFarland, 1995.

LLOYD CORRIGAN

Lloyd Corrigan was born in San Francisco, California, on October 16, 1900, the son of actress Lillian Elliott (1875–1959). He was educated at Hollywood High School and the University of California. He was on stage at seven and appeared in stock at Phoenix, Arizona, during his university days. Immediately after graduation he entered films as an actor in 1924. From 1926 to 1930 and occasionally thereafter he worked as a screenwriter. From 1930 to 1938 he was a movie director. From 1939 onwards he was a popular character actor. Among others, he played Arthur Manleder in the *Boston Blackie* series of the 1940s.

From 1955 onwards he acted mainly on television, frequently as a regular in series with one-word titles. He had an occasional but recurring role as Ned Buntline in the Western television series *The Life and Legend of Wyatt Earp* throughout its run. Buntline was the writer who presented Earp with his twin "Buntline Specials," which were pistols with extra long barrels. Corrigan made a memorable contribution to another Western series. This was the *Rawhide* episode called "Incident of the Running Man," originally aired in 1961, in which he played an apparently benign undertaker with a very sinister secret. It was one of the most suspenseful episodes of this series.

On November 5, 1969, 69-year-old Corrigan died at the Motion Picture Country Home and Hospital in Woodland Hills, California, where arthritis had confined him for many years. There were no reported survivors.

Lloyd Corrigan Filmography

1925: *The Splendid Crime.*
1927: *It.*
1939: *The Great Commandment.*
1940: *High School, The Ghost Breakers, Queen of the Mob, Sporting Blood, Captain Caution, The Return of Frank James, Dark Streets of Cairo, The Lady in Question, Two Girls on Broadway, Public Deb No. 1, Young Tom Edison.*
1941: *Men of Boys' Town, Mexican Spitfire's Baby, North to the Klondike, Whistling in the Dark, Kathleen, A Girl a Guy and a Gob.*
1942: *Confessions of Boston Blackie, Tennessee Johnson, The London Blackout Murders, Alias Boston Blackie, Bombay Clipper, Treat 'Em*

Portrait of Lloyd Corrigan, who appeared in *The Life and Legend of Wyatt Earp*.

Rough, The Great Man's Lady, The Wife Takes a Flyer, Boston Blackie Goes Hollywood, Mystery of Marie Roget, Lucky Jordan, The Mantrap, Maisie Gets Her Man.
1943: *Captive Wild Woman, Hitler's Children, After Midnight With Boston Blackie, Stage Door Canteen, Nobody's Darling, Tarzan's Desert Mystery, Secrets of the Underground, King of the Cowboys, Song of Nevada.*
1944: *Since You Went Away, Rosie the Riveter, Passport to Adventure, Gambler's Choice, Lights of Old Santa Fe, Goodnight Sweetheart, Reckless Age, The Thin Man Goes Home.*
1945: *Bring on the Girls, Boston Blackie Booked on Suspicion, The Fighting Guardsman, Lake Placid Serenade, Crime Doctor's Courage.*
1946: *She-Wolf of London, The Bandit of Sherwood Forest, Lady Luck, Two Smart People, The Chase, Alias Mr. Twilight.*
1947: *Blaze of Noon, Stallion Road, The Ghost Goes Wild, Shadowed.*
1948: *A Date with Judy, Adventures of Casanova, The Return of October, Mr. Reckless, The Bride Goes Wild, Strike It Rich, The Big Clock, Homicide for Three.*
1949: *Blondie Hits the Jackpot, Home in San Antone, Dancing in the Dark, The Girl from Jones Beach.*
1950: *Father Is a Bachelor, And Baby Makes Three, My Friend Irma Goes West, Cyrano de Bergerac, When Willie Comes Marching Home.*
1951: *The Last Outpost, Sierra Passage, Her First Romance, New Mexico, Ghost Chasers.*
1952: *Rainbow 'Round My Shoulder, Son of Paleface, Sound Off.*
1953: *Marry Me Again, The Stars Are Singing.*
1954: *Return from the Sea, The Bowery Boys Meet the Monsters.*
1955: *Paris Follies of 1956.*
1956: *Hidden Guns.*
1962: *The Manchurian Candidate.*
1963: *It's a Mad Mad Mad Mad World.*

As Director

1930: *Follow Thru, Along Came Youth.*
1931: *Daughter of the Dragon, The Beloved Bachelor.*
1932: *The Broken Wing, No One Man.*
1933: *He Learned About Women.*
1934: *By Your Leave.*
1935: *Murder on a Honeymoon.*
1936: *The Dancing Pirate.*
1937: *Night Key.*
1938: *Lady Behave.*

Television Series

1954–1955: *Willy* as Papa Dodger.
1955–1961: *The Life and Legend of Wyatt Earp* as Ned Buntline.
1960–1961: *Happy* as Charlie Dooley.
1965–1966: *Hank* as Professor McKillup.

Sources

Brooks, Tim. *The Complete Directory to Prime Time TV Stars 1946-Present.* New York: Ballantine Books, 1987.
Quinlan, David. *Illustrated Directory of Film Character Actors.* London: Batsford, 1995.

JEROME COURTLAND

Some players are very driven and have a career plan, while others drift into acting by accident. One of the latter was the tall, gangling Jerome Courtland, who starred as a mountain man in Walt Disney's least memorable 1950s Western television series, *The Saga of Andy Burnett.* Courtland was never particularly fond of acting, but he later became a highly successful producer and director. He obviously felt much happier behind the camera than in front of it.

He was born Courtland Jourolmon, Jr., in Knoxville, Tennessee, on December 27, 1926. Early on his interest lay in architecture, so while visiting Hollywood on a summer vacation his family took him to a party being thrown for designer Hal Pereira. The host, director Charles Vidor, spotted him and persuaded him to test for his next film. Courtland agreed to do the test because he did not believe he would win the part, but that it would be something to boast about when he returned to Tennessee.

Vidor changed his name to Jerome Courtland and directed him in his debut, *Together Again* (1944), as Gilbert Parker, an awkward, lovesick adolescent. The movie starred Charles Boyer and Irene Dunne. Courtland registered strongly enough to be signed to a seven-year contract by Columbia Pictures. His second film turn, *Kiss and Tell* (1945), as a faithful, bewildered admirer of the star really put him across since she was Shirley Temple. He was, however, unable to capitalize on this wave of popularity because shortly afterwards he was drafted into the army, where he served as an ordnance sergeant. He was shipped to Japan where he was injured in a train wreck.

Like many others, his career never really regained its initial momentum. Upon his discharge he was cast in *The Man from Colorado* (1948) which enabled him to obtain a foothold in the industry again. This led to him being cast in several other films, primarily Westerns. *The Palomino* (1950) was intended as a starring vehicle for him, but lightning did not strike twice. Max Arnow, Columbia's head of casting, liked him, so when Courtland expressed interest in other aspects of filmmaking, Arnow let him spend time in all the other departments on the lot. This experience served him in good stead when it came to a career switch. Courtland also had a fine singing voice. He appeared in cabaret in New York City's Latin Quarter. Back in Hollywood he had a nightclub act. This led to him making his Broadway debut with Yma Sumac in the shortlived musical *Flahooley* in 1951.

After his Columbia contract expired, Courtland formed an association with Walt Disney, who was looking for a property which would overwhelm the nation in the same way as *Davy Crockett.* Disney believed that he had found one in *The Saga of Andy Burnett* and that Jerome Courtland was the ideal hero. This series was based on the writings of Stewart Edward White (1873–1946), one of the most prolific and entertaining writers of the early 20th century. Disney turned to a collection of four White novels in a volume titled *The Saga of Andy Burnett.*

White's own life was packed with adventure. He spent his early years in his native Michigan and on a California ranch. He began to write at Columbia University and, after a trip to Hudson Bay country, established his reputation nationally with "The Blazed Trail." He became a Californian, camped and hunted in California, Wyoming and Arizona, and followed Theodore Roosevelt into Africa. Andy Burnett never lived, but White used him as a composite of the indomitable mountain men who abounded during the Western expansion of the 18th century. The series was hour-length, in color and there were six episodes. These told of the adventures of Andy and his companions on their trek from Pittsburgh to the Blackfoot Indian Territory.

The series was not a Western in the traditional sense, but more dramatization of historical novels. The hero faced every conceivable danger from Indians to badmen to natural disasters on the journey. The scripts were written by Tom Blackburn. The episodes were shown as segments of *Walt Disney Presents.* The first three were shown in October 1957, and the second three during February and March 1958. Although the series was well written with good production values, it was the least successful of the Disney Westerns of the 1950s. The ratings did not warrant the episodes being edited into feature films.

Courtland continued his association with Walt Disney by singing the title song of *Old Yeller* (1957); narrating the male voices in the cartoon *Noah and the Ark;* and narrating and singing for the television show *The Boy and the Falcon.* After this he abandoned America for a few years. He emerged in Europe as the star of some feature films shot in Germany and Italy. He was not dubbed in either language, but these films were little seen outside of their countries of origin. He was also the star of an obscure European series, *Tales of the Vikings,* which consisted of 39 half-hour episodes.

Upon his return to Hollywood in the mid–1960s, he switched careers and became an associate producer of feature films for the Walt Disney Organization. He began directing episodes of such television series as *The Flying Nun, The Partridge Family* and later *Dynasty.* He tested for the role of Baron von Trapp in *The Sound of Music,* but lost the part to Christopher Plummer. In 1975 he produced and directed the feature film *Escape to Witch Mountain.* He has since directed features, telemovies and TV episodes. In 1950 he married actress Polly Bergen in Las Vegas. They had long been separated when they divorced in Los Angeles on February 18, 1955. The same year he wed his current wife, Janet. At last report they were residing on a ranch in Thousand Oaks, California. By his second wife he has three sons and two daughters.

Jerome Courtland Filmography

1944: *Together Again.*
1945: *Kiss and Tell.*
1948: *The Man from Colorado.*
1949: *The Walking Hills, Tokyo Joe, Make Believe Ballroom, Battleground.*
1950: *A Woman of Distinction, The Palomino, When You're Smiling.*
1951: *Santa Fe, The Texas Rangers, Sunny Side of the Street, The Barefoot Mailman.*
1952: *Cripple Creek.*
1953: *Take the High Ground.*
1955: *The Bamboo Prison.*
1958: *Tonka.*
1960: *O Sole Mio.*
1961: *The Adventures of Mary Read (*a.k.a. *Hell Below Deck), Tharus Son of Attila.*
1962: *Cafe Oriental.*
1965: *Black Spurs, The Restless Ones.*

Television Series

1957–1958: *Walt Disney Presents: The Saga of Andy Burnett* as Andy Burnett.
1960: *Tales of the Vikings* as Leif Ericson.

Sources

Lamparski, Richard. *Whatever Became Of? Seventh Series.* New York: Bantam, 1977.
Picture Show Annual. London: Amalgamated Press, 1947.
Quinlan, David. *Illustrated Directory of Film Stars.* London: Batsford, 1986.
Speed, F. Maurice. *The Western Film and Television Annual.* London: MacDonald, 1960.

CHUCK COURTNEY

Chuck Courtney was discovered and put under contract by MGM at the age of nine. Some years later he joined the cast of *The Lone Ranger* as the hero's nephew Dan Reid, a role which he played occasionally for six years. A contract with Allied Artists followed and he began acting in Western films. While appearing in films with John Wayne, he found himself doing many of the stunts. He soon realized that he enjoyed stuntwork, and after appearing in *The War Lord* with Charlton Heston, he decided to become a professional stuntman.

Courtney was taught all the tricks of the trade by Yakima Canutt. Intense training made him an expert in fighting, horsemanship, saddle falls, high falls, motorcycling and car stunt driving. He served as stunt coordinator on such films as *Santee, Murph the Surf* and *Sudden*

Death. He has had a successful association with actor Robert Conrad for many years, serving as stunt coordinator and second unit director on all of Conrad's projects, including the movies-of-the-week *The Wild Wild West Revisited* and *Will, G. Gordon Liddy.* As an actor he appeared in *The Virginian* and *Laramie,* the latter of which initiated a friendship with Robert Fuller that has lasted for over three decades. His later credits as stunt coordinator include such television series as *Bring 'Em Back Alive* and *The Wizard.* He suffered a stroke in the early 1990s, but recovered to receive a Golden Boot Award at the 1993 ceremony. He is married to stuntwoman Jeri Courtney and is the father of two children.

Chuck Courtney Filmography

1950: *The Asphalt Jungle, Louisa.*
1952: *It Grows on Trees, Francis Goes to West Point.*
1953: *Born to the Saddle, Cow Country.*
1954: *Two Guns and a Badge.*
1955: *The Long Gray Line, At Gunpoint.*
1956: *Meet Me in Las Vegas.*
1958: *Some Came Running, The Line-up.*
1960: *Spartacus.*
1965: *The War Lord.*
1966: *Billy The Kid Versus Dracula.*
1967: *Code Name: Heraclitus* (TV), *El Dorado.*
1968: *The Green Berets.*
1970: *Rio Lobo.*
1972: *The Cowboys.*
1976: *The Gumball Rally, Food of the Gods.*
1986: *Assassin* (TV).
1989: *Pet Cemetary*
1990: *Rich Girl, Peacemaker.*

Television Series

1950–1956: *The Lone Ranger* as Dan Reid.

Sources

Eleventh Annual Golden Boot Awards program. August 1993.

WALTER COY

Walter Coy was born in Great Falls, Montana, on January 31, 1906. Aside from one abortive attempt to enter films in the mid-1930s, he served a long apprenticeship on stage at the New York Theater Guild and The Group Theater and in vaudeville. He came to films permanently in 1950, primarily as a character actor. His most distinguished film role was as Aaron, the brother of Ethan Edwards (John Wayne), in the classic John Ford Western *The Searchers* (1956).

He served as the host and narrator of the Western anthology series *Frontier.* "*Frontier* tells stories about average people," said executive producer Worthington Miner. Out of 200 years of American history of exploration and settlement, many legends grew up. Some grew too big. Often people came to accept a romantic untruth for a more arresting fact. The facts of men and history had suspense and drama enough. Truth, Miner believed, would create the unique drama of the stories of *Frontier.*

The series included stories with humor as well as heroism. There were also romantic stories; stories seen through children's eyes; stories of women facing hardships on the frontier; and stories which showed that there were villains other than Indians, cattle rustlers and badmen (space, wind, rain, cold, loneliness and isolation). He believed that *Frontier* would be unique and authentic. "The West is an idea," he said. "It is expressive of American individual courage, adaptability, stubbornness and pride. There is no dead end to the frontier. These stories will be stories of hope."

There were no regulars in the cast aside from Coy, who introduced and concluded each episode and starred in a few episodes himself. His opening lines were, "This is the West. This is the land of beginning again. This is the story of men and women facing the frontier. This is the way it happened." His final line was, "It happened that way ... moving West." The series began on NBC on September 25, 1955.

It was a half-hour, black and white series. Despite Miner's enthusiasm, it proved too bleak for wide acceptance and only lasted one season. It ended after 39 episodes on September 9, 1956.

Coy's career declined in stature after this series and he drifted into obscurity. He played supporting roles in a few episodes of other Western series and briefly returned to the limelight when he played a leading role in a soap called *A Time for Us*. He died on December 11, 1974, at age 68.

Walter Coy Filmography

1936: *Love Letters of a Star.*
1950: *Barricade, Tyrant of the Sea, Saddle Tramp, Colt .45, Under Mexicali Skies.*
1951: *FBI Girl.*
1952: *The Lusty Men, Flat Top.*
1953: *So Big.*
1954: *Sign of the Pagan, Phantom of the Rue Morgue.*
1955: *Cult of the Cobra, Wichita, Running Wild.*
1956: *Pillars of the Sky, On the Threshold of Space, The Searchers, The Young Guns.*
1957: *Johnny Tremain.*
1958: *Juvenile Jungle.*
1959: *Gunmen from Laredo, The Gunfight at Dodge City, Warlock, North by Northwest.*
1961: *Five Guns to Tombstone, Gun Fight.*
1971: *Catlow.*

Television Series

1955–1956: *Frontier*—host and narrator.
1964–1966: *A Time for Us/Flame in the Wind* as Jason Farrell.

Sources

Speed, F. Maurice. *The Western Film and Television Annual.* London: MacDonald, 1959
Truitt, Evelyn Mack. *Who Was Who On Screen Illustrated Edition.* New York: Bowker, 1984.

JOHNNY CRAWFORD

Johnny Crawford was born John Ernest Crawford in Los Angeles, California, on March 26, 1946, the son of film editor Robert Crawford. He has one older brother, Robert Crawford, Jr. Educated at Hollywood High School, he comes from a musical family and was involved with show business from an early age. Television roles came his way from the mid–1950s onwards, but his first big break was when he was one of the original Mickey Mouse Club Mouseketeers from 1955 to 1956. He then landed the role for which he is most famous, namely that of Chuck Connors' son in *The Rifleman,* which he played for a full five years. In 1959 he received an Emmy nomination as Best Supporting Actor (Continuing Character) in a Dramatic Series.

In the early 1960s he parlayed his television fame into a brief stint as a pop heartthrob, landing five Top 20 singles including "Cindy's Birthday" (which made it to No. 8 in 1962) and "Your Nose Is Gonna Grow" (which reached No. 14). When the series came to an end he took time off to travel and pursued his interest in rodeo roping. Much to the frustration of his agents who were trying to launch his adult acting career, he spent ten years on the professional rodeo circuit. "It really bugged them I wasn't around," he recalled, "but I was distracted by the rodeos and although I got the occasional acting part between rodeos, I was more likely to pass up an audition so I could compete."

In 1970 he starred in *The Resurrection of Bronco Billy,* a student film by John Longnecker that earned the pair an Academy Award for best live action short film. He spent a few years in New York singing songs of the 1920s and 1930s with Vince Giodiano's Nighthawks. Since 1991 he has led the 1928 Society Dance Orchestra which has become extremely popular in all the upmarket Los Angeles niteries. They play the music of Louis Armstrong, Guy Lombardo and Red Nichols (which is technically from the decade before the Big Band era).

In 1992 he bought a 65-year-old house in the Hollywood Hills, which he has been restoring to its original state, complete with period furniture. He was married (for the first time) in 1995 to Charlotte McKenna, whom he first met in the school choir in 1963. They went out together for six months, drifted apart, but were reunited in 1990. They were wed on the grounds of Will Rogers' historic estate in Pacific Palisades, California, with a reception at the trendy Beverly Hills nightspot Tatou, where his orchestra was performing.

Johnny Crawford Filmography

1958: *The Space Children.*
1964: *Indian Paint.*
1965: *Village of the Giants.*
1973: *The Naked Ape.*
1977: *The Great Texas Dynamite Chase.*
1983: *The Gambler: The Adventure Continues* (TV).
1991: *The Gambler: The Luck of the Draw* (TV).

Television Series

1958–1963: *The Rifleman* as Mark McCain.

Sources

Keck, William. "Rifleman TV Star Weds High School Sweetheart." *National Enquirer,* January 1995.
Sandler, Adam. "Lost and Found." *Variety.* May 2, 1994.
Where Are They Now? A Globe Special. Boca Raton, FL: Globe International Inc., 1993.

ROBERT CRAWFORD, JR.

Born in Quantico, Virginia, on May 13, 1944, this child actor was originally launched as a Mouseketeer on *The Mickey Mouse Club.* He received an Emmy nomination for Best Single Performance by an Actor in a CBS *Playhouse 90* production entitled "A Child Of Our Time" during the 1958–1959 season. He became very popular as Andy Sherman, the 14-year-old brother of Slim Sherman (John Smith) in the Western series *Laramie.* Andy left the ranch at the end of the first season, appeared occasionally the following season, but by the third season had been written out completely and was not referred to again.

Robert Crawford, Jr., in *Laramie.*

In 1961 it was said that the actor planned more film and television work, wanted to go to college, was interested in all sports and went to the movies whenever he could. Allegedly he made a difficult transition to adulthood, but at last report he was residing in Los Angeles, where he writes. He is the older brother of Johnny Crawford and the son of film editor Robert Crawford, Sr.

Robert Crawford, Jr., Filmography

1961: *The Great Imposter.*
1962: *The Wonderful World of the Brothers Grimm.*
1964: *Indian Paint.*

Television Series

1959–1961: *Laramie* as Andy Sherman.

Sources

Brooks, Tim. *The Complete Directory to Prime Time TV Stars.* New York: Ballantine Books, 1987.

Lance, Steven. *Written Out of Television: A TV Lover's Guide to Cast Changes 1945–1994.* Lanham, MD: Madison, 1996.

Speed, F. Maurice. *The Western Film and Television Annual.* London: MacDonald, 1960.

Who's Who in Hollywood. New York: Dell, 1961.

ROBERT CULP

When it came time for Robert Culp to decide on a career, he was split two ways. He recalled at the peak of his career on *I Spy*, "I was keen on both acting and writing. It's been that way ever since I was 14. I've tried to do both, but I find myself acting more than writing today." Before he found lasting fame, he was the star of an offbeat Western television series called *Trackdown*. He has rather too cynical a personality for top rank movie stardom, but he has certainly appeared in some outstanding television productions.

Robert Culp was born in Berkeley, California, on August 16, 1930, the son of an attorney. He was educated at the College of the Pacific at Stockton, Washington University and San Francisco State University. He was once a champion pole vaulter. Commencing acting at the age of 14, he went to New York in 1951 where he studied with Herbert Berghof, making his Broadway debut in *The Prescott Proposals* in 1953. He was in the off-Broadway productions of *He Who Gets Slapped* and *Diary of a Scoundrel* (both 1956) and *A Clearing in the Woods* (1957).

Culp was in some live television dramas before he uprooted his family to go to Los Angeles to star in the Western television series *Trackdown*. This was a most odd series which tried to replicate on the small screen the intensity of the rather static psychological Western films of the 1950s. Most of it was shot inside the studio with very few exterior shots. Culp played Hoby Gilman, a fictional Texas Ranger, although the stories were allegedly based on authentic files of real-life Texas Rangers. The series was set during the 1870s when Gilman was attached to the headquarters in Austin, Texas, from where he ventured all over the state to tackle the cases depicted in the series.

Gilman appeared in nearly all of the scenes, but there were a few other regulars in the series: Henrietta Porter (Ellen Corby), who edited the Porter, Texas, newspaper; Tenner Smith (Peter Leeds), a saloon owner and gambler; and Ralph (Norman Leavitt), the town handyman. It was advertised by sponsor Lucky Strike Cigarettes as "Human—Vivid—Memorable," but there was no mention of action or even of the West itself. It was still one of the more successful Westerns from Four Star Television. It made its debut on CBS on October 4, 1957, and had a healthy run of 71 half-hour black and white episodes before ending on September 23, 1959.

Trackdown appeared to have little beneficial effect on Culp's career. It did not lead to film offers; instead the actor spent several years guest-starring in other series such as *The Fugitive, Rawhide, Ben Casey* and *The Virginian.* One of his most impressive assignments was as the hero of the classic "Demon With a Glass Hand" episode of the anthology series *The Outer Limits*. After a while he took to calling himself "the highest paid actor still doing difficult character parts in other people's TV series." He also appeared in feature films, making his screen debut in *PT 109* (1963).

In 1965 he was cast with Bill Cosby in the adventure series *I Spy,* in which he played professional tennis player turned spy Kelly Robinson. The series executive producer and creator Sheldon Leonard recalled, "I'd been aware of Robert Culp for many years as a comedy actor and also as a writer. I detected the deft comedy touch in the man that I wanted. It was also important that privately these two should be highly compatible if their screen performance was to be effective. I'm glad to say that this has worked out." At the time Culp was a much more experienced actor than Bill Cosby, but he helped the budding actor to the best of his ability, which Cosby remembers with appreciation to this day.

Culp undertook a course in tennis before starting the series. "Strange!" he mused at the time. "I've always been keen on sport, but tennis was a game I never really played. So I just had to start learning. I mean, how could I be a top tennis star and not be able to play the game myself? But now I love to play. It's a great game." He wrote some of the *I Spy* scripts and admitted that he would like to keep on writing, adding, "There may come a time when I might consider giving up acting to concentrate more on being a writer, but I just don't know. At the moment things are going very well for me as an actor. I enjoy playing the role of Kelly Robinson. And it has certainly given me and Bill Cosby a wonderful opportunity to see quite a lot of the world." This is rather an ironic comment in view of the claustrophobic nature of his previous series *Trackdown.*

He received three Emmy nominations for Outstanding Continued Performance by an Actor in a Leading Role in a Dramatic Series in 1965, 1966 and 1967. On each occasion he lost out to Cosby. He also received one nomination for Outstanding Writing Achievement in Drama for *I Spy* in 1966, but lost out to Bruce Geller for *Mission Impossible.* After three years of *I Spy,* Culp wanted out. The amount of travel and difficulties of shooting had become insurmountable obstacles to a quality show. The series had begun on NBC on September 15, 1965, and ended on September 2, 1968.

In the late 1960s he became active in the civil rights movement. He was a supporter of Martin Luther King and spent a year shooting a documentary *(Operation Breadbasket)* about black economics which he also financed. This aired twice on network television in 1969. His most commercially successful film was *Bob and Carol and Ted and Alice* (1969), although it appears quite dated now. During the 1970s he was a frequent television guest-star, most notably as one of the definitive villains in the *Columbo* series on which he appeared three times. In the new *Columbo* series he appeared again in "Columbo Goes to College" (1990), this time playing the martinet father of one of the student murderers. He also starred in several movies for television, a couple of which have a reputation as classics of the genre. *A Cold Night's Death* dealt with a controlled experiment with chimpanzees which goes seriously wrong. In *A Cry for Help* he played a humane disc jockey who enlists the aid of listeners to find a suicidal girl. In real life the actor admitted that he was finding alimony and child support payments a problem and for a while would accept nearly any part that came along to keep ahead financially.

In 1981 he turned up in the series *The Greatest American Hero,* this time in a subordinate role as a world-weary FBI agent. Some of these later television appearances (such as *The Calendar Girl Murders* and *The Gladiator*) gave the impression that they could have been played by anyone. Of his work so far during the 1990s, his most impressive was in the film version of John Grisham's *The Pelican Brief* (1993) in which he gave a very shrewd characterization as a president of the United States enmeshed in a trail of corruption. He also appeared in the first three episodes of *Lonesome Dove: The Series* in 1994 as Farnsworth, a railroad promoter.

Culp married Nancy Wilner during the 1950s. By her he has three sons: Joshua, born in 1961; Jason, born in 1962; Joseph, born in 1963; and a daughter, Rachel, born in 1964. They divorced in 1967. Culp married the beautiful actress France Nuyen in 1967, but they divorced in 1969. Since 1971 he has been married to Sheila Sullivan.

Robert Culp Filmography

1963: *PT 109, Sunday in New York, The Raiders.*
1964: *Rhino!, The Hanged Man* (TV).
1969: *Bob and Carol and Ted and Alice, If It's Tuesday This Must Be Belgium* (cameo).
1970: *The Grove.*
1971: *See the Man Run* (TV), *Hannie Caulder.*
1972: *A Cold Night's Death* (TV), *Hickey and Boggs* (also directed).
1973: *Outrage!* (TV), *A Name for Evil.*
1974: *The Castaway Cowboy, Houston We've Got a Problem* (TV), *Strange Homecoming* (TV).
1975: *Inside Out, A Cry for Help* (TV).
1976: *Sky Riders, Flood* (TV), *The Great Scout and Cathouse Thursday, Breaking Point.*
1977: *Spectre* (TV).

1978: *Last of the Good Guys* (TV).
1979: *Golden Girl, Hot Rod* (TV).
1980: *The Night the City Screamed* (TV).
1981: *Killjoy* (TV), *National Lampoon Goes to the Movies.*
1982: *Thou Shalt Not Kill* (TV).
1984: *The Calendar Girl Murders* (TV), *Her Life as a Man* (TV), *Turk 182!*
1986: *The Gladiator* (TV), *Combat High* (TV), *The Blue Lightning* (TV).
1987: *Big Bad Mama II.*
1988: *What Price Victory?* (TV).
1989: *Silent Night Deadly Night III: Better Watch Out!*
1990: *Perry Mason: The Case of the Defiant Daughter* (TV), *Columbo Goes to College* (TV), *The Arrival, Pucker Up and Bark Like a Dog.*
1991: *That's Action, Murderous Vision* (TV).
1992: *Timebomb.*
1993: *The Pelican Brief.*
1994: *I Spy Returns* (TV), *XTRO3—Watch The Skies.*
1995: *Panther.*
1996: *Mercenary, Spy Hard* (cameo).

Television Series

1957–1959: *Trackdown* as Hoby Gilman.
1965–1968: *I Spy* as Kelly Robinson.
1981–1983: *The Greatest American Hero* as Bill Maxwell.

Miniseries

1979: *Roots The Next Generation.*
1980: *The Dream Merchants.*
1985: *The Key to Rebecca.*
1990: *Voyage of Terror—The Achille Lauro Affair.*

Sources

Brooks, Tim. *The Complete Directory to Prime Time TV Stars 1946–Present.* New York: Ballantine Books, 1987.
Ferguson, Ken. *Television Stars.* London: Purnell, 1966.
Skinner, John Walter. *Who's Who on the Screen.* Worthing, England: Madeleine, 1983.

HOWARD CULVER

Born in Colorado on June 4, 1918, Howard Culver was raised in Los Angeles. He played Matt Dillon on the audition record for the radio *Gunsmoke* and was the last Ellery Queen. He lost his hearing in the mid 1950s and ran a hobby shop for seven years. A successful ear operation restored his hearing. He played the hotel clerk on *Gunsmoke* for 20 years.

He provided voices for cartoons and commercials and was a newscaster at radio station KGIL in the San Fernando Valley. He lived with his second wife, Lois Hayes (whom he married in 1951) in the San Gabriel Valley, and their twin daughters were born in 1954. Howard Culver died on August 5, 1984, at age 66 in Hong Kong after a vacation in China.

Howard Culver Filmography

1956: *The Black Whip, Hot Rod Girl.*
1958: *Cattle Empire.*
1969: *The D.A.: Murder One* (TV).
1970: *The Computer Wore Tennis Shoes.*
1971: *The Barefoot Executive, $1,000,000 Duck.*
1975: *Shampoo.*
1976: *The Bad News Bears.*
1978: *The Swarm, Secrets of Three Hungry Wives* (TV), *Little Mo* (TV).
1979: *Friendly Fire* (TV), *Blind Ambition* (TV).
1980: *Guyana Tragedy: The Story of Jim Jones* (TV), *Night the Bridge Fell Down* (TV).
1981: *Home Safe, Halloween II.*

Television Series

1955–1975: *Gunsmoke* as Howie.

Sources

Raddatz, Leslie. "The Dodge City Gang." *Radio Times* magazine, June 15, 1972.
Brooks, Tim. *The Complete Directory to Prime Time TV Stars.* New York: Ballantine Books, 1987.

Susan Cummings with Jeff Morrow in *Union Pacific.*

SUSAN CUMMINGS

Susan Cummings is of mixed French and German parentage. As a child she came to the United States to escape the Nazis. She studied music, dance and drama, becoming proficient at all three. Subsequently she became a resident singer with the Clyde Lucas Band, later moving on to Broadway shows. She seemed to be a fixture of many 1950s Western shows such as *Cheyenne,* but her only regular role was in the syndicated series *Union Pacific,* in which she played Georgia, the glamorous young owner of the Golden Spike gambling hall and saloon that moved along with the end of the track. Of her films, the most memorable role was as Helga, the heroine of Sam Fuller's arresting movie of postwar Germany *Verboten!,* which deliberately deglamorized her.

Susan Cummings Filmography

1956: *The Secret of Treasure Mountain.*
1957: *Utah Blaine, Tomahawk Trail.*
1958: *The Man from God's Country.*
1959: *Verboten!*

Television Series

1957–1958: *Union Pacific* as Georgia.

Sources

Hardy, Phil. *Samuel Fuller.* London: Studio Vista, 1970.

Speed, F. Maurice. *The Western Film and TV Annual.* London: MacDonald, 1960.

Summers, Neil. *The First Official TV Western Book.* Vienna, WV: Old West Shop Publishing, 1987.

Barry Curtis in *The Adventures of Champion.*

BARRY CURTIS

Born in 1943, this child star had the leading human role of Ricky North in the popular *The Adventures of Champion* series. This program was produced by Gene Autry's Flying A Productions and originally shown on CBS. Champion the Wonder Horse was the leader of a herd of wild horses. Ricky lives on a ranch owned by his Uncle Sandy (Jim Bannon). When a foal slips and Ricky rescues it, Champion permits Ricky to ride him, but he is the only human permitted to do so. Ricky also owns a German Shepherd named Rebel, and both horse and dog help him to escape from the dangers in which the boy frequently finds himself.

Thirteen episodes were shot in six weeks, with a week's break in October 1955, before another 13 were shot; filming was completed before the end of 1955. Jim Bannon expressed this verdict of his costar: "Barry Curtis is a nice enough little guy, but his mother may be a shade hard to take. She gets almost panicky every time he is even near the horse, which is embarrassing as hell for the kid. He hasn't been around livestock a whole lot, but is more than willing and eager to learn what he needs to know." The series began on September 30, 1955, and lasted until February 3, 1956. Although its initial American airing was short-lived, it has had a long life in syndication overseas.

Curtis appeared in other series such as *The Lone Ranger* and in feature films, but has latterly been posted as one of the lost child players of the screen.

Barry Curtis Filmography

1952: *The Marrying Kind.*
1955: *One Desire.*
1957: *The Missouri Traveler, 3:10 to Yuma.*

Television Series

1955–1956: *The Adventures of Champion* as Ricky North.

Sources

Bannon, Jim. Collected letters 1937—1961 of Jim Bannon, published privately.

Dye, David. *Child and Youth Actors: Filmographies of Their Entire Careers, 1914–1985.* Jefferson, NC: McFarland, 1988.

RAY DANTON

Raymond Danton was born in New York City on September 9, 1931, the son of Jack and Mikael (Menkin) Danton. He was an only child. He attended Horace Mann School; the University of Pittsburgh between 1948 and 1949; and Carnegie Technical School between 1949 and 1950. His show business career began when he was a child performer on the radio show *Let's Pretend* in 1943. Between 1951 and 1954 he served in the U.S. Army infantry in Korea.

He went on to appear on live television in New York in such series as *Studio One* and *The Philco Playhouse.* Eventually he moved to Hollywood where he made his screen debut in *Chief Crazy Horse* (1955). After he appeared with Susan Hayward in *I'll Cry Tomorrow* (1955), he became in demand as a heavy. His most acclaimed screen appearance was in the title role in *The Rise and Fall of Legs Diamond* (1960). Both Danton and director Budd Boetticher have claimed the credit for his success in this role. He reprised the role doing a cameo in the biopic of Dutch Schultz, *Portrait of a Mobster* (1961), which starred Vic Morrow. Warner Bros. valiantly tried to revive the cycle of gangster films which had been so popular during the 1930s, but the attempt was doomed. After that they appeared to have little use for Danton.

Less successfully he played movie star tough guy George Raft in *The George Raft Story* (1961). The problem lay in his being unable to submerge his own distinctive personality within that of the legendary star whom he was portraying. In addition, the movie badly lacked the kind of bullet-strewn climax which successful movies about real life or fictional gangsters usually have.

For a few years during the 1950s and early 1960s he was a ubiquitous villain in Warner Bros. Western and crime television series. It comes as something of a surprise that his only semi-regular role was as Nifty Cronin, an unscrupulous saloon owner of the 1890s, in the series *The Alaskans.* He appeared in an esti-

Ray Danton and Julie Adams. Danton appeared in *The Alaskans*.

mated nine of the 36 episodes playing an infinitely nastier villain than the confidence trickster heroes. His main aim in life was to fleece miners of their gold by any means at his disposal, and he did not stop short of murder. He was enamored of Rocky Shaw (Dorothy Provine), the chanteuse in his saloon, but she wanted no part of him.

His stage roles included *Tiger at the Gate* with Robert Ryan; *Carnival;* the title role in a production of *Becket;* and Starbuck in the musical *110 in the Shade* in 1966. He later moved to Italy to act, and directed his first feature film *(Corrida for a Spy)* there. From 1968 to 1975 he directed 17 films and ran his own production company in Barcelona. In some of the films which he directed he had featured roles. In 1975 he returned to the United States where he directed the bicentennial stage production of *South Pacific* in Hawaii. He also directed the independent feature *Psychic Killer* (1975). Universal hired him as a television director in 1976, and he worked frequently in this capacity and later as supervising producer on the television series *The New Mike Hammer* during the 1980s. He also contributed to the scripts of the *McCloud* series. He won an ACE Award for director of a dramatic special for *Home,* which aired on HBO in 1987. He also directed a stage production of *Come Back Little Sheba* at Los Angeles Theater Center in 1986–1987.

Danton, 60, died in a Los Angeles hospital on February 11, 1992, after a lifelong bout with kidney disease. He met the beautiful actress Julie Adams while they were both working on the 1955 feature *The Looters.* They wed that same year. Although they were one of film-land's most attractive and popular couples, they divorced in 1974. They had two sons, Steven Richard and Mitchell Raymond, who survived him. Adams was prominent amongst the mourners at his memorial service held at noon on February 29, 1992, in the main theater at the Los Angeles Headquarters of the Directors Guild of America. Among others, director Leo Penn spoke and there were videotaped remembrances from Tyne Daly and Stacy Keach. Danton's longtime companion was Jeannie Austin.

Ray Danton Filmography

1955: *Chief Crazy Horse, The Looters, The Spoilers, I'll Cry Tomorrow.*
1956: *Outside the Law.*
1957: *The Night Runner.*
1958: *Too Much Too Soon, Onionhead, Tarawa Beachhead.*
1959: *The Big Operator, Yellowstone Kelly, The Beat Generation.*
1960: *The Rise and Fall of Legs Diamond, Ice Palace, A Fever in the Blood.*
1961: *The George Raft Story (*a.k.a. *Spin of a Coin), Portrait of a Mobster, A Majority of One.*
1962: *The Chapman Report, The Longest Day.*
1963: *FBI Code 98, Sandokan Fights Back.*
1964: *Sandokan Against the Leopard of Sarawak.*
1965: *The Spy Who Went Into Hell.*
1966: *New York Chiama Superdrago, Ballata Da Milliardo.*
1968: *The Candy Man, L'ultima Mercenario.*
1971: *Triangle, Banyon* (TV).
1972: *The Ballad of Billie Blue, A Very Missing Person* (TV), *The Sagittarius Mine.*
1973: *Runaway* (TV).
1974: *Mystic Mountain Massacre, Centerfold Girls.*

1976: *Our Man Flint: Dead On Target* (TV), *Pursuit* (TV), *Six-Pack Annie.*

Television Series

1959–1960: *The Alaskans* as Nifty Cronin.

Sources

Adams, Julia. *The Film Show Annual.* London: Robinson, 1957.

The Annual Obituary. Detroit, MI: St. James Press, 1992.

Cameron, Ian. *The Heavies.* London: Studio Vista, 1967.

Picture Show Annual. London: Amalgamated Press, 1957 and 1958.

Woolley, Lynn, Robert W. Malsbary and Robert Strange, Jr. *Warner Bros. Television.* Jefferson, NC: McFarland, 1985.

GAIL DAVIS

Gail Davis was born Betty Jeanne Grayson in Little Rock, Arkansas, on October 5, 1925. She was the daughter of Dr. and Mrs. W.B. Grayson and was raised until the age of seven in McGehee, where her father built the first hospital. When her father was appointed State Health Officer, the family relocated to Little Rock, the state capital.

She attended Harkum Junior College for Girls in Bryn Mawr, Pennsylvania, and the University of Texas, majoring in drama in both schools. While attending the latter she became one of the Texas Blue Bonnet Belles and participated in camp shows for the military stationed nearby. In 1945 she wed an army captain who had aspirations towards an acting career. In 1946 the couple relocated to Hollywood. She was sunbathing and exercising on the roof of her hotel one day when she was spotted by actor John Carroll and his wife, who was also his agent. They arranged a screen test for her at MGM.

To her surprise she passed the test and was put under contract. Her married name was Betty Davis, but this was unacceptable to the studio because of confusion with Bette Davis; her maiden name was equally unacceptable because the studio also had Kathryn Grayson under contract. The publicity department came up with Gail Davis. She took lessons in singing, dancing and drama at MGM and stayed long enough to make her screen debut in a virtually nonspeaking part in *The Romance of Rosy Ridge* (1947), a bucolic tale.

Gail Davis in *Annie Oakley.*

MGM did a clearout of their contract players after a few months and sold her contract to RKO Radio, where she appeared in some bit roles for about a year. There she gained valuable experience in movement, lighting and photography, but they let her go. From then on she freelanced. Her first Western film was *Far Frontier* (1948), in which she costarred with Roy Rogers; she landed the role because Rogers' regular leading lady, Dale Evans, was pregnant at the time. Davis then went on to costar with Jimmy Wakely, Monte Hale, Allan "Rocky" Lane and Charles Starrett. Producer Armand Schaefer, who was also Gene Autry's business partner, saw her in *Brand of Fear* (1949) and urged Autry to put her under contract.

Sons of New Mexico (1950) was the film which began her association with Gene Autry, and she appeared as the heroine in a total of 14 of his films. She also made movies with Tim Holt, Kirby Grant and Johnny Mack Brown. Davis made her television debut in "The Buried Treasure" episode of *The Lone Ranger* in 1950. She went on to appear in other episodes of this series as well as *The Gene Autry Show, The Cisco Kid, The Range Rider, Death Valley Days* and *The Adventures of Kit Carson.*

In January 1952, Gene Autry and his Flying A Productions acquired all the rights to the Annie Oakley comic strip by Eli H. Leslie. Initially Davis was not a leading contender for the role, but she battled for it. There was a contest held all over America to find a girl who could act, ride, shoot and play the part of a 17- or 18-year-old. Two hundred girls were tested, but none seemed quite right. Davis was not considered because she was too familiar as Autry's leading lady. She went home, donned a pair of jeans and boots with a gingham skirt, put her hair in pigtails and penciled her nose with freckles. She then went to see Armand Schaefer, who reluctantly agreed to let her test for the role. She passed the test with flying colors and signed the contract in April 1952.

The first episode, which served as a pilot, was called "Bull's Eye," in which after the death of Annie's parents, she and her younger brother Tagg go to live with their uncle Sheriff MacTavish in the town of Diablo. After that he always seemed to be out of town, leaving Annie and his deputy Lofty Craig (Brad Johnson) in charge. She rode a horse called Target. After the initial pilot the role of Tagg was played by Jimmy Hawkins. He was the catalyst for many of the stories.

Even though she had practiced extensively and become an excellent horsewoman and crack shot, the sponsors were reluctant to buy the series because they did not believe that a female lead would be strong enough to carry it. A second pilot called "Annie Gets Her Man" was shot. Immediately afterwards she left for London to do an eight-week tour with Gene Autry and his entourage. While there she received word that the series had been sold. After flying back, she commenced filming the series in September 1953. For the next few years she spent six months filming *Annie Oakley* and then six months on the road touring throughout the United States and Canada.

Despite the derision of skeptics, *Annie Oakley* was a smash hit with merchandising sales in excess of $10,000,000 per year. At one point it was being seen on 200 stations. In the sense that it was the only Western series to have a female lead during the 1950s it was light years ahead of its time. In the only year when the award was presented, *Annie Oakley* received an Emmy nomination for Best Western Or Adventure Series in 1954. The actress thoroughly enjoyed playing the role though it meant rising at 4 A.M., being in front of the cameras by six and filming until sunset. The main locations were Vasquez Rocks, the Gene Autry Ranch, Apple Valley and Pioneer Town. Three episodes per week were shot and the crew worked seven days a week for seven weeks. Although facilities were primitive, morale was always high. Although Davis did many of the stunts herself, she had an excellent double named Donna Hall when the risk of serious injury was possible

Annie Oakley ceased production after 81 half-hour black and white episodes in December 1956. Although the series might have continued, Jimmy Hawkins grew so tall that Davis could not pat him on the head anymore. He had to stand in a ditch while she had to mount steps for the last few episodes. After this she toured for a few years and made scattered appearances on television variety shows. Her final film was a cameo as Annie Oakley in the Western spoof *Alias Jesse James* (1959).

By the time she returned to Hollywood to resume working again, she was so hopelessly typecast both in terms of looks and voice that producers refused to cast her even for voice-overs in commercials. For several years she was a partner in a personal management firm in Hollywood handling celebrity clients, but later worked for a computer sales firm in Los Angeles. She also had her own public relations company, Gail Davis Enterprises. She was an extremely popular winner of a Golden Boot Award in 1994. A widow, she was married three times and had a daughter, Terrie Manning, of Irving, Texas. Gail Davis died March 15, 1997, at a Burbank hospital, of brain cancer; she was 71. She is buried at Forest Lawn.

Gail Davis Filmography

1947: *The Romance of Rosy Ridge, Merton of the Movies.*
1948: *If You Knew Susie, They Live by Night, The Judge Steps Out, The Far Frontier.*
1949: *Brand of Fear, Death Valley Gunfighter, Frontier Investigator, Law of the Golden West, South of Death Valley.*
1950: *Sons of New Mexico, Cow Town, Indian Territory, Trail of the Rustlers, West of Wyoming, Six Gun Mesa.*
1951: *Two Tickets to Broadway, Operation Pacific, Flying Leathernecks, Take Care of My Little Girl, Texans Never Cry, Whirlwind, Silver Canyon, Yukon Manhunt, Valley of Fire, Overland Telegraph.*
1952: *The Old West, Blue Canadian Rockies, Wagon Team.*
1953: *Winning of the West, On Top of Old Smoky, Goldtown Ghost Riders, Pack Train.*
1959: *Alias Jesse James* (cameo).

Television Series

1954–1958: *Annie Oakley* as Annie Oakley.

Sources

Goldrup, Tom, and Jim Goldrup. *Feature Players: The Stories Behind the Faces Volume #2.* Published privately, 1992.
Holland, Ted. *B Western Actors Encyclopedia: Facts, Photos and Filmographies for More than 250 Familiar Faces.* Jefferson, NC: McFarland, 1989.
Lamparski, Richard. *Whatever Became Of? Fifth Series.* New York: Crown, 1975.
Picture Show Annual. London: Amalgamated Press, 1953.
Speed, F. Maurice. *The Western Film Annual.* London: MacDonald, 1955.
Turner, Steve, and Edgar M. Wyatt. *Saddle Gals.* Madison, NC: Empire, 1995.

JIM DAVIS

Actors peak at different times, but one actor whose greatest fame came at the end of his career was Jim Davis. He spent more than 30 years as an actor before attaining stardom as Jock Ewing in *Dallas.* He appeared in many Westerns both in film and television, including *Stories of the Century.* He was an unpretentious journeyman actor throughout most of his career. In real life Davis, silver-haired and with a seamed, craggy face, had no illusions about the series *Dallas,* which caught viewers' imaginations throughout the world. He dismissed it with the words, "We all know that this show's just a damned glorified soap opera."

Jim Davis was born Marlin Davis either in Edgerton or Dearborn, Missouri (which is where he acquired his slow, drawling speech), on August 26, 1915. He was educated at William Jewell College in Liberty, Missouri. Initially he set out to be a fireman, but was sidetracked along the way into working as a railway hand, oil field laborer and circus tent rigger before arriving in California as a car salesman in 1940. A customer who was a talent scout for MGM arranged a screen test with another newcomer, Esther Williams, and Davis landed a contract with that studio.

His best-remembered starring role was opposite Bette Davis at Warner Bros. in *Winter Meeting* (1948), which was one of her least successful films. Somewhat ruefully he recalled, "When *Winter Meeting* flopped, I couldn't get another acting job for a year. Things got so bad, I ended up wheeling concrete on construction sites for a while." Before long he sank into the steady but unspectacular work of supporting roles, primarily in Westerns, where his fine physique stood him in good stead. In 1954 he became the star of the Western TV series *Stories of the Century,* which incorporated authentic facts and Western figures into its scripts. Each week's episode was the case history of a Western outlaw such as Billy the Kid or Jesse James.

Fictional hero Matt Clark (Jim Davis), who worked for the railroad, was added to the

Jim Davis with Mary Castle in *Stories of the Century*.

story, along with a female operative. Their job was to track down and apprehend these desperadoes. She usually came to town in some undercover guise, mingling with the townsfolk and feeding information back to Clark, who rode in alone later. This was a half-hour black and white syndicated series with Chatsworth standing in for towns in many states of America. The series was produced by Republic, using generous amounts of exciting stock footage from their library for the action scenes, together with actors who were familiar faces in their motion pictures. In 1954, the only year when the award was presented, *Stories of the Century* won an Emmy as Best Western or Adventure Series.

By the time of his selection for *Dallas* in 1978, Davis had made nearly 100 films and 300 television appearances, including a couple of other forgettable series. He once admitted that in between jobs he had been flat broke about 500 times and had held just about that many jobs to supplement his income as an actor during periods when he was resting. He finally attained stardom as the ruthless patriarch Jock Ewing in the television series *Dallas*.

For almost the whole of the last season in which he appeared, he had been in excruciating pain from a number of ailments, but in an amazing display of professionalism, he soldiered on. Davis was almost incapacitated on the set, with an inoperable brain tumor, severe migraine headaches and an almost ruptured stomach. In March 1981, he underwent emergency surgery for a perforated ulcer. He had been so close to death earlier in 1981 from his other ailments that the *Dallas* scriptwriters were ordered to script the show so that he could be written out at one week's notice. He was convalescing at his San Fernando home, having completed the season, when he died in his sleep of a heart attack on April 29, 1981, at age 65. He was found dead by his wife Blanche, a former professional swimmer, whom he married in 1949. They had a daughter, Tara.

The show's executive producer Paul Caprice said, "He was an extremely brave man. He was in considerable pain, yet he insisted on finishing the present series. We knew that he desperately needed medical attention, but it was his own decision to keep working. After a convalescent period, he fully expected to be back in the next series, and so did we. His death has come as a shock to all of us." Larry Hagman, who was touring the Scottish Highlands at the time of his partner's death, said, "It is very sad indeed. This is the end of an era as far as the television series is concerned."

Davis received a posthumous Emmy nomination for Outstanding Lead Actor in a Drama Series for *Dallas* in 1981. He was cremated at Forest Lawn Memorial Park in Glendale, California.

Jim Davis Filmography

1942: *White Cargo, Riding Through Nevada.*
1943: *Frontier Fury, Salute to the Marines, Swing Shift Maisie.*
1944: *Cyclone Prairie Rangers, Thirty Seconds Over Tokyo.*
1945: *What Next Corporal Hargrove?*
1946: *Up Goes Maisie, Gallant Bess.*
1947: *The Fabulous Texan, Merton of the Movies, The Beginning or the End?, The Romance of Rosy Ridge.*
1948: *Winter Meeting.*
1949: *Brimstone, Hellfire, Yes Sir That's My Baby, Red Stallion in the Rockies.*
1950: *California Passage, The Showdown, The Cariboo Trail, Hi-Jacked, The Savage Horde.*
1951: *Silver Canyon, Oh! Susanna, Cavalry Scout, Little Big Horn, The Sea Hornet, Three Desperate Men.*
1952: *Woman of the North Country, Rose of Cimarron, The Big Sky, The Blazing Forest.*
1953: *Ride the Man Down, The Woman They Almost Lynched.*
1954: *The Outcast, Jubilee Trail, Hell's Outpost, The Big Chase, The Outlaw's Daughter.*
1955: *Timberjack, Last of the Desperadoes, The Vanishing American, The Last Command.*
1956: *Blonde Bait* (U.S. version of British film *Women Without Men* with additional scenes), *The Bottom of the Bottle, The Maverick Queen, The Wild Dakotas, Frontier Gambler.*
1957: *The Quiet Gun, Duel at Apache Wells, The Restless Breed, Raiders of Old California, Apache Warrior, Last Stagecoach West, Monster from Green Hell, Guns Don't Argue.*
1958: *Toughest Gun in Tombstone, Flaming Frontier, The Badge of Marshal Brennan, Wolf Dog.*
1959: *Noose for a Gunman, Alias Jesse James.*
1961: *Frontier Uprising, The Gambler Wore a Gun.*
1965: *Zebra in the Kitchen, Iron Angel, They Ran for Their Lives.*
1966: *Fort Utah, Jesse James Meets Frankenstein's Daughter, Hondo and the Apaches* (TV).
1967: *Border Lust, El Dorado.*
1969: *The Road Hustlers.*
1970: *Dracula vs. Frankenstein, Five Bloody Graves (*a.k.a. *Gun Riders), Rio Lobo, Vanished* (TV), *Monte Walsh.*
1971: *Big Jake, The Trackers* (TV).
1972: *The Honkers, Bad Company.*
1973: *Fire Eaters, Deliver Us from Evil* (TV), *One Little Indian.*
1974: *The Parallax View.*
1975: *Satan's Triangle* (TV).
1976: *The Deputies (*a.k.a. *The Law of the Land)* (TV).
1977: *The Choirboys, Just a Little Inconvenience* (TV).
1978: *Comes a Horseman, Stone (*a.k.a. *Killing Stone)* (TV).
1979: *The Day Time Ended.*
1981: *Don't Look Back* (TV).

Television Series

1954–1955: *Stories of the Century* as Matt Clark.
1958–1959: *Rescue 8* as Wes Cameron.
1974: *The Cowboys* as U.S. Marshal Bill Winter.
1978–1981: *Dallas* as Jock Ewing.

Sources

Brodie, Ian. *Daily Telegraph* newspaper. April 1981.
McClelland, Doug. *Hollywood Talks Turkey.* Boston, MA: Faber and Faber, 1989.
Paterson, Graham. *Daily Express* newspaper. April 1981.
Willis, John. *Screen World.* London: Muller, 1982.

Note

Davis is frequently credited with appearances in the movies *Louisiana* (1947), *Mississippi Rhythm* (1949) and *Square Dance Katy* (1950), but these were another Jimmie Davis, the one-time Governor of Louisiana.

EDDIE DEAN

Eddie Dean was born Edgar Dean Glosup in Posey, Texas, on July 9, 1907, one of seven brothers. Even as a child he enjoyed music, so he bought himself a guitar and sang at social functions. His first professional engagement was as part of a singing quartet which toured the Midwest in the late 1920s. From there he sang on WIBW radio in Topeka for two years beginning in 1930. After acting in radio soap operas in Chicago during the early 1930s, he performed on the famous *National Barn Dance.* When the CBS radio coast-to-coast soap opera in which he had a leading role ended, he flipped a coin to decide whether to go to New York or Hollywood. It came up heads, so he went to Hollywood where he arrived in late 1937.

In Tinseltown he found it difficult to obtain the elusive break. He sang in a few small nightclubs before being tested at Republic, where he managed to obtain a membership in the Screen Actors Guild in 1938. He played numerous bit parts in horse operas before stardom came. He had a prominent featured role in *Harmony Trail* (1944), Ken Maynard's last film. This brought him to the attention of Bill Crespinel, who had developed a process called Cinecolor. Crespinel was trying to interest the major studios in using it but had no success, so he went to Dean and offered him an exclusive one-year contract if he could sell a Western series as a singing cowboy in Cinecolor. Dean accepted the challenge with backing from Producers Releasing Corporation. His first starring role was in *Song of Old Wyoming* (1945), which was shot on a budget of $36,000 in ten days. Since Dean was the only star shooting color B Westerns, the film was an enormous commercial success. PRC picked his option up and he was named one of the Ten Top Money Making Stars in the *Motion Picture Herald* Fame Poll in 1946 and 1947. He rode horses called Copper, Flash and White Cloud. He also wrote many of the songs which he sang in his films.

Eddie Dean (seated) with Roscoe Ates in *The Marshal of Gunsight Pass.*

He stayed with PRC for three years until they were absorbed by Eagle-Lion in 1947. At that time the budgets were trimmed and the movies reverted to black and white. By then many of the top Western stars were shooting in color and the additional expense could not be justified. Dean lasted one year at Eagle-Lion.

When Russell Hayden left the ABC-TV series *The Marshal of Gunsight Pass* in 1950 after only a few episodes, Dean replaced him in the hero's role. Andy Parker and the Plainsmen provided him with musical backing for his occasional songs. The series was broadcast live from a Los Angeles studio and shown via kinescope in the remainder of the country. The series was so lacking in the production values necessary to establish him as a small screen Western star that it folded after only four months.

In 1944 Dean was the featured male vocalist on radio's *Judy Canova Show* and on *The Western Varieties* show on station KTLA from 1944 to 1955. As a performer he remained active singing at rodeos, state fairs and upmarket niteries for decades. He was the yodeling cop in *The Beverly Hillbillies* television series. He continued his career as a successful songwriter with over 100 songs to his credit, of which the best known are "One Has My Name, The Other Has My Heart," which made the Country Charts in 1948, and "I Dreamed of a Hillbilly Heaven," which made the Country Top Ten in 1955. At last report he resided in West Lake Village, about 40 miles from Los Angeles. He has been married to wife Lorene (known as Dearest) since September 11, 1931.

Eddie Dean Filmography

1938: *Western Jamboree.*
1939: *The Lone Ranger Rides Again* (serial), *Range War, Law of the Pampas, The Llano Kid, Renegade Trail.*
1940: *Santa Fe Marshal, The Showdown, The Light of Western Stars, Hidden Gold, The Golden Trail, Stagecoach War, Oklahoma Renegades, Rollin' Home to Texas.*
1941: *Trail of the Silver Spurs, Kansas Cyclone, Down Mexico Way, Gaucho of Eldorado, Sierra Sue, Fighting Bill Fargo, Pals of the Pecos, Sunset in Wyoming, Outlaws of Cherokee Trail, West of Cimarron.*
1942: *Raiders of the West, Stagecoach Express, Arizona Stagecoach, The Lone Rider and the Bandit.*
1943: *King of the Cowboys.*
1944: *Harmony Trail.*
1945: *Wildfire, Song of Old Wyoming.*
1946: *Romance of the West, The Caravan Trail, Colorado Serenade, Down Missouri Way, Driftin' River, Tumbleweed Trail, Stars Over Texas, Wild West.*
1947: *Wild Country, Range Beyond the Blue, West to Glory, Black Hills, Shadow Valley.*
1948: *Check Your Guns, Tornado Range, The Westward Trail, The Hawk of Powder River, The Tioga Kid.*
1951: *Varieties on Parade.*

Television Series

1950: *The Marshal of Gunsight Pass* as Marshal Eddie Dean

Sources

Corneau, Ernest N. *The Hall of Fame of Western Film Stars.* N. Quincy, MA: Christopher, 1969.
Holland, Ted. *B Western Actors Encyclopedia: Facts, Photos and Filmographies for More than 250 Familiar Faces.* Jefferson, NC: McFarland, 1989.
Rothel, David. *The Singing Cowboys.* La Jolla, CA: Barnes, 1978.

Note

Eddie Dean is sometimes credited with starring in a film called *Prairie Outlaws* (1948), but this was a reedited rerelease of *Wild West* (1946).

CYRIL DELEVANTI

Born in England on February 23, 1887, this character actor, who was primarily a stage actor, drama coach, and musical hall performer, became much more familiar to movie audiences after 1940. He is probably best known for playing the poet Nonno in *Night of the Iguana* (1964). His sole regular role on television was in the Western series *Jefferson Drum,* in which he played the printer who was not only an employee of the hero, but also a loyal aide. He was 88 years old when he died in Hollywood on December 13, 1975, of lung cancer.

Cyril Delevanti Filmography

1931: *Devotion.*
1938: *Red Barry* (serial).
1940: *A Dispatch from Reuter's.*
1941: *Man Hunt.*
1942: *Journey for Margaret, Night Monster.*
1943: *Adventures of Smilin' Jack* (serial), *Frankenstein Meets the Wolf Man, Son of Dracula, Phantom of the Opera.*
1944: *The Lodger, The Invisible Man's Revenge, Ministry of Fear.*

1945: *Jade Mask, The Phantom of 42nd Street, Captain Tugboat Annie, This Love of Ours, Kitty, Confidential Agent, Jungle Queen* (serial), *The House of Fear, The Daltons Ride Again.*
1946: *The Shadow Returns, Deception, I'll Be Yours, Lost City of the Jungle* (serial), *Mysteries M&M* (serial).
1947: *Forever Amber, Monsieur Verdoux.*
1948: *The Emperor Waltz.*
1951: *David and Bathsheba.*
1952: *The Voice of Merrill, Limelight.*
1955: *Land of the Pharaohs.*
1956: *D-Day, The Sixth of June.*
1957: *Les Girls, Ride Out for Revenge, Trooper Hook.*
1958: *Gun Fever, Teacher's Pet, I Bury the Living.*
1960: *From the Terrace.*
1962: *Paradise Alley.*
1963: *Bye Bye Birdie.*
1964: *Mary Poppins, Night of the Iguana, Dead Ringer.*
1965: *The Greatest Story Ever Told.*
1967: *Oh Dad, Poor Dad, Mama's Hung You in the Closet and I'm Feeling So Sad.*
1968: *The Killing of Sister George, Counterpoint.*
1970: *Macho Callahan, Crowhaven Farm* (TV).
1971: *Bedknobs and Broomsticks.*
1973: *Soylent Green, The Girl Most Likely To ...* (TV).
1974: *Black Eye.*

Television Series

1958–1959: *Jefferson Drum* as Lucius Coin.

Sources

Brooks, Tim. *The Complete Directory to Prime Time TV Stars 1946–Present.* New York: Ballantine Books, 1987.
Truitt, Evelyn Mack. *Who Was Who On Screen Illustrated Edition.* New York: Bowker, 1984.

TERENCE de MARNEY

Portrait of Terence de Marney, who appeared in *Johnny Ringo*.

The actor who was known as "the Valentino of the air" because of his outstanding radio work was born in London on March 1, 1909, the son of Edouard de Marney and his wife, Eileen Concanen. He had one brother, actor Derrick de Marney (1906–1978). He was educated privately. He started his acting career at the age of 11 for half a crown a week and made his first appearance on the stage at the London Coliseum in 1923 as a pageboy in a sketch called *The Crown Jewels.* He was writing and producing plays before he was 19. He was best remembered for his pre-war radio serial role as the Count of Monte Cristo, and later as the hard-drinking private investigator Slim Callaghan, hero of the Peter Cheyney novels, whom he played at London's Garrick Theater.

After a string of successes writing, directing and acting in stage murder plays, a play in which he had heavily invested flopped in 1953. De Marney was broke. He left the British theater and spent two years in America, living from dollar to dollar as janitor, navvy and bottle washer. Then he got a break in television, and in seven years he played in 300 live and filmed Hollywood television shows including *Thriller, Wagon Train* and *Hawaiian Eye.* The role of the general store owner and father of the heroine in the Western series *Johnny Ringo* (1959–1960) was his only regular series role.

Nostalgia for London's theaterland took him back to Britain in 1962. He continued his career on television and occasionally in films, mainly playing eccentrics. He resided at Holland Street, Kensington. Plagued by ill health, he died on May 25, 1971, at age 62, when he jumped in front of a tube train at Kensington High Street Underground Station, London. Westminster coroner Gavin Thurston said the actor had left a note which clearly indicated that he intended to take his own life. Robin Lefever, de Marney's personal physician for five years, said about the actor, "He had a certain amount of depression, but he had an inner sadness of the creative artist and he was a great artist." He was married and divorced from actress Diana Hope Dunbar, and was later married to actress Beryl Meason, who died in 1965.

Terence de Marney Filmography

1931: *The Eternal Feminine.*
1932: *Heroes of the Mine, Merry Men of Sherwood.*
1933: *Little Napoleon, Eyes of Fate.*
1934: *The Unholy Quest.*
1935: *Immortal Gentleman, The Mystery of the Marie Celeste.*
1936: *Born That Way.*
1937: *House of Silence, Thunder in the City.*
1939: *I Killed the Count.*
1943: *They Met in the Dark.*
1946: *Dual Alibi.*
1949: *No Way Back.*
1954: *The Silver Chalice.*
1955: *Desert Sands, Target Zero.*
1956: *23 Paces to Baker Street.*
1957: *Pharaoh's Curse, My Gun Is Quick.*
1959: *The Wreck of the Mary Deare.*
1960: *The Secret of the Purple Reef, Spartacus, Midnight Lace.*
1961: *On the Double.*
1962: *Confessions of an Opium Eater.*
1965: *Monster of Terror,* (a.k.a. *Die Monster Die).*
1966: *Death Is a Woman.*
1967: *The Hand of Night.*
1968: *The Strange Affair.*
1969: *All Neat in Black Stockings.*

Television Series

1959–1960: *Johnny Ringo* as Case Thomas.

Sources

Daily Telegraph newspaper. May 1971.
Picture Show's Who's Who On Screen. London: Amalgamated Press, c. 1956.
Who's Who in the Theater Twelfth Edition London: Pitman, 1957.

Note

De Marney is frequently credited with an appearance in *Uneasy Terms* (1949), a notoriously poor British production in which Michael Rennie played the part of private eye Slim Callaghan. De Marney does not appear in this film, but since the script is uncredited, it is possible that he contributed to this.

ANDY DEVINE

Andy Devine was a jovial, humorous and outgoing person in real life. He possessed a very rotund figure, but he had been a star football player and could move with grace and agility. Although early on he was looked upon as star material, his real forte as a supporting player was comedy. He was also surprisingly effective in serious roles. A notable scene stealer, his other very memorable feature was his high-pitched, rasping voice.

There are alternate versions of how he came by it. The most commonly told is of how he was pretending that a curtain rod was a trumpet. As he was imitating playing the instrument, he tripped up and jammed the rod into the roof of his mouth, damaging the tissues of his palate and vocal chords. The other version is that he was out walking in a wood and picked up a stick to play with. When he accidentally fell down, the stick rammed into his throat and permanently injured his vocal chords. In later years certain reporters noted that in interviews he spoke in an ordinary, conversational tone, which prompted the actor to comment that his voice only rose when he had to project in acting. Whatever the origin, it turned out to be a decided asset in his acting career.

Andy Devine was born in Flagstaff, Arizona, on October 7, 1905, the son of Tom and Amy Ward Devine. His father was a hotel owner. His grandfather Admiral James Harmon Ward was one of the founders of Annapolis. Some reference books credit Devine with the real name of Jeremiah Schwartz, but this does not appear to have been substantiated. He received his early education at St. Mary and St. Benedict's College. When his father died, he was only 16. His father was virtually bankrupt, so Andy had to care for his mother and younger brother.

It was only through an athletic scholarship that he was able to continue with his education, first at Arizona Teacher's College and then later Santa Clara University, where he played football. After he graduated, he played professional football briefly, but he had his heart set on an acting career. After journeying to Hollywood in 1925, he made the rounds of the studios, but enjoyed little success. His first role was as an extra in the silent two-reeler series *The Collegians* at Paramount.

During a slack period he briefly joined the U.S. Lighthouse Service and sailed to the Bering Sea. Upon his return to Hollywood he became friendly with the popular actor Richard Arlen. The connecting link between the two of them was their mutual interest in flying (they later made a series of films with this theme). Arlen was instrumental in helping him to land his first important role, in *The Spirit of Notre Dame* (1930). In this film he played a dumb ballplayer who has to be intensively coached for his exams so that he can play for his college in an important match. It proved to be catnip to the masses, many of whom responded so favorably to Devine's characterization that they wrote to Universal asking that he be given better roles. He was signed to a contract by that studio where he remained until 1947, being loaned out from time to time.

It was with the coming of talking pictures that Devine really came into his own. He was particularly memorable in *Law and Order* (1932), a gritty Western in which he played a slightly retarded young man who is hanged for an accidental killing. Director John Ford used him to good effect in the classic Western *Stagecoach* (1939) in which he played Buck, the stagecoach driver. He was also highly successful on radio, notably as a regular on the Buck Benny sketches on *The Jack Benny Show*. A spinoff film, *Buck Benny Rides Again* (1940), was derived from this. Devine owned a flying school called Provo Devine which was used for the training of pilots by the government during World War II. When he quit Universal in 1947, he went to Republic where he appeared as Sheriff Cookie Bullfincher, the sidekick of Roy Rogers, in a series of nine feature films.

"James Butler Hickok," the hero would announce. Jingles Jones would shriek, "That's Wild Bill Hickok, mister! The bravest, strongest, fightingest U.S. Marshal in the whole West!" In 1951 producer William Broidy made a pitch to Devine to costar as Jingles, the sidekick of Guy Madison's *Wild Bill Hickok* in a television series. The offer was only $250 an episode, but the contract stipulated that the actor was to receive ten percent of the profits. Devine inked the deal, which was one of the shrewdest financial moves he ever made. Broidy shot the pilot, took it to New York, obtained sponsorship from Kelloggs, and signed one of the most lucrative deals in television history.

Between 1952 and 1956 there were 100 episodes shown ad nauseam in syndication so that the actor became a wealthy man. Between 1957 and 1958 there were a further 13 episodes shot in color and broadcast on ABC. Simultaneously, a highly successful *Wild Bill Hickok* radio series ran on the Mutual Network with the same two actors. The essence of the series was teamwork, although there is a widely held opinion that without Devine, it would not have been sold as a series. He contributed many comedy routines to the show, rehearsing beforehand and then having them incorporated into the script. In the series Jingles rode a horse

Andy Devine (right) with Guy Madison in *Wild Bill Hickok.*

called Joker. Jingles' catchphrase was, "Hey, Wild Bill, wait for me."

When Smilin' Ed McConnell died in 1954, Devine was asked to take over his kids' television show, which he did (the new title was *Andy's Gang*). It ran on NBC from 1954 to 1955. Despite negligible production values, it proved popular with the youngsters. He appeared as Sergeant Posey in *Two Rode Together* (1961) and as Link Appleyard in *The Man Who Shot Liberty Valance* (1962), both feature films directed by John Ford. Starting in 1957, Devine did a considerable amount of summer stock and played Captain Andy in several stage productions of *Showboat* (including the 1957 Broadway revival). He also appeared as Hap Gorman in the *Flipper* television series during the 1964–65 season lensed in Florida. He was the voice of Friar Tuck in Disney's animated *Robin Hood.*

A community activist, he served as mayor of Van Nuys, California, for 17 years. When he and his family relocated to Newport Beach in 1957, he became an active figure in community life there. In December 1975, he was rushed to a California hospital suffering from pneumonia and leukemia. He recovered and, as a steadfast Republican, campaigned aggressively for Ronald Reagan in 1976 when he was bidding for the Republican presidential nomination. In early 1977 Devine fell ill while camping near Santa Rosa, California. He died in a hospital there on February 18, 1977, of kidney failure and pneumonia. The 71-year-old actor was cremated and his ashes were scattered at sea.

While appearing with Will Rogers in *Dr. Bull* (1933), Devine was introduced (by Rogers) to actress Dorothy Irene House, whom he married on October 28, 1933, in Las Vegas. They had two sons, Tod, born in November 1934, and Denny, born in January 1939. They appeared with their father in *Canyon Passage* (1946). In real life Devine was a devoted husband and father who strongly believed in the family unit.

Andy Devine Filmography

1928: *We Americans, Lonesome, Red Lips.*
1929: *Hot Stuff, Naughty Baby.*
1930: *The Spirit of Notre Dame.*
1931: *The Criminal Code, Danger Island* (serial).
1932: *Law and Order, The Man from Yesterday, The Impatient Maiden, Destry Rides Again, Three Wise Girls, Radio Patrol, Tom Brown of Culver, Fast Companions (*a.k.a. *Information Kid), The All-American.*

1933: *Saturday's Millions, The Cohens and Kellys in Trouble, Midnight Mary, Horse Play, Chance at Heaven, Song of The Eagle, The Big Cage, Dr. Bull.*
1934: *The Poor Rich, Let's Talk It Over, Upper World, Gift of Gab, Wake Up and Dream, Million Dollar Ransom, Stingaree, Hell in the Heavens.*
1935: *The President Vanishes, Hold 'Em Yale, Chinatown Squad, Straight from the Heart, The Farmer Takes a Wife, Way Down East, Fighting Youth, Coronado.*
1936: *Flying Hostess, Romeo and Juliet, The Big Game, Yellowstone, Small Town Girl.*
1937: *Mysterious Crossing, A Star Is Born, Double or Nothing, You're a Sweetheart, The Road Back.*
1938: *Yellow Jack, Swing That Cheer, Personal Secretary, Strange Faces, The Storm, Men With Wings, In Old Chicago, Dr. Rhythm.*
1939: *Never Say Die, The Spirit of Culver, Mutiny on the Blackhawk, Stagecoach, Tropic Fury, Legion of Lost Flyers, Geronimo, The Man from Montreal.*
1940: *Little Old New York, Black Diamonds, Hot Steel, Torrid Zone, Margie, Danger on Wheels, The Leather Pushers, When the Daltons Rode, Trail of the Vigilantes, Buck Benny Rides Again, The Devil's Pipeline.*
1941: *A Dangerous Game, South of Tahiti, Lucky Devils, Road Agent, Men of the Timberland, The Kid from Kansas, The Flame of New Orleans, Mutiny in the Artic, Badlands of Dakota, Raiders of the Desert.*
1942: *Top Sergeant, North to the Klondike, Timber, Unseen Enemy, Sin Town, Danger in the Pacific, Between Us Girls, Escape from Hong Kong.*
1943: *Rhythm of the Islands, Frontier Badmen, Corvette K-225, Crazy House, Ali Baba and the 40 Thieves.*
1944: *Follow the Boys, Ghost Catchers, Babes on Swing Street, Bowery to Broadway.*
1945: *Sudan, Frontier Gal, That's the Spirit, Frisco Sal.*
1946: *Canyon Passage.*
1947: *The Michigan Kid, The Vigilantes Return, Bells of San Angelo, Springtime in the Sierras, The Marauders, On the Old Spanish Trail, The Fabulous Texan, Slave Girl.*
1948: *The Gallant Legion, The Gay Ranchero, Montana Belle* (released 1952), *Under California Skies, Old Los Angeles, Grand Canyon Trail, The Far Frontier, Eyes of Texas, Nighttime in Nevada.*
1949: *The Last Bandit, The Traveling Saleswoman.*
1950: *Never a Dull Moment.*
1951: *Slaughter Trail.*
1953: *Island in the Sky.*
1954: *Thunder Pass.*
1955: *Pete Kelly's Blues.*
1956: *Around the World In 80 Days.*
1960: *The Adventures of Huckleberry Finn.*
1961: *Two Rode Together.*
1962: *How the West Was Won, The Man Who Shot Liberty Valance.*
1963: *It's a Mad Mad Mad Mad World.*
1965: *Zebra in the Kitchen.*
1968: *The Ballad of Josie, The Road Hustlers.*
1969: *The Over-the-Hill Gang* (TV), *The Phynx.*
1970: *Myra Breckinridge, The Over-the-Hill Gang Rides Again* (TV).
1973: *Robin Hood* (voice only).
1975: *Won Ton Ton, the Dog Who Saved Hollywood.*
1976: *A Whale of a Tale.*
1977: *The Mouse and His Child* (voice only).

Television Series

1951–1958: *Wild Bill Hickok* as Jingles Jones.
1954–1955: *Andy's Gang* as himself.
1964–1965: *Flipper* as Hap Gorman.

Sources

Corneau, Ernest N. *The Hall of Fame of Western Film Stars.* N. Quincy, MA: Christopher, 1969.
Quinlan, David. *Illustrated Directory of Film Character Actors.* London: Batsford, 1995.
Rothel, David. *Those Great Cowboy Sidekicks.* Waynesville, NC: World of Yesterday Publications, 1984.
Willis, John. *Screen World.* London: Muller, 1978.

BOBBY DIAMOND

Bobby Diamond was born in Los Angeles on August 23, 1943, one of three children born to a real estate executive father and a musician mother. He attended stage schools, and as a toddler was on the cover of various national magazines. His mother pushed him into a show business career, but he was a very willing pupil. He was seen on other television series and in movies before he won the coveted role of Joey Newton in the Western adventure series *Fury*.

In the first episode of the series, some boys are playing baseball in the street. When a window is broken, the boys try to pin the blame on Joey, who is innocent but suspected of being a troublemaker. After the disturbance he is taken into custody by a cop. Jim Newton (Peter Graves) witnessed the incident and helps his courtroom defense. When the judge discovers that Joey is an orphan, he allows Jim to take him to live with him on his ranch, The Broken Wheel in Arizona, and start adoption proceedings. Fury is a magnificent wild black stallion which only Joey can ride. Jim gives him to Joey to give him some sense of responsibility.

The series was set in the contemporary West and concerned the problems faced with running a ranch and dealing with such problems as crooks, animals and juvenile delinquency. The series was produced primarily for children by the Independent Television Corporation. Most of the episodes had a moral, although they were so entertaining that the preaching seldom detracted from the story. Diamond played Joey in all 114 black and white episodes. The series was shown in syndication for decades.

Diamond continued his career after *Fury* was given the axe. He made the greatest professional mistake of his career when he rejected the role of one of Fred MacMurray's sons in *My Three Sons* in favor of a situation comedy called *Yes Yes Nanette*. The series he accepted lasted six months. The one he rejected lasted 12 years. He then had a regular role on another situation comedy, *The Many Loves of Dobie Gillis*. Around this time his mother (the business brains behind her son) died. He had little desire to deal personally with the agents and producers who wield the power in the Hollywood scene.

Since 1971 he has been a practicing attorney with offices in Woodland Hills, California, specializing in criminal law and personal injury. He has frequently professed not to miss acting since appearing before a jury is performing in a somewhat similar vein. He has very occasionally continued to act, being seen in an episode of *Banyon* in 1972, several commercials, and in a supporting role in a low-budget horror movie which remained on the shelf for years. For three years he had a recurring role as a lawyer on *Divorce Court*. He is very heavily into physical fitness and is an accomplished oil painter.

At last report Diamond was single and residing in Thousand Oaks, California.

Bobby Diamond Filmography

1947: *The Mating of Millie*.
1952: *Young Man with Ideas*.
1953: *The Glass Slipper, The Silver Whip, The Lady Wants Mink*.
1955: *Untamed, To Hell and Back*.
1962: *Airborne*.
1969: *The Silent Gun* (TV).
1981: *The Outing* (a.k.a. *Scream*).

Television Series

1955–1958: *Fury* as Joey Newton.
1961: *The Westinghouse Playhouse* (a.k.a. *Yes Yes Nanette*) as Buddy.
1962–1963: *The Many Loves of Dobie Gillis* as Duncan Gillis.

Sources

Dye, David. *Child and Youth Actors: Filmographies of Their Entire Careers*. Jefferson, NC: McFarland, 1988.
Lamparski, Richard. *Whatever Became Of? Eighth Series*. New York: Crown, 1982.
Taylor, Delphine. "Growing Pains—Where Are They Now?" *Memories* magazine, June 1989.

DON DIAMOND

Don Diamond has played costarring roles in three successful television series, done some 25 movies and appeared in over 100 television series. His true *metier,* however, lies as much in the vocal as in the physical side of acting. He speaks fluent Spanish and can simulate in excess of 20 authentic dialects from all over the world. He has been much in demand for providing the voices of characters in cartoons and can truly be called "The Man of a Thousand Voices."

Diamond was born in Brooklyn, New York, on June 4, 1921. His father, who was born in Russia, served in the U.S. Army in the First World War and was awarded the Purple Heart and the Silver Star medals. His mother was born in New Jersey. As a teenager she won the New Jersey Typewriter Championship. They were excellent parents who encouraged their son to earn some money selling soda pop at the local ballpark, mowing lawns and shoveling snow.

He lived some of his teen years in the Mohawk Valley town of Little Falls. From 1938 to 1942 he studied drama at the University of Michigan, where he waited tables and scrubbed pots in order to finance his studies, eventually graduating with a B.A. degree. During the summers he was a waiter at children's and adult camps.

While awaiting induction into the air corps, Diamond spent three months in New York City and worked a number of radio shows. These included the famous *March of Time* series where he did dialect roles in the Spanish language. He learned more Spanish while serving in the U.S. Military in the Southwest (notably in Arizona and Colorado) as well as increasing his understanding of the Mexican culture.

He was honorably discharged from the service in 1946 as a first lieutenant. Breaking into radio acting, he gained a reputation as an excellent portrayer of Latins and Mexicans. This led to his costarring role in 104 episodes of *The Adventures of Kit Carson* as El Toro, Carson's sidekick. Of this experience he recalls, "It was a pleasure to work with the late Bill Williams, but the two-day schedules for each half-hour show were tough. The horses couldn't read the scripts or the stagecoaches. We became so tired at the end of a long day that upon fluffing our lines, he and I would break into uncontrollable laughter and they would have to shoot the scene over and over again. Once the director told me to do the Mexican stereotype by sitting at the base of a large cactus and feign sleeping. In spite of the fact that I had no power or money, I defied the director and refused to malign any group—for instance, Mexicans."

Diamond is equally well-known for playing Corporal Reyes in 50 episodes of Disney's *Zorro* television series. "In the late 1950s I didn't get a running role when they screen-tested the first *Zorro* show. In about episode eight, I did a bit as a Spanish soldier. Subsequently they tested for a corporal to be a foil for Sgt. Garcia. I won the screen test, downplaying the role because I knew Mr. Disney wanted Sgt. Garcia to get the big laughs. I enjoyed working with Guy Williams and Henry Calvin. We truly became close friends."

Diamond made his motion picture debut in *Borderline* (1950) playing the role of Deusik. He subsequently went on to appear in over 25 other films and over 100 television series, sometimes in multiple appearances. He has also provided the voices of characters in cartoon series. He was Sgt. Gonzalez in *Zorro,* Toro in *Tijuana Toads* and Fatso in *Texas Toads.* From 1965 to 1967 he played Crazy Cat in *F Troop,* a very popular comedy Western series. He recalls, "I broke the stereotype of the deep bass voice Indian and did Crazy Cat in a high pitched voice. The role caught on."

For recreation he plays four-wall handball at the Hollywood Wilshire YMCA three times a week. He has been a member there for 45 consecutive years. He reads a lot, is an enthusiastic amateur radio operator and loves to tell jokes in English and Spanish. Of his family he says, "My wife Louisa is a Spanish teacher in an L.A. high school. She's from Mexico. Our lovely daughter Roxanne makes us so proud of her high grades at a local university, plus the fact that she's been invited into so many honorary societies."

Don Diamond Filmography

1950: *Borderline.*
1957: *Omar Khayyam, The Tijuana Story.*
1958: *Fraulein.*
1959: *Holiday for Lovers.*
1960: *The Story of Ruth.*
1963: *Irma La Douce.*
1964: *The Carpetbaggers.*
1967: *Double Trouble.*
1968: *How Sweet It Is!*
1969: *Viva Max!*
1971: *Mrs. Polifax—Spy, What's a Nice Girl Like You?* (TV).
1972: *The Judge and Jake Wyler* (TV), *Hit Man, Pete 'n' Tillie, The Scavengers (*a.k.a. *How to Steal an Airplane, Only One Day Left Before Tomorrow)* (TV).
1973: *Hawkins on Murder* (TV), *Breezy.*
1975: *The Apple Dumpling Gang.*
1976: *The Shaggy D.A.*
1978: *The Toolbox Murders.*
1980: *Hog Wild, Herbie Goes Bananas.*
1982: *The Kid with the Broken Halo* (TV).

Television Series

1951–1955: *The Adventures of Kit Carson* as El Toro.
1957–1959: *Zorro* as Corporal Reyes.
1965–1967: *F Troop* as Crazy Cat.

Don Diamond in *The Adventures of Kit Carson.*

Sources

Correspondence between Diamond and the author.

MASON ALAN DINEHART III

This young actor played the important role of Bat Masterson in the television Western series *The Life and Legend of Wyatt Earp* for a couple of seasons. When Wyatt Earp was Marshal of Dodge City, Masterson was his deputy before he left to become a county sheriff with his own jurisdiction. The actor also appeared in episodes of various other Western series such as *The Lone Ranger* and *The Texan.* He starred in a few movies, usually with youth-orientated themes suitable for drive-ins. His acting career virtually ended with the 1950s, and he has latterly been posted as one of the lost players of the screen.

Mason Alan Dinehart III Filmography

1948: *Superman* (serial).
1949: *Blondie's Big Deal, The Sun Comes Up, Easy Living.*
1950: *Copper Canyon, The Happy Years, Never a Dull Moment.*
1957: *The Careless Years.*
1958: *The Hot Angel.*
1959: *Road Racers.*
1960: *Platinum High School.*

Mason Alan Dinehart III (right) with Hugh O'Brian in *The Life and Legend of Wyatt Earp.*

Television Series

1955–1957: *The Life and Legend of Wyatt Earp* as Bat Masterson.

Sources

Brooks, Tim. *The Complete Directory to Prime Time TV Stars 1946–Present.* New York: Ballantine Books, 1987.

Speed, F. Maurice. *The Western Film and TV Annual.* London: MacDonald, 1957.

GEORGE DUNN

George Dunn had minor supporting roles in films and on television. He played one semi-regular role in *Cimarron City,* a Western series of the 1950s. He died on April 27, 1982.

George Dunn Filmography

1953: *How To Marry a Millionaire.*
1955: *Good Morning Miss Dove, Daddy Long Legs, Prince of Players.*
1956: *Away All Boats.*
1957: *Joe Dakota, The Kettles on Old MacDonald's Farm.*
1958: *The Long Hot Summer.*
1959: *Operation Petticoat.*
1965: *Baby the Rain Must Fall.*
1967: *Stranger on the Run* (TV).
1971: *The Beguiled.*

Television Series

1958–1959: *Cimarron City* as Jesse Williams.
1965–1966: *Camp Runamuck* as the Sheriff.

Sources

Brooks, Tim. *The Complete Directory to Prime Time TV Stars 1946–Present.* New York: Ballantine Books, 1987.
Ragan, David. *Who's Who in Hollywood.* New York: Facts on File, 1992.

PETE DUNN

Born in 1922, this bit player and stuntman appeared in a semi-regular role in a Western television series of the 1950s, *Cimarron City.* He died on April 14, 1990, at age 68, of a heart attack.

Pete Dunn Filmography

1951: *Soldiers Three.*
1953: *Invaders from Mars.*
1956: *Giant.*
1957: *Band of Angels.*
1961: *The Monster of Piedras Blancas* (title role).
1970: *Chisum.*
1972: *The Poseidon Adventure.*
1976: *The Shootist.*

Television Series

1958–1959: *Cimarron City* as Dody Hamer.

Sources

Brooks, Tim. *The Complete Directory to Prime Time TV Stars 1946–Present.* New York: Ballantine Books, 1987.
Ragan, David. *Who's Who in Hollywood.* New York: Facts on File, 1992.

DON DURANT

Don Durant was an American television Western series star of somewhat obscure origins. After leaving high school, he drifted to Hollywood in the early 1950s determined on a show business career. He was active in various little theater groups and studied music. He had an act that was playing in Las Vegas when he was drafted in 1952. After his honorable discharge he returned to show business, where he had a break on television. His film career was

Don Durant in *Johnny Ringo.*

negligible apart from the lead in a Roger Corman quickie called *She Gods of Shark Reef* (1956), shot on location in Hawaii.

In 1958 he was spotted by Dick Powell in a busted television pilot called *MacGreedy's Woman* with Jane Russell. The *Johnny Ringo* series began life as a 1959 episode of *Zane Grey Theater* called "Man Alone," in which Durant was fourth-billed although he was the hero of the segment. Powell was so impressed with Durant and the quality of the segment that he ordered a series with Durant as the star. Allegedly based on the exploits of a notorious real-life gunfighter, the Johnny Ringo character was now the sheriff of Velardi, Arizona, during the 1880s. On his first day in town he warned the locals, "The next man I find wearing a gun better know how to use it." He and his less experienced deputy Cully (Mark Goddard) handled the day to day crises and crimes which came to the town. Laura Thomas (Karen Sharpe) was the daughter of drunken Case Thomas (Terence de Marney), the owner of the general store. She found herself falling in love with Johnny Ringo. He is married to actress Trudy Wroe.

Johnny Ringo, however, was an action series and not a romance. Ringo frequently found himself up against gunfighters eager to kill him. The gimmick of this series lay in the weapon which they faced. Ringo's handgun was no ordinary weapon. The barrel underneath had been restructured to shoot a single shotgun bullet, which made it deadly. *Johnny Ringo* was a half-hour black and white series which debuted on CBS on October 1, 1959. It ended after a short run of 38 episodes; the last aired on September 29, 1960. Durant's musical training came in handy because he wrote and sang the theme song of the series. While the series was efficiently shot with attractive and talented players, it was not one of the classics of the genre and there was too little to distinguish it from other Western series playing on television at the same time.

After the demise of the series, Durant found himself at a career crossroads. On the one hand, there was show business with all of the insecurities attached thereto. On the other there was a more secure career, so he elected to become a realtor, at which he appears to have done extremely well. He did, however, continue to appear on television occasionally (for instance, the "No Place To Run" episode of *Laramie* aired in 1963). At last report he was living in comfort in Encino, California. Once asked about his affluence, he replied modestly, "I ain't hurting."

Don Durant Filmography

1956: *She Gods of Shark Reef.*

Television Series

1959–1960: *Johnny Ringo* as Johnny Ringo.

Sources

Goldberg, Lee. *Unsold Television Pilots 1955 through 1989.* Jefferson, NC: McFarland, 1990.

Quotation from a Western convention in the early 1990s.

Summers, Neil. *The Official TV Western Book Volume #2.* Vienna, WV: Old West Publishing Shop, 1989.

RICHARD EASTHAM

Richard Eastham was born Dickinson Swift Eastham in Opelousas, Louisiana, on June 22, 1918. He began singing as a boy soprano in St. Louis, Missouri, where he grew up. A few years after his soprano settled to baritone, he found himself singing small roles with the St. Louis Grand Opera Company and the Grand Opera in Havana, Cuba. This was followed by a voice scholarship from the famous Percy Rector Stephens in New York. World War II interrupted his studies and Eastham, entering the army as a private, served four years in the European Theater of Operations and worked his way up to the rank of Major,

Richard Eastham (left) with Pat Conway in *Tombstone Territory.*

the Executive Officer of a Signal Corps Battalion. Upon his return he studied acting and singing at the American Theater Wing and was later awarded a New York State Scholarship.

His first job on Broadway was singing in the orchestra pit of *A Flag Was Born* (1946). He later carried a spear in Judith Anderson's *Medea* (1947) and performed a variety of leading roles in summer theater. He first came into national prominence when as understudy to Ezio Pinza in *South Pacific* in 1951, he replaced the star as the romantic French planter opposite Mary Martin. Originally cast as a Seabee, he was thought to be too young to understudy the Pinza role, but his makeup and characterization were so convincing that the producers gave him the chance. His performance engendered such enthusiasm from the critics, the public and the show's producers (Rodgers and Hammerstein, Joshua Logan and Leland Hayward) that when the national company of *South Pacific* was organized, he was starred with Janet Blair for a record-breaking two-year tour. Riding high on this achievement, he was then recalled to Broadway to play opposite Ethel Merman in *Call Me Madam*, replacing Paul Lukas.

Offers quickly followed, and he did guest appearances on television including the prestigious *Ed Sullivan Show* and the recording of the *South Pacific* show album for RCA. He donned a beard to play Heidi's grandfather in the Max Liebman television special. Determined to try his hand at comedy, he starred with Marjorie Lord in *Anniversary Waltz* for many months, breaking the all-time record for San Francisco. They later teamed for *The Girl in the Freudian Slip* and *Mary Mary*. His many stage musical roles include *The Sound of Music, Fanny, Carousel, Annie Get Your Gun, Show Boat* and Leonard Bernstein's *Trouble in Tahiti* and *Wonderful Town*.

He made his screen debut as Marilyn Monroe's manager in *There's No Business Like Show Business* (1954). Subsequently he played Bing Crosby's rival in *Man On Fire* (1957), and the dynamic Colonel Castle in Walt Disney's *Toby Tyler* (1960). On television he starred as the editor of the *Tombstone Epitaph* on the popular Western series *Tombstone Territory* for three years. He also narrated the series. He appeared as a regular on *Wonder Woman* and for one season on *Falcon Crest.* He has appeared on dozens of shows such as *Hart to Hart, The Waltons, Kojak* and *Quincy.* He has also provided stalwart support in movies for television (such as playing Shirley Jones's husband in 1969's *Silent Night, Lonely Night*), and miniseries and specials such as the acclaimed *Missiles Of October* (1974). Eastham resides in Los Angeles.

Richard Eastham Filmography

1954: *There's No Business Like Show Business.*
1957: *Man on Fire.*
1960: *Toby Tyler.*
1965: *That Darn Cat.*
1966: *Not With My Wife You Don't!*
1967: *Murderers' Row.*
1969: *Silent Night, Lonely Night* (TV).
1971: *The President's Plane Is Missing* (TV).
1973: *Tom Sawyer, Battle for the Planet of the Apes.*
1974: *McQ.*
1975: *Attack On Terror* (TV).
1980: *Condominium* (TV).
1982: *A Wedding on Walton's Mountain* (TV).

Television Series

1957–1960: *Tombstone Territory* as Harris Claibourne.
1969–1972: *Bright Promise* as Red Wilson.
1976–1977: *Wonder Woman* as General Philip Blankenship.
1982–1983: *Falcon Crest* as Dr. Howell.

Sources

Correspondence between Eastham and the author.

CLINT EASTWOOD

One intriguing aspect of Clint Eastwood is that he established himself as a movie star at a time when the American film industry was in steep decline. This in itself was quite an achievement, although it was the foreign Western rather than the American variety which did the trick. Some authorities draw comparisons between the monosyllabic monolith which is Eastwood's forte and stars of a former era such as Gary Cooper and John Wayne. Such comparisons are spurious because the era of Cooper and Wayne was completely different from the era which spawned Clint Eastwood. He would probably never have made it during the golden era of Hollywood. A more valid comparison can be drawn between Eastwood and his *Rawhide* costar Eric Fleming. Both men were loners, fiercely independent men who struggled for years to make the grade in Hollywood. Both came from similar backgrounds of families struggling for survival during the Depression years. Eastwood's background was more tolerable since there appears to be no history of physical abuse. Both were equally talented. After *Rawhide,* both gravitated to low-budget movies. Fleming died an ignominious death in Peru and is seldom remembered today, while Eastwood went on to become a rich and powerful Hollywood megastar.

Clint Eastwood is the most successful actor ever to have made the transition from small to big screen. Nobody seeing him as soft-voiced Rowdy Yates would have predicted that big a future for him. His celebrity status really stems from two characters he played, "The Man with No Name" from the spaghetti Westerns and detective "Dirty" Harry Callahan with his .44 Magnum. Both have become part of movie legend. In general, his better films tend to be those which he has not directed himself.

The world which his characters inhabit tends to be a very macho one. Although he has said that he likes strong female roles in his pictures, it is to his detriment that the roles of women in many of them have either been downplayed or are virtually nonexistent. The actresses who have played major roles in his films have not tended to be particularly striking either in terms of ability or looks. He admits, "The women's roles have often been built up these days."

Eastwood himself has always been a very

Clint Eastwood in *Rawhide*.

private man, choosing to live in Carmel, hundreds of miles from Hollywood. A sportsman and conservationist, he admits he goes "through periods of liking to be around people and other times when I don't want to be around anyone. It's very easy for me to go off by myself for long periods of time. Sometimes you just don't want to think or talk or listen." He adds, "I guess I am shy. I don't really like drawing attention to myself. I also hate being stared at and it doesn't turn me on when members of the public take notice of me."

About the Western he has said, "I guess I am pretty committed to the continuation of the Western, not only because of my background—I've had some notoriety from Westerns—but also because it's a genre in which you can analyze new subject matter and moralities; you can take it in different directions, otherwise it gets into a rut." It's common knowledge that he works quickly and cheaply, mainly due to his insistence on retaining the same team from movie to movie. Actor Richard Harris said about him, "Clint is a terrific guy, very charming and laid back, [and] he's so organized it's unbearable! He knows exactly what he wants, and the crew know exactly what he wants—one guy on wardrobe has been with him since *Rawhide*—so nobody raises their voice on the set; Clint doesn't like aggravation or temperament."

Clinton Eastwood, Jr., was born in San Francisco, California, on May 31, 1930, the older child of Clinton and Ruth Eastwood. His father was of Scottish-English descent and his mother of Irish ancestry. He also has a younger sister, Jeanne. During the Great Depression, his father had immense problems finding a job. He was reasonably well-educated and a qualified cost accountant, but at one point he was pumping gas at a petrol station. The family moved from one town in Northern California to another. As a result the future star attended at least ten different high schools. Their most permanent home was their grandmother's small chicken ranch near Sonol, California. He was crazy about his hardy, independent grandmother, and now acknowledges that she had as much influence on his early years as his young parents. It was there he learned to ride a horse.

Eventually his father obtained an executive post with the Container Corporation of America in Oakland, California. Clint took up competitive swimming at the various schools he attended and played basketball for Oakland Technical High School. His major hobby was jazz, and at the age of 15 he was playing the piano for free meals at a club in Oakland. After graduating from Oakland Technical High School in 1948, he worked as a lumberjack with the Weyhauser Lumber Company, as a forest firefighter in Springfield, Oregon, and as a steelworker at the Bethlehem Steel Plant in Seattle. He moved to Renton (near Seattle) where he worked as a lifeguard and in the parts department at the Boeing Aircraft Plant.

In 1951 during the Korean War he was drafted into the army, but he never saw combat. En route to Korea, his plane ditched into the Pacific, forcing him to swim a couple of miles to shore. On the strength of this he was made a swimming instructor at Fort Ord in California. While there he met some actors such as David Janssen and Martin Milner who encouraged him to try acting. When he was discharged in 1953, he enrolled in business administration at Los Angeles City College under the G.I. Bill. Simultaneously he began making the rounds of various studios. An ex-army buddy, who was now a cameraman at Universal, persuaded him to take a screen test and he landed a $75-a-week contract with Universal in 1955.

After 18 months of playing bit parts, he was dropped by the studio after making a request for a salary increase. According to Burt Reynolds (who was fired on the same day), "He wasn't good-looking enough and his Adam's Apple stuck out too much." Lean times followed; he drew unemployment benefits and worked as a lifeguard and as a swimming pool digger. He was contemplating giving up acting and returning to college when fate took a hand. He was cast as the Ramrod, second in command to the trail boss in *Rawhide,* a series about cattle drives on the Great Plains in the 1870s. Eastwood was in Hollywood one day to see a story consultant, a friend of his wife Maggie. While talking to her, a man named Robert Sparks noticed him. Sparks had been discussing the show's casting with producer Charles Marquis Warren. When he saw Eastwood, he shouted, "Rowdy Yates!" The actor was rushed into the office to meet the producer, who began asking him all sorts of questions. Eastwood told them that he had had acting experience in films. He was then invited for a test, which he passed.

The first dozen episodes were shot in the fall of 1958, but soon afterwards the CBS network wondered if it had made a dreadful mistake and considered shelving the series. At Christmas, however, Eastwood received a telegram from his agent informing him that network executives had decided to broadcast the program after Christmas. *Rawhide* premiered on January 9, 1959, and the last episode was aired on January 4, 1966, almost seven years to the day later. The series stressed authenticity. The first episodes were shot on location in Arizona using real cowboys in the action sequences. Eastwood's own horsemanship improved considerably, and he went on record as saying that his years spent in the series were some of the most rewarding of his career.

"One thing a series affords somebody is great security," he said. "In a series you're going to work every week and if you try something one week and it doesn't work, you're going to be employed the next week so it doesn't make any difference. So you can ... try anything you want and file all the things that work for you in your brain and discard what doesn't work—it's a great training ground." In 1960–1961 *Rawhide* ranked as high as sixth in the Nielsen ratings, but by 1963–1964, it had slumped to number 44. For the final half season, Eastwood was elevated to the position of trail boss, but this did not work out. It was later reported that Eastwood refused to renew his contract when the producers reneged on a promise to let him direct some episodes. He also probably shrewdly realized that the series was pretty well played out.

In 1964, during a four-month break in the *Rawhide* production schedule, Eastwood went to Spain to star for $15,000 in a spaghetti Western directed by Sergio Leone. It was eventually called *A Fistful of Dollars* and was shot on a budget of $200,000. While Eastwood admitted that part of his reason for agreeing to work with Leone was the chance of a free trip to Europe, he was also intrigued with the script the Italian director had sent to him. The plot for the movie was a shameless reworking of *Yojimbo,* a Japanese film about a 14th-century samurai. This later resulted in litigation which caused a delayed release of the film in America, although the case was settled out of court. As "The Man with No Name," Eastwood manipulates for profit two families warring against each other in the same town. He played a Western hero without the usual heroic attributes. Although his character originally had more dialogue, Eastwood persuaded Leone to pare down the script because he believed there should be much more mystery to the character of the gunfighter. He emerged as a poncho-clad, unshaven, cigar-smoking hombre who was homeless, lawless and fearless.

A Fistful of Dollars firmly established Eastwood as an international star; the movie grossed $7 million in Europe and $4 million in Italy. He returned to Spain for two sequels: 1965's *For a Few Dollars More,* in which he costarred with Lee Van Cleef, and 1966's *The Good, the Bad and the Ugly,* in which Van Cleef and Eli Wallach costarred. For the former he received $50,000, for the latter $250,000 plus a percentage of the profits. Eastwood and Leone later had an irreconcilable difference of opinion when Leone blew up a bridge Eastwood had just crossed in *The Good, the Bad and the Ugly* allegedly because it improved the shot. Eastwood also appeared in the "Night Like Any Other" segment of *The Witches* (1966) in Italy opposite Silvana Mangano.

Eastwood was held in low esteem in America until the spaghetti Western trilogy was finally released there and grossed a fortune. As a result he found himself a bankable star in America, where he was approached by European distributors who were keen for him to star in an American film for the first time. As a consequence Eastwood formed his own production company (Malpaso Productions) in 1968 and signed a contract to make a Western for $40,000 in addition to 25 percent of the profits. "Malpaso" is an amalgam of two Spanish words meaning "bad step," but in fact this was one of the best steps he had ever taken. In *Hang 'Em High* (1967), a crude American parody of the crude foreign parodies of the American Western, Eastwood plays a man who survived his own hanging and seeks revenge on the nine men responsible. Distributor United Artists recouped its investment within ten weeks.

Coogan's Bluff (1968) was the first of several films to be directed by Don Siegel. It ultimately served as the basis for the television series *McCloud.* Eastwood played an Arizona lawman who tracks down a criminal in New York City. The Siegel-Eastwood relationship turned out to be one of the most fruitful in Hollywood history, but it almost didn't happen at all. Eastwood, whom Siegel allegedly had never met or seen, was at Universal trying to decide between two directors for *Coogan's Bluff,* Alex Segal and Don Taylor. The new computer in the basement of the Black Tower (a Universal building) was fed these two names, but the name which magically came out was Don Siegel. Eastwood asked, "Who the hell is Don Siegel?" (Eastwood, a self-professed movie buff, had never heard of him.) On seeing some of Siegel's films, Eastwood was enthusiastic and requested that Siegel be hired.

Eastwood then went on to appear in *Where Eagles Dare* (1968), a World War II adventure story in which his role was very much subordinate to that of Richard Burton. Eastwood moved completely away from his customary roles to essay the romantic lead and croon a couple of tunes in *Paint Your Wagon* (1969). This was a Paramount film based on Lerner and Loewe's Broadway musical comedy of the California Gold Rush. The extravagance which he witnessed on this film was instrumental in making Eastwood want to produce his own films at a fraction of the cost.

He was back on more familiar territory in *Two Mules for Sister Sara* (1969) in which he portrayed an American soldier of fortune in Mexico who is reluctantly pressed into helping a prostitute (Shirley MacLaine) disguised as a nun. The film was originally the idea of Elizabeth Taylor, who gave the script to Eastwood with the intention of it being a vehicle for herself and him. She insisted, however, that it should be shot in Spain, so that she could be close to her then-husband Richard Burton, but Universal said no and substituted Shirley MacLaine. In *Kelly's Heroes* (1970) he was the leader of a band of larcenous American soldiers who steal millions of dollars worth of gold bullion from the Nazis. This is another film which he was bitterly disappointed with because it eschewed Vietnam parallels and satire in favor of bullets and explosions. In *The Beguiled* (1971), a gloomy Gothic tale set during the American Civil War, Eastwood played a wounded union officer seeking refuge in a Southern girls' school where he is eventually murdered by the sex-starved students. Director Don Siegel has gone on record as saying that this is his favorite film, but it is one of the few Eastwood films from this period not to do well commercially.

By 1971 his films had collectively grossed an estimated $200 million, and he was able to command a salary of about $1,000,000 per movie plus a percentage of the profits. Repelled by the waste which he had witnessed during the production of some of his films, he turned director for *Play Misty for Me* (1971) in which he played a radio disc jockey hounded by a psychopathic fan (Jessica Walter). The movie borrowed heavily from Alfred Hitchcock in general and *Psycho* in particular in that it replicated some similar characters and incidents. The film has latterly acquired a reputation as a cult classic, and the idea later provided the basis for *Fatal Attraction* (1987).

Don Siegel directed *Dirty Harry* (1971), which established the quintessential Eastwood persona: a cynical hardcase prepared to bend the law (or break it) in order to protect society. As Inspector Harry Callahan, Eastwood tracked a homicidal maniac who was on the loose because of the stupidity of Callahan's ineffectual superiors. Of *Dirty Harry* he has said, "All Dirty Harry has ever wanted is to make some sense of the system. Originally the part was written for an older man than I was when I first played it. He was a guy who had been on the force a long time, a mature guy who was fed up with what he saw happening to people. The laws are crazy, he was saying. A lot of people felt that way. That's one reason the films are so popular."

In contrast to the sequels, the original movie maintains an excellent pace and tension throughout. It was very successful at the box office, but Eastwood found himself attacked by critics who accused him of being a fascist. His response in the first sequel *Magnum Force* (1973), directed by Ted Post, was to let Callahan defend the system against some renegade cops who were using their uniforms as an excuse to waste lowlife criminals who could not legally be touched. Although *Magnum Force* outgrossed its predecessor, artistically it is a much lesser film.

Eastwood returned to the Western genre as *Joe Kidd* (1972), a gunfighter who protects oppressed Mexican peasants. It was one of director John Sturges's lesser efforts. In *High Plains Drifter* (1973) he again directed himself as a ghost who returns from beyond the grave to avenge himself on townsfolk who have given sanctuary to his killers. *Thunderbolt and Lightfoot* (1974), a crime drama centered around a bank heist in Montana, was notable as the first movie directed by Michael Cimino and about his only economical one in that it came in on schedule and under budget. This owed more to Eastwood's watchful eye than Cimino. Eastwood then directed himself in *The Eiger Sanction* (1975), a very disappointing version of the bestselling novel by Trevanian. It was notable for Eastwood doing his own stunt work, which included mountain climbing in Switzerland. This was definitely an occasion in which a better film would have emerged if Eastwood had left the directing to a top action director of the John Sturges kind.

He took over the directorial reins when Phil Kaufman quit *The Outlaw Josey Wales* (1976). Set in the era of the post–American Civil War, he played the title character of a Missouri farmer forced to defend himself when union marauders massacre his wife and children. This was probably his most accomplished film as a director. It was while filming this movie that Eastwood became involved with his leading lady Sondra Locke. They became live-in lovers and their relationship would later erupt into a volcano of headlines. This was the first of half a dozen films which he made with Locke, some of them *(The Gauntlet* and *Sudden Impact)* among his worst films.

He played Dirty Harry again in *The Enforcer* (1976) in which Tyne Daly costarred as his partner. He directed *The Gauntlet* (1977) and starred as a disgraced Arizona police officer assigned to bringing a prostitute (Sondra Locke) from Las Vegas to Phoenix to give testimony at the trial of a mobster. This film fell to a new low, seeming to consist of a series of shootouts, each one more ridiculous than the last. The acting was so minimalistic as to be almost nonexistent. He was back on form with *Every Which Way But Loose* (1978), a lighter film in which he played a California trucker who makes ends meet by competing in bare knuckle boxing matches. His sidekicks are a foul-mouthed hag played by Ruth Gordon and a foul-smelling orangutan named Clyde. This proved to be his biggest hit up to that time, grossing $87,000,000 by 1982. The sequel, *Any Which Way You Can* (1982), also proved to be very popular.

Escape from Alcatraz (1979) was the last of his films to be directed by Don Siegel and one of his best. Eastwood played the leader of a small group of prisoners who appeared to make the only successful escape from Alcatraz Prison. In *Bronco Billy* (1980) Eastwood again directed himself as a former New Jersey shoe salesman who owns a Wild West show in which he performs as a trick rider and sharpshooter. This is reportedly the star's favorite of his own films. *Firefox* (1982) followed the pattern of *The Eiger Sanction* in that it was based on a bestselling thriller (in this case by Craig Thomas). Eastwood played an American pilot hired to steal a technologically advanced Soviet aircraft. This was an extremely disappointing film, fatally compromised by a total lack of female interest.

Honkytonk Man (1982) was a longwinded and personal odyssey in which he directed himself as a washed-up, consumptive country-western singer who travels to Nashville to audition during the Depression years. His 14-year-old nephew was played by his real-life son Kyle. There was so much of himself in this film that it began to resemble a self-indulgent home movie and was financially a loser. Even more repulsive was *Sudden Impact* (1983), the fourth Dirty Harry film, in which he directed himself. Sondra Locke played a woman who revenges herself on the gang who brutally raped her and her sister. The violence was so gratuitous and over the top that it is hard to imagine anyone being entertained, but it was his biggest hit up to that time, grossing $120 million. In this one he first issued his catchphrase, "Go ahead, make my day!" He went on to team with then-megastar Burt Reynolds in the thriller called *City Heat* (1984) which attempted to recapture the flavor of the *film noir* school of the 1940s, but neither the clever lines nor the atmosphere were there.

Tightrope (1984) featured one of Eastwood's most complex characterizations. He played Wes Block, a detective and single parent of two children (one played by his own daughter Alison) who becomes involved with a social worker (Genevieve Bujold). The case he is working on involves investigating the murders of several women. Block is deeply troubled sexually and the murders to some degree mirror his own sexual fantasies. *Pale Rider* (1985), which he directed as well as starred in, was heavily criticized for being a clumsy and vulgar parody of the classic Western *Shane* (1953). He subsequently went on the direct and star in *Heartbreak Ridge* (1986) as a marine sergeant with the usual domestic problems who has the duty of leading his squadron into combat one last time in Grenada. The United States Marine Corps originally cooperated with Eastwood by allowing him to shoot at Camp Pendleton. This support was later unilaterally withdrawn when the military objected to the violence and tone of language used in the film. He returned as Dirty Harry for the fifth time in *The Dead Pool* (1988) and as a vaguely similar character in *The Rookie* (1990), both of which proved the law of diminishing returns.

A real-life role which he appeared to play

with relish was that of the mayor of Carmel. He was elected on April 8, 1986, to the job, which paid a scant $200 a month—peanuts compared to the millions which he earned from his films. "I only took the job because it's in the community where I live," he said later. The specific reason he ran for election was because of his anger in trying to obliterate an abandoned building next door to the Hog's Breath Inn, the actor's Carmel restaurant. (He wanted to erect an office and shops in place of the derelict building.) He spent a record $25,000 campaigning for office and won in a landslide of 2,166 votes against incumbent mayor Charlotte Townsend's 799 votes. During his two-year term of office, he appointed new members to the planning commission and approved the purchase of a 22-acre ranch in Carmel for $5 million to prevent it from being exploited by land developers. Eastwood declined to run for reelection in 1988 because of his expressed desire to spend more time with his children and the adverse effect, in terms of publicity on the community, which his celebrity status had caused.

Eastwood had directed but did not star in *Breezy* (1973). As director only he helmed another personal film, *Bird* (1988), a biography of the jazz saxophonist Charlie Parker (Forest Whitaker) commonly known as Bird. His career as an actor appeared to be in decline when several vehicles in a row *(The Rookie, Pink Cadillac* and *White Hunter, Black Heart* [1990]) flopped. The latter told the story of John Huston and the making of the 1951 film classic film *The African Queen*. He played the Huston role of an Ahab-type character obsessed with the idea of killing an elephant because it's "the only sin you can buy a license to commit."

He returned to much more familiar territory with *Unforgiven* (1992), his tenth Western, which he directed and starred in as Bill Munny, a single-parent pig farmer who reluctantly agrees to join a bounty hunt for the hides of two men who gruesomely sliced up a prostitute. It was dedicated to "Sergio and Don." Of this movie he said, "If I was ever going to do a last Western, this would be it." The movie portrays a realistic, unromanticized view of the Wild West with all of its grime, poverty and violence. He added, "It kind of sums up what I feel. I bought the script ten years ago, but figured I had to age into it. Maybe that's why I didn't do it right away. I was kind of savoring it as the last of that genre—maybe the last film of that type for me." This film was his most commercially successful in a long time and won him an Oscar as Best Director. *Unforgiven* was also a very significant film with a very broad impact because it almost single-handedly resurrected the Western to the point where several major Westerns were made and released afterwards.

Almost equally well-received was *In the Line of Fire* (1993), directed by Wolfgang Petersen, a thriller in which Eastwood plays Frank Horrigan, a veteran Secret Service agent who tracks down a presidential assassin (played with relish by John Malkovitch). Horrigan has a secret sorrow that he didn't save President Kennedy from an assassin's bullet when he was in charge of security in Dallas. The film (budgeted at $30,000,000) was shot in 60 to 65 days in Washington, Chicago and Los Angeles. The script more successfully balanced the romantic and thriller elements (in the former case with fellow Secret Service agent Rene Russo) than some of his other films.

Eastwood followed a precedent set in *City Heat* by costarring with another megastar, in this case Kevin Costner, in *A Perfect World* (1993). Eastwood, who also directed, had the role of a sheriff in pursuit of a convict (Costner), but the film almost appeared like two separate films since the two stars seldom shared any scenes. Business was not as brisk as expected considering the names involved. Eastwood then went on to direct and star in an adult love story, *The Bridges of Madison County,* based on the best-selling novel by Robert James Waller. He played Robert Kincaid, with Meryl Streep as Francesca Johnson. Whatever the problems of his private life, he remained as professional and economical as ever. The 1995 film was finished in six weeks, ten days ahead of schedule.

Clint Eastwood married Maggie Johnson, a swimsuit designer and model, on December 19, 1953, and they have two children: Kyle Clinton, a musician, born on May 19, 1968, and Alison, who has studied acting, born on May 22, 1972. After Alison checked into a drink dependency clinic in 1992, Eastwood acknowledged that his fame may have damaged them, adding, "My profession was so time-consuming, it was hard to spend the proper amount of time with them. I think it was tough for my daughter." The couple separated in 1979 and were divorced in 1984 after 31 years. She received a $25 million divorce settlement including a redwood and glass house built on 12 ocean-front acres in Carmel, California. He himself lives in a small stone house on the same estate. He first discovered Carmel when he was a recruit at a military base near Monterey; he and Maggie spent their honeymoon there in 1953. She has never revealed intimate details about her life with Eastwood. All she confessed is that marriage made her feel like the woman with no name. She said, "I was this big Hollywood star's wife yet I never had any identity of my own." She later married Henry Wynberg, car salesman and former flame of Elizabeth Taylor. Eastwood has also lent support money to his eldest daughter Kimber, whom he fathered out of wedlock in 1964 with actress Roxanne Tunis.

He left his wife for actress Sondra Locke in 1980, whom he first met in 1973. Although they never married, they lived together for nine years and acquired four opulent homes and a ranch. On April 26, 1989, she filed a multimillion dollar palimony suit, claiming that the actor had persuaded her to have two abortions and evicted her from their home in Los Angeles along with her pet parrot. She received a letter from his lawyers telling her that he had put all of her possessions in storage and changed the locks on their Bel Air home. The actress, who had two operations for breast cancer in 1990, said that she fainted on the set of the movie she was directing (1990's *Impulse)* when she read the lawyer's letter.

She said, "I had to move in with friends. I had to borrow clothes and I had no idea where my pet parrot Putty was or my car." In court papers Eastwood denied that he forced her to have two abortions and a sterilization operation. The battle dragged on for two years before an alleged settlement was reached with Locke receiving the title deeds to two houses in Los Angeles and a substantial sum of money. One of the homes involved in the settlement was occupied by the actress's former husband, 43-year-old Gordon Anderson, a sculptor whom she married in 1967. According to the court papers, the marriage was never consummated and Eastwood accepted Anderson as a surrogate brother of Sondra Locke. Subsequent interviews with Locke have revealed that she dropped her original lawsuit in favor of a deal whereby she could resume her career as a director with Warner Bros. over a three-year period. Warners, however, refused to green light any of the 30 projects and scripts which she submitted to them. In October 1995, Locke admitted that she was once again involved in litigation against both them and Eastwood.

Despite the settlements, Eastwood was not left strapped for cash. His remaining fortune was estimated at over $100,000,000 and he still has four homes. He maintains one in the Los Angeles suburb of Sherman Oaks (close to the offices of Malpaso Productions on the Warner studio lot) and a 2,000-acre ranch in Northern California which was once the property of Bing Crosby. His wealth is legendary. According to one insider, "He has vast real estate holdings, ranches and businesses and owns the production company that makes his movies." He allegedly prefers a casual lifestyle and he is more inclined to drive his pickup truck than the Mercedes which he owns. Politically, he is known to be conservative.

British-born actress Frances Fisher, who was born in 1952, subsequently became his live-in lover. Their relationship began when they met during the filming of *Pink Cadillac* (1989). Physically she is remarkably similar to Sondra Locke. She was previously wed, but had no children. She played the prostitute Strawberry Alice in *Unforgiven.* By her he has a daughter Francesca Ruth, who weighed in at just over six pounds at 5:30 A.M. on August 7, 1993. The couple split in April 1995, and Fisher became a resident of Vancouver Island, Canada, with her daughter. On March 31, 1996, the star married television news journalist Dina Ruiz, 30, at a private ceremony in Las Vegas. It was her first marriage.

Clint Eastwood Filmography

1955: *Revenge of the Creature, Francis in the Navy, Lady Godiva, Tarantula.*

1956: *Away All Boats, Never Say Goodbye, Star in the Dust, The First Traveling Saleslady.*

1957: *Escapade in Japan.*

1958: *Lafayette Escadrille, Ambush at Cimarron Pass.*

1964: *A Fistful of Dollars.*

1965: *For a Few Dollars More.*

1966: *The Good, the Bad and the Ugly; The Witches.*

1967: *Hang 'Em High.*
1968: *Coogan's Bluff, Where Eagles Dare.*
1969: *Paint Your Wagon, Two Mules for Sister Sara.*
1970: *Kelly's Heroes, The Beguiled.*
1971: *Dirty Harry, Play Misty for Me.*
1972: *Joe Kidd, High Plains Drifter.*
1973: *Magnum Force.*
1974: *Thunderbolt and Lightfoot.*
1975: *The Eiger Sanction.*
1976: *The Outlaw Josey Wales, The Enforcer.*
1977: *The Gauntlet.*
1978: *Every Which Way but Loose.*
1979: *Escape from Alcatraz.*
1980: *Bronco Billy, Any Which Way You Can.*
1982: *Firefox.*
1983: *Honkytonk Man, Sudden Impact.*
1984: *City Heat, Tightrope.*
1985: *Pale Rider.*
1986: *Heartbreak Ridge.*
1988: *The Dead Pool.*
1989: *Pink Cadillac.*
1990: *White Hunter, Black Heart; The Rookie.*
1992: *Unforgiven.*
1993: *In the Line of Fire; A Perfect World.*
1995: *Casper* (uncredited cameo), *The Bridges of Madison County.*
1997: *Absolute Power.*

As Director

1971: *Play Misty for Me.*
1972: *High Plains Drifter.*
1973: *Breezy.*
1975: *The Eiger Sanction.*
1976: *The Outlaw Josey Wales.*
1977: *The Gauntlet.*
1980: *Bronco Billy.*
1982: *Firefox.*
1983: *Honkytonk Man, Sudden Impact.*
1985: *Pale Rider.*
1986: *Heartbreak Ridge.*
1988: *Bird.*
1990: *White Hunter, Black Heart; The Rookie.*
1992: *Unforgiven.*
1993: *A Perfect World.*
1995: *The Bridges of Madison County.*
1997: *Absolute Power.*

Television Series

1959–1966: *Rawhide* as Rowdy Yates.

Sources

Andrews, Geoff. "Friday's People." *Daily Mail* newspaper, August 21, 1992.

Bamigboye, Baz. "Taking Dirty Harry to the Cleaners." *Daily Mail* newspaper, April 28, 1989.

Bonilla, Kristina. "Dina Ruiz at Home on His Ranch in Carmel." *Hello* magazine, July 1996.

Clinch, Minty. *Clint Eastwood: A Biography.* London: Hodder & Stoughton, 1994.

"Clint Eastwood with His Mother Ruth." *Hello* magazine, July 1992.

Coz, Steve. "Clint's Baby Could Be the Wealthiest Love Child Ever." *National Enquirer* magazine, August 1993.

Current Biography. New York: H.W. Wilson, 1971 and 1989.

De Alcahud, Victoria. "Sondra Locke." *Hello* magazine, October 1995.

Docherty, Cameron. "Friday's People." *Daily Mail* newspaper, July 23, 1993.

Duffy, David, and Alan Braham Smith. "Superstar's real-life drama is right out of the movies." *National Enquirer* magazine, August 1993.

Gibson, Gil, and Keith Kokino. "Hollywood's Reclusive Superstar." *Hello* magazine, February 1993.

Goodman, John, and Mike Bygrave."Clint Comes Clean." *Sunday Telegraph* magazine, February 1989.

Gristwood, Sarah. "Clint Eastwood Building Bridges." *You* magazine, September 10, 1995.

Kek, William, Marc Cetner, Suzanne Ely and Tony Brenna. "Clint Eastwood's Secret Wedding." *National Enquirer* magazine, April 1996.

Larson, Virginia. "Clint pays £20m to Lover He Threw Out." *Daily Mail* newspaper, March 1991.

McCarthy, Todd. *Unforgiven* review. *Variety,* July 1992.

Moye, Hedda. "Frances Fisher." *Hello* magazine, November 1995.

Parish, James Robert. *Great Western Stars.* New York: Ace, 1976.

Siegel, Don. "The Man Who Made Harry So Dirty." *Daily Mail* newspaper, October 8, 1993.

Woodward, Ian. "Clint Eastwood's Secret Daughter Kimber Tunis." *Hello* magazine, August 1993.

Buddy Ebsen struggles with an Iroquois warrior in *Northwest Passage.*

BUDDY EBSEN

"There's nothing mysterious about the show's appeal. It's the ancient theme of the Wise Fool. It's the country folk who make fools of the rich and sophisticated." So speaks Buddy Ebsen when describing his most famous television series *The Beverly Hillbillies.* Ebsen really had three show business careers. The first was as a hoofer in stage musicals; the second was as an entertainer in musical feature films; and the last was as a television megastar. Prior to his later television series, the tall, lanky Ebsen had costarred as a frontiersman in two television Western series of the 1950s.

Ebsen was born Christian Rudolf Ebsen in Belleville, Illinois, on April 2, 1908, the son of Christian and Frances Ebsen. He had four sisters, Helga, Norma, Vilma and Leslie; he was in the middle. His father ran a natatorium and became head of physical education at Belleville Township High School. On account of his mother's health, he moved with his family to Orlando, Florida, at the age of 12. Although he learned to dance at the Orlando dancing academy run by his father, he initially rejected a career as a dancer in favor of studying medicine at the University of Florida in 1926. He then switched to local Rollins College where he studied drama. Financial problems in his family forced him to quit his studies in favor of journeying to New York, where he was virtually broke until he landed a Broadway role as a dancer in the 1928 Ziegfeld production *Whoopee,* which starred Eddie Cantor. His sister Vilma became his dancing partner and for years they appeared together in nightclubs and on tour. Their biggest hit was in a musical revue called *Flying Colors* in 1932.

Ebsen then felt the lure of Hollywood. He traveled West to appear for MGM in such lavish musicals as *Born to Dance* (1936) and *Broadway Melody of 1936.* He also appeared for 20th Century–Fox in such musicals as *Banjo on My Knee* (1936) and *Captain January* (1936), in which he partnered Shirley Temple. His film career terminated prematurely and nearly permanently when he was chosen to play the Tin Man in the classic MGM film *The Wizard of Oz* (1939). Three weeks into filming he became seriously ill after inhaling the aluminum powder makeup used to paint his face and body silver. His lungs were coated and at one stage it was feared that he might die. When he recovered, MGM punished him by pushing him into B films and then abruptly terminating his contract.

In 1942 he and another Hollywood fugitive, Skeets Gallagher, teamed in a hilarious farce called *Good Night Ladies* which was a smash hit in Chicago. This led to him making his television debut at an experimental Chicago station owned by a theater chain. It was so hideous that he had little faith in the medium. He served in the U.S. Coast Guard for two years at the end of World War II, rising to the rank of lieutenant. Afterwards he returned to Broadway in a revival of the musical *Showboat* in 1946 which ran for a year. *Honest John,* a play he wrote, was produced at Las Palmas Theater in Hollywood. He then must have broken a mirror because after that he endured seven lean years in show business during which his lot was one-night performances and summer stock. His lowest ebb was reached when Milton Berle refused to have him on his television show because he was a has-been. Years later when *The Beverly Hillbillies* was riding high in the ratings, he actually felt grateful to Berle since Berle had made him so angry that he decided to remain in show business rather than quit as he was advised to do. He wrote and acted in a busted series pilot, *Elmer Fox.* This was seen by executives at Republic, who in 1950 chose him to play the sidekick of their new Western star Rex Allen in a series of B oaters. He appeared in five of these. His role was virtually the same throughout, although the name of his character varied in each film.

Ebsen was a leading contender for the role of Davy Crockett because he appeared in "The House," a segment of a television miniseries derived from three short stories by John Steinbeck. His acting so impressed Walt Disney that Ebsen believed the Crockett role was his. However, once Disney had seen Fess Parker, the part was filled, while Ebsen was relegated to his sidekick George Russel. This he managed to make his own by sheer exuberance, which served as a marked contrast to Parker's dry, understated characterization. The Disney production people were ignorant when it came to location shoots and sent only one stuntman along. He was too short so the stars wound up doing their stunts, which led to some hair-raising incidents. Although only three episodes were shot, they took the country by storm and created a national sensation. The series was one of the greatest overnight hits in television history, but it took Disney by surprise. Both of the leading characters had been killed at the Alamo, thereby preventing further episodes.

Disney initially solved the problem by editing the original three episodes into the feature film *Davy Crockett, King of the Wild Frontier* (1955), which grossed handsomely. Disney then shot two other episodes derived from incidents in the earlier lives of Crockett and

Russel. These were edited into a prequel film called *Davy Crockett and the River Pirates* (1956), another hit. Ebsen wrote novelty songs which were issued by the Walt Disney Publishing Company.

Ebsen's other television series of the 1950s was *Northwest Passage* (1958–1959), based on the MGM film of 1940 about the search for an inland waterway which could be used to enable boats to traverse the breadth of America during the French and Indian War (1754–1759). Keith Larsen played Major Robert Rodgers, with Ebsen as his Indian fighter comrade. MGM was very impressed with some leftover footage of a spectacular attack on an Indian village. This was used up in the first episode and the quality declined rapidly thereafter. Although the series was shot in color, most viewers saw it in black and white. The English wore red coats while the French wore blue. On black and white television sets, both colors came out gray, so viewers were confused and had no idea who to root for. Its time-slot was opposite the very popular *Maverick*, which ensured its rapid extinction. Although the series lasted only one season, various episodes were edited together into feature films which were profitably released abroad.

Ebsen very effectively played a hillbilly called Doc Golightly in the movie *Breakfast at Tiffany's* (1961). Writer Paul Henning caught him in that and created the role of Jed Clampett in a forthcoming television comedy series, *The Beverly Hillbillies,* specifically with Ebsen in mind. Jed Clampett was the widower patriarch of a family of backwoods rustics who relocated to Beverly Hills after they struck oil on their land and received $25,000,000. The CBS series was instantly successful and landed in the top ten; it remained there for most of its nine year, 212 episode run. In 1993 it was revamped into the feature film *The Beverly Hillbillies,* which was generally considered dire but did good business. Ebsen had a supporting role as another character. The role of Jed Clampett is still the one with which the actor is most closely identified and which made him in real life a millionaire.

In the early 1970s television was saturated with crime series, but when two half-hour comedy series on the CBS Sunday night lineup flopped simultaneously in the fall of 1972, Fred Silverman (head honcho of the CBS program department) decreed that the spots should be filled by another crime series. He contacted executive producer Quinn Martin and told him he wanted the series on the air by January of 1973. They decided that the series should be called *Barnaby Jones* and the leading role should be played by Buddy Ebsen. It was intended that an episode of *Cannon* starring William Conrad would guest-star Buddy Ebsen, but instead this served as the first episode of the series. In it, ex-private eye Jones comes out of retirement to avenge the murder of his son. Once he has solved the crime, he decides to carry on actively running the agency he had given to his late son with the aid of his son's widow Betty (Lee Meriwether). The geriatric detective remained a popular fixture on television for eight years.

Away from acting, Buddy Ebsen is a published playwright and author, and an avid painter who enjoys politics and literature. He has a deep and abiding interest in American history with a particular bias toward Abraham Lincoln. In 1993 he wrote and had published a highly entertaining memoir, *The Other Side of Oz.*

In 1933 he wed Ruth Cambridge, Walter Winchell's energetic Girl Friday, by whom he has two daughters, Elizabeth (born in 1936) and Alix (born in 1943). After divorcing her while in the services, he wed Nancy Wolcott, by whom he has five children: Susannah (born in 1947), Catherine (1949), Bonnie (1951), Kirsten (1958) and Dustin (1959). His third wife is businesswoman Dorothy Knott, whom he wed in a romantic ceremony in Hawaii in March 1985. He has a lavish oceanfront home at Newport Beach and a ranch at Malibu Canyon, California.

Buddy Ebsen Filmography

1935: *Broadway Melody of 1936.*
1936: *Captain January, Banjo on My Knee, Born to Dance.*
1937: *Broadway Melody of 1938.*
1938: *Yellow Jack, My Lucky Star, The Girl of the Golden West.*
1939: *Four Girls in White, The Kid from Texas.*
1941: *Parachute Battalion, They Met in Argentina.*
1942: *Sing Your Worries Away.*

1950: *Under Mexicali Stars.*
1951: *Silver City Bonanza, Thunder in God's Country, Rodeo King and the Señorita, Utah Wagon Train.*
1954: *Red Garters, Night People.*
1955: *Davy Crockett—King of the Wild Frontier.*
1956: *Davy Crockett and the River Pirates, Between Heaven and Hell, Attack!*
1959: *Fury River* (NP), *Frontier Rangers* (NP), *Mission of Danger* (NP).
1961: *Breakfast at Tiffany's.*
1962: *The Interns.*
1964: *Mail Order Bride.*
1968: *The One and Only Genuine Original Family Band.*
1971: *The President's Plane Is Missing* (TV).
1972: *The Daughters of Joshua Cabe* (TV).
1973: *The Horror at 37,000 Feet* (TV), *Tom Sawyer* (TV).
1976: *Smash-up on Interstate Five* (TV).
1978: *Leave Yesterday Behind* (TV), *The Critical List* (TV).
1979: *The Paradise Connection* (TV).
1981: *Fire on the Mountain* (TV), *The Return of the Beverly Hillbillies* (TV).
1987: *Stone Fox* (TV).
1990: *Working Trash* (TV).
1993: *The Beverly Hillbillies.*

Television Series

1954–1955: *The Adventures of Davy Crockett* as George Russel.
1958–1959: *Northwest Passage* as Sgt. Hunk Marriner.
1962–1971: *The Beverly Hillbillies* as Jed Clampett.
1973–1980: *Barnaby Jones* as Barnaby Jones.
1984–1985: *Matt Houston* as Roy Houston.

Miniseries

1978: *The Bastard.*

Sources

Cox, Stephen. *The Beverly Hillbillies.* New York: Harper Perennial, 1993.
Ebsen, Buddy. *The Other Side of Oz.* Newport Beach, CA: Donovan Publishing, 1993.
Rothel, David. *Those Great Cowboy Sidekicks.* Waynesville, NC: World of Yesterday Publications, 1984.

Note

NP denotes episodes of the television series *Northwest Passage,* which were edited into feature films and released theatrically.

DALE EVANS

Dale Evans was born Frances Octavia Smith in Uvalde, Texas, on October 31, 1912. She is the daughter of Walter Hillman Smith, a cotton farmer, and Bettie Sue Wood. She has one brother, Walter Hillman Smith, Jr. Her family moved to Osceola, Arkansas, where she attended high school. She met Thomas Fox, a senior at the school with whom she eloped to Blitheville, Arkansas, in January 1927. On November 28, 1927, she gave birth to Thomas Frederick Fox, Jr. Her first husband died prematurely in 1929. Music proved to be her salvation because she found singing jobs to support herself and Thomas, Jr., using the name of Frances Fox.

When she obtained employment on radio station WHAS in Louisville, Kentucky, program director Joe Eaton insisted she change her professional name to Dale Evans. She returned to Dallas, Texas, as a vocalist on *The Early Birds,* a show on radio station WFAA. She met and married pianist and composer Robert Dale Butts in 1930. Two years later the family moved to Chicago where she found work as a vocalist with the orchestra of Anson Weeks, touring the country with that group for a year prior to returning to Chicago as staff singer for station WBBM. By 1940 she had her own show *(That Girl from Texas)* on that radio station and was simultaneously singing at some of the better-class Chicago niteries.

Paramount tested her in 1941 for the female lead in the movie *Holiday Inn,* which starred Bing Crosby, but nixed her because she

Dale Evans flanked by Roy Rogers (left) and Gabby Hayes.

could not dance. She did, however, obtain a job as a resident vocalist on the Edgar Bergen radio show for a 43-week run and did other guest shots on the programs of other stars. 20th Century–Fox signed her to a one-year contract at $400 a week, but after two bit roles, her option was not picked up.

Allegedly her agent Art Rush warned the actress that a big barrier to her advancement in Hollywood was the presence of her 14-year-old son and that she would be much more likely to achieve her ambitions if she pretended that he was her brother. She accepted this advice, but they still became members of Westwood Baptist Church as mother and son. She was a tireless worker for the U.S.O. and the Hollywood Victory Committee. She inked a one-year pact with Republic Studios where her initial film for them was *Swing Your Partner* (1943).

Evans made several other entertaining films for Republic before being fortuitously teamed with Roy Rogers in *The Cowboy and the Señorita* (1944), which was heavily endorsed by the public. Over the next few years she and Rogers were teamed in other films which gave them the premier status in the B Western market, usually aided by the musical group "The Sons of the Pioneers." Dale Evans herself also cut some records, some of which were successful. Her marriage to Robert Butts ended in divorce in 1945. In 1946 Arlene Rogers, wife of Roy Rogers, died of an embolism eight days after giving birth to a son, Roy Rogers, Jr.

Rogers returned to a heavy workload of films and personal appearances, invariably accompanied by Dale Evans. Love blossomed and on December 31, 1947, they became "King and Queen of the Cowboys" off screen as well as on. They initially moved into a rambling Spanish-style house in the Hollywood Hills where they lived with Rogers' three children Linda Lou, adopted daughter Cheryl and son Roy, Jr. (nicknamed Dusty), and Dale's son Tom. They later lived in the San Fernando Valley. In 1948 they began the successful *Roy Rogers Show* for the Mutual radio network under the sponsorship of Quaker Oats. Their final feature together at Republic was *Pals of the Golden West* (1951).

They then entered television. *The Roy Rogers Show* was first broadcast on NBC on December 30, 1951, and lasted until June 23, 1957, through 104 episodes under the sponsorship of General Foods. The format was simple but engaging. Roy Rogers was based at the Double R Bar Ranch just outside of Mineral City. With his faithful horse Trigger and dog Bullet he maintained law and order in the contemporary West around Mineral City. Dale Evans was the owner of the town cafe and rode a horse called Buttermilk. She also wrote Rogers' theme tune "Happy Trails." Pat Brady provided comic relief with his Jeep Nellybelle. A short-lived musical variety program, *The Roy Rogers and Dale Evans Show,* was presented on ABC in 1962. The couple also occasionally hosted *Kraft Music Hall* on NBC from 1967 to 1971.

On August 26, 1950, Dale Evans became the mother of a baby girl, Robin Elizabeth, but she was a Down's Syndrome baby and died two days before her second birthday of complications following a case of mumps. Distraught at the tragedy, Evans wrote a book entitled *Angel Unaware,* which became a bestseller. All the profits from this volume were donated to the National Association for Retarded Children. They adopted two other children, Sandy and Dodie.

In 1954 they made a highly successful tour of the British Isles and were part of Billy Graham's Crusade at London's Harringay Arena. In 1958 they participated in Billy Graham's Crusade at a sunrise Easter Service in Washington D.C. and did two television specials for Chevrolet from their Chatsworth, California, ranch. While in the British Isles, they adopted a daughter, 11-year-old Marion, and in 1955 they adopted another daughter, a Korean orphan named Debbie.

On August 17, 1964, Debbie was killed in a bus crash six miles south of San Clemente. Dale wrote a book, *Dearest Debbie* (1965), with all the royalties donated to World Vision Incorporated. That same year (1965) there was another tragedy when their adopted son Sandy, Pfc. John David Rogers, died on October 31, 1965, while stationed with the Third Armored Division at Gelhausen, Germany. He had just been promoted when his alleged buddies goaded him into consuming too much alcohol for his system to cope with at a celebratory party. This prompted Evans to write another book, *Salute to Sandy* (1965). In 1966 they entertained troops in Vietnam and Evans received "The Texan of the Year Award" from the Texas Press Association. She was selected as California's "Mother of the Year" in 1967 and they opened a huge museum close to their home in Apple Valley, full of memorabilia from their respective careers. They are members of the Cowboy Hall of Fame and recipients of The National Film Society's Humanitarian Award and the Golden Boot Award. In 1977 they became the first husband and wife team to serve as Grand Marshals of the Tournament of Roses Parade in Pasadena and in 1981 they were Grand Marshals of the National Cherry Blossom Festival Parade in Washington D.C. Dale Evans has a strong faith in God and has written several other books which all reflect a strong Christian message. Once asked the secret of his long and successful marriage, Roy Rogers replied, "We still like and respect each other. She is my sweetheart and hunting and fishing partner all rolled into one." At last report they have 14 grandchildren. In 1996 she was rushed to Loma Linda University Medical Center where she was admitted and treated for a stroke. On May 17, she underwent surgery to unblock an artery in one side of her neck and came through with flying colors.

Dale Evans Filmography

1940: *The East Side Kids.*
1942: *Orchestra Wives, Rhythm Hits the Ice, Girl Trouble.*
1943: *Swing Your Partner, Here Comes Elmer, Hoosier Holiday, The West Side Kid, In Old Oklahoma.*
1944: *Casanova in Burlesque, The Cowboy and the Señorita, San Fernando Valley, Yellow Rose of Texas, Song of Nevada.*
1945: *Utah, Lights of Old Santa Fe, The Big Show-Off, The Man from Oklahoma, Don't Fence Me In, Hitchhike to Happiness, Bells of Rosarita, Sunset in Eldorado, Along the Navajo Trail.*
1946: *Song of Arizona, My Pal Trigger, Under Nevada Skies, Roll on Texas Moon, Home in Oklahoma, Rainbow Over Texas, Out California Way, Heldorado.*
1947: *Apache Rose, Bells of San Angelo, The Trespasser.*
1948: *Slippy McGee.*
1949: *Down Dakota Way, Susanna Pass, The Golden Stallion.*
1950: *Twilight in the Sierras, Bells of Coronado, Trigger Jr.*
1951: *South of Caliente, Pals of the Golden West.*

Television Series

1951–1957: *The Roy Rogers Show* as Dale Evans.
1962: *The Roy Rogers and Dale Evans Show.*

Sources

Butterfield, Alan, and John South. "Dale Evans, 83, Fit as a Fiddle After Stroke." *National Enquirer*, June 1996.
Current Biography article on Roy Rogers. New York: H.W. Wilson, 1983.
Holland, Ted. *B Western Actors Encyclopedia Facts, Photos and Filmographies for More than 250 Familiar Faces.* Jefferson, NC: McFarland, 1989.
Parish, James Robert, and Lennard DeCarl. *Hollywood Players: The Forties.* New Rochelle NY: Arlington House, 1976.
Rothel, David. *The Singing Cowboys.* San Diego, CA: Barnes, 1978.
Russell, Sue. "Roy Rogers and Trigger: The Legend Lives On." *Hello* magazine, February 1996.
Turner, Steve, and Edgar M. Wyatt. *Saddle Gals.* Madison, NC: Empire, 1995.

GENE EVANS

Gene Evans was born in Holbrook, Arizona, on July 11, 1922, but from the age of seven lived in Colton, California. His father was a grocer with a store close to the Navajo reservation. He acted in some plays in high school, but spent more time playing football. Obtaining a work scholarship to the Pasadena Playhouse, he studied there from 1941 to 1942. In November 1942, he enlisted in the army as an engineer on the strength of a promise, which was later reneged upon, that he would easily obtain a commission. Once he was discharged, using the G.I. Bill, he returned to the Playhouse. He did not enjoy the experience, so he started his own business performing plays at a theater in the round.

Gene Evans (right) with his television family—Johnny Washbrook, "Flicka," and Anita Louise—in *My Friend Flicka*.

He made his motion picture debut in a B Western called *Under Colorado Skies* (1947). From the early 1950s he began to appear on television and later did many episodes of *The Lone Ranger* and *Gunsmoke,* although the pay was not good. He enjoyed doing *Gunsmoke* because of the high quality of the scripts, and he had a long-standing friendship with James Arness. He never earned more than $1,000 a year as an actor until he shot the war film *The Steel Helmet* (1951), produced and directed by Sam Fuller. Although it was shot in ten days, it elevated his standing as an actor. He also starred in other films for Fuller, notably *Park Row* (1952), which was the only movie which Fuller financed entirely himself. In it Evans starred as a crusading newspaper editor in turn-of-the-century New York. It has been stated that this is the favorite of Evans' own movies.

The actor has gone on record several times as saying that his favorite genre is the Western. Eventually he landed the opportunity to star in a TV series of his own, *My Friend Flicka.* This was a somewhat derivative series involving a boy and his horse. It was located in Montana around the turn of the century and concerned the McLaughlin family and their struggles to make a living on a ranch. Evans was top-billed as the father Rob, Anita Louise played the mother Nell and their son Ken was played by Johnny Washbrook. Ken's best friend was his horse Flicka. The series was based on novels by Mary O'Hara which had previously served as the basis for three highly successful motion pictures during the 1940s. Although this half-hour series was shot in color, it originally aired on CBS in black and white. The original 39 episodes were shown between February 1956 and February 1957.

The series was filmed at the Fox Western street and the Fox ranch at Malibu Canyon. Evans worked six days a week on each episode, frequently from sunrise to sunset. The show was good family entertainment, although occasional episodes were rather frightening for children. The remuneration was good and gave the actor a measure of economic security for the first time in his life. Although it only lasted one season, he was given the opportunity to continue for a couple more, but declined because he hated the experience of working with Anita Louise, whom he considered a lazy and decorative leading lady rather than a professional actress.

Afterwards Evans continued to appear in feature films and guest shots on television. He has also admitted that he would have liked another shot at a series, but he enjoyed little success in that department in recent times. In 1972 he went to Tennessee to shoot the feature film *Walking Tall* and fell in love with the place. During the writers' and actors' strikes of the 1970s, he became disillusioned with the entertainment industry and settled permanently in Medon, Tennessee, where he worked the land and pursued his hobbies, including fishing. In 1976 he had bought 40 acres of woods with a seven-acre lake and a small house. He has been back to Hollywood for occasional jobs as an economic measure and has been a guest at Western conventions.

Gene Evans Filmography

1947: *Under Colorado Skies.*
1948: *Assigned to Danger, Criss Cross, Larceny, Berlin Express.*
1949: *Mother Is a Freshman, It Happens Every Spring.*
1950: *Jet Pilot* (released 1957), *Never a Dull Moment, Dallas, The Asphalt Jungle, Wyoming Mail, Storm Warning, Armored Car Robbery.*
1951: *Sugarfoot, Steel Helmet, I Was an American Spy, The Big Carnival (*a.k.a. *Ace in the Hole), Fixed Bayonets!, Force of Arms.*
1952: *Park Row, Thunderbirds, Mutiny.*
1953: *Donovan's Brain, The Golden Blade.*
1954: *Cattle Queen of Montana, The Long Wait, Hell and High Water.*
1955: *Crashout, Wyoming Renegades.*
1957: *The Helen Morgan Story, The Sad Sack.*
1958: *Money Women and Guns, Revolt in the Big House, Young and Wild, The Bravados, The Giant Behemoth (*a.k.a. *Behemoth the Sea Monster), Damn Citizen!*
1959: *The Hangman, Operation Petticoat.*
1961: *Gold of the Seven Saints.*
1963: *Shock Corridor.*
1965: *Apache Uprising.*
1966: *Waco, Nevada Smith, Dragnet* (TV).
1967: *The War Wagon.*
1969: *Support Your Local Sheriff!*
1970: *The Ballad of Cable Hogue, The Intruders* (TV), *There Was a Crooked Man.*
1971: *Support Your Local Gunfighter!*
1972: *The Bounty Man* (TV).
1973: *Pat Garrett and Billy the Kid, Walking Tall.*
1974: *Shootout in a One-Dog Town* (TV), *Sidekicks* (TV), *Devil Times Five (*a.k.a. *Peopletoys), A Knife for the Ladies.*
1975: *The Last Day* (TV), *Matt Helm* (TV).
1976: *The Mahacans* (TV).
1977: *Fire!* (TV).
1978: *The Magic of Lassie, Kate Bliss and the Ticker Tape Kid* (TV).
1979: *The Sacketts* (TV), *The Last Ride of the Dalton Gang* (TV), *The Concrete Cowboys* (TV).
1980: *Casino* (TV).
1981: *California Gold Rush* (TV).
1982: *Travis McGee: The Empty Copper Sea* (TV), *The Shadow Riders* (TV).
1987: *The Alamo: 13 Days to Glory* (TV).
1988: *Once Upon a Texas Train* (TV).

Television Series

1956–1957: *My Friend Flicka* as Rob McLaughlin.
1975–1976: *Matt Helm* as Sgt. Hanrahan.
1976: *Spencer's Pilots* as Spencer Parish.

Miniseries

1977: *The Rhineman Exchange.*
1980: *Wild Times.*

Sources

Goldrup, Tom, and Jim Goldrup. *The Feature Players: The Stories Behind The Faces Volume #1.* Published privately, 1986.
Picture Show's Who's Who On Screen. London: Amalgamated Press, c. 1956.
Quinlan, David. *Illustrated Directory of Film Character Actors.* London: Batsford, 1995.
Summers, Neil. *The Official TV Western Book Volume #3.* Vienna, WV: Old West Shop Publishing, 1991.
Who's Who in Hollywood. New York: Dell, 1961.

TOM FADDEN

Born in 1895, Tom Fadden became an actor in 1915 when he joined a stock company in Omaha, Nebraska. Between 1923 and 1939 he was based in New York, where he appeared at the Palace Theater in 1926, played in vaudeville and was a regular in Broadway plays. He relocated to Hollywood and made his screen debut in 1939, amassing a long list of movie credits. He had two minor supporting roles in Western series of the 1950s: *Broken Arrow,* as Duffield; and *Cimarron City,* in which he played Silas Perry. He retired to Florida in the 1970s where he insisted that he was still a jobbing actor. He died in Vero Beach, Florida, on April 14, 1980, at age 85. His wife Genevieve died in 1959.

Tom Fadden Filmography

1939: *I Stole a Million, Destry Rides Again.*
1940: *Winners of the West* (serial), *Congo Maisie, Zanzibar, The Captain Is a Lady, The Man from Dakota.*
1941: *Come Live with Me, The Shepherd of the Hills, Kiss the Boys Goodbye.*
1942: *The Glass Key, Sundown Jim, The Lone Star Ranger, The Remarkable Andrew, Wings for the Eagle, Pardon My Sarong, The Night Before the Divorce, My Favorite Blonde.*
1943: *Edge of Darkness, Riding High, The Good Fellows, Frontier Badmen, A Lady Takes a Chance, Northern Pursuit.* 1944: *The Thin Man Goes Home, In Society, The Hairy Ape, Henry Aldrich's Little Secret, Three Little Sisters, Tomorrow the World.*
1945: *A Medal for Benny, The Naughty Nineties, The Royal Mounted Rides Again* (serial), *Murder He Says, State Fair, The Great John L.*
1946: *The Big Sleep, Dragonwyck, Trail to Vengeance, The Strange Love of Martha Ivers, The Well Groomed Bride, A Stolen Life, Cross My Heart.*
1947: *Easy Come Easy Go, Cheyenne, Dragnet, That Hagen Girl, Dark Passage.*
1948: *A Miracle Can Happen, State of the Union, Inside Story, The Dude Goes West, B.F.'s Daughter.*
1949: *Bad Men of Tombstone, Moonrise.*
1950: *Singing Guns, Dallas.*
1951: *Drums in the Deep South, Vengeance Valley.*
1953: *Kansas Pacific, The Lawless Breed, El Paso Stampede.*
1954: *Jesse James vs. the Daltons.*
1955: *Thy Neighbor's Daughter, The Tall Men, Prince of Players.*
1956: *Invasion of the Body Snatchers.*
1957: *Baby Face Nelson.*
1959: *Edge of Eternity.*
1960: *Toby Tyler.*
1961: *Pocketful of Miracles, Paradise Alley.*
1969: *Flareup, They Shoot Horses Don't They?*
1970: *Dirty Dingus Magee.*
1977: *Empire of the Ants.*

Television Series

1956–1958: *Broken Arrow* as Duffield.
1958–1959: *Cimarron City* as Silas Perry.

Sources

Brooks, Tim. *The Complete Directory to Prime Time TV Stars 1946–Present.* New York: Ballantine Books, 1987.
Ragan, David. *Who's Who in Hollywood 1900–1976.* New Rochelle, NY: Arlington House, 1976.
Twomey, Alfred E., and Arthur F. McClure. *The Versatiles.* South Brunswick and New York: Barnes, 1969.

TOMMY FARRELL

Tommy Farrell was born Thomas Richards, Jr., during the 1920s. He is the son of actress Glenda Farrell and her first husband Thomas Richards, a World War I veteran. His parents had a struggling vaudeville act and had virtually no money. She had to return to live with her family until her son was born. The couple soon divorced, and at the age of ten his name was legally changed to Tommy Farrell. He first attracted attention as the juvenile lead in a few Whip Wilson features. He also played heavies in some movies. Then he had an unsuccessful nightclub act with Peter Marshall.

He played Corporal Carson in *The Adventures of Rin Tin Tin,* appropriately commencing with an episode called "Corporal Carson." When this ended he had a regular role in the sitcom *The Many Loves of Dobie Gillis* for a season. Although he continued to act on television during the 1960s (e.g., *Lost in Space*), he later became a scriptwriter of sitcoms and dramas. He currently resides in Los Angeles. He has been married three times and has a daughter.

Tommy Farrell Filmography

1950: *Pygmy Island, Pirates of the High Seas* (serial), *Gunfire, Outlaws of Texas, Duchess of Idaho, At War with the Army.*
1951: *Colorado Ambush, Abilene Trail, The Strip, Strangers on a Train, Starlift, A Yank in Korea.*
1952: *Night Raiders, Wyoming Roundup, Flesh and Fury, You for Me, Meet Danny Wilson.*
1954: *Gunfighters of the Northwest* (serial).
1959: *A Woman Obsessed, North by Northwest.*
1961: *Breakfast at Tiffany's.*
1962: *Swingin' Along, Saintly Sinners.*
1963: *My Six Loves, Kissing Cousins.*
1967: *A Guide for the Married Man.*

Television Series

1954–1959: *The Adventures of Rin Tin Tin* as Corporal Carson.
1959–1960: *The Many Loves of Dobie Gillis* as Riff Ryan.

Sources

Cooper, Jackie, and Dick Kleiner. *Please Don't Shoot My Dog.* New York: William Morrow, 1981.
Parish, James Robert, and William Leonard. *Hollywood Players: The Thirties.* Carlstadt NJ: Rainbow, 1976.
Rothel, David. *Those Great Cowboy Sidekicks.* Waynesville, NC: World of Yesterday Publications, 1984.

WILLIAM FAWCETT

William Fawcett was born William Fawcett Thompson in High Forest, Minnesota, on September 8, 1894, the son of a minister. His original ambition was to enter the ministry, and he attended Hamline University where he took appropriate courses. His career was sidetracked by World War I when he served in the armed forces. He was decorated with the Medaille D'Honneur for work with the French wounded.

Upon being discharged he decided to become an actor, so he became a member of various stock companies until the advent of talking pictures virtually brought about their demise. He studied English and drama at the University of Nebraska where he graduated with an M.A. and doctorate. Later he taught these subjects at the same university and at Michigan State University for five years.

World War II intervened and found him working in the shipyards of San Francisco and Oakland in California. After this he went to Hollywood where he became a writer for commercial films. He reverted to his original profession, making his motion picture debut in 1946. He subsequently appeared in many movies in a wide assembly of character parts. He was also active in television and appeared in hundreds of episodes. His sole regular role was as the ranch foreman in the popular horse-and-boy series *Fury.* In contrast to his precise real-life diction, his command of language in this role was full of slang and highly original. Ironically he frequently went on record as saying that this was his favorite role.

William Fawcett died on January 25, 1974, at age 79.

William Fawcett Filmography

1946: *Stars Over Texas, Driftin' River, Tumbleweed Trails.*
1947: *The Michigan Kid, Wild Country, Black Hills, Green Dolphin Street, High Wall, Ghost Town Renegades, The Beginning or the End?, Sea Hound* (serial), *Pioneer Justice.*
1948: *Tex Granger* (serial), *Words and Music, An Act of Murder, The Tioga Kid, Check Your Guns, Superman* (serial).
1949: *The Kid from Texas, Ride Ryder Ride!, Roll Thunder Roll, Barbary Pirate, Batman and Robin* (serial), *Adventures of Sir Galahad* (serial).
1950: *Tyrant of the Sea, State Penitentiary, Cody of the Pony Express* (serial), *Pirates of the High Seas* (serial), *Chain Gang, House By the River.*
1951: *Comin' Round the Mountain, Valley of Fire, Ace in the Hole, The Hollywood Story, Wanted—Dead Or Alive, Honeychile, Oklahoma Annie, Hills of Utah, The Magic Carpet, The Mating Season, Captain Video* (serial), *Montana Incident, Mysterious Island* (serial).
1952: *The Longhorn, Roar of the Iron Horse* (serial), *King of the Congo* (serial), *Springfield Rifle, The Lion and the Horse, Kansas Territory, Barbed Wire, Jungle Jim in the Forbidden Land, Blackhawk* (serial).
1953: *The Star of Texas, The Homesteaders, The Marksman, Has Anybody Seen My Gal?, The Raiders, A Man's Country, The Neanderthal Man, Gunsmoke, Canadian Mounties Vs. Atomic Invaders* (serial), *Run for the Hills, Sweethearts on Parade.*
1954: *Dawn at Socorro, The Law vs. Billy the Kid, Alaska Seas, Riding with Buffalo Bill* (serial).
1955: *Seminole Uprising, Pirates of Tripoli, Tall Man Riding, Lay That Rifle Down, Timberjack, The Spoilers, Gangbusters.*
1956: *The Kettles in the Ozarks, Dakota Incident, The Proud Ones, Canyon River, The First Traveling Saleslady.*
1957: *The Storm Rider, The Tijuana Story, Band of Angels, Tension at Table Rock.*
1958: *Damn Yankees, No Time for Sergeants, Go Johnny Go!*
1959: *The Wild and the Innocent, Good Day for a Hanging.*
1960: *The Walking Target.*
1961: *Claudelle Inglish, The Comancheros.*
1962: *The Interns, Saintly Sinners, Gypsy, The Music Man.*
1963: *The Wheeler Dealers.*
1964: *Sex and the Single Girl, The Quick Gun.*
1965: *Dear Brigitte, King Rat.*
1966: *Jesse James Meets Frankenstein's Daughter.*
1967: *Hostile Guns, The Gnome-Mobile.*
1968: *Blackbeard's Ghost.*

Television Series

1955–1958: *Fury* as Pete.

Sources

McClure, Arthur F., and Ken D. Jones, *Heroes, Heavies and Sagebrush.* South Brunswick and New York: Barnes, 1972.
Truitt, Evelyn Mack. *Who Was Who on Screen Illustrated Edition.* New York: Bowker, 1984.

FRANK FERGUSON

Born on December 25, 1899, Frank Ferguson acquired years of experience in stock and on Broadway before gravitating to Hollywood in 1940. After making his screen debut he appeared in numerous films in small roles. Surprisingly, his only semi-regular series role for a long time was a minor one, that of the McLaughlin ranch foreman in *My Friend Flicka.* His other recurring role was toward the end of his career when he played Eli Carson, Elliott Carson's father in the popular soap opera *Peyton Place.* He died in Los Angeles on September 12, 1978, at age 78, of cancer.

Frank Ferguson Filmography

1940: *Father Is a Prince, Gambling on the High Seas.*
1941: *They Died With Their Boots On, You'll Never Get Rich, The Body Disappears.*
1942: *Spy Ship, You Were Never Lovelier, City of Silent Men, Boss of Big Town, My Gal Sal,*

Portrait of Frank Ferguson, who appeared in *My Friend Flicka*.

Broadway, Reap the Wild Wind, Ten Gentlemen from West Point, This Gun for Hire, Moonlight Masquerade.
1943: *Truck Busters, Mission to Moscow, Pilot No. 5.*
1945: *The Dolly Sisters, Rhapsody in Blue.*
1946: *Little Miss Big, Swell Guy, Night and Day, Canyon Passage, Cross My Heart, The Searching Wind, Lady Chasers, Secrets of a Sorority Girl, If I'm Lucky, Blonde for a Day, The Perfect Marriage, OSS, The Man I Love, California.*
1947: *They Won't Believe Me, T-Men, Variety Girl, The Beginning or the End?, The Farmer's Daughter, The Perils of Pauline, Blaze of Noon, Cass Timberlane, The Fabulous Texan, Welcome Stranger, Road to Rio, Killer at Large.*
1948: *Fort Apache, They Live by Night, Abbott and Costello Meet Frankenstein, The Hunted, Miracle of the Bells, The Vicious Circle, The Walls of Jericho, Walk a Crooked Mile, The Inside Story, That Wonderful Urge, Rachel and The Stranger, Fighting Father Dunne, T-Men.*
1949: *Caught, The Barkleys of Broadway, Follow Me Quietly, Free for All, State Department—File 649, Slightly French, Dynamite, Shockproof, Roseanna McCoy, Dancing in the Dark.*
1950: *He's a Cockeyed Wonder, The West Point Story, Frenchie, Under Mexicali Stars, Tyrant of the Sea, The Good Humor Man, The Great Missouri Raid, The Furies, Right Cross, Key to the City, Louisa.*
1951: *Thunder in God's Country, Santa Fe, Elopement, Warpath, The People Against O'Hara, On Dangerous Ground, The Barefoot Mailman, The Cimarron Kid, The Model and the Marriage Broker, Boots Malone.*
1952: *Rancho Notorious, Wagons West, Rodeo, It Grows on Trees, The Lone Hand, Bend of the River, Has Anybody Seen My Gal?, Ma and Pa Kettle at the Fair, The Marrying Kind, Oklahoma Annie, The Winning Team, Million Dollar Mermaid, Stars and Stripes Forever, Models Inc., Room for One More.*
1953: *Main Street to Broadway, The Beast from 20,000 Fathoms, The Big Leaguer, The Marksman, Star of Texas, The Woman They Almost Lynched, Wicked Woman, Trouble Along the Way, House of Wax, Powder River, Outlaw Territory (*a.k.a. *Hannah Lee), Texas Badman, The Blue Gardenia.*
1954: *Johnny Guitar, A Star Is Born, The Shanghai Story, The Outcast, Young at Heart, Drum Beat, Moonfleet, The Violent Men, Riding Shotgun.*
1955: *Battle Cry, New York Confidential, A Lawless Street, The Eternal Sea, The McConell Story, At Gunpoint, City of Shadows, Moonfleet, The Violent Men.*
1956: *Tribute to a Bad Man.*
1957: *This Could Be the Night, The Phantom Stagecoach, The Iron Sheriff, Gun Duel in Durango, The Lawless Eighties.*
1958: *The Light in the Forest, Cole Younger Gunfighter, Andy Hardy Comes Home, Terror in a Texas Town, Man of the West.*
1959: *The Big Night.*
1960: *Sunrise at Campobello, Raymie.*
1961: *Pocketful Of Miracles.*
1964: *Those Calloways; Hush ... Hush, Sweet Charlotte; The Quick Gun.*
1965: *The Great Sioux Massacre.*
1969: *Along Came a Spider* (TV).

Television Series

1956–1957: *My Friend Flicka* as Gus Broeberg.
1964–1969: *Peyton Place* as Eli Carson.

Sources

Brooks, Tim. *The Complete Directory to Prime Time TV Stars 1946–Present.* New York: Ballantine Books, 1987.

Quinlan, David. *Illustrated Directory of Film Character Actors.* London: Batsford, 1995.

Willis, John. *Screen World.* London: Muller, 1979.

PAUL FIX

Paul Fix was born Paul Fix Morrison in Dobbs Ferry, New York, on March 13, 1901, the son of a brewer. He toured with stock companies in the eastern states and appeared in numerous stage productions in the 1920s and 1930s on the West Coast. His motion picture debut came in 1922, but his appearances were sporadic until the arrival of sound. Since then he more than compensated in that he may have played more sheriffs, doctors and ranchers than any other thespian. He averaged at least half a dozen movie appearances each year. He was a close friend of John Wayne and appeared in many of his films. He is probably best known for playing Sheriff Micah Torrence in *The Rifleman* television series throughout its entire run. His hobbies were golf and yachting. He died in Santa Monica, California, on October 14, 1983, of kidney failure. The 82-year-old actor had been married twice. By his first marriage he had a daughter, who is married to Harry Carey, Jr.

Paul Fix Filmography

1922: *The Adventuress.*

1926: *Hoodoo Ranch.*

1927: *Chicago.*

1928: *The First Kiss.*

1929: *Lucky Star, Trial Marriage.*

1930: *Ladies Love Brutes, Man Trouble.*

1931: *Bad Girl, Three Girls Lost, The Fighting Sheriff, The Avenger, Good Bad Girl.*

1932: *The Last Mile, Dancers in the Dark (*a.k.a. *Dance Palace), Scarface, South of the Rio Grande, Back Street, Fargo Express, The Racing Strain, Sky Devils.*

1933: *Zoo in Budapest, Hard to Handle, The Sphinx, The Important Witness, The Woman Who Dared, The Avenger, The Mad Game, Gun Law, Somewhere in Sonora, Emergency Call, The Devil's Mate.*

1934: *Little Man What Now?, Rocky Rhodes, The Crosby Case, The Woman Who Dared, Flirtation Walk, The Count of Monte Cristo, The Westerner.*

1935: *The Desert Trail, The Eagle's Brood, Let 'Em Have It, Men Without Names, Bar-20 Rides Again, Miss Pacific Fleet, The Crimson Trail, The World Accuses, His Fighting Blood, The Throwback, Mutiny Ahead, Living on Velvet, Valley of Wanted Men, Bulldog Courage, Millions in the Air, Don't Bet on Blondes, Reckless.*

1936: *Road to Glory, Charlie Chan at the Race Track, The Phantom Patrol, Yellowstone, Straight from the Shoulder, Navy Born, The Prisoner of Shark Island, The Ex-Mrs. Bradford, Winterset, The Plot Thickens, Two in a Crowd, Wanted! Jane Turner, After the Thin Man, The Bridge of Sighs, 15 Maiden Lane, 36 Hours to Kill.*

1937: *Souls at Sea, Western Gold, Armored Car, Paid to Dance, King of Gamblers, The Game That Kills, Woman in Distress, Daughter of Shanghai, Border Cafe, Her Husband Lies, On Such a Night, Conquest, Hot Water.*

1938: *King of Alcatraz, Gun Law, The Buccaneer, Mannequin, Penitentiary, When G-Men Step In, Crime Ring, Mr. Moto's Gamble, The Saint in New York, Smashing the Rackets, The Night Hawk, Crime Takes a Holiday.*

1939: *Mutiny on the Blackhawk, Two Thoroughbreds, Disbarred, Wall Street Cowboy, They All Come Out, The Girl and the Gambler, News Is Made at Night, Heritage of the Desert, Those High Gray Walls, Star Reporter, Behind Prison Gates, Code of the Streets, Undercover Doctor.*

1940: *The Ghost Breakers, Outside the Three-*

Paul Fix in *The Rifleman*.

Mile Limit, The Crooked Road, Black Friday, Dr. Cyclops, Triple Justice, Black Diamonds, Virginia City, Glamour for Sale, Queen of the Mob, Strange Cargo, The Fargo Kid, Virginia City, Trail of the Vigilantes, The Great Plane Robbery.

1941: *A Missouri Outlaw, Citadel of Crime, Down Mexico Way, H.M. Pulham Esq., Unfinished Business, Public Enemies, Hold That Ghost, The Roar of the Press.*

1942: *Pittsburgh, Highways by Night, That Other Woman, South of Santa Fe, Sherlock Holmes and the Secret Weapon, Jail House Blues, Escape from Crime, Kid Glove Killer, Alias Boston Blackie, Youth on Parade, Sleepytime Gal, Dr. Gillespie's New Assistant.*

1943: *Hitler—Dead Or Alive, Mug Town, Captive Wild Woman, Bombardier, In Old Oklahoma (*a.k.a. *War of the Wildcats), The Unknown Guest.*

1944: *The Fighting Seabees, Tall in the Saddle.*

1945: *Flame of Barbary Coast, Grissly's Millions, Back to Bataan, Dakota.*

1947: *Tycoon.*

1948: *Wake of the Red Witch, Angel in Exile, Red River, Strange Gamble, Force of Evil, The Plunderers.*

1949: *The Fighting Kentuckian, She Wore a Yellow Ribbon, Hellfire, Fighting Man of the Plains.*

1950: *California Passage, Surrender, Jet Pilot, The Great Missouri Raid.*

1951: *Warpath.*

1952: *What Price Glory?, Ride the Man Down, Denver and the Rio Grande.*

1953: *Star of Texas, Fair Wind to Java, Island in the Sky, Devil's Canyon, Hondo.*

1954: *Johnny Guitar, The High and the Mighty, Ring of Fear.*

1955: *Top of the World, The Sea Chase, Blood Alley.*

1956: *Giant, Santiago, Toward the Unknown, Star in the Dust, Man in the Vault, The Bad Seed, Stagecoach to Fury.*

1957: *Night Passage, The Devil's Hairpin, Man in the Shadow.*

1958: *Guns Girls And Gangsters, Lafayette Escadrille, The Notorious Mr. Monks.*

1962: *To Kill a Mockingbird.*

1963: *Mail Order Bride.*

1964: *The Outrage.*

1965: *Baby the Rain Must Fall, The Sons of Katie Elder, Shenandoah.*

1966: *Nevada Smith, An Eye for an Eye, Ride Beyond Vengeance, Incident at Phantom Hill, Welcome to Hard Times.*

1967: *El Dorado, The Ballad of Josie, Winchester '73* (TV).

1968: *Day of the Evil Gun.*

1969: *The Undefeated, The Profane Comedy (*a.k.a. *Set This Town on Fire)* (TV), *Young Billy Young, Zabriskie Point.*

1970: *Dirty Dingus Magee, House on Greenapple Road* (TV).

1971: *Something Big, Shoot Out.*

1972: *Night of the Lepus.*

1973: *Cahill US Marshal, Pat Garrett and Billy the Kid.*

1975: *Guilty or Innocent: The Sam Shepherd Murder Case* (TV). 1977: *Grayeagle, The City* (TV).

1978: *Just Me and You* (TV).

1979: *Hanging by a Thread* (TV), *Wanda Nevada.*

Television Series

1958–1963: *The Rifleman* as Sheriff Micah Torrence.

Miniseries

1979: *The Rebels.*

Sources

Carey, Harry, Jr. *Company of Heroes.* Metuchen, NJ: Scarecrow, 1994.
McClure, Arthur F., and Ken D. Jones. *Heroes, Heavies and Sagebrush.* South Brunswick and New York: Barnes, 1972.
Parish, James Robert. *Hollywood Character Actors.* New Rochelle, NY: Arlington House, 1978.
The Picturegoer's Who's Who and Encyclopedia. London: Odhams, 1933.
Quinlan, David. *Illustrated Directory of Film Character Actors.* London: Batsford, 1995.

ARTHUR FLEMING

Arthur Fleming was born Art Fazzin in the Bronx, New York, on May 1, 1924. A veteran of stock and Broadway, his first foray into series television was as the lead in a syndicated version of *Flying Tigers* in 1953. He starred as Major Dell Conway, the leader of a group of fliers during World War II.

After the Western series *The Californians* was revamped, he played attorney Jeremy Pitt, who it sometimes seemed was the only friend of Marshal Matt Wayne (Richard Coogan). He was introduced at the start of the second season in an episode entitled "Dishonor for Matt Wayne." When asked to comment on this series, he gave a wry reply: "Tough? Boy, you can really suffer. Just growing sideburns is a problem. I had mine for nearly two years. When I shaved them off, I couldn't stand the cold." Another favorite recollection concerned his horse. He said, "For *The Californians* I picked a horse because I felt sorry for her. Out of 400 she looked the worst. Her name was Goldie. She was 23 years old and looked ready for the boneyard. Yet the handler told me, 'You've got the best of the bunch.' She'd done so many pictures, she saved her action until the sound of the clapper boards."

Julia Arnall and Arthur Fleming. Fleming appeared in *The Californians.*

When this series ended, Fleming played the agent hero of *International Detective,* a popular syndicated series lensed at Elstree Studios in England. Fleming made relatively few films, but achieved his greatest success as the host of the daytime game show *Jeopardy!,* which he fronted for a decade. He contributed a memorable cameo as the host of *Jeopardy!* in the movie *Airplane II: The Sequel* (1982).

This personable actor retired from television and lived in St. Louis, Missouri, where he had a two-hour chat show on radio five days a week, with a quiz show on Saturdays. In his spare time he lectured on motivation and enthusiasm. At age 70 he died at Crystal River, Florida, on April 25, 1995, of pancreatic cancer.

Arthur Fleming Filmography

1957: *A Hatful of Rain.*
1977: *MacArthur.*
1982: *Airplane II: The Sequel*

Television Series

1953: *The Flying Tigers* as Major Dell Conway.
1958–1959: *The Californians* as Jeremy Pitt.
1959: *International Detective* as Ken Franklin.
1964–1975: *Jeopardy!*—host.
1978–1979: *The All New Jeopardy!*—host.

Sources

Lentz, Harris M. *Obituaries in the Performing Arts, 1995.* Jefferson, NC: McFarland, 1996.
Stoddart, Sarah. "How They Suffer—Those TV Western Idols." *Picturegoer* magazine, September 12, 1959.

ERIC FLEMING

A key role in *Rawhide* was that of trail boss Gil Favor, who was once described as a "tough man of action who possessed good judgment, compassion and an iron will." Eric Fleming was excellent in the part because he was lean, rugged and taciturn, with a deep, resonant voice which commanded respect. As a television Western star Fleming enjoyed enormous popularity, but as a man he was a loser from birth to death.

Although the man himself claimed never to have known when or where he was born, Eric Fleming was born Edward Heddy, Jr., on July 4, 1925, in Santa Paula, California. He was the son of Edward Heddy, Sr., an itinerant carpenter, oil field worker and cook. His mother, Mildred Anderson, was a housewife. His father was an extremely savage man, prone to fly into violent rages during which he frequently beat his son with a belt or rope. His father could not hold a job long on account of his temper, and the family only survived because his mother usually obtained work as a cook in the labor camps where they stayed. When Fleming was nine, his leg swelled with osteomyelitis. He had to have an operation, which landed him in the hospital for six months. His father never once came to see him.

When he was 11, Fleming ran away. During the years of the Depression runaway boys were a common sight on the highways and railroads of America. Their plight was brilliantly depicted in William Wellman's classic movie *Wild Boys of the Road* (1933). Twice Fleming was picked up by the police and returned to his parents, who were living in abject poverty in the Los Angeles area. He ran away again, going as far afield as New York and Chicago.

He recalled, "I was an ugly child.... My first recollection of any place was Mexico. My dad was a roustabout, a man who'd go anywhere, anyplace for a buck. He went to where the work was. He fought to stay alive and did everything: gold miner, inventor, oil well rigger, blaster on Boulder Dam, lumberjack, cop and fisherman. He was like so many during the Depression days, maybe more so.

"By the time I was 14, I had lived in all of the then 48 states. I was already a work veteran, having first been employed at the age of six running errands, standing look-out for floating crap games and selling papers. Actually, it was a matter of survival ... no place and everywhere were my home. By the time I was nine, I was on my own completely. Few know my story. I spent much time with racket boys because they were kind to me and I didn't know better. Tired of being constantly on the run, I went legit so to speak in my teens and worked as a longshoreman, cook, truck driver and so many jobs of this sort."

Other employment included work as a miner, ambulance driver, carpenter, waiter, ditchdigger, oil field roustabout, soda jerk, hod carrier, backlot laborer and grip at Paramount studios. At the age of 17 Fleming joined the Seabees and saw four years of service during World War II as a construction worker build-

Eric Fleming (foreground) in *Rawhide*. Clint Eastwood is behind him at left.

ing bases throughout the South Pacific. After the war, he was shipped back to a naval base in California.

While supervising a building project one afternoon, on a bet he tried to demonstrate how to insert a 200 pound counterbalance block of steel. He lay on his back and started juggling the big block into place with his feet. The massive block teetered uncertainly for a second, then slipped off and crashed down on his face. His first lucky break came a few hours after the catastrophe as he was lying unconscious in the base hospital. A plastic surgeon touring the wards stopped to look at his hideously mangled face. "I'd like to treat this man personally," he said. "This boy has nothing to lose!"

The surgeon began by sewing 38 stitches in Fleming's face, but the matter of his nearly obliterated nose looked hopeless. It had been mashed and torn until it almost covered his right eye. His left eyebrow had been completely gouged out and his forehead smashed in so he could hardly see. Years later doctors still feared he might eventually lose his vision. His new face started to take shape with the second and third operations. By rebuilding whole areas with wire, the skilled surgeon was able to restore the forehead, chin and cheekbones. The treatment was so severe the doctor advised Fleming to recuperate for a while before going any further.

Still minus a nose, he left the hospital and the navy. He eventually saved enough money for two more plastic surgery operations, and by the end of the second operation his face was completely restored. He still bore marks from his dread ordeal. His left eyebrow, which was grafted on, had to be shaved daily. He used a makeup pencil to cover facial scars left by the stitches, and the area of skin around his left eye was smaller and lower than on the right eye. "My only trouble," Fleming joked, "is every time I look in the mirror, I still have trouble recognizing myself!" One curious insight is provided by Marilyn Fix, now Mrs. Harry Carey, Jr. She had dated Fleming in the early 1940s prior to his accident. She also knew him in Hollywood in later years. She claims that his appearance was substantially the same.

During the recuperation period, he made so little progress that for a while he contemplated studying to be a doctor. He recalled, "I was working at Paramount studios as a stagehand, going with a girl who was enrolled in an acting school. One night I picked her up at the school and I saw her do a scene with another student. I mentioned that I could do better and made a hundred dollar bet to that effect with my girlfriend. So they let me attempt the scene. I was so bad it was unbelievable and [I] lost the bet. I couldn't let a thing like that pass. It was a challenge. So I, too, began to study acting. Two years later, I got my first acting job, a road company of *Happy Birthday* starring Miriam Hopkins. I toured the West with the play for two months, but it was my passport to the Broadway stage."

He had a premature taste of series stardom when he played the leading role in *Major Dell Conway of the Flying Tigers* (1951) for the now defunct Dumont network. This was a live action series shot on a shoestring about a heroic pilot who served with the Flying Tigers squadron in China during World War II. He was replaced in the leading role very rapidly and became something of a misfit around the studios in Hollywood. He never worked more than a couple of days at a time, and his income during the early 1950s from acting never reached $2,000 a year. He is also believed to have had a regular role in a shortlived NBC daytime soap called *Golden Windows* (1954).

Fleming made his screen debut in *Conquest of Space* (1955). Subsequently he played leading roles in three other low-budget science fiction and horror films. One of the best remembered was *Queen of Outer Space* (1958), which starred Zsa Zsa Gabor. Director Edward Bernds recalled Fleming as "a consummate professional, always prepared with lines memorized." His first venture into the Western format was a *Studio One* television presentation called "The Strong Man" (1958) in which he played Jace Farrow, a foreman for a powerful cattle baron. Then there was the *Rawhide* pilot, "Incident at Barker Springs." He also starred in the theatrical feature *Curse of the Undead* (1959) as Preacher Dan, a cattle town man of the cloth; Michael Pate played Drake Robey, a vampire, in this horror Western. Ironically, Fleming never actually starred in a conventional Western feature film.

Fleming recalled, "I was just about making a passable living in New York, having had about a dozen plays under my belt, when I decided to quit the whole thing and go to Hawaii. I had saved $2,000 and wanted to forget chasing rainbows and do a bit of living. I booked passage on the *Lurline* and was waiting in Hollywood for the next Los Angeles sailing when I was asked to test for *Rawhide*. I did, got the part, but didn't know it was the lead role until I saw the pilot show. I canceled my trip to Hawaii and for the next seven years starred in the series."

Debuting in January 1959, as a mid-season replacement, *Rawhide* was the brainchild of Charles Marquis Warren, who had directed a film called *Cattle Empire* (1958). This implanted in Warren the seed for a series based on the great cattle drives of the 1870s. The series followed the men from Texas to the railheads of the Midwest. Although some believe that it substituted cattle for the wagons in *Wagon Train, Rawhide* set out to explore the myths and legends of the working West of the cattle kingdom and the people who inhabited it. Despite the fact that the cattle were paramount, the series still found time to incorporate the problems of many of Hollywood's best loved stars who turned up along the way, frequently in episodes beginning with the word "Incident..." Warren derived most of his source material and the unique terminology which peppered the series from a journal written by George Duffield, who had served as a drover on just such a cattle drive from San Antonio, Texas, to Sedalia, Missouri, in 1866. A highlight of the series was the Warren soliloquies beautifully delivered at the start of the first three seasons' episodes by Eric Fleming.

One episode which showcased him to advantage was "Incident of the Night on the Town," where the progress of the cattle drive is impeded by litigation when it is claimed that a proportion of the cattle were stolen. Favor goes to court to prove that this is a falsehood, but in the course of the story he enters a refined club in full evening clothes and even trips the light fantastic. It was a highly unusual episode based on an idea by the star himself. In other episodes which showed his more human side, Favor was revealed to be a widower with two daughters who were living with their aunt in Philadelphia.

The series proved to be a tremendous hit with viewers; it ranked as high as sixth during the 1960–1961 season. Although the guest-stars were impressive, it was the grit of Fleming and Clint Eastwood which kept the series riding high in the ratings. Some television historians have tried to diminish Fleming's contribution to *Rawhide* by stating that Eastwood stole every scene between the two actors by underplaying, but this is a judgment based on hindsight. By this stage of his career, Fleming had accumulated considerable experience and was no slouch as an actor, so that he could more than hold his own against almost any other star in the television Western genre.

Fleming's private life, however, remained as miserable and troubled as ever. He was a bachelor who lived quietly by himself in a Hollywood Hills garage which had been transformed into a small, seedy apartment. When publicists tried to convince him to move into an upmarket apartment or house more in keeping with his status as a top television star, he refused, saying, "I've lived out of a suitcase and a paper bag all my life and I'm staying footloose. This acting business is liable to blow up on me at any time and I'll wind up broke the way I always was."

Although his salary rose to high in the five figure bracket, he saved nearly all of it after taxes. He drove a modest car and was known by the girls he dated as adding a new dimension to the word "tightwad." He took them to rundown cafes or hamburger stands because he was chronically afraid that if he spent any money he would end up penniless. He refused to marry because he reasoned that if he brought a child into the world, it might suffer the same deprivations as himself, a thought he found unbearable. He also suffered from a continuing nightmare that his was going to be a short life and that he was going to die violently.

In the fall of 1965, Fleming parted company with the herd and the series. He and Clint Eastwood, who had previously enjoyed a good relationship, had not been getting on too well for a while. Fleming's decision to leave was more of a manifestation of a desire to move on to other projects than an outright feeling of hostility to Eastwood, and they parted amicably enough at the end. Eastwood had just begun the ascent to stardom through the spaghetti Westerns, which may have been a cause of friction. According to *Company of Heroes,* by Harry Carey, Jr., Fleming was the first choice of Sergio Leone to play the lead in the film *A Fistful of Dollars,* the original spaghetti Western. Allegedly he turned it down, whereupon Leone went after Eastwood.

By this time, however, Fleming was not looked upon too favorably by some of his directors. Gene Fowler, Jr., recalled him as "arrogant, hard to handle and undirectable." This view was supported by Ted Post, who remembers, "Eric, in self-centered and unrelated stentorian tones, overcooked the emotional delivery of his dialogue." However, an indication of how integral Fleming's contribution was to the success of *Rawhide* is that it failed to last a full season without him.

Once Fleming quit *Rawhide,* his career did not fare well. He played guest shots on a few television series, notably *Bonanza.* He also gave an excellent account of himself in *The Glass Bottom Boat* (1966), a spy spoof starring Doris Day, in which he played it straight as the villain rather than camping it up. Fleming finally made Hawaii his home, saying that he was through with Hollywood films and television. The life he envisaged for himself in Hawaii was to study, paint, sculpt and roam the beaches. He believed that his career was on the skids, but he received reassurance from his business managers who told him that if he hung in there, he would become a star in movies like Clint Eastwood.

It was for this reason that Fleming readily signed with a small independent outfit, McGowan Productions, for a costarring role in *High Jungle,* a two-part episode of MGM-TV's new ABC series *Off to See the Wizard.* His remuneration was much less than he had enjoyed as a television star on *Rawhide,* and the job required him to work on the rugged locations of the Andes in Peru. It was the kind of filming which years before would have been shot in the comparative safety of a studio back lot. No stuntmen were included in the Metro unit. Fleming had signed two separate contracts, one covering the telefilm and the other for the theatrical movie for foreign release which was to have been made. He was guaranteed ten weeks' work and a $25,000 salary, with the remainder of the planned 14-week schedule to call for remuneration on a pro rata basis.

On July 19, 1965, Fleming's business advisor, Irving Leonard, filed a will in which he was named as executor. In this bizarre document, Fleming bequeathed his eyes to the Estelle Doheny Foundation of Los Angeles for use in cornea transplants and his body to the medical research department at UCLA. A final clause stipulated that if he died, there were to be no funeral services.

On September 28, 1966, the 41-year-old actor was paddling a jungle canoe through the rapids in the Huallaga River with costar Nico Minardos when the canoe capsized. Minardos managed to swim safely to shore. Fleming tried to do the same, but the current proved too strong and he was swept away. His leading lady Anne Heywood looked on helplessly while 20 men in the film crew prepared to save him. His last recorded words were "C'mon, Nico, now or never."

His body was recovered four days later. It was carried with great difficulty along a tortuous jungle trail to the Tingo Maria village morgue and then flown back to the United States. When it reached America, doctors discovered that it was so badly decomposed it could not be used for medical operations or research. His remains were cremated and interred without a religious service or mourners. The bulk of Fleming's $125,000 estate was left to his mother, Mildred Anderson Heddy. The 69-year-old Mrs. Heddy was willed $30,000 plus the remainder of the estate after three $10,000 bequests and other costs. The smaller bequests went to a cousin, Barbara Dodge of Marina del Rey; Chris Miller; and actress Lynne Garber, both of Los Angeles. Garber, a longtime friend of the actor, was working with the film company in Peru and witnessed Fleming's death. The actor specifically disinherited his father, whom he had not seen since his parents were divorced in 1935.

In a February 1966, interview, Fleming had indicated he was ready to settle down for the first time in his life. He said, "I was never a great actor. I never expected to be. I'd like to settle down on the beach in Hawaii, possibly around Maui. For the first time, I've found a place to put down roots ... the Islands. Nowhere has had the meaning for me like Hawaii has. I hope to marry an Island girl. I have that family feeling and am hoping maybe in the not-too-distant future to start one of my own. To me Island children are like a bouquet of flowers." He had maintained an apartment on Lemon Road in Waikiki for awhile. He didn't frequent the Waikiki night spots, but he did occasionally drop in at the Honolulu Press Club. His plans were to retire to a ranch he purchased in Hawaii not long before he died.

Ironically, in many studio biographies of Eric Fleming which list his hobbies, swimming is prominent among them.

Eric Fleming Filmography

1955: *Conquest of Space.*
1957: *Fright.*
1958: *Queen of Outer Space.*
1959: *Curse of the Undead.*
1966: *The Glass Bottom Boat.*

Television Series

1951: *Major Dell Conway of the Flying Tigers* as Major Dell Conway.
1954: *Golden Windows.*
1959–1965: *Rawhide* as Gil Favor.

Sources

"Eric Fleming: Head 'Em Up ... Move 'Em Out." *Trail Dust* magazine, spring 1993.
Thomey, Tedd. *The Glorious Decade.* New York: Ace, 1971.

HENRY FONDA

Henry Fonda became the epitome of the honest, liberal American. His personality and physical appearance suggested the pioneer spirit, and he was well cast as a frontiersman. There were flashier performers, but few more genuine and sincere. He was virtually the only cinema star with a flourishing career who agreed to do a half-hour Western series at a time when his career was still close to its peak. He admitted his fear: "Never being asked to work again, no one wanting me. No matter how many calls I get, it's still there. Sounds ridiculous, but that's why I take jobs I probably should pass by."

He managed to resolve the problem of the degree of commitment needed for episodic television by not making himself the focal point of *The Deputy* as the title implied. Fonda was a man of strong principle both on and off camera. Although a well-known liberal, he never agreed with the radicalism of his daughter Jane. He detested Darryl F. Zanuck because of the disputes over poor material when he was under contract at Fox, and Ward Bond because of his extreme right wing political views.

Henry Jaynes Fonda was born in Grand Island, Nebraska, on May 16, 1905, the eldest child and only son of Herberta Jaynes Fonda and William Brace Fonda. His father was a commercial printer. When Henry Fonda was six months old, his parents moved to Omaha, Nebraska, where his father owned the W.B. Fonda Printing Company. Two sisters, Harriet and Jayne, were born there. His mother died in 1934 and his father in 1935. The family were Christian Scientists.

In 1923 he graduated from Omaha Central High School and subsequently enrolled at the University of Minnesota where he studied journalism. After two years he dropped out of college. Some accounts say that the reason was because he failed his exams, while others state that he had realized by that time that journalism was not his vocation in life. This decision was possibly made for him when his father's printing company ran into financial difficulties.

He returned to Omaha where he was soon contacted by Dorothy Brando, the mother of Marlon, who was a friend of Fonda's mother. She helped to run an amateur theatrical group called the Omaha Community Playhouse and asked Fonda to join the company. He agreed, but his family was against his desire to become an actor. Since there was no salary, he obtained a job as an office boy with the Retail Credit Company. In the season of 1926 Fonda played the title role of *Merton of the Movies* to rave reviews and standing ovations. After this he obtained various jobs with lowly theatrical companies.

In 1928, at Falmouth on Cape Cod, he joined the University Players a group which consisted mainly of Princeton and Harvard undergraduates. He remained with them for three seasons and played a variety of roles. In the course of his work he met the talented but tempestuous actress Margaret Sullavan, whom

Henry Fonda in *The Deputy*.

he married on Christmas Day, 1931, at the Kernan Hotel in Baltimore. There were monumental arguments before they split in February 1932, and they divorced in 1933. The autumn of 1932 found him in New York sharing an apartment with fellow University Players Joshua Logan, James Stewart and Myron Mc-Cormick. He did work in the theater, but none of it amounted to very much until he landed a role in a Broadway revue called *New Faces* in February 1934. On the strength of this he signed a personal management agreement with agent Leland Hayward, who urged him to go to Hollywood. The thought of working in Hollywood did not appeal to Fonda at all. Nevertheless, he inked a contract with producer Walter Wanger for two movies a year at $1,000 a week.

Fonda was acting in a play in Mount Kisco, New York. June Walker, the wife of a member of the cast, had been signed to star in the Broadway play *The Farmer Takes a Wife.* She suggested to the producers that Fonda would be ideal in the role of the farmer. The play opened in October 1934. While it was scarcely a success, the property was sold to Fox Films as a vehicle for Janet Gaynor. It was intended that either Gary Cooper or Joel McCrea should play the male lead, but when they proved unavailable, it was arranged with Wanger that Fonda should inherit the role in the film. Fonda thus became a star in his first film and stayed that way throughout his career. The director, Victor Fleming, was instrumental in pointing out to Fonda the differences between film and stage acting, lessons which Fonda readily absorbed.

His friend from the University Players, James Stewart, arrived in Hollywood almost simultaneously. The two actors shared a house together for a while. Stewart recalled, "His career just took off. It really happened pretty quick and in a year or so he was recognized as a very important leading man in pictures." Fonda made three films in 1935, three in 1936 and four in 1937. While in Europe working on *Wings of the Morning,* Fonda met Frances Seymour Brokaw, a beautiful, socially prominent widow with a daughter. They wed at Christ Church on Park Avenue in New York on September 17, 1936. They had two children, Jane (born December 21, 1937) and Peter (born February 23, 1939).

Fonda played the title role in *The Virginian* at the Westchester Playhouse and went on to star in *Blow Ye Winds* on Broadway, but it folded after 36 performances. Fonda returned to Hollywood where he shot five films in 1938. His status improved considerably when John Ford cast him in the title role of *Young Mr. Lincoln* (1939). Initially he was reluctant to play the part of Abraham Lincoln because he did not consider himself worthy enough. Ford convinced him by saying that he was playing a young country lawyer, not the great emancipator.

Darryl F. Zanuck, the head of 20th Century–Fox, acquired the rights to the novel *The Grapes of Wrath* by John Steinbeck, which dealt with the plight of migrants from the Dust Bowl in Oklahoma. Fonda made no secret of the fact that he wished to play the part of Tom Joad. Zanuck agreed to cast him, but only on the condition that he sign a seven-year contract with the studio. *The Grapes of Wrath* (1940), as directed by John Ford, became one of *the* classic movies, and Fonda earned himself an Academy Award nomination. It did much to establish his screen persona indelibly as a liberal, idealistic American. Ironically, he lost out on the Oscar to James Stewart in *The Philadelphia Story,* but Stewart voted for Fonda. The downside was that Fonda was forced into servitude by this contract. As he later expressed it, "I made all kinds of movies I hated at Fox. My gorge rises when I remember them."

When he was 14, Fonda's father had taken him to witness the lynching of a black because he wanted his son to understand what bigotry and racism could lead to. This made such a vivid impression on him that he fought to play the role of Gil Carter in a classic Western about the lynching of three innocent men, *The Ox Bow Incident* (1943). Although the film was not a box office success, Fonda recalled, "This was the only good picture at Fox in five years, and that was made against Zanuck's wishes because director William Wellman agreed to do another that Zanuck wanted him to do."

This proved to be his final film for three years because in August 1942, he enlisted in the United States navy. He first saw active service as a quartermaster third class on a destroyer in the Pacific. He was later commissioned back into the navy as a lieutenant, junior grade. He spent the balance of the war with Air Combat Intelligence before being honorably discharged in October 1945. He did not want to return to Hollywood, but he was still under contract to 20th Century–Fox. For recreation he was a keen gardener and built model airplanes with James Stewart.

His initial film back from the war reestablished him as a cinema actor of the front rank: He played Wyatt Earp in *My Darling Clementine* (1946), directed by John Ford, an account of the feud between the Earps and the Clantons which eventually led to the gunfight at the OK Corral. Once free of the Fox contract, he gave a memorable performance as the martinet soldier Col. Owen Thursday in *Fort Apache* (1948), another outstanding Western directed by Ford.

While Fonda was in New York to see Joshua Logan, Logan read him a play he had written called *Mister Roberts.* It centered on the crew of a ship called the *Reluctant* during the war. Mister Roberts, the most normal of the bunch, obtains a transfer to active service, but is killed in action off stage. The actor was so entranced with the play that he immediately shouted, "I'm going to do it!" Although Fonda was committed to doing another film, his tough agent extricated him from it. After 11 years away from the legitimate stage, with Logan directing, Fonda opened on Broadway in the title role on February 18, 1948, at the Alvin Theater. The play was a smash hit, with Fonda earning the reviews of a lifetime.

After the opening, Fonda moved his family to Greenwich, Connecticut. Fonda himself lived in an apartment on East 64th Street in Manhattan where he was rumored to be having an affair with Susan Blanchard, 21, whose mother was the wife of Oscar Hammerstein II. Frances Brokaw had been suffering from increasing mental disorder. When Fonda told her that he wanted a divorce to marry Blanchard, she agreed readily enough and began proceedings, but on April 14, 1950, while in a Beacon, New York, sanitarium, she committed suicide by slashing her throat with a razor blade. On December 28, 1950, Fonda and Susan Blanchard were wed in New Hope, Pennsylvania. On November 9, 1953, they adopted an eight-week-old girl named Amy from a foster home in Connecticut.

Fonda played Mister Roberts for three years through 1,671 performances in New York and on tour. He opened in John P. Marquand's *Point of No Return* on December 13, 1951. Although it was a less distinguished production, it lasted until 1953 through 364 performances. He then played Lt. Barney Greenwald in *The Caine Mutiny Court-Martial,* derived from the final part of the novel by Herman Wouk. It opened in New York on January 20, 1954, and he played in it until May of that year. Fonda continued to rejuvenate himself by returning to the theater throughout the rest of his career.

Fonda had been away from the screen for eight years. When Warner Bros. purchased the screen rights to *Mister Roberts*, there was a widespread debate about who should play the leading role. Joshua Logan wanted Marlon Brando, but producer Leland Hayward held out for Fonda. When Warner Bros. went with Fonda, John Ford replaced Logan as director. Shooting began, but after rows and a fistfight, Ford quit and was replaced by Mervyn LeRoy, who claimed to have shot 90 percent of the finished product. The movie was as successful as the play and gave Fonda credibility as a bankable cinema star again.

He subsequently went on to play Pierre in

War and Peace (1956), shot on location in Rome. While there he became acquainted with Afdera Franchetti, a 22-year-old Italian known as "The Countess." In May 1956, Susan Blanchard obtained a divorce in Reno, Nevada, on the grounds of intense mental pain. On March 9, 1957, "The Countess" and Fonda were married in New York City. That marriage lasted until 1960, when she obtained a Mexican divorce on the grounds of incompatibility. Fonda went on the appear in the acclaimed film *Twelve Angry Men* (1957), which he also produced for tax reasons, but he found the experience nightmarish. He played Juror Number Eight in this film about a group of men who come into conflict before delivering a verdict in a trial. The movie was shot in Manhattan in 20 days at a cost of $314,000. It was not a commercial success because it was under-distributed by United Artists. Since then, like *The Ox-Bow Incident,* it has become a cult classic, reshown at countless retrospectives.

In *The Tin Star* (1957), a Western directed by Anthony Mann, Fonda played a bounty hunter who was once a sheriff. When he rides into town, he discovers the sheriff (Anthony Perkins) is an inexperienced tenderfoot. He stays to instill courage in the young man and give him the benefit of his experience. The film is important because it served as the basis for *The Deputy,* a Western television series which starred Fonda with Allen Case in the title role. It made its debut on NBC on September 12, 1959. Fonda starred as Simon Fry, Territorial Marshal in Arizona during the 1880s. Fry was a hardnosed marshal whose dedication to law and order was so total that he would just as soon shoot the bad guys as lock them up. There was a certain element of Fonda jumping on the band wagon in making this series, but it was certainly efficiently done.

In the second season, when Fonda was less of the focal point of the stories than Case, the network found themselves inundated with letters from irate viewers complaining. This situation was then remedied by having Fry written more prominently into the episodes. Fonda said, "My first reaction was to resist it because I still feel I have a future and I didn't want to be identified with one character. I found a way for me to limit my appearances in the weekly series. In some of them I appeared in just one scene. I did the series because the show is something I produced and partly owned. If I didn't do things like that, I wouldn't be able to live the way I do." He did, though, narrate each episode. The series lasted for two seasons until September 16, 1961. It consisted of 76 half-hour, black and white episodes for Revue Productions. It ended at the insistence of its star, who had movie commitments, although the network would have been happy to continue for a third season. As with some of Fonda's other work, it was not a tremendous audience grabber, but it was regarded as a prestigious series.

Fonda continued to straddle two lines in his career very successfully. On the one hand he was the star of some very commercially successful films such as *Spencer's Mountain* (1963), which became the basis of the long-running television series *The Waltons.* On the other hand, he appeared in a number of uncommercial but critically acclaimed movies. Along with these he continued to balance stage and television work. Toward the end of the 1960s and into the 1970s he continued to appear in films of much lower quality than he was used to. Indeed, some of them would rank among the worst films of all time, but these were not good years for many stars.

In 1960 he met airline stewardess Shirlee Mae Adams at a cocktail party. On December 3, 1965, they married in Minneola, New York. She was 33, and this marriage endured happily until his death. In 1968 he signed a lucrative contract to market GAF products on television. He also starred in another television series, *The Smith Family,* about the private life of a plainclothes detective, but it was not a success. He practiced painting as a hobby and his canvases were acknowledged as excellent by the critics.

On March 26, 1974, he opened on Broadway in a one-man show called *Clarence Darrow,* which was a remarkable personal triumph. On April 23, he collapsed in his dressing room from total exhaustion. Rushed to hospital, he had a pacemaker fitted to stabilize a heart disorder. He continued to appear in the show in New York and later in Los Angeles and London. John Houseman directed it and admitted there were problems caused by Fonda's drive towards perfection. Fonda's final Broadway appearance was in 1978 in *First Monday in October* in which he played a Supreme Court judge. He toured with the play until Chicago, when he was forced to drop out because of a recurring ailment which eventually turned out to be cancer.

Despite, or perhaps because of, the consistently fine quality of his work, major awards had eluded him until the late 1970s. He was lauded by the American Film Institute for his lifetime contribution to the cinema. He was awarded a special Tony Award for his outstanding contribution to the theater, and in 1981 the Academy gave him a Special Oscar in recognition of his enduring contribution to the art of motion pictures.

Jane Fonda acquired the screen rights to *On Golden Pond,* a Broadway play, as a vehicle for the talents of Henry Fonda, Katharine Hepburn and herself. It was turned into a movie about a long-married couple and their daughter who resolves her differences with her father. It turned out to be a case of life imitating art. One curious fact is that not only had Henry Fonda and Katharine Hepburn never appeared in a movie together, they had never met before shooting this film. The film did excellent business and earned glowing reviews. In March 1982, Fonda was awarded the Oscar for Best Actor. The award was accepted on his behalf by his daughter because he was too ill to attend.

On August 12, 1982, Henry Fonda, 77, died in Los Angeles after a long fight against heart disease. He had asked that there be no funeral services and that he be cremated. His fifth wife Shirlee said, "That was his wish and I have to honor that." She had seldom left her ailing husband's side during the previous 18 months, and he died comfortably in hospital and was not in pain. Jane and Peter Fonda and their sister Amy, now a Colorado housewife, joined Mrs. Fonda in the seclusion of her home soon after the death. Among the few visitors were actors James Stewart and Robert Wagner. "I've lost my best friend," Stewart said as he left the house. "I think people all over the world have lost the man I think was the finest actor in the world." Peter Fonda said that his father had been a fair and just man, "and I believe this was reflected in his art as well as his life." Fonda was cremated at Glenview Memorial Park in Glendale, California.

Henry Fonda had one more surprise in store, stunning the Hollywood community by leaving his fortune to his fifth wife and adopted daughter. Jane and Peter Fonda were omitted. Friends of the family were shocked that the actor did not even leave a memento to the two children. In his will he said, "I have made no provision in this will for Peter or Jane or their families solely because, in my opinion, they are financially independent and my decision is not in any sense a measure of my deep affection for them." Everything apart from $200,000 for Amy went to his wife.

A close family friend said, "I know Hank had his rows with Jane and Peter, but after he got his Oscar for *On Golden Pond* it looked like all had been forgiven." Attorney William Stinehart, who filed the three-page will, refused to put a figure on Fonda's fortune. He would only say, "It is in excess of $20,000." According to a Beverly Hills estate agent, his house was worth at least $1,500,000. It was also full of valuable works of art estimated to be worth more than $1,000,000.

Fonda was bitterly upset by his daughter's outspoken condemnation of America's involvement in the Vietnam War. Peter Fonda's alleged involvement with the underworld in the movie business and his easygoing lifestyle also upset the actor. Jane Fonda admitted of her father during the making of *On Golden Pond* in 1980, "The grouchiness is real. And the difficulty in seeing that one can cause suffering for someone else, that's true of my Dad. He doesn't know when he has hurt someone."

Peter Fonda had originally been made a coexecutor of his father's will. On July 7, 1981, the actor then changed the will, naming his wife Shirlee and an attorney as the only executors. In the new will he asked that if his wife died within 90 days of him, his fortune should be given to the Community Playhouse in Omaha, Nebraska, where he was raised.

Henry Fonda Filmography

1935: *The Farmer Takes a Wife, Way Down East, I Dream Too Much.*

1936: *The Trail of the Lonesome Pine, Spendthrift, The Moon's Our Home.*

1937: *Slim, Wings of the Morning, That Certain Woman, You Only Live Once.*

1938: *Blockade, I Met My Love Again, The Mad Miss Manton, Jezebel, Spawn of the North.*

1939: *Jesse James, The Story of Alexander Graham Bell, Let Us Live, Young Mr. Lincoln, Drums Along the Mohawk.*
1940: *The Grapes of Wrath, The Return of Frank James, Lillian Russell, Chad Hanna.*
1941: *The Lady Eve, Wild Geese Calling, You Belong to Me.*
1942: *Rings On Her Fingers, The Male Animal, The Magnificent Dope, The Big Street, Tales of Manhattan.*
1943: *The Immortal Sergeant, The Ox-Bow Incident.*
1946: *My Darling Clementine.*
1947: *The Fugitive, Daisy Kenyon, The Long Night.*
1948: *Fort Apache, A Miracle Can Happen (*a.k.a. *On Our Merry Way).*
1949: *Jigsaw* (cameo).
1955: *Mister Roberts.*
1956: *War and Peace.*
1957: *The Wrong Man, 12 Angry Men, The Tin Star.*
1958: *Stage Struck.*
1959: *Warlock, The Man Who Understood Women.*
1962: *Advise and Consent, The Longest Day, How the West Was Won.*
1963: *Spencer's Mountain.*
1964: *The Best Man, Fail Safe, Sex and the Single Girl.*
1965: *The Rounders, In Harm's Way, Battle of the Bulge, The Dirty Game.*
1966: *A Big Hand for the Little Lady, Welcome to Hard Times.*
1967: *Firecreek, Stranger on the Run* (TV).
1968: *Yours Mine and Ours, Madigan, The Boston Strangler.*
1969: *Once Upon a Time in the West, Too Late the Hero.*
1970: *There Was a Crooked Man, The Cheyenne Social Club.*
1971: *Sometimes a Great Notion.*
1972: *The Serpent.*
1973: *The Alpha Caper* (TV), *Ash Wednesday, The Red Pony* (TV), *My Name Is Nobody.*
1974: *Mussolini: The Last Act (*a.k.a. *Mussolini: The Last Four Days).*
1976: *Midway, Collision Course, Tentacles.*
1977: *Rollercoaster, The Last of the Cowboys (*a.k.a. *The Great Smokey Roadblock), The Biggest Battle.*
1978: *The Swarm, Fedora* (cameo), *Wanda Nevada, City on Fire, Home To Stay* (TV).
1979: *Meteor.*
1980: *Gideon's Trumpet* (TV), *The Oldest Living Graduate* (TV).
1981: *On Golden Pond, Summer Solstice* (TV).

Television Series

1955: *The Star and the Story*—host
1959–1961: *The Deputy* as Marshal Simon Fry
1971–1972: *The Smith Family* as Detective Sgt. Chad Smith.

Miniseries

1976: *Captains and the Kings.*
1979: *Roots: The Next Generation.*

Sources

McCullough, Erskine. "Not A Cent Of Fonda's Money Goes To Peter And Jane." *Daily Express* newspaper, August 23, 1982.
Norman, Barry. *The Film Greats.* London: Futura, 1985.
Parish, James Robert, and Don E. Stanke. *The All-Americans.* Carlstadt, NJ: Rainbow, 1978.
Shipman, David. *The Great Movie Stars: The Golden Years.* Feltham, England: Hamlyn, 1970.
Speed, F. Maurice. *The Western Film And Television Annual.* London: MacDonald, 1960.
Willis, John. *Screen World.* New York: Crown, 1983.

SCOTT FORBES

Conrad Scott Forbes was born in High Wycombe, Buckinghamshire, England, on September 11, 1920, the son of a psychiatrist. He was raised in England. His education was obtained at Repton public school; University College, London; Balliol College, Oxford; and the Sorbonne, Paris. His original ambition was to be a diplomat, but the war intervened. During World War II he served in the RAF until he was invalided out in 1943. At the suggestion of impresario Binkie Beaumont he changed his name. Under the name of Julian Dallas, he made his stage debut in 1945 at the Intimate Theater in Palmers Green, North London, where he won rave reviews. Appearances in little theaters led to stage plays opposite Anna Neagle and Wendy Hiller; performances under the direction of John Gielgud and Peter Ustinov; and several seasons with the Old Vic in classical drama.

He made his screen debut in *Night Boat to Dublin* (1945). He appeared in British films over the next five years, but caused little sensation until his swashbuckling performance with Jean Kent in *The Reluctant Widow* secured him a contract with Warner Bros. in 1950. His best remembered film role was as the Union officer Lt. Rickey in Errol Flynn's last Western, *Rocky Mountain* (1950). Forbes did not succeed in ingratiating himself with the Warner Bros. hierarchy and was dropped from contract the following year. Active on the New York stage scene for a while, he surfaced on television as the hero of a CBS soap called *The Seeking Heart* (1954), which came and went in six months.

Producer Louis F. Edelman was searching for a suitable leading man for a television series called *The Adventures of Jim Bowie*. Noticing that Forbes was ambidextrous and athletic while watching him play at a charity tennis match, he tested him and cast him in the leading role. Initially Forbes proved to be somewhat overzealous in his interpretation of the part. He pored over every article he could find about the real Bowie, insisting on portraying him as a surly and unkempt hero, wanting to show his character defects rather than his virtues. This realistic approach would no doubt have been much more acceptable in the current climate than it was in those days, so Forbes was forced to clean up the appearance and behavior of Bowie.

The Adventures of Jim Bowie made its debut on ABC on September 7, 1956. It was based very loosely on the genuine historical character. According to the television scriptwriters, Jim Bowie invented his favorite knife after an encounter with a grizzly bear, when his ordinary knife snapped at a vital moment. The series was adapted from the book *Tempered Blade* by Monte Barrett. The locale was the Louisiana Territory of the 1830s, which allowed for backdrops of French-American New Orleans and backwoods settings. Bowie was presented as a wealthy young planter and soldier of fortune. On his travels he encountered several famous historical characters in incidents which appeared to have escaped the history books, most notably with the naturalist painter John James Audubon.

Scott Forbes in *The Adventures of Jim Bowie.*

A major artistic defect of this series was that it was nearly all studio-bound, which did not sit too well with fans. In addition, children who for years had enjoyed galloping along and shooting cap pistols in imitation of Western heroes saw no reason why they should not likewise imitate Jim Bowie. Since his weapon was the famous long knife which he used most freely, the potential dangers of childish imitation were obvious. This produced a flood of protests, and in later episodes Bowie used his knife much less frequently. Nevertheless, the series ran for a healthy two seasons, ending on August 29, 1958. It might have continued except for a minor scandal involving Forbes and his wife, which also had the effect of terminating the series after 78 half-hour, black and white episodes.

Afterwards Forbes was seen in episodes of some anthology series, his last U.S. credits dating from the early 1960s. He also had an interest in at least one fashionable Hollywood nightclub. During the 1960s he relocated to England where he appeared on television, notably in one of the BBC's numerous attempts at filming Robert Louis Stevenson's classic novel *Treasure Island.* He also guest-starred in episodes shot in exotic locales with British financing ("Moving Target," a 1964 episode of *Crane,* for example). He toured with the National Theatre Company as the Earl of Essex in "Elizabeth the Queen" in 1961 and in London played the husband in Harold Pinter's "The Lover," directed by the author in 1963. Forbes himself began to write. His imitation Pinter play "The Meter Man," first performed in 1964, became the basis of the film *The Penthouse* (1967). His final acting appearance was in a television thriller, *Someone at the Top of the Stairs,* in 1973. There are some indications that he also spent time in Italy and Spain when the film industry boomed there during the 1960s. This served as an authentic background when he contributed a script to *The Saint* television series in 1967.

Increasingly reclusive in later years, he devoted himself to composing and listening to classical music. He died in Swindon, Wiltshire, England, on February 25, 1997, at age 76. He is buried in a country churchyard close to his last home. He married Jeanne Moody in 1954 and had two daughters, Elena and Jessica.

Scott Forbes Filmography

1945: *Night Boat to Dublin.*
1947: *Mrs. Fitzherbert, This Was a Woman.*
1948: *But Not in Vain.*
1950: *The Reluctant Widow, Rocky Mountain.*
1951: *Inside the Walls of Folsom Prison, Raton Pass, Operation Pacific, The Highwayman, The Desert Fox.*
1952: *What Price Glory?*
1953: *Charade.*
1959: *Seventy Times Seven.*
1968: *Subterfuge.*
1969: *The Mind of Mr. Soames.*
1990: *Mirror Mirror* (voice).

Television Series

1954: *The Seeking Heart* as Dr. John Adam.
1956–1958: *The Adventures of Jim Bowie* as Jim Bowie.

Sources

The Daily Telegraph newspaper, May 1997.
The Independent newspaper, May 1997.
Inman, David. *The TV Encyclopedia.* New York: Perigee, 1991.
Noble, Peter. *Picture Parade.* London: Burke, 1952.
Picture Show Annual. London: Amalgamated Press, 1952.
Ragan, David. *Who's Who in Hollywood.* New York: Facts on File, 1992.
Speed, F. Maurice. *The Western Film and Television Annual.* London: MacDonald, 1957.
Speed, F. Maurice. *The Western Film Annual.* London: MacDonald, 1951.

WALLACE FORD

Wallace Ford was born in Bolton, Lancashire, England, on February 12, 1898. His real name was Sam Grundy and he was the son of Samuel Grundy and his wife Catherine Jones. Although his parents were not deceased, he was separated from them at an early age. He hit the headlines in the mid–1930s after seeking and finding his long-lost parents on an English trip. After living for a time at an orphanage in England, he was shipped to Canada where he was a Dr. Barnardo's boy. He made his first appearance on the stage in a stock company at Winnipeg in 1908 in *Under Two Flags.* After living in 17 foster homes, he ran away at the age of 11, and joined a vaudeville troupe called the Winnipeg Kiddies, with whom he remained from 1911 to 1914.

Still using his real name, he joined a

friend named Wallace Ford on the road and hoboed into the United States. His friend was crushed to death in a railroad accident, so Grundy assumed the name of Wallace Ford. Joining the American Navy during World War I, he was looking forward to the prospect of regular meals when the Armistice was declared. His discharge came through exactly two days after he had donned his uniform.

He made his first appearance on the New York stage at Booth's Theater on January 21, 1918, in a minor role in *Seventeen.* By December 1919, he was appearing at the Cort Theater in *Abraham Lincoln,* which lasted for 18 months. He appeared in other Broadway plays until 1924, when he spent some years in stock companies and in vaudeville. He appeared in Chicago in 1928 as Willie Burton in *The Nut Farm.* It lasted a year before it went to New York, where Ford later played the same role.

In 1930 he went to Hollywood where he made his screen debut in *Swellhead* (1930). By 1932 he was under contract to MGM, his most infamous film for them being the horror *Freaks* (1932). Remaining in Hollywood shooting films for the next six years, he reappeared on the New York stage in November 1937, playing George in *Of Mice and Men.* He appeared in several films directed by John Ford, including *The Informer* (1935) and *The Last Hurrah* (1958).

From the early 1950s onwards he was active in anthology television series. Although he guest-starred in several Westerns, his only regular series role was as Herk Lamson, the Marshal of Silver City during the first season of *The Deputy.* He was the person whom the title character helped out when there was trouble in the town. Ford left the series at the end of the first season, although he continued to be an active television performer. His final film appearance was as the kindly grandfather in *A Patch of Blue* (1965).

Sixty-eight years old, Wallace Ford died in Woodland Hills, California, on June 11, 1966, of a heart ailment. He married Martha Haworth in 1922. They had a daughter, Patricia, born in 1928. His wife predeceased him by a short time in 1966. One of Hollywood's well-known drinkers, Ford listed his hobbies as golf, tennis and arguing.

Wallace Ford in *The Deputy.*

Wallace Ford Filmography

1930: *The Swellhead.*

1931: *Possessed, Skyscraper Souls, X Marks The Spot.*

1932: *Freaks, Beast of the City, Prosperity, Hypnotized, Central Park, Are You Listening?, The Wet Parade, The Big Cage, City Sentinel.*

1933: *Goodbye Again, East of Fifth Avenue, Employees' Entrance, Headline Shooter, My Woman, Night of Terror, Three Cornered Moon, She Had to Say Yes.*

1934: *Money Means Nothing, A Woman's Man, Men in White, The Man Who Reclaimed His Head, I Hate Women, The Lost Patrol.*

1935: *The Whole Town's Talking, Another Face, The Nut Farm, The Informer, Swell-Head, In Spite of Danger, She Couldn't Take It, Men of the Hour, Get That Man, Mary Burns—Fugitive, One Frightened Night, The Mysterious Mr. Wong, Sanders of the River.*

1936: *OHMS* (a.k.a. *You're in the Army Now*), *Rogues' Tavern, Two in the Dark, Absolute Quiet, A Son Comes Home.*

1937: *Jericho* (a.k.a. *Dark Sands*), *Mad About Money* (a.k.a. *He Loved an Actress*), *Swing It Sailor, Exiled to Shanghai.*

1939: *Back Door to Heaven.*

1940: *Isle of Destiny, Two Girls on Broadway, Love Honor and Oh Baby!, Give Us Wings, The Mummy's Hand, Scatterbrain.*

1941: *A Man Betrayed, The Roar of the Press, Blues in the Night, Murder by Invitation.*

1942: *Scattergood Survives a Murder, Inside the*

Law, X Marks the Spot, All Through the Night, Seven Days' Leave, The Mummy's Tomb.
1943: *The Marines Come Through, Shadow of a Doubt, The Cross of Lorraine, The Ape Man.*
1944: *Secret Command, Machine Gun Mama.*
1945: *The Great John L, Spellbound, They Were Expendable, Blood on the Sun, On Stage Everybody.*
1946: *The Green Years, A Guy Could Change, Rendezvous with Annie, Crack-Up, The Black Angel, Lover Come Back, Dead Reckoning.*
1947: *Magic Town, T-Men.*
1948: *Shed No Tears, Coroner Creek, The Man from Texas, Embraceable You, Belle Starr's Daughter.*
1949: *Red Stallion in the Rockies, The Set-Up.*
1950: *The Breaking Point, Dakota Lil, The Furies, Harvey.*
1951: *Warpath, He Ran All the Way, Painting the Clouds With Sunshine.*
1952: *Flesh and Fury, Rodeo.*
1953: *She Couldn't Say No, The Nebraskan, The Great Jesse James Raid.*
1954: *The Boy from Oklahoma, Destry, Three Ring Circus.*
1955: *The Man from Laramie, The Spoilers, Lucy Gallant, A Lawless Street, Wichita.*
1956: *Johnny Concho, The Maverick Queen, The First Texan, Stagecoach to Fury, Thunder Over Arizona, The Rainmaker.*
1958: *The Last Hurrah, The Matchmaker, Twilight for the Gods.*
1959: *Warlock.*
1961: *Tess of the Storm Country.*
1965: *A Patch of Blue.*

Television Series

1959–1960: *The Deputy* as Marshal Herk Lamson.

Sources

Jones, Ken D., Arthur F. McClure and Alfred E. Twomey. *Character People.* Secaucus, NJ: Citadel, 1979.
Quinlan, David. *The Illustrated Directory of Film Character Actors.* London: Batsford, 1995.
Speed, F. Maurice. *The Western Film and TV Annual.* London: MacDonald, 1960.
Who's Who in the Theater Tenth Edition. London: Pitman, 1947.
Winchester, Clarence. *The World Film Encyclopedia.* London: The Amalgamated Press, 1933.

WILLIAM H. FORREST

Born in 1902, William H. Forrest was a star footballer while studying at Princeton University. He commenced his acting career in 1938 at the Pasadena Playhouse, making his screen debut in 1940. With his patrician looks, he frequently played men of authority on screen such as judges, diplomats and high ranking military types. Not surprisingly he graduated to similar roles on television, his best known part being as the fort commander in the television Western series *The Adventures of Rin Tin Tin.* He died in Santa Monica, California on January 26, 1989, at age 86, of natural causes.

William H. Forrest Filmography

1940: *The Man Who Talked Too Much, The Lone Wolf Meets a Lady, Nobody's Children, The Secret Seven, Gangs of Chicago..*
1941: *Barnacle Bill, Dive Bomber, Down in San Diego, Flight from Destiny, Here Comes Mr. Jordan, Hold That Ghost, International Lady, Keep 'Em Flying, Life Begins for Andy Hardy, The Lone Wolf Takes a Chance, Lucky Devils, Meet John Doe, Million Dollar Baby, The Phantom Submarine, Sun Valley Serenade, Doctors Don't Tell, The Pittsburgh Kid, Mercy Island.*
1942: *Flight Lieutenant, In This Our Life, Joe Smith American, Lucky Jordan, My Favorite*

Blonde, My Favorite Spy, Priorities on Parade, Sleepytime Gal, Spy Ship, They Died with Their Boots On, Wake Island, Yankee Doodle Dandy, Spy Smasher (serial), *Pardon My Stripes, Bells of Capistrano.*

1943: *Air Force, Du Barry Was a Lady, Hitler's Children, Flight for Freedom, The Iron Major, It Ain't Hay, Mission to Moscow, G-Men vs. the Black Dragon* (serial), *Mug Town, So Proudly We Hail, The Masked Marvel* (serial).

1944: *Abroad with Two Yanks, The Fighting Seabees, Follow the Boys, Here Come the Waves, Laura, Marine Raiders, Mr. Skeffington, Mr. Winkle Goes to War, Wilson.*

1945: *Anchors Aweigh, Behind City Lights, The Caribbean Mystery, Gangs of the Waterfront, Girls of the Big House, God Is My Co-Pilot, Road to Alcatraz, Rough Tough and Ready, Salty O'Rourke, Without Love, Youth on Trial, Adventures of Kitty O'Day, Captain Eddie, Love, Honor and Goodbye.*

1946: *Dangerous Business, The Jolson Story, The Kid from Brooklyn, Meet Me on Broadway, Nobody Lives Forever, Till the Clouds Roll By, Till the End of Time, The Well-Groomed Bride, Behind Green Lights, Three Little Girls in Blue.*

1947: *The Corpse Came C.O.D., Dead Reckoning, Devil on Wheels, Devil Ship, The Guilt of Janet Ames, Miracle on 34th Street, Mother Wore Tights, Sarge Goes to College, The Senator Was Indiscreet, The Spirit of West Point, Blind Spot, The Fabulous Texan.*

1948: *Alias a Gentleman, Fort Apache, The Gentleman from Nowhere, Homecoming, Race Street, Three Daring Daughters, Trapped by Boston Blackie.*

1949: *Angels in Disguise, Arson Inc., The Devil's Henchman, The Girl from Jones Beach, The Story of Seabiscuit, Trail of the Yukon, The Younger Brothers.*

1950: *Emergency Wedding, Square Dance Katy, Hit Parade of 1951.*

1951: *Flight to Mars, Follow the Sun, Fort Dodge Stampede, Gasoline Alley, The Harlem Globetrotters, I Was a Communist for the FBI, I'll See You In My Dreams, Missing Women, Smuggler's Gold, Spoilers of the Plains, Let's Go Navy.*

1952: *Deadline USA, Jet Job, Night Without Sleep, One Minute to Zero, The Rose Bowl Story, The Story of Will Rogers.*

1953: *Bandits of Corsica, Destination Gobi, Invaders from Mars, Winning of the West, Private Eyes, The Eddie Cantor Story.*

1954: *Demetrius and the Gladiators, The French Line.*

1955: *The Court-Martial of Billy Mitchell, Francis in the Navy, The Girl in the Red Velvet Swing, A Man Called Peter, New York Confidential, One Desire, Rage at Dawn.*

1956: *Behind the High Wall, The First Traveling Saleslady, Pardners, These Wilder Years, You Can't Run Away from It.*

1957: *Band Of Angels, Jailhouse Rock, Loving You, The Monster That Challenged the World.*

1958: *The Last Hurrah, Toughest Gun in Tombstone.*

1959: *The Horse Soldiers.*

1961: *One-Eyed Jacks.*

1962: *Sweet Bird of Youth, Paradise Alley (*a.k.a. *Stars in Your Backyard).*

1964: *Good Neighbor Sam.*

1966: *Billy the Kid vs. Dracula.*

1971: *The Marriage of a Young Stockbroker.*

Television Series

1954–1959: *The Adventures of Rin Tin Tin* as Major Swanson.

Sources

Motion Picture Annual. Evanston, IL: Cinebooks, 1990.

Picture Show's Who's Who On Screen. London: Amalgamated Press, c. 1956.

ROBERT FOULK

This character actor was a dialogue coach before becoming a thespian. He entered movies during the 1940s and made appearances in numerous films and later was very active in television. He played the role of the bartender of the local saloon in the Western series *Wichita Town.* He died in 1989 in his 70s.

Robert Foulk Filmography

1948: *Road House, That Wonderful Urge.*
1949: *Thieves Highway, Johnny Stool Pigeon, White Heat.*
1950: *Between Midnight and Dawn, Mystery Street, Where the Sidewalk Ends.*
1951: *The Mob, The Strip, The Unknown Man, The Guy Who Came Back.*
1952: *Carrie, The San Francisco Story, The Sniper, Carbine Williams, My Pal Gus, Don't Bother to Knock.*
1953: *The 49th Man, Remains to Be Seen, Valley of Head Hunters.*
1955: *The Far Country, Apache Ambush, Rebel Without a Cause, Strange Lady in Town, The Blackboard Jungle.*
1956: *Backlash, The Rawhide Years, Hot Blood, Indestructible Man, The Great Man.*
1957: *My Man Godfrey, Last of the Badmen, Sierra Stranger, The Tall Stranger, Untamed Youth, Hold That Hypnotist, Raintree County.*
1958: *Day of the Bad Man, Quantrill's Raiders, The Left Handed Gun, Hell's Five Hours, Go Johnny Go!*
1959: *Cast a Long Shadow, Born to Be Loved.*
1960: *Ocean's 11.*
1962: *State Fair, The Wonderful World of the Brothers Grimm.*
1963: *Tammy and the Doctor, A Ticklish Affair.*
1964: *Robin and the Seven Hoods.*
1968: *The Split.*
1969: *The Love Bug.*
1971: *Skin Game.*
1972: *Bunny O'Hare.*
1973: *Emperor of the North Pole.*
1977: *Pete's Dragon.*

Television Series

1955-1959: *Father Knows Best* as Ed Davis.
1959-1960: *Wichita Town* as Joe Kingston.

Sources

Ragan, David. *Who's Who in Hollywood.* New York: Facts on File, 1992.
Thomas, Tony. *Joel McCrea: Riding The High Country.* Burbank, CA: Riverwood Press, 1991.

DOUGLAS FOWLEY

Douglas Fowley was born Daniel Vincent Fowley in Greenwich Village, New York City, on May 30, 1911, and had ambitions to be an actor from childhood. After completing his education at St. Francis Xavier Military Academy in New York, he appeared in nightclubs as a song and dance man and acquired experience in stock. For a time he ran his own drama school. There were also many odd jobs before he gravitated to Hollywood, where he made his screen debut in 1933. At one point he was under contract to 20th Century–Fox. Throughout the 1930s and '40s, he was seen in numerous motion pictures, frequently as a ruthless gangster in crime films and as the leader of the outlaw gang in Westerns.

With the dearth of suitable leading men in Hollywood during the war years, he occasionally played romantic leads, as in *Lady in the Death House* (1944). In later years he was sometimes seen as a toothless old codger. He played many character roles on television. For the first season of *The Life and Legend of Wyatt Earp* he played Doc Fabrique. He returned to the series in the third season playing a different role, namely that of Doc Holliday. He later had a regular role of Grandpa in the comedy Western series *Pistols 'n' Petticoats.* At last report he was retired and living in Hot Springs, California. He has been married eight times and has four children.

Douglas Fowley Filmography

1933: *The Mad Game.*
1934: *The Gift of Gab, Operator 13, The Thin Man, The Woman Who Dared, Student Tour, I Hate Women, Let's Talk It Over, The Girl from Missouri.*
1935: *Miss Pacific Fleet, Straight from the Heart, Transient Lady, Night Life of the Gods, Two For Tonight, Old Man Rhythm.*
1936: *Ring Around the Moon, Dimples, Small Town Girl, Big Brown Eyes, Navy Born, Crash Donovan, Sing Baby Sing, Thirty Six Hours to Kill, 15 Maiden Lane.*

1937: *Woman Wise, Time Out for Romance, On the Avenue, Fifty Roads to Town, Wake Up and Live, This Is My Affair, One Mile from Heaven, Wild and Woolly, Charlie Chan on Broadway, She Had to Eat, Love and Kisses, City Girl, Passport Husband.*
1938: *Mr. Moto's Gamble, Walking Down Broadway, Alexander's Ragtime Band, Keep Smiling, Time Out for Murder, Inside Story, Submarine Patrol, Arizona Wildcat.*
1939: *Lucky Night, Dodge City, The Boy Friend, It Could Happen to You, Charlie Chan at Treasure Island, Slightly Honorable, Henry Goes Arizona.*
1940: *Cafe Hostess, Twenty Mule Team, Wagons Westward, Pier 13, The Leather Pushers, Cherokee Strip, East of the River, Ellery Queen Master Detective.*
1941: *The Great Swindle, The Parson of Panamint, Tanks a Million, Doctors Don't Tell, Dangerous Lady, Secrets of the Wasteland, Mr. District Attorney in the Carter Case.*
1942: *Mississippi Gambler, The Devil with Hitler, Pittsburgh, Somewhere I'll Find You, Mr. Wise Guy, Hay Foot, So's Your Aunt Emma, I Live On Danger, The Man in the Trunk, Stand By for Action, Sunset on the Desert.*
1943: *Jitterbugs, Johnny Doesn't Live Here Anymore, Gildersleeve's Bad Day, Chance of a Lifetime, Bar 20, Minesweeper, Colt Comrades, The Kansan, Sleepy Lagoon, Riding High, Lost Canyon.*
1944: *Racket Man, Rationing, One Body Too Many, See Here Private Hargrove, Shake Hands with Murder, And the Angels Sing, Detective Kitty O'Day, Lady in the Death House.*
1945: *Don't Fence Me In, Life with Blondie, Along the Navajo Trail, Behind City Lights.*
1946: *Chick Carter Detective* (serial), *'Neath Canadian Skies, Her Sister's Secret, Driftin' Along, In Fast Company, The Glass Alibi, Rendezvous 24, North of the Border, Larceny in Her Heart, Freddie Steps Out, Blonde Alibi, High School Hero.*
1947: *Wild Country, Undercover Maisie, Backlash, Three on a Ticket, Yankee Fakir, The Sea of Grass, Jungle Flight, Desperate, The Hucksters, The Trespasser, Gas House Kids in Hollywood, Fall Guy, Scared to Death, Ridin' Down the Trail, Roses Are Red, Merton of the Movies, Rose of Santa Rosa.*

Portrait of Douglas Fowley, who appeared in *The Life and Legend of Wyatt Earp.*

1948: *Docks of New Orleans, Waterfront at Midnight, If You Knew Susie, The Dude Goes West, Black Bart, Coroner Creek, Joe Palooka in Winner Take All, Behind Locked Doors, Gun Smugglers, The Denver Kid, Badmen of Tombstone.*
1949: *Flaxy Martin, Massacre River, Battleground, Susanna Pass, Arson Inc., Search for Danger, Mighty Joe Young, Take Me Out to the Ball Game, Satan's Cradle, Renegades of the Sage, Joe Palooka in the Counter Punch.*
1950: *Bunco Squad, Rider from Tucson, Armored Car Robbery, Hoedown, Edge of Doom, Killer Shark, He's a Cockeyed Wonder, Mrs. O'Malley and Mr. Malone, Rio Grande Patrol, Stage to Tucson, Beware of Blondie.*
1951: *Chain of Circumstance, Tarzan's Peril, Callaway Went Thataway, Across the Wide Missouri, Criminal Lawyer, South of Caliente.*
1952: *Just This Once, Singin' in the Rain, This Woman Is Dangerous, Room for One More, Horizons West, The Man Behind the Gun.*
1953: *A Slight Case of Larceny, The Band Wagon, Cruisin' Down the River, Kansas Pacific, Red River Shore.*
1954: *Deep in My Heart, The Naked Jungle, Casanova's Big Night, Cat Women of the Moon, The Lone Gun, The High and the Mighty, Three Ring Circus, Untamed Heiress.*
1955: *The Girl Rush, Texas Lady.*
1956: *Bandido!, The Broken Star, The Man from Del Rio, Rock Pretty Baby.*

1957: *Bayou, Kelly and Me, The Badge of Marshal Brennan, Raiders of Old California.*
1959: *These Thousand Hills.*
1960: *Desire in the Dust, Macumba Love* (director only).
1961: *Barabbas.*
1962: *Miracle of the White Stallions.*
1963: *Who's Been Sleeping in My Bed?*
1964: *Seven Faces of Dr. Lao, Guns of Diablo.*
1965: *Nightmare in the Sun.*
1969: *The Good Guys and the Bad Guys.*
1972: *Seeta the Mountain Lion.*
1973: *Walking Tall, Homebodies.*
1975: *Starsky and Hutch* (TV).
1976: *Black Oak Conspiracy, The Oregon Trail* (TV).
1977: *From Noon Till Three, Sunshine Christmas* (TV), *The White Buffalo.*
1978: *The North Avenue Irregulars.*

Television Series

1955–1956: *The Life and Legend of Wyatt Earp* as Doc Fabrique.
1957–1961: *The Life and Legend of Wyatt Earp* as Doc Holliday.
1966–1967: *Pistols 'n' Petticoats* as Grandpa Hanks.
1979: *Detective School* as Robert Redford.

Miniseries

1976: *The Moneychangers.*

Sources

Brooks, Tim. *The Complete Directory to Prime Time TV Stars 1946-Present.* New York: Ballantine Books, 1987.
McClure, Arthur F., and Ken D. Jones. *Heroes, Heavies and Sagebrush.* South Brunswick and New York: Barnes, 1972.
Parish, James Robert. *Hollywood Character Actors.* New Rochelle, NY: Arlington House, 1978.
Quinlan, David. *Illustrated Directory of Film Character Actors.* London: Batsford, 1995.
Twomey, Alfred E., and Arthur F. McClure. *The Versatiles.* South Brunswick and New York: Barnes, 1969.

EDUARD FRANZ

Eduard Franz was born in Milwaukee, Wisconsin, on October 31, 1902, the son of a sea captain. He was one of ten children. He enrolled in Milwaukee's Layton Art School, which was located close to a little theater company. He found himself divided between wanting to be an actor or an artist, so he split his time between the two.

Upon graduating from art college, he spent a little under a year following the profession of commercial artist and then joined a stock company in Chicago. He made his professional bow at the Provincetown Playhouse. By the mid–1920s he had relocated to New York and appeared on Broadway. At the heart of the Depression, he abandoned acting in favor of farming in a couple of states. In the mid–1930s he went back to New York where he appeared as Shylock in *The Merchant of Venice.* After this he remained based in that city as a theatrical actor for the next ten years. He played a Jack the Ripper type in a disastrous Broadway play. His acclaimed performance as the doctor in *Home of the Brave* was seen by a talent scout, and Hollywood beckoned.

20th Century–Fox offered him a role in a prestigious film, *The Iron Curtain* (1948), so he relocated to California where he remained for the rest of his career. He appeared in many movies, typically cast as an academic, diplomat, psychiatrist or civic leader. Usually he was a pillar of integrity, but occasionally, as in *The Unknown Man* (1951), his suavity masked a villainous heart. Of his films he numbered two Westerns (*Broken Lance* [1954] and *White Feather* [1955]) among his personal favorites.

He also had regular roles in two television series. In the second season of *Zorro,* he played the father of the romantic interest Anna Maria Verdugo (Jolene Brand). In *The Breaking Point* he played the director of York Hospital's psychiatric unit. He also played numerous guest-starring roles on television. Until his death he remained active as an actor. In later years he renewed his interest in painting and had exhibitions staged in a couple of Los Angeles art galleries. He died in Century City, Los Angeles, on February 10, 1983, at age 80, survived by his wife of many years, Margaret.

Eduard Franz Filmography

1948: *The Iron Curtain, Hollow Triumph, Wake of the Red Witch.*
1949: *Madame Bovary, The Doctor and the Girl, Outpost in Morocco, Francis, Oh You Beautiful Doll, Whirlpool.*
1950: *The Vicious Years, Molly (*a.k.a. *The Goldbergs), Tarnished, The Magnificent Yankee, Emergency Wedding.*
1951: *The Great Caruso, The Thing from Another World, The Desert Fox, The Unknown Man, Shadow in the Sky.*
1952: *Because You're Mine, One Minute to Zero, The DuPont Story, Everything I Have Is Yours.*
1953: *Dream Wife, Latin Lovers, Sins of Jezebel, The Jazz Singer.*
1954: *Sign of the Pagan, Broken Lance, Beachhead.*
1955: *Lady Godiva, The Last Command, White Feather, The Indian Fighter.*
1956: *The Ten Commandments, Three for Jamie Dawn, The Burning Hills.*
1957: *Man Afraid.*
1958: *Day of the Bad Man, Last of the Fast Guns, A Certain Smile.*
1959: *The Miracle, The Four Skulls of Jonathan Drake.*
1960: *The Story of Ruth.*
1961: *Francis of Assisi, The Fiercest Heart.*
1962: *Hatari!, Beauty and the Beast.*
1966: *Cyborg 2087.*
1967: *The President's Analyst.*
1970: *The Brotherhood of the Bell* (TV).
1971: *Johnny Got His Gun.*
1974: *Panic on the 5:22* (TV), *The Sex Symbol* (TV) (voice only).

Portrait of Eduard Franz, who appeared in *Zorro*.

1983: *Twilight Zone—The Movie.*

Television Series

1958–1959: *Zorro* as Senor Gregorio Verdugo.
1963–1964: *The Breaking Point* as Dr. Edward Raymer.

Sources

Brooks, Tim. *The Complete Directory to Prime Time TV Stars 1946–Present.* New York: Ballantine Books, 1987.
Jones, Ken D., Arthur F. McClure, and Alfred E. Twomey. *Character People.* Secaucus, NJ: Citadel Press, 1979.
Quinlan, David. *Illustrated Directory of Film Character Actors.* London: Batsford, 1995.
Who's Who in Hollywood. New York: Dell, 1961.

ROBERT FULLER

Robert Fuller is an actor who is struggling to meet the challenge of acting in the 1990s, but who dates from a time when there was a Western on television every night of the week. He once admitted, "I should have lived 100 years ago, back in the days of the real Old West." Many of his greatest achievements date from his early years, and his career decline mirrors the decline of the Western on television and in film. In recent years, when only a trickle of Westerns have been in production, his name is still one which is automatically thought of because he has been so closely identified with the genre. At one time he was very popular with surviving oldtime Western stars who believed him the best of the crop of television Westerners.

He frequently played a reformed badman, trying to atone for some crime which he committed in his youth when he was on the wrong side of the law. When he reformed, he became even more fanatical about upholding the law than most legitimate peace officers. With his grim visage, it is easy to imagine him pursuing some vendetta through all kinds of adversity. Although he cuts a stylish figure in contemporary dramas, he is nowhere near as convincing. It would have been interesting to see him as a cop with a conscience in a '40s film noir. When he says, "I would rather play a Western role than eat," there is no reason to disbelieve him. He is a tough hombre in real life. Burt Reynolds called him "wilder than a March hare," typified by an oft-told story that when the studio refused to give him a door between dressing rooms, he knocked the wall down!

Robert Fuller in *Laramie*.

Robert Fuller was born Leonard Leroy Lee on July 29, 1933, in Troy, New York. His parents were divorced when he was ten years old. Afterwards his mother married Robert Simpson, whom he came to regard as his real father. He later assumed the name Robert Chalmers Simpson. He went through several changes of name when searching for a stage name, settling on Robert A. Fuller because it was virtually the only one not already belonging to an existing member of the Screen Actors Guild. He named himself after ancestor Deacon Fuller, who sailed from England on the Mayflower and landed at Plymouth Rock. The "A." appears to stand for nothing.

Robert Simpson was a naval officer initially, and Fuller's mother was a professional dancer. He had a gypsy childhood, moving from New York to Florida and then to Chicago and back to Florida, where his parents (now using the names of Bob and Betty Cole) opened a dance academy. Fuller attended 11 different schools, including Miami Military Academy, and graduated in Florida. In 1950 the Simpsons moved to Los Angeles where Robert Fuller started work as an usher at Grauman's Chinese Theater and the Paramount Hollywood Theater. The show business bug bit around this time and he studied dancing. On the strength of this, his father secured him bit roles in some musicals. His career was put on hold in 1953 when he joined the army. He undertook basic training at Fort Ord, California, before being involved in the Korean conflict with the 24th Infantry Division. He was honorably discharged as a Sergeant First Class in 1955.

He drifted into acting, attending the drama school run by actor Richard Boone. Boone suggested that he go to New York City and study under Sanford Meisner. When he returned, he worked as an extra and stuntman. His proper screen debut came in 1956 when director William Wyler cast him as a union soldier in *Friendly Persuasion,* allegedly because he was impressed with Fuller's sideburns. He then became a stalwart of the numerous Western series which were being shown on television in those days. He also starred in a shortlived sci-fi series which was never aired. In 1959 he was signed to play the role of Jess Harper in the series *Laramie,* which costarred John Smith. Jess was the drifter who rode into the Sherman relay station in the first episode and stayed. This proved to be an immense success worldwide. Fuller was especially popular in Japan (where Emperor Hirohito gave him the Golden Order of Merit) and West Germany (where he was awarded five Ottos, the equivalent of an Emmy). He once admitted, however, "I've never actually been to Laramie. Filming was mainly done in California and Arizona."

The offscreen relationship between John Smith and Robert Fuller was once good, but it went sour. Their original animosity stemmed from Smith's belief that he would one day become an enduring top flight motion picture star and Fuller's instinct that his own star would soon outshine that of his rival and costar. His view was upheld when *Picturegoer* magazine held a competition in England in which viewers were encouraged to vote to determine which of the two of them was the more popular. Although Smith polled a significant number of votes, twice as many voted for Fuller. For two men who did not enjoy each other's company offscreen, they teamed extremely well on camera. They had not met or spoken in many years before Smith's demise.

Laramie also changed Fuller's personality. One of his then-girlfriends said, "You've no idea what a difference *Laramie* has made to Bob. He used to be a dullish boy, but since his success he's opened out so much. At a party there's no one like him for getting things going. I think his success has given him confidence as a personality. It has also broadened his outlook." A contrasting view of his personality was provided by an unnamed coworker around this time: "Bob was a rare guy. He would go out on fantastic expeditions—shark hunting, mountain lion hunting—and he even tried bronco busting at rodeos. As a result of his adventures he was an interesting guy. He had lots of stories to tell because he did things that not many other people had tried. Now what with the television series, he doesn't get time and he has got himself involved with so many show business people, he only talks shop. I suppose that's the price he has to pay for his success."

Part of the reason Fuller became so much a part of the show business scene is that he liked to keep abreast of what was going on because he did not wish to spend the rest of his acting days playing Jess Harper. When *Laramie* ended in 1963, he almost immediately found himself in another popular Western series, *Wagon Train,* although this was one which had seen better days. He assumed the role of Cooper Smith, the chief scout. When that series ended, his stock slumped, mainly because of his too-rigid adherence to wanting to continue as a Western star. He rejected the leads in at least three series: *The Rounders,* a short-lived comedy Western series; *Run for Your Life,* which proved to be a big hit for Ben Gazzara; and *The Rat Patrol.* The reason he rejected the last of these was because this was a World War II series which involved him killing Germans, but he was afraid that it would place his popularity there in jeopardy.

He went to Spain where he starred opposite Yul Brynner in *Return of the Seven* (1967), a routine sequel to *The Magnificent Seven* (1960). It is Fuller's favorite of his own films. Subsequently he made other films abroad, notably in Germany and Israel. He admitted that there had been some lean years when he had not been working much while his wife earned some money by selling saddles in a Western store.

He began doing commercials in 1969 and earned as much as $65,000 per annum from them. For seven years he was the National Spokesperson for Teledyne Water-Pik and Budweiser Malt Liquor. He also appeared on stage scoring notable successes in *Chapter Two* and *Wait Until Dark. The Hard Ride* (1971) was a low-budget movie in which Fuller played a

Vietnam veteran bringing home the body of his black buddy who has been killed in the war. He encounters trouble when he tries to accomplish his dead buddy's wishes. The film dealt with racism, sex, violence, drugs and bikers, and like many of these films was undermined by its low budget. This movie was very important because it was seen by producer Jack Webb, who was so impressed with Fuller's performance that he cast him as Dr. Kelly Brackett in the NBC series *Emergency,* which ran for five seasons. Although not a particularly characteristic role for him, the part involved him in doing meticulous research into the medical aspects of the scripts so that he felt comfortable with the character.

He also appeared in some telemovies, the most interesting one being *Donner Pass: The Road to Survival* (1978). Fuller narrated and starred as pioneer James Reed, who struggles to save his family and others in a wagon train when they find themselves trapped in deep mountain snow and turn to cannibalism to survive. At one point Fuller was buried in snow for a day while filming. The crew were concerned that he would suffer frostbite, but it turned out that Fuller was wearing both long johns and his then-wife's sauna suit under his clothes to keep warm.

In the early 1980s Fuller and his family relocated to the Bahamas for two years while shooting a syndicated series called *Fishing Fever,* which made the most out of his longstanding interest in the sport of deep sea fishing. He hosted the series and invited guests from Hollywood to participate, but it sometimes became hazardous, as when he and actress Lynda Day George hand-fed sharks underwater. Although this series greatly appealed to him, it was not widely seen. It had an extremely detrimental effect on his career because it kept him out of circulation. Upon his return to Hollywood, he found that the parts had dried up and he virtually had to start his career again from scratch.

Since his return he has been seen from time to time guest-starring in series like *Murder She Wrote, The Fall Guy, Tour of Duty* and *Paradise.* His most impressive work in many years was in an expensive pilot for a recycled version of *Bonanza* called *Bonanza: The Next Generation* (1987) in which he starred with John Ireland and Barbara Anderson. He played Charley Poke, the ranch foreman with a shady past who was rescued from a hangman's noose by Ben Cartwright. The reason is not revealed. It was up in the air for a long time whether it would turn into a series. Eventually a similar series was picked up in syndication, but with the exception of Mike Landon, Jr., the cast was completely different.

Since then Robert Fuller has worked on an episode of *Goldrush* which was shot in Russia in 1991, an experience which he found particularly distasteful. He existed on a diet of soup and lost several pounds. He has also shot a movie in Japan appropriately called *Comeback* (1991), which apart from his dialogue was all in Japanese. In 1994 he played host to a series of celebrity guests in another syndicated series, *River Colorado Adventures.* This consisted of 13 half-hour episodes showing the special people and natural wonders of the 1,400 mile Colorado River that runs through Colorado, Utah, Arizona and Nevada.

Offscreen he is an expert rider and prize-winning marksman, which has enabled him to participate in and judge celebrity trap and skeet charity events. He also plays tennis for various charities. While "resting" he also has a half share and spends time on a deep sea fishing boat in Florida. On December 29, 1962, he eloped with television actress Patricia (Patty) Lyons, who was ten years his junior. They were married in a secret wedding ceremony in Las Vegas. He has a son, Robert John, who was born on April 8, 1964; a daughter, Christine Ann, born November 11, 1965; and son Patrick Daniel, born in January 1975. He was divorced in 1984 after 22 years of marriage. His ex-wife (with whom he remained close), died in June 1993, of lung cancer. Of the series *Laramie* which made his name he said, "I wouldn't say *Laramie* made me wealthy—I was earning $650 a week from the show in 1959—but it certainly enabled me to live well. I guess I've been very fortunate for a man who never got past the ninth grade."

Robert Fuller Filmography

1953: *Gentlemen Prefer Blondes, I Love Melvin, Latin Lovers.*
1956: *Friendly Persuasion.*
1957: *Teenage Thunder.*
1958: *The Brain from Planet Arous.*

1966: *Incident at Phantom Hill.*
1967: *Return of the Seven, Midsummer Night.*
1968: *Sinai Commandos.*
1969: *Whatever Happened to Aunt Alice?, King Gun (*a.k.a. *The Gatling Gun*—released 1972).
1971: *The Hard Ride.*
1976: *Mustang Country.*
1978: *Donner Pass: The Road to Survival* (TV).
1979: *Disaster on the Coastliner* (TV).
1982: *Megaforce, Separate Ways.*
1987: *Bonanza: The Next Generation* (TV).
1989: *All Dogs Go to Heaven* (voice only).
1990: *Repossessed.*
1991: *Comeback.*
1993: *Adventures of Brisco County Junior* (TV), *The Program.*
1994: *Maverick.*

Television Series

1955: *Strange Intruder.*
1959–1963: *Laramie* as Jess Harper.
1963–1965: *Wagon Train* as Cooper Smith.
1972–1977: *Emergency* as Dr. Kelly Brackett
1982–1984: *Fishing Fever*—host/narrator.
1994–1995: *River Colorado Adventures*—host

Sources

Barton, Dick. "Where Are They Now?" *Sunday Express* newspaper, 1986.
Ferguson, Ken. *The Boy's Western Film and Television Annual.* London: Purnell, 1963.
The Laramie Trail Fanzine. 1988–1990.
Miller, Lee O. *The Great Cowboy Stars of Movies and Television.* New Rochelle, NY: Arlington House, 1979.
"TV Westerns: A Ten Page Special Feature." *Photoplay* magazine, July 1960.

JAMES GARNER

James Garner tends to mount scenes rather than appear in them. He has been in the forefront of movies and television for decades now and his achievements have been formidable, but there are some indications that he has never been quite as popular as his publicists maintain. He did not make the superstar category in movies in the Clint Eastwood mold, which rankles him. As Bret in *Maverick* he demonstrated a neat sense of humor. He ducked out early from a series that was too cluttered with other Mavericks to be remembered as uniquely his own. He has a likable, relaxed personality which makes him an ideal series lead. He is not, however, an actor of the breadth and dimension to be considered alongside Gable, Tracy, or his own self-professed idol Henry Fonda. One senses with these legends that they could rise to any occasion. Garner has never really indicated either the ability or the desire to stray much outside the clearly defined perimeters of his own cozy personality. One point in his favor is that he has proven to be the most durable star of all the numerous Warner Bros. television leading men of the late 1950s. He is also extremely capable of handling satire, one form of humor at which many actors and writers consistently fail.

James Garner was born James Scott Baumgarner in Norman, Oklahoma, on April 7, 1928, the son of Weldon and Mildred Baumgarner. He has two brothers. Jack was a former professional baseball pitcher and subsequently played the minor role of the bartender in the revival of *Bret Maverick* in the early 1980s; Charles became a schoolteacher in Norman. His father was a carpenter and upholsterer in Norman. His mother died in 1933. After that, Garner and his brothers spent three years being shuttled between various relatives until his father remarried a sadistic woman who allegedly beat the three boys regularly. James Garner was riding a horse to school when only six years old, and much of his childhood was spent amongst horses and ranchhands. At Norman High School he excelled in football, basketball and track. At 16 he left high school and spent a year as a merchant seaman aboard a seagoing tug out of New Orleans. Next he moved to Los Angeles (where his father was working as a carpeting contractor) and resumed his education at Hollywood High School.

Before long he returned to Norman to complete his high school education until he joined the Oklahoma State National Guard. He stayed in Norman until 1950 and then went to Hollywood to work with his father installing carpets. Shortly afterwards the Korean war broke out and Garner, who was still a legal resident of Oklahoma, became the first draftee from that state to be called for active service. He served 14 months in Korea with the Fifth Regimental Combat Team of the 24th Division and was awarded a Purple Heart for gallantry in action. He was honorably discharged in June 1952.

Back in Norman, Garner began to study business administration at the University of Oklahoma but left after one semester. He went to Hollywood and over the years he held nearly 50 jobs, including waiter, oil driller, lifeguard, janitor, chauffeur, hod carrier, dishwasher, truck driver, window decorator, grocery clerk, golf ball retriever, pool room manager, insurance salesman and swimming trunks model. The one which was to have the most significant influence on his life was as a gas station attendant. While employed at the gas station, he became acquainted with a soda jerk across the street called Paul Gregory. Years later in Hollywood Garner happened to see Gregory's name on an office building. He went inside, renewed the friendship and found out that Gregory was now a theatrical producer.

Gregory found Garner a job feeding cues to star Lloyd Nolan during rehearsals for his production of *The Caine Mutiny Court Martial* which opened on Broadway in January 1954. When a vacancy arose for a small nonspeaking role as one of the six military judges, Garner leapt at the chance to play the part. He took advantage of the opportunity to study the leading players, particularly Henry Fonda, and admitted in later years that he modelled his own style on that of Fonda. He stayed with the play for 512 performances. At the same time he attended Herbert Berghof's Studio in New York where he studied drama.

Richard L. Bare, a director at Warner Bros., spotted him in a Hollywood restaurant bar. Bare began a conversation with him by asking him if he was an actor. Garner admitted that he was, but had done little. Bare liked him, told him that Warners wanted to do more television series and would like him to join them. Garner had just done an extended test for 20th Century–Fox and was waiting to hear whether he was going to be offered a contract with them. Fox did not sign him, so he went to Warners, tested and was placed under contract immediately. He did a few episodes of *Cheyenne* and some supporting roles in movies. When *Maverick* was devised, he was the first and only choice for the crafty Bret Maverick so the pilot was shot. His salary around this time was $175 to $200 a week. From the very start of his exposure, he began to receive fan mail.

Garner's first big opportunity came when Warner Bros. cast him in the role of Bailey, the marine captain who is befriended by Marlon Brando, in the film version of *Sayonara* (1957), from the novel by James A. Michener. Director Joshua Logan had intended to use an established name in the part until he was introduced to Garner, who made a favorable impression on him and subsequently proved effective in the role. *Sayonara* was being shot on location in Japan. During this time the pilot for *Maverick* was accepted. There was some question over whether he would return from Japan in time to start the series, but in true cliffhanger tradition he did.

Garner has contended that the origin of *Maverick* lay in the film *San Antonio* (1945) which starred Errol Flynn. He dressed like a dandy on the range because his garb had to match stock shots of Errol Flynn. He even claimed that some of his outfits were the same as those worn by Flynn. The sponsor of *Maverick* was searching for a program which would give stiff competition to *The Ed Sullivan Show* and *The Steve Allen Show* on Sunday evening. The series represented a radical departure from the traditional Western in that leading character Bret Maverick was not the highly principled, hardy, heroic Westerner who placed his trust in his gun and his horse, but a conniving cardsharp who lived by his wits and was more likely to win the West by a dazzling repertoire of confidence tricks, most of which were as old as the hills, than by a show of steely determination and bravery. When *Maverick* had its premiere on September 22, 1957, public reaction was overwhelmingly positive. Shortly afterwards it surpassed both the Sullivan and Allen shows in the ratings, which shocked Garner. Roy Huggins, who created and produced the series, found the explanation for its success in a mass cultural acceptance of the anti-hero, a literary type first found in the novels of the 19th-century French writer Stendhal. Garner believed that *Maverick* only really

James Garner vaults over Jack Kelly in *Maverick*.

emerged as a spoof after the fourth or fifth episode. One particular writer, Marion Hargrove, observed Garner's offscreen personality traits and incorporated them into his script directions. This led to Garner clowning around and improvising so that *Maverick* developed into a satire.

Many of the best *Maverick* episodes were derived from stories contained in *Yellow Kid Weil*, a book about the exploits of a notorious conman at the turn of the century. Much of the mystique surrounding Garner and Bret Maverick arose from a single episode called "Shady Deal at Sunny Acres," telecast in 1959. In a late night poker game Bret wins $15,000 which he deposits with John Bates, the banker, until morning. He is given a receipt, but when he arrives the following day to collect his money, Bates claims he has never seen him before. Bret promptly displays the receipt, but is told it is not official. Bret warns Bates that he is not leaving town without his money. Except for two scenes at the beginning and one at the end, Bret spends the rest of the time seated in a chair either whittling a piece of wood or, with his hat pulled low over his eyes, assuring the guffawing townsfolk that he is working on his problem. Meanwhile brother Bart (Jack Kelly) arrives in town and by an elaborate scam involving a fake stock deal and several cohorts succeeds in swindling the banker out of the money. Once the loot has been returned to Bret, he closes his knife, walks to the stagecoach and climbs aboard, whereupon it rolls away. His display of the light touch in this episode made it a classic. He received an Emmy nomination during 1958–1959 for Best Actor in a Leading Role in a Dramatic Series. In the same year *Maverick* won for Best Western Series.

By 1960 Garner was champing at the bit. He considered himself woefully underpaid and bound hand and foot by his seven-year contract. He compared his own salary of $1,500 a week with Ed Sullivan's $20,000. He also believed that although *Maverick* still did well in the ratings, the series declined in quality with the departure of Roy Huggins during the 1959–1960 season. When Warner Bros. suspended him for eight weeks after the outbreak of the writers' strike in March 1960, he saw the opportunity to free himself and sued the studio, maintaining that the suspension was a breach of contract. Warner Bros. filed a countersuit, claiming that the contract was still in effect. In December 1960, after a bitter court battle, a superior district court ruled in Garner's favor. In November 1961, a district court of appeals upheld the decision. Although his legal fees were $100,000, Garner considered the money well spent. His first acting job after winning his release was a summer stock tour for eight weeks of *John Loves Mary* in 1960.

The first film company to hire him after his rebellion was the Mirisch Brothers at United Artists who signed him to a three-picture pact. He also made deals with Universal and MGM. He showed a relaxed comedy style reminiscent of Cary Grant in a couple of comedies with Doris Day: *The Thrill of It All* (1963), which has a classic scene where he drives a car into a swimming pool, and *Move Over Darling* (1963), but his best work is contained elsewhere.

In *The Great Escape* (1963), a very popular war adventure film directed by John Sturges, he played an American who managed through elaborate scams to supply his fellow prisoners in a German concentration camp with almost anything they desired. *The Americanization of Emily* (1964), a satire set in World War II London, cast Garner as an aide to an admiral who supplied the Navy top brass with broads and booze. The basic message of the film, that pacifism rather than military heroism is the highest virtue, caused Garner to receive hate letters from people who objected to his role in the film. Nevertheless his favorite memory is working on this film with Julie Andrews. They were later teamed to rather less effect in *Victor/Victoria* (1982).

Garner also fared extremely well in Westerns during this period. *Duel at Diablo* (1966), directed by Ralph Nelson, with a memorable score by Neal Hefti, was a vivid recycling of the cavalry vs. Indians story with some new twists. Sidney Poitier costarred. *Support Your Local Sheriff!* (1968) and *Support Your Local Gunfighter!* (1971), its sequel, were very amusing, broadly played comedy Westerns. *Skin Game* (1971), which many consider to be one of his best films, concerned an elaborate con game involving an alleged master and slave relationship. This movie possibly endeared itself to audiences because it was the closest of his films to the spirit of *Maverick.* He also established his own production company ("Cherokee"), which had an interest in several of his films and the later television series *The Rockford Files.* His movies were sometimes less than he had hoped. He said, "Everybody has their films which after they're done, they wish they'd never done them. I've got a couple in the closet, just like everybody else." He cites *The Pink Jungle* (1968) and *A Man Called Sledge* (1971) as his all-time worst, but *Health* (1979) and *The Glitter Dome* (1984) could easily be added for good measure. Some of these turkeys explain the reason he appeared on *Variety*'s list of overpriced stars in 1968.

Garner came a cropper with his next television series *Nichols* (1971–1972). This was the season in which stars came before substance. Many much-touted vehicles for veteran stars were aired and rapidly sent to television's graveyard. NBC signed him to a contract paying him $40,000 per episode, with a guarantee of at least $1,000,000, which gave him carte blanche to develop any series which he felt would suit him. This soon proved to be a costly mistake, especially when within a few weeks of production commencing, no format had been decided. He assured everyone breezily, "We aren't concerned with situation. It's more of an attitude we're interested in." If so, he had an attitude problem.

He played Nichols, a man without a first name. This was a shade of Clint Eastwood, but any resemblance to that manly hero ends there. Nichols leaves the army in 1914 after 18 years to return to the small town in Arizona which bears his surname. He finds it has been taken over by the Ketchum family. He is blackmailed into becoming sheriff, but is a very apathetic one, preferring to spend his time trying to strike it rich. The apathy spread to the viewers, so the title was changed to *James Garner as Nichols*. The ratings continued to plummet. In a last ditch attempt to energize Nichols, the network had him killed off in the final episode of the season, only to have him resurrected immediately in the guise of his twin brother Jim, who had more grit in him. This ploy did not work, and after being counted out in the ratings *Nichols* did not emerge for a second season. The compensation which Garner must have had, in addition to his salary, was that just about every other veteran star's show, with the notable exception of Rock Hudson, croaked in the same way that season. Some of these had even more hopeless premises than *Nichols*. Garner commented at the time that the series was just beginning to find its feet when it was axed. Over the years he has become ever more defensive about this series and one senses that it equates to Patrick McGoohan's *The Prisoner* in his personal philosophy. It has, however, never developed a cult status with the public, most of whom have forgotten that he ever appeared in such a series.

He returned briefly to the bleak environment of theatrical films with a pair of Disney movies costarring Vera Miles, *One Little Indian* (1973) and *The Castaway Cowboy* (1974). Of more relevance was his appearance as private investigator Philip Marlowe in MGM's *Marlowe* (1969), derived from the novel *The Little Sister* by Raymond Chandler. This was not in itself a particularly distinguished film, nor a commercially successful one. It was updated to contemporary Southern California, but the gallery of lowlifes and grotesques which had memorably peopled Chandler's Los Angeles in the 1940s had become relatively commonplace and scarcely way out by '60s standards. *Marlowe* and *They Only Kill Their Masters* (1972), in which he played an official police chief investigating a slaying in Southern California, were interesting as dry runs for his second successful television series *The Rockford Files* (1974–1980).

When Roy Huggins initially asked him if he wished to do another television series, Garner refused. The *Nichols* experience had gutted him. When Huggins heard via the grapevine that Garner had changed his mind, he created *The Rockford Files* almost overnight. Universal, equally sickened by the *Nichols* fiasco, cautiously funded a pilot which was a ratings winner and NBC elected to go for a series. The noxious stench created by *Nichols* still polluted the atmosphere, which remained hostile between the two camps throughout the duration of the series.

Every episode of *The Rockford Files* opened with the sound of a telephone answering machine: "Hello, this is James Rockford. At the sound of the tone, please leave your name and number. I'll get back to you as soon as possible." Jim Rockford (Garner) is the sole operative of the Rockford Private Detective Agency. He is an ex-con who served five years for a crime of which he was innocent, living alone in a shabby, static beachfront trailer. He keeps his gun in a biscuit tin and exists on junk food. He is a persuasive talker, ever ready with the wisecracks. He takes on cases which the regular police force have given up on, and his clients are frequently on welfare. Like Marlowe, he is an honest but cynical guy in a nihilistic, violent, predatory society. Rockford was really an odyssey about a middle-aged man of integrity adrift in a sea of corruption and how he copes. Garner felt completely at ease playing Rockford. He said, "I had no second thoughts about doing the series. I'm not the heroic type and I don't believe in heroic types. That's why I love the character." Another reason was that it enabled Garner to collaborate again with Roy Huggins and attack the conventions of yet another solidly established genre, the private eye thriller.

Integral to the series was Rockford's relationship with this pop, Joseph "Rocky" Rockford (Noah Beery, Jr.), who drops by to share a pizza, watch the news on television and whine about the state of civilization. This grates on his son. Rockford's attractive attorney Beth Davenport (Gretchen Corbett) is Garner's recurring love interest in all but the final season. Rockford also has a friendship which is plausible, but at times rather moving, with Police Sgt. Dennis Becker (Joe Santos). *The Rockford Files* was peopled with all kinds of fascinating and bizarre characters tossed into the maelstrom of life. Since they were all jazzed up for latter-day consumption, they emerge as infinitely less dated than their equivalent Chandler counterparts.

In its first season *The Rockford Files* finished twelfth in the ratings. In 1977 Garner won the Emmy for Outstanding Lead Actor in a Drama Series, while the series itself won in 1978. He also received a nomination in 1976, 1978, 1979 and 1980. His salary was reported to be $100,000 an episode. The series began on NBC on September 13, 1974, and finished somewhat abruptly on July 25, 1980. When queried on the reason for its ending, Garner recalled that rolling out of moving cars, leaping from windows and making flying tackles had caused permanent injury to his knees. He explained, "Too many hours on concrete, too many falls. I've had six operations and I just can't take any more pain. The series has already made a lot of money, so who needs more? I don't. What I need is my health. I've worked six days a week and then been kept awake at night with pain." According to a story in *The National Enquirer* (January 1994), Garner faced further surgery to unblock a major artery in his leg. According to the actor, "This is just a temporary setback. It won't stop me from doing anything or change my life at all. I hate the thought of surgery, but it looks like I've got no choice, so I'm just going to get it over with."

The noted thriller writer John D. MacDonald wrote of the series, "In believability, dialogue, plausibility of character, plot coherence, *The Rockford Files* comes as close to meeting the standards of the written mystery as anything I found." Another writer, Donald E. Westlake, pinpointed its weakness. After admitting it was the best series of its type around, he added that the episodes were too complicated for the amount of time the writers had, leading to unconvincing but tidy tie-ups. Simultaneously Garner did a memorable series of Polaroid camera commercials with Mariette Hartley where their rapport was so great that many viewers wrongly assumed they were husband and wife in real life.

Despite his alleged fatigue, Garner was soon back in another series, *Bret Maverick*. He remained intrigued with the character of Bret Maverick and in 1981 decided to revive the character for a new series. Bret was now older and less of a wanderer. The series was located in Sweetwater, Arizona, in the late 1880s. Bret owned a ranch outside of town and was co-owner of the Red Ox Saloon in Sweetwater. The town was trying to rid itself of its wide open image and move into civilization. Although the series was acceptable for diehard Garner fans and *Maverick* buffs, it died after one season and failed to produce classic episodes like the earlier series. Nevertheless, he received an Emmy nomination as Outstanding Lead Actor in a Drama Series. Earlier Garner had inaugurated and starred in the pilot of a one-season spinoff from *Maverick* called *The New Maverick* (1978) which conclusively proved that viewers preferred the old one.

Unlike many stars of long-running series who become so closely identified with a particular role that they cannot find other work, Garner has maintained a high profile as a star since the demise of *Bret Maverick*. By common consent he was at his most impressive in and won an Oscar nomination for *Murphy's Romance* (1985) opposite Sally Field, directed by Martin Ritt. It was these two who pushed for Garner's casting as the free-wheeling philosopher Murphy when executives at Columbia were against him. It details the relationship between a divorcee and a widowed pharmacist in a small town. Garner said, "Murphy really knows what he's about, and that's what I like about him.... I feel very comfortable playing the character." Of some interest was *Sunset* (1988), in which he played a flamboyant Wyatt Earp to Bruce Willis's less than charismatic Tom Mix. Garner had earlier played the same role in *Hour of the Gun* (1967).

During the 1980s Garner found himself enmeshed in the kind of labyrinthine conspiracy plot which would have done justice to an episode of *The Rockford Files.* In 1985 he filed suit against MCA/Universal over what he claimed should have been his share of the profits of *The Rockford Files* series. He explained, "I have been disillusioned with the business for a long time, with all the corrupt people who would rather lie than tell the truth. They'll tell you anything to get you to do what they want with no intention of keeping their word. That's how they operate. Honor has nothing to do with it. Pride and self-esteem have nothing to do with it. That's about all I've found as far as executives go in the 30 years I've worked in Hollywood. I feel guilty in a way doing business with them. I feel like I'm contributing to a corrupt system." In 1989, after years of protracted litigation, he eventually won an extra $9,000,000 from Universal Studios for reruns and foreign sales of *The Rockford Files.*

However, his problems did not finish there. He has had nine operations on his knees and suffered broken ribs and slipped discs from doing his own stunts. In 1987 he suffered a coronary, while in 1988 he had major heart surgery and an operation on his stomach. He made a slow recovery, but by 1991 felt sufficiently well to star in another television series for NBC, *Man of the People,* a sitcom in which he played a con man who inherits his late wife's seat on a city council. It was rapidly placed on hiatus after an abysmal showing. This was an example of the wrong star being wed to the wrong series. Nobody wanted to see James Garner play a modern conman. Instead viewers tune in to see him in a crime show or riding his trusty steed in the Old West, the kind of strenuous programs which were a no-go from the standpoint of his health at this time.

In 1994 he played Zane Cooper, a character described as "a smooth talking stranger," in a feature film revival of *Maverick* which starred Mel Gibson. He scored heavily in *Barbarians at the Gate* (1993), a superlative telepic based on the rise and fall of Nabisco CEO F. Ross Johnson (Garner). In 1995 he signed to revive the character of Jim Rockford in a series of six movies for television. Indications were that there was still an audience out there for this character. In the same year he assumed the role of Cpt. Woodrow Call in *Streets of Laredo.* This was a gritty, violent miniseries which served as a sequel to *Lonesome Dove* (from the novel by Larry McMurtry). It was also a ratings grabber. Garner has been Emmy-nominated on other occasions for his various television movies and specials and has been inducted into the ATAS Hall of Fame for his outstanding contribution to television.

Garner married Lois Clarke, a former television actress, on August 17, 1956, in the courthouse at Beverly Hills after a two-week courtship. They have two daughters: Kimberley (born in 1947), from Mrs. Garner's first marriage, and Greta Scott (born on January 4, 1958). In recent times she has achieved some chart success as a gospel singer based in Nashville.

James Garner Filmography

1956: *Toward the Unknown, The Girl He Left Behind.*
1957: *Sayonara, Shoot-Out at Medicine Bend.*
1958: *Darby's Rangers.*
1959: *Up Periscope!, Alias Jesse James* (cameo).
1960: *Cash McCall.*
1961: *The Children's Hour.*
1962: *Boys' Night Out.*
1963: *The Thrill of It All, Move Over Darling, The Great Escape, The Wheeler Dealers.*
1964: *The Americanization of Emily, 36 Hours.*
1965: *The Art of Love, Mister Buddwing.*
1966: *A Man Could Get Killed, Duel at Diablo, Grand Prix.*
1967: *Hour of the Gun.*
1968: *The Pink Jungle, How Sweet It Is!, Support Your Local Sheriff!*
1969: *Marlowe.*
1970: *A Man Called Sledge.*
1971: *Skin Game, Support Your Local Gunfighter!*
1972: *They Only Kill Their Masters.*
1973: *One Little Indian.*
1974: *The Castaway Cowboy.*
1978: *The New Maverick* (TV).
1979: *Health.*
1981: *The Fan, The Long Hot Summer of George Adams* (TV).
1982: *Victor/Victoria.*
1983: *Tank.*
1984: *The Glitter Dome* (TV), *Heartsounds* (TV).
1985: *Murphy's Romance.*
1986: *Promise* (TV).
1988: *Sunset.*
1989: *My Name Is Bill W* (TV).

1990: *Decoration Day* (TV).
1992: *The Distinguished Gentleman* (cameo).
1993: *Fire in the Sky, Barbarians at the Gate* (TV).
1994: *Breathing Lessons* (TV), *Maverick.*
1996: *My Fellow Americans.*
1997: *Dead Silence.*

Miniseries

1985: *Space.*
1995: *Streets of Laredo.*

Television Series

1957–1960: *Maverick* as Bret Maverick.
1971–1972: *Nichols* as Nichols.
1974–1980: *The Rockford Files* as Jim Rockford.
1981–1982: *Bret Maverick* as Bret Maverick.
1991: *Man of the People* as Jim Doyle.
1995–: *The Rockford Files* as Jim Rockford.

Sources

Beck, Marilyn. *Hollywood.* New York: Hawthorn, 1973.
Beck, Marilyn. "*Rockford Files:* A Lawsuit." January 1986.
Current Biography. New York: H.W. Wilson, 1966.
Meyers, Richard. *The TV Detectives.* San Diego, CA: Barnes, 1981.
Miller, Lee O. *The Great Cowboy Stars of Movies & Television.* New Rochelle, NY: Arlington House, 1979.
Moseley, Roy. *Roger Moore: A Biography.* London: New English Library, 1985.
Norman, Barry. "Film Week." *Radio Times* magazine, April 15, 1989.
Quinlan, David. *Illustrated Directory of Film Stars.* London: Batsford, 1991.
Robertson, Ed. *Maverick: Legend of the West.* Beverly Hills, CA: Pomegranate, 1994.
Stallings, Penny. *Forbidden Channels.* New York: Harper Perennial, 1991.

NANCY GILBERT

This child actress played Calamity Bridger, the orphan sister of Buffalo Bill, Jr. (Dick Jones), whose adventures in and around Wileyville provided the basis of that television series *Buffalo Bill, Jr.* (1955). This appears to be her only recorded credit.

Television Series

1955: *Buffalo Bill, Jr.* as Calamity Bridger

Sources

Speed, F. Maurice. *The Western Film and TV Annual.* London: MacDonald, 1957.

GINA GILLESPIE

Born in Los Angeles in 1952, this child actress was the younger sister of Mickey Mouse Club Mouseketeer Darlene Gillespie. She appeared in feature films and had regular roles in two series. One of these was the offbeat and shortlived *Law of the Plainsman* in which she played an eight-year-old orphan whom Sam Buckhart (Michael Ansara) rescued after a stagecoach mishap. She roomed at the boarding house run by Martha Commager (Nora Marlowe), who acted as a surrogate mother.

Gina Gillespie Filmography

1958: *The Lost Missile, Andy Hardy Comes Home.*

1959: *Face of a Fugitive, It Happened to Jane.*
1962: *What Ever Happened to Baby Jane?*

Television Series

1959–1960: *Law of the Plainsman* as Tess Logan.
1964–1965: *Karen* as Mimi Scott.

Sources

Brooks, Tim. *The Complete Directory to Prime Time TV Stars 1946–Present.* New York: Ballantine Books, 1987.
Dye, David. *Child and Youth Actors: Filmographies of Their Entire Careers, 1914–1985.* Jefferson, NC: McFarland, 1988.
Ragan, David. *Who's Who in Hollywood.* New York: Facts on File, 1992.

MARK GODDARD

Mark Goddard, whose real name is Charles Goddard, was born in Lowell, Massachusetts, on July 24, 1936, the son of a clothing store owner. He is the youngest of five children. At high school he was a proficient basketball and baseball player. He applied to Holy Cross, a Jesuit Catholic College in Wooster, Massachusetts, because he loved basketball and they had a good team. When he was not considered good enough for the team, he became interested in dramatics instead. He was in the dramatic society at Holy Cross. In his junior year (1956) he took a one-year leave of absence with the option that he would return to Holy Cross if he failed in his endeavor to become an actor in New York.

He studied with Lee Strasberg at the American Academy of Dramatic Arts in New York where he enjoyed acting so much that he decided not to return to Holy Cross. Instead he went to Florida, where he did summer stock, and New England, where he appeared in stock. He then thought he was ready to gatecrash Hollywood, so he journeyed to California where he stayed with relatives at Long Beach. He found Hollywood, but was denied entrance to Paramount Studios.

Across the street from there was a restaurant called O'Blatts. The actor was having a cup of coffee when he ran into fellow actor Frank Dana, who was playing a bit in the movie *Career* (1959). He suggested that Goddard write to the director Joseph Anthony, which the young actor did. Shortly afterwards Anthony set up an interview with Goddard at Paramount Studios, the outcome of which was for Goddard to see agents at the William Morris Agency and MCA. The William Morris Agency signed him and sent him to see Dick Powell and Aaron Spelling. The following week he was tested and within three weeks he signed to play the deputy Cully in the Western series *Johnny Ringo* starring Don Durant.

Of this series he says, "It was only on for one year and it was something I really loved doing. Aaron Spelling was great to work for." When the series ended, Dick Powell gave Goddard the choice of a couple of series to do. He chose *The Detectives Starring Robert Taylor* because he wanted to work with the famous Hollywood star. In this he played a police officer, the junior member of the team. When that series ended in 1962, he played guest shots on other television series such as *Perry Mason,* did a couple of movies and had a role in a sitcom before being cast in *Lost in Space.*

In this series he played Major Don West. He landed this role because he was with the same agency as Irwin Allen and they packaged it. The series lasted three seasons, but Goddard grew unhappy during the third season. There was much tension on the set because he believed that he should have become a much bigger star on the strength of it and that the show was going to be a much bigger hit. Largely because of superstition, he quit acting and became an agent for seven years from 1967 to 1974.

He then returned to acting, doing a successful musical called *The Act* with Liza Minnelli on Broadway. He had regular roles in three soaps, one of which (Ted Clayton in *One*

Mark Goddard in *Lost in Space*, his *Johnny Ringo* days behind him.

Life to Live) ranks amongst his personal favorites because he played a contract killer. He did this for a year. Later he appeared on *General Hospital* for two years. He has been an active supporter of Head Start programs and Parents Anonymous Groups (combating child abuse). At the Sloane Kettering Center in New York City he worked with children suffering from cancer. This led to appearances on a couple of shows on Continental Cable called *Not So Strictly Speaking with Kids* and *Imagination.*

Becoming somewhat bored with his existence in 1988, he quit acting again, returning to Massachusetts where he graduated magna cum laude from Bridgewater State College in 1990 with a Bachelor of Arts in Communication with the intention of working with children. As he expressed it, "That was a dream I had, someday it will come true. Right now I have to go back to California because after two years, my funds ran out and I have to go back to work." At the Dixie Trek Convention 1990, he gave a rather sad commentary on his life when he said, "What is it with actors? What's wrong with us? No friends, no family, we run around doing conventions. I could die in my hotel room. I could be here six weeks before they found me."

Since then he has become a behavioral specialist dealing with disturbed children at Longview Farm School in his native Massachusetts. In August 1992, he obtained a Master's Degree in elementary school education and later studied for a Master's Degree in special education.

Goddard has been married and divorced twice. By his first marriage he has two children, one of whom (Melissa) has been active in show business. His second wife was actress Susan Anspach.

Mark Goddard Filmography

1965: *The Monkey's Uncle, A Rage to Live.*
1967: *The Love-Ins.*
1972: *Play It Again Sam.*
1973: *The Death Squad* (TV).
1976: *Blue Sunshine.*
1979: *Roller Boogie.*
1983: *Strange Invaders.*

Television Series

1959–1960: *Johnny Ringo* as Cully.
1960–1962: *The Detectives Starring Robert Taylor* as Sgt. Chris Ballard.
1964–1965: *Many Happy Returns* as Bob Randall.
1965–1968: *Lost in Space* as Major Don West.
1981: *One Life to Live* as Ted Clayton.
1982: *The Doctors* as Paul Reed.
1984–1986: *General Hospital.*

Sources

Mitchell, Flint, and William E. Anchors, Jr. *The Lost in Space 25th Anniversary Celebration 1965–1990.* Alpha Control Press, 1991.

Van Hise, James. *Lost in Space 25th Anniversary Tribute Book.* Las Vegas, NV: Pioneer Books, 1990.

Weaver, Tom. *They Fought in the Creature Features: Interviews with 23 Classic Horror, Science Fiction and Serial Stars.* Jefferson, NC: McFarland, 1995.

LEO GORDON

Leo V. Gordon was born in New York City on December 2, 1922. He worked in the construction industry prior to being drafted into the army during World War II. Upon his discharge he attended the Academy Of Dramatic Arts in New York. He appeared in stage plays in the United States and in the London production of *Mister Roberts.* Gravitating to Hollywood, he made his screen debut in 1953. He has always claimed that nothing much happened before he sold a script, *Black Patch.* Since he made his screen debut in 1953, and *Black Patch* was not filmed until 1957, one assumes there was a considerable time lapse between selling the script and shooting the film.

He had a minor semi-regular role as Hank Miller in a marginal Western, *Circus Boy.* His most active period was during the 1950s and 1960s when he became steadily employed, turning in several chilling studies in savage villainy. In real life he has penned several scripts (which have been filmed) and written novels. He has also directed for television. He married Lynn Cartwright and has a daughter Tara.

Leo Gordon Filmography

1953: *All the Brothers Were Valiant, Gun Fury, Hondo, City of Bad Men, China Venture.*
1954: *Riot in Cell Block 11, The Yellow Mountain, Sign of the Pagan, The Bamboo Prison.*
1955: *Ten Wanted Men, Santa Fe Passage, Seven Angry Men, Soldier of Fortune, Robbers' Roost, The Man with the Gun, Tennessee's Partner.*
1956: *The Conqueror, Red Sundown, Great Day in the Morning, Johnny Concho, The Steel Jungle, The Man Who Knew Too Much, 7th Cavalry.*
1957: *The Restless Breed, Black Patch, The Lonely Man, Lure of the Swamp, The Tall Stranger, Baby Face Nelson, Man in the Shadow (*a.k.a. *Pay The Devil).*
1958: *The Notorious Mr. Monks, Quantrill's Raiders, Ride a Crooked Trail, Apache Territory, The Cry Baby Killer.*
1959: *The Big Operator, Escort West, The Jayhawkers.*
1960: *Noose for a Gunman.*
1961: *The Intruder (*a.k.a. *I Hate Your Guts!).*
1962: *The Nun and the Sergeant, Tarzan Goes to India.*
1963: *The Haunted Palace, Kings of the Sun, McLintock!*
1964: *L'Arme a Gauche, The Dictator's Guns, Kitten with a Whip.*
1965: *Girls on the Beach.*
1966: *Tobruk, Night of the Grizzly, Beau Geste.*
1967: *The Devil's Angels, Hostile Guns, The St. Valentine's Day Massacre.*
1968: *Buckskin.*
1970: *You Can't Win 'Em All.*
1971: *The Trackers* (TV).
1972: *Bonnie's Kids.*
1973: *My Name Is Nobody.*
1975: *Barbary Coast* (TV).
1976: *Nashville Girl.*
1978: *Hitler's Son, Bog.*
1980: *Rage* (TV).
1982: *Fire and Ice* (voice only).
1985: *Savage Dawn.*
1988: *Saturday the 14th Strikes Back, Big Top Pee-wee.*
1989: *Alienator.*
1990: *Mob Boss.*
1994: *Maverick.*

Television Series

1956–1958: *Circus Boy* as Hank Miller.
1980–1981: *Enos* as Sgt. Theodore Kick.

Miniseries

1983: *The Winds of War* as General Benton.

Sources

Cameron, Ian, and Elisabeth Cameron. *The Heavies.* London: Studio Vista, 1967.
Parish, James Robert. *Hollywood Character Actors.* New Rochelle, NY: Arlington House, 1978.
Quinlan, David. *Illustrated Directory of Film Character Actors.* London: Batsford, 1995.
Summers, Neil. *The Official TV Western Book Volume #4.* Vienna, WV: Old West Shop Publishing, 1992.

WILLIAM D. GORDON

This actor played the supporting role of one of the crew members during the first season of the troubled *Riverboat* series. He had left (along with several other members of the cast) by the time the series returned for a second season. Although he continued to accept acting assignments (e.g., 1971's *Powderkeg*), his name was much more frequently seen as a scriptwriter for acclaimed series such as *The Lawyers* and *Ironside*.

Television Series

1959–1960: *Riverboat* as Travis.

Sources

Brooks, Tim. *The Complete Directory to Primetime TV Stars 1946–Present.* New York: Ballantine, 1987.

Martindale, David. *Television Detective Shows of the 1970s.* Jefferson, NC: McFarland, 1991.

KIRBY GRANT

The name of Kirby Grant became synonymous with the television series *Sky King.* His background was in music but he was also keen on flying, which helped him in the role. As with several other personalities, he became consumed by the character he played. As he once expressed it, "The whole thing has a tendency to make a better person of me. I tried to live up to the character I portrayed."

Kirby Grant Hoon, Jr., was born in Butte, Montana, on November 24, 1911, of Scottish and Dutch descent. When he was ten years old, he began violin lessons. At the age of 12, he gave his first concert with the Seattle Symphony Orchestra where he was regarded as a child prodigy. Winning a musical scholarship to the University of Washington, he followed his vocation in music by attending Whitman University, the Chicago Institute of Art and the American Conservatory of Music.

After two years of performing classical music in concerts, he became convinced that a career in that direction did not appeal to him. He organized his own dance band and toured the country performing in night clubs. After a stint with a Midwest stock company, in 1937 he seized an opportunity to appear on radio, winning first prize on the popular *Gateway to Hollywood* program which fostered fresh talent. On the strength of this he was given a six-month contract with RKO. While there he played bits in George O'Brien Westerns using the name Robert Stanton.

After RKO failed to pick up his option, he was drafted into the armed forces, serving as an Air Force flight instructor. He later found himself entertaining the troops in Europe and North Africa. After an honorable discharge in 1944, he signed a contract with Universal Pictures. They cast him in comedies, musicals and the occasional drama until their B Western star Rod Cameron was given a buildup in A features. Then Grant was given the lead in Universal's B Western series, but he did not care for them. He rebelled against them because he had been promised better things, but was threatened with a suspension. The service had left him virtually without funds, so he was in no position to be suspended. His costar was Fuzzy Knight. Grant appeared in these until 1946 when the changing policies and fortunes of Universal dictated a halt on all B films. This effectively ended the series, and his contract was not renewed.

He had some difficulty finding another berth. Producer Lindsley Parsons had seen and liked him in Monogram's *Law Men* (1944) and decided that he would be the ideal star of an unusual series of outdoor dramas. These were Canadian Mountie adventures based on stories by James Oliver Curwood and featuring a canine discovery called Chinook. Grant played a mountie. These features, ten in all, were released by Monogram/Allied Artists and enabled Grant to keep a respectable footing in the industry. He continued to appear in this film series until 1954.

Simultaneously Grant turned to television

in 1951 with a very successful contemporary juvenile Western series called *Sky King*. This had been heard on radio from 1946 to 1954. The actor was a lifelong flying fanatic who had been taught to fly by barnstorming in the 1920s. In the series he starred as Schuyler King, an Arizona millionaire who flew a twin engine Cessna (nicknamed "The Songbird") to patrol his Flying Crown Ranch. King was aided by his niece Penny (Gloria Winters) and nephew Clipper (Ron Hagerthy). The stories were straightforward ones of good vs. evil, sometimes with an ecological theme. What made the series unusual was the use of electronic gadgets and modern scientific methods. Villains were frequently undone by such latter-day devices as Geiger counters, tape recorders and antennae.

The series was seen on all three networks at various times and ended in 1954. It was a half-hour black and white series. There were a total of 130 episodes filmed. Unfortunately, negatives, masters and prints of all the episodes were stored in one New York City vault. When a fire broke out, episodes were destroyed in the inferno and only 72 segments were saved. Ironically, when the series was originally broadcast, the star was living at Highland Park, Illinois, and commuting to the Hollywood studio where they were shot. By the time it was rebroadcast in the late 1950s, he was residing in Los Angeles. Next he spent several years on tour with the Carson and Barnes Circus before retiring in 1970 and settling in Winter Springs, Florida.

He bought the rights to the series and established "The Sky King Youth Ranch," which provided food, clothing and shelter for a number of underprivileged children. This nonprofit enterprise led to the star being declared bankrupt. It must also seriously have affected his health because he suffered two heart attacks and had to undergo bypass surgery. He later found himself a job acting in a public relations capacity firstly for an insurance company in Austin, Texas, and then for Sea World in Florida. He also dabbled in real estate.

Kirby Grant died on October 30, 1985, at age 73, in an automobile accident en route to watch the launch of the Challenger space shuttle at Cape Canaveral, Florida. He went at the specific request of the astronauts, who had watched his exploits on television as children. His vehicle was involved in a collision which sent it plunging off the highway and into a ditch. He drowned in several feet of water before help could free him. At the time of his death he was working on a revival of his television series and a replica of the Flying Crown Ranch as part of a Sky King Theme Park. He was survived by his wife Caroline and three children.

Kirby Grant Filmography

1935: *I Dream Too Much*.
1938: *Lawless Valley, Red River Range*.
1939: *Three Sons*.
1940: *Bullet Code, The Marines Fly High*.
1941: *Blondie Goes Latin*.
1942: *My Favorite Blonde, Dr. Kildare's Victory*.
1943: *Hello Frisco Hello, Bombardier, The Stranger from Pecos*.
1944: *Destination Tokyo, Law Men, Hi Good Lookin', Babes on Swing Street, Ghost Catchers, In Society*.
1945: *Easy to Look At, I'll Remember April, Penthouse Rhythm, Trail to Vengeance, Bad Men of the Border, Code of the Lawless, Blondie's Lucky Day*.
1946: *The Spider Woman Strikes Back, She Wrote the Book, Gun Town, Gunman's Code, The Lawless Breed, Rustlers' Roundup*.
1948: *Song of Idaho, Singin' Spurs*.
1949: *Black Midnight, Feudin' Rhythm, Trail of the Yukon, Wolf Hunters*.
1950: *Snow Dog, Indian Territory, Call of the Klondike*.
1951: *Comin' Round the Mountain, Rhythm Inn, Yukon Manhunt, Northwest Territory*.
1952: *Yukon Gold*.
1953: *Northern Patrol, Fangs of the Arctic*.
1954: *Yukon Vengeance*.
1955: *The Court-Martial of Billy Mitchell*.

Television Series

1951–1954: *Sky King* as Schuyler King.

Sources

Corneau, Ernest N. *The Hall of Fame of Western Film Stars*. North Quincy, MA: Christopher, 1969.
Fitzgerald, Michael G. *Universal Pictures*. New Rochelle, NY: Arlington House, 1977.

Lamparski, Richard. *Whatever Became Of? Tenth Series* New York: Crown, 1986.
Picture Show Annual. London: Amalgamated Press, 1947.
Speed, F. Maurice. *The Western Film Annual.* London: MacDonald, 1952.
Willis, John. *Screen World.* New York: Crown, 1986.
Yoggy, Gary A. *Riding the Video Range: The Rise and Fall of the Western on Television.* Jefferson, NC: McFarland, 1995.

PETER GRAVES

There is an old show business adage about never acting with either animals or children. Peter Graves is an actor who did both in *Fury* (1955–1958) and survived to tell about it. He has done extremely well to sustain a career which in a sense has gone nowhere. He has always been relatively successful and is still relatively successful. With his fair hair and tall, imposing figure, he looks as if he belongs in series television as a leading man. Of the four television series in which he has starred, *Fury* was the earliest and *Mission Impossible* was the most successful. He is regarded by his peers as a totally professional actor.

Peter Graves was born Peter Aurness at Minneapolis, Minnesota, on March 8, 1925, the son of Rolf C. Aurness, a businessman, and Ruth O. Duesler, a journalist. He is of German descent. He has one brother, actor James Arness. One question which intrigues people is the nature of their relationship. They have both dismissed rumors of feuds as being totally untrue and nonsensical. "The important thing," Graves has stressed, "is that we be true brothers in every sense, without making public displays of it." Ruth Duesler once said, "My sons are very different... Jim likes to be patted and told everything will be all right. Peter will pat you and say that everything will be okay. ... They each got where they wanted to be in such divergent ways; Jim, the elder, almost by adventuresome accident; Peter by calculated design."

As a young high school boy, Peter was a talented musician. At 15 he was one of the youngest full-fledged members of the Musicians' Union, and he regularly played clarinet and saxophone with local dance bands. At 16 he was employed as a radio announcer, one of the world's youngest. Although busy, he still found time to reign as the state hurdles champion of Minneapolis.

Upon graduating from high school he enlisted in the U.S. Air Force, being sorely disappointed on receiving his discharge two years later (in 1945) without ever having left the United States. Taking advantage of the G.I. Bill, he enrolled at the University of Minnesota as a drama major. There he played leading roles in many plays, including *The Wild Duck, Macbeth, Death Takes a Holiday* and *Of Mice and Men.* Dr. Drank Whiting, Director of Speech and Drama at the university, has said of his pupil, "I believe he has as much talent as any of our young actors on stage or screen." During his college days he also appeared in summer stock, continued radio announcing part-time and earned extra money by playing the saxophone.

On completing his university studies, he headed directly for Hollywood where he made his television debut in an episode of *Fireside Theater* in 1951. Motion picture producer Frank Melford saw him performing in his first television program, and almost before he knew what was happening, Graves had been signed to costar with Rory Calhoun in *Rogue River* (1950). Then he costarred with Dane Clark in *Fort Defiance* (1951).

Producers began to take note of his appeal and strength of performance, and he landed the important part of the spy in *Stalag* 17 (1953). More important roles followed in *Beneath the 12-Mile Reef* (1953) and *The Long Gray Line* (1955). Independent producer Leonard Goldstein sought and signed Graves for a big assignment in *The Raid* (1954), which starred Van Heflin. On seeing the finished print Goldstein immediately signed him to a long-term contract and cast him in the second male role in *Black Tuesday* (1954). The untimely death of Goldstein spelled *finis* to this contract, but the actor costarred immediately afterwards in *Robbers' Roost* (1955), produced by Goldstein's brother Robert. He was one of several actors who were tested for the lead in *Gunsmoke*, but rejected because after *Stalag 17*, it was considered that he did not look American enough.

Films such as *Wichita* (1955) and *Fort Yuma* (1955) followed before he was cast in the leading role in the television series *Fury* (1955–1958). *Fury* premiered on September 15, 1955, on the NBC morning lineup. It was half an hour in length and shot in black and white. *Fury* was located in the modern west and dealt with contemporary themes with which young audiences were able to identify. The focus of the series was on tough orphan Joey (Bobby Diamond), adopted by widower Jim Newton (Peter Graves) who owned the Broken Wheel Ranch. Fury was a magnificent coal black stallion played by a horse called Beauty. Fury only allowed Joey to ride him. The series was produced by the Independent Television Corporation primarily for children, and there was always some lesson to be derived from each episode. It won numerous awards from various civic groups. It ran for a total of 114 episodes over a four-year period and was seen by millions. During breaks between seasons, Graves continued with his film career.

Almost immediately after *Fury* ended, he was signed to do another television series, *Whiplash* (1960). This was Australia's contribution to the Western television series genre, although producer Ben Fox, director John Meredith and star Graves were all American. It was to Australia that the 22-strong unit went to shoot this series of 39 half-hour episodes, depicting the exciting days of the Gold Rush in the 1850s when the Cobb and Company stageline opened up thousands of miles of the outback. The country was still only emerging from the worst days of its penal colony history, and bushranging was still rife.

Alice Springs, which is more than a thousand miles from the sea in any direction, was the center of the unit's activities for location shooting. Producer Fox said, "We have in our series not the familiar visual and audio clichés to be found in so many outdoor adventure television series, but instead the changing countryside of the Central Australian area, aborigines and stock routes, the Macdonnell Ranges, the Ormiston Gorge and Ayer's Rock with its aboriginal myths and legends, the Ross River and other scenic spots around Alice Springs."

Graves played Christopher Cobb, the founder of the stageline. The star loved to swim and surf, which influenced his choice of place to live in Sydney. He chose Bilgola, a lovely beach about 20 miles from Sydney and a little more than half that distance from Artransa Studios in French's Forest, where the interiors of *Whiplash* were shot.

He was subsequently offered the role of the army lawyer Major Frank Whittaker in the television series *Court Martial* (1966). Graves and Bradford Dillman played officer lawyers of the U.S. Army Judge Advocate General's Office, headquartered in England, who prosecuted crimes committed in wartime. This series of 26 episodes for Lew Grade was shown on ABC and originated as a 1963 episode of *The Kraft Suspense Theater.* It was shot at Pinewood Studios which entailed Graves relocating to England, an experience which he enjoyed very much.

Steven Hill, star of the CBS series *Mission Impossible* during the first season, left the show, and Graves replaced him as Jim Phelps, head of the Impossible Missions Force. This group of undercover operatives worked for a top secret government agency which executed secret missions with an incredible array of gadgets. Their instructions were usually relayed via a tape recorder which self-destructed five seconds afterwards. This left the series open to parody, and even Graves himself (when making public appearances) sometimes burlesques this. The 1966–1973 series became very successful. Even prior to its ending, Graves shot a few different pilots for new television series. Although some of them had potentially interesting premises, none of them were picked up for various reasons. In 1988 ABC resurrected the series with a new production lensed in a couple of states of Australia. Graves returned to play his former role. This lasted two seasons before it self-destructed in dismal ratings. He has narrated documentaries and provided the voices of two Civil War generals for a cable

Peter Graves (right) with William Fawcett (left) and Bobby Diamond in a publicity pose for *Fury*.

television series. A marketing consultant for Mel Gibson's film *Braveheart,* he currently hosts and narrates the cable series *Biography.*

While at college Graves met a vivacious coed named Joan Endress whom he married on December 16, 1950. She has been described as a community activist. They have three daughters: Kelly Jean (born October 19, 1951), Claudia (born November 1, 1954) and Amanda Lee (born May 21, 1958). He has said that the best relaxation for him is reading a book, adding, "Anything worthwhile." He and his wife live in Santa Monica, California.

Peter Graves Filmography

1950: *Rogue River.*
1951: *Fort Defiance, Up Front.*
1952: *Red Planet Mars.*
1953: *East of Sumatra, War Paint, Stalag 17, Beneath the 12-Mile Reef, Killers from Space.*
1954: *The Raid, The Yellow Tomahawk, Black Tuesday.*
1955: *The Naked Street, Robbers' Roost, The Long Gray Line, Wichita, The Night of the Hunter, The Court-Martial of Billy Mitchell, Fort Yuma.*
1956: *Hold Back the Night, Canyon River, It Conquered the World.*
1957: *Death in Small Doses, Bayou, Beginning of the End.*
1958: *Wolf Larsen.*
1959: *Stranger in my Arms.*
1963: *The Case Against Paul Ryker* (TV) (shown in cinemas as *Sergeant Ryker* in 1968).
1965: *A Rage to Live.*
1966: *Texas Across the River.*
1967: *The Ballad of Josie, Valley of Mystery.*
1969: *The Five Man Army.*
1971: *The President's Plane Is Missing* (TV).
1972: *Call to Danger* (TV).
1974: *Sidecar Racers, Where Have All the People Gone* (TV), *The Underground Man* (TV), *Scream of the Wolf* (TV).
1975: *Dead Man on the Run* (TV), *Bigfoot: The Mysterious Monster* (narrator only).
1976: *Spree.*
1977: *SST Death Flight* (TV).
1978: *Teheran Incident* (a.k.a. *Missile X*), *High Seas Hijack.*
1979: *The Clonus Horror, Death Car on the Freeway* (TV).
1980: *Trieste File, Airplane!, Survival Run, The Memory of Eva Ryker* (TV).
1981: *300 Miles for Stephanie* (TV), *The Guns and the Fury.*
1982: *Savannah Smiles, Airplane II: The Sequel.*
1986: *Number One with a Bullet.*
1987: *The Law and Harry McGraw* (TV), *If It's Tuesday It Must Still Be Belgium* (TV).
1993: *Addams Family Values.*

Television Series

1955–1958: *Fury* as Jim Newton.
1960–1961: *Whiplash* as Christopher Cobb.
1966: *Court Martial* as Major Frank Whittaker.
1967–1973: *Mission Impossible* as Jim Phelps.
1988–1990: *Mission Impossible* as Jim Phelps.

Miniseries

1979: *The Rebels.*
1983: *The Winds of War.*
1989: *War and Remembrance.*

Sources

Ferguson, Ken. *Television Stars.* London: Purnell, 1966.
Nelson, Jim, and Barbara Koskie. "*Mission Impossible Cast*—Where Are They Now?" *National Enquirer* magazine, 1996.
Skinner, John Walter. *Who's Who on the Screen.* Worthing, England: Madeleine Productions, 1983.
Speed, F. Maurice. *The Western Film and TV Annual.* London: MacDonald, 1961.

LORNE GREENE

Lorne Greene was a solidly built actor with a resonant voice, prematurely white hair and a "take charge" demeanor. To Canadians he represented "the voice of Canada," giving reassurance during the dark days of World War II. To generations of Western fans he was the patriarch Ben Cartwright of *Bonanza,* embodying the wisdom of Solomon with the strength of Samson. To sci-fi fans he was the resolute commander of an intergalactic star ship. As for his offscreen personality, his second wife once said, "He is the mildest, most thoughtful of

Lorne Greene as he appeared in *Bonanza*.

men." He also had a terrific sense of humor and was always joking on the set.

Lorne Greene was born in Ottawa, Canada, on February 12, 1915, the son of Daniel and Dora Greene. They were Jewish immigrants from Imperial Russia. His father had a business making orthopedic boots and shoes; he was 19 when his son Lorne was born. Greene was named after his father's first customer, a man named Lorne MacKenzie. Lorne Greene, whose older brother died in infancy, grew up as an only child. He enjoyed a very happy relationship with his parents. At Lisgar Collegiate Institute he had his first taste of theatricals when his French teacher cast him in the comedy *Les Deux Sourds* as one of two deaf characters who had to shout at one another.

From 1932 to 1937 he attended Queen's University, Kingston, Ontario, where he acted in and directed plays for the Drama Guild. He began studying chemical engineering, but switched to languages in the hope of having more time to devote to the theater. After his graduation with a BA degree, he accepted a fellowship to the Neighborhood Playhouse School of the Theater in New York City. His training as an actor also included lessons at the Martha Graham School of Contemporary Dance to learn stage movement. When Greene returned to Canada in 1939 after two years' study in New York, he began his professional career. There was little work for actors, but he subsequently became Canada's leading broadcaster for the Canadian Broadcasting Corporation, his voice being familiar across the land. In 1941 he narrated the documentary film *Churchill's Island.* Later he saw active service with the Royal Canadian Air Force.

After the war he established the Academy of Radio Arts in 1946 to serve as a training ground for young Canadian talent. His school had some 400 graduates. He cofounded a repertory theater, the Jupiter Group, and directed and acted in over 50 productions. On a trip to New York in 1953 to demonstrate a special stopwatch he had invented (it ran backwards so a radio director would know how much time was left), he had a chance encounter with a producer friend, Fletcher Markle, who was producing the successful dramatic television anthology series *Studio One.* Markle gave him roles in different episodes. His role in "1984" as a Thought Police official earned him glowing reviews. He became so crazy about acting that he liquidated the Academy of Radio Arts to concentrate on a thesping career.

From 1953 to 1954 he appeared opposite the legendary Katharine Cornell on Broadway in *Prescott Proposals,* which ran 125 performances. He also appeared in two Shakespearean plays back in his native Canada in 1955, but they were among his least successful work. He liked movies and television more than the stage. Film and more television work followed, often on anthology series like *Climax* and *Alfred Hitchcock Presents.* He was frequently villainous in films and not conspicuously successful. His best role was probably as the prosecuting attorney in *Peyton Place* (1957). He gained a foretaste of series stardom when he starred as a freighter captain in an early Anglo-Canadian television series, *Sailor of Fortune* (1956), which lasted for 30 black and white episodes. One of these segments, "The Crescent And The Star," marked an early role for Sean Connery. Greene eventually objected to the dismal quality of the scripts, and when there were no signs of things improving he quit in disgust and returned to Hollywood.

A guest role on *Wagon Train* in early 1959 caught the eye of producer David Dortort, who was casting *Bonanza* for NBC. Greene as Ben Cartwright presided over the 100,000 acre Ponderosa ranch from 1959 to 1973 through 430 episodes. It was set in Virginia City, Nevada, during the Civil War period, soon after the discovery of the fabulous Comstock Silver Lode. Ben's strongwilled sons by different wives were played by Pernell Roberts, Dan Blocker and Michael Landon. This combination resulted in one of the most successful television series of all time, the anchor of NBC's Sunday night lineup for more than a decade. It received one Emmy nomination as Outstanding Dramatic Series in 1966, but didn't win.

Bonanza, which was shot in color, was partly intended by NBC as a vehicle for marketing color television sets on behalf of RCA. NBC was also influenced by psychological studies which claimed that young American males were obsessed with "monism," an excessive identification with their mothers. This was said to have led to defection by U.S. soldiers in Korea, and NBC conceived it their patriotic duty to offer viewers a strong father and son relationship.

When *Bonanza* was first aired in 1959, it was slotted opposite *Perry Mason* on Saturday nights and was faring badly in the ratings war. According to Greene the show was nearly axed before it found its feet. They were shooting the sixth show when gossip began to spread that the man with the sharpened pencil at NBC in New York had declared *Bonanza* cost too much and should end after 13 episodes. The NBC people in California objected, but it was touch and go until December 1959, when a rumor was printed that *Bonanza* had been axed. The network was deluged with complaint mail, and it was then they knew they had an audience. The show was moved to Sundays at nine P.M. and ranked high in television's Top Ten for years thereafter. From 1964 to 1967 it was the number one show on the air. At its peak *Bonanza* was being shown in 80 countries with an estimated viewing audience of 400 million. President Lyndon Johnson reputedly did not dare make television announcements of his own at the same time for fear of being ignored.

Greene based his characterization on his father, whom he admired above all men because he would listen to the other fellow's point of view. His father had warned him of the insecurities of the acting profession, but never opposed him. Greene softened his characterization of Ben Cartwright from the first few episodes. Originally he was asked to play the role of a stern patriarch, but he objected. He did not want to play Ben Cartwright as a man with a rifle in one hand and a Bible in the other, who ruled his sons with a rod of iron. He wanted Cartwright to be more human, to grow with his sons and to invite strangers into his home instead of warning them off his property with a shotgun.

Greene recalled, "I felt the Cartwrights should make nice nice, say to people, 'Hey, you're on the Ponderosa, but that's all right. C'mon in. You hungry? You want to stay with us for a couple of weeks?' There were no radios or television, and I thought that would be a great way for the Cartwrights to find out what was happening in the world." He also reasoned that for Ben Cartwright to have been married three times, he could not have been too much of a tyrant. He must have had the charm to attract women.

Bonanza relied on historical events and characters to develop its storylines. References to the Civil War, the statehood of Nevada and the discovery of the Comstock Lode were common in the early years of the series, as were appearances by such historical figures as Mark Twain, Cochise, Charles Dickens and Lotta Crabtree. Many of the events and characters could not have appeared within the alleged time frame of the stories. The most glaring mistake was the map which appeared in the opening sequence, then burst into flame to reveal the Cartwrights astride their horses. An identical map was shown behind Ben Cartwright's desk in the Ponderosa. Most of the distances shown were ludicrously inaccurate, but this was fairly common on early maps. The town of Reno was shown on the map, yet it was not named until May 1868. Many of the incidents taking place in the stories occurred long before that. For a series based around the Comstock Lode, there was a complete dearth of miners and mining activity in Virginia City. It is a tribute to *Bonanza* and its stars that none of this mattered at all.

Characteristically, Lorne Greene attributed the success of *Bonanza* to teamwork. During the show's run Greene and his costars toured extensively in rodeos, fairs and other attractions, and he was seen on numerous variety shows and specials. He was Master of Ceremonies at the Royal Command Performance for Queen Elizabeth on her visit to Canada in 1964 and presided over the televised memorial tribute to President Kennedy. He was Canada's Man of the Year in 1965. He spent ten months of each year playing the same part, but claimed the role never bored him since there was a new script with fresh characters and circumstances regularly.

Bonanza made Lorne Greene a multimillionaire. The residual rights for the first ten years' programs were sold for millions; his fee per episode climbed to $17,000 (plus a third of the residuals for the episodes filmed during the last four years of production, which eventually doubled his salary to $34,000 per week). Greene's other income derived from such diverse investments as potato sacking and belt-making factories; office buildings in downtown Los Angeles; and a $2,000,000 half-mile stretch of Malibu Beach property. He also invested his earnings in a stable of thoroughbred horses at Santa Anita and Del Mar racetracks. He built a replica of the Ponderosa in Arizona which for complete authenticity even had a staircase leading nowhere.

Bonanza ceased production in January 1973, mainly because of Dan Blocker's death; other factors included a move to Tuesday nights which led to a low ratings performance, and the fact that Greene had suffered a minor heart attack. When he recovered, he tried again, this time with a crime show called *Griff* in 1973. It was strange that the pilot, *Man on the Outside,* was not aired until more than a year after the series went off the air. He played Los Angeles Police Captain Wade Griffin, whose son is shot down before his eyes and whose grandson is kidnapped. Griff sets out in hot pursuit on his own after witnessing the bureaucracy of the official police department.

The series opened after the killing and the kidnapping had taken place. Griff had resigned from the force after 30 years over a matter of principle and had set up his own private investigation business, Wade Griffin Investigations. The series was set in the swinging Westwood section of Los Angeles, and Griff's assistant was Mike Murdoch (Ben Murphy). *Griff* was as big a flop as *Bonanza* had been a success and was axed after three months. (A similar series which enjoyed higher ratings and a longer run was *Barnaby Jones* with Buddy Ebsen.) Michael Landon later attributed the failure of *Griff* to Lorne Greene being too much the gentleman. He had the pick of any show he cared to do, but the climate of the industry had changed since *Bonanza* started. Greene listened to the advice of freeloaders and hillbillies instead of relying on his own gut instinct about what was right for him.

One consequence of this was that when James Stewart rejected the role of Sam Royce in Universal's all-star disaster movie *Earthquake* (1974), Greene was available to play the part. *Earthquake* told of the various people trapped in Los Angeles after a mammoth earthquake. It offered viewers excellent special effects as well as some tremors of their own because the film was originally shown in Sensurround (which wired up shocks to cinema seats so patrons believed they were really experiencing an earthquake). The actors took a backseat to the mayhem, but Universal needed reassuring stars around the edges of the drama who could quickly gain audience empathy. Greene played Charlton Heston's father-in-law and Ava Gardner's father, but it was commented upon that he looked much too young. His acting was top notch as usual, and the film was the most commercially successful he ever appeared in.

Greene was deeply committed to environmental and wildlife causes, having served as chairman of the National Wildlife Federation and on the board of the American Horse Protection Association. He remained primarily in television where he executive-produced and narrated two syndicated series, *Last of the Wild* (1974–1979) and *New Wilderness* (1982–1986); the Bicentennial specials *What Do You Want To Be When You Grow Old?* and *Ballad of America;* and hosted *A Gift of Music* and *A Fantasy on Ice.* He starred in some movies made for television and miniseries. He reunited with his *Bonanza* sons Pernell Roberts on the "Aloha, You're Dead" episode of *Vegas* in 1978 and with Mike Landon on a segment of *Highway to Heaven.* He also appeared in the short films *George Washington* and *Lorne Greene's Canada;* hosted the videocassette programs *The Pritkin Promise* and *The Fifth Pritkin Promise;* and did voice characterizations for the animated feature *Heidi's Song* (1982) and the television series *The Greatest Adventure Stories from the Bible.* He also did many commercials for Alpo dog food and medical insurance plans.

From 1978 to 1980 Greene played the stoic, silver-haired Commander Adama of *Bat-*

tlestar Galactica, a *Star Wars* clone. In the seventh millennium A.D., Galactica was the only surviving battlestar after a surprise attack by the evil Cylons had shattered interplanetary peace and wiped out most of humankind. The Cylons pursued Galactica and her attendant fleet of 220 smaller spacecraft as they sped through space towards a last refuge, a distant, unknown planet called Earth. Galactica was reputed to have cost $1,000,000 per episode to produce, the highest budget ever up to that time, and was so close to the concept of *Star Wars* that the producers of that movie sued ABC for stealing their film. The series was first judged a flop, but then became a cult hit after an edited version enjoyed considerable success when released theatrically.

Greene also starred in *Code Red* (1981), dubbed by one wiseacre "Lorne Greene with fire trucks," but this series flopped too. The pilot, which was "warmly dedicated to firefighters all over the world," with Greene playing an arson investigator, was possibly the most woefully inept ever filmed. After the alarm is raised and Greene *et al.* rush to the scene, it becomes very apparent that the firefighting techniques were being applied to the wrong house! When he received his first script of the series, it had changed beyond recognition. He was now cast as a battalion chief with two sons, which was old hat. Apparently ABC had changed the timeslot from eight to seven in the evening, which meant the show had to be a straight action format because it was the kiddies' hour. This is precisely what Greene had been trying to escape from, and he lashed out at the producers who he felt had betrayed him. He refused to do any publicity for the revamped show. This boycott was so effective that it insured the demise of the series overnight.

Greene made his last appearance in cameo as Sam Houston in the superfluous telefilm *The Alamo: 13 Days to Glory* (1987). At the time of his death, he was slated to appear in *Bonanza: The Next Generation* (1988), but his health began to fail. Even when producer David Dortort arranged to have the script rewritten so that it made his role less strenuous, Greene was unable to play it. John Ireland replaced him. He underwent abdominal surgery for a perforated ulcer on August 19, 1987, and subsequently developed pneumonia. He occasionally had required an oxygen tank to help him breathe, but over Labor Day weekend rallied sufficiently to be removed from intensive care and given a private room. He was put back on the critical list on September 10. Greene died on September 11, 1987, at age 72, of a heart attack in hospital in Santa Monica, California. He is buried at Hillside Memorial Park in Los Angeles, California.

Greene was married in 1940 to Rita Hands, whom he divorced in 1960. With her he had twins, daughter Belinda Susan and son Charles (born in 1945). In 1960 he married actress Nancy Anne Deale of Toronto (professionally known as Lisa Cummings) with whom he had daughter Gillian Donna, born in 1968. He was survived by his wife, three children and two grandchildren.

Lorne Greene Filmography

1954: *The Silver Chalice.*
1955: *Tight Spot.*
1956: *Autumn Leaves.*
1957: *The Hard Man, Peyton Place.*
1958: *The Gift of Love, Last of the Fast Guns, The Buccaneer.*
1959: *The Trap, The Hangman.*
1961: *The Errand Boy* (cameo).
1966: *Waco* (sang title song only).
1969: *Destiny of a Spy* (TV).
1971: *The Harness* (TV).
1974: *Earthquake.*
1975: *Tidal Wave, Nevada Smith* (TV), *Griff: Man on the Outside* (TV).
1977: *SST—Death Flight (*a.k.a. *SST: Disaster in the Sky)* (TV), *The Trial of Lee Harvey Oswald* (TV).
1979: *Battlestar Galactica* (TV).
1980: *Klondike Fever, A Time for Miracles* (TV).
1981: *Code Red* (TV).
1986: *Vasectomy: A Delicate Matter.*
1987: *The Alamo: 13 Days to Glory* (TV).

Television Series

1956: *Sailor of Fortune* as Captain Grant Mitchell.
1959–1973: *Bonanza* as Ben Cartwright.
1973–1974: *Griff* as Wade Griffin.
1978–1980: *Battlestar Galactica* as Commander Adama.
1981–1982: *Code Red* as Battalion Chief Joe Rorchek.

Miniseries

1976: *The Moneychangers.*
1977: *Roots.*
1978: *The Bastard.*

Sources

Barton, Dick. "Where Are They Now?" *Sunday Express* newspaper, October 1985.
Current Biography. New York: H.W. Wilson, 1967.
Miller, Lee O. *The Great Cowboy Stars of Movies and Television.* New Rochelle, NY: Arlington House, 1979.
Picture Show Annual. London: Amalgamated Press, 1958.
Rovin, Jeff. *TV Babylon.* New York: Signet, 1987.
Shapiro, Melany. *Bonanza: The Unofficial Story of the Ponderosa.* Las Vegas, NV: Pioneer Books, 1993.
Thomey, Tedd. *The Glorious Decade.* New York: Ace, 1971.
Willis, John. *Screen World.* New York: Crown, 1988.

DABBS GREER

Dabbs Greer was born William Greer in Fairview, Missouri, on April 2, 1917, but was raised in Anderson, Missouri. He is the only son of a pharmacist father and a drama teacher mother. He made his stage debut in a Children's Theater Production of *Cinderella* in 1925. After graduating from Drury College in Springfield, Missouri, in 1939, he went on to become head of the drama department in Mountain Grove, Missouri, for four years. Next he joined the staff of the Pasadena Playhouse for the next seven years.

He made his screen debut in *The Black Book* (1949). On television he played the role of a Dodge City storekeeper for the first five seasons of *Gunsmoke.* He has made in excess of 500 television appearances of which his best known role was playing the Reverend in *Little House On The Prairie.* At last report he was residing in Pasadena.

Dabbs Greer Filmography

1949: *Reign of Terror (*a.k.a. *The Black Book).*
1950: *Try and Get Me, Storm Warning, The Damned Don't Cry, Trial Without Jury, California Passage.*
1951: *Call Me Mister, The Unknown Man, The Lady from Texas, Father's Little Dividend.*
1952: *Room for One More, Million Dollar Mermaid, Because of You, The Bad and the Beautiful, Scarlet Angel, Sally and St. Anne, Deadline—U.S.A., Monkey Business, Diplomatic Courier, We're Not Married.*
1953: *Dream Wife, House of Wax, Affair with a Stranger, Half a Hero, China Venture, Mission Over Korea, Mister Scoutmaster, A Slight Case of Larceny, Trouble Along the Way, Remains to Be Seen, Above and Beyond.*
1954: *Living It Up, Riot in Cell Block* 11, *Bitter Creek, The Desperado, Private Hell 36, She Couldn't Say No, Lucky Me, Rose Marie.*
1955: *Foxfire, An Annapolis Story, The Scarlet Coat, At Gunpoint, Seven Angry Men, Hit the Deck, The Seven Little Foys, The McConnell Story.*
1956: *Invasion of the Body Snatchers, D-Day the Sixth of June, Hot Rod Girl, Hot Cars, Tension at Table Rock, Meet Me in Las Vegas.*
1957: *My Man Godfrey, Pawnee, The Vampire, Young and Dangerous, Baby Face Nelson, Chair of Evidence, The Spirit of St. Louis.*
1958: *It! The Terror from Beyond Space, I Want to Live!*
1959: *The Lone Texan, Day of the Outlaw, Last Train from Gun Hill, Cash McCall, Edge of Eternity.*
1963: *Showdown, Palm Springs Weekend.*
1964: *Roustabout.*
1965: *Shenandoah.*
1970: *The Cheyenne Social Club, The Boy Who Stole the Elephant.*
1972: *Rage.*
1973: *White Lightning.*
1974: *The Greatest Gift* (TV), *God Damn Dr. Shagetz.*
1978: *The Winds of Kitty Hawk* (TV).
1981: *Chu Chu and the Philly Flash.*

1983: *Little House on the Prairie: Look Back to Yesterday* (TV).
1985: *Evil Town.*
1988: *Two Moon Junction.*
1989: *Sundown—the Vampire in Retreat.*
1990: *Pacific Heights.*
1992: *House IV.*
1994: *Runaway Daughters* (TV), *Little Giants.*

Television Series:

1955–1960: *Gunsmoke* as Mr. Jones.
1965–1966: *Hank* as Ossie Weiss.
1974–1983: *Little House on the Prairie* as Reverend Robert Alden.
1992: *Picket Fences* as Reverend Henry Novotny.

Sources

Brooks, Tim. *The Complete Directory to Prime Time TV Stars 1946–Present.* New York: Ballantine Books, 1987.

Jones, Ken D., Arthur F. McClure, and Alfred E. Twomey. *Character People.* Secaucus, NJ: Citadel, 1979.

Valley, Richard. "Character Actor." *Scarlet Street* magazine, winter 1995.

JAMES GRIFFITH

James Jeffrey Griffith was born in Los Angeles, California, on February 13, 1916, the son of a boat builder. He had one sister. He was of mixed Scotch, Irish, Welsh and English ancestry. He was raised in San Pedro, California, where as a child he made his stage debut as Santa Claus in a play staged at the local Methodist church. His family moved to Balboa where he was educated at Newport Beach Grammar School. He was very musical and played many instruments.

With the stock market crash of 1929 and the Great Depression that followed, the family relocated to Tahiti and then returned in 1931 to Balboa, where his parents were divorced. After this the mother and children lived in Santa Monica. Griffith's later education was attained at Huntington Beach High School and Santa Monica High School where he focused on music, playing the clarinet. During that time he and his boyhood friend Gwyllyn Ford (later actor Glenn Ford) went around town trying out for all the plays. On occasion they spread their territory beyond Santa Monica and would hitchhike over to Pasadena where they auditioned at the Pasadena Playhouse. By the time he was 17, Griffith had acted in 70 plays and graduated from high school.

After high school he joined the Marine Corps, serving from 1934 to 1938. During that time he was bandmaster and music arranger. He wrote, coproduced and coarranged the musical *Stand By for Music,* which was presented to marines stationed in major North China cities. Upon his discharge he obtained a job as a reporter, but spent most of his time working with little theater groups in San Diego. He was also screen-tested by 20th Century–Fox, but nothing came of it.

In 1944 he was recalled into the marines where he became supervisor in production planning at Douglas Aircraft Factory. In 1947 he was discharged, after which he worked at a gas station for a short while. This continued even after a chance encounter with band leader Spike Jones won him a job playing with the band. With friend John Russell Daly he penned a couple of screenplays including *Whodunnit?,* which they sold to Paramount in 1948. They were doing a reading of one of these in an agent's office which was attended by a producer and writer named Martin Mooney. On the strength of this Mooney gave the actor a lead in a quickie movie he was producing, *Blonde Ice* (1948). The actor called in sick to the gas station while he was shooting the film. Afterwards he re-turned to pumping gas, but when the film was released and was seen by his supervisor, he was fired.

This scarcely mattered because this movie had given him the necessary exposure and roles as a character actor, usually villainous, that kept him in demand for some years. He had a hand in the scripting of some of these as well. His favorite role was as Doc Holliday in *Masterson of Kansas* (1954). Active in television from its early days, he appeared in several Western series such as *The Lone Ranger, Frontier* and *Trackdown,* where he had an occasional recurring role as the town barber.

His face appeared in excess of 400 television episodes, notably as arrow straight Deputy Tom Ferguson in the Western series *U.S. Marshal* which starred John Bromfield in the title role. The two men preserved law and order in modern-day Arizona where there were high-speed car chases and fistfights galore. The shooting schedule involved filming two episodes every week. Since he and Bromfield were good friends off-camera, they were always well rehearsed and had considerable chemistry together. Despite the grueling pace, it was a very professional set and frequently in advance of schedule. It was also enormously popular. Bromfield recalls, "Jim Griffith, one of my dearest friends, kept me and everyone else in stitches pulling tricks mostly on me. He loved to ask me who someone was with a sketchy description, just before we were about to film so that it would bother me throughout the filming."

With Hal Hopper he penned a couple of screenplays *(Lorna* and *Motor Psycho)* which became exploitation films that he also acted in. He also wrote scripts based on Louis L'Amour novels which were filmed as *Shalako* (1968) and *Catlow* (1971), but failed to receive the recognition which he deserved for them. He continued to work as an actor until 1978 when he was diagnosed with papillary cancer, which drastically curtailed his career. He underwent a successful operation and lived for a long time afterwards, but producers became wary of casting him.

James Griffith, 77, died at his home at Avila Beach, California, on September 17, 1993, of cancer; his body was cremated. He was survived by his second wife Elizabeth T. Griffith (known as Betsy); a daughter and son-in-law, Cynthia and David McColl; and two granddaughters, Angela and Colleen McColl. Shortly before he died he wrote a farewell letter to his friends which read in part, "I have lived a wonderfully full life. You name it, I've done it. I've made a living doing what I wanted to do."

James Griffith Filmography

1944: *Pardon My Rhythm.*
1948: *Blonde Ice, Appointment with Murder, Every Girl Should Be Married.*
1949: *Holiday Affair, Search for Danger, Daughter of the West, Fighting Man of the Plains, Oh You Beautiful Doll!, Alaska Patrol.*
1950: *The Petty Girl, The Breaking Point, Indian Territory, Bright Leaf, The Cariboo Trail, Double Deal, The Great Missouri Raid, In a Lonely Place, Young Man with a Horn.*
1951: *As Young as You Feel, Apache Drums, The Lady Pays Off, Rhubarb, Al Jennings of Oklahoma, Chain of Circumstance, Inside the Walls of Folsom Prison, Goodbye My Fancy, Payment on Demand, Drums in the Deep South.*
1952: *Eight Iron Men, Ma and Pa Kettle at the Fair, Wait 'Til the Sun Shines Nellie, No Escape, Red Skies of Montana.*
1953: *Botany Bay, Kansas Pacific, Son of Sinbad, The Kid from Left Field, A Lion Is in the Streets, Powder River.*
1954: *The Boy from Oklahoma, Jesse James Vs. the Daltons, The Black Dakotas, The Law Vs. Billy The Kid, The Shanghai Story, Masterson of Kansas, Dragnet, Day of Triumph, Rails Into Laramie, Ride Clear of Diablo, Drum Beat.*
1955: *The Kentuckian, I Cover the Underworld, Apache Ambush, Count Three and Pray, At Gunpoint, Phantom of the Jungle.*
1956: *The Killing, Anything Goes, Tribute to a Bad Man, The First Texan, Rebel in Town.*
1957: *Raintree County, The Guns of Fort Petticoat, The Vampire, Omar Khayyam, The Domino Kid.*
1958: *Return to Warbow, The Man from God's Country, Bullwhip, Seven Guns to Mesa.*
1959: *Frontier Gun, The Big Fisherman.*
1960: *The Amazing Transparent Man, North to Alaska.*
1961: *Pocketful of Miracles.*
1963: *How the West Was Won.*
1964: *Advance to the Rear.*
1965: *Lorna, Motor Psycho.*
1966: *A Big Hand for the Little Lady.*
1968: *Eve (*a.k.a. *The Face Of Eve), Day of the Evil Gun.*
1969: *Heaven with a Gun, Seven in Darkness* (TV), *Hail Hero.*
1970: *Dial Hot Line* (TV).
1971: *Vanishing Point.*

1974: *Seven Alone, Hitchhike!* (TV).
1975: *Not My Daughter, Babe* (TV).
1976: *Flood!* (TV), *Law of the Land* (TV).
1977: *Speedtrap.*
1978: *Desperate Women* (TV), *The Legend of Sleepy Hollow.*
1979: *The Main Event.*
1981: *The Adventures of Huckleberry Finn* (TV).

Television Series

1959–1960: *U.S. Marshal* as Deputy Tom Ferguson.

Sources

Correspondence between John Bromfield and the author.
Goldrup, Tom, and Jim Goldrup. *Feature Players: The Stories Behind the Faces Volume #2.* Published privately 1992.
McClure, Arthur F., and Ken D. Jones. *Heroes, Heavies and Sagebrush.* South Brunswick and New York: Barnes, 1972.
Magers, Boyd. *Western Clippings* magazine, 1993
Twomey, Alfred E., and Arthur F. McClure. *The Versatiles.* South Brunswick and New York: Barnes, 1969.

KEVIN HAGEN

Kevin Hagen was born Don Thomas Hagen in Chicago, Illinois, in 1928, the son of professional dancers. During World War II his family relocated to Portland, Oregon, where he attended Jefferson High School. He sang in a choir, took voice lessons and was taught dancing. After graduating from the University of Southern California with a B.A. degree in International Relations, he worked for the government in Wiesbaden, Germany.

Upon his return to America, he resided in California where he entered U.C.L.A. Law School. After a while he dropped out and tried a number of different jobs including banking, insurance and sportswriting. Buddy Ebsen's sister Vilma had a dance studio which doubled as a little theater in Santa Monica. Hagen read about a play called *Blind Alley* which was being staged there. He auditioned and wound up with a bit role as a policeman. He also worked extensively behind the scenes, an experience which he enjoyed. Subsequently he went on to appear in a number of plays. The turning point came when he played the role of Ephraim in *Desire Under the Elms* in which he was spotted by agent Meyer Mishkin, who signed him. From that time onwards he began to appear professionally in movies and television.

One of his earliest roles was in the television series *Yancy Derringer* in which he played John Colton, the civilian administrator of New Orleans after the Civil War. He is the man who employs Derringer as an undercover agent and to whom Derringer reports. He appeared in several 1950s Western series, first encountering Michael Landon in an episode of *Tales of Wells Fargo* in which Hagen played the leader of a gang of outlaws. He was not an experienced horseman, but he learned in a hurry. It turned out to be a baptism of fire when his horse ran away while shooting one scene.

Hagen subsequently went on to guest-star in a number of very popular television series, becoming part of the Irwin Allen repertory company and appearing in all his sci-fi shows. In this genre he is most fond of his appearances in "Elegy" and "You Drive" episodes of *The Twilight Zone.* His favorite film role was in *Rio Conchos* (1964) because of the beautiful shooting locations in Utah. He accepted the role on two days' notice while auditioning for a play in New York.

He was resting, selling cars at Beverly Hills Lincoln Mercury, when he was offered the role of Inspector Dobbs Kobick in the television series *Land of the Giants.* His character was introduced as a new adversary to the little folk after the seven-month gap in filming during the first season. He was hired because Irwin Allen was familiar with his work from other episodes in his series. Hagen appeared in six episodes during season one and a further three episodes during season two.

Then he became Doc Baker on *Little House on the Prairie.* This is his favorite television role because he was given the latitude to develop the character as he saw fit. Walnut Grove was built in the Simi Valley, northwest of Los Angeles, on vacant land which was built for Westerns. A later outgrowth of this was a one-man show which he has performed all over America called *A Playful Dose of Prairie Wisdom,* depicting prairie life in the late 1800s in general and the limitations faced by doctors in the 19th century in particular. He has also done two other one-man shows: *An Evening with Kevin: Songs and Stories* (1986), including songs by Billy Joel and Harry Chapin, and *Up Close and Personal* (1989). Disillusioned with the California lifestyle, he relocated to the country where he has been active in community theater, notably playing Judge Andrew Carnes in *Oklahoma.* He has also appeared in commercials to promote a local bank.

During the 1960s Hagen married the beautiful cover girl and actress Suzanne Cramer, who was born in Wiesbaden, Germany on December 3, 1937. She died prematurely in Hollywood on January 7, 1969, at age 31, of pneumonia; single parent Hagen has raised their son Kristopher, who graduated from high school in 1988 and later from college.

Kevin Hagen Filmography

1958: *The Light in the Forest, Gunsmoke in Tucson.*
1959: *Pork Chop Hill.*
1962: *Rider on a Dead Horse.*
1964: *Rio Conchos.*
1965: *Shenandoah.*
1967: *The Last Challenge* (a.k.a. *The Pistolero of Red River).*
1969: *The Learning Tree.*
1970: *Weekend of Terror* (TV), *Vanished* (TV).
1971: *Dead Men Tell No Tales* (TV).
1972: *The Delphi Bureau* (TV).
1973: *The Soul of Nigger Charlie.*
1975: *Gentle Savage.*
1976: *The San Pedro Bums* (TV).
1980: *Simon and Simon* (TV), *The Hunter.*
1987: *Bonanza: The Next Generation* (TV).

Television Series

1958–1959: *Yancy Derringer* as John Colton.
1969–1970: *Land of the Giants* as Inspector Dobbs Kobick.
1974–1984: *Little House on the Prairie* as Doc Baker.

Miniseries

1980: *Beulah Land.*

Sources

Georgala, Jeanette, Carole Lewin, William E. Anchors, Jr., and Cynthia Liljeblad. *The Giants Are Coming 1968–1993: A 25th Anniversary Celebration* of Land of the Giants, 1992.

RON HAGERTHY

Ron Hagerthy was born in South Dakota on March 9, 1932. He turned his attention to dramatics while at college, taking part in a large number of productions. Seen by a talent scout in one of the college plays, he was given a screen test and a role in *I Was a Communist for the FBI* (1951). He was briefly under contract to Warner Bros. For the first 25 episodes of the *Sky King* television series he played Clipper, the nephew of Kirby Grant. During the Korean War he was drafted, but not replaced in the series. Once he returned from active duty, he only resumed his career in a minor key. He eventually retired from acting and went into real estate where for many years he has been a successful salesman with his own company in Newport Beach. At last report he was residing with his family in Encino, California.

Ron Hagerthy (right) with Kirby Grant and Gloria Winters in *Sky King*.

Ron Hagerthy Filmography

1951: *I Was a Communist for the FBI, Starlift, Force of Arms.*
1953: *The Charge at Feather River, City That Never Sleeps.*
1954: *Make Haste to Live.*
1957: *Eighteen and Anxious.*
1959: *The Horse Soldiers.*
1962: *Saintly Sinners.*
1964: *Guns of Diablo.*
1966: *The Hostage.*

Television Series

1951–1952: *Sky King* as Bud "Clipper" King.

Sources

Lamparski, Richard. *Whatever Became Of? Tenth Series.* New York: Crown, 1986.
Picture Show's Who's Who on the Screen. London: The Amalgamated Press, c. 1956.
Summers, Neil. *The Official TV Western Book Volume #2.* Vienna, WV: Old West Shop Publishing, 1989.

DON HAGGERTY

Don Haggerty was born in Poughkeepsie, New York, on July 3, 1914. As a child he enjoyed sports. He was educated at Brown University where he became a champion boxer. He became interested in dramatics while attending a summer school for theater at Basser College, a famous girl's school. From there he obtained a job in the Federal Theater. He then played leads in summer stock at Woodstock New York, Worcester, Massachusetts and Suffield, Connecticut, among others. To supplement his income he also worked in New York as a male model.

After serving in military intelligence in

Don Haggerty in *The Life and Legend of Wyatt Earp*.

the army for three-and-a-half years, he appeared in a *March of Time* film series short about Alcoholics Anonymous called "Problem Drinker." This was highly regarded and resulted in him being sent to California to test for a role in *Pursued* (1947) which he did not win. Nevertheless he stayed in Hollywood and persevered. Some of his earliest roles were in Hopalong Cassidy Westerns. His personal favorites among his films were *Cattle Empire* (1958) and *Night of the Grizzly* (1966). In the former he played a blind man. In the latter he played Clint Walker's ranch foreman whom Nancy Kulp has designs on until his character is killed off by the beast of the title.

He was active in television from its very early days and racked up numerous episodics. He did a brace of syndicated series called *The Cases of Eddie Drake* (1949) and *The Files of Jeffrey Jones* (1952), playing a private eye in both. He also had the semi-regular role of Marsh Murdock, the newspaper editor, in the first season of *The Life and Legend of Wyatt Earp*. He made a memorable contribution to other Western series such as *Rawhide* in which he had guest appearances. Of all the series and features in which he appeared, Westerns were his favorites.

He retired in 1986 to Florida, where he died on August 19, 1988, at age 74.

Don Haggerty Filmography

1947: *The Gangster.*

1948: *Silent Conflict, The Dead Don't Dream, Sinister Journey, False Paradise, Gun Smugglers, Train to Alcatraz, Act of Violence, The Gentleman from Nowhere, Command Decision, Borrowed Trouble, Fighting Father Dunne, That Lady in Ermine, Pitfall, Angel in Escile.*

1949: *Scene of the Crime, Malaya, Side Street, Sands of Iwo Jima, The Cowboy and the Prizefighter, King of The Rocket Men* (serial), *South of Rio, The Crooked Way, Canadian Pacific, Rustlers.*

1950: *Mystery Range, The Sundowners, Dynamite Pass, The Kid from Texas, Storm Over Wyoming, The Vanishing Westerner, Armored Car Robbery, Gambling House, Vigilante Hideout, The Asphalt Jungle, Shadow on the Wall, Jet Pilot* (released 1957), *Sands of Iwo Jima.*

1951: *Mr. Imperium, Go for Broke, Quebec, Cause for Alarm, Rhubarb, Fighting Coast Guard, Spoilers of the Plains, Force of Arms, Angels in the Outfield, Callaway Went Thataway, Starlift, The Strip.*

1952: *Bronco Buster, Hoodlum Empire, Denver and the Rio Grande, Wild Stallion, The Stooge, Skirts Ahoy!, The Narrow Margin.*

1953: *The Roar of the Crowd, City of Bad Men, Combat Squad, Hannah Lee (*a.k.a. *Outlaw Territory).*

1954: *Loophole, The Rocket Man, Return from the Sea, Jubilee Trail, Phantom Stallion, Naked Alibi, Cry Vengeance, The Atomic Kid.*

1955: *The Desperate Hours, An Annapolis Story, Strategic Air Command, The Private War of Major Benson, Texas Lady, Mobs Inc., Air Strike, The Eternal Sea, I Cover the Underworld.*

1956: *Crashing Las Vegas, Calling Homicide, Somebody Up There Likes Me.*

1957: *Spring Reunion, Chain of Evidence, Footsteps in the Night, The Sad Sack, The Crooked Circle, Spoilers of the Forest, Back from the Dead.*

1958: *Day of the Bad Man, Cattle Empire, Blood Arrow, The Man Who Died Twice.*

1959: *Gunfight at Dodge City, Some Came Running.*

1960: *The Purple Gang, Seven Ways from Sundown.*
1962: *Hell Is for Heroes.*
1964: *Muscle Beach Party, The Killers.*
1965: *The Loved One, The Great Sioux Massacre, That Funny Feeling.*
1966: *Night of the Grizzly.*
1971: *Dirty Harry, The Skin Game, The Resurrection of Zachary Wheeler.*
1977: *The Incredible Rocky Mountain Race* (TV).
1981: *California Gold Rush* (TV), *The Adventures of Huckleberry Finn* (TV).

Television Series

1949: *The Cases of Eddie Drake* as Eddie Drake.
1952: *The Files of Jeffrey Jones* as Jeffrey Jones.
1955–1956: *The Life and Legend of Wyatt Earp* as Marsh Murdock.

Sources

Goldrup, Jim, and Tom Goldrup. *Feature Players: The Stories Behind the Faces Volume # 2.* Published privately, 1992.
Ragan, David. *Who's Who in Hollywood.* New York: Facts on File, 1992.

PETER HANSEN

Peter Hansen was born in Oakland, California, on December 5, 1921, but was raised and educated in Michigan. He was the son of Sydney and Lee Hansen. He attended Cranbrook Academy of Arts at Michigan and the University of Michigan for two years (1940–1941) with the intention of becoming an artist. He learned to fly before World War II with the Civilian Pilot Training Program. Consequently, when World War II was declared, he became a marine fighter pilot in the South Pacific, where he flew 80 combat missions and was awarded three air medals including the Distinguished Flying Cross. He finished the war as a flying instructor in Texas.

Once he had been discharged from the service, he and his wife decided to head for the West Coast because his father lived there. A close friend had been killed in a flying accident and Hansen went to visit the friend's guardian, who had once been a leading lady on stage to Tyrone Power, Sr. Hansen had a family and needed a job, so she set up an appointment with film star Tyrone Power. On the strength of the advice he received, he enrolled at the Pasadena Playhouse in 1946 and studied for two-and-a-half years. This was funded through the G.I. Bill. He earned extra money to support his family by working in a laundry.

All together he appeared in about 40 productions at the Pasadena Playhouse, but *This Happy Breed* by Noël Coward (in which he played a Cockney sailor) was the one which secured him a contract with Paramount, who put him in their "Golden Circle" of young talent. He made his motion picture debut in *Branded* (1950) and was making some headway when television boomed and he was dropped from contract along with dozens of others. He returned to the Pasadena Playhouse where he appeared in the play *Berkeley Square.*

This brought him to the attention of millionaire Huntington Hartford, who allowed him to stay in his penthouse in New York while he appeared in a play called *The Bat.* When that folded, he returned to Hollywood where an influential casting director landed him a role in a half-hour anthology television series. From that point he was off and running on television with appearances in several series. He had a semi-regular role in the Western television series *The Adventures of Jim Bowie* as Bowie's brother, but this was not one of the best of the bunch, and he has no especially fond memories of either it or the star Scott Forbes. He is much fonder of *Matinee Theater,* a live television series in color; he appeared in over 20 during a three-year period. The discipline instilled in him through this experience served him in good stead when it came to appearing in soap opera later on.

A chance meeting in church with the wife of Jack Parker of Grey Advertising ignited the next phase of his career. He was invited to

Portrait of Peter Hansen, who appeared in *The Adventures of Jim Bowie.*

audition to become the next commercial announcer for Plymouth cars. He was awarded this prestigious job and signed a contract for three years. Afterwards he had difficulty obtaining employment as a legitimate actor. Then a friend at television station KCOP invited him to audition as a newsman. He passed with flying colors and became Director of News and Special Events, writing and editing news items. This lasted for about six months until the station was taken over by a Texas conglomerate who brought in their own team, so he was out of a job.

He had a semi-regular role as a schoolteacher on *Mr. Novak.* During the 1963–1964 season he did a very shortlived daytime serial called *Ben Jerrod Attorney at Law.* The same production company was initiating a new daytime serial, *General Hospital.* He agreed to play a lawyer for a couple of weeks, but when they wanted to make the role a permanent one, he had to decline because of his other commitments. Another actor played the role for a couple of years, but when he left, Hansen assumed the role because his other shows were no longer on the air.

He first joined the daytime serial in 1965, winning an Emmy in 1979 for Best Supporting Actor on a Daytime Drama. He left the serial in 1985, but briefly returned. Later he rejoined the cast permanently in 1992. In addition to these acting chores he has guest-starred in several prime time series including *Police Woman, Cagney and Lacey* and *Golden Girls.* He and his wife Betty, to whom he has been married since the 1940s, have three grown-up children. At last report the Hansens were residing in Tar-zana, California.

Peter Hansen Filmography

1950: *Branded, Molly (*a.k.a. *The Goldbergs).*
1951: *When Worlds Collide, Passage West, Darling How Could You?, The Last Outpost.*
1952: *Something to Live For, The Savage.*
1954: *Drum Beat.*
1955: *The Violent Men, A Bullet for Joey, Top of the World.*
1956: *Hell on Frisco Bay, Three Violent People, A Cry in the Night, The Proud and the Profane.*
1957: *Five Steps to Danger.*
1958: *The Deep Six.*
1964: *Apache Rifles.*
1965: *Harlow* (Paramount version).

Television Series

1956–1958: *The Adventures of Jim Bowie* as Rezin Bowie.
1963: *Ben Jerrod Attorney at Law* as Peter Morrison.
1964–1965: *Mr. Novak* as Mr. Parkson.
1965–: General Hospital as Lee Baldwin.

Sources

Goldrup, Tom and Jim Goldrup. *Feature Players: The Stories Behind The Faces Volume # 1.* Published privately, 1986.
Modern Screen's Who's Who on TV. New York: Sterling Magazines, 1983.
Picture Show Annual London: Amalgamated Press, 1953.

TY HARDIN

In one episode of an obscure Australian television series called *Riptide,* a bikini-clad beach bimbo turned to her female friend and said, "I wish they held beauty contests for men." The object of this profound remark was the hero of that series, Moss Andrews, better known as actor Ty Hardin, who looked as though he was born to be a Western series star. He was tall and handsome with a prominent Adam's apple, muscular without being musclebound. He is best remembered for the television series *Bronco.* In a recent interview, actress Diane McBain described him as the star who least impressed her, noting that his nickname was "Ty Hard-on!" Veteran independent producer Sidney Pink recalls him as a great personality and a charmer but no actor, spending most of his nights in Rome and Madrid in the 1960s lustily bedding starlets in innumerable one-night stands.

Ty Hardin was born Orson Whipple Hungerford, Jr., in New York City on January 1, 1930. His father was an acoustical engineer who moved his family to Austin, Texas, in June 1930. Four years later he abandoned them. Hardin attended schools in Houston and Austin where his childhood was one of poverty. He then attended Blinn College in Brenham, Texas, where he spent a year on a football scholarship. After a four-year stretch with the U.S. Army, he returned to Texas A&M. University to obtain a degree in electrical engineering, again on a football scholarship. A severe leg injury spelled *finis* to his football aspirations so he turned to acting instead, playing his first major role in *Ah Wilderness* by Eugene O'Neill.

He had by this time married his childhood sweetheart, by whom he had a son and daughter, but when he decided to relocate to Los Angeles in 1957, his family did not accompany him. He worked for a while for Douglas Airport in Los Angeles in its acoustical research department. He decided to go to a Halloween party dressed as a cowboy. While he was looking for the prop department at Paramount to rent some authentic six-guns, he blundered into the offices of a talent scout who gave him a script and a screen test. A few days later he signed a contract which commenced at $300 a week, which was twice what he earned as an engineer. At Paramount he had bit parts in five movies, was a male model for a day on *Queen for a Day* and appeared briefly on *Playhouse 90.*

One day he dropped into Warner Bros. studios to see William T. Orr, Executive Producer for Television and son-in-law of Jack Warner. When he walked in, Orr screamed for his underling Hugh Benson. Benson exclaimed, "Lock the door!" which was the code for, "Let's sign him!" They bought his contract from Paramount, signed him for seven years and changed his name to Ty Hardin. Ty was derived from a childhood nickname, "Typhoon." When Clint Walker was involved in a contract dispute with Warners, Hardin was imported into *Cheyenne* as Bronco to replace him. *Bronco* made its debut on ABC on September 23, 1958. At first Hardin was insecure, which made him aggressive, but he had confidence in the studio and enjoyed his work. When mail arrived criticizing him for usurping the throne of Walker, this made him work all the harder to make *Bronco* a hit. When Walker returned to the fold, Hardin was rewarded by being given a series of his own called *Bronco.*

Bronco Layne was an ex–Confederate captain who was discharged from the army and returned to Texas only to find himself stripped of honor and his home confiscated. Bronco proved himself to be very much a jack-of-all-trades, working for anyone from the federal government on a secret mission to a humble ranch hand. His travels led him all over the state of Texas and elsewhere. There were 68 black and white hour-length episodes of *Bronco,* which was last broadcast on August 20, 1962. Although ratings-wise it was consistently the least successful of the *Cheyenne/Sugarfoot/Bronco* trio, they were still very high. "Duel at Judas Basin" (shown during the 1960–1961 season) was unique because it was the only one to feature all three heroes.

He made some features for Warners, but in the sixth year of his contract, when the studio had nothing to offer him, he went to Europe to shoot some movies. The most notable of these was *The Battle of the Bulge*

Ty Hardin in a beefcake publicity shot for *Bronco*.

(1965) in which he played Schumacher, the Nazi soldier who disguises himself as an American M.P. guarding the River Ut bridge so that he could mislead American forces when they come along. He shot films in such diverse places as South America and Africa. In *Riptide* (1965), an enjoyably straightforward action series lensed in Australia, he played Moss Andrews, a Madison Avenue executive who after the premature death of his wife journeys to Australia where he operates Riptide Incorporated, a charter boat service. It was produced by Ralph Smart, and the ubiquitous Chips Rafferty guested every other week in different roles. Hardin did virtually all his own stunts in this series.

He did not hit it off with Joan Crawford, his costar in *Berserk* (1967). He recalled her as a dominating woman who constantly invited him over to her place. Since he liked choosing his own women, he refused, which led to a falling-out. He scarcely fared much better when he did a British theatrical tour of *A Streetcar Named Desire* in 1969 with Veronica Lake. She nicknamed him "Try Harder." (Writer Raymond Chandler once dubbed *her* "Moronica Lake.") He now regards his European exile as a mistake because he had not really established himself in America as a big-name movie star with a string of hit movies. Although he worked steadily in Europe making between $35,000 and $40,000 a movie, few of them had much exposure Stateside. He blew his biggest opportunity when he rejected a paltry fee of $10,000 to star in a spaghetti Western entitled *A Fistful of Dollars* in 1964. He was also up for the lead in the *Batman* television series which Adam West won, but it did little for his career. Another reason he did not fulfill his promise was his formidable reputation as a ladies' man. Some producers believed they should have had the first pick of the nubile starlets, but when Hardin was around there were not many left. Many producers were so incensed in this direction that they refused to cast him in their movies.

When his film career petered out in the early 1970s, he lived mainly in Spain running a chain of laundromats. He allegedly had a gargantuan appetite. During a lunch bash held at Warner Bros., he consumed two shrimp cocktails, a 16-ounce steak, a salad, and still found room for a plate of avocado pears and two large apple pies. Perhaps this obsession with food is what led him to dabble in the restaurant business. He ran one called "The Fat Black Pussycat" on the Costa Brava and a bar called "Los Alamos" which served hamburgers and chili.

In the summer of 1974 he was jailed for a month in Madrid on a drug trafficking charge, Spanish police claiming they had found 25 kilos of hashish hidden in his car. Tried in court in the spring of 1975 after being released on bail, he was given a $9,200 fine. He sold his various businesses and returned to America shortly afterwards. He admitted later, "I had lost my drive to live. I was into smoking dope and drinking. I was just short of suicide when the Lord found me."

He was ordained as a minister and preached in tents. He filmed a 30-minute religious program *(Going Home)* that aired three times a week in 39 states on the Trinity Broadcasting Network. He lived in Prescott, Arizona, where he headed a small nondenominational congregation, his church being a room in the Hassaycamp Hotel. Eventually conflict between money and his principles led to a split, al-though he maintains that his dedication to Christ is intact. He also became involved in extreme right wing politics and published a magazine called *The Arizona Patriot* which at one stage was under investigation by the FBI. In 1984 he announced his intention of running for President of the United States on the Populist Party ticket, but nothing came of it.

Acting-wise his career has not fared well since his return to the United States. His first television job back in Hollywood was an episode of a failed Western series, *The Quest.* Many casting directors chose not to remember him because of his long absence, so he had to read for parts despite his experience. He became so frustrated that he formed his own production company ("Bookends") to make Westerns. His contention was that even though producers were making Western pilots, they were not selling them because the leading men were no good. He was one of several veterans in the telemovie remake of the classic *Red River* (1988). He played a sinister sheriff in a survival movie, *Born Killer,* released direct to video. His last film to date is the slowly paced *Bad Jim* (1989), about three badmen who buy Billy the Kid's horse and pretend to be Billy's gang. Hardin's unfulfilled ambition is to play a running role in a successful prime time soap opera.

He claims to have been married "around eight times," but history seems only to have recorded six of them, although it may be that he married the same woman in more than one ceremony. He married nonprofessional Nancy Jean Hunt in 1951; beautiful Warner Bros. starlet Andra Martin in 1958 (they had twin sons); former Miss Universe of 1961 Marlene Schmidt in 1962; Francine Nebel in 1966; and model Jeanette Atkins in 1971. He met his latest wife Judy, a divorcee with three children, when he was an evangelist, and they married in 1978. While they lived in Arizona they bred a small amount of livestock, but have since relocated to Grass Valley, Northern California, where a near-neighbor is Clint Walker.

Although he has several children, he has no idea of the number of his grandchildren since, with the exception of his youngest daughter, he never hears from any of his offspring. At last report he and his current wife were running an organic orchard, growing a variety of pesticide-free fruits and vegetables.

Ty Hardin Filmography

1958: *As Young as We Are, The Space Children, I Married a Monster from Outer Space, The Buccaneer.*
1959: *Last Train from Gun Hill.*
1961: *The Chapman Report.*
1962: *PT 109, Merrill's Marauders.*
1963: *Palm Springs Weekend, Wall of Noise.*
1964: *Boudine* (also directed), *L'Uomo Della Valle Muledetta.*
1965: *The Battle of the Bulge.*
1966: *Savage Pampas, Custer of the West.*
1967: *Berserk!* (a.k.a. *Circus of Blood), One Step to Hell* (a.k.a. *King Of Africa), Death on the Run, Ragan* (a.k.a. *Devil's Angel).*
1970: *Sacramento, The Last Rampage* (a.k.a. *Last Train to Berlin).*
1971: *Acquasanta Joe, The Last Rebel.*
1974: *Drums of Vengeance.*
1977: *Fire!* (TV).
1986: *The Zoo Gang.*
1988: *Red River* (TV), *Born Killer.*
1989: *Bad Jim.*

Television Series

1958–1962: *Bronco* as Bronco Layne.
1965: *Riptide* as Moss Andrews.

Sources

Ferguson, Ken. *The Boy's Western Television and Film Annual.* London: Purnell, 1963.
Globe Special: Where Are They Now? Boca Raton, FL: Globe International Incorporated, 1993.
Lamparski, Richard. *Whatever Became Of? Ninth Series.* New York: Crown, 1985.
Ragan, David. *Who's Who in Hollywood.* New York: Facts on File, 1992.
Woolley, Lynn, Robert W. Malsbury, and Robert G. Strange. *Warner Bros. Television.* Jefferson, NC: McFarland, 1985.

Note

A 1988 announcement in *Variety* stated he was returning to the screen to direct as well as star in *The Peace Officer* opposite some of his former Western cronies, namely Peter Brown, William Smith, Will Hutchins and Don Haggerty. After some stills were taken of these stars in Western costume at Hardin's house, the production was abandoned.

JOHN HARPER

Born in Columbus, Ohio, in 1929, John Harper originally worked as a busboy and house detective while studying at the American Theater Wing in New York. Later he took riding and fast-draw lessons so that he could work in Westerns. He played the part of Christ in the Hollywood Pilgrimage Play. At a comparatively young age he found himself frequently playing older men. For 20 years he played the Dodge City undertaker on *Gunsmoke.* The demand for less violence on television gradually reduced the call for his services. He married in 1957 and has two sons, born in 1962 and 1964.

Television Series

1955–1975: *Gunsmoke* as Percy Crump.

Sources

Raddatz, Leslie. "The Dodge City Gang." *Radio Times* magazine, June 15, 1972.

The supporting cast of *Gunsmoke*. From left, first row: Hank Patterson, Charles Seel, Woody Chambliss, Sarah Shelby. From left, second row: Howard Culver, Charles Wagenheim. From left, top row: Roy Roberts, Ted Jordan, Tom Brown and John Harper.

JOHN HART

John Hart was a tall, handsome actor with considerable athletic ability and a background which incorporated stage experience. He was the hero of two well-remembered television series of the 1950s which have been revived recently on television and video. In retrospect he was an actor who should have won more recognition, but as he explains it, "You'd get stuck making serials and little low-budget movies and you'd never get a shot at doing anything really good."

John Hart was born in Los Angeles, California, on December 13, 1917. He grew up in San Marino near Pasadena, where his mother was drama critic on the local newspaper. Since she reviewed all the productions at the Pasadena Playhouse, he was introduced to drama at a very early age. As a child he worked on cattle ranches, so he became an excellent rider. From the early 1930s onwards he enjoyed surfing at Malibu which is where he encountered Jackie Coogan, who became a close friend. He decided to become an actor at an early age, so he appeared in some productions at South Pasadena High School and later at the Pasadena Playhouse. A friend introduced him to an agent for the influential Myron Selznick agency, who signed him. Cecil B. De Mille knew him socially, so he made his screen debut in *The Buccaneer* (1938).

On the strength of that film he was signed to a contract at Paramount where he appeared in several films between 1937 and 1939. After this his option was not picked up, so he remained a freelance actor for the remainder of his career. World War II intervened when he

John Hart in *Hawkeye and the Last of the Mohicans.*

was drafted into the army, where he became a first sergeant in the artillery for a couple of years. Then he was transferred to the Air Service Command where he made some recruiting films before being moved to the film unit at the Hal Roach Studio in Culver City. Later he was sent to Japan where he saw active service in Leyte, Luzon and Okinawa, returning to the United States where he was discharged.

Once out of the service, he had to rebuild his career from scratch. He happened to be at a party at the home of actor Jon Hall and his wife Frances Langford when Hall suggested he appear as one of the villains in *The Vigilantes Return* (1947), a Western which was shooting at Universal. On the strength of this, he was invited by producer Sam Katzman at Columbia to double for Jon Hall in another film which involved stunt work. Hart proved so adept that Katzman cast him in the leading role of a serial, *Jack Armstrong—The All American Boy* (1947). This had a five-week shoot, which was a long time for a serial, and a generous budget. Although it did very well commercially, it did not lead to more leading roles immediately. He later starred in another Columbia serial, *The Adventures of Captain Africa* (1955).

He appeared in some of the "Red Ryder" films for Eagle Lion which starred Jim Bannon. He then moved into the early days of television, appearing in some episodes of *The Lone Ranger*. When Clayton Moore became involved in a contract dispute over money with producer Jack Chertok, a substitute actor was sought to replace him as the Lone Ranger. Chertok ran footage of Hart from these other Westerns and signed him to play thc Lone Ranger for a season.

He shot 52 episodes of *The Lone Ranger*, each one being shot in two days. He rose at five A.M., went over his lines again and was at the studio being made up by 7:30. There were two directors, Paul Landres and Hollings-worth Morse, whom he worked with. While one was shooting an episode, the other one was preparing the next episode. The scripts ran approximately 34 pages, of which they endeavored to shoot 16 or 18 pages a day. Since Hart was in virtually every scene, his workload was overwhelming. The salary he was being paid was negligible, but he was glad of the continuous employment. When Clayton Moore resolved his contract dispute with Chertok, he was reinstated as the character. Hart did not harbor a grudge because he was not looking to make a career out of the character, and the schedule was punishing. His association with the character did not end there, however. He has appeared as the Lone Ranger three times since on episodes of the television series *Happy Days* and *The Greatest American Hero* and in the film *The Phynx* (1969).

Although he had worn a mask while playing the character, he had become so closely associated with the role in the minds of some casting directors that they refused to cast him, so that he was largely unemployed for 12 months after that. His career revived when he was chosen to play Hawkeye in the syndicated television series *Hawkeye and the Last of the Mohicans,* with Lon Chaney, Jr., as his faithful Indian companion Chingachgook. It was inspired by the novel by James Fenimore Cooper. The series was shot in Canada, near Toronto, on a financial arrangement called "The E Plan," where several of the production side of the series had to be of either Canadian or English nationality.

He spent 12 months in Canada shooting the series. Most of the actors who appeared in it lived around Toronto, the center of the Canadian television industry. In contrast to his previous television series, the shooting schedule was an easy one, one episode being shot every four days. The series is generally deemed to be the first filmed Canadian television series of the fledgling industry there. Although it proved to be extremely popular, it lasted for only 39 episodes. It was produced by the Independent Television Corporation and the Canadian Broadcasting System and was a half-hour, black and white series. The problem which he then faced was that, having been out of circulation for a year in Hollywood, he virtually had to begin his career all over again.

Later he appeared in episodes of television series such as *Fury, The Adventures of Rin Tin Tin, Highway Patrol* and *Sgt. Preston of the Yukon.* He appeared mostly as a drover on some episodes of *Rawhide,* but in "Incident of the Champagne Bottles" he played a sinister gunman. He directed and photographed a film called *Sloane* in the Philippines. During the 1970s he moved over to the production side of the business and had a behind-the-scenes job on the television series *Quincy M.E.* with Jack Klugman.

His last major acting appearance came in *the Legend of the Lone Ranger* (1981), an extremely poor attempt to revive the character in which Hart played a frontier newspaper editor who is murdered. He was cast in the role on short notice and shot his scenes in Santa Fe. Although his actual work involvement was only four to five days, he was actually on salary for closer to four or five weeks. In contrast to his meager earnings from his original involvement with the series, he was paid a substantial wage on this film. At last report Hart was living in Warner Springs, northern San Diego County, California, with his wife Beryl, whom he met while working on *Hawkeye and the Last of the Mohicans.*

John Hart Filmography

1937: *Daughter of Shanghai.*
1938: *The Buccaneer, Dangerous to Know, Tip Off Girls, Hunted Men, King of Alcatraz, Prison Farm.*
1939: *Union Pacific, Disbarred, Million Dollar Legs, $1,000 A Touchdown.*
1940: *North West Mounted Police.*
1942: *Wake Island.*
1947: *The Vigilantes Return, Jack Armstrong—The All American Boy* (serial), *Vacation Days, Brick Bradford* (serial).
1948: *Tex Granger* (serial), *The Plunderers.*
1949: *Joe Palooka in the Counterpunch, The Cowboy and the Prizefighter, The Fighting Redhead.*
1950: *State Penitentiary, Champagne For Caesar, Hit Parage of 1951.*
1951: *Belle Le Grand, The Wild Blue Yonder, Warpath, Stagecoach Driver, The Longhorn, Texas Lawmen, Stage to Blue River, Colorado Ambush, Fury of the Congo.*
1952: *Texas City, Kansas Territory, Waco, Dead Man's Trail.*
1953: *Gunfighters of the North West* (serial).
1954: *The Man Who Loved Redheads.*
1955: *The Adventures of Captain Africa* (serial), *The Crooked Web, Dial Red 0, Last of the Desperadoes.*
1956: *The Ten Commandments, Perils of the Wilderness* (serial).
1959: *The Shaggy Dog.*
1960: *Noose for a Gunman.*
1961: *Ada.*
1962: *Billy Rose's Jumbo.*
1963: *Captain Newman M.D.*
1965: *The Cincinnati Kid.*
1969: *The Phynx.*
1971: *Simon King of the Witches.*
1972: *Santee.*
1975: *The Gemini Affair.*
1976: *The Astral Factor (*released as *Invisible Strangler* in 1984*).*
1981: *The Legend of the Lone Ranger.*

Television Series

1952–1954: *The Lone Ranger* as The Lone Ranger.
1956–1957: *Hawkeye and the Last of the Mohicans* as Hawkeye.

Sources

Harmon, Jim, and Donald F. Glut. *The Great Movie Serials: Their Sound and Fury.* New York: Doubleday, 1972.
Inman, David. *The TV Encyclopedia.* New York: Perigee, 1991.
Speed, F. Maurice. *The Western, Film and TV Annual.* London: MacDonald, 1958.
Van Hise, James. *Who Was That Masked Man? The Story of the Lone Ranger.* Las Vegas, NV: Pioneer, 1990.

HARRY HARVEY, SR.

Harry Harvey, Sr., was born in Indian Territory, Oklahoma, on January 10, 1901. With an inclination towards music he commenced his show business career in 1918 in Gus Hill's Honey Boy Minstrels. After this he appeared in many minstrel and burlesque shows. This led to assignments in stock and on Broadway. He relocated to Hollywood in 1934 and appeared in supporting roles in numerous films, mainly Westerns. He was sidekick to Fred Scott in four B Westerns from the 1939–1940 period. He is well known for his work in shorts with Leon Errol and Edgar Kennedy. He was also active on television. A semi-regular role on television was as the mayor in the Western series *Man Without a Gun*. Another was as the marshal of Mineral City on *The Roy Rogers Show*. He died in Sylmar, California, on November 27, 1985, at age 84.

Harry Harvey, Sr., Filmography

1935: *The Lone Wolf Returns, Ticket to Paradise, Dr. Socrates, One More Spring, Streamline Express.*

1936: *The Oregon Trail, Public Enemy's Wife, The Moon's Our Home, Under Your Spell, Theodora Goes Wild, Hitch Hike to Heaven, Ghost Town Gold, Country Gentlemen, Born to Fight, The Gentleman from Louisiana, The President's Mystery.*

1937: *Mysterious Pilot* (serial), *High Hat, Here's Flash Casey, Headline Crasher, Kid Galahad.*

1938: *Six Shootin' Sheriff, Man's Country, Rolling Caravans, Phantom Gold, Man from Music Mountain, The Painted Trail, Under the Big Top, The Spy Ring, Romance of the Limberlost, Held for Ransom, Gangster's Boy, Prison Nurse, Born to Be Wild.*

1939: *Code of the Fearless, In Old Montana, Rollin' Westward, Two Gun Troubadour, Lone Star Pioneers, Stanley and Livingstone, Pirates of the Skies, Daughter of the Tong, Street of Missing Men.*

1940: *Texas Renegades, Phantom Rancher, Pals of the Silver Sage, Ridin' the Trail, Deadwood Dick* (serial), *The Fargo Kid, Rollin' Home to Texas, Men Against the Sky, Mercy Plane, Wagon Train, Strike Up the Band, Sky Bandits, The House Across the Bay, The Fatal Hour.*

1941: *Robbers of the Range, Six-Gun Gold, Bad Man of Deadwood, The Spider Returns* (serial), *Obliging Young Lady, Double Cross.*

1942: *It Ain't Hay, Bullets for Bandits, The Rangers Take Over, Pride of the Yankees, The Mexican Spitfire's Elephant, The Strange Case of Doctor RX.*

1943: *The Return of the Rangers, So's Your Uncle, The Heat's On.*

1944: *Spook Town, Gangsters of the Frontier, Black Arrow* (serial), *Lady Let's Dance, Youth Runs Wild, I'm from Arkansas.*

1945: *Patrick the Great, Nob Hill.*

1946: *Cross My Heart, Sunset Pass, Crack-Up, Nocturne, Step by Step, The Falcon's Alibi, The Bamboo Blonde, The Falcon's Adventure, Genius at Work, Bedlam.*

1947: *Woman on the Beach, Code of the West, Trail Street, Thunder Mountain, Under the Tonto Rim, The Arizona Ranger, They Won't Believe Me, Beat the Band, Crossfire, Sinbad the Sailor, The Secret Life of Walter Mitty, Night Song, Dick Tracy's Dilemma, Dick Tracy Meets Gruesome.*

1948: *They Live by Night, All My Sons, If You Knew Susie, Train to Alcatraz, The Paleface, My Dog Rusty, He Walked by Night, The Arizona Ranger.*

1949: *He Walked by Night, Death Valley Gunfighter, Stagecoach Kid, Calamity Jane and Sam Bass, The Reckless Moment, Arctic Manhunt, Leave It to Henry, Dear Wife, Miss Grant Takes Richmond, Rusty Saves a Life, I Cheated the Law, Francis.*

1950: *Convicted, Cow Town, Beyond the Purple Hills, Rio Grande Patrol, Hoedown, Tea for Two, Emergency Wedding, Unmasked, Key to the City.*

1951: *Silver City Bonanza, Whirlwind, Rodeo King and the Señorita, Arizona Manhunt, The Big Carnival (*a.k.a. *Ace in the Hole), Footlight Varieties, Hometown Story, Storm Warning, Take Care of My Little Girl, Let's Make It Legal, The Hills of Utah, The Guy Who Came Back, The Day the Earth Stood Still, Superman and the Mole Men.*

1952: *Target, Barbed Wire, Wagon Train, Colorado Sundown, High Noon, The Cimarron Kid, Outcasts of Poker Flat, The Narrow Margin, The Sniper, Scarlet Angel, We're Not Mar-*

ried, Ma and Pa Kettle at the Fair, Thunderbirds.

1953: *Old Overland Trail, Bandits of the West, Last of the Comanches, City of Bad Men, Tumbleweed, Law and Order.*

1954: *Man with the Steel Whip* (serial), *The Outlaw Stallion, The Glenn Miller Story, Highway Dragnet, 20,000 Leagues Under the Sea.*

1955: *Murder Is My Beat, Wyoming Renegades, The Naked Street, The Second Greatest Sex, The Twinkle in God's Eye.*

1956: *Showdown at Abilene, Fury at Gunsight Pass.*

1957: *Man in the Shadow, Shootout at Medicine Bend.*

1958: *The Return of Dracula, The Sheepman.*

1960: *Polyanna.*

1965: *Cat Ballou.*

1966: *Ride Beyond Vengeance, The Trouble with Angels.*

Television Series

1951–1957: *The Roy Rogers Show* as Sheriff Blodgett.

1954–1956: *It's a Great Life* as Mr. Russell.

1957–1959: *Man Without a Gun* as Mayor George Dixon.

1962–1963: *It's a Man's World* as Houghton Stott.

Sources

Brooks, Tim. *The Complete Directory to Prime Time TV Stars 1946–Present.* New York: Ballantine Books, 1987.

McClure, Arthur F,. and Ken D. Jones. *Heroes, Heavies and Sagebrush.* South Brunswick and New York: Barnes, 1972.

Parish, James Robert. *The Hollywood Death Book.* Las Vegas, NV: Pioneer, 1992.

JIMMY HAWKINS

Born in Los Angeles in 1941, this child actor was one of Hollywood's busiest since he made his screen debut in 1944. He played Tagg Oakley, the brother of Annie Oakley (Gail Davis), in the Western television series *Annie Oakley.* It was his activities which frequently started the action. The series virtually ended when he grew too tall for Annie to pat on the head. He later appeared in the semi-regular role of Mary Stone's boyfriend in *The Donna Reed Show.* The connection with this star continued when he sat on the board of the Donna Reed Foundation, which awards college scholarships in performing arts. In recent times, however, his main source of income has been as a producer of movies for television in which capacity he has reportedly been extremely successful.

Jimmy Hawkins Filmography

1944: *The Seventh Cross.*

1946: *It's a Wonderful Life.*

1947: *The Sea of Grass.*

1948: *Moonrise.*

1949: *Caught, The Red Menace.*

1950: *Love That Brute.*

1951: *The Blue Veil.*

1953: *Mister Scoutmaster, Savage Frontier, The Women They Almost Lynched.*

1954: *Private Hell 36, Destry, Yankee Pasha.*

1955: *Count Three and Pray.*

1962: *Zotz!*

1965: *Girl Happy.*

1966: *Spin Out.*

Television Series

1949–1952: *The Ruggles* as Donald Ruggles.

1954–1958: *Annie Oakley* as Tagg Oakley.

1961–1962: *Ichabod and Me* as Jonathan Baylor.

1962–1963: *The Donna Reed Show* as Scotty Simpson.

Sources

Dye, David. *Child and Youth Actors: Filmographies of Their Entire Careers, 1914–1985.* Jefferson, NC: McFarland, 1988.

Ragan, David. *Who's Who in Hollywood.* New York: Facts on File, 1992.

Jimmy Hawkins with Gail Davis in *Annie Oakley*.

VINTON HAWORTH

Born in 1906, Vinton J. Haworth was active in films, radio and television. He commenced his acting career in Washington in 1925 and became well known as Jack Arnold in the *Myrt and Marge* radio series which lasted six years. In the 1930s he had a stab at a movie career with RKO Radio under his real name of Vinton Haworth, but then used the name of Jack Arnold from *Hitting a New High* (1937) until well into the 1940s. During the early 1940s he was at Universal where he mainly played bits.

Later he reverted back to his real name when he played the part of Magistrate Galindo, one of the foremost adversaries of the hero in the Disney television series *Zorro.* He continued to be active on television until his death. He died in Van Nuys, California, on May 21, 1970, at age 63, of a heart attack.

Vinton Haworth Filmography

1936: *That Girl from Paris, Without Orders, Night Waitress.*
1937: *We're on the Jury, China Passage, You Can't Buy Luck, Riding on Air, Danger Patrol, Hitting a New High.*
1938: *Law of the Underworld, Blind Alibi, Crime Ring, The Mad Miss Manton, Vivacious Lady, Tarnished Angel, This Marriage Business.*
1939: *Fixer Dugan, The Day the Bookies Wept, Sued for Libel, When Tomorrow Comes, That's Right You're Wrong.*
1940: *Millionaires in Prison, Enemy Agent, Danger on Wheels, Mexican Spitfire Out West, Cross Country Romance, Margie, Oh Johnny How You Can Love, Framed, Love Honor and Oh Baby!*
1941: *Two Faced Woman, Lucky Devils, The Mexican Spitfire's Baby, Tillie the Toiler, New York Town, The Saint in Palm Springs, Playmates.*
1942: *Juke Box Jenny, Mexican Spitfire's Elephant, Junior G-Men of the Air* (serial), *You're Telling Me, Spy Smasher* (serial), *Saboteur, Behind the Eight Ball.*
1943: *Ladies Day.*
1956: *The Girl He Left Behind, The Great Man.*
1961: *The Police Dog Story.*
1964: *Quick Let's Get Married (*a.k.a. *The Confession).*
1966: *Chamber of Horrors.*

Television Series

1957–1959: *Zorro* as Magistrate Galindo.
1969–1970: *I Dream of Jeannie* as General Winfield Schaeffer.

Sources

Brooks, Tim. *The Complete Directory to Prime Time TV Stars 1946–Present.* New York: Ballantine Books, 1987.
Jones, Ken D., Arthur F. McClure, and Alfred E. Twomey. *Character People.* Secaucus, NJ: Citadel, 1979.
Ragan, David. *Who's Who in Hollywood.* New York: Facts on File, 1992.

RUSSELL HAYDEN

Russell Hayden was born either Pate or Hayden Michael Lucid on a large spread in Chico, California, on June 10, 1910. He had an itinerant childhood, moving all over the West. As a teenager he left home and eventually found his way to Hollywood. His first job in the movie industry was as a studio grip at Universal, after which he became a member of the sound recording department at Paramount. He graduated to the position of film cutter, was promoted to assistant cameraman, and finally became a production manager for producer Harry "Pop" Sherman (creator of the Hopalong Cassidy series which starred William Boyd).

When James Ellison, who played the young sidekick of Cassidy, left the series, Sherman chose Pate Lucid to replace him. Since Russell Harlan had been assistant cameraman on many of these films, Lucid changed his name to one which was a derivation of Harlan's. Under the name of Russell Hayden, he made his screen debut as Lucky Jenkins riding a horse called Banjo in *Hills of Old Wyoming* (1937). There were numerous Cassidy films following that benefited from good plotting, exciting action sequences and picturesque locations. In later years Hayden recalled these films and the camaraderie on the sets with great fondness. Hayden also appeared in Western remakes which Harry Sherman produced from Zane Grey novels.

Columbia Pictures lured him away from Sherman on the strength of additional remuneration together with a series of his own. Instead, he found himself supporting Charles Starrett in eight Westerns before landing his own series. This enabled Hayden to be voted among the top ten moneymaking Western stars of 1943 and 1944 in the *Motion Picture Herald* Fame Poll. During World War II he was drafted and served in the U.S. Army until 1946. Upon his discharge, he returned to Hollywood to star in a series of four films for Screen Guild in which he played a Royal Canadian Mounted Policeman. These were based on stories by James Oliver Curwood and were short on running time. In 1950 he costarred with James Ellison and coproduced an extremely low budget series of six Westerns. Costs were rigidly controlled by identical casts wearing the same clothes in the same locations, which made the films virtually indistinguishable from another.

As early as 1950 Hayden was starring on ABC in a shortlived Western series called *The Marshal of Gunsight Pass* in the title role. This was a cheap series with the sets and stunting at a primitive level. It was shown live on the West Coast. Hayden had come and gone within a few episodes. He abdicated his declining movie career and instead concentrated on being the producer and star of television Western series, becoming executive producer and vice president of his own company, Quintet.

He starred along with Jackie Coogan in a series called *Cowboy G Men* (1954–1955). This was a syndicated series which Hayden coproduced along with Henry Donovan in which he and Coogan played two undercover agents working for the government. There were 39 half-hour, black and white shows (shot on location in Chatsworth) which proved to be extremely popular, particularly with younger audiences. Hayden's background in all aspects of production proved to be advantageous here because it had substantially better production values than his previous television effort. He also understood the merit of publicity because he and Jackie Coogan made constant personal appearances all over the country to the delight of fans. As a performer, this was Hayden's most memorable contribution to television.

He later produced two other Western series. There was *Judge Roy Bean* (1955–1956) which starred Edgar Buchanan, where Hayden had the semi-regular role of Steve, a Texas Ranger. There was also *26 Men* (1957–1959) starring Tristram Coffin, shot on location in Arizona. He also directed some episodes of this series. There were ugly but unconfirmed reports that this series ended in acrimony when the backers went bust and failed to pay Hayden the salary he was due. Afterwards he became an assistant director with Malcolm Howard Television Productions.

He divided his time between a home in North Hollywood and a 200-acre ranch near Palm Springs. This was later opened to the public as Old Pioneer Town and boasted over $250,000 worth of genuine Western memorabilia which were used in the making of his films and television series. Towards the end of his life the actor was virtually blind. He died in Palm Springs on June 9, 1981, of viral pneumonia the day before his 71st birthday. In 1939 he married the actress Jan Clayton, but they were divorced in 1946. With her he had a daughter, Sandra Jane, who was born in 1940. She died tragically in 1956 when the new Cadillac which her parents had bought her collided with another car. In 1946 he wed 20th Century–Fox starlet Lillian Porter, known as "Mousie," who died in 1997.

Russell Hayden Filmography

1937: *Hills of Old Wyoming, Rustler's Valley, North of the Rio Grande.*

1938: *Partners of the Plains, Cassidy of the Bar 20, Heart of Arizona, Bar 20 Justice, Pride of the West, In Old Mexico, Sunset Trail, The Frontiersman, Mysterious Rider (*a.k.a. *Mark of the Avenger).*

1939: *Silver on the Sage, Renegade Trail, Range War, Law of the Pampas, Heritage of the Desert.*

1940: *Santa Fe Marshal, The Showdown, Hidden Gold, Stagecoach War, 3 Men from Texas, Knights of the Range, The Light of Western Stars.*

1941: *Doomed Caravan, In Old Colorado, Border Vigilantes, Pirates on Horseback, Wide Open Town, The Royal Mounted Patrol, Riders of the Badlands, Two in a Taxi.*

1942: *West of Tombstone, Lawless Plainsmen, Down Rio Grande Way, Riders of the North Land, Bad Men of the Hills, Overland to*

Russell Hayden (left) with Stanley Ridges in *Silver on the Sage*. Russell Hayden later appeared in *Marshal of Gunsight Pass*, *Cowboy G Men* and *Judge Roy Bean*.

Deadwood, The Lone Prairie, A Tornado in the Saddle.
1943: *Riders of the Northwest Mounted, Saddles and Sagebrush, Silver City Raiders, Frontier Law, Minesweeper.*
1944: *Marshal of Gunsmoke, The Vigilantes Ride, Wyoming Hurricane, The Last Horseman, Gambler's Choice.*
1946: *'Neath Canadian Skies, North of the Border, Rolling Home, Lost City of the Jungle* (serial).
1947: *Where the North Begins, Trail of the Mounties, Seven Were Saved.*
1948: *Albuquerque, Sons of Adventure.*
1949: *Apache Chief, Deputy Marshal.*
1950: *Hostile Country, Marshal of Heldorado, Colorado Ranger, West of the Brazos, Crooked River, Fast on the Draw.*
1951: *Texans Never Cry, Valley of Fire.*

Television Series

1950: *The Marshal of Gunsight Pass* as the Marshal.
1954–1955: *Cowboy G Men* as Pat Gallagher.
1955–1956: *Judge Roy Bean* as Steve.

Sources

Corneau, Ernest N. *The Hall of Fame of Western Film Stars.* North Quincy, MA: Christopher, 1969.
Holland, Ted. *B Western Actors Encyclopedia: Facts, Photos and Filmographies for More than 250 Familiar Faces.* Jefferson, NC: McFarland, 1989.
Lamparski, Richard. *Whatever Became Of? Fifth Series.* New York: Crown, 1974.
Ragan, David. *Who's Who in Hollywood 1900–1976.* New Rochelle, NY: Arlington House, 1976.
Tuska, Jon. *The Filming of the West.* Garden City, NY: Doubleday, 1976.
Willis, John. *Screen World.* London: Muller, 1982.

MYRON HEALEY

Myron Daniel Healey was born in Petaluma, California, on June 8, 1923, the son of Dr. Robert Healey and California Penney. His father was a noted proctologist and sportsman. As a child Healey performed on radio as a vocalist and actor and gave concert recitals playing the piano and violin. He was educated at East Central State Teachers College, Oklahoma. From 1940 to 1941 he acted in the legitimate theater and roadshow productions under the auspices of the Victory Committee. In 1941 he studied with Maria Ouspenskaya; by August 1942, he had signed a contract with MGM, appearing in some of the *Crime Does Not Pay* shorts and a few features.

In 1943 he volunteered as an air force cadet and graduated from the U.S. Army Aviation Corps. During World War II he served with the U.S. Air Corps and saw combat in France and Germany as a navigator and bombardier, being twice decorated. He was shot down by one of Germany's first rocket-powered fighters, but avoided serious injury. After the war he served in the United States Air Force Reserve, from which he retired in 1962 with the rank of captain. When he returned from the war in 1946, he resumed his acting career, going on to appear in over 500 television episodes. *The Man from Colorado* (1948) marked his first appearance in a Western, a genre with which he is particularly associated.

He has also written scripts, notably *Outlaw Gold* (1950), *Colorado Ambush* (1951) and *Lone Star Lawman* (1951). On the legitimate stage he has appeared in many plays produced in the Los Angeles area and has directed for the Santa Monica Theater Guild. He had a regular role on television for one season as Doc Holliday in *The Life and Legend of Wyatt Earp*, which ranks as one of his favorites. He also played Major Harvey, right-hand man of Colonel Francis Marion, in the short-lived Walt Disney series *The Swamp Fox*. (Healey replaced actor George Wallace, whose back was broken when a horse reared and fell over on him.)

His favorite feature film roles were as Andy in *The Longhorn* (1952), as the Sheriff in *The Son of Belle Starr* (1953) and as Rault in *Monsoon* (1953). He has been married three times, with two daughters by his first marriage and a son by his second. He is also a grandfather. One of his daughters, Ann, is a former Oklahoma beauty queen. In 1971 he married actress Adair Jameson. He has gone on record several times as saying of his career, "It has been most rewarding, not by measure of success, but by association with many wonderful coworkers." At last report he was residing in Simi Valley, California.

Myron Healey Filmography

1943: *Swing Shift Maisie, Salute to the Marines, I Dood It, Thousands Cheer, The Iron Major.*

1944: *See Here Private Hargrove, Meet the People.*

1946: *The Time of Their Lives, The Crime Doctor's Man Hunt, That Brennan Girl.*

1947: *The Corpse Came COD, It Had to Be You, Buck Privates Come Home, Down to Earth.*

1948: *Blondie's Reward, The Man from Colorado, Hidden Danger, Across the Rio Grande, Wake of the Red Witch, I Jane Doe, You Gotta Stay Happy, Ladies of the Chorus, Range Justice.*

1949: *Trail's End, Knock on Any Door, South of Rio, Lawless Code, Haunted Trails, Western Renegades, Gun Law Justice, Riders of the Dusk, Slightly French, Rusty's Birthday, I Was an American Spy, Brand of Fear, Laramie, The Wyoming Bandit.*

1950: *Salt Lake Raiders, Trail of the Rustlers, Pioneer Marshal, Emergency Wedding, Over the Border, A Woman of Distinction, My Blue Heaven, Abbott and Costello in the Foreign Legion, Johnny One Eye, The Fuller Brush Girl, I Killed Geronimo, Outlaw Gold, Between Midnight and Dawn, West of Wyoming, Fence Riders, Law of the Panhandle, Hot Rod, In a Lonely Place, Short Grass.*

1951: *Colorado Ambush, Montana Desperado, Bonanza Town, The Big Night, The Texas Rangers, Roar of the Iron Horse* (serial), *The Longhorn, Lorna Doone, The Hoodlum, Bomba and the Elephant Stampede, Silver City, The Wild Blue Yonder* (voice only), *Slaughter Trail, Night Riders of Montana, Drums in the Deep South.*

1952: *The Kid from Broken Gun, Rodeo, Desperadoes' Outpost, West of Wyoming, The Maverick, Fort Osage, Storm Over Tibet, Montana Territory, Apache War Smoke, Monsoon, Fargo.*
1953: *White Lightning, Vigilante Terror, Texas Bad Man, Kansas Pacific, Private Eyes, Saginaw Trail, Son of Belle Starr, Combat Squad, The Fighting Lawman, Hot News.*
1954: *Cattle Queen of Montana, Silver Lode, Rails Into Laramie.*
1955: *Man Without a Star, Panther Girl of the Kongo* (serial), *Rage At Dawn, Gang Busters, Ma and Pa Kettle at Waikiki, Tennessee's Partner, Jungle Moon Men, African Manhunt, The Man from Bitter Ridge, Count Three and Pray.*
1956: *Magnificent Roughnecks, Dig That Uranium, Thunder Over Sangoland, Slightly Scarlet, The First Texan, The Young Guns, The White Squaw, Calling Homicide, Running Target.*
1957: *The Restless Breed, Guns Don't Argue, Shoot-out at Medicine Bend, Hell's Crossroads, Crime Beneath the Sea (*a.k.a. *Undersea Girl), The Hard Man, The Unearthly, Cavalry Command* (released 1965).
1958: *Quantrill's Raiders, Escape from Red Rock, Cole Younger Gunfighter, Apache Territory.*
1959: *Gunfight at Dodge City, Rio Bravo.*
1960: *The Sign of Zorro* (TV).
1961: *The George Raft Story.*
1962: *Convicts Four, Varan the Unbelievable.*
1964: *He Rides Tall.*
1965: *Harlow* (Carroll Baker version), *Mirage* (voice only).
1967: *Journey to Shiloh.*
1968: *Shadow on the Land* (TV).
1969: *True Grit, The Over-the-Hill Gang* (TV).
1970: *The Cheyenne Social Club, Which Way to the Front?*
1975: *Goodbye Franklin High, Devil Bear, Smoke in the Wind.*
1977: *The Incredible Melting Man.*
1978: *The Other Side of the Mountain Part 2.*
1983: *V The Movie* (TV).
1986: *Ghost Fever.*
1987: *Pulse.*

Television Series

1959: *The Life and Legend of Wyatt Earp* as Doc Holliday.
1959–1960: *The Swamp Fox* as Major Harvey.

Sources

Goldrup, Jim, and Tom Goldrup. *Feature Players: The Stories Behind the Faces Volume #1.* Published privately, 1986.
McClure, Arthur F. and Ken D. Jones. *Heroes, Heavies and Sagebrush.* South Brunswick and New York: Barnes, 1972.
Parish, James Robert. *Hollywood Character Actors.* New Rochelle, NY: Arlington House, 1978.
Quinlan, David. *Illustrated Directory of Film Character Actors.* London: Batsford, 1995.

KELO HENDERSON

In 1905 a report was written by Joseph H. Kibbey, Governor of the Arizona Territory, to the United States Secretary of the Interior. It read: "Under an act of the Legislature approved March 21, 1901, an armed force of men known as the Arizona Rangers is maintained for the preservation of law and order in the territory of Arizona. The force consists of one Captain, one Lieutenant, four Sergeants and 20 privates, who provide at their own expense, their arms, horses and equipment. The members of the Ranger Force are authorized and empowered to make arrests and seizures of criminals in any part of the territory. Upon the arrest of criminals, the Ranger effecting the arrest is required to deliver him to the nearest Peace Officer in the county where the crime was committed."

The series *26 Men* dealt with these rangers, in particular two of them: Captain Tom Rynning and a new eager recruit, Ranger Clint Travis. It was a straightforward Western, full of action and rugged riding. The stories were obviously tailored for television, but historical facts were interwoven into each episode. What

Kelo Henderson in *26 Men*.

made *26 Men* unique in its time was that it was shot entirely on location in Arizona. It was extremely unusual for a television series to base outside of Hollywood. It gave *26 Men* an air of authenticity few shows could boast of in the early days of television. Arizona was the last state to enter the union (except for Alaska and Hawaii) and *26 Men* dramatized the last fading days of the lusty Old West. The part of Ranger Clint Travis was played by Kelo Henderson.

Henderson was born Paul Henderson, Jr., in Pueblo, Colorado, on August 8, 1923, the son of a rancher. At the age of nine he moved to Daggett, California, in the Mojave Desert area. From infancy he loved the outdoors and ranched with his father in Blyth, California. It was his father, Paul, Sr., who taught him to ride, rope and brand cattle, and how to handle a six-gun. They grew alfalfa and raised horses, cattle and buffalo. After leaving school he did a hitch in the Merchant Marines and then obtained a job as a foreman of a 450-acre cattle ranch in Malibu, California.

A friend who worked for Republic kept urging him to seek a career in movies and television. A couple of years slipped by, and it was only at the end of 1956 that he paid a visit to his friend at Republic. This friend introduced him to Harold Rossmore, a casting director, who in turn introduced him to an agent. This agent persuaded him to quit his job and move to the San Fernando Valley where he would be closer to interviews. The agent also arranged for him to have drama lessons with Josephine Dillon, who had been Clark Gable's first wife.

Soon he began to obtain small film roles. He appeared in *Gun Glory* (1957) with Stewart Granger, whom he helped to improve his gundrawing skills. Then he did *Saddle the Wind* (1958) with Robert Taylor, performing a similar function for John Cassavetes. (In this movie, Henderson's real-life son played the son of Royal Dano.) Henderson was so proficient at this that he was called upon to help other stars develop a fast draw. In particular, Warner Bros. asked him to coach Will Hutchins with a gun and rope before he played *Sugarfoot*.

The agent set up an interview for Henderson with actor-producer Russell Hayden. Hayden and George Shubert of ABC Film Syndication met him at a hotel in Beverly Hills where he showed them a short film of his equestrian and gun skills. Then he did some fancy gun twirling there and then which served as an audition. The two producers were so impressed that they virtually signed him on the spot. He inked a five-year deal to do *26 Men* with ABC. The two men were so impressed that they rewrote the pilot script of *26 Men* ("The Recruit") to incorporate some of his skills.

It was also Russell Hayden who changed Henderson's name from Paul to Kelo. The pilot episode was shot in Placerita Canyon in the San Fernando Valley in California. The balance of the series was filmed on location in Arizona. He started filming *26 Men* in Phoenix in July 1957. He did all of his own stunts in the series because Russell Hayden liked it that way. Many of the required skills he had already learned from his father. Others he acquired by speaking with the four survivors of the original Arizona Rangers. In the series he rode a horse called Travis, obviously named after the character he played (Clint Travis). Although Henderson's character was fictitious, the episodes dramatized were based on real incidents.

Henderson was a natural actor who enjoyed being in front of the camera. He recalls, "I had no trouble because I totally ignored it. When you are in the wardrobe and you have the armament under you, you really fall into the role." It lasted for two seasons for a total of 78 episodes, ending in 1959. It was one of the most popular syndicated shows in the world for years and in June 1962, the star was made an honorary citizen of the state of Arizona. The series was shot with the full cooperation of the Governor of Arizona and the Chamber of Commerce and did wonders for tourism. Each episode took two-and-a-half days to shoot, and they shot two episodes a week. Two of his personal favorite episodes were "The Avenger" and "Cave In." Once the series ended, he never saw either Tristram Coffin or Russell Hayden again.

He appeared in "The Brand," a 1957 episode of *Cheyenne;* "The Target," an episode of *Tales of Wells Fargo;* and "Escape to the North," an episode of *Sergeant Preston of the Yukon.* He enjoyed television much more than film because the pace of shooting was faster.

In the 1960s he accompanied actor Lex Barker to Germany, where he shot two films based on novels by the German author Karl May. The two movies were called *Der Schatz Der Azteken* and *Die Pyramide Des Sonnengottes,* both released in 1964. Barker played Dr. Sternau and Henderson was an American cowboy. The movies were shot in color, produced by Arthur Brauner, president of Central Cinema Company in West Berlin, and were coproduced with Avala Film Studios in Belgrade, Yugoslavia. They were shot on location in Yugoslavia and released in Europe but not in the United States. Henderson also served as technical consultant on these films.

Kelo Henderson has been married twice. By his first marriage he has two sons. Since the early 1980s he and his wife Gail have managed a mobile park home in the desert town of Ridgecrest, about 150 miles from Los Angeles. His hobbies (which reflect his abiding interest in the Western) are collecting oil paintings of the West and photography. He has kept up his prowess with guns and has a video released by Rimrock Video of Arizona which shows his skills. He is an extremely popular guest at Western conventions all over the United States; he also won first prize in the first international fast-draw contest ever held in America.

Kelo Henderson Filmography

1957: *The Last Stagecoach West, Gun Glory.*
1958: *Saddle the Wind.*
1964: *Der Schatz Der Azteken, Die Pyramide Des Sonnengottes.*

Television Series

1957–1959: *26 Men* as Ranger Clint Travis.

Sources

Correspondence between Henderson and the author.
Fagen, Herb. "Kelo Henderson: A Real Live Cowboy." *Classic Images* magazine, #228.

MICHAEL HINN

This small-part actor had one regular role on television: the scout, the ears and eyes of the army defending the Arizona frontier during the 1870s in *Boots and Saddles.* Many of his film parts were so small that they do not appear to have ever been recorded. He produced and directed a short Western called *Night Rider* (1962). He was in his 70s when he died in 1988.

Michael Hinn Filmography

1957: *The Halliday Brand.*
1958: *Escape from Red Rock, Gun Fever.*
1965: *The Bounty Killer.*
1969: *The Reivers.*
1971: *Valdez Is Coming.*
1972: *The Mechanic.*

Television Series

1957–1958: *Boots and Saddles—The Story of the Fifth Cavalry* as Luke Cummings.

Sources

Ragan, David. *Who's Who in Hollywood.* New York: Facts on File, 1992.

Speed, F. Maurice. *Western Film and TV Annual.* London: MacDonald, 1959.

EARL HOLLIMAN

Earl Holliman was born in Tennasas Swamp near Delhi, Louisiana, on September 11, 1928, the seventh son of a Louisiana farmer who died shortly before Earl was born. When he was one week old, he was adopted by Henry and Velma Holliman. Even as a child he was starstruck. When his foster father also died, he quit school at the age of 14 and waited on tables for $5 a week. At the age of 15, he hitchhiked his way to Hollywood to try his luck. His money ran out after one week, so he was forced to make his way home.

For a short while he returned to school but then enlisted in the navy by lying about his age. A year later the navy discovered his real age and sent him home. Back in high school, he studied hard and was first introduced to drama when he played a lead in the class play. After graduating from high school, he rejoined the navy. While attached to the base at Norfolk, he essayed the lead in a number of plays at the Norfolk Navy Theater. Upon his discharge he studied drama at Louisiana State University, but soon relocated to California where he attended U.C.L.A. under the G.I. Bill and joined the Pasadena Playhouse. He was spotted while there and made appearances in films from 1952 onwards.

His screen debut came in the Martin and Lewis feature *Scared Stiff* (1953) in which he had one line. His second film was *Girls of Pleasure Island* (1953) in which he was given a G.I. hair cut which he retained for 15 films. Small film parts eventually came his way and after Holliman gave an impressive performance as Charles Bassett in *Gunfight at the OK Corral* (1957), producer Hal Wallis placed him under contract and gave him the role of Jim Curry in *The Rainmaker* (1956), which brought him much acclaim.

His first television series was *Hotel de Paree* in which he played a gunslinger called Sundance who had killed a man in Georgetown, Colorado. He had been imprisoned for 17 years, but upon his release he nevertheless returned to the town to discover that the hotel was being run by relatives of the dead man, Annette Deveraux (Jeanette Nolan) and her beautiful niece Monique (Judi Meredith). The two ladies were running the hotel in such a refined way as if it were in Europe rather than on the Western frontier. This gave the series its rather odd title for a Western.

Since they were constantly being badgered and manhandled and made the butt of jokes by the rowdy cowhands and lawless elements who were present in the town, the two women were in desperate need of someone to protect them. This was where Sundance and his legendary fast draw came in. The gimmick of this series was that Sundance wore a black hat circled with bright silver coins which dazzled his opponents in a showdown. This series first appeared on CBS on October 2, 1959. It lasted for 33 half-hour black and white episodes until September 23, 1960.

As well as continuing his career in films, Holliman had two other television series. The first was *The Wide Country* (1962), a modern, hour-length Western which lasted only 28 episodes in which he played a rodeo rider who tries to dissuade his younger brother (Andrew Prine) from following in his footsteps. His best-known role was as Det. Sgt. William Crowley, the boss of Pepper Anderson (Angie Dickinson), in the extremely popular *Police Woman* series. In the 1980s he is best remembered for playing Luddie Mueller in *The Thorn Birds* miniseries.

Off-screen he is a tireless worker for animal welfare and is the president of Actors and Others for Animals, an organization dedicated to finding homes and taking care of animals. One privilege he treasures is the time he traveled to Africa to shoot a documentary for ABC's *American Sportsman* and spent two weeks with Dian Fossey and the mountain gorillas in the Rwandan rain forests.

Earl Holliman is single and resides in Los Angeles.

Earl Holliman Filmography

1953: *Scared Stiff, The Girls of Pleasure Island, Destination Gobi, East of Sumatra, Devil's Canyon.*
1954: *Tennessee Champ, The Bridges at Toko-Ri, Broken Lance.*
1955: *I Died a Thousand Times, The Big Combo.*
1956: *Forbidden Planet, Giant, The Burning Hills, The Rainmaker.*
1957: *Don't Go Near the Water, Gunfight at the OK Corral, Trooper Hook.*
1958: *Hot Spell.*
1959: *Last Train from Gun Hill, The Trap.*
1960: *Visit to a Small Planet.*
1961: *Armored Command, Summer and Smoke.*
1965: *The Sons of Katie Elder.*
1967: *A Covenant with Death, The Power.*
1968: *Anzio.*
1969: *Desperate Mission* (TV) (a.k.a. *Joaquin Murieta).*
1970: *Tribes* (TV) (a.k.a. *The Soldier Who Declared Peace)*
1971: *Alias Smith and Jones* (TV), *Cannon* (TV).
1972: *The Biscuit Eater.*
1973: *Trapped* (TV) (a.k.a. *Doberman Patrol).*
1974: *I Love You, Goodbye* (TV), *Cry Panic* (TV).
1977: *Alexander: The Other Side of Dawn* (TV).
1978: *Good Luck Miss Wyckoff.*
1979: *The Solitary Man* (TV).
1980: *Where the Ladies Go* (TV).
1981: *Sharky's Machine.*
1982: *Country Gold* (TV).
1987: *American Harvest* (TV), *Gunsmoke: Return to Dodge* (TV).

Television Series

1959–1960: *Hotel de Paree* as Sundance.
1962–1963: *The Wide Country* as Mitch Guthrie.
1974–1978: *Police Woman* as Det. Lt. Bill Crowley.
1991: *P.S. I Have You as Darning.*
1992–1993: *Delta as Darden.*
1995–: *Caroline in the City.*

Earl Holliman as he appeared in *Hotel de Paree.*

Miniseries

1983: *The Thorn Birds.*

Sources

Brooks, Tim. *The Complete Directory to Prime Time TV Stars 1946–Present.* New York: Ballantine Books, 1987.
Hyem, Janette. "Earl Holliman meets the real Gorillas in the Mist." *TV Scene* magazine, issue #3, 1989.
Picture Show Annual. London: Amalgamated Press, 1956 and 1958.
Skinner, John Walter. *Who's Who on the Screen.* Worthing, England: Madeleine, 1983.

Note

Some authorities credit Holliman with making his screen debut in *Pony Soldier* (1952) in the role of Tyrone Power's adopted son, but they seem to be confusing him with Indian child actor Anthony Earl Numkeena.

HAL HOPPER

Born Harold Stevens Hopper in Oklahoma on November 11, 1912, he played one of the corporals in *The Adventures of Rin Tin Tin*. He also wrote the musical score of this series and others (including *Circus Boy* and *Colt .45*). Hopper was a singer with the Pied Pipers. He collaborated with his friend James Griffith on motion picture title songs, and they wrote a screenplay which became the film *Shalako* (1968). He ended up one of four credited scribes on the movie. He later descended into pornographic movies. Hopper is reported to have been the uncle of child star Jay North and was instrumental in guiding his career. He died in Sylmar, California, on November 2, 1970, at age 57, of emphysema.

Hal Hopper Filmography

1964: *Kitten with a Whip, Lorna.*
1966: *Beau Geste.*
1969: *Mud Honey (*a.k.a. *Rope of Flesh).*

Television Series

1954 1959: *The Adventures of Rin Tin Tin* as Corporal Clark.

Sources

Goldrup, Tom, and Jim Goldrup. *Feature Players: Stories Behind the Faces Volume #2.* Published privately, 1992.
Miller, Maud. *Girl Television and Film Annual.* London: Longacre Press, 1963.
Perry, Jeb H. *Screen Gems: A History of Columbia Pictures Television from Cohn to Coke, 1948–1983.* Metuchen, NJ: Scarecrow, 1991.
Truitt, Evelyn Mack. *Who Was Who On Screen Second Edition.* New York: Bowker, 1977.

ROBERT HORTON

"My name is Flint McCullough. I ride scout for Major Adams's wagon train." Those familiar words were frequently spoken in the television series *Wagon Train* by Flint McCullough, alias actor Robert Horton. Of the character he played, Horton has said, "In the desire to know what made Flint McCullough tick, I have done a great deal of research. It has not been easy to plumb the depths of this man—at times so gentle and soft-spoken; at others like a caged beast, violent and unpredictable." Flint was the brave, handsome, dashing scout who supplied a big measure of romantic appeal, a feature which made *Wagon Train* adult enough to attract an enthusiastic, mixed-aged audience. Robert Horton is an intelligent, personable, physically robust actor, and one of his major attributes was his ability to play convincing romantic scenes with some of the screen's prettiest leading ladies. About this he once said, "Well, I'm certainly aware of it. I've been told I have lots of sex appeal."

Robert Horton was born Meade Howard Horton in Los Angeles on July 29, 1924. His family were predominantly professional people. He attended high school in Los Angeles. He volunteered at the start of World War II for the Air Force, but was turned down because of their stiff physical requirements. He tried the Coast Guard and was accepted. His interest in the theater was stimulated when he functioned as troop trainer for various actors. There was no worry about the future until he was discharged. He did all sorts of odd jobs until 1946, when he decided to study drama and entered the University of Miami, later transferring to U.C.L.A. in Los Angeles. After graduation he played a few minor television parts. He then decided to study at the American Theater Wing in New York. Later he appeared with stock companies. Eventually he returned to Los Angeles, where he settled down to build a career in films. He made his screen debut in *The Tanks Are Coming* (1951).

He was signed to a contract by MGM in 1952 and stayed there until 1954. His first Western was the studio's *Apache War Smoke* (1952). While under contract he did two films *(Pony Soldier* and *Return of the Texan,* both 1952) for 20th Century–Fox. Of *Return of the Texan* he recalls, "That was a very nice film with an excellent cast written and directed by Delmer Daves. Dale Robertson, Joanne Dru and myself were the triangle. Walter Brennan, a high powered and wonderful character actor was also in it."

He does not, however, have particularly fond memories of most of the films he made at MGM. He recalls, "The best film I ever appeared in was *The Story of Three Loves* [1953], an excellent film in which I had a charming scene with Leslie Caron." *Code Two* (1953), about the motorcycle division of the Los Angeles Police Force, he dismisses as "action adventure, not a very good film." Asked his feelings concerning *Bright Road* (1953), a story about Negroes in which he was the sole white member of the cast, he says, "This was a good idea, but they made two mistakes. Firstly, they let Harry Belafonte sing. He had the lead in the film and the singing was against his will because it threw the focus back again onto him as a calypso singer. The second big mistake was the character I played was a doctor willing to make house calls. After a discussion he goes to visit a black family, but the family looks like a middle-class family in Los Angeles. Half the plot went out of the window."

Horton continues, "At that time the studio signed actors who they believed had star appeal. I had the lead in a big film and received wonderful reviews. I was penciled in to do *All the Brothers Were Valiant* [1953], an epic directed by Richard Thorpe. Stewart Granger was to play the older brother with me as the younger brother. That was the first year that television began to impact on the picture business. When MGM made the movie it was with Robert Taylor and Stewart Granger."

By 1955 he was under contract to Warner Bros. where he did the television series *King's Row.* From 1957 to 1962 he was under contract to Universal where he did the television series *Wagon Train.* In spite of the fact that he had appeared in a few Westerns, he did not expect to play the part of Flint McCullough because it was said that he was not the Western type. Asked how he won the coveted role, he replies succinctly, "They tested nine guys and selected me."

Robert Horton as he appeared in *Wagon Train.*

It was while he was in the East that a call came through telling him that he had been signed for *Wagon Train.* "When I learned I was going to star in the show, I read through all the Western history books I could find to discover as much as possible about the frontier scouts," he said. Curiosity made him set off on a tour to find out exactly where the last century's wagon trains really went. He first motored to St. Joseph, Missouri, the original starting point of most of the wagon trains of the 1870s. Then he set out for Hollywood via a historic route touching Dodge City, Denver, Salt Lake City, Reno via the Donner Pass and on to San Francisco. "The trip," he recalls, "had a romantic appeal to me. I'm a great one for poking around, looking at plaques and cemetery inscriptions, and the whole journey gave me a good solid feel for the terrain our wagon train followed in the series." He also learned to speak the native tongue of the Sioux Indian. During this time he learned to walk as he imagined Flint did after long hours in the saddle—a sort of smooth-muscled rolling gait.

Horton was an unassuming man when he first started the series, and he was grateful for his good luck in landing such a break. When he flew to England in 1960 for a Royal Command Performance, a party of his fans met him at London Airport and presented him with a gold pen. One of his girlfriends said of him at the time, "Robert has always been involved in his work—that is why his first two marriages didn't work. He works very hard and never seems to relax when he's away from it. Sometimes when you're with him, you can't help feeling that he would rather be at a script conference or planning a new show." Even the actor himself admitted that he had changed when he saddled success. As he expressed it at the time, "Many people think I have changed in many different ways. As for me, I feel I'm more steady and certain of myself. I feel I have mastered myself. I am far more in control of my emotions."

Asked which were his favorite episodes of *Wagon Train,* he recalls, "I appeared in about 240 episodes. 'The Sister Rita Story' with Vera Miles was very indicative of the character I played. 'The Jennifer Churchill Story' with Rhonda Fleming was a charming story, a reworking of *It Happened One Night.* 'The Larry Hanify Story' with Tommy Sands was a very good script. It was directed by Ted Post and was very well done. 'The Old Man Charvanaugh Story' with J. Carrol Naish was a classic Western story with lots of action. 'The Earl Packer Story' with Ernie Borgnine was another favorite. Those five were about as good as they got."

Wagon Train ranked as high as second most popular series on television. Then star Ward Bond died in November 1960. Horton continues, "There was no wagon master *per se.* They didn't do a story that he had died. We got along without him. For several weeks I did scripts which had been earmarked for him until they got this idea of introducing John McIntire. In one show Lee Marvin played a wagonmaster who was none too trustworthy so they let the actor who replaced him top him in the story. John McIntire came in the spring of 1961 about a year before I left the series. He was a very good actor, but the chemistry was not the same as between Ward and myself which was about as good as it got." There are stories, though, that off-screen the hellraising Bond did not get along with his more conservative costar.

In the 1961–1962 season *Wagon Train* finally became the most popular series on television. "I left in May 1962, to do stage work," Horton says. "The crew wanted to give me a farewell party, but the studio didn't want that. They wanted as little publicity as possible. They were not very gracious when I left the show. In fact, I didn't work for Universal again until I did an episode of *Murder She Wrote* in 1989. I know Angela Lansbury very well and her husband used to be my agent. It's a very popular show, but this was not a particularly good script. It involved a priest who can't tell what a little girl has told him in the confessional. I played a close friend of Jessica Fletcher's. I was a red herring. Maybe I did it. They took out the only moment of the show which made you think that so I don't know why the role was in there."

After leaving *Wagon Train* Horton was under contract to Richard Rodgers and Alan Lerner to do the musical which subsequently became *On a Clear Day, You Can See Forever.* He was subsequently under contract to David Merrick for *110 Degrees in the Shade,* the musical version of *The Rainmaker.* He then came back to MGM to do the TV series *A Man Called Shenandoah* (1965–1966). "When I left *Wagon Train* in 1962, I thought I'd had enough of TV Westerns. I wanted to be in the theater, but I've learned a lot since then." This series turned out to be a somewhat bitter experience. Of horses he says, "I've ridden all my life and I became quite expert during my years on *Wagon Train.* I've always been fond of horses and I keep several at a stable about 15 miles from my home. In *A Man Called Shenandoah* I rode my own horse Smoky throughout the series." The actor was also heard singing behind the credits of the series.

Shenandoah was a quiet man with restless eyes who was constantly asking, "Who am I?" He searched for an answer by wandering from place to place, from face to face. He was always asking, seeking, searching and listening for any clue to his past. He was seriously wounded in a gunfight. He fled wounded and in agony from his assailants on a bitter winter's night in 1877. Taken to New Mexico by buffalo hunters, his life was saved by a doctor who had no idea of his identity. He was a man who wandered through life hoping one day to be welcomed back by those who once knew him. He had no memory of the past, no memory of his earlier life. Shenandoah was not his real name, and could not remember ever having had another.

Of the character he portrayed in the series, Horton said at the time, "I always play Shenandoah with a worried look in my eyes. For the poor guy is not only searching for an identity, he wonders on which side of the law he was in the days before he lost his memory. Was he a gunslinger? Will he ever recover his memory or did it go along with the two bullets which the doctor removed from him in a rough and ready operation on a billiard table?"

A Man Called Shenandoah ended after 34 episodes without a solution. Asked the reason behind its abrupt finish, the actor replies, "Who the hell knows why they decided to take it off before the end? The people who were running the studio, the head of MGM television, were stunned. It was up against *The Andy Griffith Show* and *Andy Williams,* the number one and number two most popular shows, it had a very poor lead in *Legend of Jesse James* and it had a very, very good share of the audience. The concept of the series was very good, but the majority of the stories were all alike, all did a disservice to me as the leading character. All except three started with me riding into town, dismounting and going into a bar. Some guy comes up to me and hits me on the head because he thinks I killed his mother. Everything was very somber, which is not my cup of tea. The executive structure at the ABC network changed about three weeks before it was canceled. I was going along with the concept that it was going to be picked up and then on the last day to renew the option, MGM called me and said the show had been canceled. I did not do a final episode like *Cheers* or *The Fugitive. A Man Called Shenandoah* just faded away."

He did a Western telemovie called *The Dangerous Days of Kiowa Jones* (1966), which was shot in the rugged, rocky region of 80 acres in Southern California known as Vasquez Rocks. He then became extremely busy in the theater and nightclubs from 1966 to 1969. He also shot a U.S.-Japanese coproduction between MGM and the Toei studios called *The Green Slime* (1968). Asked how this came about, he recalls, "The plot of the movie was the same as *Alien* and *Marooned* which were very well done. It was originally called *Battle Beyond the Stars.* I read the script and had cocktails with the producer and my agent. The producer told me, 'It is a film about the agony of command.' I said, 'It's really a kind of hokey science fiction film with a very good title. I don't really know if I should be doing this kind of film or not. It's fun to spend three months in Tokyo and Japan and the money's right, but I don't think the script is very good and I don't think it's going to get any better.' Then when I got to Japan and saw the Goddamn monsters! There's a photograph of me someplace feeding one of them a cookie ... ludicrous. Eventually it became a cult film and is frequently shown over here so I was quite glad I did it."

He shot two telemovies *(The Spy Killer* and *Foreign Exchange)* back-to-back in 1969. In them he played a James Bond–type character called John Smith, an ex-spy turned private eye. "I loved them," he smiles, "both acting in them and for the experience of working in England, which was a very civilized experience compared to the United States. They were designed as features abroad and in the U.S. as ABC Movies of the Week. The producer/director Jimmy Sangster was very successful at that time and there was some hope at one time that maybe they would become a series." He became very active in the theater again until 1982, when he went to CBS and spent a couple of years on the daytime soap opera *As the World Turns.*

His first two marriages (which included one to actress Barbara Ruick [1932–1974]) ended in divorce. In December 1960, he wed Marilynn Bradley, his leading lady in a 1959 theatrical production of *Guys and Dolls.* They appeared in nightclubs together and toured the country in shows like *Oklahoma, Carousel, Man of La Mancha, There's a Girl in My Soup* and *Zorba the Greek. I Do I Do* was their last together in 1982. They live in a ranch-style house in Encino, California, where he is semi-retired. Most of his hobbies were once sports- and body building-oriented, but although he keeps in shape, he prefers to concentrate on his interests of cars and flying his plane. He has eight cars, including an Astin Martin, a Morgan, a '57 Thunderbird and a '57 Chrysler, that he takes to auto shows. He has no children.

Financially he is very well off, mainly through earnings and investments. One fan whom he never met left him her entire estate, which was a substantial sum of money. Of his life and career ambitions, he says, "I can't say they have been fulfilled on the level I would like them to have been, but I did most of the things that I wanted to along the way. Most actors never even earn enough money to support themselves, so I've done well. I've been successful both professionally and financially."

Robert Horton Filmography

1951: *The Tanks Are Coming.*
1952: *Apache War Smoke, Return of the Texan, Pony Soldier.*
1953: *Code Two, Bright Road, Arena, The Story of Three Loves.*
1954: *Men of the Fighting Lady, Prisoner of War.*
1956: *The Man Is Armed.*
1966: *The Dangerous Days of Kiowa Jones* (TV).
1968: *The Green Slime.*
1969: *The Spy Killer* (TV), *Foreign Exchange* (TV).
1988: *Red River* (TV).

Television Series

1955–1956: *King's Row* as Drake McHugh.
1957–1962: *Wagon Train* as Flint McCullough.
1965–1966: *A Man Called Shenandoah* as Shenandoah.
1982–1984: *As the World Turns* as Whit McCall.

Sources

Ferguson, Ken. *Western Stars of Television and Film.* London: Purnell, 1967.
Globe Special: Where Are They Now? Boca Raton, Florida: Globe International, 1993.
Horton, Robert. *The Film Show Annual.* London: Robinson, 1960.
Hyem, Janette. "What Are They Doing Now?" *Photoplay* magazine, July 1988.
Interview with Robert Horton, 1993.
Picture Show Annual. London: Amalgamated Press, 1954 and 1955.
Salisbury, Lesley. "Dateline America: Why Flint Ain't Finished Yet." *TV Times* magazine, April 1989.
Speed, F. Maurice. *The Western Film and TV Annual.* London: MacDonald, 1960.
"TV Westerns: A Ten Page Special Feature." *Photoplay* magazine, July 1960.

Note

Wagon Train received three Emmy nominations, twice in 1957 (as Best New Program Series of the Year and as Best Dramatic Series with Continuing Characters) and in 1958–1959 (as Best Western Series), but failed to secure victory in any of these categories.

OLIN HOWLIN

Olin Howlin was born Olin Howland in Denver, Colorado, on February 10, 1886. He was the brother of actress Jobyna Howland (1881–1936). He started in show business as a vaudeville comedian. He appeared on the New York stage in legitimate plays and in many musicals. Although he made his screen debut in 1918, he did not become a permanent fixture in movies until the mid–1930s. Numerous films followed, but his only semi-regular television role was a minor one, that of Swifty in the marginal Western series *Circus Boy.* Ironically, his best-remembered film role was also his last: He played the first victim of *The Blob* (1958). Seventy-three years old, he died in Hollywood on September 19, 1959.

Olin Howlin Filmography

1918: *Independence B'Gosh.*
1924: *The Great White Way, Janice Meredith.*
1925: *Zander the Great.*
1931: *Over the Hill.*
1932: *Cheaters at Play, So Big.*

1933: *Blondie Johnson, Little Women.*
1934: *Treasure Island, Wagon Wheels, Behold My Wife!, Private Scandal, Marie Galante.*
1935: *Dr. Socrates, The Case of the Lucky Legs, The Case of the Curious Bride, Folies Bergere, Love Me Forever, Under Pressure.*
1936: *The Widow from Monte Carlo, Man Hunt, Satan Met a Lady, Road Gang, I Married a Doctor, Boulder Dam, The Big Noise, The Case of the Velvet Claws, Snowed Under, Earthworm Tractors, Country Gentlemen, Love Letters of a Star, The Longest Night, Gold Diggers of 1937.*
1937: *A Star Is Born, Mountain Music, Marry the Girl, Stand-In, Stella Dallas, Wife Doctor and Nurse, Nothing Sacred, Men in Exile, The Bad Man of Brimstone.*
1938: *The Mad Miss Manton, Swing Your Lady, The Adventures of Tom Sawyer, Girl of the Golden West, Sweethearts, Kentucky Moonshine, Little Tough Guy, Brother Rat, Mr. Moto's Gamble, When Were You Born, A Trip to Paris.*
1939: *Nancy Drew—Detective, Blondie Brings Up Baby, The Return Of Dr. X, Days of Jesse James, Zenobia, Gone with the Wind, Disbarred, Boy Slaves, Made for Each Other, One Hour to Live, Ambushed, Four Wives, Henry Goes Arizona, The Kid from Kokomo.*
1940: *Lucky Partners, Comin' Round the Mountain, Young People, Chad Hanna, The Doctor Takes a Wife, Young Tom Edison.*
1941: *You're in the Army Now, Shepherd of the Hills, Buy Me That Town, One Foot in Heaven, Ellery Queen and the Murder Ring, The Great Lie, Belle Starr.*
1942: *Almost Married, Henry and Dizzy, Dr. Broadway, When Johnny Comes Marching Home, The Man Who Wouldn't Die, Home in Wyomin', This Gun for Hire, Blondie's Blessed Event, You Can't Escape Forever, Orchestra Wives, Joan of Ozark, Ridin' Down the Canyon.*
1943: *Lady Bodyguard, Young and Willing, Secrets of the Underground, A Stranger in Town, The Good Fellows, Jack London, The Falcon and the Coeds, The Sky's the Limit.*
1944: *Allergic to Love, Since You Went Away, Sing Neighbor Sing, Bermuda Mystery, Can't Help Singing, I'll Be Seeing You, The Man from Frisco, The Town Went Wild, Twilight on the Prairie, Goodnight Sweetheart, In the Meantime Darling, Nothing But Trouble.*
1945: *She Gets Her Man, Sheriff of Cimarron Gap, Captain Eddie, Her Lucky Night, Colonel Effingham's Raid, Dakota, Fallen Angel, Señorita from the West, Santa Fe Saddlemates, Grissly's Millions.*
1946: *The Strange Love of Martha Ivers, Home Sweet Homicide, The Crime Doctor's Manhunt.*
1947: *Wyoming, Easy Come Easy Go, The Angel and the Badman, The Wistful Widow of Wagon Gap, Apache Rose, For the Love of Rusty, The Tenderfoot, The Fabulous Texan.*
1948: *Isn't It Romantic?, The Dude Goes West, Return of the Whistler, My Dog Rusty, The Paleface, The Last of the Wild Horses, Station West, Bad Men of Tombstone.*
1949: *Anna Lucasta, Massacre River, Grand Canyon, Leave It to Henry, Little Women, Hellfire.*
1950: *The Nevadan, Father Makes Good, Rock Island Trail, A Ticket to Tomahawk, Stage to Tucson.*
1951: *Fighting Coast Guard, Santa Fe.*
1952: *The Fabulous Señorita, Gobs and Gals.*
1954: *Them!*
1957: *The Spirit of St. Louis.*
1958: *The Blob.*

Television Series

1956–1958: *Circus Boy* as Swifty.

Sources

Perry, Jeb H. *Screen Gems: A History of Columbia Pictures Television from Cohn to Coke, 1948–1983.* Metuchen, NJ: Scarecrow, 1991.
Truitt, Evelyn Mack. *Who Was Who On Screen Illustrated Edition.* New York: Bowker, 1984.
Vazzana, Eugene Michael. *Silent Film Necrology: Births and Deaths of Over 9000 Performers, Directors, Producers, and Other Filmmakers of the Silent Era Through 1993.* Jefferson, NC: McFarland, 1995.

WILL HUTCHINS

Will Hutchins once said about his most famous character Tom Brewster, "I see him as a kid who can't help involving himself deeply when someone tells him a story about injustice. He doesn't go looking for trouble. That finds him easily enough. But there's a strong and dominant feeling for justice in him. After all, he's studying to be a lawyer and there's nothing like putting into practice the things you do learn."

When he first arrived in show business, Hutchins reminded a number of older fans of the late Will Rogers, his own self-professed idol. He talked like him and had the same kind of laid-back manner and personality. Physically he resembled Gary Cooper and James Stewart more. Warner Bros. was always trying to clone existing stars with young actors on the rise. There is no telling how high his star might have risen with good direction and the right, carefully chosen vehicles. The collapse of the studio system, which generated stars so efficiently, meant that he did not endure as well as earlier stars.

His fame, therefore, rests squarely on his stardom in one of Warners' most successful Western television series, *Sugarfoot* (1957–1961), in which he played Tom Brewster. This established him as a star at a time when most of the actors who were to dominate in succeeding decades were still struggling to obtain a foothold. It is ironic that his most successful role was in a Western series, when he feels that his real forte was physical comedy of a type seldom seen since silent days. Harold Lloyd once told him that he was the only contemporary actor who could successfully do that kind of stuff. His television luck ran out with two unsuccessful television comedy series and no less than three busted pilots. He did however make five pilots that sold. Academically he is the best trained of all the Warner Bros. Western stars. (Others, like Clint Walker and Ty Hardin, had little formal dramatic training). He is also the acting fraternity's most knowledgeable movie buff.

Will Hutchins was born Marshall Lowell Hutchason in the Atwater Village section of Los Angeles on May 5, 1932, the son of a prominent Los Angeles dentist and socialite. His father was married four times and died in 1947. He has one half-brother, Bill Hutchason, who is ten years older and who subsequently became an architect. His parents divorced when he was small. At school he was the class clown, and an early ambition was to be a burlesque comic and to play jazz alto saxophone. He studied drama at Pomona College and graduated with a B.A. honors degree in speech and drama in 1952. At college he excelled at basketball. After graduation he produced and starred in a musical called *Run for Cover* at the Ivar Theater in Hollywood. Richard Chamberlain was in the cast and Hutchins recalls him as "a very funny fellow in those days."

Drafted, Hutchins was stationed at Fort Lewis, Washington, for a brief spell. He undertook basic training at Camp San Luis Obispo, California, before going on to Fort Mason, San Francisco, and then SHAPE Head-quarters in Paris where he spent the duration, being honorably discharged in 1954 as a corporal. Of this experience he recalls, "I loved the army." He had a variety of jobs for a while including special delivery messenger, busboy, grocery store clerk and hand bill passer. Attendance at the cinematography department at U.C.L.A. followed for one year only. He was on the G.I. Bill with thoughts of be-coming a professional student when NBC's *Matinee Theater* came along.

He was discovered for the screen when he auditioned for the lead in an all-student production ("The Young and the Damned") for live television anthology series *Matinee Theater.* He won the role of a man who suffered the trauma of accidentally killing a young woman and then hiding her body. He tries to anesthetize himself into believing that he has not done it. The episode came off very well, largely thanks to his acting. This was one of four Matinee Theaters he did.

Various studios bid for his services, but he chose to sign a contract with Warner Bros. not only because he liked the style of their early films, but also because he wanted to do an episode of *Conflict* ("The Magic Brew") directed by Fred de Cordova, whom he ran into

Will Hutchins in *Sugarfoot.*

frequently when they both worked for NBC. *Sugarfoot* was expressly written for him, which was rare in Hollywood. Generally a series was planned and then a search followed for the right actor to fit the part. "I guess I was very lucky," he says. "The show's executive producer William T. Orr devised it for me. At the time I wasn't at all well known, but thanks to *Sugarfoot* I have had an exciting career." When asked where his change of name came from, he recalls, "Warners dubbed me Will Hutchins, I suppose after Will Rogers. They reckoned Marshall Lowell Hutchason was too long. My choice for a new name was Hutch McDuff, a burlesque comic at heart, but they were having none of that." *Sugarfoot* was first broadcast on ABC on September 17, 1957.

"Sugarfoot" means young, untried and inexperienced, one rung lower than a tenderfoot. Tom Brewster was one of the most gentle Western heroes ever to be written into a television script. He was a young man who preferred to use brains rather than fists or guns, but if he was forced to use physical violence, he could be as tough as any other television Western hero. By profession he was a law student who roamed the West while studying law by correspondence course. Generally in his travels he found trouble and a pretty girl. Executive producer William T. Orr said of Tom Brewster, "He's rather an anti-hero in a way, almost timid. He's slow to anger, but he has a strong sense of justice, and there's no holding him when he finds law and order being violated." Hutchins adds, "Today I'm as fast as ever on the draw—jes' takes me a leetle longer to get on my hoss."

Sugarfoot derived not from the movie *Sugarfoot* (1951) which starred Randolph Scott, but from the movie *The Boy from Oklahoma* (1954). The theme music by Paul Sawtell from the movie *Sugarfoot* was the only aspect of this film which was used in the television series. Hutchins explains, "Merry Anders played the leading lady in 'Brannigan's Boots.' Nancy Olson originally created the role in *The Boy from Oklahoma* starring Will Rogers, Jr., the feature flick directed by Michael Curtiz from which we spun off the TV pilot. Dennis Hopper played Billy the Kid in our show. Merv Griffin essayed the role in the Rogers, Jr., version. Slim Pickens played the same part in both versions."

It ran on an alternate weekly basis with *Cheyenne* from 1957 to 1959 and with *Bronco* from 1959 to 1960. For its final season it became one of three rotating elements of the *Cheyenne* anthology. Its greatest popularity came in the 1958–1959 season when it finished number 21 in the Nielsen ratings. It was never as popular as *Cheyenne,* but always more popular than *Bronco.* A favorite question which Hutchins was constantly asked around this time was, "When not busy working, what does he like to do for relaxation?" He replied, "I write poetry and do yoga and the five mystic rites of Tibet, 8mm home movies, jogging and bike riding (21 Speed). I love boxing and can think of nothing better than sitting in a cozy chair at home watching a title fight on television. I always wanted to be a boxer. Now and again I like to shadow box—you know, just fool around in the ring with other guys. Keeps me fit too." To this list he has latterly added writing a column for a magazine. He is also a jazz fanatic and at one time had a collection of over 800 records. Duke Ellington was his hero.

Hutchins recalls one amusing incident that took place on the set of *Sugarfoot:* "When I was practicing my fast-draw during the filming of the pilot, Slim Pickens snuck up behind me and shot off a full load blank cartridge from his .45. I jumped in the air pretty high, you bet, to the hoots and hollers of those assembled. Slim told me that he'd pulled that stunt on Audie Murphy and Audie didn't so much as blink." He also had to do plenty of hard riding in the series. Asked where he acquired this skill, he says, "I learned to ride one summer on a dude ranch in Colorado when I was ten. By the time we shot the pilot of *Sugarfoot,* I was once again a rank amateur. I had to fake it. When the pilot sold, it was back to serious lessons. The secret of good horseback riding? Hours in the saddle."

When asked which episode was the worst and which episodes he liked the most, he recalls, "Richard Long worked with me on an episode called 'The Vultures,' one of my worst efforts at Warner Bros.—it was sheer meller drama with not a hint of humanity nor humor—it wasn't horse opera, it was soap opera. Long, pro that he was, emerged unscathed. I, on the other hand, am still licking my wounds. ... I enjoyed working on 'MacBrewster the Bold,' my dad being a Scot [McHutchason] and all, our ancestral Scot name. I thought I created a good comedy line of action in that one. 'Apollo With a Gun' costarring the beauteous and charming Mari Blanchard was another favorite. Robert Altman did a bang-up job of direction and they spent a bit of money on it for a change. It was imaginative and had a lot of visual comedy. I got to play Shakespeare in tights. Another show I like is 'Captive Locomotive.' I saw it again recently and I thought it captured the spirit of *Sugarfoot* to the nth degree." The series eventually ended after 69 black and white hour-length episodes; the last original one aired on July 3, 1961.

By this time he had become bitterly disillusioned with the Warner Bros. sweatshop. He says, "Each episode took six days to shoot. One took seven, one took five—all the rest were six. We worked all hours with no overtime." He does however have some pleasant memories of working on *Lafayette Escadrille* (1958) with director "Wild Bill" Wellman. "He called me Shelley—he said my hair reminded him of Shelley Winters. In my first scene in the flick I wake up in the Air Force barracks in France in World War I and spot my old Stateside buddies. Jubilantly, I run over to them for a big welcome. I was quite skinny in those days and I asked Mr. Wellman if I could wear a T shirt over my skivvies. He said no, he liked me that way, bare-chested in droopy underwear, wearing an air force cap. A few nights later I was taking a bath in our garage apartment when the phone rang—it was 'Wild Bill' telling me how much he liked my work in the flick. He'll always be one of my favorites—they don't make 'em like that any more. Wellman told me that while directing *Wings* [1927], Gary Cooper came up to him after a shot and asked to do it again. 'Why?' 'I picked my nose.' 'Coop, just keep picking that nose and one day you'll be a big star,' replied Wellman."

Hutchins' final feature at Warner Bros. was *Merrill's Marauders* (1962) of which he recalls, "I loved working with Sam Fuller and Jeff Chandler. We shot it in the Philippines at Clark Air Force Base. Sam was indeed a wild man. He brought in hard-as-nails special forces soldiers to work as actors and extras and we were required to do all the stuff they did—no stunt men allowed." He was with Warners from 1956 to 1961. He was in the Philippines working on *Merrill's Marauders* in 1961 when his character was killed off halfway through the film. He was immediately taken off salary and sought employment elsewhere. After he left Warners, his first job was a $55-a-week role in *Will Success Spoil Rock Hunter?* at the 99-seat Horseshoe Theater in Hollywood. The only one from Warners to come and see him was his stand-in Chuck Hibbs. Hutchins adds, "They wouldn't allow my horse Penny inside despite the theater's name."

Since then he has made numerous stage appearances in *Mister Roberts, Here Lies Jeremy Troy, Paisley Convertible, Sweet Charity, Everybody Loves Opal* and *Bus Stop.* He worked with William Bendix and Nancy Carroll in the national road company version of *Never Too Late.* He is one of very few players who enjoyed working with Miss Carroll. In 1964 he replaced Orson Bean on Broadway in the same show and worked with Martha Scott and Dennis O'Keefe.

Interspersed with this show, there were some feature films, notably *The Shooting* (1965) with Jack Nicholson, Millie Perkins and Warren Oates. Hutchins recalls, "We shot *The Shooting* in Kanab, Utah, in 1965. It took us three weeks. It would have been two, but it rained one week and we got stuck in the mud. We shot it in sequence. Once I was in Paris in 1970 and *The Shooting* was double-billed at a little theater. I paid half price under the proviso that I not stay to see the second half of the bill. I enjoyed working out there in that weirdly beautiful prehistoric location. The best thing about the flick was Greg Sandor's smashing photography. Most folks don't seem to understand it. It's become something of a cult classic. ... I wasn't asked to be in *Ride the Whirlwind,* which was shot directly after *The Shooting.* Jack Nicholson rode the Whirlwind on the horse I rode in *The Shooting.* It was much the fastest horse I ever rode and I was plum scared, but I rode like the wind and looked good doing it."

He made two feature films with Elvis Presley. When questioned about Elvis, he recalls, "The camera loved him and vice versa. It all came so easily to him. Working on *Spinout* and *Clambake* was not work at all. They were just like going to parties, and Elvis, ever the Southern gentleman, was the perfect host. Once he invited me into his dressing room to listen to an LP. I thought I was going to hear the King's latest. Instead he treated me to Charles Boyer's reciting love poetry."

There were also two short-lived comedy series, *Hey Landlord* (1966–1967) and *Blondie* (1968–1969). Of the latter he says, "I loved playing Dagwood in *Blondie.* I loved the producer Joe Connelly. I loved two of the directors, Norm Abbott and Peter Baldwin. I loved the scripts. I loved my costars especially Jim Backus and I loved that I got to play physical comedy. ... We were on CBS and NBC's *Daniel Boone* was beating us so off we went, although we were beating our competition on ABC." He then went on to shoot one of his most obscure feature film credits, *Shangani*

Patrol (1970). "This was a flick I made in what was then Rhodesia, now Zimbabwe, in 1970. Brian O'Shaughnessy, South Africa's leading movie star, was in it as well. It did well in Africa, but never made it to the States. On the salary I made on it I took a trip round the world. The last stop was Tahiti."

He then traveled for two years throughout the USA and Canada as a clown and ringmaster, creating a character called "Patches." It was while doing this that he came to appear in one of the *Dirty Harry* films. He explains, "I was traveling with a small circus in Walla Walla, Washington, when I got a call from my manager to fly to San Francisco to talk about playing a part in *Magnum Force.* My boss let me go for a couple of days and I did what I was told. The director told me I was to play an extra role at poolside at the beginning of the flick. A few months later I was with another circus in Boston, Massachusetts, when I got a call to fly to Frisco to begin work on *Magnum Force.* I paid for my own transportation as well as lodging and meals in Frisco. We shot for three nights at a store near Fisherman's Wharf. I actually played a cop who got shot during a thwarted robbery in a store. Luckily I wore a bullet-proof vest, so that I was merely stunned, although I don't think the audience was aware of the vest. I was paid $350 for my efforts. In other words I lost money at the time, but over the years I have received residuals for my three nights on the Frisco Wharf."

Over the years he has made numerous guest starring appearances on television; one of the most unusual stemmed directly from "Patches the Clown." This was when he guested on the "Clown of Death" episode of *The Streets of San Francisco* in 1976. He recalls, "This was a unique experience for me in that while I was performing as a clown in a circus in San Francisco, I was at the same time working on 'Clown Of Death.' The circus scenes in the show are examples of my being paid twice for doing one job." For five years during the 1970s he joined the Theater Arts Program of Los Angeles which he thoroughly enjoyed. They did free shows all over L.A. for schools, recreation centers, hospitals, libraries and senior citizens homes. Actor Anthony Caruso was his boss. About this experience he recalls, "Best darn job I ever had."

He spent 1980 to 1982 touring Australia and New Zealand as a clown in Ashton's 160-plus-year-old circus. Then once again he traveled the world, returning to Los Angeles in 1983. From 1984 he worked for NBC in Hollywood and has been a celebrity guest at numerous conventions and functions. His recent activity in features and television has been limited, but he was in three Westerns. The first was called *The Great Bar 20* (1989), a Hopalong Cassidy story. "I played a character called 'Judge.' I guess I was the judge of the town. Anyway, all I did was announce the rodeo. It was written and directed by Chris Coppola, Francis Ford Coppola's nephew." He shot a surrealist Western in Pioneertown for the same outfit, intended for a Japanese audience. It was called *Gunfight at Red Dog Corral* (1992) with Clu Gulager and Michu, the world's smallest Hungarian. Of this he says, "I play Bumbalo Bill, the sheriff, and for one brief moment in time I got to be a visual screen comic. I helped out in devising some of the gags. My wife Babs did the choreography—we tried to emulate Laurel and Hardy's dance in *Way Out West,* but we lacked grace." This also has a bearing on his biggest show business disappointment. He explains, "I was to do a comedy television series about a small town veterinarian to be produced by Harold Lloyd. It was loosely based on [Lloyd's silent film] *Dr. Jack.* Sadly the project never got off the ground." He also made an appearance in the feature film *Maverick* (1994). Of this he says, "They put me to the back of the pack on the gambling boat. They didn't have enough parts to go around."

Hutchins was married and divorced during the 1960s to the former Chris Burnett, Carol's sister. He has a daughter Jennifer, who resides in Arizona. Since May 1988, he has been wed to the former Barbara Torres. They resided in the Los Feliz district of Los Angeles until 1995, when he retired from NBC and went to live in Glen Head, New York.

Will Hutchins Filmography

1957: *Bombers B-52.*
1958: *No Time for Sergeants, Lafayette Escadrille.*
1961: *Claudelle Inglish.*
1962: *Merrill's Marauders.*
1965: *The Shooting.*

1966: *Spinout.*
1967: *Clambake.*
1970: *Shangani Patrol.*
1973: *Magnum Force, The Horror at 37,000 Feet* (TV).
1976: *The Quest* (TV).
1977: *Slumber Party '57, The Happy Hooker Goes to Washington.*
1981: *Roar.*
1989: *The Great Bar 20.*
1992: *Gunfight at Red Dog Corral.*
1994: *Maverick* (uncredited).

Television Series

1957–1961: *Sugarfoot* as Tom Brewster.
1966–1967: *Hey Landlord!* as Woody Banner.
1968–1969: *Blondie* as Dagwood Bumstead.

Sources

Correspondence between Hutchins and the author.

Note

Hutchins is sometimes credited with an appearance in a movie called *The Peace Officer* (1988), but production was abandoned after some publicity and preproduction stages.

SELMER JACKSON

Selmer Adolph Jackson was born in Lake Mills, Iowa, on May 7, 1888. In movies from silent days, he appeared in the role of the Mayor of Dodge City for a single season in the Western series *The Life and Legend of Wyatt Earp.* Jackson died in Burbank, California, on March 30, 1971, at age 82, of heart disease.

Selmer Jackson Filmography

1921: *The Supreme Passion.*
1929: *Thru Different Eyes, Why Bring That Up?*
1930: *Lovin' the Ladies.*
1931: *Subway Express, Dirigible, The Secret Call, Leftover Ladies.*
1932: *You Said a Mouthful, Doctor X, Big City Blues, Three on a Match, The Mouthpiece, Winner Take All.*
1933: *Forgotten, Hell and High Water, After Tonight, The Working Man, The Little Giant* (voice only), *Picture Snatcher, Blood Money.*
1934: *I've Got Your Number, Let's Fall in Love, Sisters Under the Skin, The Witching Hour, The Defense Rests, I'll Fix It, Bright Eyes, Jealousy, Now I'll Tell, The Richest Girl in the World, Sadie McKee, Murder in the Clouds, Fog Over Frisco, Stand Up and Cheer, The Secret Bride.*
1935: *Devil Dogs of the Air, Living on Velvet, Broadway Gondolier, Carnival, Paddy O'Day, Don't Bet on Blondes, She Married Her Boss, Alibi Ike, Red Salute, Page Miss Glory, Black Fury, Traveling Saleslady, Public Hero Number One, Front Page Woman, This Is the Life, Grand Exit, A Night at the Opera.*
1936: *Bridge of Sighs, Public Enemy's Wife, Ace Drummond* (serial), *My Man Godfrey, Parole, Easy Money, The Magnificent Brute, Robinson Crusoe of Clipper Island* (serial), *The Golden Arrow, Libeled Lady, The Singing Kid, Charlie Chan at the Opera, The Great Ziegfeld, Revolt of the Zombies, Charlie Chan at the Racetrack, Show Boat, Gold Diggers of 1937, It Had to Happen, Next Time We Love, Sing Baby Sing, Stage Struck.*
1937: *Girl Overboard, Breezing Home, Charlie Chan at the Olympics, Two Wise Maids, A Family Affair, The Case of the Stuttering Bishop, The Man in Blue, The Thirteenth Man, Meet the Boy Friend, The Westland Case, The Wrong Road, Federal Bullets, Manhattan Merry-Go-Round, Hot Water, The Duke Comes Back, West of Shanghai, Jungle Jim* (serial), *The Man Who Cried Wolf, Three Smart Girls, My Dear Miss Aldrich, Behind the Headlines, Reported Missing.*

1938: *You're Only Young Once, Prison Nurse, Midnight Intruder, Arson Gang Busters, Arson Racket Busters, Alexander's Ragtime Band, The Missing Guest, Gambling Ship, Flight to Fame, The Gangster's Boy, Personal Secretary, Rhythm of the Saddle, Secrets of an Actress, Down In "Arkansaw," The Law West of Tombstone, The Chaser, Crime Ring, Gateway, Little Tough Guy, Prison Nurse, Garden of the Moon, Four Men and a Prayer, Too Hot to Handle, Rhythm of the Saddle.*

1939: *Off the Record, Stand Up And Fight, Inside Information, The Star Maker, On Dress Parade, Calling All Marines, South of the Border, Naughty But Nice, Espionage Agent, Each Dawn I Die, Confessions of a Nazi Spy, The Green Hornet* (serial), *The Forgotten Woman, Gambling Ship, The Escape, Blondie Brings Up Baby, Outside These Walls, Pacific Liner, Private Detective, 20,000 Men a Year, Sorority House, Two Thoroughbreds, Society Lawyer, The Under-Pup, Full Confession, Five Came Back, Undercover Agent, Union Pacific, Wings of the Navy, 6,000 Enemies.*

1940: *Scandal Sheet, The Grapes of Wrath, Honeymoon Deferred, I'm Still Alive, The Man from Dakota, On Their Own, Son of the Navy, Johnny Apollo, Wagons Westward, Millionaires in Prison, Babies for Sale, Sailor's Lady, Men Against the Sky, Hired Wife, City for Conquest, Brigham Young, Public Deb. No. 1, The Ape, The Lady with Red Hair, Queen of the Mob, If I Had My Way, Invisible Stripes, Santa Fe Trail, Florian, The Man Who Wouldn't Talk, Military Academy, No Time for Comedy, Murder in the Air, Abe Lincoln in Illinois, Bowery Boy, Forty Little Mothers, Gallant Sons, Glamour for Sale, Girls Under 21.*

1941: *Here Comes Mr. Jordan, Back Street, International Squadron, The Man Who Lost Himself, Tight Shoes, Paper Bullets, Parachute Battalion, Navy Blues, Remember The Day, Buck Privates, Play Girl, They Died With Their Boots On, Sergeant York, Love Crazy, It Started with Eve, Nice Girl?, Dick Tracy Vs. Crime Inc.* (serial), *International Lady, Shepherd of the Hills, Hold Back the Dawn, Meet John Doe, She Knew All the Answers; The Devil Pays Off.*

1942: *The Road to Happiness, Secret Agent of Japan, Ten Gentlemen from West Point, Miss Annie Rooney, Through Different Eyes, The Falcon Takes Over, Cairo, Joe Smith American, Thunder Birds, True to the Army, My Favorite Spy, Romance on the Range, Powder Town, Madame Spy, Saboteur, Dr. Kildare's Wedding Day, The Secret Code* (serial).

1943: *Honeymoon Lodge, Around the World, Margin for Error, It Ain't Hay, Adventures of the Flying Cadets* (serial), *You Can't Beat the Law, Harrigan's Kid, Margin for Error, Guadalcanal Diary, Someone to Remember, What a Woman!*

1944: *The Sullivans, Roger Touhy—Gangster, Hey Rookie!, Stars on Parade, The Big Noise, Sheriff of Las Vegas, The Big Noise, Since You Went Away, Destiny, Heavenly Days, Wing and a Prayer, Marine Raiders.*

1945: *They Shall Have Faith (*a.k.a. *Forever Yours), Circumstantial Evidence, The Caribbean Mystery, A Sporting Chance, Dakota, This Love of Ours, The Royal Mounted Rides Again* (serial), *Allotment Wives, Dillinger, Black Market Babies, First Yank into Tokyo, Thrill of a Romance, Out of This World; Along the Navajo Trail.*

1946: *Johnny Comes Flying Home, The Glass Alibi, The French Key, Child of Divorce, Wife Wanted, Boston Blackie and the Law, Dangerous Money, The Time of their Lives, Shock, San Quentin, Girl on the Spot, She Wrote the Book.*

1947: *Magic Town, Sarge Goes to College, Stepchild, Her Husband's Affairs, The Pretender, Key Witness, Headin' for Heaven, The Fabulous Texan, Cass Timberlane, The 13th Hour, High Wall.*

1948: *King of the Gamblers, The Fuller Brush Man, Pitfall, The Girl from Manhattan, Stage Struck, Blonde Ice, Sealed Verdict, Dream Girl, Every Girl Should Be Married, The Gentleman from Nowhere.*

1949: *Alaska Patrol, Forgotten Women, Renegades of the Sage, The Crime Doctor's Diary, Mighty Joe Young, The Fountainhead, Sorrowful Jones, Tulsa.*

1950: *Gunmen of Abilene, Mark of the Gorilla, Buckaroo Sheriff of Texas, Lucky Losers, The Magnificent Yankee, No Man of Her Own; Mardi Gras.*

1951: *Elopement, That's My Boy, Bowery Battalion, Purple Heart Diary.*

1952: *Sudden Fear, Young Man with Ideas, We're Not Married, Deadline USA.*

1953: *The President's Lady, Sky Commando, Rebel City, Jack McCall Desperado.*

1954: *Demetrius and the Gladiators; Crazylegs.*

1955: *Devil Goddess; The Eternal Sea.*
1956: *Autumn Leaves.*
1957: *Hellcats of the Navy, Three Brave Men.*
1958: *The Lost Missile.*
1959: *The Atomic Submarine.*
1960: *The Gallant Hours.*

Television Series

1956–1957: *The Life and Legend of Wyatt Earp* as Mayor Hoover.

Sources

Brooks, Tim. *The Complete Directory to Prime Time TV Stars 1946–Present.* New York: Ballantine Books, 1987.
Quinlan, David. *Illustrated Directory of Film Character Actors.* London: Batsford, 1995.

BRAD JOHNSON

Born in 1924, this tall actor appeared in some minor Western films and played a reporter in the circus extravaganza *The Greatest Show on Earth.* Then he was cast as Lofty Craig, the deputy sheriff who was enamored of Annie Oakley and usually became embroiled in her adventures in the television series of that name. When the series ended, he appeared in supporting roles in some other Western series during the years 1959–1961. One of his last recorded appearances was in an episode of *Gunsmoke* ("Cattle Barons") dating from 1967. By this time he had switched careers and dealt in stocks and bonds, a profession at which he was reportedly successful. He died prematurely on April 4, 1981, at age 56, a victim of cancer.

Brad Johnson with Gail Davis in a publicity pose for *Annie Oakley*.

Brad Johnson Filmography

1951: *Bedtime for Bonzo.*
1952: *Outlaw Women, The Greatest Show on Earth.*
1953: *The Marksman, The Lady Wants Mink.*
1954: *Taza Son of Cochise.*
1955: *Last of the Desperadoes.*
1958: *The Buccaneer.*

Television Series

1954–1958: *Annie Oakley* as Deputy Sheriff Lofty Craig.

Sources

Conversation with Gail Davis in 1993.
Inman, David. *The TV Encyclopedia.* New York: Perigee, 1991.

Russell Johnson with Anna-Lisa in *Black Saddle.*

RUSSELL JOHNSON

Russell Johnson was born in Ashley, Pennsylvania, on November 9, 1924. He commenced drama studies at school when he was 13 years old. Educated at Girard College, he served in the Army Air Corps during World War II before gravitating to Los Angeles. He was associated with the Actors Lab for about four years. This was both a theater and a dramatic school started by a group of actors from New York. The school was founded in the late 1940s, and Johnson was in the first class that was held in 1947. He joined the venture on the strength of the G.I. Bill. He also financed himself by taking odd jobs on the side. The Actors Lab was considered one of the best schools in the country, and frequently talent scouts from various studios would come to see the productions staged there.

He made his screen debut in *For Men Only* (1952), which Paul Henreid produced, directed and starred in. Although it was a small independent film, it was an influential one. A talent scout from Universal-International saw this movie and signed him to a contract. This led to two of his best-remembered film appearances: as George, the telephone linesman captured by aliens, in *It Came from Outer Space* (1953), and as scientist Steve Carlson in *This Island Earth* (1955).

He then went on to costar in the television Western series *Black Saddle.* In this he played the role of cynical Marshal Gib Scott who keeps a watchful eye on reformed gunslinger turned lawyer Clay Culhane (Peter Breck) because he doubts that Culhane has really reformed. The actor retains particularly fond memories of this series because of the high quality of the writing, and he believes that the part he played was a good one. He concludes, "I honestly enjoy Westerns and *Black Saddle* was probably my favorite. It showed some real craftsmanship."

One person whom he worked for several times, but whom he disliked, was Jack Webb. This was not only because Webb had a reputation as a tightwad and refused to negotiate over low salaries, but also because he insisted on his actors using teleprompters, a situation which stage trained Johnson could not adjust to. Most of his television work on numerous series, however, has been overshadowed by his participation as the Professor in the static situation comedy *Gilligan's Island.*

This came about because he was part of a theatrical group which worked out of the former Desilu Studios. This group produced evenings of one- and three-act plays for public consumption. At one point he was appearing in a one-act play with Hal Cooper, who knew Sherwood Schwartz, creator of *Gilligan's Island.* Johnson became acquainted with Schwartz, who offered him the role of the Professor. The actor turned him down because he had two other pilots shooting at the time, but neither of them came to anything.

A *Gilligan's Island* pilot was shot and sold, but it was felt that the actor who played the Professor was unsuitable and should be replaced. Johnson told his agent that if the producers would improve the money slightly, he would be prepared to talk to them again. He tested for the role, and a few days later his agent rang to say that he had landed the part and shooting would commence in a couple of months. Years later he still feels the presence of the Professor in his life because of all the reunion movies and because he provided the voice of the Professor in *The New Adventures of Gilligan* and *Gilligan's Planet* cartoons.

After the demise of the series, the pickings were slim because he had become typecast. His career revived when he played a district attorney in one episode of *Owen Marshall, Counselor at Law.* The producers were so impressed with the quality of his work that they invited him back. Over a three-year period he did 18 episodes of that series in a recurring role. This opened the floodgates for dozens of other television guest starring roles including *Dynasty, Dallas, Wonder Woman* and *Cannon.* He has also done a considerable amount of dinner theater, ranging from classics such as *Hamlet* and *Romeo and Juliet* to lighter works such as *Bell, Book and Candle.* In more recent years he has relocated to a rural country home on an island off Washington State's Puget Sound, where he has penned his autobiography and done voiceovers in commercials and supplied narration for documentaries for the Defense Department.

He married and had two children, David and Kimberly. His wife died of cancer in 1980. The actor remarried a lady named Constance who already had a son named Courtney. Johnson attracted a considerable amount of publicity when his son David died of AIDS in Los Angeles on October 27, 1994, at age 39.

Russell Johnson Filmography

1952: *For Men Only, Loan Shark, Willie and Joe Back at the Front, The Turning Point, Rancho Notorious.*
1953: *Seminole, Tumbleweed, It Came from Outer Space, Law and Order, Column South, The Stand at Apache River.*
1954: *Rogue Cop, Ride Clear of Diablo, Black Tuesday, Johnny Dark.*
1955: *Ma and Pa Kettle at Waikiki, This Island Earth, Many Rivers to Cross, Strange Lady in Town.*
1957: *Courage of Black Beauty, Attack of the Crab Monsters, Rock All Night.*
1958: *Badman's Country, The Space Children, The Saga of Hemp Brown.*
1964: *A Distant Trumpet.*
1965: *The Greatest Story Ever Told.*
1970: *The Movie Murderer* (TV).
1971: *Vanished* (TV).
1973: *Beg, Borrow or Steal* (TV), *The Horror at 37,000 Feet* (TV).
1974: *Aloha Means Goodbye* (TV).
1975: *You Lie So Deep My Love* (TV), *Adventures of the Queen* (TV).
1977: *MacArthur, Nowhere to Hide* (TV).
1978: *Rescue from Gilligan's Island* (TV), *The Ghost of Flight 401* (TV), *Hitch Hike to Hell; The Great Skycopter Rescue.*
1979: *The Castaways on Gilligan's Island* (TV).
1981: *The Harlem Globetrotters on Gilligan's Island* (TV).
1988: *Blue Movies.*
1992: *With a Vengeance* (TV).

Television Series

1959–1960: *Black Saddle* as Marshal Gib Scott.
1964–1967: *Gilligan's Island* as Professor Roy Hinkley.
1984: *Santa Barbara* as Roger Wainwright.

Miniseries

1978: *The Bastard.*

Sources

Interview. *Filmfax* magazine, issue #33.
Keck, William. "Heartbreak as *Gilligan's Island* star watches his son die of AIDS." *National Enquirer* magazine, November 1994.
Picture Show Annual. London: Amalgamated Press, 1955.

DICK JONES

Dick Jones was a child player. Ironically his most famous role was one in which he was never seen, namely the title role in the animated feature *Pinocchio* (1940). As an adult his career largely consisted of two Western television series, *The Range Rider* and *Buffalo Bill, Jr.* Far from the most glittering career that any child star ever had, it was all over by the age of 30.

Dick Jones was born in Snyder, Texas, on February 25, 1927, the son of a local newspaper editor. He learned to ride and had his own pony almost before he learned to walk. By the age of five he was performing in rodeos billed as the "Youngest Trick Rider and Roper in the World." At the Dallas Centennial Rodeo in 1933, the famous Western star Hoot Gibson spotted him and encouraged him to enter movies. Dick Jones' parents were divorced when his mother accompanied her son to Hollywood. They stayed with Hoot Gibson, who helped Jones gain a foothold in the movie industry. They appeared in a circus, but never actually made a movie together.

Dick Jones starred with the circus for a year touring the United States and Canada before making his motion picture debut in *Wonder Bar* (1934). He went on to play in dozens of movies. He appeared in shorts with Edgar Kennedy and five *Our Gang* comedies. His best chance came when Walt Disney selected him to provide the voice for the title role of *Pinocchio* (1940) in the feature length cartoon. When Ezra Stone was conscripted into the armed services, Dick Jones assumed the role of Henry Aldrich in the popular national radio show. Although he aspired to more important roles in A budget features, he lost all the decent roles to Dickie Moore.

He entered the U.S. Army in 1944, serving in Alaska until his discharge from active service in December 1946. He was no longer in demand as an actor, and apart from minor roles, he earned his living for a while as a carpenter. His career picked up when he was signed to a five-year contract with Gene Autry's Flying A Productions. He had appeared in movies with Autry and starred in two syndicated television series, *The Range Rider* with Jock Mahoney and *Buffalo Bill, Jr.* Both series were noted for their plentiful action scenes. Jones performed all of his own stunts. Although he was only a sidekick in *The Range Rider,* he preferred it to *Buffalo Bill, Jr.,* where he was the legitimate star. The latter series was set in Wileyville, Texas, in the 1890s and told of Buffalo Bill, Jr. (Dick Jones) and his sister Calamity (Nancy Gilbert), orphans adopted by Judge Ben Wiley, the founder of the town. When appointed sheriff, Buffalo Bill, Jr., attempted to maintain law and order. While it seemed like a big break, the series type-cast him to the point where few roles came his way afterwards. He kept in contact with Jock Mahoney until Mahoney died and receives a Christmas card every year from Gene Autry.

For many years when acting jobs were scarce, he owned a working ranch near Salinas, California. His final screen appearance was in *Requiem for a Gunfighter* (1965). After this he went into real estate on a full-time basis and became senior loan officer with Home Savings and Loan. He is enamored of neither horses nor show business. His permanent home nowadays is in Northridge, California. He married his childhood sweetheart Betty Bacon and has four children: Melody (born in 1950), Ricky "Buck" (born in 1953) and twins Jeffrey and Jennifer (born in 1956).

Dick Jones Filmography

1934: *Wonder Bar, Little Men, Strange Wives.*
1935: *Westward Ho!, Moonlight on the Prairie, Three Women, The Hawk.*
1936: *Black Legion, Daniel Boone, The First Baby, Little Lord Fauntleroy, Life Begins at Twenty, The Man I Marry, Pepper.*
1937: *Stella Dallas, Love Is in the Air, Blake of Scotland Yard, Renfrew of the Royal Mounted, Hollywood Roundup, Border Wolves, Flying Fists, Don't Pull Your Punches.*
1938: *The Devil's Party, The Kid Comes Back, A Man to Remember, Sergeant Madden, The Great Adventures of Wild Bill Hickok* (serial), *The Frontiersman, Woman Doctor.*
1939: *Nancy Drew Reporter, City in Terror (*a.k.a. *The Man Who Dared), Destry Rides Again, Sky Patrol, Young Mr. Lincoln, Mr. Smith Goes to Washington, On Borrowed Time, Beware Spooks.*
1940: *Pinocchio* (voice only), *Virginia City, Maryland, Brigham Young, The Howards of Virginia, Knute Rockne—All American.*
1941: *The Vanishing Virginian, Adventure in Washington.*
1942: *Mountain Rhythm.*
1943: *Heaven Can Wait.*
1944: *The Adventures of Mark Twain.*
1948: *Strawberry Roan.*
1949: *Sands of Iwo Jima.*
1950: *Military Academy, Redwood Forest Trail, Rocky Mountain, Sons of New Mexico, The 10th Avenue Gang.*
1951: *Fort Worth.*
1952: *The Old West, Wagon Team.*
1953: *Last of the Pony Riders.*
1955: *Bamboo Prison.*
1956: *The Wild Dakotas.*
1958: *The Cool and the Crazy.*
1965: *Requiem for a Gunfighter.*

Television Series

1951–1952: *The Range Rider* as Dick West.
1955: *Buffalo Bill, Jr.* as Buffalo Bill Junior.

Sources

Corneau, Ernest N. *The Hall of Fame of Western Film Stars.* North Quincy, MA: Christopher, 1969.

Dye, David. *Child and Youth Actors: Filmographies of Their Entire Careers, 1914–1985.* Jefferson, NC: McFarland, 1988.

Lamparski, Richard. *Whatever Became Of? Ninth Series.* New York: Crown, 1985.

L.Q. JONES

"Three or four years ago my agent called and told me there was a good part and it was between three of us—Tab Hunter, the pretty boy heartthrob of the 1950s; Rosie Greer, the gigantic black ex-football player; and me. I told him to say, 'Thank you very much, but no thank you.' They obviously didn't know what they were talking about." So speaks L.Q. Jones, who took his name from the character he played in his first film, *Battle Cry* (1955). He is a rebel actor with a rapier wit and a Rabelaisian turn of phrase. He usually plays villains. As he expresses it, "I've been described as having pig eyes and snake eyes. I believe both were meant as compliments."

L.Q. Jones was born Justus Ellis McQueen in Belmont, Texas, on August 19, 1927, the son of Justus Ellis McQueen, Sr., and Pat Stephens. He was an only child and grew up in Texas. He was educated at Lamar Junior College until 1944 and Lon Morris College until 1949. He served with the United States Navy from 1945 to 1946. His ambition to be an actor was not encouraged. "I've been an actor since I was 30 seconds old. Well, now, sports fans, in my family you could be the neighborhood pimp or con man, but not an actor," he says. This was the reason he went to the University of Texas to study law from 1950 to 1951. He was sidetracked into being a standup comedian and did over 800 live shows before students and servicemen in the area. It was his only acting training. He roomed with Fess Parker, who later enjoyed television success as *Davy Crockett* and *Daniel Boone.* Parker met actor Adolphe Menjou, who urged him to try his luck in Hollywood. Jones, meanwhile, bought a ranch in Nicaragua.

He spent one Christmas in Hollywood with Fess Parker and then returned to his ranch. About two months later Parker sent him a copy of a book called *Battle Cry* by Leon Uris. Parker was up for a part in the film. McQueen read the novel and decided he would like to play the part of L.Q. Jones. He flew to Hollywood where he stayed with Fess Parker. He sneaked into Warner Bros. where he made his way to the office of Hoyt Bowers, who was casting *Battle Cry.* Neither Bowers nor Warners' head of casting Solly Biano was impressed. Eventually his persistence paid off, for he was summoned to meet the director Raoul Walsh, who insisted on Jones being tested. They had already tested 250 other actors for the role. Walsh wanted him for the part, but the top brass at Warners wanted an actor with experience. At length Walsh threatened to resign from the picture unless Jones was cast, so he won the role.

At the end of the first day's shooting, Walsh told him that he didn't like the way his first scene had been written and to polish it overnight. He duly obliged and Walsh shot the scene as the actor had rewritten it. He recalls, "Walsh had amalgamated four other actors' roles into the L.Q. Jones part. I rewrote two-thirds of my own scenes. I ended up with more screen time than the star Van Heflin!" *Battle Cry* was one of the top-grossing films of its year. Halfway through shooting, Walsh signed Jones to a personal contract which he later sold to Warner Bros.

Who suggested he change his name to L. Q. Jones? The actor explains, "It was Leon Uris. He was not doing too well at the time. He told me to change it so he could sue and we could get ourselves some publicity. Uris soon became so busy on the film he never did get around to suing. I still ring him up occasionally and scream, 'Yahoo, you forgot to sue!'"

Next Warners assigned him to a television series, *Cheyenne,* in which he played Cheyenne's sidekick and mapmaker in a few early episodes. Of this experience he recalls, "They signed me to do *Cheyenne* before they signed Clint Walker. I only did the first season. The director was the only human being in this business I couldn't get along with. I wouldn't spit in his mouth if his brains were on fire. I could tell it wasn't going to work out. *Cheyenne* was a one-person show. At my request they put me in a movie instead. That decision cost me three or four million dollars. I never claimed I was very smart, sports fans!"

Jones found himself in a procession of military pictures in which he mainly played comic relief. "It got so they didn't hire and fire me. They just drafted and discharged me." He talked his way out of his Warners contract. Once he cast himself adrift, he was free to do television. "If you made yourself available and stayed busy, you were given the gambit. Most of the series were Westerns so if you didn't do Westerns you didn't work." Andrew J. Fenady was preparing *The Rebel* (1959–1961), starring Nick Adams, and told Jones there was a marvelous role for him in one episode as comic relief. The actor pleaded with him, "I want to play the heavy." Fenady relented, "Go ahead, screw it up!" Far from screwing up, he romped away with the best notices of his career.

He became part of a "crazy heavy" repertory company which included Warren Oates, Strother Martin, Jack Elam and Slim Pickens. About them he says, "You really had to act when those guys were around. Otherwise you got left behind." He believes that playing the heavy is the other side of the coin from being comic relief. He admired director Sam Peckinpah and appeared in nine television and film productions for him, including the celebrated Westerns *Ride the High Country* (1962) and *The Wild Bunch* (1969). "Sam only really told one story. It is about men who are tough, fight for a living, but who have outlived their time. They are fighting to make the transition, but can't so they have to resort to violence. They have crossed over the line and gone to the bad." He remembers Peckinpah as a perfectionist. "The first cut of *The Wild Bunch* ran eight hours. He would still be editing it today if it hadn't been taken out of his hands."

He is particularly proud of *A Boy and His Dog* (1974), which he scripted, directed and financed with his own money. He received a Hugo award for his adaptation of Harlan Ellison's novella which focused on the relationship between young scavenger Vic (Don Johnson) and his telepathic dog Blood as they roam the earth circa 2024 after a nuclear holocaust. Jones says, "You either adore or detest it. There is no middle ground. It is a brutal, funny, one-of-a-kind movie." He believes it was years ahead of its time. "It had two total releases in 1975–1976 and again in 1982–1983. It was seen by more people and made more money second time around." In 1996 *Variety* reported him to be hard at work supervising the laserdisc release of this movie.

He is caustic about the current state of television. "Television once presented the greatest opportunity to educate, to entertain and to build an audience by capturing the imagination. Instead they opted for the almighty buck. Something's wrong out there, sports fans!" He cites as an example the puerile 1988 remake of the classic Western *Red River* (1948). "The director had never seen a cow, much less a stampede. We shot it in four and a half weeks. We were tight on budget. Our cows looked like Great Danes with horns! They spliced in a lot of stock footage of longhorns—all spots, browns and greys—with our mice, a few itty bitty cows roaming loose. They totally missed the point of the story, which was the cattle drive. They should have left *Red River* alone and saved their money. They should have called their trash 'Up the Creek Without a Paddle.'"

Jones has appeared in over 700 television shows, including 40 episodes of *The Virginian.* Asked about his most challenging role, he replies, "It was an episode of *Cimarron Strip* [1967] called 'The Search' in which I played a character called Rummy. Rummy as written was the scum of the earth. He owned the general store and talked to his mule. I said to the director Burt Kennedy, 'Let's do something completely wild here.' So we changed it. Rummy became a split personality. He talked to himself. I even created two different voices and sets of mannerisms. One scene where Rummy nursed Marshal Jim Crown [Stuart Whitman] back to health was classic. Rummy's house looked like a junkyard. I came shambling from way in back, talking as both characters through all this junk until I reached him.

I had a monologue lasting six or seven pages and relished every word of it. I won the best notices of my career. Of course they don't give Emmy awards to actors in Westerns, sports fans!"

In 1995 he returned to prominence when Martin Scorsese cast him as the redneck county commissioner in the prestigious film *Casino.*

L.Q. Jones married Sue Helen Lewis on October 10, 1950. She is deceased. He has three children: Marlin Randolph, Marilyn Helen and Steven Lewis; none of them works in show business. He subsequently remarried in 1974, but divorced after 21 years of marriage. He is a Republican and a Methodist. In 1995 he was described as living mainly in a Central Hollywood house where he also maintains a production office.

L.Q. Jones Filmography

1954: *Battle Cry.*
1955: *Target Zero, An Annapolis Story.*
1956: *Santiago, Toward the Unknown, Between Heaven and Hell, Love Me Tender.*
1957: *Men in War, Operation Mad Ball.*
1958: *The Young Lions, The Naked and the Dead, Buchanan Rides Alone, Torpedo Run.*
1959: *Warlock, Hound Dog Man, Battle of the Coral Sea.*
1960: *Ten Who Dared, Cimarron, Flaming Star.*
1961: *The Deadly Companions.*
1962: *Ride the High Country (*a.k.a. *Guns In The Afternoon), Hell Is for Heroes!*
1963: *Showdown.*
1964: *Apache Rifles.*
1965: *Major Dundee.*
1968: *Hang 'Em High, Stay Away Joe, The Counterfeit Killer* (TV), *Backtrack* (TV).
1969: *The Wild Bunch.*
1970: *The Ballad of Cable Hogue, The McMasters, The Brotherhood of Satan* (also coproduced).
1971: *The Hunting Party.*
1972: *Fireball Forward* (TV), *The Bravos* (TV).
1973: *Pat Garrett and Billy the Kid, Smash-Up Alley (*a.k.a. *43: The Petty Story).*
1974: *Mrs. Sundance* (TV), *Manhunter* (TV), *Mother Jugs and Speed* (released 1976), *The Strange and Deadly Occurrence* (TV).
1975: *White Line Fever, Winterhawk, Attack on Terror: The F.B.I. Versus the Ku Klux Klan* (TV).
1976: *Banjo Hackett: Roamin' Free* (TV).
1977: *Grayeagle (*a.k.a. *Sacred Ground).*
1978: *Fast Charlie—The Moonbeam Rider, Standing Tall* (TV).
1979: *The Sacketts* (TV).
1980: *Wild Times* (TV).
1982: *The Beast Within, Timerider—The Adventures of Lyle Swann, Melanie.*
1983: *Lone Wolf McQuade.*
1988: *Bulletproof, Red River* (TV).
1989: *River of Death.*
1990: *The Legend of Grizzly Adams.*
1994: *Lightnin' Jack.*
1995: *Casino.*
1996: *Tornado* (TV).

As director only

1964: *The Devil's Bedroom.*
1974: *A Boy and His Dog.*

Television Series

1955–1956: *Cheyenne* as Smitty.
1964–1967: *The Virginian* as Belden.

Miniseries

1996: *In Cold Blood.*

Sources

Alexander, Max. "Above the Line: A Jones for evil." *Variety,* January 8, 1996.
Interview with L.Q. Jones in 1989.
Quinlan, David. *Illustrated Directory of Film Character Actors.* London: Batsford, 1995.

STAN JONES

Born in Douglas, Arizona, on June 5, 1914, Stanley D. Jones was originally a ranger with the National Park Service for 15 years, living all over the West with his wife Olive. More importantly he was a composer and singer. He was introduced by actor George O'Brien to John Ford, who was so impressed that he used his songs in the film *Rio Grande* (1950). Thereafter his music became an integral part of the Ford Westerns. Many regard his finest composition as "Ghost Riders in the Sky," but film buffs rate his ballad of *The Searchers* (1956) as his greatest achievement. He wrote and sang songs for some Walt Disney pictures.

He was also a supporting actor. He played Deputy Olsen for two seasons in the Western television series *Sheriff of Cochise.* On film he played General Grant in Ford's *The Horse Soldiers* (1959). Jones died prematurely (at 49) in Los Angeles on December 13, 1963. Of his contribution to Western music, Marilyn Carey said it all: "There is Stan Jones all by himself and then they're [*sic*] the other guys."

Stan Jones Filmography

1950: *Rio Grande.*
1951: *Whirlwind.*
1952: *The Last Musketeer.*
1956: *The Great Locomotive Chase, The Rainmaker.*
1959: *The Horse Soldiers.*
1960: *The Alamo, Ten Who Dared.*
1964: *Invitation to a Gunfighter.*

Television Series

1956–1958: *Sheriff of Cochise* as Deputy Olsen.

Sources

Carey, Harry, Jr. *Company of Heroes: My Life As an Actor in the John Ford Stock Company.* Metuchen, NJ: Scarecrow, 1994.
Correspondence between John Bromfield and the author.
Truitt, Evelyn Mack. *Who Was Who On Screen Second Edition.* New York: Bowker, 1977.

BETTY LOU KEIM

Betty Lou Keim was born Elizabeth Louise Keim in Malden, Massachusetts, on September 27, 1938. She gained a considerable knowledge of theater because she had been an actress from the age of six. At that age she was chosen to appear in a documentary short subject for schools. From then on she continued acting, becoming a veteran of six Broadway shows and making over 50 television appearances over a period of 14 years. Eventually she made her screen debut as Suzie Keller, a pregnant teenager, in *These Wilder Years* (1956). She went on to repeat her Broadway performance in *Teenage Rebel* (1956) opposite her future husband Warren Berlinger.

Her best remembered television performance was in the regular role of Fran McCord, sister of the title character, in the prestigious Western series *The Deputy* during its first season. Her studio biography listed her hobbies as horseback riding, swimming, dancing and collecting pictures of clowns. She married actor Warren Berlinger on February 18, 1960, which seemed to mark her retirement from show business. With him she has a son and a daughter, and at last report was residing with her family in Chatsworth, California.

Betty Lou Keim Filmography

1956: *These Wilder Years, Teenage Rebel.*
1957: *The Wayward Bus.*
1958: *Some Came Running.*

Television Series

1953: *My Son Jeep* as Peggy Allison.
1959–1960: *The Deputy* as Fran McCord.

Sources

Brooks, Tim. *The Complete Directory to Prime Time TV Stars 1946–Present.* New York: Ballantine Books, 1987.

Picture Show Annual. London: Amalgamated Press, 1958.

Who's Who in Hollywood. New York: Dell, 1961.

JACK KELLY

There are some actors who never made the front rank. Such a one was Jack Kelly, who is still best remembered in his own words as "Maverick's brother" in the long-running spoof Western series *Maverick.* The characteristics which he brought to the character were a wry sense of humor and smug charm. Although he was a competent actor in his own right, in that series he was overshadowed by the contribution of James Garner. Kelly tended to be self-deprecating about his ability: "Maverick was fairly one dimensional and within that one dimension I was super. But it wore thin enough that I didn't have a career." In real life he was a gregarious and convivial man who loved to drink and to party. There is one theory that his acting career really ended because he had to choose between being a thespian and his other life. He preferred his alternative lifestyle.

Jack Kelly was born John Augustus Kelly, Jr., in Astoria, New York, on September 16, 1927. He was the son of John Augustus Kelly, a theatrical ticket broker, and Ann Mary Walsh, who used the stage name Nan Kelly Yorke (1895–1978). She was a model for the artist James Montgomery Flagg and later for the John Robert Powers model agency. Kelly was one of four children. His sisters were actress Nancy Kelly (1921–1995) and sometime thespian Carole Elizabeth Kelly. His younger brother was named Clement. As a baby Kelly modeled in an Ivory Soap commercial. In New York he appeared in five Broadway plays and 300 radio dramas. His family moved to Hollywood where he appeared in numerous two-reel pictures and a couple of features. In 1945 he entered the Air Force as a private and was discharged in 1946 as a sergeant after serving in the 7th Weather Group of the 11th Air Force in Alaska.

Studying at U.C.L.A. in 1945 and 1947, Kelly toyed with the idea of becoming an attorney, but somehow his ambition died. He hitched a ride back to New York City where he soon found a job flipping announcement cards on a pioneer television show. He made his screen debut as an adult in an uncredited bit in *Fighting Man of the Plains* (1949). The notorious agent Henry Willson arranged for him to return to Hollywood for a screen test for a leading role in the movie *Saturday's Hero.* Although he did not win the part, he was signed to a contract with Universal. He was seen thereafter in several motion pictures, but the size of his roles and his billing varied considerably. In some he was barely glimpsed, while in others he had quite substantial roles. He was frequently villainous, but somehow never seemed entirely at ease as a bad guy.

In 1955 he played a physician in the syndicated television series *Dr. Hudson's Secret Journal.* His biggest break appeared to come when he was cast in the leading role of another physician in the Warner Bros. television series *Kings' Row,* but this series lasted only seven episodes. It was one of four rotating elements in *Warner Bros. Presents.* Two years later when producers were looking for an actor to costar with James Garner in *Maverick,* they remembered him. When it was calculated that each episode of *Maverick* took a week and a day to shoot, it was decided that a second star was needed for the series. Two episodes would be shot simultaneously, with the actors sometimes leaping from one set to another to put in appearances in each other's segments.

Several actors were suggested as possible choices, but Kelly was the one who outshone the others. Executive producer William T. Orr recalled that no proper test was ever made of him. He was simply taken on to the set, introduced to Garner and then left to improvise. From the resulting dialogue, he was cast. His problem was that even though he started shooting episodes before the debut of the series, Warner Bros. came out with ten shows in a row which Garner already had in the can. The excuse from the studio was that Kelly's episodes were rough and unready. From an audience perspective, it put Kelly into a secondary status and he never really recovered the lost ground.

Kelly first appeared with Garner in "Hostage," followed by two more episodes with both brothers, "The Jeweled Gun" and "The Wrecker." Bart Maverick's solo debut was "The Naked Gallows," in which he attempted to clear the name of a friend who had escaped from jail after being wrongly accused of murder. His ability as an actor and his personality overcame initial hostility from viewers. Some even wrote to complain that Kelly was not being given scripts as good as James Garner's. Warner Bros. defended themselves by saying that scripts were tailored to fit the personality of each actor. The more romantic stories were written for Bart, the more humorous ones for Bret. Kelly insisted that he could handle some of the wittier scripts as well. It was an episode which Jack Kelly starred in which beat out ratings champ *The Ed Sullivan Show.* Although Garner received the lion's share of the kudos from the series, it was actually the Kelly episodes which had a very slight edge in the ratings during the first and second seasons of the show. It was only during the third and final season of Garner's association with the series that more viewers tuned in to his episodes by a wide margin.

Kelly believed that the character of Bart Maverick was ripe for development, but heavy production schedules prevented this. Scripts were frequently delivered to him the night before shooting, and he wanted more time to develop Bart within each episode. He also wanted to work with a drama coach before each episode, so that he could present the director with some fresh ideas. After three years of *Maverick,* Kelly claimed that while initially he had not seen himself as a cowboy, he found the experience very satisfying and added that he would not object to playing Maverick forever. In later years he looked back on *Maverick* as the high point of his career. He said, "I whistled all the way to work on that one."

An ongoing joke between the two stars was that whenever they encountered each other on the Warner Bros. lot, they drew with prop guns. The one drawing first would yell, "Bang!" The other would have to drop what he was holding. Kelly proved to be somewhat more adept when playing this game and allegedly drew on Garner in the studio commissary so that Garner dropped his lunch. On another occasion Garner was in process of trying on a new suit when Kelly caught him and Garner dropped his trousers. Although they had a good relationship, Garner frequently kidded Kelly about his weight and the consequent difficulty of buckling on his gunbelt.

By 1960 Garner was dissatisfied with the slave charter which masqueraded as a contract with Warner Bros. and wanted out. He used as a pretext a writers' strike by the Screen Writers Guild in Hollywood. Both actors kept receiving scripts which were signed by "W. Hermanos." "Hermanos" was the Spanish word for brothers. The initial "W" stood for Warner. These scripts had been filmed before for *The Alaskans* and only the location and the name of the characters had been changed. By filming these, Warners could still deliver the segments which they were contractually committed to produce. When they figured out what was going on, the actors walked out in the middle of production.

They hired an outstanding attorney and battled Warner Bros. About two months later Jack Warner personally called Jack Kelly and invited him to talk at the studio. At the meeting, Warner offered him a substantial raise in salary if he would return. Kelly agreed because he wanted to avoid a costly lawsuit and he realized he did not have the formidable drawing power of Garner. He returned to work and at Warner's personal request tried to persuade James Garner to do the same, but Garner refused, persevered with the lawsuit and won his freedom.

Bret was replaced by cousin Beau (Roger Moore) and later, in two episodes, by a younger brother and James Garner clone Brent (Robert Colbert). Jack Kelly was now the top star of the series, but despite his efforts the show quickly spiraled into decline and the 124th and last episode aired on July 8, 1962. Virtually every series that Warner Bros. made at the time was shown on the ABC network. This was fine for a while when the series were of consistently high quality, but ABC rebelled when presented with series like *The Alaskans.* Dissatisfied ABC executives went to Jack Warner and demanded a say in the series that were shot and a better deal. Warner flatly refused. ABC retaliated by changing the time slot of *Maverick* from Sunday at 7:30 P.M., where it was still a hit, to 6:30 P.M. where *Dennis the Menace* savaged it in the ratings. Shortly afterwards Henry Kaiser (the sponsor) dropped the series because of the change in the time slot. Ironically, Jack Kelly was never officially told that the series had ended.

In *Love and Kisses* (1965) he supported Rick Nelson under the direction of Ozzie Nelson. Kelly was starring in the comedy at a dinner theater in Chicago when he was told that Ozzie Nelson had bought it as a vehicle for Ricky Nelson and his wife. He visited Kelly after the show and complimented him on his performance. He had already cast Fred MacMurray and Joan Caulfield in the movie, however, because they were bigger names.

Kelly had been home in California for a few weeks when he received a call from his agent who said that Ozzie Nelson wanted to see him. When he arrived, Nelson told him he would like to do a screen test of him in the role. Fred MacMurray had given up the part and Nelson wanted Kelly to substitute for him. The film was being shot at Universal and there was a week's rehearsal for the cast before shooting. While they were waiting for Joan Caulfield to arrive on the first day, Nelson received a phone call telling him that she had been hospitalized with appendicitis. Kelly rescued Nelson from this predicament when he suggested substituting Madelyn Hines, who had done the play in Chicago with him.

Kelly appeared on stage in musicals such as *Guys and Dolls, The Music Man* and *The Pajama Game* and on Broadway in shows including *Night Life* and *Family Way.* He continued to guest star in dramas and Westerns during the 1960s and appeared several times on *Bob Hope's Chrysler Theater.* Some of these were attempts to star him in a series in which he played a insurance investigator, but the pilots did not sell. He dropped in on *The Lucy Show* in 1964 and *Batman* in 1967. During the 1970s for three years he hosted the daytime game show *The Sale of the Century* from New York. Upon his return to Los Angeles he continued to guest star in prime time series such as *Quincy M.E., McCloud, Vegas, B.J. and the Bear, Ironside, Wagon Train, The Bionic Woman, The Name of the Game,* and *The Rockford Files* with James Garner.

He was again professionally reunited with Garner when he livened up the last quarter-hour of *Young Maverick* (1978), a television movie pilot which starred the husband-and-wife team of Charles Frank and Susan Blanchard. Kelly reprised his old role of Bart Maverick. He was one of those actors who had considerable difficulty in controlling his girth. He had gained considerable weight since, spry and slender, he had originally played the role. The point was made even clearer by the insertion of some tantalizing black and white footage of the two from earlier episodes of *Maverick.* Kelly was not present even as a guest star when the subsequent series was aired and quickly scuttled. He did, however, appear in two short-lived series, *Get Christie Love!* (1975) and *The Hardy Boys Mysteries* (1978–1979), but by this time he had slipped into character parts. For many years the greater part of his performing income was derived from numerous voiceovers on television commercials including Lowenbrau Beer, General Tires and Aurora Toys.

In 1981 he appeared on "The Hidalgo Thing" episode of the *Bret Maverick* series which starred James Garner. Originally Kelly wanted to pass on this because of the hassles of wardrobe and shooting (a day each), together with his dislike of going to Los Angeles, but Garner called him personally and insisted he come because they needed him badly. When he arrived on the set, he was greeted by Garner and Meta Rosenberg, his executive producer. They then showed him six completed scripts in which Bart Maverick is shown running the saloon where Bret carries out his confidence tricks. A stumbling block was salary. The offer on the table was $27,000 an episode. At his insistence, Kelly's agent William Morris wanted $45,000. They were still negotiating when Kelly discovered the series was not going to be picked up. He recalled, "That was one of the major disappointments of my life." His final appearance as Bart Maverick was in the telemovie *The Gambler IV: The Luck of the Draw* (1991). He spent about a week on that show which he enjoyed immensely, primarily because it enabled him to meet and talk to several of his contemporaries.

In his private life his hobby was cooking,

but he also enjoyed outdoor pursuits such as golf and sailing. His salary during his peak years was almost entirely invested. He once claimed that he could not afford a particular sailing ship he wanted because it was too expensive and beyond his budget. He had been investing in California real estate since 1950 and had become an authority on it. He ran his own August 2nd Investment Firm and had become extremely wealthy. At one time a business manager and three lawyers aided him in overseeing all of his various business interests, making sure that no money was spent on items which were not tax deductible. One of his few bad investments was his purchase of the *Huntington Beach News,* which folded early in 1992.

By 1980 acting had taken a backseat to politics. He was a volunteer in the presidential campaigns of Adlai Stevenson and John F. Kennedy. Originally he was campaign chairman for a friend who was running for county supervisor in Huntington Beach in 1978. People who worked on behalf of his candidate interested him in running for the city council. He was elected in 1980 and sat as city councilor for two consecutive four-year terms. His salary was $176 a month. He was elected Mayor for the Democratic Party from 1983 to 1984. He was forced to take a two-year sabbatical under the rules, but was reelected in 1990. Of this he said, "I enjoy what I'm doing as a city councilman here to some degree, although I get frustrated with civic work because you can't see the conclusion of an act that you put in motion." He was a member of the Screen Actors Guild; the American Federation of TV and Radio Artists; Artists Equity Association; The Sea Cliff Country Club and Balboa Bay Club.

In the mid–1950s he married May Wynn (born Donna Lee Hickey in 1930), a beautiful actress who lifted her stage name from the character she played in *The Caine Mutiny* (1954). They appeared together in many films during the 1950s and were thought to be an ideal couple until they divorced in the early 1960s. A contributory factor was his heavy drinking in those days, together with the fact that he was seldom home. He remarried in 1970 to Jo Ann Roberta Smith, who helped to run his real estate firm. They had one child, Nichole Christine (born in 1971), who has been a local television anchorwoman.

In April 1992, he suffered a heart attack and underwent heart bypass surgery in May, but he never fully recovered. He was separated from his wife and living alone when he collapsed after suffering a massive brain hemorrhage. His estranged wife found him six hours later and called paramedics who rushed him to Humana Hospital. In a vain attempt to help him recover, his daughter played tapes of his favorite singer Ella Fitzgerald, hoping that he would be able to hear it. His family and friends prayed for his death as he lay connected to a life support machine. On November 7, 1992, doctors disconnected the machine with the consent of his family and he died shortly after noon at age 65. His daughter said, "He was such a vital, energetic man. In the end he slipped away peacefully. I can't even begin to tell you how much I will miss him. He was the best dad in the whole world." Memorial services were held in the amphitheater of the city hall complex. Chris Alcaide, May Wynn, Denver Pyle and Paul Burke were all there, but the only two of the Warner Bros. players who attended were Will Hutchins and Robert Colbert. James Garner was a notable absentee.

Jack Kelly Filmography

1938: *Young Mr. Lincoln.*
1940: *The Story of Alexander Graham Bell.*
1949: *Fighting Man of the Plains* (uncredited).
1950: *Where Danger Lives, Peggy, The West Point Story.*
1951: *Submarine Command, The Wild Blue Yonder, People Will Talk, Call Me Mister.*
1952: *The Redhead from Wyoming, No Room for the Groom, Red Ball Express, Sally and St. Anne.*
1953: *The Stand at Apache River, Gunsmoke, Law and Order, Column South, The Glass Web.*
1954: *Drive a Crooked Road, Black Tuesday, They Rode West, The Bamboo Prison, Magnificent Obsession.*
1955: *The Night Holds Terror, Double Jeopardy, To Hell and Back, Cult of the Cobra, The Violent Men.*
1956: *Julie, Forbidden Planet.*
1957: *She Devil, Taming Sutton's Gal.*
1958: *The Hong Kong Affair.*
1961: *A Fever in the Blood.*
1964: *FBI Code 98.*
1965: *Love and Kisses.*
1968: *Commandos.*

1969: *Young Billy Young.*
1978: *Vegas* (TV), *Young Maverick* (TV).
1991: *The Gambler IV: The Luck of the Draw* (TV).

Television Series

1955: *Dr. Hudson's Secret Journal* as Dr. Bennett.
1955–1956: *King's Row* as Dr. Parris Mitchell.
1957–1962: *Maverick* as Bart Maverick.
1975: *Get Christie Love!* as Captain Arthur P. Ryan.
1978–1979: *The Hardy Boys Mysteries* as Harry Hammond.

Sources

Coates, Julia. "How *Maverick* Star Lost His Gamble With Death." *National Enquirer* magazine, November 1992.
Lamparski, Richard. *Whatever Became Of? Tenth Series.* New York: Crown, 1986.
Martin, Mick. "Memoirs of a Maverick." *Filmfax* magazine, issue #40, August/September 1993.
Moseley, Roy. *Roger Moore: A Biography.* London: New English Library, 1985.
Robertson, Ed. *Maverick: Legend of the West.* Beverly Hills, CA: Pomegranate, 1994.
Variety. Obituary, November 16, 1992.
Woolley, Lynn, Robert W. Malsbary, and Robert G. Strange, Jr. *Warner Bros. Television.* Jefferson, NC: McFarland, 1985.

Note

Jack Kelly is often credited with an appearance in *The Country Girl* (1954), but this appears to be erroneous (perhaps a mixup with the character actor Jack Kenney).

ADAM KENNEDY

Adam Kennedy was born near Lafayette, Indiana, on March 10, 1922. He was born in the middle of winter in a farmhouse without central heating or electricity. Two-and-a-half months premature and weighing less than three pounds, he was kept in a peach box incubator (heated by waterfilled fruit jars). Beginning work as a small boy, he later had such jobs as butcher, mortician's assistant, teacher, sign painter, singer, commercial artist, farm and construction worker, photographer's model and radio announcer.

He received a B.A. cum laude from DePaul University and was later awarded a D.Litt from there in 1974. He also studied at Chicago Professional School of Art, Academie de la Grande Chaumiere, Alliance Francaise and the Neighborhood Playhouse. He won an oil painting prize from John Herron Museum and was named outstanding American painter in Paris by the Society for American Art in Paris in 1951. He was an account executive with Grant Advertising Incorporated in Chicago and later an art director and illustrator for *Esquire* and *Coronet* magazines.

Switching careers, he became a professional actor, appearing on stage in Europe and on Broadway and performing in more than 300 television programs and several feature films during the 1950s. He starred in the television serial *The Doctors* and the series *The Californians* in 1957. In the latter he briefly played the lead of Dion Patrick, a two-fisted newspaperman during the San Francisco Gold Rush of the 1850s.

After his tenure as an actor, he reverted back to his original interest in art and studied painting. He has enjoyed some success with group and solo shows in the United States and Paris, being considered an abstract painter of some distinction. He also became a successful published novelist with over a dozen novels to his credit from 1967 onwards. Initially he wrote under the pseudonym of John Redgate, although from 1971 onwards he has been using the name of Adam Kennedy. Many of these are in the thriller genre; possibly his best known is *The Domino Principle,* which was filmed in 1977 with Gene Hackman and Candice Bergen. The reviews of his fiction have generally been very favorable. He has also written historical fiction.

He has been a screenwriter, most notably of *The Dove* (1973) and *Raise the Titanic* (1980). The latter was somewhat unfortunate because the film was one of the biggest flops in Hollywood history up to that time. Kennedy lists his hobby as traveling and has done a considerable amount of it in Europe, South America, New Zealand, Barbados and Trinidad. He is married to Susan, a professional actress, and has two sons, Regan and Jack. At last report he was residing with his wife in Connecticut.

Adam Kennedy Filmography

1953: *Act of Love.*
1955: *The Court-Martial of Billy Mitchell.*
1957: *Men in War, Until They Sail, Bailout at 43,000, The Tall Stranger.*

Television Series

1957–1958: *The Californians* as Dion Patrick.
1963: *The Doctors* as Brock Hayden.

Sources

Contemporary Authors. Volume 107. Detroit, MI: Gale Research Company.
Summers, Neil. *The First Official TV Western Book.* Vienna, WV: Old West Shop Publishing, 1987.

DOUGLAS KENNEDY

Douglas Kennedy was born Harve Garrison in New York City on September 14, 1915, the son of a composer and musician. After attending high school in Larchmont, New York, he graduated from Deerfield Academy and Amherst College in Massachusetts. He became an expert rider during summer vacations in the Catskill Mountains of New York State. His original ambition was to enter the diplomatic service, but he was sidetracked by the lure of motion pictures.

He journeyed to California where he taught at the Thatcher School for Boys in Ojai. While there he endeavored to obtain employment at Hollywood studios, but was rejected and had a hard struggle to establish himself. He began making screen appearances from 1940 onwards, initially using the name of Keith Douglas. The momentum of his career was interrupted by World War II. He enlisted as a private in the army, serving with distinction as a major in the Signal Corps and working with the O.S.S. and Military Intelligence overseas.

Upon his discharge, he signed a contract with Warner Bros. where he made several motion pictures. Later he worked at other studios where he appeared in Westerns, sometimes as famous historical figures with varying

Douglas Kennedy in *Steve Donovan—Western Marshal.*

degrees of authenticity. These included Wild Bill Hickok in *Jack McCall—Desperado* (1953) and General Custer in *Sitting Bull* (1954). Many of his characterizations were villainous, but sometimes he was sympathetic, such as his forceful wagon train boss in *The Last Wagon* (1956).

Kennedy's sole television series was the syndicated *Steve Donovan—Western Marshal* in which he played a peace officer who tried to bring law and order to the West. This series seemed to go overboard at times to bring the marshal out to be rather inept. Although mildly popular, it did little to enhance its star's reputation and is hardly remembered today. There were 39 half-hour black and white episodes.

Kennedy was the kind of personable, strapping actor that television frequently latched onto and turned into heroes in a long-running television series, but this was not his fate. Instead, he continued to ply his craft in predominantly villainous roles in prime time Westerns such as *Rawhide* and *Wagon Train.* He was particularly memorable in an episode of the latter called "Charlie Wooster Wagonmaster" where, as a seemingly honest traveler, he turns out to be the leader of a vicious band of white slave traders. Kennedy had the occasional role of the sheriff in the last couple of seasons of the Western television series *The Big Valley* during the 1960s.

After this he semi-retired to live in Hawaii. Among his last recorded appearances were a trio of roles in episodes of *Hawaii Five-O* in which his physical decline was very evident and which were telecast posthumously. Douglas Kennedy died in Kailua, Hawaii, at age 57, of cancer on August 10, 1973. He was survived by his widow and four children, including twin daughters.

Douglas Kennedy Filmography

1940: *Those Were the Days, Opened By Mistake, Love Thy Neighbor, Arise My Love, The Way of All Flesh, North West Mounted Police, Women Without Names, The Ghost Breakers, The Mad Doctor.*

1941: *The Roundup, The Great Mr. Nobody, Affectionately Yours, The Bride Came C.O.D., The Nurse's Secret, Passage from Hong Kong.*

1947: *Life with Father, Possessed, The Unfaithful, Dark Passage, That Hagen Girl, Always Together, Deep Valley, Nora Prentiss, Stallion Road, The Unsuspected, Voice of the Turtle.*

1948: *To the Victor, The Decision of Christopher Blake, Adventures of Don Juan, Whiplash, Embraceable You, Johnny Belinda, Romance on the High Seas.*

1949: *South of St. Louis, Look for the Silver Lining, One Last Fling, Fighting Man of the Plains, East Side West Side, Rangers of Cherokee Strip, The Fountainhead, Flaxy Martin, South of Rio, John Loves Mary.*

1950: *The Next Voice You Hear..., Montana, The Cariboo Trail, Convicted, Chain Gang.*

1951: *Oh Susanna!, I Was an American Spy, Revenue Agent, The Texas Rangers, Callaway Went Thataway, The Lion Hunters, China Corsair.*

1952: *For Men Only, Ride the Man Down, The Du Pont Story, Fort Osage, Indian Uprising, Last Train from Bombay, Hoodlum Empire.*

1953: *War Paint, Gun Belt, Torpedo Alley, Invaders from Mars, Safari Drums, San Antone, Sea of Lost Ships, Mexican Manhunt, Jack McCall—Desperado, All American.*

1954: *Massacre Canyon, Sitting Bull, The Big Chase, The High and the Mighty, The Lone Gun, Cry Vengeance, Rails into Laramie.*

1955: *The Eternal Sea, Wyoming Renegades, Strange Lady in Town.*

1956: *Wiretapper, The Last Wagon, Strange Intruder.*

1957: *Chicago Confidential, Rockabilly Baby, The Land Unknown, Last of the Badmen, Hell's Crossroads.*

1958: *The Lone Ranger and the Lost City of Gold, The Bonnie Parker Story.*

1959: *The Lone Texan, The Alligator People.*

1960: *The Amazing Transparent Man.*

1961: *Flight of the Lost Balloon.*

1966: *The Fastest Guitar Alive.*

1967: *Valley of Mystery.*

1968: *The Destructors.*

Television Series

1951–1952: *Steve Donovan—Western Marshal* as Steve Donovan.

Sources

Quinlan, David. *Illustrated Directory of Film Character Actors.* London: Batsford, 1995.

Speed, F. Maurice. *The Western Film and TV Annual.* London: MacDonald, 1957.
Summers, Neil. *The Official TV Western Book Volume #4.* Vienna, WV: Old West Shop Publishing, 1994.

JACK LAMBERT

Jack Lambert was born in Yonkers, New York, in 1920. He studied to be a professor of English and won a degree from a Colorado college before switching careers and acquiring stock and Broadway experience. He gravitated to Hollywood where he made his screen debut in 1941. He became very familiar as a heavy over the next 20 years both in films and on television. His sole regular role in a television series was as Joshua, the first mate on *Riverboat.* He drifted away from show business in the late 1960s. At last report he and his wife were living in some splendor in Carmel, California, where among other activities he has been running a shop.

Jack Lambert Filmography

1942: *About Face.*
1943: *Swing Fever, Follies Girl, The Lost Angel, Bomber's Moon, The Cross of Lorraine.*
1944: *The Canterville Ghost.*

Jack Lambert, who appeared in *Riverboat.*

1945: *Duffy's Tavern, The Hidden Eye, The Harvey Girls, Abilene Town.*
1946: *Specter of the Rose, The Hoodlum Saint, The Killers, The Plainsman and the Lady.*
1947: *The Vigilantes Return, Dick Tracy's Dilemma, The Unsuspected.*
1948: *Force of Evil, Belle Starr's Daughter, River Lady, Montana Belle* (released 1952), *Disaster.*
1949: *The Great Gatsby, Border Incident, Big Jack, Brimstone.*
1950: *Stars in My Crown, Dakota Lil, North of the Great Divide.*
1951: *The Secret of Convict Lake, The Enforcer.*
1952: *Blackbeard the Pirate, Bend of the River.*
1953: *Scared Stiff, 99 River Street.*
1954: *Vera Cruz.*
1955: *Run for Cover, Kiss Me Deadly, At Gunpoint*
1956: *Backlash, Canyon River.*
1957: *Chicago Confidential.*
1958: *Hot Car Girl, Machine-Gun Kelly, Party Girl.*
1959: *Day of the Outlaw, Alias Jesse James.*
1960: *Freckles.*
1961: *The George Raft Story (*a.k.a. *Spin of a Coin).*
1962: *How the West Was Won.*
1963: *4 for Texas.*
1967: *Winchester 73* (TV).

Television Series

1959–1961: *Riverboat* as Joshua.

Sources

Mitchum, John. *Them Ornery Mitchum Boys.* Pacifica, CA: Creatures at Large Press, 1989.
Quinlan, David. *Illustrated Directory of Film Character Actors.* London: Batsford, 1995.
Ragan, David. *Who's Who in Hollywood.* New York: Facts on File, 1992.

DUNCAN LAMONT

This character actor was born Duncan William Ferguson Lamont in Lisbon, Portugal, on June 17, 1918. He was raised in Scotland. He commenced acting at a repertory company in Margate, England, after winning a drama cup in the National Eisteddfod at the age of 15. He then trained at the Royal Academy of Dramatic Art and completed four years' repertory work and touring before entering the army and serving six years as a glider pilot.

After World War II he did another four years in repertory. Then he came to London and also played in the Festival Company at Stratford-upon-Avon. This led to his screen debut in 1950. He was also very active on television in England from its embryo days. His most memorable film role was as the villain Count William De La Marck in *The Adventures of Quentin Durward* (1955), in which he battled it out in a bell tower with Robert Taylor.

Lamont and his actress wife Patricia Driscoll, best known as Maid Marian in the later seasons of the television series *The Adventures of Robin Hood,* then decided to emigrate to America to pursue their careers in 1959. Once there they appeared jointly in the first episode of *Hawaiian Eye.* His subsequent American career was limited to appearances in episodic Westerns such as *The Alaskans* and *The Life and Legend of Wyatt Earp,* for he shot no feature films. In the second and final season of *The Texan* he had a semi-regular role as Mac from December 1959, onwards. He must have been one of the least credible Westerners both to himself and others because disconsolately he and his wife packed their bags and returned to England in 1960.

Duncan Lamont remained a moderately high profile supporting actor averaging at least one film a year and multiple television programs throughout most of the next two decades. His somewhat humorless style of acting tended to lend itself to playing villains. His hobbies were listed as wood carving, collecting antiques and salmon fishing. He also ran a small farm with livestock at Blackham near Tunbridge Wells, Kent, where he and his family had settled. Although no obituary of him was ever published and reference books list him as being alive, in actuality he died at Tunbridge Wells in 1978 at age 60. He was survived by his widow and two daughters.

Duncan Lamont Filmography

1950: *Waterfront* (a.k.a. *Waterfront Women),* *The Woman in Question* (a.k.a. *Five Angles on Murder), She Shall Have Murder.*

1951: *The Galloping Major, The Man in the White Suit, Night Without Stars.*

1952: *Emergency Call* (a.k.a. *100 Hour Hunt), The Brave Don't Cry, The Lost Hours* (a.k.a. *The Big Frame), The Golden Coach, The Night Won't Talk, Song of Paris* (a.k.a. *Bachelor in Paris).*

1953: *The Final Test, The Intruder, Meet Mr. Malcolm.*

1954: *Burnt Evidence, Time Is My Enemy, The End of the Road, The Teckman Mystery, The Passing Stranger.*

1955: *The Adventures of Quentin Durward, The Quatermass Experiment.*

1956: *The Baby and the Battleship.*

1957: *High Flight.*

1958: *A Tale of Two Cities, I Was Monty's Double.*

1959: *The 39 Steps, Ben-Hur, A Touch of Larceny.*

1960: *Circle of Deception, The Queen's Guards.*

1961: *Macbeth.*

1962: *Mutiny on the Bounty.*

1963: *Murder at the Gallop, The Scarlet Blade* (a.k.a. *The Crimson Blade), Panic, The Devil-Ship Pirates.*

1964: *The Evil of Frankenstein.*

1965: *The Brigand of Kandahar, The Murder Game.*

1966: *Arabesque.*

1967: *Frankenstein Created Woman, Quatermass and the Pit.*

1968: *Decline and Fall ... of a Birdwatcher, Dr. Jekyll and Mr. Hyde* (TV).

1969: *Battle of Britain.*

1971: *Burke and Hare, Mary Queen of Scots.*

1972: *Pope Joan, Nothing but the Night, The Creeping Flesh.*

1976: *Escape from the Dark* (a.k.a. *The Littlest Horse Thieves).*

Television Series

1959–1960: *The Texan* as Mac.

Sources

Andrews, Cyrus. *Radio and Television Who's Who Third Edition.* London: George Young, 1954.
Death verified at St. Catherine's House, London, England.
Gianakos, Larry James. *Television Drama Series Programming: A Comprehensive Chronicle, 1980–1982.* Metuchen, NJ: Scarecrow, 1983.
Picture Show's Who's Who On Screen. London: Amalgamated Press, c. 1956.
Quinlan, David. *Illustrated Directory of Film Character Actors.* London: Batsford, 1995.

Portrait of Duncan Lamont, who appeared in *The Texan.*

MICHAEL LANDON

Michael Landon enjoyed an unprecedented 28 years of continuing success on television, during which time he matured in front of viewers' eyes. He had a clean and well-scrubbed look which endeared him to the public. He threw the javelin a long way, but he pitched his television career even further. He started out as an actor. Later he became an accomplished writer and director. The old-fashioned virtues expressed in his work were a major factor in his success. All three of his most successful series were done in association with the NBC network. His relationship with them was believed to be the longest in the history of network television.

It was not always the happiest of relationships, however. In contrast with the sweetness and light which was his professional trademark, colleagues at the network branded him arrogant and difficult. He relentlessly interfered with all aspects of production. He had a novel way of dealing with temperamental actresses. He kept a live tarantula under his hat and at the appropriate moment, he tipped the brim to allow the hairy creature to walk all over his face. Brandon Tartikoff, head honcho at NBC, rallied to his defense: "My dream network would be 22 hours of talent like his. I liked him a lot." Landon himself said, "I am a driven man, because ever since I was a kid I wanted to show myself and others that I was somebody."

Michael Landon was born Eugene Maurice Orowitz on October 31, 1936, in Forest Hills, New York, to publicist Eli Maurice Orowitz and his wife Peggy O'Neill, a former Broadway musical comedy actress. He had one older sister named Evelyn who eventually performed professionally under the name of Victoria King. Michael Landon recalled, "My father was a Jew who didn't care for Catholics and my mother was a Catholic who was anti-Semitic." He described his childhood as "wretched." Shortly after his birth his family moved to Collingswood, New Jersey, a small town on the outskirts of Philadelphia where Eli Orowitz worked as a theater manager and press agent. It was a predominantly WASP community and not overly kind to Jewish families.

He attended both elementary and high schools in Collingswood. He earned national recognition as a javelin thrower by tossing it nearly 212 feet, a national high school record.

He spent so much time practicing his throw that he graduated 300th in a class of 301, but his athletic prowess won him several offers of athletic scholarships; and in the mid–1950s he enrolled at the University of Southern California at Los Angeles. He was obliged to bribe another student $10 to take his entrance exam for him.

He had seen the movie *Samson and Delilah* (1949), which so impressed him that he grew his hair long to give him strength. Three weeks after he arrived at USC, some sadistic jocks cornered him and administered an improvised crewcut. The following day he discovered that every toss was at least 50 feet short of his average. Finally he tore the ligaments in his arm, which effectively ended his career as a javelin thrower. He dropped out of college after his freshman year.

He worked at a variety of jobs including blanket salesman, canner in a soup factory and car wash attendant. When unloading freight at a North Hollywood warehouse, he encountered an aspiring thespian who requested his assistance in preparing to audition in a scene from *Home of the Brave.* He found the experience so rewarding that he decided to take lessons at the Warner Bros. acting school. Although the class was terminated after four months, he gained a role on *Telephone Time,* a dramatic anthology television series which aired from 1956 to 1958 on both CBS and ABC. The name Michael Landon was chosen at random from the Los Angeles telephone book. He began to obtain television roles in anthology series and Westerns. His first important motion picture role was the title character of *I Was a Teenage Werewolf* (1957). It cost $100,000 to make and grossed $2,000,000 for American International Pictures. He was ashamed of it, but it gave him some necessary exposure and is considered a camp classic today.

Producer David Dortort had seen Landon in the pilot episode of *The Restless Gun* (1957) starring John Payne. Intrigued by Landon's personality and versatility, Dortort requested him to read for the role of Little Joe Cartwright in *Bonanza* when he was casting for the series in 1959. He was virtually hired then and there. Landon initially had less faith than his costars in the success of *Bonanza,* but he was later very perceptive in analyzing the success of the show. He attributed it to the fact that *Bonanza* gave the viewers at home a sense of security in the old-fashioned values. In 1964 he won the Silver Spurs Award as the most popular TV Western star. Often told is the story of how he spent a day in 1962 with a U.S. Marine unit on a toughening-up course and the battalion commander was so impressed with the way he behaved "under fire" that he was made an honorary first sergeant on the spot.

Landon began writing and directing occasional episodes of *Bonanza* from 1962 onwards. By the time the series ended, he had written 30 original teleplays and directed a dozen episodes. He began to write out of necessity when a shortage of suitable scripts forced production to cease temporarily. He had been mulling over an idea for a script, in which the Cartwrights are mistaken for bank robbers. Over a weekend he wrote the script, which he described as functional rather than inspired, gave it to David Dortort on Monday, and shooting on "The Gambler" began a few days later.

His later scripts were more professional and he was proudest of "The Wish," an episode he wrote and directed, in which a well-intentioned Hoss (Dan Blocker) attempts to befriend a family of black settlers, but merely adds to their problems. He also liked "Forever," a two-part love story originally written for Blocker which Landon rewrote for Little Joe, adding a couple of scenes indicating the death of Hoss mainly by a kind of stillness. During the last five years of *Bonanza* there was increasing friction on the set caused by Landon's questioning the competence of other directors and writers, much to the consternation of David Dortort. On his lavish estate in Beverly Hills, Landon installed a *Bonanza* room featuring mementos from the Ponderosa set—including the privy!

When *Bonanza* expired in January 1973, all three television networks tried to sign him. By his own estimate he was offered 36 crime series, six medical shows and one sci-fi. He rejected all of them. Finally in late 1973, Ed Friendly, one of the creators of *Laugh-In,* approached him with the idea of doing a television series based on Laura Ingalls Wilder's children's classics about 19th century frontier life. Although he was at first reluctant, he changed his mind when he discovered that his wife had read the books as a girl and was rereading them with their 12-year-old daughter. He directed and starred in the two-hour pilot *The Little House on the Prairie,* which was broadcast in April 1974, and was an immense success. He played Charles Ingalls, a farmer trying to make a living for his family in a community called Walnut Grove, Plum Creek, Minnesota. Stories related experiences of family life, growing children, natural disasters and relating to other members of the community in which they live.

To ensure authenticity he researched frontier life in Minnesota in the 1870s. Every building on the show was an exact replica of one that actually existed. By the end of its first season *Little House on the Prairie* was a top-rated series and one of the most popular NBC shows in years. Coproducer Ed Friendly withdrew from active participation in mid-1974 after he came into creative conflict with Michael Landon. Friendly wanted to follow the incidents depicted in the original books to the letter, whereas Landon insisted upon weaving fictional plots around incidents mentioned in the books. From then onwards Mike Landon was king of the hill. He nixed one projected episode in which his character is suspected of having murdered a pregnant girl and delayed another in which Ingalls' nine-month-old baby son died.

Landon had a deep-rooted mistrust of Hollywood sycophants and believed that taking advice from them was tantamount to taking lessons in sailing from the captain of the *Titanic.* On several occasions he asserted, "If Mike Landon flops, I don't want anyone else to take the blame but Mike Landon." As a director his skill at visual storytelling had sharpened over the years, and his work had been likened to that of the great romantic director Frank Borzage. In 1981 Landon created and produced *Father Murphy,* a short-lived spinoff of the *Little House* which starred Merlin Olsen. Landon also directed the pilot. He decided to leave the original series in 1982, so the title was changed to *Little House: A New Beginning,* but it lasted only a single season.

Landon continued with yet another hit series, *Highway to Heaven,* which began in 1984 and lasted five years. In it he played Jonathan Smith, a probationary angel whose quest was to bring love and understanding to

Michael Landon in *Bonanza.*

troubled people everywhere. He gave chosen people a chance to redeem their lives. Despite having supernatural powers, most often he relied on giving advice and examples to guide people. Although deceased, Jonathan traveled around the country in the guise of an itinerant laborer, complete with denim jacket and bouffant hair do. Only ex-cop and reformed deadbeat Mark Gordon (Victor French) assisted him in his mission. This series was the least successful of the three series in which Landon starred. Levity was in short supply and the series highlighted Landon's greatest weakness, a tendency for sentimentality to get the better of him.

By the mid–1980s he was spending most of his time with his new family. He admitted that during that decade he had increased his weight and stopped exercising. He began dieting and working out, dying his gray locks in anticipation of a new television series which was not to be. CBS had picked up the pilot of *US,* a series which he was set to produce and star in as a traveling columnist. The series (which was to have been produced in association with Columbia Pictures TV) was abandoned after his death. He had also inked a deal to make theatrical movies, and he was writing the script for his first picture when he became ill. His long-standing business association with NBC ended in acrimony when the actor publicly stated that executives there had insulted him, although network officials subsequently repudiated this.

He had been having bad stomach pains for several weeks when in March 1991, he went skiing with his family in Park City, Utah. When the pain became unbearable, he flew back to Los Angeles a day early and checked into Cedars Sinai Medical Center. He was diagnosed on April 5, 1991, as having cancer, but stated his determination to fight the disease and had undergone experimental treatment. On May 9 he appeared on his friend Johnny Carson's *Tonight Show* where he talked freely and with some humor about his illness. It was the most watched *Tonight Show* since 1981 and the second most highly rated segment since Carson began hosting in 1962.

Michael Landon, 54, died on Monday, July 1, 1991, at 1:20 P.M. of liver and pancreatic cancer on his ten-acre ranch in Malibu Canyon, California. He was cremated on the same day, and his ashes were placed in a private room at Hillside Memorial Park Cemetery in Los Angeles. He was married three times. He married former legal secretary and widow Dodie Levy in 1957 when she was 26 and he was 19. She had a son named Mark by a previous marriage, whom he adopted. They divorced late in 1960. He also adopted a second son named Josh during this marriage. There was also another son, Jason Smith, who was adopted by the Landons when he was one week old and spent his first three years as their son. He was subsequently handed back for adoption by others when their marriage crumbled.

He then married Lynn Noe, an actress and model, when they eloped to Mexico on January 12, 1961. She was then 27. When they divorced in December 1981, she publicly abused him for ending their marriage. Landon adopted Cheryl, her daughter by a previous marriage, who was born in 1953. They also had four children of their own: Michael, Jr., Leslie Ann, Shawna Leigh and Christopher Beau. In 1983 he wed Cindy Clerico, a stand-in and makeup artist, who was born in 1957. They met while working on *Little House on the Prairie.* With her he had two children: Jennifer (born in 1984) and Sean (born in 1986). Landon was survived by his widow and all nine children.

He left an estate of $100,000,000. Under the terms of his will, his widow received 45 percent of his estate, his nine children received 40 percent, and 15 percent went to charity. In effect this meant that his seven children by his first two marriages each inherited about $4,500,000. His two youngest children each inherited about $4,500,000 together with a small extra amount to pay for their education.

In 1967 the Ponderosa was built on the shores of Lake Tahoe, Nevada, where the show's interiors were shot from then onwards. Aside from the ranch, the Ponderosa included the town featured in all the episodes. The cowboy hat and jacket worn by Little Joe Cartwright hang on a wooden peg inside the ranch house. Within one month after Landon's death, 80,000 fans had visited the Ponderosa to pay their last respects to Little Joe.

Michael Landon Filmography

(as actor only)

1956: *These Wilder Years.*
1957: *I Was a Teenage Werewolf.*
1958: *God's Little Acre, Maracaibo, High School Confidential!*
1959: *The Legend of Tom Dooley.*
1961: *The Errand Boy* (cameo).
1974: *The Little House on the Prairie* (TV).
1976: *The Loneliest Runner* (TV).
1983: *Love Is Forever (*a.k.a. *Comeback)* (TV).
1984: *Sam's Son, Highway to Heaven* (TV), *Look Back to Yesterday* (TV).
1989: *Where Pigeons Go to Die* (TV) (cameo).

Television Series

1959–1973: *Bonanza* as Little Joe Cartwright.
1974–1982: *Little House on the Prairie* as Charles Ingalls.
1984–1989: *Highway to Heaven* as Jonathan Smith.

Sources

Current Biography. New York: H.W. Wilson, 1977.
Daily Telegraph newspaper. Obituary, July 1991.
Shapiro, Melany. *Bonanza: The Unofficial Story of the Ponderosa.* Las Vegas, NV: Pioneer, 1993.

Sternig, Barbara, and Tony Brenna. "Landon's widow reveals Michael's inspiring last message." *National Enquirer* magazine, July 23, 1991.

Variety. Obituary, July 8, 1991.

Wilson, Cheryl Landon. *I Promised My Dad: An Intimate Portrait of Michael Landon by His Eldest Daughter.* New York: Simon and Schuster, 1992.

KEITH LARSEN

Keith Larsen was a virile leading man who starred in four television series of the action adventure variety so popular in the 1950s. He had a particularly incisive acting style and magnificent physique which made him a good hero for series of this sort. Of the four series in which he had the lead, two *(Brave Eagle* and *Northwest Passage)* could be classified as Westerns, but none were long-lasting. His career as an actor did not long survive the 1950s, but he reestablished himself as a director. In this respect he was rather like a poor man's Cornel Wilde. He was generally well-liked by his costars.

Keith Larsen was born in Salt Lake City, Utah, on June 17, 1925, the son of a traveling salesman. Once, he reckoned that in the course of his childhood he was a pupil at over 20 different schools. He attended high school in Glendale, California, where he became an excellent athlete and tennis player. His original ambition was to be a top criminal lawyer. At the age of 16 in 1942, with World War II raging, he enlisted in the navy. It was while he was convalescing from injuries received when his ship was bombed that he became interested in acting. In 1944 he was discharged when it was discovered that he had lied about his age.

He enrolled at the University of Utah, but transferred to the University of Southern California. After Larsen spent some time as a professional tennis player, his stage debut came when he appeared in *Golden Boy* in Santa Monica. Agent Walter Mirisch spotted him there and was so impressed that he signed him to a personal contract which led to his screen debut in *The Rose Bowl Story* (1952).

He never became a big name in either films or television, but he enjoyed some success in both until the end of the decade. In TV's *The Hunter* he briefly replaced Barry Nelson as Bart Adams, a handsome, successful entrepreneur whose adventures take place in exotic locales all over the world. He then played the title role in the *Brave Eagle* series. *Brave Eagle* was somewhat unusual in that Larsen played the hero who was a full-blooded Indian, but a benign one. He was a young 19th century chief who wanted peace with the white man. Despite this there were situations of conflict where Brave Eagle and his tribe had to resort to weapons to defend themselves against evil white men who sought to rob and destroy them. Keena (Anthony Numkeena) was his young foster son. Morning Cloud (Kim Winona), a beautiful Indian maiden, provided the romantic interest. Each week Brave Eagle taught his ward a lesson in charity or justice in a setting virtually free of stereotypes. The Indians all spoke good English and were depicted as the possessors of an old but still great culture.

Brave Eagle was produced by Roy Rogers Frontier Productions, with location shooting in Chatsworth, California. It was shown on CBS from September 28, 1955, and lasted for 26 half-hour black and white episodes until June 6, 1956. Although movies like *Dances with Wolves* would enjoy resounding success, possibly this series was a little too far ahead of its time to win wide popular acceptance.

One person whom Larsen's characterization impressed was producer Adrian Samish, who remembered him when casting the television series *Northwest Passage,* in which Larsen starred as Major Robert Rogers. This was the character played by Spencer Tracy in the classic MGM film *Northwest Passage: Rogers' Rangers* (1940), from which this series was derived. The locale of this series was the

Keith Larsen as *Brave Eagle.*

area which became New York State and Eastern Canada at the time of the French and Indian War of 1754–1759. The Northwest Passage was a mythical inland waterway which would enable ships to traverse the breadth of America. The original film was conceived in two parts, but the second part was never shot. The Northwest Passage was not found and seldom referred, to so the film was subtitled *Rogers' Rangers.*

In the television series it was not found either, but there were constant skirmishes with the French and Red Indians. The experienced Indian fighter and explorer Major Rogers called upon men to volunteer and organized them into an efficient fighting force called Rogers' Rangers, the main purpose of which was to aid him in his exploration. The other regulars in the series were his sidekick and cohort Hunk Marriner (Buddy Ebsen) and mapmaker Langdon Towne (Don Burnett), a Harvard graduate from an affluent Eastern family. His men were generally a very tough bunch, with Rogers himself regarded as history's first commando since he penetrated deep into enemy territory.

Northwest Passage was an extremely well-made series, shot by MGM in color mainly on their studio back lot. Location shooting was kept to a minimum. It made its debut on NBC on September 14, 1958, but lasted for only 26 half-hour episodes until September 8, 1959. There was a general feeling that it should have lasted longer, but no appropriate timeslot was ever found for it. Consequently it was in competition with some immensely popular programs which quickly scuttled its chances. The series did turn in a profit for MGM when individual episodes were stitched together into feature films, released to maximum advantage during the school holidays.

Larsen went on to star in another adventure series, *The Aquanauts,* in which he played Drake Andrews, one of two professional salvage divers in Southern California. He was last seen in the episode dated January 18, 1961. He was forced to depart the series after a sinus operation that made him bleed profusely when he submerged 30 feet. This more or less spelled *finis* to his acting career. He continued as a director, primarily of television episodes. He had ambitions to direct in the early 1950s and helmed episodes of his own television series. He later directed a few low-budget feature films, usually with outdoor themes. Directing is the vocation which he prefers. Once asked about this, he replied, "What appeals to me about directing as opposed to acting is that you have more creative control and more opportunity to express your imagination." His career as a director was similar to his career as an actor in that he never made the "A list" of either. The Screen Directors Guild no longer has a listing for him, and he has latterly been posted among the lost players of the screen.

Formerly wed to Susan Larsen, Larsen was married to actress Vera Miles from 1960 until their divorce in 1973. They have one son, Erik, born in 1960.

Keith Larsen Filmography

1952: *The Rose Bowl Story, Flat Top, Hiawatha.*
1953: *Fort Vengeance. Son of Belle Starr, War Paint.*
1954: *Arrow in the Dust, Security Risk.*
1955: *Dial Red O, Chief Crazy Horse, Night Freight, Wichita, Desert Sands.*
1957: *Last of the Badmen, Badlands of Montana, Apache Warrior.*
1959: *Frontier Rangers (*a.k.a. *Northwest Rangers* (TV:NP).
Fury River (TV:NP), *Mission of Danger* (TV: NP).
1965: *Women of the Prehistoric Planet.*
1967: *Caxambu!*
1968: *Mission Batangas* (also directed), *The Omegans.*
1970: *Night of the Witches* (also wrote and directed).
1972: *Run to Cougar Mountain* (also directed).
1976: *White Water* (also wrote and directed).

Television Series

1954: *Hunter* as Bart Adams.
1955–1956: *Brave Eagle* as Brave Eagle.
1958–1959: *Northwest Passage* as Major Robert Rogers.
1960–1961: *The Aquanauts* as Drake Andrews.

Sources

Essoe, Gabe. *The Book of Movie Lists.* Westport, CT: Arlington House, 1981.
Picture Show Annual. London: Amalgamated Press, 1955.
Quinlan, David. *Illustrated Directory of Film Stars.* London: Batsford, 1996.
Rovin, Jeff. *The Great Television Series.* South Brunswick and New York: Barnes, 1977.
Speed, F. Maurice. *The Western Film Annual.* London: MacDonald, 1955.

Note

Feature films derived from the *Northwest Passage* series are denoted NP in the filmography.

"LASH" LARUE

Since he spent so much time emulating Humphrey Bogart, it always comes of something of a surprise to realize that "Lash" LaRue did not hail from New York. The idea of a reformed bad man goes back to the time of William S. Hart and became an overworked cliché during the more morally ambivalent climate of the 1960s, but "Lash" LaRue was an early character in this mode. In the days when there was a sharp delineation between the white-hatted hero of virtue and the black-hatted villain, LaRue blurred the distinction by being a hero who dressed entirely in black. His period of stardom was brief and he would scarcely rate more than a footnote in most histories of film and television, but he strove to be different and, on account of his longevity, he has become something of a cult hero.

Alfred "Lash" LaRue was most likely born in Gretna, Louisiana, on June 14, 1917, the son of a salesman. His early life is somewhat obscure, but he is known to have spent much time as an itinerant traveling in the South. After military school, he drifted to California where he attended the College of the Pacific in Stockton, California, originally studying speech and drama to help correct a couple of speech defects. After leaving, he became a real estate salesman for a short time, but soon decided that he would prefer to be an actor. He obtained some experience with little theater groups, where he showed enough charisma for Warner Bros. to test him. They rejected him, however, because of his too-close resemblance to Humphrey Bogart. Another star there, George Brent, suggested that he try Universal.

He was tested in a scene from *Christmas Holiday,* a film which starred Deanna Durbin. She saw the test and was sufficiently impressed to recommend that Universal sign him. During his brief tenure there, he appeared in a Universal serial called *The Master Key* (1945) and the Deanna Durbin feature *Lady on a Train* (1945) in which he played a waiter. LaRue credited Robert Tansey with creating the character of "Lash" LaRue. This producer-director arranged for LaRue to be trained in the use of a bullwhip for a forthcoming film. Although it was originally intended only to be a gimmick for one film, LaRue became extremely proficient at it, a skill which he maintained into the 1990s.

LaRue was introduced as "The Cheyenne Kid" in the film *Song of Old Wyoming* (1945). It was in the Eddie Dean film *Caravan Trail* (1946), however, that he rose to fame. Producers Releasing Corporation (PRC) were deluged with fan mail; as a result, LaRue was rewarded with a series of his own in which he was partnered with comic sidekick Al "Fuzzy" St John. He rode a black stallion called Rush, but is one of a large band of television Western stars who did not like horses. Although the series was extremely low budget, the producers had no difficulty earning a profit. When PRC metamorphosed into Eagle-Lion in 1947, LaRue shot more Westerns for them, but by this time he had dropped "The Cheyenne Kid" and become the more familiar "Lash" LaRue. When Eagle-Lion went bust, LaRue signed another contract with Screen Guild, with whom he remained until 1951. His final two Western features were released by Realart in 1952.

When B Westerns came to an end, he hosted a television series called *Lash of the West.* This was originally a syndicated quarter-hour series in which he was shown as a modern marshal who did a brief introduction about some adventure of his grandfather. This was a cue for a rehash of one of his old movies in a heavily edited format. It was shown briefly on ABC. There is a very strong body of opinion that it would have been much better if some enterprising producer had shot a new series of adventures featuring this character specifically designed for television.

Although he had made a considerable amount of money through the films and merchandising, it went as fast as it had come in and he ran into trouble with the I.R.S., who hounded him for back taxes. To pay them off, he embarked on an endless round of circuses, fairs and carnivals. He lost control of his life after this and fought a losing battle against booze and drugs. In 1956 he was arrested in Memphis for receiving stolen property. In 1958 he attempted suicide when his estranged wife

"Lash" LaRue, who appeared in *The Life and Legend of Wyatt Earp*.

refused a reconciliation and sued for divorce. His most substantial acting work of the late 1950s came when he landed the role of shady Sheriff Johnny Behan in the television series *The Life and Legend of Wyatt Earp*. This job ended in acrimony because of his intense antipathy to the star Hugh O'Brian, and the role was recast. He made scattered appearances in other series such as *26 Men*. After this he became *persona non grata* in the film and television world.

By the early 1960s he and another wife were reliably reported to be running a motel cum restaurant in Reno, Nevada, but he allegedly lost this in a costly divorce settlement and shortly afterwards all his personal belongings were stolen. In 1964 he paid for an advertisement in a Hollywood trade paper in which he begged forgiveness for past misdemeanors and wanted work. In 1966 he was arrested for vagrancy in Tampa, Florida. A friendly policeman introduced him to Mission Power Headquarters and Home of the Apostles, where for several years he became an evangelist until a spectacular falling out. There were still brushes with the law and in September 1974, he was arrested in Georgia for public drunkenness and later convicted of attempting to exchange a Bible for marijuana. He appeared wearing clothes in a hard core pornographic film, *Hard on the Trail* (1971), an experience he had mixed feelings about. On the one hand he did not approve of it, but the money came in useful.

He drove around in a convertible marked "Lash" and habitually still wore black. He was married 12 times and divorced 11 times. His wives included Eloise Mulhall, actress Barbra Fuller and Western heroine Reno Browne. For years he existed on Social Security and handouts. In more recent years he became involved in a successful business and, in his new reformed state, he became a popular figure at Western conventions held all over the United States.

"Lash" LaRue, 79, died at the Providence St. Joseph Medical Center in Burbank, California, on May 21, 1996. A chain smoker for decades, he died of a heart attack. His body was cremated on May 22, and his remains were placed in a vault at Forest Lawn Cemetery.

"Lash" LaRue Filmography

1945: *The Master Key* (serial), *Lady on a Train, Song of Old Wyoming.*
1946: *The Caravan Trail, Wild West.*
1947: *Border Feud, Ghost Town Renegades, Law of the Lash, Pioneer Justice, Cheyenne Takes Over, Return of the Lash, The Fighting Vigilantes, Stage to Mesa City, Heartaches.*
1948: *Dead Man's Gold, Frontier Revenge, The Enchanted Valley.*
1949: *Mark of the Lash, Outlaw Country, Son of the Bad Man, Son of Billy the Kid.*
1950: *King of the Bullwhip, The Dalton's Women.*
1951: *The Thundering Trail, Vanishing Outpost.*
1952: *Black Lash, Frontier Phantom.*
1953: *Please Don't Touch Me.*
1955: *Gang Busters* (a.k.a. *Guns Don't Argue*).
1971: *Hard on the Trail.*
1985: *Dark Power.*
1986: *Stagecoach* (TV), *Alien Outlaw.*
1987: *Escape.*
1990: *Pair of Aces* (TV).

Television Series

1953: *Law of the Lash* as "Lash" LaRue.
1959: *The Life and Legend of Wyatt Earp* as Sheriff Johnny Behan.

Sources

Conversation with "Lash" LaRue in 1993.
Dellinger, Paul. "Remembering 'Lash' LaRue." *Classic Images* magazine, issue #253, July 1996.
Lamparski, Richard. *Whatever Became Of? Eighth Series.* New York: Crown, 1982.
Miller, Lee O. *The Great Cowboy Stars of Movies and Television* New Rochelle, NY: Arlington House, 1979.
Ragan, David. *Who's Who in Hollywood.* New York: Facts on File, 1992.

HARRY LAUTER

Harry Lauter was born in New York City on June 19, 1914, the son of a graphic artist. His mother, who wrote for *The Literary Digest,* died when he was four years old, so he was sent to live with his grandmother in rural Colorado. His grandparents were once highly successful trapeze artists. While in his teens he rodeoed in Wyoming and Montana where he became a skilled rider and first acquired an interest in the West. These skills served him well in later years when it came to shooting Westerns because he could do his own stunts and riding. He attended high school in San Diego, California, and later studied for a few years at the Balboa Academy of Fine Arts before deciding to become an actor.

He did summer stock at Martha's Vineyard in Maine and at Elitch Gardens in Denver, Colorado. After this he was drafted for the duration of World War II. Upon his discharge he went to New York where he appeared on Broadway in *The Story of Mary Surratt* (1947), which starred Dorothy Gish. A talent scout from 20th Century–Fox spotted him in that play and the studio brought him to Hollywood, where they tested and signed him but offered him nothing in the way of roles. After resting for a year, he insisted on being released because the idleness did not sit well. Since little was happening in New York, he decided to stay in Hollywood, but his problem was lack of credits.

He attended an open audition and won a role in *Hit Parade of 1947,* which marked his screen debut. After taking some advice, he was told that Westerns would always be in vogue, which suited his talents down to the ground. Consequently he did multiples of television Western series such as *The Lone Ranger* and *Death Valley Days.* He was also a member of the Gene Autry and Russell Hayden stock companies which used actors regularly in the oaters they produced for television. He was sometimes on the right side of the law but most frequently played villains which he freely admitted that he enjoyed the most.

Lauter had two television series in which he was a regular. In *Waterfront* he was a member of the crew and the son of a tugboat captain played by Preston Foster, an actor whom he admired tremendously. In *Tales of the Texas Rangers* he costarred with Willard Parker as members of the highly respected law enforcement agency. Originally this series was seen on children's television (where it had an enormous following) before being switched to prime time television. There were 52 half-hour black and white shows in all. It was dubbed into various languages and shown all over the world. Some of the stories were part of Western history while others were contemporary in their settings. Ironically, for a man who had spent much of his career playing villains, in his own series he was decidedly heroic. In all he reckoned that he shot over 900 Western episodes.

He continued to work actively in the industry for many years before chain smoking caught up with him, and he suffered from emphysema and asthma. Many of the people whom he had enjoyed working with had either died or retired, so he switched professions and became a highly successful artist, painting oils of dramatic scenes in the High Sierras and Rocky Mountains, rugged locations where he had shot films. These paintings he sold at exhibitions all over America. His other hobby was cooking. He lived in a mobile home park in California's Ojai Valley. He died on October 30, 1990, in Ojai, California, of heart failure, at age 76. He was survived by his wife Doris Gilbert, a seascape artist, and daughter Brooke.

Harry Lauter Filmography

1947: *Hit Parade of 1947, The Magnificent Rogue.*

1948: *Moonrise, The Gay Intruders, A Foreign Affair, Let's Live Again, Jungle Patrol.*

1949: *Prince of the Plains, White Heat, Tucson, Slattery's Hurricane, The Great Dan Patch, Zamba, Incident, Frontier Marshal, Bandit King of Texas, Alimony, I Was a Male War Bride, Without Honor, Too Late for Tears, State Department File 649, Twelve O'Clock High, Parole, Inc.*

1950: *The Blue Grass of Kentucky, Experiment Alcatraz, Between Midnight and Dawn, I'll Get By, No Way Out, The Flying Missile, Bunco Squad, Counterspy Meets Scotland Yard, The Great Jewel Robber, When Willie Comes Marching Home, 711 Ocean Drive.*

1951: *Silver City Bonanza, Roadblock, Call Me Mister, Thunder in God's Country, Let's Go Navy, Flying Disc Man from Mars* (serial), *Lorna Doone, Whirlwind, The Mob, Hills of Utah, The Day the Earth Stood Still, According to Mrs. Hoyle, The Kid from Amarillo, Valley of Fire, The Racket, I Want You, Bowery Battalion, Flying Leathernecks, Come Fill the Cup, Inside Straight, Operation Pacific.*

1952: *Night Stage to Galveston, This Woman Is Dangerous, Apache Country, The Sea Tiger, The Steel Fist, Talk About a Stranger, Yukon Gold, Red Ball Express, Androcles and the Lion, Sound Off, Battle Zone, Rancho Notorious, Bugles in the Afternoon.*

1953: *Canadian Mounties vs. Atomic Invaders* (serial), *The Marshal's Daughter, Prince of Pirates, Topeka, The Big Heat, The Fighting Lawman, Forbidden, Fighter Attack, Pack Train, I Love Melvin, Flight Nurse.*

1954: *Dragonfly Squadron, Trader Tom of the China Seas* (serial), *Crime Wave, Yankee Pasha, The Bob Mathias Story, Return to Treasure Island, The Forty Niners, Riot in Cell Block 11, Captain Kidd and the Slave Girl, Dragnet, The Boy from Oklahoma, They Rode West.*

1955: *It Came from Beneath the Sea, King of the Carnival* (serial), *Creature with the Atom Brain, Lord of the Jungle, The Crooked Web, At Gunpoint, Apache Ambush, Outlaw Treasure, Not as a Stranger, The Eternal Sea.*

1956: *Earth Vs. the Flying Saucers, The Werewolf, The Man in the Gray Flannel Suit, Miami Exposé, Dig That Uranium, Tension at Table Rock, Blonde Bait, Gun Brothers, The Three Outlaws.*

1957: *The Women of Pitcairn Island, The Badge of Marshal Brennan, Hellcats of the Navy, Death in Small Doses, The Oklahoman, Raiders of Old California, Shoot-Out at Medicine Bend, Jet Pilot.*

1958: *Return to Warbow, Toughest Gun in Tombstone, The Cry Baby Killer, Tarzan's Fight for Life, Good Day for a Hanging, Girl on the Run* (TV), *The Last Hurrah, The Lawless Eighties, Buffalo Gun, The Case Against Brooklyn.*

1959: *The Gunfight at Dodge City, Louisiana Hussy, A Date with Death.*

1960: *Key Witness.*

1961: *Posse from Hell.*

1962: *The Wild Westerners, Lonely Are the Brave.*

1963: *It's a Mad Mad Mad Mad World, Showdown.*

1965: *Fort Courageous, Convict Stage, Harlow* (Carroll Baker version), *The Satan Bug.*

1966: *Ambush Bay, Fort Utah, For Pete's Sake!, Batman.*
1967: *Return of the Gunfighter* (TV).
1968: *Massacre Harbor.*
1969: *More Dead than Alive, Paint Your Wagon, Barquero, Superbeast* (released 1972).
1970: *Zig Zag.*
1971: *The Todd Killings, Escape from the Planet of the Apes.*
1980: *Cade County* (unreleased).

Television Series

1953–1956: *Waterfront* as Jim Herrick
1955–1958: *Tales of the Texas Rangers* as Ranger Clay Morgan.

Sources

Goldrup, Tom, and Jim Goldrup. *Feature Players: The Stories Behind the Faces Volume #1.* Published privately, 1986.
Lamparski, Richard. *Whatever Became Of? Ninth Series.* New York: Crown, 1985.
Quinlan, David. *Illustrated Directory of Character Actors.* London: Batsford, 1995.

NORMAN LEAVITT

For the record, this supporting actor had the semi-regular role of the town handyman in the *Trackdown* Western series of the 1950s. Leavitt is understood to be deceased, but the details are not available.

Norman Leavitt Filmography

1946: *The Idea Girl, The Harvey Girls, The Spider Woman Strikes Back.*
1947: *If Winter Comes. Daisy Kenyon.*
1948: *Yellow Sky, The Big Clock, Music Man, The Walls of Jericho, The Luck of the Irish.*
1949: *The Reckless Moment, Slattery's Hurricane, The Inspector General.*
1950: *Mule Train, Side Street, Harvey.*
1951: *Comin' Round the Mountain, Vengeance Valley, Showboat.*
1952: *The Bushwackers, Mutiny.*
1953: *Hannah Lee (*a.k.a. *Outlaw Territory), The Moonlighter, Stars and Stripes Forever.*
1954: *Living It Up, The Long Long Trails.*
1955: *Inside Detroit.*
1956: *Stagecoach to Fury, The Brass Legend, Friendly Persuasion.*
1957: *Fury at Showdown, The Girl in Black Stockings, Rockabilly Baby.*
1958: *Showdown at Boot Hill, Teenage Monster.*
1959: *The Rookie.*
1960: *Young Jesse James.*
1962: *Billy Rose's Jumbo, Saintly Sinners, The Three Stooges in Orbit.*
1963: *Summer Magic.*
1964: *The Patsy.*
1971: *The Marriage of a Young Stockbroker.*
1975: *The Day of the Locust.*

Television Series

1958–1959: *Trackdown* as Ralph.

Sources

Summers, Neil. *The First Official TV Western Book.* Vienna, WV: Old West Shop Publishing, 1987.

PETER LEEDS

Peter Leeds was born in Bayonne, New Jersey, on May 30, 1917, and graduated from the Neighborhood Playhouse. Afterwards he appeared on Broadway in such shows as *Johnny*

Johnson, My Heart's in the Highlands, Gypsy and *Sugar Babies.* An accomplished voiceover artist, he appeared in over 3,000 radio broadcasts.

He was perhaps best remembered as a straight man for Bob Hope. Their working relationship began in 1954 on one of Hope's television specials and extended until 1991. He also completed 14 tours with Hope as part of the Army Air Corps special services unit visiting G.I.'s during the Vietnam War. He acted as straight man for several other comedians and made thousands of television appearances on nearly every popular sitcom and variety show. He played the semi-regular supporting role of a saloon owner and gambler in the Western series *Trackdown* during the 1950s. He later had a regular role in the sitcom *Pete and Gladys.*

Offcamera he served as president of the Los Angeles AFTRA local for five years during the 1970s and was a member of the national and local AFTRA Board of Directors. He received AFTRA's highest honor, the Gold Card, in 1992. He was on the Board of Governors for the Academy of Television Arts and Sciences and was Vice President of the Eddie Cantor Lodge B'nai B'rith.

Leeds died in Los Angeles on November 12, 1996, at age 79, of cancer. He was survived by his wife Pat, whom he married in 1962, and a granddaughter.

Peter Leeds Filmography

1941: *Don Winslow of the Navy* (serial), *Public Enemies.*
1942: *Treat 'Em Rough.*
1943: *Crash Dive, Lady Bodyguard.*
1949: *The Lady Gambles.*
1950: *Ma and Pa Kettle Go to Town, Saddle Tramp.*
1951: *The Frogmen, Katie Did It, Ma and Pa Kettle Back on the Farm.*
1952: *Come Back Little Sheba.*
1953: *99 River Street, Stalag 17.*
1954: *The Last Time I Saw Paris, The Atomic Kid, The Long Long Trailer.*
1955: *Interrupted Melody, Tight Spot, Love Me or Leave Me, I'll Cry Tomorrow, Bobby Ware Is Missing, Hit the Deck, Six Bridges to Cross, It's Always Fair Weather.*
1956: *Behind the High Wall, The Best Things in Life Are Free.*
1957: *Kiss Them for Me.*
1959: *Girls Town, The Rookie, The Thirty Foot Bride of Candy Rock.*
1960: *The Facts of Life, Please Don't Eat the Daisies.*
1962: *The Scarface Mob.*
1963: *The Wheeler Dealers.*
1965: *Harlow.*
1967: *Eight on the Lam.*
1968: *With Six You Get Egg Roll.*
1974: *Nine Lives of Fritz the Cat* (voice).
1987: *Dragnet.*

Television Series

1958–1959: *Trackdown* as Tenner Smith.
1960–1962: *Pete and Gladys* as George Colton.

Sources

Summers, Neil. *The First Official TV Western Book.* Vienna, WV: Old West Shop Publishing, 1987.
Torres, Vanessa. *Variety.* Obituary, November 25, 1996.

NAN LESLIE

Nan Leslie was born in Los Angeles on June 4, 1926. A photograph of her on the cover of *Liberty* magazine at the wheel of a sailboat led to her becoming an RKO contract player. She is best remembered for the six films she made with Western star Tim Holt. She and Holt were unofficially engaged for 18 months, but broke off because he dated other women.

She had regular roles in three series. In *Fury* (the horse and boy Western series) she played the sister of Jim Newton (Peter Graves). In the short-lived soap opera *King's Row* she played the role which Ann Sheridan had originated in the feature film. In *The Californians* she played the wife of storekeeper and vigilante leader Jack McGivern (Sean McClory).

Leslie married in 1949, but divorced in the early 1950s. She remarried in 1969 and unofficially retired from acting. Widowed in 1990, she currently resides in San Juan Capistrano, California.

Nan Leslie Filmography

1945: *George White Scandals, Under Western Skies, I'll Remember April.*
1946: *Sunset Pass, Sister Kenny, The Bamboo Blonde, The Falcon's Alibi, From This Day Forward, Bedlam.*
1947: *The Devil Thumbs a Ride, Woman on the Beach, Under the Tonto Rim, Wild Horse Mesa.*
1948: *The Arizona Ranger, Guns of Hate, Western Heritage, Indian Agent.*
1949: *Rim of the Canyon, Pioneer Marshal.*
1950: *Train to Tombstone.*
1953: *Problem Girls, Iron Mountain Trail.*
1959: *Miracle of the Hills.*
1960: *The Crowded Sky.*
1969: *The Bamboo Saucer.*

Television Series

1955–1958: *Fury* as Harriet Newton.
1955–1956: *King's Row* as Randy Monaghan.
1957–1958: *The Californians* as Martha McGivern.

Sources

Brooks, Tim. *The Complete Directory to Prime Time TV Stars 1946–Present.* New York: Ballantine Books, 1987.
Rothel, David. *Tim Holt.* Madison, NC: Empire, 1994.
Turner, Steve, and Edgar M. Wyatt. *Saddle Gals.* Madison, NC: Empire, 1995.

GEORGE J. LEWIS

George Jorge Lewis was born in Guadalajara, Mexico, on December 10, 1903, to an American father and Spanish mother. He was one of three brothers. His father was an executive with a typewriter company. When civil war broke out in Mexico in 1911, the family fled Mexico and relocated initially to Chicago and then to Princeton, Illinois. His father was then transferred, and so the family moved to Rio de Janeiro, Brazil. Upon their return to the United States, the family lived in Indiana and then near Milwaukee, Wisconsin.

At the start of World War I his father was commissioned and sent to Long Beach, California, with his family to protect the shipyards. At the end of the war, since he spoke fluent Spanish, his father was sent to work in Nogales, Arizona, on the U.S.-Mexican border. After this stint the family returned to California to live near San Diego. As a teenager George Lewis had the ambition to be an actor. When he was in high school in Coronado, California, he appeared in several plays. A Hollywood screenwriter attended one of these performances and encouraged him to try the movies.

When he graduated from school in 1923, he announced to his family that he was heading for Hollywood. His father gave him a year to make good. He started out as an extra in silent films in 1923 and did reasonably well during his first year, so he decided to stay. He made his screen debut in *The Spanish Dancer* (1923), which starred Pola Negri. His big break came when he was interviewed by a casting director for one film which came to nothing, but the same person recommended him for an important role as a prizefighter in *His People* (1925). This remains his favorite role. It was shot at Universal, who were so impressed with him that they signed him to a five-year contract.

The studio was searching for an actor to play the lead in a series of shorts which dealt with college life, appropriately to be called *The Collegians.* They readily cast Lewis in the lead of Bob Wilson, and he appeared in 45 shorts between 1926 and 1929. Simultaneously he continued to appear in feature films. He made his first feature-length talkie, *College Love* (1929), as a spinoff from the original series, but the series ended rather abruptly in 1929 when his character graduated from college.

When his contract expired, he found himself at liberty, but in 1930 Fox signed him to a contract to appear in the Spanish versions of some of their movies. They dropped him when it became more economical to dub the original version rather than shoot versions in different languages. By 1932 he found himself in quickies for independent studios and appearing in serials. This trend continued until 1936 when he became disenchanted with the industry for a while because he did not feel he was playing the kind of roles which his abilities merited.

He temporarily abandoned the Hollywood scene for New York, where he appeared in several stage plays and on radio. When he returned to Hollywood in 1939, he found himself in demand to play character roles of the kind which he craved. For the next two decades he did these parts (primarily in Westerns) from which he derived considerable satisfaction. He also appeared in a number of serials of which *Zorro's Black Whip* (1944) was his favorite. He appeared in several films which starred Alan Ladd, an off-screen friend (as was Ladd's wife Sue Carol).

Active on television from its pioneer days, he appeared in several Western series including *The Range Rider, Annie Oakley, The Adventures of Rin Tin Tin* and the premiere episode of *The Lone Ranger.* His sole regular role on television was as the father of Zorro in the Walt Disney television series *Zorro.* His appearances in this series he found very satisfying, and he liked and respected Walt Disney himself very much as a person. He believed that this might have brought him further offers of work, but oddly it typed him instead. In the harsher climate of the 1960s he received relatively few offers of work.

To counteract this he opened his own real estate business which he ran successfully until 1972 when he retired. Most of his contemporaries were deceased, and consequently he had no contact with show business. His hobbies were listed as reading and playing golf. In March 1928, he married Mary Louise Lohman, the daughter of a leading insurance executive, a marriage which endured happily. They had two children, a son Jimmy who died in infancy, and a daughter Mary Louise who was born in 1938. He has two grandchildren. He went on record as saying several times that he believed his best roles dated from the silent period, while his best acting dated from the talkies. Neither he nor his contemporaries understood, however, why he did not become a bigger name. George J. Lewis died of a stroke at his home in Rancho Santa Fe, California, on December 10, 1995, at age 92.

Early portrait of George Lewis, who much later appeared in *Zorro.*

George J. Lewis Filmography

1923: *The Spanish Dancer.*
1924: *Captain Blood.*
1925: *His People, The Lady Who Lied.*
1926: *Devil's Island, The Old Soak.*
1928: *The Fourflusher, Give and Take, Honeymoon Flats, Jazz Mad, 13 Washington Square, We Americans.*
1929: *College Love, Tonight at Twelve.*
1930: *Last of the Duanes* (Spanish version), *The Big Trail (Spanish version).*
1931: *A Body and Soul* (Spanish version).

1932: *Bad Girl* (Spanish version), *Heart Punch, A Parisian Romance, South of the Rio Grande.*
1933: *Her Resale Value, Pleasure Cruise* (Spanish version), *Whispering Shadow* (serial), *The Wolf Dog* (serial).
1934: *Lazy River, The Merry Widow, The Pecos Dandy, Two Heads on a Pillow.*
1935: *The Headline Woman, Red Morning, Storm Over the Andes* (and Spanish version), *Under the Pampas Moon.*
1936: *Captain Calamity, Ride Ranger Ride.*
1939: *Back Door to Heaven, Beware Spooks!, The Middleton Family at the New York World's Fair, Say That You Love Me.*
1940: *Men Against the Sky, Outside the 3-Mile Limit.*
1941: *Death Valley Outlaws, Kansas Cyclone, No Hands on the Clock, Outlaws of the Desert, Riders of the Badlands, They Met in Argentina.*
1942: *The Falcon's Brother, Gang Busters* (serial), *Outlaws of Pine Ridge, Perils of Nyoka* (serial), *Spy Smasher* (serial), *Phantom Killer, Sin Town, A Yank in Libya.*
1943: *Black Hills Express, The Blocked Trail, Daredevils of the West* (serial), *Flesh and Fantasy, G-Men vs. the Black Dragon* (serial), *The Masked Marvel* (serial), *Secret Service in Darkest Africa* (serial).
1944: *Black Arrow* (serial), *Captain America* (serial), *Charlie Chan in the Secret Service, The Falcon in Mexico, Haunted Harbor* (serial), *The Laramie Trail, Oh! What a Night, Shadows of Suspicion, The Texas Kid, The Tiger Woman* (serial), *Zorro's Black Whip* (serial), *Brazil.*
1945: *Federal Operator 99* (serial), *Lady on a Train, Song of Mexico, South of the Rio Grande, Wagon Wheels Westward, Mexicana.*
1946: *Beauty and the Bandit, The Missing Lady, Passkey to Danger, The Phantom Rider* (serial), *Rainbow Over Texas, South of Monterey, Tarzan and the Leopard Woman, The Thrill of Brazil, Under Nevada Skies, Gilda.*
1947: *Blackmail, Pirates of Monterey, Slave Girl, Twilight on the Rio Grande, The Wistful Widow Of Wagon Gap, Web of Danger.*
1948: *Adventures of Frank and Jesse James* (serial), *Casbah, Docks of New Orleans, The Feathered Serpent, Lulu Belle, Oklahoma Blues, One Touch of Venus, Renegades of Sonora, The Sheriff of Medicine Bow, Silver Trails, Tap Roots.*
1949: *Bandits of El Dorado, The Big Sombrero, Crashing Thru, The Dalton Gang, Ghost of Zorro* (serial), *The Lost Tribe.*
1950: *Captain Carey U.S.A., Cody of the Pony Express* (serial), *Colorado Ranger, Crisis, Crooked River, Fast on the Draw, Hostile Country, Marshal of Eldorado, One Way Street, Radar Patrol vs. Spy King* (serial), *Short Grass, West of the Brazos.*
1951: *Abbott and Costello Meet the Invisible Man, Al Jennings of Oklahoma, Appointment with Danger, The Kid from Amarillo, King of the Bullwhip, Saddle Legion, South of Caliente.*
1952: *The Bad and the Beautiful, Hold That Line!, The Iron Mistress, The Prisoner of Zenda, The Raiders, Viva Zapata!, Wagon Team.*
1953: *Bandits of Corsica, Cow Country, Desert Legion, Devil's Canyon, Shane, Thunder in the East, The Veils of Bagdad.*
1954: *Border River, Drum Beat, Saskatchewan, Phantom of the Rue Morgue.*
1955: *The Prodigal.*
1956: *A Cry in the Night, Davy Crockett and the River Pirates, Hell on Frisco Bay, Santiago, Lust for Life.*
1957: *The Big Land, Jeanne Eagels, The Tall Stranger, The Brothers Rico.*
1960: *The Sign of Zorro* (TV:Z), *Zorro the Avenger* (TV:Z).
1961: *The Comancheros.*
1965: *Indian Paint.*

Television Series

1957–1959: *Zorro* as Don Alejandro.

Sources

Ankerich, Michael G. *Broken Silence: Conversations with 23 Silent Film Stars.* Jefferson, NC: McFarland, 1993.
Goldrup, Tom, and Jim Goldrup. *Feature Players: The Stories Behind The Faces Volume #1.* Published privately, 1986.
Lentz, Harris M., III. *Obituaries in the Performing Arts, 1995.* Jefferson, NC: McFarland, 1996.
Lyden, Pierce. *The Movie Badmen I Rode With.* Mario DeMarco, 1980s.

Note

Feature films edited from episodes of the Zorro television series are denoted Z in the filmography.

MICHAEL LIPTON

After service in World War II, Michael Lipton trained for the stage and became a classical actor, primarily on the New York theater scene. He was on the road appearing in *Separate Tables* in Los Angeles when he was spotted and approached by a prominent agent who offered to put his name forward for suitable projects. Although he had no experience in this genre, the first offer which came his way was to appear in the Western series *Buckskin* in 1958. A pilot was shot which was unofficially derived from the play *They Knew What They Wanted* about a middle-aged man who obtains a bride by mail order. It was decided, however, to make the character younger, so Lipton played the part of schoolteacher Ben Newcomb.

Several of the episodes of the series were unofficially derived from classics such as *Hamlet* and *Lysistrata*. "In fact," he recalls, "we had great fun each week deciding which of the classics was being pillaged." Once the pilot was accepted, they shot 13 episodes of the series as a summer replacement for Tennessee Ernie Ford. There were many well-known guests on the series, notably Pernell Roberts. They shot an episode every two days and it was on Friday afternoon while shooting an episode of *Buckskin* that Pernell Roberts was told officially that he had won the part of Adam Cartwright in *Bonanza*.

After the initial set of episodes was shot in 1958, everyone assumed that would be it. The series however was a minor hit, but when it was decided that new episodes were going to be shot in 1959, panic ensued and there was plenty of scrambling around to try to reassemble the same cast and crew. Every episode was a little morality play. The series was shot at the old Republic lot, by then renamed Revue Studios, where so many television Westerns were then being filmed. The adult stars of the series all came from similar backgrounds of the classical theater and consequently were very congenial. Lipton recalls child star Tommy Nolan as "a great little actor."

In between takes Lipton would wander over to the sets of other Westerns being shot there and chat with the guest stars such as Bette Davis and Mary Astor. He was also used as a player in some of the other Westerns shot at the same studio. He recalls appearing in an episode of *The Restless Gun* with John Payne. It was the episode where Payne played twins, one good, the other evil. Lipton was due to be shot by the evil twin. In those days a raspberry sauce concoction was applied to simulate blood. He was lying down waiting for this to be put on his clothes when an assistant director from *Buckskin* ran up yelling, "You can't do that. We need him dressed like that for our show." So they compromised: They smeared it on his hair instead!

Lipton appeared in episodes of other television series such as *Then Came Bronson* and *I Dream of Jeannie*. He did not adjust too well to the California lifestyle, preferring the New York theater scene and being on the road in classical plays. He once summed up his attitude about his career when he said, "I would jump a ferry to Manitoba to play Chekhov for a dollar and a half." His most high-profile job was the five years he spent appearing in the soap opera *As the World Turns*. He has also very occasionally appeared in feature films, notably *Hercules in New York* (1970) which costarred Taina Elg and marked the screen debut of Arnold Schwarzenegger, both of whom he found very pleasant to work with. Lipton continues to reside in New York.

Michael Lipton Filmography

1970: *Hercules in New York*.
1976: *Network*.
1980: *Windows*.
1990: *Invasion of the Space Preachers*.
1993: *Intent to Kill*.

Television Series

1958–1959: *Buckskin* as Ben Newcomb.
: *As the World Turns* as Neil Wade.
1962–1967: *As the World Turns*.

Sources

Interview with Lipton in 1995.

ROBERT LOGGIA

There is a caste system which operates in Hollywood so that thespians who are television-orientated are virtually automatically precluded from landing major movie roles. This has proven to be the reason why a number of successful TV stars never made a successful transition to movies. One actor who overcame the taboo, no doubt by shrewd career management, is Robert Loggia. He graduated from playing the offbeat lead in a couple of television series in the 1950s and 1960s to being one of the most ubiquitous character actors in Hollywood films of the 1980s and 1990s.

Robert Loggia, whose surname is pronounced "Lowjah," was born in New York City on January 3, 1930, the son of Benjamin Loggia, a shoe designer, and Elena Blandino. His parents were Italian immigrants. He attended Wagner College on Staten Island from 1947 to 1949 where at the Wagner College Theater he made his stage debut as Petruchio in *The Taming of the Shrew*. Then he transferred to the University of Missouri School of Journalism from where he graduated in 1951 with a degree. He paid his way through college on the strength of a football scholarship. After a season of summer stock, he was drafted. He entered the army where he served with the Panama Caribbean Forces Network from 1951 to 1953.

After his discharge, he was looking for work in New York when he met a friend who persuaded a producer to cast him in a bit role in a live television drama. The star, Hume Cronyn, was so impressed with what Loggia did with the role that he encouraged him to study acting. Loggia enrolled at the Actors' Studio in New York City where he studied under Stella Adler. He appeared in several plays and television roles. He made his off-Broadway debut in *The Man with the Golden Arm* in 1955. He made an inauspicious screen debut as Frankie Peppo in *Somebody Up There Likes Me* (1956). It was his performance in "Rumors of Evening" on *Playhouse 90* which brought him to the attention of Walt Disney and led to him being cast in *The Nine Lives of Elfego Baca.*

The Nine Lives of Elfego Baca was a Western series which was shown as part of *Walt Disney Presents* on the ABC network. Elfego Baca was a real-life sheriff of Socorro County, New Mexico, during the 1880s. When the legend began, Baca was 20. He stood alone against 80 gunslingers in a gun battle. The battle raged for 33 hours and over 4,000 bullets were fired at Baca, but at the end he emerged unscathed. This began the story of him having nine lives. Baca was a man of action. He killed four men and was twice acquitted of murder. When his father was jailed and held for murder, he engineered a jailbreak.

Among his friends were Billy the Kid and Pancho Villa. Later Villa became his enemy and put a $30,000 bounty on Baca's head. So feared was Baca that he once sent a letter to wanted men in Socorro County which is reported to have read, "Dear Sir, I have a warrant for your arrest. Please come in by the 15th and give yourself up. If you don't, I will feel justified in coming after you and shooting you on sight. Very truly yours, Elfego Baca, Sheriff." Many of them surrendered, while others left the territory. Baca was 80 when he eventually died in Albuquerque in 1945.

The first four episodes of this series were shown between October and December 1958, and commenced with the story of the 33-hour siege. They were an hour in length and shot in color on location at Santa Fe and Cerrillos, New Mexico. The next two episodes were shown in February 1959, with two more in November 1959. The final two segments were shown in March 1960, which made ten episodes in all. Two theatrical features were edited together from episodes of the television series. Although the series was not as popular as some of the other Disney Westerns, it still did well in the ratings.

Over the next few years Loggia appeared in over 100 television roles as well as stage and occasional film parts. He had a second short lived series called *T.H.E. Cat* (1965–1966). Thomas Hewitt Edward Cat, to give him his full name, was a professional bodyguard who offered protection to those in need of it (generally people marked for death). He was a man who relied on his amazing agility and wits, developed in the days when he was a cat burglar, to protect his clients' lives and his own. He operated out of the Casa del Gato, a jazz club. Despite an interesting premise, the series lasted only one season of 26 episodes.

In 1973–1974 he appeared in *Boom Boom Room* on Broadway. He continued to appear as guest star on several television series and even directed some episodes. During the 1970s he appeared in a couple of daytime soaps and had a regular role in the short-lived prime time soap *Emerald Point N.A.S.* A highlight of his television career was when he played Anwar Sadat to Ingrid Bergman's Golda Meir in the miniseries *A Woman Named Golda* (1982). He played a somewhat unusual FBI agent, Nick Mancuso, in the miniseries *Favorite Son* (1988). A spinoff from this was a television series, *Mancuso F.B.I.* (1989–1990). For this series (which was not an audience pleaser), he received an Emmy nomination as Outstanding Lead Actor in a Drama Series in 1989, but one senses he was there to make up the numbers. From the early 1980s he began to appear in important feature films, notably as drug baron Frank Lopez in *Scarface* (1983); Oscar-nominated as Sam Ransom, Glenn Close's foul-mouthed legman, in the courtroom thriller *Jagged Edge* (1985); and as the department store head Mac MacMillan in *Big* (1988).

By his first marriage, he has three children, Tracey, John and Kristina. He next married his business manager Audrey O'Brien in Switzerland on December 27, 1982. She has a daughter, Cynthia Marlette, by a previous marriage. Loggia is a Roman Catholic.

Robert Loggia Filmography

1956: *Somebody Up There Likes Me.*
1957: *The Garment Jungle.*
1958: *Cop Hater, The Lost Missile.*
1959: *The Nine Lives of Elfego Baca* (TV:EB).
1962: *Six Gun Law* (TV:EB).
1963: *Cattle King (*a.k.a. *The Guns of Wyoming).*
1964: *The Three Sisters.*
1965: *The Greatest Story Ever Told.*
1969: *Che!*
1976: *Raid on Entebbe* (TV), *Scott Free* (TV), *Street Killing* (TV), *Mallory: Circumstantial Evidence* (TV).
1977: *Speedtrap, First Love.*
1978: *The Revenge of the Pink Panther, The Sea Gypsies.*
1979: *The Ninth Configuration (*a.k.a. *Twinkle, Twinkle Killer Kane), No Other Love* (TV).
1980: *Casino* (TV).
1981: *SOB.*
1982: *An Officer and a Gentleman, The Trail of the Pink Panther.*
1983: *The Curse of the Pink Panther, Psycho II, Scarface.*
1984: *A Touch of Scandal* (TV).
1985: *Jagged Edge, Prizzi's Honor, Streets of Justice* (TV).
1986: *Armed and Dangerous, That's Life.*
1987: *Over the Top, Hot Pursuit, Gaby—A True Story, The Believers, Oliver and Company* (voice only), *Echoes in the Darkness* (TV).
1988: *Big, Intrigue* (TV).
1989: *Triumph of the Spirit, Relentless, Two Women (*a.k.a. *Running Away), Dream Breakers* (TV), *White Hot, Code Name Chaos (*a.k.a. *Spies, Lies, Alibis and Spooks).*
1990: *Opportunity Knocks.*
1991: *The Marrying Man, First Force.*
1992: *The Gladiator, Necessary Roughness, Innocent Blood, Afterburn* (TV).
1993: *Nurses on the Line* (TV), *Lifepod* (TV), *Mercy Mission: The Rescue of Flight 771* (TV), *Taking Liberties.*
1994: *Bad Girls, The Last Tattoo, I Love Trouble, White Mile* (TV).
1995: *Between Love and Honor* (TV), *Cold-blooded, Man with a Gun, Picture Windows* (TV: "Armed Response" episode only).
1996: *Lost Highway, Mistrial, Independence Day, Wide Awake.*

Television Series

1958–1960: *Walt Disney Presents: The Nine Lives of Elfego Baca* as Elfego Baca.
1966–1967: *T.H.E. Cat* as Thomas Hewitt Edward Cat.
1972: *The Secret Storm* as Frank Carver.
1973: *Search for Tomorrow* as Anthony Vincente.
1983–1984: *Emerald Point N.A.S.* as Admiral Yuri Bukharin.
1989–1990: *Mancuso F.B.I.* as Nick Mancuso.

Miniseries

1976: *The Moneychangers.*
1982: *A Woman Named Golda.*
1988: *Favorite Son.*

1993: *Wild Palms.*
1996: *Pandora's Clock.*

Sources

Contemporary Theater, Film and Television Volume 11. Detroit, MI: Gale Research Inc., 1993.
Ferguson, Ken. *The Boy's Western Television and Film Annual.* London: Purnell, 1963.
Ferguson, Ken. *Television Stars.* London: Purnell, 1966.
Maltin, Leonard. *The Disney Films.* New York: Crown, 1973.
Quinlan, David. *Illustrated Directory of Character Actors.* London: Batsford, 1995.

Note

Films denoted EB in the filmography were derived from episodes of *The Nine Lives of Elfego Baca.*

BRITT LOMAND

This American actor was a Walt Disney discovery. He is best remembered for playing the evil but incompetent Captain Monastario in the Disney television series *Zorro* in which he was the chief enemy of the hero. His sole film role of note was Disney's *Tonka* (1957) in which he played General George Armstrong Custer. One of his most sympathetic roles was as the circus aerialist in love with Gloria Talbott in "The Prairie Elephant" episode of *Rawhide* during the 1961 season. After a regular role for one season on *The Life and Legend of Wyatt Earp,* he largely abandoned acting for a career on the production end of the business at which he was still active decades later. He and his wife Diane reside in Los Angeles.

Britt Lomond Filmography

1957: *Tonka.*
1960: *The Sign of Zorro* (TV:Z).

Television Series

1957–1959: *Zorro* as Captain Monastario.
1960–1961: *The Life and Legend of Wyatt Earp* as Johnny Ringo.

Sources

Maltin, Leonard. *The Disney Films.* New York: Crown, 1973.
Speed, F. Maurice. *The Western Film and TV Annual* London: MacDonald, 1960.
Yenne, Bill. *The Legend of Zorro.* Greenwich, CT: Brompton, 1991.

Note

TV:Z in the filmography denotes a feature film derived from episodes of the *Zorro* television series.

DIRK LONDON

Dirk London was born Raymond Eugene Boyle in Ambridge, Pennsylvania, on August 24, 1925. He was a stage producer and director. He changed his name to Dirk London when he began appearing in Westerns. He played Morgan Earp, the brother of Wyatt Earp, during the last two seasons of *The Life and Legend of Wyatt Earp.* In later years he became a successful artist and at last report was residing in Wisconsin. He married actress Jan Shepard.

Dirk London Filmography

1952: *Zombies of the Stratosphere* (serial).

1957: *That Night, The Lonely Man.*
1958: *Ambush at Cimarron Pass.*
1960: *The Purple Gang.*

Television Series

1959–1961: *The Life and Legend of Wyatt Earp* as Morgan Earp.

Sources

Brooks, Tim. *The Complete Directory to Prime Time TV Stars 1946–Present.* New York: Ballantine Books, 1987.
Magers, Boyd. "Claudia Barrett: Shy Persistence." *Western Ladies Volume #2.* November 1996.
Ragan, David. *Who's Who in Hollywood.* New York: Facts on File, 1992.

JACKIE LOUGHERY

Born in Brooklyn, New York, in 1930, this beauty queen was crowned Miss New York State and won the title of Miss America in 1952. She originally went to Hollywood to compete in the Miss Universe contest of 1952, but was beaten in the finals. She stayed on to make a fair stab at an acting career. She appeared in a few feature films and played regular supporting roles in two syndicated television series. One of these was as the niece of the title character in the *Judge Roy Bean* Western series.

She always made better copy for her husbands and boyfriends than for her thesping. She met and married singer Guy Mitchell, but divorced him in less than a year. In obtaining her divorce she testified that he thought more of his horse than of her. After the divorce (which brought her $1,500 a month alimony), she became an item with Vince Edwards, but broke off the relationship. From 1958 until their divorce in 1964 she was the third wife of Jack Webb, with whom she appeared in *The D.I.* (1957) as Annie, the object of his romantic attentions. She once said, "I'm looking for a guy who wants a wife and 12 kids." At last report she had remarried and was still living in the Los Angeles area.

Jackie Loughery Filmography

1953: *Abbott and Costello Go to Mars, The Mississippi Gambler, The Veils of Bagdad, Take Me to Town.*
1955: *The Naked Street.*
1956: *Pardners.*
1957: *The D.I., Eighteen and Anxious.*
1958: *The Hot Angel.*

Television Series

1954: *Mr. District Attorney* as Miss Miller.
1955–1956: *The Adventures of Judge Roy Bean* as Letty Bean.

Sources

Brooks, Tim. *The Complete Directory to Prime Time TV Stars 1946–Present.* New York: Ballantine Books, 1987.
Carpozi, George, Jr. *Vince Edwards.* New York: Belmont Books, 1962.

ANITA LOUISE

She was born Anita Louise Fremault in New York City on January 9, 1915, to Louis and Anne Fremault, her parents both being born in Alcace-Lorraine. Her father was an

Portrait of Anita Louise, who appeared in *My Friend Flicka*.

antiques dealer. A child model, she first became famous as "The Post Toasties Girl." She was educated at the Professional Children's School in New York. Her Broadway debut came with a version of *Peter Ibbetson* in 1921. Under her real name she made her screen debut in a bit in *Down to the Sea in Ships* (1922). In 1927 her mother, now Mrs. Anne Beresford, took her to Hollywood where she studied at the famous Lawlor Prep School and later graduated from Greenwood School for Girls.

She used the name Anita Louise from 1929 onwards. A Wampas Baby Star of 1931, at different times in the 1930s and 1940s she was under contract to Warner Bros. and Columbia. She first appeared on live television in 1947. In the summer of 1957 and 1958, she hosted reruns of Loretta Young's television series. The only television series in which she appeared as a regular was as Nell McLaughlin in *My Friend Flicka*. She played the wife of Rob (Gene Evans) and the mother of Ken (Johnny Washbrook) in this horse-and-boy Western series. It was shot by the television arm of 20th Century–Fox, and since Louise was married to a bigwig in the Fox Corporation, she could choose her own hours. This fact did not please her costar Gene Evans, one of the few men who found her charms very resistible, and was one reason why he would not continue with the series beyond the first season. Louise continued to act, appearing on an episode of *Mannix* as late as 1969.

Anita Louise was one of Hollywood's most lavish partygivers. On May 17, 1940, she wed Buddy Adler, a former actor who became production chief at 20th Century–Fox. They had a daughter Melanie (born August 10, 1947) and a son Anthony (born in 1950). Adler died of lung cancer in Los Angeles on July 12, 1960, at age 51, leaving his widow millions. On April 21, 1962, she remarried to importer Henry L. Berger. She became very active in philanthropic causes and they were close friends of Richard Nixon. On April 25, 1970, the day on which she was due to attend a charity ball, she was felled by a massive stroke at her home in Holmby Hills, West Los Angeles, at age 55. She is buried alongside her first husband at Forest Lawn Cemetery in Glendale, California.

Anita Louise Filmography

1922: *Down to the Sea in Ships.*
1924: *The Sixth Commandment, Lend Me Your Husband.*
1927: *The Music Master.*
1928: *Four Devils, A Woman of Affairs.*
1929: *The Spirit of Youth, Wonder of Women, Square Shoulders, The Marriage Playground.*
1930: *What a Man!, The Florodora Girl, Just Like Heaven, The Third Alarm.*
1931: *Millie, The Great Meadow, The Woman Between, Everything's Rosie, Heaven on Earth.*
1932: *The Phantom of Crestwood.*
1933: *Our Betters.*
1934: *Most Precious Thing in Life, Are We Civilized?, I Give My Love, Cross Streets, Judge Priest, Madame Du Barry, The Firebird, Bachelor of Arts.*
1935: *Lady Tubbs, Here's to Romance, A Midsummer Night's Dream, Personal Maid's Secret, The Story of Louis Pasteur.*
1936: *Brides Are Like That, Anthony Adverse.*
1937: *Call It a Day, Green Light, The Go-Getter, That Certain Woman, First Lady, Tovarich.*

1938: *My Bill, Marie Antoinette, Going Places, The Sisters.*
1939: *The Gorilla, Hero for a Day, Reno, These Glamour Girls, Main Street Lawyer, The Little Princess.*
1940: *Wagons Westward, The Villain Still Pursued Her, Glamour for Sale.*
1941: *The Phantom Submarine, Two in a Taxi, Harmon of Michigan.*
1943: *Dangerous Blondes.*
1944: *Nine Girls, Casanova Brown.*
1945: *Love Letters, The Fighting Guardsman.*
1946: *Shadowed, The Bandit of Sherwood Forest, The Devil's Mask, Personality Kid.*
1947: *Blondie's Big Moment, Bulldog Drummond at Bay.*
1952: *Retreat Hell.*

Television Series

1956–1957: *My Friend Flicka* as Nell McLaughlin.

Sources

Dye, David. *Child and Youth Actors: Filmographies of Their Entire Careers, 1914–1985.* Jefferson, NC: McFarland, 1988.
McClure, Arthur F., and Ken D. Jones. *Star Quality.* South Brunswick and New York: Barnes, 1974.
Parish, James Robert, and William T. Leonard. *Hollywood Players: The Thirties.* Carlstadt, NJ: Rainbow Books, 1976.
Picture Show Annual. London: Amalgamated Press, 1947.

ROBERT LOWERY

Robert Lowery was born Robert Lowery Hanks in Kansas City, Missouri, on October 17, 1914, the son of an attorney and a concert pianist. He was educated at Bancroft Grammar School and Paseo High. After the death of his father, he and his mother Leah relocated in the mid–1930s to California where he appeared in little theater productions. He sang with Slate Randall's Orchestra and was a radio announcer before being spotted by a 20th Century–Fox talent agent and signed to a contract.

His career as a movie star probably reached its peak with them, one of his best roles being as one of the sons of Eugenie Leontovich in the poignant drama *Four Sons* (1940), about a Czech family swept into the maelstrom of the Nazi rise to power. Once he left Fox, his career drifted almost exclusively into action-orientated B pictures, particularly those of Pine-Thomas. He also starred in serials of which the most fondly remembered is *Batman and Robin* (1949) in which he played Batman. His career stagnated in low-budget films, so he returned to stage touring in *The Caine Mutiny Court Martial,* for which he drew excellent notices.

He was one of dozens of actors tested and rejected for the role of Matt Dillon in *Gunsmoke.* He did however play Big Tim Champion, circus owner and guardian of Corky (Mickey Braddock), in the marginal Western series *Circus Boy* which lasted two seasons. This was a rather backhanded opportunity for him since the focal points of this series were a child and animals, which largely overshadowed his contribution. There are those who have suggested that his left wing political views harmed his career and made some conservative right wing producers reluctant to hire him. This was parodied in one of his last roles in a major film *McLintock!* (1963), in which he played John Wayne's political opponent. Offscreen he had a reputation as a tippler and general good time Charlie, but this did not spill over into his acting style, which was at times rather wooden and insipid.

He was very active on television between 1956 and 1966, usually playing suave villains or misguided men of principle on the Western and private eye shows which predominated during those years. He had a supporting role as the beau of Ann Sheridan in the comedy Western series *Pistols 'n' Petticoats,* which lasted a season. He attended Christmas festivities in 1971 at his mother's house and then returned to his own Hollywood apartment. On Decem-

Robert Lowery in *Circus Boy*.

ber 26, he died of an apparent heart attack at age 57. He was stricken while talking on the phone to his mother, telling her how much he had enjoyed the party. She also lived in Hollywood and called an ambulance, but when it reached his apartment the actor was dead.

He was married and divorced from actresses Vivian Wilcox, Barbara "Rusty" Farrell and Jean Parker, by whom he had a son (Robert Hanks, Jr., born in 1953).

Robert Lowery Filmography

1936: *Come and Get It, Great Guy.*
1937: *You Can't Have Everything; Wife, Doctor and Nurse; Second Honeymoon, Life Begins in College, Charlie Chan on Broadway, City Girl, Wake Up and Live, Big Town Girl, The Lady Escapes, The Jones Family in Hot Water.*
1938: *Passport Husband, Submarine Patrol, Tail Spin, The Baroness and the Butler, Always Goodbye, A Trip to Paris, Kentucky, Gateway, Straight Place and Show, Alexander's Ragtime Band, Kentucky Moonshine, Four Men and a Prayer, Josette, Happy Landing, Island in the Sky, Keep Smiling, One Wild Night, Safety in Numbers.*
1939: *Wife Husband and Friend, Daytime Wife, Second Fiddle, Charlie Chan in Reno, Young Mr. Lincoln, Hollywood Cavalcade, Drums Along the Mohawk, Mr. Moto in Danger Island, Everybody's Baby, The Escape.*
1940: *City of Chance, Free Blonde and 21, Shooting High, Four Sons, Maryland, The Mark of Zorro, Star Dust, Charlie Chan's Murder Cruise, Murder Over New York.*
1941: *Private Nurse, Ride On Vaquero!, Cadet Girl, Great Guns.*
1942: *Dawn on the Great Divide, My Gal Sal, Criminal Investigator, Who Is Hope Schuyler?, She's in the Army, Lure of the Islands, Rhythm Parade.*
1943: *Tarzan's Desert Mystery, So's Your Uncle, The North Star (*a.k.a. *Armored Attack), Campus Rhythm, Revenge of the Zombies.*
1944: *The Navy Way, Hot Rhythm, A Scream in the Dark, Dark Mountain, Dangerous Passage, The Mummy's Ghost, The Mystery of the Riverboat* (serial).
1945: *Homesick Angel, Thunderboat, Road to Alcatraz, Fashion Model, High Powered, Prison Ship, The Monster and the Ape* (serial).
1946: *Sensation Hunters, They Made Me a Killer, House of Horrors, God's Country, The Lady Chaser, Gas House Kids.*
1947: *Big Town, Danger Street, I Cover Big Town, Killer at Large, Queen of the Amazons, Jungle Flight.*
1948: *Death Valley, Heart of Virginia, Mary Lou, Highway 13.*
1949: *Shep Comes Home, Batman and Robin* (serial), *Arson Inc., The Dalton Gang, Call of the Forest.*
1950: *Gunfire, Border Rangers, Western Pacific Agent, Train to Tombstone, Everybody's Dancing.*
1951: *Crosswinds.*
1953: *Jalopy, Cow Country, The Homesteaders.*
1955: *Lay That Rifle Down.*
1956: *Two Gun Lady.*
1957: *The Parson and the Outlaw.*
1959: *The Rise and Fall of Legs Diamond.*
1962: *The Deadly Duo, When the Girls Take Over, Young Guns of Texas.*
1963: *McLintock!*
1964: *Stage to Thunder Rock, Johnny Reno.*
1965: *Zebra in the Kitchen.*
1966: *Waco.*
1967: *The Undertaker and his Pals, The Ballad of Josie.*

Television Series

1956–1958: *Circus Boy* as Big Tim Champion.
1966–1967: *Pistols 'n' Petticoats* as Buss Courtney.

Sources

Krivello, Kirk. *Passing Parade.* Obituary, 1972.
Quinlan, David. *Illustrated Directory of Film Stars.* London: Batsford, 1996.
Summers, Neil. *The Official TV Western Book Volume #4.* Vienna, WV: Old West Shop Publishing, 1992.
Truitt, Evelyn Mack. *Who Was Who on Screen Illustrated Edition.* New York: Bowker, 1984.

DAYTON LUMMIS

Dayton Lummis was born in Summit, New Jersey, in 1903. He attended Carlton Academy and Georgetown University and studied drama at the Martha Oatman School in Los Angeles. His first professional engagement was with the Russell Stock Company in Redlands, California, in 1927. Through the late 1920s and early 1930s he acted with various stock companies in California, Salt Lake City and Canada. In 1936 he began a career as a radio actor in New York City, eventually expanding his activities to announcing, producing and directing.

In 1943 he began appearing on Broadway, playing in such shows as *Peepshow, Catherine Was Great* with Mae West, *Miracle in the Mountains, Anthony and Cleopatra* with Katharine Cornell, *Edward My Son* and *As You Like It* with Katharine Hepburn. He toured in *Ten Little Indians.* In 1950 he moved to Los Angeles where he was seen in numerous films and television series. His sole regular role in a television series was the Western *Law of the Plainsman* in which he played the veteran marshal under whom Sam Buckhart (Michael Ansara) served in 1885 New Mexico.

Dayton Lummis, 84, died in Santa Monica, California, on June 23, 1988, survived by his son.

Dayton Lummis Filmography

1952: *The Winning Team, Androcles and the Lion, Les Miserables, Ruby Gentry, Bloodhounds of Broadway.*
1953: *All I Desire, China Venture, The Glenn Miller Story, The Golden Blade, How to Marry a Millionaire, Julius Caesar, Man in the Dark, The Mississippi Gambler, Port Sinister, The President's Lady, Tangier Incident.*
1954: *Demetrius and the Gladiators, Dragon's Gold, Loophole, Return to Treasure Island, 20,000 Leagues Under the Sea, The Yellow Mountain, The Caine Mutiny.*
1955: *The Cobweb, The Court-Martial of Billy Mitchell, High Society, A Man Called Peter, My Sister Eileen, Prince of Players, The Prodigal, The Spoilers, Sudden Danger, The View from Pompey's Head.*
1956: *The Bad Seed, A Day of Fury, The First Texan, Over-Exposed, Showdown at Abilene, The Wrong Man.*
1957: *Monkey on My Back.*
1958: *From Hell to Texas.*
1959: *Compulsion.*
1960: *Spartacus, Elmer Gantry, The Music Box Kid.*
1961: *The Flight That Disappeared.*
1962: *The Deadly Duo, Jack the Giant Killer.*
1963: *Beauty and the Beast.*
1970: *Moonfire.*

Television Series

1959–1960: *Law of the Plainsman* as Marshal Andy Morrison.

Sources

Brooks, Tim. *The Complete Directory to Prime Time TV Stars.* New York: Ballantine Books, 1987.
The Motion Picture Annual. Evanston, IL: Cinebooks, 1989.
Twomey, Alfred E., and Arthur F. McClure. *The Versatiles.* South Brunswick and New York: Barnes, 1969.

John Lupton (right) with Michael Ansara in *Broken Arrow*.

JOHN LUPTON

"I am a blue collar actor. This means that I sometimes play roles which other actors wouldn't. That's just me. I would rather work than read scripts." So spoke John Lupton, who is probably still best remembered for playing Tom Jeffords in the Western television series *Broken Arrow* (1956–1958). His career was hampered early on because he looked much younger than his real age. Later he seemed to lack a distinct on-camera personality, and most frequently he has been confused with another actor, Marshall Thompson.

John Lupton was born in Highland Park, Illinois, on August 22, 1926, the son of a reporter. He had one sister. He lived just outside of Chicago until he completed junior high school. His father secured a better job with the *Milwaukee Journal*, so Lupton was raised and educated in Milwaukee where he appeared in high school plays which made him determine to be an actor. He worked with a local stock company called the Port Players during summer vacations. After graduation from Shorewood High School, he appeared with Edwin Strawbridge Children's Theater for a couple of years. He subsequently studied at the American Academy of Dramatic Arts in New York City.

He made his Broadway debut in *Diamond Lil* as a Keystone Kop. This lasted about two weeks until the star Mae West noticed him, inquired who the little boy standing behind her was, and had him transferred. He toured with Susan Peters in *The Glass Menagerie* and then went on the road with Katharine Hepburn in *As You Like It*. She brought him to the attention of MGM. Although he had intended to join one of America's most prestigious stock companies, he opted instead to go under contract with MGM in 1950. The movie money together with the Californian lifestyle attracted him.

Asked about his preference for stage, television or films, he replied, "Most actors like the theater because of the gratification. Television is so quick particularly nowadays when it is run by the bank who couldn't care less whether it's artistic or not. If you turn your back and goof a line, sometimes they leave it in. With movies, there is a little extra time. It is however like comparing apples and oranges. Stage acting in front of audiences is a different art. It's great to work in the theater because if you have a funny line, people laugh."

Life at MGM proved to be particularly frustrating because he was not given the roles which he desired. In addition there was a clause in his contract which forbade him from doing television. After a couple of years under contract, his option was not picked up. He was soon brought back on a freelance basis for some additional films. One of these, *Diane* (1955), possibly cost him a role he wanted very badly, that of Martin Pawley in *The Searchers* (1956). He recalled, "I had done a live television show with Ward Bond when I was called for interview by John Ford to do *The Searchers*. At the time I went to see John Ford, I was living with Fess Parker. Fess lent me his boots. His shoe size was 13. Mine was nine. I put a wadded sock in each boot. So I clumped in to see John Ford wearing Fess Parker's boots. I think he must have caught on because during the interview, he kept mentioning these boots. When it came time to do the test, I was still stuck at MGM in a picture called *Diane*. Taina Elg and I played Lana Turner's man and woman servants. I had one scene left and they wouldn't let me out of it to test for *The Searchers*. It would have been great to work with Wayne and Ford. That was one that got away. It was a good one for Jeff Hunter, but you never know..."

Director Raoul Walsh's *Battle Cry* (1955) was one of Lupton's favorite roles. In it he played a soldier named Marion Hodgekiss, who is killed in battle shortly after learning that the girl he has fallen in love with (Anne Francis) is a prostitute. He explained, "I went straight over to Warner Bros. from MGM. This was one of my favorites because of the way in which it was written. He was called Sister Mary because he had glasses. He might have written the great American novel. There was a lot to the guy and his relationship with Anne Francis. It was a great book and a great movie for all the guys in that. Warner Bros. bought the rights to the novel and assigned three writers to write the script. When we left to go on location to Puerto Rico, we left without a completed script. Van Heflin was writing his own lines. James Whitmore was writing his own dialogue. L.Q. Jones was writing his own lines. On location we never really seemed to know what we were doing. It all came right in the end though because the movie turned out to be one of Warner Bros.' biggest grossers."

Lupton believed that he gave some of his best performances on the many live dramatic shows he did on television in the 1950s. One he particularly remembers was called "The Mojave Kid" on *Climax* in 1955. "I played the Mojave Kid. Ward Bond was the old sheriff. Ricardo Montalban was a gunslinger who had seen the light. Ricardo did not like live television because he was used to another take if something went wrong. A guy was hired to help us at gunslinging. Two weeks before we began rehearsing, we went to his house to practice. All of us had to learn. Ward Bond had been around Westerns all his career and was not too worried. It was necessary to draw and cock a six gun. If your finger slips off the hammer, then *bam,* it shoots before you want it to. At the dress rehearsal Ricardo was pulling the gun out of his holster when his thumb slipped off the hammer and, even though it was only a blank, it caused an explosion. I could see the fear in Ricardo's eyes in case that happened when it was on live, but it worked out fine..."

In the television series *Broken Arrow* he was Tom Jeffords, a United States Government mail rider who became the first-ever Indian Commissioner. He helped keep peace with the Chiracahua Apaches by making friends with Chief Cochise (Michael Ansara). It was based on authentic incidents of the Apache uprising in the second half of the 19th century. On account of his courage and constant desire for peace between white man and Apache, Jeffords had the privilege of being called "Blood Brother" by the Apache. Jeffords and Cochise tried to put a stop to Geronimo's Indian renegades who were a major obstruction in the cause of peace. The series was derived from an Elliott Arnold novel called *Blood Brother* which served as the basis for the film *Broken Arrow* (1950), starring James Stewart as Jeffords and Jeff Chandler as Cochise. Arnold spent years of research on Indian warfare and contributed many unusual story ideas in the series, which were based on historical fact. Lupton appeared in 72 half-hour black and white episodes between 1956 and 1958.

Asked how he won the lead in the series, he recalled, "Irving Asher was a producer at Paramount, where I had assisted in a test for Carol Ohmart whom the studio was about to place under contract. Asher remembered the test when it came to casting the hour-length television version of *Broken Arrow* under the banner of *20th Century-Fox Presents.* These were remakes of old movies using stock footage. In the hour-length version, Ricardo Montablan played Cochise. Irving Asher wanted me for Tom Jeffords, but for some reason the network representative at ABC said no. Irving Asher said, 'In that case, you're not doing the show.' Asher held out for me. Thank goodness he did because I got to do it."

Broken Arrow was immensely popular, and at one time Lupton was receiving approximately 1,000 fans letters a day. The salary, however, was much lower than he had been used to in motion pictures and the conditions were primitive. He explained, "There was no comparison between film and television salaries. Fortunately Fox did a television deal for *Broken Arrow.* Warner Bros. stars were on television contracts so they did not even get residuals. We were able to negotiate a contract with residuals. On location we had maybe a couple of limos and trailers hitched on back. There was no heating in the dressing rooms."

Asked where the series was shot, he said, "My homestead scenes were shot on the Fox Ranch at Malibu Canyon. It was supposed to be in Arizona. One time they were shooting a feature there, *The True Story of Jesse James* [1957] with Robert Wagner. One Monday they had painted all the ground green like it was the Middle West. Here we were supposed to be in Arizona with green grass! We had to go up in the hills and shoot other stuff until it had grown brown again. The locations were shot at Vasquez Rocks, an interesting rock formation with slatted rocks jutting out of the earth. Fox thought the television arm was like kindergarten and we were treated like second cousins. Every year at Christmastime they would remove our crew and put the movie crews to work on our show because they didn't have anything for them to do. We could end up a whole day behind schedule because they were not used to television being so quick. They would set the lighting as if for a feature."

Asked why the series ended, he explained, "It was right on the edge of color. It was only on the air for two years. It has been rerun a lot. I've even seen it dubbed in French and Japanese. Someone told me that we were on the 21st or 22nd go-round. If it had been done in color, it would probably have lasted at least a couple more years.... I had lunch with Michael Ansara about a year ago. He's become a big golfing fan, taking part in all the celebrity golfing tournaments."

As regards prime time television series, luck did not appear to smile on Lupton again. He shot several busted pilots for other series.

K-Nine Patrol (1961) was a story about the Baltimore Police Department. He was a lieutenant with a police dog in the canine corps of police. *Me and Benjie* was a *Leave It to Beaver* situation about two couples (one white and the other black), their nine-year-old sons, and their interrelationship. Lupton explained, "It was really too early for that. In those days the affiliates in the South refused to agree to broadcast it. No one wanted black families as series leads then."

Lupton appeared in supporting and guest-starring roles on numerous television series. Off and on for over a decade in the 1960s and 1970s he played Tommy Horton, Jr., on the daytime soap opera *Days of Our Lives*. It started out as an independent half-hour serial from Corday Productions when Columbia Television came on board as a partner to improve the production values by providing extra finance. As a result its length was increased to an hour in April 1975. This is also one of his favorite roles. He expanded on this: "There are a lot of ups and downs, blacks and whites because they keep changing your story line. For that reason there is an awful lot more to play."

One spinoff which delighted him was a soap opera stage version of Neil Simon's *Plaza Suite*. He explained, "For about a year we went out every weekend. Emily McLaughlin and I did the first act. Two kids from *The Young and the Restless* did the second act. James Sikking and Jeanne Cooper did the third act. It's a very funny play. It turned out to be a heck of a thing. It didn't do great business because soap opera fans are not necessarily theater fans, but we did pretty well."

For a few years he had a full time job with a computer company. He expounded, "I used to build radios as a kid. My neighbor was president of a small company that did electronic, technical kind of stuff. It was like working in a candy store. No assembly line stuff. Everyday was a new project. Eventually they moved to San Diego when it was taken over by a larger company. I tried to commute for a while, but it was just impossible. I really didn't want to get into assembly line stuff."

John Lupton continued to be a jobbing actor. Asked about his career in later years he said, "Mostly commercials and regional stuff shown only on the West Coast. I did a commercial for Missouri Lotteries which played only in Missouri. I did a movie *Body Shot!* [1993] in which I played this little old guy. I didn't have much to do." Did he still love show business? "Absolutely!" he cried. "How could you not? It's such an interesting business to be in. Every time you get a job, it's a new project, a new experience."

He was married twice. He was married to the former wife of Kenton Sills, son of silent stars Milton Sills and Doris Kenyon. With her he had a daughter Rollin, but he and his wife were divorced. His second wife Dian, with whom he had two stepsons Ed and Tony, is the granddaughter of composer Rudolf Friml.

John Lupton died of a massive heart attack on November 3, 1993, at age 67.

John Lupton Filmography

1951: *Shadow in the Sky.*
1952: *Rogue's March.*
1953: *Scandal at Scourie, All the Brothers Were Valiant, Escape from Fort Bravo, The Story of Three Loves, Julius Caesar, The Band Wagon.*
1954: *Dragonfly Squadron, Prisoner of War.*
1955: *Diane, Battle Cry, The Man with the Gun, Seven Angry Men.*
1956: *Glory, The Great Locomotive Chase.*
1957: *Drango, Taming Sutton's Gal.*
1958: *Gun Fever.*
1959: *The Man in the Net, The Rebel Set, Blood and Steel.*
1960: *Three Came to Kill.*
1962: *The Clown and the Kid.*
1965: *The Greatest Story Ever Told.*
1966: *Jesse James Meets Frankenstein's Daughter.*
1972: *The Astronaut* (TV), *All My Darling Daughters* (TV), *The Judge and Jake Wyler* (TV), *Napoleon and Samantha, Cool Breeze, Private Parts.*
1973: *Day of the Wolves, The World's Greatest Athlete.*
1974: *Airport 1975, The Phantom of Hollywood* (TV).
1975: *The Dream Makers* (TV).
1976: *Midway.*
1978: *Doctors' Private Lives* (TV).
1981: *Sidney Shorr: A Girl's Best Friend* (TV), *Miracle on Ice* (TV).
1982: *Bare Essence* (TV).
1985: *Anna Karenina* (TV).
1988: *Red River* (TV).
1993: *Body Shot!*

Television Series

1954–1955: *The Halls of Ivy.*
1956–1958: *Broken Arrow* as Tom Jeffords.
1965–1966: *Never Too Young* as Frank Landis.
1965–1979: *Days of Our Lives* as Dr. Tommy Horton, Jr.

Sources

Doyle, Billy. *Films in Review* magazine. Obituary, November 1993.
Interview with John Lupton in 1993.
Rout, Nancy E., Ellen Buckley, and Barney M. Rout. *The Soap Opera Book: Who's Who in Daytime Drama.* West Nyack, NJ: Todd Publications, 1992.

SEAN McCLORY

Sean Joseph McClory was born in Dublin, Ireland, on March 8, 1924, the son of Hugh Patrick McClory, an architect and civil engineer, and Mary Margaret Ball, a model. He made his professional stage debut at the age of eight in 1932 in the government sponsored Gaelic Theater of Galway. He continued acting with them while attending St. Ignatus Jesuit College at Galway between 1932 and 1941 and the National University of Ireland Medical School between 1942 and 1945. He served in the maritime inscription service of the Irish Army Medical Corps during World War II.

Sean McClory in *The Californians.*

During a visiting appearance with the Gaelic Theater at the famed Abbey Theater in Dublin, he was invited to join the Abbey Players who were the National Theater Company. While acting there from 1945 to 1946 he was spotted by an RKO talent scout and given a seven-year contract without a test by that studio. Billed as "The Rogue with a Brogue," he made his screen debut as an Irish cop in *Dick Tracy's Dilemma* (1947) before making his United States stage debut as Mickey Linden in *The Shining Hour* at La Jolla Playhouse, California. He took time out to be a gold miner in Grass Valley between 1947 and 1948.

Since that time he has been under contract to Warner Bros. from 1948 to 1949 and John Wayne's Batjac Productions. He has appeared as a featured player and costar in many motion pictures, notably John Ford's *The Quiet Man* (1952), which led to him becoming a member of Ford's celebrated stock company. Asked his opinion of the celebrated director, he replies, "John Ford was a son of a bitch, but he was *our* son of a bitch!" In 1953 he was considered for a Best Supporting Actor Academy Award nomination for his lead heavy in *Plunder of the Sun* and received acclaim for his first starring role in *Ring of Fear* (1954).

He did a series of filmed poetry readings with James Mason and Richard Burton, and a television anthology with James Mason. His television debut was in *The O'Branigans of Boston* in 1950. Since 1952 he has performed in

600 television series, appearing on nearly every major series and in many varied roles. The first series in which he had a recurring role was *The Californians.* This was set in San Francisco at the peak of the Gold Rush during the 1850s and told the story of a few honest citizens trying to maintain law and order in a city where criminals abounded. Dion Patrick (Adam Kennedy) was an adventurous reporter who joined the vigilantes who were the only law enforcement around. They were led by businessman Jack McGivern (McClory). Asked how he won the role he replies succinctly, "I auditioned for it." Part way through the first season, Kennedy was replaced by Richard Coogan as Marshal Matt Wayne. McClory explains, "The producers thought Kennedy's acting stank so they fired him. To my mind Coogan wasn't much better."

McClory himself left the series at the end of the first season. He continues, "I stopped playing Jack McGivern because the sponsors, Lipton Tea and Singer Sewing Machines, wanted Coogan to be the sole star. This did not sit too well with me—to have an unknown paramount in a series I helped to originate—so I quit. However I did stay on as a director and helm some ten episodes." Despite this, the role of Jack McGivern is one of his two favorites. He adds, "Incidentally I did scads of Westerns other than *The Californians.*"

Later he played the genial manager of the Raffles Hotel in *Overland Trail* and costarred as Anne Meara's father in the series *Kate McShane.* As his worst acting experience he recalls, "While shooting a *Tarzan* episode in Mexico, the leading lady, who was a well-known Italian actress of the period [Gia Scala], went bonkers and couldn't finish the flick. Consequently I was forced to play our love scene with the actress's Mexican stand-in, who neither understood nor spoke English, and who just sat there, rolling her eyes at me, while I declared my undying love for her."

In between film and television assignments, he managed to keep his stage career alive and active, appearing for eight seasons during the heyday of the La Jolla Playhouse in such plays as *The Lady's Not for Burning, The Shining Hour, The Winslow Boy* and *Billy Budd.* He also toured with Maurice Evans in *Dial M for Murder* and did a tour of West Coast cities in *The Lady's Not for Burning.* On the local scene he appeared in *Shadow of a Gunman, Anna Christie,* and *Juno and the Paycock* with the original Juno Sara Allgood, to name but a few. On Broadway he was Rory Commons in *King of Friday's Men,* which lasted three performances in 1951. In 1984 and 1985 he garnered kudos for his scintillatingly delightful portrayal of that quintessential gorgon, Lady Bracknell, in Oscar Wilde's *The Importance of Being Earnest,* which he says is undoubtedly his favorite role. He received a Dramalogue Award as Best Actor in 1984 for his hilarious portrayal of Seamus Shields in *Shadow of a Gunman.* Both of these were productions of the California Artists Repertory Theater, an organization founded by Sean McClory and his current wife, actress Peggy Webber.

He has gained a considerable reputation as a theatrical producer, having coproduced as well as starred in the World Premiere Production of Steve Allen's play *The Wake* (which received three nominations from the Los Angeles Drama Critics Circle in 1971) and coproduced Jerry Devine's *A Frog He Would A-Wooing Go* which subsequently went to Broadway under the title *Children of the Wind.* In addition he received wide acclaim as an actor-manager of his own theater company, the Tara Theater Guild, which he founded in San Francisco in 1948. He has also been active for many years in producing theatrical events for the Annual Festival of St. Andrews Priory in Valyermo, California. Asked about his recent activities he replies, "I write plays which have been produced and adapt radio dramas. My wife Peggy runs C.A.R.T. (California Artists Radio Theater). To date I have appeared in some 30 ninety-minute radio plays. Currently we present a show a month, in front of an audience, at the Hollywood Roosevelt Hotel, a landmark spot in Hollywood since the 1920s. I also dabble in photography." His long one-act play *Moment of Truth* was produced by the Masquers Theater in Hollywood in 1970, and he has written articles and edited magazines.

Sean McClory married firstly P. Souris and secondly M.B. Morrison, and is divorced from both. He then married Sue Alexander, who died in 1979. By these marriages he has two sons, Duane (born in 1947) and Kevin (born in 1949), and a daughter Cathleen (born in 1954). He has five grandchildren. He married actress and producer Peggy Webber on

March 17, 1983. They reside in the Mecca of Old Hollywood, historic Whitley Heights, where many Hollywood celebrities and theatrical colleagues are their neighbors and friends. McClory, who is a Roman Catholic, is a lay reader at mass for the Blessed Sacrament Church in Hollywood.

Sean McClory Filmography

1947: *Dick Tracy's Dilemma, Dick Tracy Meets Gruesome.*
1948: *Beyond Glory.*
1949: *Roughshod, My Dog Rusty.*
1950: *Daughter of Rosie O'Grady, The Glass Menagerie.*
1951: *Anne of the Indies, Lorna Doone, Storm Warning, The Desert Fox.*
1952: *Face to Face, The Quiet Man, Rogues March, Les Miserables, What Price Glory?*
1953: *Island in the Sky, Plunder of the Sun, Botany Bay, Niagara, Charade.*
1954: *Them!, The Long Gray Line, Ring of Fear, Man in the Attic.*
1955: *Moonfleet, I Cover the Underworld, The King's Thief.*
1956: *Diane.*
1957: *The Guns of Fort Petticoat.*
1961: *Valley of the Dragons.*
1964: *Cheyenne Autumn.*
1965: *Mara of the Wilderness.*
1966: *Follow Me Boys.*
1967: *The Gnome Mobile, The Happiest Millionaire, The King's Pirate.*
1968: *Bandolero!*
1973: *Day of the Wolves.*
1976: *The New Daughters of Joshua Cabe* (TV).
1979: *Roller Boogie.*
1983: *Two of a Kind.*
1986: *My Chauffeur.*
1987: *The Dead.*
1990: *Fools of Fortune.*
1993: *Body Bags* (TV).

Television Series

1957–1958: *The Californians* as Jack McGivern.
1960: *Overland Trail.*
1975: *Kate McShane* as Pat McShane.
1980: *General Hospital.*
1982–1983: *Bring 'Em Back Alive* as Myles Delany.

Miniseries

1976: *Captains and the Kings.*
1976–1977: *Once an Eagle.*

Sources

Correspondence between McClory and the author.

JODY McCREA

Jody McCrea was born Joel Dee McCrea in Los Angeles, California, on September 6, 1934, the son of Joel McCrea and Frances Dee. Spending very little time in Hollywood as a youth, he was brought up mainly on his father's working ranch in Camarillo, California. He earned his first money as a cowboy for neighbors. At school and college he achieved considerable distinction at athletics and at one time actually had ambitions to become a professional footballer. Upon leaving university life he took dramatic training and eventually landed small parts on several television shows.

After a two-year interruption in the army, he was signed to do a television series straight away. His father Joel McCrea was planning on retiring from show business, but was convinced to do a weekly Western series *Wichita Town* in which he played a marshal. It was well-known in Hollywood circles that his real incentive was so that his son Jody could acquire some additional credits by costarring as his deputy. The series was believed to be a surefire hit, but oddly it failed and lasted only one season.

Jody McCrea insisted, however, that while he worked on the series, he receive no special concessions or treatment because of his famous father. "On the set we maintain a professional attitude toward each other," said Jody. "We play as actor to actor rather than father to son." Although father sometimes gave son advice, he did not do so unless it was solicited. He did not want to threaten his son's strong feelings of independence. "I tell him exactly the same things I would tell anyone else seeking my advice. Most often he asks my opinion about such things as how to wear his hat, or if he looks uncomfortable with his gunbelt at a certain angle."

Since Joel McCrea was the star of *Wichita Town,* he was granted certain privileges not accorded to other actors, including his son. His dressing room was large and furnished with comfortable early American pieces while Jody's small cubicle boasted two straight back chairs and a dressing table. "When we first started filming the show I offered him the use of my dressing room, but he preferred to use his own. I even have a heck of a time buying him lunch when we're working!"

When the series ended, Jody McCrea busily pursued his screen career during the 1960s in a series of lightweight, youth-oriented films, sometimes in the company of other offspring of famous Hollywood stars. In 1970 he formed a production partnership with Harold Roberts to make an adult Western *(Cry Blood Apache)* as a starring vehicle for himself. This brutal and misguided Western flopped and spelled *finis* to his screen ambitions. At last report he was understood to be single and managing one of his late father's ranches in New Mexico.

Jody McCrea Filmography

1956: *The First Texan, The Naked Gun.*
1957: *Gunsight Ridge, The Monster That Challenged the World.*
1958: *Lafayette Escadrille, The Restless Years.*
1961: *Force of Impulse, All Hands on Deck.*
1962: *The Broken Land, Young Guns of Texas.*
1963: *Beach Party, Operation Bikini.*
1964: *Law of the Lawless, Muscle Beach Party, Bikini Beach, Pajama Party.*
1965: *How to Stuff a Wild Bikini, Young Fury, Beach Blanket Bingo.*
1967: *The Glory Stompers.*
1969: *Free Grass.*
1970: *Cry Blood Apache.*

Television Series

1959–1960: *Wichita Town* as Deputy Ben Matheson.

Sources

Rogers-Cowan. Press release, September 1959.
Speed, F. Maurice. *Film Review.* "Rising Stars." London: MacDonald, 1964/1965.
Thomas, Tony. *Joel McCrea: Riding the High Country.* Burbank, CA: Riverwood Press, 1992.

JOEL McCREA

Joel McCrea was once described as "the idealized American." Modest about his abilities as an actor, McCrea often played roles in the 1930s that had been rejected by Gary Cooper or Cary Grant and freely admitted that he did not consider himself their equal. He could have been Cooper's younger brother, for he projected the same dignified, peace-loving image. His only handicap was his slightly monotonous voice. The director Preston Sturges was once reputed to have told McCrea that a great pianist does not reprise one note continuously, but varies the tone of the instrument. McCrea replied, "Well, the way I look at it, Rubenstein and those other guys are looking for their one note. I've already found mine."

He showed tremendous loyalty towards certain directors and vice versa, numbering his favorites as Gregory La Cava, Jacques Tourneur, George Stevens, Frank Lloyd and Preston Sturges. McCrea was well-liked by almost all his leading ladies, most of whom wanted to

Joel McCrea (left) and Jody McCrea in *Wichita Town*.

work with him on many occasions. One of them, actress Frances Dee, he married. It was actress Maureen Stapleton, however, who provided the best tribute to him when she said, "There are men you dream of, there are men you fall in love with, there are men you marry and there is real life—and Frances Dee got it all."

Joel McCrea was a leading actor in Hollywood for seven years before Frank Lloyd cast him in *Wells Fargo* (1937). It was McCrea's first Western, a genre to which he was ideally suited. The delay was probably a reflection of the low esteem in which Westerns were then held. It was only after World War II that he concentrated on them, a reflection of the growing trend toward adult Westerns together with the then-proven box office of that genre. His television series *Wichita Town* (1959–1960) marked a top Western star riding into television, but it was a rare occasion when he was outdrawn by the sharpshooter of ratings failure. Of Westerns he once said, "I always felt so much more comfortable in a Western. The minute I got a horse with a hat and a pair of boots on, I felt like I was the guy out there doing it."

Joel Albert McCrea was born in South Pasadena, California, on November 5, 1905, the son of Thomas P. McCrea and Lou Whipple. He had one brother and one sister. He came from pioneer stock: His paternal grandfather drove a stagecoach and fought Apaches, and his maternal grandmother moved to California during the 1849 Gold Rush in a covered wagon. His father was an executive with the Los Angeles Gas and Electric Company. McCrea moved with his family to Hollywood in 1914, his father buying a house at the west end of Hollywood Boulevard where it links with Nichols Canyon. He attended public school on Gardner Street about a mile away. As a boy he delivered newspapers to celebrities like Cecil B. DeMille and rode a bicycle around Hollywood watching *Intolerance* being shot.

In 1919 he entered Hollywood High School and encountered the children of many of the leading lights in the movie industry. Some of these contacts were later very useful to him, including director Jacques Tourneur. During the summer vacations he worked as a stableboy in local riding schools and as a ranch hand at the King Cattle Company in the Tehachapi mountains. His intention was to become a rancher, and this continued to be his ambition when he enrolled at Pomona College at Claremont, California, in 1924.

While there he took courses in public speaking and drama. It was Benjamin David Scott, the head of the drama department, who invited him for an interview and suggested that he become a movie actor. At college McCrea played leads and supporting roles in plays. He graduated in 1928 and gained some legit experience at the Pasadena Community Playhouse. He then tried to gate-crash the movie industry. Even though he had influential friends, this turned out to be little advantage initially when it came to obtaining his first break. He played bits in some movies, but they led nowhere.

McCrea was trying to find acting work at the same time as K.T. Stevens, the daughter of director Sam Wood. He gave McCrea a note of introduction to actress Gloria Swanson. In turn she sent him to producer William LeBaron at FBO just before it became RKO Radio Pictures. This was during the first wave of talking pictures. RKO Radio was about to shoot a film on location called *The Silver Horde* (1930), based on a Rex Beach story of the Alaska fishing industry. LeBaron cast McCrea in the lead of Boyd Emerson.

While under contract to RKO, McCrea was loaned to Fox to play the juvenile lead of John Marvin in the movie *Lightnin'* (1930) which starred Will Rogers. Rogers befriended McCrea and became a father figure to him. It was he who insisted that McCrea borrow money and buy a ranch. Rogers said, "Git yourself a piece of land, boy, and you'ss never going to worry. Land in California can't go any place but up." It was while making his second film with Rogers (*Business and Pleasure* [1932]) that McCrea bought a thousand acres of land in the Santa Rosa Valley for $4,600. He stocked his ranch with cattle and planted the land with oats and barley. He later bought ranches in Northern California, Nevada and New Mexico.

In 1931 RKO renegotiated the actor's contract for the next four years and used him to support their top female stars, some of whom (like Constance Bennett) were only too pleased to have him make multiple appearances with them. McCrea found himself for the most part in drawing room comedies and dramas. He usually managed to talk himself out of roles which he did not feel himself suited for, and in none of his films was he cast as a nationality other than American. The best-remembered of his early films was *The Most Dangerous Game* (1932), in which he and Fay Wray were chased on a remote island by madman Count Zaroff, played by Leslie Banks. McCrea also starred in King Vidor's highly erotic *Bird of Paradise* (1932), lensed in Hawaii, which costarred the beautiful Dolores Del Rio.

When his contract with RKO expired, McCrea refused to sign with them again because he had not liked the loan-outs, nor was he happy with all the films they had cast him in. One of the last and most successful of the films he made under contract was *The Richest Girl in the World* (1934) which costarred him with Miriam Hopkins. She took an immediate liking to him and was instrumental in having him signed to a contract with mogul Sam Goldwyn in 1935. His first film for Goldwyn was *Barbary Coast* (1935), which also costarred Hopkins. This was the first of seven films which he shot for that producer over the next three years. These greatly increased McCrea's prestige in Hollywood. Although they mostly did well commercially and enhanced McCrea's reputation, they seem somewhat pretentious now and date rather badly.

While the later persona of Joel McCrea became synonymous with making Westerns, it was 1937's *Wells Fargo* which started this association. In this account of the famous express and transportation company founded by Henry Wells and William Fargo in 1852, McCrea played Ramsay McKay, an agent for the company. Producer-director Frank Lloyd had specifically asked Paramount to obtain his services from Goldwyn. Although it is somewhat slow in parts and was heavily cut in reissue, it was an important film for the star. Two years later he scored a resounding hit with *Union Pacific* (1939) where he was paired with Barbara Stanwyck for the fourth of six times. This Western epic was produced and directed by Cecil B. DeMille.

Espionage Agent (1939), an undistinguished spy film for Warner Bros., was instrumental in landing him the title role of *Foreign Correspondent* (1940) as Johnny Jones. This superb thriller was notable as the second American film directed by Alfred Hitchcock, although largely set in Europe. In one memorable scene he narrowly escaped death after being pushed off the top of Westminster Cathedral in London. Ironically McCrea had been assigned to do another De Mille epic, *North West Mounted Police,* and Gary Cooper had been intended for *Foreign Correspondent.* Neither star liked his assignment and agreed to change places, which turned out to be for the benefit of all.

When Sam Goldwyn put Gary Cooper under contract, McCrea asked to be released. Although the association with Goldwyn had initially been beneficial, it turned out to have its shortcomings. McCrea felt it better to move on, particularly after the success of *Union Pacific.* He found a congenial haven for a while at Paramount, where he developed a rapport with the eccentric but talented Preston Sturges. He appeared in three Sturges films, one of which (*Sullivan's Travels* [1941]) is considered a classic. In it he played a director of frivolous comedies who takes to the road to learn about real life. Another prestigious film was *The More the Merrier* (1943), a character comedy directed by George Stevens, which poked fun at the housing shortage in Washington D.C. during the war years. Excellent roles were provided for McCrea, Jean Arthur and Charles Coburn. Stevens later wanted McCrea for the role of Joe Starrett in the classic Western *Shane* (1953), but McCrea rejected the role. He felt it was Alan Ladd's film and was not ready to play a secondary part. One could also question whether any woman would have rejected him convincingly in favor of Ladd.

During World War II McCrea appeared in only six films, very few for any leading actor not involved in military service (particularly at a time when there was a shortage of leading men in Hollywood). He also refused to appear in any flag-waving propaganda films, saying, "If I was too old to be called, I was too old for that kind of film." His major contribution to the war effort came in the area of beef producing. As a rancher he was asked to increase productivity, which reached a plain of approximately 200,000 pounds a year.

There were many changes in Hollywood after the war. Many influential actors, directors and writers who had been in the services returned and expressed a desire to make more realistic movies. This had a profound effect on Westerns, which now frequently dealt with more adult themes and became darker in mood. They became geared to adults as well as children and, in terms of story content, were less like fairy tales. Joel McCrea had not been particularly well-served by a couple of non-Westerns he had made in recent years. Commencing with *The Virginian* (1946), McCrea resolved to devote the rest of his career to shooting Westerns. *The Virginian* was not a particularly good version of the book by Owen Wister, but it was the star's top-grossing film. He commented, "The big advantage for me with Westerns is that I could go on and on. When you're young it's all right to romance young ladies on the screen, but not when you become mature."

McCrea became one of the most prolific leading men on the screen during the period until he retired in 1959. Of all the films he made after the war, only one (the British-lensed thriller *Shoot First* [1953]) was not a Western. These Westerns were extremely efficiently shot, and McCrea became one of the most authoritative Westerners on screen. All of these films returned a profit. His best roles were probably *Colorado Territory* (1949), as outlaw Wes Hardin; *Wichita* (1955), as Wyatt Earp; and *Fort Massacre* (1958), as embittered cavalry sergeant Vinson. McCrea's personal favorite, *Stars in My Crown* (1950), was directed by Jacques Tourneur. It was set in a Southern town after the Civil War. McCrea played Josiah Doziah Gray, a minister who settles there after the war with his wife and son. He initially solves problems by using his fists and a six-gun, but later by his wits and compassion. His final crisis is facing up to the Ku Klux Klan after an attempted lynching. McCrea also starred in a moderately successful radio series, *Tales of the Texas Rangers* (1950–1952). On television he became one of the original founders of Four Star Television, but backed out early.

Immediately after the war McCrea shot two Westerns for the Enterprise Company, established by Harry Sherman, and released through United Artists. He then went to Warner Bros. and MGM. In the early 1950s most of his films were released by Universal. In the mid–1950s he signed a contract with producer Walter Mirisch and shifted his base of operations to Allied Artists. Towards the end of this period, Mirisch began to release his product through United Artists.

After the release of the last of these Westerns (*The Gunfight at Dodge City* [1959]), McCrea contemplated retirement, but Mirisch talked him into coproducing and starring in the television series *Wichita Town* (1959–1960), which borrowed the title from one of his best films of the 1950s. It was a weekly half-hour, black and white NBC series which was first broadcast on September 30, 1959. In it McCrea played Marshal Mike Dunbar, who is responsible for law and order in Wichita, Kansas, in the years after the Civil War. The role of his deputy was played by McCrea's son Jody.

NBC had such enormous faith in the series that it was sold without a pilot being shot. Surprisingly it flopped and only 24 episodes were shot, the last of which was aired on September 23, 1960. McCrea had once been an innovator, but this series was too repetitive of what he and others had been doing for years on the big screen. It also came along at a time when there were numerous other Westerns which were doing extremely well on television. The time slot for the series was Wednesday nights at 10:30 P.M., traditionally a very difficult time to hold an audience. Insiders in the industry have said that McCrea only agreed to do it because he felt it would help his son's career. This was one of his few errors of judgment. Of this experience he said, "*Gunsmoke* and *Bonanza* were marvelous series. I enjoy watching them myself. With *Wichita Town* failing to make much of an impression, I thought it best to quit. I had nothing to prove and I didn't need the money or the exposure."

He came out of retirement to shoot *Ride the High Country* (1962) in which he played Steve Judd and was paired with another giant of the genre, Randolph Scott, as Gil Westrum. It was directed by Sam Peckinpah. They played two veteran lawmen who have been swept to one side by the advance of civilization, but who team up one more time to transport a gold shipment. Although the film was not adequately promoted by MGM, word of mouth elevated it to the status of a classic and it has been much revered by movie buffs over the years. McCrea had a memorable death scene in which he expressed his lifelong wish "to enter my father's house justified."

McCrea again returned to his ranch. He did a cameo in the brutal *Cry Blood Apache* (1970) and narrated two documentaries, *Sioux Nation* (1970), lensed in the Pine Ridge Indian Reservation at South Dakota, and *The Great American Cowboy* (1974). He also appeared in two others, *George Stevens: A Filmmaker's Journey* (1980) and *Preston Sturges: The Rise and Fall of an American Dreamer* (1990). Writer/director John Champion obtained backing from Universal and asked McCrea to play Dan, an old cowboy, in *Mustang Country* (1976). He tries to capture a wild stallion with the help of an Indian boy (Nika Mina). The film was beautifully shot on location in Banff National Park at Alberta, Canada, but it was a bland film with a paper thin story, the least impressive and interesting of all McCrea's starring Westerns.

In 1959 he sold 540 of the 3,000 acres occupied by his ranch in Thousand Oaks near Camarillo. In the 1960s and 1970s he sold more. He also owned 20,000 acres in Nevada which he sold in the 1960s, but he continued to supervise the operation of his 2,600-acre spread at Paso Robles near San Luis Obispo, the remaining acres at Thousand Oaks together with the two ranches in New Mexico. He later admitted that he had made more money out of selling off parcels of his land than in his entire career as an actor.

His last public appearance was at a Beverly Hills fundraiser for Republican California gubernatorial candidate Pete Wilson on October 1, 1990. At this event, First Lady Barbara Bush greeted him as "my hero." He had been in robust health for his age, but was hospitalized on October 3 when a case of the flu worsened into pneumonia. He died at the Motion Picture Country Home and Hospital in Woodland Hills, California, on October 20, 1990, of pulmonary complications. He was 84 years old. Frances Dee, his wife of precisely 57 years, was with him at the time.

Joel McCrea met actress Dee on the set of the film *The Silver Cord* in 1933. They were married at the White Methodist Church in Rye, New York, on October 20, 1933. They appeared together on screen four times, the other films being *One Man's Journey* (1933), *Wells Fargo* (1937) and *Four Faces West* (1948). They had three sons: Jody (born September 6, 1934), David (born November 15, 1936) and Peter (born in April 1955). Both his two eldest sons became ranchers in New Mexico, but Peter became a land planner and real estate developer in Los Angeles.

Joel McCrea Filmography

1927: *The Fair Co-Ed.*

1928: *The Freedom of the Press, The Enemy, The Jazz Age.*

1929: *So This Is College, The Five O'Clock Girl, The Single Standard, Dynamite.*

1930: *The Silver Horde, Lightnin', Once a Sinner.*

1931: *Born to Love, Kept Husbands, Girls About Town, The Common Law.*

1932: *Business and Pleasure, Bird of Paradise, Rockabye, The Lost Squadron, The Sport Parade, The Most Dangerous Game (*a.k.a. *The Hounds of Zaroff).*

1933: *The Silver Cord, One Man's Journey, Bed of Roses, Chance at Heaven, Scarlet River* (cameo).

1934: *Half a Sinner, Gambling Lady, The Richest Girl in the World.*

1935: *Private Worlds, Our Little Girl, Splendor, Barbary Coast, Woman Wanted.*

1936: *Adventure in Manhattan, Come and Get It, Banjo on My Knee, These Three, Two in a Crowd.*

1937: *Interns Can't Take Money, Woman Chases Man, Wells Fargo, Dead End.*

1938: *Three Blind Mice, Youth Takes a Fling.*

1939: *They Shall Have Music, Espionage Agent, Union Pacific.*

1940: *He Married His Wife, The Primrose Path, Foreign Correspondent.*

1941: *Sullivan's Travels, Reaching for the Sun.*

1942: *The Palm Beach Story, The Great Man's Lady.*

1943: *The More the Merrier.*

1944: *The Great Moment, Buffalo Bill.*

1945: *The Unseen.*

1946: *The Virginian.*

1947: *Ramrod.*

1948: *Four Faces West.*

1949: *Colorado Territory, South of St. Louis.*

1950: *Stars in My Crown, The Outriders, Saddle Tramp, Frenchie.*

1951: *The Hollywood Story* (cameo), *Cattle Drive.*

1952: *The San Francisco Story.*

1953: *Lone Hand, Shoot First (*a.k.a. *Rough Shoot).*

1954: *Border River, Black Horse Canyon.*
1955: *Wichita, Stranger on Horseback.*
1956: *The First Texan.*
1957: *The Oklahoman, Trooper Hook, Gunsight Ridge, The Tall Stranger.*
1958: *Fort Massacre, Cattle Empire.*
1959: *Gunfight at Dodge City.*
1962: *Ride the High Country (*a.k.a. *Guns in the Afternoon).*
1970: *Cry Blood Apache.*
1976: *Mustang Country.*

Television Series

1959–1960: *Wichita Town* as Marshal Mike Dunbar.

Sources

The Annual Obituary. Detroit, MI: St. James Press, 1990.
Corneau, Ernest N. *The Hall of Fame of Western Film Stars.* Quincy, MA: Christopher, 1969.
The Daily Telegraph newspaper. Obituary, October 1990.
Lamparski, Richard. *Whatever Became Of? Third and Eighth Series.* New York: Crown, 1970 and 1982.
McBride, Joseph. *Variety.* Obituary, October 1990.
Miller, Lee O. *The Great Cowboy Stars of Movies and Television.* New Rochelle, NY: Arlington House, 1979.
Parish, James Robert. *Great Western Stars.* New York: Ace, 1976.
Thomas, Tony. *Joel McCrea: Riding the High Country.* Burbank, CA: Riverwood Press, 1992.

DARREN McGAVIN

There is an old saying about acting: "Television is where the recognition lies, movies are where megabucks can be earned and the stage is where the actor finds greatest satisfaction." Darren McGavin has striven to prove this by being active in all media. He has an aggressive acting style which has been usefully deployed at times. He has been one of the most ubiquitous players on the small screen in the past 30 years, leading one critic to describe him as "The Gene Hackman of TV." McGavin's quotes, often tinged with irony, and some of his actions lead one to suppose that he does not believe that he has yet fulfilled his potential as an actor. He is underrated and no doubt his talent has been abused and exploited at times. He once expressed his personal philosophy as, "Do nothing you are ashamed of, honor all commitments and hope for the best."

Darren McGavin was born William Richardson in Spokane, Washington, on May 7, 1922, son of Reid Delano Richardson and Grace Bogart. He was raised in the small town of Galt in the San Joaquin Valley not far from San Francisco and attended the College of the Pacific for one year, making his first stage appearance in a college production of *Lady Windermere's Fan* in 1941. He gate-crashed Hollywood a couple of times without making much impact. On the first occasion he retired to a lumber camp in northwest California to work and nurse his wounds after numerous rebuffs by agents. When he returned it was as a scene painter at Paramount Studios, working in his spare time in small theater productions such as playing the Judge Advocate in *Liliom* for the controversial but acclaimed Actors' Lab in Hollywood in 1945.

He recalled, "When I saw all the activity at Paramount, the costumes and most especially the warm lights—it was cold where I was—I knew that I wanted to be not only in the scene, but in the center of it." He landed a contract with Columbia Pictures, where he made his screen debut in *A Song to Remember* (1945). He made three other appearances for them before being abruptly dropped from contract. Smarting, he disappeared from Hollywood. In 1946 he did a U.S.O. tour in *The Late Christopher Bean* playing the juvenile. Then he went East and worked as a drug store assistant, truck driver and messenger.

In 1948 he studied acting for six months at the Neighborhood Playhouse and made an inauspicious return doing a walk-on in *The Old Lady Says No* at the Mansfield Theater, New York City. After a few more modest acting parts, he was cast as one of the leads in a production of *Death of a Salesman.* Initially he played the role of Happy at the Morosco Theater, New York City, in 1949, but was subsequently in the national tour until 1951. He studied acting for six months at the Actors' Studio. Among his fellow students were Marlon Brando, Rod Steiger and James Dean.

Parts began to come his way after that. After several successful stage parts in New York, Philadelphia and playing the King in *The King and I* at the St. Louis Municipal Opera in 1955, he headed back to Hollywood. He played the part of a flyer, Gary Cooper's friend, in *The Court-Martial of Billy Mitchell* (1955), and the young painter Eddie Yaeger in *Summertime* (1955). By far his best remembered film part was as the flashy drug pusher Louie in *The Man with the Golden Arm* (1955).

His television career began with the live *Crime Photographer* series shot in New York, and he was the original tough television detective *Mike Hammer.* He then landed the main starring role in *Riverboat,* which was set on the Mississippi River in the 1840s. This weekly one-hour black and white series told of the adventures aboard *The Enterprise,* one of the riverboats which traveled the length of the great waterway. Among its passengers were gamblers, merchants, lawbreakers and immigrants, some seeking a new life, others trying to escape from the past, many in search of a fortune. Historical research was carried out for two years before production of *Riverboat* began. A full-sized replica of a two-funneled stern wheel riverboat, complete with engine room and machinery, was built for the series.

McGavin starred as Grey Holden, a polished gentleman adventurer, who was captain and part owner of *The Enterprise* (which he won in a poker game). Burt Reynolds costarred as Ben Frazer, the tough and experienced river pilot who was Grey Holden's partner. The content of the series has been overshadowed by the highly publicized feud which developed between the two stars. It seems apparent that McGavin wanted to permanently undermine Reynolds' confidence as an actor, for he rode roughshod over the fledgling star. Before a take he would make disparaging remarks about Reynolds' performance. After a take he would belittle him in front of the crew and other actors. In their scenes together he ran the entire repertoire of tricks to upstage his costar. If it were time for a Reynolds closeup, he would rampage to such a degree that the shot was either ruined or never filmed. In the end it had become so bad that McGavin did not show up for work and the studio substituted Dan Duryea as Captain Brad Turner in two episodes, "The Wichita Arrows" and "Fort Epitaph." McGavin found that little sympathy accrued to him on account of this. There was a general feeling that McGavin was such a gifted actor anyway that he scarcely need to indulge in these tricks to assert himself.

By the time of the second season, the series had been revamped. Burt Reynolds had departed and was replaced by another veteran, Noah Beery, Jr. The list of guest stars on this series was extremely impressive and included names who previously had avoided television altogether. There were 44 episodes of *Riverboat* shown on NBC between September 13, 1959, and January 16, 1961, with most of the shooting being done on the back lot lake at Universal. The series was set to emulate *Wagon Train* and *Rawhide* as one of the classiest shows on television and would no doubt have run much longer if the two original stars had been more harmonious.

McGavin continued to be very active and was a frequent guest star on numerous action-orientated series during the 1960s and 1970s. Once the movie-for-television became a genre in itself he embraced this, and the frequency with which he turned up on these indicates that he was trying to compensate for all of the years of relative obscurity and anonymity. He came very close to hitting the jackpot when he starred in the telemovie *The Night Stalker* (1972), a unique blend of horror and humor in which he played the cynical, hard-boiled reporter Carl Kolchak.

The character was created by author Jeff Rice in the novel *The Kolchak Papers* (1970). ABC bought the rights but did nothing with

Darren McGavin (center) with Burt Reynolds and guest star Nancy Gates in *Riverboat*.

it until producer Dan Curtis handed it to writer Richard Matheson to adapt as a television movie. It told of reporter Kolchak tracking down the mysterious Janos Skorzeny (Barry Atwater), who turns out to be a vampire in Las Vegas. When it was originally broadcast on March 17, 1972, it was a ratings bonanza. This prompted a follow-up the following year, *The Night Strangler* (1973), in which Kolchak confronts Dr. Malcolm Reynolds (Richard Anderson), an alchemist who lives in the city beneath the streets of Seattle. This was even more witty and there were plenty of thrills along the way. It was another ratings winner.

Although the ABC network was initially somewhat ashamed of such a lowbrow concept being such a success, they were convinced that a series would be a ratings grabber. McGavin agreed and coproduced it with his own Francy Productions, filming being done at Universal Studios. Each week Kolchak tackled a monster, but most of these were cleverly suggested rather than explicitly shown; many times they skulked in the shadows. The blend of scares and comedy, along with eerie photography and atmospheric music, was adroitly balanced in the same way as in the two telemovies, but oddly the series failed to repeat their success. It disappeared without a ripple in 1974 after only 20 episodes were shot. Network programming head Fred Silverman, who personally disliked sci-fi and horror series, zapped *Kolchak: The Night Stalker* in a way that none of the monsters ever could.

McGavin's film *Hangar 18* (1980), which dealt with UFOs, was another big hit in this genre. His experience on *The Natural* (1984), in which he played the leading heavy, was rather characteristic of this actor and his place in the Hollywood galaxy. His name was inexplicably missing from the credits. Initially critics speculated that this was an in-joke, until McGavin publicly admitted that after the producers refused to accede to his salary and billing demands, his reaction was to insist that his name be removed. He appeared on stage many times during the 1960s both on Broadway and on tour, reemerging after a long absence as Vern in *California Dog Fight* at the Manhattan Theater Club at the New York City Center in 1985. He has directed a considerable number of stage plays and has helmed episodes of such television series as *Buckskin, Riverboat* and *Death Valley Days,* all dating from the 1959–1960 period. He does not appear to have too many ambitions in that direction. In 1990 he received an Emmy nomination as Outstanding Guest Actor in a Comedy Series for his work as the father of *Murphy Brown* (Candice Bergen).

McGavin married actress Melanie York on March 20, 1944. They have four children, York, Megan, Bridget and Bogart. Trivia buffs may note that they appeared together in the film *Queen for a Day* (1951), but in different episodes. After their divorce in the 1960s, he married statuesque actress Kathie Browne on December 31, 1969. She has also made a solid contribution to television, and they have appeared together. She was particularly memorable as a police chief in "The Sentry" episode of *Kolchak: The Night Stalker.* They reside in Beverly Hills, but McGavin also owns a 250-acre farm at Livingston Manor, a two-hour drive from New York City. He is also president of his own production company.

Darren McGavin Filmography

1945: *A Song to Remember, Kiss and Tell, She Wouldn't Say Yes, Counter-Attack.*
1946: *Fear.*
1951: *Queen for a Day.*
1955: *Summertime (*a.k.a. *Summer Madness), The Court-Martial of Billy Mitchell, The Man with the Golden Arm.*
1957: *Beau James, The Delicate Delinquent.*
1958: *The Case Against Brooklyn.*
1964: *Bullet for a Badman.*
1965: *The Great Sioux Massacre, Ride the High Wind.*
1967: *The Outsider* (TV).
1968: *The Challengers* (TV), *Mission Mars.*
1969: *Anatomy of a Crime.*
1970: *Mrs. Pollifax—Spy, The Challenge* (TV), *Berlin Affair* (TV), *Tribes (*a.k.a. *The Soldier Who Declared Peace)* (TV), *The 48 Hour Mile.*
1971: *The Birdmen (*a.k.a. *Escape of the Birdmen)* (TV), *Banyon* (TV), *The Death of Me Yet* (TV).
1972: *The Night Stalker* (TV), *Something Evil* (TV), *The Rookies* (TV), *Say Goodbye Maggie Cole* (TV), *Smash-Up Alley (*a.k.a. *43: The Petty Story).*
1973: *The Night Strangler* (TV), *B Must Die, Happy Mother's Day Love George* (also produced and directed), *The Six Million Dollar Man* (TV).
1976: *No Deposit No Return, Brinks: The Great Robbery* (TV), *Law and Order* (TV).
1977: *Airport '77.*
1978: *Zero to Sixty, The Users* (TV), *Hot Lead and Cold Feet.*
1979: *Love for Rent* (TV).
1980: *Waikiki* (TV), *Hangar 18.*
1981: *Firebird 2015 A.D.*
1983: *A Christmas Story.*
1984: *The Natural, The Return of Marcus Welby M.D.* (TV), *The Baron and the Kid* (TV), *Turk 182!*
1985: *My Wicked Wicked Ways: The Legend of Errol Flynn* (TV).
1986: *Raw Deal.*
1987: *From the Hip.*
1988: *Dead Heat, Inherit the Wind* (TV), *The Diamond Trap* (TV).
1989: *Captain America.*
1990: *By Dawn's Early Light* (TV), *Grand Tour (*a.k.a. *Disaster in Time)* (TV), *A Child in the Night* (TV).
1991: *Blood and Concrete, Perfect Harmony* (TV).
1993: *The American Clock* (TV).
1994: *A Perfect Stranger* (TV).
1995: *Fudge-A-Mania* (TV), *Derby* (TV), *Billy Madison.*

Television Series

1951: *Crime Photographer* as Casey.
1957–1959: *Mike Hammer* as Mike Hammer.
1959–1961: *Riverboat* as Grey Holden.
1968–1969: *The Outsider* as David Ross.
1974–1975: *Kolchak: The Night Stalker* as Carl Kolchak.
1983: *Small and Frye* as Nick Small.

Miniseries

1979: *Ike.*
1980: *The Martian Chronicles.*
1989: *Around the World in 80 Days.*

Sources

Brooks, Tim. *The Complete Directory to Prime Time TV Stars.* New York: Ballantine Books, 1987.

Contemporary Theater, Film and Television Volume 5. Detroit, MI: Gale Research Inc., 1987.

Picture Show Annual. London: Amalgamated Press, 1953 and 1959.

Speed, F. Maurice. *The Western Film and Television Annual.* London: MacDonald, 1961.

Stallings, Penny. *Forbidden Channels.* New York: Harper Perennial, 1991.

FRANK McGRATH

Born in Mound City, Missouri, on February 2, 1903, Frank McGrath was of mixed Irish and Indian origin. He became a top stuntman, double and wrangler, and was particularly associated with the films of John Ford. He was equally cantankerous and a hellraiser, although his drinking never affected the quality of his work. He appeared in several Ford pictures, but never had any dialogue. Through Ford he came to know the equally ornery Ward Bond.

When Ward Bond accepted the role of Major Seth Adams on *Wagon Train,* he demanded that Frank McGrath and Terry Wilson be hired too. Allegedly McGrath had some misgivings because he did not consider himself to be a proper actor, but Bond persuaded him and taught him how to play the cook Charlie Wooster. Wooster does not appear in the first few episodes, but McGrath grew into the role until eventually he virtually carried the occasional episode. An example of this was "Charlie Wooster Wagonmaster," originally shown in 1959, where he is the only regular character left to take command of the wagon train after all the others mysteriously vanish. A helpful type played by Douglas Kennedy assists him. It turns out that Kennedy is the leader of a band of white slavers who have kidnapped the other regulars and intend to sell them into servitude. It is only the quick thinking of Wooster which saves the day.

Most of the time, however, he functioned as low comedy relief in much the same way as Shakespeare's fools. In that capacity he was invaluable. McGrath lasted throughout the run of the series. When the series ended, he quickly found himself another berth as a regular in the sitcom *Tammy.* Years of hard living eventually caught up with the 64-year-old actor when he died in Beverly Hills, California, of a heart attack on May 13, 1967.

Frank McGrath Filmography

1931: *The Cisco Kid.*
1932: *The Rainbow Trail.*
1933: *Robbers' Roost.*
1934: *Broadway Bill, Call It Luck, Elinor Norton.*
1935: *Under the Pampas Moon.*
1937: *Vogues of 1938.*
1940: *High School.*
1941: *Riders of the Purple Sage.*
1942: *Sundown Jim.*
1943: *The Ox Bow Incident.*
1945: *They Were Expendable.*
1948: *Three Godfathers, Alias a Gentleman.*
1949: *She Wore a Yellow Ribbon, Big Jack.*
1951: *Across the Wide Missouri.*
1953: *Ride Vaquero!*
1956: *The Searchers.*
1957: *Hell Bound, The Tin Star.*
1965: *The Sword of Ali Baba.*
1967: *The War Wagon, Gunfight in Abilene, The Reluctant Astronaut, The Last Challenge.*
1968: *The Shakiest Gun in the West.*

Television Series

1957–1965: *Wagon Train* as Charlie Wooster.
1965–1966: *Tammy* as Uncle Lucius.

Sources

Brooks, Tim. *The Complete Directory to Prime Time TV Stars 1946–Present.* New York: Ballantine Books, 1987.

Carey, Harry, Jr. *Company of Heroes: My Life as an Actor in The John Ford Stock Company.* Metuchen, NJ: Scarecrow, 1994.
Truitt, Evelyn Mack. *Who Was Who on Screen Illustrated Edition.* New York: Bowker, 1984.

MIKE McGREEVEY

This child actor played the cabin boy on the troubled *Riverboat* series during its first season. His character has disappeared by the second season. The son of John McGreevey, he made a stab at an adult acting career. He appeared in *The Waltons* before becoming a scriptwriter for four seasons. He cowrote the screenplay (with his father John) of the telemovie *Ruby and Oswald* (1978). He was the head writer for the short-lived series *Palmerstown USA* and was producer and story editor on the *Fame* series. During the 1990s he contributed television scripts, notably to *Star Trek: Deep Space Nine* and the revamped version of *Bonanza.*

Mike McGreevey Filmography

1959: *Man in the Net, Day of the Outlaw.*
1960: *The Chartroose Caboose.*
1961: *The Clown and the Kid.*
1967: *The Way West.*
1968: *The Impossible Years.*
1969: *Death of a Gunfighter.*
1970: *The Computer Wore Tennis Shoes.*
1972: *Now You See Him Now You Don't, Snowball Express.*
1974: *For the Love of Willadean.*
1975: *The Strongest Man in the World.*
1976: *The Shaggy DA.*
1977: *Michael O'Hara the Fourth.*

Television Series

1959–1960: *Riverboat* as Chip.

Sources

Gillis, Steve. *The Gillis Guide to Star Trek.* Published privately, 1996.
Summers, Neil. *The Official TV Western Book Volume #3.* Vienna, WV: Old West Shop Publishing, 1991.

GARDNER McKAY

Gardner McKay was born George Cadogan Gardiner McKay in New York City on June 10, 1932, the son of an advertising executive. He had a peripatetic childhood, living in several places with his family and attending in excess of a dozen different schools. His education was completed at Cornell University where he contributed articles to the campus newsletter. Afterwards he lived in Manhattan where he became a male model and sculptor.

A photograph of him surrounded by his sculpture in *Town and Country* magazine during the early 1950s resulted in him being signed by an agent who obtained him roles in television series. He appeared in *The Thin Man* and "The Big Rendezvous" segment of *Death Valley Days* in 1956 as a psycho. Then he had a secondary role as a cavalry lieutenant in the syndicated Western series *Boots and Saddles.* He was signed to a contract by 20th Century–Fox. A 1959 *Life* magazine cover story about him caused a blaze of publicity just after he was cast in the lead of the TV series *Adventures in Paradise,* which lasted three seasons. He played a schooner captain plying the South Pacific in search of cargo, business or passengers. Most of the filming was done on the back lot of 20th Century–Fox, but during the last season there were location shots of the South Pacific. This lightweight show featured his physique to maximum advantage and won him the image of heartthrob and male sex symbol.

When the series folded in 1962, he disappeared from the Hollywood scene. He acted for financial reasons, but it was not a vocation he felt comfortable with and he preferred writing. The series, however, must have given him the wanderlust in real life. Eventually he was tracked down to the desert wastes of Libya and Egypt and later the jungles of Venezuela. This served to break the armlock which the press had upon him. Upon his return, he received little media coverage and his television roles were minimal. Around this time he lived on an estate in Coldwater Canyon, where he kept a menagerie of wild animals which periodically escaped and caused his neighbors' blood pressure to rise.

He appeared in a couple of feature films, one of which—*I Sailed to Tahiti with an All Girl Crew* (1968)—had a kinky title, but the plot did not deliver. He reverted back to writing, but *Me,* a play which he wrote and directed in 1973, won him little lasting acclaim. For three years in the 1970s he was drama critic for *The Los Angeles Herald Examiner* and taught a recreational class in playwriting at UCLA. Another of his plays, *Sea Marks,* won the Los Angeles Drama Critics Award for Best Play of 1979. It was briefly produced professionally off Broadway in 1981, and another version was produced for television.

During his halcyon years as an actor, McKay had a reputation as a playboy keeping company with several nubile starlets, but when he married in 1984 it was to a nonprofessional who came from Ireland. At the same time he also became a stepfather. The McKays, whose most permanent home is in Beverly Hills, have since spent long periods living in Southern Ireland, Northern California and Hawaii.

Gardner McKay Filmography

1959: *Holiday for Lovers.*
1964: *The Pleasure Seekers.*
1968: *I Sailed to Tahiti with an All Girl Crew.*

Television Series

1957–1958: *Boots And Saddles—The Story of the 5th Cavalry* as Lt. Kelly.
1959–1962: *Adventures in Paradise* as Captain Adam Troy.

Sources

Brooks, Tim. *The Complete Directory to Prime Time TV Stars 1946–Present.* New York: Ballantine Books, 1987.
Inman, David. *The TV Encyclopedia.* New York: Perigee, 1991.
Lamparski, Richard. *Whatever Became Of? Eleventh Series.* New York: Crown, 1989.

STEVE McQUEEN

Steve McQueen was one of the most fashionable stars of the 1960s. He was one of a number of actors from the late 1950s who made his name in a Western television series. His series *Wanted: Dead or Alive* was not the best, but it was one of the more unusual ones and it relied heavily on his personality. He was laconic and streetwise. Although he could be placid, there was something in his ice blue eyes which indicated menace. He was one actor who fulfilled his promise. Surprisingly, in view of his reputation in his own lifetime and his premature death, it might be assumed that a cult would have grown up around him, fueled by a deluge of biographies. In death he might have rivaled Marilyn Monroe and James Dean as an object of worship. But his stature has not been enhanced by death, which indicates that he was an actor of his time.

He had a fair, wedge-shaped head resting on a wiry frame of middling height. He could have been a character created by John Steinbeck: the footloose, restless boy from a farming community, none too honest, none too gentle, hustling his way across America to a distant dream. "When I act, I am digging up little pieces of myself," he once said. He summed up his own philosophy: "When you get to see the light at the end of the tunnel, it is most likely to be an oncoming train."

Steve McQueen was born Terrence Steven McQueen either in Indianapolis, Indiana, or Slater, Missouri, on March 24, 1930. He was the son of William McQueen and Julia Crawford. His father was a former pilot in the U.S. navy who later became a stunt pilot with a flying circus. His son was named after one of his gambling pals. McQueen, Sr., deserted his family six months after his son was born. His mother dumped the three-year-old on her uncle Claude Thomson, who owned a farm in Indiana. She subsequently remarried and took her son at the age of 12 to live with them in a rundown section of Los Angeles. He missed most of his schooling and "graduated" to petty crime.

Eventually his stepfather (whose surname was Berri and whom McQueen detested) insisted that he was unmanageable and had him committed to the Junior Boys' Republic at Chino, a reform school where he was known as No. 3188. Discipline was very strict there so he ran away twice. Lloyd Panter, one of the instructors, took an interest in him, warning him that he would be in trouble for the rest of his life. McQueen adjusted to life there, which ended after 14 months in 1946. By this time Berri was dead and McQueen's mother had relocated to Greenwich Village in New York. He lived with her for a while, becoming interested in motorbikes before taking a job as a seaman aboard a Greek tanker. He jumped ship and made his way slowly back to America, where he enlisted in the marines in September 1947.

He became a mechanic and truck driver, but continuous infractions of the rules meant that he was unable to make much progress. During part of his spell he worked in the engine room of ships in the San Diego docks. Asbestos dust in the atmosphere there is generally believed to have contributed to his death years later. He obtained his discharge papers in April 1950.

He did some odd jobs before deciding to go to the Neighborhood Playhouse drama school under the G.I. Bill. This decision was made on the basis that there were more girls there. He stayed at the Playhouse before moving to the Uta Hagen-Herbert Berghof Dramatic School in Manhattan, where he studied for two more years. His tuition fees he paid by modeling and driving for the post office.

He made his professional stage debut in New York State with a touring company's production of *Peg o' My Heart,* followed by a touring version of *Time Out for Ginger.* When he asked for a raise in salary, he was fired. Nevertheless, he was one of only five people chosen from thousands of applicants to join Lee Strasberg's Actors' Studio in 1955. Since better roles began to come his way rapidly, he did not attend for too long. He made his Broadway bow in a short-lived play called *The Gap.* An early success was scored when he assumed the lead from Ben Gazzara in the Broadway play *A Hatful of Rain.* He made his screen debut as an extra in *Somebody Up There Likes Me* (1956), which made a star of Paul Newman. There was always a certain amount of rivalry between these two actors in later years.

In New York in July 1956, he met Neile Adams, an up-and-coming young dancer and actress who was then dancing in the chorus of *The Pajama Game.* When she went to Hollywood to play a featured role in *This Could Be the Night* (1957), he pursued her and they married on November 2, 1956, at Mission San Juan Capistrano, Mission Viejo, California. With her he had two children, daughter Terri Leslie (born on June 6, 1959) and son Chad (born on December 28, 1960). She said of him, "Steve was a far-out guy from Endsville. When I first met him, he had a heart like steel. But I could also recognize in him a great yearning to be tender." His movie career picked up, and he had his first starring role in *Never Love a Stranger* (1958). He also had the lead in a tacky but extraordinarily commercially successful sci-fi film, *The Blob* (1958).

McQueen became a star via the television series *Wanted: Dead or Alive* (1958–1961). It was a Dick Powell-Four Star Production which was spun off from "The Bounty Hunter" episode of a series called *Trackdown,* first aired in March 1958. This episode served as the pilot and starred McQueen as Josh Randall, a bounty hunter. Producer Vincent Fennelly wanted him for the role from the outset because he was

Steve McQueen in *Wanted: Dead or Alive.*

small and offbeat with a feral instinct which rendered him dangerous and unpredictable. He also brought to the character a brooding, lonesome quality. McQueen preferred feature films, but nonetheless accepted the role after reading a sample script.

The gimmick of this series was that Randall carried a .30-40 sawed-off carbine which he called a "Mare's Leg," a cross between a handgun and a rifle. He did not have to draw it, but could swivel and fire it. Bullets from this gun had a much more explosive impact when they hit a target. Randall tried to bring his quarry in alive where possible. In spite of the rushed look of the series, he strove valiantly to bring credibility to his characterization. He observed, "I try to think what Randall would do in a situation and I also try to put in some of my own ingredients—what I would do."

His input in every facet of the character (including what he thought of Randall's clothes) led to a series of showdowns with the producers. At one point he even seriously contemplated emigrating to Australia to become a sheep farmer. For a while in 1960 Randall was joined by sidekick Jason Nichols (Wright King), but this did not work out. When the series was nearing the end of its second season, McQueen made it plain that he wanted out to return to making feature films. Some compromises were made and McQueen stayed on for a third season. His salary for the series was $90,000 per annum. The CBS series finally ended after 94 black and white half-hour episodes in March 1961. It was number 16 in the ratings during its first season, rose as high as number nine during the 1959–1960 season, but was nowhere in the top 25 during its last season. The final episode of this series was virtually the last appearance on episodic television McQueen ever made. There is an unconfirmed story that in order to extricate himself from the series, he had to engineer a car crash in which he suffered injuries.

McQueen made two films during this period. *Never So Few* (1959), a World War II story set in the Burmese Jungle, was the first of several films to be directed by John Sturges. Sturges' *The Magnificent Seven* (1960), in which McQueen played Vin, was the one which really put him over. This was a runaway box office hit, a reworking in a Western setting of Akira Kurosawa's *Seven Samurai,* about a group of seven gunfighters who ride to the rescue of some Mexican villagers. He earned $50,000 in salary for this film. The movie which elevated him to the superstar category was *The Great Escape* (1963), also directed by Sturges. In it he played "Cooler King" Hilts, so called because he is an American prisoner of war in Germany who is perpetually trying to escape, but is always recaptured and sentenced to solitary confinement. Particularly memorable to film buffs is the scene where he makes a desperate dash for freedom by motorbike, hotly pursued by the Nazis. For recreation McQueen liked biking. At all hours of the day and night he would take off into the California desert. "Speeding drains me," he once said. "It cleans me out. I ride off all the anger that is in my gut at the phonies I have to meet and work with."

The Cincinnati Kid (1965) was similar in theme to *The Hustler* (1961) in that it involved the challenge of an older expert (Edward G. Robinson) by a younger one (McQueen). In this case the game was stud poker. *The Sand Pebbles* (1966) secured him his only Oscar nomination. Initially he refused to play the leading role of a cop in *Bullitt* (1968) because he felt the role ran contrary to his anti-establishment image. He eventually relented only because his wife begged him to. It is not a particularly distinguished film, but it was an enormously successful one (primarily because of a stunningly executed car chase).

Fast though he was on his motorcycle, greed overtook him somewhere along the way. His fee escalated to the point where he would not read a script without a $5,000,000 fee being attached. This alienated some producers and directors, notably John Sturges (they did not work together again in a completed movie). *Le Mans* (1971), the movie that Sturges walked out on, turned out to be his biggest dud. Minus any story line, it consisted of endless footage of McQueen racing round a circuit. He also became embroiled in the hippy youth culture of the late 1960s and early 1970s, which meant that he experimented with drugs, causing his weight to balloon. His wife, Neile Adams, filed for divorce in Los Angeles on September 10, 1971, on the grounds of irreconcilable differences. In March 1972, the divorce became final.

The Getaway (1972), an irritating and flashy crime thriller directed by Sam Peckinpah, was a big hit. His costar was Ali MacGraw, a classy New Yorker who became his second wife on July 12, 1973, in a city park at Cheyenne, Wyoming. They lived for a while in Malibu, but apart from an intense physical passion, their interests were totally incompatible. They divorced in 1978. *The Towering Inferno* (1974), which told of a blazing skyscraper and of the different characters caught up in it, is generally regarded as the best of the disaster cycle of films. McQueen played Fire Chief Michael O'Hallorhan. This was the movie in which he shared top billing with Paul

Newman. It also turned out to be his last good film.

His career began to decline when he starred in a film version of Ibsen's *An Enemy of the People* (1977). Allegedly he had a commitment to make a film for a company called First Artists, in which he was also a partner. He picked up a book which his wife happened to be reading at the time and insisted it be filmed. Naturally there were no takers, particularly when he rejected several much more commercial projects such as Alistair MacLean's *The Way to Dusty Death*. After years of tantrums which kept him offscreen, the film was made and promptly sank. This was the closest to a character acting job that the star ever did. He made two final films, *Tom Horn* (1980) and *The Hunter* (1980). Ironically, in the latter he played a modern-day bounty hunter so that it seemed his career had come full circle. For this he received a salary of $3,000,000 plus a share of the profits. It was not a success. He looked a shadow of his former self even though he had shed his excess weight.

He bought a ranch called the Last Chance Ranch and met Barbara Jo Minty, a New York model, whom he married in January 1980. He became interested in flying and religion. He also adopted an underprivileged 13-year-old girl, Karen Wilson. While shooting his last film, he was troubled with a persistent cough. By the time he had completed the movie, he was seriously ill. Tests conducted in a Los Angeles hospital revealed that he was suffering from mesothelioma, a rare form of lung cancer caused by exposure to asbestos. There were several times when racing his bike that he had exposed himself to asbestos.

Doctors at Cedars Sinai hospital told him that there was no cure. He undertook various unorthodox remedies, but to little avail. In October 1980, he admitted to friends and fans that he had cancer. In November he checked in to the Santa Rosa clinic at Juarez, Mexico, under the alias of Samuel Sheppard to have a five-pound tumor removed from his stomach. Although it was extracted, he was so weakened that he suffered a heart attack and died at 3:50 A.M. on November 7, 1980, with his third wife and two children at his side. He was 50. "His body was just not strong enough to withstand the shock," the hospital said. His body was cremated at Ventura, California, and his ashes scattered over the Pacific Ocean. His estate amounted to approximately $9,000,000 mostly divided between his last wife and two children, with specific bequests to Karen Wilson and the Junior Boys' Republic at Chino.

Steve McQueen Filmography

1956: *Somebody Up There Likes Me.*
1958: *Never Love a Stranger, The Blob.*
1959: *Never So Few, The Great St. Louis Bank Robbery.*
1960: *The Magnificent Seven.*
1961: *The Honeymoon Machine.*
1962: *Hell Is for Heroes!, The War Lover.*
1963: *The Great Escape, Soldier in the Rain.*
1964: *Love with the Proper Stranger.*
1965: *Baby, the Rain Must Fall, The Cincinnati Kid.*
1966: *Nevada Smith, The Sand Pebbles.*
1968: *The Thomas Crown Affair, Bullitt.*
1969: *The Reivers.*
1971: *Le Mans.*
1972: *The Getaway, Junior Bonner.*
1973: *Papillon.*
1974: *The Towering Inferno.*
1976: *Dixie Dynamite* (uncredited).
1977: *An Enemy of the People.*
1980: *Tom Horn, The Hunter.*

Television Series

1958–1961: *Wanted: Dead or Alive* as Josh Randall.

Sources

Benson, Ross. "The Tragedy of Steve McQueen." *Daily Express* newspaper, November 8, 1980.
Norman, Barry. *The Hollywood Greats.* London: Futura, 1985.
Shipman, David. *The Great Movie Stars: The International Years.* London: Angus and Robertson, 1972.

PATRICK McVEY

Born in 1910, Patrick McVey graduated from Indiana University in 1931 and later from its law school. In 1938 he joined the Pasadena Playhouse, which was the start of a successful career. He was later a member of the Actors' Studio and the Players. He was also a successful Broadway actor and appeared in such plays as *Detective Story* and *Bus Stop*.

He had leading roles in three successful television series: *Big Town*, in which he played a crusading reporter; *Boots and Saddles*, in which he played a cavalry officer; and *Manhunt*, in which he played yet another reporter. He was also a prolific television performer in other series, including multiple episodes of *Perry Mason*. He died in New York on July 6, 1973, at age 63.

Patrick McVey Filmography

1941: *They Died with Their Boots On, The Man Who Came to Dinner, Navy Blues.*
1942: *Calling Dr. Gillespie, To the Shores of Tripoli, Pierre of the Plains, The Mummy's Tomb, Snuffy Smith Yard Bird, Moonlight in Havana, Invisible Agent, The Talk of the Town, Murder in the Big House.*
1946: *Two Guys from Milwaukee, Swell Guy, The Show-Off.*
1947: *Dark Passage, Welcome Stranger, Easy Come Easy Go, Swell Guy, Suddenly It's Spring.*
1957: *The Big Caper.*
1958: *Party Girl.*
1959: *North by Northwest.*
1968: *The Detective.*
1971: *Desperate Characters.*
1972: *The Visitors.*
1973: *Bang the Drum Slowly.*

Television Series

1950–1954: *Big Town* as Steve Wilson.
1957–1958: *Boots and Saddles—The Story of the Fifth Cavalry* as Lt. Col. Hayes.
1959–1961: *Manhunt* as Ben Andrews.

Sources

Brooks, Tim. *The Complete Directory to Prime Time TV Stars 1946–Present.* New York: Ballantine Books, 1987.
Jones, Ken D., Arthur F. McClure, and Alfred E. Twomey. *Character People.* Secaucus, NJ: Citadel, 1979.
Truitt, Evelyn Mack. *Who Was Who on Screen Illustrated Edition.* New York: Bowker, 1984.

GUY MADISON

"James Butler Hickok, mister," the hero introduced himself. On cue his rotund sidekick Jingles (Andy Devine) would explain, "That's Wild Bill Hickok, mister! The bravest, strongest, fightingest U.S. Marshal in the whole West!" The hero of this juvenile Western series was a handsome but bland actor by the name of Guy Madison. Although some fame sprang up early in his career (fanned by the magazines of the period), *Wild Bill Hickok* was the most successful venture which he ever appeared in. Tallulah Bankhead once said about him, "He made all the other cowboys look like fugitives from Abercrombie and Fitch" (the New York gentlemen's outfitters).

Guy Madison was born Robert Ozelle Mosely in Bakersfield, California, on January 19, 1922, the son of Benjamin J. Mosely. He had two brothers and a sister. He attended Bakersfield Junior College and was working as a telephone lineman prior to being drafted for active duty during World War II. He was serving at a U.S. naval base in San Diego where he attended a radio broadcast starring Janet Gaynor. He was sitting in the audience when he was noticed by agent Henry Willson. Willson brought him to the attention of Selznick International Pictures, who signed him to a contract.

He made his screen debut while still in uniform in *Since You Went Away* (1944), a blockbuster in which he played a young marine who heckles Jennifer Jones and Robert Walker in a bowling alley. The navy even granted him a two-week furlough for his shooting schedule. Even though he was only on screen for three minutes, the studio received 43,000 fan letters. This film established him as catnip to young female viewers and the fan magazines. Willson made him change his name to Guy Madison. The name derived from the Dolly Madison Ice Cream signs because as Willson explained, "You never saw a guy who liked to eat so much ice cream."

Producer David O. Selznick secured his release from the services six months early and loaned him to various other studios for considerable fees. Madison averaged to make one movie a year. Although he studied diligently at drama school, he never became more than a barely competent leading man. Ironically, his most animated performance was his first, made before he studied.

When Madison's contract with Selznick expired, his stock slumped. With his career at its lowest ebb, he and his agent Helen Ainsworth created a television series especially for him, *Wild Bill Hickok* (1951–1958), which restored his popularity. The syndicated half-hour series was shown at various times on both CBS and ABC. There was a real life Wild Bill Hickok (1837–1876), but the series borrowed only his name and occupation and had no basis in historical fact.

According to the series, Hickok was Marshal of Abilene, Kansas, but rode his horse Buckshot in the Old West of the 1870s capturing desperadoes. He was accompanied by his sidekick Jingles Jones (Andy Devine), who rode a horse called Joker. Madison was extensively doubled in the series by David Sharpe. The series (produced by William F. Broidy Productions and shot on the Monogram/ Allied Artists lot) originally ran to 100 black and white episodes between 1951 and 1956. Subsequently, Screen Gems Incorporated, who had acquired the rights, shot a further 13 episodes in color between 1957 and 1958.

Madison was part-owner of the series and made a fortune from the deal. Simultaneously he did a radio version. Rodeo appearances and royalties from merchandising were also very rewarding financially. Several episodes were edited together and released theatrically in Europe. The series also proved to be beneficial from a career standpoint. Madison was able to stay employed in some surprisingly good films until the end of the decade. He starred in two Warner Bros. Westerns, *The Charge at Feather River* (1953), the first 3D western, and *The Command* (1954). *The Beast of Hollow Mountain* (1956), although hampered by poor special effects, was an intriguing amalgam of Western and horror. In *Bullwhip* (1958) he played a character who had the choice of either marrying gorgeous Rhonda Fleming or being hanged!

Guy Madison as Wild Bill Hickok.

Relocating to Europe during the early 1960s, he starred in many features lensed in Italy, Germany and Spain in various genres. In the early 1970s he returned to live alone in Hollywood, where he occasionally appeared on television and in commercials. In 1973 he toured the Midwest in a play. Most of his earnings were lost in a series of bad investments. His private life was quiet, and his recreations were fishing and hunting. He made his own hunting bows and arrows. He appeared at conventions, film premieres and the Golden Boot Awards during the 1990s. He later lived in Morongo Valley, California.

Madison married actress Gail Russell on July 31, 1949, but they were divorced in Los Angeles on October 6, 1954. In 1955 he wed another actress, Sheila Connolly. They separated in 1960 and divorced in 1963. With her he had a son and three daughters with whom he remained close: Bridget Catherine (born in 1955), Erin Patricia (born in 1956) and Dolly (born in 1957).

Guy Madison died of emphysema at Desert Hospital Hospice in Palm Springs, California, on February 6, 1996, at age 74. His children, brothers and sister survived him. Actor Rory Calhoun, a neighbor and longtime hunting companion, said of him, "We shared a lot of campfires together. It is another empty saddle and I will really miss him."

Guy Madison Filmography

1944: *Since You Went Away.*
1946: *Till the End of Time.*
1947: *Honeymoon.*
1948: *Texas, Brooklyn and Heaven.*
1949: *Massacre River.*
1951: *Drums in the Deep South.*
1952: *Red Snow.*
1953: *The Charge at Feather River.*
1954: *The Command.*
1955: *Five Against the House, The Last Frontier.*
1956: *Hilda Crane, Reprisal!, On the Threshold of Space, The Beast of Hollow Mountain.*
1957: *The Hard Man.*
1958: *Bullwhip!*
1959: *Jet Over the Atlantic.*
1960: *Slaves of Rome.*
1961: *Sword of the Conqueror.*
1962: *Women of Devil's Island.*
1963: *Sandokan the Great, Hangman of Venice.*
1964: *Sandokan Strikes Back, The Return of Sandokan, The Mystery of Thug Island, Shatterhand.*
1965: *Adventurer from Tortuga, Gunmen of the Rio Grande.*
1966: *Five Giants from Texas, LSD—Flesh of the Devil.*
1967: *Winchester for Hire, The Son of Django, The Devil's Man, Hell in Normandy.*
1968: *Superargo and the Faceless Giants, I Lunghi Giorni Dell'odio, The Bang Bang Kid.*
1969: *Commando all'infierno, A Place in Hell, La Batalla Del Ultimo Panzer.*
1970: *Retroguardia, This Man Can't Die, Reverendo Colt.*
1975: *Hatcher Bodine, Won Ton Ton the Dog Who Saved Hollywood, The Pacific Connection.*
1977: *Where's Willie?*
1988: *Red River* (TV).

Television Series

1951–1958: *Wild Bill Hickok* as Wild Bill Hickok.

Sources

Lamparski, Richard. *Whatever Became Of? Fifth Series.* New York: Crown, 1974.
Parish, James Robert. *Great Western Stars.* New York: Ace, 1976.
Perry, Jeb H. *Screen Gems: A History of Columbia Pictures Television from Cohn to Coke 1948–1983.* Metuchen, NJ: Scarecrow, 1991.
Shipman, David. *The Independent* newspaper. Obituary, February 8, 1996.
Variety. Obituary, February 12, 1996.

JOCK MAHONEY

Stunting is an extremely hazardous and specialized branch of show business. Good stuntmen are always very much in demand. Consequently, there are very few who step from their ranks to become stars in their own right. Chief among those who made the transition was Jock Mahoney, whose name became synonymous with playing the Range Rider on television and Tarzan in the cinema. He was a thinking Tarzan who gave the impression of being literate and intelligent, and was almost the only actor to play the part who had anything like a decent career outside the narrow confines of the role.

Jock Mahoney was born Jacques O'Mahoney in Chicago, Illinois, on February 7, 1919, of French and Irish parents with a strain of Cherokee Indian, which accounts for his unusual name. As a child his parents took him to live in Davenport, Iowa, where he attended school and earned himself an athletic scholarship to the University of Iowa. An all-around athlete, he distinguished himself in swimming, football, baseball, track, gymnastics and boxing.

He endured two years of pre-medical school before he decided to accept an offer to be a lifeguard and swimming coach at Long Beach Pacific Coast Club. He had various other jobs such as grease monkey. In 1941 he joined the U.S. Marine Corps. He had a distinguished service record as a drill instructor in San Diego, and was then promoted to Corporal at Ordinance School in Norman, Oklahoma. After promotion to Tech Sergeant, he served on board the U.S.S. *Guadalcanal*; was a Carrier Fighter Pilot; and was finally honorably discharged as a Second Lieutenant.

After the war, for a while he bought, certified and sold surplus war planes; and bred, raised and trained Arabian horses in Chatsworth, California. He simultaneously made the rounds of the movie studios hoping to obtain a chance to act, but instead landed a job as a stuntman doubling for stars like Errol Flynn, Randolph Scott and Gregory Peck. By 1946 he was among the most active stuntmen in Hollywood, earning as much as $20,000 in one year for risking his neck.

He was performing some extremely dangerous stunts in a couple of Charles Starrett Westerns at Columbia when Starrett realized his potential in action roles and helped him to land a featured role in a film called *Fighting Frontiersman* (1946), which resulted in a contract with Columbia. He became a fixture of the Durango Kid series which starred Starrett; the films were shot in eight days. Although he was first cast as a heavy, Mahoney later switched type and played supporting roles as a good guy and starred in some exciting serials. In some of these Durango Kid Westerns, he played a character called Jock Mahoney. He had absolutely no idea why he should have played himself. "I was young and good looking enough to kiss the girl," he recalled. "The hero, Charlie Starrett, a great guy, was older and only got to kiss his horse. There was no special reason why I played myself. Nothing about those B Westerns had much reason to it, but they were great fun to do."

While working as a stuntman on *The Gal Who Won the West* (1949), he met star Yvonne De Carlo. She tried to help him in the industry because he was desperate to be a star. They were engaged. She became pregnant with his child, but had an abortion. They quarreled and split up. The romance effectively ended when he took up with actress Maggie Field, whom he later married.

In 1949, Gene Autry became the first cowboy star to enter the field of television when he started producing series exclusively for the small screen under the banner of "Flying 'A' Productions." He decided to begin a new one called *The Range Rider* (1951–1952), a half-hour black and white show set in California during the 1860s about a wandering defender of justice. He chose Mahoney for the title role and gave the secondary part of Dick West to Dick Jones. The series suffered from script malnutrition, but it was compensated for by plentiful action, which made it an enormous success worldwide. The duo performed all their own stunts, and a highlight of the show was the riding and fighting.

Mahoney remained on the best of terms with his costar Dick Jones over the years and regarded him as a salt of the earth. One of his last public appearances was at the 1989 Golden Boot Awards, where he presented an award to his former sidekick. About the only disagreement the duo ever had was over the number of *Range Rider* episodes that were made. Mahoney believed it was 96, and Dick Jones claimed 104 and that he had a script for each one. The reference books list 78. Each episode was shot in three days.

When the show was at the peak of its popularity, the duo found time to give personal exhibitions while touring with the Gene Autry Rodeo. It was in one of these that Mahoney broke a leg and collar bone, forcing him to take time to recuperate. The star did endure his fair share of injuries over the years, including having his nose broken four times and his chest crushed three times. One shoulder broken years

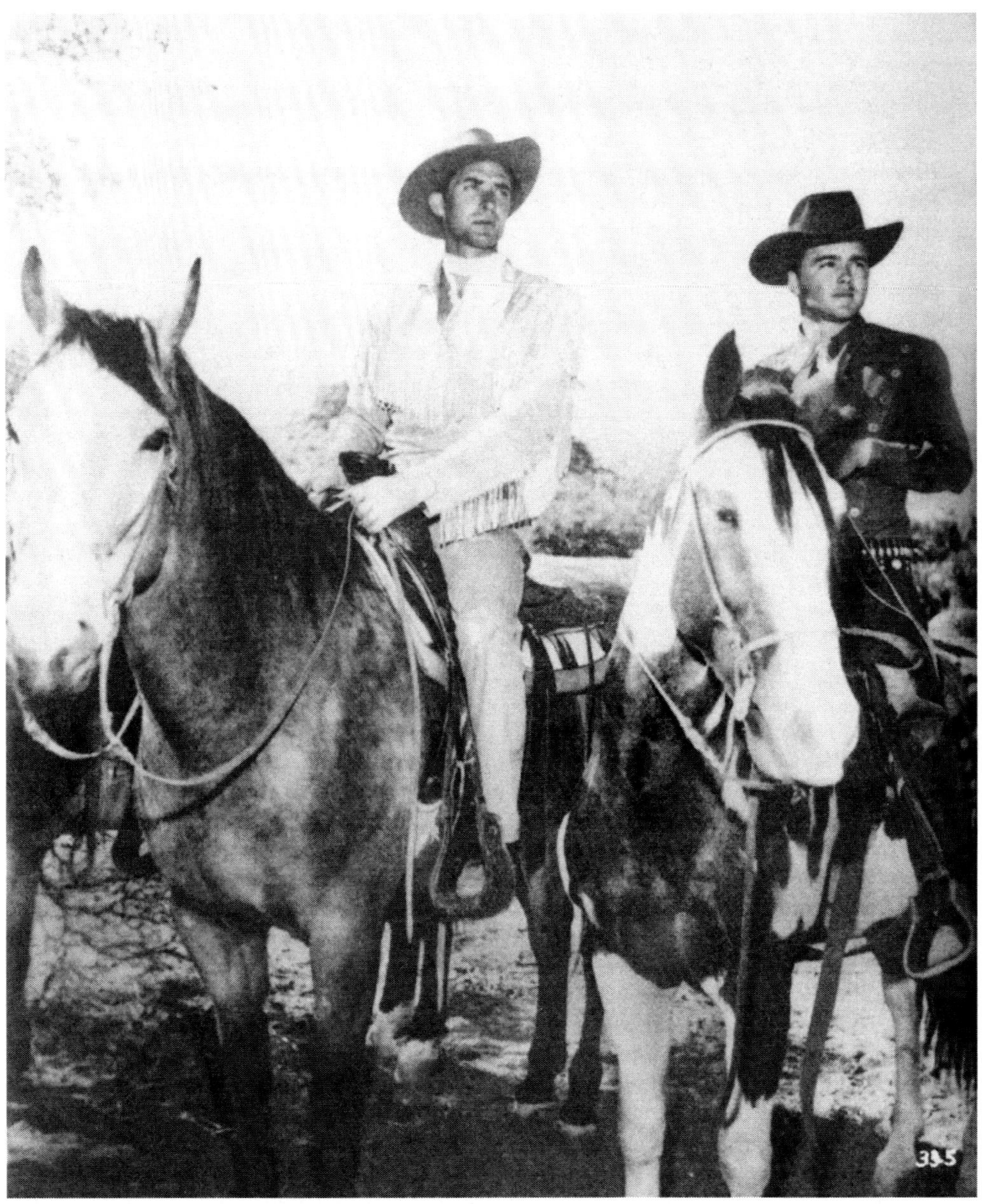

Jock Mahoney (left) and Dick Jones in *The Range Rider*.

earlier never knitted together. He quoted an old saying in stunting that if the injury is nowhere near your heart, remount your horse and ride on.

The Range Rider ended because after playing in virtually every country of the world, the network arbitrarily decided the market was saturated and there was no need to make any more. Mahoney believed the network made a mistake because a switch to color would have given the series a fresh lease on life and made it run for years.

Although he was recognized as primarily a Western star, he proved himself a capable straight dramatic actor on seven segments of *The Loretta Young Show*. It was this exposure which enabled him to secure a contract with Universal-International in 1956. He appeared in almost a dozen features for them, sometimes as the star of interesting, offbeat minor A and

B pictures, while simultaneously lending support in more prestigious films.

Joe Dakota (1957) was a *Bad Day at Black Rock* clone cleverly combining elements of Western and thriller. Mahoney starred in the title role of the cavalry officer who searches for the Indian who was once his scout. He is too late since Cal Moore (Charles McGraw) organized the lynch mob that hanged the Indian in order to gain possession of his oil-rich land. Luana Patten played the girl who helps Joe Dakota. The direction by Richard Bartlett is atmospheric, and the film is thought-provoking and entertaining. Like the earlier Joel McCrea oater *Four Faces West* (1948), not a shot is fired throughout.

As a change, Mahoney did *Slim Carter* (1957), an amusing spoof on the Western myth and the superhuman heroes who star in them, allegedly based on episodes in the life of William Boyd, star of *Hopalong Cassidy*. Mahoney played an egotistical singing star, Slim Carter, who is transformed into a star in his first movie. Clover Doyle (Julia Adams) is the publicist who discovered him and is given the job of nursemaid to him when the studio discovers how temperamental he is. Leo Gallagher (Tim Hovey) is the orphan child who wins a month's stay with the star as a prize in a competition and reforms him, whereupon Clover agrees to marry Slim and adopt Leo. As a novelty the credits of the movie were autographed with the stars signing their own names, rather than the names being displayed in print on the screen as usual. A further credit assures the audience that the star did all his own singing and stunts for the film. His wife Maggie has a cameo, as do Barbara Hale and William Hopper (then enjoying success on television's *Perry Mason*).

In 1958 Mahoney starred in another popular half-hour black and white series, *Yancy Derringer*. This CBS program was set in New Orleans in the years immediately following the war between the states. It told of the exploits of the ex–Confederate soldier turned gambler Yancy Derringer, who is really a special agent working under John Colton, Civil Administrator of New Orleans, to rid the city of its criminal element. Yancy was smooth and had one eye on the ladies and the other on his hat, which concealed a tiny pistol. His faithful companion was Pahoo-Ka-Ta-Wah (X Brands), a full-blooded Indian who carried a dagger and a sawed-off shotgun with a hair trigger, both of which made him most formidable.

Mahoney remembered the series with enormous affection because it enabled him to wear fancy clothes and to appear with some of the most beautiful actresses in Hollywood. One episode of which he was particularly fond cast Beverly Garland as a female river pirate! Mahoney recalled, "The scripting was a major plus factor in the success of the show. Richard Sale and Mary Loos, the husband and wife writing team, were the inspiration behind the series. Richard had a central story in each half-hour episode, but simultaneously interwove the plot of a second story with the germ of a third being introduced." They were overjoyed with the series. It was a hit and they assured Mahoney that it would run forever. On the strength of this he bought a mansion. Instead it ended after just 34 episodes, a victim of network politics. The mansion was sold soon afterwards.

When Universal announced in 1959 that they were no longer going to make B features, his contract was not renewed. On the strength of his performance as a heavy in the film *Tarzan the Magnificent* (1960), he was chosen by producer Sy Weintraub to be the 13th Tarzan. Weintraub wanted a slimmer, more cerebral Tarzan than his current Atlas, Gordon Scott. Mahoney's acquaintance with Tarzan went back to 1948, when Johnny Weissmuller left the role. He was tested as Weissmuller's replacement, but lost out to Lex Barker.

Mahoney made two Tarzan features, *Tarzan Goes to India* (1962) and *Tarzan's Three Challenges* (1963). He insisted on doing all his own stunts such as riding elephants, getting jerked in the air upside down in an animal snare and wrestling a live leopard. Both features were shot in color on exotic locations, India and Thailand respectively. Halfway through production of the second the actor contracted amoebic dysentery and dengue fever which led to pneumonia. His weight shrank dramatically from 220 pounds to 175 pounds. He rose from his sick bed and completed his role against all medical advice, but looked so tired and emaciated that it was impossible to believe he would genuinely have beaten his muscle-bound adversary Khan (Woody Strode) in combat. It took him 18 months to regain the lost weight.

He returned to Hollywood to recuperate, but after two months was called by producer Sy Weintraub, who informed him that his services were needed urgently in London. A technical fault had wiped out all the recorded dialogue from the film and he was required to post-synchronize all his lines. He was on an early flight to London, a city he loved, where he became a popular celebrity. On one occasion he met members of the British Royal Family, treating them to a discourse on UFOs, a subject he was much interested in at the time. He made a tour of 50 cities for MGM (distributors of the *Tarzan* films), and because this was so successful he toured 60 more. *Tarzan Goes to India* made more money for MGM than any other *Tarzan* film up to that time, but was outgrossed by *Tarzan's Three Challenges.* Mahoney believed he would become an in-demand star at MGM. Instead, he never worked for them again.

He tried to maintain the momentum of his career by shooting films in such far-flung places as the Philippines where he shot three features, but the era for the kind of films which were his forte was passing. While there he made the acquaintance of John Derek and his then-wife Ursula Andress, who were shooting a film called *Once Before I Die* (1964). In the cast was an arrogant young Adonis named Ron Ely who was constantly ribbing him about the fact that after playing Tarzan twice, his career had gone down the tubes and there was no way he (Ely) would fall victim to the same syndrome. A couple of years later, Mahoney was contacted by Sy Weintraub, who asked him to go to South America to play the heavy in a new *Tarzan* television series. "Sure I'll go," he promised, "but if I play the baddie, who's playing Tarzan?" "Ron Ely," came the reply.

Jock Mahoney costarred with Lili St. Cyr in the exploitation movie *Runaway Girl* (1966) and invited ridicule as the world's oldest biker in *The Glory Stompers* (1967). By 1968 he was reduced to playing a bit in *Bandolero!* (1968) as Raquel Welch's husband, with low billing, one line of dialogue and death by bullet before the opening credits, even though he still looked just as capable of dealing with the bad guys as he had when he was the Range Rider. It was clearly time to find some other line of work. He proved he was just as capable an administrator as he was an actor and stuntman. He subsequently held various senior posts in leisure industry.

From 1968 to 1970 he was General Manager and Publicity Director at VC Lodge, Lake City, Colorado, where he was responsible for the promotion and successful operation of the guest and dude ranch supervising 30 employees, including a cordon bleu chef! From 1970 to 1972 he was vice president and general manager of Paradise Park, Honolulu, Hawaii, where his brief was to oversee all functions related to the successful operation of the largest collection of Citicene (parrot family) birds in the United States, a 250-seat restaurant, 15 acres of tropical flora, a gift shop and a fleet of trams and busses.

While guesting on the television series *Kung Fu* in 1973, he suffered a stroke on the set which temporarily put him in a wheelchair. A firm believer in the saying "if life hands you a lemon, make lemonade," he soon learned how to do a perfect stunt fall from it. His final film appearances were in *Their Only Chance* (1976) followed by the prophetically titled *The End* (1978), his only movie with stepdaughter Sally Field, directed by and costarring her then-flame Burt Reynolds. He furthered his career association with John Derek when he acted as stunt coordinator on the remake of *Tarzan, the Ape Man* (1981) starring Bo Derek, and subsequently chose the leading man Miles O'Keeffe. He later guest-starred on television in episodes of *BJ and the Bear* and *The Fall Guy,* the latter in 1984. He made over 200 appearances on the small screen.

His most responsible post since the mid-1970s was as Advertising Manager for Gallant Charger Productions located at Capistrano Beach, California, where he sold and placed advertising for *Gun World*, *Horse and Horseman*, *Bow and Arrow* and other related magazines. He did a very considerable amount of public relations work, handling numerous delicate situations with tact and diplomacy, thereby saving accounts which would otherwise have been lost.

He held important, active posts with various associations over the years. He was a member of the Board of Directors of the Screen Actors Guild for nine years and Vice-President of the Lancaster, California, chapter of the Stuntman's Hall Of Fame. During his last years he directed three musical stage productions. He was a regular fixture at various stunting and Western competitions and conventions where he was welcomed as a celebrity judge and ambassador of good will. He believed that people make their own luck in life and consequently did not gamble. He regarded himself as a leader, not a joiner.

He was operated on by surgeons for five-and-a-half hours in 1988 for an aneurysm, from which he recovered. His only concession to illness and injury was that he did not ride his horse as frequently as he used to. He chose to go under the knife in the comparative safety of a modern Hollywood hospital, rather than run the risk of having the aneurysm burst while on some rough location where medical help was remote. After this he lived in retirement in Sherman Oaks, California, where his next-door neighbor and closest friend was Pat Buttram.

In 1989 he relocated to Poulsbo, Washington. He suffered an apparent stroke at the wheel of his car. He was hospitalized at Harrison Memorial Hospital at Bremerton, Washington, but died two days later on December 14, 1989, at age 70. He had two children from an early marriage which had been dissolved. He married the statuesque American leading lady Maggie Field, subsequently Maggie Mahoney, in 1951, and was stepfather to her two children: a son Jim who was born in 1942 and a daughter Sally who was born in 1946. (Sally Field went on to become a TV and motion picture star.) They also had a daughter of their own, Princess Melissa, born in November 1952. After divorcing his second wife, he married actress Autumn (Patricia) Russell, who survived him. After his death all of his contemporaries gathered at the Sportsman's Lodge in the San Fernando Valley where they held a memorial roast for him, drinking to his memory and telling funny stories about this larger-than-life stuntman turned actor.

Jock Mahoney Filmography

1946: *The Fighting Frontiersman, South of the Chisholm Trail.*
1947: *Stranger from Ponca City.*
1948: *Smoky Mountain Melody, Blazing Across the Pecos.*
1949: *The Doolins of Oklahoma, Bandits of El Dorado, The Blazing Trail, Renegades of the Sage, Horsemen of the Sierras, Rim of the Canyon, Jolson Sings Again.*
1950: *The Nevadan, David Harding—Counterspy, Cow Town, Texas Dynamo, Pecos River, Hoedown, Lightning Guns, Frontier Outpost, Cody of the Pony Express* (serial).
1951: *The Kangaroo Kid, Santa Fe, The Texas Rangers, Roar of the Iron Horse* (serial).
1952: *The Rough Tough West, Smoky Canyon, Junction City, The Kid from Broken Gun, The Hawk of Wild River, Laramie Mountains.*
1953: *Gunfighters of the North West* (serial).
1954: *Overland Pacific.*
1956: *A Day of Fury, Away All Boats, I've Lived Before, Battle Hymn, Showdown at Abilene.*
1957: *Joe Dakota, Slim Carter, The Land Unknown.*
1958: *Last of the Fast Guns, A Time to Love and a Time to Die.*
1959: *Money Women and Guns.*
1960: *Three Blondes in His Life, Tarzan the Magnificent.*
1962: *Tarzan Goes to India.*
1963: *Tarzan's Three Challenges, California.*
1964: *Walls of Hell, Moro Witch Doctor.*
1965: *Marine Battleground.*
1966: *Runaway Girl.*
1967: *The Glory Stompers.*
1968: *Bandolero!*
1972: *Spirits of the Wild.*
1973: *Tom, The Bad Bunch.*
1976: *Their Only Chance.*
1978: *The End.*

Television Series

1951–1952: *The Range Rider* as The Range Rider.
1958–1959: *Yancy Derringer* as Yancy Derringer.

Sources

Associated Press obituary, December 16, 1989.
Courneau, Ernest N. *The Hall of Fame of Western Film Stars.* North Quincy, MA: Christopher, 1969.
Interview with Jock Mahoney in 1988.
Willis, John. *Screen World.* London: Muller, 1990.

NORA MARLOWE

Born in 1915, this character actress made feature films and television appearances. She had regular roles in three television series. In *Law of the Plainsman,* a short-lived Western series, she ran the boarding house where Deputy Marshal Sam Buckhart (Michael Ansara) and his young ward Tess Logan (Gina Gillespie) lived. She acted as surrogate mother to them both when necessary. Her best-known role was as the neighbor Flossie Brimmer in the highly successful series *The Waltons.* Nora Marlowe, 62, died in harness on December 31, 1977, after a long illness. She was survived by her husband, actor James McCallion, a son and daughter.

Nora Marlowe Filmography

1955: *I'll Cry Tomorrow.*
1957: *An Affair to Remember, Designing Woman.*
1959: *North by Northwest.*
1964: *The Brass Bottle, Kitten with a Whip.*
1966: *Texas Across the River.*
1967: *The Hostage.*
1968: *The Thomas Crown Affair.*
1973: *Westworld.*
1975: *Mr. Ricco.*

Television Series

1959–1960: *Law of the Plainsman* as Martha Commager.
1969–1970: *The Governor and JJ* as Sara Andrews.
1972–1977: *The Waltons* as Flossie Brimmer.

Sources

Brooks, Tim. *The Complete Directory to Prime Time TV Stars 1946–Present.* New York: Ballantine Books, 1987
Ragan, David. *Who's Who in Hollywood.* New York: Facts on File, 1992.
Willis, John. *Screen World.* London: Muller, 1978.

EDDIE MARR

This character actor had small roles in several films from the late 1930s to the 1950s. He appeared in several films produced and directed by Andrew L. Stone. His sole semi-regular role on television was the minor one of the barker in the marginal Western series *Circus Boy.* He was in his 70s when he died in 1987.

Eddie Marr Filmography

1937: *Forty Naughty Girls, The Last Gangster.*
1938: *The Affairs of Annabel, Sky Giant, Mr. Moto's Gamble, City Girl, Garden of the Moon, Spawn of the North, Time Out for Murder, Dangerous to Know, King of Alcatraz, Gateway, Road Demon.*
1939: *Mr. Moto on Danger Island, Tail Spin, Torchy Plays with Dynamite, Grand Jury Secrets, Disbarred, It Could Happen to You, Judge Hardy and Son, King of Chinatown, Scandal Sheet, Our Neighbors—the Carters, Sudden Money, Waterfront.*
1940: *Charlie Chan at the Wax Museum, Johnny Apollo, The House Across the Bay, City of Chance, Queen of the Mob, Parole Fixer, Opened by Mistake, Women Without Names, Youth Will Be Served, The Earl of Chicago.*
1942: *The Glass Key, Star Spangled Rhythm.*
1943: *One Dangerous Night, Hi Diddle Diddle.*
1944: *Hollywood Canteen.*
1945: *Rhapsody in Blue, Tell It to a Star.*
1946: *Deadline for Murder.*
1947: *It Happened on Fifth Avenue.*
1950: *The Damned Don't Cry.*
1951: *Close to My Heart, On Moonlight Bay.*

1952: *Carrie, Confidence Girl, The Steel Trap.*
1953: *The Clown.*
1954: *20,000 Leagues Under the Sea.*
1955: *The Night Holds Terror.*
1956: *Julie, Dance with Me Henry.*
1957: *I Was a Teenage Werewolf.*
1958: *How to Make a Monster.*
1964: *Roustabout.*

Television Series

1956–1958: *Circus Boy* as Barker.

Sources

Brooks, Tim. *The Complete Directory to Prime Time TV Stars 1946–Present.* New York: Ballantine Books, 1987.
Perry, Jed. *Screen Gems: A History of Columbia Pictures Television from Cohn to Coke, 1948–1983.* Metuchen, NJ: Scarecrow, 1991.
Ragan, David. *Who's Who in Hollywood.* New York: Facts on File, 1992.

EUGENE MARTIN

This child actor played the role of Joey Drum, the son of Jefferson Drum (Jeff Richards), in the television series *Jefferson Drum* (1958–1959). He appeared in a few feature films and in "The Captain's Wife" and "The Deserters' Patrol" episodes of *Rawhide,* both in 1961. He was still appearing in television series in the 1970s, such as "The Brown Horse Connection" episode of *Bert D'Angelo Superstar* (1976).

Eugene Martin Filmography

1958: *Terror in a Texas Town.*
1960: *This Rebel Breed.*
1962: *Tower of London.*

Television Series

1958–1959: *Jefferson Drum* as Joey Drum.

Sources

Brooks, Tim. *The Complete Directory to Prime Time TV Stars 1946–Present.* New York: Ballantine Books, 1987.

STROTHER MARTIN

Strother Martin was born in Kokomo, Indiana, on March 26, 1919, and graduated from high school in Indianapolis. During World War II he enlisted in the United States navy where he was commissioned as an officer. Upon his discharge he enrolled at the University of Michigan where he studied drama but was also a top class swimmer and diver. Originally he arrived in Hollywood as a swimming coach in 1948, with a tremendous drive to be a professional actor, but made little headway. He did some little theater work and made his screen debut in *The Asphalt Jungle* (1950).

He played in minor roles in feature films and on television, most notably in *Gunsmoke.* Over the 21 year run of that series, he is reckoned to have been one of the two actors who appeared more frequently than any others aside from the regulars. He had a continuing but minor supporting role in the unsuccessful Western series *Hotel De Paree.* During the 1960s he became part of a "crazy heavy" repertory company and generally played neurotic villains. His career gained enormous impetus when he played the captain of a prison farm in *Cool Hand Luke* (1967).

Thereafter he had many important supporting roles in films. He occasionally essayed leads in low-budget films to less effect. On television he was seen as James Stewart's cousin in another unsuccessful series, *Hawkins on Murder.* He was a rare example of a minor supporting player in a Western series of the 1950s who subsequently attained considerable success, frequently stealing scenes from accomplished stars. He was still at it when he died suddenly from a heart attack in Thousand Oaks, California, on August 1, 1980, at age 61. He is buried at the Courts of Remembrance Section of Forest Lawn—Hollywood Hills Cemetery.

Strother Martin Filmography

1950: *The Asphalt Jungle, The Damned Don't Cry.*
1951: *The People Against O'Hara, Rhubarb.*
1952: *Storm Over Tibet.*
1953: *The Magnetic Monster, South Sea Woman.*
1954: *A Star Is Born, Drum Beat.*
1955: *The Big Knife, Strategic Air Command, Kiss Me Deadly, Target Zero.*
1956: *Johnny Concho, Attack!, World Without End.*
1957: *Copper Sky, The Black Whip, Black Patch.*
1958: *Cowboy.*
1959: *The Shaggy Dog, The Wild and the Innocent, The Horse Soldiers.*
1961: *Sanctuary, The Deadly Companions.*
1962: *The Man Who Shot Liberty Valance.*
1963: *McLintock!, Showdown.*
1964: *Invitation to a Gunfighter.*
1965: *Brainstorm, Shenandoah, The Sons of Katie Elder.*
1966: *Harper, An Eye for an Eye, Nevada Smith.*
1967: *The Flim Flam Man, Cool Hand Luke.*
1969: *True Grit, Butch Cassidy and the Sundance Kid, The Wild Bunch.*
1970: *The Brotherhood of Satan, The Ballad of Cable Hogue.*
1971: *Fool's Parade, Red Sky at Morning.*
1972: *Pocket Money, Hannie Caulder.*
1973: *Sssssss.*
1975: *Rooster Cogburn, Hard Times, One of Our Own* (TV).
1976: *The Great Scout and Cathouse Thursday.*
1977: *Slap Shot.*
1978: *Up in Smoke, The Champ, Steel Cowboy* (TV), *Love and Bullets, The End.*
1979: *Nightwing, The Villain, Better Late Than Never* (TV).
1980: *Hotwire, The Secret of Nikola Tesla.*

Television Series

1959–1960: *Hotel De Paree* as Aaron Donager.
1973–1974: *Hawkins* as R.J. Hawkins.

Sources

Jones, Ken D., Arthur F. McClure, and Alfred E. Twomey. *Character People.* Secaucus, NJ: Citadel, 1979.
Quinlan, David. *The Illustrated Directory of Film Character Actors.* London: Batsford, 1995.
Summers, Neil. *The Official TV Western Book Volume #2.* Vienna, WV: Old West Shop Publishing, 1989.

CAROLE MATHEWS

"I want to go on making Westerns. Quite apart from the fact that I owe them a great deal for giving me that first big break, I like Westerns. Too, they're probably the most reliable of all kinds of motion pictures." So spoke Carole Mathews, who proved her point when she played Wilma Fansler in *The Californians* television series.

Born in Montgomery, Illinois, on September 13, 1920, Mathews was educated at Aurora High School, Illinois. In spite of being voted "Miss Chicago" in a beauty contest, she found no takers at the studios when she gatecrashed Hollywood in the late 1930s, so she hit the road to gain experience in dramatics and in every facet of show business.

Following a course in drama in Chicago, which she financed by appearing as a nightclub entertainer and conductor of her own radio show, she headed south for night club stints in Miami, Havana and South America. The trip brought her considerable success, and in 1944 she returned to Hollywood where she made her screen debut. Stock contracts with Columbia and Paramount followed. Despite fierce determination and an independent personality, she had a slow rise from bit roles. A showy part in *The Great Gatsby* (1949) did a great deal toward establishing her as a dramatic actress of note, and she came over to England with the film to assist in the publicity campaign. By 1950 she was established in leading roles but in programmer-type pictures, few of which showcased her dominant personality to advantage. She is one actress who would probably have fared better in the more permissive climate of later decades. Her studio biography indicates that she had golden hair, hazel eyes and stood 5'6" tall.

From 1955 to 1961 she appeared as guest in many series of the mystery and Western genres which were very popular then. Her sole regular role was in the revamped version of *The Californians* in which she played the young widow and saloon hostess Wilma Fansler, who becomes the romantic interest of Marshal Matt Wayne (Richard Coogan). Even here she proved to be unlucky because the series folded after a season.

Carole Mathews with Richard Coogan in *The Californians*.

Mathews was allegedly very shrewd with finance in real life and invested her money in multiple businesses in Hollywood and New York, which enabled her to retire from show business in the early 1960s. She developed such a fondness for England that in the middle 1950s she bought a large interest in a British restaurant in the heart of New York. Called "Mike's Pub," it was thoroughly British in decor and cuisine and became a regular haunt of English actors in New York. Between acting assignments she hopped a plane for London, Paris or Rome. This love of travel possibly led her to open her own travel agency in California which she ran successfully for years.

A one-time resident of Reseda and later Sherman Oaks, California, she has latterly been posted among the lost players of the screen.

Carole Mathews Filmography

1944: *Together Again, Girl in the Case, Swing in the Saddle, The Missing Juror, She's a Sweetheart, Strange Affair, Tahiti Nights.*
1945: *Outlaws of the Rockies, Blazing the Western Trail, I Love a Mystery, Over 21, A Thousand and One Nights, Sing Me a Song of Texas, Ten Cents a Dance, The Monster and the Ape* (serial).
1946: *Stars Over Texas.*
1948: *Sealed Verdict, The Accused.*
1949: *Massacre River, Special Agent, Chicago Deadline, The Great Gatsby, Amazon Quest, Cry Murder.*
1950: *No Man of Her Own, Paid in Full.*
1951: *The Man with My Face.*
1952: *Red Snow, Meet Me at the Fair.*
1953: *City of Bad Men, Shark River.*
1954: *Port of Hell, Treasure of Ruby Hills.*
1955: *Betrayed Women.*
1956: *Assignment Redhead* (a.k.a. *Requiem for a Redhead*), *Swamp Women.*
1957: *Showdown at Boot Hill.*
1958: *Strange Awakening* (a.k.a. *Female Fiends*).
1960: *13 Fighting Men.*
1961: *Tender Is the Night, Look in Any Window.*

Television Series

1958–1959: *The Californians* as Wilma Fansler.

Sources

Correspondence between Sean McClory and the author.
Picture Show's Who's Who on Screen. London: Amalgamated Press, c. 1956.
Quinlan, David. *Illustrated Directory of Film Stars.* London: Batsford, 1996.
Speed, F. Maurice. *The Western Film Annual.* London: MacDonald, 1956.
Turner, Steve, and Edgar M. Wyatt. *Saddle Gals.* Madison, NC: Empire, 1995.

Note

Carole Mathews is sometimes credited with an appearance in *Rabbit Run* (1970), but this appears to be a mistake and should be Carmen Mathews.

DONALD MAY

Donald May was born in Chicago, Illinois, on February 22, 1928, but moved with his family to Houston, Texas, in 1936. He was raised there, but moved again in his teens to Cleveland, Ohio, where he graduated from high school in 1944. He attended the University of Oklahoma, graduating with a B.A. degree in 1949. He studied drama at Yale and did a season of summer stock before playing a lead in the play *Yellow Jack* at Albany, New York. In 1951 he was conscripted into the U.S. navy during the Korean War, serving as a gunnery officer aboard destroyers until his honorable discharge in 1955.

Afterwards he returned to New York to resume his acting career. He amassed 250 stage credits and appeared in many live television series. He briefly served as the host of the military anthology series *The West Point Story,* which dramatized actual events and persons from the files of West Point. He signed a contract with Warner Bros. When Wayde Preston became involved in an increasingly bitter dispute with that studio and walked off the set of *Colt .45,* the solution was to substitute Donald May as his cousin Sam Colt, Jr., and make him the focal point of the series. It could scarcely be said that the switch of actor augured well, and the series ended a short while later with a whimper rather than a bang.

Donald May was then cast as reporter Pat Garrison in the television series *The Roaring Twenties* which, like the more successful *The Untouchables,* was set during the Prohibition era of the 1920s. This is probably his best-known role. He made a successful transition into daytime soap operas where he had a decade-long run as attorney Adam Drake on *The Edge of Night.* During the 1980s he had roles on such soaps as *Texas, As the World Turns* and *Falcon Crest.* He is married to Carla Borelli, a soap opera actress, with whom he has sometimes acted.

Donald May Filmography

1956: *The Wrong Man.*
1960: *The Crowded Sky.*
1964: *A Tiger Walks, Kisses for My President.*
1966: *Follow Me Boys!*
1985: *O.C. & Stiggs.*
1987: *Dirty Laundry.*

Television Series

1956: *The West Point Story* as Cadet Charles C. Thompson.
1959–1960: *Colt .45* as Sam Colt, Junior.
1960–1962: *The Roaring Twenties* as Pat Garrison.
1967–1977: *The Edge of Night* as Adam Drake.
1980–1982: *Texas* as Grant Wheeler.

Donald May in *Colt .45*.

Sources

Brooks, Tim. *The Complete Directory to Prime Time TV Stars.* New York: Ballantine Books, 1987.

Woolley, Lynn, Robert W. Malsbury, and Robert G. Strange, Jr. *Warner Bros. Television* Jefferson, NC: McFarland, 1985.

JUDI MEREDITH

Judi Meredith was born Judith Clare Boutin in Portland, Oregon, on October 13, 1936. At school she was good at mathematics and ice skating. By the age of 15, she was starring in an ice show when she fell through a window and broke her back. Once she had recovered and was skating again, she broke her knee cap. Neither accident proved a handicap because she learned how to skate on ice and on rollers as well as before and enjoyed water skiing. This led to her decision to try for a movie career.

She became enormously popular on television playing the girlfriend of Ronnie Burns (the real-life son of George Burns and Gracie Allen) on *The George Burns and Gracie Allen Show.* Her sole other regular series role was in the oddly-titled Western series *Hotel De Paree,* which was not a success. She played Monique, the niece of Annette Deveraux, who helps to run a European-style hotel in the Old West. Once the pilot was shot, it was decided not to continue with her character, so she was packed off to college. After only a few episodes, she was brought back. Routine plotlines and poor dialogue meant that her character was finally written out again.

Meredith's studio biography listed her hobbies as buying shoes and lingerie. She continued her film and television career until the early 1970s. She married director Gary Nelson.

Judi Meredith Filmography

1958: *Summer Love, Wild Heritage.*
1959: *Money Women and Guns.*
1962: *Jack the Giant Killer.*
1964: *The Night Walker, The Raiders.*
1965: *Dark Intruder.*
1966: *Queen of Blood.*
1971: *Something Big.*

Television Series

1957–1958: *The George Burns and Gracie Allen Show* as Bonnie Sue McAfee.
1958–1959: *The George Burns Show* as herself.
1959–1960: *Hotel De Paree* as Monique Deveraux.

Sources

Picture Show Annual. London: Amalgamated Press, 1960.

Ragan, David. *Who's Who in Hollywood.* New York: Facts on File, 1992.

Who's Who in Hollywood. New York: Dell, 1961.

JAN MERLIN

Jan Merlin played the son of John Loder in the film *Woman and the Hunter,* shot on location in Africa. Filming commenced at a farmhouse a couple of miles outside Nairobi. When the production staff assembled on the first morning, among them there was a stunning Kenyan girl who was responsible for continuity. Merlin headed straight for her, put his face close to hers, looked her straight in the eye and asked, "When?" Everyone laughed. She replied, "You must get an awful lot of slaps in the face!" "Sure," he replied with a grin, "but I get an awful lot of lovin' too." Jan Merlin was the star of *Rough Riders*, one of the more unusual Westerns of the 1950s.

Merlin was born in New York City on April 3, 1925. His real name is Jan Wasylewski, and he is the son of Peter, a mechanic, and Theresa Guziak. His parents were Polish, but he adopted the surname of Merlin after he left the navy, since he believed his real last name was more suitable for a ballet dancer. He was educated at Grace Church Choir School for Boys, a private school based on the English form system. After enlisting in the U.S. Navy in April 1942, he served aboard various destroyers as a torpedo man, participating in the taking of Casablanca. The remainder of the war he served in the Pacific, participating in all the major actions from Wake Island to Okinawa and the occupation of Japan. He received the usual medals for those theaters of operations (including the Liberation of the Philippines, Navy Commendation Ribbon and the Good Conduct Ribbon) before being honorably discharged in April 1946.

After apprenticeship as a scenic designer in a summer theater at Fishkill, New York, in 1946, he entered the Neighborhood Playhouse School of the Theater in New York City as an acting student studying with Sanford Meisner and Martha Graham. This was a two-year course during which he spent summers acting in various summer theaters on the East Coast.

He made his Broadway debut when he replaced an actor in the hit play *Mister Roberts* in the fall of 1948. He remained with the show for two years, playing several different roles as each actor left for other assignments. He made his motion picture debut in *Fourteen Hours* (1951). Of this experience, he recalls, "When casting me for a minute role, my first film appearance, director Henry Hathaway asked me if I was a good actor. I replied that I was at the time working on Broadway as one of the sailors in *Mister Roberts,* the Henry Fonda hit of the season. Mr. Hathaway nodded and repeated his question. I felt stupid ... it was a one-line part he had asked me to read for him consisting of the words, 'Jump! Jump!'" He finally left the play in October 1952, to be one

Jan Merlin on the set of *Rough Riders*.

of the three stars of *Tom Corbett, Space Cadet* on live coast-to-coast television. Remaining in the cast for three years, he quit once in 1953 in order to indulge himself with a honeymoon safari throughout East Africa and the Belgian Congo. Returning to the series, he quit permanently in 1954 to do off-Broadway plays.

He was well-received by the New York critics for his outstanding portrayal of the lead murderous student in Patrick Hamilton's *Rope.* A scout from Universal-International spotted him, and he found himself with a part in *Six Bridges to Cross* (1955). For this he journeyed to Hollywood, where he has remained to this day. He played numerous menacing roles in television and films after he arrived in Hollywood and was seldom without employment for more than a week. He appeared for four months at the Circle Theater in Hollywood in a production of a new play called *The Woman with Red Hair.* Warner Bros. heard of his performance and sent their talent scout, which led to his being tested and accepted for the role of the killer in *Illegal.*

In 1957 he was surprised to be asked to test for a romantic lead role, that of Lt. Cullen Kirby, for a new series to be done by Ziv Studios (who had earlier hired him to play heavies in their other series). He explains, "As I had recently done a film in East Africa, playing Ann Sheridan's husband in *Woman and the Hunter,* that may have suggested I could play a more likable character." He was tested and hired to star in the series *Rough Riders* along with Kent Taylor and Peter Whitney. The series told of the adventures of three Civil War veterans, each of whom planned to move west in search of a new life. The veterans decided to join forces for mutual companionship and protection on the journey. Two of the veterans had fought on the union side, but Lt. Kirby was from the Confederacy.

Despite the fact that they traveled through country where the northerners were often unfriendly, Lt. Kirby rigidly wore his army uniform. One item of uniform which he dispensed with was a hat. When asked about this, Merlin explains, "I did not wear a hat because I didn't want to have one. Hats are a bother when doing chase scenes and fights and I was humored by the studio, thereby creating that rare character, a cowboy without a hat." Of his costars Merlin says, "We did 39 episodes and relished working together, remaining close friends. Both have since died and I miss them dearly."

Most of the episodes were shot in Simi Valley and out in Chatsworth, Newhall and Placerita Canyon, California, with various excursions to more familiar nearby locations such as the Edgar Rice Burroughs ranch and the Bronson caves. The interiors were done at Ziv Studios on Santa Monica Boulevard. Each episode took five days to shoot, seldom going over a day longer. Although a conscious attempt was made to feature one of the stars more prominently in rotation in each episode, the character Merlin played seemed to capture the affection of the fans to such an extent that he won the lion's share of the scripts in the long run. *Rough Riders* was dropped because it was on late at night, opposite the *Tennessee Ernie Ford Show,* and failed to win decent ratings until it was offered in syndication at about six o'clock in the evening, which was a far better time for the show to be seen. By that time, however, the three stars had gone on to other films and were unwilling to return to the series, so it was lost altogether.

Merlin has appeared in many movies and 1,500 live and film television episodes. "My favorite roles were usually as bad types, such as the teenaged rowdy in *A Day of Fury* for Universal or as Charles Bronson's nemesis in *Guns of Diablo* which was originally aired on television as episodes of *The Travels of Jamie McPheeters,* a series starring Dan O'Herlihy and Kurt Russell. I particularly liked working with Audie Murphy in *Hell Bent for Leather.* Although it wasn't up to snuff, I enjoyed doing the African film with Ann Sheridan most, as we spent three grand months roughing it in the Northern Frontier District of Kenya with those two fine actors David Farrar and John Loder and the delightful Ronald Adam. This film was the last one Sheridan was to make."

Quizzed about his worst acting experience, he replies, "This was the year I spent on *The List of Adrian Messenger,* playing several roles underneath masks which barely disguised me, knowing I would never be credited for the performances." The whole thing started out as a gimmick. The idea was that the five famous guest stars (Kirk Douglas, Burt Lancaster, Robert Mitchum, Frank Sinatra and Tony Curtis) would play their parts disguised in rubber masks. The audience was invited to guess which star was playing which part. Then at the end of the film, the five guest stars were seen peeling off their masks to give the answer. The parts Douglas, Lancaster and Sinatra were supposedly playing behind masks, however, were played by other actors. All but one of those disguises supposedly done by Douglas was actually performed by Merlin. He continues, "I managed to get one laugh out of all the painful hours I spent under the masks and that was to receive a letter from a friend in England asking to know if I had been in a strange film she had just seen, for it very much looked and sounded like me. My voice was not redubbed."

Continuing to act in films and television, though with less enthusiasm about playing similar roles over and over again, he took to writing scripts and novels. *Brocade*, a novel about the occupation of Japan, later published by Avon Books in 1982, led to an offer from Harding Lemay, head writer for the NBC television soap *Another World,* to write scripts for the show between 1974 and 1979. Merlin earned an Emmy in 1975 and another Emmy nomination in 1977. He later contributed scripts to *Little House on the Prairie* and wrote unpublished novels such as *Gunbearer* (based in Africa) and *Jack in the Green* (set in upstate New York). He is currently revising his latest novel manuscript and has avoided writing for television and films altogether. He has not abandoned acting completely and still consents to do a film or television part occasionally. Appearances at Western film festivals keep him traveling throughout the year to most of the United States, since he is best known for his work in that genre. He is an expert at several dialects and languages and has provided voiceovers for foreign and domestic productions. He has also been a volunteer at the Braille Institute, reading and recording books for their lending library for the visually impaired.

Jan Merlin married actress Patricia Ann Datz on August 17, 1951; they had a son, Peter. She died of cancer after a six-month illness some years ago. Subsequently he married Barbara Doyle. He adds, "We now share a family of eight children, all fully grown and pursuing careers of their own in exciting fields."

Jan Merlin Filmography

1951: *Fourteen Hours.*
1955: *Six Bridges to Cross, Running Wild, Illegal, Big House USA.*
1956: *Screaming Eagles, Strange Adventure, A Day of Fury, The Peacemaker.*
1957: *The Woman and the Hunter.*
1958: *Cole Younger Gunfighter.*
1960: *Hell Bent for Leather.*
1963: *The List of Adrian Messenger* (uncredited), *Gunfight at Comanche Creek.*
1964: *Guns of Diablo.*
1966: *The Oscar.*
1967: *The St. Valentine's Day Massacre.*
1969: *Take the Money and Run.*
1972: *Twilight People (*a.k.a. *Beasts).*
1973: *The Slams, I Escaped from Devil's Island.*
1975: *The Hindenburg.*
1987: *Nowhere to Hide.*
1988: *Permanent Record.*
1989: *Time Trackers, Caddo Lake, Silk II.*
1990: *Buried Alive* (TV). *False Identity (*a.k.a. *Yesterday's Heroes), After the Shock* (TV).
1992: *A Child Lost Forever* (TV).

Television Series

1952–1954: *Tom Corbett, Space Cadet* as Roger Manning.
1958–1959: *Rough Riders* as Lt. Cullen Kirby.

Sources

Correspondence between Merlin and the author.

KRISTINE MILLER

Kristine Miller was born Jacqueline Olivia Eskeson in Buenos Aires in 1925, the daughter of an oil executive. She only spent the first five years of her life in Argentina until her father's job took the family to Denmark. She was educated in Copenhagen, where she became a model and was given the title "The Viking Girl" by a group of Royal Danish Illustrators because of her good looks, stunning figure and athletic ability. She was also fluent in several languages. With her family she escaped from Denmark at the time of the Nazi invasion and eventually made her way to San Francisco, where she commenced her acting career in little theaters.

While appearing in a production of *The Doll's House*, she was spotted by producer Hal B. Wallis, who placed her under personal contract and developed her potential as an actress before she made her screen debut in 1946. She developed into a competent actress who excelled in roles as a femme fatale. Most of her physical attributes suited her character well in her only regular television series, *Stories of the Century.* In this syndicated series she played Margaret Jones ("Jonesy"), a beautiful undercover railroad detective who worked as assistant to Matt Clark (Jim Davis). Few realized that they worked together because she normally came into town ahead of him, settled down and endeavored to discover the whereabouts of the villain they were hunting.

Miller left the series part way through to marry a television executive and retired from the screen. At last report she was residing in Northern California.

Portrait of Kristine Miller, who appeared in *Stories of the Century*.

Kristine Miller Filmography

1946: *Suspense.*
1947: *Desert Fury, I Walk Alone, The Trouble with Women.*
1948: *Jungle Patrol.*
1949: *Paid in Full, Too Late for Tears.*
1950: *Shadow on the Wall, Young Daniel Boone, High Lonesome.*
1952: *The Steel Fist, Tropical Heat Wave.*
1953: *Flight Nurse, Geraldine, From Here to Eternity, Blades of the Musketeers.*
1954: *Hell's Outpost.*
1956: *Thunder Over Arizona.*
1957: *The Persuader, Domino Kid.*

Television Series

1954–1955: *Stories of the Century* as Margaret "Jonesy" Jones.

Sources

Picture Show's Who's Who on Screen. London: Amalgamated Press, c. 1956.

Summers, Neil. *The Official TV Western Book Volume #2.* Vienna, WV: Old West Shop Publishing, 1989.

Winchester, Clarence. *Who's Who on Screen.* London: Winchester Publications, 1948.

MORT MILLS

Born in 1919, this enigmatic American character actor and former Marine paratrooper made his screen debut in 1952. Over the next decade he became an extremely familiar face to both film and television audiences. His best-remembered big-screen role was as the cop in dark glasses who stops Janet Leigh in the classic Hitchcock film *Psycho* (1960). Given that television frequently made stars out of actors who were not conventionally handsome, it seems reasonable to suppose that it could have done the same for Mort Mills if he had landed the right series.

His only regular role was as stalwart U.S. Marshal Frank Tallman in the syndicated television Western series *Man Without a Gun.* He was the minder of courageous frontier newspaper editor Adam MacLean (Rex Reason). He despised his role in this series and wanted out to pursue more meaty assignments. Possibly he overrated himself because the better roles went elsewhere and his career stagnated.

Mills also had an occasional role as the sheriff in the early seasons of *The Big Valley* and as Lt. Ben Landau on *Perry Mason.* His last credits date from the early 1970s. One

Mort Mills (left) and Rex Reason in *Man Without a Gun*.

report states that after this he became despondent about his career, severed his connections with show business and retired to live in Oxnard, California, where there were several reported sightings of him. In later years he became a sales representative for a wholesale manufacturer of nuts and bolts.

Mort Mills died on June 6, 1993, at age 74.

Mort Mills Filmography

1952: *Affair in Trinidad, No Holds Barred.*
1953: *Hannah Lee (*a.k.a. *Outlaw Territory), The Farmer Takes a Wife, Texas Bad Man.*
1954: *Pushover, Drive a Crooked Road, Cry Vengeance.*
1955: *Jupiter's Darling, Trial, Desert Sands, Dial Red O, The Marauders, To Hell and Back.*
1956: *Davy Crockett and the River Pirates, Crashing Las Vegas, The Harder They Fall.*
1957: *Man in the Shadow, The Iron Sheriff, Shadow on the Window.*
1958: *Touch of Evil, Ride a Crooked Trail.*
1960: *Psycho.*
1961: *Twenty Plus Two.*
1963: *Gunfight at Comanche Creek.*
1964: *Bullet for a Badman, The Quick Gun.*
1965: *The Outlaws Is Coming.*
1966: *Torn Curtain, Blindfold.*
1967: *Return of the Gunfighter* (TV).
1968: *The Name of the Game Is Kill.*
1970: *Breakout* (TV), *Soldier Blue.*

Television Series

1957–1959: *Man Without a Gun* as U.S. Marshal Frank Tallman.

Sources

"In Memoriam." *Screen Actor* magazine, March 1995.
Magers, Boyd. "Empty Saddles." *Western Clippings* magazine, issue #6, July/August 1995.
Summers, Neil. *The Official TV Western Book Volume #4.* Vienna, WV: Old West Shop Publishing, 1992.

EWING MITCHELL

Born in 1911, Ewing Young Mitchell played small roles in films. He was the sheriff on a couple of Western series of the 1950s. He died in La Jolla, California, on September 2, 1988, at age 77, following a stroke.

Ewing Mitchell Filmography

1950: *Tripoli.*
1951: *Francis Goes to the Races, The Last Outpost.*
1952: *Horizons West, Springfield Rifle, The Blazing Forest.*
1953: *Winning of the West, Above and Beyond.*
1954: *Black Horse Canyon, Drums Across the River.*
1955: *Man Without a Star, The Court-Martial of Billy Mitchell.*
1956: *Behind the High Wall.*
1957: *Band of Angels.*

Television Series

1951–1954: *Sky King* as the Sheriff of Grover.
1955–1956: *The Adventures of Champion* as Sheriff Powers.

Sources

Ragan, David. *Who's Who in Hollywood.* New York: Facts on File, 1992.
Summers, Neil. *The Official TV Western Book Volumes 2 and 3.* Vienna, WV: Old West Shop Publishing, 1989 and 1991.

JOHN MITCHUM

John Mitchum was born in Bridgeport, Connecticut, on September 6, 1919, the son of James Thomas Mitchum and Ann Harriet Gunderson. He has one brother, the late actor Robert Mitchum (born August 6, 1917), and one sister, Annette (born July 23, 1914). His father was killed in an accident in 1919. He was raised on a farm in Woodside, Delaware, and attended Felton High School. During the Depression the family relocated to Manhattan where he attended P.S. 59, but economic problems forced a return to rural Delaware. In 1934 the two brothers decided to strike out on their own and head for California.

In Los Angeles he attended the Long Beach Polytechnic High School, from which he graduated in 1936. Most of the time he and his brother lived at the beach. In 1937 he enrolled briefly at Long Beach Junior College. He also obtained some experience as a deckhand on various boats. Through his brother's influence he joined the Long Beach Players Guild and acted small roles in plays which starred his brother. Always good at music, he sang in the choir of the First Presbyterian Church of Long Beach. With the outbreak of World War II, he went to work at Ryan Aircraft in San Diego, learning the sheet metal business, and then toiled at Lockheed.

In 1944 he was drafted into the army, serving in the 361st Harbor Craft Company until 1946, when he was discharged. He became a professional actor when he was stopped on Santa Monica Boulevard by an agent who took him to producer-director Frank Wisbar, who cast him right away in a feature called *The Prairie* (1947). It sank without trace. He began working for the Los Angeles Bureau of Music as a youth worker and also attended the Herbert Wall School of Music. Wisbar used him in some early television series such as *Fireside Theater*, and he had small roles in a few feature films.

After marrying for a second time, he relocated in 1951 to Dallas, Texas, where he became a sheet metal worker at Collins Radio Company, but the lure of the camera proved to be too strong. Shortly before his son was born, he moved his family back to Hollywood in 1953 to pursue a precarious career as an actor. He supplemented his income by working for a contractor who built and hung garage doors and later by selling policies for the Prudential Life Insurance Company. He appeared in several films and in one of the last serials ever made, and played small roles in several action-orientated television series.

He had a semi-regular role on television as Pickalong, a guitar-strumming crew member and boat's cook, in the first season of *Riverboat.* He liked the regularity of the work, but did not get on with some of his costars, notably Jack Lambert. He appeared in 11 episodes, but it was a troubled series which expired prematurely. During the 1960s he worked on numerous television series; toured the country with James Drury; did a political tour with Senator Barry Goldwater; acted in a half dozen movies; and cut a patriotic RCA record album ("Our Land Our Heritage") recorded in 1964. He had a semi-regular role as Hoeffen Mueller, a German who spoke no English but acted as translator for the Indians, in the comedy Western series *F Troop* for two seasons. He also contributed substantially to the record "America Why I Love Her" by John Wayne.

Professional extra George Fargo, known as Grey Cloud, recommended Mitchum to Clint Eastwood to play Frank di Georgio, Inspector Harry Callahan's partner in *Dirty Harry* (1971). He also played the same role in the first two sequels. This trio of movies represent his most prestigious movie credits and his most memorable character until he was killed off to make way for Tyne Daly. At last report he was residing with his current wife in Nevada City, Northern California, where he still acts primarily in plays staged at the Nevada Theater. He also penned an excellent memoir about his life and that of his brother, *Them Ornery Mitchum Boys,* published in 1989.

In 1941 he married Joy Grahame, elder sister of actress Gloria Grahame. With her he had a daughter Victoria, born on December 18, 1941. They divorced in 1951. In 1951 he married Nancy Munro with whom he had a son, Jack, Jr., born in August 1953, and a daughter, Cindy, born in May 1958. His wife died in 1976. Shortly afterwards he married Dorothy McCoy in 1976, but divorced her in 1984. He wed Bonnie Duff in 1986.

John Mitchum Filmography

1947: *The Prairie.*
1949: *Knock on Any Door.*
1950: *In a Lonely Place, When Willie Comes Marching Home, Submarine Command, Born to Be Bad.*
1951: *Flying Leathernecks, One Minute to Zero, Right Cross.*
1952: *The Lusty Men.*
1953: *Stalag 17.*
1955: *The Man in the Vault, The Big Combo.*
1956: *Perils of the Wilderness* (serial), *The Man Is Armed.*
1957: *Up in Smoke, Operation Mad Ball, Five Steps to Danger.*
1961: *Hitler.*
1963: *Cattle King.*
1964: *My Fair Lady.*
1965: *Brainstorm.*
1967: *The Way West, El Dorado.*
1968: *Bandolero!*
1969: *Bigfoot.*
1970: *Paint Your Wagon, Chisum.*
1971: *Dirty Harry, Do Not Fold Spindle or Mutilate* (TV).
1973: *High Plains Drifter.*
1974: *Magnum Force, The Hanged Man* (TV).
1975: *Breakheart Pass.*
1976: *The Enforcer, The Outlaw Josey Wales.*
1977: *Telefon.*
1984: *Escapes.*
1989: *Jake Spanner Private Eye* (TV).
1990: *A Family for Joe* (TV).

Television Series

1959–1960: *Riverboat* as Pickalong.
1965–1967: *F Troop* as Hoeffen Mueller.

Sources

Mitchum, John. *Them Ornery Mitchum Boys.* Pacifica, CA: Creatures at Large Press, 1989.

Note

Mitchum used the name John Mallory in some of his early films such as *Flying Leathernecks.*

ROGER MOBLEY

Born in 1951, this child actor played the role of Joey Newton's friend Packy on *Fury*. He is the brother of Mary Ann Mobley, Miss America of 1959.

Roger Mobley Filmography

1960: *A Dog's Best Friend.*
1961: *The Comancheros, The Silent Call, The Boy Who Caught a Crook.*
1962: *Jack the Giant Killer.*
1963: *Dime with a Halo.*
1964: *Gallagher V, Emil and the Detectives.*
1968: *The Mystery of Edward Sims.*
1974: *For the Love of Willadean.*
1979: *The Apple Dumpling Gang Rides Again.*

Television Series

1955–1958: *Fury* as Packy Lambert.

Sources

Lance, Steven. *Written Out of Television: A TV Lover's Guide to Cast Changes 1945–1994.* Lanham, MD: Madison, 1996.
Ragan, David. *Who's Who in Hollywood.* New York: Facts on File, 1992.
Terrace, Vincent. *The Complete Encyclopedia of Television Programs 1947–1976.* South Brunswick and New York: Barnes, 1976.

GEORGE MONTGOMERY

At one time it was commonplace in Hollywood for a star to start out as a bit player in Westerns, be boosted to stardom as a Western hero and then abandon Westerns in favor of straight roles in more prestigious productions. This was the route which George Montgomery took before World War II. Afterwards he returned to the Western plains where he played the rugged, handsome hero of numerous sagebrush movies, exhibiting the necessary physical presence and riding skills. When many of the B Western heroes departed the scene in the 1950s, he and a handful of others continued on alone in programmer Westerns. He also starred in a television series *(Cimarron City)* at a time when the genre reached its zenith on the small screen. His Westerns produced no classics, but there was a lot of action-packed entertainment on the trail.

George Montgomery Letz was born on a ranch in Brady, Montana, on August 29, 1916, the son of George G. Letz and his wife Dena, Russian immigrants. He was the youngest of eight brothers and five sisters. He was brought up on rangeland where horsemanship was a staple requirement. As a child he raised pigeons and chickens for sale, for food and for entry in competitions. He built his own coops and did some woodcarving, activities which stood him in good stead later on in his life.

They were an itinerant family, but they had settled near Great Falls where he attended high school. Upon graduation he attended the University of Montana for two years, studying interior decorating. Throughout his limited academic life he excelled in sports (baseball, football, track and especially boxing). He became collegiate heavyweight boxing champion for the areas of Montana, Idaho, Washington and Oregon. He decided that it would be a good idea to put his athletic ability and enthusiasm for acting to practical use. A career in the movies seemed the obvious answer for him.

He went to visit a brother who was working as an engineer in Los Angeles. While pursuing his ambition, he obtained a menial job as a decorator. He did the rounds of the studios virtually without success aside from playing a bit in Republic's *The Singing Vagabond* (1935), which starred Gene Autry. He later had a one-day job riding a horse as a Cossack in *Conquest*

George Montgomery in *Cimarron City.*

(1937), which starred Greta Garbo. Republic hired him to play one of the fake Lone Rangers in the classic serial *The Lone Ranger* (1938). He also doubled for virtually everyone else in the cast, and long after he was officially killed in the chapterplay it was not hard to spot him stunting in the fight scenes.

He appeared in minor roles under his real name in some other Republic Westerns over the next few months before he decided that his career was not advancing anywhere and promptly returned to work on his father's ranch. The following year he decided to gate-crash Hollywood again. This time he acquired an aggressive agent in Benny Medford, who put his career on ice until a studio contract could be arranged. The actor filled in time as a bartender and dishwasher at a Hollywood cafe.

Medford arranged an interview for him with 20th Century–Fox casting executive Lou Schreiber, who looked at Montgomery's physique and thought he would be ideal for cowboy movies. The studio signed him to a contract. A supporting role in *The Cisco Kid and the Lady* (1940) convinced the studio executives that they really had a find in him. The studio groomed him for stardom in a series of Westerns based on Zane Grey stories (they had served William Farnum and Tom Mix well in their silent days at the same studio, and had been dusted off for George O'Brien in the early 1930s). They also shortened his name to George Montgomery.

The first of his Westerns, *Riders of the Purple Sage* (1941), was an unusually fine subject, fast, snappy, full of action, and produced with care with a good cast. Backed by Zane Grey's suspenseful story, it was an extremely promising start. The follow-up, *Last of the Duanes* (1941), was less entertaining, but still well-done. Ironically, William Farnum, star of the original, played a supporting role in it.

Montgomery so far exceeded expectations, and the studio was so deluged with fan mail, that they promptly removed him from the series and proceeded to build him up as a "new Gable." A mustache was cultivated and a similar wave introduced into his haircut. He was given a lead in *Cadet Girl* (1941) in which he had to choose between Carole Landis or attending West Point. After this he found himself in some very choice assignments opposite some of the screen's most famous leading ladies. His name was also linked romantically with most of them and others like Hedy Lamarr.

He provided the romantic interest for Ginger Rogers in *Roxie Hart* (1942), a very broadly played burlesque set in Chicago in the 1920s, about a murder and subsequent trial. In the Technicolor film *Ten Gentlemen from West Point* (1942) he was paired opposite Maureen O'Hara in a fictional story about the first class to graduate from the Academy. The drama was finely balanced with comedic elements. In *China Girl* (1942) he won Gene Tierney, but although he fancied her in real life, she only had eyes for Oleg Cassini, who became her first husband. *Coney Island* (1943) starred him opposite Betty Grable in a Technicolor musical located at that famous resort.

The momentum of his career was slowed down when he was drafted into the Army Signal Corps, where he remained for three years. Upon his discharge he returned to 20th Century–Fox. He remembers it somewhat ruefully this way: "When I was due for a discharge, Victor Mature was doing *Three Little Girls in Blue.* It had already been in production three weeks when Darryl Zanuck heard I was coming out and decided to take Mature out of the film and put me in. He had already fired Mature from the part by the time I got home. My agent, Ben Medford, said, 'Now we've got Zanuck over a barrel. I'll get you a lot of money. He'll have to pay it.' I sat in a car and waited while Medford was up in Zanuck's office arguing with him. He finally got me $2750 a week—but Zanuck was furious. He said, 'I'm going to see that he's killed in this business.' He did a pretty good job of it."

The studio cast him as Raymond Chandler's private detective Philip Marlowe in *The Brasher Doubloon* (1947). This had as decidedly B-picturish look to it, lacking the production values which had distinguished his earlier movies. It was based on one of Chandler's best novels *(The High Window)*, but ironically it became one of the weakest films. Montgomery made an indifferent showing as the shamus. He did not appear as convincing as Humphrey Bogart in the role. He departed from the studio because of dissatisfaction over the roles which he was being offered.

Determined to regain prominence in the field which was his true forte, he specialized in action roles once again, predominantly but not exclusively in Westerns. By the early 1950s he found himself at Columbia Studios as a reigning Western hero. By the mid–1950s he had changed his base to Allied Artists, but he also shot films for United Artists and Republic. Along with Randolph Scott, Joel McCrea and Audie Murphy, he completed the quartet of stars from that period whose names were instantly associated with the genre. His films were generally not of the same standard as theirs, and he was the least acclaimed of the four. Some of his Westerns tended towards the offbeat, and he coproduced some of them.

Like many other actors at the end of the 1950s, he moved over to television where he shot 26 hour-length episodes of a series entitled *Cimarron City*. This was produced by Revue Productions for NBC. It made its debut on October 11, 1958, and the last original episode was shown on September 26, 1959. Cimarron City was an oil town in the Oklahoma Territory during the 1890s. Its citizens hoped that it would become the capital of the future state of Oklahoma. Montgomery played Mayor Matthew Rockford, son of the town's founder and the leading citizen. Beth Purcell (Audrey Totter) ran the boarding house and was the female interest. Although the series had its admirers, there are those who believe it might have proven more popular if Montgomery had played the proactive role of the sheriff Lane Temple instead of the passive one of Rockford. John Smith played Temple. Most of the episodes involved these three characters, although several others had running roles in the series. The lineup of guests was impressive, with Montgomery's then-wife Dinah Shore turning up in one episode, "Cimarron Holiday." The star narrated the series, relating the stories from the perspective of an older man, recalling the tales of his younger days.

Later Montgomery signed a contract with Warner Bros. to produce, direct, script and star in movies. They were primarily low-budget war films shot in the Philippines. As the 1960s continued, he shot an ever-increasing number of films in a similar vein where he was frequently the only name star. The locations of these films changed. As his acting career wound down, he turned to other avenues as an outlet for his energy and creativity where he proved to be immensely successful. He designed and built homes for a great many movie-related personalities and also established a flourishing furniture manufacturing business. His art has been exhibited throughout the country, and he is the creator of the Hollywood Western Hall of Fame Award. He is also the founder of the George Montgomery Foundation of the Arts, dedicated to perpetuating the history and culture of America's frontier.

During the 1970s he became commercial spokesperson for Johnson's Wax, in which capacity he appeared in their advertisements and toured extensively for the company. In the 1980s he starred in two international coproductions which appeared to be trying to set some kind of record for the number of different countries involved in them. He also played the President of the United States in a children's serial. At last report he resides alone in a magnificent three-level, Spanish-style house in California's exclusive Trousdale Estates. He designed and built the mansion by himself; he also designed the furniture.

George Montgomery met singer Dinah Shore at the Hollywood Canteen in 1942. They corresponded while he was stationed in the services in Alaska. They wed while he was on leave in Las Vegas on December 5, 1943. They had two children: daughter Melissa Ann, born in 1948, and son John David, nicknamed Jody, whom they adopted in 1954. Even though they divorced after 19 years in Santa Monica on May 9, 1962, they remained close, and Montgomery was at the 76-year-old Shore's bedside when she died on February 24, 1994, of cancer. At last report he has three grandchildren.

George Montgomery Filmography

1935: *The Singing Vagabond.*
1937: *Conquest, Springtime in the Rockies.*
1938: *The Lone Ranger* (serial), *Gold Mine in the Sky, Come on Rangers, Billy the Kid Returns, Hawk of the Wilderness* (serial), *Shine on Harvest Moon.*
1939: *Man of Conquest, Rough Riders Round-Up, Frontier Pony Express, Wall Street Cowboy.*
1940: *Cisco Kid and the Lady, Jennie, Charter Pilot, Young People, Star Dust.*
1941: *The Cowboy and the Blonde, Accent on Love, Riders of the Purple Sage, Last of the Duanes, Cadet Girl.*
1942: *Roxie Hart, Ten Gentlemen from West Point, China Girl, Orchestra Wives.*
1943: *Coney Island, Bombers' Moon.*
1946: *Three Little Girls in Blue.*
1947: *The Brasher Doubloon (*a.k.a. *The High Window).*
1948: *The Girl from Manhattan, Lulu Belle, Belle Starr's Daughter.*

1949: *Dakota Lil.*
1950: *Davy Crockett Indian Scout, The Iroquois Trail.*
1951: *The Sword of Monte Cristo, The Texas Rangers.*
1952: *Indian Uprising, Cripple Creek.*
1953: *Jack McCall Desperado, The Pathfinder, Fort Ti, Gun Belt.*
1954: *The Lone Gun, Battle of Rogue River.*
1955: *Masterson of Kansas, Robbers' Roost, Seminole Uprising.*
1956: *Huk, Canyon River.*
1957: *Last of the Badmen, Street of Sinners, Gun Duel in Durango, Pawnee.*
1958: *Black Patch, Badman's Country, Toughest Gun in Tombstone. Man from God's Country.*
1959: *Watusi, King of the Wild Stallions.*
1961: *The Steel Claw* (also directed).
1962: *Samar* (also directed).
1964: *From Hell to Borneo* (also directed), *Guerillas in Pink Lace* (also directed).
1965: *Battle of the Bulge.*
1966: *Outlaw of Red River, Hallucination Generation, Bomb at 10:10.*
1967: *Hostile Guns, Warkill.*
1968: *Strangers at Sunrise.*
1969: *Satan's Harvest* (also directed).
1970: *Ride the Tiger* (also directed).
1971: *The Daredevil.*
1972: *The Leo Chronicles.*
1986: *Wild Wind.*
1988: *Ransom in Blood.*

Television Series

1958–1959: *Cimarron City* as Matthew Rockford.

Sources

Corneau, Ernest N. *The Hall of Fame of Western Film Stars.* North Quincy, MA: Christopher, 1969.
Eleventh Annual Golden Boot Awards Program. August 21, 1993.
McClelland, Doug. *Forties Film Talk: Oral Histories of Hollywood, with 120 Lobby Posters.* Jefferson, NC: McFarland, 1992.
Parish, James Robert, and Lennard DeCarl. *Hollywood Players: The Forties.* New Rochelle, NY: Arlington House, 1976.
Ragan, David. *Movie Stars of the '40s.* Englewood Cliffs, NJ: Spectrum, 1985.
Speed, F. Maurice. *The Western Film and TV Annual.* London: MacDonald, 1957 and 1961.

CLAYTON MOORE

A masked figure is galloping at full speed astride a magnificent white horse to the strains of "The William Tell Overture" while a voice intones, "A fiery horse with the speed of light, a cloud of dust and a hearty 'Hi Yo, Silver!' This is the story of one of the most mysterious characters to appear in the early days of the West. He was a fabulous individual whose presence brought fear to the lawless and hope to those who wanted to make this frontiersland their home. He was known as the Lone Ranger." The actor who became the definitive Lone Ranger is Clayton Moore. He brought tremendous physical grace and incisiveness to the part. He was an expert horseman and gun twirler who performed most of his own fight and action routines and did his own stunts throughout his career.

Clayton Moore was born Jack Carlton Moore in Chicago, Illinois, on September 14, 1914, the son of a realtor. He had two older brothers. He was raised in that city and was on the gymnastics team in high school. He became a trapeze artist as one of the Flying Behrs in a circus which toured the U.S. and appeared in the World's Fair in Chicago in 1934. He left that city in 1934 and headed for New York. From 1935 to 1938 he was a male model for the prestigious John Robert Powers Agency. He gravitated to Hollywood and was under contract to Warner Bros. in 1938 and MGM in 1939. Around this time he was using the name Jack Carlton. In 1940 he signed with Edward Small Productions and had excellent roles in two films, *Kit Carson* and *The Son of Monte Cristo.* It was Small who changed his Christian name to Clayton.

He had been playing bit parts in serials since the late 1930s. His career as a serial star fluctuated between playing hero and chief villain, and he played both with aplomb. He attained stardom in a Republic chapterplay called *Perils of Nyoka* (1942) which is regarded as a classic and is Moore's personal favorite of his serials. Kay Aldridge starred as Nyoka Gordon, a jungle girl. Clayton Moore costarred as Dr. Larry Grayson, her boyfriend, who has acquired a papyrus which will enable them to locate the lost tablets of Hippocrates. His career would probably have gone forward (if not with the speed of light, then at least much more rapidly) if World War II had not intervened. From 1943 to 1945 he served in the air force. Upon being honorably discharged he made features at Columbia, Republic and RKO and was generally regarded as "King of the Serials" at Republic from 1946 to 1949. Producers tended to ignore him when it came to providing him with a Western film series of his own. On the rare occasions when he did star in a feature such as *Buffalo Bill in Tomahawk Territory* (1952), the results were lackluster.

His first serial after the war was *The Crimson Ghost* (1946) for Republic. The title character was a skull-masked malefactor after an invention called the Cyclotrode which could short circuit electric current. The Ghost's chief henchman was the evil gangster Ashe (Clayton Moore) who used all his underworld contacts to obtain it for his masked boss. In 1947 he was the hero of *Jesse James Rides Again* and followed this with other heroic roles in Republic serials before switching to villainy once again in *Radar Men from the Moon.* The serial roles at Republic overlapped with his early work in the role of the Lone Ranger. His final Republic serial was *Jungle Drums of Africa* (1953), which was reckoned to be the weakest of all 66 Republic serials. He also slipped across to Columbia to appear in serials such as *Son of Geronimo* (1952), in which he was billed as Clay Moore, and *Gunfighters of the Northwest* (1954).

The Lone Ranger was a character who was originally created for radio, where the series debuted in January 1933. He was the brainchild of Detroit station owner George W. Trendle and writer Fran Striker. Although it started as a local show, it was an almost instant smash and quickly spread nationwide via the Mutual Radio Network. It was first brought to the screen in the very exciting Republic chapterplay *The Lone Ranger* (1938), starring Lee Powell. It was so successful that a sequel was immediately ordered; *The Lone Ranger Rides Again* (1939) starred Bob Livingston.

In 1949 the Lone Ranger was brought to television in a series of half-hour films. The cost of the series was borne by General Mills, the long-time sponsor of the radio series, but Trendle still handled the creative aspects of the series (writing, casting and directing). The radio Lone Ranger, Brace Beemer, was desperate to play the role on television. He was an excellent horseman and a crack shot, and he slimmed down considerably to play the part, but lost the role to Clayton Moore because of his lack of film experience. Moore's voice resembled that of Beemer. It was thought that Moore won the role because of his performance in the serial *Ghost of Zorro* (1949), in which he wore a mask. The radio Tonto was an elderly gentleman past 80 named John Todd, so Jay Silverheels assumed that role. This was the first Western series shot specifically for television. Although *Hopalong Cassidy* arrived there first, the early episodes of this series were the original feature films edited for television. The series received two Emmy nominations in 1949 and 1950.

Clayton Moore played the role for the first three seasons. After requesting a substantial increase in salary in 1952, Moore was dropped from the role. He was temporarily replaced by John Hart, a competent, personable actor who had played supporting roles in a couple of earlier *Lone Ranger* episodes. The producers' thinking was that the mask would hide his identity well enough, but the ploy did not work and public opinion forced the return of Moore after a couple of years. There may have been a couple of other factors which influenced his decision to return. The Gene Autry/Roy Rogers features which had long been a second string to his bow wound up in the early 1950s. The serials had also dried up, the pickings were lean and his billing was low, so Clayton Moore assumed the role again and played it until the demise of the series in 1957.

Although he was a fictional character, the Lone Ranger came into being as a result of a true incident in the Old West. Six Texas Rangers rode into an ambush. All except one were killed. The surviving ranger was seriously wounded, but was nursed back to health by an Indian called Tonto who found him close to death. When the Ranger recovered, he swore to Tonto he would avenge the death of his five friends, one of whom was his brother. The Ranger fashioned a mask out of his dead brother's vest, so that he would not be recognized by the outlaws who ambushed them. Along with the silver bullets, this mask became a symbol of truth and justice. True to his word, the Lone Ranger brought them all to justice.

While searching for the killers, the Lone Ranger and Tonto saw a wild steed being gored by a bison. The Ranger shot and killed the bison, then tended the horse's serious wounds. The horse recovered and was tamed by the Ranger, who called it "Silver." A silver mine left to him by his dead brother provided the ore for the famous silver bullets and the money he needed to carry on his quest.

The Lone Ranger was the biggest hit of the ABC network. In the first national poll taken by A.C. Nielsen in 1950, it came in at seventh and was the only ABC program to reach the top 15. The abundance of action made it a great success with children, while adults enjoyed the show because of the lack of explicit violence together with the high moral code by which the Lone Ranger lived. At its peak the show was carried by 177 American television stations and had an audience of 65,000,000 viewers a week in the United States. It was simultaneously being televised to millions more in England, Canada, Puerto Rico and Japan.

Clayton Moore played the Lone Ranger in 169 half-hour episodes out of 221. The total breakdown was 182 in black and white and 39 in color. The color episodes had a much different look to them mainly because of the extensive location shooting. The series was so popular on television that Warner Bros. decided to film a full-length color feature called *The Lone Ranger* (1956) with Moore and Silverheels in their regular roles. It was shot in Kanab, Utah. Bonita Granville, former child actress, had a big part. She was the wife of Jack Wrather, whose corporation had acquired the rights to the series. The film was such a smash hit that another equally successful film, *The Lone Ranger and the Lost City of Gold* (1958), was made. This was shot in Tucson, Arizona. Moore and Silverheels repeated their roles, with United Artists releasing. Apart from a commercial, it was the last original work which both actors did together. The series ended when it lost its sponsor in 1957.

Moore and Silverheels also appeared together in two features in which they did not play the Lone Ranger and Tonto. They were *The Cowboy and the Indians* (1950), a Gene Autry Western in which Moore played the heavy and Silverheels an intelligent, college-educated Indian, and *The Black Dakotas* (1954). While shooting the first feature the two actors did not meet. They only met for the first time in the office of George W. Trendle and Fran Striker just prior to shooting the series.

Hollywood continued to beckon Moore back for television commercials for automobiles (in which he wore his famous mask) and aftershave (for which he discarded it). He also took to the road as a celebrity turn at rodeos, county fairs and supermarket openings. In 1984 he was reported to be drawing fees of thousands of dollars for each appearance, plus expenses and a bonus if required to ride a horse. He rode "Silver" in the 1969 Hollywood Santa Claus Parade and at the opening of many of the Lone Ranger franchise restaurants. There were two Silvers. The first one died while shooting the original series. The replacement died in 1973.

When producers wanted to make a new feature film version of *The Lone Ranger* in 1979, Moore was taken to court by the Wrather Corporation. They wanted to obtain an injunction preventing him from appearing in public as the Lone Ranger. He turned up in court wearing his black mask and white Stetson. The first judge excused himself on the grounds that he was too much of a fan to be unbiased. A second judge was made of sterner stuff. He ordered the actor to remove his hat in court and awarded the case to the Wrather Corporation.

The movie was called *The Legend of the Lone Ranger* (1981). Moore believed that he should have played the title role. In much the same way as he had once won out over Brace Beemer, Moore was passed over in favor of Klinton Spilsbury, whose acting experience on camera was limited to two minor television

Clayton Moore (left) as *The Lone Ranger*, with Jay Silverheels as Tonto.

assignments. Spilsbury quickly acquired quite a reputation for all the wrong reasons while on location in Santa Fe. He beat up waitresses; busted glasses while trying to play with the house band; tossed drinks around the room yelling, "Hey, I'm the Lone Ranger"; could not mount his horse or recall his lines; and caused extras to walk off the set in protest after he blew his lines in excess of a dozen times in succession.

Clayton Moore had this to say: "They offered me a bit part in the movie, and said they'd let me wear the mask again if I'd go out on the road and promote the movie. I sure want no part of it, not after the shocking behavior by the young fellow who has the starring role.

I just can't endure the thought of anyone damaging the image of such a great person as the Lone Ranger." He could derive some satisfaction from the critical and commercial failure of the film. Moore subsequently made appearances in dark wrap-around sunglasses until the restraining order was quietly lifted in January 1985, after Jack Wrather's death.

Clayton Moore has always been very reticent about his private life. Intriguing photographs from the early 1940s contained in the notorious underground classic movie book *Hollywood Babylon,* by Kenneth Anger, showed him cavorting by a swimming pool in gaudy bathing trunks, having his pectorals stroked by Lupe "Mexican Spitfire" Velez. Firstly he married and divorced dancer Mary Francis within a year (1940). His second wife, however, was Sally Allen, whom he married in 1943 and who died in 1986. By her he has an adopted daughter Dawn (born in 1958) who works in the fashion business. Of his current lifestyle he has said, "I'm a great believer in physical exercise and try to walk between five and seven miles every day. I also swim and do a lot of fishing. But I plan to keep working and never hang up my spurs."

Iron Eyes Cody stressed in his memoirs that there was friction between Clayton Moore and Jay Silverheels, but this was a figment of his imagination. One factor which did little to help his credibility was that he was confused between the actor who played the role of the Lone Ranger on television (Moore) and the actor in the original serial (Lee Powell, who was killed in the war). Indian expert Col. Tim McCoy dismissed alleged Indian expert Iron Eyes Cody as "a complete fraud."

Clayton Moore remembers it this way: "Every show I worked on was a real pleasure and I enjoyed my partnership with Jay Silverheels, who played Tonto. It's had a great influence on my life to be able to play the Lone Ranger, an American hero. I wouldn't say he has made me wealthy, but my wife and I live very well and we're very happy." Together he and Silverheels represented truth, honesty and decency, and the Lone Ranger's efforts to encourage these qualities among youngsters were officially recognized when he was invited to the White House by Richard Nixon, then vice president.

It was widely trumpeted in 1989 that there was to be a theatrical movie of *The Lone Ranger* released by Universal and a new syndicated series produced by Palladium, the company which acquired the rights to the character, both to be delivered in the autumn to Christmas period. For ill-defined reasons, both were shelved.

In February 1989, Moore was reported to be swathed in bandages after an operation on his nose. He explained, "I spent too much time in the sun. I'm an old man now, but I'd like people to remember me the way that I was." His third wife, Connie, a nurse whom he married in 1986 and divorced in 1989, added, "It's skin cancer, but it's not serious. You can tell all his fans that he's enjoying a well deserved rest." He appeared to be very much his old self at the "Golden Boot" ceremonies which have been held since. He married Clarita Petrone, a widow, in Los Angeles on January 18, 1992. He resides in Calabasas at the eastern end of the San Fernando Valley.

Clayton Moore Filmography

1938: *The Cowboy from Brooklyn, Dick Tracy Returns* (serial), *Go Chase Yourself, Where Were You Born?, Crime School.*

1939: *Daredevils of the Red Circle* (serial), *Tell No Tales, Sergeant Madden, Mesquite Buckaroo.*

1940: *Kit Carson, The Son of Monte Cristo.*

1941: *International Lady, Tuxedo Junction.*

1942: *Perils of Nyoka* (serial), *Black Dragons, Outlaws of Pine Ridge, Hello Annapolis.*

1946: *The Crimson Ghost* (serial), *Bachelor's Daughters, Heldorado.*

1947: *Jesse James Rides Again* (serial), *Along the Oregon Trail.*

1948: *G Men Never Forget* (serial), *Adventures of Frank and Jesse James* (serial), *Marshal of Amarillo, The Far Frontier, The Plunderers, El Dorado Pass.*

1949: *Ghost of Zorro* (serial), *Frontier Marshal* (a.k.a. *Frontier Investigator*), *Sheriff of Wichita, The Gay Amigo, South of Death Valley, Riders of the Whistling Pines, Masked Raiders, Bandits of El Dorado, Cowboy and the Indians, Bride of Vengeance.*

1950: *Sons of New Mexico.*

1951: *Cyclone Fury, Flying Disc Man from Mars* (serial) (Moore is seen only in stock footage from *The Crimson Ghost*).

1952: *Night Stage to Galvaston, Mutiny, Hawk of Wild River, Buffalo Bill in Tomahawk Territory, Desert Passage, Montana Territory, Barbed Wire, Captive of Billy the Kid, Son of Geronimo* (serial), *Radar Men from the Moon* (serial), *The Raiders.*
1953: *Jungle Drums of Africa* (serial), *Kansas Pacific, Down Laredo Way, Bandits of Corsica, City of Bad Men.*
1954: *Black Dakotas, Gunfighters of the North West* (serial).
1955: *Apache Ambush.*
1956: *The Lone Ranger.*
1958: *The Lone Ranger and the Lost City of Gold.*

Television Series

1949–1957: *The Lone Ranger* as the Lone Ranger.

Sources

Barton, Dick. "Whatever Happened To?" *Sunday Express* newspaper, June 17, 1984.
Corneau, Ernest N. *The Hall of Fame of Western Film Stars.* North Quincy, MA: Christopher, 1969.
Culp, Lisa-Anne. "Clayton Moore." *Filmfax* magazine #30, Dec./Jan. 1992.
Essoe, Gabe. *The Book of Movie Lists.* Westport, CT: Arlington House, 1981.
Hamilton, Mick. "Old Lone Ranger Has the Big C." *News of the World* newspaper, February 26, 1989.
Hyem, Janette. "The Lone Ranger." *TV Scene* magazine, 1989.
McClure, Arthur F., and Ken D. Jones. *Heroes, Heavies and Sagebrush.* South Brunswick and New York: Barnes, 1972.
Miller, Lee O. *The Great Cowboy Stars of Movies and Television.* New Rochelle, NY: Arlington House, 1979.
Quinlan, David. *The Illustrated Directory of Film Stars.* London: Batsford, 1996.
Smith, David James. "The Lone Ranger Unmasked." *TV Times* magazine, July 29, 1989.
Van Hise, James. *Who Was That Masked Man? The Story of the Lone Ranger.* Las Vegas, NV: Pioneer, 1990.

ROGER MOORE

Roger Moore is one of the more incongruous names to crop up in any survey of the personalities in Westerns of the 1950s. He always seemed ill-suited to the genre, and the genre did not serve him particularly well. He did television Westerns only because they were prevalent in Hollywood at the time when he was under contract to Warner Bros., a studio which mass produced them. With his impeccable British accent and stylish clothes, he was much better served by the British television crime series *(The Saint)* and the later role of James Bond in the cinema.

Roger George Moore was born in London on October 14, 1927, the son of George Moore and Lily Pope. His father was a London policeman. Roger was an only child. It was a happy childhood, and he had an excellent relationship with his parents. He was educated at Hackford Road Elementary School in London where he excelled at art and drawing. He passed the entrance examination to Battersea Grammar School, but was not able to take advantage of this because World War II broke out. He was evacuated three times, but returned to London in 1941 where he attended Vauxhall Central School until 1943.

He left school at the age of 15 without any particular qualifications and went to work as a junior trainee and office boy at Publicity Picture Productions, a cartoon studio, with the intention of making a career as an animator. For somewhat ill-defined reasons he was fired from this job. Subsequently he obtained some work as an extra in *Caesar and Cleopatra* in 1944. His father's work had brought him into contact with leading film director Brian Desmond Hurst, whom he was introduced to on the set of that film. Hurst became his patron and secured extra work for him in two other films. The director was also responsible for sending him to the Royal Academy of Dramatic Art, where to conceal his lack of confidence he clowned around as much as he studied. He left after a year and did a season of repertory at Cambridge.

In 1945 he was called up to do National Service, in the course of which he was commissioned a second lieutenant in the Royal Army Service Corps. He was put in charge of a supply depot in Germany. While on leave, on December 9, 1946, at Wandsworth Registry Office, he married Doorn Van Steyn, a 24-year-old professional ice skater and actress whom he had met at the Royal Academy. Later, at his own request, he was transferred to the Combined Services Entertainments Unit for which he was much better suited.

His National Service completed, he and his new bride were forced to lodge with relatives because the large scale destruction of housing in London during the war meant that there was a shortage of living space. There was little work and they were always broke. Briefly a stage manager for the BBC at their studios in Alexandra Palace, he went on to small parts in London stage productions, augmenting this sporadic work by doing some modeling. The actor and his wife spent much of their time apart, mainly because of her work commitments, and their marriage crumbled; they eventually divorced in March 1953. In 1952 he was invited to a party which was held at the home of the entertainer Dorothy Squires, who was born in 1915. She assumed the role of his mentor, and they occasionally appeared on stage together.

He accompanied her to America where she was promoting one of her records. Four days after arriving he was signed to appear in an episode of the anthology series *Robert Montgomery Presents.* On July 6, 1953, he married Squires in New Jersey. She had to return to England, but he stayed on to make his Broadway debut in *A Pin to See the Peepshow,* which folded after a single performance on September 17, 1953. Journeying to Hollywood, he appeared in various television productions for the prestigious *Hallmark Theater.* These in turn were seen by talent scouts at MGM who insisted that he make a screen test. Back in England while appearing in a flop play called *I Capture the Castle,* he received news that his test had been successful so he returned to America.

When he arrived at MGM early in 1954, the studio tried to groom him as a swashbuckling star. After some lesser roles, he was given the star treatment in *Diane* (1955), the last film at MGM of Lana Turner. When it flopped, he was dropped by MGM in 1956 and returned somewhat disconsolately to England, where there was little demand for his services. He appeared briefly on stage at Worthing, Sussex, in August 1956, in *The Family Tree,* his most recent stage appearance to date.

After the best part of a year's idleness, he signed a contract to star in a swashbuckling television series called *Ivanhoe* for Columbia's Screen Gems in December 1956. Shooting began early the following year with interiors being lensed at Elstree Studios and later Beaconsfield Studios. Curiously, because of winter shooting and the lack of appropriate English vegetation, the exteriors were shot in California on suitable locations at the Columbia Ranch. There were 39 half-hour episodes shot until June 1958.

The following month he flew to Hollywood at the invitation of Warner Bros. to star in a major feature called *The Miracle.* It enjoyed little success, but nevertheless Warners signed him to a long-term contract. He shot a pedestrian Western for them called *Gold of the Seven Saints* which had a delayed release in 1961. It costarred Clint Walker. Roger Moore played Shaun Garrett, an Irish cowboy from Dublin. It had been the policy of Warners since the days of Errol Flynn to cast British actors in Westerns, excusing their accents by giving them a strong Irish background. Much of the film was shot in the overwhelming heat of Utah where he suffered from dehydration. This was a direct cause of him being ill with kidney stones, an ailment which plagued him for many years.

Warner Bros. decided to shift their new contract actor away from feature films and into television, a sure sign of declining status. He was given the starring role of Silky Harris in an ABC television series called *The Alaskans,* set in and around Skagway during the 1898 Gold Rush. The character was a light-hearted con man and fur trapper. The first of 36 hour-length black and white episodes was seen on October 4, 1959, and the last original episode was shown on September 25, 1960. Most of the Warners series were shown all over the world, but this one was considered such a turkey that it did not travel. The chief complaint was that the scripts were poor. Although it was set in Alaska, it was shot in the blazing heat of the

California sun. The worst aspect was that snowstorms were simulated by airplane engines. The snow (salt and gypsum) was blown into the faces of the actors by the machines. At the end of each day, the actors had to wash out their eyes, which were frequently scratched by the gypsum. The only compensation was that during the course of the shooting, Moore became extremely friendly with his leading lady Dorothy Provine.

Once this experience was over, Moore was keen to return to the big screen, but Warners insisted on casting him as Beau Maverick in their long-running satirical Western series *Maverick.* James Garner had quit and Warner Bros. wanted Moore as a replacement. He refused to accede to their requests and was suspended. He withdrew to the gaming tables of Las Vegas and only returned to shoot the series when Jack L. Warner himself personally called him. Moore did not like the series because the scripts were recycled episodes of other series, including *The Alaskans.* While he tried to bring humorous qualities to the character, the *Maverick* experience was not a high point of this career. With the prospect of nothing more than television work on the horizon, he asked for his release and the contract was terminated by mutual consent.

Deeply disillusioned with Hollywood, he returned in 1961 to England, where he signed with a new agent. He intended to concentrate on a cinema career, but the only offers he received were from Italian and French companies specializing in cut rate epics with semi-names. He selected one of them, *The Rape of the Sabine Women,* to be shot in Italy. Although Mylene Demongeot was his costar, it was a striking actress called Luisa Mattioli who caught his eye. They became immediate friends and later lovers. His marriage to Dorothy Squires had broken down, but because of complications they were not divorced until November 1968. Roger Moore and Luisa Mattioli (32 years old) were finally wed at Caxton Hall, London, on April 11, 1969. They have three children: Deborah (born October 27, 1963), an actress whose stage name is Deborah Barrymore; Geoffrey (born July 28, 1966); and Christian (born August 18, 1973).

Robert Baker and Monty Berman, partners in a production company called New World, acquired the television rights to the

Roger Moore in *The Alaskans.*

"Saint" novels by Leslie Charteris. There was considerable speculation about who would be cast in the leading role. Moore was told that he had won the part while in Italy. Between 1962 and 1968 he played Simon Templar in 114 hour-length and two feature-length episodes which were an enormous success worldwide and catapulted him to the top level of television stardom. Afterwards he tried to return to the big screen, but a couple of efforts sank without a trace. He did another escapist series called *The Persuaders* in 1971 with Tony Curtis. Although it was well-received in Britain, it only lasted for 24 episodes because it was not a success in the American market. This is attributed to the fact that it was scheduled against the very successful *Mission Impossible.* Away from acting he became a director of the perfume company Fabergé and the clothing company Pearson and Foster.

On August 1, 1972, he was signed by Harry Saltzman and Albert Broccoli to take over the role of James Bond from the departing Sean Connery. This rewarded him with the successful cinema career that he had long craved. Although there was some concern that (being a television star) he had become overexposed, he was able to take the Bond character and give it a new interpretation. His first Bond film was *Live and Let Die,* and he went on to play the role in six other adventures, the last of which was *A View to a Kill* (1985). This gave him the necessary visibility to star in other big-budget adventure films, usually playing tough adventurers, which usually did well at the box office.

Since the end of his James Bond films, he has not pursued an acting career at full throttle. He has appeared in some indifferent films. In January 1989, he made headlines when he won the coveted role of Sir George Dillingham in the Andrew Lloyd Webber stage musical *Aspects of Love,* but by March 1989, he had bowed out because he was having nightmares and could not cope with the technical side of the singing. He said that he would love to return to the West End in another musical, "but I need to learn to sing with an orchestra first." He has also been very active in recent years as a special ambassador for UNICEF, the United Nations Agency which helps children around the world.

In November 1993, he underwent surgery for prostate cancer. Shortly afterwards he was first seen in the company of Christina "Kiki" Tholstrup, 54, a Danish former air hostess and millionairess, in the South of France. He was introduced to the twice-widowed Mrs. Tholstrup by his third wife Luisa when they were Tholstrup's neighbors in St. Paul de Vence on the French Riviera. He split from Luisa, and the pending divorce may cost the star a third of his £30,000,000 (thirty million pounds) fortune.

Roger Moore Filmography

1945: *Caesar and Cleopatra, Perfect Strangers* (a.k.a. *Vacation from Marriage).*
1946: *Gaiety George, Piccadilly Incident.*
1949: *Paper Orchid, Trottie True* (a.k.a. *Gay Lady).*
1954: *The Last Time I Saw Paris.*
1955: *Interrupted Melody, The King's Thief, Diane.*
1959: *The Miracle.*
1960: *The Sins of Rachel Cade.*
1961: *Gold of the Seven Saints, Rape of the Sabine Women* (a.k.a. *Romulus and the Sabines).*
1962: *No Man's Land.*
1969: *Crossplot.*
1970: *The Man Who Haunted Himself.*
1973: *Live and Let Die.*
1974: *Gold, The Man with the Golden Gun.*
1975: *That Lucky Touch.*
1976: *Shout at the Devil, The Sicilian Cross* (a.k.a. *Street People), Sherlock Holmes in New York* (TV).
1977: *The Spy Who Loved Me.*
1978: *The Wild Geese, Escape to Athena.*
1979: *Moonraker, North Sea Hijack* (a.k.a. *ffolkes).*
1980: *The Sea Wolves, Sunday Lovers.*
1981: *The Cannonball Run, For Your Eyes Only.*
1983: *Octopussy, Curse of the Pink Panther.*
1984: *The Naked Face.*
1985: *A View to a Kill.*
1987: *The Magic Snowman* (voice only).
1989: *Bed and Breakfast.*
1990: *Bullseye, Fire Ice and Dynamite.*
1993: *The Man Who Wouldn't Die* (TV).
1996: *The Quest.*

Television Series

1957–1958: *Ivanhoe* as Ivanhoe.
1959–1960: *The Alaskans* as Silky Harris.
1960–1961: *Maverick* as Beau Maverick.
1962–1968: *The Saint* as Simon Templar.
1971–1972: *The Persuaders* as Lord Brett Sinclair.

Sources

Current Biography. New York: H.W. Wilson, 1975.
Donovan, Paul. "The Saint That Ain't." *Daily Mail* newspaper, November 28, 1994.
Jones, Geraint. "Low for Moore as he quits musical." *Daily Mail* newspaper, March 14, 1989.
Moore, Christian. "Our torn family, by Moore's son." *Daily Mail* newspaper, April 10, 1996.
Moseley, Roy. *Roger Moore: A Biography.* London: New English Library, 1986.
Robertson, Ed. *Maverick: Legend of the West.* Beverly Hills, CA: Pomegranate, 1994.
Susman, Ed. "Roger Moore's secret battle with cancer." *National Enquirer* magazine, December 1993.
Woolley, Lynn, Robert W. Malsbary, and Robert G. Strange, Jr. *Warner Bros. Television.* Jefferson, NC: McFarland, 1985.

JEFF MORROW

Jeff Morrow was born in Brooklyn, New York, on January 13, 1907, the youngest of four children. He was introduced to drama via recordings of stage stars at an early age by his parents. This led to him playing the lead in high school plays. Later he attended Pratt Institute (where he studied art), and for a while he was a freelance commercial illustrator. His interest in acting never waned, and he studied voice, mime, singing and dancing at a New York drama school. While there he was seen by the head of a Chester, Pennsylvania, stock company who needed a young leading man. This being the heart of the Depression, the company soon went bust, but this experience coupled with some fictitious credits enabled him to obtain employment in a little stock company in Connecticut.

After this he returned to New York where for a season he was associated with the Jolson Theater, appearing in about 15 Shakespearean productions. He toured with Katharine Cornell and did further work on the New York stage before World War II broke out. He had been about to sign a movie contract with Paramount, but this was aborted. After service in the war he returned to New York where he appeared in several plays which generated great notices, but not great box office. He worked extensively on radio where he made over 2,000 broadcasts, including the leading role of Dick Tracy for two years. He also did live television out of New York.

At the time when he was set to appear in the television version of *Billy Budd,* his agent sent him to see director Henry Koster, who was casting for a few roles in the film *The Robe* (1953) at 20th Century–Fox offices in New York. His test was satisfactory so he was cast in the role of Paulus, which won him some of the best notices of his career. He decided to remain in Hollywood and concentrate on feature films because he figured that the days of live television were numbered. He did his most impressive work at Universal where he shot *Captain Lightfoot* (1955), his favorite among his own films. This was because it was the first CinemaScope color film shot entirely on location in Ireland. Morrow had the title role, and he, Rock Hudson and Barbara Rush were supported by a splendid cast of stage-trained British character actors.

His work as the Irish rebel leader so impressed executives at Universal that he was signed to a two-picture-a-year nonexclusive contract. He became a favorite of science fiction buffs when he appeared in *This Island Earth* (1955), in which his forehead was built up for the part of the friendly alien Exeter. He also starred in the last and weakest of the Creature trilogy, *The Creature Walks Among Us* (1956), where he played a neurotic scientist. Rex Reason was his costar in both films. Morrow also acted in plays on the West Coast, of which the best known was the 1956 Los Angeles production of the Lincoln-Douglas debates. He played the role of Abraham Lincoln at the Circle Theater in a semi-theater-in-the-round.

He had a busy television career playing guest roles in series such as *Wagon Train* and *Bonanza.* He also starred in the syndicated

Jeff Morrow in *Union Pacific.*

Western series *Union Pacific* (1957–1958). It was in 1862 that the President Lincoln approved the Act Of Congress which gave permission for the original Union Pacific Railroad Company to construct lines from the Missouri River to the Pacific Ocean. It was primarily done as a war measure and also to preserve the Union. After the first length of rail was laid, the railway's Western progress was delayed by every kind of incident from bitter quarrels over the right kind of gauge to be used, to deadly attacks by Indians.

Almost impossible terrain, desperate shortages of supplies, funds which ran out, scheming politicians and ruthless financiers all did their bit to make the progress of the line a slow, arduous and sometimes seemingly impossible business. Even at the end of the Civil War, the troubles were not over, for outlaw bands and train robbers were everywhere. Yet in the end, victory crowned the struggle and in May 1896, the last of the line's 9,800 miles of railroad was laid and the job was completed. There was an original movie called *Union Pacific* (1939), but the building of this great railroad offered limitless story possibilities for a television series, for it was thrust Westward into little-known, still untamed country, and almost every mile of the way produced an adventure of some sort.

Two men figured prominently in the television series *Union Pacific,* namely former Union Cavalry Major Bart McClelland, Executive Operations Manager in charge of the project (Jeff Morrow), and his right hand man, former Cavalry Sergeant Billy Kincaid (Judson Pratt). The other leading character was Georgia (Susan Cummings), the beautiful owner of "The Golden Spike" gambling hall and saloon that moved along with the end of the track. The series was produced by California National Productions and ran to 39 black and white episodes. Along with many of his contemporaries, Morrow found shooting a series extremely hard work, particularly because each episode was shot in three days. Although he was an diligent actor, he was not a quick study.

In later years his career faded, but he continued to guest star on television and did commercials (notably for Suntory Whiskey) shot in the U.S. for Japanese television. He briefly had another regular role as an affable but fraudulent surgeon in the short-lived medical sitcom *Temperatures Rising* (1973–1974). For many years he owned a ranch in the San Fernando Valley where outdoor life was the order of the day.

Morrow, 86, died at a nursing home in Canoga Park, California, on December 26, 1993, after a long illness. He was survived by his widow, actress Anna Karen, whom he married in the 1940s, and by daughter Lisa, who was born in 1946.

Jeff Morrow Filmography

1953: *The Robe, Flight to Tangier.*
1954: *Tanganyika, Siege at Red River, Sign of the Pagan.*
1955: *Captain Lightfoot, This Island Earth.*
1956: *World in My Corner, The Creature Walks Among Us, Pardners, The First Texan.*
1957: *Kronos, The Giant Claw, Hour of Decision, Copper Sky.*
1960: *Five Bold Women, The Story of Ruth.*
1963: *Harbor Lights.*
1970: *A Normal Young Man.*
1971: *Octaman, Legacy of Blood.*

Television Series

1957–1958: *Union Pacific* as Bart McClelland.
1973–1974: *Temperatures Rising* as Dr. Lloyd Axton.

Sources

Goldrup, Tom, and Jim Goldrup. *Feature Players: The Stories Behind the Faces Volume #2.* Published privately, 1992.
Picture Show Annual. London: Amalgamated Press, 1956.
Speed, F. Maurice. *The Western Film and Television Annual.* London: MacDonald, 1960.
Variety. Obituary, January 3, 1994.
Weaver, Tom. *They Fought in the Creature Features: Interviews with 23 Classic Horror, Science Fiction and Serial Stars.* Jefferson, NC: McFarland, 1995.

JAMES MURDOCK

James Murdock provided some of the comic relief in the Western series *Rawhide,* in which he played the cook's louse Mushy. He was frequently the object of the barbs of Wishbone, the cook. The episode which showcased him to best advantage was "Incident of the Captive," which reveals much about the life of his character. He joined the drive to escape a domineering mother (Mercedes McCambridge). When Mushy's father dies, the mother goes to the trail drive to persuade Mushy to return with her. A plot is concocted whereby she is kidnapped so that Mushy can rescue her, but it backfires when she is kidnapped for real by some evil miscreants and Mushy really does come to her aid. This is not, however, one of the best episodes of the series simply because Mushy is not a dominant character. Murdock later played some bit parts in movies under the name of David Baker. He died in California of pneumonia on December 24, 1981, at age 50. Television buffs may note that he died within three weeks of another *Rawhide* regular, Rocky Shahan.

James Murdock Filmography

1971: *Some of My Best Friends Are ...*
1974: *The Godfather Part II.*

Television Series

1959–1965: *Rawhide* as Harkness "Mushy" Mushgrove.

Sources

Ragan, David. *Who's Who in Hollywood.* New York: Facts on File, 1992.

GEORGE NEISE

George N. Neise was born in Chicago in 1916. In the early 1940s he gravitated to Hollywood where he made his screen debut. Shortly afterwards he was drafted in World War II and he served as a colonel in the Army Air Corps. Later he worked as a character actor in several films before embarking on a career in television. He had a rather supercilious personality which at times he made very effective use of, as in the Western film *Fort Massacre* (1958). He played the role of Nat Wyndham, the first town doctor, in the Western series *Wichita Town.* He also essayed numerous roles on *The Jackie Gleason Show, The Red Skelton Show* and *The Loretta Young Show.*

Neise, 79, died at his home in Hollywood on April 14, 1996, of natural causes. He was survived by his wife Edy, two daughters from a previous marriage, five grandchildren and four great grandchildren.

George Neise Filmography

1942: *He's My Old Man, They Raid by Night, Valley of Hunted Men, War Dogs, Flight Lieutenant.*
1943: *Air Force, Chetniks, Bomber's Moon, Sahara.*
1944: *The Man from Frisco* (narrated only), *Experiment Perilous, Once Upon a Time, Ladies of Washington.*
1948: *One Sunday Afternoon, Romance on the High Seas.*
1949: *My Dream Is Yours.*
1951: *I'll See You in My Dreams.*
1956: *The Sharkfighters.*
1957: *Tomahawk Trail, The Tall Stranger, Pharaoh's Curse, Jeanne Eagels.*
1958: *Fort Massacre, Outcasts of the City, No Time for Sergeants.*
1962: *The Three Stooges in Orbit, The Three*

Stooges Meet Hercules, Twenty Plus Two, Rome Adventure.
1963: *Johnny Cool.*
1964: *Looking for Love.*
1965: *Brainstorm.*
1967: *A Guide for the Married Man.*
1968: *Now You See It, Now You Don't* (TV), *Did You Hear the One About the Traveling Saleslady?*
1970: *On a Clear Day You Can See Forever.*
1971: *The Barefoot Executive.*

Television Series

1959–1960: *Wichita Town* as Doctor Nat Wyndham.

Sources

Magers, Boyd. "Empty Saddles." *Western Clippings* magazine, Sept./Oct. 1996.
Thomas, Tony. *Joel McCrea: Riding the High Country.* Burbank, CA: Riverwood Press, 1992.

BEK NELSON

Born in Goin, Tennessee, but raised in Canton, Ohio, this good-looking blonde starlet played the role of Dru Lemp, the cafe owner, during the first season of *Lawman.* Allegedly she left the series voluntarily and was replaced by a much stronger personality in Lily Merrill (Peggie Castle). Nelson appeared in a few films and continued to play television roles into the 1960s. She was at one time the wife of actor Don Gordon.

Bek Nelson Filmography

1957: *Pal Joey.*
1958: *Crash Landing, Cowboy, Bell Book and Candle.*
1965: *Lollipop Cover.*

Television Series

1958–1959: *Lawman* as Dru Lemp.

Sources

Brooks, Tim. *The Complete Directory to Prime Time TV Stars 1946–Present.* New York: Ballantine Books, 1987.

LESLIE NIELSEN

"I do have a wonderful time doing comedy. There's a special feeling when you're doing something that you always wanted, but for so long never had the courage to do. The door opens to something that is filled with delight and fascination as it is for me with comedy." So speaks Leslie Nielsen, who can understandably be complacent, since he has emerged well into middle age from years of relative anonymity and continuous employment to be a success as a comedy film star. Somewhere among his 60 films and 1,200 television appearances he has played some other leads, notably for Walt Disney in the television series *The Swamp Fox.*

Nielsen was born in Regina, Saskatchewan, Canada, on February 11, 1926, the son of a constable in the Royal Canadian Mounted Police. He has two brothers, one of whom (Erik Nielsen) became Canadian Deputy Prime Minister. Nielsen was educated at Victoria High School, Edmonton, Alberta. Then he

Left-right: Leslie Nielsen, Myron Healey, and Richard Erdman in *The Swamp Fox.*

served for a short spell as an aerial gunner in the Royal Canadian Air Force. After the war he returned to Canada where he became a disc jockey and announcer on a Calgary radio station. He then studied at Lorne Greene's Academy of Radio Arts in Toronto.

Soon he realized that he wanted to act. After his first year he won a scholarship, so in 1948 he went to study at the Neighborhood Playhouse. There he was taught acting by Sanford Meisner and took dancing lessons with Martha Graham. He appeared in several radio shows followed by a season of stock. Of this period he recalled, "I once did a decent Richard III in the back of a kosher deli."

His break came in television where he made his debut in a *Studio One* production for which he was paid $75 for ten days' work. He became one of six leading men who worked nonstop in the days of live television. In 1950 alone he appeared in 45 live television shows. By the time he moved to Hollywood in 1954 he had appeared in over 400. He came to Hollywood initially at the invitation of Paramount, but they only used him in one film which was released after some of the others. Initially there was a misguided attempt by MGM to make him a star. He was third billed in his screen debut *Ransom!* (1956) in which he played Charlie Telfer, a reporter helping a couple recover their kidnapped child. He then played an astronaut, Commander Adams, who lands on the *Forbidden Planet* (1956), a classic sci-fi version of *The Tempest.* Walt Disney saw him in a *Playhouse 90* production called "The Right Hand Man" (1958) and cast him in the lead of *The Swamp Fox,* based on the exploits of a real-life character.

This nickname was bestowed on Col. Francis Marion by the British during the Revolutionary War. Marion was active in the state of South Carolina and, with most of the other forces defeated, he and his band of guerrillas were the only effective fighting men left in the South. His mission was to carry out lightning raids against the British which would give the Northern forces time to build up their numbers and organize themselves properly. Marion's attacks against the British were devastatingly effective. After each raid, Marion and his cohorts would disappear into the swamps.

The first two episodes of *The Swamp Fox*

were seen in October 1959, commencing with "The Birth of the Swamp Fox" as part of *Walt Disney Presents.* Four further episodes were shown in January 1960. The final two episodes were seen in January 1961. The series was in color, hour-length and endowed with excellent production values. It was highly rated, but the problem lay in the extensive scope of its subject. It was such an expensive series to produce that its budget was too great for Disney to carry, so the series was short-lived. Curiously, the episodes were never edited into a feature film.

In 1979 Nielsen toured U.S. cities in the one-man show *Darrow.* More familiarly throughout the 1960s and 1970s he was seen as guest star in numerous television series of the action variety, usually playing villains. Of this trend he explains, "Here in Hollywood, if you weren't playing the guy who was in the show every week, then the next best part was as the villain. Therefore I sought out villains to play. I have played some lulus." He starred in several drama series of his own, but none was remotely successful. Ironically, a comedy cop spoof called *Police Squad* (in which he played a bungling police officer) was one of his biggest flops, lasting only six episodes in 1982. His characterization did net him an Emmy nomination, however.

It might have been supposed that he would never outrun the treadmill of television typecasting, but the tide turned. In *Airplane!* (1980) he enjoyed more acclaim than he had received in a long time as Dr. Rumack, on board a threatened airliner in this spoof of disaster films. Eventually this led to a big-screen revival of his flop series called *The Naked Gun* (1988) in which he was hilarious as inept plainclothes cop Frank Drebin. This proved to be so successful that it spawned two successful sequels and a series of cider commercials. Of his late success, he says, "All I know is that I'm having a lot of fun and I really enjoy doing comedy. All I want to do is to keep working enough within my profession so as to maintain whatever celebrity status I have, so they'll keep inviting me to golf tournaments." He released a golf video in 1993 called "The Nielsen Method: Bad Golf Made Easier." In 1994 his unreliable memoirs (entitled *The Naked Truth*) were published.

Nielsen has been married three times. His first marriage to Monica Boyer in the early 1950s lasted five years. He has two daughters, Thea (born in 1962) and Maura (born in 1964), from his second marriage to Sandy Ullman, which lasted 16 years. His third marriage to Brooks Oliver lasted two years in the 1980s. Of these experiences he quips, "My wives were all good housekeepers—when we split up, they all kept the house." He has been romantically involved for many years with career consultant Barbaree Earle, who was born in 1953. They first met in 1983 during his third marriage.

Leslie Nielsen Filmography

1956: *Ransom!, Forbidden Planet, The Opposite Sex, The Vagabond King.*

1957: *Hot Summer Night, Tammy and the Bachelor.*

1958: *The Sheepman.*

1964: *Night Train to Paris, See How They Run* (TV).

1965: *Harlow, Dark Intruder.*

1966: *Beau Geste, The Plainsman.*

1967: *Gunfight in Abilene, Rosie!, The Reluctant Astronaut, Counterpoint, Code Name: Heraclitus* (TV), *Companions in Nightmare* (TV).

1968: *Shadows Over Elveron* (TV), *Dayton's Devils, Hawaii Five-O* (TV).

1969: *Four Rode Out, How to Commit Marriage, Change of Mind, Deadlock* (TV), *Trial Run* (TV).

1970: *The Aquarians* (TV), *Hauser's Memory* (TV), *Night Slaves* (TV), *Happiness Is a Warm Clue* (TV) (a.k.a. *The Return of Charlie Chan).*

1971: *They Call It Murder* (TV), *The Resurrection of Zachary Wheeler, Incident in San Francisco* (TV).

1972: *The Poseidon Adventure, The Letters* (TV), *Snatched* (TV).

1973: *And Millions Will Die.*

1974: *Can Ellen Be Saved?* (TV).

1976: *Day of the Animals, Project: Kill, Brink's: The Great Robbery* (TV), *The Siege* (TV), *Grand Jury.*

1977: *Viva Knievel!, The Amsterdam Kill, Sixth and Main.*

1978: *Institute for Revenge* (TV), *Little Mo!* (TV).

1979: *City on Fire, The Mad Trapper, Riel, Cave In!* (TV), *The Night the Bridge Fell Down* (TV).

1980: *Prom Night, Airplane!, OHMS* (TV).
1981: *The Creature Wasn't Nice, A Choice of Two.*
1982: *Creepshow, Wrong Is Right (*a.k.a. *The Man with the Deadly Lens), Foxfire Light.*
1985: *Reckless Disregard* (TV), *Blade in Hong Kong* (TV), *Striker's Mountain.*
1986: *The Patriot, Soul Man, Home Is Where the Hart Is.*
1987: *Nuts, Calhoun (*a.k.a. *Night Stick), Fatal Confession: A Father Dowling Mystery* (TV).
1988: *Dangerous Curves, The Naked Gun: From the Files of Police Squad.*
1990: *Repossessed.*
1991: *The Naked Gun 2½: The Smell of Fear, All I Want for Christmas, Chance of a Lifetime* (TV).
1993: *Surf Ninjas, Digger.*
1994: *The Naked Gun 33⅓: The Final Insult, S.P.Q.R. 2,000 and a Half Years Ago.*
1995: *Dracula: Dead and Loving It, Rent-A-Kid.*
1996: *Spy Hard, Harvey* (TV).

Television Series

1959–1961: *Walt Disney Presents: The Swamp Fox* as Gen. Francis Marion.
1961–1962: *The New Breed* as Lt. Price Adams.
1963–1964: *Channing* as Prof. Paul Stafford.
1965: *Peyton Place* as Dr. Vincent Markham.
1969–1970: *The Bold Ones: The Protectors (*a.k.a. *The Law Enforcers)* as Sam Danforth.
1970: *Bracken's World* as John Bracken.
1982: *Police Squad* as Lt. Frank Drebin.
1984: *Shaping Up* as Buddy Fox.

Miniseries

1979: *Backstairs at the Whitehouse.*

Sources

Contemporary Theater, Film, and Television Volume 11. Detroit, MI: Gale, 1993.
"Leslie Nielsen Tells: Why I Won't Wed Love of My Life." *National Enquirer* magazine, 1994.
Maltin, Leonard. *The Disney Films.* New York: Crown, 1973.
Mehas, Michael W. "Leslie Nielsen: My Life Is One Long Vacation." *OK! Magazine,* June 1994.
Skinner, John Walter. *Who's Who on the Screen.* Worthing, England: Madeleine, 1983.
Summers, Neil. *The Official TV Western Book Volume #3.* Vienna, WV: Old West Shop Publishing, 1991.

JEANETTE NOLAN

Jeanette Nolan was born in Los Angeles on December 30, 1911. This dominant actress was a leading radio performer of the 1930s who made a comparatively late start in films. Her best known role was as Lady Macbeth in Orson Welles' version of *Macbeth* (1948). Since then she has played character roles in numerous films and television series. She has also had regular roles in four television series of which the first was *Hotel De Paree.*

In this short-lived Western series she played Annette Deveraux, the owner (along with her niece Monique [Judi Meredith]) of the rather oddly named *Hotel De Paree.* Although the hotel was situated in the wild West, these two cultured ladies tried to run it as if it were in Europe. They encountered difficulties, but Sundance (Earl Holliman) was around to assist them.

In real life Nolan is the widow of versatile character actor John McIntire and was the mother of two sons, one of whom was the late actor Tim McIntire. She and John McIntire met while they were both on radio, married in 1936 and remained wed until his death in 1991. She and her husband had a 480-acre ranch in Montana where they escaped from the pressures of Hollywood. At last report she was residing in retirement in her other home in Laguna Beach, California.

Jeanette Nolan Filmography

1948: *Words and Music, Macbeth.*

1949: *Abandoned.*
1950: *Saddle Tramp, No Sad Songs for Me.*
1951: *The Secret of Convict Lake.*
1952: *The Happy Time, Hangman's Knot.*
1953: *The Big Heat.*
1955: *A Lawless Street.*
1956: *Tribute to a Bad Man, Everything but the Truth, The Seventh Cavalry.*
1957: *The Halliday Brand, Guns of Fort Petticoat, April Love.*
1958: *The Deep Six, Wild Heritage.*
1959: *The Rabbit Trap.*
1960: *The Great Imposter, Psycho* (voice).
1961: *Two Rode Together.*
1962: *The Man Who Shot Liberty Valance.*
1963: *Twilight of Honor, Sergeant Ryker* (TV).
1965: *My Blood Runs Cold.*
1966: *Chamber of Horrors.*
1967: *Sullivan's Empire, The Reluctant Astronaut.*
1968: *Did You Hear the One About the Traveling Saleslady?*
1970: *Alias Smith and Jones* (TV).
1971: *Longstreet* (TV).
1972: *Say Goodbye Maggie Cole* (TV), *Nightmare Honeymoon.*
1973: *Hijack!* (TV).
1975: *The Desperate Miles* (TV), *Babe* (TV).
1976: *The Winds of Autumn, The New Daughters of Joshua Cabe* (TV).
1977: *The Rescuers.*
1978: *Avalanche, The Awakening Land* (TV), *The Manitou.*
1979: *Better Late Than Never* (TV).
1980: *The Hustler of Muscle Beach* (TV).
1981: *True Confessions, Goliath Awaits* (TV), *The Fox and the Hound* (voice).
1982: *The Wild Women of Chastity Gulch* (TV).
1984: *Cloak & Dagger.*
1989: *Street Justice.*

Television Series

1959–1960: *Hotel De Paree* as Annette Deveraux.
1963–1964: *The Richard Boone Show.*
1967–1968: *The Virginian* as Holly Grainger.
1974: *Dirty Sally* as Sally Fergus.

Sources

Brooks, Tim. *The Complete Directory to Prime Time TV Stars.* New York: Ballantine Books, 1987.
Inman, David. *The TV Encyclopedia.* New York: Perigee, 1991.

TOMMY NOLAN

Tommy Nolan was born Bernard Maurice Joseph Girouard, Jr., of French Canadian parents in Montreal, Canada, on January 15, 1948. He also used the name of Butch Bernard. He was trained from an early age at stage school. At the age of four he made his stage debut in a pantomime where he registered so strongly that he became part of a company which toured hospitals. At the age of five he moved with his parents to Los Angeles for the sake of his mother's health. One day mother and son went to NBC studios for tickets to a television show when the pair were approached by the mother of Mexican child actor Ricky Vera. She was so impressed with the boy that she gave them the name of agent Lola Moore. This agent thought he had talent and began to send him out for auditions.

Mother and son did the rounds for about a year before he landed his first role. This was as the Prince of Wales, the son of King Henry VIII, in the prestigious *Hallmark Hall of Fame* television show. This opened up other doors for him so that he became a familiar television face by frequent exposure on popular series of the time. He worked often because he was regarded as a professional who was particularly good in emotional scenes.

In 1957 he became a naturalized citizen. His ambition was to star in a series of his own, and this was fulfilled when he was chosen from 200 applicants to play Jody O'Connell, the leading character in the NBC Western series *Buckskin.* In the 1880s, in the frontier town of Buckskin, Montana, Jody's widowed mother Annie O'Connell (Sallie Brophy) ran a board-

Tommy Nolan and Sallie Brophy in *Buckskin*.

ing house which became the focal point of the community. Stories depicted Jody's involvement with the guests staying at the boarding house and residents of the town. This series was not the average "shoot 'em up," but depicted stories of human interest which sometimes were more character studies. It began on July 3, 1958, and was only intended as a summer replacement for Tennessee Ernie Ford's show, but drew such high ratings that it remained on the air until the end of August 1959. There were 39 half-hour, black and white episodes. Nolan became a celebrity and did a great deal of promotional work for the series as well as endorsing merchandise.

Once the series left the air, however, his stock slumped. For a while he continued to appear on other television series such as *Wagon Train* and *Rawhide*. As he grew up he encountered difficulties with people in the business who had once professed to be friends or well disposed toward him, but who now did not want to know him. His acting career as a child ended circa 1961. His heart was no longer in acting. Under the name of Tom Nolan, he persevered for over a decade until the rejection and politics of show business finally reached a level he could no longer abide, so he virtually quit in 1970. Between 1962 and 1966 he attended UCLA. His knowledge of the folklore of show business, however, was put to good use when he switched career and became a successful freelance writer, a vocation which he found more gratifying than being an actor. His articles have been published in a wide variety of popular newspapers and magazines. He has also written books about popular music and rock stars.

At last report he was married and living in the San Fernando Valley.

Tommy Nolan Filmography

1954: *A Star Is Born.*
1955: *The Seven Year Itch.*
1957: *All Mine to Give, An Affair to Remember, Jeanne Eagels.*
1964: *Kiss Me Stupid.*
1969: *Chastity.*
1970: *The Moonshine War.*
1985: *School Spirit.*

Television Series

1958–1959: *Buckskin* as Jody O'Connell.
1959–1960: *The Dennis O'Keefe Show.*

Sources

Contemporary Authors Volume 14. Detroit, MI: Gale, 1979.
Lamparski, Richard. *Whatever Became Of? Ninth Series.* New York: Crown, 1985.

ANTHONY NUMKEENA

Anthony Earl Numkeena was born in Culver City, California, in 1943, where he was also raised. He is the son of Anthony Numkeena, Sr., and is of genuine Hopi and Yakima ancestry. He was one of 500 children tested for the role of Tyrone Power's adopted son Comes Running in *Pony Soldier* (1952). After winning the role, he underwent several months of training in riding, archery and singing. This served him in good stead when he played a similar role (that of Keith Larsen's adopted son) in *Brave Eagle,* his only regular series role.

Anthony Numkeena Filmography

1952: *Pony Soldier.*
1954: *Secret of the Incas, Alaska Seas.*
1955: *Escape to Burma, Strange Lady in Town.*
1956: *Westward Ho! The Wagons.*

Television Series

1955–1956: *Brave Eagle* as Keena.

Sources

Picture Show Annual. London: Amalgamated Press, 1954.
Summers, Neil. *The Official TV Western Book Volume #2.* Vienna, WV: Old West Shop Publishing, 1989.

JAMES NUSSER

Born in 1905, this actor played bit parts in films, many of which do not ever appear to have been recorded. He had a regular role as the town drunk for 20 years in *Gunsmoke.* He died in 1979 at age 74.

James Nusser Filmography

1953: *It Should Happen to You.*
1957: *Hell Canyon Outlaws.*
1973: *Cahill United States Marshal.*

Television Series

1955–1975: *Gunsmoke* as Louie Pheeters.

Sources

Brooks, Tim. *The Complete Directory to Prime Time TV Stars 1946–Present.* New York: Ballantine Books, 1987.
Ragan, David. *Who's Who in Hollywood.* New York: Facts on File, 1992.

HUGH O'BRIAN

When Hugh O'Brian made an early appearance in a film called *Never Fear* (1950), the movie's director Ida Lupino said of him, "I thought he was awfully good then and I think so now. Hugh has a beautiful speaking voice, wonderful facial bone structure and a great pair of eyes for the screen. He's ambitious, but he never steps on anyone to get where he wants." All of these qualities came to serve him well when he played his greatest television role of Wyatt Earp, he of the natty, floral vest and the Buntline Specials. Some might attribute his casting to luck, but O'Brian dismisses this, saying, "Luck is a thing which happens when preparation meets opportunity."

Hugh O'Brian was born Hugh Charles Krampe in Rochester, New York, on April 19, 1925. He was the son of Hugh John Krampe and his wife Edith. His father was a retired captain in the U.S. Marine Corps who was later a sales executive with the Armstrong Cork Company, Inc. His mother died in 1950. His father remarried but died in July 1958. O'Brian is of mixed French, German and Irish descent. He has one younger brother named Don who was born in 1929. He had a gypsy childhood, growing up in such varied places as Lancaster, Pennsylvania; Long Island, New York; Chicago and Evanston, Illinois.

His father was given the Chicago territory while his son was in his teens. Hugh O'Brian attended New Trier High School in Winnetka, Chicago, and afterwards Hirsch High School in Chicago. He won letters in football, basketball, wrestling and track events. Once he expressed a desire to attend a military school, he was sent to Roosevelt Military Academy in Aledo, Illinois, and afterwards to Kemper Military School in Boonville, Missouri.

Prior to graduating from the latter school, he enrolled at the University of Cincinnati, Ohio, the university his father attended. His studies were interrupted by the outbreak of World War II. He left the university in his sophomore year to enlist in the U.S. Marine Corps in 1941. At 18 he became one of the youngest drill instructors in the history of the Marine Corps. In the hopes of being sent overseas, he applied for a transfer to a tank company. Instead of being assigned an overseas post, he was selected to apply for admission to the U.S. Naval Academy at Annapolis, Maryland. He failed the entrance requirements by only about one percent, but was given the chance to rectify this the following year. Along the way he danced with glamorous actresses at the Hollywood Canteen, which sparked his interest in show business. He was also keen on boxing and did a lot of it when he was in the Marine Corps. Out of 29 official fights, he won 23, drew two and lost four. The war ended in 1945, and by this time he had decided not to pursue a military career.

When he was discharged from the marines as a corporal, he made plans to apply to Yale University in New Haven, Connecticut, to study law. (His father retired to live in California.) While in Los Angeles, he went out with a girl who was a member of the Playmakers, a little theater group based in Los Angeles. She asked him if he would drop her at the theater the following evening. They were due to start rehearsals for a new play and she wanted to be in good time. He obliged, but when they arrived they discovered that panic reigned backstage. The leading man had been taken ill and a replacement was desperately needed. O'Brian looked like a leading man, so the frenzied producer cast him. He learned the part in four days. The critics did not rave about the newcomer, but they were kind. "Hugh Krampe has a lot of promise, but he also has a lot to learn," one wrote. He was so thrilled with the stimulation which he received from acting that he decided to become a professional actor.

His father was so dead set against his career choice that he refused all financial assistance. O'Brian undertook a series of odd jobs (including landscape gardening and collecting garbage) to subsidize his drama studies. Later he earned money by door-to-door selling of men's and women's clothes. He gained experience performing with little theater companies. Around this time he used Jaffer Gray as a stage name. While studying acting at Los Angeles City College during the day, he appeared in the first live dramatic television shows to be seen on the West Coast. For this nighttime exposure, he worked without pay because he considered it imperative that he gain experience in the new medium. In 1949 producer Arch Oboler offered him his first paying role on television playing a number of roles on the anthology series *Mystery Theater.* He also appeared in his first film, a one-day bit in *Kidnapped* (1948) for Monogram.

He built up a regular string of clients among the big actors and agents in Los Angeles. They were all perfectly willing to talk clothes, but if ever he mentioned himself as an actor, they froze up. At last he hit upon the idea of how to sell himself. Every agent who bought a pair of socks or a tie from him was given a pair of tickets for the opening night of his play. One of them was a prestigious agent named Milo Frank who saw him perform with a little theater group at the Lobero Theater in Santa Barbara, California.

After the final curtain came down there was a knock on his dressing room door. It was Frank. "What did you think of it?" O'Brian asked. "You know," said Frank, "we might make an actor out of you yet." He told O'Brian that he would come back the following night with a producer who might be interested. After the second show, Frank was again knocking at his door. With him was actress Ida Lupino, whom O'Brian greatly admired. When Frank introduced her as the producer, O'Brian was surprised. Ida Lupino said, "That's right. I'm in the middle of casting a film for my own pro-

Hugh O'Brian in *The Life and Legend of Wyatt Earp.*

duction company. Would you be interested in a part?"

He jumped at the chance. In Lupino's film *Never Fear* he was cast as a polio patient. This was a role close to his own heart, as his own brother had suffered from the disease as a child. To prepare for this part, he applied to the local Kabat-Kaiser Institute for Polio and asked if he could spend a few weeks with the patients. The Institute agreed, and he spent three weeks there in a wheelchair learning what it felt like to be afflicted with polio. By the end of this period there he had become so proficient that he could play basketball and do a square dance in a wheelchair. It was at this time that he changed his name to Hugh O'Brian for professional purposes.

His sound and sensitive performance in *Never Fear* was seen by executives at Universal-International, who signed him to a seven-year pact. When under contract to this studio from 1951 to 1954, he appeared in 18 movies. They were usually featured roles. Dissatisfaction in 1954 with these parts led to him seeking a meeting with the top brass where he requested his release. Despite a promise from them that they had plans for a star build-up, he declined to continue with them and they gave him his release. Afterwards he was under contract to 20th Century–Fox. Then he freelanced. For a few months he was unemployed. Then he met Tom Lewis, husband of Loretta Young and producer of the anthology television series *The Loretta Young Show.* He saw O'Brian's potential and signed him up. He gave him a few small roles to play in the series. His roles gradually improved, but despite this he remained largely unknown. Frequently there were long gaps between parts, and sometimes he was forced to go without proper meals.

In 1955 opportunity galloped up. Along with nearly every other unemployed actor in Hollywood, he auditioned for the title role in *The Life and Legend of Wyatt Earp.* ABC network executives rejected actor after actor. Eventually they accepted O'Brian not only because of his uncanny resemblance to the young Wyatt in real life, but also because he was the only choice of Stuart Lake, the author who made a lifetime study of the character and upon whose book the series was based.

O'Brian was duly signed, but when the publicity machine was cranked up and a team dispatched to his bachelor quarters at Malibu Beach, they discovered that the actor was flat broke. The one bedroom shack was shabby and littered with dirty clothes which he could not afford to have cleaned, and there was no food or drink in the house. They departed for a nearby beach cafe, where O'Brian enjoyed the first proper meal he had eaten in some time.

The Life and Legend of Wyatt Earp made its debut on ABC on September 6, 1955, and after a few weeks the ratings soared. It was ranked in the Nielsen Top 20 for three out of six years and reached sixth during the 1957-1958 season. The series initiated the adult Westerns of the late 1950s. According to research undertaken at the time, two-thirds of the audience were adults. The series evolved over a period of six years in a continuing saga of family relationships and politics against a background of the Wild West, rather like a serial. In the premiere episode "Mr. Earp Becomes a Marshal," Earp pinned on a badge and avenged the death of his friend Marshal Whitney of Ellsworth, Kansas. Wyatt's biographer, Ned Buntline, presented him with two "Buntline Special" pistols (pistols with extra long barrels). Their recoil was horrendous, but their extra length allowed the marshal to shoot his opponents from a greater distance. In the first season he fought foes in and around Ellsworth, and from the second season onwards he became Marshal of Dodge City. By the fifth season Earp had become Marshal of Tombstone, Arizona, which led to the running feud between the Earps and the Clantons. For two seasons Earp battled the Clantons, who had a stranglehold on the town, by legal and political means. Finally this led to the celebrated showdown at the OK Corral. The events leading up to this climax were dramatized in a five-part episode shown at the end of the final season in 1961.

ABC executives were delighted with the way in which the actor assumed the stance and mannerisms of the famous lawman. The effect was even enhanced by the childhood scar which the actor had on his lower lip. In 1956 he received an Emmy nomination for Best Continuing Performance by an Actor in a Dramatic Series. He was exclusively Wyatt Earp for five months of the year. In that time they shot 39 episodes in five-day weeks which kept him busy from 5:30 A.M., when he rose. The normal time he returned home was 7:30 P.M. He reported to the ranch by 7:30 A.M., was made up, worked throughout the day, drove home to dictate letters to his secretary and then learned 18 pages of dialogue for the next day's shooting. Initially learning his lines took three hours, but by the end he had it down to half an hour. By Friday night he was exhausted. His favorite weekend recreation was skin diving to 100 feet below the surface where the fish had never heard of Wyatt Earp!

He also made a very deep and detailed study of Earp. Earp (1848–1929) never looked for trouble, although when it came he never backed off. He went through 140 gunfights, was never wounded, and killed only four men. According to Stuart Lake, they only died because the position reached the point of no return. Earp had to kill to survive. Usually he wounded the trouble makers. O'Brian said that the Wyatt Earp series bible was Stuart Lake's biography. "It is well worth studying," he enthused. "Wyatt accomplished unbelievable feats. He must have had nerves of iron. And the more one reads about the gunfighting period, the more one appreciates the strength of his courage and control."

O'Brian spent long hours practicing a fast draw. After over a hundred hours of repeated draw and fire action, he could whip both six shooters out of their holsters and fire them in a fraction of a second. However, contemporary comparisons indicate that he was not the fastest draw amongst the screen stars and was in fact beaten on some occasions. He once issued a challenge to other stars. Two who picked up the gauntlet were Audie Murphy and Al "Lash" LaRue. Murphy wanted to draw using live ammunition. LaRue, a lifelong critic of O'Brian, agreed to the challenge if he could use his bullwhip instead of a pistol. On both occasions O'Brian backed off hastily.

The actor himself was not immune to danger. While appearing in person in a Western show, he was giving demonstrations of his fast draw in theaters in the South and Midwest. While giving a performance in Wilmington, North Carolina, one of his six-guns failed to clear his holster. O'Brian squeezed the trigger prematurely, causing a blank cartridge to explode. This burned a hole in his trousers and broke the skin. After receiving first aid, he went on with the show.

The tours, royalties from the sale of merchandising and his salary and residuals from the series made him a millionaire. He also had a financial interest in real estate, a sports gun rental service and a sports equipment business. The series did, however, take its toll on him personally. A blonde actress who befriended O'Brian before the television series started said later, "Hugh takes the whole business far too seriously. As Wyatt Earp he's not allowed to kiss any girl because Earp wasn't the type. But it seems to me he keeps up the act in private life too. He's become cold."

Before he became a Western hero, Hugh O'Brian would gladly have settled for married life. After he became a success, he admitted, "Women frighten me. I'm uneasy with them. I know I'm going to wind up being married to one and it terrifies me." "He's just one of those dull actors who puts his career before his private life," said one disappointed girlfriend when the series was at its zenith. "Do you know what he says about romance? 'No time'!" A close friend of O'Brian's put it another way: "Hugh has to drive himself hard. He spends five months of the year filming the series and the rest of the time making personal appearances. The result is we never see the real Hugh. As he said himself, 'I only see myself when I'm shaving.' Hugh was such a likable character. I'm not saying he isn't now, but somehow it's different. He's become an out-and-out businessman and I think he's lost a lot of his charm."

"He was a down-to-earth sort of chap," explained an actress friend. "But today he is difficult to pin down. He's up in the clouds and you don't know where you stand with him. I expect it's the strain of playing the same character day after day." People who watched him work on the series predicted that he had become tired of it and would quit. They were right. When the series was still highly successful, O'Brian himself called an end to it. He explained, "I want more out of life than that. I don't want to be known simply as that man on the little screen who can draw a revolver faster than anyone else. I think I'm a better person than that and a better actor. And now I've got the chance to find out if I am. The hardest part of acting is yet ahead—to strive for a bigger goal." Even though the network sent their most persuasive emissaries offering to fill his pockets and chests with dollars, he rejected them all. His salary alone for the final season was $105,000 with clauses for escalations if he would continue, but he was adamant; he wanted out after 266 half-hour black and white episodes. He expanded on this theme by saying, "Each week the same lines of dialogue, more or less. The same fast draws, the same situations with slight variations. There's got to be more to life than this. A man doesn't spend a fourth of his life working his tail off for that kind of achievement. I think I can do better."

After this he seemed to deliberately pick roles which distanced him as much as possible from Earp. He made his New York debut at the Imperial Theater in the summer of 1959 when he took over from Andy Griffith in the title role of *Destry.* He has appeared in numerous stage plays and musicals including *Guys and Dolls* as Sky Masterson; *Cactus Flower* as Julian; *A Thousand Clowns* as Murray Burns; *1776; The Desperate Hours;* and as Walter Burns in *The Front Page.* These were in Los Angeles, New York, and on the road throughout the 1960s and 1970s. On television he sang and danced on the shows of such diverse personalities as Frances Langford, Ed Sullivan and Dinah Shore. In a television musical he wore a scarecrow costume and clowned with Jane Powell. In *Great Adventures from the Bible* he had a religious role as Joseph, who wore the coat of many colors. He played leads and supporting roles in several features. One of his most showy roles was as Pulford, one of the opponents who participates in the showdown against John Wayne in *The Shootist* (1976).

He has been a president of the Thalians, a group of entertainers (including Debbie Reynolds) who raised money for charity and served on the board of the Southern California Mental Health Foundation. The encounter which changed his life was in 1958 when he met Dr. Albert Schweitzer. He spent nine days at Dr. Schweitzer's clinic in Africa working in the kitchen, building, plumbing and carrying supplies. With the aid of an interpreter at night, he learned much of his mentor's philosophy. When he returned Stateside he founded the Hugh O'Brian Youth Foundation (HOBY), in which he invested a great deal of time and money. In 1993 he was reported to be still putting in a 70-hour week as its head. The Foundation operates from an office block on Wilshire Boulevard. HOBY's purpose is to bring select groups of high school sophomores with demonstrated leadership qualities together with groups of distinguished people from all walks of life and let the groups interact. About 14,000 young people from all over the world participate annually. He explains, "These kids are concerned about today's world. There's so much tragedy, but I want them to learn that for every tragedy, there's a triumph, and for every mishap there's a miracle—and they can be one of those miracles." Once nicknamed "Knight in a Satin Vest" on account of his charity work, he says, "A lot of people give money to their own favorite charity. That's easy. It isn't so easy to give time. Well, I've had a lot out of this life and this is the only way I know to give something back."

He still accepts a couple of acting jobs a year not only to fund the foundation, but also because he still enjoys acting. His only other series was *Search* (1972–1973), in which he played one of three secret agents working for the World Securities Organization. It was not a success. He appeared on *Fantasy Island* and *Police Story* in the 1970s and *Murder She Wrote* and *LA Law* in the 1980s. He reprised his role of Wyatt Earp on an episode of *Paradise* (1989) and in *The Gambler Returns: The Luck of the*

Draw (1991). A big screen assignment was playing Arnold Schwarzenegger's father in *Twins* (1988). He has also been a commercial spokesperson for McDonald's. He claims never to have regretted quitting *The Life and Legend of Wyatt Earp,* although none of his other roles has ever brought him the same acclaim.

In 1993 in the wake of the free publicity from such film releases as *Tombstone* and *Wyatt Earp,* CST Entertainment Imaging colorized and reedited the original television series into feature length movies for television. CST Featurizations Division pacted with the owner of the series (Wyatt Earp Enterprises) for the initial project, which called for the creation of between three and six Earp movies, each using between 10 and 12 episodes from the series. O'Brian reprised the role in flashback wraparounds that were shot in black and white, then colorized to more closely resemble the original episodes. Rob Word was the creator and producer.

A lifelong bachelor, Hugh O'Brian lives in a Cape Cod style house in Beverly Hills with his two dogs.

Hugh O'Brian Filmography

1948: *Kidnapped.*
1950: *D.O.A., Never Fear, Rocketship X-M, Kansas Raiders, Beyond the Purple Hills, The Return of Jesse James.*
1951: *On the Loose, Buckaroo Sheriff of Texas, Vengeance Valley, Fighting Coast Guard, Little Big Horn, Cave of Outlaws, The Cimarron Kid.*
1952: *Red Ball Express, Battle at Apache Pass, Sally and Saint Anne, Son of Ali Baba, The Raiders, The Lawless Breed, Meet Me at the Fair.*
1953: *Seminole, The Man from the Alamo, The Stand at Apache River, Back to God's Country.*
1954: *Fireman Save My Child!, Saskatchewan, Drums Across the River, There's No Business Like Show Business, Broken Lance.*
1955: *White Feather, The Twinkle in God's Eye.*
1956: *Brass Legend.*
1958: *The Fiend Who Walked the West.*
1959: *Alias Jesse James* (cameo).
1962: *Come Fly With Me.*
1963: *Assassin ... Made in Italy (*a.k.a. *Assassination in Rome), Il Segreto Del Vestito Rosso.*
1964: *Love Has Many Faces, Strategy of Terror* (TV).
1965: *In Harm's Way, Ten Little Indians.*
1966: *Ambush Bay.*
1967: *Africa—Texas Style.*
1970: *Wild Women* (TV).
1971: *Harpy* (TV).
1972: *Probe* (TV).
1975: *Killer Force (*a.k.a. *The Diamond Mercenaries), Murder on Flight 502* (TV).
1976: *The Shootist.*
1977: *Murder at the World Series* (TV), *Fantasy Island* (TV), *Benny and Barney: Las Vegas Undercover* (TV).
1978: *Game of Death, Cruise into Terror* (TV).
1987: *Doin' Time on Planet Earth.*
1988: *Twins.*
1990: *Gunsmoke: The Last Apache* (TV).
1991: *The Gambler Returns: The Luck of the Draw* (TV).

Television Series

1955–1961: *The Life and Legend of Wyatt Earp* as Wyatt Earp.
1972–1973: *Search* as Hugh Lockwood.

Sources

Current Biography. New York: H.W. Wilson, 1958.
Globe Special: Where Are They Now? Boca Raton, Florida: Globe International, 1993.
Hugh O'Brian Fan's Star Library No. 22. London: Amalgamated Press, 1959.
Speed, F. Maurice. *The Western Film and TV Annual.* London: MacDonald, 1959.
Thomey, Tedd. *The Glorious Decade.* New York: Ace, 1971.
Weissberg, Brad. "Hugh O'Brian back as Wyatt Earp after 33 years." *National Enquirer* magazine, April 1994.

DAMIAN O'FLYNN

This supporting actor (who also performed under the name Damon Ford) made his screen debut in 1936 and was active in motion pictures until 1963. He had the semi-regular role of Doc Goodfellow during the last two seasons of *The Life and Legend of Wyatt Earp*. O'Flynn retired to live in Idaho where he is believed to have died in the late 1970s, survived by his widow.

Damian O'Flynn Filmography

1936: *Wedding Present.*
1937: *Marked Woman.*
1941: *Victory, The Gay Falcon, Lady Scarface.*
1942: *Broadway, Powder Town, Wake Island, X Marks the Spot, The Great Man's Lady.*
1943: *Flight for Freedom, Sarong Girl, So Proudly We Hail!.*
1944: *Winged Victory.*
1946: *The Bachelor's Daughters, Crack-Up.*
1947: *The Beginning or the End?, The Devil on Wheels, Philo Vance Returns, Saddle Pals, Web of Danger.*
1948: *Half Past Midnight, A Foreign Affair, Disaster, The Snake Pit.*
1949: *Black Magic, Outpost in Morocco, Riders of the Whistling Pines.*
1950: *Young Daniel Boone, Pioneer Marshal, Gambling House, Bomba and the Hidden City.*
1951: *Fighting Coast Guard, Yellow Fin, You're in the Navy Now, Inside the Walls of Folsom Prison.*
1952: *The Half-Breed, Hoodlum Empire, The Pride of St. Louis, Plymouth Adventure.*
1954: *The Glenn Miller Story, The Miami Story, Two Guns and a Badge.*
1955: *Daddy Long Legs, The Far Country.*
1956: *Hidden Guns, D-Day The Sixth of June, Daniel Boone Trail Blazer.*
1957: *Drango, Apache Warrior, Eighteen and Anxious.*
1963: *Gunfight at Comanche Creek.*

Television Series

1959–1961: *The Life and Legend of Wyatt Earp* as Doc Goodfellow.

Sources

Brooks, Tim. *The Complete Directory to Prime Time TV Stars.* New York: Ballantine Books, 1987.
Conversation with Walter Reed in 1997.
Picture Show's Who's Who on Screen. London: Amalgamated Press, c. 1956.

FESS PARKER

The life of Fess Parker was magically changed by a coonskin cap. A major factor in his success story was his sincerity, which made him a perfect choice for the role of Davy Crockett. It is small wonder that in his least successful series *Mr. Smith Goes to Washington,* he repeated on television a role played by James Stewart in a movie because both actors project the same homespun qualities. His later roles revealed him to be a competent and extremely likable actor, but one of limited range. Director Norman Foster expressed it: "I found if I didn't do something to get adrenaline in his system, he would get slower and slower." His well-liked personality and scandal-free private life pay testimony to the influence playing such men as Davy Crockett and Daniel Boone have had on him.

Fess Parker was born in Fort Worth, Texas, on August 16, 1924, the son of Fess Parker, Sr., and Mackie Allen. His father owned a small ranch. The actor was raised around San Angelo. Graduating from the University of Texas, where he majored in business administration, he was conscripted almost immediately and served aboard a minesweeper during World War II. While in the navy, he was on leave in California in 1943, so he decided to look around 20th Century–Fox studio. There he saw *State Fair* being shot. He liked the environment so much that he decided to pursue a career as an actor.

Upon his discharge from the navy, he enrolled at the University of Southern California where he studied drama. He began his acting career with a touring company of *Mister Roberts.* Then he made his screen debut in *Untamed Frontier* (1952), in which he had one line of dialogue and seven weeks' work. Other small film and television roles followed. Walt Disney was searching for an actor to play Davy Crockett, and he chanced to look in on a televised version of *Them* (1954). Although legend has it that he originally considered James Arness for the role, when he saw Fess Parker he switched allegiance, believing that he was a more appropriate choice.

Disney immediately contacted Parker's agent, and Parker found himself on his way to an interview with him. The reason for the interview was not explained to the actor. He had always associated Disney with animated films and could not understand what Disney wanted. At the interview, Disney outlined his intention to shoot some live-action adventure films. Parker became the first adult actor signed to a long term contract with Disney. At the time, work as an actor was slow and rumor has it that Parker had been contemplating giving up his acting ambition to go into business.

Disney shot three segments of his anthology series *Disneyland* based on the life of the frontiersman Davy Crockett, with Parker in the title role. These were called "Davy Crockett Indian Fighter" (aired on CBS December 15, 1954); "Davy Crockett Goes to Congress" (aired January 26, 1955) and "Davy Crockett at the Alamo" (aired February 23, 1955). Before the organization knew what was happening, the whole country had become crazy about the character. Disney reaped a fortune from the merchandising rights, as seemingly every American boy bought a coonskin cap and other items. The episodes brought Parker overnight fame, and he found himself the most talked-about character in America. Its success was also helped by the theme tune "The Ballad of Davy Crockett" by Tom Blackburn and George Burns.

Parker became concerned that his fame might be transitory because the public only knew him as Davy Crockett and not Fess Parker. Disney helped him to establish an identity of his own by sending him on a personal appearance tour of the United States. He went out dressed as Davy Crockett, but met the fans as Fess Parker. Fortunately this worked, and he was reassured when fans started asking for the autograph of Fess Parker and not Davy Crockett. He traveled all over America and met thousands of people.

As Disney later recalled, "We had no idea what was going to happen to Crockett. Why, by the time the first show finally got on the air, we were already shooting the third one and calmly killing Davy off at the Alamo. It became one of the biggest overnight hits in TV history and there we were with just three films and a dead hero." Disney astutely took advantage of the boom and spliced the three color hour-length episodes into a feature called *Davy Crockett, King of the Wild Frontier* (1955). Disney's policy was to create quality television, and this paid dividends because the 90-minute feature film scarcely betrayed its television origins.

While the film was smashing many box office records in the United States, it was decided to release it in Europe. To coincide with this, Disney sent the star on a personal appearance tour of Britain and Europe. When Parker recovered from the shock, he consoled himself with the thought that Britain was smaller than the United States. He changed his mind when he was mobbed by 10,000 children in a Scottish city. In two months he covered 35,000 miles, visiting literally hundreds of hospitals, cinemas, stores and dance halls. Along the trail he met thousands of people, including civic dignitaries of all the big towns in Britain, France, Italy, Norway, Sweden and other continental countries. There was no rest, only a few hours' snatched sleep before catching an early train to the next destination. It was a dawn to dusk round of activity with scarcely time to grab a meal. Back in Hollywood, it was the actor's first vacation since the sensation had begun.

Anxiety set in again with the release of a second film for Disney called *The Great Locomotive Chase* (1956). In this Parker played James J. Andrews, a Union spy who stole a huge locomotive during the American Civil War and tried to stop the war by cutting the supply lines to the South. His attempt is foiled by the persistence of a young conductor on the train, William A. Fuller (Jeffrey Hunter). Although Parker felt the story stood up well on its own merits, he feared that he was on trial as an actor. As he recalled, "The character of Andrews was quiet and dignified without any coonskin gimmicks or robust humor to help it over." He only overcame his nerves when the reviews came out with the consensus solidly in favor of his acting performance.

Walt Disney could scarcely drop the *Davy Crockett* phenomenon. Even though Crockett had died at the Alamo in the original television episodes, Disney resurrected him for two further segments originally aired as "Davy Crockett's Keelboat Race" on November 16, 1955, and "Davy Crockett and the River Pirates" on December 14, 1955. These two episodes were subsequently edited together to make another successful feature film, *Davy Crockett and the River Pirates* (1956). Disney later recalled, "We tried to come back later with two more called *The Legend of Davy Crockett*, but by that time the fever had run its course. Those two never did catch on the way the original three did."

When he came to shoot another Disney film (1956's *Westward Ho! The Wagons*), Parker approached it with new confidence. It is an extremely handsome film which consists of a series of random episodes bridged by pioneer songs, with a background of gorgeous scenery. The episodes center around the struggle between whites and Indians when the Oregon trail was being pioneered. Parker liked the movie because it was a family film with plenty of children and animals. The other reason was because it was the first time he had been given a leading lady (Kathleen Crowley) throughout the film. Parker played John "Doc" Grayson. The actor ended his association with Disney after *The Light in the Forest* (1958). There was still five years to run on his contract, but he left after a dispute over billing and the size of his intended role in the feature film *Tonka*.

He did not fare particularly well initially. He alternated television appearances with feature films. His purpose as Sheriff Buck Weston in *The Hangman* (1959) was to be Robert Taylor's rival for the hand of Tina Louise. In *The Jayhawkers* (1959), one of several lackluster vehicles for Jeff Chandler after he quit Universal, Parker was the hero. He did a half-hour situation comedy called *Mr. Smith Goes to Washington*, aired for one season on ABC during 1962–1963. This was one of his few contemporary roles (he played a freshman senator) but the approach was the same, that of a small-town guy coping with the urban political jungle of Washington by using crackerbarrel philosophy.

The actor hit the jackpot again when *Daniel Boone* made its debut on ABC on September 24, 1964. The actor recalled, "I very much wanted to do a series based on Davy Crockett, but Mr. Disney said he wasn't interested. My lawyers told me Disney might sue if we proceeded, so we fastened on Daniel Boone instead." The series was a resounding success and lasted for 165 episodes, the final one of which was aired on August 27, 1970. Parker shot two other pilots, *Climb an Angry Mountain* (1972) and *The Fess Parker Show* (1974), but neither was picked up. He has not faced the cameras since.

He had made a great deal of money out of the series and subsequently became a business tycoon as owner of Santa Barbara's highly successful Red Lion Resort and Parker Winery. The winery (which he began in 1988) is producing many different varieties of wine. Its product sells in 30 states, is available at Disney World and was served by President Reagan at the opening of the Reagan Library and by Elizabeth Taylor at her Santa Barbara wedding. Despite this success, however, he has been somewhat downcast by the dearth of acting offers in recent years: "I like to joke that even though I haven't made a movie in 20 years, I am still between pictures, but it's not really a joke. I don't think I'd like to do a Davy Crockett film. I haven't anything to gain from reprising that character, but I would sure love to do something."

Fess Parker married Marcella Rinehart in 1960. They have a son, Fess Parker III (born in 1961), and a daughter, Ashley Allen Parker (born in 1964).

Fess Parker Filmography

1952: *Untamed Frontier, Springfield Rifle, No Room for the Groom.*

1953: *Thunder Over the Plains, Island in the Sky, The Kid from Left Field, Take Me to Town.*

1954: *Them!, The Bounty Hunter, Battle Cry.*
1955: *Davy Crockett King of the Wild Frontier.*
1956: *The Great Locomotive Chase, Davy Crockett and the River Pirates, Westward Ho! The Wagons.*
1957: *Old Yeller.*
1958: *The Light in the Forest.*
1959: *Alias Jesse James* (cameo), *The Hangman, The Jayhawkers!*
1962: *Hell Is for Heroes!*
1966: *Smoky.*
1972: *Climb an Angry Mountain* (TV).

Television Series

1954–1955: *Disneyland Presents Davy Crockett* as Davy Crockett.
1962–1963: *Mr. Smith Goes to Washington* as Senator Eugene Smith.
1964–1970: *Daniel Boone* as Daniel Boone.

Sources

Brooks, Tim. *The Complete Directory to Prime Time TV Stars 1946–Present.* New York: Ballantine Books, 1987.
Fleming, Charles. "Lost and Found." *Variety,* 1992.
Maltin, Leonard. *The Disney Films.* New York: Crown, 1973.
Speed, F. Maurice. *The Western Film and TV Annual.* London: MacDonald, 1957.
Summers, Neil. *The Official TV Western Book Volume #3.* Vienna, WV: Old West Shop Publishing, 1991.

WILLARD PARKER

Willard Parker was born Worster Van Eps on February 5, 1912, in New York City, the son of a vice consul. He changed his name because he was tired of people giving the "Van" a German "Von." When he first set foot in Hollywood, he was a tennis ace attached to the teaching staff of Ellsworth Vines. A chance encounter with agent Zeppo Marx led to a screen test, and he suddenly found that he had switched career. He was a Warner Bros. contract player for a little over a year, but made little headway and was dropped.

Undaunted, he returned to New York and won a part on Broadway with Gertrude Lawrence in *Lady in the Dark* before trying Hollywood again in 1943, this time under contract to Columbia Studios. He made one film before being drafted, which kept him offscreen for a while. When he resumed his acting career, Columbia endeavored to give him a star buildup, but his stodgy personality found little permanent favor with the public. *Renegades* (1946) was intended as a star vehicle for him, but the movie was stolen by Larry Parks, who became a star as a result.

Willard Parker (right) and Harry Lauter in ***Tales of the Texas Rangers.***

Parker was gradually relegated into that

bracket of players known in Hollywood cliché terms as "the other man," continuing to play these kind of parts well into the 1950s. He was also one of several leading men tested for the role of Tarzan after Johnny Weissmuller left it in 1948. Parker's physique and 6'4" height made him a possible candidate, but he lacked charisma so he lost out to Lex Barker.

Parker's one television series, *Tales of the Texas Rangers,* was a juvenile Western adventure about the exploits of two Texas Rangers, Jace Pearson and Clay Morgan, working for the famed law enforcement authority. Although the series was set in the Lone Star State, many of the exteriors were shot at the Corriganville Movie Ranch. The novelty was that it leapt back and forth in time in alternate weeks between the Old West and the current one. It started on radio in 1950 with Joel McCrea as Jace Pearson and ran for two years. In the television series, Parker replaced McCrea as Jace Pearson and Harry Lauter played Clay Morgan.

Tales of the Texas Rangers made its debut on CBS as an afternoon show on September 3, 1955, and lasted until May 25, 1957. It then switched networks to ABC where it was a prime time series, beginning on September 22, 1957, and lasting until March 22, 1958. There were 52 black and white half-hour episodes produced by Screen Gems, the television arm of Columbia Pictures. Appropriately, the theme song of the series was "The Eyes of Texas Are Upon You."

Willard Parker ended his acting career in B pictures in the early 1960s when he became a successful realtor in Indian Wells near Palm Springs. This career terminated abruptly when he suffered a serious stroke in 1974. He married actress Marion Pierce, with whom he had a son who became a banker. After his divorce, he married actress Virginia Field in 1951. Although they had no children of their own, she had daughter Margaret by a previous marriage to actor Paul Douglas. This child was awarded to Field so that she lived with her mother and Willard Parker. When Field died on January 2, 1992, of lung cancer, her husband was listed among the survivors. Willard Parker died in Rancho Mirage, California, on December 4, 1996, at age 84, of heart failure.

Willard Parker Filmography

1937: *That Certain Woman, Over the Goal, Back in Circulation, China Passage, The Devil's Saddle Legion, Love Is on the Air.*
1938: *Accidents Will Happen, A Slight Case of Murder.*
1939: *Zero Hour.*
1943: *What a Woman!*
1945: *The Fighting Guardsman, One Way to Love.*
1946: *Renegades.*
1948: *Relentless, The Mating of Millie, The Wreck of the Hesperus, You Gotta Stay Happy.*
1949: *Slightly French, Calamity Jane and Sam Bass.*
1950: *David Harding—Counterspy, Bodyhold, The Secret Fury, Emergency Wedding, Bandit Queen.*
1951: *Hunt the Man Down, Apache Drums, My True Story.*
1952: *Caribbean.*
1953: *The Vanquished, Sangaree, Kiss Me Kate.*
1954: *The Great Jesse James Raid.*
1956: *The Naked Gun.*
1957: *Lure of the Swamp.*
1959: *The Lone Texan.*
1960: *Walk Tall, The High-Powered Rifle, Young Jesse James.*
1962: *Air Patrol.*
1964: *The Earth Dies Screaming.*
1966: *Waco.*

Television Series

1955–1958: *Tales of the Texas Rangers* as Jace Pearson.

Sources

Lamparski, Richard. "Virginia Field." *Whatever Became Of? Fifth Series.* Crown: New York, 1974.
Picture Show Annual. London: Amalgamated Press, 1947 and 1954.
Summers, Neil. *The Official TV Western Book Volume #2.* Vienna, WV: Old West Shop Publishing, 1989.
Winchester, Clarence. *Screen Encyclopedia.* London: Winchester Publications, 1948.

BART PATTEN

When Burt Reynolds was experiencing difficulties on the series *Riverboat* and made an unscheduled exit, Bart Patten was one of the actors drafted in to fill the void. He played the role of the cub pilot for a short while during the first season. By the time the series returned for the second season, he was gone. This appears to have been his only regular series role, and he has latterly been posted among the lost players of the screen.

Bart Patten Filmography

1960: *Strangers When We Meet.*

Television Series

1959–1960: *Riverboat* as Terry Blake.

Sources

Brooks, Tim. *The Complete Directory to Prime Time TV Stars 1946–Present.* New York: Ballantine Books, 1987.

HANK PATTERSON

Hank Patterson was born Elmer Calvin Patterson in Alabama on October 9, 1888. He started out as a serious musician in Texas where he was raised, but signed on as a piano player with a road show in 1910. Soon he began filling in as an actor, "when somebody got drunk or sick or something." By 1912 he was acting full time in tent shows. During the 1920s he settled in the Los Angeles area, breaking into vaudeville. He had been in show business 30 years when he came to movies in 1940.

Of his many films his particular favorites were *Duel in the Sun* (1945) and *Abilene Town* (1946). On television he played the role of Hank the stableman on *Gunsmoke* in 1957 and continued in that role until he died. He was the oldest of the townsfolk of Dodge City, describing him as "an old guy who's playing an old guy." This role was overshadowed by his droll character Fred Ziffel in the comedy series *Green Acres.*

He was residing at the Motion Picture Country Home in Woodland Hills, California, recovering from a stroke, when he died of complications from bronchial pneumonia and the stroke on August 23, 1975, at age 86. He was survived by his wife, Daisy M. Sheeler, a former vaudeville dancer whom he married in 1916.

Hank Patterson Filmography

1939: *The Arizona Kid, Sabotage, The Covered Trailer.*
1940: *Three Faces West.*
1941: *The Phantom Cowboy, Gangs of Sonora.*
1945: *Duel in the Sun.*
1946: *Abilene Town, The El Paso Kid, Wild Beauty, Santa Fe Uprising, The Scarlet Horseman* (serial), *I Ring Doorbells.*
1947: *Bells of San Angelo, Springtime in the Sierras, Robin Hood of Texas, Under Colorado Skies.*
1948: *Relentless, Oklahoma Badlands, Night Time in Nevada, The Denver Kid, The Plunderers.*
1949: *Outcasts of the Trail, Red Canyon, The Cowboy and the Indians, Riders in the Sky.*
1950: *The James Brothers of Missouri* (serial), *Code of the Silver Sage, The Gunfighter, Desperadoes of the West* (serial), *The Return of Jesse James.*
1951: *Silver City Bonanza, Don Daredevil Rides Again* (serial), *Al Jennings of Oklahoma.*
1952: *Indian Uprising, California Conquest.*
1953: *Canadian Mounties Vs. Atomic Invaders* (serial), *Jack Slade, Blades of the Musketeer, Woman They Almost Lynched.*
1954: *Southwest Passage, Ride Clear of Diablo.*
1955: *Tarantula.*
1956: *Julie.*
1957: *The Storm Rider, Gunsight Ridge, Begin-*

ning of the End, Man of a Thousand Faces, The Amazing Colossal Man.
1958: *Terror in a Texas Town, The Decks Ran Red, Day of the Bad Man, Monster on the Campus, Earth vs. the Spider, Attack of the Puppet People, Escape from Red Rock.*
1959: *No Name on the Bullet.*
1960: *Gunfighters of Abilene.*

Television Series

1957–1975: *Gunsmoke* as Hank.
1965–1971: *Green Acres* as Fred Ziffel.

Sources

Cox, Stephen. *The Hooterville Handbook: A Viewer's Guide to Green Acres.* New York: St. Martin's Press, 1993.
Raddatz, Leslie. "The Dodge City Gang." *Radio Times* magazine, June 15, 1972.
Truitt, Evelyn Mack. *Who Was Who On Screen Illustrated Edition.* New York: Bowker, 1984.

EUGENIA PAUL

Born in Dearborn, Michigan, this starlet was once under contract to 20th Century–Fox and appeared in some films and episodes such as *The Lone Ranger.* She played the daughter of political prisoner Nacho Torres in the television series *Zorro.* By the 1990s she had turned to religion and made appearances on *The Living Christ Series.*

Eugenia Paul Filmography

1954: *Jivaro.*
1956: *Bigger Than Life, The Revolt of Mamie Stover.*
1957: *Man on the Prowl, The Disembodied, Apache Warrior.*
1960: *Gunfighters of Abilene, The Sign of Zorro* (TV:Z).

Television Series

1957–1959: *Zorro* as Elena Torres.

Sources

Brooks, Tim. *The Complete Directory to Prime Time TV Stars 1946–Present.* New York: Ballantine Books, 1987.
Yoggy, Gary A. *Riding the Video Range: The Rise and Fall of the Western on Television.* Jefferson, NC: McFarland, 1995.

Note

TV:Z in the filmography denotes a film derived from episodes of the television series *Zorro.*

JOHN PAYNE

The career of John Payne rather neatly divides itself into two distinct parts. He was a virile, dependable and tuneful leading man in many musicals made by 20th Century–Fox in the early 1940s. With his honest face, dimpled chin and thatch of dark wavy hair, he introduced many songs which have since become standards. He looked good in a tuxedo with one of the studio's reigning blondes on his arm. In the dramatic interludes he was convincing enough to emote his way through the conventions which spun these movies out to the required screen length, before he and his leading lady came together for the clinch at the fadeout. When he went independent in the late 1940s he was adept as a boxer, cowboy, crime czar or swashbuckler in movies of an altogether tougher sort.

John Payne and an unnamed fallen cowboy in *The Restless Gun*.

He was a rarity in Hollywood in that he seemed to be universally well-liked and respected by everyone. The only exceptions were probably his two ex-wives and director Oliver Drake, whom he clashed with on the feature *They Ran for Their Lives* (1965). He fired Drake and took over the directorial reins himself in addition to starring. Everyone else, whether male or female, seems to have had nothing but praise for him. Actor Pierce Lyden recalled, "John Payne was a sober and serious minded actor." While working on the television series *The Restless Gun* actor Don C. Harvey reported, "Our star John Payne is talented, dependable and cooperative." Veteran independent producer Sidney Pink recalled, "I knew John Payne and he was always cooperative, pleasant and professional." Actress Maureen O'Hara, who costarred with him in four features, said, "John Payne was a particular favorite of mine."

Payne was an astute businessman and very farsighted. In an interview with *TV Guide* in 1958 he commented, "The producer who says pay TV isn't coming is like a man sitting on a railroad track insisting that the steam engine bearing down on him from just one mile away isn't an engine at all and that he can sit there as long as he wants to."

John Howard Payne was born in Roanoke, Virginia, either on May 23, or May 28, 1912, the son of George Washington Payne, a gentleman farmer, and Ida Hope Schaeffer, an opera singer. He had two brothers, Peter and William. His father lost his fortune in the stock market crash of 1929. Nevertheless, John Payne attended Mercerberg Academy in Pennsylvania; Roanoke College in Virginia; and finally he studied acting at Columbia University and singing at the Juilliard School of Music in New York. To pay his tuition fees he supported himself with radio jobs and toured in Shubert shows. He was also briefly a professional wrestler and did sundry other occupations.

By 1935 he was an understudy in the revue *At Home Abroad* at the Winter Garden Theater in New York City. A talent scout for Sam Goldwyn saw him perform one night when Reginald Gardiner was indisposed and brought him to Hollywood, where he was placed under contract to Goldwyn. He stayed there for a year, during which time he made his motion picture debut as Harry, the son of Walter Huston, in *Dodsworth* (1936). This was his only film for the legendary producer.

He was under contract to Paramount for a year where he made two pictures. By 1938 he was at Warner Bros. where he made six films, usually in roles which had been rejected by Dick Powell. When his option was not picked up there, he signed with 20th Century–Fox. His career received a big boost when he was chosen to play opposite Claudette Colbert in *Remember the Day* (1941). Subsequently he played opposite most of the blonde film actresses at that studio such as Alice Faye, Betty Grable and June Haver in a string of escapist musicals which made him good box office. His career was interrupted by World War II, where he served as a pilot in the U.S. Army Corps.

Unlike many war veterans who returned from service in the armed forces but were unable to regain their former stature in the industry, Payne became even more successful. He bought a short story from a magazine and sold it to Fox, who offered the lead to Cary Grant. Payne collared studio head Darryl F. Zanuck in the men's room and insisted on testing for the leading role. He won the part, which became one of his most commercially successful films, *Sentimental Journey* (1946). This is also reputed to be his favorite film from the Fox years. In similar fashion he bought the studio a magazine story about a little girl who refused to believe in Santa Claus from which the Christmas classic *Miracle on 34th Street* (1947) was made, starring Payne, Maureen O'Hara, Edmund Gwenn and Natalie Wood.

Payne did not like the treatment which his studio had dished out to him, and he figured correctly that he could make more money as a freelance. In 1948 he set up his own company (Window Glen Productions) and inked deals with Paramount and Universal. He released several pictures through United Artists, shot movies for the Pine-Thomas unit at Paramount and was involved with the mildly eccentric independent producer Benedict Bogeaus. The films which he made were in many genres such as Westerns, thrillers and swashbucklers. They were among the most entertaining films of the period, and nearly all returned large profits.

Payne produced, starred and coscripted *The Boss*, a dramatization of the life and times of politician Tom Pendergast, but it upset the State Department, who branded it subversive and not characteristic of American society. It did poor business in the United States where it received only a limited release some time after it was made and was not shown overseas. Allegedly it was Payne's personal favorite of his post–Fox films. He had a piece of the action on thc films he made and was regularly earning in excess of $300,000 per annum during the 1950s.

In contrast to many leading stars who had a deep-rooted mistrust of television, he embraced it. His first appearance on the small screen was in "Double Eyed Deceiver," an episode of *The Nash Airflyte Theater* in 1950. He continued to appear in episodes of anthology series throughout the 1950s. The most significant of these was when he played Britt Ponset in "Six Shooter," an episode of CBS's *Schlitz Playhouse of the Stars* in March 1957. The format was revamped and the name of the title character changed when the pilot was picked up and became a series called *The Restless Gun.*

The Restless Gun made its debut on NBC on September 23, 1957. Payne starred as Vint Bonner, a drifter who rides from town to town but cannot settle in the post–Civil War West. An idealist with a formidable reputation as a gunfighter, he found himself in situations of conflict and drama where he frequently ended up defending those less able to take care of themselves. With his television series Payne wanted total control. He was the executive producer, star, narrator and occasional scriptwriter. In a sense this was his strength, but also his downfall. The workload was so daunting that when NBC offered him the option of making the series an hour in length, he could not face this and canceled the series instead.

As with most of the other ventures which Payne turned his hand to, this series was very popular and was ranked as high as number eight in the Nielsen ratings during its first season on television. He retained 50 percent of the rights for his own company, Window Glen Productions. It is generally believed that the biggest demerit of the series was that it was largely studio-bound and there was virtually no location shooting. *The Restless Gun* ended, after two seasons and 77 half-hour black and white episodes, on September 14, 1959. It was coproduced by David Dortort for Revue Productions (which was Universal Television).

When Payne called an end to the series, he tried to return to feature films but discovered that the climate of the times had changed and that there were no offers. He had also grown older. He produced and starred in a half-hour pilot called *O'Connor's Ocean* for NBC in 1960, but this was not picked up. In 1961 he nearly died when he was hit by a car and flung through the windshield. He required extensive plastic surgery and physiotherapy. He recovered sufficiently to tour in a play called *Here's Love* in 1964, but detested the experience. During the 1960s he wrote television scripts and an unproduced play. Dealing in real estate made him an extremely wealthy man and enabled him to buy a flourishing ranch in Montana. He made four more guest starring appearances on television: *The Name of the Game* (1968), *Gunsmoke* (1970), *Cade's County* (1971) and *Columbo* (1975). The episode of *Columbo* was entitled "Forgotten Lady" and costarred him with Janet Leigh as former movie star dancing partners. There are those who believe he stole the show.

In 1973 Alice Faye, who had not seen Payne in 17 years, insisted on him as her leading man for a stage revival of the musical *Good News,* which was a box office smash in New York. He played Bill Johnson, the football coach, who sang, "You're the Cream in My Coffee." Faye recalled, "*Tin Pan Alley* [1940] was the first of several times I worked with John Payne, whom I loved. More than 30 years later we costarred together on Broadway in a revival of *Good News.* That wasn't as much fun, especially for John who sometime before had been badly injured when hit by a car in New York. His leg hurt a great deal, making it very difficult for him to sing and dance and just move around the stage. John was a very intelligent person and a fine businessman, the least actorish of all the men I worked with." John Payne was relieved when his contract ended and he could return home to ply his trade as a property speculator.

He married actress Anne Shirley on August 22, 1937, in Santa Barbara, California. Their daughter, Julie Anne, was born on August 10, 1940. On February 19, 1942, Anne divorced him in Los Angeles on the grounds of cruelty. The actor married actress Gloria De Haven in Beverly Hills on December 28, 1944. The couple had two children, Kathie (born in 1945) and Thomas (born in 1948). De Haven divorced him in Los Angeles on February 9, 1950, because their careers clashed. She obtained custody of their children. In 1953 he married Alexandra "Sandy" Curtis, an artist and widow of B picture leading man Alan Curtis.

John Payne died at his home in Malibu on December 6, 1989, at age 77, of congestive heart failure, survived by his wife, three children and two grandchildren.

John Payne Filmography

1936: *Dodsworth.*
1937: *Hats Off, Fair Warning.*
1938: *College Swing, Garden of the Moon, Love on Toast.*
1939: *Indianapolis Speedway, Bad Lands, Wings of the Navy, Kid Nightingale.*
1940: *Tear Gas Squad, King of the Lumberjacks, The Great Profile, Star Dust, Maryland, Tin Pan Alley.*
1941: *Remember the Day, The Great American Broadcast, Weekend in Havana, Sun Valley Serenade.*
1942: *Iceland, Springtime in the Rockies, To the Shores of Tripoli, Footlight Serenade.*
1943: *Hello Frisco Hello.*
1945: *The Dolly Sisters.*
1946: *Wake Up and Dream, The Razor's Edge, Sentimental Journey.*
1947: *Miracle on 34th Street.*
1948: *Larceny, The Saxon Charm.*
1949: *The Crooked Way, El Paso, Captain China.*
1950: *The Eagle and the Hawk, Tripoli.*
1951: *Passage West, Crosswinds.*
1952: *The Blazing Forest, Caribbean, Kansas City Confidential.*
1953: *Raiders of the Seven Seas, The Vanquished, 99 River Street.*
1954: *Rails Into Laramie, Silver Lode.*
1955: *Hell's Island, Santa Fe Passage, The Road to Denver, Tennessee's Partner.*
1956: *Slightly Scarlet, The Boss, Rebel in Town, Hold Back the Night.*
1957: *Bailout at 43,000, Hidden Fear.*
1965: *They Ran for Their Lives* (also directed).
1970: *The Savage Wild.*
1978: *Go West Young Girl* (TV).

Television Series

1957–1959: *The Restless Gun* as Vint Bonner.

Sources

Goldrup, Tom, and Jim Goldrup. *Feature Players: The Stories Behind the Faces Volume #1.* Published privately, 1986.

Lamparski, Richard. *Whatever Became Of? Third Series.* New York: Crown, 1970.

Lyden, Pierce. *The Movie Badmen I Rode with Volume #4.* West Boylston, MA: Mario DeMarco, 1988.

McClelland, Doug. *Forties Film Talk: Oral Histories of Hollywood with 120 Lobby Posters.* Jefferson, NC: McFarland, 1992.

Ragan, David. *Movie Stars of the '40s.* Englewood Cliffs, NJ: Spectrum, 1985.

Willis, John. *Screen World Volume 41.* Obituary. New York: Crown, 1990.

Yoggy, Gary A. *Riding the Video Range: The Rise and Fall of the Western on Television.* Jefferson, NC: McFarland, 1995.

Note

Payne is sometimes credited with an appearance in a film called *Gift of the Nile* in 1968, but no details of this film can be traced.

WILLIAM PHIPPS

Born in St. Francisville, Illinois, in 1922, William Edward Phipps was an actor from childhood. He appeared in several plays in high school and at Eastern Illinois University. Hitchhiking to Hollywood in 1941, he almost immediately landed a role in a play called *Families Are Like That.* When World War II broke out, he was drafted into the navy where he spent three years. Upon his discharge, he enrolled at the Actors' Lab on the G.I. Bill.

He provided the voice of Prince Charming in the Walt Disney cartoon *Cinderella* (1950). During these years he lived at a rooming house for fledgling actresses called the "House of the Seven Garbos." He was part of Charles Laughton's acting class, and Laughton recommended him to producer Arch Oboler for a science fiction film called *Five* (1951). He made a number of science fiction films and Westerns for various producers. He did a considerable amount of television including four regular roles in television series, most of which were short-lived. For the last two seasons of *The Life and Legend of Wyatt Earp* he played flamboyant gunslinger Curley Bill Brocius.

When his career reached something of a plateau because he had outgrown younger character roles but not matured into older character parts, he withdrew from the industry. He exiled himself to Hawaii in 1969 and remained until March 1975, when he returned to Hollywood. During this hiatus he had a couple of commercial fishing boats and did a radio and cable television program. His first role upon his return was as Teddy Roosevelt in the made-for-television movie *Eleanor and Franklin* (1976). In the short-lived television series *Time Express* (1979) he played the train engineer. Although he has been less active in films lately, he has established a solid reputation as a character actor on television and stage. A longtime Hollywood resident, he has done numerous voiceovers and commercials and provided the narration for many productions.

William Phipps Filmography

1947: *Crossfire.*

1948: *The Arizona Ranger, Train to Alcatraz, Desperadoes of Dodge City, Belle Starr's Daughter, Station West, They Live by Night.*

1949: *The Man on the Eiffel Tower, Scene of the Crime.*

1950: *Cinderella* (voice only), *Key to the City, The Outriders, Rider from Tucson, The Vanishing Westerner.*

1951: *The Red Badge of Courage, No Questions Asked, Five.*

1952: *Fort Osage, Rose of Cimarron, Loan Shark, Flat Top.*
1953: *Invaders from Mars, Julius Caesar, The Twonky, Fort Algiers, Northern Patrol, The War of the Worlds, Savage Frontier, Cat Women of the Moon, The Blue Gardenia* (voice only), *Red River Shore, The Boss* (released 1956).
1954: *Francis Joins the Wacs, Riot in Cell Block 11, Executive Suite, Jesse James Vs. the Daltons, Two Guns and a Badge, The Snow Creature.*
1955: *The Indian Fighter, Rage at Dawn, The Violent Men, Smoke Signal, The Far Horizons, The Eternal Sea, Lord of the Jungle.*
1956: *The Man in the Gray Flannel Suit, Away All Boats, The First Texan, Great Day in the Morning, Lust for Life, The Wild Party.*
1957: *Kiss Them for Me, Badlands of Montana, The Brothers Rico, Cavalry Command* (released 1965).
1958: *Escape from Red Rock.*
1959: *The F.B.I. Story.*
1963: *Black Gold, Showdown.*
1964: *The Kidnappers.*
1965: *Harlow* (Carroll Baker version).
1966: *Dead Heat on a Merry-Go-Round, Not with My Wife, You Don't!, Incident at Phantom Hill.*
1967: *Gunfight in Abilene, Valley of Mystery.*
1976: *Eleanor and Franklin* (TV).
1993: *Homeward Bound: The Incredible Journey.*

Television Series

1959–1961: *The Life and Legend of Wyatt Earp* as Curley Bill Brocius.
1976: *Sara* as Claude Barstow.
1979: *Time Express* as Engineer Callahan.
1983–1984: *Boone* as Uncle Link.

Sources

Brooks, Tim. *The Complete Directory to Prime Time TV Stars.* New York: Ballantine Books, 1987.
Picture Show's Who's Who On Screen. London: Amalgamated Press, c. 1956.
Weaver, Tom. *Attack of the Monster Movie Makers: Interviews with 20 Genre Giants.* Jefferson, NC: McFarland, 1994.

JOHN PICKARD

John Pickard was born on a farm at Murfreesboro (near Nashville), Tennessee, in 1913. The farm had been in his family since 1829. During his teen years he lived and worked on the farm. In high school and college he appeared in plays. After winning a Major Bowes Amateur Contest as a singer, he obtained a week's engagement at the Princess Theater in Nashville. From this he won a regular spot as a singer on local radio in Nashville. He saved some money and rode to Hollywood on a bus in the hope of becoming a professional actor.

Instead he became a male model during World War II, appearing on recruitment posters in New York. In 1942 he enlisted in the navy in Washington D.C. and served for three-and-a-half years (primarily in the Welfare and Recreation Program). Once he was honorably discharged, he tried to resume his career as a male model, but there was little call for his services. He obtained a job as a stage manager in *The Diamond Jubilee Show* located in Vancouver, British Columbia.

After this stint, he returned to Hollywood where he appeared in plays at the Pasadena Playhouse and elsewhere. A director saw him act and asked if he would like to appear in motion pictures. This led to his screen debut in *Wake of the Red Witch* (1948), starring John Wayne. He later appeared in the classic Western *The Gunfighter* (1950), which starred Gregory Peck. Pickard played one of the brothers of Richard Jaeckel. This was allegedly his favorite film. He played Vint McCloud in *Little Big Horn* (1951), about the events surrounding the massacre of Custer and his men, which was his favorite role.

This started him out on a cycle in which he appeared predominantly in Westerns with stars such as Charles Starrett and Wild Bill

Elliott. Elliott was the star and a very fast draw in real life, but on one occasion Pickard (playing the bad guy) outdrew Elliott. This earned him the star's enmity for a while. Another classic Western in which Pickard appeared was *True Grit* (1969), shot on beautiful locations in Colorado, in which he played Kim Darby's father (killed by Jeff Corey in the opening scenes).

Pickard racked up an enormous number of Western television credits, particularly multiples of *The Lone Ranger, Gunsmoke* and *Rawhide.* He auditioned twice for the role of Matt Dillon in *Gunsmoke,* but lost to James Arness. His only Western television series lead was as Captain Shank Adams in the syndicated *Boots and Saddles: The Story of the Fifth Cavalry.* The Fifth Cavalry was an experienced regiment that had served during the American Civil War with the Army of the Potomac, and afterwards in Kansas and Nebraska against the Cheyenne and the Sioux. Robert E. Lee once commanded it with the rank of Lieutenant-Colonel, and Buffalo Bill Cody had served with it as Chief Scout.

In the autumn of 1871, the unit was posted to the Arizona Territory with its headquarters at Fort Lowell. The series dealt with the regiment from that time on and was concerned with its directive, namely to break the backbone of Indian resistance in general, and the Apache tribes in particular. Although the stories themselves were fictional, the makers of the series took immense care to present an accurate and intelligent portrait of the period in terms of Apache customs and appropriate cavalry dress. The half-hour black and white series was shot on breathtakingly beautiful locations at Kanab, Utah, because of the presence of a near-century-old fort which was a replica of the one at Fort Lowell.

Pickard himself loved the scenery, shot several movies and television episodes there, and became a frequent visitor. He made numerous personal appearances in connection with the series. It lasted only 39 episodes despite frequently ranking in the Top Ten most popular syndicated series. It was produced by California National Productions. Although it was set to be renewed, it was abruptly canceled. Pickard was disappointed and attributed its demise to dirty politics within the television industry.

He later had a regular role in another even more short-lived series, *Gunslinger,* in which he played a veteran army officer attached to the fort where Cord (Tony Young) receives his assignments. Young said about Pickard, "I never saw him angry. He seemed to be at ease with life. A very genuine warm guy. He was very helpful to me because I was pretty green. We were under tremendous pressure ... 12–14 hour days were not uncommon. It took the cooperation of everybody and John was just terrific."

Pickard died in a freak accident on the farm at Murfreesboro, Tennessee, on August 4, 1993. He was killed as he fell and broke his neck when a 1,300 pound bull knocked him down. Sheriff's authorities said the 80-year-old Pickard was killed as he was crossing a field to open a gate so the animals could have access to a spring. His friend Gene Evans recalled of him, "He was a straight-up guy and there aren't many straight-up guys in that business that we could afford to lose one. He could play anything—good guys, bad guys. He was really a good actor ... much better than he ever got the chance to show." He was survived by his wife, Ann McLaurine, and a son.

John Pickard Filmography

1948: *Wake of the Red Witch.*
1949: *Once More My Darling, City Across the River.*
1950: *Bright Leaf, The Gunfighter, Stage to Tucson, David Harding—Counterspy, Twilight in the Sierras, Prisoners in Petticoats, California Passage.*
1951: *The Desert Fox, Three Guys Named Mike, Little Big Horn, Snake River Desperadoes, Government Agents Vs. Phantom Legion* (serial), *Oh! Susanna.*
1952: *Bandits of Corsica, Willie and Joe Back at the Front, Red Ball Express, Bugles in the Afternoon, The Lawless Breed, Hellgate, Trail Guide, Androcles and the Lion, Hoodlum Empire.*
1953: *Arrowhead, The Charge at Feather River, The Fighting Lawman, Above and Beyond, Flight to Tangier, Story of Three Loves.*
1954: *Human Desire, Bitter Creek, Two Guns and a Badge, Return from the Sea, Black Horse Canyon, Massacre Canyon, Arrow in the Dust, Rose Marie.*
1955: *The McConnell Story, Shotgun, Francis Joins the Navy, Flame of the Islands, Away All*

Boats, At Gunpoint, Seven Angry Men, Seminole Uprising, Fort Yuma, To Hell and Back.
1956: *Tension at Table Rock, The Great Locomotive Chase, Walk the Proud Land, Kentucky Rifle, The Lone Ranger, Crime Against Joe, The Broken Star, The Black Whip, Friendly Persuasion; A Strange Adventure.*
1957: *The Oklahoman, Ride a Violent Mile, Badlands of Dakota, War Drums, Copper Sky, Outlaw's Son.*
1960: *Cimarron.*
1961: *Gun Street.*
1963: *A Gathering of Eagles.*
1967: *Hondo and the Apaches* (TV).
1969: *True Grit, Charro!*
1970: *Chisum.*
1973: *Shootout in a One Dog Town* (TV).
1974: *Act of Vengeance.*
1976: *Mayday at 40,000 Feet* (TV).
1981: *Legend of the Lone Ranger.*

Television Series

1957–1958: *Boots and Saddles: The Story of the Fifth Cavalry* as Captain Shank Adams.
1961: *Gunslinger* as Sgt. Major Murdock.

Sources

DeMarco, Mario. *Donald "Red" Barry: The Kid from Texas.* West Boylston, MA: Mario DeMarco, 1992.
Goldrup, Jim, and Tom Goldrup. *Feature Players: The Stories Behind the Faces Volume #1.* Published privately, 1986.
Magers, Boyd. "Empty Saddles." *Western Clippings* magazine, September 1993.
Speed, F. Maurice. *The Western Film and Television Annual.* London: MacDonald, 1959.

DICK POWELL

The path of Dick Powell from crooner to business tycoon was a long and difficult one. He had to fight hard to escape from typecasting, but eventually directors and producers realized that he could do more than sing; and the result was a series of really tough roles in the *film noir* cycle of the 1940s. On television he made a big success as a star-producer-director in the popular anthology series *Four Star Playhouse, Zane Grey Theater* and *The Dick Powell Show.* On top of this, Powell was the business brains of the company which made the series.

Richard Ewell Powell was born on November 14, 1904, in Mountain View, Arkansas, the son of Ewing Powell and Sally Thompson. His father was a machinist, but he inherited his musical talent from his mother. He had one older brother called Howard and one younger brother called Luther. In 1914 he moved with his family to Little Rock, Arkansas, where he grew up. He was a boy soprano who performed in many local churches and at local events.

While attending Little Rock College, he organized a dance band called the Peter Pan. He worked his way through college by doing odd jobs such as soda jerk and by accepting any musical engagements which came his way. After college he worked for 18 months for the telephone company collecting coins from pay phones. In September 1925, he received an offer to join the Royal Peacocks, a touring dance band based in Louisville, Kentucky. In 1926 the group disbanded, leaving Powell stranded in Anderson, Indiana. By taking an intensive course, he became a banjo player with the Charlie Davis Orchestra in Indianapolis.

In 1927 he quit and went to work as a solo act, singing in the Midwest, but this flopped and he was forced to rejoin the Charlie Davis Orchestra (now playing at the major movie houses). Powell sensed that being master of ceremonies for the live acts that preceded the main pictures might put him on the road to fame and fortune. From Indianapolis he moved to the Enright Theater in Pittsburgh and later to the prestigious Stanley Theater. While there he began singing on the radio and making records.

The Stanley Theater was one of a chain of theaters owned by Warner Bros. In late 1931 he was sent to New York to test for a film called

Dick Powell in *Zane Grey Theater.*

Crooner. He flunked the test, thereby losing the role, but was still signed to a contract by Warner Bros. The salary was only half of what he had been earning, and with the Depression it kept on reducing, but he stayed with them because he had faith in movie musicals. He had constant battles over salary and later on over the quality of his material. Initially he did little work for Warner Bros., but his appearance in the classic backstage musical *42nd Street* (1933) made him a sensation. He became a fixture of their musicals of the period, many of them featuring unique songs and dances which were created by choreographer Busby Berkeley. With the exception of *Convention City* (1933), Powell sang in every Warner Bros. picture in which he appeared. Throughout the 1930s he appeared in an average of four films a year, had a successful weekly radio show and recorded songs from his films.

Desperate to escape the rut of typecasting as the pleasant, juvenile singing lead in these musicals, he severed his connections with Warner Bros. at the end of 1938. He believed that he was overworked and underpaid and that these musicals had run their course. In this he possibly made an error of judgment because at least a year elapsed before he appeared in another film. In the meantime he devoted his considerable talent and energies to his business interests, primarily real estate. By 1939 his income derived from these was greater than his earnings from show business.

He resumed his film career when Preston Sturges offered him the leading role in a satire called *Christmas in July* (1940). This was a cult hit which resulted in Paramount signing him to a contract. Although some of the films he made for them were amusing, he found the contract with them as restrictive as the Warner Bros. one in terms of material. He eventually went on suspension when he was assigned a lightweight film called *Bring on the Girls.* Instead, he campaigned to win the lead of the crooked insurance agent in *Double Indemnity* but lost out to Fred MacMurray, which made him very bitter. A chance encounter in an elevator with Frank Freeman, the head of production at Paramount, led to the termination of his contract.

He appeared in a fantasy comedy called *It Happened Tomorrow* (1944), splendidly directed by Rene Clair, which became a cult classic, but elsewhere the pickings were lean. In May 1944, he went to see Charles Koerner, the head of production at RKO, and begged him for a more substantial role. Koerner gave him the script of *Farewell My Lovely,* a novel by Raymond Chandler. Powell read the script and agreed to do it the same day. Director Edward Dmytryk was skeptical because he considered Powell over the hill with a very limited image, but Powell put on his most persuasive act and Dmytryk took a chance on him. The film was retitled *Murder My Sweet* (1944) to avoid confusion with Powell's previous musicals. In it he played the cynical private eye Philip Marlowe. It was a critical and commercial success and made his reputation all over again.

Tough guy roles became his forte in *film noir* which revealed the dark side of the American way of life. Powell starred in some of the best of the genre. His sole bona fide Western film was called *Station West* (1948), which emerged as a *film noir* on the range. It was adapted from a novel by Luke Short, an author noted for his dramatic and violent plots. Powell starred as Haven, an undercover U.S. Army Intelligence Officer sent to investigate the murder of two soldiers while guarding a ship ment of gold. This brought him into contact with an assortment of bizarre characters, notably beautiful female saloon owner and chanteuse Charlie (Jane Greer). The film was notable for its snappy dialogue, all contributed by screenwriter Frank Fenton, and its brutal fistfight between Haven and Mick (played by the hulking Guinn "Big Boy" Williams). By the early 1950s, this cycle had also wound down and Powell was looking for new horizons. His final feature was *Susan Slept Here* (1954), his worst film in years and not greatly different from the type of picture he had fled from at Warner Bros. and Paramount.

Powell became a producer and director. This step was closely linked to the eccentric multimillionaire Howard Hughes, who acquired RKO in 1948. When producer Edmund Grainger suggested that Powell should be the director of a thriller called *Split Second* (1953), Hughes readily agreed. Powell subsequently went on to produce and direct four other films. None were particularly successful, but the one which is best remembered was an epic called *The Conqueror* (1956). The subject was Genghis Khan (John Wayne), the 12th century Mongol warlord who rose to power after defeating the Tartars in the Gobi Desert. It was shot on location in southwest Utah near the city of St. George. The location proved to be unfortunate because it was less than 200 miles from the atomic testing grounds of Yucca Flats. In the years that followed there has been conjecture that the remarkably high degree of cancer-related deaths among the cast and crew (including Powell and John Wayne) could be attributed to this. A more logical explanation was provided by Pilar Wayne in her book, *John Wayne: My Life with the Duke,* when she wrote that all of them were chain smokers. There was also talk that Dick Powell might take over as head of production at RKO, but this idea came to nothing when Howard Hughes sold the studio in 1955.

Powell moved into television in a big way when he formed Four Star Television in 1952. Unlike many movie stars who refused to accept television, he embraced it. His partners were David Niven and Charles Boyer, but Powell was the financial genius behind the operation. It started with *Four Star Playhouse,* a weekly half-hour anthology series which made its debut on CBS on September 25, 1952. Four Star was really a three star company, but Powell justified this by explaining that the fourth star would always be a guest. There were 129 episodes of this series; Powell appeared in 31 of them. The last episode was aired on July 26, 1956. It was called "Success Story" and starred Powell.

The next Four Star series in which Powell was producer, host and occasional star and director was *Dick Powell's Zane Grey Theater.* He claimed that Grey was his favorite author and that he had read all of Grey's novels and short stories. He obtained the rights to all the stories with the provision that scripts could be devised from characters and incidents in them. Of all the headaches he had, the biggest was to find the right stories. Grey wrote an enormous number of Western tales, but not all were suitable for television. One of the problems was that there was often too much in a book to squeeze into 30 minutes of visual television time. "If you have ever tried to compress a novel into half an hour on television, you'll know what I mean," Powell said. He added, "We cannot depend on the script alone, it must be complemented by the finest of actors and actresses." He was able to obtain the services of stars who otherwise disdained television.

Most viewers agreed that Powell did extremely well. The series offered a high level of quality drama. It captured the exciting color and drama of life on the American frontier. It presented credible characters, realistic drama, authentic settings and mature, adult themes. After a while the connection with the original Grey material became more tenuous, but Powell stressed that the shows were always in the spirit of Zane Grey. Each episode began with Powell in Western garb introducing the story by informing the audience of some aspect of Western folklore which related to the yarn about to unfold. This CBS series made its debut on October 5, 1956. Powell starred two weeks later in "The Long Road Home." Over the next five seasons he starred in 13 other episodes, the last of which was "The Silent Sentry," shown on February 16, 1961. The anthology series lasted for 147 episodes, and was last broadcast on May 18, 1961.

Powell liked Westerns and believed that virtually any kind of story could be adapted to a Western setting. Four Star Television created seven other Western series: *Trackdown, Wanted*

—*Dead or Alive, The Rifleman, Johnny Ringo, Black Saddle, Law of the Plainsman* and *The Westerner.* Powell's final personal television venture was NBC's *The Dick Powell Show,* an anthology of original stories; he hosted and also starred in at least one out of every four episodes. The first season ran to 30 episodes of which Powell starred in six. The first episode ("Who Killed Julia Greer?") was the best-remembered because Powell starred as Amos Burke, a millionaire police captain, a character who became very popular in a later television series, *Burke's Law,* starring Gene Barry.

The second season of *The Dick Powell Show* opened on September 25, 1962, with "Special Assignment" starring Powell. On November 20, 1962, he starred in "In Search of a Son" and on December 11 in "The Court Martial of Captain Wycliff," which was his final appearance as an actor. It was completed two months before his death, but by this time he was stricken with cancer. His final broadcast as host was on January 1, 1963, the day before he died. In deference to his family, the introductions he had already filmed for future telecasts were omitted and a succession of guest stars substituted as hosts for the remaining 16 episodes. The title of the series was also changed to *The Dick Powell Theater.*

In the summer of 1962, after returning from a vacation, he complained of fatigue and back pains. When he went to his doctor, tests confirmed that he had cancer of the lymph glands. In November he resigned as Chairman of Four Star Television and became Chairman of the Board. As the cancer spread throughout his body, he was moved into an apartment on Wilshire Boulevard where he received close friends. He had a perfectly normal Christmas, but on January 2, 1963, with his head cradled against his wife June Allyson's shoulder, he said, "I'm sorry. Oh, I'm so sorry," and died at age 58. His estate ran into millions. He was awarded a posthumous Emmy (a Trustees' Award) "in grateful memory of his conspicuous contribution to and reflections of credit upon the industry as an actor, director, producer and executive."

He married Mildred Maund in 1925, but they divorced in 1927 because she did not share his show business ambitions. On September 19, 1936, aboard the cruise ship *San Paula* moored in the harbor of San Pedro, California, he wed Joan Blondell, a frequent costar. He adopted her son Norman (born November 2, 1934) by a previous marriage. On July 1, 1938, they had a daughter named Ellen who was born in Los Angeles. The divorce hearing in Los Angeles on July 14, 1944, took four minutes. She divorced him because his intense devotion to business took priority over family life. He then wed June Allyson, an actress and longtime fan, whom he met on the set of *Meet the People.* They wed on August 19, 1945, at the Los Angeles home of composer Johnny Green. Louis B. Mayer gave the bride away. They adopted a two-month-old daughter named Pamela on August 10, 1948, and had a son Richard, Jr., born on Christmas Eve, 1950. On March 31, 1961, Allyson won a $2,500,000 divorce settlement and custody of their children. The decree, which was granted in Los Angeles, would have become final in one year. Although Dick Powell moved out, he spent as much time with his wife as before and consequently they were reconciled.

Dick Powell Filmography

1931: *Street Scene.*
1932: *Big City Blues* (voice only), *Blessed Event, Too Busy to Work.*
1933: *The King's Vacation, 42nd Street, Gold Diggers of 1933, Footlight Parade, College Coach, Convention City.*
1934: *Wonder Bar, 20 Million Sweethearts, Dames, Happiness Ahead, Flirtation Walk.*
1935: *Gold Diggers of 1935, Broadway Gondolier, Page Miss Glory, A Midsummer Night's Dream, Shipmates Forever, Thanks a Million.*
1936: *Colleen, Hearts Divided, Stage Struck, Gold Diggers of 1937.*
1937: *On the Avenue, Singing Marine, Varsity Show.*
1938: *Hollywood Hotel, Cowboy from Brooklyn, Hard to Get, Going Places.*
1939: *Naughty But Nice.*
1940: *Christmas in July, I Want a Divorce.*
1941: *Model Wife, Abbott and Costello in the Navy.*
1943: *Star Spangled Rhythm, Happy Go Lucky, True to Life, Riding High.*
1944: *It Happened Tomorrow, Murder My Sweet, Meet the People.*
1945: *Cornered.*
1947: *Johnny O'Clock.*

1948: *To the Ends of the Earth, The Pitfall, Station West, Rogues' Regiment.*
1949: *Mrs. Mike.*
1950: *The Reformer and the Redhead, Right Cross.*
1951: *Cry Danger, The Tall Target, You Never Can Tell, Callaway Went Thataway* (cameo).
1953: *The Bad and the Beautiful.*
1954: *Susan Slept Here.*

As Director Only

1953: *Split Second.*
1956: *The Conqueror, You Can't Run Away from It.*
1957: *The Enemy Below.*
1958: *The Hunters.*

Television Series

1952–1956: *Four Star Playhouse.*
1956–1961: *Zane Grey Theater.*
1961–1963: *The Dick Powell Show.*

Sources

Houseman, Victoria. *Made in Heaven.* Chicago, IL: Bonus, 1991.
Shipman, David. *The Great Movie Stars: The Golden Years.* London: Hamlyn, 1970.
Speed, F. Maurice. *The Western Film and TV Annual.* London: MacDonald, 1958.
Thomas, Tony. *The Dick Powell Story.* Burbank, CA: Riverwood Press, 1993.

JUDSON PRATT

Born in 1916, this character actor played Billy Kincaid in the syndicated Western series *Union Pacific.* He was the "right-hand" man of Bart McClelland, Executive Operations Manager. Kincaid was an ex–U.S. Army Cavalry Sergeant Major, so it was small wonder that he was tough and such a help to his boss. The Screen Actors Guild no longer carries a listing for this actor, and at last report he was living in retirement in Northridge, California.

Judson Pratt Filmography

1953: *I Confess.*
1956: *Somebody Up There Likes Me, Toy Tiger, Outside the Law, Four Girls in Town, The Great American Pastime.*
1957: *Man Afraid.*
1958: *Flood Tide, Monster on the Campus.*
1959: *The Horse Soldiers.*
1960: *The Rise and Fall of Legs Diamond, Sgt. Rutledge.*
1961: *The Crimebusters.*
1962: *Kid Galahad, A Public Affair.*
1963: *The Ugly American.*
1964: *A Distant Trumpet, Cheyenne Autumn.*
1971: *The Barefoot Executive.*
1976: *Futureworld, Vigilante Force.*

Television Series

1957–1958: *Union Pacific* as Billy Kincaid.

Sources

Speed, F. Maurice. *The Western Film and TV Annual.* London: MacDonald, 1960.

Judson Pratt in *Union Pacific.*

WAYDE PRESTON

There was a standing joke between strapping, six-foot-four Western star Wayde Preston and his double, Bill Monaghan, when Preston was starring as Christopher Colt in the successful Warner Bros. Western series *Colt .45* back in the 1950s. When Preston came on the set in the morning, he would say, "Howdy, Monaghan." "Howdy, Wayde," came the reply. "How would you like to be the star of a series, Monaghan?" "No, thanks. I couldn't afford the cut in salary, Wayde." This was Preston's recollection of the series in which he made his name.

Wayde Preston was an actor who, given the right opportunities and the correct management, could have hit the jackpot. He did not play the Hollywood game at all well, was blacklisted, and squandered his talent in a succession of inferior films shot in Europe. Once he had had a taste of stardom, however, he found it a heady brew and was convinced that the world owed him a living. It was a wasted life. Unlike many dandies who become Western stars, however, he was the genuine article. He was actually born and raised on a ranch.

Wayde Preston was born William Erskine Strange in Steamboat Springs, Colorado, on September 10, 1929. He was the adopted son of a high school teacher and had two sisters with whom he was not close. He grew up on horseback on a ranch in Laramie, Wyoming. "Ranching," he recalled, "is not glamorous, just hard work." After World War II his family moved back to town. He entered the University of Wyoming in 1947 where he graduated with a degree in pharmacy in 1950. He played bass fiddle and vibraharp with a jazz quartet and began to develop his acting talent by appearing in school plays. Subsequently he was drafted and spent three years in the army, including one-and-a-half years in Korea as a captain and pilot flying artillery planes. After being honorably discharged, he did a stint in a guided missile plant as an electronics technician and became a commercial pilot for Trans World Airlines.

When asked how he became an actor, he recalled, "Partly by chance. I went to parties with some pilots who were living out in Malibu. There were movie people at those parties. One thing led to another. I was signed by Charlie Feldman, who was head of Famous Artists Agency." He spent six months under contract to 20th Century–Fox and then seven years under contract to Warner Bros. He was given a tryout in an episode of *Cheyenne* which proved successful, so he was given the lead in his own Western series.

Colt .45 debuted on ABC on October 18, 1957. It was a half-hour black and white show in which Preston starred as Christopher Colt, a U.S. federal agent working undercover as a gun salesman to rid the West of desperadoes. It was inspired by the very successful Warner Bros. film of the same name starring Randolph Scott. Preston, who was given his new name by the Warner Bros. publicity department, found Warner Bros. television a sweat shop and had bitter memories of his time there.

He recalled, "We did 39 shows a year. It was all done on the Warners' back lot. I did 16 to 18 hours a day, five days a week. That's 40 to 50 setups a day. For the first few years, I had no stuntman. I did all my own stunts. I was the only star of the show. That meant I had to be in virtually every scene. Weekends I would take off on a twin-deck city tour to Detroit, Baltimore, Chicago or Boston and do local television shows to publicize the series. The pace was terrible. I could not work like that now." He even turned up playing Christopher Colt on episodes of other Warner Bros. television series such as *Sugarfoot*. "Warners hated to see any of us sitting around idle. I used to wish I could get to appear in a feature film because I needed a vacation!"

Did he make much money out of the series? "Not a cent. I couldn't afford to be a star. There were no residuals. It was a total loss." According to recently released statistics, he was put under contract for $200 a week and earned a couple of $50 raises. The most he ever earned was $750 a week after four years. It was a pitifully low salary even for television (which at that time was nowhere near as lucrative as films). Nevertheless, *Colt .45* was a big hit. As the actor said, "If they had kept their people happier, those shows would still be running."

At the time when he was still on negotiating terms with Warner Bros., he guest starred in a 1959 *Maverick* episode called "The Saga of Waco Williams" with James Garner. Preston played Waco, and years later this character provided the basis for a whiter than white P.I. in *The Rockford Files* played by Tom Selleck. This was probably Preston's best acting job and was the highest rated episode of the series. Warners were so pleased with his work that they intended to close down *Colt .45* and place him in an hour-length series as this character. There were, however, a series of well-documented disputes over salary, use of stuntmen, clothes and sponsorship. After one walkout he was temporarily replaced without explanation by cousin Sam Colt, Jr., played by Donald May. Even though they appear together in one scene of one episode, it was faked and the two actors never actually met.

Wayde Preston in *Colt .45*.

Wayde Preston married actress Carol Ohmart in late 1956. The marriage lasted about six years and left him extremely bitter about both marriage and children. The particular issue which brought matters to a head with the studio was when he complained about being unable to make ends meet because he was now a married man. Warners refused to increase his salary, but thinking it would increase their hold over him, gave him a loan. They neglected, however, to have him sign a note until the following day, when he denied the transaction ever took place. Despite threats, he never did pay them back. To some employees this episode made him a hero, but it also led to him being blacklisted. Eventually he quit for good in 1960. There is a splendidly ironic moment in the "Hadley's Hunters" episode of *Maverick* in 1960 which featured all the Warners' Western stars in cameo except Wayde Preston. Instead, the camera flashes on the gun and hat of Christopher Colt, which are shown hanging on a peg. Preston would fly his airplane overhead and buzz the sets when Warners were shooting outdoors. The noise forced them to cease filming temporarily.

He sat out the remainder of his Warner Bros. contract and then headed for Europe. "I went to Rome, liked it and stayed for ten years. I traveled all over Europe and Africa working." He made an estimated 42 movies costarring in spaghetti Westerns, war films and James Bond-type spy spoofs. He was often the only member of the cast who spoke English and the films were dubbed. Later he became fluent in Italian. "Sometimes the entire plot was changed afterwards to fit the lips of the actors saying the dialogue," he laughs. He achieved his ambition of being a legitimate movie star and enjoyed a very affluent lifestyle with a villa and servants. He traveled to London where he fraternized with other actors who frequented the swank Colony Club, which was being fronted by the famous American tough guy actor George Raft. He was also a close friend of Guy Elmes, a successful scriptwriter for the J. Arthur Rank Organization. His marriage long over, Preston indulged in his other hobby of pursuing women, of whom there were a superabundance in the European film industry in those days.

It was a period of his life which he very much enjoyed. Why did it end? "The Italian unions decided that we were taking work away from Italian actors and decreed no more Americans! I didn't want to come back, but it was too expensive to live there without working," was his story at the time. Later he admitted that this was not the whole story. He had been stricken with cancer and went to America to a veterans' hospital for an operation because he trusted the doctors there. Although the operation was a success, he admitted that he felt like a human timebomb afterwards because he knew the cancer would recur and kill him. He wanted to return to Europe, but never had enough money again.

He tried to return to acting, but one hurdle which he had to overcome was that while any of his films were big hits in Europe, few were given much exposure Stateside. He survived on unemployment benefits, handouts from friends and occasional bit roles in series like *Starsky and Hutch* and *The Hardy Boys.* Some accounts of his life indicate that he was a charter pilot between America and Australia, but he never visited Australia. There were also reports that he owned land and property in California and Nevada, but this is fiction. He rented one room from a landlady in a rundown section of Los Angeles.

Later he doubled for Charlton Heston on *The Colbys* and appeared in the film *Captain America* (1989) from the famous comic strip. He played the husband of Captain America's ex-girlfriend. Captain America was frozen for decades. When he was revived, his girlfriend had aged and was now married to Wayde's character. He had high hopes for that film, believing that he was on the verge of a whole new career as a character actor, but it did not materialize. Instead, in 1989 he relocated to Lovelock, Nevada, where he died virtually destitute on February 6, 1992, of cancer. The 62-year-old actor was buried in a quiet private service in that state.

Wayde Preston Filmography

1963: *The Man on the Spying Trapeze.*
1968: *A Long Ride from Hell, Anzio.*
1969: *Today It's Me Tomorrow You!*
1970: *A Man Called Sledge.*
1989: *Captain America.*

Television Series

1957–1960: *Colt .45* as Christopher Colt.

Sources

Interview with Wayde Preston, 1988.
Jarvis, Everett G. *Final Curtain: Deaths of Noted Film and TV Personalities.* New York: Citadel Press, 1995.

Note

These are the only Preston films which were ever shown outside of Europe.

DOROTHY PROVINE

Michelle Dorothy Provine was born in Deadwood, South Dakota, on January 20, 1937, while her parents were visiting her mother's family. Her early years were spent in San Francisco before the family relocated to Seattle, where she attended Lincoln High School. She was acting and appearing in musicals in school which enabled her to win a four-year scholarship to the University of Washington. While there she starred in 35 shows and did summer musicals such as *South Pacific* at Seattle Equity Musical Theater. There was also a popular local television show in which she starred daily.

Immediately after graduating from college in 1957, she headed for Hollywood where in rapid succession she acquired a reputable agent and some work, making her screen debut in 1958. In her first 15 months in Hollywood, she is reckoned to have guest starred on television 31 times. Warner Bros. signed her because they wanted her for the female lead in *The Alaskans,* but she declined initially because she did not want to do a series. The studio improved the offer and promised a series with the same comedy hijinks as *Maverick,* so she accepted.

She played Rocky Shaw, chanteuse of various saloons and one of three soldiers of fortune looking for easy pickings in the Klondike and

Dorothy Provine as she appeared in *The Alaskans.*

Yukon territories around the turn of the century. Her initial joy turned to dismay when she found the quality of the scripts was poor and the series was not of the caliber originally described to her. The only compensation was the presence of Roger Moore, an actor with whom she felt great rapport. According to Hollywood folklore, she had a romantic relationship with him. The series lasted only a single season.

With the demise of *The Alaskans* she played another female lead as flapper Pinky Pinkham in *The Roaring Twenties,* which attempted to capture the spirit of the zesty Warner Bros. crime melodramas of a previous era. It was generally felt that her singing and dancing was the best element of the series and the one which brought it closest to its goal. Although this series lasted longer than her previous one, it only gave her a brief taste of stardom. She also seemed dogged by ill luck in other ways. She was set to make her London debut in a spectacular stage musical which had to be postponed when she put out her back while working on a film. When she recovered, a sudden attack of laryngitis in London prevented her from appearing in that city. She made a memorable contribution to other Warner Bros. series such as *77 Sunset Strip* as a guest star.

Unlike many other Warner contract artists, she had a moderately successful career in films. She continued to be active until 1967, after which her output greatly diminished. One of her last recorded credits was "The Big Walk" episode of *Police Story* in 1973. In 1967 she married the British director Robert Day, by whom she has a son born in 1970. Since 1981 they have resided on Bainbridge Island, Washington State, where the actress has indicated that she has no desire to perform again, adding that she is very happy in domestic anonymity. Unlike many of the brash extroverts she played on screen, in real life Miss Provine is reported to be reserved and sensitive.

Dorothy Provine Filmography

1958: *The Bonnie Parker Story, Live Fast Die Young.*
1959: *Riot in Juvenile Prison, The 30 Foot Bride of Candy Rock.*
1963: *It's a Mad Mad Mad Mad World, Wall of Noise.*
1964: *Good Neighbor Sam.*
1965: *That Darn Cat!, The Great Race, One Spy Too Many* (TV).
1966: *Kiss the Girls and Make Them Die.*
1967: *Who's Minding the Mint?, Never a Dull Moment.*
1968: *The Sound of Anger* (TV).

Television Series

1959–1960: *The Alaskans* as Rocky Shaw.
1960–1962: *The Roaring Twenties* as Pinky Pinkham.

Sources

ATV Television Show Book. London: Purnell, 1962.
Ragan, David. *Who's Who in Hollywood.* New York: Facts on File, 1992.
Woolley, Lynn, Robert W. Malsbary, and Robert G. Strange, Jr. *Warner Bros. Television.* Jefferson, NC: McFarland, 1985.

DENVER PYLE

Denver Pyle was born in Bethune, Colorado, on May 11, 1920, the son of a homesteader. He was named after the capital of the state in which he was born. He has one older brother named Willie and an older sister named Skippy. He attended school in Bethune and later in Boulder, Colorado. As a child he did odd jobs. He attended the University of Colorado for two years before dropping out to pursue a career as a drummer in a dance band. When he decided that he did not wish to do this either, he drifted around, eventually landing in the oil fields of Texas and Oklahoma. He had been working in a refinery for about 18 months when on impulse he decided to head for Hollywood to look up his brother and sister who were working there.

His stay was short-lived because he returned to Boulder, obtained some more education and then went back to Hollywood where his sister helped him to obtain a job as a page boy at NBC. When World War II broke out, he worked at Lockheed by night. Later he joined the Merchant Marines and through this served in the navy during the war. When it was over, he married and went back to work at Lockheed. An actor friend of his wife suggested that he try out for a play. He landed the part and did so well with it that he studied acting with various drama teachers, notably Maria Ouspenskaya.

She suggested he join the American Repertory Theater as an actor and set builder. He was involved in much little theater activity for six years. To supplement his meager earnings he worked as a waiter and as a hearing aid and insurance salesman. While appearing in *Ring Around Elizabeth* at the Glendale Center Theater, he was seen by director Henry Levin who cast him in two films, *The Guilt of Janet Ames* (1947) and *The Man from Colorado* (1948).

Although he became established as a character actor, it was only in the mid–1950s that he was able to derive all of his income from acting and quit his various other jobs. He has had several regular or semi-regular roles on television, one of the earliest being as outlaw Ben Thompson for the first season of *The Life and Legend of Wyatt Earp.* Since the mid-1950s, he has appeared in numerous episodes of various television series in an enormous variety of different roles. Unlike many actors he is very fond of working in the television medium, although he considers that his best opportunity came in the movie *Bonnie and Clyde* (1967) of which he has said, "I played the Texas Ranger Frank Hamer like a B Western sheriff." In later years his most familiar role was as Uncle Jesse in the television series *The Dukes of Hazard.*

Denver Pyle Filmography

1947: *The Guilt of Janet Ames, Devil Ship, Where the North Begins.*

1948: *The Man from Colorado, Train to Alcatraz, Marshal of Amarillo.*

1949: *Captain China, Hellfire, Flame of Youth, Streets of San Francisco, Too Late for Tears, Red Canyon.*

1950: *Dynamite Pass, Federal Agent at Large, The Flying Saucer, Singing Guns, Customs Agent, The Old Frontier, Jet Pilot* (released 1957).

1951: *Rough Riders of Durango, Million Dollar Pursuit, Hills of Utah.*

1952: *Oklahoma Annie, Desert Passage, The Lusty Men, Fargo, The Man from the Black Hills, The Maverick.*

1953: *Gunsmoke, Texas Bad Man, Vigilante Terror, Canyon Ambush, Rebel City, Topeka, Goldtown Ghost Riders, A Perilous Journey.*

1954: *The Boy from Oklahoma, Drum Beat, Ride Clear of Diablo, Johnny Guitar, The Forty-Niners.*

1955: *To Hell and Back, Rage at Dawn, Run for Cover, Ten Wanted Men, Top Gun.*

1956: *Please Murder Me, I Killed Wild Bill Hickok, The Naked Hills, 7th Cavalry, Yaqui Drums.*

1957: *The Lonely Man, Gun Duel in Durango, Destination 60,000, Domino Kid.*

1958: *The Left Handed Gun, Fort Massacre, The Party Crashers, China Doll, A Good Day for a Hanging.*

1959: *The Horse Soldiers, King of the Wild Stallions, Cast a Long Shadow.*

1960: *The Alamo, Home from the Hill.*

1962: *Bearheart, Geronimo, The Man Who Shot Liberty Valance.*

1963: *Mail Order Bride.*
1964: *Cheyenne Autumn.*
1965: *The Rounders, Mara of the Wilderness, Shenandoah, The Great Race.*
1966: *Gunpoint, Incident at Phantom Hill.*
1967: *Welcome to Hard Times, Bonnie and Clyde.*
1968: *Bandolero!, 5 Card Stud.*
1971: *Something Big.*
1972: *Who Fears the Devil (*a.k.a. *Legend Of Hillbilly John).*
1973: *Hitched* (TV), *Cahill United States Marshal.*
1974: *Sidekicks* (TV), *Murder or Mercy* (TV), *The Life and Times of Grizzly Adams, Escape to Witch Mountain.*
1975: *Winterhawk, Death Amongst Friends* (TV).
1976: *Buffalo Bill and the Indians, or Sitting Bull's History Lesson; Hawmps; Welcome to LA; Guardian of the Wilderness; The Adventures of Frontier Fremont.*
1978: *Return from Witch Mountain.*
1981: *Legend of the Wild.*
1987: *Discovery Bay.*
1994: *Maverick, Father and Scout* (TV).

Television Series

1955–1956: *The Life and Legend of Wyatt Earp* as Ben Thompson.
1957: *Code 3* as Sgt. Murchison.
1965–1966: *Tammy* as Grandpa Tarleton.
1968–1970: *The Doris Day Show* as Buck Webb.
1977–1978: *The Life and Times of Grizzly Adams* as Mad Jack.
1979–1985: *The Dukes of Hazzard* as Uncle Jesse Duke.

Sources

Eleventh Annual Golden Boot Awards program. August 21, 1993.
Goldrup, Tom, and Jim Goldrup. *Feature Players: The Stories Behind The Faces Volume #1.* Published privately, 1986.
McClure, Arthur F., and Ken D. Jones. *Heroes, Heavies and Sagebrush.* South Brunswick and New York: Barnes, 1972.
Quinlan, David. *Illustrated Directory of Film Character Actors.* London: Batsford, 1995.

BILL QUINN

Bill Quinn was born in New York City on May 6, 1912, the son of a supervisor in the copying department of the United States Shipping Board. His mother was a silent screen bit player and Broadway chorine. Through this connection he started out as a child, making his acting debut in vaudeville in New York in 1917. He was also active in silent movies shot in New York in the teens. His Broadway debut came in 1918 in *Daddies,* which starred Jeanne Eagels. He joined stock companies and toured with them during the 1920s.

During the depths of the Depression in 1933 he was persuaded by an old friend to enter the medium of radio. He played on radio shows from New York until the industry declined in the late 1950s, when he ventured to Hollywood. It is estimated that during this time he made in excess of 6,000 broadcasts on every conceivable program. After arriving in Hollywood he appeared as the bartender on *The Rifleman* throughout the duration of the series. His best-known television role in later years was as Mr. Van Ranseleer in *All in the Family.* His best-known film appearance was as McCoy's father in *Star Trek V: The Final Frontier* (1989).

Bill Quinn married in 1942 and had three daughters, one of whom is married to comedian Bob Newhart (whom Quinn supported in roles on television).

Quinn died in Camarillo, California, after a long illness, on April 29, 1994, at age 81.

Bill Quinn Filmography

1959: *The Flying Fontaines, The Last Angry Man.*
1960: *From the Terrace, The Mountain Road.*
1961: *The Young Savages, Cry for Happy, Ada.*

Portrait of Bill Quinn, who appeared in *The Rifleman.*

1962: *Five Finger Exercise, Advise and Consent.*
1963: *The Birds.*
1964: *FBI Code 98.*
1965: *Dark Intruder, When the Boys Meet the Girls.*
1967: *The Reluctant Astronaut.*
1969: *The Pigeon* (TV), *Set This Town on Fire* (TV), *Pendulum.*
1970: *Love Is a Funny Thing, The Challenge* (TV).
1971: *How to Frame a Figg, Ace Eli and Rodger of the Skies, The Sheriff* (TV), *Dead Men Tell No Tales* (TV), *Incident in San Francisco* (TV).
1972: *The Mad Bomber.*
1973: *The Magician* (TV), *Savages* (TV), *Satan's School for Girls* (TV), *Sweet Jesus Preacher Man.*
1974: *The Rockford Files* (TV).
1975: *Death Scream* (TV), *Psychic Killer.*
1976: *Sherlock Holmes in New York* (TV), *The Lindbergh Kidnapping Case* (TV).
1977: *Tail Gunner Joe* (TV), *Delta County USA* (TV).
1978: *Crisis in Sun Valley* (TV), *Terror Out of the Sky* (TV), *Matilda.*
1980: *Rage* (TV).
1981: *Bustin' Loose, Dead and Buried.*
1982: *The Mysterious Two* (TV).
1983: *Twilight Zone—The Movie.*
1984: *Velvet* (TV), *The Dark Mirror* (TV).
1988: *Lucky Stiff.*
1989: *Star Trek V: The Final Frontier.*

Television Series

1958–1963: *The Rifleman* as Sweeney.
1966–1967: *Please Don't Eat the Daisies* as Dean Gerald Carter.
1978–1983: *All in the Family* as Mr. Van Ranseleer.

Miniseries

1976: *Captains and the Kings.*
1979: *Backstairs at the Whitehouse.*
1980: *Scruples.*

Sources

Jones, Ken D., Arthur F. McClure, and Alfred E. Twomey. *Character People.* New York: Citadel, 1979.
Lentz, Harris M., III. *Obituaries in the Performing Arts, 1994.* Jefferson, NC: McFarland, 1996.

STEVE RAINES

Born in 1916, Steve Raines was an expert wrangler and stuntman who first found movie work at Republic in the late 1940s. He doubled Alan Ladd in *Shane* (1953). His performance in the film *Cattle Empire* (1958) led to him being cast in a regular role in the television series *Rawhide.* For several seasons he played one of the drovers, Jim Quince. His character was seen to particular advantage in the 1960 episode "Incident at Rojo Canyon," which related to Quince's experiences during the Civil War; Raines helped write the script himself. He lasted throughout the duration of the series. He also appeared in numerous episodes in the same genre. Raines died of a stroke in Grants Pass, Oregon, on January 4, 1996, at age 79.

Steve Raines Filmography

1947: *Under Colorado Skies, Along the Oregon Trail.*
1948: *Frontier Revenge, Oklahoma Badlands, Desperadoes of Dodge City, Sundown in Santa Fe.*
1949: *Sheriff of Wichita, Son of a Badman.*
1951: *Border Fence.*
1953: *Shane.*
1955: *Count Three and Pray.*
1956: *The Naked Gun.*
1958: *Cattle Empire, Street of Darkness.*

Television Series

1959–1966: *Rawhide* as Jim Quince.

Sources

Lentz, Harris M., III. *Classic Images.* Obituaries, May 1996.

STUART RANDALL

This supporting actor made his screen debut in 1950 and was active in motion pictures until 1965. He played Art Sampson in the Western series *Cimarron City,* but is better remembered as Marshal Mort Corey, a semi-regular role in *Laramie.* At last report he was retired and residing in Oxnard, California.

Stuart Randall Filmography

1950: *Bells of Coronado, Rider from Tucson, Rustlers on Horseback, Storm Warning.*
1951: *Tomahawk, Wells Fargo Gunmaster, Rough Riders of Durango, The Hoodlum, Tomorrow Is Another Day, Arizona Manhunt, Fixed Bayonets.*
1952: *Bugles in the Afternoon, Diplomatic Courier, This Woman Is Dangerous, Carbine Williams, Kid Monk Baroni, The Pride of St. Louis, The Bushwackers, Rancho Notorious, Hurricane Smith, Park Row, O. Henry's Full House* ("The Clarion Call" episode), *Captive Women, Hia-watha, Pony Soldier.*
1953: *Sword of Venus, Pony Express, Arena, Vicki, Captain John Smith and Pocahontas, Pickup on South Street, Mexican Manhunt, Champ for a Day.*
1954: *This Is My Love, Southwest Passage, Naked Alibi, They Rode West, The Man with the Steel Whip* (serial).
1955: *Chief Crazy Horse, Female on the Beach, Headline Hunters.*
1956: *Pardners, Indestructible Man.*
1957: *Run of the Arrow.*
1958: *Verboten!*
1959: *From the Terrace.*
1961: *Frontier Uprising, Posse from Hell.*
1964: *Taggart!*
1965: *Fluffy.*

Television Series

1959–1960: *Cimarron City* as Art Sampson.
1960–1963: *Laramie* as Mort Corey.

Sources

Brooks, Tim. *The Complete Directory to Prime Time TV Stars 1946–Present.* New York: Ballantine Books, 1987.
Picture Show's Who's Who on Screen. London: Amalgamated Press, c. 1956.

GIL RANKIN

This character actor, who was born Gilman Warren Rankin, played the part of Deputy Charlie Riggs in the first season of *Tombstone Territory.* He appeared in a few feature films and some television episodes, most dating from the late 1950s. He died on October 31, 1993, at age 82.

Gil Rankin Filmography

1949: *Champion, Bride of Vengeance Special Agent, My Foolish Heart.*
1950: *The Story of Seabiscuit, Union Station Three Secrets, Cyrano de Bergerac.*
1951: *The Day the Earth Stood Still, The Men.*
1952: *The Big Sky.*
1953: *The Greatest Show on Earth Houdini, Fort Algiers, Rear of the Crowd.*
1954: *Phffi.*
1955: *Illegal.*
1956: *Ghost Town, The Broken Star, Dance with Me Henry.*
1957: *Black Patch.*
1964: *Your Cheatin' Heart.*
1969: *Midnight Cowboy.*
1976: *Assault on Precinct 13.*

Television Series

1957: *Tombstone Territory* as Deputy Charlie Riggs.

Sources

Brooks, Tim. *The Complete Directory to Prime Time TV Stars 1946–Present.* New York: Ballantine Books, 1987.
Magers, Boyd. "Empty Saddles." *Western Clippings* magazine, issue #6, July/August 1995.
Ragan, David. *Who's Who in Hollywood.* New York: Facts on File, 1992.

REX REASON

Rex Reason was born in Berlin, Germany, on November 30, 1928. He was one of twin sons born to a representative for the General Motors Acceptance Corporation. His brother Rhodes also became an actor. The family returned to America in 1930. When his parents divorced, he was raised in Glendale, California, by his grandfather, the first mayor of Glendale. His grandfather owned a stable of horses which enabled his grandsons to become proficient riders at an early age.

Subsequently he went to live with his mother, a practicing Christian Scientist, in Hollywood, where he was educated at Hollywood High School and Hoover High. At the age of 16 he was chosen to play the lead of Chico in the school play version of *Seventh Heaven.* A year later he entered the army, underwent basic training, received his high school diploma and was discharged in 1947. After this he had to choose between careers in civil engineering and acting, so he chose the latter.

Under the G.I. Bill he enrolled at the Pasadena Playhouse, where he spent 12 months. From there he moved on to the Ben Bard Players where he played leads for about a year-and-a-half. He auditioned for a role in a play which was to run on Broadway. Although he won the part, an agent approached him and suggested that he would be right for a leading role in an independent film to be shot at MGM called *Storm Over Tibet* (1952), a nine-day quickie. Although MGM passed on releasing the film, his personality and professionalism so impressed them that they tested and signed him to a six-month contract.

When there were no roles forthcoming they let him go, so he sallied over to Columbia, who had released *Storm Over Tibet.* They signed him to a seven-year contract in 1952. He appeared in a few features for them before they failed to pick up his option about 12 months later. He was then tested at Universal where he inked a seven-year contract. For his first two Universal releases he was billed as Bart Roberts, but he strongly objected because he thought his real name was fine, so the studio relented and let him revert back to it. He spent three

Rex Reason on the set of *Man Without a Gun*.

years at Universal where he shot eight feature films. These were definitely his best movies, including *This Island Earth* (1955), which ranks as a sci-fi classic and is the actor's favorite film.

When Universal dropped him from their roster of contract players, he freelanced at other studios. At Warner Brothers he shot *Band of Angels* (1957), which he particularly recalls because of the charisma of star Clark Gable. Next he starred as Adam MacLean, a two-fisted newspaperman, in the Western series *Man Without a Gun* (1957–1959). This was a syndicated half-hour, black and white series produced by 20th Century–Fox. His character edited the *Yellowstone Sentinel* in that town in the rugged Dakota Territory of the 1880s. The drama in this series derived from a young and partially lawless town struggling to become a decent and respectable community. MacLean did not carry a gun, thus the title of the series. His only real ally was the official peace officer, U.S. Marshal Frank Tallman (Mort Mills). MacLean believed that the pen was mightier than the gun, and consequently ran blistering editorials attacking the evil crooks and corrupt politicians who controlled the area. If the occasion demanded, he was quick to defend himself with his fists. Initially 39 episodes of this rugged series were shot, each segment being filmed in two days.

This schedule was extremely punishing since the actor was in virtually every scene. He also agreed to do most of his own stunts, which made considerable demands upon him both mentally and physically. He came down with brain fever, commonly known as sleepy sickness (encephalitis lethargic), in which inflammatory changes, accompanied by edema and hemorrhages, take place in parts of the brain, causing a serious and often fatal disorder. He spent ten months in bed and had to learn how to speak, write and other commonplace acts again. Fortunately the series was extremely popular, and the deal which had been made was very lucrative so that he had no monetary worries during this period. When he recovered there were 13 new episodes shot, which made a total of 52.

After this he was offered a new series called *The Borderline* in which he would have played a casino manager. Although he was initially intrigued by this, Warner Bros. came up with what he thought was a better offer. They had liked his characterization of a newspaperman in his previous series so much that they invited him to play Scott Norris, an investigative reporter, in the television series *The Roaring Twenties.* Set during the Prohibition Era in New York City, this was the series which came closest to capturing the spirit of the Warner Bros. crime melodramas of the 1930s. It has been said that he appeared in fewer series as a guest than other Warner Bros. contract artists, but the converse is true. When he signed with them there was a writers' strike in progress, so the series production was postponed until it was settled. Warners hated to see any of their players idle, so they used him to play heavies in several of their other series such as *Sugarfoot* and *The Alaskans.* There is another story told about him that he rejected the lead in the *Maverick* television series when James Garner left and the studio was searching for a substitute.

When *The Roaring Twenties* ended in 1962, he bought out his contract with Warner Bros. nine months before it was due to expire. He experienced some difficulty with his agent, the notorious Henry Willson, who threatened to blacklist him throughout the industry, but since he planned on leaving show business by that time, this did not perturb him unduly. A prime reason for his decision to quit was his desire to prove himself in other areas, since up to that time show business had been his entire life. He has since admitted on several occasions, however, that quitting show business was extremely traumatic.

Although he had no idea then what he wished to do, a chance meeting with a real estate broker convinced him that his vocation lay in that direction. He won sponsorship, went to college, passed the examination and became a real estate salesman. He lived in Glendale, but moved in 1971 to Diamond Bar, where he ran a real estate office until 1984. Since then he has been a loan broker. He currently resides in Walnut, California. Rex Reason has been married three times and divorced twice. By his second wife he has a son and daughter. His third wife Shirley was a supermarket cashier whom he met through his real estate job. She has three daughters by a former marriage. They subsequently fostered an additional child.

Rex Reason Filmography

1952: *Storm Over Tibet.*

1953: *Salome, China Venture, Mission Over Korea.*

1954: *Sign of the Pagan* (narrated only), *Taza Son of Cochise, Yankee Pasha, Saskatchewan* (voice only).

1955: *Lady Godiva, Smoke Signal, This Island Earth, Kiss of Fire.*

1956: *The Creature Walks Among Us, Raw Edge.*
1957: *Band of Angels, Under Fire, Badlands of Montana.*
1958: *Thundering Jets, The Rawhide Trail.*
1959: *The Miracle of the Hills, The Sad Horse.*

Television Series

1957–1959: *Man Without a Gun* as Adam MacLean.
1960–1962: *The Roaring Twenties* as Scott Norris.

Sources

Goldrup, Tom, and Jim Goldrup. *Feature Players: The Stories Behind the Faces.* Published privately, 1986.
Lamparski, Richard. *Whatever Became Of? Seventh Series.* New York: Bantam, 1977.
Picture Show Annual. London: Amalgamated Press, 1954.
Weaver, Tom. *They Fought in the Creature Features: Interviews with 23 Classic Horror, Science Fiction and Serial Stars.* Jefferson, NC: McFarland, 1995.
Woolley, Lynn, Robert W. Malsbary, and Robert G. Strange, Jr. *Warner Bros. Television.* Jefferson, NC: McFarland, 1985.

DUNCAN RENALDO

"Fame would be an empty triumph without my family. My nationwide work—and I haven't been the Cisco Kid all my life—has shown me that his family must be the pivotal part of a father's work. Family breakups eventually break up the community because a family is the unit which makes a nation. Its real success must be measured in terms of its number of happy families." So spoke Duncan Renaldo, who made a later career for himself by playing the Cisco Kid on film and television. His life story was certainly one of the most curious of any sagebrush hero.

His studio biography listed him as born in Camden, New Jersey, on April 23, 1904, but the truth was that he genuinely had no idea when or where he was born. He was most likely born in Valladolid, Spain, or in Romania, of a Scottish father and Romanian mother, but was abandoned by them as a child. He was raised as a foundling primarily among agricultural and cattle people in rural districts of Spain and Central Europe. His real name was Renault Renaldo Duncan. He was educated at Madame de Burrier's School at Versailles, France.

He joined the Brazilian Merchant Marine and sailed ships to ports in Turkey, Italy, Greece, Egypt, France, Brazil, Argentina, Africa, Siam and Indo-China. He entered the United States in 1921 on a temporary 90-day seaman's permit when the ship he was a stoker on caught fire in Baltimore docks. While in town he encountered a movie director who showed him sketches of Havana docks which were going to be used in a film. Renaldo was a gifted artist. As his ship had just arrived from Cuba, he informed the director that the sketches were incorrect and offered to redraw them.

He was a portrait painter from 1921 to 1925 and was hired at $15.00 a week as a stage designer at the Metropolitan Opera Company in New York. He developed an interest in movies and made an early appearance in *The Bright Shawl* (1923), thereafter playing many bits. He became an actor, writer and director for Famous Lovers Film Productions at Long Island, New York, from 1923 to 1925, as well as a performer on the legitimate stage. His first big hit was a stage play called *My Son,* which started him on his way to Hollywood.

From 1925 to 1928 he was an actor and writer with Colorart Productions in Hollywood where he produced and played the title role in a series of shorts on famous composers. When a distribution deal did not materialize, he nearly went broke because of a huge debt he owed to Herbert J. Yates, who owned the company which had printed the films. Renaldo was saved from bankruptcy at the last minute by an offer from Pathe to buy them outright. The price came to within one dollar of what he owed Yates.

In 1927 he scored a big hit in a stage play called *Her Cardboard Lover* in Los Angeles which starred Edward Everett Horton. This enabled him to play his first important movie role in *Fifty Fifty* (1927). He had read Thornton Wilder's novel *The Bridge of San Luis Rey,* which he enjoyed so much he took an option on it. No studio would finance it. At last he sold it to director Charles Brabin, who sold the property to MGM for $50,000. Brabin honored his promise by paying Renaldo $5,000, together with a role as Esteban in the film shot in 1929.

His performance was so good that he won a contract with MGM and was given a leading role as Peru in *Trader Horn* (1931), a primitive but classic African adventure which starred Harry Carey and beautiful Edwina Booth. Renaldo and Booth later costarred in a quickie called *Trapped in Tia Juana* (1932). Louis B. Mayer was physically attracted to Edwina Booth, but was rejected by her. He chose to believe that she and Renaldo were having a torrid affair. Mayer, who was insanely jealous, persuaded Renaldo's first wife to start an alienation of affection suit. To further her case, she exposed her husband to the U.S. immigration department for illegal entry, stemming from his original 90-day permit in 1921.

This cost Renaldo his first marriage, and he spent his entire savings fighting the case in the courts. Nevertheless, he was found guilty and served nearly two years at McNeill Island Penitentiary before being pardoned by President Roosevelt. After his release Mayer continued his persecution by having him blacklisted within the film industry. Although Duncan Renaldo told this story many times in later years, he did not relate it with any bitterness.

Ironically it was Herbert J. Yates, the President of Republic whom he had fallen out with years before, who saved him. In 1939 Republic was in the process of reorganizing the popular "Three Mesquiteers" Westerns and the producers chose Renaldo to play the part of Rico in a new series of features which starred Bob Livingston and Raymond Hatton. After making seven movies in the series, Renaldo appeared in several other features and serials mainly for Republic, but also for other studios.

His characterization so impressed producer Philip N. Krasne that in 1945, he signed Renaldo to play the Cisco Kid in a new series for Monogram. 20th Century–Fox was jettisoning some of their properties such as Charlie Chan and the Cisco Kid and they were picked up by Monogram. It is generally accepted that their movies with Renaldo were among the best of this low-grade company's output. The Cisco Kid was created by O. Henry in the short story "The Caballero's Way." He was originally a disreputable bandit who stole from the rich and aided the poor. He was not the first character to be whitewashed in the movies and emerge in a much more handsome form. Renaldo was the third of four actors to play the role and the one who was most associated with the character in later years. He brought the requisite dash and vitality to the part.

As depicted in the movies and television, the Cisco Kid was a Mexican soldier of fortune who roamed the Southwest with his trusty sidekick Pancho. He was impeccably dressed in hand-embroidered black garb and was endowed with an abundance of Latin charm. Usually he swept a señorita off her feet in the course of dealing with the bad guys. He also broke her heart when he rode away. Cisco rode a horse called Diablo while Pancho rode one called Loco. Renaldo had two horses which he used interchangeably.

After the Monogram series, Renaldo quit the role allegedly because he was involved in government work. He had acted as cameraman to George Weeks Incorporated on a propaganda short called *Mission to America* (1943). With backing from Frederick Ziv, Krasne obtained the rights to the Cisco Kid from Monogram and produced a new series for United Artists starting in 1948. Part of the deal was that Renaldo play the leading role. There were five further adventures which were highly regarded because Renaldo teamed with the most famous Pancho, played by Leo Carrillo. The Cisco Company had Ziv as its head, Krasne as producer and Renaldo as associate producer. Renaldo worked on the scripts of many of the later Ciscos, frequently using the pseudonym of Renault Duncan.

The series then went to television where

Duncan Renaldo (left) with Leo Carrillo in *The Cisco Kid*.

it ran as a syndicated series from 1950 to 1956. It proved to be an enormous hit partly because of the charisma of the leads, Renaldo and Carrillo, but also because it was shot in color. Most stations showed them in black and white during the 1950s, but color kept them running for years afterwards. At its peak it was being watched by 42 million viewers, and the revenues generated ran into millions. Renaldo himself claimed to have shot 176 episodes, although the reference books list 156. *The Cisco Kid* received a single Emmy nomination as Best Children's Show in 1950.

After the series ceased production, Renaldo

continued to be active, making personal appearances as the character at service clubs and community events; and giving lectures in schools and the places he preferred (namely children's hospitals). He served on the board of directors of the Hope Ranch Association; the old Spanish Days of Santa Barbara fiesta; and the Research Park Association. He worked on scripts for a projected new television series called *Son of the Cisco Kid* as a vehicle for one of his sons.

He resided on a 40-acre estate next to a State Park called Rancho Mi Amigo, in a replica of a Spanish hacienda overlooking the Pacific Ocean in the hills of Santa Barbara. His living room alone measured 60 feet by 30 feet. His garden was wide and extensive, full of flowers, orange trees and lemon trees. On his land deer and horses roamed free. One interesting feature of his estate was that, being high up, he had installed a water tank holding 35,000 gallons of water.

Duncan Renaldo was married three times. His second wife was Lea Rosenblatt, whom he married in 1939. By her he had a daughter named Stephanie Marisa Consuelo, who was born in 1942. She is currently a music teacher. He also had three sons: Jeremy, born in 1945; Richard, born in 1947; and Edwin, born in the late 1950s. His third and final wife was Audrey Madalene Leonard, whom he married in 1956. He died of a combination of lung cancer and heart failure at Goleta, California, on September 3, 1980, at the apparent age of 76.

Duncan Renaldo Filmography

1923: *The Bright Shawl.*
1927: *Fifty Fifty.*
1928: *Gun Runner, The Devil's Skipper, Clothes Make the Woman, The Naughty Duchess, Marcheta, Romany Love.*
1929: *Pals of the Prairie, The Bridge of San Luis Rey.*
1931: *Trader Horn.*
1932: *Trapped in Tia Juana.*
1934: *The Moth, Public Stenographer.*
1936: *Moonlight Murder, Rebellion, Lady Luck.*
1937: *Mile a Minute Love, Two Minutes to Play, Jungle Menace* (serial), *The Painted Stallion* (serial), *Zorro Rides Again* (serial).
1938: *Spawn of the North, Crime Afloat, Rose of the Rio Grande, Tropic Holiday.*
1939: *The Lone Ranger Rides Again* (serial), *Rough Rider's Roundup, Juarez, The Kansas Terrors, Zaza, Cowboys from Texas, South of the Border, The Mad Empress* (Mexican).
1940: *Heroes of the Saddle, Pioneers of the West, Covered Wagon Days, Gaucho Serenade, Rocky Mountain Rangers, Oklahoma Renegades.*
1941: *Gaucho of Eldorado, Outlaws of the Desert, King of the Texas Rangers* (serial), *South of Panama, Down Mexico Way, Bad Men of Missouri.*
1942: *King of the Mounties* (serial), *A Yank in Libya, We Were Dancing.*
1943: *Secret Service in Darkest Africa* (serial), *For Whom the Bell Tolls, Mission to Moscow, Border Patrol, Tiger Fangs, Hands Across the Border, The Desert Song, Around the World.*
1944: *The Tiger Woman* (serial), *The Fighting Seabees, The San Antonio Kid, Call of the South Seas, Sheriff of Sundown.*
1945: *Adventure, The Cisco Kid Returns, The Cisco Kid in Old Mexico, South of the Rio Grande* (CK).
1947: *Jungle Flight, Bells of San Fernando.*
1948: *Sword of the Avenger, The Valiant Hombre* (CK).
1949: *The Gay Amigo* (CK), *The Daring Caballero* (CK), *Satan's Cradle* (CK), *We Were Strangers.*
1950: *The Girl from San Lorenzo* (CK), *The Capture.*
1951: *The Lady and the Bandit.*

Television Series

1950–1956: *The Cisco Kid* as the Cisco Kid.

Sources

Corneau, Ernest N. *The Hall of Fame of Western Film Stars.* N. Quincy, MA: Christopher, 1969.
Lamparksi, Richard. *Whatever Became of? Eighth Series.* New York: Crown, 1982.
Marx, Kenneth S. *Star Stats Who's Whose in Hollywood.* Los Angeles, CA: Price/Stern/Sloan, 1979.
Quinlan, David. *Illustrated Directory of Film Stars.* London: Batsford, 1996.
Speed, F. Maurice. *The Western Film and TV Annual.* London: MacDonald, 1959.

Tuska, Jon. *The Filming of the West.* Garden City, NY: Doubleday, 1976.

Note

CK in the filmography denotes an entry in the *Cisco Kid* series.

BURT REYNOLDS

Burt Reynolds was born Burton Leon Reynolds, Jr., in Waycross, Georgia, on February 11, 1936. He is the son of Burton Reynolds, Sr., who was born and raised on an Indian reservation in North Carolina. His grandmother was a full-blooded Cherokee. His mother Fern was an Italian. He has one older sister, Nancy Ann, born in 1930. There was also an adopted brother named Jimmy Hooks. At the age of ten, Burt moved with his family to Riviera Beach, Florida, where his father became police chief. He was educated at Central Junior High School in Palm Beach, where he became an outstanding athlete but was always rebellious.

On the strength of a football scholarship, he enrolled at Florida State University. While there he was badly injured in a car accident which spelled *finis* to his academic and sporting careers. Since he won a $5,000 settlement, he decided to go to New York where he resided in Greenwich Village and fell into the company of actors. Inspired by this, he enrolled at the School of Theater at Florida University in March 1956, remaining there until December 1957. While there he won the Florida Drama Award for his performance in *Outward Bound,* and with it a scholarship to Hyde Park Playhouse in New York.

A season of summer stock took him on the road with Linda Darnell in the play *Tea and Sympathy.* There was little money, and he supplemented his income by working on the New York docks. Actress Joanne Woodward was so impressed with his acting that she introduced him to her agent, who signed him as a client. He made his Broadway debut in a revival of *Mister Roberts* in the role of Mannon at the New York City Center.

Stardom seemed to have arrived when he went to Hollywood in the summer of 1958 and signed with the prestigious MCA talent agency. He inked a seven-year contract with Universal Studios. Universal's president Lew Wasserman personally selected him for Ben Frazer, the second lead of a river pilot, in a marginal Western series called *Riverboat.* The antipathy between nominal star Darren McGavin and Burt Reynolds became part of the folklore of American television. According to Reynolds, McGavin's intention was to sabotage him every time he stepped in front of the camera. As Reynolds explained it, "We'd run through a scene a couple of times and then just before the cameras rolled, McGavin would say to me, 'You're not going to play it that way, are you?' What little confidence I had would go right down the drain. ... He destroyed me."

By way of escape, Reynolds haunted the bars of Los Angeles where he started brawls at the drop of a hat. Subsequently he became so despondent that he did not show up for work, and other actors filled in for him. It was only when he threatened to blow up the riverboat, which was moored in the Universal lake, that he was dropped from the series and the role was renamed and recast. Years later he still bore a grudge against his erstwhile costar, saying darkly, "McGavin's going to be very disappointed on the first Easter after his death." He appeared in one season of 26 episodes. Although it was not his fault, his behavior caused him to be labeled a troublemaker and to be blacklisted at many Hollywood studios.

He switched agents to Dick Clayton, who encouraged him and had faith in his abilities. Reynolds divided his time between B movies, short-lived Broadway plays and stunt work. Series television beckoned again and he played Quint Asper, the half-breed Indian blacksmith, on *Gunsmoke* for three years. There is at least one published account that Reynolds was fired from this, but the version which he likes to tell is that he resigned because the part was not developing. A lean period followed, but eventually he won the lead in *Hawk,* a television series about a resentful New York Indian detective named John Hawk. There were only four out of 17 episodes aired when the series was canceled, although the ABC network was bombarded with complaints from irate viewers who wanted it to continue. His macho image made him in demand to play the hero in B movies which were usually shot on foreign locations. Producer Quinn Martin offered him the lead in *Dan August,* a series in which he played the upholder of the law in a small town, but this proved no more successful than his other ventures into series television and was axed after only 26 episodes.

His career zoomed when he made the first of several appearances on April 2, 1971, on *The Tonight Show* with Johnny Carson, where his sense of humor and verbal sparring with his host won him numerous fans. Carson invited him to become a guest host in May and he was seen by director John Boorman, who cast Reynolds as Lewis in the film *Deliverance* (1972) simply on the strength of his ability to manipulate people. The movie, shot on location in Clayton, Georgia, was a big hit and contains the best performance of his career. One night on *The Tonight Show* he found himself sitting next to Helen Gurley Brown, the editor of *Cosmopolitan* magazine, who was searching for the first nude male centerfold celebrity for the magazine. Reynolds fitted the groove in the April 1972, issue which caused a sensation and was a sellout.

With the success of *Deliverance* Reynolds became a superstar, moving quickly from one movie to another. He became America's number one box office star for five consecutive years, but even then there were several major flops along the way. He scored his biggest hit in *Smokey and the Bandit* (1977), in which the combination of country boy personality and screeching tires proved irresistible to everyone except the more discriminating who wanted a decent script.

His films degenerated into star vehicles in which he gave smug, egocentric performances, and the public, which had once endorsed his films, began to stay away. Reynolds became bedeviled with problems during the 1980s. When John Boorman quit *Sharky's Machine* (1981), Reynolds assumed the directing chores himself, but it was his last unqualified hit. While a major project *(The Bourne Identity)* collapsed and could not be resuscitated, there were numerous other projects which could not be lifted off the ground. Although his career paralleled that of Clint Eastwood, he proved not to have the staying and rejuvenative powers of his rival. Their only film together, *City Heat* (1984), was no credit to either of them, although this was not Reynolds' fault. While shooting a brawl in it, he suffered a serious injury when an inexperienced stunt man clobbered him on the side of the head with a heavy metal chair which fractured his jaw and caused severe inner ear damage. He lived with the pain for years before he eventually found a doctor who cured him. Speculation in the press about whether the star had AIDS proved much more newsworthy than any of his later films.

In his debilitated state he gave power of attorney to a new business manager who invested heavily in a chain of restaurants called "Poor Folks" which crashed spectacularly and depleted his fortune. Virtually his only offer once he had recovered his health was a thriller called *Heat* (1987), which ended up with Reynolds and the nominal director Dick Richards coming to blows. To appease him, Reynolds bought him a car and apologized in front of the whole crew, but a lawsuit still followed. There were several more poor thrillers which suffered the ignominy of going straight to video.

Television remained the only avenue to go down and, not surprisingly, Reynolds explored it thoroughly. *B.L. Stryker,* in which he played a private eye, proved at an hour-and-a-half to be overlong for its content. His career was temporarily saved by the successful sitcom *Evening Shade,* in which he played Wood Newton, a high school football coach. This lasted for four seasons and netted him an Emmy in 1990 as Outstanding Lead Actor in a Comedy Series. In June 1993, MTM, the company producing the series, sold the syndication rights to the Family Channel for the paltry sum of $150,000 per episode. He had expected the sum to be much higher and to reap millions from the deal, but instead this caused the series to be canceled and left him strapped for cash once again.

He returned to feature films in supporting roles. It was said that he was offered only

$170,000 when he accepted the role of a sex-crazed congressman who chases Demi Moore in the film *Striptease* in the hopes that this surefire hit would resuscitate his career.

Burt Reynolds married Judy Carne on June 28, 1963, at a tiny church in Burbank. She is best remembered as the "sock it to me" girl on television's *Rowan and Martin's Laugh-In*. On October 25, 1966, the couple divorced. Reynolds then had long-standing and highly publicized relationships with actresses Miko Mayama, Sally Field, Dinah Shore and tennis player Chris Evert. On April 29, 1988, he wed actress Loni Anderson in Jupiter, Florida. In September 1988, they adopted a boy, Quinton, named after the character Reynolds played on *Gunsmoke*. This proved insufficient to cement the couple's relationship and in 1994 they were divorced, their antics providing endless fodder for tabloid newspapers. In 1994 his autobiography *My Life* was published, detailing the vicissitudes of his private life and career.

Burt Reynolds Filmography

1961: *Angel Baby, Armored Command.*
1965: *Operation CIA.*
1966: *Navajo Joe.*
1967: *Shark!*
1968: *Impasse, 100 Rifles, Fade In (*a.k.a. *Iron Cowboy).*
1969: *Skullduggery, Sam Whiskey.*
1970: *Run Simon Run* (TV), *Hunters Are for Killing* (TV).
1972: *Everything You Always Wanted to Know About Sex but Were Afraid to Ask, Deliverance, Fuzz.*
1973: *Shamus, White Lightning, The Man Who Loved Cat Dancing.*
1974: *The Longest Yard (*a.k.a. *The Mean Machine).*
1975: *W.W. and the Dixie Dancekings, At Long Last Love, Hustle, Lucky Lady.*
1976: *Nickelodeon, Silent Movie* (cameo), *Gator* (also directed).
1977: *Smokey and the Bandit, Semi-Tough.*
1978: *Hooper, The End* (also directed).
1979: *Starting Over.*
1980: *Smokey and the Bandit II, Rough Cut, The Cannonball Run.*
1981: *Sharky's Machine* (also directed), *Paternity.*
1982: *The Best Little Whorehouse in Texas, Best Friends.*
1983: *Stroker Ace, Cannonball Run II, The Man Who Loved Women, Smokey and the Bandit III* (cameo).
1984: *City Heat.*
1985: *Stick* (also directed), *Uphill All the Way* (cameo).
1987: *Heat, Malone.*
1988: *Rent-A-Cop, Switching Channels, All Dogs Go to Heaven* (voice only).
1989: *Physical Evidence, Breaking In, Modern Love.*
1992: *The Player* (cameo).
1993: *Cop and a Half, The Man from Left Field* (TV: also directed).
1995: *The Maddening.*
1996: *Precious, Citizen Ruth, Striptease.*

Television Series

1959–1960: *Riverboat* as Ben Frazer.
1962–1965: *Gunsmoke* as Quinton Asper.
1966: *Hawk* as Lt. John Hawk.
1970–1971: *Dan August* as Detective Lt. Dan August.
1988–1990: *B.L. Stryker* as B.L. Stryker.
1990–1994: *Evening Shade* as Wood Newton.

Sources

Mitchum, John. *Them Ornery Mitchum Boys.* Pacifica, CA: Creatures at Large Press, 1989.
Resnick, Sylvia Safran. *No. 5 Film Fan Library Series: Burt Reynolds.* London: W.H. Allen, 1983.
Reynolds, Burt. *My Life.* London: Hodder and Stoughton, 1994.
Speed, F. Maurice. *The Western Film and TV Annual.* London: MacDonald, 1961.
Stallings, Penny. *Forbidden Channels: The Truth They Hide from TV Guide.* New York: Harper Perennial, 1991.

ADDISON RICHARDS

This actor was born Addison Whitaker Richards, Jr., in Zanesville, Ohio, on October 20, 1887. He graduated with a BA degree from Washington State University and did postgraduate work at Pomona College. He began his acting career in *The Pilgrimage Play* in 1926. In 1931 he became associate director of the Pasadena Playhouse and acted there as well. He made his screen debut in 1933 and went on to amass dozens of credits as a freelance character actor. Among his television roles was one as Martin Kingsley, a semi-regular role in the Western series *Cimarron City*. He was married and had one daughter. The 76-year-old actor died in Los Angeles on March 22, 1964, after a heart attack. He is buried at Forest Lawn Memorial Parks at Glendale, California.

Addison Richards Filmography

1933: *Lone Cowboy, Riot Squad.*

1934: *Let's Be Ritzy, The Love Captive, The Case of the Howling Dog, Beyond the Law, Our Daily Bread, Gentlemen Are Born, Babbitt, The St. Louis Kid, British Agent, 365 Nights in Hollywood, The Girl from Missouri, A Lost Lady, Love Captive.*

1935: *Black Fury, Only Eight Hours, G-Men, Home on the Range, The Eagle's Brood, The Frisco Kid, A Dog of Flanders, Sweet Music, Society Doctor, Here Comes the Band, The White Cockatoo, Front Page Woman, Little Big Shot, Dinky, Alias Mary Dow, The Crusades, Freckles, Ceiling Zero, The Petrified Forest.*

1936: *Bullets or Ballots, Sutter's Gold, Public Enemy's Wife, Trailin' West, Road Gang, Song of the Saddle, The Law in Her Hands, Jail Break, Anthony Adverse, The Case of the Velvet Claws, Hot Money, China Clipper, Smart Blonde, God's Country and the Woman, Man Hunt, Colleen, The Walking Dead, Black Legion, Draegerman Courage.*

1937: *Ready Willing and Able, Her Husband's Secretary, White Bondage, Dance Charlie Dance, The Singing Marine, Love Is on the Air, The Barrier, Wine Women and Horses, Empty Holsters.*

1938: *Flight into Fame, Alcatraz Island, The Black Doll, The Last Express, Accidents Will Happen, Valley of the Giants, Boys Town, Prison Nurse, The Devil's Party, Gateway.*

1939: *Whispering Enemies, They Made Her a Spy, Twelve Crowded Hours, Off the Record, Inside Information, Burn 'Em Up O'Connor, Andy Hardy Gets Spring Fever, They All Come Out, Thunder Afloat, Geronimo, Espionage Agent, Nick Carter Master Detective, Bad Lands, Exile Express, The Gracie Allen Murder Case, I Was a Convict, Tell No Tales, When Tomorrow Comes, Mystery of the White Room.*

1940: *Santa Fe Trail, Andy Hardy Meets Debutante, Boom Town, Northwest Passage, The Man from Dakota, The Man from Montreal, The Lone Wolf Strikes, Edison the Man, Charlie Chan in Panama, South to Karanga, Wyoming, Gangs of Chicago, The Girl from Havana, Arizona, Flight Command, Moon Over Burma, Black Diamonds, Cherokee Strip, Slightly Honorable, Public Deb No. 1, Island of Doomed Men, Give Us Wings, Flight Angels, My Little Chickadee.*

1941: *Ball of Fire, Dive Bomber, Western Pacific, Tall Dark and Handsome, Back in the Saddle, Sheriff of Tombstone, The Great Lie, Men of Boys Town, Mutiny in the Arctic, International Squadron, Texas, Her First Beau, Badlands of Dakota, Andy Hardy's Private Secretary, I Wanted Wings, Strawberry Blonde, The Trial of Mary Dugan, Design for Scandal, Sealed Lips, Our Wife, They Died with Their Boots On, Western Union.*

1942: *My Favorite Blonde, The Lady Has Plans, Cowboy Serenade, Pacific Rendezvous, A-Haunting We Will Go, Secrets of a Coed, Man with Two Lives, Secret Agent of Japan, The Pride of the Yankees, Seven Days' Leave, Men of Texas, Top Sergeant, Secret Enemies, Flying Tigers, War Dogs, A Close Call for Ellery Queen, Friendly Enemies, Mystery of Marie Roget, Pride of the Army, Ship Ahoy!, Ridin' Down the Canyon, Underground Agent, War Dogs.*

1943: *Destroyer, Headin' for God's Country, Corvette K-225, Where Are Your Children?, The Mystery of the 13th Guest, Mystery Broadcast, The Deerslayer, Air Force, A Guy Named Joe, Always a Bridesmaid, Smart Guy, The Mad Ghoul, Salute to the Marines, Hit Parade of 1943.*

1944: *Raiders of Ghost City* (serial), *The Fighting Seabees, Follow the Boys, Three Men in White, Moon Over Las Vegas, Roger Touhy—Gangster, A Night of Adventure, Marriage Is a Private Affair, Since You Went Away, The Mummy's Curse, The Sullivans, Are These Our Parents?, Barbary Coast Gent, Three Little Sisters, Border Town Trail, Grissly's Millions.*
1945: *The Master Key* (serial), *Duffy's Tavern, The Royal Mounted Rides Again* (serial), *Lady on a Train, The Chicago Kid, God Is My Co-Pilot, Betrayal from the East, Rough Tough and Ready, Bells of Rosarita, Come Out Fighting, I'll Remember April, Black Market Babies, Danger Signal, The Shanghai Cobra, Men in Her Diary, Strange Confession, The Adventures of Rusty, Spellbound, Bewitched, Leave Her to Heaven, Divorce, The Tiger Woman.*
1946: *Secrets of a Sorority Girl, Angel on My Shoulder, The Criminal Court, The Hoodlum Saint, Step by Step, Renegades, Don't Gamble with Strangers, The Mummy's Curse, Anna and the King of Siam, Love Laughs at Andy Hardy, Dragonwyck, Courage of Lassie.*
1947: *The Millerson Case, Monsieur Verdoux, Call Northside 777, Reaching from Heaven,*
1948: *Lulu Belle, The Saxon Charm, A Southern Yankee.*
1949: *The Rustlers, Henry the Rainmaker, Mighty Joe Young.*
1950: *Davy Crockett Indian Scout.*
1955: *Illegal, High Society, Fort Yuma.*
1956: *Walk the Proud Land, Reprisal!, Everything but the Truth, When Gangland Strikes, Fury at Gunsight Pass, The Ten Commandments, The Broken Star, The Fastest Gun Alive.*
1957: *Last of the Badmen, Gunsight Ridge.*
1958: *The Saga of Hemp Brown.*
1959: *The Oregon Trail.*
1960: *All the Fine Young Cannibals, The Dark at the Top of the Stairs.*
1961: *The Gambler Wore a Gun, Frontier Uprising, The Flight That Disappeared.*
1962: *Saintly Sinners.*
1963: *The Raiders.*
1964: *For Those Who Think Young.*

Television Series

1953: *Pentagon USA* as the Colonel.
1958–1959: *Cimarron City* as Martin Kingsley.
1959–1960: *Fibber McGee and Molly* as Doc Gamble.

Sources

Brooks, Tim. *The Complete Directory to Prime Time TV Stars 1946–Present.* New York: Ballantine Books, 1987.
Parish, James Robert. *Hollywood Character Actors.* New Rochelle, NY: Arlington House, 1978.
Quinlan, David. *Illustrated Directory of Film Character Actors.* London: Batsford, 1995.
Twomey, Alfred E. and Arthur F. McClure. *The Versatiles.* South Brunswick and New York: Barnes, 1969.

JEFF RICHARDS

Jeff Richards was born Richard Mansfield Taylor in Portland, Oregon, on November 1, 1924, of mixed French, Irish and Scottish parentage. Educated at Tacoma, Washington High School, he was an outstanding athlete. While studying at the University of California, his ambition was to be a professional baseball player. Subsequently he served with the U.S. Navy from 1943 to 1946. His first acquaintance with Hollywood occurred during a visit arranged for a group of servicemen.

After the war he became a promising baseball star, appearing with both the New York Yankees and Brooklyn Dodgers. A talent scout had told him to return to Hollywood if he ever wanted to become an actor, but he only did so when a torn leg ligament received while playing basketball cost him his career in baseball. After arriving in Hollywood in 1948, he played bits for a while. In 1950 he signed a seven-year contract with MGM, who groomed him for stardom hoping that he might one day become a replacement for Clark Gable.

Although he made over a dozen films for

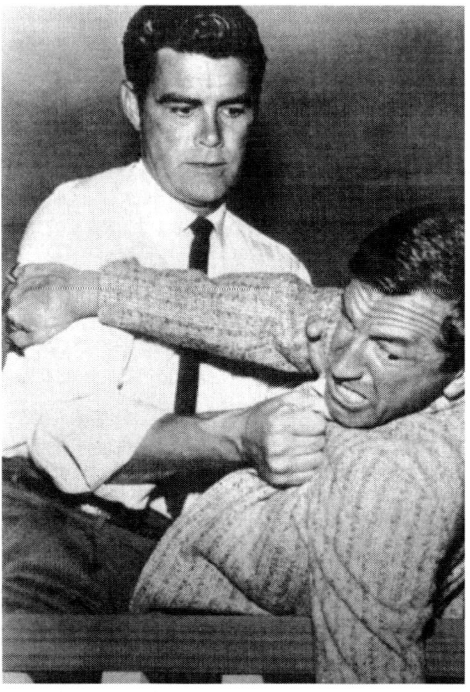

Jeff Richards (top) and Buddy Lester in an episode of the anthology series *Producers' Choice*. Richards was also appearing in the Western series *Jefferson Drum*.

that studio and there was a very considerable investment in him, he did not succeed in coming anywhere close to usurping the throne of "The King." One film in which he costarred with Howard Keel was the classic *Seven Brides for Seven Brothers* (1954). Keel remembers him this way: "Jeff Richards was my second in command, my second brother. He was a tough kid, he wound up being a bouncer in a bar. There was always a kind of competition about whether he could lick me or not. That came across in the film. He was the only one that really stood up against me every once in a while." Russ Tamblyn added, "And he hated musicals. He absolutely hated them! He was actually rebellious about being a part of it! If you remember, we were all prancing round in the countryside, all walking around picking flowers—he hated that! This was a rough and tumble baseball player." Julie Newmar, who was paired with Richards, was no fonder of him. She says, "He was the only one who didn't dance. I'm almost six feet tall and Jeff was big in the other direction." Unable to adjust to the demands of a career perpetually in the spotlight, he sought solace in alcohol.

At this time his home was a ketch moored in San Pedro harbor. Once cast adrift by his home studio in 1957, his only consistent work afterwards as an actor was in *Jefferson Drum*, an NBC Western series shown during the 1958–1959 season. In it Richards played the title character, a frontier newspaperman. Located in the wide open town of Jubilee during the 1850s, Drum took over as editor and owner of the *Star* newspaper when the original proprietor was savagely murdered. Drum was endowed with more principle than many of the characters depicted in the teleplays. A widower with a young son, he was aided by Lucius Coin, his printer, and Big Ed, who ran the local saloon. Many of his articles carried sentiments which he aimed squarely at his son. Although he believed that the pen was mightier than the gun, he was capable of using both revolver and fists when the need arose.

The series was a production of executive producers Mark Goodson and Bill Todman, who graduated from game shows to filmed dramas. They experienced difficulty acquiring influential sponsors and maintaining satisfactory relations with the networks and studios. Therefore, there were only 26 half-hour black and white episodes of *Jefferson Drum* shown between April 25, 1958, and April 23, 1959. He also turned up in the episode of *Rawhide* called "Incident of His Brother's Keeper," originally aired in 1961, in which he acquitted himself well as the brother of Jack Lord. Richards made a few quickies before vanishing from the screen. In later years he became a carpenter, ironically working construction at Hollywood studios where once he had been regarded as star material.

The last years of his life were spent in an apartment at Hisperia, California. He died at Victor Valley Community Hospital in Victorville, California, on July 28, 1989, at age 64, of acute respiratory failure due to acute respiratory distress syndrome due to diffuse pneumonia. He is buried at Riverside National Cemetery at Riverside, California. Twice divorced, he had one child.

Jeff Richards Filmography

1948: *Johnny Belinda, Fighter Squadron.*

1949: *The Girl from Jones Beach.*
1950: *Kill the Umpire.*
1951: *The People Against O'Hara, The Tall Target, The Strip, Angels in the Outfield, The Sellout.*
1952: *Above and Beyond, Desperate Search.*
1953: *Code Two, The Big Leaguer, Battle Circus.*
1954: *Crest of the Wave (*a.k.a. *Seagulls Over Sorrento), Seven Brides for Seven Brothers.*
1955: *Many Rivers to Cross, The Marauders, It's a Dog's Life (*a.k.a. *Bar Sinister).*
1956: *The Opposite Sex.*
1957: *Don't Go Near the Water.*
1959: *Island of Lost Women, Born Reckless.*
1960: *Secret of the Purple Reef.*
1966: *Waco.*

Television Series

1958–1959: *Jefferson Drum* as Jefferson Drum.

Sources

Ciaccia, Maria. *Dreamboats: Hollywood Hunks of the '50s.* New York: Excalibur, 1992.
Death certificate, 1989.
Perry, Jeb H. *Screen Gems: A History of Columbia Pictures Television from Cohn to Coke 1948–1983.* Metuchen, NJ: Scarecrow, 1991.
Picture Show Annual. London: Amalgamated Press, 1954 and 1957.
Summers, Neil *The Official TV Western Book Volume #3.* Vienna, WV: Old West Publishing Shop, 1991.

STEVEN RITCH

Steven Ritch was born in Providence, Rhode Island, on December 26, 1921. He arrived in Hollywood after serving as a staff sergeant in the First Marine Division and the tank battalion during World War II. On the G.I. Bill he attended Brown University intending to become a lawyer but switching to drama instead. After some stage experience he gravitated to Hollywood where he made his screen debut in *Valley of Head Hunters* (1953). He had a brief acting career when he was under contract to Columbia during the 1950s. He did much of his movie work for producer Sam Katzman. His biggest claim to cinematic fame was playing the title role in Katzman's *The Werewolf* (1956).

He became typecast as an Indian because he was most convincing. When he grew a beard to escape the rut, he was soon cast as Nakaya in the Western series *Broken Arrow,* so he had to shave his beard off. The role lasted ten episodes. After this he appeared frequently in Western television episodes; wrote some film scripts; and became a dialogue coach between 1957 and 1962.

After retiring from films, Ritch became an ordained minister with a chapel in Canoga Park, California. He died in Oregon on July 20, 1995, at age 73.

Steven Ritch Filmography

1953: *Valley of the Head Hunters, Conquest of Cochise.*
1954: *The Battle of Rogue River, Massacre Canyon, Riding with Buffalo Bill* (serial).
1955: *Seminole Uprising, The Crooked Web.*
1956: *The Werewolf.*
1957: *Plunder Road, Bailout at 43,000.*
1958: *Murder by Contract.*
1959: *City of Fear* (also scripted).
1960: *Studs Lonigan.*

Television Series

1956–1958: *Broken Arrow* as Nakaya.

Sources

Hirschhorn, Clive. *The Columbia Story.* London: Pyramid, 1989.
Magers, Boyd. "Empty Saddles." *Western Clippings* magazine, Nov./Dec. 1996.

MICHAEL ROAD

Born during the 1920s, Michael Road began his acting career as a teenager in Boston working with a little theater group. From there he relocated to New York, where he did various odd jobs while working in off-Broadway plays. He made his Broadway debut in *Doodle Dandy of the USA,* which flopped, but later landed a leading role in *Dear Ruth* which lasted six months. He acquired substantial Broadway experience in other plays. He directed some famous names in stock and Signe Hasso in the Swedish lensed *The True and the False* (1955).

His best opportunity was when he landed the role of Marshal Tom Sellers in the Western series *Buckskin* in 1958. His character was the mentor of young Jody O'Connell (Tommy Nolan). In August 1960, Warner Bros. signed him to a contract. On the strength of this he was cast as confidence trickster Pearly Gates in a couple of episodes of *Maverick*. In another *Maverick* episode he ironically played a character called Buckskin. Under this contract, however, his best-known role was as the police lieutenant in *The Roaring Twenties* series. He later provided the voice of "Race" Bannon in the prime-time cartoon adventure series *Jonny Quest.* For a single episode of *Alias Smith and Jones* ("Shootout at Diablo Station," 1971), he assumed the role of Sheriff Tom Trevors. He was still seen on television during the rest of the 1970s and did voiceovers in commercials. At last report he was residing in Los Angeles. He was married with a family.

Michael Road Filmography

1943: *Gildersleeve on Broadway, The Iron Major.*
1950: *The Halls of Montezuma.*
1952: *Androcles and the Lion.*
1966: *Destination Inner Space.*

Television Series

1958–1959: *Buckskin* as Marshal Tom Sellers.
1960–1962: *The Roaring Twenties* as Lt. Joe Switolski.
1964–1965: *Jonny Quest* as Roger "Race" Bannon (voice only).

Sources

Brooks, Tim. *The Complete Directory to Prime Time TV Stars 1946–Present.* New York: Ballantine Books, 1987.
Interview with Michael Lipton in March 1995.
Woolley, Lynn, Robert W. Malsbary, and Robert G. Strange, Jr. *Warner Bros. Television.* Jefferson NC: McFarland, 1985.

PERNELL ROBERTS

Pernell Roberts had all the attributes of top stardom—good looks, a fine physique, mellifluous voice and a sense of humor. Somehow he missed the boat. His fans believe he is talented and professional in his approach, but his critics insist he is rebellious and uncooperative. One fact is certain. He waited a long time between success as the clean-cut Adam Cartwright and his career revival, bald and bearded, as *Trapper John M.D.* Few of his television appearances have been much acclaimed despite his talent and drive for better parts. In spite of craving quality, he has seldom, aside from his long-running successes, commanded good material. He is also the last surviving star of the original cast of *Bonanza.*

Pernell Roberts was born in Waycross, Georgia, on May 18, 1928, the son of a soft drink salesman. He was educated at Waycross High School, Georgia Institute of Technology and the University of Maryland, where he was flunked three times during the late 1940s for refusing to pay attention to his studies. He decided to become a professional actor after appearing in plays at the University of Maryland Theater. He held many odd jobs, including a stint in the U.S. Marines where he learned to play the tuba. He became bored with them all. He joined the Arena Stage in Washington where he was a member from the end of 1950 to the middle of 1952. He made his professional debut in *The Man Who Came to Dinner*, one of four plays in which he appeared with them.

He did some summer stock in Cleveland before heading to New York, where he appeared with a number of theater companies both on and off Broadway. His first Broadway appearance was in *Tonight at Samarkand* in 1953. In 1955 while with the Shakespeare-wrights, he won the Drama Desk Award for the Best Actor Off-Broadway for his appearances in *Macbeth* and *Romeo and Juliet*. He also appeared in classical plays and musicals such as *Kismet, The King and I, Guys and Dolls* and *The Music Man*. A part on Broadway in *The Lovers* with Joanne Woodward led to his move West.

Once there he made his screen debut in *Desire Under the Elms* (1958). He stayed to find more work in television and films. His big break came when he was cast as Adam Cartwright in *Bonanza*. Adam was somewhat mysterious, wore black and was slow to anger. During its early years Adam dominated the action because his resolute character offered an interesting contrast to the levity of Hoss and Little Joe. He frequently received more fan mail than the others, but Pernell Roberts rapidly came to despise the role which he felt was a lie. When there was so much misery and poverty in the real world, he could not understand how the Cartwrights could be looked upon as heroes. He objected because the series showed men forging ahead with their guns and fists rather than their brains. The scripts, he reasoned, suggested that women existed simply as sex objects for the male characters. The part also failed to challenge him as an actor. "Give the silly asses half of what the scene requires and they think it's great," he asserted.

The antagonism between Roberts and the other members of the cast was no secret. In particular Michael Landon and Roberts despised each other. Apparently they did not speak for the first couple of years. Mike Landon believed Roberts made little effort, saying, "You can imagine how it is for an actor to be delivering his lines and get nothing but a blank stare from the person he is talking to." Pernell Roberts believed that his costar was untrained and perpetuating bad acting habits. He has since expressed regret over these remarks and stated that Landon misunderstood the nature of his comments.

Pernell Roberts as he appeared in *Bonanza*.

In 1965 Pernell Roberts quit. It was originally intended that he would be written out of the series when Adam married in a 1964 telecast. He made a controversial suggestion to the network that Adam's bride should be an Indian played by a Negro actress, but he was overruled. Producer David Dortort later said that he thought the actor's suggestion was well-meaning but confused. Instead, beautiful blue-eyed actress Kathie Browne was chosen to play schoolmarm Laura Dayton, Adam's romantic interest. It was intended that he should be replaced by a cousin, Will Cart-wright (Guy Williams). Roberts and Kathie Browne appeared in four very highly-rated episodes, but the network was overwhelmed with letters from fans who insisted that the four Cartwrights should stay unmarried. This caused the producers to exercise a clause in his contract which meant that Roberts was forced to play the character for another year, while Laura and Will rode hand-in-hand into the Western sunset. There was no farewell episode, but Adam was said to be looking after the Cartwrights' business interests abroad.

In the interim, star Lorne Greene urged Roberts not to be a damn fool. He told him not to quit, but to continue as Adam and enjoy the money and prestige. At the time his fee was an estimated $10,000 an episode. Subsequently he could open his own studio and make his own projects. Roberts listened to his onscreen father, but did not heed his advice. He was sure that *Bonanza,* like most of television's other long-running series, would soon dwindle and die. His prediction did appear to be coming true when the other two networks put up some strenuous competition in 1967 and the ratings faltered. Greene refused to listen, saying, "We're good and we're clean as well as exciting. I think we'll last a lot more years." His assessment proved correct. *Bonanza* climbed back to the top of the ratings and stayed there.

Roberts' decision was rumored to have cost him over $1,000,000. He spent the next 14 years in limbo playing in stock companies and doing guest shots on dozens of action shows mostly of inferior quality to the one he had left. His credits included *The Girl from U.N.C.L.E.; The Wild Wild West; Mission Impossible; Marcus Welby, M.D.; Most Wanted* and *The Six Million Dollar Man.* No matter how tacky the show, there was Pernell Roberts. He believed that *Bonanza* would make him in demand for better quality parts, but he soon learned differently. He appeared as Rhett Butler in the musical version of *Gone with the Wind* at the Los Angeles Civic Light Opera. It was a critically lambasted production which he landed because no one else would touch it. He was cast in a pacifist stage musical called *Mata Hari,* but it never ran despite rave personal notices. By 1972 he was quoted as saying, "I take work whenever I can find it." He admitted that not much had happened to him professionally since leaving *Bonanza.* He had spent the intervening years wondering where his next paycheck was coming from, while his former costars had difficulty finding enough places to stash their loot.

By 1979 he had learned his lesson. He came in from the cold to star in the comeback series *Trapper John M.D.* to raise money to pay the mortgage. He asserted, "I now want security. It's called covering your rear end." The series was a spinoff from *M*A*S*H* and told of the experiences of Korean War veteran Dr. "Trapper" John McIntyre, who is now Chief of Surgeons at San Francisco Memorial Hospital. He won the role because he agreed to accept a lower paycheck than other stars who were up for the part. It was also an edict from the CBS network that if he became too temperamental, he would be fired. Although he complained about the poor quality of the scripts, the unconvincing sets and the inaccurate props, he generally toed the line. He did, however, have a battle with guest star Jessica Walter three days into shooting the first episode, when he believed the director favored her over him in one scene. He received an Emmy nomination in 1981 as Outstanding Lead Actor in a Drama Series.

Once *Trapper John M.D.* ended in 1986, he reverted to the same old dross, although he was less frequently seen for a while. He turned up in *Night Train to Kathmandu* (1988), shot in India for cable television. The critics were none too kind. "OK for kids, spins its wheels for adults," said *Variety.* In *Perry Mason: The Case of the All Star Assassin* (1989), he was the murder victim, a sports entrepreneur. He was so obnoxious that his murderer deserved a medal, except that the wrong party was accused. In the superior telemovie *Donor* (1990) he gave one of his patented performances as a testy medical chief of staff. In 1991 he returned to prime time television on a regular basis as the frontman for a half-hour docudrama series, *The FBI: The Untold Stories.* It was competently done, but against the formidable competition of *Cheers,* it was a nonstarter in the ratings war. It did, however, improve its performance appreciably when it was moved to a different day and timeslot. The epithets "affable" and "charming" could scarcely be applied to his personality.

Pernell Roberts married Kara Knack in 1972, and they have a son, Christopher. In February 1995, it was announced that they were divorcing on the grounds of irreconcilable differences. He guards his privacy like the legendary Garbo used to do. He has long been obsessed by speed and for many years was a fixture of the stock car racing circuit in California. His other hobbies are listed as swimming, photography, running, riding, tennis and—surprisingly for a man who no longer gives interviews—conversation.

Pernell Roberts Filmography

1958: *Desire Under the Elms, The Sheepman.*
1959: *Ride Lonesome.*
1961: *The Errand Boy* (cameo).
1969: *Four Rode Out, The Kashmiri Run, The Silent Gun* (TV).
1970: *San Francisco International Airport* (TV).
1972: *The Bravos* (TV), *The Adventures of Nick Carter* (TV), *Assignment: Munich* (TV).
1975: *Dead Man on the Run* (TV), *The Lives of Jenny Dolan* (TV), *Alien Lover* (TV), *The Deadly Tower* (TV).
1977: *Charlie Cobb: Nice Night for a Hanging* (TV).
1978: *The Magic of Lassie.*
1979: *Night Rider* (TV), *Hot Rod* (TV).
1980: *High Noon: Part II* (TV).
1981: *Incident at Crestridge* (TV).
1987: *Desperado* (TV).
1988: *Night Train to Kathmandu* (TV).
1989: *Perry Mason: The Case of the All Star Assassin* (TV).
1990: *Donor* (TV), *The Checkered Flag.*

Television Series

1959–1965: *Bonanza* as Adam Cartwright.
1979–1986: *Trapper John MD* as Dr. "Trapper" John McIntyre.
1991–1993: *The FBI: The Untold Stories*—host.

Miniseries

1976: *Captains and the Kings.*
1978: *Centennial, The Immigrants.*
1989: *Around the World in 80 Days*

Sources

Beck, Marilyn. *Hollywood.* New York: Hawthorn, 1973.
Brooks, Tim. *The Complete Directory to Prime Time TV Stars 1986–Present.* New York: Ballantine Books, 1987.
Essoe, Gabe. *The Book of TV Lists.* Westport, CT: Arlington House, 1981.
Rovin, Jeff. *TV Babylon.* New York: Signet, 1987.
Shapiro, Melany. *Bonanza: The Unofficial Story of the Ponderosa.* Las Vegas, NV: Pioneer, 1993.
Thomey, Tedd. *The Glorious Decade.* New York: Ace, 1971.

DALE ROBERTSON

Western heroes are supposed to ride tall in the saddle, but few ever rode taller, fired faster or spoke straighter than Dale Robertson, who is best known for playing Jim Hardie in the classic Western series *Tales of Wells Fargo* (1957–1962). He possessed a ramrod back, splendid physique and a rich, distinctive Oklahoma accent. He is an authentic Westerner, born and raised on a ranch, and it has remained in his blood. As a horseman, he has few equals. Offscreen, unlike the authoritative roles he generally plays, he is noted for his sense of humor. Actor Tony Young, who worked with him on episodes of *The Iron Horse* (1966–1968), said, "There was always plenty of fun on the sets of the series he worked on. He absolutely refused to take anything seriously."

Dayle LeMoine Robertson was born in Harrah, Oklahoma, on July 14, 1923, the son of Melvin and Varvel Robertson. He has two older brothers, Chester (Chet) and Roxy, and an older sister. An aunt gave him the name Dayle from a novel she was reading, but he spelled it Dale even in childhood. His father was a ranch owner. His parents were friends of Will Rogers, who wanted to take him to Hollywood even as a boy, but his parents refused on the grounds that it might interfere with his education. In 1927 the family moved to Oklahoma City, where he attended Eugene Field Grade School, Roosevelt Junior High School and Classen High School. He studied law at Oklahoma City Military College and gained a reputation for being a top athlete, winning no less than 28 letters in athletic events. When he left school he worked as a shipping clerk, construction laborer and cowpuncher before becoming a professional boxer. He had over 40 legitimate fights, and for each bout he earned between $40 and $200.

In September 1942, he entered the army, first in the Horse Cavalry at Fort Riley, Kansas, then the Armed Forces at Fort Knox, Kentucky, and Fort Belvoir, Virginia. He attended engineering school and joined the 322nd Combat Engineers Battalion attached to General Patton's Third Army in Europe, fighting in Africa, Italy and France. He received several medals, including the Bronze and Silver Stars and the Purple Heart from the United States and the Cross of Lorraine from France. His boxing career came to an end when he was wounded in the knee by enemy mortar fire. He was sent home where he was honorably discharged as a first lieutenant in June 1945.

It was after the war he decided he wanted to become an actor, so he journeyed to Hollywood ten times looking for work. Sometimes he stayed there for a few months, working for photographers who were illustrating clothes advertisements for Los Angeles department stores. On other occasions he would return to Oklahoma disillusioned after only a couple of weeks in Tinseltown. Allegedly he was once a schoolteacher, but this seems to be a mistake started by film historian Leslie Halliwell. (Halliwell seems to have confused him with another actor, Douglas Kennedy, who *was* a former schoolteacher. Oddly, the star himself has never denied it.) Producer Lee Brooks took a liking to him and introduced him to two agents. After he signed with Charles Feldman and Ned Marin, he did the rounds of the studios. 20th Century–Fox tested him, but he had no acting experience and failed the test miserably. On the recommendation of director Edwin L. Marin, his agent's brother, producer Nat Holt cast him in the role of Jesse James in the Western *Fighting Man of the Plains* (1949), which starred Randolph Scott. Although he only appeared in the last half-hour, the audience reaction at the Long Beach Crest Theater where the film was previewed was very positive. The young actor made a personal appearance there and was nearly mobbed on leaving. As Nat Holt recalled, "It had to be genuine. No one could have that many relatives!" This was followed by a featured role in another Randolph Scott Western, *The Cariboo Trail* (1950), which caused a very favorable reaction.

He signed a contract with 20th Century–Fox on November 9, 1949, for seven years. There he was given a build-up as a romantic leading man opposite stars such as Betty Grable in *Call Me Mister* (1951) and *The Farmer Takes a Wife* (1953), Jeanne Crain in *Take Care of My Little Girl* (1951) and Mitzi Gaynor in *Golden Girl* (1951). By 1951 he was voted one of the "Stars of Tomorrow" and was well on his way to becoming a big star at the Fox studio. Executives wanted him to modulate his strong Oklahoma accent, but he objected, saying, "I don't want to put my voice in a dinner jacket. I'm a horseman, not a cafe society fellow." However, he did study film editing, stage designing and script writing in evening classes at UCLA.

To some degree Fox granted him his wish and cast him in a number of lower-case Westerns, most of which have points of interest. A sudden fit of temperament led to a major argument with the studio over contracts and choice of scripts, and his contract was abruptly terminated in 1954. Once he had cast himself adrift, he found himself in a particularly precarious position in view of the revolutionary changes which were taking place in the industry in the mid–1950s. His films were a somewhat bizarre lot. He even turned up as the star of an Arabian Nights adventure, *Son of Sinbad* (1953), which is one of his most frequently revived films on television. He scarcely seemed ideal for the role, but he proved himself a lithe and handsome hero, and his horsemanship came in useful during the extensive riding sequences. The film was not a commercial success, but costar Sally Forrest recalled recently that the only problems encountered while shooting were caused by his pronounced Oklahoma accent, which was at first thought incongruous in the old Bagdad setting. (It actually turned out to be a great plus, adding to the satirical approach of the production.) She added, "Vincent Price and Dale were joys to work with." A few years later when he came to do *Anna of Brooklyn* (1957) with Gina Lollobrigida, he was cast as an Italian!

In 1852, when pioneers began moving further West, Wells Fargo went with them. As the frontier moved toward the Pacific Coast, Wells Fargo linked the many hundreds of new towns which sprang up overnight in the prairie and desert. The business of the agency was to safeguard travelers, goods and gold. The company hired special agents whose job was to protect shipments, investigate robberies and track down the culprits. Such a man was Jim Hardie, whose exploits became the basis of the long-running Western series *Tales of Wells Fargo.*

Nat Holt had thought up the idea of making a television series about Wells Fargo. He acquired maximum cooperation from the Wells Fargo Bank Museum in San Francisco, and his stories were based on genuine incidents. Robertson was his first and only choice to play the role of Hardie. Holt explained, "His great love of the outdoors and his interest in the West made him the perfect choice." When he showed Robertson the pilot script in 1955, the actor rejected it because he believed there was a surfeit of Westerns on television. At the time he was a contender for the role of *Perry Mason* until the producers decided his voice was wrong for the part. He later accepted, and the pilot aired as an episode of *Schlitz Playhouse of the Stars* on December 14, 1956.

Tales of Wells Fargo made its debut without fanfare on NBC in March 1957, and was almost immediately an enormous success. It came at an opportune time for Robertson, whose film career was at a virtual standstill. He felt that he had been pushed into a rut and desperately wanted to do something different. Its most successful season was 1957–1958, when it finished third in the Nielsen ratings; in 1958–1959 it finished seventh. The question arises as to how this success affected him as a person. An associate recalled, "Dale had a tough time before *Wells Fargo.* Money didn't come easily to him at one stage and he was terribly careful with it. We used to call him 'meany.' You see, none of us had much, but we all used to chip in. But since his pockets have been bulging, he has learned to become a very generous man. He does a lot for charity and will help out any associate who is down on his luck. Maybe he remembers the days when he didn't have it so good."

Robertson rode his own horse (named Jubilee) throughout the run of the series. His contract called for a six-day week for 46 weeks of the year with time off every third week. He allegedly owned 50 percent of the rights to the series and at one point even wrote a nonfiction book about the real Wells Fargo. For its first five seasons the series ran half an hour, and Robertson appeared as sole star. For its final season it was expanded to a full hour. Although still retaining his job, Jim Hardie had acquired a ranch outside of San Francisco and with it a crusty caretaker, Jeb Gaines (William Demarest), and a young assistant, Beau McCloud (Jack Ging). In spite of the best efforts of all concerned, fans somehow did not take to this new format and the series ended after 167 25-minute episodes and 34 50-minute episodes. One distinctive feature of *Wells Fargo* was its theme music, which sounded like a train or stagecoach in rapid motion. This also disappeared in the hour-length episodes.

Once clear of television, Robertson returned to the declining feature film market. When agent-turned-producer A. C. Lyles was hired by Paramount in the 1960s to make a series of low budget westerns, the first and best of these was *Law of the Lawless* (1964), in which Robertson played a judge. *Coast of Skeletons* (1964) was a typical, scrappy Harry Alan Towers production deal, in this case a reworking of *Sanders of the River,* with Robertson an unlikely villain called Magnus. *Blood on the Arrow* (1964) was one of the cheapest looking Westerns ever made, but the star and his leading lady Martha Hyer kept it well afloat by good acting.

He returned to television with another Western series, *The Iron Horse,* in 1966. His own production company, Dagonet, was a major partner. Its pilot, *Scalplock,* left much to be desired, but the series itself was solid and well-regarded without ever reaching the popularity or classic status of *Wells Fargo.* In this hour-length series, the star played Ben Calhoun, a hellraising highroller who won a railroad in a poker game. The Buffalo Pass, Scalplock and Defiance Line was only half built and virtually bankrupt, so Calhoun was left with the task of raising sufficient capital to finish the job. Along

Dale Robertson in *Tales of Wells Fargo*.

the way he and his associates encountered Indians, badmen and crooked businessmen, all of whom sought to delay or prevent the task. *The Iron Horse* lasted through 47 episodes until 1968. Robertson gravitated in real life toward those members of the profession who were ranchers by avocation. He was a close friend of the much-loved actor Robert Taylor. When Taylor died, Robertson assumed his chores as the host and occasional star of the cheapjack, syndicated but very popular anthology Western series *Death Valley Days* until the early 1970s.

After its demise he turned up in the occasional telemovie and guest star in television series, of which the best remembered were his appearances as a flamboyant G-man in the telemovies *Melvin Purvis G-Man* (1974) and *The Kansas City Massacre* (1975), the sequel being better than the original. The star diversified his interests during the 1970s. He traveled extensively, notably to Japan, where he allegedly made a movie called *The Walking Major.* He spent years studying film editing, scoring and cinematography, possibly in anticipation of producing movies. He participated in celebrity golfing tournaments and did particularly well in the 1970s. A country and western music enthusiast, he recorded an album in 1973.

He returned to prominence in 1981 when he became one of the first actors to costar in both *Dynasty* and *Dallas.* He also turned his back on both. He quit *Dynasty* after only 13 episodes as crusty, wildcatting oil rigger Walter Lankershim. He retired after only three episodes of *Dallas* in which he played Miss Ellie's boyfriend Frank Crutcher. Asked the reason for leaving *Dynasty,* he recalls, "I did not like the direction the show was taking. I thought *Dynasty* was going to be an interesting show about big business, but it kind of wound up as nothing but a story about monkey business." It was hard to imagine him having much patience with the conventions of soap opera. His character in *Dynasty* was the only one who actively seemed to be working for a living. The actor preferred to return to Oklahoma. He added, "I didn't really want to be a part of either. I'd like to see them bring back good, wholesome shows where people still have a good, wonderful outlook on life. We don't have good story tellers anymore, that's the problem."

The first person to be inducted into Oklahoma's Motion Picture Hall of Fame, he was voted into the National Cowboy Hall of Fame in 1983. He was described as "a millionaire racehorse breeder with a 430-acre ranch in Yukon, Oklahoma, and a partnership in Haymaker Farms with his brother, Chet. This vast expanse of land, covering over a thousand acres, is situated in the beautiful country of the Canadian River County, not far from the center of Oklahoma City." The actor pronounced himself a happy man. "I have a good life right now and enjoy every day and everything I do. Why it's fun just getting out of bed every morning."

His good fortune did not last. He suffered a series of reverses in the late 1980s which included breaking his hip and filing for bankruptcy in a Tulsa court in 1986 with debts of over $1,000,000. He had been offered megabucks to continue with *Dallas,* and he must have wished he had accepted. To pay off his creditors he made another assault on the citadel of series television with *J.J. Starbuck* (1987) as a folksy, Texas billionaire. At home in San Antonio, Texas Starbuck keeps his eye on his billion dollar corporation, Marklee Industries, while his longtime friend and business partner Charlie Bullets (Jimmy Dean) runs the day-to-day operation as chairman of the giant conglomerate. Starbuck lives with his niece Jill Starbuck (Shawn Weatherly), who is studying to be a CPA. Home is an unpretentious but comfortable lodging in a ranch house, surrounded by good neighbors. Using his wits, guile and common sense, Starbuck tries to correct "situations that jest don't appear quite right." He drives around the country in his 1964 Lincoln Continental, which boasts steerhorns on the hood and a horn which blares "The Eyes of Texas" whenever he cares to honk it. He never charges a fee and frequently helps people whom society has given up on. *J.J. Starbuck,* which was described by one critic as "Matt Houston grown old," was created by Stephen J. Cannell.

Early in 1988 J.J. picked up a super conman and disguise artist, Tenspeed Turner (Ben Vereen, who had played the same character in a failed 1980 series). Unlike some other television series which starred veterans around the same time, it was a ratings hit. At the time he went bust, his agents were negotiating for his remuneration for this series. When the news became public, his salary offer dropped by half. Financially, he would have been out of trouble if the series had lasted two seasons. Its cancellation after just one season sent shock waves through the television industry, not to mention Robertson's creditors. Ironically, at least one series *(Jake and the Fatman)* which started at the same time and had consistently worse ratings ran much longer. Since then Robertson has been relatively little seen, but he did turn up (oddly unbilled) in a prominent role as Lee Goddard in two of the best-scripted episodes of *Murder She Wrote* in 1988: "The Last Flight of Dixie Damsel" and "Prediction: Murder." He was as strong and charming as ever and even proposed to Jessica Fletcher! More recently he played Lloyd Bridges' brother in the CBS television series *Harts of the West.*

When Robertson was young he met and married an older career lady from Oklahoma. By all accounts this marriage lasted only a short time, and they divorced shortly after he returned home from the war. Secondly he married a young and beautiful 19-year-old debutante named Jacqueline Wilson, who came from a very affluent family. They wed in 1951 after a whirlwind five-day romance. They had a daughter, Rochelle, who was born on July 10, 1952, and who now lives in France. The Robertsons lived in a modest, two-bedroom bungalow in Reseda, California. Their different upbringing made them incompatible, so they divorced in 1954. In June 1956, he eloped to Yuma with actress Mary Murphy, whom he first met when they costarred in *Sitting Bull* (1954). Acting commitments drove them apart, and when their marriage was annulled in 1957 it was estimated that of their nine months as man and wife, they had spent only six of them together. Murphy, who in recent years has worked for Greenpeace and in a Los Angeles art gallery, recalls him with affection: "Dale is a lovely man. We're still good friends. There are a lot of men like that. They're great until they become your husband." In 1959 he married Lulu Mae Harding. With her he has an adopted daughter Rebel Lee, who was born in 1961 and resides in Oklahoma City. A son was stillborn. They divorced after 17 years in 1977. The divorce settlement cost him a million dollars. Asked about those failed marriages, he replies, "Joe Louis was the greatest champion who ever lived and he lost his first 13 fights." Since then he has found happiness with his fifth wife, Susan Dee. He is still an optimist. He says, "My hip is fine and as far as finances go, you never lose anything until you give up and I never want to know how to give up!"

Dale Robertson Filmography

1948: *The Boy with Green Hair, Johnny Belinda.*
1949: *The Girl from Jones Beach, Flamingo Road, Fighting Man of the Plains.*
1950: *The Cariboo Trail, Two Flags West.*
1951: *Call Me Mister, Golden Girl, Take Care of My Little Girl.*
1952: *Lydia Bailey, Return of the Texan, The Outcasts of Poker Flat, O. Henry's Full House* ("The Clarion Call" sequence).
1953: *The Silver Whip, The Farmer Takes a Wife, City of Bad Men, Devil's Canyon, Son of Sinbad* (released 1955).
1954: *The Gambler from Natchez, Sitting Bull.*
1955: *Top of the World.*
1956: *The High Terrace, A Day of Fury, Dakota Incident.*
1957: *Hell Canyon Outlaws, Anna of Brooklyn (*a.k.a. *Fast and Sexy).*
1964: *Law of the Lawless, Blood on the Arrow, Coast of Skeletons.*
1965: *The Man from Button Willow* (cartoon, voice only, also produced).
1966: *One Eyed Soldiers, Scalplock* (TV).
1974: *Melvin Purvis G-Man* (TV).
1975: *Kansas City Massacre* (TV).
1979: *The Last Ride of the Dalton Gang* (TV).

Television Series

1957–1962: *Tales of Wells Fargo* as Jim Hardie.
1966–1968: *The Iron Horse* as Ben Calhoun.
1968–1972: *Death Valley Days*—host and occasional star.
1981: *Dynasty* as Walter Lankershim.
1987–1988: *J.J. Starbuck* as J.J.Starbuck.
1993–1994: *Harts of the West.*

Sources

Corneau, Ernest N. *The Hall of Fame of Western Film Stars.* North Quincy, MA: Christopher, 1969.
Correspondence between Robertson and the author.*Picture Show Annual.* London: Amalgamated Press, 1953 and 1959.
Dacre, Peter. "Where Are They Now?" *Sunday Express* newspaper, May 5, 1985.
"Dale Goes Bust." *Sunday Express* newspaper, November 2, 1986.
The Fans' Star Library No. 10: The Real Dale Robertson. London: The Amalgamated Press, 1958.

Ferguson, Ken. *Western Television and Film Annual.* London: Purnell, 1963 and 1964.
Miller, Lee O. *The Great Cowboy Stars of Movies and Television.* New Rochelle, NY: Arlington House, 1979.
Photoplay magazine. Special TV Western issue, July 1960.
Picture Show Annual. London: Amalgamated Press, 1953 and 1959.

ANN ROBINSON

Ann Robinson was born in Hollywood on May 25, 1929, the daughter of a bank official. Even as a child at Hollywood High School, she was very keen on dramatics and appeared in plays. Initially she broke into films as a stunt girl and double. For a while she used the name of Ann Robin because there was a stuntwoman by the name of Ann Robinson. Her first film role as an actress was a bit in *A Place in the Sun* (1951). She auditioned for a play called *The Wind Without Rain* and won a part. It was staged at the Circle Theater and lasted about ten weeks. Milt Lewis, a talent scout from Paramount, saw her in this and asked her to read for the studio.

Despite this, she had no real test until Robert Walker fell seriously ill while shooting *My Son John* (1952); Lewis called her and said, "We have a whole crew standing by. Come over. We'd like to do a screen test of you." They tested her and she signed a contract with Paramount in late 1951, becoming one of the Golden Circle of stars of the future. She was tested by producer George Pal for *The War of the Worlds* (1953), a classic sci-fi movie which starred Gene Barry. Since physically she looked wrong for the role, Pal changed her appearance. The movie was shot on a soundstage and back lot, with some location shooting in Arizona. She made no other films at Paramount, and they dropped her from their list of contract players. However, when it came time to do a promotional tour for *The War of the Worlds,* the studio hired her back (at a much greater salary) as a freelance.

She then went to Warner Bros. where she shot *Dragnet* (1954), the feature film version of the television series starring Jack Webb. Warner wanted her for the role of Randy Monaghan in the television series *King's Row,* but she had already signed with independent producer Edward Small to do the Western television series *Fury* in which she played Helen Watkins, the schoolteacher girlfriend of Jim Newton (Peter Graves). She had another semi-regular role as an alien queen in *Rocky Jones Space Ranger.* She also appeared in two Western features for Edward Small and did a large number of television shows.

On July 7, 1957, she attended a bullfight in Mexico City. On a whim she met and married Jaime Bravo, a famous Mexican matador, the same day. With him she had two children, Jaime (a director with ABC Sports) and Estefan (a back up singer with a singing group called Human Drama). She lived for many years in Mexico City, followed the bullfighting circuit and virtually retired from acting. Her only work in several years was an episode of *Gilligan's Island* in 1963. They divorced in 1967. Bravo was killed in a car crash in Mexico in 1970. In 1987 she married Joseph Valdez, a real estate broker.

In 1977 Paramount decided to reissue *The War of the Worlds.* This was orchestrated as a media event and kickstarted her career again. She had a guest shot on *Police Woman,* did a part in the soap opera *Days of Our Lives* and appeared in a Canadian-lensed television series of *The War of the Worlds.* She also shot a feature film of *Space Patrol,* but because of technical problems, it was re-edited and became a film-within-a-film in the low-budget *Midnight Movie Massacre* (1988). She has also done a number of voiceovers and commercials. At last report she was residing with her husband in Los Angeles.

Ann Robinson Filmography

1949: *The Story of Molly X, Black Midnight.*

Ann Robinson and Peter Graves in *Fury*.

1950: *Frenchie, Peggy, Abbott and Costello in the Foreign Legion.*
1951: *An American in Paris, A Place in the Sun, Goodbye My Fancy, Callaway Went Thataway, I Want You, The Cimarron Kid.*
1952: *Son of Ali Baba.*
1953: *The War of the Worlds, The Glass Wall, Bad for Each Other.*
1954: *Dragnet.*
1956: *Gun Brothers, Julie.*
1957: *Gun Duel in Durango* (a.k.a. *Duel in Durango).*
1958: *Damn Citizen.*
1959: *Imitation of Life.*
1988: *Midnight Movie Massacre.*

Television Series

1954–1955: *Rocky Jones Space Ranger* as Juliandra.
1955–1958: *Fury* as Helen Watkins.

Sources

Fagen, Herb. "The Hollywood Girl: An Interview With Ann Robinson." *Classic Images* magazine, no. 216, June 1993.
Weaver, Tom. *Attack of the Monster Movie Makers: Interviews with 20 Genre Giants.* Jefferson, NC: McFarland, 1994.

ROBERT ROCKWELL

Robert Rockwell was born in Chicago, Illinois, on October 5, 1921. His father died when he was four years old. He was raised in Lake Bluff, Illinois, by his mother, who was principal of the local grade school. He was educated at Highland Park High School where he appeared in school plays. Enrolling at the University of Illinois to study business, he gradually realized that his primary interest was in the theater, so he dropped out. He switched to the Pasadena Playhouse where he studied for three-and-a-half years. Almost immediately after this he was drafted during World War II and served in the navy until his discharge, when he went to New York to act.

His big break came in 1947, when he was cast in the Broadway production of *Cyrano de Bergerac* which starred Jose Ferrer. From there he relocated to Hollywood where he made his screen debut in *You Gotta Stay Happy* (1948). He signed a contract with Republic, for whom he turned out a number of B pictures. *Our Miss Brooks* began in 1948 as a radio series and was transferred to television, where it ran from October 3, 1952, until September 21, 1956. Miss Brooks was a high school teacher played by Eve Arden. One theme of the series dealt with the relationship between her and the shy biology teacher Philip Boynton, originally played by Jeff Chandler. When he left to pursue a film career, he was replaced by Robert Rockwell both in the radio and television versions. In the Warner Bros. feature film of *Our Miss Brooks* (1956) he again played Boynton. When the series ended, Rockwell was so typecast that he was unemployed for a year.

He appeared several times in the anthology series *The Loretta Young Show,* where he invariably played her husband. The actor then had his own television series called *The Man from Blackhawk.* This was a rather unusual Western series in which he played Sam Logan, an investigator for the Blackhawk Insurance Company in the late 1880s. Logan traveled the West wearing a business suit and string tie and carrying a carpetbag with a Blackhawk bird logo on it. His primary target was crooks who tried to swindle the company. At the same time he tried to honor legitimate claims. He seldom carried a gun, but was quick to use his fists if the need arose. He mainly traveled by stagecoach but would ride a horse if necessary. The range of his cases covered the entire West from sophisticated cities such as San Francisco to rough frontier towns. *The Man from Blackhawk* made its debut on ABC on October 9, 1959, and lasted through 37 half-hour black and white episodes until September 23, 1960. It was a production of Screen Gems, Columbia's television arm.

The series was created and produced by Herb Meadow, who had a very clear vision of what he wanted in the series. He hired excellent writers, directors and supporting casts, and initially it did extremely well in the ratings. Part way through the first season, Rockwell was sent on personal appearance tours to promote the series. When he returned he found that Herb Meadow had been fired. The writers' strike was on at the time, and Columbia recycled old scripts from other series and films and reshot them to reach the needed quota of episodes. They sliced the budget by half, shot only interiors and used generous lumps of stock footage to simulate exteriors. Audiences, like Sam Logan, were not so easily deceived and the series was not renewed for a second season.

Rockwell has appeared in a wide range of other television series from the early 1950s onwards. He is particularly well remembered for playing Jor-El, the father of Superman (George Reeves), in the premiere episode of *The Adventures of Superman* in 1951. He made multiple appearances on *Lassie* and *Perry Mason.* He played the head coach on a few episodes of *The Bill Cosby Show* and had a regular role on the daytime soap *Search for Tomorrow* for one year in the late 1970s. This led to appearances on 1980s prime time soaps such as *Flamingo Road, Dallas* and *Dynasty.* More recently he has appeared in comedy series such as *Private Benjamin* and *Benson,* and he played Jane Powell's husband on *Growing Pains.* He has also done numerous voiceovers and commercials. He continued his stage career appearing with Ginger Rogers and in the two-hander *I Do, I Do.* His film career never really took off, his only later role being as David McCallum's boss in the tough thriller *Sol Madrid.* His image in that 1968 film was far removed from that of Philip Boynton, the role which has continued to haunt him.

He built a house in Pacific Palisades, where he has resided since 1956 with his wife. They have three sons, two daughters and several grandchildren. A civic-minded person active in community affairs, he has served as honorary mayor of that area.

Robert Rockwell Filmography

1948: *You Gotta Stay Happy.*

1949: *Task Force, Alias the Champ, The Red Menace, Blonde Bandit.*

Robert Rockwell in *The Man from Blackhawk.*

1950: *Federal Agent at Large, Belle of Old Mexico, Unmasked, Destination Big House, Woman from Headquarters, Trial Without Jury, Lonely Hearts Bandits, Prisoners in Petticoats.*
1951: *The Frogmen, The Prince Who Was a Thief.*
1952: *The Turning Point.*
1953: *The War of the Worlds.*
1956: *Our Miss Brooks.*
1968: *Sol Madrid.*

Television Series

1952–1956: *Our Miss Brooks* as Philip Boynton.
1959–1960: *The Man from Blackhawk* as Sam Logan.
1977–1978: *Search for Tomorrow.*

Sources

Brooks, Tim. *The Complete Directory to Prime Time TV Stars 1946-Present.* New York: Ballantine Books, 1987.
Inman, David. *The TV Encyclopedia.* New York: Perigee, 1991.
Lamparski, Richard. *Whatever Became Of? Ninth Series.* New York: Crown, 1985.
Magers, Boyd. "Empty Saddles." *Western Clippings* magazine, Herb Meadow, May/June 1995.
Perry, Jeb H. *Screen Gems: A History of Columbia Pictures Television from Cohn to Coke, 1948–1983.* Metuchen, NJ: Scarecrow, 1991.
Summers, Neil. *The Official TV Western Book Volume #2.* Vienna, WV: Old West Publishing Shop, 1989.

ROY ROGERS

Ralph Edwards, the host of *This Is Your Life,* once admitted that he received more requests to present the life of Roy Rogers than any other person. Rogers has for decades been known as "King of the Cowboys." To millions of fans he was the hero in the white hat who, astride his palomino horse Trigger, vanquished the bad guys. From 1943 to 1955 he was America's number one cowboy star at the box office. After making numerous motion pictures, he became a television star in the appropriately titled *The Roy Rogers Show* (1951–1957). Once quizzed on whether it was a burden to be Roy Rogers all the time, he replied, "Why, no, it's a real good responsibility, all those kids, lookin' up to me." Of his offscreen personality Rex Allen has said, "He's just a fantastic individual and I think a lot of him. He paid his dues and he damn well deserves everything good that's happened to him."

Roy Rogers was born Leonard Franklin Slye in Cincinnati, Ohio, on November 5, 1911. He was one of four children and the only son of Andrew E. and Martha "Mattie" (Womack) Slye. His father worked in the factory of the United States Shoe Company in Cincinnati.

His mother enjoyed music and could play several instruments. Early in his life he took a trip by houseboat down the Ohio River from Cincinnati to Portsmouth, where the family lived for several years.

In 1919 Andy Slye moved his family to a small farm in Duck Run, Ohio, where his son learned to tend cows, chickens and hogs, and to do planting and plowing. He became proficient at playing the guitar, sang very well and was a popular square dance caller. When he was 17, his father gave up the farm and the family moved back to Cincinnati. Leonard Slye dropped out of high school after the tenth grade and went to work alongside his father in the shoe factory.

One of his sisters (Mary) had married and gone to live in California. He had saved $100 and persuaded his father, who was fed up with the shoe factory, to visit her in California along with the rest of his immediate family. They packed their belongings in a battered 1923 Dodge and went there on vacation. The journey was long and difficult. In an oft-quoted remark, he has said regarding *The Grapes of Wrath* by John Steinbeck, "There are parts of that book that make me wonder if maybe Mr. Steinbeck wasn't looking over the shoulders of the Slye family." Although the family later returned to Ohio, Leonard Slye chauffeured his sister's father-in-law back to California a few months later and stayed. Initially he drove a truck and picked peaches to earn money.

At the insistence of his sister Mary, he appeared on radio on an amateur talent show called *Midnight Frolic* from Inglewood, California, in which he strummed his guitar and sang. On the strength of his radio appearances, he was engaged as a guitarist and occasional vocalist with an instrumental group known as the Rocky Mountaineers. He has since recalled, "The Depression forced me into the entertainment field due to the scarcity of other employment." When the Rocky Mountaineers disbanded, he formed a group called the International Cowboys. This group evolved into the O-Bar-O Cowboys. The group was hired for a barnstorming tour of the Southwest, supplementing their virtually nonexistent fees by hunting jack rabbits and cottontail and accepting food contributions from their audiences.

When appearing on radio in Roswell, New Mexico, there was a phoned promise of lemon meringue pie if he would do "The Swiss Yodel." When Slye did this, the following day a Mrs. Wilkins and her pretty daughter Arlene turned up at the radio station to present him with a couple of pies. Slye instantly fell in love with the daughter. They continued to write to each other and eventually married on June 14, 1936, at her family's home in Roswell. Returning home to Los Angeles in September 1933, the group dissolved. He was briefly and unhappily part of Jack Lefevre and His Texas Outlaws. With two former Rocky Mountaineers, he formed the Pioneer Trio. They rehearsed diligently and were joined by two new members.

They won fame as the Sons of the Pioneers, a name given to them inadvertently by a radio announcer. In 1934 the group broadcast from coast to coast and recorded four songs for Delta Records including "Tumbling Tumbleweeds," which became their theme song. The Sons of the Pioneers remained with station KFWB until 1936, when they joined the *Hollywood Barn Dance* on radio station KNX. From 1935 onwards the Sons of the Pioneers were also seen in motion pictures. They appeared in some Charles Starrett and Gene Autry westerns and the Bing Crosby musical *Rhythm on the Range* (1936).

In 1937 Slye was in a hat shop in Glendale dropping off his Stetson which needed to be cleaned and reblocked. While there he overheard a young cowboy who rushed in and bought a new hat for an audition which Republic was having the next day for singing cowboys. Although Slye had difficulty sneaking past the guard, he managed to slip in with some returning employees after lunch. By pure coincidence he was glimpsed by Sol Siegel, the producer who was auditioning the singing cowboys. Fortunately, Siegel was familiar with his singing as one of the Sons of the Pioneers. Although he had auditioned 17 cowboys, none of them seemed right. At the audition Slye sang "Hadie Brown," a song with a fast yodel in it which impressed Siegel.

Although he passed the audition, he was not screen tested. As part of the Sons of the Pioneers, he was hired to do background singing on a Gene Autry Western at Republic. He mentioned to director Joseph Kane that he had never been screen tested. Kane replied, "Let me see what I can do." He was screen

Roy Rogers and Trigger.

tested the following day and passed with flying colors. On October 13, 1937, he signed a contract with Republic. He appeared briefly in a couple of their Westerns under a new name (Dick Weston), but fame did not come overnight.

In early 1938 Gene Autry failed to report for shooting at the start of filming his new feature, which was tentatively called *Washington Cowboy.* In it he was to play a cowboy who confronts Congress with the suffering of ranchers and farmers whose fields and cattle were being destroyed by conditions in the Dust Bowl. Slye/Weston was cast in the leading role, but a further name change was dictated. The big brass were in the office of Republic president Herbert J. Yates, where they were running through prospective surnames. Slye chose Rogers because of his deep-rooted admiration for Will Rogers. Roy was chosen because it fitted well with Rogers. The cowboy star only legally changed his name in 1942.

Roy Rogers was shown several horses from which he chose a palomino originally called Golden Cloud. He recalled, "I got on him and rode him 100 yards and never looked at another horse." Although the horse originally came from Hudkins Stables, Rogers subsequently bought him. The horse was tough, fast and was seldom doubled except in long shots. Although he received billing in the movies, he was not under separate contract. He was dubbed "Trigger" by Smiley Burnette because of his speed. Rogers made all of his films astride the same horse. The original animal retired in 1957 and died in 1965 at age 33. Rogers had his remains stuffed and enshrined in his museum.

The title of the movie was changed to *Under Western Stars* (1938) and turned out to be a box office smash. The initial series of Rogers Westerns were set in the period from the Civil War to the late 1880s, so they were historical Westerns. Although Rogers sang a minimum of two songs per film, they were always introduced within the context of the movie. The character Roy Rogers played was almost always given a famous name such as "Billy the Kid" or "Buffalo Bill." He supported John Wayne in *Dark Command* (1940) and bucolic comedians the Weaver Brothers in two of their comedies. After 1942, Rogers became known as "King of the Cowboys" and even made a film with this title in 1943. His films reverted to modern times with more songs and lavish production numbers, and budgets were increased.

When Gene Autry entered the armed forces in 1942, Rogers became the number one Western box office champ in the world. Regarding military service he passed his physical examination, but before he was called up for service V-E Day came and the services stopped inducting anyone over 30. There was a monumental blaze of publicity to promote him which scored a bull's eye. *Idaho* (1943) was his first vehicle to play the prestigious Loew chain of first-run theaters. He was invited by President Franklin Delano Roosevelt to the White House in 1943 for a March of Dimes ball on the occasion of the President's 61st birthday. He gave Roosevelt a gift of silver spurs engraved "To F.D.R. from Roy Rogers" on that occasion. The climax of this attention probably came when Rogers made the cover of *Life* magazine on July 12, 1943.

His initial salary was $75 a week. Throughout his first contract Herbert Yates reduced the amount of the raise he was supposed to receive. After five years he was still only earning $400 a week. Despite his enormous popularity, he could not afford to answer his fan mail. Yates refused to allow him to charge this to the studio, so on one occasion Rogers took a five-ton dump truck full of answered fan mail over to Republic, backed the truck onto the lawn of the studio and dumped it all. This made Yates fume. To supplement his meager income, Rogers did one-night stands. On one occasion he played 138 dates in 20 days. In 1943, while he was playing Madison Square Garden, he met some businessmen who wanted him for some commercial endorsements, but he had to secure a release from Yates. The president of Republic did give him such a paper, but only because he was not giving him a raise that year.

In 1943 at Edwards Air Force Base in Lancaster, California, he was introduced by his agent Art Rush to singer Dale Evans. Although romance did not ignite immediately, she became his leading lady and they made their first film together, *The Cowboy and the Señorita* (1944). Rogers inked a new seven-year pact with Republic in 1944. In the same year he inaugurated a network radio program called *The Roy Rogers Show* sponsored by Goodyear. While it did moderately well in the ratings, Goodyear did not pick up the option and the show went off the air in the spring of 1945. At the peak of his popularity in 1945, he was receiving 75,000 fan letters in one month alone. Tragedy struck, however, when his wife Arlene died suddenly of a blood clot on November 3, 1946. Left with three children to raise on his own, he became increasingly close to Dale Evans and they were wed on December 31, 1947, at the Flying L Ranch in Davis, Oklahoma.

In all his years at Republic, Rogers was directed by only four men (Joseph Kane, Frank McDonald, John English and William Witney). Of these the one who made the single greatest impact was Witney, who liked action and violence. In *The Bells of San Angelo* (1947) the hero took a savage beating at the hands of the villains. This marked a new departure for a Rogers feature, and the trend continued in his other Witney-directed vehicles such as *Twilight on the Sierras* (1950), where Rogers rescues a man and woman bound and gagged inside a burning runaway stagecoach. Of his own films he is most fond of *Under Western Stars* (1938), *My Pal Trigger* (1946), *The Golden Stallion* (1949) and *Trigger Jr.* (1950). *My Pal Trigger* is his all-time favorite.

In the fall of 1948 he began another radio series sponsored by Quaker Oats on the Mutual Broadcasting System. When Quaker Oats declined to renew his contract in 1951, the show was later sponsored by General Foods and Dodge Motors. His contract with Republic expired on May 27, 1951, and it was widely assumed that he would re-sign with them, but he insisted that his new contract include clauses allowing him television rights plus a percentage from the sale of his old movies to television. Herbert Yates refused to allow him such rights and announced the imminent sale of a package of his old movies to TV. Lawyers acting on behalf of the star threatened Yates with an injunction since Rogers had retained all rights to his own image, which was interpreted to mean television. Simultaneously, Rogers' manager was negotiating with potential sponsors for a half-hour television series. The contract expiry date came and went without a new contract being signed. Republic sold the Rogers films to television in June 1951, and Rogers' attorney obtained a temporary restraining order, forbidding the use of the Rogers name for commercial purposes. Soon a contract was signed with General Foods allowing Rogers to do a television series.

On September 13, 1951, the hearing began on the lawsuit filed by Rogers against Republic. After over a month of testimony, the court ruled in favor of Rogers. Republic announced immediately that it would appeal. In June 1954, the United States Court of Appeals reversed a portion of the original verdict, which allowed the sale of the old movies to television. The Gene Autry and Roy Rogers features were both involved in the litigation, and Wall Street experts calculated that the studio would garner at least $20,000,000 in revenue from this sale. The star himself did not make a cent.

The benefit from the original verdict was that Rogers was now free to do television. The premiere of *The Roy Rogers Show* on NBC was on December 30, 1951. The first half-hour was a live show from the El Capitan Theater in Hollywood with regulars Roy Rogers, Dale Evans and Pat Brady, and special guest star Bob Hope. The second half of the program consisted of the first episode of the regular 30-minute black and white adventure series. In it Rogers played the owner of the rambling Double R Bar Ranch located in Paradise Valley in the modern West. Close to the ranch was Mineral City, where Dale Evans operated the Eureka Cafe. The animal stars of the series were horses Trigger and Buttermilk and a German Shepherd dog called Bullet. A Jeep named Nellybelle run by Pat Brady was also prominent in the series. The show lasted in its original run for 104 episodes on NBC, the last episode being aired on June 23, 1957. Although the series was a big success, it did not duplicate his popularity in movies and was not the winner that *Hopalong Cassidy* and *The Lone Ranger* were.

On television Rogers did 14 specials, sponsored by the Chevrolet Division of General Motors, which were top guns ratings-wise. He and Dale Evans were the stars of the short-lived musical variety series *The Roy Rogers and Dale Evans Show* presented on ABC in 1962. On NBC the couple occasionally hosted *Kraft Music Hall* from 1967 to 1971. In 1977 Rogers hosted and narrated the TV special *The Great Movie Cowboys*. In 1966 they went on a USO tour of American bases in Vietnam. Aside from *Son of Paleface* (1952) and a cameo in *Alias Jesse James* (1959), both starring Bob Hope, he was offscreen until *Mackintosh and T.J.* (1975), where he played an aging ranch hand who befriends a homeless teenage boy. Rogers made the film (shot on location in the Texas Cap Rock high plains country) because it represented solid, family-style entertainment. He has occasionally guested on television series, most recently on *The Fall Guy* in 1984.

In 1964 Rogers and Evans moved to Apple Valley, California, where they opened the Roy Rogers Museum. In 1976 they relocated to Victorville, California, where they live today, every aspect of the move being supervised by the duo. His business interests include extensive real estate holdings, the Paramount-Roy Rogers music publishing company and a chain of over 500. Roy Rogers Family Restaurants. Rogers has been the recipient of numerous civic honors and has penned and recorded numerous popular songs. He underwent successful triple cardiac bypass surgery in 1978.

His hobbies include bowling, hunting, fishing and collecting minerals. He is a strong Republican who campaigned vigorously on behalf of Ronald Reagan, but declined to run for Congress in 1970 on the grounds that he numbered Democrats and Republicans among his fans and did not want to lose the support of either. They have toured with Billy Graham and other leading evangelists. His personal wealth is estimated to be in the vicinity of $100 million.

By his first wife Roy Rogers has two children, Linda Lou (born April 18, 1943) and Roy, Jr., nicknamed Dusty (born on October 28, 1946, six days before his mother died). There is another daughter, Cheryl Darlene, adopted at four months old from Hope Cottage, Louisville, Kentucky, in 1941, at a time when it was wrongly believed that Rogers and his first wife could not have children. The only child born to Rogers and Dale Evans was Robin Elizabeth, born August 26, 1950, stricken with Down's Syndrome and a heart condition. She died August 24, 1952, two days before her second birthday, of complications from mumps. To help them overcome their grief, they adopted Mary Little Doe, nicknamed Dodie, a Choctaw Indian from Hope Cottage, Dallas, in October 1952. In 1952, they adopted a six-year-old son, Harry, from a foster home in Covington, Kentucky. They changed his name to John David, nicknamed Sandy. On October 31, 1965, he choked to death while serving in the United States Army in Germany. Marion Fleming was an 11-year-old native of Scotland who was adopted in 1954. In 1955, they adopted a Korean war orphan named Deborah, but she died in a church bus accident in San Clemente, California, on August 17, 1964, at age 12. Evans also has a son, Thomas Frederick Fox, Jr., born on November 28, 1927, from a previous marriage. Over the years they have stated many times that only their deep religious convictions have helped to sustain them in the face of these tragedies. At last report they have 15 grandchildren and 30 great-grandchildren. Once asked the essence of Roy Rogers' appeal, his son Dusty responded, "He says, 'I am what I am!' He's like Popeye. What you see is what you get; very honest, very straightforward. He never tries to be anything other than what he is. People like that."

Roy Rogers Filmography

1935: *The Old Homestead, Way Up Thar, Tumbling Tumbleweeds, Gallant Defender.*

1936: *The Big Show, Rhythm on the Range, The Mysterious Avenger, The Old Corral.*

1937: *The Old Wyoming Trail, Wild Horse Rodeo.*

1938: *The Old Barn Dance, Under Western Stars, Come on Rangers, Shine on Harvest Moon, Billy the Kid Returns.*

1939: *Rough Riders' Roundup, Frontier Pony Express, Southward Ho, In Old Caliente, The Arizona Kid, Wall Street Cowboy, Saga of Death Valley, Days of Jesse James, Jeepers Creepers.*

1940: *Dark Command, The Carson City Kid, The Ranger and the Lady, Colorado, Young Buffalo Bill, Young Bill Hickok, Border Legion.*

1941: *Robin Hood of the Pecos, In Old Cheyenne, Arkansas Judge, Nevada City, Sheriff of Tombstone, Bad Men of Deadwood, Jesse James at Bay, Red River Valley.*

1942: *Man from Cheyenne, South of Santa Fe, Sunset on the Desert, Romance on the Range, Sons of the Pioneers, Sunset Serenade, Heart of the Golden West, Ridin' Down the Canyon.*

1943: *King of the Cowboys, Idaho, Song of Texas, Silver Spurs, Man from Music Mountain, Hands Across the Border.*

1944: *The Cowboy and the Señorita, The Yellow Rose of Texas, Song of Nevada, San Fernando Valley, Lights of Old Santa Fe, Brazil, Hollywood Canteen, Lake Placid Serenade.*

1945: *Bells of Rosarita, Utah, Sunset in El Dorado, The Man from Oklahoma, Don't Fence Me In, Along the Navajo Trail.*

1946: *Song of Arizona, Rainbow Over Texas, My Pal Trigger, Under Nevada Skies, Roll on Texas Moon, Home in Oklahoma, Out California Way, Heldorado.*

1947: *Hit Parade of 1947, Apache Rose, Bells of San Angelo, Springtime in the Sierras, On the Old Spanish Trail.*

1948: *The Gay Ranchero, Under California Skies, Eyes of Texas, Nighttime in Nevada, Grand Canyon Trail, The Far Frontier.*

1949: *Susanna Pass, Down Dakota Way, The Golden Stallion, Bells of Coronado.*

1950: *Twilight in the Sierras, Trigger Jr., Sunset in the West, North of the Great Divide, Trail of Robin Hood.*

1951: *Spoilers of the Plains, Heart of the Rockies,*

In Old Armarillo, South of Caliente, Pals of the Golden West.
1952: *Son of Paleface.*
1959: *Alias Jesse James* (cameo).
1975: *Mackintosh and T.J.*
1983: *The Gambler: The Adventure Continues* (TV).

Television Series

1951–1957: *The Roy Rogers Show* as Roy Rogers.
1962: *The Roy Rogers and Dale Evans Show.*

Sources

Corneau, Ernest N. *The Hall of Fame of Western Film Stars.* North Quincy, MA: Christopher, 1969.
Current Biography. New York: H.W. Wilson, 1983.
Miller, Lee O. *The Great Cowboy Stars of Movies and Television.* New Rochelle, NY: Arlington House, 1979.
Parish, James Robert. *Great Western Stars.* New York: Ace, 1976.
Rothel, David. *The Singing Cowboys.* San Diego, CA: Barnes, 1978.
Russell, Sue, and Roy Rogers, Jr. "Roy Rogers: The Legend Lives On." *Hello!* magazine, February 1996.
Tuska, Jon. *The Filming of the West.* Garden City, NY: Doubleday, 1976.

CARLOS ROMERO

Born in 1927, this character actor played the part of Rico Rodriguez, a reformed Mexican gun-fighter turned deputy marshal, in the Western series *Wichita Town.*

Carlos Romero Filmography

1958: *The World Was His Jury, The Gun Runners.*
1959: *They Came to Cordura.*
1962: *The Deadly Duo.*
1964: *Island of the Blue Dolphins.*
1966: *The Professionals.*
1969: *The D.A. Murder One* (TV).
1973: *Soylent Green.*

Television Series

1959–1960: *Wichita Town* as Deputy Marshal Rico Rodriguez.
1982: *Falcon Crest* as Carlo Agretti.

Sources

Summers, Neil. *The Official TV Western Book Volume #2.* Vienna, WV: Old West Publishing Shop, 1989.
Thomas, Tony. *Joel McCrea: Riding the High Country.* Burbank, CA: Riverwood Press, 1991.

HERBERT RUDLEY

Herbert Rudley was born in Philadelphia, Pennsylvania, on March 22, 1910. He graduated from high school there and entered Temple University to study law. He became active in a little theater group and then auditioned for Eva Le Gallienne's classical studio company, The Civic Repertory Theater. He passed the audition, dropped out of Temple University at the end of his second year, and went to New York to join the group on the strength of a scholarship. After a three-month trial he was accepted into the permanent company, which netted him $25 a week. He remained there for three years, appearing in several plays from 1928 onwards.

Feeling somewhat constricted with the company, but being much freer when doing summer stock elsewhere, he reluctantly decided to move on. Shortly afterwards he landed the juvenile lead in a critically acclaimed (but commercially unsuccessful) Broadway play, *We the People* by Elmer Rice. He was approached one evening by Lee Stewart, casting director for Warner Bros. short subjects in New York, who offered him a job. Not being impressed with movies, Rudley turned him down. It was the heart of the Depression. Unemployment and a lean period followed so, remembering Stewart's offer, he went to see him. Eventually this led to an appearance in a short subject for which he was paid $50.

When the WPA was formed, he obtained a nonperforming job in its theater wing, where he remained for a couple of years. When the Depression lifted, he obtained acting jobs again, earning excellent reviews for *Macbeth* and *Abe Lincoln in Illinois*. The latter brought him to Hollywood where he recreated his role in the film version of 1940. He appeared in a number of other plays on Broadway, but when it appeared he was likely to be drafted into the armed forces during World War II, he decided to relocate to California. There he hoped to earn enough money to support his wife and infant child while he was gone. However, he was not drafted.

In Hollywood he obtained representation from George Chasin, who became a powerful agent. Chasin was instrumental in securing him the role of Ira Gershwin in the Warner Bros. musical *Rhapsody in Blue* (1945), based on the life of George Gershwin. Production began on this movie in 1942, but release was delayed until 1945. This was his personal favorite of his many films. Warners offered him a seven-year contract, but he turned it down in favor of being a freelance, an erroneous decision which continued to haunt him down through the years. In retrospect he believed that with the exposure and promotion of a major studio behind him, he might have become a bigger name.

Nevertheless, he appeared in several other films until 1948. In that year he encountered another fallow period when the studios failed to call him for work. Even a switch of agent did not help. He was not, however, blacklisted. He started a theater called The Players Theater in which he invested a great deal of time and mounted some highly regarded productions, but it ran into financial difficulties. During this period he wrote a play, so he and his then-wife relocated to New York in order to find the necessary financial backing to mount a production. The play, which he wrote and directed, had a controversial theme and opened and closed out of town in two weeks.

A role as Linus in the major motion picture *The Silver Chalice* (1954) brought him back to Hollywood. Even though it flopped, it revived his reputation and he was cast in other feature films. With the decline in the number of movies being shot because of television, he began to work increasingly in the latter medium. He had regular roles in four series. The first was a Western series, *The Californians,* in which he played Sam Brennan, the newspaperman who employs Dion Patrick at the time when only vigilantes maintained law and order in San Francisco. To Rudley's chagrin, he was dropped after the first season when his role became largely redundant.

Another was a crime series, *Michael Shayne,* in which he played a Miami police chief. On the sitcom *Mona McCluskey* he played a general. His final regular role, also his most successful, was in the sitcom *The Mothers in Law,* in which he played the husband of Eve Arden. This was very well received and lasted two seasons before its demise at the hands of network politics. He also had an occasional recurring role on *Dallas* as J.R.'s attorney, but when he lost a case, his character had to be eliminated.

His final film dates from 1983, shortly after which he retired. Since then he has penned unpublished novels, polished his game of golf and pursued an active social life. He has been married four times, his latest marriage dating from the late 1950s. At last report he was residing in Marina Del Rey, California.

Herbert Rudley Filmography

1940: *Abe Lincoln in Illinois.*

1944: *Marriage Is a Private Affair, The Seventh Cross, The Big Noise, The Master Race.*

Portrait of Herbert Rudley, who appeared in *The Californians*.

1945: *Rhapsody in Blue, A Walk in the Sun, Brewster's Millions.*
1946: *Decoy.*
1948: *Hollow Triumph (*a.k.a. *The Scar), Casbah, Joan of Arc.*
1954: *The Silver Chalice.*
1955: *Artists and Models.*
1956: *The Black Sleep, The Court Jester, Raw Edge, That Certain Feeling.*
1958: *Tonka, The Bravados, The Young Lions.*
1959: *The Big Fisherman, The Jayhawkers, Beloved Infidel.*
1960: *The Great Imposter, Hell Bent for Leather, Who Was That Lady?*
1962: *Follow That Dream.*
1972: *Call Her Mom* (TV).
1980: *Falling in Love Again.*
1983: *Forever and Beyond.*

Television Series

1957–1958: *The Californians* as Sam Brennan.
1960–1961: *Michael Shayne* as Will Gentry.
1965–1966: *Mona McCluskey* as General Crone.
1967–1969: *The Mothers in Law* as Herb Hubbard.

Sources

Goldrup, Tom, and Jim Goldrup. *Feature Players: The Stories Behind the Faces Volume #2.* Published privately, 1992.
Twomey, Alfred E. and Arthur F. McClure. *The Versatiles.* South Brunswick and New York: Barnes, 1969.
Weaver, Tom. *Attack of the Monster Movie Makers: Interviews with 20 Genre Giants.* Jefferson, NC: McFarland, 1994.

JOHN RUSSELL

John Russell was stern, resolute, even intimidating when he played Dan Troop in *Lawman.* Even though he was only in his late thirties when he came to the role, he seemed to be much older, a comparison reinforced by his paternal mustache, string tie and graying hair. He was unusual in that, for the most part, Warner Bros. specifically created stars for their television series, whereas John Russell came to Warner Bros. after a successful ten-year career elsewhere.

Offscreen he was a sensitive man and a pillar of integrity. He seemed to have rather too much principle and too little talent for self-promotion for lasting success in the world of films and television. He stayed a jobbing actor all his life, although in later years the jobs were fewer and much less prestigious. His hobbies also tended to reveal the complexity of the man. In the extremely modest Hollywood apartment where he lived during the last part of his life, he read widely and voraciously and his shelves were crammed with books. On the other hand, he was a sportsman as well. He was placed by Robert Stack as among the top skeet shooters in Hollywood. Russell was also dedicated to the outdoors and the Western. As he expressed it once, "A look at the blue sky above and the reassuring feel of a horse underneath, that's all a man needs."

John Lawrence Russell was born in Los Angeles, California, on January 8, 1921, one of five children who were descended from a California pioneer family. He attended the University of California where he studied drama. He later said, "Dramatics was taken as an easy credit. If I'd known how hard I've had to work, I would have done something else." From 1942 to 1944 he served with the Marine Corps. He received a battlefield commission for valor at Guadalcanal and was honorably discharged as a second lieutenant. After the war he was spotted at a Beverly Hills restaurant and made his screen debut in *A Bell for Adano* (1945). He was under contract to 20th Century–Fox, Universal, Republic and Warner Bros. He was mainly typecast as a handsome heavy. When Ben Johnson's agent raised his asking price too high for John Ford, Russell inherited the role of Ashby Corwin in *The Sun Shines Bright* (1953). Russell delighted in telling stories about how irascible director Ford was.

His first stab at series television was the syndicated adventure series *Soldiers of Fortune* (1955–1956), which ran to 52 black and white episodes. He played Tim Kelly, and Chick Chandler was his sidekick Toubo Smith. They were of the "go anywhere, do anything" mentality as the title of the series implied. This was strictly backlot stuff, with sets and scenery which perpetually seemed to be on the point of falling down. Offscreen, however, Russell acknowledged his debt to Chandler, who he claimed added immensely to his knowledge and experience of acting.

He was excellent in the offbeat United Artists feature *Fort Massacre* (1958) as the somewhat ineffectual army recruit who is eventually forced to kill an Indian-hating cavalry sergeant (Joel McCrea) when he comes to realize that he is as crazed as some of the other men claim he is. He appeared in only two films during his Warner Bros. contract. They were *Yellowstone Kelly* (1959) and the classic *Rio Bravo* (1959), in which he played a smooth cattle baron and the brother of Claude Akins.

Russell played the role of a heavy in an episode of *Cheyenne* called "The Empty Gun" in 1958. He was a gunslinger with an injured hand who suffers an attack of conscience and wants to set matters right with the widow of one of his victims. His performance was so good that Warners wanted to create a series in which he would be the embodiment of law and order. Out of this came the *Lawman* series, which made its debut on ABC on October 5, 1958, and ran for four seasons. Its most successful season was its second, when it ranked 15th in the Nielsen ratings above all the other Warner Bros. Westerns.

The old West needed tough and dedicated sheriffs. One of them was Marshal Dan Troop (Russell), to whom maintaining law and order in Laramie, Wyoming, was a full-time job demanding a lifetime's dedication. A man of few words, Troop was a professional lawman who took his responsibilities with deadly seriousness. If there were citizens in his territory who needed help, they knew to whom they could turn. Once satisfied that a cause was a just one, he was a firm ally. Lawbreakers were his enemies and their days were numbered.

Of the character Russell said, "Troop doesn't laugh very often because he reckons that law and order is a serious business. But he is sympathetic and friendly, even fatherly. In one episode he had to deal with a gang of roughnecks who swooped into town. Maybe they caused some trouble, but they weren't vicious. Troop used an understanding approach here. He figured it was the best way to keep the town clean and peaceful. Although the Marshal has a first class deputy in Johnny McKay, he doesn't believe in letting a sidekick do all the work. The Troop fist will swing with the best, if there is a fight on."

The series was produced by Jules Schermer, a producer with a spare style, who referred to *Lawman* as a thinking Western. Troop was supported by Deputy Johnny McKay (Peter Brown). In the second season Lily Merrill (Peggie Castle), owner of the Birdcage Saloon, appeared. She helped the marshal unwind a little. Offscreen he was extremely proud of the efficiency with which the show was run. He was also somewhat consumed by the character of Troop. Will Hutchins said of him, "Even though we did a *Sugarfoot* together, he was always so serious about his work on *Lawman* at Warners that I didn't get too close."

There were problems, however, Russell, like most of the other Warner television stars, became very disenchanted with the dismal industrial relations which prevailed at the time. This took the form of endeavoring to keep salaries at rock bottom, refusing to grant pay increases, cheating stars out of residual payments and demanding a large percentage of fees for personal appearances. So repressive was the regime that whenever he went on personal

John Russell (left) with Peggie Castle and Peter Brown in *Lawman*.

appearance tours, notes were kept and reports were typed up on the standards which he and the other Warner stars maintained. It was only years later that he ever saw them.

The studio tried to conceal from their stars how popular they were and did not let them see their fan mail. One year Russell was the only Western star to obtain a pay increase when he produced evidence that *Lawman* was riding high in the ratings. The studio granted him the increase, but paid him back later. When *Lawman* was dropped from the schedules after 156 half-hour black and white episodes on October 2, 1962, they kept his costars on salary for a while afterwards, but terminated Russell's contract the following day.

Russell confided in Clint Walker, who urged him to get tough with the studio and walk out like himself and other Warner stars. He refused because his personal code, which was as pronounced as that of Dan Troop, forbade him to renege on a contract. He also had a family to provide for and could not afford to jeopardize their security. The sponsor of the series was a tobacco company. When Russell was stressed out, his first urge was to reach for a cigarette. That urge, which made him a chain smoker, later cost him his life.

Once free of his contract, his career fell away to nothing. He appeared in no films and did little television between late 1962 and 1965. Indeed it is possible to believe that he was on some kind of unofficial blacklist. Gradually he began to appear again, but his career was in much lower gear than he had been used to. He did an episode of *Daniel Boone* in 1965. This was followed by multiples of *It Takes a Thief* and *Alias Smith and Jones*. He played the head of Star Command on the daytime live action series *Jason of Star Command* (1979–1981). He guested on about a dozen other series until 1984. On the big screen, his appearances were equally unimpressive. He was a stalwart of the A.C. Lyles group in the 1960s, acting in Westerns made on a minuscule budget. He later appeared in three films which starred Clint Eastwood, his best-remembered appearance being in *Pale Rider* (1985) as the evil Marshal Stockburn.

It might be supposed that he had some other job aside from acting, but this is erroneous. He frequently lamented his inability to turn his hand to other jobs during the lean periods as other actors did. When not working he lived off welfare benefits. During his last years, he suffered increasingly from emphysema, a legacy of his heavy smoking, which forced him to turn down a couple of roles. This finally claimed his life in Los Angeles on January 19, 1991, at age 70. He had a military funeral and lies buried at the Santelle Military Cemetery in Westwood, California. Among others, his handsome son and daughter attended; his brother, a state senator, spoke well and humorously of his memories of John; and a crusty old marine buddy had warm remembrances as well.

John Russell was twice married and divorced. He had a long-standing marriage which crumbled in the 1960s and a marriage to a much younger woman (circa 1970) which was over almost as soon as it had begun. He was a dedicated family man. During his *Lawman* years he rose early and studied his lines diligently so that he could set aside time in the evenings for his family. He was survived by three children, two brothers and two sisters.

John Russell Filmography

1945: *A Bell for Adano, A Royal Scandal, Don Juan Quilligan, Within These Walls.*
1946: *Three Little Girls in Blue, Somewhere in the Night, The Dark Corner, Wake Up and Dream.*
1947: *Forever Amber.*
1948: *Sitting Pretty, Yellow Sky.*
1949: *Slattery's Hurricane, The Gal Who Took the West, The Story of Molly X, Undertow.*
1950: *Saddle Tramp, Frenchie.*
1951: *The Fat Man, Man in the Saddle, The Barefoot Mailman, Fighting Coast Guard, Hoodlum Empire.*
1952: *Oklahoma Annie.*
1953: *The Sun Shines Bright, Fair Wind to Java.*
1954: *Jubilee Trail.*
1955: *Hell's Outpost, The Last Command.*
1957: *Untamed Youth, The Dalton Girls, Hell Bound.*
1958: *Fort Massacre.*
1959: *Rio Bravo, Yellowstone Kelly.*
1965: *Apache Uprising.*
1966: *Fort Utah.*
1967: *Hostile Guns.*
1968: *Buckskin, If He Hollers Let Him Go!*
1970: *Cannon for Cordoba.*
1971: *Smoke in the Wind, Noon Sunday, Legacy of Blood, Alias Smith and Jones* (TV).
1975: *Lord Shango.*
1976: *The Outlaw Josey Wales, Six Tickets to Hell.*
1977: *Kino, the Padre on Horseback.*
1981: *Uncle Scam.*
1982: *Honkytonk Man.*
1985: *Pale Rider.*
1986: *Under the Gun.*

Television Series

1955–1956: *Soldiers of Fortune* as Tim Kelly.
1958–1962: *Lawman* as Dan Troop.

1979–1981: *Jason of Star Command* as Commander Stone.

Sources

Cameron, Ian, and Elisabeth Cameron. *The Heavies*. London: Studio Vista, 1967.
Correspondence between Will Hutchins and the author.
Inman, David. *The TV Encyclopedia*. New York: Perigee, 1991.
Parish, James Robert. *The Hollywood Death Book*. Las Vegas, NV: Pioneer, 1992.
Quinlan, David. *Illustrated Directory of Film Stars*. London: Batsford, 1996.
Woolley, Lynn, Robert W. Malsbary, and Robert G. Strange, Jr. *Warner Bros. Television*. Jefferson, NC: McFarland, 1985.

RALPH SANFORD

Born in Springfield, Massachusetts on May 21, 1899, this character actor made his screen debut in 1937. He played Jim "Dog" Kelly during one season of *The Life and Legend of Wyatt Earp*. Sixty-four years old, he died in Van Nuys, California, on June 20, 1963, of a heart ailment.

Ralph Sanford Filmography

1937: *Prescription for Romance, Sea Racketeers, Escape by Night.*
1938: *Broadway Musketeers, Blondes at Work, If I Were King, Angels with Dirty Faces, The Great Waltz, The Patient in Room 18, Give Me a Sailor, The Devil's Party, Girls on Probation, Reckless Living, Ride a Crooked Mile, Sweethearts.*
1939: *Undercover Agent, Little Accident, The Star Maker, They Asked for It, Kid Nightingale, Smashing the Money Ring, You Can't Cheat an Honest Man, Two Bright Boys, Torchy Blane Playing with Dynamite, Jeepers Creepers.*
1940: *Tear Gas Squad, Cross-Country Romance, Gaucho Serenade, Alias the Deacon, So You Won't Talk, Carolina Moon, Three Cheers for the Irish, Girls Under 21, Sandy Is a Lady, Stranger on the Third Floor, They Drive by Night, Black Diamonds, East of the River, In Old Missouri.*
1941: *High Sierra, Mr. and Mrs. Smith, Arkansas Judge, Mr. District Attorney, Country Fair, No Hands on the Clock, Sun Valley Serenade.*
1942: *Wildcat, I Live on Danger, My Favorite Spy, Torpedo Boat, The Old Homestead, The Wrecking Crew.*
1943: *Alaska Highway, The Heavenly Body, Minesweeper, High Explosive, Ladies' Day, Aerial Gunner, Submarine Alert, A Night for Crime, No Place for a Lady.*
1944: *The Doughgirls, Cover Girl, Lost in a Harem, Barbary Coast Gent, Sweethearts of the USA.*
1945: *Nob Hill, Thunderhead Son of Flicka, The Bullfighters, High Powered, Where Do We Go from Here?, Army Wives, Adventures of Kitty O'Day, There Goes Kelly, State Fair.*
1946: *They Made Me a Killer, The Best Years of Our Lives, Girl on the Spot, It Shouldn't Happen to a Dog, Sioux City Sioux, My Pal Trigger, That Brennan Girl.*
1947: *Out of the Blue, Linda Be Good, Hit Parade of 1947, Copacabana, Web of Danger.*
1948: *Let's Live Again, French Leave, Shaggy, Winner Take All, Smart Woman, Easter Parade.*
1949: *Champion.*
1950: *Cow Town, Father's Wild Game, The Glass Menagerie, Hi-Jacked, Rogue River, Union Station.*
1951: *Danger Zone, Behave Yourself, My Favorite Spy, Bright Victory, Fort Defiance, Kentucky Jubilee, Let's Make It Legal, Appointment with Danger, Rhythm Inn, Missing Women, Fighting Coast Guard.*
1952: *Carrie, A Girl in Every Port, Somebody Loves Me, Sea Tiger, The Turning Point, Springfield Rifle, Rancho Notorious.*
1953: *Count the Hours.*
1954: *The Forty Niners, River of No Return, Silver Lode.*
1955: *The Seven Year Itch, To Hell and Back, The Lieutenant Wore Skirts, Night Freight, Shotgun, The Road to Denver.*
1956: *Blackjack Ketchum Desperado, Uranium Boom, Friendly Persuasion.*

1957: *Up in Smoke, All Mine to Give, Beginning of the End.*
1958: *Alaska Passage, The Big Country.*
1959: *The Oregon Trail, The Remarkable Mr. Pennypacker.*
1960: *Cage of Evil, The Purple Gang.*

Television Series

1958–1959: *The Life and Legend of Wyatt Earp* as Jim "Dog" Kelly.

Sources

Brooks, Tim. *The Complete Directory to Prime Time TV Stars 1946–Present.* New York: Ballantine Books, 1987.
Truitt, Evelyn Mack. *Who Was Who on Screen Illustrated Edition.* New York: Bowker, 1984.

JOE SAWYER

Born in Ontario, Canada, in 1901, his real name was Joseph Sauers. In the United States from childhood, he was a professional football player in college. He would move from school to school and be well paid for his trouble. When he gave this up, he gravitated to Hollywood where he was employed as an appraiser at a building society while simultaneously studying drama at the Pasadena Playhouse by night. Active from the dawn of talking pictures, he became one of the screen's busiest supporting players. Until 1935 he used his real name on screen. One of his most memorable roles was as the sadistic army sergeant Humphrey Bogart kills when he encounters him in civilian life in *The Roaring Twenties* (1939). He also shot a series of comedies with William Tracy for Hal Roach.

For six years he played the gruff but goodhearted Sgt. Biff O'Hara in the popular television Western series *The Adventures of Rin Tin Tin.* It was a happy series to shoot, and all the cast were extremely congenial together. When the series ended, he virtually retired from show business, apart from an occasional cameo, and went on a round-the-world trip. Upon his return he settled in Ashland, Oregon, where he died from liver cancer on April 21, 1982, at age 81. He was survived by three sons and a daughter, actress Patricia Sauers (1940–1989).

Joseph Sawyer Filmography

1931: *Surrender.*
1932: *Huddle, Forgotten Commandments, Arsene Lupin.*
1933: *College Humor, Saturday's Millions, Three Cornered Moon, College Coach, Blood Money, The Stranger's Return, Ace of Aces, Son of a Sailor, Hold Your Man, Jimmy and Sally, Olsen's Big Moment.*
1934: *Eskimo, Death on the Diamond, Looking for Trouble, Behold My Wife, College Rhythm, The Prescott Kid, The Band Plays On, Stamboul Quest, Jimmy the Gent, The Notorious Sophie Lang, The Westerner, The Whole Town's*

Joe Sawyer in *The Adventures of Rin Tin Tin.*

Talking, Against the Law, Wharf Angel, Gridiron Flash, Sing and Like It.
1935: *Broadway Gondolier, Car 99, Special Agent, The Arizonian, The Informer, I Found Stella Parish, Little Big Shot, Man of Iron, The Frisco Kid, Moonlight on the Prairie, The Man on the Flying Trapeze, The Revenge Rider, Air Hawks, Eight Bells.*
1936: *Big Brown Eyes, The Petrified Forest, And Sudden Death, Murder with Pictures, Crash Donovan, The Leathernecks Have Landed, Two in a Crowd, Freshman Love, The Country Doctor, The Last Outlaw, The Walking Dead, High Tension, Special Investigator, Pride of the Marines, Black Legion, The Accusing Finger, Rose Bowl, A Son Comes Home.*
1937: *Great Guy, Slim, Midnight Madonna, The Lady Fights Back, They Gave Him a Gun, Navy Blues, Reported Missing, Motor Madness, San Quentin, A Dangerous Adventure.*
1938: *Always in Trouble, Tarzan's Revenge, Stolen Heaven, Gambling Ship, Heart of the North, The Storm, Passport Husband.*
1939: *You Can't Get Away with Murder, The Lady and the Mob, I Stole a Million, Union Pacific, Sabotage, Inside Information, Confessions of a Nazi Spy, Frontier Marshal, The Roaring Twenties.*
1940: *The Man from Montreal, The Grapes of Wrath, King of the Lumberjacks, Women Without Names, The Long Voyage Home, Border Legion, Santa Fe Trail, The House Across the Bay, Dark Command, Lucky Cisco Kid, Melody Ranch, Wildcat Bus.*
1941: *Tanks a Million, The Lady from Cheyenne, Last of the Duanes, Down in San Diego, Swamp Water, You're in the Army Now, Sergeant York, Belle Starr, Down Mexico Way, They Died with Their Boots On.*
1942: *The McGuerins from Brooklyn, Wrecking Crew, Sundown Jim, Hay Foot, Brooklyn Orchid.*
1943: *Buckskin Frontier, Fall In, Prairie Chickens, Taxi Mister, Yanks Ahoy, Let's Face It, Tarzan's Desert Mystery, The Outlaw, Cowboy in Manhattan, Hit the Ice, Tornado, Alaska Highway, Sleepy Lagoon.*
1944: *Moon Over Las Vegas, Hey Rookie, Raiders of Ghost City* (serial), *The Singing Sheriff, South of Dixie.*
1945: *The Naughty Nineties, High Powered, Brewster's Millions.*
1946: *Joe Palooka—Champ, Deadline at Dawn, G.I. War Brides, The Runaround, Gilda, Inside Job.*
1947: *Big Town After Dark, Christmas Eve, A Double Life, Roses Are Red.*
1948: *Half Past Midnight, If You Knew Susie, Fighting Back, Coroner Creek, The Untamed Breed, Here Comes Trouble, Fighting Father Dunne.*
1949: *The Gay Amigo, Deputy Marshal, And Baby Makes Three, Curtain Call at Cactus Creek, Kazan, The Lucky Stiff, The Stagecoach Kid, Tucson.*
1950: *Blondie's Hero, Operation Haylift, The Traveling Saleswoman, The Flying Missile.*
1951: *Pride of Maryland, Comin' Round the Mountain, As You Were.*
1952: *Red Skies of Montana, Indian Uprising, Mr. Walkie Talkie.*
1953: *It Came from Outer Space.*
1954: *Taza Son of Cochise, Johnny Dark, Riding Shotgun.*
1956: *The Kettles in the Ozarks, The Killing.*
1960: *North to Alaska.*
1962: *How the West Was Won.*
1973: *Harry in Your Pocket.*

Television Series

1954–1959: *The Adventures of Rin Tin Tin* as Sgt. Biff O'Hara.

Sources

Perry, Jeb H. *Screen Gems: A History of Columbia Pictures Television from Cohn to Coke, 1948–1983.* Metuchen, NJ: Scarecrow, 1991.
Quinlan, David. *Illustrated Directory of Film Comedy Stars.* London: Batsford, 1992.
Willis, John. *Screen World Volume 34.* London: Muller, 1983.

JAMES SEAY

James Seay was born in Pasadena, California, on September 9, 1914. He desired to be an actor from childhood, but upon graduating from high school joined an insurance company as a clerk. He met a friend who was attending the Pasadena Playhouse on a scholarship. This friend introduced him to a director there who gave him a walk-on in a play called *Judgment Day.* This led him to do several bits with a few lines in different productions. Subsequently he joined a postgraduate class where he performed plays in a space behind the managing director's home. After a performance an agent invited him to be the leading man for a season at the Chapel Playhouse in Connecticut.

After this he returned to the Pasadena Playhouse where he appeared in leading roles in two prestigious historical plays. On the strength of these he was spotted by Jeanette McPherson, assistant to Cecil B. DeMille. She was instrumental in him obtaining a contract at Paramount, where he appeared in a number of films before turning freelance. World War II intervened while (appropriately) he was shooting a film for the Air Force. An officer invited him to join their unit, which he did, spending the years until 1945 shooting training films for the Air Force.

On account of this experience, 20th Century–Fox signed him to a one-year contract, and he stayed to shoot three films. Thereafter he freelanced in character roles both in films and on television. He had semi-regular roles in two television series of the 1950s. In *Fury* he played the sheriff. In *The Life and Legend of Wyatt Earp* he played a judge in the Tombstone, Arizona, episodes. Seay retired in 1970 and died at Capitol Beach, California, on October 10, 1992, at age 78.

James Seay as he appeared in *Fury*.

James Seay Filmography

1940: *Emergency Squad, Golden Gloves, North West Mounted Police, Oklahoma Renegades, Queen of the Mob, The Son of Monte Cristo, Those Were the Days, The Way of All Flesh, Women Without Names, The Green Hornet Strikes Again* (serial), *I Want a Divorce, Love They Neighbor, Flight Command, Opened by Mistake.*

1941: *Mr. Celebrity, The Face Behind the Mask, In Old Colorado, Keep 'Em Flying, The Kid from Kansas, Two in a Taxi, Meet Boston Blackie, Flying Blind, Power Dive, The Mad Doctor.*

1942: *Ten Gentlemen from West Point, Dangerously They Live, Eagle Squadron, Enemy Agents Meet Ellery Queen, Highways by Night, Home in Wyoming, The Man from Cheyenne, Ride 'Em Cowboy, Ridin' Down the Canyon, They Died with Their Boots On, Timber, Time to Kill, Tramp Tramp Tramp, Flight Lieutenant, Joe Smith American.*

1943: *Flight for Freedom.*

1945: *The Return of Monte Cristo.*

1946: *Home Sweet Homicide.*

1947: *Heartaches, Miracle on 34th Street, T-Men, The Brasher Doubloon* (a.k.a. *The High Window).*

1948: *The Checkered Coat, The Cobra Strikes, Don't Trust Her Husband* (a.k.a. *An Innocent*

Affair), The Secret Beyond the Door, Slippy McGee, The Strange Mrs. Crane.
1949: *I Cheated the Law, Prejudice, Red Canyon.*
1950: *The Asphalt Jungle, The Flying Missile, Military Academy, Union Station.*
1951: *Close to My Heart, The Day the Earth Stood Still, When the Redskins Rode, Hunt the Man Down, Up Front, When Worlds Collide.*
1952: *Brave Warrior, Models Inc., Voodoo Tiger.*
1953: *Captain John Smith and Pocahontas, Fort Ti, The Homesteaders, Jack McCall Desperado, Phantom from Space, Problem Girls, Son of Belle Starr, Torpedo Alley, Sea of Lost Ships, The War of the Worlds, Off Limits.*
1954: *Captain Kidd and the Slave Girl, Return to Treasure Island, Killers from Space, The Steel Cage, Vera Cruz.*
1955: *I Died a Thousand Times, Kiss Me Deadly, The Kentuckian.*
1956: *Friendly Persuasion, Gun Brothers, I've Lived Before, Man in the Vault.*
1957: *The Amazing Colossal Man, Man of a Thousand Faces, The Big Land, Bombers B-52, Pal Joey, Beginning of the End.*
1958: *The Buccaneer, Street of Darkness, Flood Tide.*
1960: *The Threat.*
1961: *Secret of Deep Harbor.*
1962: *What Ever Happened to Baby Jane?*
1965: *Brainstorm.*
1967: *First to Fight.*
1968: *The Destructors, Panic in the City, The Green Berets.*
1969: *The D.A.: Murder One* (TV).
1970: *There Was a Crooked Man.*

Television Series

1955–1958: *Fury* as the Sheriff.
1959–1961: *The Life and Legend of Wyatt Earp* as Judge Will Spicer.

Sources

Goldrup, Tom, and Jim Goldrup. *Feature Players: The Stories Behind The Faces Volume #2.* Published privately, 1992.
Jarvis, Everett G. *Final Curtain: Deaths of Noted Movie and TV Personalities.* New York: Citadel Press, 1995.

CHARLES SEEL

Born in the Bronx, New York, in 1897, this character actor originally worked for a glove company. While there he spotted a silent movie company shooting on the streets of New York, requested a job as an actor and was given one. He made his debut as an office boy in a Biograph film, the title of which he could not remember. He subsequently appeared in films in such small roles that frequently they were not recorded.

In television since its pioneer days, he is remembered as Mr. Krinkle in some episodes of *Dennis the Menace.* He admitted to being on *Gunsmoke* "for generations" as the Dodge City telegraph agent. Simultaneously he played the grandfather on *The Road West,* another Western series that only lasted a season. The pilot was later released theatrically. His wife, whom he met in vaudeville and married in 1922, died in 1964. After her death he lived alone in the Burbank house they had bought in 1941. Seel died in 1980 at age 83.

Charles Seel Filmography

1937: *Off the Record.*
1938: *Comet Over Broadway.*
1949: *Not Wanted.*
1955: *The Man with the Golden Arm.*
1957: *I Was a Teenage Frankenstein.*
1959: *The Horse Soldiers.*
1960: *Sergeant Rutledge, North to Alaska, The Dark at the Top of the Stairs, Please Don't Eat the Daisies.*
1962: *The Man Who Shot Liberty Valance, Flashing Spikes.*
1963: *Donovan's Reef, Tammy and the Doctor.*

1964: *Lady in a Cage, Cheyenne Autumn.*
1965: *The Great Race.*
1966: *Mister Buddwing, This Savage Land* (TV), *Chamber of Horrors.*
1969: *Winning.*
1971: *Duel* (TV), *The Priest Killer* (TV).
1973: *Westworld.*

Television Series

1955–1975: *Gunsmoke* as Barney.
1966–1967: *The Road West* as Grandpa Pride.

Sources

Raddatz, Leslie. *Radio Times* magazine. "The Dodge City Gang," June 15, 1972.

ROCKY SHAHAN

Rocky Shahan was an expert wrangler and stuntman. For many seasons he played drover Joe Scarlett in the Western series *Rawhide.* He died in Texas on December 8, 1981, while in his 50s.

Rocky Shahan Filmography

1947: *Son of Zorro* (serial).
1949: *Roll Thunder Roll.*
1950: *The James Brothers of Missouri* (serial).
1954: *Jubilee Trail.*
1957: *The Storm Rider, The Deerslayer, Copper Sky, Ride a Violent Mile.*
1958: *Blood Arrow, Cattle Empire.*

Television Series

1959–1964: *Rawhide* as Joe Scarlett.

Sources

Brooks, Tim. *The Complete Directory to Prime Time TV Stars.* New York: Ballantine Books, 1987.
Ragan, David. *Who's Who in Hollywood.* New York: Facts on File, 1992.

KAREN SHARPE

Born Karen Kay Sharpe in San Antonio, Texas, on September 20, 1934, she made her screen debut in 1952. She appeared in some feature films and had regular roles in two television series. One of these was *Johnny Ringo,* an early and unsuccessful Western series produced by Aaron Spelling. In this she played Laura Thomas, the daughter of the general store owner, who is in love with the title character of a reformed gunman turned sheriff (Don Durant).

In 1966 she retired from acting when she became the wife of producer-director Stanley Kramer. She and Kramer have three children, Casey, Katharine and Jennifer. Mr. Kramer, who was frequently at the forefront of motion picture excellence for decades, seemed to lose his way in the 1970s. In 1978 the family relocated to Seattle, Washington, where they enjoyed an extremely affluent lifestyle. Since 1985, however, they have resided in Beverly Hills, California, where Kramer has been trying to resume his career, although there appears to have been little of note to report so far.

Karen Sharpe Filmography

1952: *Strange Fascination, Army Bound, Bomba and the Jungle Girl.*
1953: *Mad at the World.*

Karen Sharpe with Don Durant in *Johnny Ringo.*

1954: *The High and the Mighty.*
1955: *Man with the Gun.*
1956: *The Man in the Vault.*
1958: *Tarawa Beachhead.*
1964: *The Disorderly Orderly.*

Television Series

1959–1960: *Johnny Ringo* as Laura Thomas.
1965–1966: *I Dream of Jeannie* as Melissa Stone.

Sources

Ragan, David. *Who's Who in Hollywood.* New York: Facts on File, 1992.
Summers, Neil. *The Official TV Western Book Volume #2.* Vienna, WV: Old West Publishing Shop, 1989.

GENE SHELDON

Born in 1909, Gene Sheldon was a veteran vaudevillian who made some appearances in 20th Century–Fox films. His best-remembered role was as the loyal but mute manservant Bernardo in the television series *Zorro* for Walt Disney. He pretended to be deaf as well as mute in order to facilitate eavesdropping for his master Zorro. Zorro alone knew that Bernardo could really hear. Sheldon went on to appear in other Disney films such as *Toby Tyler* and *Babes in Toyland.* He had something of a comic double act in these movies with his

Zorro costar Henry Calvin. Sheldon was little heard from after his stint with Disney and died in obscurity on May 1, 1982, at age 73.

Gene Sheldon Filmography

1935: *Roberta.*
1938: *Star of the Circus* (a.k.a. *Hidden Menace*).
1945: *Where Do We Go from Here?, The Dolly Sisters.*
1951: *Golden Girl.*
1954: *Three Ring Circus.*
1960: *Toby Tyler, The Sign of Zorro* (TV:Z).
1961: *Babes in Toyland.*

Television Series

1957–1959: *Zorro* as Bernardo.

Sources

Brooks, Tim. *The Complete Directory to Prime Time TV Stars 1946–Present.* New York: Ballantine Books, 1987.
Maltin, Leonard. *The Disney Films.* New York: Crown, 1973.
Yenne, Bill. *The Legend of Zorro.* Greenwich, CT: Brompton, 1991.

Note

TV:Z denotes a movie derived from episodes of the television series *Zorro.*

FRED SHERMAN

Born in 1905, Frederick E. Sherman was a character actor of stage, screen and television. His sole semi-regular role on television was in the Western series *Cimarron City.* Of interest to television trivia buffs is that in real life Sherman was married to actress Claire Carleton, who played his wife in this series. Sherman died of a stroke in Woodland Hills, California, on May 20, 1969, at age 64. His wife survived him.

Fred Sherman Filmography

1942: *Shepherd of the Ozarks, Wrecking Crew.*
1946: *Behind Green Lights, Lady in the Lake.*
1947: *The Hucksters.*
1950: *Mystery Street, Chain Lightning.*
1951: *Valley of Fire.*
1956: *Stranger at My Door.*
1957: *The Tall T, War Drums, Gun Battle at Monterey, Dino, Lust to Kill.*
1959: *Westbound, Some Like It Hot, Alaska Passage.*
1961: *Twist All Night.*

Television Series

1958–1959: *Cimarron City* as Burt Purdy.

Sources

Brooks, Tim. *The Complete Directory to Prime Time TV Stars 1946–Present.* New York: Ballantine Books, 1987.
Truitt, Evelyn Mack. *Who Was Who On Screen Second Edition.* New York: Bowker, 1977.

JAY SILVERHEELS

Hollywood seemed to take a perverse delight in casting actors in roles far removed from their own ethnic origins, but one actor who was the genuine article was Jay Silverheels, a Native American who subsequently became most closely identified with television's most famous Indian character, Tonto. He was a Mohawk Indian of the Iroquois nation who portrayed American Indians to cinema and television audiences in a career which spanned 35 years.

Jay Silverheels was born Harold J. Smith

Jay Silverheels in *The Lone Ranger.*

on May 26, 1918, on the Six Nations Indian Reservation, Ontario, Canada. He was given the name of "Silverheels" by a tribal elder. He was brought up in the traditions of his tribe. He left high school to become a professional lacrosse player. Under his real name he emigrated in 1935 with his family, to Buffalo, New York, where he became a champion middleweight boxer. Although he wanted to use his tribal name, he was forced to use his real one by the Canadian government. He legally changed his name to Jay Silverheels in the 1940s.

In 1937–1938 he was runner-up in the

national finals of the Golden Gloves Boxing Tournament, having won the Eastern finals in Madison Square Garden, New York. Comedian Joe E. Brown was responsible for planting the seed of acting in Jay Silverheels' mind. Brown spotted him at a lacrosse game in Hollywood in 1937 and encouraged him to try acting. An injury to Silverheels's eye ended his career as a boxer, and he journeyed to Hollywood with his personal possessions in a battered suitcase. He roomed at the home of the brother of actor Iron Eyes Cody, where he nurtured the ambition of combining acting with professional gambling.

Cody introduced him to Tyrone Power and Errol Flynn. He became a drinking buddy of theirs, and they in turn gave him bit parts in a few of their films under a variety of different names. Having made his screen debut in 1938 as a stuntman and bit player, he did not achieve any notice until he was given his first important role as the Aztec warrior Coatl in *Captain from Castile,* which starred Tyrone Power. Released in 1947 by 20th Century–Fox, the picture was a costume epic that had a cast headed by name performers. In spite of all the stiff competition, the Indian was able to distinguish himself in several key scenes that elevated his professional standing. The money he earned from this film enabled him to buy a home of his own and to pursue gambling, at which he dropped thousands. Fortunately, with Hollywood's changing attitude toward Indian characters, notably in movies like *Broken Arrow* (1950), he was able to play sympathetic Indians as well as bellicose ones.

During the 1950s he made a specialty of playing the Bendonkohe Apache chief Geronimo in *Broken Arrow* (1950), *Battle at Apache Pass* (1952) and *Walk the Proud Land* (1956). He became best known for his television role as Tonto, the faithful Indian sidekick of the Lone Ranger. Both characters were invented by Fran Striker for a radio show of the 1930s.

Silverheels played Tonto and appeared in all 221 episodes of the television series, apart from four episodes in 1954 when he was recovering from a heart attack. In order not to disrupt the flow of the series, production was suspended for a few weeks, while episodes intended for him were rewritten for Dan Reid (Chuck Courtney). He ended up missing only four episodes which were spread out throughout the season so that when aired, his absence would not be conspicuous. The series originally ran from 1949 to 1957. He and Clayton Moore as the Lone Ranger also appeared in two features which grew out of the series, *The Lone Ranger* (1956) and *The Lone Ranger and the Lost City of Gold* (1958). He also appeared with Moore in two films in which they did not play the Lone Ranger and Tonto, *Cowboy and the Indians* (1949) and *The Black Dakotas* (1954).

After *The Lone Ranger* ceased production, Silverheels found himself typecast. He ended up with so firm an image in the minds of the public and casting directors that for many years he found little acting work. The changing attitude in the United States towards Indians (which originally helped him) subsequently hindered his career development. Many feel that the Tonto role was equivalent to Uncle Tom. Tonto may have taken as many chances as the Lone Ranger and called him "Kimosabe" (faithful friend), but throughout the series Tonto was always subservient as the faithful Indian companion.

During the 1960s he became increasingly dissatisfied with the portrayal of Indian characters on television and spoke out against the subordinate part he had played. "I resented being hit over the head all the time. When they didn't know what to do with me, the story department would just hit me over the head. How was it that out in the forest I could hear a rabbit on tiptoes a mile away, and yet a villain in big boots could creep up and surprise me with a club?" Although there is some truth in his remarks, a recent analysis of the episodes shows that on several occasions Tonto came to the rescue and saved the Lone Ranger's life.

In 1961 he had a brief featured role on the short-lived CBS series *Frontier Circus* and he made occasional appearances on *Rawhide, The Mike Douglas Show, Pistols and Petticoats, Gentle Ben, Texas John Slaughter, Laramie, The Virginian* and *Cade's County.* On several of his television chat show appearances he read some of his poetry, which was strongly influenced by his life as a boy on the reservation. His last acting assignment appears to have been a guest-starring role on an episode of *Cannon* in 1974. He supplemented his income by work as a salesman and spent much time at the Indian Actors' Workshop. He helped to found this in

1963 as a means of helping aspiring Indian actors in the profession. In August 1979, he became the first American Indian to have a star set for him in Hollywood's Walk of Fame along Hollywood Boulevard.

After his retirement from the screen, Silverheels continued as an enthusiastic sportsman. In 1974 he obtained a harness racing license and became a familiar figure at tracks across the United States. This terminated abruptly in 1977, when he suffered a stroke from which he never fully recovered. This caused him to lose weight dramatically. When he attended a party in his wheelchair, he tottered to his feet to sing a rousing rendition of "Home, Home on the Range" which earned him a standing ovation. His death at the Motion Picture and Television Country Home and Hospital in Woodland Hills, California, was caused by complications arising from pneumonia on March 5, 1980. He was 61 years old. According to his family, his ashes were scattered over the Indian Reservation where he was born.

He married Mary Diroma in 1946 and had four children: Marilyn, a teacher; Pamela; Karen; and Jay Anthony. His son Jay, Jr., did voices for Saturday morning cartoons in the 1970s. They lived in Canoga Park, California. His wife was at his bedside when he died. Clayton Moore, who visited him in the hospital a week earlier, was on his way to Texas when his partner died. He wept openly at the funeral and recalled, "I enjoyed my partnership with Jay Silverheels. He was a wonderful man and a good friend."

Marriage to an Italian did nothing to weaken Silverheels' ties to his Indian background. He described his four children as, "Indalian." All were raised in the strict Mohawk tradition of honesty, respect for elders and respect for the natural environment as the universal provider. When his children complained of the inaccurate, often malicious representation of American Indians in film and television, Silverheels responded with his own philosophy: "Let me remind you that the people who write these things don't know the truth. But don't be angry. Remember our Indian proverb: 'Let me never condemn my brother until I have walked sun-up to sun-down in his moccasins.' Be slow to judge, respect the traditions and practices of others. Never be afraid to tell the truth; obey the laws wherever you live; show courtesy to all fellow human beings and tenderness to animals. What has endured is good and will be made better as we move, generation after generation towards perfection."

Jay Silverheels Filmography

1939: *Geronimo.*
1940: *The Sea Hawk, Too Many Girls.*
1941: *Western Union.*
1942: *Valley of the Sun.*
1943: *Good Morning Judge, The Girl from Monterey, Daredevils of the West* (serial).
1944: *Northern Pursuit.*
1945: *Song of the Sarong.*
1946: *Singin' in the Corn, Canyon Passage.*
1947: *Gas House Kids Go West, The Last Round-up, Vacation Days, Captain from Castile, Northwest Outpost, Unconquered.*
1948: *Indian Agent, The Feathered Serpent, Key Largo, Fury at Furnace Creek, The Prairie, Singing Spurs, Yellow Sky, Family Honeymoon.*
1949: *Sand, Trail of the Yukon, For Those Who Dare, Laramie, Lust for Gold, The Cowboy and the Indians, Song of India.*
1950: *Broken Arrow.*
1951: *Red Mountain, The Wild Blue Yonder.*
1952: *Brave Warrior, The Battle at Apache Pass, Yankee Buccaneer, The Will Rogers Story, The Pathfinder, Last of the Comanches.*
1953: *War Arrow, Jack McCall—Desperado, The Nebraskan.*
1954: *The Black Dakotas, Masterson of Kansas, Saskatchewan, Drums Across the River, Four Guns to the Border.*
1955: *The Vanishing American.*
1956: *Walk the Proud Land, The Lone Ranger.*
1958: *Return to Warbow, The Lone Ranger and the Lost City of Gold.*
1959: *Alias Jesse James* (cameo).
1965: *War Paint.*
1969: *Smith!, True Grit, The Phynx* (cameo).
1972: *Santee.*
1973: *One Little Indian, The Man Who Loved Cat Dancing.*

Television Series

1949–1957: *The Lone Ranger* as Tonto.

Sources

The Annual Obituary. Detroit, MI: St. James Press, 1981.
Corneau, Ernest N. *The Hall of Fame of Western Film Stars.* North Quincy, MA: Christopher, 1969.
Ferguson, Ken. *The Boy's Western TV and Film Annual.* London: Purnell, 1963.
Smith, David James. "The Lone Ranger Unmasked." *TV Times* magazine, July 29, 1989.
Van Hise, James. *Who Was That Masked Man? The Story of the Lone Ranger.* Las Vegas, NV: Pioneer, 1990.

RICHARD SIMMONS

Richard Simmons was born in St. Paul, Minnesota, on August 19, 1918, and was educated at the University of Minnesota. As a student he paid his way by doing radio announcing and also learned to fly. After graduation he decided to relocate to California where job prospects seemed brighter. Upon arriving in Los Angeles, he became a radio and band announcer. He started playing parts in little theater productions and gradually drifted into films. Since things were still slow and he could not earn enough to make ends meet, he became a commercial pilot. When World War II began, he was drafted almost immediately and spent the war years as a fighter pilot.

After his honorable discharge, he returned to Hollywood, where he was under contract to MGM for many years as a utility actor but was also loaned out to other studios. Many of his films were of the action genre, and he is particularly fond of *Man with the Steel Whip* (1954), a Republic serial in which he played the title role. He was master of ceremonies at all the MGM premieres and hosted a couple of MGM radio series. When his motion picture career began to ebb in the mid–1950s, he turned to television where he appeared in several anthology series.

The role with which he is most associated was the title role in *Sergeant Preston of the Yukon.* This series was set in the Yukon Territory of Alaska at the turn of the century when legitimate gold prospectors and settlers were threatened by rogues and bandits. The Royal Canadian Mounted Police were represented in this wilderness by Sgt. Preston (Simmons), who was aided by his magnificent black stallion Rex and his malamute dog Yukon King. The dog had been raised by a she-wolf and rescued by Preston during a lynx attack. It often seemed that Preston was the sole representative of law and order on the Canadian frontier.

Sergeant Preston of the Yukon had started out as a radio series in 1947 and was created by George W. Trendle and Fran Striker. This lasted until 1955, but the CBS television series made its debut on September 29, 1955. There were 78 half-hour, color episodes which aired until September 25, 1958. Simmons was initially reluctant to shoot such a series because he was afraid of typecasting; versatility had been the keynote of his career until then. Later he relented, saying, "This is the series I was meant for." He also admitted that it was his ability to ride rather than his thespian talent which had won him the role. The spectacular location shooting in California and Colorado greatly enhanced the series, which was well-written and acted and scored highly with fans of the genre. The Wrather Corporation produced the series, and the theme music was "The Donna Diana Overture" by Emil Von Reznicek. Since the shows were shot at the rate of two a week, Simmons found the schedule grueling. He was also doing other television work such as *The Loretta Young Show* and *Death Valley Days* simultaneously, which further exhausted him.

When *Sergeant Preston of the Yukon* ended, Simmons appeared in a daytime soap opera (CBS's *Clear Horizon*) about Cape Canaveral. Later, producer Robert Stabler hired him to shoot another action-orientated series. Simmons was flying a helicopter when the rotary flew apart and the machine touched the side of

Richard Simmons in *Sergeant Preston of the Yukon.*

a mountain. While he escaped death, his back and both legs were broken, which caused an enforced idleness for three years. When he recovered, he decided to make his temporary retirement a permanent one. Consequently he sold his lavish Encino home and moved into a mobile home park in Carlsbad, California, where he served as manager of the complex until retiring in the early 1980s. His chief recreations are playing golf and attending Western conventions.

He has been married to his wife Jonni since 1941 and has two children. He is one individual who harbors no bitterness towards the entertainment industry, saying, "I have no complaints because it has been very good to me."

Richard Simmons Filmography

1937: *A Million to One.*
1940: *King of the Royal Mounted* (serial).
1941: *King of the Texas Rangers* (serial), *Sergeant York.*
1942: *Yukon Patrol, Stand by for Action.*
1943: *Pilot No. 5, Thousands Cheer, The Youngest Profession.*
1946: *Love Laughs at Andy Hardy.*
1947: *Lady in the Lake, Undercover Maisie, This Time for Keeps.*
1948: *On An Island with You, The Three Musketeers, Act of Violence, Easter Parade.*
1949: *The Great Sinner* (voice only), *Look for the Silver Lining.*
1950: *The Duchess of Idaho, Dial 1119.*
1951: *The Well, No Questions Asked, I'll See You in My Dreams.*
1952: *I Dream of Jeannie, Desperate Search, Glory Alley, Thunderbirds.*
1953: *Woman They Almost Lynched, Battle Circus, Flight Nurse, Three Sailors and a Girl, Above and Beyond, Remains to Be Seen.*
1954: *Man with the Steel Whip* (serial), *Rogue Cop, Men of the Fighting Lady, Dragonfly Squadron.*
1955: *You're Never Too Young, Love Me or Leave Me, Interrupted Melody.*
1962: *Sergeants Three.*
1964: *Robin and the 7 Hoods.*
1971: *The Resurrection of Zachary Wheeler.*

Television Series

1955–1958: *Sergeant Preston of the Yukon* as Sgt. William Preston.
1962: *Clear Horizon.*

Sources

Goldrup, Tom, and Jim Goldrup. *Feature Players: The Stories Behind the Faces Volume #1.* Published privately, 1986.

Lamparski, Richard. *Whatever Became Of? Sixth Series.* New York: Bantam, 1976.

Speed, F. Maurice. *The Western Film and TV Annual.* London: MacDonald, 1960.

JOHN SMITH

John Smith was the tall, slim, boyish-looking, Dutch-American actor who achieved his greatest fame as Slim Sherman, the owner of the relay station, in the very popular television series *Laramie.* Although in recent years he has been unjustly neglected, he was a competent and personable actor who fitted the bill for that role. The qualities which he exhibited were scarcely those for either enduring stardom or sterling character work. There is little correlation between series popularity and a long-term acting career. He has been cited as an example of the kind of young actor of the 1950s whose career nosedived into oblivion in the rougher climate of the 1960s. He was never convincing in his occasional forays into screen villainy such as *Fury at Showdown* (1957). His later life and career were blighted by chronic alcoholism.

John Smith was born in the Crenshaw area of Los Angeles on March 6, 1931, with the real name of Robert Earl Van Orden. He was the son of Earl and Margaret Van Orden. Although he was raised in the city, he spent much of his boyhood at his uncle's ranch in El Monte, where he became an expert horseman. While in high school, he acquired early screen exposure by singing in the choir of St. Agatha's, his local Roman Catholic church. He became a member of the Bob Mitchell Boys Choir, appearing with them in the films *Going My Way* (1944) and *The Bells of St. Mary's* (1945), which starred Bing Crosby. At Dorsey Senior High School and El Camino Junior College, he was a football star. At that stage he wanted to become an engineer and even enrolled at UCLA as an engineering major, but settled on being an actor instead.

He dropped out of college to become a messenger at MGM. His daily rounds used to take him through the casting department where he was spotted one day by casting director Jimmy Broderick, who recommended him to play the younger brother of James Stewart in *Carbine Williams* (1952), where he was billed under his real name. Once his part was over he returned to the mail room. He decided to make a serious study of acting and, with Debbie Reynolds, started dramatic training lessons on the lot. This resulted in him being fired.

After a period of unemployment, he obtained various selling jobs for silverware, china and, later, cars. He also delivered and repaired television sets. On his day off he dropped into MGM to look up Jimmy Broderick. While there he was introduced to the influential homosexual agent Henry Willson, who had a reputation for turning young male actors into minor stars and heartthrobs with memorable names, Rock Hudson being his greatest success. The new name which he settled on for Robert Van Orden was John Smith. Willson later claimed that he chose this name to dispel the myth that his discoveries made the grade through their oddball names rather than through talent. Willson accompanied the actor to court to change his name. "You mean you've got a good name like Robert Van Orden and you want to take a common name like John Smith?" the judge asked. "Yes, just plain John Smith," the actor said. "I'm the only one in the business."

He was given his first important role by John Wayne in *The High and the Mighty* (1954) as a young honeymooner on board a doomed plane. He was signed by Wayne's Batjac Productions. He seldom appeared for them but was loaned out to other studios. He played leads in some B movies and featured roles in A pictures. One film in which he appeared, *Friendly Persuasion* (1956), was notable because it marked an early appearance of Robert Fuller, who later became Smith's costar in *Laramie.* Smith's role in this is unsatisfactory since he disappears halfway into the movie. Possibly there were possible additional scenes of his filmed that were left on the cutting room floor.

Smith starred in two television Western series. The first was *Cimarron City* (1958–1959) in the costarring role of Sheriff Lane Temple. He hit the peak of his career when he essayed the part of Slim Sherman in *Laramie* (1959–1963). It was set in the Wyoming Territory of the 1870s. After the death of Slim's father, the responsibility of running their ranch fell to Slim and his 14-year-old brother Andy (Bobby Crawford, Jr.). The ranch was neglected and barely provided a living for the Shermans. In their efforts to revive the ranch they were helped by Jonesy (Hoagy Carmichael), who had helped to raise them, and later Daisy Cooper (Spring Byington). In the first episode they were joined by drifter Jess Harper (Robert Fuller), who settled down with them.

The Shermans used the ranch as a relay station, changing the horses of stagecoaches passing through; this provided added scope for stories. Episodes usually featured either him or Robert Fuller as the pivotal character around whom alternate episodes revolved. Frequently in the early days they had equal footage in some episodes. Increasingly towards the end of the series, Smith and Fuller appeared in episodes alone, a reflection of their personal feelings toward one another. Smith also tested for other roles while *Laramie* was on the air, notably *Overland Trail, Rawhide* and *The Virginian,* but the roles went to Doug McClure and Clint Eastwood instead.

By the end of the fourth season in 1963, both actors wanted to go on to fresh projects, so *Laramie* ended after 128 episodes. Initially Smith fared the better of the two with an important role in a major movie, John Wayne's *Circus World* (1964). Smith played Steve McCabe, an ex-rodeo rider starring in a Wild West show. In the same year he headed the cast of a stage production of *The World of Suzie Wong.* Although he left *Laramie* believing that he was going to become a major star, as it turned out his days of stardom were over.

He drifted into the twilight world of the has-been celebrity who is only fodder for trivia questions and "whatever became of...?" columns. The answer appears to be that not much happened to him professionally. He appeared in a few very low-budget films and guested on a few television series. He played Ed Dow, the husband of Angie Dow, who was killed in the first episode of the short-lived *Hondo* series in 1967. His last recorded television appearances were in a 1974 episode of *Police Woman* in which he played a hitman very unconvincingly, and a 1975 episode of *Marcus Welby M.D.*

Smith, who was reputedly bisexual in later years, also had a serious drink problem. He lived for a time in the same bungalow in the Crenshaw district of Los Angeles where he was raised. During the 1990s he was reported to be unemployed and living in a Los Angeles apartment with a male companion where the phone was frequently disconnected for non-payment of the bill. Allegedly he armed himself with a new agent and was considering scripts with a view to reactivating his career. His only professional work in years was doing voiceovers in commercials. His final public appearance is understood to have been in March 1994, when he was presented as a guest member of the Cauliflower Alley Club, an association of pugilists and wrestlers who invite some members of the entertainment industry to be members since they have been pictured in so many brawls on screen.

None of this did him any good, and he continued to live in the same wretched state until he died in his Los Angeles home on January 25, 1995, at age 63, of what was probably a combination of cirrhosis of the liver and heart problems. His funeral was attended by very few of his former colleagues, but it is believed that Robert Fuller was among them.

Smith was popular with the ladies during the 1950s. His dates with nubile starlets provided constant items to fill up the fan magazines of the period. In 1958 he met the actress Luana Patten on the set of an episode of *Cimarron City.* They were wed in a highly publicized Roman Catholic ceremony in 1960. They moved into a lavish hilltop aerie close to the Errol Flynn estate. They were divorced in 1964 with no children. Smith did have a daughter born in the 1960s, but not with either of his wives. He subsequently married and divorced an equestrienne in the 1970s. Later he lived with Elaine M. Conte, a former Miss Ohio and sometime wife of the late Edward G. Robinson, Jr. She died in her sleep in April 1987. Later he became very friendly again with Luana Patten, and the couple, now virtually unrecognizable, were spotted together at some Hollywood bars. Patten, who was born on July 6, 1938, outlived her ex-husband by just over 12 months and died on May 1, 1996, at age 57.

John Smith Filmography

1944: *Going My Way.*
1945: *The Bells of St. Mary's.*
1952: *Carbine Williams.*

1954: *The High and the Mighty.*
1955: *Seven Angry Men, We're No Angels, Wichita, Desert Sands, Ghost Town.*
1956: *The Bold and the Brave, Quincannon Frontier Scout, Rebel in Town, Friendly Persuasion, Women of Pitcairn Island, Hot Rod Girl.*
1957: *Tomahawk Trail, Fury at Sundown, The Kettles on Old MacDonald's Farm, The Lawless Eighties, The Crooked Circle.*
1958: *Handle with Care.*
1959: *Island of Lost Women.*
1964: *Circus World* (a.k.a. *The Magnificent Showman*).
1966: *Waco.*
1971: *Legacy of Blood* (a.k.a. *Blood Legacy; Will to Die*).
1978: *Legend of Lady Blue* (a.k.a. *Confessions of Lady Blue*).

Television Series

1954–1955: *That's My Boy* as Bill Baker.
1958–1959: *Cimarron City* as Lane Temple.
1959–1963: *Laramie* as Slim Sherman.

Sources

Ferguson, Ken. *The Boy's Western TV and Film Annual.* London: Purnell, 1963.
Lamparski, Richard. *Whatever Became Of? Eleventh Series.* New York: Crown, 1989.
The Laramie Trail fanzine. All issues, 1988–1990.
Lentz, Harris M., III. *Obituaries in the Performing Arts, 1995.* Jefferson, NC: McFarland, 1996.

John Smith in *Cimarron City*.

Miller, Maud. *Girl Television and Film Annual.* London: Longacre Press, 1963.

Note

Smith is sometimes incorrectly credited with appearances in *No Holds Barred* (1952) and *Personal Best* (1982), but these were sportsmen with similar names.

ROBERT J. STEVENSON

Born in 1915, this supporting actor had multiple careers as a newsreader, actor and even ran for public office. His only regular role on television was in the Western series *Jefferson Drum,* in which he played the saloon owner, a loyal friend of the hero. He died in Northridge, California, on March 4, 1975, at age 60, of cardiac arrest.

Robert Stevenson Filmography

1934: *Operator 13.*
1936: *God's Country and the Woman.*
1939: *Beasts of Berlin, The Lady's from Kentucky, Invitation to Happiness.*
1940: *Till We Meet Again, The Mortal Storm.*
1942: *Always in My Heart, Valley of Hunted Men.*
1943: *Background to Danger.*
1944: *Frenchman's Creek, A Voice in the Wind.*
1949: *The Great Sinner, The Gal Who Took the West, I Was a Male War Bride.*
1950: *Where Danger Lives.*

1951: *All That I Have.*
1952: *Radar Men from the Moon* (serial).
1954: *Fangs of the Wild.*
1957: *Zero Hour!*
1958: *Gun Fever, When Hell Broke Loose.*
1959: *Have Rocket—Will Travel.*
1960: *Spartacus.*
1961: *The Four Horsemen of the Apocalypse.*

Television Series

1958–1959: *Jefferson Drum* as Big Ed.

Sources

Perry, Jeb H. *Screen Gems: A History of Columbia Pictures Television from Cohn to Coke, 1948–1983.* Metuchen, NJ: Scarecrow, 1991.
Truitt, Evelyn Mack. *Who Was Who on Screen Second Edition.* New York: Bowker, 1977.

CAROL STONE

Carol Stone was born Fredeline Montgomery Stone in New York City on February 1, 1915, the daughter of actor Fred Stone and his wife Allene Crater. She was one of three sisters, the others being Paula and Dorothy. Carol was educated at Kew-Forest School, Forest Hills, Long Island, New York. She made her first stage appearance at the John Drew Memorial Theater, Easthampton, Long Island, on July 20, 1933, as Sissie Prohack in *Mr. Prohack.* Her first New York stage appearance was at the Henry Miller Theater on November 13, 1933, as Augusta Bastida in *Spring In Autumn.*

Her sole recorded screen credit was *Freckles* (1935), an RKO release, in which she and Tom Brown supplied the romantic interest. She appeared in many stage plays in New York, touring and summer stock well into the 1950s. She also did an extensive amount of television (primarily live plays) out of New York. She journeyed to California where she played the role of Kate Holliday in the television series *The Life and Legend of Wyatt Earp* during one season. At last report she was residing in retirement in New York. She married Robert W. McCahon, but the marriage ended in divorce.

Carol Stone Filmography

1935: *Freckles.*

Television Series

1957–1958: *The Life and Legend of Wyatt Earp* as Kate Holliday.

Sources

Brooks, Tim. *The Complete Directory to Prime Time TV Stars 1946–Present.* New York: Ballantine Books, 1987.
Who's Who in the Theater Twelfth Edition. London: Pitman, 1957.

MILBURN STONE

Most actors have few friends because of the itinerant nature of the profession, but one notable exception was Milburn Stone, who had time for everyone. He was the stocky, grizzled actor who achieved immortality playing Doc Adams in *Gunsmoke.* He once said, "My father wanted me to be a doctor. Playing Doc in the series is the closest I've ever come to being what my father wished. I like Doc. He is a bit of a ruffian as well, you know, but you can't help liking him." In an acting career spanning 40 years he appeared in numerous movies. Nevertheless, in a sea of reliable character actors he would probably have remained relatively anonymous except for the intervention of television. Ken Curtis, one of his closest friends, recalled of him, "He is one of the most entertaining fellows I have ever been around. When he decides to do something, he doesn't pull any punches. You've got to admire him for it, because he really stands up and fights. He's one of the most honest guys I've ever met."

Milburn Stone was born in Burrton, Kansas, on July 5, 1904, the son of storekeeper John Stone and his wife, a Kansas pioneer who had been raised in a sodhouse. When his father was a child, *his* father moved the family to Larned, Kansas, to obtain a job. Although Dodge City was only 30 miles away, it had scant influence on young Milburn Stone. He was much more interested in his uncle Fred Stone, a noted Broadway headliner. His outstanding scholastic achievements while attending elementary and high school in Burrton earned him a congressional appointment to the U.S. Naval Academy at Annapolis. He rejected the appointment in favor of joining the Helen B. Ross stock company to tour the Midwest as a fledgling actor.

He made his stage debut in a tent show in Kansas in 1919. In the late 1920s Stone abandoned stock for vaudeville. In 1930 he teamed in a song and dance act, "Stone and Strain." In 1932 he made his debut on the Great White Way at the Cort Theater in *The Jayhawker*, a Sinclair Lewis play set in post–Civil War Kansas. This initial role on the New York stage led to numerous other parts on Broadway.

He had a terrible struggle establishing himself as a motion picture actor. His motivation was to earn sufficient money to support his family. Few people were interested in seeing live plays when they could see a movie, and Broadway was also suffering. Since he knew he could never be happy except as an actor, he came to Hollywood where competition was fierce. In 1935 he made his first film, playing opposite Marie Wilson in *Ladies Crave Excitement*. Before getting into films and in between movie assignments he worked in a gas station seven days a week, 12 hours a day for $15 a week. He had his hours arranged so that he could audition for roles at the Pasadena Playhouse. He landed a part, did the play and was fired from the gas station. He talked his way back into the job, which lasted until he had enough movie roles to quit. He was under contract to Universal from 1943 to March 1947, and since 1935 had featured parts in over 125 motion pictures. His personal favorites were *Young Mr. Lincoln* (1939), in which he played Stephen A. Douglas, because it was directed by John Ford and had a great cast, and *The Savage* (1952) because it was great fun to shoot and it established a lifelong friendship with Charlton Heston. Alternating with his motion picture roles, Stone appeared in television in numerous characterizations since 1951.

His greatest popular success came in 1955 when he essayed the role of gruff but compassionate Doc Adams from the start of *Gunsmoke* to the demise of the series in 1975. In 1968 he received an Emmy as Outstanding Performance by an Actor in a Supporting Role in a Drama. He freely admitted that he patterned the character on his own grandfather, who had fought in the Civil War. Of the character he once said, "Except for my immediate family, Milburn Stone no longer exists. To everyone else, I'm Doc. Good old Doc Adams. Getting so I have to restrain myself from making house calls."

His favorite episode was one in which Doc was the lone witness to a killing outside the Long Branch Saloon. He had come out for a breath of air on the upstairs landing. Seeing the killing, he yelled for Dillon, who appeared and shot the killer. The killer was brought into Doc's surgery where he was operated upon to remove the bullet. Doc knew that he would subsequently be called upon to give evidence against the man, who would be hanged for murder. During the operation, a young man walked into the doctor's surgery and begged him to come at once as the man's wife was having a breech birth and would surely die. Doc refuses because of the Hippocratic oath saying that he cannot leave a patient on the table. The baby died instead. The actor loved the script because it showed the need to learn the priorities in a man's life.

He liked the stage and live audiences. He formed various song, dance and comedy acts with Dennis Weaver, Amanda Blake and Ken

Curtis barnstorming the country on weekends, performing at rodeos and state fairs. Offscreen in 1955 his life-long hobby of furniture designing and creating developed into a successful business. He and a partner opened a thriving business specializing in custom-built furniture and antique reproductions. He became the self-appointed, unofficial guardian of *Gunsmoke* and fought anyone whom he believed was undermining the series. He openly criticized Dennis Weaver for being tardy and for his hijinks on the set. He was also against the appointment of British producer Philip Leacock, which led to scripts being written by people with no understanding of the Western. After CBS canceled *Gunsmoke* in 1967, Stone said that he got an avalanche of angry, sorrowful mail. When the network subsequently reinstated the show, Stone said that it felt like coming off death row with a full pardon.

He suffered heart attacks in 1968, 1970 and 1971, and underwent open heart surgery. Nevertheless, he recovered and continued with the series until the end. He was quoted as saying around this time, "Acting has been my life and it's been good to me. It's brought me a wealth of friends and finally with this show, enough money in the bank to take care of my family comfortably for long after I'm gone. ... The studio is unbelievably considerate. I work when I want and when I get tired, I don't have to work. I pray I will last as long as *Gunsmoke*, but you'll never find me quitting." He achieved his ambition.

Afterwards he moved from his home in Van Nuys to Rancho Santa Fe, north of San Diego, where he found another career raising prize livestock. While in retirement, he sorely missed the show and other acting parts. In 1977 he came to Hollywood and attended a reunion of some cast members to celebrate the 50th anniversary of CBS Television. He said, "Damn, it was good to see those guys again. I really miss *Gunsmoke* and I'd dearly love to go back to work. I'm really getting bored with retirement." He spent his retirement puttering about the house and going fishing for bass and trout. He said that he gave up golf because he couldn't beat anybody at the frustrating game. He told a reporter, "It's true what they say about retirement killing people. My God, it's awful not having something to keep you going. Everyone tells me I look great which makes me wonder why I feel so bad." One night he complained of feeling ill and his wife took him to nearby Scripps Memorial Hospital. He died in his sleep at La Jolla, California, on June 12, 1980, at age 75, of heart failure. He was survived by his wife Jane, a former secretary whom he married in 1940. By his first wife, who preceded him in death, he had a daughter, Mrs. Patrick Gleason of Costa Mesa, California, who also survived him along with four grandchildren. Other survivors were brother Joseph, a retired San Diego newspaperman, and sister Glennis Ellis of San Francisco. He lies buried at El Camino Memorial Park at La Jolla, California. Dennis Weaver said about him, "He was one of my dear friends and associates and just the ultimate professional actor."

Milburn Stone Filmography

1935: *Ladies Crave Excitement, His Night Out, The Fighting Marines* (serial), *Rendezvous.*

1936: *The Milky Way, China Clipper, The Three Mesquiteers, The Princess Comes Across, Two in a Crowd, The Accusing Finger, Banjo on My Knee, The Man I Marry, Murder with Pictures, Rose Bowl, Nobody's Fool.*

1937: *A Doctor's Diary, Atlantic Flight, Federal Bullets, Wings Over Honolulu, Blazing Barriers, Music for Madame, Swing It Professor, Youth on Parole, The Thirteenth Man, The Man in Blue, Port of Missing Girls, Mr. Boggs Steps Out, Reported Missing, You Can't Beat Love.*

1938: *Wives Under Suspicion, The Storm, Sinners in Paradise, Crime School, Paroled from the Big House, California Frontier.*

1939: *Mystery Plane (*a.k.a. *Sky Pilot), King of the Turf, Society Smugglers, Fighting Mad, Blind Alley, Young Mr. Lincoln, Tail Spin, Tropic Fury, Stunt Pilot, When Tomorrow Comes, Sky Patrol, Made for Each Other, Danger Flight, Nick Carter Master Detective, Crashing Through, Charlie McCarthy Detective.*

1940: *Chasing Trouble, Enemy Agent, Johnny Apollo, An Angel from Texas, Framed, Give Us Wings, Lillian Russell, Colorado, The Great Plane Robbery, Elsa Maxwell's Public Deb No. 1.*

1941: *The Phantom Cowboy, The Great Train Robbery, Death Valley Outlaws.*

1942: *Reap the Wild Wind, Eyes in the Night,*

Rubber Racketeers, Invisible Agent, Frisco Lil, Police Bullets, Pacific Rendezvous.
1943: *Keep 'Em Slugging, You Can't Beat the Law, Get Going, Sherlock Holmes Faces Death, Captive Wild Woman, Corvette K-225, Gung Ho!, The Mad Ghoul.*
1944: *The Imposter, Hi Good Looking, Hat Check Honey, Moon Over Las Vegas, Jungle Woman, Phantom Lady, Twilight on the Prairie, The Great Alaskan Mystery* (serial).
1945: *The Master Key* (serial), *The Beautiful Cheat, The Daltons Ride Again, The Frozen Ghost, I'll Remember April, On Stage Everybody, She Gets Her Man, Strange Confession, Swing Out Sister, The Royal Mounted Rides Again* (serial).
1946: *Danger Woman, Inside Job, Smooth as Silk, Little Miss Big, The Spider Woman Strikes Back, Strange Conquest, Her Adventurous Night.*
1947: *Cass Timberlane, Killer Dill, The Michigan Kid, Headin' for Heaven, Buck Privates Come Home.*
1948: *Train to Alcatraz, The Judge.*
1949: *The Green Promise, Calamity Jane and Sam Bass, Sky Dragon.*
1950: *No Man of Her Own, The Fireball, Snow Dog, Branded.*
1981: *The Racket, Road Block, Flying Leathernecks.*
1952: *The Atomic City, The Savage, Behind Southern Lines* (compiled from episodes of the *Wild Bill Hickok* TV series).
1953: *The Sun Shines Bright, Invaders from Mars, Second Chance, Arrowhead, Pickup on South Street.*
1954: *The Siege at Red River, Black Tuesday.*
1955: *White Feather, The Long Gray Line, Smoke Signal, The Private War of Major Benson.*
1957: *Drango.*
1972: *The World of Sport Fishing* (documentary).

Television Series

1955–1975: *Gunsmoke* as Dr. Galen (Doc) Adams.

Sources

The Annual Obituary. Detroit, MI: St. James Press, 1981.
Dorst, Gary D. "A Lost Interview with Milburn Stone Blazing the *Gunsmoke* Trail." *Filmfax* magazine, issue No. 36, Dec./Jan. 1993.
Newcomb, Horace, and Robert S. Alley. *The Producer's Medium: Conversations with Creators of American TV.* New York: Oxford University Press, 1983.
Speed, F. Maurice. *The Western Film and TV Annual.* London: MacDonald, 1957.

RANDY STUART

Born in Iola, Kansas, on October 12, 1924, this actress started out at the age of three with her parents in their touring company. She had every kind of show business experience in vaudeville, stock, radio and television. After Randy relocated to California, her appearance in a college play caught the eye of a 20th Century–Fox talent scout and she was signed to a contract in 1947. She made her screen debut in *The Foxes of Harrow* (1947) as Rex Harrison's mother in the prologue scene in which his character, Stephen Fox, is born. She was seen in supporting roles in some major Fox features dating from the late 1940s. Her studio biography indicated that she had blue eyes, blonde hair and stood 5'4½" tall. By far her best-known film role was at Universal when she played Louise Carey, the wife of *The Incredible Shrinking Man* (1957).

Her first regular series role was in *This Is the Life,* the religious series produced by the Lutheran Church which depicted a Christian family's attempts to deal with the problems of everyday life. The family was called the Fishers, and Stuart played the eldest daughter. She was seen in a rather more mature role in *Biff Baker USA.* Biff Baker (Alan Hale, Jr.) traveled the world in search of merchandise for his import business, but usually met trouble along the way. Stuart played his capable wife and partner in this short-lived CBS series.

For a single season she brought romance into the life of Wyatt Earp when she played the owner and operator of the Birdcage Saloon in the famous television Western series. She was also active at Warner Bros. in the late 1950s, particularly in the television series *Bourbon Street Beat* in the occasional role of a female private eye. Some of her last recorded appearances were in the revival of *Dragnet* in the late 1960s, in which she had the occasional role of the wife of Officer Bill Gannon (Harry Morgan).

Offscreen in 1964, she was involved in Project Prayer, a movement dedicated to allowing voluntary prayer in public schools. In the same year she was active in the unsuccessful Goldwater presidential campaign. She was a founder of a Celebrity Speakers Bureau and wrote speeches for Ronald Reagan when he ran for governor of California.

Although she had had a family, Randy Stuart lived the last part of her life as a recluse in Bakersfield, California, where she wanted neither publicity nor correspondence. She died there on July 20, 1996, at age 71, of lung cancer.

Randy Stuart Filmography

1947: *The Foxes of Harrow.*
1948: *Sitting Pretty, The Street with No Name, Apartment for Peggy.*
1949: *I Was a Male War Bride, The Fan, Whirlpool, Dancing in the Dark.*
1950: *All About Eve, Stella.*
1951: *I Can Get It for You Wholesale.*
1952: *Room for One More.*
1956: *Star in the Dust.*
1957: *The Incredible Shrinking Man.*
1958: *The Man from God's Country.*

Television Series

1952–1953: *Biff Baker USA* as Louise Baker.
1952–1956: *This Is the Life* as Emily Fisher.
1959–1960: *The Life and Legend of Wyatt Earp* as Nellie Cashman.

Sources

Magers, Boyd. "Empty Saddles." *Western Clippings* magazine, Sept./Oct. 1996.
Picture Show Annual. London: Amalgamated Press, 1951.

HOPE SUMMERS

Hope Summers was born in Mattoon, Illinois, in 1901, the daughter of a congressman. She had two brothers, both of whom entered the diplomatic service. After graduating from Northwestern University, she spent one year with the Harry Duffy Stock Company in Seattle, Washington. In 1927 she temporarily abandoned show business to become a teacher at her alma mater. In 1939 she entered radio in Chicago, where she acted in dozens of broadcasts. She also founded two stock companies, producing and acting in both. She toured in a one-woman show called *Backstage of Broadway.*

In the early 1950s she appeared in a local video soap called *Hawkins Falls.* With the demise of this she gravitated in 1956 to Hollywood, where she soon found herself much in demand for character parts in feature films and television. Her television career began with roles on *Alfred Hitchcock Presents.* She played the role of storekeeper Hattie Denton throughout the run of *The Rifleman* series. Summers remained a busy actress until she died in Woodland Hills, California, on July 22, 1979, of heart failure. She was 77.

Hope Summers Filmography

1956: *Storm Fear.*
1957: *Zero Hour, Black Patch.*
1958: *I Want to Live!, The Return of Dracula.*
1959: *Hound Dog Man, Edge of Eternity.*
1960: *Inherit the Wind.*

1961: *Parrish, Claudelle Inglish, Homicidal, The Children's Hour.*
1962: *Rome Adventure, The Couch.*
1963: *Spencer's Mountain.*
1961: *One Man's Way.*
1965: *The Hallelujah Trail.*
1966: *The Ghost and Mr. Chicken.*
1968: *Rosemary's Baby, The Shakiest Gun in the West, 5 Card Stud.*
1969: *The Learning Tree.*
1970: *Get to Know Your Rabbit.*
1972: *Where Does It Hurt?, Ace Eli and Rodger of the Skies.*
1973: *Charley Varrick.*
1974: *Our Time, Death Sentence* (TV).
1978: *Foul Play, Smokey and the Goodtime Outlaws.*

Television Series

1951–1955: *Hawkins Falls* as Mrs. Catherwood.
1958–1963: *The Rifleman* as Hattie Denton.
1960–1968: *The Andy Griffith Show* as Clara Edwards.
1978: *Another Day* as Olive Gardner.

Sources

Beck, Calvin Thomas. *Scream Queens: Heroines of the Horrors.* New York: Collier, 1978.
Brooks, Tim. *The Complete Directory to Prime Time TV Stars.* New York: Ballantine Books, 1987.
Jones, Ken D., Arthur F. McClure, and Alfred E. Twomey. *Character People.* Secaucus, NJ: Citadel Press, 1979.

GLORIA TALBOTT

Gloria Talbott was born in Glendale, California, on February 7, 1931, the daughter of a dry cleaning shop owner. As a very young child, she learned to sing and dance. While at high school she became interested in dramatics, acting in plays and winning prizes. She also did bit parts in a few major films as a child. In 1947 she was voted Miss Glendale in a bathing beauty contest. She appeared in stock, notably at the Eagle Rock Theater where she met and married a young actor named Sandy Sanders in 1948. In the same year she appeared in support of Charles Ruggles and Mary Boland in *One Fine Day,* a stage vehicle for the duo, which brought her to the attention of talent scouts.

She and Sanders had a son, Mark Parrish, born in 1950. She was absent from show business for three years before she and her husband divorced in 1953. Although she appeared on television anthology programs extensively during the 1950s and did live television plays from the West Coast, her sole regular TV role was as Abbie Crandall in *The Life and Legend of Wyatt Earp* for one season. This is some of her least-remembered work. She guest-starred on other Western series, notably *Rawhide* and *Wanted: Dead or Alive.* Later she landed a regular role on the *Mr. Novak* series, but injury forced her to withdraw.

She had plum roles in a few big-budget films of the 1950s, but missed out on top stardom. Instead she fell into the rut of science fiction B movies and occasional Westerns, some of which are highly regarded by film buffs. In 1961 she married a physician by whom she has a daughter, Mia Mullally, born in 1966. This marriage ended in divorce in 1967. Shortly afterwards, she voluntarily retired from show business to raise her daughter. In 1970 she remarried to a dentist. At last report she is a grandmother residing in Glendale, where she is very content with her life.

Gloria Talbott Filmography

1937: *Maytime.*
1944: *Sweet and Lowdown.*
1945: *A Tree Grows in Brooklyn.*
1952: *Border City Rustlers, We're Not Married.*
1953: *Northern Patrol, Desert Pursuit.*
1955: *We're No Angels, Crashout, Lucy Gallant, All That Heaven Allows.*
1956: *The Young Guns, Strange Intruder.*
1957: *The Oklahoman, The Cyclops, Daughter of*

Jack Lord and Gloria Talbott guest-starring on *Rawhide*. Talbott also appeared in *The Life and Legend of Wyatt Earp*.

Dr. Jekyll, The Kettles on Old MacDonald's Farm, Taming Sutton's Gal.
1958: *Cattle Empire, I Married a Monster from Outer Space.*
1959: *Alias Jesse James, Girls' Town, The Oregon Trail.*
1960: *The Leech Woman, Oklahoma Territory.*
1965: *Arizona Rangers.*
1966: *An Eye for an Eye.*

Television Series

1955–1956: *The Life and Legend of Wyatt Earp* as Abbie Crandall.

Sources

Lamparski, Richard. *Whatever Became Of? Eleventh Series.* New York: Crown, 1989.
Picture Show Annual. London: Amalgamated Press, 1957 and 1958.
Weaver, Tom. *Interviews with B Science Fiction and Horror Movie Makers: Writers, Producers, Directors, Actors, Moguls and Makeup.* Jefferson, NC: McFarland, 1988.

WILLIAM TANNEN

William Tannen was born in New York City on November 17, 1911, the son of actor Julius Tannen (1881–1965) and the brother of actor Charles Tannen (1915–1980). He made his screen debut in 1934. In *The Life and Legend of Wyatt Earp,* he played Deputy Hal Norton. During Wyatt's Dodge City years, Bat Masterson was his first deputy. After he left he was replaced by his brother Ed for a short while. When he departed, stability was restored for a season in the form of Hal Norton, who remained until Earp departed for Tombstone. Tannen died in Woodland Hills, California, on December 2, 1976, at age 65.

William Tannen Filmography

1934: *The Band Plays On.*
1935: *It's in the Air, She Couldn't Take It, Biography of a Bachelor Girl, Murder in the Fleet.*
1936: *Crash Donovan, Tough Guy, Exclusive Story, Speed.*
1937: *When Love Is Young.*
1938: *The Devil's Party, Dramatic School, The Mad Miss Manton.*
1939: *Stand Up and Fight, Broadway Serenade, It's a Wonderful World, Judge Hardy and Son, The Secret of Dr. Kildare, Within the Law, Another Thin Man.*
1940: *Bitter Sweet, New Moon, Sky Murder, Flight Command, Wyoming, Sporting Blood, I Love You Again, Broadway Melody of 1940, Gallant Sons, Phantom Raiders.*
1941: *Two Faced Woman, The Big Store, Whistling in the Dark, Dr. Jekyll and Mr. Hyde, I'll Wait for You, The Trial of Mary Dugan, Love Crazy, Forbidden Passage.*

1942: *Joe Smith American, Fingers at the Window, Nazi Agent, Woman of the Year, Pacific Rendezvous, Stand by for Action.*
1943: *Air Raid Wardens, Pilot No. 5, Three Hearts for Julia, The Youngest Profession.*
1944: *Maisie Goes to Reno, The Canterville Ghost.*
1945: *Abbott and Costello in Hollywood, Weekend at the Waldorf.*
1946: *Two Smart People.*
1947: *This Time for Keeps, It Happened in Brooklyn.*
1948: *An Innocent Affair (*a.k.a. *Don't Trust Your Husband), Homecoming, Walk a Crooked Mile, A Southern Yankee, B.F.'s Daughter.*
1949: *Lust for Gold, The Gal Who Took the West, Alaska Patrol, The Mysterious Desperado, Riders of the Range, Abandoned, Scene of the Crime, The Barkleys of Broadway.*
1950: *Convicted, Armored Car Robbery, Annie Get Your Gun, Chain Gang, Sunset in the West, Pygmy Island, Father Is a Bachelor, Three Little Words.*
1951: *A Yank in Korea, New Mexico, Insurance Investigator, Roaring City, Blue Blood, Rhythm Inn, The Strip, Flame of Araby.*
1952: *Loan Shark, Road Agent, Jungle Jim in the Forbidden Land, Jet Job, Talk About a Stranger, The Bad and the Beautiful.*
1953: *Raiders of the Seven Seas, Jack McCall Desperado, 99 River Street, El Paso Stampede, Dangerous Crossing, Eyes of the Jungle.*
1954: *Sitting Bull, Jesse James Vs. The Daltons, Captain Kidd and the Slave Girl, The Law Vs. Billy the Kid, The Golden Idol, Woman's World.*
1955: *Dial Red O, Devil Goddess, Jupiter's Darling.*
1956: *Blackjack Ketchum Desperado.*
1957: *The Tijuana Story, Jailhouse Rock.*
1960: *Noose for a Gunman.*
1965: *The Great Sioux Massacre.*
1968: *Panic in the City.*

Television Series

1957–1958: *The Life and Legend of Wyatt Earp* as Deputy Hal Norton.

Sources

Brooks, Tim. *The Complete Directory to Prime Time TV Stars 1946–Present.* New York: Ballantine Books, 1987.
Truitt, Evelyn Mack. *Who Was Who on Screen Illustrated Edition.* New York: Bowker, 1984.

FORREST TAYLOR

Forrest Taylor was born in Bloomington, Illinois, on December 29, 1883. Active in films since silent days, he amassed numerous credits, many of them Western features in which he cropped up on either side of the law. He also appeared on television, notably a semi-regular role as the doctor in the Western series *Man Without a Gun.* He died at age 81 in Garden Grove, California, on February 19, 1965.

Forrest Taylor Filmography

1915: *Man Afraid of His Wardrobe, The Terror of Twin Mountains, Two Spot Joe, The Sheriff of Willow Creek, The Trail of the Serpent, The Valley Feud, In the Sunset Country, There's Good in the Worst of Us, The Idol.*
1916: *The Thunderbolt, Wild Jim, Reformer, The Wild Rosette, April, The Disappearance of Helen Mintern, The Abandonment, The Music Swindlers, The Social Pirates, In the Service of the State, The Madonna of the Night, The Fighting Heiress, Black Magic.*
1926: *No Man's Gold, A Poor Girl's Romance.*
1933: *Riders of Destiny.*
1935: *Mississippi, Rider of the Law, Courageous Avenger, Between Men, Big Caliber, Trail of Terror.*
1936: *Rio Grande Romance, Too Much Beef, Kelly of the Secret Service, West of Nevada, Prison Shadows, Men of the Plains, Put on the Spot, Headin' for the Rio Grande, Shadow of Chinatown* (serial), *Phantoms of the Range, Rip Roarin' Buckaroo, Two Minutes to Play, Song of the Gringo.*
1937: *The Mystery of the Hooded Horsemen,*

Arizona Days, The Red Rope, Riders of the Dawn, Where Trails Divide, Island Captives, Courage of the West, Moonlight on the Range, Lost Ranch, The Roaming Cowboy, Orphan of the Pecos, Tex Rides with the Boy Scouts.

1938: *Fighting Devil Dogs* (serial), *Heroes of the Hills, California Frontier, Durango Valley Raiders, The Feud Maker, The Painted Trail, The Last Stand, Desert Patrol, Outlaw Express, Gun Packer, Black Bandit, Law of the Texan, Frontier Town, Ghost Town Riders, Guilty Trails, Man's Country, Lightning Carson Rides Again, The Story of Dr. Carver, Prairie Justice, Western Trails, King of the Newsboys, Dick Tracy Returns* (serial).

1939: *The Phantom Creeps* (serial), *Riders of Black River, Rovin' Tumbleweeds, Chip of the Flying U, Trigger Fingers, Trigger Smith, Texas Wildcats, Stand Up and Fight, The Phantom Stage, Outlaws' Paradise, The Lone Ranger Rides Again* (serial), *Street of Missing Men, S.O.S. Tidal Wave, Dick Tracy's G-Men* (serial).

1940: *The Green Hornet* (serial), *The Ghost Creeps, Terry and the Pirates* (serial), *Straight Shooters, Rhythm of the Rio Grande, Wild Horse Range, Frontier Crusader, West of Abilene, The Durango Kid, The Kid from Santa Fe, Trailing Double Trouble, Under Texas Skies, The Trail Blazers, Friendly Neighbors.*

1941: *Flying Wild, The Iron Claw* (serial), *Ridin' on a Rainbow, Billy the Kid's Fighting Pals, Kansas Cyclone, Wranglers Roost, Ridin' on the Cherokee Trail, The Lone Star Vigilantes, Pals of the Pecos, Hurricane Smith, The Singing Hill, King of the Texas Rangers* (serial), *Dick Tracy Vs Crime Inc.* (serial).

1942: *The Spoilers, Perils of the Royal Mounted* (serial), *Cowboy Serenade, Home in Wyoming, Sunset in the Desert, A Night for Crime, Sons of the Pioneers, King of the Stallions, The Yanks Are Coming, The Pay Off, The Living Ghost, Outlaws of Pine Ridge, Code of the Outlaw, In Old California, Perils of Nyoka* (serial), *King of the Mounties* (serial), *Ridin' Down the Canyon.*

1943: *Air Raid Wardens, Thundering Trails, Dead Men Walk, The Rangers Take Over, Man of Courage, Corregidor, Fighting Buckaroo, Silver Spurs, Sleepy Lagoon, Song of Nevada, Idaho, King of the Cowboys, Song of Texas.*

1944: *Haunted Harbor* (serial), *Mystery Man, Lady in the Death House, Song of Nevada, Shake Hands with Murder, Three Little Sisters, Sundown Valley, The Last Horseman, Sonora Stagecoach, Mojave Firebrand, Cyclone Prairie Rangers, Sagebrush Heroes, Outlaws of Santa Fe, Beneath Western Skies, Cheyenne Wildcat, Zorro's Black Whip* (serial).

1945: *Federal Operator 99* (serial), *Rockin' in the Rockies, Manhunt of Mystery Island* (serial), *Identity Unknown, Dangerous Intruder, Strange Voyage, Bandits of the Badlands, Rough Ridin' Justice, Steppin' in Society.*

1946: *The Caravan Trail, The Glass Alibi, Romance of the West, Colorado Serenade, Texas Panhandle, Santa Fe Uprising, The Crimson Ghost* (serial), *Driftin' River, Strange Impersonation.*

1947: *The Black Widow* (serial), *Stagecoach to Denver, Yankee Fakir, The Pretender, Rustlers of Devil's Canyon, Along the Oregon Trail, The Stranger from Ponca City, Buckaroo from Powder River.*

1948: *Superman* (serial), *The Golden Eye, Four Faces West, Coroner Creek, The Plunderers.*

1949: *Bruce Gentry* (serial), *Deputy Marshal, Navajo Trail Riders, Death Valley Gunfighter, Stallion Canyon, The Fighting Redhead.*

1950: *Cherokee Uprising, The Cowboy and the Prizefighter, Rustlers on Horseback, Forbidden Jungle, The Fighting Stallion, Code of the Silver Sage, The Arizona Cowboy.*

1951: *Prairie Roundup, Wells Fargo Gunmaster, Blazing Bullets, Don Daredevil Rides Again* (serial), *Utah Wagon Train.*

1952: *Night Riders, Smoky Canyon, Border Saddlemates, Park Row, South Pacific Trail.*

1953: *The Lost Planet* (serial), *Iron Mountain Trail, The Marshal's Daughter.*

1954: *Bitter Creek.*

1959: *The FBI Story.*

Television Series

1952–1956: *This Is the Life* as Grandpa Fisher.

1957–1959: *Man Without a Gun* as Doc Brannon.

Sources

Brooks, Tim. *The Complete Directory to Prime Time TV Stars 1946–Present.* New York: Ballantine Books, 1987.

McClure, Arthur F., and Ken D. Jones. *Heroes, Heavies and Sagebrush.* South Brunswick and New York: Barnes, 1972.

KENT TAYLOR

Kent Taylor once worked with director W.S. Van Dyke in *I Take This Woman* (1940). He had a big scene with Hedy Lamarr in a nightclub where there were lots of extras. He had to ask her for a dance, trip the light fantastic around the floor, remember his lines, avoid colliding with the extras and dance to no music. (Music would have interfered with the dialogue, so it was to be dubbed in later.) It was a complicated shot with no coverage or other angles. Van Dyke did not do much rehearsing, either. So Taylor was presented with his greatest challenge. He had to do that complicated maneuver plus get Miss Lamarr back to her table at the proper time with no rehearsal. He accomplished it in one take.

Kent Taylor's trademark was his pencil-thin mustache. He played leads in so many minor films that he was once dubbed "King of the B's." During the 1950s he starred in a couple of television series, one of which was a Western called *Rough Riders.*

Kent Taylor was born Louis William John Henry Von Weiss on May 11, 1906, on a ranch outside Nashua, Iowa. He was raised on a farm and educated at a local high school, where he first performed in plays and as a teenager played sax in a dance band. At the Darrah Institute of Technology in Chicago, he studied engineering for two years. The acting bug bit, so he joined a touring repertory company.

When his father retired from farming, the family relocated to California at the heart of the Depression in 1931. Kent Taylor supported himself for a while as a salesman for the canvas business which his father had started in their new state. While applying for work as an extra at Paramount, he was noticed by a casting director who was so impressed with his physique and appearance that he cast him as a dress extra. Shortly afterwards the same casting director asked him to appear in a screen test opposite Claire Dodd. Despite the fact that there was no pay, Taylor readily agreed. So well did he photograph that studio executives signed him to a long-term contract with Paramount.

He spent seven years under contract at Paramount, two at Universal and two at Twentieth Century–Fox. During World War II he entertained troops in North Africa. Although he was almost continuously employed, he did not rise to top stardom. He accepted every role assigned to him, never complaining about the quality of the scripts nor the size of his roles. He was an extremely self-effacing person who sought to overcome his shyness by drinking. Alcohol had the effect of dampening his ambition. Although he quit drinking in the early 1950s, one detrimental long-term effect was that he gradually lost the faculty for remembering his lines.

When the cinema's Boston Blackie Chester Morris refused to appear in the television series, Taylor took over. Boston Blackie was created by Jack Boyle in 1919. Originally he was a gentleman safecracker, but by the time Taylor came to play him in a syndicated television series, he had become an ex-thief turned New York private eye. The series (which ran for 58 episodes from 1951–1953) was very successful, but typecast him. His other television series for Ziv was *Rough Riders* (1958–1959), in which he played a veteran Union officer in the Civil War. After the Civil War ended, three soldiers who had intended to travel West in search of a new life joined forces for mutual companionship and protection on the journey. En route they encountered Indians, bandits and other assorted cutthroats. This ABC series lasted for 39 episodes.

After the series ended, Taylor returned to irregular work in feature films. He appeared in B pictures produced by such characters as Maury Dexter and Al Adamson. Taylor's final appearance was a telemovie called *The Phantom of Hollywood* (1974). Ironically, he played one of a couple of buyers of a once-famous studio. For recreation in real life he was a keen golfer.

In the 1980s Kent Taylor underwent several heart operations. He had been under the care of a nurse at his North Hollywood home before being hospitalized for the last time on April 9, 1987. He died in his sleep at the Motion Picture Country Home and Hospital in Woodland Hills, California, on April 11, 1987, at age 80. He was survived by his widow

Kent Taylor (right) with Peter Whitney (far left) and Jan Merlin in *Rough Riders*.

Augusta Kulek (whom he wed in 1932) and children Kay, Judy and Bill. He lies buried at Westwood Village Memorial Park in Los Angeles.

Kent Taylor Filmography

1931: *Road to Reno.*
1932: *Dancers in the Dark, Forgotten Commandments, Two Kinds of Women, Husband's Holiday, The Devil and the Deep, Merrily We Go to Hell, The Sign of the Cross, Make Me a Star, If I Had a Million, Sinners in the Sun, Blonde Venus.*
1933: *Mysterious Rider, A Lady's Profession, The Story of Temple Drake, Sunset Pass, I'm No Angel, White Woman, Cradle Song, Under the Tonto Rim.*
1934: *Death Takes a Holiday, Many Happy Returns, David Harum, Double Door, Mrs. Wiggs of the Cabbage Patch, Limehouse Blues.*
1935: *The County Chairman, College Scandal, Smart Girl, Without Regret, Two-Fisted, My Marriage.*
1936: *The Sky Parade, Florida Special, Ramona, The Accusing Finger.*
1937: *When Love Is Young, Wings Over Honolulu, The Lady Fights Back, A Girl with Ideas, Prescription for Romance, Love in a Bungalow.*
1938: *The Jury's Secret, The Last Express.*
1939: *Four Girls in White, Pirates of the Skies, The Gracie Allen Murder Case, Five Came Back, Three Sons, Escape to Paradise, I Take This Woman.*
1940: *Sued for Libel, Two Girls on Broadway, The Girl in 313, Men Against the Sky, I'm Still Alive, The Girls from Avenue A.*
1941: *Washington Melodrama, Repent at Leisure.*
1942: *Mississippi Gambler, Tombstone the Town Too Tough to Die, Army Surgeon, Halfway to Shanghai, Frisco Lil, Gang Busters* (serial).
1943: *Bombers' Moon.*
1944: *Roger Touhy—Gangster, Alaska.*
1945: *The Daltons Ride Again.*
1946: *Smooth as Silk, Young Widow, Tangier, Deadline for Murder, Dangerous Millions.*
1947: *Second Chance, The Crimson Key.*

1948: *Half Past Midnight.*
1950: *Federal Agent at Large, Western Pacific Agent, Trial Without Jury.*
1951: *Payment on Demand.*
1954: *Playgirl, Track the Man Down.*
1955: *Secret Venture, Ghost Town, The Phantom from 10,000 Leagues.*
1956: *Slightly Scarlet, Frontier Gambler.*
1957: *The Iron Sheriff.*
1958: *Fort Bowie, Gang War.*
1960: *Walk Tall.*
1961: *The Purple Hills.*
1962: *The Broken Land, The Firebrand.*
1963: *The Day Mars Invaded Earth, Harbor Lights, The Crawling Hand.*
1964: *Law of the Lawless.*
1968: *Brides of Blood.*
1970: *Hell's Bloody Devils (*a.k.a. *The Fakers* and *Smashing the Crime Syndicate), Satan's Sadists.*
1971: *The Mighty Gorga.*
1974: *Girls for Rent, The Phantom of Hollywood* (TV).

Television Series

1951–1953: *Boston Blackie* as Boston Blackie.
1958–1959: *Rough Riders* as Cpt. Jim Flagg.

Sources

Imber, Larry. "Forgotten Man." *Films of the Golden Age* magazine, number 5, summer 1996.
Lamparski, Richard. *Whatever Became Of? Seventh Series.* New York: Bantam, 1977.

GUY TEAGUE

This character actor was usually seen in Westerns. He had one semi-regular role as the deputy sheriff in the television series *Fury.* He died in Texas on January 24, 1970, while in his 60s. He was the father of actor Brian Teague (1937–1970), who was killed in a road accident.

Guy Teague Filmography

1949: *The Gal Who Took the West.*
1950: *The Showdown, Vigilante Hideout, Desperadoes of the West* (serial), *The Invisible Monster* (serial).
1951: *Don Daredevil Rides Again* (serial), *Honeychile, The Kid from Amarillo, Flying Disc Man from Mars* (serial).
1952: *Radar Men from the Moon* (serial), *Carson City, Cattle Town, Harem Girl.*
1953: *The Stranger Wore a Gun.*
1954: *Man with the Steel Whip* (serial), *The Outlaw Stallion, The Bounty Hunter.*
1955: *Wyoming Renegades, A Lawless Street.*
1956: *Fury at Gunsight Pass, The White Squaw, Giant.*

Television Series

1955–1958: *Fury* as The Deputy Sheriff.

Sources

Terrace, Vincent. *The Complete Encyclopedia of Television Programs 1947–1976.* South Brunswick and New York: Barnes, 1976.
Truitt, Evelyn Mack. *Who Was Who on Screen Second Edition.* New York: Bowker, 1977.

Richard Boone and Carol Thurston in *Frontier*. Thurston also appeared in *The Life and Legend of Wyatt Earp*.

CAROL THURSTON

Born in Forsyth, Montana, in 1923, this actress attended Montana University and the Bliss Hayden School of Acting in Hollywood. She initially appeared with her father in amateur theatricals from an early age. She began her professional acting career in local stock companies and later appeared in road shows. She was an unknown when she won the much coveted role of the beautiful native girl Tremartini in Cecil B. DeMille's *The Story of Dr. Wassell* (1944). Although this remains her best performance, her career as an actress never really developed much beyond that point and she seemed to find herself typed in variations on that role.

Active in television Western series from the early 1950s, she played a loyal pioneer wife in an episode of *Frontier* and loyal Indian squaws in episodes of *The Lone Ranger* and *Rawhide*. Her sole regular series role was in one of the later seasons of *The Life and Legend of Wyatt Earp* in which she played the daughter of evil Old Man Clanton. Her last screen appearance came in *Showdown* (1963), a very inferior Audie Murphy Western, in which she had low billing with but one scene and minimal dialogue. She is believed to have had an unhappy private life compounded by a drink problem.

Carol Thurston committed suicide in obscurity on December 31, 1969, at age 46.

Carol Thurston Filmography

1944: *The Story of Dr. Wassell, The Conspirators.*
1945: *China Sky.*
1946: *Swamp Fire.*
1947: *The Jewels of Brandenburg, The Last Round-Up.*
1948: *Rogue's Regiment.*
1949: *Arctic Manhunt, Apache Chief.*
1951: *Flaming Feather.*

1952: *Arctic Flight.*
1953: *Conquest of Cochise, Killer Ape.*
1954: *Yukon Vengeance.*
1955: *Pearl of the South Pacific.*
1956: *The Women of Pitcairn Island.*
1960: *The Hypnotic Eye.*
1963: *Showdown.*

Television Series

1959–1960: *The Life and Legend of Wyatt Earp* as Emma Clanton.

Sources

Brooks, Tim. *The Complete Directory to Prime Time TV Stars 1946–Present.* New York: Ballantine Books, 1987.
Truitt, Evelyn Mack. *Who Was Who on Screen Second Edition.* New York: Bowker, 1977.

KAM TONG

Born in 1907, Kam Tong played the part of Hey Boy, the Oriental working at the Carlton Hotel, who was seen at the start of many episodes of *Have Gun Will Travel,* bringing the newspaper and a message from a likely but desperate client to Paladin (Richard Boone). A more lucrative television offer (to costar in *The Garlund Touch*) presented itself, and Kam Tong departed to be replaced by Hey Girl (Lisa Lu). When his new venture sank after only half a season, Hey Boy was back.

Kam Tong also appeared in a number of films from his debut onwards. The best known of these roles was as Dr. Li, the father of Miyoshi Umeki in *Flower Drum Song* (1961). Kam Tong, 62, died at Costa Mesa, California, on November 8, 1969.

Kam Tong Filmography

1936: *The General Died at Dawn.*
1937: *The Good Earth.*
1938: *International Settlement, City Girl.*
1939: *The Real Glory.*
1942: *Joan of Ozark, Rubber Racketeers, China Girl, The Hidden Hand, Across the Pacific.*
1953: *Target Hong Kong.*
1954: *This Is My Love.*
1955: *Love Is a Many Splendored Thing, The Left Hand of God, Soldier of Fortune.*
1960: *Who Was That Lady?*
1961: *Flower Drum Song.*
1963: *It Happened at the World's Fair.*
1965: *Women of the Prehistoric Planet.*
1966: *Dimension 5, Mister Buddwing.*
1967: *Kill a Dragon.*

Television Series

1957–1960: *Have Gun Will Travel* as Hey Boy.
1960–1961: *Mr. Garlund (*a.k.a. *The Garlund Touch)* as Kam Chang.
1961–1963: *Have Gun Will Travel* as Hey Boy.

Sources

Brooks, Tim. *The Complete Directory to Prime Time TV Stars 1946–Present.* New York: Ballantine Books, 1987.
Truitt, Evelyn Mack. *Who Was Who on Screen Illustrated Edition.* New York: Bowker, 1984.

PHILIP TONGE

Philip Tonge was born in London on April 26, 1892, the son of H. Asheton Tonge and Lillian Brennard. He made his first stage appearance at His Majesty's Theater, London, on October 2, 1902, as Joseph in *The Eternal City.* As a child actor he appeared on tour and in London with some of the best-known theatrical names such as Ellen Terry and Sir Henry Irving. He appeared in plays in England until 1914.

By October 1914, he had emigrated to America to avoid serving in World War I and was appearing as Tommy Traddles in *The Highway of Life* at Wallack's Theater, New York. He followed this up by making numerous appearances on the New York stage during the 1920s, punctuated by a spell with the Boston Repertory Theater between 1924 and 1925. His stage career continued without interruption during the 1930s and 1940s, including seasons at the Casino Theater, Newport, Rhode Island. As late as 1954 he was touring as Linus Larrabee in *Sabrina Fair.*

His offscreen hobbies were listed as skating, cycling and outdoor sports. Although he toyed with films in 1915 and 1933, he did not become a regular until after World War II. One of his best film roles was as Inspector Hearne in *Witness for the Prosecution* (1958). His sole regular role on television was as Gen. Amherst in the series *Northwest Passage.* He was the commanding officer of the fort from which Rogers' Rangers undertook their missions. Tonge died in Hollywood on January 28, 1959, at age 66, while the series was still in production.

Philip Tonge Filmography

1915: *Still Waters.*
1933: *His Double Life.*
1947: *Love from a Stranger, Miracle on 34th Street.*
1952: *Hans Christian Andersen, O. Henry's Full House* ("The Cop and the Anthem" episode).
1953: *House of Wax, Scandal at Scourie, Small Town Girl.*
1954: *Elephant Walk, Khyber Patrol, Ricochet Romance, Track of the Cat.*
1955: *Desert Sands, The Prodigal, The Silver Chalice.*
1956: *Pardners, The Peacemaker.*
1957: *Les Girls.*
1958: *Witness for the Prosecution, Darby's Rangers, Macabre.*
1959: *This Earth Is Mine, Invisible Invaders.*

Television Series

1958–1959: *Northwest Passage* as Gen. Amherst.

Sources

Truitt, Evelyn Mack. *Who Was Who On Screen, Second Edition.* New York: Bowker, 1977.
Who's Who in the Theatre Twelfth Edition. London: Pitman, 1957.

AUDREY TOTTER

Audrey Totter was born in Joliet, Illinois, on December 20, 1917, the eldest of five children of an Austrian father and a Swedish mother. When she saw a circus perform in her home town at the age of seven, she tried to run away and join it. Her ambition to be a star was not encouraged by her parents, but they relented and allowed her to do some amateur dramatics while at high school. She also played bass fiddle with her school band.

Upon graduating she went to Chicago where she won a lead opposite Ian Keith in a play *(The Copperhead)* in 1938. She spent the following year in his stock company, which led to a tour of *My Sister Eileen.* She became extremely active in Chicago's flourishing radio soap operas and later in New York, where she developed a reputation for being able to imitate any accent. While there she was tested by Warner Bros. and 20th Century–Fox, but without success.

Then she was tested and signed by MGM

for seven years, making her screen debut in *Main Street After Dark* (1944) as Selena Royle's daughter who entices and rolls servicemen. She is best remembered, however, as the female lead in *Lady in the Lake* (1946), an unexciting version of a Raymond Chandler thriller, more notable for its use of subjective camera in place of the hero Philip Marlowe (Robert Montgomery). There are those who believe that she and Robert Ryan gave the best performances of their careers in the boxing melodrama *The Set-Up* (1949), which she made on loan-out to RKO.

As a freelance, she starred in *Meet Millie,* a CBS radio comedy series, from 1951 to 1954, but other commitments prevented her from playing the lead in the television series. She made two USO tours of Korea in the early 1950s. After marriage and motherhood, she downscaled her career. She did, however, do television. She played the boarding house owner in *Cimarron City,* a one-season Western series which starred George Montgomery. Although she was the main female interest, she allegedly departed the series before the end because her character was not sufficiently integral to the plotlines. She later had a regular role on *Our Man Higgins,* a one-season but very funny sitcom in which she played the employer of a British butler (Stanley Holloway). In 1972 she came out of a self-imposed retirement at the urging of Frank Glicksman, executive producer of the soap opera *Medical Center,* to play the tough but tenderhearted Nurse Wilcox.

In 1952 Totter married Dr. Leo Fred, chief physician at the Los Angeles Veterans' Hospital and Assistant Dean of UCLA's School of Medicine. They had one daughter, Mary Elizabeth Ann, who was born in 1954. Her husband died in March 1995. Audrey Totter lives in West Los Angeles.

Portrait of Audrey Totter, who appeared in *Cimarron City.*

Audrey Totter Filmography

1944: *Main Street After Dark, Ziegfeld Follies* (released 1946).
1945: *Bewitched* (voice only), *The Sailor Takes a Wife, The Hidden Eye, Her Highness and the Bellboy, Adventure, Dangerous Partners.*
1946: *The Postman Always Rings Twice, The Cockeyed Miracle, The Secret Heart* (voice only), *The Lady in the Lake.*
1947: *The Beginning or the End?, The High Wall, The Unsuspected.*
1948: *Tenth Avenue Angel, The Saxon Charm.*
1949: *Alias Nick Beal, The Set-Up, Any Number Can Play, Tension.*
1950: *Under the Gun.*
1951: *The Sellout, The Blue Veil, FBI Girl.*
1952: *My Pal Gus, Assignment—Paris.*
1953: *Man in the Dark, The Woman They Almost Lynched, Cruisin' Down the River, Mission Over Korea, Champ for a Day.*
1954: *Massacre Canyon.*
1955: *Women's Prison, A Bullet for Joey, The Vanishing American.*
1957: *Ghost Diver.*
1958: *Jet Attack, Man or Gun.*
1964: *The Carpetbaggers.*
1965: *Harlow* (the Carol Lynley version).
1967: *The Outsider* (TV).
1968: *Chubasco.*
1978: *The Magnificent Hustle.*
1979: *The Apple Dumpling Gang Rides Again.*
1984: *City Killer* (TV).

Television Series

1958–1959: *Cimarron City* as Beth Purcell.

1962–1963: *Our Man Higgins* as Alice MacRoberts.
1972–1976: *Medical Center* as Nurse Wilcox.

Sources

Lamparski, Richard. *Whatever Became Of? Tenth Series.* New York: Crown, 1986.
Parish, James Robert, and Ronald L. Bowers. *The MGM Stock Company.* London: Ian Allan, 1973.

TOM TRYON

Despite the plaudits he won for acting in such movies as *The Cardinal* and in the Walt Disney television series *Texas John Slaughter,* Tom Tryon found his achievements in Hollywood to be unrewarding. During his lifetime he changed careers three times, but they blended perfectly. His knowledge of Hollywood and the movie business gave him the background for two books. His familiarity with scripts for both stage and screen gave him a flair for dialogue and his actor's presence and charisma were a great sales boost when he went on promotional tours. He drew on his artist's palette to make his writing more visual. Painting and acting were useful tools, but writing was his great love. He once told an interviewer, "When I began writing all I had going for me was that I could type 80 words per minute. I could spell and I liked words. But in doing it, I found that the real reward was the writing itself, working at it day by day and finally accomplishing something. To have a book published is one of the most exciting things that can happen to you. Infinitely more rewarding than acting."

Thomas Tryon was born in Hartford, Connecticut, on January 14, 1926, the son of Arthur Lane Tryon, a clothier, and Elizabeth Lester. He was descended from Gov. William Tryon of North Carolina and later of New York, a leading Tory during the Revolutionary War. He grew up and attended schools in Wethersfield, one of the oldest towns in Connecticut. When he was 17, he enlisted in the United States Navy, serving from 1943 to 1946 in the South Pacific as a radio specialist third class. After being honorably discharged, he enrolled at Yale University where he majored in fine arts and obtained a B.A. degree in 1949, graduated with honors.

While preparing for a career in art at the Art Students League in New York City, he spent a summer painting scenery at Richard Aldrich's Cape Playhouse in Dennis, Cape Cod, Massachusetts. His stage debut was made when he was asked by the director to substitute in a walk-on part as a centurion in a production of *Caesar and Cleopatra.* At the suggestion of Aldrich's wife, Gertrude Lawrence, he returned to New York to study acting under Sanford Meisner at the Neighborhood Playhouse. While there he lived on the $75 a week benefit from the G.I. Bill, supplemented by occasional work as an extra on television shows. His Broadway debut came in 1952 when he was an understudy in the musical *Wish You Were Here.* When he joined the Jose Ferrer Repertory Company at the New York City Center in 1953, he played a lackey in *Cyrano de Bergerac* and Tressel in *Richard III.*

By the end of 1955, his career was stagnating. He had been playing "nice small parts," but there was no hope of anything major. Discovered by the New York representative of film producer Hal Wallis, he ventured to Hollywood, where he was tested and put under joint contract to Hal Wallis and Paramount Pictures. He made his screen debut in *The Scarlet Hour* (1956), but many of his subsequent roles proved to be disappointing. He was Charlton Heston's black sheep brother in *Three Violent People* (1956), a Western in which the loss of his arm has left him with an inferiority complex. Heston, in his book *The Actor's Life,* recalled, "I was nervous about Tom Tryon playing my brother in this film. Actually ...

he was very good in the part. We were lucky to have him." In the cult sci-fi classic *I Married a Monster from Outer Space* (1958) he played an Earthman duplicated by an alien invader. On the negative side he suffered several disappointments along the way, most notably when Universal-International reneged on a promise to cast him in the lead of *A Time to Love and a Time to Die*. The male lead in *Marjorie Morningstar* went to Gene Kelly instead of Tryon.

In late 1958 his career appeared to be on the upswing when Walt Disney chose him to play the colorful title character in the hour-long Western series *Tales of Texas John Slaughter*. Slaughter was a real-life character who was a cowboy, scout and peace officer. He had a fearsome reputation in Arizona, where he cleaned up the lawless elements. He established the cattle route which eventually became known as the Slaughter Trail. As a tracker he pursued Geronimo and was in on his eventual capture. The *Texas John Slaughter* episodes were shot in color and shown as segments of *Walt Disney Presents*. The first episode was shown on October 31, 1958, and the last on April 23, 1961. There were 17 of them in total. Several of these episodes were subsequently edited together and shown as theatrical features in Europe.

Tryon enjoyed the relaxed atmosphere of the Disney Studios where, during his college days, he had once intended to work as a cartoonist. He was very pleased to be appearing in a series which was action-packed with scripts which had obviously been written with care. Most of the shooting was done at the Disney Studios in Burbank. To prepare for the role he trained for two months with Dick Farnsworth, one of the best stunt men in Hollywood. Farnsworth also doubled for Tryon in the series. *Slaughter* became the biggest success on the show since *Davy Crockett*. Walt Disney said, "Every time it goes on the air, the ratings go up. So I guess we'll stick with it for a while."

Tryon then signed a contract in 1960 with 20th Century–Fox, who agreed to share his contract with Walt Disney on the basis of six months each for three years. Potentially his most interesting role under the Fox banner turned out to be an abortive one. He was one of the last actors to work with Marilyn Monroe in 1962 in *Something's Got to Give*, production of which was abandoned when she died.

Tryon achieved his greatest screen recognition as Father Stephen Fermoyle in *The Cardinal* (1963), produced and directed by Otto Preminger from the Henry Morton Robinson novel. There were several contenders for the role, but Preminger went with Tryon primarily because "he could be made to age beautifully," a necessity since the movie followed the title character through over 30 years of his career. Although initially Tryon regarded the film as his best opportunity, it ended in disaster because of the tyrannical attitude of Preminger. On the second day of shooting, Preminger fired and rehired Tryon within the space of one hour. Tryon recalled, "He repeatedly berated me in front of the whole company, calling me a lousy actor." Subsequent clashes with the director ruined acting for Tryon, causing a nervous collapse, the psychological effects of which lingered on for years. He was hospitalized and spent several years in analysis.

Surprisingly, Tryon did work for Preminger again in *In Harm's Way* (1965), a turgid account of the bombing of Pearl Harbor. It was one of the very few failures of John Wayne. Considerably better was *The Glory Guys* (1965), a spirited Western in which he played the lead. He had guest-starring roles in such television series as *The Virginian*, *The Big Valley* and *The Men from Shiloh*.

After 1968 he seldom acted again. For many years he had been interested in writing and directing. He recalled, "It seemed to me the best thing to do was to write something and try to get to direct it." He taught himself to write by simultaneously reading Dickens, Tolstoy, Jane Austen and Colette, and working on a script. In 1967 he read *Rosemary's Baby* by Ira Levin. That novel had such a tremendous impact on him that he decided to write one in a similar vein. After two years of hard work he had a first draft of *The Other*, which he revised with the help of an editor at Alfred A. Knopf.

An American gothic, it was published in 1971, sold 3,500,000 copies and was on the best-selling lists for seven months. When it was filmed by 20th Century–Fox in 1972, Tryon was credited with the screenplay and as executive producer. Tryon was extremely clever in realizing the value of publicity, and his Hollywood personality was invaluable when it came to promoting the book on tours. He had continued to accept occasional acting assignments up to that time, but the success of his book enabled him to concentrate completely on writing, to his enormous relief. Tryon's second novel, *Harvest Home,* became the basis for a long movie-for-television, *The Dark Secret of Harvest Home* (1978) with Bette Davis. His third novel, *Lady,* was published in 1975.

His first three books were located in New England but for his fourth, *Crowned Heads* (1976), he used his knowledge of Hollywood as a background for a collection of novellas, each based on a typical Hollywood character. One of these became the basis of the disappointing film *Fedora* (1978). Nothing more of his writing was published for a decade, but he used a similar format of five Hollywood novellas for the book *All That Glitters* (1986). His habit was to rise at 5:50 A.M. and write for eight hours at a stretch, a discipline which he attributed to the Protestant work ethic on which he was reared.

In the mid–1970s, Tryon moved from Beverly Hills to Manhattan, where he lived and wrote for many years in a Central Park West apartment. As the years rolled by, he looked very little different from his days as a Hollywood star. He later moved back to California. At the time of his death, Tryon was working on a four-volume historical series collectively titled *Kingdom Come.* The first book in the series, *The Wings of the Morning,* was published in 1990. The second volume *(By the Rivers of Babylon)* (1992) and a children's book *(The Adventures of Opal and Cupid),* (1992) were both published posthumously.

Tom Tryon died of stomach cancer on September 4, 1991, at age 65, in his Los Angeles home. He was survived by two brothers. He married Ann Lilienthal (a.k.a. Ann Noyes) in 1955. They divorced in 1958, she is known to be deceased.

Tom Tryon Filmography

1956: *The Scarlet Hour, Screaming Eagles, Three Violent People.*
1957: *The Unholy Wife.*
1958: *I Married a Monster from Outer Space, Texas John Slaughter* (TV:TJS).
1959: *Gunfight at Sandoval* (TV:TJS).
1960: *Geronimo's Revenge* (TV:TJS), *The Story of Ruth.*
1961: *Showdown at Bitter Creek* (TV:TJS), *Marines Let's Go!*
1962: *Moon Pilot, The Longest Day.*
1963: *The Cardinal.*
1965: *In Harm's Way, The Glory Guys.*
1967: *The Narco Men, Winchester '73* (TV).
1969: *Color Me Dead.*

Television Series

1958–1961: *Walt Disney Presents: Tales of Texas John Slaughter* as Texas John Slaughter.

Sources

The Annual Obituary. Detroit, MI: St. James Press, 1992.
Current Biography. New York: H.W. Wilson, 1977.
Maltin, Leonard. *The Disney Films.* New York: Crown, 1973.
Picture Show Annual. London: Amalgamated Press, 1957.

Note

Films derived from the *Texas John Slaughter* television series are denoted TV:TJS in the filmography.

CLINT WALKER

The script of the Western feature *Night of the Grizzly* (1966) describes Big Jim Cole as "tall and rugged." It is doubtful whether any actor was better equipped to play the role than Clint Walker, one of the tallest, most rugged and convincing of Western stars. Earlier he was the hero of the Warner Bros. television series *Cheyenne,* the part for which he is best remembered. His size, together with his matching deep, resonant voice, made him a convincing Westerner. He had next to nothing in the way of dramatic training. It scarcely mattered.

Clint Walker was born Norman Eugene Walker on May 30, 1927, in Hartford, Illinois, the son of Mr. and Mrs. Paul Arnold Walker. His father was half-Indian and an engineer. He has a twin sister, Lucille Neoma. He was educated at Roosevelt Grammar School in Alton, Illinois, and Alton Grammar School. At school he excelled in sports. At the age of 16 he quit high school to go to work in a local factory in Alton. In 1944 he joined the Merchant Navy and for three years sailed the Great Lakes and the North American Pacific coastline with the Army Transportation Service as an able-bodied seaman. In 1947 he was discharged from the navy and returned to Alton, where he held a number of jobs including sheet metal worker, carpenter, vacuum cleaner salesman, insurance salesman and truck driver. On September 5, 1948, he married his childhood sweetheart, the former Verna Lucille Garber. Daughter Valerie Jean was born on February 28, 1950. She became one of the first U.S. female commercial airlines pilots and has made the actor a grandfather.

In November 1950, he decided that the prospects in Alton were few indeed for an ambitious man. When he heard from a friend that a fortune could be made in Texas, they packed their bags and headed for the Lone Star State oilfields. He bought a Model A Ford for $65 and drove his family through dust storms, snow, sleet and hail, but Texas proved to be a disappointment. The only place he could find to house his family was a shack situated six miles outside the town of Brownwood. There was no electricity, and they bathed by pouring water into a bucket punched full of holes and standing under a makeshift shower. By working on several construction jobs he just about made ends meet. He also did a little prospecting for silver and oil which amounted to nothing. He spent his last few months in Texas working on a large ranch as a cowboy.

In December 1952, he and his wife decided to uproot themselves again and move to California, where his wife had a sister. In Long Beach he did not exactly become an overnight success, either. He worked as a nightclub bouncer, oil field worker, a shipyard worker, in a saw mill and as a private investigator. He heard that fortunes were to be made in Las Vegas, so he moved again and headed for the Neon City where he homesteaded a two-and-a-half acre spread. He became a deputy sheriff working at the Sands Hotel. "I never thought about becoming an actor until I got to Las Vegas," he recalls, "but I was always being told that I'd be good in pictures. Van Johnson and I met one day and he introduced me to an agent named Henry Willson. Willson told me that if ever I decided I wanted to become an actor I should look him up in Hollywood." When Walker moved to Hollywood, Willson signed him as a client and even changed his name to Jett Norman for a while, but things were slow.

The question arises as to how he won the role of Cheyenne Bodie. Walker himself takes up the story: "I had done a couple of screen tests at Paramount. They were Westerns. Producer Hal Wallis put me under contract for six months which was set up for me by a fine man called Henry Wilcoxon. Henry took a liking to me and felt that I would fit in well in Westerns. They were just setting up for *The Ten Commandments* [1956] and I wound up with a role in it. DeMille was going to give me a bigger role in it, but Warner Bros. I guess saw the tests and bought my contract from Hal Wallis. Then I tested along with 30 or 40 other actors for the part of Cheyenne. I had a bit of an edge inasmuch as I was already under contract. The first day I tried hard, but didn't feel good about what I did. On the second day I felt there were so many guys I had seen before who had been in the business a long time whereas I was a Johnny Come Lately. I didn't think that I would get it so I just had fun with the part and that was what I think got me the part. I relaxed with it and had much more fun."

Cheyenne was first broadcast by ABC in September 1955, shortly after *Gunsmoke* and *The Life and Legend of Wyatt Earp.* Around this time he changed his name to Clint, which had been a childhood nickname. The series was Warners' entry in the adult Western sweepstakes and was a resounding success largely thanks to Walker's physique and personality. The first episode, "Mountain Fortress," used stock footage from Errol Flynn's western *Rocky Mountain* (1950), while the second episode

Clint Walker in *Cheyenne.*

"Julesburg" was partially based on the Randolph Scott film *Colt .45* (1950). The premise of the series was simple but effective. Cheyenne Bodie who was of Indian descent, full of knowledge of both the white and Indian worlds. He was a drifter who along the way encountered villains, fights and beautiful girls aplenty. His job varied from episode to episode. He could be a humble cowboy, a deputy or the foreman of a ranch. When *Cheyenne* made its debut, it was one of four rotating elements on *Warner Bros. Presents,* the others being *Conflict, Casablanca* and *King's Row.* A myth is that *Cheyenne* was loosely based on a 1947 film which starred Dennis Morgan. In truth, the series borrowed the title, but nothing else. In the film the title referred to a town, not the character played by Morgan. Ironically, the less remembered movie harvested the most successful of the television series, *Cheyenne.*

Walker would arrive at the studio at six in the morning and work through until late evening. It was not unusual for him to work a 15- or 16-hour day. During the first year of the series he had only one week's holiday. Frequently he was given a script one day before they started shooting, and then there were multiple changes afterwards typed on different-colored paper. In 1958 Walker walked out on Warner Bros. after they refused to release him from some onerous terms of his contract, which had been signed before *Cheyenne* became such a hit. Walker wanted a deal similar to those which James Arness and Hugh O'Brian enjoyed on their TV series. He asked for a much higher salary; participation in the program's profits; the right to make public appearances without having to give the studio half his fee; the right to use his name for advertising; the right to make records for labels other than Warners'; and payment for reruns. The studio refused, their argument being that since they had made him a star, they were entitled to the money.

The studio replaced him with Ty Hardin as a new character called Bronco Layne. Warners obtained an injunction preventing Walker from working elsewhere. In early 1959 the actor and the studio finally made peace. He continued with the series and made the occasional feature while Hardin spun off in a series of his own, *Bronco.* Walker remained unhappy about the settlement, complaining to reporters, "I am like a caged animal."

Nevertheless, his favorite episode dates from the period after his return. "It was a spoof comedy called 'The Durango Brothers' which started the seventh season," he recalls. "This family supposedly runs a boarding house, but they were killing people. When I beat one of the brothers in a test of strength, the other brothers decide I'd make a good husband for their sister Lottie. Sally Kellerman was the girl. I guess it was about the first thing that she did. Mickey Simpson and Jack Elam were two of the brothers. I liked it. It was real cute and I got a kick out of it. When executive producer Bill Orr saw it, he laughed himself silly and then said, 'We can't make any more of these because we should be making serious stuff.'"

For part of the 1959–1960 season, *Cheyenne* alternated with *Shirley Temple's Storybook.* Then, in the 1960–1961 season *Cheyenne* became *The Cheyenne Show,* a rotating anthology in which Walker was seen a majority of weeks, interspersed with episodes of Ty Hardin in *Bronco* and Will Hutchins in *Sugarfoot.* In the 1961–1962 season *Sugarfoot* was dropped and only *Cheyenne* and *Bronco* were shown. In the fall of 1962 the series consisted of episodes of *Cheyenne* alone. Although it was in the Top 20 consistently from 1958 to 1960, it was canceled after 108 episodes, the last original episode being aired in December 1962.

When his contract expired, Walker went on an extended vacation to hunt sharks in Mexico and visit the Rocky Mountains. Upon his return his services were not greatly in demand, but an appearance clowning on *The Jack Benny Show* convinced producers that he was suitable to play the role of Doris Day's former sweetheart, a Texas millionaire, in *Send Me No Flowers* (1964). He became in demand again and signed a two-picture deal with Paramount. The first film was a war movie, *None but the Brave* (1964). "Frank Sinatra directed it partially," he says. "Frank Sinatra is a very unique individual, talented in many ways. I don't think the public realizes how talented the man is. I was invited to his home one evening in Hawaii where he spent three hours telling stories to keep you in stitches. He was very nice to me and my family and I consider it a privilege to have worked with him. Howard Koch directed the rest of it. I think Frank Sinatra got bored with directing it. He was certainly a capable director."

The second feature was called *Night of the Grizzly* (1966). In this film he played Big Jim Cole, who inherited from his grandfather 640 acres located in the little town of Hope, Wyoming. Big Jim, for ten years a lawman in Utah, now wants to retire to raise cattle, crops and his family. A dangerous grizzly bear stalks the area and causes devastation and destruction among his cattle and his men. Ironically, the producers of this film chose for their location scenes a resort named Big Bear nestled in the towering San Bernardino range. This was the sight of Southern California's greatest gold discovery in 1860, and pits in the earth remain where pioneers trapped the marauding bears that came down from the hills. It was the bear which gave its name to the area. The cast (which included Martha Hyer in the role of Big Jim's wife) spent three tough weeks in the mountains for the film's exciting outdoor sequences and then returned to the Hollywood studios about 100 miles away to finish the picture.

Walker recalls, "The story was my idea. I had a two-picture commitment with Paramount. At the time Howard Koch was the boss. I did one picture with Frank Sinatra, but they couldn't come up with another story. I was reading a book about Howard Hill who was probably one of the finest bow and arrow men. One-and-a-half pages of this book told of a grizzly bear that waded into a herd of sheep, killing 60 of them because it enjoyed killing. I told the story to Howard Koch, who liked it a lot. He told me to find a writer I liked and see what he could do with it. Out of it came *Night of the Grizzly*.

"This is my favorite movie. It's been shown so many times, it's positively embarrassing. It was very well cast. It started out in a light vein, but it did get more serious as the grizzly was doing more damage. The more damage it did, the more jeopardy for me and my family because I had to get loans from the bank and the banker Jed Curry [Keenan Wynn] was after my property. Then Cass Dowdy [Leo Gordon], a killer I had once sent to jail, blamed me and wanted to get the grizzly so he could stop me from getting the reward so that I would lose my ranch. Then one of my men, played by Don Haggerty, was killed by the grizzly..."

One incident while shooting this film reveals that the drama was not confined to the movie itself. The actor continues, "I cut my foot with an axe. I was doing a scene which involved chopping logs. It involved swinging an axe and landing it in a spot on a log which was sitting on another log. There was a prop man down below holding the logs. I swung the axe headed for the wood when suddenly I saw the prop man down below—he had unwittingly put his hand right where the axe was headed. I turned the axe to miss his hand. It struck the wood, bounced off, but rebounded into my boot on the inside of the instep. I could see the blood inside my boot, but I didn't know how bad it was. My brain was calculating how best to get the scene done because we had to move onto a different set tomorrow. I just continued to do the scene. I had to have four or five stitches. The funny thing is that viewing the scene, you could never tell that anything was wrong."

He continued to appear in feature films until 1971. While he was skiing, a ski pole pierced his chest and punctured his heart. The pole (which bent at 90 degrees) decorates the fireplace of his living room. He was pronounced dead by two doctors, but a third one revived him. *Snowbeast* (1977), a highly rated telemovie, concerned a mysterious giant figure on the rampage in America's snowbound Midwest. It is one movie which he is unlikely to forget. It had been a difficult shoot because personality clashes with one player had led to several of the original cast walking out. Walker was one of the substitutes in the role of Sheriff Paraday. Following arduous winter shooting in the Colorado Rockies, he returned to his ranch where he was felling trees when he felt short of breath and unable to rest. He drove himself to hospital, where he collapsed. Doctors found that he not only had pneumonia in both lungs, but also a tumor in his heart which was choking off his blood supply. It transpired that scar tissue had built up after the ski pole accident and had to be removed by open heart surgery. Doctors later said they had given him a one percent chance of survival, but he beat the odds and fully recovered. Of this experience he says, "I guess I'm one of the luckiest guys alive. I owe my life to the skill of the doctors, their assistants and to modern technology. And, of course, to God."

His only other television series, *Kodiak* (1974), was set in Alaska. It was a half-hour series shot mostly on location in Oregon. The star played Cal "Kodiak" McKay, a member of the Alaska State Patrol, responsible for 50,000 square miles of rough territory. He was called Kodiak after the bear. He usually worked alone, traveling by four-wheel drive truck. There were only four episodes aired before the ABC network swung their axe. It was trampled in the ratings by *Sanford and Son*. The star owned a percentage of the show, but this was one of a number of occasions when a deal went sour. He suffered other professional disappointments. He had a prominent role as Joe Bean in the miniseries *Centennial* (1978–1979), but was rung up out of the blue by the producers who told him that, with several of his major scenes still to be shot, there was to be no more filming. He has also rejected roles if they contain scenes he considers distasteful.

During the 1980s his name gradually faded from prominence and, aside from a couple of television appearances and rock bottom budget features, he was not seen. He has, however, been slightly more active recently. He reprised his most famous role as Cheyenne Bodie in a cameo in *The Gambler Returns: The Luck of the Draw* (1991), which starred Kenny Rogers. He also appeared as Bodie in "Gunfighters," an episode of *Kung Fu* aired in 1995. He guested in the television series *Sweating Bullets* in 1992. Of this he says, "I went to Israel and did an episode as an older Western actor. Evidently the French Canadian director is a great fan and asked for me. It was pretty cute. I enjoyed working for them. They were nice people."

Divorced from his first wife, Walker married French-born dancer-singer-actress Giselle Camille D'Arc in 1974. She had two daughters by a previous marriage. They resided on a small ranch at Grass Valley in Northern California where he designs exercise equipment, invents and is also much into organic natural food. Of this later lifestyle he mused, "I think it's kinda sad the way so many of us get involved with scrambling around for money and success that we don't take time to smell the flowers and watch the hummingbirds and look at the true reality of life. We are happy and thankful for the good fortune we had in finding this place." Gigi Walker died at age 65 in Fresno, California, on January 1, 1994, of cancer. She is buried in a family plot in Culver City, California. Walker married for the third time in Sparks, Nevada on March 7, 1997.

Clint Walker Filmography

1954: *Jungle Gents*.
1956: *The Ten Commandments*.
1958: *Fort Dobbs*.
1959: *Yellowstone Kelly*.
1961: *Gold of the Seven Saints*.
1964: *Send Me No Flowers*.
1965: *None but the Brave*.
1966: *Night of the Grizzly, Maya*.
1967: *The Dirty Dozen*.
1968: *Sam Whiskey, More Dead Than Alive*.
1969: *The Great Bank Robbery, The Phynx* (cameo).
1971: *Pancho Villa, Yuma* (TV).
1972: *Hardcase* (TV), *The Bounty Man* (TV).
1974: *Killdozer* (TV), *Scream of the Wolf* (TV).
1975: *Death Harvest*.
1976: *Baker's Hawk*.
1977: *Snowbeast* (TV), *The White Buffalo*.
1979: *The Mysterious Island of Beautiful Women* (TV),
1982: *Hysterical*.

1983: *Serpent Warriors.*
1991: *The Gambler Returns: The Luck of the Draw* (TV).

Television Series

1955–1962: *Cheyenne* as Cheyenne Bodie.
1974: *Kodiak* as Cal "Kodiak" McKay.

Miniseries

1978–1979: *Centennial.*

Sources

"Empty Saddles." *Trail Dust* magazine, spring, 1994.
Fans' Star Library No. 17: Clint Walker. London: Amalgamated Press, 1959.
Ferguson, Ken. *The Boy's Western Television and Film Annual.* London: Purnell, 1963.
Globe Special: Where Are They Now? Boca Raton, FL: Globe International Limited, 1993.
Interview with Clint Walker, 1993.
Lamparski, Richard. *Whatever Became Of? Tenth Series.* New York: Crown, 1986.
Salisbury, Lesley. "Clint's tickled to death at being alive." *TV Times* magazine, November 14, 1987.
Woolley, Lynn, Robert W. Malsbary, and Robert G. Strange, Jr. *Warner Bros. Television.* Jefferson, NC: McFarland, 1985.

EDDY WALLER

Eddy C. Waller was born in Chippewa Falls, Wisconsin, in 1889. He was the son of a preacher. His family were very much opposed to him going into show business. He was living in New York where at the age of 14 he debuted on Broadway in the play *Of Human Hearts.* He was then offered the juvenile lead by a stock company. To bribe him against the stage, his parents offered to pay his way through college. Nevertheless, after graduation he returned to the stage. He appeared with numerous stock companies in an acting capacity but also worked behind the scenes. Gravitating to Hollywood when sound was taking over in 1927, he had an extensive apprenticeship as an assistant director before making his screen debut as an actor in *Rhythm on the Range* (1936).

Thereafter, he appeared in numerous films frequently as a leathery Westerner. His movies ran the gamut from MGM to Poverty Row. The highlight of his movie career was when he played Nugget Clark, sidekick of Allan "Rocky" Lane, in 32 films between 1947 and 1953 at Republic Studios. Unlike some other saddle pals, Nugget was not just used as comic relief but was integrated into the storyline. He frequently did not know Lane as the film started, but backed him up in the climactic shootout.

He also appeared as a regular in two syndicated television series of the 1950s. In *Steve Donovan—Western Marshal* he played Rusty Lee, deputy to the title character. This early series is generally regarded as one of the weakest of the genre. In *Casey Jones* he played Red Rock, the conductor of the train driven by the title character. Although his last film dated from 1958, he continued in harness (literally) when he played the veteran stagecoach driver Mose, an occasional recurring role, in the Western series *Laramie.* After this he appeared at various Western conventions. He was married to the stage actress Doris Brownlea and lived in the San Fernando Valley.

Eddy Waller died in Los Angeles on August 9, 1977, at age 88, after a stroke. He is buried at Forest Lawn Cemetery in the Hollywood Hills.

Eddy Waller Filmography

1936: *Rhythm on the Range, Meet Nero Wolfe, Banjo on My Knee, Poppy.*
1937: *Sweetheart of the Navy, Small Town Boy, The Bad Man of Brimstone, Secret Agent X-9* (serial), *Off to the Races, Wild and Woolly.*
1938: *Stablemates, Stand Up and Fight, State Police, Call the Mesquiteers, Flaming Frontiers* (serial), *The Great Adventures of Wild Bill*

Portrait of Eddy Waller, who appeared in *Steve Donovan—Western Marshal* and made semi-regular appearances on *Laramie*.

Hickok (serial), *Out West with the Hardys, State Police, Strange Faces.*
1939: *Rough Riders Round-Up, Geronimo, I'm from Missouri, Jesse James, The Return of the Cisco Kid, Legion of Lost Flyers, Allegheny Uprising, New Frontier, Two Bright Boys, Mutiny on the Blackhawk, The Cisco Kid and the Lady, Man from Missouri, Young Mr. Lincoln, Stand Up and Fight, The Story of Alexander Graham Bell, North of the Yukon.*
1940: *Carolina Moon, The Devil's Pipeline, Legion of the Lawless, The Grapes of Wrath, The Man from Montreal, The Blue Bird, Brigham Young, Enemy Agent, The Girl from Avenue A, Viva Cisco Kid, Santa Fe Trail, Youth Will Be Served, Konga the Wild Stallion, You're Not So Tough, Stagecoach War, Gold Rush Maisie, Texas Terrors, Love Honor and Oh-Baby!, 20 Mule Team.*
1941: *Public Enemies, In Old Colorado, The Son of Davy Crockett, Six Gun Gold, The Bandit Trail, Bad Men of Missouri, Honky Tonk, Road Agent, Double Date, Hands Across the Rockies.*
1942: *Junior G-Men of the Air* (serial), *My Gal Sal, A-Haunting We Will Go, Call of the Canyon, Scattergood Survives a Murder, The Mummy's Tomb, The Lone Star Ranger, Sundown Jim, Night Monster, Shut My Big Mouth, Sin Town, Don't Get Personal.*
1943: *Cinderella Swings It, Headin' for God's Country, A Lady Takes a Chance, My Kingdom for a Cook, The Kansan, Silver Spurs, Frontier Badmen, Destroyer, Sweet Rosie O'Grady.*
1944: *The Adventures of Mark Twain, Home in Indiana, The Mummy's Ghost, Raiders of Ghost City* (serial), *Tall in the Saddle, Rationing, The Man from Frisco, Mystery of the River Boat* (serial).
1945: *Lady on a Train, The Affairs of Susan, The Missing Corpse, The Man Who Walked Alone, Dakota, Under Western Skies, Rough Riders of Cheyenne, Steppin' in Society, San Antonio.*
1946: *Little Giant, Sun Valley Cylone, Abilene Town, Renegades, Avalanche, Sing While You Dance, Singing on the Trail, Rustler's Round-Up, In Old Sacramento, The Plainsman and the Lady, Lover Come Back, The Magnificent Doll, Rendezvous with Annie.*
1947: *Wild Harvest, Wyoming, The Millerson Case, The Michigan Kid, Louisiana, Bandits of Dark Canyon, The Wild Frontier, The Beginning or the End?, Dangerous Years, Pursued, Nightmare Alley.*
1948: *Secret Beyond the Door, The Strawberry Roan, Oklahoma Badlands, River Lady, The Bold Frontiersman, Carson City Raiders, The Return of the Whistler, The Girl from Manhattan, Marshal of Amarillo, The Denver Kid, Sundown in Santa Fe, Renegades of Sonora, Desperadoes of Dodge City, Black Bart, Whispering Smith, Adventures of Silverado, The Wreck of the Hesperus.*
1949: *Massacre River, Death Valley Gunfighter, Sheriff of Wichita, Frontier Marshal, Lust for Gold, The Wyoming Bandit, Bandit King of Texas, Navajo Trail Raiders, Powder River Rustlers, Ma and Pa Kettle.*
1950: *Gunmen of Abilene, Code of the Silver Sage, Salt Lake Raiders, Covered Wagon Raid, Vigilante Hideout, Traveling Saleswoman, Frisco Tornedo, He's a Cockeyed Wonder, Rustlers on Horseback, California Passage, Curtain Call at Cactus Creek, The Furies.*
1951: *Cavalry Scout.*
1952: *Indian Uprising, Leadville Gunslinger, Black Hills Ambush, Montana Territory, Thundering Caravans, Desperadoes Outpost.*
1953: *Marshal of Cedar Rock, It Happens Every*

Thursday, Bandits of the West, Savage Frontier, 99 River Street, Champ for a Day, El Paso Stampede, The Last Posse.
1954: *Make Haste to Live.*
1955: *Man Without a Star, The Far Country, Foxfire, The Man from Laramie.*
1957: *The Night Runner, The Phantom Stagecoach, The Restless Breed.*
1958: *Day of the Bad Man.*

Television Series

1951–1952: *Steve Donovan—Western Marshal* as Rusty Lee.
1956–1957: *Casey Jones* as Red Rock.

Sources

Rothel, David. *Those Great Cowboy Sidekicks.* Waynesville, NC: World of Yesterday, 1984.
Summers, Neil. *The Official TV Western Book Volume #4.* Vienna, WV: Old West Shop Publishing, 1992.

JOHNNY WASHBROOK

Johnny Washbrook was born in Toronto, Canada, on October 16, 1944. He has one older brother. Their theatrical ambitions were encouraged by their parents. When he was ten, this child actor was brought to New York City where he soon won a role on the prestigious *U.S. Steel Hour.* Other television roles followed before he went to Hollywood and starred in the series *My Friend Flicka,* one of the most popular boy-and-horse Western adventure series of the 1950s. Set in the ranchlands of Montana around the turn of the century, the series featured Washbrook as Ken McLaughlin, son of Rob McLaughlin (Gene Evans) and Nell McLaughlin (Anita Louise). His best friend was his magnificent horse Flicka.

The actor made personal appearance tours in connection with the series and also starred in a television special called *The Prince and the Pauper.* He tested for but lost the role of Deborah Kerr's son in *The King and I* because of conflicting schedules. During the 1960s he had the occasional role of Eddie Burke on the *Hazel* television series. In 1970 he relocated to New York, where he became a stage actor. At last report he was married and residing in Canoga Park, California.

Johnny Washbrook Filmography

1958: *Lonelyhearts, The Space Children.*

Television Series

1956–1957: *My Friend Flicka* as Ken McLaughlin.

Sources

Dye, David. *Child and Youth Actors: Filmographies of Their Entire Careers, 1914–1985.* Jefferson, NC: McFarland, 1988.
Lamparski, Richard. *Whatever Became Of? Sixth Series.* New York: Bantam, 1976.

DENNIS WEAVER

Although he is primarily known nowadays for his characterization of Sam McCloud, Dennis Weaver had earlier been a great success in the role of Chester Goode, the limping deputy of Marshal Matt Dillon in the long-running Western series *Gunsmoke.* Tall and lanky, Weaver showed considerable versatility in being able to play both roles so convincingly. Although the two characters were vastly different, they both had a homespun quality which made them endearing. Not content to be solely an actor, Weaver has brought energy, personal magnetism and genuine social concern to a variety of issues outside of the acting arena.

Dennis Weaver was born on June 4, 1924, in Joplin, Missouri, of Irish, Scottish, English and Indian origin. His father worked for the electrical company. The family also farmed ten acres of land near Joplin during the Depression. Both he and his brother were keen movie buffs from childhood. His ambition to be an actor was encouraged by his mother, who taught him to recite poems. Upon graduation from high school, where he was a top athlete, Weaver attended Joplin Junior College for one year. In 1943 he enlisted in the United States Naval Reserve and spent over two years in the Navy Air Force. He established records for speed and agility as a member of the navy's track and field squad. He was honorably discharged with the rank of ensign.

He enrolled at the University of Oklahoma as a drama major. He brought his university team to first place in an all–Midwest competition in track and field events. In 1948 he qualified for the United States Olympic trials in decathlon, but although he came in sixth out of 36, he failed to make the Olympic team. He graduated with a B.A. degree in 1949.

He moved to New York City to pursue a career as an actor. His first acting job was as an understudy in the role of the college athlete Turk in the 1950 Broadway production of *Come Back Little Sheba.* He later assumed the role of Turk and embarked on the company's national tour. Back on Broadway in 1951, he was featured in a comedy *(Out West of Eighth)* which folded after four performances.

He enrolled at the Actors' Studio for further study under Lee Strasberg. His outstanding performance there in a scene from *27 Wagons Full of Cotton,* by Tennessee Williams, attracted the attention of Shelley Winters, who was instrumental in persuading Universal to sign him to a stock contract. The studio at that time was interested in boosting the careers of other actors, and Weaver was reduced to playing villainous roles in films which usually starred Tony Curtis, Rock Hudson and Audie Murphy. He eventually left the studio in disgust, but as a freelance he fared little better. Winters coaxed him to appear as Stanley Kowalski in a Los Angeles stage production of *A Streetcar Named Desire.* Some critics asserted that his acting was superior to that of Marlon Brando, who had originated the role on Broadway. For three years in the 1950s he ran his own drama workshop in Hollywood.

Despite amassing screen credits, Weaver found his early years in Hollywood to be unpromising. In 1955 he was working as a deliveryman at his aunt's florist shop. Then Charles Marquis Warren auditioned him for the role of the deputy Chester Goode in *Gunsmoke.* His initial reading was uninspiring, but he concentrated on developing the character and appearance. He spoke with an authentic Western drawl, had a hunched look and wore suspenders. At the eleventh hour he decided to give Chester a limp. When he next read for the part he was so convincing that he landed the role immediately, signing a contract which commenced at $400 a week. Of the limp he once said, "It's a put-on job for the series. At times I forget myself and start limping when I'm not in front of the cameras. But you can take it from me, it's not easy to act the part of a cripple. Have you ever tried running or jumping while trying to keep one leg as stiff as possible? Try it some time and you'll see what I mean."

Gunsmoke began on CBS in 1955, and although Weaver's role was secondary the series made him an instant star. His fan mail was enormous, many letters suggesting genuine cures for his assumed limp. His unique delivery of the line "Mister Dillon" was anticipated weekly by millions of fans. His portrayal of Chester won him an Emmy in 1959 as Best Supporting Actor (Continuing Character) in a Dramatic Series. He had also been nominated in 1957. His popularity increased with personal appearances at state fairs and rodeos which added to his income by an estimated $60,000 per annum. In 1958, Milburn Stone, Amanda Blake and Weaver created a singing act for their public appearances. In 1960 they broke the house record for the Albuquerque Arena during the New Mexico State Fair. He recalled,

"We had a lot of fun and we were in demand for personal appearances."

Weaver was eager to prove himself in other roles and won rave reviews for his performances in some of television's top dramatic anthology series of the 1950s, such as *Playhouse 90* and *Climax*. When the 1960s dawned, he was anxious to move on. Although he loved the role of Chester, he was keen to escape the rut into which the industry had typecast him. Nothing came of his initial efforts in this direction, so he returned to the series for its 1961–1962 season. He also directed six of its episodes, commenting, "It makes quite a change, getting behind the cameras. Kind of a challenge too. I found the experience very exciting." He shot two pilots as the star of his own television series, but neither of them sold.

His salary on *Gunsmoke* had climbed to $7,000 per week. On January 4, 1964, after nine seasons and 233 episodes, he shot the last of his ten contracted episodes for the 1963–1964 season and left *Gunsmoke* permanently. People thought that he was crazy to quit a hit series and he was deluged with letters to this effect, but as he explained, "This time I'm severing the umbilical cord for good. ... I want to grow as an actor, to create, to expand. I know I'll never be lucky enough to find another show like *Gunsmoke*, but in all fairness to myself I can't afford to make it my whole life's work."

When comedian Jack Carson died, NBC actively sought Weaver as a replacement in a new television series *(Kentucky Jones)* which Carson was set to star in. When the series made its bow in 1964, Weaver had undergone a transformation. He was now the title character, a veterinarian-horsetrainer who adopts a Chinese orphan. He was a snappy dresser who owned a ranch in Southern California. Although Weaver's personal notices were fine, the series proved unpopular and was axed after 26 episodes.

In 1967, CBS wooed him back for a more successful series entitled *Gentle Ben* lensed in Florida. He starred as a wildlife officer with a wife and young son. The real hero and title role was a pet black bear who lived in the Everglades and weighed 650 pounds. Although the star lashed out at critics who derided the premise of making a pet out of a wild bear, he was not pleased about playing straight man to an animal and was not sorry when the series ended in 1969 after two seasons and 56 episodes. Of this period he recalled, "I think that had I known in 1964 what I know now, I probably would have thought long and hard about leaving *Gunsmoke*. See I thought that every series you got into was a hit. That was the only experience I'd had. So when *Kentucky Jones* folded in one year, it was an eye opener. I was lucky that I got a couple of pictures, and *Gentle Ben* and then *McCloud*. You know, *McCloud* was the kind of part that I left *Gunsmoke* to get. I wanted to be a leading man, instead of a second banana."

He rejected an offer to star in a Broadway play and instead spent 1969 guest-starring in a number of well-established television series. Later that year he went to New York to film the pilot for a rotating NBC television series called *The Bold Ones*. The series was to consist of four shows, each running for six continuous episodes. The element starring Weaver premiered in 1970 and was called "McCloud: Who Killed Miss USA?" He played a lawman from Taos, New Mexico, who comes to New York to extradite a subpoenaed witness only to see the witness kidnapped and find himself handcuffed to a fence along a highway. It was loosely based on the Clint Eastwood film *Coogan's Bluff* (1968). After capturing the villain, McCloud was temporarily transferred to Manhattan's 27th Precinct under exasperated Chief Peter B. Clifford (J.D. Cannon), ostensibly to study the police methods employed by a huge urban police department. He was a maverick in New York with his sheepskin jacket, Stetson hat and walnut-handled six-guns. His catchphrase this time around was, "There you go." He had some memorable moments, notably riding a horse down 42nd Street. He grew a moustache for the role.

Of the four series, *McCloud* proved to be the only ratings winner. It was continued in the 1971–1972 season as part of the *NBC Sunday Mystery Movie* series along with *Columbo* and *McMillan and Wife*. Despite the fact that nominally he was still playing a cowboy, the role afforded him a broader acting range and opportunities for humor and romance. Of McCloud the actor has said, "He's a rural character in a complex metropolitan environment and therefore a fish out of water. But he has bite and a dry sense of humor and he always sees things with fresh eyes. He's a character I can live with." He twice received Emmy nominations as Outstanding Lead Actor in a Limited Series (in 1974 and 1975).

He made an amusing cameo guest appearance as the character in an episode of the *Hardy Boys-Nancy Drew* series in 1977. *McCloud* ended after a run of 46 episodes in 1977. Weaver returned to the role in *The Return of Sam McCloud* (1989), a one-shot telemovie in which McCloud found himself up against an evil company intent on causing pollution by dumping chemical waste and damaging the ozone layer. Although his return was welcome, McCloud's elevation to senator generally did not convince. The original series gave the star very high visibility, and he found himself deluged with offers of leading roles in telemovies of which the most outstanding was *Duel* (1971), Steven Spielberg's eerie suspense yarn of an average motorist menaced by an anonymous killer trucker who turns out to be the Devil.

After the demise of *McCloud* the star returned in three attempts at series television, all of them unsuccessful. In *Stone* (1980) he played Detective Sgt. Daniel Stone, a police officer who is also a best-selling novelist (loosely based on Joseph Wambaugh). In the much-hyped soap opera *Emerald Point N.A.S.* (1983–1984) he played Rear Admiral Thomas Mallory, commanding officer of a naval air station. *Buck James* (1987–1988) sought to combine elements of medical drama and soap opera; the actor played a Texan surgeon who also owns a ranch and has an unhappy family life. In *Lonesome Dove: The Series* (1994) he had an occasional but recurring guest role as Buffalo Bill Cody.

He is one actor who has also been very active in community affairs. In 1972 he was guest speaker at a fund raising banquet in Joplin that raised $1,000,000 for a new hospital. The town named one of its streets after him. He is a member of Hollywood for Sane, which supports a ban on nuclear testing. In 1972 he journeyed and spoke in 17 states on the campaign trail for Democratic presidential candidate George McGovern. The following year he ran as an independent for the office of president of the Screen Actors Guild on a platform in favor of improving of work rules and benefits for thespians. In November 1973, he was elected by an overwhelming majority, ousting the incumbent John Gavin and creating the single biggest upheaval in the union's 40 year history. He held the post for two years.

Dennis Weaver and Geraldine Stowell, who met in junior college, were married on October 20, 1945, and have three sons: Richard (born in 1948), Robert (born in 1953) and Rustin (born in 1959). He has been a vegetarian since the late 1950s and does not smoke or drink. In 1958 he was introduced by his father-in-law to the Self Realization Fellowship, a nonsectarian church. The Weavers used to live in Calabasas on the west end of the San Fernando Valley in a mansion which he personally designed and decorated with Spanish-American motifs. In 1964 the Weavers were honored as Family of the Year for "outstanding moral, social and civic leadership" by their San Fernando Valley neighbors. They now live in Tellwide, Colorado, with a vacation home near Taos Ski Valley, New Mexico.

Dennis Weaver Filmography

1952: *The Raiders, Horizons West, The Lawless Breed.*

1953: *The Redhead from Wyoming, The Mississippi Gambler, Law and Order, Column South, It Happens Every Thursday, The Man from the Alamo, The Golden Blade, The Nebraskan.*

1954: *War Arrow, Dangerous Mission, Dragnet.*

1955: *Ten Wanted Men, The Bridges at Toko-Ri, Seven Angry Men, Chief Crazy Horse.*

1956: *Storm Fear.*

1958: *Touch of Evil.*

1960: *The Gallant Hours.*

1966: *Duel at Diablo, Way ... Way Out.*

1967: *Gentle Giant.*

1968: *Mission Batangas.*

1969: *The Great Man's Whiskers* (TV).

1970: *Sledge, McCloud: Who Killed Miss USA?* (TV).

1971: *The Forgotten Man* (TV), *What's the Matter with Helen?, Duel* (TV).

1972: *Rolling Man* (TV), *Female Artillery* (TV).

1973: *Terror on the Beach* (TV).

1977: *Intimate Strangers* (TV) (a.k.a. *Battered!).*

1978: *The Islander* (TV), *Ishi: The Last of His Tribe* (TV).

1979: *The Ordeal of Patty Hearst* (TV), *Stone* (TV).

1980: *Amber Waves* (TV), *The Ordeal of Dr. Mudd* (TV).
1981: *The Day the Loving Stopped* (TV).
1982: *Cocaine: One Man's Seduction* (TV), *Don't Go to Sleep* (TV).
1985: *Going for Gold: The Bill Johnson Story* (TV).
1986: *A Winner Never Quits* (TV).
1987: *Bluffing It* (TV).
1988: *Walking After Midnight, Disaster at Silo 7* (TV).
1989: *The Return of Sam McCloud* (TV).
1993: *Earth and the American Dream* (voice only).
1994: *Greyhounds* (TV).
1995: *Two Bits and Pepper.*

Television Series

1955–1964: *Gunsmoke* as Chester Goode.
1964–1965: *Kentucky Jones* as Kentucky Jones.
1967–1969: *Gentle Ben* as Tom Wedloe.
1970–1977: *McCloud* as Deputy Marshal Sam McCloud.
1980: *Stone* as Detective Sgt. Daniel Stone.
1983–1984: *Emerald Point NAS* as Rear Admiral Thomas Mallory.
1987–1988: *Buck James* as Dr. Buck James.

Miniseries

1978: *Pearl.*
1978–1979: *Centennial.*

Sources

Current Biography. New York: H.W. Wilson, 1977.
Essoe, Gabe. *The Book of TV Lists.* Westport, CT: Arlington House, 1981.
Miller, Lee O. *The Great Cowboy Stars of Movies and Television.* New Rochelle, NY: Arlington House, 1979.
"The Ozone Friendly Marshal Blazes Into Town." *Daily Mail* newspaper, 1989.
Picture Show Annual. London: Amalgamated Press, 1955.
Speed, F. Maurice. *The Western Film and TV Annual.* London: MacDonald, 1957.

DICK WESSEL

Born in 1913 in Wisconsin, this character actor was a very familiar face in motion pictures. He was also active on stage, television and radio. He had one semi-regular role on television as one of the crew members (Carney) in *Riverboat* for both seasons. He died in Studio City, California, on April 20, 1965, at age 52, after a heart attack.

Dick Wessel Filmography

1935: *In Spite of Danger, Bonnie Scotland, Eight Bells.*
1936: *Ace Drummond* (serial), *Fury, Adventures of Frank Merriwell* (serial).
1937: *Prescription for Romance, Vogues of 1938, Round-up Time in Texas, The Game That Kills, Slim, Borrowing Trouble, San Quentin, Submarine D-1, Slim, They Gave Him a Gun, White Bondage.*
1938: *Yellow Jack, Hawk of the Wilderness* (serial), *Arson Gang Busters, Angels with Dirty Faces, The Crowd Roars, Racket Busters, A Slight Case of Murder, Over the Wall.*
1939: *The Roaring Twenties, Beasts of Berlin, Dust Be My Destiny, Missing Daughters, They Made Me a Criminal, The Kid from Kokomo, I Stole a Million, Cafe Hostess, Cowboy Quarterback, Blackwell's Island, They All Come Out, Main Street Lawyer.*
1940: *Framed, They Drive by Night, Brother Orchid, So You Won't Talk, The Border Legion, Flight Command, Sandy Is a Lady, Castle on the Hudson, City for Conquest.*
1941: *Dive Bomber, Manpower, The Great Train Robbery, Desert Bandit, Tanks a Million, Red River Valley, Model Wife, Lucky Devils, Penny Serenade, The Strawberry Blonde.*
1942: *X Marks the Spot, Dudes Are Pretty People, Yankee Doodle Dandy, The Traitor Within, You Can't Escape Forever, Gentleman Jim, Highways by Night, Romance on the Range, Sunset Serenade, Bells of Capistrano, Sunday Punch, About Face, Enemy Agents Meet Ellery Queen.*

1943: *Silver Spurs, Action in the North Atlantic, King of the Cowboys, False Faces, A Gentle Gangster.*
1944: *Crime by Night.*
1945: *Scarlet Street, Dakota.*
1946: *Black Angel, California, In Old Sacramento, Dick Tracy vs. Cueball, In Fast Company, Young Widow, Little Miss Big.*
1947: *Blondie's Big Moment, Merton of the Movies, The High Wall.*
1948: *The Pitfall, Unknown Island, When My Baby Smiles at Me, The Fuller Brush Man, River Lady, Hollow Triumph (*a.k.a. *The Scar), Good Sam, A Southern Yankee.*
1949: *Thieves Highway, Blondie Hits the Jackpot, Slattery's Hurricane, Frontier Outpost, Canadian Pacific, Badmen of Tombstone, Tulsa, Take Me Out to the Ball Game.*
1950: *Blondie's Hero, Wabash Avenue, Beware of Blondie, Watch the Birdie, Father of the Bride, Frontier Outpost, Sands of Iwo Jima, Harvey.*
1951: *The Wild Blue Yonder, An American in Paris, Francis Goes to the Races, The Scarf, Reunion in Reno, Texas Carnival, Corky of Gasoline Alley, Honeychile, Strangers on a Train, Flying Leathernecks.*
1952: *Love Is Better Than Ever, The Belle of New York, Blackbeard the Pirate, The Wac from Walla Walla, Young Man with Ideas, Rancho Notorious, Hoodlam Empire.*
1953: *Gentlemen Prefer Blondes, Champ for a Day, Let's Do It Again, The Caddy, The Lawless Breed.*
1954: *Untamed Heiress, Them!, Flight Nurse*
1955: *Bowery to Bagdad, The Eternal Sea.*
1956: *The Desperadoes Are in Town, Around the World in 80 Days.*
1958: *No Time for Sergeants.*
1960: *The Gazebo.*
1961: *Pocketful of Miracles.*
1963: *Wives and Lovers, Who's Minding the Store?*
1965: *The Ugly Dachshund.*

Television Series

1959–1961: *Riverboat* as Carney.

Sources

Brooks, Tim. *The Complete Directory to Prime Time TV Stars 1946–Present.* New York: Ballantine Books, 1987.
Truitt, Evelyn Mack. *Who Was Who on Screen Illustrated Edition.* New York: Bowker, 1984.

BERT WHEELER

Bert Wheeler was born Albert Jerome Wheeler in Paterson, New Jersey, on April 7, 1895. As a boy, he sold newspapers in New York. Involved in show business from childhood, he served an apprenticeship as a property boy and stage assistant in the stock company of his home town. Impresario Gus Edwards spotted him and cast him in his schoolboy act with George Jessel. As a teenage dancer in vaudeville from 1911, he broke an ankle one night. This seemed a setback at the time, but ultimately proved a blessing because it forced him to switch the direction of his career and become a comedian. By 1914 he was a comedy headliner and spent 11 years with his first wife Betty as a top star in vaudeville.

He twice worked for Florenz Ziegfeld, which he regarded as his finest hour. His first show for the famed producer was *The Ziegfeld Follies of 1923.* During the Roaring Twenties Wheeler was one of the most famous names in show business, topping the bill at the prestigious Palace Theatre in New York many times and one of the stars guaranteed to fill theaters wherever he appeared. Wheeler and Robert Woolsey (1889–1938) worked together for the first time in Ziegfeld's smash musical *Rio Rita* in 1927. The duo were the only members of the original cast who went to Hollywood for the movie version.

On the strength of the enormous success of the film version of *Rio Rita* (1929), the comedy team signed a contract with RKO. They shot films very cheaply throughout the 1930s.

The heroine of many of their films was Dorothy Lee, which made them a trio rather than a duo. Although Wheeler did not particularly like the movies in which the duo found themselves, he prided himself on the fact that in the depths of the Depression, their movies always made money. It is doubtful whether movies ever showcased his formidable talent to best advantage in the way that live musical comedy did.

Wheeler was extremely close to his partner and was deeply upset when Woolsey died in 1938 of chronic kidney failure. Although he made a couple of solo movies which flopped badly, Wheeler never felt at ease in Hollywood as a solo act and returned to the stage. He mainly worked on Broadway and in summer stock during the 1940s and 1950s. His last Broadway musical was *Three Wishes for Jamie* in 1952. Active on television, his best-remembered television appearance was on an episode of *Robert Montgomery Presents* in 1950 which reprised *Rio Rita*. His sole regular television role was in the Western series *Brave Eagle* as an eccentric Indian medicine man. His eccentricity was explained away by the fact that he was a half-breed. His function was to provide light relief in a series that was badly in need of it. One of his last recorded television roles was "The Invisible Badge" episode of *The Defenders,* aired in 1962. In 1963 he teamed with a fresh partner, Tommy Dillon, and performed a new routine, singing, dancing and exchanging comic patter in Las Vegas and some of the niteries in Manhattan's Latin Quarter. His last performances came in 1966.

Despite a volatile private life, Wheeler was one of the most popular men in the profession. An honorary lifetime member of both the Friars and the Lambs Clubs, he was a resident of the latter in New York City. When his health began to deteriorate, Dorothy Lee became increasingly concerned about him to the extent that she was making arrangements for him to be flown to stay with her and her husband in Winnetka, Illinois, on a permanent basis. Before this could happen, 72-year-old Wheeler died in New York City on January 18, 1968, of chronic emphysema. Despite the fact that he had once been amongst the highest paid artists in the world, earning in excess of $1,500 a week during the 1920s, he died flat broke and alone. His four marriages had all ended in divorce, and it was believed that the alimony payments had crippled him financially. His wives were Betty Wheeler, Bernice Speer, Sally Haines and Patty Orr. His only child, Patricia Walters, predeceased him by a couple of weeks, dying on December 31, 1967. She was not the actress of the same name who appeared in Jean Renoir's *The River* (1951).

Bert Wheeler Filmography

1922: *Captain Fly-by-Night* (a).
1929: *Rio Rita.*
1930: *The Cuckoos, Half-Shot at Sunrise, Hook Line and Sinker, Dixiana.*
1931: *Cracked Nuts, Caught Plastered, Peach O'Reno, Too Many Cooks* (a).
1932: *Girl Crazy, Hold 'Em Jail.*
1933: *So This Is Africa, Diplomaniacs.*
1934: *Hips Hips Hooray!, Cockeyed Cavaliers, Kentucky Kernels.*
1935: *The Nitwits, The Rainmakers.*
1936: *Silly Billies, Mummy's Boys.*
1937: *On Again Off Again, High Flyers.*
1939: *Cowboy Quarterback* (a).
1941: *Las Vegas Nights* (a).

Television Series

1955–1956: *Brave Eagle* as Smokey Joe.

Sources

Jones, Ken D., Arthur F. McClure, and Alfred E. Twomey. *Character People.* Secaucus, NJ: Citadel, 1979.
Lamparski, Richard. *Whatever Became Of? First Series.* New York: Crown, 1967.
Maltin, Leonard. *Movie Comedy Teams.* New York: Signet, 1970.
Miller, Mark A. "Wheeler and Woolsey Part Two." *Filmfax* magazine, issue No. 30, Dec./Jan. 1992.
Vazzana, Eugene Michael. *Silent Film Necrology: Births and Deaths of Over 9,000 Performers, Directors, Producers and Other Filmmakers of the Silent Era, Through 1993.* Jefferson, NC: McFarland, 1995.

Note

All of these films were with Robert Woolsey unless marked (a), which means alone.

PETER WHITNEY

Peter Whitney was born Peter King Engle in Long Branch, New Jersey, in 1916. He came from an affluent family and was educated at Exeter Academy, where he studied economics and business with the intention of embarking on a career on Wall Street. This ambition was thwarted when his family's finances were wiped out with the crash of 1929 and the Depression. The family relocated to California where eventually he enrolled as a student at the Pasadena Playhouse.

Later he went for a year to London, where he gained valuable stage experience. Returning to California, he did summer stock where he was seen by a scout from Warner Bros., who signed him to a contract. He made his motion picture debut in *Underground* (1941). Although he made many films for them over a five-year period, his best roles were as the hillbilly twins Mert and Bert Fleagle in *Murder He Says* (1945), a hilarious black comedy for Paramount, and as Ed Bannister in *The Man from Del Rio* (1956), an offbeat Western.

Although his solid build lent itself naturally to playing heavies, his sole series lead was as a hero in *Rough Riders* for Ziv Productions. He played Sgt. Buck Sinclair, one of a trio of former Civil War servicemen who join forces to ride West in search of a new and hopefully better life. Along the way they encountered all manner of hostiles in the country which they rode through. The series lasted for 39 half-hour black and white episodes.

Whitney remained a jobbing actor throughout the rest of his career. One of his last recorded credits was "Harlequin's Gold," an episode of *Mannix* telecast in 1970. He died prematurely of a heart attack on March 30, 1972, at his Santa Barbara home. He was 55 years old. His widow and six children survived him.

Peter Whitney Filmography

1941: *Underground, Nine Lives Are Not Enough, Blues in the Night.*
1942: *Rio Rita, Valley of the Sun, Busses Roar, Spy Ship, Whistling in Dixie, Reunion in France.*
1943: *Action in the North Atlantic, Destination Tokyo.*
1944: *Mr. Skeffington.*
1945: *Murder He Says, Hotel Berlin, Bring on the Girls.*
1946: *Three Strangers, The Notorious Lone Wolf, Blonde Alibi, The Brute Man, Canyon Passage.*
1947: *The Gangster, Northwest Outpost, Violence.*
1948: *The Iron Curtain.*
1953: *The Great Sioux Uprising, The Big Heat, All the Brothers Were Valiant.*
1954: *Day of Triumph, The Black Dakotas, Gorilla at Large.*
1955: *The Sea Chase, The Last Frontier.*
1956: *The Man from Del Rio, Great Day in the Morning, The Cruel Tower.*
1957: *Domino Kid.*
1958: *Buchanan Rides Alone.*
1962: *The Wonderful World of the Brothers Grimm.*
1965: *The Sword of Ali Baba.*
1967: *In the Heat of the Night, Chubasco.*
1969: *The Great Bank Robbery.*
1970: *The Ballad Of Cable Hogue.*

Television Series

1958–1959: *Rough Riders* as Sgt. Buck Sinclair.

Sources

Quinlan, David. *The Illustrated Directory of Film Character Actors.* London: Batsford, 1995.
Summers, Neil. *The Official TV Western Book Volume #3.* Vienna, WV: Old West Shop Publishing, 1991.
Willis, John. *Screen World Volume 24.* Obituary. London: Muller, 1973.

BILL WILLIAMS

Bill Williams is best remembered as the hero of the kiddies' Western series *The Adventures of Kit Carson.* He was equally well known for another long-running role which probably meant more to him, namely that of being the real-life husband of Barbara Hale, television's Della Street in *Perry Mason.* He was an athletic, competent but uninspired leading man during the 1940s and early 1950s. When his series turned to reruns, he struggled. He was not individualistic enough as an actor to have the career longevity which he no doubt craved. Long before the end of his life, he had virtually given up acting in favor of real estate, in which he was much more successful. His son, actor William Katt, who has admitted that his father only struck him once in his childhood, said, "Physically, he was a very strong man."

Bill Williams was born William Herman Katt in Brooklyn, New York, on May 15, 1915, the son of German Jews. His father died when his son was only four years old. His mother was a waitress who left him an orphan at 16. His was a poverty-stricken childhood in the notorious Hell's Kitchen district of New York, where he was fostered by a series of Jewish families. He was educated at Brooklyn Technical High School, then attended Pratt Institute preparing for a career in construction engineering. In 1934 and 1935 he was junior scholastic champion in the 220/440 meter swim meet. He became a professional swimmer in aquatic revues in the 1930s. He was intending to enter the Olympic trials when he was noticed by Stuart Morgan, a vaudeville producer, who signed him as part of an adagio act appearing in St. Louis.

In 1935 he sang baritone with the Municipal Opera Company in St. Louis before he left to form his own adagio act touring Europe and playing for some time at the London Palladium. Then he went to Hollywood for a long stay at Earl Carroll's theater. Some experience was obtained in acting when he appeared in stock, stimulating his desire to be an actor. He made his motion picture debut in *Murder in the Blue Room* (1944) at Universal. The impact was sufficient for him to be signed to a stock contract with RKO at a starting salary of $100 a week.

In his spare time he studied navigation with the intention of becoming a pilot. He was drafted into the U.S. Army Air Force, but after less than a hundred days' service he was given a medical discharge. He was given a publicity buildup as RKO's answer to Van Johnson. Probably his most impressive role was as Perry Kincheloe, the handicapped friend of Guy Madison, in *Till the End of Time* (1946). His salary eventually rose as high as $1,200 a week. He was not temperamental and accepted almost any role which was offered to him, but he still spent long periods in idleness when he was not shooting a picture.

His ability with music enabled him to host several television musical variety shows as early as 1949. He came to the attention of director Lew Landers, who used him in a radio Western series which became a television series tied up with a seven-year Coca Cola sponsorship contract. *The Adventures of Kit Carson* was a half-hour series which told of the exploits of Christopher "Kit" Carson, frontiersman and Indian scout, and his Mexican sidekick El Toro (Don Diamond) on the Western frontier during the 1880s. There were 104 episodes of this syndicated series filmed between 1951 and 1955. According to *Variety,* this series was the most popular program on children's television in 1954, although it has not been revived much since it went off the air. At one time in the late 1950s, Williams declared, "I never want to see or hear of Kit Carson again!" In later years he mellowed on this subject considerably.

Don Diamond has said of him, "Bill was a very fine gentle man and a gentleman also. I never had a harsh word with him. We went our separate ways after the series. They moved towards the desert. I saw him when they had a special show on oldtime Western series called *When the West Was Fun* in 1979. It was always a pleasure to work with Bill and see him—a very competent, hard-working actor."

Williams costarred with Betty White in *A Date with the Angels,* a domestic sitcom on ABC. His judgment was definitely lacking when he rejected the lead in the television series *Sea Hunt* because he believed that the public would not go for an underwater adventure series. When it turned into a megahit for Lloyd Bridges, Williams belatedly did a similar series called *Assignment Underwater* (1960). This syndicated series of 39 episodes sank without trace. Set in Florida, it featured him and Diane Mountford as father-daughter sea-diving owners of a charter boat called *The Lively Lady*. Its lack of success proved conclusively that there was room for only one such series on television.

Williams slipped into the ranks of supporting players by the 1960s. He kept an apartment in Horace Heidt's residential complex in Van Nuys, California, and owned a mobile home in Palm Desert. At the time they married, he and Barbara Hale agreed to invest one-third of all their earnings in real estate. Since his hobby was building and repairing, much of his later time was spent maintaining their extensive holdings. Although he had a fairly modest home and cars, the constant purchasing of real estate, particularly in Palm Springs, had made him extremely wealthy. He had retired from acting completely by the 1980s because he no longer enjoyed the grind of making movies and television and his career was at a standstill.

An early marriage ended in divorce in the mid–1940s. He met actress Barbara Hale when they were shooting a Western *(West of the Pecos)* in 1944. They were married at her hometown of Rockford, Illinois, on June 22, 1946. They subsequently appeared in four features together. They had two daughters and a son. Barbara Willa Johanna, now Jody Katt Coulter, was born on July 24, 1947. William Katt was born on February 16, 1951. Laura Lee Juanita, now Nita Katt King, was born on December 22, 1953.

One of his most frequent costars was actress Jane Nigh. She remembers him thus: "The reason I liked him is because he and Barbara were so warm, so good ... I loved being with him. Our sense of humor was similar. We used to laugh a lot. ... They were very good to each other and they loved their family."

A slightly different view is provided by William Katt, who remembers, "Our home was filled with love and understanding, but it was not always totally serene. There is a lot of tension in the entertainment business. There were jealousies when one was working and the other wasn't. ... I saw the friction. ... There were times when Mom and Dad would go for months without really being together."

Bill Williams died on September 21, 1992, at age 77, of complications from a brain tumor at St. Joseph Medical Center in Burbank, California. He was survived by his wife, children and four grandchildren.

Bill Williams Filmography

1944: *Murder in the Blue Room, Thirty Seconds Over Tokyo, Those Endearing Young Charms.*
1945: *The Body Snatcher, Back to Bataan, Johnny Angel, West of the Pecos.*
1946: *Deadline at Dawn, Till the End of Time.*
1947: *A Likely Story, Smoky River Serenade.*
1949: *A Woman's Secret, The Clay Pigeon, The Stratton Story, Fighting Man of the Plains, Range Justice, A Dangerous Profession.*
1950: *Blue Grass of Kentucky, The Cariboo Trail, Operation Haylift, Rookie Fireman, The Great Missouri Raid.*
1951: *The Last Outpost, Blue Blood, Havana Rose.*
1952: *The Pace That Thrills, Bronco Buster, Son of Paleface, Rose of Cimarron.*
1953: *Torpedo Alley.*
1954: *Racing Blood, The Outlaw's Daughter.*
1955: *Apache Ambush, Hell's Horizon.*
1956: *The Broken Star, Wiretapper, The Wild Dakotas.*
1957: *The Halliday Brand, Slim Carter, Pawnee.*
1958: *Space Master X-7, Legion of the Doomed.*
1959: *The Scarface Mob, Alaska Passage.*
1960: *Hell to Eternity, Oklahoma Territory.*
1961: *The Sergeant Was a Lady, A Dog's Best Friend.*
1963: *Creatures of Darkness* (also directed).
1964: *Law of the Lawless.*
1965: *Tickle Me, The Hallelujah Trail, Space Flight IC1.*
1967: *Trial by Error.*
1968: *Buckskin.*
1970: *Rio Lobo, Carter's Army* (TV).
1971: *Scandalous John.*
1974: *The Phantom of Hollywood* (TV).
1975: *The Giant Spider Invasion.*
1977: *69 Minutes.*
1981: *Goldie and the Boxer Go to Hollywood* (TV).

Television Series

1951–1955: *The Adventures of Kit Carson* as Kit Carson.
1957–1958: *A Date with the Angels* as Gus Angel.
1960: *Assignment Underwater* as Bill Greer.

Sources

Brooks, Tim. *The Complete Directory to Prime Time TV Stars 1946–Present.* New York: Ballantine Books, 1987.
Jarvis, Everett G. *Final Curtain: Deaths of Noted Movie and TV Personalities.* New York: Citadel Press, 1995.
Lamparski, Richard. *Whatever Became Of? Ninth Series.* New York: Crown, 1985.
Strait, Raymond. *Hollywood's Star Children.* New York: Spi Books, 1992.

GUINN WILLIAMS

Guinn "Big Boy" Williams was born on a ranch in Decatur, Texas, on April 26, 1899, the son of Texas Congressman Guinn Williams, Sr., and his wife Minnie Lee. He had three sisters. He was educated at Decatur Military Academy (where he was an all-around athlete) and later studied law for a spell at North Texas State College. During World War I he volunteered for the army and was commissioned as a second lieutenant. When he returned home after the armistice, he discovered his father had arranged for him to go to West Point, but he rebelled and joined the Chicago White Sox baseball team instead. He flopped as a ballplayer and instead drifted around the country, riding in rodeos.

Eventually he gravitated to Hollywood where he first encountered Larry Semon and his company digging a ditch for a comedy. Williams joined in. Semon was so impressed with the enthusiasm that Williams displayed that he gave him a job in movies as a stuntman. He made his screen debut in *Almost a Husband* (1919), which starred Will Rogers. It was Rogers who dubbed him "Big Boy" on account of his strapping physique, a nickname which stuck ever afterwards. Williams liked Westerns and believed that this was where his appeal lay, so he wrote and starred in one, *The Jack Riders* (1921). In 1922 he signed a three-year contract for six films a year at $250 a movie with Frederick Herbst Productions. He later made Westerns for Hal Roach Productions and Aywon's Charles R. Seeling Productions in the 1920s. He played supporting roles in A pictures and other movies with a sporting background.

He made a successful transition to talking pictures and had a voice which matched his physique. He is best remembered as one of Errol Flynn's tough cohorts in Western films such as *Dodge City* (1939). He contributed memorably to another Western film, *Station West* (1948), in which the highlight was an extended brawl between him and hero Dick Powell. Offscreen he was a prodigious drinker and a ferocious polo player, at one time owning a string of polo ponies. He had small semi-regular roles in two Western series of the 1950s. He played the town blacksmith in *My Friend Flicka* and was Pete the canvasman in the marginal Western *Circus Boy*.

Williams semi-retired from the screen in 1945 to become a prosperous fruit grower in San Diego, but the cyclamen mite decimated his fruit crop. He later ran a hotel in Needles, Arizona, but this venture too proved less than successful when a new highway on which most traffic traveled bypassed his property. He died at his home in Van Nuys, California, on June 6, 1962, at age 63, of uremic poisoning. He was survived by his widow and son Tyler. His first wife was actress Kathleen Collins, one of his silent leading ladies, whom he later divorced. In January 1943, he wed Dorothy Patterson, who survived him.

Guinn Williams Filmography

1919: *Almost a Husband, Jubilo.*

Portrait of Guinn Williams, who appeared in *Circus Boy*.

1920: *Jes' Call Me Jim, Cupid the Cowpuncher.*
1921: *Western Firebrands, The Jack Rider, The Vengeance Trail, Doubling for Romeo.*
1922: *Trail of Hate, Blaze Away, The Freshie, The Cowboy King, Across the Border, Rounding Up the Law.*
1923: *$1000 Reward, Cyclone Jones, Riders of the Night, End of the Rope.*
1924: *The Avenger, The Eagle's Claw.*
1925: *The Big Stunt, Black Cyclone, Fangs of Wolfheart, Riders of the Sandstorm, Sporting West, Wolfheart's Revenge, Bad Man from Bodie, Courage of Wolfheart, Red Blood and Blue, Rose of the Desert, Whistling Jim.*
1926: *Brown of Harvard, The Desert's Toll.*
1927: *Arizona Bound, The Down Grade, Babe Comes Home, Backstage, Slide Kelly Slide, The Woman Who Did Not Care, The College Widow, Quarantined Rivals, Lightning, Snowbound.*
1928: *Ladies Night in a Turkish Bath, Beggars of Life, Burning Daylight, Lucky Star, Vamping Venus, My Man.*
1929: *From Headquarters, Forward Pass, Noah's Ark.*
1930: *College Lovers, The Big Fight, City Girl, The Bad Man, Liliom.*
1931: *Bachelor Father, The Great Meadow, The Phantom.*
1932: *70,000 Witnesses, Polly of the Circus, The Devil Is Driving, Ladies of the Jury, Drifting Souls, Heritage of the Desert, You Said a Mouthful.*
1933: *Mystery Squadron* (serial), *The Phantom Broadcast, Laughing at Life, Man of the Forest, College Coach.*
1934: *Half a Sinner, Rafter Romance, The Cheaters, Flirtation Walk, Thunder Over Texas, Palooka, Our Daily Bread, Romance in the Rain, Here Comes the Navy, Silver Streak.*
1935: *Private Worlds, One in a Million, Village Tale, Gun Play, Danger Trail, The Law of the .45's, Miss Pacific Fleet, Cowboy Holiday, The Glass Key, Society Fever, Powdersmoke Range, Big Boy Rides Again, The Littlest Rebel, Lucky Boots.*
1936: *The Big Game, Muss 'Em Up, End of the Trail, Career Woman, The Vigilantes Are Coming* (serial), *Grand Jury, Kelly the Second, North of Nome.*
1937: *A Star Is Born, You Only Live Once, The Singing Marine, She's No Lady, My Dear Miss Aldrich, Bad Man of Brimstone, Girls Can Play, Don't Tell the Wife, Dangerous Holiday, Big City, Wise Girl.*
1938: *Down in Arkansas, Everybody's Doing It, Professor Beware, I Demand Payment, Flying Fists, Army Girl, You and Me, Hold That Co-Ed, The Marines Are Here, Crashin' Thru Danger.*
1939: *6,000 Enemies, Pardon Our Nerve, Fugitive at Large, Mutiny on the Blackhawk, Bad Lands, Dodge City, Blackmail, Street of Missing Men, Legion of Lost Flyers.*
1940: *Virginia City, The Fighting 69th, Santa Fe Trail, Dulcy, Castle on the Hudson, Money and Women, Alias the Deacon, Wagons Westward.*
1941: *Billy the Kid, Six Lessons from Madame La Zonga, Swamp Water, Riders of Death Valley* (serial), *Country Fair, You'll Never Get Rich, The Bugle Sounds.*
1942: *American Empire, Mr. Wise Guy, Lure of the Islands, Between Us Girls, Silver Queen.*
1943: *Buckskin Frontier, The Desperadoes, Hands Across the Border, Minesweeper.*
1944: *Swing in the Saddle, Belle of the Yukon, The Cowboy and the Señorita, Nevada, Thirty Seconds Over Tokyo, Cowboy Canteen.*
1945: *The Man Who Walked Alone, Rhythm*

Roundup, Sing Me a Song of Texas, Song of the Prairie.
1946: *Throw a Saddle on a Star, Cowboy Blues, That Texas Jamboree, Singing on the Trail.*
1947: *King of the Wild Horses, Singin' in the Corn, Road to the Big House, Over the Santa Fe Trail.*
1948: *Bad Men of Tombstone, Station West, Smoky Mountain Melody.*
1949: *Brimstone.*
1950: *Hoedown, Rocky Mountain.*
1951: *Al Jennings of Oklahoma, Man in the Saddle.*
1952: *Springfield Rifle, Hangman's Knot.*
1954: *Southwest Passage, Massacre Canyon, The Outlaw's Daughter.*
1956: *Hidden Guns, The Man from Del Rio.*
1957: *The Hired Gun.*
1959: *Five Bold Women.*
1960: *Home from the Hill, The Alamo.*
1961: *The Comancheros.*

Television Series

1956–1957: *My Friend Flicka* as the Blacksmith.
1956–1958: *Circus Boy* as Pete the Canvasman.

Sources

Courneau, Ernest N. *The Hall of Fame of Western Film Stars.* North Quincy, MA: Christopher, 1969.
Katchmer, George A. *Eighty Silent Film Stars: Biographies of the Obscure to the Well Known.* Jefferson, NC: McFarland, 1991.
Perry, Jeb H. *Screen Gems: A History of Columbia Pictures Television from Cohn to Coke 1948–1983.* Metuchen, NJ: Scarecrow, 1991.
Quinlan, David. *The Illustrated Directory of Film Character Actors.* London: Batsford, 1995.
Rothel, David. *Those Great Cowboy Sidekicks.* Waynesville, NC: World of Yesterday, 1984.

GUY WILLIAMS

To play a swashbuckler on television requires good looks, dash, fencing skill and equestrian ability. One actor who had this combination was Guy Williams, who essayed the role of *Zorro,* a swashbuckling Mexican aristocrat. The part was equivalent to that of the Lone Ranger or Robin Hood. Feats of derring-do were required rather than feats of acting ability, but the series was successful and Williams fitted the cape and mask and wielded his rapier with panache.

Guy Williams was born Guido Armando Catalano in New York City on January 14, 1924, the son of Italian immigrants. His father was an insurance broker. He was educated at the Peekskill Military Academy in New York, where he went with the intention of entering West Point. Instead, an agent spotted him walking on Fifth Avenue and took some photographs of him which resulted in his first trip to Hollywood in 1952. He was signed to a one-year contract with Universal-International, making his screen debut in *Bonzo Goes to College* (1952). He adopted the name of Guy Williams to avoid being typecast in ethnic parts.

He played the role of the policeman who guns down Michael Landon in the cult classic *I Was a Teenage Werewolf* (1957), but after appearing in the film he returned to New York. He studied at the Neighborhood Playhouse, acted on the New York stage and supplemented his income by modeling and toothpaste commercials. Believing that television offered a more secure future than the declining feature film market, he returned to California when he heard that a casting call had gone out from Walt Disney, who was planning on shooting a television series called *Zorro.*

Zorro was the fictional creation of Johnston McCulley (1883–1958) in a series of stories commencing with "The Curse of Capistrano" in 1919. The character had been played numerous times in movies and serials. In 1950 McCulley sold all his rights to the *Zorro* property to Mitchell Gertz, a leading Hollywood agent. Gertz brought *Zorro* to the attention of Disney, who was looking for a suitable property to fill a void following the enormous success of *Davy Crockett.*

Once Disney elected to make the series, he chose to shoot it in black and white, an unwise decision because it limited the potential of the show. When it came to casting the star, the studio decided to go with an unknown. Williams was one of a hundred actors who tested. He won the role mainly because of his dashing good looks but also because of his fencing ability. His father had been a keen fencer who had taught his son since childhood. *Zorro* was an extremely demanding role because the star was in nearly every scene and had to be very athletic.

The television series was written so that while each episode was complete in itself, most belonged to multiple episodes of continuing plotlines. The series opened with Don Diego De La Vega (Williams) leaving Spain in 1820, at the request of his father Don Alejandro, to return to Pueblo de Los Angeles in his native California, where the people are being oppressed by the villainous Cpt. Monastario. While Don Diego pretends to be bookish and ineffectual, he disguises himself as Zorro and rides forth on his horse from a secret cave to do battle with the evil tyrant. Only his mute servant Bernardo knows his true identity.

Behind the camera, the talent Disney employed was first rate. Norman Foster was hired to direct. The famous fencing master Fred Cavens was put on the payroll to make the swordsmanship of the star second to none. Dave Sharpe was responsible for the stunts. William Lava wrote the background music, which had a special theme for each member of the regular characters, played when that character entered the scene. The theme song (written by George Bruns and Norman Foster) was a big hit of 1958. Johnston McCulley was hired as script supervisor.

Disney built a replica of a city on the back lot of the studio, where the episodes were filmed, at a cost of $500,000. The half-hour series began on ABC on October 10, 1957, with the episode "Presenting Senor Zorro." It ran for two seasons, each of 39 episodes. The cost of the first season was $3,200,000 and the second season was $2,700,000. The second season cost less than the first because the major set had already been built. The original episodes of the series ended on July 2, 1959, with "Finders Keepers," although repeats continued to run until September 24.

The series was an enormous hit which rode high in the ratings. However, it was canceled somewhere near the peak of its popularity. The reason was that Disney wished to move all his series to the NBC network, who offered a better deal. NBC, who had just introduced their logo of a peacock with a multi-colored tail, wished to show all their series in color. Since *Zorro* was in black and white, a compromise was impossible. Disney chose to axe the series rather than remain with ABC.

There were a tremendous number of commercial tie-ins with the series. As a result of this, Disney kept Williams and others on salary for a further two years for publicity purposes. There were also four hour-long *Zorro* specials, shown on *Walt Disney Presents,* shot in 1960 and 1961. Two films, *Zorro the Avenger* and *The Sign of Zorro,* compilations of episodes from the series, were theatrically released. When the series finally ended, Williams became a resident of Europe for two years, shooting features such as *Captain Sindbad* in Germany and *Damon and Pythias* in Italy.

Upon his return he appeared in four key episodes of *Bonanza* as Will Cartwright, a cousin of the Cartwrights. Williams had been the original choice for Adam Cartwright, but by the time the series was ready to roll, he was unavailable because he was playing Zorro. By 1964 Pernell Roberts was threatening to quit the series, so it was intended to marry him off to the schoolteacher Laura Dayton (Kathie Browne) and replace him with Williams. The outcry was such that it was decided to abandon this idea and keep Roberts on contract for another 12 months. Instead it was Williams and Kathie Browne who rode off into the distant sunset, never to be referred to again. Williams is reputed not to have cared much for the *Bonanza* experience because he believed that he was being used as a pawn in network politics.

In late 1964 the pilot script for the sci-fi television series *Lost in Space* was offered to him and he accepted. The series could just as easily have been called *Space Family Robinson,* but that title had to be discarded when the Disney organization planned on using it for a series of their own. Williams played the patriarch of a family marooned in space. The actor recalled, "I wasn't taken with the script. It was typical television. If I had been asked to do *Richard III,* that would have been a surprise, but to go into *Lost in Space* after having done *Zorro,* it was just standard television subject matter."

Williams was rumored to have become especially disenchanted with the series when his character became relegated to the background. He was constantly being upstaged by the robot and the character of Dr. Zachary Smith, the sneering comic villain, played by scene-stealing Jonathan Harris. Nevertheless, the Irwin Allen series which made its debut on CBS on September 15, 1965, lasted for 83 episodes and was last broadcast on March 6, 1968. Some of the scripts for this series were extremely dim, but it has become something of a cult classic which is frequently revered at sci-fi conventions.

After the series was canceled because of declining ratings, the star was invited to appear in a charity show in Buenos Aires, Argentina, by the wife of Argentine president Juan Peron. *Zorro* was enjoying a revival there, and Mrs Peron was a great fan of his. He made numerous personal appearances all over the country. Liking the laid-back lifestyle of the country, the actor decided to divide his time between California and Argentina. In an interview he once admitted that he had had an up-and-down career as an actor but that he believed something would turn up. The "something" he referred to, presumably a good role, did not materialize. Williams faced serious financial problems in California caused by betting on the ponies and a divorce. He had to sell his large house and the yacht which had been his pride and joy.

When he visited California in 1983 he was invited by the Disney organization to consider reprising the role of *Zorro* in a series called *Zorro and Son.* The actor was disgusted with the scripts presented to him and rejected the series. Although it did make it to the prime time lineup, it was quickly scuttled after just six episodes in 1983. Back in Hollywood in 1986, Williams guested with *Lost in Space* costars June Lockhart, Marta Kristen, Angela Cartwright and Bob May on the game show *Family Feud.* It was his final television appearance.

The former actor suffered a stroke and became something of a recluse. He was found dead on May 6, 1989, in a Buenos Aires apartment where he had been living for several months. Police said that he had been dead for about a week, apparently from a heart attack. He was 65 years old. He had been married since the early 1950s to model Janice Cooper, from whom he was later divorced. With her he had a son Steve and a daughter Toni. In an eloquent tribute to him, actor Mark Goddard, who costarred with him in *Lost in Space,* said, "I liked working with Guy. Guy was very intelligent and had a great taste in things like wine. He was nice. I miss Guy a lot. Once Dr. Smith started stealing Guy's lines, Guy started taking mine. That was not so nice." Goddard had not seen his onetime costar for many years. "It had been a long while. I ran into him at the racetrack in L.A. We talked. We spoke about handicapping horses, that's all. It was in the middle 1970s maybe."

Guy Williams Filmography

1952: *Bonzo Goes to College, Willie and Joe Back at the Front.*
1953: *All I Desire, The Golden Blade, The Man from the Alamo, The Mississippi Gambler.*
1955: *The Last Frontier, Seven Angry Men, Sincerely Yours.*
1957: *I Was a Teenage Werewolf.*
1958: *The Sign Of Zorro* (TV:Z)
1959: *Zorro The Avenger* (TV:Z)
1962: *Damon and Pythias, The Prince and the Pauper* (TV:WD).
1963: *Captain Sindbad.*
1973: *General Massacre.*

Television Series

1957–1959: *Zorro* as Don Diego De La Vega/ Zorro.
1965–1968: *Lost in Space* as Prof. John Robinson.

Sources

Mitchell, Flint, and William E. Anchors, Jr. *The Lost in Space 25th Anniversary Celebration.* Alpha Control Press, 1991.
Van Hise, James. *Lost in Space 25th Anniversary Tribute Book.* Las Vegas, NV: Pioneer, 1990.

Willis, John. *Screen World Volume 41.* London: Muller, 1990.
Yenne, Bill. *The Legend of Zorro.* Greenwich, CT: Brompton, 1991.

Note

Films denoted TV:Z and TV:WD denote feature films compiled from episodes of either *Zorro* or *Walt Disney Presents.*

DAVE WILLOCK

Dave Willock was born in Chicago, Illinois, in 1909, of a non-show business family. He was educated at the University of Wisconsin, where he first became interested in drama. From 1931 to 1935 he appeared in vaudeville as one half of the team of Willock and Carson, partnering Jack Carson. He appeared on radio from 1931 to 1945 in a variety of different shows and guises. He made his screen debut in 1938 and played numerous bellhops, elevator boys, hotel pages, reporters and gormless sailors. He usually supplied comic relief.

In the late 1940s and early 1950s he began working in television. He was a regular on *Pantomime Quiz* and had a local do-it-yourself show titled *Willock's Workshop.* One of his rare straight roles was as a cavalry lieutenant in the Western series *Boots and Saddles.* Since his real forte was comedy, this was rather anomalous to the rest of his career. He continued to be an active film and television performer well into the 1970s. Even when middle-aged he contrived to look years younger. He died in Woodland Hills, California, on November 12, 1990, at age 81, from complications following a stroke. He was survived by his wife Rae, a former dancer; five daughters; nine grandchildren; and five great-grandchildren.

Dave Willock Filmography

1939: *Good Girls Go to Paris, Legion of Lost Flyers, Three Texas Steers, The Amazing Mr. Williams, Blondie Takes a Vacation, Golden Boy, Little Accident, Mr. Smith Goes to Washington.*

1940: *Framed, Brother Rat and a Baby, Argentine Nights, Black Friday, Honeymoon Deferred, Granny Get Your Gun.*

1941: *Caught in the Draft, Never Give a Sucker An Even Break, Playmates, Cracked Nuts, The Monster and the Girl, Great Guns, Louisiana Purchase, The Chocolate Soldier.*

1942: *Sunday Punch; Ice Capades Review; The Fleet's In; Priorities on Parade; Lucky Jordan; Yankee Doodle Dandy; Two Yanks in Trinidad; The Male Animal; Frisco Lil; Flying Tigers; You Were Never Lovelier; Take a Letter, Darling.*

1943: *Let's Face It, Princess O'Rourke, The Gang's All Here, Dixie Dugan.*

1944: *Pin-up Girl, She's a Sweetheart, Wing and a Prayer, Four Jills in a Jeep.*

1945: *Pride of the Marines, Spellbound, This Love of Ours, It's in the Bag.*

1946: *Joe Palooka—Champ, The Runaround, The Searching Wind.*

1947: *The Fabulous Dorseys, Stork Bites Man.*

1948: *So This Is New York, State of the Union.*

1949: *Chicago Deadline.*

1950: *Belle of Old Mexico, Louisa, No Man of Her Own.*

1951: *Darling How Could You!, Call Me Mister, Rodeo, Let's Go Navy!, Roadblock.*

1952: *Love Is Better Than Ever, Flat Top, Jet Job, Battle Zone, The Merry Widow, A Girl in Every Port, Just for You.*

1953: *It Came from Outer Space, Remains to Be Seen, Roar of the Crowd, Ma and Pa Kettle on Vacation.*

1955: *Revenge of the Creature.*

1957: *The Buster Keaton Story, The Delicate Delinquent.*

1958: *Queen of Outer Space.*

1959: *Ten Seconds to Hell.*

1962: *What Ever Happened to Baby Jane?*

1963: *Wives and Lovers, 4 for Texas, The Nutty Professor.*

1964: *Send Me No Flowers, The Patsy.*

1965: *Hush ... Hush, Sweet Charlotte.*
1967: *The Adventures of Bullwhip Griffin.*
1968: *The Legend of Lylah Clare.*
1970: *The Barefoot Executive.*
1971: *The Grissom Gang.*
1972: *Now You See Him, Now You Don't.*
1973: *Emperor of the North Pole.*
1974: *Framed.*
1975: *Hustle.*

Television Series

1953–1954: *Pantomime Quiz.*
1955: *Willock's Workshop.*
1957–1958: *Boots and Saddles—The Story of the Fifth Cavalry* as Lt. Binning.
1961–1962: *Margie* as Harvey Clayton.
1968: *The Beautiful Phyllis Diller Show.*
1969: *The Queen and I* as Ozzie.

Sources

Brooks, Tim. *The Complete Directory to Prime Time TV Stars 1946–Present.* New York: Ballantine Books, 1987.
Jarvis, Everett G. *Final Curtain: Deaths of Noted Movie and TV Personalities.* New York: Citadel Press, 1995.
Twomey, Alfred E., and Arthur F. McClure. *The Versatiles.* South Brunswick and New York: Barnes, 1969.

TERRY WILSON

Born in Huntington Park, California, on September 3, 1923, Terry Wilson was a stuntman, wrangler and double for John Wayne who became a close friend of Ward Bond. When Bond was cast as Major Seth Adams on *Wagon Train,* he insisted that his friends Wilson and Frank McGrath be signed as well. Initially, Wilson as Bill Hawks was presented as a rather belligerent ordinary member of the wagon train, but within a few episodes his character was softened and made more reliable. He became the deputy wagonmaster who took over whenever Major Adams was absent. Later episodes showed in flashback that he and Adams had fought together in the Civil War. Even after Ward Bond's death, Bill Hawks functioned in the same capacity for another wagonmaster.

Wilson had a good run in the role, scripting a few episodes. He stayed with the series until its demise. After this he was occasionally seen on television and in films, but still primarily in Westerns. In real life, most of the rest of his time was spent managing a working ranch in the Simi Valley which doubled as a movie location.

Terry Wilson Filmography

1956: *Pillars of the Sky, The Last Hunt, The Searchers.*
1966: *The Plainsman.*
1967: *The War Wagon.*
1968: *The Shakiest Gun in the West.*
1969: *A Man Called Gannon.*
1970: *Dirty Dingus Magee.*
1971: *Support Your Local Gunfighter.*
1973: *One Little Indian, Westworld.*
1975: *The Daughters of Joshua Cabe Return* (TV), *Escape to Witch Mountain.*
1976: *The Treasure Seekers.*

Television Series

1957–1965: *Wagon Train* as Bill Hawks.

Sources

Inman, David. *The TV Encyclopedia.* New York: Perigee, 1991.
Summers, Neil. *The First Official TV Western Book.* Vienna, WV: Old West Shop Publishing, 1987.

Left to right: Frank McGrath, John McIntire, Terry Wilson, and Robert Fuller in *Wagon Train*.

KIM WINONA

Kim Winona was born on the Rosebud Reservation, South Dakota, in the early 1930s and is of Sioux ancestry. The producers of the television series *Brave Eagle* were having an extremely hard time casting the role of Morning Star, the romantic interest of Brave Eagle (Keith Larsen). They needed a beautiful Indian who was very graceful, athletic and an excellent horserider. They tested and cast her almost immediately. Winona fit the bill perfectly, but in spite of this the series was short-lived, lasting only one season from 1955 to 1956. This was her only recorded credit.

Television Series

1955–1956: *Brave Eagle* as Morning Star.

Sources

Brooks, Tim. *The Complete Directory to Prime Time TV Stars 1946–Present.* New York: Ballantine Books, 1987.

Summers, Neil. *The Official TV Western Book Volume #2.* Vienna, WV: Old West Shop Publishing, 1989.

GLORIA WINTERS

Gloria Winters was born in Los Angeles, California, on November 28, 1932. She acted in films from childhood and played Babs, the daughter of Jackie Gleason, for one season of *The Life of Riley.* The role of Penny, the niece of Kirby Grant in the television series *Sky*

King, is the one which she regards as the most rewarding of her career. She made numerous personal appearances in connection with the series in the company of Grant, who was an offscreen friend and rather like a real-life uncle.

She rode her own horse in the series and wrote a book *(Penny's Guide to Teenage Charm and Popularity)* which was a bestseller. She made a few other scattered episodes after the demise of the series and married the sound engineer on *Sky King.* At last report she was residing extremely happily with her husband in Northridge, California. She keeps German Shepherds, is an active gardener and is an executive with their family company, which leases sound equipment to movie and television studios.

Gloria Winters Filmography

1950: *Hot Rod, Gambling House, The Lawless.*
1951: *Darling How Could You!, Stagecoach Driver.*
1952: *Hold That Line.*
1954: *She Couldn't Say No.*

Television Series

1949–1950: *The Life of Riley* as Babs.
1951–1954: *Sky King* as Penny.

Sources

Lamparski, Richard. *Whatever Became Of? Tenth Series.* New York: Crown, 1986.
Summers, Neil. *The Official TV Western Book Volume #2.* Vienna, WV: Old West Shop Publishing, 1989.

MORGAN WOODWARD

Thomas Morgan Woodward was born in Fort Worth, Texas, on September 16, 1925, the son of Dr. Valin Woodward and Frances McKinley. He is the middle of five brothers. He spent his childhood and was educated at nearby Arlington, graduating from high school in 1944. He was a keen football player in high school and began flying lessons in 1941. He served in the Army Air Corps during World War II before being discharged in December 1945. He enrolled in junior college at Arlington State in January 1946.

While he was there, he devoted much of his time to theater work and performed regularly for one year with Margo Jones' "Theatre 47." His ambition was to join the Metropolitan Opera, but because of a slump in opera in America around this time, he switched to the University of Texas in 1948, graduating with a BBA degree in corporation finance. Afterwards he attended law school there. Simultaneously he was a talk show host on a local radio station and was involved in singing with a dance band and barbershop quartet.

His studies were interrupted by the outbreak of the Korean conflict, during which he was recalled to active service as a lieutenant

Morgan Woodward in *The Life and Legend of Wyatt Earp.*

assigned to special services. He spent the next couple of years overseas. Upon his discharge he returned to a more sedate life as a junior executive with the Lone Star Steel Company in Dallas. He rapidly grew disenchanted with this and decided to relocate to California where he felt that he could fulfill his creative aspirations.

Arriving in Hollywood in 1955, he contacted college roommate Fess Parker, who arranged for him to be tested by the Walt Disney organization. He passed the test with flying colors and made his screen debut in *The Great Locomotive Chase* (1956), followed shortly afterwards by a second film, *Westward Ho the Wagons!* (1956). Since it was several months before these movies were set to be released, the actor found odd jobs of one sort and another to support himself.

When the Disney films were released, they were very successful and opened some doors for him. After appearing in three other movies and 23 television shows, he was signed for small parts in three episodes of *The Life and Legend of Wyatt Earp.* His characterizations were so sharp and convincing that the role of Wyatt Earp's unofficial deputy "Shotgun" Gibbs was created for him. His buckskins, 15-gallon hat, moustache and corn cob pipe became regular trademarks for three seasons along with Gibbs' faithful mule Roscoe. In his spare time the actor studied singing with former Metropolitan Opera star Mario Chamlee with the ambition of using his bass-baritone voice in musical comedy, but again he was thwarted.

By the time the series came to an end, he had become very typecast in Westerns as an older man, which made producers and casting directors reluctant to hire him. They could see him only in one part, and they had a rather supercilious attitude toward Westerns like *Wyatt Earp.* The actor endured lean times professionally and virtually had to start his career again. Oddly it was another Western series, *Gunsmoke,* in which he guested a record 16 times from 1965 onwards that rekindled awareness of his abilities. His cause was aided by landing a good movie role in *Cool Hand Luke* (1967).

With the decline of the Western, he had to look further afield. His contribution to the Western genre was recognized in 1988 when he won a Golden Boot. He has remained active in television. His greatest exposure on television in later years was playing the regular role of Punk Anderson in *Dallas,* a role which he enjoyed if for no other reason than it took him back to his home state. His parts as this character gradually became fewer, and he was not even on the guest list for the final party.

He has since made a memorable contribution as a guest-star to an episode of the cult television series *The X Files.*

Morgan Woodward Filmography

1956: *The Great Locomotive Chase, Westward Ho the Wagons!*
1957: *Gunsight Ridge, Slaughter on 10th Avenue.*
1958: *Ride a Crooked Trail.*
1962: *The Gun Hawk.*
1965: *The Sword of Ali Baba.*
1966: *Gun Point.*
1967: *Cool Hand Luke, Firecreek.*
1968: *Death of a Gunfighter.*
1969: *The Wild Country.*
1971: *Yuma* (TV).
1972: *One Little Indian, Running Wild.*
1973: *The Midnight Man, Ride in a Pink Car.*
1975: *The Killing of a Chinese Bookie, A Small Town in Texas, The Last Day* (TV), *The Hatfields and the McCoys* (TV).
1976: *Moonshine County Express, The Quest* (TV).
1977: *Supervan, Walking Tall—The Final Chapter, Which Way Is Up.*
1978: *Speed Trap.*
1980: *Battle Beyond the Stars.*
1985: *Girls Just Want to Have Fun.*
1989: *Dark Before Dawn.*
1991: *Gunsmoke III: To the Last Man* (TV).

Television Series

1958–1961: *The Life and Legend of Wyatt Earp* as Shotgun Gibbs.
1980–1988: *Dallas* as Punk Anderson.

Miniseries

1978–1979: *Centennial.*

Sources

Anderson, Janette, and Bob Anderson. "I Traded Grand Opera For Horse Opera!" *Trail Dust* magazine, spring, 1995.

Goldrup, Tom, and Jim Goldrup. *Feature Players: The Stories Behind the Faces Volume #1.* Published privately, 1986.

Speed, F. Maurice. *The Western Film and TV Annual.* London: MacDonald, 1960.

SHEB WOOLEY

If prizes were handed out for versatility, Sheb Wooley would win one. During the course of his career, there have been few avenues of show business that he has not ridden down, from penning country-western songs to costarring in the top-rated Western series *Rawhide.* Carrying versatility a stage further, he was equally well known under both his real name of Sheb Wooley and by his assumed one of Ben Colder.

Shelby F. Wooley was born on April 10, 1921, near Erick, Oklahoma. Part Cherokee Indian, he was raised on the family farm, learning to ride as a child and riding in rodeos in his teen years. His father exchanged a shotgun for a guitar, which he promptly gave to his son. While still at high school he formed a band which played at dances and on local radio. Upon graduating he obtained a job as a welder in an oil field, but soon grew tired of this and relocated to Nashville.

He appeared on the WLAC and WSM radio stations and recorded for the Bullet label. In 1946 he relocated to Fort Worth, where for the next three years he became the master of ceremonies for a major show on WBAP sponsored by Calumet Baking Powder. He moved to Los Angeles where he signed a contract with MGM Records. Intending to combine singing with acting, he took drama lessons at the Jack

Sheb Wooley (left) and Walter Pidgeon in *Rawhide*.

Koslyn School of Acting. He made his screen debut as Kay Rawlins in the film *Rocky Mountain* (1950), which starred Errol Flynn. His most memorable appearance was as Ben Miller, one of four killers plotting to shoot down Marshal Will Kane (Gary Cooper) in the classic Western *High Noon* (1952). He is also famous for his running role as Pete Nolan, the scout for the trail drive, in the television series *Rawhide.* He wrote some scripts for the series and recorded an album, "Songs from the Days of Rawhide" (1961). His scripts, such as "Incident of the Blackstorms," usually featured his character prominently. Pete Nolan left the trail drive part way through the fourth season in 1962. The episode was "The Deserters' Patrol," and his character returned to the U.S. Army to help reach a solution to an Indian conflict. He was temporarily replaced by the slightly unscrupulous Clay Forrester (Charles Gray). Nolan returned to the trail drive in 1963 and stayed with it for another couple of seasons.

Other artists began to record songs he had penned, and in 1953 Hank Snow had a huge hit with a parody of two hit songs entitled "When Mexican Joe Met Jole Blon." In 1958, Wooley's novelty number "Purple People Eater" became a million seller. He derived the inspiration from a schoolboy joke he heard from the son of Don Robertson, a composer friend of Wooley's. MGM initially thought the song was such a dud that they did not consider it to be worth releasing. "Sweet Chile" was another major U.S. hit. His first appearance in the U.S. country charts was in 1962 when the novelty number "That's My Pa" became a number one hit. This was probably the reason for his absence from *Rawhide* for a season.

When he was prevented by film commitments from recording "Don't Go Near the Indians" before a version by Rex Allen proved a hit, Wooley jokingly told MGM executives that he would write a sequel. Instead he penned and recorded a parody, "Don't Go Near the Eskimos." Subsequently he developed a drunken character who served as his alter ego and whom he has lived with ever since. Wooley offered MGM a choice of three names, which were Ben Freezin, Klon Dyke and Ben Colder, which was the one they chose.

He had some further minor hits with serious songs such as "Blue Guitar." It was as Colder, however, that he recorded humorous parodies of pop and country songs which frequently made the charts. In 1968 Ben Colder was voted Comedian of the Year by the Country Music Association. In 1969 he joined the CBS country show *Hee Haw,* wrote the theme music and remained with it for some years. Throughout the 1960s and 1970s he maintained an extensive touring schedule, appearing all over America and overseas. He also owned two music publishing companies. His last chart success was in 1971. Ironically, the parodies by the drunken Ben Colder have proven to be more enduring than the serious recordings by Sheb Wooley and have accounted for the majority of his sales. As a legitimate actor he was much less frequently seen after the 1960s. He still turns up occasionally, however: appropriately in the movie *Purple People Eater* (1988) and in an episode of *Murder She Wrote* set in Nash-ville.

Sheb Wooley Filmography

1950: *Rocky Mountain.*
1951: *Inside the Walls of Folsom Prison, Distant Drums, Little Big Horn.*
1952: *High Noon, Bugles in the Afternoon, Cattle Town, Sky Full of Moon, Hellgate, Toughest Man in Arizona, The Lusty Men.*
1953: *Texas Bad Man.*
1954: *The Boy from Oklahoma, Johnny Guitar, Rose Marie.*
1955: *Man Without a Star, The Second Greatest Sex, Trial.*
1956: *Giant.*
1957: *The Black Whip, Trooper Hook, Ride a Violent Mile, The Oklahoman.*
1958: *Terror in a Texas Town.*
1963: *Hootenanny Hoot.*
1966: *Country Boy.*
1967: *The War Wagon.*
1976: *The Outlaw Josey Wales.*
1985: *Uphill All the Way, Silverado.*
1986: *Hoosiers.*
1988: *Purple People Eater.*

Television Series

1959–1962: *Rawhide* as Pete Nolan.
1963–1965: *Rawhide* as Pete Nolan.

Sources

Inman, David. *The TV Encyclopedia.* New York: Perigee, 1991.

Larkin, Colin. *The Guinness Encyclopedia of Popular Music.* Enfield, England: Guinness, 1993.

Marschall, Rick. *The Encyclopedia of Country and Western Music.* London: Bison, 1985.

JEFF YORK

Jeff York was born in Los Angeles in 1912, but was raised in San Jose, California. His original ambition was to become a journalist, but he dropped out part way through his college course. A friend told him that he could make money as an actor, so he relocated to Hollywood where he struggled for some time. He auditioned for and won some stage roles at the Pasadena Playhouse, simultaneously working during the day as a salesman.

Under the name of Granville Owen, he made some film appearances in the late 1930s. His height and strapping build lent themselves to productions where the action content was high. After war service in the army, he returned to the screen using the name of Jeff York. For several years he played bit roles in films, but Walt Disney spotted him playing boxer John L. Sullivan in an anthology series on television.

He made several appearances for the Disney organization, for whom he did most of his best work. His first role for them was as Mike Fink, the self proclaimed King of the River in the later episodes of the *Davy Crockett* television series starring Fess Parker. Although York is nominally the heavy, his characterization was so broad that much of the rivalry between Crockett and Fink emerged as more comic than sinister. York was also memorable in the more serious role of James Otis in *Johnny Tremain* (1957), the Disney story of the Revolutionary War. York played the sidekick of Andy Burnett in the television series *The Saga of Andy Burnett.*

He signed a contract with Warner Bros. where he played the role of Reno McKee in *The Alaskans* television series. McKee was one of three soldiers of fortune and benign confidence tricksters who embark on a series of adventures in and around Skagway during the Alaskan gold rush of the 1890s. *The Alaskans* was one of the few unsuccessful Warners series of the period. If it been shot today, it would probably have been scuttled after only a few episodes, but it managed a reasonably healthy 36 episodes during its only season. A forthright individual in real life, York was particularly contemptuous of the series, complaining about the lack of authenticity and the poor quality of the scripts. He allegedly left the series after 23 episodes when his contract expired, but oddly his name appears in the production notes for the series until the end.

York continued to guest-star on television during the 1960s. One of his last recorded movie credits was *Savage Sam* (1963), an unrelated sequel to Disney's *Old Yeller* (1957) in which he reprised the character of Bud Searcy. The actor retired to live with his family in Santa Cruz, California. At last report, however, he had suffered a serious stroke and became a permanent resident of the Motion Picture Country Home and Hospital in Woodland Hills, California.

Jeff York Filmography

1937: *The Adventurous Blonde, That Certain Woman, The Devil's Saddle Legion, Expensive Husbands, Kid Galahad.*

1938: *Alcatraz Island, Start Cheering.*

1940: *The Great Plane Robbery, Li'l Abner, Terry and the Pirates* (serial).

1945: *They Were Expendable.*

1946: *Alias Mr. Twilight, Little Miss Big, The Postman Always Rings Twice, Up Goes Maisie, The Yearling.*

1947: *Fear in the Night, Blondie's Holiday, Unconquered.*

1948: *Panhandle, Isn't It Romantic?, The Paleface.*

1949: *Knock on Any Door, Samson and Delilah, Special Agent.*

1950: *Father of the Bride, Surrender, Short Grass, Kill the Umpire.*

1951: *The Unknown Man, The Lady Says No.*
1954: *Demetrius and the Gladiators.*
1956: *The Great Locomotive Chase, Davy Crockett and the River Pirates, Westward Ho the Wagons!*
1957: *Johnny Tremain, Old Yeller.*
1963: *Savage Sam.*

Television Series

1955: *Davy Crockett* as Mike Fink.
1957–1958: *The Saga of Andy Burnett* as Joe Burke.
1959–1960: *The Alaskans* as Reno McKee.

Sources

Maltin, Leonard. *The Disney Films.* New York: Crown, 1973.
Woolley, Lynn, Robert W. Malsbary, and Robert G. Strange, Jr. *Warner Bros. Television.* Jefferson, NC: McFarland, 1985.
Summers, Neil. *The Official TV Western Book Volumes #3 and #4.* Vienna, WV: Old West Shop Publishing, 1991 and 1992.
Ragan, David. *Who's Who in Hollywood.* New York: Facts on File, 1992.

VICTOR SEN YUNG

Victor Sen Yung was one of Hollywood's favorite Orientals. He must have felt he was appearing in series throughout his career since he stepped from Charlie Chan's son in movies to Hop Sing the cook in *Bonanza* on television. It was not, overall, a career of much light and shade. There was little versatility. He had two ambitions in real life, and neither was realized. The first was to be an international lawyer; he became successively a chemical salesman, an actor and a cook. The other was to visit mainland China; the closest he ever came was a trip to Hong Kong.

He was born in San Francisco on October 18, 1915. His real name was Sen Yew Cheung. His parents had emigrated from China late in the 19th century. Shortly after his mother died in the flu epidemic of 1919, his father placed him and his sister in a shelter for children and returned to China. In the mid–1920s his father returned and his children went back to live with him and his new wife. It was then that Victor Sen Yung first learned to speak Cantonese. He majored in veterinary science at the College of Agriculture at Berkeley, intending to work in China. Later he changed to economics.

He made his motion picture debut as one of the peasants who kill the locusts in *The Good Earth* (1937), but worked simultaneously as a salesman for a chemical firm. When he obtained his big break into motion pictures, he was trying to interest technicians at Fox studios in a flame-proofing compound. It was suggested he audition for the role of one of Charlie Chan's sons.

The series about the Oriental sleuth created by Earl Derr Biggers was undergoing a major change in the cast upon the death of the celebrated Warner Oland, who was long associated with the role. Keye Luke, a close personal friend of Oland's, was so distressed he could not continue playing Chan's son. The new star, Sidney Toler, approved of Victor Sen Yung as Luke's successor. Although Yung was at first labeled incompetent, his characterization improved when Toler took him in hand and gave him some intensive coaching. Subsequently he enrolled in an actors' studio and to round out his knowledge of motion pictures attended courses at the California Graduate School of Cinema Arts.

In his first Charlie Chan feature, *Charlie Chan in Honolulu* (1938), he played Lee. In *Charlie Chan in Reno* (1939) and in 11 subsequent episodes he played Jimmy. When Roland Winters assumed the part of Charlie Chan for Monogram after Toler's death in 1947, Yung played Tommy. He did not appear in the final episode *Sky Dragon* (1949), which is considered unwatchable.

Although he was under contract to Fox, he also made features for Warners and MGM. His favorite film roles were as the scheming solicitor's clerk Ong Chi Seng in *The Letter* (1940) and as Sammy Fong in the stage and film productions of *Flower Drum Song* (1961). At Warners he appeared as Joe Totsuiko, a character who is not quite all he seems, in the excellent Humphrey Bogart thriller *Across the Pacific* (1942).

During World War II, Victor Sen Yung served as a Captain in the U.S. Air Force Intelligence. The account of how he did not make it to China almost plays like a black comedy. He missed a transfer to the 22nd Field Hospital Unit by two days. Instead he was assigned to the "Winged Victory" unit of the air force. When he was informed that a China-bound intelligence unit was being formed, he applied and was sent to Berkeley's Chinese Language School to learn the Mandarin dialect. He received his orders to go to China, but the war ended before he was shipped out.

He had two running parts on television. On *Bachelor Father* he played Cousin Charlie Fong, the race track tout who dropped by frequently to visit with John Forsythe's houseman Peter Tong and try to persuade him to bet on a horse. He was best-known, however, as Hop Sing, houseboy and cook to the Cartwright family on *Bonanza*. The episode in which he was seen to best advantage was the one where Hop Sing lost his pigtail.

In 1972 he was returning to Los Angeles from Sacramento when his plane was skyjacked by terrorists. The passenger in the seat in front of him was shot dead in a confrontation between the terrorists and FBI agents, but Yung escaped with a flesh wound. He later sued the airline for $500,000, but settled out of court for much less.

From the mid–1970s onward, most of his income was derived from his cooking. He even wrote a book on the subject of Chinese food, *The Great Wok Cookbook*, published in 1974. He also gave cooking demonstrations in department stores and on television. Although the stars of *Bonanza* were millionaires, he appeared in only 20 percent of the shows over 14 seasons, which was not enough to support him. To supplement his income he did a variety of jobs including waiter, truck driver, sales assistant of men's clothing and frozen food promotion.

He was working on his second cookbook when he was found dead at his San Fernando Valley home on November 9, 1980, at age 65. He had been heating his small home with the kitchen stove when he was overcome by gas fumes. The weather had been inclement, the house was difficult to heat, and the actor had become careless. Family and friends testified that he was not depressed at the time and the coroner accepted this, recording a verdict of accidental death. Yung did, however, die broke. He was survived by a sister, his son and two grandchildren who were then living in Ohio. His only marriage had ended in divorce some years before.

Portrait of Victor Sen Yung, who appeared in *Bonanza*.

Victor Sen Yung Filmography

1937: *The Good Earth, Lost Horizon, The General Died at Dawn.*
1938: *Charlie Chan in Honolulu* (ST), *Shadows Over Shanghai.*
1939: *Charlie Chan in Reno* (ST), *Charlie Chan at Treasure Island* (ST), *20,000 Men a Year.*
1940: *The Letter, Charlie Chan at the Wax Museum* (ST), *Murder Over New York* (CC:ST), *Charlie Chan in Panama* (ST), *Charlie Chan's Murder Cruise* (ST).
1941: *Dead Men Tell* (CC:ST), *Charlie Chan in Rio* (ST).
1942: *Manila Calling, Across the Pacific, Moon-*

tide, A Yank on the Burma Road, Little Tokyo USA, Secret Agent of Japan, Castle in the Desert (CC:ST), *The Mad Martindales.*
1943: *China, Night Plane from Chungking.*
1945: *Betrayal from the East.*
1946: *Shadows Over Chinatown* (CC:ST), *Dangerous Money* (CC:ST), *Dangerous Millions.*
1947: *The Crimson Key, The Trap* (CC:RW), *The Chinese Ring* (CC:RW) (a.k.a. *The Red Hornet), Web of Danger, The Flame, Intrigue.*
1948: *Docks of New Orleans* (CC:RW), *The Shanghai Chest* (CC:RW), *Golden Eye* (CC:RW), *The Feathered Serpent* (CC:RW), *Half Past Midnight.*
1949: *Oh You Beautiful Doll!, Red Light, State Department File 649, And Baby Makes Three.*
1950: *The Breaking Point, A Ticket to Tomahawk, Chinatown at Midnight, Woman on the Run, Key to the City.*
1951: *Peking Express, The Groom Wore Spurs, Valley of Fire, The Law and the Lady.*
1952: *Target Hong Kong, The Sniper.*
1953: *Forbidden.*
1954: *Jubilee Trail, The Shanghai Story, Port of Hell, Trader Tom of the China Seas* (serial).
1955: *Blood Alley, The Left Hand of God, Soldier of Fortune.*
1956: *Accused of Murder.*
1957: *Men in War.*
1958: *The Hunters, She Demons, Jet Attack.*
1959: *The Saga of Hemp Brown.*
1961: *Flower Drum Song.*
1962: *Confessions of an Opium Eater.*
1968: *A Flea in Her Ear.*
1970: *The Hawaiians* (a.k.a. *Master of the Islands).*
1972: *Kung Fu* (TV).
1973: *The Red Pony* (TV).
1975: *The Killer Elite.*
1980: *The Man with Bogart's Face* (a.k.a. *Sam Marlow Private Eye).*

Television Series

1961–1962: *Bachelor Father* as Cousin Charlie Fong.
1959–1973: *Bonanza* as Hop Sing.

Sources

Jones, Ken D., Arthur F. McClure, and Alfred E. Twomey. *Character People.* Secaucus, NJ: Citadel, 1979.
Lamparski, Richard. *Whatever Became Of? Ninth Series.* New York: Crown, 1985.
Picture Show's Who's Who on Screen. London: Amalgamated Press, c. 1956.
Shapiro, Melany. Bonanza: *The Unofficial Story of the Ponderosa.* Las Vegas, NV: Pioneer, 1993.
Tuska, Jon. *The Detective in Hollywood.* Garden City, NY: Doubleday, 1978.

Notes

1. In many of the above movies Victor is billed simply as Sen Yung. He added "Victor" in the early 1940s.
2. Charlie Chan movies whose titles do not contain the words "Charlie Chan" are denoted CC.
3. Charlie Chan movies with Sidney Toler are denoted ST.
4. Charlie Chan movies with Roland Winters are denoted RW.

APPENDIX: TELEVISION SERIES CATALOG

Information on television series is presented in the following order:

Title; any alternative titles; original air dates; production company or producer; whether network or syndicated; number of episodes; whether black and white or color; length of each episode; plot synopsis; prime-time series time of airing; and players in the series who appear in this book.

1. *The Adventures of Champion;* a.k.a. *Champion the Wonder Horse;* Sept. 30, 1955–Feb. 3, 1956, Flying A Productions

CBS 26 episodes B/W ½ hour

Adventures of a wonder horse, dog and little boy in the American Southwest of the 1880s.

9/55—2/56 Friday 7:30—8:00

Barry Curtis, Jim Bannon, Ewing Mitchell.

2. *The Adventures of Jim Bowie;* Sept. 7, 1956—Aug. 29, 1958 Louis F. Edelman

ABC 78 episodes B/W ½ hour

Stories of a wealthy young planter and adventurer in the Louisiana Territory of the 1830s.

9/56—8/58 Friday 8:00—8:30

Scott Forbes, Robert Cornthwaite, Peter Hansen.

3. *The Adventures of Kit Carson;* 1951–1955 Revue

Syndicated 104 episodes B/W ½ hour

The famous scout and his Mexican sidekick right wrongs in the Old West.

Bill Williams, Don Diamond.

4. *The Adventures of Rin Tin Tin;* Oct. 15, 1954—Aug. 28, 1959 Screen Gems/Herbert B. Leonard

ABC 164 episodes B/W ½ hour

Stories of a dog and small orphan boy adopted by the cavalry soldiers at Fort Apache Arizona in the 1880s.

10/54—8/59 Friday 7:30—8:00

Lee Aaker, James Brown, Joe Sawyer, Rand Brooks, Hal Hopper, Tommy Farrell, William Forrest.

5. *The Alaskans;* Oct. 4, 1959—Sept. 25, 1960 Warner Bros.

ABC 36 episodes B/W Hour

Adventures of two benevolent confidence tricksters and a singer during the Alaskan gold rush of the 1890s.

10/59—9/60 Sunday 9:30—10:30

Roger Moore, Dorothy Provine, Jeff York, Ray Danton.

6. *Annie Oakley;* 1954–1958 Flying A Productions

Syndicated 81 episodes B/W ½ hour

Adventures of female sharpshooter around her hometown of Diablo.

Gail Davis, Brad Johnson, Jimmy Hawkins.

7. *Bat Masterson;* Oct. 8, 1958—Sept. 21, 1961 Ziv/United Artists

NBC 108 episodes B/W ½ hour

Adventures of a debonair gunfighter in the Southwest.

10/58—9/59 Wednesday 9:30—10:00

10/59—9/60 Thursday 8:00—8:30
9/60—9/61 Thursday 8:30—9:00
Gene Barry

8. *Black Saddle;* Jan. 10, 1959—Sept. 30, 1960 Four Star

NBC/ABC 44 episodes B/W ½ hour

A former gunfighter turned attorney has a roving commission in the post Civil War New Mexico territory.

1/59—9/59 NBC Saturday 9:00— 9:30
10/59—9/60 ABC Friday 10:30—11:00
Peter Breck, Russell Johnson, Anna-Lisa.

9. *Bonanza;* Sept. 12, 1959—Jan. 16, 1973 David Dortort

NBC 430 episodes Color Hour

Stories of the Cartwright family on the Ponderosa spread near Virginia City.

9/59—9/61 Saturday 7:30— 8:00
9/61—9/72 Sunday 9:00—10:00
9/72—1/73 Tuesday 8:00— 9:00
Lorne Greene, Pernell Roberts, Dan Blocker, Michael Landon, Victor Sen Yung.

10. *Boots and Saddles: The Story of the 5th Cavalry;* 1957–1958 California National Productions

Syndicated 39 episodes B/W ½ hour

Life of the cavalry men stationed at Fort Lowell, Arizona, in the 1870s.

John Pickard, John Alderson, Michael Hinn, Gardner McKay, Patrick McVey, Dave Willock.

11. *Brave Eagle;* Sept. 28, 1955–June 6, 1956 Roy Rogers Frontier Productions

CBS 26 episodes B/W ½ hour

The expansion of the white man across the Indian lands in the Southwest during the middle of the 19th century, told from the viewpoint of a young Cheyenne chief.

9/55—6/56 Wednesday 7:30—8:00
Keith Larsen, Anthony Numkeena, Kim Winona, Bert Wheeler.

12. *Broken Arrow;* Sept. 25, 1956–Sept. 23, 1958 20th Century–Fox

ABC 78 episodes B/W ½ hour

The efforts of mail rider Tom Jeffords and Apache chief Cochise to keep peace in the Arizona territory.

9/56—9/58 Tuesday 9:00—9:30
John Lupton, Michael Ansara, Tom Fadden, Steven Ritch.

13. *Bronco;* Sept. 23, 1958—Aug. 20, 1962 Warner Bros.

ABC 68 episodes B/W Hour

Adventures of an ex-Confederate army captain who roams the post–Civil War West.

9/58—9/60 Tuesday 7:30—8:30
10/60—8/62 Monday 7:30—8:30
Ty Hardin.

14. *Buckskin;* July 3, 1958–Sept. 14, 1959 Revue

NBC 39 episodes B/W ½ hour

Morality tales centering around a boarding house in Buckskin, Montana, during the 1880s.

7/58—9/58 Thursday 9:30—10:00
10/58—1/59 Friday 7:30— 8:00
1/59—9/59 Monday 7:30— 8:00
Tommy Nolan, Sallie Brophy, Michael Road, Michael Lipton.

15. *Buffalo Bill, Jr.;* 1955 Flying A Productions

Syndicated 40 episodes B/W ½ hour

Title character tries to maintain law and order in Wileyville, Texas, in the 1890s.

Dick Jones, Nancy Gilbert, Harry Cheshire.

16. *The Californians;* Sept. 24, 1957–Aug. 27, 1959 Louis F. Edelman

NBC 69 episodes B/W ½ hour

Format 1: Crusading reporter and vigilantes try to maintain law and order in San Francisco during the 1850s at the height of the gold rush.

Format 2: Official marshal fights crime and corruption with new police force during the same period.

9/57—3/59 Tuesday 10:00—10:30
4/59—6/59 Tuesday 9:00— 9:30
7/59—8/59 Thursday 7:30— 8:00

Format 1: Adam Kennedy, Sean McClory, Nan Leslie, Herbert Rudley, Howard Caine.

Format 2: Richard Coogan, Carole Mathews, Arthur Fleming.

17. *Cheyenne;* Sept. 20, 1955–Sept. 13, 1963 Warner Bros.

ABC 108 episodes B/W Hour

Wandering soldier of fortune roams the West in the post–Civil War period.

9/55– 9/59	Tuesday	7:30–8:30
9/59–12/62	Monday	7:30–8:30
4/63– 9/63	Friday	7:30–8:30

Clint Walker, L.Q. Jones.

18. *Cimarron City;* Oct. 11, 1958–Sept. 26, 1959 Revue/George Montgomery

NBC 26 episodes B/W Hour

Stories of mayor and cattle rancher in the tough environment of a boom town in the Oklahoma Territory of the 1890s.

10/58–9/59 Saturday 9:30–10:30

George Montgomery, Audrey Totter, John Smith, Stuart Randall, Addison Richards, Fred Sherman, Claire Carleton, Dan Blocker, George Dunn, Pete Dunn, Tom Fadden, Wally Brown.

19. *Circus Boy;* Sept. 23, 1956–Sept. 11, 1958 Screen Gems/Herbert Leonard

NBC/ABC 49 episodes B/W ½ hour

Circus life on the frontier at the turn of the century as seen through the eyes of a 12-year-old orphan boy.

9/56–9/57	NBC	Sunday	7:30–8:00
9/57–9/58	ABC	Thursday	7:30–8:00

Mickey Braddock, Noah Beery, Jr., Robert Lowery, Guinn Williams, Leo Gordon, Billy Barty, Olin Howlin, Eddie Marr.

20. *The Cisco Kid;* 1950–1956 Ziv/United Artists

Syndicated 156 episodes Color ½ hour

Legendary Mexican adventurer and his sidekick have adventures in the Southwest.

Duncan Renaldo, Leo Carrillo.

21. *Colt .45;* Oct. 18, 1957–Sept. 27, 1960 Warner Bros.

ABC 67 episodes B/W ½ hour

A government agent in the guise of a gun salesman tracks down outlaws on the Western frontier of the 1870s.

10/57–12/57	Friday	10:00–10:30
1/58– 4/58	Friday	8:30– 9:00
10/58– 9/59	Sunday	9:00– 9:30
10/59–3/60	Sunday	7:00– 7:30
4/60–9/60	Tuesday	9:30–10:00

Wayde Preston, Donald May.

22. *Cowboy G Men;* 1954–1955 Russell Hayden/Henry B. Donovan

Syndicated 39 episodes Color ½ hour

Two government undercover agents hunt various outlaws.

Russell Hayden, Jackie Coogan.

23. *Davy Crockett;* Dec. 15, 1954–Dec. 14, 1955 Walt Disney

ABC 5 episodes Color Hour

Various exploits in the life of the legendary frontiersman. Shown as episodes in the anthology series *Disneyland.*

12/54–12/55 Wednesday 7:30–8:30

Fess Parker, Buddy Ebsen, Jeff York.

24. *Death Valley Days;* 1952–1975 Twenty Mule Team Borax/Madison Productions

Syndicated 558 episodes B/W Color ½ hour

Anthology series revolving round the legends and folklore of Death Valley, California.

Stanley Andrews.

25. *The Deputy;* Sept. 12, 1959–Sept. 16, 1961 Revue/Top Gun

NBC 76 episodes B/W ½ hour

Conflict between a veteran marshal and a young storekeeper turned peace officer in the Arizona territory of the 1880s.

9/59–9/61 Saturday 9:00–9:30

Henry Fonda, Allen Case, Wallace Ford, Betty Lou Keim.

26. *Frontier;* Sept. 25, 1955–Sept. 9, 1956 Worthington Miner

NBC 39 episodes B/W ½ hour

Gritty anthology series depicting the hardships faced by pioneers traveling West.

9/55–9/56 Sunday 7:30–8:00

Walter Coy.

27. *Frontier Doctor;* a.k.a. *Man Of The West / Unarmed;* 1957–1958 Studio City Television Productions

Syndicated 39 episodes B/W ½ hour

Stories of a medical doctor on the Western frontier.
Rex Allen.

28. *Fury;* 1955–1958 Independent Television Corporation

Syndicated 114 episodes B/W ½ hour
Adventures of a boy and a wild horse on the Broken Wheel Ranch in the contemporary West.
Peter Graves, Bobby Diamond, William Fawcett, Ann Robinson, Nan Leslie, Jimmy Baird, Roger Mobley, James Seay, Guy Teague.

29. *The Gene Autry Show;* July 23, 1950–Aug. 7, 1956 Flying A Productions

CBS 108 episodes 95 B/W ½ hour
13 Color
A singing marshal with a roving commission upholds justice in the contemporary West.

7/50—7/53	Sunday	7:00—7:30
7/53—9/54	Tuesday	8:00—8:30
9/54—8/56	Saturday	7:00—7:30

Gene Autry, Pat Buttram.

30. *The Gray Ghost;* 1957 Lindsley Parsons Productions

Syndicated 39 episodes B/W ½ hour
Exploits of the quick-witted Confederate hero during the Civil War.
Tod Andrews, Phil Chambers.

31. *Gunsmoke;* Sept. 10, 1955–Sept. 1, 1975 Charles Marquis Warren/ Norman MacDonnell/John Mantley

CBS 633 episodes 233 B/W ½ hour
400 Color Hour
U.S. Marshal Matt Dillon maintains law and order in Dodge City, Kansas, during the 1880s.

9/55—9/61	Saturday	10:00—10:30
9/61—9/67	Saturday	10:00—11:00
9/67—9/71	Monday	7:30— 8:30
9/71—9/75	Monday	8:00— 9:00

James Arness, Milburn Stone, Amanda Blake, Dennis Weaver, Hank Patterson, Tom Brown, Howard Culver, John Harper, Dabbs Greer, James Nusser, Charles Seel, Robert Brubaker.

32. *Have Gun Will Travel;* Sept. 14, 1957–Sept. 21, 1963 Frank Pierson

CBS 225 episodes B/W ½ hour
A mysterious black-clad gunfighter operating out of a San Francisco hotel sells his services in the post–Civil War West.

9/57—9/63	Saturday	9:30—10:00

Richard Boone, Kam Tong.

33. *Hawkeye and the Last of the Mohicans;* 1956–1957 Independent Television Corporation/The Canadian Broadcasting System/ Normandie Productions of Canada

Syndicated 39 episodes B/W ½ hour
Famous scout and his Indian companion attempt to maintain peace on the Eastern frontier.
John Hart, Lon Chaney, Jr.

34. *Hopalong Cassidy;* June 24, 1949–Dec. 23, 1951 William Boyd Productions

NBC 54 episodes B/W Hour
1952–1954

Syndicated 52 episodes B/W ½ hour
A black-clad cowboy maintains law and order on the Western frontier.

6/49—10/49	Friday	8:00—9:00
4/50—12/51	Sunday	6:00—7:00

William Boyd, Edgar Buchanan.

35. *Hotel De Paree;* Oct. 2, 1959–Sept. 23, 1960 William Self

CBS 33 episodes B/W ½ hour
An ex-gunfighter protects two women who have inherited a hotel in Georgetown, Colorado.

10/59—9/60	Friday	8:30—9:00

Earl Holliman, Judi Meredith, Jeanette Nolan, Strother Martin.

36. *Jefferson Drum;* a.k.a. *The Pen and the Quill;* April 25, 1958–April 23, 1959 Screen Gems

NBC 26 episodes B/W ½ hour
A courageous newspaperman with a young son attempts to build up community life in the town of Jubilee in the West of the 1850s.

4/58— 9/58	Friday	8:00—8:30
9/58—10/58	Friday	7:30—8:00
10/58— 4/59	Thursday	7:30—8:00

Jeff Richards, Cyril Delevanti, Eugene Martin, Robert Stevenson.

37. *Johnny Ringo;* Oct. 1, 1959–Sept. 29, 1960 Four Star

CBS 38 episodes B/W ½ hour

A gunman turned sheriff maintains law and order in the town of Velardi, Arizona, in the 1880s.

10/59—9/60 Thursday 8:30—9:00
Don Durant, Karen Sharpe, Mark Goddard, Terence de Marney, Willis Bouchey.

38. *Judge Roy Bean;* 1955–1956 Quintet Productions/Russell Hayden

Syndicated 39 episodes B/W ½ hour
Color

A scalawag judge dispenses his own brand of justice in Texas during the 1870s.
Edgar Buchanan, Jack Buetel, Jackie Loughery, Russell Hayden.

39. *Laramie;* Sept. 15, 1959–Sept. 17, 1963 Revue

NBC 124 episodes 64 B/W Hour
60 Color

Two brothers, a family friend and a drifter encounter problems running a stagecoach relay station and ranch near Laramie, Wyoming, in the 1870s.

9/59—9/63 Tuesday 7:30—8:30
John Smith, Robert Fuller, Hoagy Carmichael, Robert Crawford, Jr.

40. *Law of the Plainsman;* a.k.a. *Tales of the Plainsman;* Oct. 1, 1959–Sept. 22, 1960 Four Star

NBC 30 episodes B/W ½ hour

Conflict in the New Mexico Territory of the 1880s where an Apache is a deputy marshal.

10/59—9/60 Thursday 7:30—8:00
Michael Ansara, Dayton Lummis, Gina Gillespie, Nora Marlowe.

41. *Lawman;* Oct. 5, 1958—Oct. 2, 1962 Warner Bros.

ABC 156 episodes B/W ½ hour

A marshal and his deputy maintain law and order on the streets of Laramie, Wyoming, during the 1870s.

10/58—4/62 Sunday 8:30—9:00
4/62—10/62 Sunday 10:30—11:00
John Russell, Peter Brown, Peggie Castle, Bek Nelson.

42. *The Life and Legend of Wyatt Earp;* Sept. 6, 1955–Sept. 26, 1961 Wyatt Earp Enterprises/ Louis F. Edelmann

ABC 266 episodes B/W ½ hour

Adventures of the legendary lawman in the various towns where he was a peace officer.

9/55—9/61 Tuesday 8:30—9:00
Hugh O'Brian, Mason Alan Dinehart III, Denver Pyle, Hal Baylor, Gloria Talbott, Don Haggerty, Douglas Fowley, Lloyd Corrigan, Paul Brinegar, Ralph Sanford, Selmer Jackson, William Tannen, Myron Healey, Carol Stone, Morgan Woodward, Dirk London, John Anderson, Randy Stuart, Trevor Bardette, Carol Thurston, Lash LaRue, Steve Brodie, William Phipps, Damian O'Flynn, James Seay.

43. *The Lone Ranger;* Sept. 15, 1949–Sept. 12, 1957 Jack Wrather/Jack Chertok/George Trendle

ABC 221 episodes 182 B/W ½ hour
39 Color

A mysterious masked rider and his Indian companion fight for justice in the Old West.

9/49—9/57 Thursday 7:30—8:00
Clayton Moore, John Hart, Jay Silverheels, Chuck Courtney.

44. *MacKenzie's Raiders;* 1958–1959 Ziv/United Artists

Syndicated 39 episodes B/W ½ hour

Conflict between cavalry officer and his men—stationed at Fort Clark, Texas, in 1873—and Mexican bandits.
Richard Carlson.

45. *The Man from Blackhawk;* Oct. 9, 1959–Sept. 23, 1960 Screen Gems

ABC 37 episodes B/W ½ hour

An insurance investigator in the Old West investigates fraudulent claims.

10/59—9/60 Friday 8:30—9:00
Robert Rockwell.

46. *Man without a Gun;* 1957–1959 20th Century-Fox

Syndicated 52 episodes B/W ½ hour

Crusading newspaper editor solves problems in the tough environment of Yellowstone, a frontier town in the Dakotas, during the 1880s.

Rex Reason, Mort Mills, Harry Harvey, Sr., Forrest Taylor.

47. *The Marshal of Gunsight Pass;* Mar. 12, 1950–Sept. 30, 1950

ABC 26 episodes B/W ½ hour

Primitive series about the title hero.

3/50—9/50	Saturday	6:30—7:00

Russell Hayden, Eddie Dean, Roscoe Ates.

48. *Maverick;* Sept. 22, 1957–July 8, 1962 Warner Bros.

ABC 124 episodes B/W Hour

Classic satirical Western about two gambler brothers attempting to fleece others in the West of the 1880s.

9/57—9/61	Sunday	7:30—8:30
9/61—7/62	Sunday	6:30—7:30

James Garner, Jack Kelly.

49. *My Friend Flicka;* Feb. 10, 1956–Aug. 28, 1957 20th Century–Fox

CBS 39 episodes Color ½ hour

Adventures of a horse and boy in the ranchlands of Montana at the turn of the century.

2/56—2/57	Friday	7:30—8:00
3/57	Saturday	7:00—7:30
4/57—5/57	Sunday	6:00—6:30
6/57—8/57	Wednesday	7:30—8:00

Gene Evans, Anita Louise, Johnny Washbrook, Frank Ferguson.

50. *The Nine Lives of Elfego Baca;* Oct. 3, 1958–Mar. 25, 1960 Walt Disney

ABC 10 episodes Color Hour

Events in the life of a real life Mexican lawman in Socorro County, New Mexico, during the 1880s. Shown as episodes in the anthology series *Walt Disney Presents.*

9/58—9/59	Friday	8:00—9:00
9/59—3/60	Friday	7:30—8:30

Robert Loggia.

51. *Northwest Passage;* Sept. 14, 1958–Sept. 8, 1959 MGM

NBC 26 episodes Color ½ hour

Maj. Robert Rogers, noted Indian fighter, and his men try to find a legendary inland waterway during the French-Indian War of the 1750s.

9/58—1/59	Sunday	7:30—8:00
1/59—7/59	Friday	7:30—8:00
7/59—9/59	Tuesday	7:30—8:00

Keith Larsen, Buddy Ebsen, Don Burnett, Philip Tonge.

52. *The Range Rider;* 1951–1952 Flying A Productions

Syndicated 78 episodes B/W ½ hour

Adventures of the Range Rider and his sidekick Dick West in California during the 1860s.

Jock Mahoney, Dick Jones.

53. *Rawhide;* Jan. 9, 1959–Jan. 4, 1966 Charles Marquis Warren

CBS 216 episodes B/W Hour

Drama on one of the great cattle drives along the Sedalia Trail during the late 1860s.

1/59—4/59	Friday	8:00—9:00
5/59—9/63	Friday	7:30—8:30
9/63—9/64	Thursday	8:00—9:00
9/64—9/65	Friday	7:30—8:30
9/65—1/66	Tuesday	7:30—8:30

Eric Fleming, Clint Eastwood, Sheb Wooley, Paul Brinegar, Steve Raines, Rocky Shahan, James Murdock.

54. *The Rebel;* Oct. 4, 1959–Sept. 17, 1961 Andrew J. Fenady/Goodson-Todman Productions

ABC 76 episodes B/W ½ hour

The adventures of Johnny Yuma, ex–Confederate soldier, on the Western frontier after the Civil War.

10/59—9/61	Sunday	9:00—9:30

Nick Adams.

55. *The Restless Gun;* Sept. 23, 1957–Sept. 14, 1959 Revue/Window Glen (John Payne)/ David Dortort

NBC 77 episodes B/W ½ hour

Adventures of a loner drifting through the post–Civil War Southwest.

9/57—9/59	Monday	8:00—8:30

John Payne.

56. *The Rifleman;* Sept. 30, 1958–July 1, 1963 Four Star

ABC 168 episodes B/W ½ hour

The story of Lucas McCain, a widower and homesteader in North Fork, New Mexico, and his struggles to raise his young son.

9/58–9/60	Tuesday	9:00–9:30
9/60–9/61	Tuesday	8:00–8:30
10/61–7/63	Monday	8:30–9:00

Chuck Connors, Johnny Crawford, Paul Fix, Hope Summers, Bill Quinn.

57. *Riverboat;* Sept. 13, 1959–Jan. 16, 1961 Revue

NBC 44 episodes B/W Hour

Drama aboard the *Enterprise,* a boat that sailed various rivers during the 1840s.

9/59–1/60	Sunday	7:00–8:00
2/60–1/61	Monday	7:30–8:30

Darren McGavin, Burt Reynolds, William D. Gordon, Richard Wessel, Jack Lambert, Mike McGreevey, John Mitchum, Bart Patten.

58. *Rough Riders;* Oct. 2, 1958–Sept. 24, 1959 Ziv/United Artists

ABC 39 episodes B/W ½ hour

After the Civil War, three soldiers join forces and ride west in search of a new life.

10/58–9/59	Thursday	9:30–10:00

Kent Taylor, Jan Merlin, Peter Whitney.

59. *The Roy Rogers Show;* Dec. 30, 1951–June 23, 1957 Roy Rogers Productions

NBC 104 episodes B/W ½ hour

Roy Rogers, his horse and dog maintain law and order in the contemporary West around Mineral City.

12/51–6/52	Sunday	6:30–7:00
8/52–6/57	Sunday	6:30–7:00

Roy Rogers, Dale Evans, Pat Brady, Harry Harvey, Sr.

60. *The Saga of Andy Burnett;* Oct. 2, 1957–Dec. 3, 1958 Walt Disney

ABC 6 episodes Color Hour

Exploits of a rugged mountain man who headed West in the early years of the 19th century. Shown as episodes in the anthology series *Walt Disney Presents.*

10/57–3/58	Wednesday	7:30–8:30

Jerome Courtland, Jeff York.

61. *Sergeant Preston of the Yukon;* Sept. 29, 1955–Sept. 25, 1958 The Wrather Corporation

NBC 78 episodes B/W ½ hour

Adventures of a dedicated Mountie, his horse and dog in the Yukon Territory at the turn of the century.

9/55–9/58	Thursday	7:30–8:00

Richard Simmons.

62. *Sheriff of Cochise;* 1956–1958 Desilu

Syndicated 78 episodes B/W ½ hour

Sheriff Frank Morgan maintains law and order in Cochise County, Arizona, in the contemporary West.

John Bromfield, Stan Jones.

63. *Shotgun Slade;* 1959–1961 Revue

Syndicated 78 episodes B/W ½ hour

A private eye solves crimes in the Old West.

Scott Brady.

64. *Sky King;* 1951–1954 Nabisco

Syndicated 130 episodes B/W ½ hour

In the contemporary West, an Arizonian ranch owner and his niece track down miscreants by flying his own plane.

Kirby Grant, Gloria Winters, Ron Hagerthy, Ewing Mitchell.

65. *Steve Donovan Western Marshal;* 1951–1952 Nabisco/Jack Chertok/Vibar Productions

Syndicated 39 episodes B/W ½ hour

A Western marshal and his deputy uphold the law.

Douglas Kennedy, Eddy Waller.

66. *Stories of the Century;* a.k.a. *The Fast Guns;* 1954–1955 Studio City TV Productions

Syndicated 38 episodes B/W ½ hour

A railroad detective and his beautiful assistant pursue outlaws all over the United States.

Jim Davis, Kristine Miller, Mary Castle.

67. *Sugarfoot;* Sept. 17, 1957–July 3, 1961 Warner Bros.

ABC 69 episodes B/W Hour

Adventures of a young correspondence school law student who rides West in search of adventure.

9/57—9/60	Tuesday	7:30—8:30
10/60—7/61	Monday	7:30—8:30

Will Hutchins.

68. *Swamp Fox;* Oct. 23, 1959–Jan. 15 1961 Walt Disney

ABC 8 episodes Color Hour

Exploits of Col. Francis Marion, a hero of the Revolutionary War. Shown as episodes of the anthology series *Walt Disney Presents.*

9/59—9/60	Friday	7:30—8:30
9/60—9/61	Sunday	6:30—7:30

Leslie Nielsen, Myron Healey.

69. *Tales of the Texas Rangers;* Sept. 3, 1955–Mar. 22, 1958 Screen Gems

CBS and ABC 52 episodes B/W ½ hour

Exploits of two Texas Rangers alternately in the old and contemporary West.

9/55—5/57	Saturday	11:30 A.M.—12:00
9/57—3/58	Sunday	5:00 P.M.— 5:30

Willard Parker, Harry Lauter.

70. *Tales of Wells Fargo;* Mar. 18, 1957–Sept. 8, 1962 Revue/Overland/Nat Holt

NBC 201 episodes 167 B/W ½ hour
34 Color Hour

Adventures of Jim Hardie, special agent for the Wells Fargo Company.

3/57—7/57	Monday	8:30—9:00
9/57—9/61	Monday	8:30—9:00
9/61—9/62	Saturday	7:30—8:30

Dale Robertson.

71. *The Texan;* Sept. 29, 1958–Sept. 12, 1960 Desilu/Rorvic (Rory Calhoun, Vic Orsatti).

CBS 78 episodes B/W ½ hour

Whitewashed adventures of a wanderer who in the years following the Civil War carved out a niche for himself as a Texas gunfighter.

9/58—9/60	Monday	8:00—8:30

Rory Calhoun, Duncan Lamont.

72. *Texas John Slaughter;* Oct. 31, 1958–April 23, 1961 Walt Disney

ABC 17 episodes Color Hour

Exploits of a legendary lawman and scout in and around Tucson, Arizona. Shown as episodes of the anthology series *Walt Disney Presents.*

9/58—9/59	Friday	8:00—9:00
9/59—9/60	Friday	7:30—8:30
9/60—9/61	Sunday	6:30—7:30

Tom Tryon.

73. *Tombstone Territory;* Oct. 16, 1957–Oct. 9, 1959, and 1960 Ziv/United Artists

ABC 91 episodes B/W ½ hour
Syndicated

Sheriff Clay Hollister and newspaper editor Harris Claybourne uphold justice in the town of Tombstone, Arizona.

10/57— 9/58	Wednesday	8:30—9:00
3/59—10/59	Friday	9:00—9:30

Pat Conway, Richard Eastham, Gil Rankin.

74. *Trackdown;* Oct. 4, 1957–Sept. 23, 1959 Four Star

CBS 71 episodes B/W ½ hour

Adventures of a Texas Ranger in the Southwest during the 1870s.

10/57—1/59	Friday	8:00—8:30
2/59—9/59	Wednesday	8:30—9:00

Robert Culp, Ellen Corby, Peter Leeds, Norman Leavitt.

75. *26 Men;* 1957–1959 Russell Hayden

Syndicated 78 episodes B/W ½ hour

Exploits of rangers stationed in Arizona just after the turn of the century.
Tristram Coffin, Kelo Henderson.

76. *Union Pacific;* 1957–1958 California National Productions

Syndicated 39 episodes B/W ½ hour

Episodes in the construction of the Union Pacific Railroad.
Jeff Morrow, Judson Pratt, Susan Cummings.

77. *U.S. Marshal;* 1958–1960 Desilu

Syndicated 78 episodes B/W ½ hour

A sequel to *Sheriff of Cochise.* Marshal Frank Morgan now has jurisdiction over the entire state of Arizona in the contemporary West.

John Bromfield, James Griffith, Robert Brubaker.

78. *Wagon Train;* Sept. 18, 1957–Sept. 5, 1965 Revue/Howard Christie

NBC/ABC 283 episodes 251 B/W Hour
32 Color

Character studies and action encountered on a classic wagon train from St. Louis to California in the post–Civil War days.

9/57—9/62	NBC	Wednesday	7:30— 8:30
9/62—9/63	ABC	Wednesday	7:30— 8:30
9/63—9/64	ABC	Monday	8:30—10:00
9/64—9/65	ABC	Sunday	7:30— 8:30

Ward Bond, Robert Horton, Terry Wilson, Frank McGrath.

79. *Wanted: Dead or Alive;* Sept. 6, 1958–Mar. 29, 1961 Four Star

CBS 94 episodes B/W ½ hour

A morose bounty hunter stalks outlaws during the 1880s.

9/58—9/60	Saturday	8:30—9:00
9/60—3/61	Wednesday	8:30—9:00

Steve McQueen.

80. *Wichita Town;* Sept. 30, 1959–Sept. 23, 1960 Revue/Mirisch/McCrea

NBC 24 episodes B/W ½ hour

Marshal and deputies attempt to establish and maintain law and order in the Kansas Territory after the Civil War.

9/59—4/60	Wednesday	10:30—11:00
6/60—9/60	Friday	8:30— 9:00

Joel McCrea, Jody McCrea, Carlos Romero, George Neise, Bob Anderson, Robert Foulk.

81. *Wild Bill Hickok;* 1951–1958 100 episodes William F. Broidy Productions
13 episodes Screen Gems

Syndicated 113 episodes 100 B/W ½ hour
13 Color

Fictional adventures of a real-life hero and his fat sidekick in the Old West.
Guy Madison, Andy Devine.

82. *Yancy Derringer;* Oct. 2, 1958–Sept. 24, 1959 Sharpe-Lewis

CBS 34 episodes B/W ½ hour

Adventures of Yancy Derringer, a riverboat gambler and undercover agent, in New Orleans in the years following the Civil War.

10/58—9/59	Thursday	8:30—9:00

Jock Mahoney, Kevin Hagen, X Brands, Frances Bergen.

83. *Zane Grey Theater;* a.k.a. *Dick Powell's Zane Grey Theater;* Oct. 5, 1956–May 18, 1961 Four Star

CBS 147 episodes B/W ½ hour

Western anthology series with many stories derived from the pen of prolific Western author Zane Grey.

10/56—7/58	Friday	8-30—9:00
10/58—9/60	Thursday	9:00—9:30
10/60—5/61	Thursday	8:30—9:00

Dick Powell.

84. *Zorro;* Oct. 10, 1957–Sept. 24, 1959 Walt Disney

ABC 78 episodes B/W ½ hour

In Spanish California of 1820, a fop has a secret identity, turning into a Mexican Robin Hood to right wrongs.

10/57—9/59	Thursday	8:00—8:30

Guy Williams, George J. Lewis, Gene Sheldon, Henry Calvin, Britt Lomond, Don Diamond, Jan Arvan, Eugenia Paul, Vinton Haworth, Jolene Brand, Eduard Franz.

BIBLIOGRAPHY

Books

Alicoate, Jack. *The Film Daily Yearbook of Motion Pictures.* New York: Film Daily, 1957.

The Annual Obituary. Detroit: St. James, various years.

Austin, John. *More of Hollywood's Unsolved Mysteries.* New York: Shapolsky, 1991.

Beck, Marilyn. *Hollywood.* New York: Hawthorn, 1973.

Bogdanovich, Peter. *John Ford.* Berkeley: University of California Press, 1978.

Brooks, Tim. *The Complete Directory to Prime Time TV Stars 1946–Present.* New York: Ballantine, 1987.

_____, and Earle Marsh. *The Complete Directory to Prime Time TV Shows 1946–Present,* 4th ed. New York: Ballantine, 1988.

Carey, Harry, Jr. *Company of Heroes: My Life As an Actor in the John Ford Stock Company.* Metuchen, NJ: Scarecrow, 1994.

Contemporary Authors. Detroit: Gale Research, various years through 1995.

Contemporary Theater, Film and Television: A Biographical Guide. Detroit: Gale Research, various years through 1995.

Corneau, Ernest N. *The Hall of Fame of Western Film Stars.* North Quincy, MA: Christopher, 1969.

Current Biography Yearbook. New York: Wilson, various years through 1995.

Dye, David. *Child and Youth Actors: Filmographies of Their Entire Careers, 1914–1985.* Jefferson, NC: McFarland, 1988.

Ebsen, Buddy. *The Other Side of Oz.* Newport Beach, CA: Donovan, 1993.

Essoe, Gabe. *The Book of Movie Lists.* Westport, CT: Arlington House, 1981.

_____. *The Book of TV Lists.* Westport, CT: Arlington House, 1981.

Fenin, George N., and William K. Everson. *The Western from Silents to Cinerama.* New York: Bonanza, 1962.

Ferguson, Ken. *The Western Television and Film Annual.* London: Purnell, 1963–1967.

Fireman, Judy. *TV Book: The Ultimate Television Book.* New York: Workman, 1977.

Garfield, Brian. *Western Films: A Complete Guide.* New York: Da Capo, 1982.

Gianakos, Larry. *Television Drama Series Programming.* Metuchen, NJ: Scarecrow, various years 1980–1987.

Goldberg, Lee. *Unsold Television Pilots 1955 Through 1989.* Jefferson, NC: McFarland, 1990.

Goldrup, Tom, and Jim Goldrup. *Feature Players: The Stories Behind the Faces,* Vols. 1 and 2. Published privately, 1986 and 1992.

Hardy, Phil. *The Western.* London: Aurum, 1983.
Hayward, Anthony, and Deborah Hayward. *TV Unforgettables.* Enfield, Middlesex: Guinness, 1993.
Heston, Charlton. *The Actor's Life: Journals 1956–1976.* London: Allen Lane Penguin, 1979.
Holland, Ted. *B Western Actors Encyclopedia: Facts, Photos and Filmographies for More than 250 Familiar Faces.* Jefferson, NC: McFarland, 1989.
Houseman, Victoria. *Made in Heaven: Unscrambling the Marriages and Children of Hollywood Stars.* Chicago: Bonus, 1991.
Inman, David. *The TV Encyclopedia.* New York: Perigee, 1991.
Jarvis, Everett G. *Final Curtain: Deaths of Noted Film and TV Personalities.* New York: Citadel, 1995.
Lamparski, Richard. *Whatever Became Of?* Series 1-11. New York: Crown, 1967–1989.
Landon, Cheryl. *I Promised My Dad: an Intimate Portrait of Michael Landon by His Eldest Daughter.* New York: Simon and Schuster, 1992.
McClure, Arthur F., and Ken D. Jones. *Heroes, Heavies and Sagebrush.* South Brunswick, NJ: Barnes, 1972.
_____, _____, and Alfred E. Twomey. *Character People.* Secaucus, NJ: Citadel, 1979.
_____, and Alfred E. Twomey. *The Versatiles.* South Brunswick, NJ: Barnes, 1969.
McDonald, Archie P. *Shooting Stars: Heroes and Heroines of Western Film.* Bloomington: Indiana University Press, 1987.
Maltin, Leonard. *The Disney Films.* New York: Crown, 1973.
______. *Movie and Video Guide.* New York: Signet, 1996.
Martindale, David. *Television Detective Shows of the 1970s: Credits, Storylines and Episode Guides for 109 Series.* Jefferson, NC: McFarland, 1991.
Marx, Kenneth. *Star Stats: Who's Whose in Hollywood.* Los Angeles: Price/Stern/Sloan, 1979.
Miller, Don. *Hollywood Corral.* New York: Big Apple, 1976.
Miller, Lee O. *The Great Cowboy Stars of Movie and Television.* New Rochelle, NY: Arlington House, 1979.
Mitchum, John. *Them Ornery Mitchum Boys.* Pacifica, CA: Creatures at Large, 1989.
Moseley, Roy. *Roger Moore: A Biography.* London: New English Library, 1986.
Newcomb, Horace, and Robert S. Alley. *The Producer's Medium.* New York: Oxford University Press, 1983.
O'Neil, Thomas. *The Emmys: Star Wars, Showdowns and the Supreme Test of TV's Best.* New York: Penguin, 1992.
Parish, James Robert. *Hollywood Death Book.* Las Vegas, NV: Pioneer, 1992.
Perry, Jeb H. *Screen Gems: A History of Columbia Pictures Television from Cohn to Coke, 1948–1983.* Metuchen, NJ: Scarecrow, 1991.
Pink, Sidney. *So You Want to Make Movies: My Life as an Independent Film Producer.* Sarasota, FL: Pineapple, 1989.
Quigley, Martin, Jr. *International Television Almanac.* New York: Quigley, 1961 and 1966.
Quinlan, David. *Illustrated Directory of Film Character Actors.* London: Batsford, 1995.
______. *Illustrated Directory of Film Stars.* London: Batsford, 1996.
Ragan, David. *Who's Who in Hollywood.* New Rochelle, NY: Arlington House, 1976; New York: Facts on File, 1992.
Rainey, Buck. *The Shoot 'Em Ups Ride Again.* Waynesville, NC: World of Yesterday, 1990.
_____, and Les Adams. *Shoot 'Em Ups.* New Rochelle, NY: Arlington House, 1978.
Reynolds, Burt. *My Life.* London: Hodder and Stoughton, 1994.
Robertson, Ed. *Maverick: Legend of the West.* Beverly Hills, CA: Pomegranate, 1994.
Rothel, David. *The Singing Cowboys.* San Diego, CA: Barnes, 1978.

______. *Those Great Cowboy Sidekicks.* Waynesville, NC: World of Yesterday, 1984.
Rout, Nancy E., Ellen Buckley, and Barney M. Rout. *The Soap Opera Book: Who's Who in Daytime Drama.* West Nyack, NJ: Todd, 1992.
Rovin, Jeff. *The Great Television Series.* South Brunswick, NJ: Barnes, 1977.
______. *TV Babylon* and *TV Babylon II.* New York: Signet, 1984 and 1991.
Sackett, Susan. *Prime Time Hits: Television's Most Popular Network Programs 1950–Present.* New York: Billboard, 1993.
Shapiro, Melany. *Bonanza: The Unofficial Story of the Ponderosa.* Las Vegas: Pioneer, 1993.
Shepherd, Donald, and Robert Slatzer, with Dave Grayson. *Duke: The Life and Times of John Wayne.* London: Sphere, 1986.
Skinner, John Walter. *Who's Who on the Screen.* Worthing, England: Madeleine, 1983.
Smith, Ron. *Comic Support: Second Bananas in the Movies.* New York: Citadel, 1993.
______. *Sweethearts of '60s TV.* New York: St. Martin's, 1989.
Speed, F. Maurice. *The Western Film and Television Annual.* London: MacDonald, various years 1952–1962.
Stallings, Penny. *Forbidden Channels: The Truth They Hide from TV Guide.* New York: Harper Perennial, 1991.
Strait, Raymond. *Hollywood's Star Children.* New York: SPI, 1992.
Summers, Neil. *The Official TV Western Book Vols. 1, 2, 3,* and *4.* Vienna, WV: Old West Publishing Shop, 1987–1992.
Terrace, Vincent. *The Complete Encyclopedia of Television Programs 1947–1976.* 2 vols. South Brunswick, NJ: Barnes, 1976.
Thomas, Tony. *The Dick Powell Story.* Burbank, CA: Riverwood, 1993.
______. *Joel McCrea: Riding the High Country.* Burbank, CA: Riverwood, 1991.
Thomey, Tedd. *The Glorious Decade.* New York: Ace, 1971.
Truitt, Evelyn Mack. *Who Was Who on Screen.* New York: Bowker, 1977 (2d ed.) and 1984 (illustrated ed.).
Tuska, Jon. *The American West in Film: Critical Approaches to the Western.* Lincoln, NE: Bison, 1988.
______. *The Filming of the West.* Garden City, NY: Doubleday, 1976.
Van Hise, James. *Who Was That Masked Man? The Story of the Lone Ranger.* Las Vegas, NV: Pioneer, 1990.
Wayne, Pilar, with Alex Thorleifson. *My Life with the Duke.* London: New English Library, 1987.
Weaver, John T. *Forty Years of Screen Credits, Vols. 1* and *2, 1929–1969.* Metuchen, NJ: Scarecrow, 1970.
______. *Twenty Years of Silents 1908–1928.* Metuchen, NJ: Scarecrow, 1971.
Weaver, Tom. *Science Fiction Stars and Horror Heroes: Interviews with Actors, Directors, Producers and Writers of the 1940s through 1960s.* Jefferson, NC: McFarland, 1991.
Woolley, Lynn, Robert W. Malsbary, and Robert G. Strange, Jr. *Warner Bros. Television: Major Shows of the Fifties and Sixties Episode-by-Episode.* Jefferson, NC: McFarland, 1985.
Yenne, Bill. *The Legend of Zorro.* Greenwich, CT: Brompton, 1991.
Yoggy, Gary A. *Riding the Video Range: The Rise and Fall of the Western on Television.* Jefferson, NC: McFarland, 1995.

Periodicals

The Big Reel
Classic Images
Filmfax
Film Review
Memories
The National Enquirer
The Radio Times
Trail Dust
TV Guide
TV Scene
The TV Times
Variety
Western Clippings
Where Are They Now? A Globe Special

INDEX

Page numbers in boldface refer to photographs